Speller's Law Relating to Hospitals

Speller's Law Relating to Hospitals

Seventh edition

John Finch

Senior Lecturer in Law,
Leicester University
Formerly member of the Mental Health
Act Commission for England and Wales

CHAPMAN & HALL MEDICAL

London · Glasgow · New York · Tokyo · Melbourne · Madras

Published by Chapman & Hall, 2–6 Boundary Row, London SE1 8HN

Chapman & Hall, 2–6 Boundary Row, London SE1 8HN, UK

Blackie Academic & Professional, Wester Cleddens Road, Bishopbriggs, Glasgow G64 2NZ, UK

Chapman & Hall Inc., One Penn Plaza, 41st Floor, New York NY10119, USA

Chapman & Hall Japan, Thomson Publishing Japan, Hirakawacho Nemoto Building, 6F, 1–7–11 Hirakawa-cho, Chiyoda-ku, Tokyo 102, Japan

Chapman & Hall Australia, Thomas Nelson Australia, 102 Dodds Street, South Melbourne, Victoria 3205, Australia

Chapman & Hall India, R. Seshadri, 32 Second Main Road, CIT East, Madras 600 035, India

First edition 1947 by H.K. Lewis & Co. Ltd. Subsequent editions 1949, 1956, 1965, 1971 and 1978

Seventh edition 1994 by Chapman & Hall

© 1994 Chapman & Hall

Typeset in 10/12pt Palatino by Photoprint, Torquay, Devon
Printed in Great Britain at the University Press, Cambridge

ISBN 0 412 41000 1

   The publisher makes no representation, express or implied, with regard to the accuracy of the information contained in this book and cannot accept any legal responsibility or liability for any errors or omissions that may be made.

A catalogue record for this book is available from the British Library

Library of Congress Cataloging-in-Publication data available

∞ Printed on permanent acid-free text paper, manufactured in accordance with the proposed ANSI/NISO Z 39.48-1992 and ANSI Z 39.48-1984

Contents

Preface

In January 1947 Dr Speller wrote that 'only last year did Mr Aneurin Bevan achieve the distinction of being the first Minister of Health to embody provisions for a comprehensive health service in a Bill that has now become law as the National Health Service Act, 1946.' That same year saw the first edition of this book.

Few in 1947 would have chanced a prediction of the changes in health services structure, and even philosophy, that have produced the conditions and priorities prevailing in 1993. This seventh edition incorporates major changes wrought in health services structure by the National Health Service and Community Care Act 1990, in particular the creation of National Health Service trusts.

Beyond the process of change in statutory structures and responsibilities lies a vast number of changes in common law and legislation affecting the delivery of personal health care in hospitals and nursing homes. Since the last edition, much of the law relating to consent to treatment has altered out of recognition. The legal liability of hospitals managed by health authorities and trusts has become so complex that a new and separate chapter in this edition is devoted entirely to the possibility of legal proceedings against them. The laws relating to employment and to professional qualifications have undergone fundamental changes. Attention to employee safety is, or should be, a major concern for the modern hospital manager, and the chapter on *Injury at work* has been significantly expanded to meet the needs of 1993. A whole new area of law relating to data protection and access to health records has emerged. Mental health law has undergone radical and far-reaching changes, starting with the Mental Health Act 1983 and continuing with the much later publication, in 1990, of the Statutory Code of Practice, already in its first revision by the Department of Health.

The interval since the publication of the previous edition has presented the opportunity to give a very different appearance to this established book. Footnote references now appear at the end of each chapter, and the text itself is left uncluttered. Material formerly contained in substantial appendices is now, so far as necessary, contained in the body of the text.

Consistent with the original spirit of this book, the seventh edition offers a legal support not only to practitioners and teachers of the law relating to hospitals but also, and importantly, to managers and health care practitioners who seek a guide to the law affecting their professional life. The changed presentation of this seventh edition aims to assist and support not only lawyers but all health care professionals and managers.

In particular, it helps to address the statutory responsibility of National Health Service trusts to conduct their activities 'effectively, efficiently and economically': National Health Service and Community Care Act 1990, Schedule 2, paragraph 6(1). But further than that, this seventh edition of *Speller* tries to make the law relating to hospitals more accessible to all those who want, and need, to know it.

John Finch
1993

Acknowledgements

The first five editions of this book were prepared single-handed by Dr Speller. It is a testament to his great knowledge and ability that such a task was executed with such success. The law relating to hospitals has, however, grown so much in complexity especially in recent years that it would be unwise to present this 1993 edition without some reference to expert consultants. This has been done in respect of a number of chapters, and those consultants are identified separately. Their input is warmly and gratefully acknowledged, and the text has benefited greatly from their expertise and experience.

In addition, thanks are due to Kirsty Keywood LL M for her assistance on a number of chapters and to Camilla Parker LL M, Solicitor, for her assistance with Chapter 29. A very substantial debt of gratitude is owed, and warmly acknowledged, to Robert Cowley, Barrister-at-law, for his hard work and valuable assistance across numerous chapters. His name is also listed among the specialist consultants, for the chapters on Data protection, and Access to medical records and reports are almost entirely his work.

Specialist consultants

Robert Cowley, Barrister-at-law, 8 Fountain Court, Birmingham. *Data protection; Access to medical records and reports.*

Ian Dodds-Smith, Solicitor, McKenna & Co., London. *Medicines and poisons.*

Mike Doyle, Oxley and Coward, Solicitors, Sheffield. *Hospitals managed under the National Health Service.*

Peter Edwards, Solicitor, Liverpool. *Mental health law.*

Clive Loyns, Solicitor, Hempsons, London. *Employment law; Professional qualifications.*

Alan Milligan, District Pharmaceutical Officer, South Durham District Health Authority. *Medicines and poisons.*

Mary Mulholland, Senior Lecturer in Law, De Montfort University, Leicester. *Taxation of hospitals.*

Paul Ridout, Solicitor, Nabarro Nathanson, London. *Nursing homes: registration, conduct and inspection.*

Amanda Wearing, Barrister, McKenna & Co., London. *Medicines and poisons.*

Table of Cases

Table of statutes

Table of statutory instruments and rules

CHAPTER 1

Hospitals: definition and classification

1.1 DEFINITION OF 'HOSPITAL'

1.1.1 General

The term 'hospital' usually means any institution maintained for the reception, care and treatment of those in need of medical, surgical or dental attention, being an institution which is not carried on for private gain.[1] It is in this general sense that the term is used throughout this book except where otherwise indicated. In an Australian case a testator bequeathed the income of part of his residuary estate to the Sisters of Charity, a voluntary association of women devoting themselves without reward to good works, for the purposes of a private hospital which they ran in Australia. Its patients were charged fees and at times there were surpluses of income over expenditure but the hospital was not run for profit. Its essential purpose was to provide a type of medical and nursing care which a nearby public general hospital could not give. The poor were not excluded and sometimes patients were treated without payment or at reduced rates. On appeal to the Privy Council, it was held that it was a valid charitable gift.[2] The following propositions can be made on the basis of their Lordships' decision:

1. A gift for the purposes of a hospital is prima facie a good charitable gift.
2. If a bequest is made on trusts requiring it to be applied for a particular charitable purpose, it is immaterial that some of the general purposes of the recipient body may not be charitable.
3. It is not a condition of validity of a trust for the relief of the sick that it should be limited to the poor sick.

The expression 'those in need of medical, surgical or dental . . . attention' is preferred to the term 'sick persons'. The former, but not the latter, includes women in childbirth (who are not necessarily *ill*), mentally disordered persons and also persons suffering from physical disability, not normally regarded as *sick persons*. A woman in normal childbirth may not need medical attention and, even in hospital, she may for her delivery be in the care of a midwife; but even then she will ordinarily have been attended by a medical practitioner both before and after birth. In *Jewish Blind Society v Henning* (1961)[3] it was decided that blindness as such is not an 'illness' for the purposes of this definition. The word 'attention' is preferred to 'treatment' because the former, but not the latter, includes hospitals and homes for the incurable and the dying where the patients need nursing care under medical supervision rather than active medical treatment.[4] The scope of this book includes hospitals popularly so called, maternity homes and psychiatric hospitals, including mental handicap hospitals, as well as homes for the dying, provided always that they are not carried on for private gain. Our definition excludes nursing homes (because they are conducted for private gain) and also charitable institutions otherwise than for the reception and treatment of those in need of medical or surgical attention; but there is nothing *in law* restricting the use of the term 'hospital' to institutions defined in this sense. The expression 'private hospital' is sometimes used as part of the name of a nursing home, to distinguish it from a public or charitable hospital. Hospitals as here defined may be classified either as being voluntary or public authority hospitals, or according to their function. Having said that, much of the law examined in this book applies equally to private hospitals and nursing homes in the independent health care sector. Such law includes principally employment laws, responsibility for the safety of staff and patients, consent to treatment and the greater part of the law relating to the treatment of mental disorder.

1.1.2 National Health Service

The National Health Service Act 1977 uses the term 'hospital' to include institutions such as nursing homes which are carried on for profit. Section 128 provides:

' "hospital" means—
(a) any institution for the reception and treatment of persons suffering from illness,
(b) any maternity home, and
(c) any institution for the reception and treatment of persons during convalescence or persons requiring medical rehabilitation,
and includes clinics, dispensaries and out-patient departments maintained in connection with any such institution or home as aforesaid, and "hospital accommodation" shall be construed accordingly.'

In *Minister of Health v General Committee of the Royal Midland Counties Home for Incurables* (1954)[4] the Court of Appeal by a majority held that an institution for incurables, where no active medical or surgical treatment was given, was a hospital within that definition in its broadly equivalent form in the National Health Service Act 1946, section 6(1). The patients required nursing and nursing was held by two of the three members of the Court of Appeal to be treatment for the purpose of the definition of 'hospital' even though the nursing is not associated with active medical or surgical treatment. Lord Justice Denning, dissenting, said:

> 'If the main purpose is to treat patients for their illnesses by the exercise of professional skill, then the institution is a hospital. But if the main purpose is only to take care of them and make life more comfortable for them, then it is not a hospital but a home, and is not caught by the Acts.'

The word 'reception' in this definition has been held to mean reception as an *in-patient*. The definition therefore excludes a clinic which provides exclusively outpatient treatment. In *Re Couchman's Will Trusts, Couchman v Eccles* (1952)[5] it was held that 'reception' means taking a person into a building and keeping him there. Any such facility, unless it is 'maintained in connection with' a facility which does receive in-patients, will therefore not fall within the statutory definition.

For the purpose of formal admission (detention) under the Mental Health Act 1983, 'hospital' is defined by section 145 as follows:

' "hospital" means—
  (a) any health service hospital within the meaning of the National Health Service Act 1977; and
  (b) any accommodation provided by a local authority and used as a hospital by or on behalf of the Secretary of State under that Act;
and "hospital within the meaning of Part II of this Act" has the meaning given in section 34 above; [application to mental nursing homes].'

Non-profit or charitable hospitals or institutions receiving mentally disordered patients for treatment are, for the purposes of the Registered Homes Act 1984[6] relating to registration and conduct, within the definition of 'mental nursing home', being premises used for the reception of and the provision of nursing or other medical treatment for one or more mentally disordered patients (whether exclusively or in common with other persons) not being (a) a hospital as defined in the Mental Health Act 1983 (above), or (b) any accommodation provided by a local authority and used as a hospital by or on behalf of the Secretary of State under the National Health Service Act 1977. Nevertheless, Part II of the Mental Health Act 1983 which sets out rules relating to the detention of mentally disordered persons in hospital, applies also to mental nursing homes, registered for the reception of patients liable to be detained, section 34(2) providing as follows:

'Except where otherwise expressly provided, this Part of this Act applies in relation to a mental nursing home, being a home in respect of which the particulars of registration are for the time being entered in the separate part of the register kept for the purposes of section 23(5)(b) [of the Registered Homes Act 1984] as it applies in relation to a hospital, and references in this Part of this Act to a hospital, and any reference in this Act to a hospital to which this Part of this Act applies, shall be construed accordingly.'

No single definition of 'hospital' will therefore suffice for all purposes. The definition in the opening paragraph points broadly to the limits of the scope of this book. Insofar as the law relating to them is different, residential homes are excluded, even though for the reception and treatment of disabled, mentally disordered or old persons. However, apart from rules as to registration and inspection, there are no significant differences in law between hospitals and residential homes or between hospitals and nursing homes, and all are covered by the laws contained in this book, except where otherwise indicated. The definition of 'hospital' may usefully be considered in a variety of practical contexts. These include (though by no means exhaustively):

1. whether a trust in favour of a hospital is valid and operating;
2. whether a person has been admitted as an in-patient so as to be open to the exercise of powers under the Mental Health Act 1983;
3. whether a hospital, for instance through its accident and emergency department, has assumed a legal duty of care to a patient.

There is no further legal definition of 'in-patient', the fact of the matter depending on administrative practice.

There are no separate and special legal rules relating to, for instance, consent to treatment or confidentiality of information, which apply solely to a 'hospital'. The law governing such issues is the general common law as decided and applied by the courts in the context of health care facilities.

1.2 VOLUNTARY AND PUBLIC AUTHORITY HOSPITALS

1.2.1 Voluntary hospitals

A 'voluntary' hospital is a hospital not carried on for private gain and having the legal status of a charity, being supported at least in part by endowments and voluntary contributions.

In the Charities Act 1993 there is no attempt at a statutory definition of 'charity' or of 'charitable purpose', 'charity' being defined in section 45 as 'any institution whether corporate or not established for charitable purposes . . .' and 'charitable purposes' as 'purposes which are exclusively charitable according to the law of England and Wales'.

The charitable status of voluntary hospitals within that definition is founded on the spirit and intention of the now repealed preamble to the

Statute of Elizabeth I[7] now surviving only in the broad guiding principles laid down by Lord Macnaghten in his judgment in *Commissioners of Inland Revenue v Pemsel* (1891)[8] when he said that 'charity' in its legal sense comprises four main divisions:

> trusts for the relief of poverty; trusts for the advancement of education; trusts for the advancement of religion; and trusts for other purposes beneficial to the community not falling under any of the preceding heads. The trusts last referred to are not the less charitable in the eye of the law because incidentally they benefit the rich as well as the poor, as indeed every charity that deserves the name must do either directly or indirectly.

While the fourth head of Lord Macnaghten's definition does not embrace every object of public utility (benevolent objects not being *necessarily* charitable), it is settled law that it includes a hospital owned by the Secretary of State for the purposes of the National Health Service.[9]

The older voluntary hospitals founded exclusively for the relief of the sick poor are clearly charities within Lord Macnaghten's 'trusts for the relief of poverty'. Non-profit voluntary hospitals established later, having power to admit paying patients as well as the sick poor, also have charitable status. The Voluntary Hospitals (Paying Patients) Act 1936[10] (still in force) authorised the Charity Commissioners, by Order, to modify the trusts of any voluntary hospital not having power to admit paying patients to permit it to do so. This modification was subject to conditions assuring that the original objects of the charity are not thereby prejudiced. Since then it has been clear that a non-profit hospital providing care for rich and poor alike is a charity falling within the fourth of Lord Macnaghten's divisions of charity, viz. 'trusts for other purposes beneficial to the community'. A non-profit nursing home for paying patients will presumably be accepted by the Charity Commissioners for registration as a charity under section 3 of the Charities Act 1993, providing its constitution is otherwise acceptable. It has been held by the Court of Appeal in *Re Adams, deceased; Gee and another v Barnet Group Hospital Management Committee* (1968)[11] that the endowment of beds for paying patients is a valid charitable bequest. The broad test of whether a hospital is a charity is whether it is a non-profit institution for the relief of sickness. Whether or not all the patients are able to pay full cost seems only marginally relevant, if at all.

Many of the voluntary hospitals in existence today, excluding non-profit nursing homes, are voluntary hospitals receiving mainly patients not able to pay the full cost of treatment. These were disclaimed by the Minister of Health in 1948 under the provisions of sections 6 and 7 of the National Health Service Act 1946. They are mainly religious foundations, mostly Roman Catholic, the patients (except paying patients) being admitted under contract with the health authority for the district which the hospital serves. The admission of patients under such contractual arrangements does not in itself bring their status as charities into question, though the trusts of the charity may have to be modified to permit it.

1.2.2   Public authority hospitals

A public authority hospital is established or carried on directly by the central government or by some other public authority. This definition includes National Health Service hospitals as well as hospitals run by the military, naval or air force authorities and the special hospitals owned and administered by the Secretary of State for Health under section 4 of the National Health Service Act 1977. However, the hospitals administered by health authorities in England on behalf of the Secretary of State for Health and in Wales on behalf of the Secretary of State for Wales, under the National Health Service Acts, are administered by statutory corporations and they are separately treated in Chapter 2. The statutory corporations are charities.[12]

1.3   FUNCTIONAL CLASSIFICATION OF HOSPITALS

1.3.1   General and special hospitals

A general hospital is one where treatment relating to a substantial range of diseases and injuries is provided, but not necessarily for certain rare conditions such as leprosy or conditions requiring neuro-surgery. Deep X-ray therapy and radium treatment are also often restricted to hospitals suitably equipped and staffed for the purpose. A general hospital serving the needs of a particular district within the national health service is referred to as a District General Hospital.

'Special hospital' sometimes refers to (a) a hospital for treatment of patients suffering from a particular type of illness, such as cancer, or from conditions requiring a particular range of treatment, such as orthopædic hospitals; or (b) a hospital for treatment of patients suffering from diseases of a particular organ or group of organs, such as diseases of the eyes or chest, or diseases special to women; or (c) a hospital for treatment of patients of a particular class, for example children or women. But for the purposes of the Mental Health Act 1983 and of the National Health Service Act 1977, an altogether different statutory meaning has been given to the term, namely 'an establishment provided by the Secretary of State for Social Services [now Health] for persons subject to detention under the 1983 Act who, in his opinion, require treatment under conditions of special security on account of their dangerous, violent or criminal propensities'. That is to say, highly difficult to manage mental patients.

A patient suffering from mental disorder,[13] even one liable to detention, may be treated at *any* hospital, not necessarily a so-called psychiatric hospital, administered under the National Health Service Act 1977 which is willing to receive him. Any voluntary hospital, private hospital or private nursing home which receives a mentally disordered patient, whether or not the patient be liable to be detained, must be registered as a mental nursing home under the Registered Homes Act 1984. Consequently, so far as the voluntary and private sectors are concerned, psychiatric hospitals having the legal status of 'mental nursing homes' are still to be distinguished from other hospitals and nursing homes.[14]

1.3.2 Specialist and general practitioner staffed hospitals

A distinction likely to be of practical importance, especially in relation to the question of liability for injuries to patients, is between a hospital where the treatment of patients is the immediate responsibility of specialists of consultant[15] rank and a small general hospital (sometimes called a 'cottage hospital') the regular staff of which consists of visiting local general practitioners but which may be visited either more or less regularly, or on request only, by specialists.

1.3.3 Changes in use of hospitals: voluntary hospitals

Whether there can be a change in the nature of the work carried on at a voluntary hospital depends on the terms of the trust and on whether that trust can, if necessary, be altered.[16] In the case of hospitals within the National Health Service there are other considerations and in 1949 the Minister of Health, in a Circular,[17] drew the attention of regional hospital boards (now health authorities) to the fact that any alteration of the user of hospitals under their control should only be made with due regard to the provisions of the National Health Service Act 1946 and is also subject to his powers of direction. Under the law now contained in section 88 of the National Health Service Act 1977, the Minister is bound, in using a hospital transferred under the Act of 1946, 'so far as practicable' to 'secure that the objects for which it was used immediately before the appointed day are not prejudiced by the provisions of this section' (providing for transfer to the Minister). The Circular states that the Minister may not ignore representations made to him by members of the public and 'the profession' (presumably the *medical* profession).

The Circular examines in detail questions involved in the decision upon changes in the user of hospitals and, presumably, therefore the considerations which will weigh with the Secretary of State in deciding whether to issue a directive to a health authority on the subject if appealed to by members of the public or of the medical profession. The Circular continues: 'The principal factors are, of course, (1) the possible loss of service to patients; (2) the disturbance of medical staff'; and in the light of those 'principal factors' discusses the things to be taken into account in (a) changing over the use of the hospital from one specialty to another or from a special to a general hospital; (b) changing it from being a general practitioner ('cottage') hospital to specialist hospital; and (c) changes in method of staffing general practitioner maternity hospitals.

It is certainly appropriate to draw attention to (what are now) the provisions of section 88 and also to the kind of consideration which will influence the Secretary of State in giving directions to health authorities. The Circular tends to confuse separate and distinct issues. It seems to be suggested that 'the disturbance of medical staff' might amount to an infringement of the obligation 'so far as practicable' to 'secure that the objects for which any such property[18] was used immediately before the appointed day are not prejudiced'. This is inappropriate in relation to what were charitable hospitals, suggesting as it does a vested interest of medical staff. The hospital was used for the treatment of *patients*, the method of staffing being wholly incidental to the attainment of that object. The Circular sought to give the inappropriate impression that 'the disturbance of medical staff' is a factor on a par with 'the possible loss of service to patients'.

A Scottish case, *Adams and others v Maclay (Secretary of State) and the South Eastern Regional Hospital Board* (1958),[19] turned on the meaning of the word 'practicable' in section 6 (4) of the National Health Service (Scotland) Act 1947, which subsection is in terms substantially identical with those of section 6 (4) the National Health Service Act 1946 (now section 88 of the 1977 Act). It seriously questioned whether the Secretary of State has the freedom to deal with transferred hospitals which had been assumed to exist. The two hospitals in question in that case had been founded for the treatment of women and children by women medical practitioners. On the retirement of a woman consultant some years after the hospitals had been transferred, the regional board proposed to open up the appointment to men as well as women. Although the board of management of the hospitals objected the Secretary of State declined to intervene. Ten women sought a declaration that by virtue of the latter part of section 6 (4) of the Scottish Act the appointment should be restricted to women.

Lord Walker, in upholding their claim, stated that under section 6 (4) it was the duty of the Secretary of State to secure, if practicable, the continued use of the hospitals for the objects for which they had been used before the 'appointed day'.[20] He did not consider it possible to determine by hearing evidence whether the appointment of a woman consultant was or was not practicable. He therefore ruled that it was the duty of the Secretary of State to secure that a male medical practitioner be not appointed consulting physician at the two hospitals unless and until, after the advertisement of the post as being open to women medical practitioners only, it should appear that no woman suitable for appointment had applied. He also ordered the regional board not to appoint a male medical practitioner to the post.

It seems clear from the judgment that if a transferred hospital *can* be used for the objects for which it was used immediately before the 'appointed day',[20] it must be. In other words *practicable* is equated with *possible*. It may be concluded that in England and Wales, under section 88 of the National Health Service Act 1977, the law is the same. In *Re Hayes' Will Trusts* (1954)[21] an English court had already, though not on the interpretation of the National Health Service Act 1946, decided that *impracticable* meant *not able to be done*.

As the Scottish decision is not binding on English courts, an English court might conceivably apply section 88 more liberally and be satisfied if the objects for which the property had been being used immediately before the appointed day were in fact being satisfactorily provided at another hospital reasonably available to the patients for whose benefit the charity had been established. Nevertheless, it has to be said that the Scottish case has raised very serious issues as the use to which the Secretary of State may put any former voluntary hospital can apparently be challenged in the courts at any length of time after its being taken over on 5 July 1948. There is no statutory restriction on change of user of any voluntary hospital which might be taken over by the Minister otherwise than under section 88 of the Act of 1977.

Two further points arising from this Scottish case would no doubt be adopted by an English court. First, the objects for which the property must be used 'if practicable' are those for which it was used immediately before the appointed day, not those for which it might have been used under the trust deed, if any. A strict interpretation of section 88 of the 1977 Act (or the Scottish Act) suggests that the objects within the protection of the 'if practicable' requirement are those for which the property was used immediately before the appointed day, even though so used in contravention of the terms of an express trust. Second, the duty of complying with the requirement that the property be used as far as practicable for the pre-appointed day objects fell on the Secretary of State who was, therefore, properly made a co-defendant. The Secretary of State for Health or the Secretary of State for Wales would likewise be a co-defendant under the National Health Service Act 1977.

After the decision in the Scottish case the Minister of Health issued fresh instructions to hospital authorities on the procedure to be adopted when it is proposed to close or change the use of a hospital, the new procedure being designed to take particular account of the duty to secure as far as practicable that the objects for which a hospital was used immediately before transfer in 1948 are not prejudiced by the change.[22]

1.3.4   Closure or change of use of National Health Service buildings and facilities

The question of closure or substantial change of use of National Health Service facilities has assumed a particular significance following the cumulative effect of two administrative and policy developments. First, the impact of the introduction of the 'general management' concept following the Griffiths Report on health services management; and second, with particular reference to the mental health and mental handicap care and treatment sectors, the programme of closure or restructuring of the large mental hospitals in the direction of 'community care'.

The duty of health authorities to consult, and the limits of that duty, are now set out in paragraph 19 of the Community Health Councils Regulations 1985[23] as follows:

'**19.**—(1) Subject to [paragraphs (1A). (2) and (2A)], it shall be the duty of each relevant District Authority and of each relevant [Family Health Service Authority] to consult a Council on any proposals which the Authority or [Family Health Service Authority] may have under consideration for any substantial development of the health service in the Council's district and on any such proposals to make any substantial variation in the provision of such service.

[((1A) Paragraph (1) shall not apply with respect to any proposal to establish an NHS trust.]

(2) Paragraph (1) shall not apply to any proposal on which the District Authority or Committee is satisfied that, in the interest of the health service, a decision has to be taken without allowing time for consultation; but, in any such case, the District Authority or [Family Health Service Authority] shall notify the Council immediately of the decision taken and the reason why no consultation has taken place.

[(2A) Where it appears to a Regional Authority that it is expedient in the interests of the health service for consultation required under this regulation to be carried out by the Regional Authority instead of a District Authority or [Family Health Service Authority], the Regional Authority shall so notify the District Authority or [Family Health Service Authority], and thereupon it shall be the duty of the Regional Authority and not of the District Authority or [Family Health Service Authority] to carry out that consultation in accordance with this regulation.]'

Circular HSC(IS)207,[24] referring to the predecessor[25] of the Community Health Councils Regulations 1985 which in this respect were framed in similar terms, deals with the procedures to be adopted in relation to what it refers to as 'closure or change of use of health buildings', as follows:

'The aim of the revised procedures is to enable resources to be redeployed with the maximum speed and simplicity consistent with adequate local (and, where relevant, national) consultations. Especially at a time of economic constraints it is essential that no unnecessary barriers should impede cost-effective use of the resources available to the National Health Service. Because local circumstances vary, the procedures should be worked out for each case in the light of individual circumstances at the time and reviewed if those circumstances change.

In general, responsibility for determining the closure or change of use of health buildings rests with the District Health Authority, subject to the formal agreement of the Community Health Council. Where sufficient local agreement exists, it should be possible to move from a proposal to close (or change use) to actual closure or change of use within a period of six months.

A closure or change of use must be justified for one of the following reasons:

(a) the service provided can more efficiently be undertaken elsewhere; (b) the facility is no longer required because of new developments; (c) redeployment of services is essential having regard to the resources of manpower and finance available; (d) it is necessitated by developments outside the National Health Service, *eg* road proposals.

The guidance emphasises the need for early, informal consultations, especially on points of possible difficulty, between Districts, [...] and Regions, and describes the consultations on planning proposals that will need to be undertaken with a wide range of interests. Any foreseeable closure or change of use will clearly need to be dealt with in the exchanges and consultations described in the Guide. The attention of Community Health Councils,[26] Local Authorities (including District Councils) through the Joint Consultative Committees, Family Practitioner Committees (now FHSAs), Local Advisory Committees, Local Medical Committees, Joint Staff Consultative Committees and other bodies, as appropriate, should be drawn particularly to any closures or changes of use required by plans, and their general reaction to the proposals sought. A final commitment is not normally required at this stage since the plan as a whole will still be subject to review.'

1.4 STATE HOSPITALS

State hospitals may be divided into two classes. First, those controlled directly by a department of state such as special hospitals under section 4(1) of the National Health Service Act 1977, owned by the Secretary of State for Health and administered directly by his department; and also naval, military and air force hospitals and prison hospitals administered by other Government departments. Second, hospitals owned by the Secretary of State under the National Health Service Act 1977 and administered on his behalf by one of the corporate health authorities established under the National Health Service Act 1977. These two classes must be treated separately not only on grounds of convenience but because the legal liabilities of the Secretary of State and of officials and the rules regarding proceedings in respect of the two classes still differ.

This section refers solely to hospitals controlled directly by central government. Hospitals managed by statutory authorities established under the National Health Service Act 1977, and NHS trusts established under the National Health Service and Community Care Act 1990, are discussed in the following chapter.

By virtue of the Crown Proceedings Act 1947, the Crown is not generally immune from liability in tort in respect of loss or damage suffered by a subject as a result of the wrongful act or omission of a public servant or other agent of the Crown. Generally speaking, under that Act anyone injured in person, property or reputation by a servant of the Crown has the same rights against the Crown as against any other principal or employer in like circumstances. There were certain exceptions, the most important being injury suffered by a person in the armed forces of the Crown and caused by some other person also so serving, and certified by the Secretary of State to have been treated or which will be treated as attributable to service for the purposes of entitlement under the Royal Warrant, Order in Council or order relating to the disablement or death of members of the force of which he was a member.[27] And where this exception applied the member of the forces causing the injury was exempt from personal liability in tort unless the court was satisfied that the act or omission was not connected with his duties as a member of those forces. This exclusion from legal liability was removed, but only in respect of any act or omission committed on or after 15 May 1987, by section 1 of the Crown Proceedings (Armed Forces) Act 1987.[28]

The Crown will not ordinarily be liable in tort for injury done to a member of the Navy, Army or Air Force at a service hospital by reason of the negligence or incompetence of another person in the forces of the Crown (such as a doctor or a ward orderly in the Royal Army Medical Corps). As the definition of armed forces is apt to include the women's nursing and auxiliary services under control of service departments the Crown immunity will extend to members of such women's services. The person responsible for the injury would also be exempt from liability in tort within the limits already indicated.

If a service patient in a service hospital is injured by someone who is a servant or agent of the Crown but not a member of the armed forces (such as a civilian doctor or nurse) within the extended meaning of armed forces in section 38 (5) of the Act, in circumstances which would give rise to a claim in tort against a private individual, then the injured person will apparently have a claim in tort both against the Crown and against the tortfeasor (wrongdoer).

Subject to what has been said in respect of persons in the armed forces, to prerogative powers[29] and to statutory exceptions, whether under the Crown Proceedings Act 1947, or otherwise, superior civil servants will seemingly be responsible in law for the acts and omissions of their subordinates in like manner and to the like extent as if they were superior and subordinate in the service of a private employer. That is, they will, in effect, be liable only for such wrongful acts and omissions of their subordinates as they have expressly authorised.

1.5   PROVISIONS AFFECTING THE PSYCHIATRIC SPECIAL HOSPITALS

Following a number of problems experienced at Rampton Hospital, one of the four special hospitals for the treatment of mental disorder, the Rampton Hospital Review Board Orders came into operation on 11 June 1981. By the Rampton Hospital Review Board (Establishment and Constitution) Order, a special health authority to be known as the Rampton Hospital Review Board was to be established. The Board was to perform such functions in relation to the special hospital known as Rampton Hospital as the Secretary of State might by regulations direct the Board to perform on his behalf.

The Rampton Hospital Review Board continued to function until the coming into operation, on 1 July 1986, of the Rampton Hospital Board (Establishment and Constitution) Order 1986[30] and the Rampton Hospital Board (Functions and Membership) Regulations 1986.[31] The Order provided for the establishment and constitution of a special health authority known as the Rampton Hospital Board for the purposes of exercising on behalf of the Secretary of State functions in relation to Rampton Hospital. By the Functions and Membership Regulations, directions were given by the Secretary of State to the Board to exercise on his behalf functions under the National Health Service Act relating to Rampton Hospital as well as his functions as the Manager of the Hospital under the Mental Health Act 1983. The Board exercised on behalf of the Secretary of State his functions in relation to the hospital as follows:

1. functions in relation to the provision of services at the hospital including appropriate professional services, and in relation to the giving of advice and support to officers employed at the hospital, to secure the implementation of such policies and programmes as may be required for the care and treatment of patients in the hospital;
2. functions as to the determination of priorities and the development of policies in relation to the use of manpower resources, revenue and capital funds allocated by the Secretary of State for the provision of services at the hospital;
3. functions in relation to the operation of an adequate procedure for the investigation of complaints made by or on behalf of any person

who is a patient in the hospital in respect of any service provided at the hospital;
4. the functions conferred upon the Secretary of State as the manager of the hospital by virtue of section 145(1) of the Act of 1983.

These Regulations also provided for the appointment and tenure of office of members of the Rampton Hospital Board and for the procedure of, and report to the Secretary of State by, that special health authority.

Regulations affecting the other three hospitals (Moss Side and Park Lane Hospitals being on the same site near Liverpool) came into operation on 1 January 1987. These were the Broadmoor Hospital Board (Establishment and Constitution) Order 1986[32] together with Regulations in relation to Functions and Membership,[33] and a corresponding Order[34] and accompanying Regulations[35] in respect of Moss Side and Park Lane Hospitals. The Chairman and other members of the Boards were appointed by the Secretary of State. The powers of the Boards were strictly limited.

With the development of the concept of general management in the National Health Service, the Special Hospitals came under an altogether different management structure in 1989. The Boards for the (then) four hospitals were abolished by the Boards for Special Hospitals (Abolition) Order 1989[36] and the governing authority became the Special Hospitals Service Authority. Paragraph 3 of the abolition order provides that any right which was enforceable by and any liability which was enforceable against any of the old boards shall be enforceable by or against the new Authority.

By the Special Hospitals Service Authority (Establishment and Constitution) Order 1989[37] there was established a Special Health Authority (that is, within the National Health Service) to have overall authority over the special hospitals. The Authority shall exercise such functions relating to the management of the special hospitals as the Secretary of State may by Regulations direct it to perform on his behalf. The new Authority was initially charged with taking the necessary action to wind up the affairs of the old boards. The new Authority shall make reports to the Secretary of State at least once a year, and must furnish to the Secretary of State such information and papers as he may from time to time require.

The Special Hospitals Service Authority was set up on 1 July 1989. It took over the running of the service from the Department of Health and what were by then the three hospital boards (following the establishment of joint management for the Liverpool hospitals, Park Lane and Moss Side). On 1 October 1989 the Special Hospitals Service Authority also became the employer of all staff in the service at that time employed by the Department of Health, with the sole exception of administrative staff in respect of whom special arrangements have been made.

The initial constitution of the Authority comprised a non-executive Chairman together with four non-executive members; and three executive members, being the Chief Executive, Services, the Head of Medical Services and the Head of Nursing Services. The Department of Health's future role will be very different and much curtailed. In essence the Department will be concerned with strategic policy and priority setting, approval of long and short-term service plans and the allocation of matching resources, monitoring of standards and progress and review of performance. These responsibilities will be discharged and the roles of the individual disciplines involved co-ordinated through a reconstituted Special Hospitals Service Board.

The relationship of the new arrangements to the historical background of changes in the overall management of the special hospitals is reflected in an information document issued by the Department of Health in October 1989 entitled *Starting Afresh*. Concern about the special hospitals which was evidenced in the Boynton Report (1980) on Rampton Hospital leading to the establishment of the Rampton Hospital Review Board continued to be recognised in the following statement in *Starting Afresh*:

'The existing three boards – the Broadmoor Hospital Board, the Rampton Hospital Board and the Moss Side and Park Lane Hospitals Board – are all presently constituted as special health authorities. By law one special health authority (i.e. the SHSA) cannot manage another (the hospital boards). So, on 1 October, when the SHSA takes over the full management of the service, the existing three hospital boards will be abolished. However, the Boynton Report on Rampton Hospital identified the need to ensure "regular and authorised public scrunity of the special hospitals"; and experience before and since shows that it is important that, at hospital level, there should be a body of impartial outsiders – in the main lay people – charged with keeping an eye on the interests and welfare of patients. While, in that role, such a body needs close contact with the unit general manager, it is the manager who is clearly responsible for the management of the hospital. So the functions of the new bodies will be different from those of their local boards; in particular, they will not have any responsibilities for hospital management.

In essence, these bodies will be a "window" outwards from the hospitals and inwards from the local community. Three new bodies – one for Broadmoor Hospital, one for Rampton Hospital and one for the Liverpool campus – with these new, more clearly defined roles, called Hospital Advisory Committees are to be constituted after 1 October 1989 as sub-committees of the SHSA. Chairmen of the Hospital Advisory Committees will be directly accountable to the Chairman of the SHSA.'

NOTES

1. *Re Smith (deceased)* [1962] 1 WLR 763.
2. *Le Cras v Perpetual Trustee Co, Far West Children's Health Scheme v Perpetual Trustee Co* [1967] 1 All ER 915, Privy Council.
3. [1961] 1 All ER 47.
4. *Minister of Health v General Committee of the Royal Midland Counties Home for Incurables* [1954] Ch 530.
5. [1952] Ch 391.
6. Section 22.
7. 43 Eliz I, c 4 (Charities).
8. [1891] AC 531 at 583.
9. *Re Frere (deceased): Kidd and another v Farnham Group HMC* [1950] 2 All ER 513.
10. Further on paying patients see Chapter 22.
11. [1968] Ch 80.
12. *Re Frere (deceased)* [1950] 2 All ER 513, footnote 9, above.
13. For the definition of 'mental disorder' see the Mental Health Act 1983, section 1.
14. On 'hospitals' and 'mental nursing homes' for the purposes of detention and treatment under the Mental Health Act 1983 see Chapter 30, p. 740, below.
15. See Chapter 5, p. 112, below, as to the meaning of 'consultant'.
16. See further Chapter 21, p. 621, below.
17. Circular RHB(49)132. The Minister's views were modified and expanded in HM(58)29 issued after the decision in *Adams v Maclay (The Secretary of State)* [1958] SC 279, discussed on p. 8, above. The functions of Regional Hospital Boards were taken over by health authorities now constituted under the National Health Service Act 1977. See also Circular HSC(IS)207.
18. That is, a hospital and its contents and equipment transferred in 1948 to the National Health Service pursuant to the Act of 1946.
19. [1958] SC 279.
20. 5 July 1948.
21. [1954] 1 WLR 22.
22. Circular HM(58)29.
23. SI 1985/304.
24. Issued October 1975.
25. National Health Service (Community Health Council) Regulations 1973, SI 1973/2217.
26. The specific function of consultation with the relevant Community Health Council(s) is discussed in Chapter 2, pp. 43–45, below.
27. Crown Proceedings Act 1947, section 10.
28. Section 1 is not retrospective, and any act or omission committed before that date continues to be excluded from liability.
29. Crown Proceedings Act 1947, section 11.
30. SI 1986/963.
31. SI 1986/964.
32. SI 1986/2004.
33. SI 1986/2005.
34. SI 1986/2006.

35. SI 1986/2007.
36. SI 1989/947.
37. SI 1989/948. Provisions relating to membership, procedure and functions of the Authority are made by the Special Hospitals Service Authority (Functions and Membership) Regulations 1989, SI 1989/949.

CHAPTER 2

Hospitals managed under the National Health Service Act 1977

2.1 OUTLINE OF THE LEGISLATIVE STRUCTURE OF HOSPITALS WITHIN THE NATIONAL HEALTH SERVICE

2.1.1 Introductory

The object of the National Health Service Act 1977 is to maintain the establishment in England and Wales of a comprehensive health service available to all in need of hospital, specialist or general practitioner or dental or optical services, or of those public health services such as maternity and child welfare clinics, midwifery, health visitors or home nursing formerly provided by local authorities. The services provided are generally free at point of use and are, subject to numerous exceptions, free of charge[1] either to the patients or to their relatives except in respect of private or part-paying hospital patients as noted elsewhere. Hospital charges are discussed in Chapter 22.

The National Health Service Act 1946 established the basis of the scheme and came into force, for all practical purposes, on 5 July 1948. The National Health Service Reorganisation Act 1973 made considerable modifications to the administration of the health service, and further major modifications, including the power to establish National Health Service trusts within the structure of the National Health Service, were introduced by the National Health Service and Community Care Act 1990. Under the old arrangements, although the Minister (and later the Secretary of State[2]) was responsible for both the hospital service and general medical, ophthalmic and dental services they were administered by separate agencies. So also local authorities had a considerable jurisdiction in the health field. The 1973 Act abolished this and brought the other health services under the same management. The 1977 Act consolidated the bulk of the legislation into a single statute.

The duty of the Secretary of State[2] in respect of the provision of health services is now laid down in section 1(1) of the National Health Service Act 1977 which reads:

'**1.**—(1) It is the Secretary of State's duty to continue the promotion in England and Wales of a comprehensive health service designed to secure improvement —
  (a) in the physical and mental health of the people of England and Wales and
  (b) in the prevention, diagnosis and treatment of illness,
and for that purpose to provide or secure the effective provision of services in accordance with this Act.'

Section 1(1) of the Act of 1977 must be read with sections 2, 3, and 4. Section 2 provides for the general powers and duties of the Secretary of State in respect of the National Health Service:

'**2.**—(1) Without prejudice to the Secretary of State's powers apart from this subsection, he has power—
  (a) to provide such services as he considers appropriate for the purpose of discharging any duty imposed on him by this Act; and
  (b) to do any other thing whatsoever which is calculated to facilitate, or is conducive or incidental to, the discharge of such a duty.'

Section 3 provides as follows:

'**3.**—(1) It is the Secretary of State's duty to provide throughout England and Wales, to such extent as he considers necessary to meet all reasonable requirements—
  (a) hospital accommodation;
  (b) other accommodation for the purpose of any service provided under this Act;
  (c) medical, dental, nursing and ambulance services;
  (d) such other facilities for the care of expectant and nursing mothers and young children as he considers are appropriate as part of the health service;[3]
  (e) such facilities for the prevention of illness, the care of persons suffering from illness and the after-care of persons who have suffered from illness as he considers are appropriate as part of the health service.
  (f) such other services as are required for the diagnosis and treatment of illness.'
(2) Where any hospital provided by the Secretary of State in accordance with this Act was a voluntary hospital transferred by virtue of the National Health Service Act 1946, and—
  (a) the character and associations of that hospital before its transfer were such as to link it with a particular religious denomination, then
  (b) regard shall be had in the general administration of the hospital to the preservation of that character and those associations.'

Section 3(3) provides that nothing in sections 2 or 3 affects the provisions of Part II of the Act (which relates to arrangements with practitioners for the provision of medical, dental, ophthalmic and pharmaceutical services).

Section 5(1) confers on the Secretary of State powers and duties in respect of the medical inspection and treatment of pupils at schools maintained by local education authorities. Section 5(1A) imposes a duty on the Secretary of State to provide to such extent as he considers necessary to meet all reasonable requirements for the dental inspection, treatment and education in dental health of pupils in attendance at schools maintained by local education authorities or at grant maintained schools. Under section 5(1)(b) he has the duty of providing a family planning service and supplying contraceptive substances and appliances to the extent which in his opinion is necessary to meet all reasonable requirements.

By virtue of section 5(2) the Secretary of State is empowered, as opposed to obliged, to provide invalid carriages (or other form of transport if so requested) for disabled persons. He also has power to arrange for the provision of treatment and accommodation outside Great Britain for persons suffering from respiratory tuberculosis. Authority for the Secretary to provide a microbiological service is contained in section 5(2)(c). The aim of this service is to control the spread of infectious diseases and carry on such other activities that, in the opinion of the Secretary of State, can conveniently be carried on in conjunction with that service. The service may include the provision of laboratories and may be subject to financial charges under section 5(2A).

The legal nature of the Secretary of State's duty to provide health services, and its non-enforceability at the instance of an aggrieved patient, is discussed in Chapter 6 pp. 153–155, below.

The effect of the 1973 Act was to impose upon the Secretary of State the duties formerly carried out by regional hospital boards, boards of governors of teaching hospitals and hospital management committees, as well as those of former local health authorities, and to provide for the discharge of those functions on his behalf and subject to his directions by Regional and Area Health Authorities and by Area Health Authorities (Teaching). Since 1982, when the Health Services Act 1980 came into force, Area Health Authorities have been replaced by District Health Authorities, some with the designation '(Teaching)', this being later discontinued.

Special hospitals for persons subject to detention under the Mental Health Act 1983 who require treatment under conditions of special security on account of their dangerous, violent or criminal propensities continued to be managed directly by the Secretary of State, but are now managed individually under the auspices of the Special Hospitals Service Authority.[4] The London postgraduate teaching hospitals named in Schedule 2 of the Act continued to be managed by Boards of Governors ('preserved Boards') but had all ceased to be so managed by 1 April 1984 at which date all preservation Orders were spent. The London teaching hospitals are now managed under the Authorities for London Postgraduate Teaching Hospitals Regulations 1990.[5]

2.1.2 The constitutional position of health authorities

The provisions relating to the management of health and hospital services provided by the Secretary of State under the National Health Service Act 1977, so far as they relate to hospital activities, are set out below. Since all the authorities so constituted were formerly regarded as operating a Crown service, it appeared that they were formerly not bound by any statutory provision not binding on the Crown[6] unless by necessary implication or expressly by the terms of the statute they are. A number of statutes were nevertheless substantially applied by administrative action. Section 60 of the National Health Service and Community Care Act has now expressly removed Crown status from health authorities within the National Health Service, with some exceptions noted elsewhere in this book.

2.1.3 Effect of the National Health Service Reorganisation Act 1973

On 1 April 1974 the responsibility for the administration of virtually the whole of the hospital and specialist services, until then provided on behalf of the Secretary of State by boards and committees established under the provisions of the 1946 Act, became the responsibility of the Secretary of State.[7] However, by delegation by him, they are to be carried on by Regional Health Authorities and District Health Authorities constituted under sections 8 and 9 of the 1977 Act, as amended.[8] Similarly, these same Authorities are, again by delegation, responsible for the administration of those health services which were formerly the responsibility of local health authorities, unless any such services were transferred to a local authority social services committee under section 2 of the Local Authority Social Services Act 1970. The responsibility for social services to hospital patients, such as had in the past been undertaken by medical social workers employed by hospital boards and committees, is now likewise the responsibility of the appropriate local authority under the 1970 Act, though medical social workers and others concerned may still be carrying out their duties at hospitals.

2.2 EXECUTIVE BODIES

2.2.1 Regional Health Authorities

Introductory

In addition to the National Health Service bodies to be examined in this section, the institution of the National Health Service trust was introduced into legislation by the National Health Service and Community Care Act 1990. Although such bodies are within the National Health Service (albeit independent of regions and districts as regards their operations) National Health Service trusts are sufficiently independent to merit separate discussion. Consideration is therefore reserved for a separate section at the end of this chapter.

A Regional Health Authority appointed by the Secretary of State under the provisions of section 8 and Part I of Schedule 5 of the 1977 Act is a body corporate with perpetual succession and a common seal.[9] Paragraph 1(2) of Part I of the Schedule imposes on the Secretary of State the duty of consulting with named bodies when appointing members, without being bound by their advice.

The regions for which Regional Health Authorities are established are determined by the Secretary of State in accordance with the National Health Service (Determination of Regions) Order 1981.[10]

The Regional and District Health Authorities (Membership and Procedure) Regulations 1990[11] provide for membership of such authorities, including joint membership and officers, non-officer membership, the period of tenure of office, termination of tenure of office, eligibility for reappointment and disqualification for appointment. The Regulations also contain provisions for the constitution and proceedings of Regional Health Authorities which relate to the appointment and powers of the vice-chairman (the appointment of chairman having been already covered by the membership provisions), the appointment of committees and sub-committees, arrangements for the exercise of functions and powers, meetings and proceedings, and the disability of chairman and members in relation to proceedings in which they have a pecuniary interest.

Admission of press and public to meetings

Regional and District Health Authorities are public bodies to which the provisions of the Public Bodies (Admission to Meetings) Act 1960 apply. The effect of the Act was summarised in a departmental Circular to regional hospital boards, a copy of that summary having since been made available to Regional and District Health Authorities under cover of a later Circular.[12] It reads as follows:

'4. Subject to what is said below, any meeting of a *Regional or District Health Authority* will be open to the public and if during a meeting the *Regional or District Health Authority* resolves itself into committee, the proceedings in committee will be treated as if they were proceedings of the *Regional or District Health Authority* (section 1(1) and 1(6)).

5. The *Regional or District Health Authority* may by resolution exclude the public from the whole or part of a meeting "whenever publicity would be prejudicial to the public interest by reason of the confidential nature of the business to be

transacted, or for other special reasons stated in the resolution and arising from the nature of that business or of proceedings"; and these special reasons may include "the need to receive or consider recommendations or advice from sources other than members, committees or sub-committees" of the *Regional or District Health Authority* "without regard to the subject or purport of the recommendations or advice" (section 1(2) and 1(3)).

6. Where a meeting is required by the Act to be open to the public in whole or in part, the *Regional or District Health Authority* has a duty under section 1(4):

(a)   to give public notice of the time and place of the meeting by posting it at the *Regional or District Health Authority* offices at least three clear days before the meeting or, if the meeting is convened at shorter notice, then at the time it is convened;

(b)   to supply, on request and on payment of postage or other necessary charge for transmission, for the benefit of any newspaper, a copy of the agenda as supplied to members of the *Regional or District Health Authority* but excluding, if thought fit, any item during which the meeting is likely not to be open to the public, together with such further statements or particulars, if any, as are necessary to indicate the nature of the items included or, if thought fit, copies of any reports or other documents supplied to *Regional or District Health Authority* members;

[In so far as the supply of this material to the Press or to a member of the public is "publication" of any defamatory matter contained therein, then that publication is privileged, unless it is proved to be made with malice.][13]

(c)   to afford so far as practicable to accredited representatives of newspapers, attending for the purpose of reporting the proceedings for those newspapers, reasonable facilities for taking their report and, unless the meeting is held in premises not belonging to the *Regional or District Health Authority* or not on the telephone, for telephoning the report at their own expense.

7. The above references to a newspaper apply also to a news agency whether it serves the Press or the broadcasting services. But the *Regional or District Health Authority* is not required to permit the taking of photographs of any proceedings, or the making of a visual or aural broadcast or recording, or the making of a running commentary (section 1(7)).

8. The above provisions are without prejudice to the *Regional or District Health Authority's* power of exclusion to suppress or prevent disorderly conduct or other misbehaviour at a meeting (section 1(8)).'

In *R v Liverpool City Council, ex parte Liverpool Taxi Fleet Operators Association* (1975)[14] it was held that there must be reasonable but not unlimited accommodation for members of the public. In that case it was held that where a public body had made reasonable arrangements to accommodate the public wishing to attend one of its meetings but in the event so many people wished to attend that it was quite impossible to accommodate them all, that would be a special reason 'arising from the nature of [the] business or of the proceedings', within section 1(2) of the Act, justifying a decision of the committee, arrived at honestly and fairly, that the only solution would be to exclude all members of the public.

Functions of Regional Health Authorities

The functions of Regional Health Authorities are imposed on them by the National Health Service Functions (Directions to Authorities and Administrative Arrangements) Regulations 1991[8] wherein those authorities are directed to carry out on behalf of the Secretary of State specific functions under particular sections of the National Health Service Act 1977, subject to such restrictions and limitations as are laid down in the Regulations. In general terms, the effect of the Regulations is to delegate to each Regional Authority in respect of its own region all the powers and duties of the former regional hospital boards, boards of governors and hospital management committees and of the former local health authorities. But this all-over delegation is coupled with a direction to the Regional Health Authorities themselves by direction to delegate almost all those same functions to District Health Authorities, also subject to certain restrictions.

Wales

In Wales, there is no regional health authority and the functions of the regional authorities are left with the Secretary of State.

2.2.2   District Health Authorities

Introductory

By sections 8 and 9 of the National Health Service Act 1977 (as subsequently amended by the Health Services Act 1980),[15] District Health Authorities constituted in accordance with the provisions of paragraphs 2 to 5 of Schedule 5 of the Act have been formed to cover in aggregate the whole of England and Wales.[16] Every such authority is a body corporate with perpetual succession and a common seal.

Determination of Districts

The National Health Service (Determination of Districts) Order 1981[17] makes provision for the following matters:

1. the determination of the new Districts (Article 3 and Schedule 1, England and Schedule 2, Wales);
2. the transfer of staff, their contracts and training arrangements; (Article 4–5 and Schedule 3);
3. trust property in old areas (Articles 6–11 and Schedule 3);
4. the enforceability of rights and liabilities (Article 12);
5. the winding-up and accounts of the old authorities (Articles 13–14);
6. the continuance of the exercise of functions (Article 14);

7. the modification of arrangements under the National Assistance Act 1948 and accommodation and services available for payment (Articles 16–17);
8. for the new arrangements in respect of the then re-constituted Family Practitioner Committees (Article 18);
9. for transitional provisions relating to the Health Service Commissioners (article 19); and
10. for the appointment of persons to act on behalf of others unable to act for themselves by reason of mental or other incapacity (article 20).

Establishment of District Health Authorities

Under the National Health Service (Constitution of District Health Authorities) Order 1981,[18] authorities were constituted for each of the districts established under the above-mentioned Determination of Districts Order.

As regards membership and procedure of District Health Authorities, parallel provision is made for them in the Regional and District Health Authorities (Membership and Procedure) Regulations 1990,[11] for details of which see p. 22 of this chapter.

2.2.3 Functions of Regions and Districts

The National Health Service Functions (Directions to Authorities and Administration Arrangements) Regulations 1991[19] provide, so far as relevant for present purposes, as follows:

'PART II

DIRECTIONS TO REGIONAL AUTHORITIES

Functions exercisable by Regional Authorities

3.—(1) Subject to paragraph (2) and regulation 4, every Regional Authority shall exercise the specified health service functions on behalf of the Secretary of State—

(a) in so far as those functions consist of providing or securing the provision of services to patients, other than the services specified in sub-paragraph (b) of this paragraph, for the benefit of—
   (i) persons usually resident in its region;
   (ii) persons resident outside the United Kingdom who are present in its region;
(b) in so far as those functions consist of providing or securing the provision of—
   (i) accident and emergency services, including ambulance services provided in connection with those services; and
   (ii) any other services which the Secretary of State may direct, for the benefit of all persons present in its region; and
(c) in so far as those functions consist of any other functions, generally as respects its region.

(2) The functions exercisable by a Regional Authority under paragraph (1)(a)

do not include providing or securing the provision of any services which are, or are to be, purchased by the members of a recognised fundholding practice in accordance with Regulations under section 15(7) of the 1990 Act.

(3) A Regional Authority shall exercise the specified health service functions in accordance with paragraph (1) at or from hospitals, establishments and facilities owned by the Secretary of State for the purposes of the health service and situated in its region or anywhere outside its region as the Secretary of State may direct, as well as by means of National Health Service and other contracts.

Restriction on the exercise of functions by Regional Authorities

4.—(1) The exercise by a Regional Authority of specified health service functions is subject to such limitations as the Secretary of State may direct and shall be in accordance with any directions which are given by the Secretary of State.

(2) Nothing in these Regulations is to be taken as giving directions for the exercise of any function conferred on or vested in the Secretary of State with respect to the making of any Order or Regulations.

(3) Nothing in these Regulations enables a Regional Authority to exercise the functions of the Secretary of State under section 87(1) of the Act with respect to—

(a)   the compulsory acquisition of land; or

(b)   land or other property where the function is exercisable by a Family Authority by virtue of regulation 11(3)(a)

or to give directions to a District Authority which would empower a District Authority to exercise those functions.

(4) The power of the Secretary of State under section 2 of the Act is exercisable by a Regional Authority only to such extent as is necessary for the proper exercise of one or more other functions which the Secretary of State has directed that Authority to exercise on his behalf.

(5) Where, in the exercise of specified health service functions, arrangements are made with medical practitioners for the vaccination or immunisation of persons against disease, every medical practitioner providing general medical services shall, so far as is reasonably practicable, be given an opportunity to participate in the arrangements.

(6) Approval of a medical practitioner for the purposes of section 12(2) of the Mental Health Act 1983 (approval of medical specialists) as having special experience in the diagnosis and treatment of mental disorder shall be given only—

(a)   after the carrying out of such consultations, and obtaining of such advice, as the Secretary of State shall direct;

(b)   for such periods as the Secretary of State shall direct.

(7) The exercise of the Secretary of State's function under section 3(1)(c) of the Act with respect to the provision of ambulance services is subject to obtaining his approval to the proposed arrangements for such exercise.

(8) In the exercise of the Secretary of State's specified health service functions under section 25 of the Act, such charges shall be made with respect to the supplies of human blood as are determined by the Secretary of State.

PART III

DIRECTIONS TO DISTRICT AUTHORITIES

Functions to be made exercisable by District Authorities in England

5.—(1) Subject to paragraph (2) and regulation 6, every Regional Authority shall secure, by a direction given by an instrument in writing, that each District Authority of which the district is included in its region shall exercise—

(a) functions exercisable under regulation 3(1)(a) for the benefit of—
    (i) persons usually resident in its district;
    (ii) persons resident outside the United Kingdom who are present in its district;
(b) functions exercisable under regulation 3(1)(b) for the benefit of persons present in its district;
(c) functions exercisable under regulation 3(1)(c) generally as respects its district;

at or from hospitals, establishments and facilities owned by the Secretary of State for the purpose of the health service and situated in its district or anywhere outside its district that the Secretary of State or the relevant Regional Authority may direct, as well as by means of National Health Service and other contracts.

(2) The functions exercisable by a District Authority under paragraph (1) do not include functions under—

(a) section 19(1) and (2) of, and paragraphs 1, 2 and 3 of Schedule 6 to, the Act (recognition of advisory committees);
(b) section 25 of the Act (supply of human blood);
(c) section 12(2) of the Mental Health Act 1983 (approval of medical specialists).

(3) Each Regional Authority shall secure that no directions are given to any District Authority directing it to exercise any functions under the enactments specified in paragraph (2)(a), (b) or (c).

Restriction on exercise of functions by District Authorities in England

6.—(1) The exercise by a District Authority in England of functions to which regulation 5(1) applies is subject to such limitations as the Secretary of State may direct and shall be in accordance with any directions which are given by the Secretary of State or, subject to any such directions, by the relevant Regional Authority.

(2) The exercise by a District Authority in England of functions to which regulation 5(1) applies is subject to the provisions of regulation 4(2), (5), (7) and (8).

(3) The power of the Secretary of State under section 2 of the Act is exercisable by a District Authority in England only to such extent as is necessary for the proper exercise of one or more other functions which the relevant Regional Authority has directed to be exercisable by that District Authority.

Functions exercisable by District Authorities in Wales

7.—(1) Subject to paragraph (2) and regulation 8, every District Authority in Wales shall exercise on behalf of the Secretary of State the specified health service functions except those under section 19(1) and (2) of, and paragraphs 1, 2 and 3 of Schedule 6 to the Act (recognition of advisory committees)—

(a) in so far as those functions consist of providing or securing the provision of services to patients under the Act, other than the services specified in sub-paragraph (b) of this paragraph, for the benefit of—
    (i) persons usually resident in its district;
    (ii) persons resident outside the United Kingdom who are present in its district;
(b) in so far as those functions consist of providing or securing the provision of—
    (i) accident and emergency services, including ambulance services provided in connection with those services; and
    (ii) any other services which the Secretary of State may direct, for the benefit of all persons present in its district; and

(c) in so far as they consist of any other functions, generally as respects its district.

(2) The functions exercisable by a District Authority in Wales under paragraph (1)(a) do not include the providing or securing the provision of any services which are, or are to be, purchased by the members of a recognized fund-holding practice in accordance with regulations under section 15(7) of the 1990 Act.

(3) A District Authority in Wales shall exercise the specified health service functions in accordance with paragraph (1) at or from hospitals, establishments and facilities owned by the Secretary of State for the purposes of the health service and situated in its district or anywhere outside its district that the Secretary of State may direct, as well as by means of National Health Service and other contracts.

Restrictions on exercise of functions by District Authorities in Wales

8.—(1) The exercise by a District Authority in Wales of the specified health service functions is subject to the provisions of regulation 4(2), (5), (6), (7) and (8) and such limitations as the Secretary of State may direct and shall be in accordance with any directions which are given by the Secretary of State.

(2) Nothing in these Regulations enables a District Authority in Wales to exercise the functions of the Secretary of State under section 87(1) of the Act with respect to—

(a) the compulsory acquisition of land; or
(b) land or other property where the function is exercisable by a Family Authority under regulation 11(3)(a).

(3) The power of the Secretary of State under section 2 of the Act is exercisable by a District Authority in Wales only to such extent as is necessary for the proper exercise of one more other functions which the Secretary of State has directed that Authority to exercise on his behalf.

PART IV

ADMINISTRATION ARRANGEMENTS

Arrangements by Regional Authorities for exercise of functions

9. Subject to any directions which may be given by the Secretary of State as to its exercise, any function exercisable by a Regional Authority pursuant to a direction given under section 13 of the Act may by arrangement with that Authority be exercised on its behalf by—

(a) another Regional Authority;
(b) a committee or sub-committee of another Regional Authority;
(c) another body of which the members consist only of that and other Regional Authorities; or
(d) an officer of another Regional Authority or of such other body.

Arrangements by District Authorities for exercise of functions

10.—(1) Subject to any directions which may be given by the Secretary of State and, in the case of a District Authority in England, to any directions given by the relevant Regional Authority as to the exercise of any function exercisable by virtue of a direction given under section 14 of the Act, functions exercisable by a District Authority by virtue of any provision of the Act may by arrangement with that Authority be exercised on its behalf by—

(a) another District Authority;
(b) a committee or sub-committee of another District Authority;
(c) another body of which the members consist only of that and other District Authorities; or

(d) an officer of another District Authority or of such other body.

(2) Subject to any directions which may be given by the Secretary of State, functions of a District Authority exercisable by virtue of an Order under section 103(1) of the Act may by arrangement with that Authority be exercised on its behalf by a Family Authority.'

2.3 RELATIONS OF HEALTH AUTHORITIES WITH OTHER STATUTORY BODIES UNDER THE NATIONAL HEALTH SERVICE ACT 1977

2.3.1 Central administration

The Health Services Act 1980 abolished the Central Health Services Council and established a new scheme of statutory advisory committees. The constitution of standing advisory committees is provided for in the National Health Service (Standing Advisory Committees) Order 1981[20] which provides, relevantly, as follows:

'Constitution of Standing Advisory Committees
2.—(1) The Standing Advisory Committees specified in column (1) of Part I of the Schedule to this Order shall continue to be constituted for the purpose of advising the Secretary of State on the services mentioned in column (2) of the Schedule opposite the names of the respective Committees.

(2) The Standing Advisory Committee specified in column (1) of Part II of the Schedule to this Order is hereby constituted for the purpose of advising the Secretary of State on the services mentioned in column (2) of the Schedule opposite the name of that Committee.

(3) The said services are services under the National Health Service Act 1977.

(4) Each of the said Committees shall consist of such number of members as the Secretary of State may from time to time determine.

Revocation of regulations
3. The National Health Service (Standing Advisory Committees) Order 1949, the National Health Service (Standing Advisory Committees) (Amendment) Order 1962, the National Health Service (Standing Advisory Committees) (Amendment) Order 1966 and the National Health Service (Standing Advisory Committees) (Amendment) Order 1974 are hereby revoked.

SCHEDULE

PART I

Column (1)	Column (2)
The Standing Medical Advisory Committee	The medical services
The Standing Dental Advisory Committee	The dental services
The Standing Pharmaceutical Advisory Committee	The pharmaceutical services including hospital pharmaceutical services
The Standing Nursing and Midwifery Advisory Committee	The nursing and midwifery services

PART II

Column (1)	Column (2)
The Standing Advisory Committee on Vaccination and Immunisation	The provision of vaccination and immunisation services being facilities for the prevention of illness

The appointment and membership of the Committees is governed by the National Health Service (Standing Advisory Committees) Regulations 1981,[21] as follows:

'Terms of office of members

3. Subject to the following provisions of these regulations, the term of office of members shall be for such period not exceeding four years, expiring on 31 March in any year, as the Secretary of State shall specify on making the appointment.

Casual vacancies

4. Where, for any reason, a person ceases to be a member before the expiration of the period for which he was appointed, the term of office of any member appointed in his place shall be the remainder of that period.

Termination of term of office

5.—(1) A member may resign his office at any time during the period for which he was appointed by given notice in writing to the Secretary of State.

(2) A person who at the time of his appointment as a member of an Advisory Committee was the holder of one of the offices specified in paragraph (3) below (in these regulations referred to as "an office-holder") shall cease to be a member of that Advisory Committee if he ceases to hold such office.

(3) The offices referred to in paragraph (2) above are—
The President of the Royal College of Physicians of London;
The President of the Royal College of Surgeons of England;
The President of the Royal College of Obstetricians and Gynaecologists;
The President of the Royal College of Psychiatrists;
The President of the Royal College of Pathologists;
The President of the Royal College of Nursing of the United Kingdom;
The President of the Royal College of Midwives;
The Chairman of the Council of the British Medical Association;
The Chairman of the Council of the British Dental Association;
The Chairman of the Council of the Royal College of General Practitioners;
The President of the Faculty of Community Medicine;
The President of the Pharmaceutical Society of Great Britain;
The President of the Royal College of Radiologists;
The Dean of the Faculty of Anaesthetists; and
The Dean of the Faculty of Occupational Medicine.

Appointment of deputies

6.—(1) Any office-holder may notify the Secretary of State in writing of another member of the body in which he holds office whom he has nominated as his deputy for such period or any part of such period as he holds that office.

(2) Any person nominated pursuant to paragraph (1) above may, if

subsequently appointed by the Secretary of State, act as a member of the Advisory Committee of which the office-holder is a member in the place of that office-holder until either—

(a) the relevant office-holder ceases to hold office, or

(b) the Secretary of State notifies such person in writing that his appointment pursuant to this paragraph is terminated, whichever is the first to occur.

(3) Without prejudice to the generality of paragraph (2)(b) of this regulation the Secretary of State may in particular terminate such appointment at the request of the relevant office-holder if that office-holder either nominates some other person to be his deputy or proposes to the Secretary of State that he wishes to attend future meetings of the Advisory Committee himself.

Eligibility for re-appointment to membership

7. A member shall, on the expiration of his term of office, be eligible for re-appointment.'

2.3.2 Clinical Standards Advisory Group

Section 62 of the National Health Service and Community Care Act 1990 established this Group, in the following manner:

'62.—(1) There shall be established in accordance with this section a Clinical Standards Advisory Group (in this section referred to as "the Advisory Group") which shall have the following functions—

(a) in accordance with a request made by the Health Ministers or any one of them, to provide advice on the standards of clinical care for, and the access to and availability of services to, National Health Service patients and, in this connection, to carry out such investigations into such matters (if any) and to make such reports in relation thereto as the Health Ministers may require;

(b) in accordance with a request made by one or more health service bodies, to provide advice on, to carry out investigations into and to report on the standards of clinical care for, and the access to and availability of services to, National Health Service patients for whom services are or are to be provided by or on behalf of the body or bodies concerned; and

(c) such other functions as may be prescribed by regulations.

(2) The Advisory Group shall consist of a chairman and other members appointed by the Health Ministers and regulations may—

(a) require that one or more members of the Advisory Group shall be appointed from persons nominated by such body or bodies as may be specified in the regulations; and

(b) provide that one or more of the members who are not appointed from persons so nominated must fulfil such conditions or hold such posts as may be so specified.

(3) Regulations may make provision as to—

(a) the appointment, tenure and vacation of office of the chairman and members of the Advisory Group;

(b) the appointment of and the exercise of functions by committees and sub-committees of the Advisory Group (including committees and sub-committees consisting wholly or partly of persons who are not members of the Advisory Group);

(c) the procedure of the Advisory Group and any committees or sub-committees thereof; and

(d)   the attendance at meetings of the Advisory Group or any committee or sub-committee thereof of persons appointed by the Health Ministers and the extent of their participation in such meetings.'

The remaining provisions of section 62 relate to proceedings of the Group and to the payment of remuneration and travelling expenses.

2.3.3   Local Advisory Committees

Regional Advisory Committees: recognition and functions

Section 19(1) of the 1977 Act provides for recognition by the Secretary of State of committees formed for the region of a Regional Health Authority (or for Wales) as representative of (a) the medical practitioners of the region; (b) the dental practitioners of the region; (c) the nurses and midwives of the region; (d) the registered pharmacists of the region; and (e) the ophthalmic and dispensing opticians of the region. These committees are called the Regional Medical, Dental, Nursing and Midwifery, Pharmaceutical and Optical Committees respectively. Provision is also made in Schedule 6, paragraph 1(1) of the Act, for the recognition by the Secretary of State of committees representative of any category of persons (other than a category mentioned above) who provide services forming part of the health service and also for the recognition of committees representative of any two or more of the categories of persons mentioned or referred to above. Schedule 6, paragraph 2 of the Act provides that the Secretary of State may withdraw recognition from a committee, recognising in its place another committee established within the above provisions of the section.

Duties of Advisory Committees: obligation of Regional Health Authority

Schedule 6, paragraph (4) of the Act provides:

'(4) It is the duty of a committee duly recognised by reference to the region of a Regional Health Authority or the district of a District Health Authority[22]—
(a)   to advise the Authority on the Authority's provision of services of a kind provided by the categories of persons of whom the committee is representative, and
(b)   to perform such other funtions as may be prescribed,
and it shall be the duty of the Authority to consult the committee with respect to such matters, and on such occasions, as may be prescribed.'

Welsh Advisory Committees: recognition and functions

There being no Regional Health Authority for Wales, provision was made in the National Health Service Reorganisation Act 1973 adapting the provisions of section 8. The special provisions for Wales are now to be found in section 19(2)(a) and Schedule 6, paragraph 3 of the 1977 Act. The other provisions of section 19(1) and Schedule 6, paragraphs 1, 2 and 5 are applicable.

The effect is that there are Welsh Medical, Dental, Nursing and Midwifery, Pharmaceutical and Optical Committees operating under the same terms as those in the Regions in England.

Expenses of Advisory Committees

Regional Health Authorities are authorised, but are not obliged unless so directed, to pay expenses etc. of members of local advisory committees within the limits laid down in Schedule 6, paragraph 5 which provides:

'(5) An Authority may defray such expenses incurred by such a committee in performing the duty imposed on the committee by paragraphs 3 and 4 above as the Authority considers reasonable, and those expenses may include travelling and other allowances and compensation for loss of remunerative time at such rates as the Secretary of State may determine with the approval of the Minister for the Civil Service.'

An Authority in the paragraph means, in Wales, the Secretary of State and, in England, the Regional or District Health Authority as the case may be.

District Advisory Committees: recognition and functions

District advisory committees in all respects corresponding with regional advisory committees under section 19 and Schedule 6 (save that their functions relate to the District Health Authority and not to the regional Health Authority) shall be recognised both in England and Wales under the provisions of section 19(3):[23]

'(3) Where the Secretary of State is satisfied that a committee formed for the district of a District Health Authority is representative of persons of any of the categories mentioned in paragraphs (a) to (e) in subsection (1) it shall be his duty to recognise the committee.'
    A committee recognised in pursuance of this subsection shall be called the District Medical, Dental, Nursing and Midwifery, Pharmaceutical or Optical Committee, as the case may be, for the district in question.'

Accordingly, the same pattern of functional advisory committees is reproduced in the districts. They have the same tasks to perform.

2.4   CO-OPERATION AND ASSISTANCE BETWEEN HEALTH AUTHORITIES, LOCAL AUTHORITIES AND VOLUNTARY BODIES

2.4.1   Local authorities and voluntary bodies

Health authorities and local authorities: establishment of consultative committees

Section 22(1) of the Act of 1977 provides as follows:

'**22.**—(1) In exercising their respective functions Health Authorities and local authorities shall co-operate with one another in order to secure and advance the health and welfare of the people of England and Wales.'

The functions of local social services authorities are set out in section 21 and Schedule 8 of the Act, and include the care of mothers and young children; prevention, care and after-care, and home help and laundry facilities.

Section 22(2) specifically requires the establishment of joint consultative committees which shall advise District Health Authorities and the corresponding local authorities there indicated on the performance of their duties under section 22(1) and on the planning and operation of services of common concern to those authorities. The Secretary of State has power by Order under section 22(4) to deal with various matters relating to the composition and functioning of such joint consultative committees. This has been done by the Health Authorities and Local Authorities Joint Consultative Committees Order 1974[24]. Practical guidance is given to health authorities on the setting up of joint consultative committees in Circular HRC(74)19. The Circular also commends the second report of the working party on collaboration.

Supply of goods and services by or on behalf of the Secretary of State

The supply of goods and services and the provision of other facilities of a kind used or available in the health service to local authorities and other public bodies is dealt with in section 26, the two main subsections reading as follows:

'26.—(1) The Secretary of State may—
   (a) supply to local authorities, and to such public bodies or classes of public bodies as he may determine, any goods or materials of a kind used in the health services;
   (b) make available to local authorities, and to those bodies or classes of bodies, any facilities (including the use of any premises and the use of any vehicle, plant or apparatus) provided by him for any service under this Act and the services of persons employed by the Secretary of State or by a health authority;
   (c) carry out maintenance work in connection with any land or building for the maintenance of which a local authority is responsible.'

Section 26(3) provides as follows:

'(3) The Secretary of State shall make available to local authorities—
   (a) any services or other facilities (excluding the services of any person but including goods or materials, the use of any premises and the use of any vehicle, plant or apparatus) provided under this Act,
   (b) the services provided as part of the health service by any person employed by the Secretary of State or a Health Authority, and
   (c) the services of any medical practitioner, dental practitioner or nurse employed by the Secretary of State or a Health Authority otherwise than to provide services which are part of the health service, so far as is reasonably necessary and practicable to enable local authorities to

discharge their functions relating to social services, education and public health.'

While under section 26(1) the Secretary of State has discretion whether or not to do any of the things he is there permitted to do, section 26(3) imposes a duty to make available to local authorities the services and facilities there referred to *so far as is reasonably necessary and practicable* to enable local authorities to discharge their functions relating to social services, education and public health.

For the purposes of section 26(1)(b) or (3)(b) or (c), the Secretary of State may give such directions to health authorities to make the services of their officers available as he considers appropriate. Except in an emergency the Secretary of State, before making the services of a person available under section 26(1)(b) or under section 26(3)(b) or (c), is under a duty to consult either the officer or the officer's representative body, e.g. union. The valid exercise of emergency powers is in turn dependent on the requirement imposed by section 27(2), namely that the Secretary of State shall have previously consulted the relevant body about the making available of services in an emergency. Section 27(3) provides that it shall be the duty of a health authority to comply with any such direction. Terms for supply of goods and services etc., under section 26(1) and (3), including financial terms, are to be as may be agreed. In default of agreement between the Secretary of State and the local authority as to charges to be made by the Secretary of State for services or facilities which under section 26(3) he is under a duty to provide, the matter will be determined by arbitration, as provided by section 27(4).

The effect of the National Health Service (Vehicles) Order 1974[25] is to make provision for National Health Service vehicles made available for the use of any person, body or local authority to be exempted from the statutory requirements in respect of vehicle excise duty and third party insurance, provided that they are used in accordance with the terms under which they are made available.

Supply of goods and materials to persons providing general medical, dental, ophthalmic or pharmaceutical services

Such goods, materials and other facilities as may be prescribed by Regulations may be provided for persons in the above categories. The supply of goods, materials and other facilities under section 26(2), like provision under section 26(1) or (3), may be subject to charges under section 27(4) and to section 27(5) in respect of vehicles excise and third party insurance.

Supply of goods and services by local authorities

Section 28(1) of the 1977 Act allows local authorities to supply goods or services to any health authority and, so far as relates to his functions under the National Health Service Acts, to the Secretary of State. The section also provides for the variation or revocation of that authorisation by an order under section 1(5) of the Local Authorities (Goods and Services) Act 1970.

The making of services available to health authorities by local authorities is obligatory to the extent laid down in section 12(2) of that Act which provides:

'(2)—Every local authority shall make available to Health Authorities acting in the area of the local authority the services of persons employed by the local authority for the purposes of the authority's functions under the Local Authority Social Services Act 1970 so far as is reasonably necessary and practicable to enable Health Authorities to discharge their functions under this Act.'

The purpose of the subsection is primarily to secure to the health service, particularly to hospitals, the continued availability of medical social workers and others who transferred to local authority employment under the 1970 Act.

2.4.2   Voluntary organisations and other bodies

Provision of services under the National Health Service Act 1977 by voluntary and other bodies and persons

Section 23(1) of the 1977 Act provides as follows:

'**23.**—(1) The Secretary of State may, where he considers it appropriate, arrange with any person or body (including a voluntary organisation) for that person or body to provide, or assist in providing, any service under this Act.'

'Voluntary 'organisation' is defined in section 128(1) of the 1977 Act as meaning 'a body the activities of which are carried on otherwise than for profit', excluding any public or local authority.

Provision of facilities (including goods or materials, premises and vehicles) to persons and bodies providing services

Subsections (2) to (5) of section 23 of the 1977 Act authorise the provision by the Secretary of State of facilities, including goods or materials, or the use of any premises and of any vehicle, plant or apparatus and of persons in connection with anything made available on such terms as may be agreed, including terms as to the making of payments by or to the Secretary of State. Such facilities may be made available by the Secretary of State:

1. to a person or body providing services under the National Health Service pursuant to section 23(1) of the 1977 Act;

2. to a voluntary organisation eligible for assistance under section 64 or section 65 of the Health Services and Public Health Act 1968.

In this latter case, however, the facilities are made available in connection with the services provided by such voluntary organisation under section 23(2)(b) of the 1977 Act, as distinct from being made available in connection with services provided by the National Health Service itself. These latter provisions are commonly relied on by District Health Authorities to enter into agreements with voluntary organisations for the provision of hostels and other accommodation and services for former hospital patients. Such agreements often also rely on the power to make capital payments under section 28A of the 1977 Act which is discussed below.

Power to make payments towards expenditure on community services

Section 28A of the National Health Service Act 1977 provides, relevantly, as follows:

'28A.—(1) This section applies to the following authorities—
  (a) a District Health Authority; and
  (b) a special health authority established for a London Post-Graduate Teaching Hospital.
  (2) An authority to whom this section applies may, if they think fit, make payments—
  (a) to a local social services authority towards expenditure incurred or to be incurred by them in connection with any function which, by virtue of section 2(1) or (2) of the Local Authority Social Services Act 1970, is to be performed through their social services committee, other than functions under section 3 of the Disabled Persons (Employment) Act 1958;
  (b) to a district council, towards expenditure incurred or to be incurred by them in connection with their functions under section 8 of the Residential Homes Act 1980 or Part II of Schedule 9 to the Health and Social Services and Social Security Adjudications Act 1983 (meals and recreation for old people);
  (c) to an authority who are a local education authority for the purposes of the Education Acts 1944 to 1981, towards expenditure incurred or to be incurred by them in connection with their functions under those Acts, in so far as they perform those functions for the benefit of disabled persons;
  (d) to an authority who are a local authority for the purposes of the Housing Act 1957, towards expenditure incurred or to be incurred by them in connection with their functions under Part V of that Act (provision of housing accommodation); and
  (e) to the following bodies, in respect of expenditure incurred or to be incurred by them in connection with the provision of housing accommodation,—
    (i) a housing association, as defined in section 189(1) of the Housing Act 1957, which is registered by the Housing Corporation under section 13 of the Housing Act 1974;
    (ii) the Commission for the New Towns;
    (iii) a new town development corporation;

(iv) an urban development corporation established under the Local Government, Planning and Land Act 1980;
(v) the Housing Corporation; and
(vi) the Development Board for Rural Wales.

(3) A payment under this section may be made in respect of expenditure of a capital or of a revenue nature or in respect of both kinds of expenditure.

(4) No payment shall be made under this section in respect of any expenditure unless the expenditure has been recommended for a payment under this section by a joint consultative committee on which the authority proposing to make the payment are represented.

(5) The Secretary of State may by directions prescribe conditions relating to payments under this section.'

Further detailed requirements are contained in various Circulars and Notices issued by the Department of Health. Among other matters these include a requirement of repayment in respect of property acquired with money paid under this section, of an amount equal to the portion of the open market value of the property which is attributable to the expenditure of the payment. Similar provisions apply to Wales under section 28B of the 1977 Act. Sections 28A and 28B were added by section 4 of the Health Services Act 1980.

2.4.3   Ancillary services provided on behalf of the Secretary of State

Microbiological services, supplies of human blood and the supply of other substances or preparations not readily obtainable may be provided by Health Authorities on behalf of the Secretary of State under sections 5(2) and 25 of the 1977 Act.

The Secretary of State's power to make such provision is expressly limited by section 62 of the Act:

'**62.**—The Secretary of State shall exercise the powers conferred on him by the provisions of section 25 above (supplies not readily obtainable) [. . .] above only if and to the extent that he is satisfied that anything which he proposes to do or allow under those powers—

(a) will not to a significant extent interfere with the performance by him of any duty imposed on him by this Act to provide accommodation or services of any kind; and

(b) will not to a significant extent operate to the disadvantage of persons seeking or afforded admission or access to accommodation or services at health service hospitals (whether as resident or non-resident patients) otherwise than as private patients.'

2.4.4   Community Health Councils

Section 20 of the National Health Service Act 1977[26] provides:

'**20.**—(1) It is the Secretary of State's duty to establish in accordance with this section a council for the area of each Area Health Authority and a council for the district of each District Health Authority or separate councils for such separate parts of the areas or districts of those Authorities as he thinks fit, and such a council shall be called a Community Health Council.

(2) The Secretary of State—

(a) may if he thinks fit discharge this duty by establishing a Community Health Council for a district which includes the areas or parts of the areas of two or more Area Health Authorities or for a district which includes the districts or parts of the districts of two or more District Health Authorities;

(b) shall be treated as not having discharged that duty unless he secures that there is no part of the area of an Area Health Authority or for the district of a District Health Authority which is not included in some Community Health Council's district.

(3) The additional provisions of Schedule 7 to this Act have effect in relation to Community Health Councils.'

Schedule 7[27] to the Act makes the following detailed provisions:

'1. It is the duty of a Community Health Council (in this Schedule referred to as a "Council")—

(a) to represent the interests in the health service of the public in its district; and

(b) to perform such other functions as may be conferred on it by virtue of paragraph 2 below.

2. Regulations may provide as to—

(a) the membership of Councils (including the election by members of a Council and a chairman of the Council);

(b) the proceedings of Councils;

(c) the staff, premises and expenses of Councils;

(d) the consultation of Councils by Regional Health Authorities, NHS trusts, District Health Authorities or relevant Family Health Service Authorities with respect to such matters, and on such occasions, as may be prescribed;

(e) the furnishing of information to Councils by Regional and District Health Authorities, NHS trusts or relevant Family Health Services Authorities, and the right of members of Councils to enter and inspect premises controlled by such health authorities or NHS trusts;

(f) the consideration by Councils of matters relating to the operation of the health service within their districts, and the giving of advice by Councils to such Authorities [. . .] on such matters;

(g) the preparation and publication of reports by Councils on such matters, and the furnishing and publication by such Authorities [. . .] of comments on the reports; and

(h) the functions to be exercised by Councils are the functions exercisable by them by virtue of paragraph 1(a) above and the preceding provisions of this paragraph.

3. It is the Secretary of State's duty to exercise his power to make regulations in pursuance of paragraph 2(a) above so as to secure as respects each Council that—

(a) at least one member of the Council is appointed by each local authority of which the area or part of it is included in the Council's district, and at least half of the members of the Council consist of persons appointed by those local authorities;

(b) at least one third of the members are appointed in a prescribed manner by bodies (other than public or local authorities) of which the activities are carried on otherwise than for profit;

(c) the other members of the Council are appointed by such bodies, and in such manner and after such consultation as may be prescribed; and

(d) no member of the Council is also a member of the Regional Health Authority or Area or District Health Authority or Family Health Service Authority.

4. Nothing in paragraph 3 above affects the validity of anything done by or in relation to a Council during any period during which, by reason of a vacancy in the membership of the Council or a defect in the appointment of a member of it, a requirement included in regulations in pursuance of that paragraph is not satisfied.

5. The Secretary of State may by regulations—

(a) provide for the establishment of a body—

   (i) to advise Councils with respect to the performance of their functions, and to assist Councils in the performance of their functions; and

   (ii) to perform such other functions as may be prescribed; and

(b) provide for the membership, proceedings, staff, premises and expenses of that body.

6. The Secretary of State may pay to members of Councils and any body established under paragraph 5 above such travelling and other allowances (including compensation for loss of remunerative time) as he may determine with the consent of the Minister for the Civil Service.

7. In this Schedule—

"local authority" means the council of a London borough, or of a county or district as defined in relation to England in section 270(1) of the Local Government Act 1972, or of a country or district mentioned in section 20(3) of that Act (which relates to Wales) or the Common Council of the City of London, and

"district", in relation to a Council, means the locality for which it is established, whether that locality consists of the area or part of the area of an Area Health Authority or the district or part of the district of a District Health Authority or for such an area or district or part thereof together with the areas or parts of the areas of other Area Health Authorities or the districts or parts of districts of other District Health Authorities and the district of a Council must be such that no part of it is separated from the rest of it by territory not included in the district.

8.—A Family Health Service Authority is a relevant Family Health Service Authority in relation to a Council's district if any part of the Authority's locality is in that district, but is only a relevant Authority in relation to that Council to the extent that the Council performs its functions in relation to that part..'

Regulation 3 of the Community Health Councils Regulations 1985[28] provides:

'Number, size and composition of Councils

3.—(1) The number of Councils to be established by an establishing authority, and the district for which each Council is to be established, shall be determined by that authority and that authority may vary the number of Councils established by it and the district for which each such Council is established.

(2) The establishing authority shall determine, in relation to each Council which it establishes, the relevant District Authority or District Authorities and may, at any time, vary that determination.

(3) The number of members and, subject to the following provisions of this regulation, the numerical proportion as between members falling to be appointed by different appointing bodies, shall be such as may be determined on the establishment of Council by the establishing authority; and, subject to those provisions, an establishing authority may at any time vary the total membership and composition of a Council.

(4) The establishing authority shall secure as respects each Council that at least one member is appointed by each relevant local authority and that at least half of the members consist of persons appointed by relevant local authorities.

(5) The establishing authority shall secure that at least one third of the members are appointed, in accordance with the provisions of regulation 6, by voluntary organisations.

(6) Any member other than a member appointed by a relevant local authority or a voluntary organisation shall be appointed by the establishing authority after consultation with the relevant District Authority, with the relevant Committee and with such other bodies as the establishing authority may consider appropriate.'

Regulation 4 provides for members' term of office (four years), and makes provision for expiry of terms of office in such a way as to ensure revolving membership of, respectively, members appointed by the relevant local authorities, members appointed by voluntary organisations, and members appointed by the establishing authority.

Regulation 5 provides:

'Appointment of members by local authorities

5.—(1) Where the number of members to be appointed to a Council by relevant local authorities allows for such members to be appointed in addition to the one member to be appointed by each relevant local authority, the appointment of such additional members shall be made by agreement between the relevant local authorities or, in default of such agreement by such date as the establishing authority may specify, by such of the relevant local authorities as the establishing authority may determine.

(2) A member appointed by a local authority may be, but need not be, a member of that local authority but, if he is a member of that authority, he shall cease to be a member two months after ceasing to be a member of that authority unless either—

(a) that authority within those two months gives notice in writing to the Secretary and to the establishing authority that the person appointed as a member is to continue as such; or

(b) the person so appointed ceased to be a member of that authority by reason of retirement and has been re-elected a member of that authority not later than the day of his retirement.'

Regulation 6 provides:

'Appointment of members of voluntary organisations

6.—(1) The establishing authority shall invite such voluntary organisations as it shall determine, being organisations which in its opinion have an interest in the health service in the district of the Council, to take part in appointing members of the Council.

(2) Subject to paragraph (3), the voluntary organisations invited to take part in making appointments to a Council shall, by agreement between them, determine which of their number, either acting alone or jointly with one or more other voluntary organisations, shall make the appointment of those members to be appointed by a voluntary organisation.

(3) In default of unanimous agreement for the purposes of paragraph (2), by such date as the establishing authority may specify for reaching agreement, by the voluntary organisations invited to take part in appointing members, the establishing authority shall determine which voluntary organisation or voluntary organisations shall make any appointment and whether the appointment should be made by such organisations acting alone or jointly with one or more other organisations.

(4) A member appointed by a voluntary organisation or by two or more such organisations acting jointly may be, but need not be, a member of an appointing body.'

Regulation 8 provides:[28]

'Disqualification for membership

8.—(1) A person shall be disqualified for appointment as a member and for being a member of a Council if he is a member of a Regional Authority, a District Authority or a director of an NHS trust.

(2) Subject to paragraph (3), a person shall be disqualified for appointment as a member of a Council if he has been dismissed, otherwise than by reason of redundancy, from any paid employment with any of the following bodies—
  (a) a health authority;
  (b) the Public Health Laboratory Service Board referred to in section 5(4) of the Act;
  (c) the Dental Practitioner Board referred to in section 37 of the Act;
  (d) the National Radiological Protection Board established by section 1 of the Radiological Protection Act 1970;
  (e) a Committee;
  (f) (g) [. . .];
  (h) an NHS trust.

(3) Subject to paragraph (4), where a person is disqualified under paragraph (2) he may, after the expiry of a period of not less than two years commencing with the dismissal, apply in writing to the Secretary of State to remove the disqualification, and the Secretary of State may direct that the disqualification shall cease.

(4) Where the Secretary of State refuses a person's application to remove a disqualification no further application may be made by that person until the expiry of two years from the date of that application.'

Regulation 9 provides for the termination of membership of Community Health Councils and Regulation 10 gives certain powers to the establishing health authority to vary or to terminate membership.

Part III of the Regulations (regulations 11–17) provide for the constitution and proceedings of Councils. Matters provided for include:

election of chairman and vice-chairman; appointment of committees and joint committees; officers; premises and other facilities; expenses; and reports. In respect of reports, regulation 17[29] provides:

'**17.**—(1) It shall be the duty of a Council as soon as practicable after the completion of one year from the date of its establishment and thereafter as soon as reasonably practicable after the completion of each successive year—
  (a) to make a report to the establishing authority on the performance of its functions during the preceding year;
  (b) to furnish copies of that report to each relevant District Authority and each relevant Family Health Service Authority; and
  (c) to take steps as appear to the Council to be necessary to secure that that report is made known to the public in its district.
(2) Upon receipt of the report each relevant District Authority and each relevant Family Health Service Authority shall furnish to the Council comments on that report and shall include in such comments a record of any steps taken by that District Authority or Family Health Service Authority in consequence of advice given or proposals made by the Council, and it shall be the duty of a District Authority or Family Health Service Authority furnishing comments on any report to secure that those comments are made known to the public in the district of the Council.'

Performance of functions by Community Health Councils

Part IV of the Regulations, as amended, contains the core of the matters contained in them so far as concerns the particular part played by Councils in the provision of health services within the National Health Service.

Regulation 18[30] provides:

'*Advising on operation of the health service*

18. It shall be the duty of each Council to keep under review the operation of the health service in its district and make recommendations for the improvement of that service or otherwise advise any relevant District Authority and any relevant Family Health Service Authority upon such matters relating to the operation of the health service within its district as the Council thinks fit.'

Regulation 19, arguably the most significant of the regulations in times of closure and change of use in the psychiatric and learning disabilities health care sectors, provides:[30]

'*Consultation of Councils by relevant District Authority or Family Health Service Authority*

19.—(1) Subject to paragraphs (1A), (2) and (2A), it shall be the duty of each relevant District Authority and of each relevant Family Health Service Authority to consult a Council on any proposals which the Authority or Family Health Service Authority may have under consideration for any substantial development of the health service in the Council's district and on any such proposals to make any substantial variation in the provision of such service.

(1A) Paragraph (1) shall not apply with respect to any proposal to establish an NHS trust.

(2) Paragraph (1) shall not apply to any proposal on which the District Authority or Committee is satisfied that, in the interest of the health service, a decision has to be taken without allowing time for consultation; but, in any such case, the District Authority or Family Health Service Authority shall notify the Council immediately of the decision taken and the reason why no consultation has taken place.

(2A) Where it appears to a Regional Authority that it is expedient in the interests of the health service for consultation required under this regulation to be carried out by the Regional Authority instead of a District Authority or Family Health Service Authority, the Regional Authority shall so notify the District Authority or Family Health Service Authority, and thereupon it shall be the duty of the Regional Authority and not of the District Authority or Family Health Service Authority to carry out that consultation in accordance with this regulation.

(3) A District Authority or Family Health Service Authority, or, in a case where a Regional Authority has given notification in accordance with paragraph (2A), that Regional Authority, may specify a date by which comments on any such proposals as are referred to in paragraph (1) should be made by the Council to be taken into consideration by the District Authority, Regional Authority or Family Health Service Authority.

(4) In any case where a Council is not satisfied that sufficient time has been allowed under paragraph (3) or that consultation on a proposal has been adequate—

(a)   the establishing authority shall have power to require a District Authority or Family Health Service Authority to carry out such further consultations with the Council as the establishing authority considers appropriate; and

(b)   the Secretary of State shall have, in a case where a Regional Authority has given notification in accordance with paragraph (2A), power to require the Regional Authority to carry out such further consultations with the Council as the Secretary of State considers appropriate, and the District Authority, Regional Authority or Family Health Service Authority shall reconsider any decision taken on the proposals having regard to such further consultations.'

Special provision for urgent closure

In 1990 the National Health Service Management Executive published its document *Consultation and Involving the Consumer*.[31] It contains a paragraph on the statutory requirements relating to consultation prior to closure or substantial change of use. The document is unspecific about closure and is more forthcoming on what it calls 'substantial changes to the services in the CHC's District'.

Referring to the current Regulation of 1985,[32] the document says: 'Regulations 19(1) and (2) do not distinguish between permanent and temporary closure – only "urgency" permits closure without consultation.' In so saying the document could be interpreted to mean that temporary and urgent elements of a health authority's decision are in some way related for legal purposes. While a measure which is urgently to be taken may in fact address a substantive problem which is only transient, or temporary, in nature, it remains as untrue as it always has been to conclude from the transient nature of the problem that its short-lived existence in some way makes a decision on its solution 'urgent' as distinct from longer-term.

The Regulations do not distinguish between permanent and temporary closure and it would have been more helpful if the National Health Service Management Executive had stated explicitly that permanent and temporary are factors which are not intrinsically relevant to the statutory equation, even though they (plus many other elements) may perfectly well enter into the application of the statutory criteria at local level in the resolution of particular cases.

Limits on the obligation of the health authority to consult other relevant bodies

A significant limitation on the obligation of a health authority to consult the hospital's League of Friends arose from the decision of the Divisional Court of the Queen's Bench Division in *R v Shropshire Health Authority and others, ex parte Duffus* (1989).[33]

The defendant health authority had proposed closure of a district general hospital, as part of a number of interdependent proposals. It consulted the hospital's League of Friends and, in consequence of its widespread consultations which included the League of Friends as just one of the consultees, put forward amended proposals. These amended proposals were not put out for further consultation, and the applicant, together with the League of Friends which he represented, sought judicial review of the authority's decision not to pursue further consultation on the proposals.

Their application failed. As Mr Justice Schiemann pointed out, the closure of the district general hospital and arrangements consequent on that closure were 'merely one of a vast number of proposals covering the District Health Authority's area, many of which were inevitably interlocking to some degree'. Furthermore, were there to be more than one consultation process then any changes could give rise to an expectation for further consultation, and so on. His Lordship said that if the courts in a case such as this were to be liberal in the exercise of their power to review administrative action, interminable consultations could result in no decisions actually being made.

The same approach will apparently apply to the judicial attitude to a health authority's consultation of community health councils.

Information to be furnished by relevant District Authority or Family Health Service Authority

'**20.**—(1) Subject to paragraph (2), it shall be the duty of a relevant District Authority and of a relevant Family Health Service Authority to provide a

Council with such information about the planning and operation of health services in the district of that Authority or locality of that Family Health Service Authority as the Council may reasonably require in order to carry out its duties.

(2) Confidential information about diagnosis and treatment of individual patients or any personnel matters relating to individual officers employed by a health authority or Family Health Service Authority shall not be given to any Council or member or officer of a Council and, subject to paragraphs (3) and (4), a District Authority or Family Health Service Authority may refuse to disclose to a Council any other information which the Authority or Family Health Service Authority regards as confidential.

(3) In the event of a relevant District Authority or relevant Family Health Service Authority refusing to disclose to a Council information requested, the Council may appeal to the establishing authority and a decision of the establishing authority as to whether the information is reasonably required by the Council in order to carry out its duties or as to whether the District Authority or relevant Family Health Service Authority may regard the information as confidential shall be final for the purposes of this regulation.'

Inspection of premises by Councils

'**21.** A Council shall have the right to enter and inspect any premises controlled by a relevant District Authority, Regional Authority or NHS trust[34] at such times and subject to such conditions as may be agreed between the Council and the District Authority, Regional Authority or NHS trust or, in default of such agreement, as may be determined by the establishing authority or, where the premises are controlled by a Regional Authority or NHS trust, by the Secretary of State; except that—
   (a) premises or part of the premises used as residential accommodation for officers employed by any health authority may not be entered by members of a Council without their having first obtained the consent of the officers residing in such accommodation; and
   (b) premises or parts of premises made available to persons providing general medical services, general dental services, general ophthalmic services or pharmaceutical services may not be entered by members of a Council without their having first obtained the consent of the persons providing such services.'

Meetings between the Council and the relevant District Authority

Regulation 22(1) states that it is the duty of each relevant District Authority to arrange, not less than once every year, a meeting between members of the Authority (or NHS trust), being not less than one third of the whole number of such members, and the members of the Council to discuss such matters relating to the functions of the Council as may be raised by the Council or the relevant District Authority.

Meetings between the Council and the Family Health Service Authority are provided for in Regulation 22(2).

Access to information

The Community Health Councils (Access to Information) Act 1988 provides for access by the public to meetings of, and to certain documents and information relating to, Community Health Councils and their committees, by applying to them the provisions of sections 100A–100D of the Local Government Act 1972.

2.5 INTERNAL ARRANGEMENTS

2.5.1 Default and emergency powers of the Secretary of State

The Secretary of State, after such enquiry as he thinks fit, may make an order declaring any of certain authorities established under the 1977 Act, including a Regional Health Authority, District Health Authority, Special Health Authority or NHS trust to be in default. In the case of any of the authorities there named the effect of such order is that the members forthwith vacate their office; the order shall provide for the appointment of new members and, if expedient, authorise any person to act in place of the body in question, pending appointment of new members.

Provision is also made for transfer to the Secretary of State in case of need of the property and liabilities of a body in default and of transfer back to the body together with any additional rights and liabilities, acquired or incurred by the Secretary of State on its behalf.[35]

The 1977 Act also makes provision for the Secretary of State, in an emergency, to direct that any function which should be carried out by any body or person under the National Health Service legislation be carried out by another body or person.[36]

2.5.2 Contracts

Regional Health Authorities, District Health Authorities, Special Health Authorities and NHS trusts, being bodies corporate with perpetual succession and a common seal, fall within the provisions of the Corporate Bodies' Contracts Act 1960, as follows:

'1.—(1) Contracts may be made on behalf of any body corporate, wherever incorporated, as follows:
  (a) a contract which if made between private persons would be by law required to be in writing, signed by the parties to be charged therewith, may be made on behalf of the body corporate in writing signed by any person acting under its authority, express or implied; and
  (b) a contract which if made between private persons would by law be valid although made by parol only, and not reduced into writing, may be made by parol on behalf of the body corporate by any person acting under its authority, express or implied.
  (2) A contract made according to this section shall be effectual in law, and shall bind the body corporate and its successors and all other parties thereto.
  (3) A contract made according to this section may be varied or discharged in the same manner in which it is authorised by this section to be made.

(4) Nothing in this section shall be taken as preventing a contract under seal from being made by or on behalf of a body corporate.

(5) This section shall not apply to the making, variation or discharge of a contract before the commencement of this Act but shall apply whether the body corporate gave its authority before or after the commencement of this Act.'

2.5.3   Conditions of employment and the appointment of officers

Officers may be appointed directly by Regional and District Health Authorities on such terms as the Authority may determine. Under the National Health Services (Remuneration and Conditions of Service) Regulations 1974[37] officers whose remuneration is the subject of negotiations by a negotiating body are to receive by way of remuneration no more and no less than has been approved by the Secretary of State whether or not it is paid out of monies provided by Parliament. However, the officers' conditions of service, other than with respect to remuneration, which have likewise been the subject of negotiations by a negotiating body and approved by the Secretary of State are to *include* the conditions so approved; and it therefore seems to follow that additional *non-approved* conditions can be provided.

The position of NHS trusts is more straightforward. Schedule 2, paragraph 16(1)(d) of the National Health Service and Community Care Act 1990 provides that, subject to Schedule 3 of that Act (which provides for finance of NHS trusts), a trust may employ staff 'on such terms as the trust thinks fit'. The Secretary of State has power by regulation or discretion to place limits on the scope of the Authority's discretion. The Schedule goes on to provide that the regulations made under this power shall not require that all consultants employed by an Authority are to be employed whole-time.

2.5.4   Protection of members and officers of health authorities and trusts

By section 125 of the National Health Service Act 1977, section 265 of the Public Health Act 1875 is extended to Regional and District Health Authorities and Special Health Authorities. The protection is extended to NHS trusts by virtue of Schedule 2, paragraph 25 of the National Health Service and Community Care Act 1990. Section 265 of the Public Health Act 1875 provides:

'**265.**—No matter or thing done, and no contract entered into by any local authority or joint board or port sanitary authority, and no matter or thing done by any member of such authority or by any officer of such authority or other person whomsoever acting under the direction of such authority, shall if the matter or thing were done or the contract were entered into *bona fide* for the purpose of executing this Act subject them or any of them personally to any action, liability, claim or demand whatsoever; and any expense incurred by any such authority, member, officer or other person acting as last aforesaid shall be borne and repaid out of the fund or rate applicable by such authority to the general purposes of this Act.

Provided that nothing in this section shall exempt any member of any such authority from any liability to be surcharged with the amount of any payment which may be disallowed by the auditor in accounts of such authority, and which such member authorised or joined in authorising.'

The proviso does not apply to members of health authorities under the National Health Service Act, since no power of surcharge is anywhere conferred on the Departmental auditors. But it must be appreciated that the section only protects an authority from an action for breach of its public duties. It does not protect a health authority in its corporate capacity against any action in respect of any contract or other matter referred to in the section, nor does it protect officers against actions in tort based on negligence or other liability in tort.

In *McGinty v Glasgow Victoria Hospitals Board* (1951)[38] in which a workman claimed damages at common law and under the Factories Act 1937, against a hospital board established under the National Health Service (Scotland) Act 1947, in respect of injury in a hospital laundry due to an unfenced machine, it was held by the Second Division of the Court of Session (Lord Mackay dissenting) that section 70 of the National Health Service (Scotland) Act 1947, corresponding with section 125 of the National Health Service Act 1977, did not bar such a claim against the authority as the present one, being based on negligence. Further it was said that the breach of common law and statutory duty in this case arose out of the private relationship of the contract of employment, and not from the duties imposed by Parliament on the board to provide health services for the public at large.

Similarly, in Scotland, in *Walker v Greenock and District Combination Hospital Board* (1951)[39] on appeal to the First Division of the Court of Session, it was held that a hospital authority could not escape the consequences of a breach of contract by reliance on section 70.

In *Bullard v Croydon Group HMC* (1953)[40] it was held that section 72 of the National Health Service Act 1946, applying section 265 of the Public Health Act 1875 to hospital authorities, did not protect a hospital management committee in its corporate capacity in respect of actions for negligence. Nor, held the House of Lords in *British Medical Association v Greater Glasgow Health Board* (1989),[41] did the Crown Proceedings Act 1947 render health boards (in England and Wales, health authorities) immune from suit. That point is now academic following the removal, by section 60 of the National Health Service and Community Care Act 1990, of Crown status from health authorities within the National Health Service.

2.5.5   Finance

Financial provision for health authorities

Section 97 of the National Health Service Act 1977 provides that every Regional Health Authority (and every Health Authority in Wales) is to receive from the Secretary of State[42] the sums needed to defray its approved expenditure. Every Regional Authority shall pay to every District Authority in its region such sums as are needed to meet the expenditure of the District Authority as the Regional Authority approves.[43] Special Health Authorities are to receive their monies from, first, a Regional or District Health Authority as provided in the order establishing the Special Health Authority (or if the order provided there should be two or more such Authorities, in such proportions as the order determined) and, second, for the balance of their expenditure, from the Secretary of State.[44] Each of the sums due under section 97 shall be payable subject to compliance with such conditions as to records, certificates or otherwise as the Secretary of State may determine.[45]

The National Health Service (Audit of Accounts of Health Authorities) Regulations 1982[46] make provision relating to the audit of accounts of all Regional and District Health Authorities, all Special Health Authorities, all special trustees of certain university or teaching hospitals and the Dental Estimates Board, and in particular for the production of documents and information.

The Regulations revoke the National Health Service Financial (No. 2) Regulations 1974.[47] Provisions of those Regulations which are not superseded by these Regulations are covered in directions given by the Secretary of State by way of Health Circulars and (now) Health Service Guidelines. Section 69 of the Charities Act 1993 requires the accounts of a charity with a permanent endowment to be transmitted annually to the Charity Commissioners unless the charity is excepted by order or regulation. Hospital authorities under the 1946 Act were so exempted,[48] and the exemption is now extended to the new health authorities.[49] Schedule 2, paragraph 16(c) of the National Health Service and Community Care Act 1990 entitles NHS trusts to receive charitable gifts and to enjoy the benefits of land or other property held on trust.

Travelling allowances for health authority members

Travelling and other allowances of and payments to health authorities including compensation in respect of loss of remunerative time, are subject to determination by the Secretary of State with the approval of the Treasury.[50]

Travelling expenses of officers

In practice scales and conditions of allowances for travelling expenses, including subsistence, for officers generally are prescribed by the General Council of the Whitley Councils for the Health Services (Great Britain) following agreement by the management and staff sides under the national negotiating procedures. On any such agreement being approved by the Secretary of State under the National Health Service (Remuneration and Conditions of Service) Regulations 1991[51] the agreed scales and conditions become binding on authorities and officers alike. For the Secretary of State's power of variation and for his other powers under the regulations see Regulation 3(3).

Travelling expenses of patients and visitors

Payment of a patient's travelling expenses out of Exchequer funds and of the expenses of a companion when the patient needs one on his journey to or from hospital is permitted only in accordance with the provisions of the National Health Service (Travelling Expenses and Remission of Charges) Regulations 1988.[52] The Regulations provide for full and part remission of expenses and payments, for the calculations of resources and requirements in order to qualify, for the claiming of remission or payment and for repayment. Under Schedule 1, Part I of the Regulations a claimant's resources are to be calculated in terms of income and capital in accordance with section 22 of the Social Security Act 1986, and eligibility is based on modified provisions of the Income Support (General) Regulations 1987.[53] Where travelling expenses are incurred, or to be incurred, in attending a hospital which is managed by an NHS trust, payment shall be made by the trust; in any other case, payment shall be made by the Secretary of State.[54]

Travelling expenses of visitors to patients detained in special hospitals may be paid out of Exchequer funds in accordance with arrangements made by the Secretary of State with the approval of the Treasury under section 66(1) of the Health Services and Public Health Act 1968.

2.5.6   Health Services Act 1980: fund raising by NHS authorities

Section 5 of the Health Services Act 1980 gives health authorities the power to engage in fund raising activities. Circular HC(80)11 (Parts I and II), and the attached Memorandum, describe the new provisions and advise authorities on the use of the new power. The power is incorporated as section 96A of the National Health Service Act 1977 and is now applicable also to NHS trusts.[55]

Health and Medicines Act 1988: income generation

Health Notice HN(89)9 advises authorities of section 7 of the Health and Medicines Act 1988, giving powers to the Secretary of State to provide additional services on a commercial basis, and covers Directions (Annex A) which devolve those powers to the extent shown therein. The Directions given to Special Health Authorities exclude exercise of the power to acquire land and manage and deal with land. The Notice also encloses a Guidance Booklet, *Income Generation – A Guide to Local Initiative*, about the implementation of the Income Generation Initiative. Appendix 1 deals with the setting of commercial charges for private patients, amenity beds and overseas visitors and Appendix 2 lists points for consideration when considering a contract.

2.5.7   Motor vehicles used for hospital purposes

Registration and licensing

Prior to 1 April 1991 all health service vehicles used solely for such purposes and solely by members and employees of health authority committees operated under a certificate of Crown ownership and no excise licence duty was payable.[56] Vehicles had, however, still to be registered and a registration mark assigned, but no registration documents were issued. The legal position remains the same despite the removal, on the above date, by section 60 of the National Health Service and Community Care Act 1990, of Crown status from health authorities within the National Health Service. By paragraph 2 of Part I of Schedule 8 to the 1990 Act, the following provision is made:

'2. In section 7 of the Vehicles (Excise) Act 1971 (miscellaneous exemptions from duty), after subsection (4) there shall be inserted the following subsection—

(4A) A mechanically propelled vehicle shall not be chargeable with any duty under this Act at a time when it is used or kept on a road by a health service body, as defined in section 60(7) of the National Health Service and Community Care Act 1990 or a National Health Service trust established under Part I of that Act or the National Health Service (Scotland) Act 1978.'

Insurance

Prior to 1 April 1991, in accordance with Government policy, health service vehicles being Crown property were not insured. Despite the removal by section 60 of the National Health Service and Community Care Act 1990 of Crown Status from health authorities, paragraph 4 of Part I of Schedule 8 to the Act maintains the former legal position by providing as follows:

'4. In section 144 of the Road Traffic Act 1988 (exceptions from requirement of third-party insurance or security) in subsection (2) after paragraph (d) there shall be inserted the following paragraphs—

'(da) to a vehicle owned by a health service body, as defined in section 60(7) of the National Health Service and Community Care Act 1990, at a time when the vehicle is being driven under the owner's control.

(db) to an ambulance owned by a National Health Service trust established under Part I of the National Health Service and Community Care Act 1990 or the National Health Service (Scotland) Act 1978, at a time when a vehicle is being driven under the owner's control.'

In departmental Circular RHB (50)121, particulars are given of arrangements for handling claims and of certain 'Forbearance and Sharing Agreements' with insurers of other vehicles. Detailed treatment of these matters is rather beyond the scope of the present work. It will be noted that privately owned vehicles, even though the expenses of their owners may (or must) be paid when they are travelling on official health service business, must still be insured.

2.5.8 Land

The subject of acquisition, leasing and disposal of National Health Service land, and the law relating to real property in general as it affects land and buildings used for the delivery of health services, is beyond the scope of this work. This section therefore restricts itself to certain principal references in the Department of Health's guidance[57] entitled *Estatecode: Property Transactions in the NHS.*

Circular HC(86)13 advised health authorities on what was expected of them in respect of estates work. This document sets out what is required of health authorities in safeguarding the Secretary of State's estate and in conducting property transactions. Part 1 comprises the mandatory requirements on property transactions with which health authorities *must* comply. Part 2 contains the procedures to be used when they are implementing Part 1. Part 3 comprises matters of general guidance which health authorities may use depending on the specific case and the views of their professional advisers. All three parts have been incorporated into the *Estatecode* in order to emphasise that property transactions are not an end in themselves but are one element, albeit an important element, of the overall policies and procedures in the management of National Health Service estate.

The *Estatecode* contains guidance on legal and practical aspects of land transactions. Part 1 contains mandatory requirements and makes reference to certain essential legislative provisions. Part 2 consists of five Procedure Papers; and Part 3 contains Advice Papers relating to the practical implementation of policies and procedures.

THE LEGAL STATUS OF THE ESTATE AND GENERAL POLICY ON LAND TRANSACTIONS

'General

1.1 All National Health Service property is vested in the Secretary of State for Health (who holds property not as beneficial owner, but as trustee for the Crown for the purposes of the Department); it is therefore Government property and subject to the policies which apply to Government property generally. National Health Service property is occupied and managed by health authorities on behalf of the Secretary of State and they must act within the instructions set out in this document.

Powers of the Secretary of State

1.2 Under section 87 of the NHS Act 1977 the Secretary of State may acquire (either by agreement or compulsorily) and maintain property required for the purposes of carrying out the functions of the Act, and under section 7(2)(b) of the Health and Medicines Act 1988 the Secretary of State may acquire land by agreement and manage and deal with land in order to make more income available to the health service.

1.3 The Secretary of State has no specific statutory power to dispose of property. The power to dispose of property which is surplus to requirements, ie no longer needed for the purposes of the health service, derives from the Crown which may dispose of such property except where prevented by Statute from so doing.

Powers of Regional and District Health Authorities

1.4 Except for the power to acquire property compulsorily, the Secretary of State has directed Regional Health Authorities to exercise his powers (relating to section 87 of the 1977 Act) by the National Health Service Functions (Directions to Authorities and Administration Arrangements) Regulations 1989,[58] subject to such limitations and directions as may be given. A Direction dated 3 July 1989 has accordingly been given, setting out the powers for and limitations on action by Regional Health Authorities. Under this Direction Regional Health Authorities may:

- acquire and dispose of property
- seal documents
- give directions to DHAs.

1.5 District Health Authorities have no authority to undertake property transactions other than within the terms of any Directions given by their Regional Health Authority. Where functions are to be delegated to District Health Authorities, they will need to be authorised to act by an instrument in writing issued by the Regional Health Authority in accordance with section 14 of the National Health Service Act 1977, having regard to the limitations set out in the Direction dated 3 July 1989 from the Secretary of State to Regional Health Authorities.

1.6 Under the Directions on Income Generation dated 23 February 1989 (reproduced as Annex A to HC(89)9) Regional Health Authorities and District Health Authorities have delegated authority to exercise the Secretary of State's power (relating to section 7(2)(b) of the 1988 Act) to acquire, manage and deal with land for the purposes of making more income available to improve the health service. This Direction is subject to, and must be read in conjunction with, the main Direction of 3 July 1989. It does not enable District Health Authorities to acquire land or property for purposes other than income generation and the words "manage and deal with land" do not convey the power to dispose. Further guidance is given in Advice Paper 5.

Professional advice

1.7 Health authorities must obtain early and regular professional advice to assist in the efficient management of the National Health Service estate and to meet their obligations to conduct property transactions in a manner which safeguards the Secretary of State's interest. Sources of advice are set out in Advice Paper 1.

Legal advice

1.8 Health authorities must have available the services of a legal adviser (either in-house or private) who can deal with all legal aspects of property transactions. The legal adviser is responsible for taking all necessary steps to safeguard the Secretary of State's legal interest whether as purchaser, vendor, lessee or lessor, including the investigation of title and of any covenants, restrictions or charges affecting the use of the property. Health authorities must not allow entry onto property or enter into a contract without taking advice from the legal adviser.

Accountability

1.9 As a recognised safeguard to public funds and to satisfy the requirements of Parliamentary accountability, all transactions must be carried out in accordance with the recommendation of the District Valuer unless the Department has authorised other arrangements. Where other arrangements have not been authorised, health authorities wishing to act other than in accordance with the District Valuer's recommendation must consult the Department who, in turn, may be required to consult the Treasury. No commitment should be given pending the Department's decision.

Status of trust property

1.10 Property vested in health authorities on trust is deemed to be private property. It should be managed by the trustees in accordance with the terms of the trust.'

Paragraph 1.11, written in 1989, dealt with the subject of Crown exemption from general legal requirements and liabilities. Crown exemption was removed by section 60 of the National Health Service and Community Care Act 1990. Schedule 8, Part II of that Act contains certain consequential amendments relating to the law affecting acqui- sition of land, town and country planning and housing, to which reference should be made when reading the *Estatecode* in the present state of the law.

'Restrictive covenants

1.12 The Secretary of State has power under section 87(1) and (5) of the 1977 Act to override restrictive covenants on land acquired by agreement after 31 March 1974 in pursuance of his statutory functions. Where he does so, action for damages, or for an injunction, cannot be taken but the person entitled to benefit under the covenant can apply for compensation under section 7 or 10 of the Compulsory Purchase Act 1965.

Compulsory purchase orders

1.13 The Secretary of State has the power to acquire property compulsorily where it is not possible to acquire by agreement, provided that the property concerned is needed for health service purposes and that there are no other suitable alternative properties available. There is no power to acquire property compulsorily to facilitate the disposal, or enhance the value, of surplus National Health Service property. Where Regional Health Authorities consider that there is justification for using compulsory powers they must consult the Department setting out the full circumstances of the case. If the Secretary of State agrees to proceed by way of compulsory purchase more detailed instructions will be given by the Department.

1.14 National Health Service land [. . .] cannot be acquired compulsorily by other bodies. Where National Health Service land is included in a compulsory purchase order, health authorities (acting on behalf of the Secretary of State) must consider whether the land can be released and if so they should agree terms after consultation with the District Valuer.'

2.5.9   The purchaser–provider relationship and the 'internal market'

Sections 3 and 4 of the National Health Service and Community Care Act 1990 give legislative effect to the management device of splitting the purchase and the provision of health care services. Health authorities are funded on the basis of their resident population and each health authority is required by the National Health Service Management Executive to carry out a systematic assessment on the health needs of its population. This assessment is effected by the Director of Public Health in each District Health Authority, who consults with clinicians in hospitals, general medical, dental and optical practitioners, and with other interested groups and parties. There is a complementary duty, imposed by section 46 of the 1990 Act, on social services authorities to produce social service plans in collaboration with health authorities, voluntary bodies and service users and their representatives.

Section 3 (1) gives the name 'primary functions' to the functions exercisable by directions under sections 11, 13 and 14 of the National Health Service Act 1977. These functions are, respectively, the establishment and direction of Special Health Authorities; the direction by the Secretary of State to Regions to perform functions under the Act; and the permission to Regions to direct health districts to perform functions within their geographical area. Section 3 (2) provides:

'(2) In addition to carrying out its primary functions, a Regional, District or Special Health Authority or a Family Health Services Authority may, as the provider, enter into an NHS contract (as defined in section 4 below) under which the goods or services to be provided are of the same description as goods or services which the authority already provides or could provide for the purposes of carrying out its primary functions.'

In relation to its resident population, each District Health Authority may secure the fulfilment of its 'primary functions' in a number of ways, including providing health care itself, as was the case before the inception of the 1990 Act. It may, as it could before the Act, make arrangements with another health service or health care body (including a trust, or another trust) to provide personal health care services, by an arrangement referred to in section 4 of the Act as a 'National Health Service contract'. A district health authority may also make such arrangements with a body which is outside the National Health Service altogether, by contracting out the care, or part of the care, of a particular patient to the private sector. (The contracting out of a patient who is 'sectioned' under the Mental Health Act 1983 to the private sector, and the powers of managers and of the Secretary of State in relation to the discharge of that patient, are specifically explained in Chapter 30 below.) Furthermore, a health authority is now empowered to make arrangements, also referred to by the term 'contract', with its own directly-managed provider units.

Section 4 of the Act provides in detail for these so-called 'NHS contracts':

'4.—(1) In this Act the expression "NHS contract" means an arrangement under which one health service body ("the acquirer") arranges for the provision to it by another health service body ("the provider") of goods or services which it reasonably requires for the purposes of its functions.

(2) In this section "health service body" means any of the following, namely,—

(a) a health authority;
(b) a health board;
(c) the Common Services Agency for the Scottish Health Service;
(d) a Family Health Services Authority;
(e) an NHS trust;
(f) a recognised fund-holding practice;
(g) the Dental Practice Board or the Scottish Dental Practice Board;
(h) the Public Health Laboratory Service Board; and
(i) the Secretary of State.

(3) Whether or not an arrangement which constitutes an NHS contract would, apart from this subsection, be a contract in law, it shall not be regarded for any purpose as giving rise to contractual rights or liabilities, but if any dispute arises with respect to such an arrangement, either party may refer the matter to the Secretary of State for determination under the following provisions of this section.

(4) If, in the course of negotiations intending to lead to an arrangement which will be an NHS contract, it appears to a health service body—

(a) that the terms proposed by another health service body are unfair by reason that the other is seeking to take advantage of its position as the only, or the only practicable, provider of the goods or services concerned or by reason of any other unequal bargaining position as between the prospective parties to the proposed arrangement, or

(b) that for any other reason arising out of the relative bargaining position of the prospective parties any of the terms of the proposed arrangement cannot be agreed,

that health service body may refer the terms of the proposed arrangement to the Secretary of State for determination under the following provisions of this section.

(5) Where a reference is made to the Secretary of State under subsection (3) or subsection (4) above, the Secretary of State may determine the matter himself or, if he considers it appropriate, appoint a person to consider and determine it in accordance with regulations.

(6) By his determination of a reference under subsection (4) above, the Secretary of State or, as the case may be, the person appointed under subsection (5) above may specify terms to be included in the proposed arrangement and may direct that it be proceeded with; and it shall be the duty of the prospective parties to the proposed arrangement to comply with any such directions.

(7) A determination of a reference under subsection (3) above may contain such directions (including directions as to payment) as the Secretary of State or, as the case may be, the person appointed under subsection (5) above considers appropriate to resolve the matter in dispute; and it shall be the duty of the parties to the NHS contract in question to comply with any such directions.

(8) Without prejudice to the generality of his powers on a reference under subsection (3) above, the Secretary of State or, as the case may be, the person appointed under subsection (5) above may by his determination in relation to an arrangement constituting an NHS contract vary the terms of the arrangement or bring it to an end; and where an arrangement is so varied or brought to an end—

(a) subject to paragraph (b) below, the variation or termination shall be treated as being effected by agreement between the parties; and

(b) the directions included in the determination by virtue of subsection (7) above may contain such provisions as the Secretary of State or, as the case may be, the person appointed under subsection (5) above considers appropriate in order satisfactorily to give effect to the variation or to bring the arrangement to an end.'

Subsections (5)–(8) of section 4 make provision for references under subsections (3) and (4) above and make provision for the determination of disputes. It is subsection (3) of section 4 which indicates the precise nature of such 'contractual' arrangements, in pointing out that these 'shall not be regarded for any purpose as giving rise to contractual rights or liabilities'. The function of an 'NHS contract' within a formerly composite health authority (as distinct from a contract to which an NHS trust is a party) is simply to act as a management device within a particular authority, which both in law and in fact is incapable of contracting with itself. The concept serves to draw attention to the concept of health care provision as a 'product' which is bought and sold on the commercially-conscious internal market of the National Health Service. Procedures for the resolution of particular disputes are contained in the National Health Service Contracts (Dispute Resolution) Regulations 1991.[59]

2.6 NATIONAL HEALTH SERVICE TRUSTS

The concept and institution of the National Health Service trust (hereafter 'NHS trust') was new to the health service on its introduction, having been initially introduced to the health service in a letter from the Chief Executive in 1989.[60] NHS trusts are provided for by section 5 and Schedule 2 of the Act, financial provision relating to NHS trusts being made by Schedule 3. The powers, and associated duties, of the Secretary of State in relation to the establishment of NHS trusts are set out in section 5, subsections (1)–(4), as follows:

'**5**.—(1) Subject to subsection (2) or, as the case may be, subsection (3) below the Secretary of State may by order establish bodies, to be known as National Health Service trusts (in this Act referred to as NHS trusts),—

 (a) to assume responsibility, in accordance with this Act, for the ownership and management of hospitals or other establishments or facilities which were previously managed or provided by Regional, District or Special Health Authorities; or

 (b) to provide and manage hospitals or other establishments or facilities.

(2) In any case where the Secretary of State is considering whether to make an order under subsection (1) above establishing an NHS trust and the hospital, establishment or facility concerned is or is to be situated in England, he shall direct the relevant Regional Health Authority to consult, with respect to the proposal to establish the trust—

 (a) the relevant Community Health Council and such other persons or bodies as may be specified in the direction; and

 (b) such other persons or bodies as the Authority considers appropriate;

and, within such period (if any) as the Secretary of State may determine, the relevant Regional Health Authority shall report the results of those consultations to the Secretary of State.

(3) In any case where the Secretary of State is considering whether to make an order under subsection (1) above establishing an NHS trust and the hospital, establishment or facility concerned is or is to be situated in Wales, he shall consult the relevant Community Health Council and such other persons and bodies as he considers appropriate.

(4) In subsections (2) and (3) above—

 (a) any reference to the relevant Regional Health Authority is a reference to that Authority in whose region the hospital, establishment or other facility concerned is, or is to be, situated; and

 (b) any reference to the relevant Community Health Council is a reference to the Council for the district, or part of the district, in which that hospital, establishment or other facility is, or is to be, situated.'

The structure of an NHS trust is set out in subsection (5) of section 5, as follows:

'(5) Every NHS trust—

 (a) shall be a body corporate having a board of directors consisting of a chairman appointed by the Secretary of State and, subject to paragraph 5(2) of Schedule 2 to this Act, executive and non-executive directors (that is to say, directors who, subject to subsection (7) below, respectively are and are not employees of the trust); and

 (b) shall have the functions conferred on it by an order under subsection (1) above and by Schedule 2 to this Act.'

2.6.1 Membership and procedure of National Health Service trusts

The membership of NHS trusts is set out in Part II of the National Health Service Trusts (Membership and Procedure) Regulations 1990[61] as follows:

'Maximum number of directors

2. The maximum number of directors of an NHS trust shall be eleven.

Appointment of directors

3.—(1) Of the non-executive directors of an NHS trust whose hospital establishment or facility is situated in England—

(a) two shall be appointed by the Regional Health Authority in whose region the hospital establishment or facility is situated, or, if it is situated in more than one region, the Regional Health Authority in whose region it principally carries out its functions; and

(b) the remainder, which shall include the person, if any, appointed pursuant to paragraph 3(1)(d) of Schedule 2 to the Act, shall be appointed by the Secretary of State.

(2) All of the non-executive directors of an NHS trust whose hospital establishment or facility is situated in Wales shall be appointed by the Secretary of State.

(3) The executive directors of an NHS trust shall be appointed by the relevant committee.

Qualifications for appointments

4.—(1) The executive directors of an NHS trust shall include—

(a) the chief officer of the trust;

(b) the chief finance officer of the trust;

(c) except in the case of a trust mentioned in paragraph (2) a medical or dental practitioner and a registered nurse or registered midwife as defined in section 10(7) of the Nurses, Midwives and Health Visitors Act 1979.

(2) Paragraph 1(c) shall not apply in the case of a trust—

(a) which does not provide services directly to patients; or

(b) whose principal function is to provide ambulance or patient transport services.

Persons to be regarded as executive directors

5. A person who is not an employee of an NHS trust but—

(a) holds a post in university with a medical or dental school, and also works for the trust; or

(b) is seconded from his employers to work for the trust,

is nevertheless, on appointment as a director, to be regarded as an executive rather than a non-executive director of the trust.

Joint directors

6. Where more than one person is appointed jointly to a post in an NHS trust which qualifies the holder for executive directorship or in relation to which an executive director is to be appointed, those persons shall become or be appointed an executive director jointly, and shall count for the purposes of regulation 2 as one person.

Tenure of office of chairman and directors

7.—(1) Subject to regulation 9, the chairman and non-executive directors of an NHS trust shall be appointed for such period not exceeding four years as the appointing authority may specify on making the appointment.

(2) Subject to regulation 8, the tenure of office of executive directors other than the chief officer and chief finance officer, shall be for such period as the appointing authority may specify on making the appointment.

Tenure and suspension of tenure of office of executive directors

8.—(1) Subject to paragraphs (2) to (4) and regulation 7(2), an executive director of an NHS trust shall hold office—
 (a) if he is not the chief officer or the chief finance officer, for as long as he holds a post in the trust;
 (b) if he is the chief officer or the chief finance officer, for as long as he holds that post in the trust.

(2) If the appointing authority is of the opinion that it is not in the interests of the NHS trust that an executive director of an NHS trust other than the chief officer or chief finance officer should continue to hold office as director the appointing authority shall forthwith terminate his tenure of office.

(3) If an executive director of an NHS trust is suspended from his post in the trust he shall be suspended from performing his functions as director for the period of his suspension.

(4) An executive director other than the chief officer or chief finance officer of an NHS trust may resign his office at any time during the period for which he was appointed by giving notice in writing to the relevant committee.

Termination of tenure of office of chairman and non-executive directors

9.—(1) The chairman or a non-executive director of an NHS trust may resign his office at any time during the period for which he was appointed by giving notice in writing to the appointing authority.

(2) Where during his period of directorship a non-executive director of a trust is appointed chairman of the trust, his tenure of office as non-executive director shall terminate when his appointment as chairman takes effect.

(3) If an appointing authority is of the opinion that it is not in the interests of the health service that a person who is appointed as chairman or non-executive director of an NHS trust should continue to hold that office the appointing authority may, subject to the consent of the Secretary of State, unless it is the Secretary of State, forthwith terminate his tenure of office.

(4) If a chairman or non-executive director of an NHS trust has not attended a meeting of the trust for a period of six months, the Secretary of State shall forthwith terminate his tenure of office unless the Secretary of State is satisfied that—
 (a) the absence was due to a reasonable cause; and
 (b) the chairman or non-executive director will be able to attend meetings of the trust within such period as the Secretary of State considers reasonable.

(5) Where a person has been appointed the chairman or non-executive director of an NHS trust—
 (a) if he becomes disqualified for appointment under regulation 11 the appointing authority shall forthwith notify him in writing of such disqualification; or
 (b) if it comes to the notice of the appointing authority that at the time of his appointment he was so disqualified it shall forthwith declare that he was not duly appointed and so notify him in writing,
and upon receipt of any such notification, his tenure of office, if any, shall be terminated and he shall cease to act as chairman or non-executive director.

(6) If it appears to the Secretary of State that the chairman or non-executive director of an NHS trust has failed to comply with regulation 20 (disclosure etc. on account of pecuniary interest) he may forthwith terminate that person's tenure of office.

(7) Where a person appointed as a non-executive director pursuant to

paragraph 3(1)(d) of Schedule 2 to the Act ceases to hold a post in the university in question the Secretary of State shall terminate his appointment as non-executive director.

Eligibility for reappointment

10.—(1) Subject to regulation 11 the chairman or non-executive director of an NHS trust shall, on the termination of the period of his tenure of office, be eligible for reappointment.

(2) An executive director of an NHS trust other than the chief officer and the chief finance officer shall on the termination of the period of his tenure of office be eligible for reappointment.

Disqualification for appointment of chairman and non-executive directors

11.—(1) Subject to regulation 12 a person shall be disqualified for appointment as the chairman or non-executive director of an NHS trust if—

(a) he has within the preceding five years been convicted in the United Kingdom, the Channel Islands or the Isle of Man of any offence and has had passed on him a sentence of imprisonment (whether suspended or not) for a period of not less than three months without the option of a fine; or

(b) he has been adjudged bankrupt or has made a composition or arrangement with his creditors; or

(c) he has been dismissed, otherwise than by reason of redundancy, from any paid employment with a health service body; or

(d) he is a person whose tenure of office as the chairman member or director of a health service body has been terminated because his appointment is not in the interests of the health service, for non-attendance at meetings or for non-disclosure of a pecuniary interest;

(e) he is a chairman, member, director or employee of a health service body; or

(f) he is a general medical practitioner or general dental practitioner or an employee of either of those; or

(g) he holds a paid appointment or office with a trade union which represents the interests of members who are employed by a health service body; or

(h) he has had his name removed, by a direction under section 46 of the National Health Service Act 1977, from any list prepared under Part II of that Act and has not subsequently had his name included in such a list.

(2) For the purposes of paragraph (1)(a) the date of conviction shall be deemed to be the date on which the ordinary period allowed for making an appeal or application with respect to the conviction expires, or if such an appeal or application is made, the date on which the appeal or application is finally disposed of or abandoned or fails by reason of it not being prosecuted.

(3) For the purposes of paragraph (1)(c) a person shall not be treated as having been in paid employment by reason only of his chairmanship, membership or directorship of the health service body.

(4) A person shall not be disqualified by paragraph (1)(e) from being the non-executive director of an NHS trust referred to in paragraph 3(1)(d) of Schedule 2 to the Act by reason of his employment with a health service body.

Cessation of disqualification

12.—(1) Where a person is disqualified under regulation 11(1)(b) by reason of having been adjudged bankrupt—

(a) if the bankruptcy is annulled on the ground that he ought not to have been adjudged bankrupt or on the ground that his debts have been paid in full, the disqualification shall cease on the date of the annulment;

(b) if he is discharged the disqualification shall cease on the date of his discharge.

(2) Where a person is disqualified under regulation 11(1)(b) by reason of his having made a composition or arrangement with his creditors, if he pays his debts in full the disqualification shall cease on the date on which the payment is completed and in any other case it shall cease on the expiry of five years from the date on which the terms of the deed of composition or arrangement are fulfilled.

(3) Subject to paragraph (4) where a person is disqualified under regulation 11(1)(c) (dismissed employees) he may, after the expiry of a period of not less than two years, apply in writing to the Secretary of State to remove the disqualification and the Secretary of State may direct that the disqualification shall cease.

(4) Where the Secretary of State refuses an application to remove a disqualification no further application may be made by that person until the expiration of two years from the date of the application.

(5) Where a person is disqualified under regulation 11(1)(d) (certain chairmen and directors whose appointments have been terminated), the disqualification shall cease on the expiry of a period of two years or such longer period as the appointing authority specifies when terminating his period of office but the Secretary of State may on application being made to him by that person or by that appointing authority, reduce the period of disqualification.'

2.6.2 Constitution and proceedings of National Health Service trusts

The constitution and proceedings of NHS trusts are set out in Part III of the above Regulations, as follows:

'Appointment of vice-chairman

13.—(1) For the purpose of enabling the proceedings of the trust to be conducted in the absence of the chairman, the directors of an NHS trust may appoint a non-executive director from amongst them to be vice-chairman for such a period, not exceeding the remainder of his term as non-executive director of the trust, as they may specify on appointing him.

(2) Any non-executive director so elected may at any time resign from the office of vice-chairman by giving notice in writing to the chairman and the directors of the trust may thereupon appoint another non-executive director as vice-chairman in accordance with paragraph (1).

Powers of vice-chairman

14. Where the chairman of an NHS trust has died or has otherwise ceased to hold office or where he has been unable to perform his duties as chairman owing to illness, absence from England and Wales or any other cause, references to the chairman in the Schedule to these Regulations shall, so long as there is no chairman able to perform his duties, be taken to include references to the vice-chairman.

Appointment of committees and sub-committees

15.—(1) Subject to regulations 17 and 18 an NHS trust may appoint committees of the trust consisting wholly or partly of directors of the trust or wholly persons who are not directors of the trust.

(2) A committee appointed under this regulation may appoint sub-committees consisting wholly or partly of members of the committee (whether or not they include the directors of the trust) or wholly of persons who are not members of the committee (whether or not they include the directors of the trust).

Arrangements for the exercise of functions

16. Subject to regulations 17 and 18 an NHS trust may make arrangements for the exercise, on behalf of the trust, of any of its functions by a committee or sub-committee appointed by virtue of regulation 15 subject to such restrictions and conditions as the trust thinks fit.

Committee for appointing chief officer as director

17. An NHS trust shall appoint a committee whose members shall be the chairman and non-executive directors of the trust whose function will be to appoint the chief officer as a director of the trust.

Committee for appointing executive directors other than chief officer

18. An NHS trust shall appoint a committee whose members shall be the chairman, the non-executive directors and the chief officer whose function will be to appoint the executive directors of the trust other than the chief officer.

Meeting and proceedings

19.—(1) The meetings and proceedings of an NHS trust shall be conducted in accordance with the rules set out in the Schedule to these Regulations and with Standing Orders made under paragraph (2).

(2) Subject to those rules and to regulation 20 an NHS trust shall make and may vary or revoke Standing Orders for the regulation of its proceedings and business and provision may be made in such Standing Orders for the suspension of them.

(3) An NHS trust may make, vary and revoke Standing Orders relating to the quorum, proceedings and place of meetings of a committee or sub-committee but, subject to regulation 20 and to any such Standing Order, the quorum, proceedings and place of meeting shall be such as the committee or sub-committee may determine.

(4) The proceedings of an NHS trust shall not be invalidated by any vacancy in its membership or by any defect in a director's appointment.

Disability of directors in proceedings on account of pecuniary interest

20.—(1) Subject to the following provisions of this regulation, if a director of an NHS trust has any pecuniary interest, direct or indirect, in any contract, proposed contract or other matter and is present at a meeting of the trust at which the contract or other matter is the subject of consideration, he shall at the meeting and as soon as practicable after its commencement disclose the fact and shall not take part in the consideration and discussion of the contract or other matter or vote on any question with respect to it.

(2) The Secretary of State may, subject to such conditions as he may think fit to impose, remove any disability imposed by this regulation, in any case in which it appears to him in the interests of the health service that the disability shall be removed.

(3) An NHS trust may, by Standing Orders made under regulation 19, provide for the exclusion of a director from a meeting of the trust while any contract, proposed contract, or other matter in which he has a pecuniary interest, direct or indirect, is under consideration.

(4) Any remuneration, compensation or allowances payable to a director by

virtue of paragraph 9 of Schedule 2 to the Act shall not be treated as a pecuniary interest for the purpose of this regulation.

(5) Subject to paragraphs (2) and (6), a director shall be treated for the purposes of this regulation as having indirectly a pecuniary interest in a contract, proposed contract or other matter if—

(a) he, or a nominee of his, is a director of a company or other body, not being a public body, with which the contract was made or is proposed to be made or which has a direct pecuniary interest in the other matter under consideration; or

(b) he is a partner of, or is in the employment of, a person with whom the contract was made or is proposed to be made or who has a direct pecuniary interest in the other matter under consideration and, in the case of married persons living together, the interest of one spouse shall be deemed for the purpose of this regulation to be also an interest of the other.

(6) A director shall not be treated as having a pecuniary interest in any contract, proposed contract or other matter by reason only—

(a) of his membership of a company or other body if he has no beneficial interest in any securities of that company or other body;

(b) of an interest in any company, body or person with which he is connected as mentioned in paragraph (5) which is so remote or insignificant that it cannot reasonably be regarded as likely to influence a director in the consideration or discussion of or in voting on, any question with respect to that contract or matter.

(7) Where a director—

(a) has an indirect pecuniary interest in a contract or other matter by reason only of a beneficial interest in securities of a company or other body; and

(b) the total nominal value of those securities does not exceed £5,000 or one hundredth of the total nominal value of the issued share capital of the company or body, whichever is the less; and

(c) if the share capital is of more than one class, the total nominal value of shares of any one class in which he has the beneficial interest does not exceed one hundredth of the total issued share capital of that class,

this regulation shall not prohibit him from taking part in consideration or discussion of the contract or other matter or from voting on any question in respect to it without prejudice however to his duty to disclose his interest.

(8) This regulation applies to a committee or sub-committee of an NHS trust as it applies to the trust and applies to any member of any such committee or sub-committee (whether or not he is also a director of the trust) as it applies to a director of the trust.'

2.6.3 Duties, powers and status of National Health Service trusts

In line with section 60 of the National Health Service and Community Care Act 1990, namely that a health authority no longer has Crown status, paragraph 18 of Part II of Schedule II of the 1990 Act provides that an NHS trust shall not be regarded as the servant or agent of the Crown or, except as provided by this Act (for instance, in the case of vehicles and insurance, for which see p. 52, above) as enjoying any status, immunity or privilege of the Crown. The property of an NHS trust is not to be regarded as Crown property.

The duties and powers of NHS trusts are set out in paragraphs 6–17 of Part II of Schedule 2 of the Act, as follows:

'Specific duties

6.—(1) An NHS trust shall carry out effectively, efficiently and economically the functions for the time being conferred on it by an order under section 5(1) of this Act and by the provisions of this Schedule and, with respect to the exercise of the powers conferred by section 5(10) of this Act and paragraphs 10 to 15 below, shall comply with any directions given to it by the Secretary of State, whether of a general or a particular nature.

(2) An NHS trust shall comply with any directions given to it by the Secretary of State with respect to all or any of the following matters—

(a) the qualifications of persons who may be employed as officers of the trust:

(b) the employment, for the purpose of performing functions specified in the direction, of officers having qualifications or experience of a description so specified;

(c) the manner in which officers of the trust are to be appointed;

(d) prohibiting or restricting the disposal of, or of any interest in, any asset which, at the time the direction is given, the Secretary of State reasonably considers to have a value in excess of such sum as may be specified in an order under section 5(1) of this Act and in respect of which the Secretary of State considers that the interests of the National Health Service require that the asset should not be disposed of;

(e) compliance with guidance or directions given (by circular or otherwise) to health authorities, or particular descriptions of health authorities; and

(f) the implementation of awards relating to the distinction or merit of medical practitioners or dental practitioners or any class or classes of such practitioners.

7.—(1) For each accounting year an NHS trust shall prepare and send to the Secretary of State an annual report in such form as may be determined by the Secretary of State.

(2) At such time or times as may be prescribed, an NHS trust shall hold a public meeting at which its audited accounts and annual report and any report on the accounts made pursuant to subsection (3) of section 15 of the Local Government Finance Act 1982 shall be presented.

(3) In such circumstances and at such time or times as may be prescribed, an NHS trust shall hold a public meeting at which such document as may be prescribed shall be presented.

8. An NHS trust shall furnish to the Secretary of State such reports, returns and other information, including information as to its forward planning, as, and in such form as, he may require.

9.—(1) An NHS trust shall be liable to pay—

(a) to the chairman and any non-executive director of the trust remuneration of an amount determined by the Secretary of State, not exceeding such amount as may be approved by the Treasury;

(b) to the chairman and any non-executive director of the trust such travelling and other allowances as may be determined by the Secretary of State with the approval of the Treasury;

(c) to any member of a committee or sub-committee of the trust who is not also a director such travelling and other allowances as may be so determined.

(2) If an NHS trust so determines in the case of a person who is or has been a chairman of the trust, the trust shall be liable to pay such pension, allowances or gratuities to or in respect of him as may be determined by the Secretary of State with the approval of the Treasury.

(3) Different determinations may be made under sub-paragraph (1) or sub-paragraph (2) above in relation to different cases or descriptions of cases.

Specific powers

10. In addition to carrying out its other functions, an NHS trust may, as the provider, enter into NHS contracts.

11. An NHS trust may undertake and commission research and make available staff and provide facilities for research by other persons.

12. An NHS trust may—
    (a) provide training for persons employed or likely to be employed by the trust or otherwise in the provision of services under the principal Act; and
    (b) make facilities and staff available in connection with training by a university or any other body providing training in connection with the health service.

13. An NHS trust may enter into arrangements for the carrying out, on such terms as seem to the trust to be appropriate, of any of its functions jointly with any Regional, District or Special Health Authority, with another NHS trust or with any other body or individual.

14. According to the nature of its functions, an NHS trust may make accommodation or services or both available for patients who give undertakings (or for whom undertakings are given) to pay, in respect of the accommodation or services (or both) such charges as the trust may determine.

15. For the purpose of making additional income available in order better to perform its functions, an NHS trust shall have the powers specified in section 7(2) of the Health and Medicines Act 1988 (extension of powers of Secretary of State for financing the Health Service).

General powers

16.—(1) Subject to Schedule 3 to this Act, an NHS trust shall have power to do anything which appears to it to be necessary or expedient for the purpose of or in connection with the discharge of its functions, including in particular power—
    (a) to acquire and dispose of land and other property;
    (b) to enter into such contracts as seem to the trust to be appropriate;
    (c) to accept gifts of money, land or other property, including money, land or other property to be held on trust, either for the general or any specific purposes of the NHS trust or for all or any purposes relating to the health service; and
    (d) to employ staff on such terms as the trust thinks fit.

(2) The reference in sub-paragraph (1)(c) above to specific purposes of the NHS trust includes a reference to the purposes of a specific hospital or other establishment or facility which is owned and managed by the trust.

17.—(1) Without prejudice to the generality of paragraph 16 above, for or in respect of such of its employees as it may determine, an NHS trust may make such arrangements for providing pensions, allowances or gratuities as it may determine; and such arrangements may include the establishment and administration, by the trust or otherwise, of one or more pension schemes.

(2) The reference in sub-paragraph (1) above to pensions, allowances or gratuities to or in respect of employees of an NHS trust includes a reference to pensions, allowances or gratuities by way of compensation to or in respect of any of the trust's employees who suffer loss of office or employment or loss or diminution of emoluments.

Status

18. An NHS trust shall not be regarded as the servant or agent of the Crown or, except as provided by this Act, as enjoying any status, immunity or privilege of the Crown; and an NHS trust's property shall not be regarded as property of, or property held on behalf of, the Crown.'

The precise meaning and content of the duty, provided for in paragraph 6 (1) of Part II of Schedule 2 of the Act, that a trust 'shall carry out effectively, efficiently and economically the functions for the time being conferred on it by an order' of the Secretary of State, is unclear. Certainly there is no similar wording in associated health care legislation. The expression is vague but potentially far-reaching. The duty imposed by paragraph 6 will no doubt encompass efficient and safe working practices, the efficient and effective use of professional and other staff within the parameters of good and lawful practice, and the proper establishment and implementation of policies and practices for the trust, their effect and purpose being properly understood by all staff to whom the policies and practices relate. The duty no doubt includes an appropriate training and staff development responsibility of the trust, particularly where management responsibilities include statutory duties such as those imposed by the Mental Health Act 1983.[62] Powers to provide staff training and to make resources available for that purpose are provided by Schedule 2, paragraph 12 of the National Health Service and Community Care Act 1990.

2.6.4   Dissolution of National Health Service trusts

Part IV of Schedule 2 to the 1990 Act provides for the dissolution of NHS trusts as follows:

'29.—(1) The Secretary of State may by order made by statutory instrument dissolve an NHS trust.

(2) An order under this paragraph may be made—
(a)   on the application of the NHS trust concerned; or
(b)   if the Secretary of State considers it appropriate in the interests of the health service.

(3) Except where it appears to the Secretary of State necessary to make an order under this paragraph as a matter of urgency, no such order shall be made until after the completion of such consultation as may be prescribed.

30.—(1) If an NHS trust is dissolved under this Part of this Schedule, the Secretary of State may by order transfer or provide for the transfer to—

(a) the Secretary of State; or

(b) a health authority; or

(c) another NHS trust,

of such of the property, rights and liabilities of the NHS trust which is dissolved as in his opinion is appropriate; and any such order may include provisions corresponding to those of section 8 of this Act.

(2) An order under this paragraph may make provision in connection with the transfer of staff employed by or for the purposes of the NHS trust which is dissolved; and such an order may include provisions corresponding to those of sections 6 and 7 of this Act, including provision for the making of a scheme by such health authority or other body as may be specified in the order.

(3) No order shall be made under this paragraph until after completion of such consultation as may be prescribed.'

31. Without prejudice to the generality of paragraph 30 above, if an NHS trust is dissolved under this Part of this Schedule, the Secretary of State or such other NHS trust or health authority as he may direct shall undertake the responsibility for the continued payment of any such pension, allowances or gratuities as, by virtue of paragraph 9(2) or paragraph 17 above, would otherwise have been the responsibility of the trust which has been dissolved.

32. An NHS trust may not be dissolved or wound up except in accordance with this Part of this Schedule.'

Schedule 3 makes provision for financial aspects of NHS trusts, including borrowing, guarantees of borrowing, limits on indebtedness, additional public dividend capital, surplus funds and investment.

2.6.5 Financial and supplementary provisions relating to National Health Service trusts

Part III of Schedule 2 of the National Health Service and Community Care Act 1990 provides[63] for the reimbursement for health services work carried out otherwise than under NHS contract; the supply of goods and services by local authorities;[64] the making of charges;[65] the power to raise money by appeals;[66] accounts and audit;[67] and for the protection of members and officers by the extension to the members and officers of NHS trusts of the protection conferred by section 125 of the National Health Service Act 1977 (for which see pp. 48–49, above.)

2.6.6 Consultation on establishment of National Health Service trusts

In the case of *R v Rochdale Health Authority, ex parte Rochdale Metropolitan Borough Council* (1992)[68] the Divisional Court of the Queen's Bench Division held that it is solely for the Secretary of State for Health, and not for local health authorities, to consider the reactions of those consulted under section 5(2) of the National Health Service and Community Care Act 1990 on proposals to establish NHS trusts. The court so held in dismissing an application by Rochdale Metropolitan Borough Council for judicial review of the decision of Rochdale Health Authority not to permit further financial information, in particular the business plan, to be available for use in such consultations.

While those consulted by the Regional Health Authority under section 5(2) are entitled to express whatever views they wish, there is no direct line of communication between them and the Secretary of State. In particular they are not 'objectors' with rights similar, for example, to those provided by legislation affecting town and country planning, and objections under that legislation. There is, the court held, nothing to prevent the Secretary of State from making arrangements to obtain further responses from any of those consulted, or to arrange for them to be provided with further information. The mere fact, however, that the response includes objections based on a perceived absence of information about part of the proposal does not of itself oblige the Secretary of State to do so.

NOTES

1. National Health Service Act 1977, section 1(2).
2. By the Secretary of State for Social Services Order, SI 1968/729, the functions of the Minister of Health under the National Health Service Acts 1946 to 1968 became the responsibility of the Secretary of State. Under the Transfer of Functions (Wales) Order, SI 1969/358, the functions of the Secretary of State for the Social Services under the above-mentioned Acts in respect of Wales passed to the Secretary of State for Wales. When used in this book in relation to functions under the National Health Service Act 1977 the expression Secretary of State must be read accordingly. Functions under the Mental Health Act 1959 (now 1983) in respect of Wales were not transferred to the Secretary of State for Wales.
3. See section 21 and Schedule 8 on distribution of these functions between the Secretary of State and the local social services authority.
4. See the Special Hospitals Service Authority (Establishment and Constitution) Order 1989, SI 1989/948 and the Special Hospitals Service Authority (Functions and Membership) Regulations 1989, SI 1989/949 (as amended by SI 1989/1611).
5. SI 1990/1526; the Authorities are constituted under SI 1990/1525.
6. *Pfizer Corporation v Minister of Health* [1965] AC 512; *Hills (Patents) Ltd v University College Hospital* [1956] 1 QB 90; *and Wood v Leeds AHA (T)* [1974] ICR 535. This view is taken throughout this book, and for convenience it is repeated elsewhere as appropriate.
7. National Health Service Reorganisation Act 1973, section 2. By the Isles of Scilly (National Health Service) Order, SI 1973/1935, the reorganisation was applied to the Scilly Isles. The local authority is the Council of the Isles.
8. See now the National Health Service Functions (Directions to Authorities and Administrative Arrangements) Regulations 1991, SI 1991/554.
9. Part III.
10. SI 1981/1836, as amended by SI 1982/343 and SI 1990/1755.

11. SI 1990/1331, as amended by SIs 1990/1755 and 1758.
12. Appendix II of HRC(73)22, quoting from HM(61)59. The latter is still applicable even though the 1973 Circular is revoked.
13. Public Bodies (Admission to Meetings) Act 1960, section 1(5).
14. [1975] 1WLR 701.
15. As amended by the Health Services Act 1980, Schedule 1, paragraph 28.
16. For Wales, see now the Welsh Common Services Authority Constitution Order 1990, SI 1990/2647.
17. SI 1981/1837, as amended by SI 1982/344, SIs, 1983/30 and 36, SI 1984/328, SI 1988/407, SIs 1990/1755 and 1756.
18. SI 1981/1837.
19. SI 1991/554.
20. SI 1981/597.
21. SI 1981/101, as amended by SI 1986/458. For detail on the functions of the Health Advisory Service see Circular HC(84)16.
22. As amended by the Health Services Act 1980, Schedule 1, paragraph 81; and see Circular HC(82)1.
23. As amended by the Health Services Act 1980, Schedule 1, paragraph 39.
24. SI 1974/190.
25. SI 1974/168.
26. As amended by the Health Services Act 1980, Schedule 1, paragraph 40; and see HC(81)15 and HC(85)11 generally.
27. As amended by the Health Services Act 1980, Schedule 1, paragraph 82 and the Health and Social Security Act 1984, Schedule 3, paragraphs 15–17.
28. SI 1985/304 as amended by SI 1990/1375.
29. The references to a Family Health Service Authority were substituted by section 2 of the National Health Service and Community Care Act 1990.
30. As amended by SI 1990/1375. The references to a Family Health Service Authority were substituted by section 2 of the National Health Service and Community Care Act 1990.
31. National Health Service Management Executive pamphlet published 1990, for guidance only.
32. SI 1985/304.
33. The Times, 16 August 1989.
34. As amended by SI 1990/1375.
35. National Health Service Act 1977, section 85.
36. National Health Service Act 1977, section 86.
37. SI 1974/296, now revoked and replaced by SI 1991/481.
38. 1951 SC 200.
39. 1951 SC 464.
40. [1953] 1 QB 511.
41. The Times, 17 March 1989.
42. Out of monies provided by Parliament.
43. National Health Service Act 1977, section 97(2).
44. National Health Service Act 1977, sections 97(6) and 97(1)(c).
45. National Health Service Act 1977, section 97(7).
46. SI 1982/277.
47. SI 1974/541.
48. Charities (Exempted Accounts) Regulations 1963, SI 1963/210, replaced by SI 1976/929.
49. Charities (Exempted Accounts) Regulations 1976, SI 1976/929, as amended by SI 1982/288.
50. National Health Service Act 1977, section 8 and Schedule 5, Part III, paragraph 9.

51. SI 1991/481.
52. SI 1988/551, as amended by SI 1991/557.
53. Regulation 5A.
54. National Health Service (Travelling Expenses and Remission of Charges) Amendment Regulations 1991, SI 1991/557.
55. National Health Service and Community Care Act 1990, Schedule 2, paragraph 23.
56. See the National Health Service (Vehicles) Order 1974, SI 1974/168.
57. HMSO 1989; ISBN 0 11 321165 1. At the time of going to press with the 7th edition of this book, NHS Estates advised that it was in the process of updating and revising the document. The document issued in 1989 applies to property managed by health authorities on behalf of the Secretary of State for Health, and not to NHS trusts which have the estate required for operational use legally conveyed to them.
58. SI 1989/51.
59. SI 1991/725. See also 'Contracts for Health Services: Operating Contracts' and EL(90)MB/26 'Contract Pricing: Cost Allocation Principles'.
60. EL(89)MB/125.
61. SI 1990/2024, as amended by SI 1990/2160.
62. In particular, section 132; see Chapter 30, p. 843 for a discussion of the duties which are effectively imposed on the Directors of an NHS trust in this regard.
63. Paragraphs 19 and 20.
64. Paragraph 21.
65. Paragraph 22.
66. Paragraph 23.
67. Paragraph 24.
68. The Times, 17 February 1992.

CHAPTER 3

Voluntary hospitals

3.1 GOVERNING BODIES AND THEIR POWERS AND DUTIES

A voluntary hospital is defined in the Voluntary Hospitals (Paying Patients) Act 1936 (as now read in the light of the National Health Service and Community Care Act 1990) as an institution, not being an institution which is carried on for profit, or which is maintained wholly or mainly at the expense of the rates, or which is vested in the Secretary of State or in a National Health Service trust which provides medical or surgical treatment for in-patients.

Such hospitals were empowered by that Act to provide accommodation for paying patients in pursuance of orders made by the Charity Commissioners, and under section 5 (1) the Commissioners were authorised to make rules in relation to such orders.

The powers of a voluntary hospital governing body as well as the effect of acts apparently *ultra vires* (that is, beyond its legal powers) depend on the constitution of the hospital. This may be in the form of a charter, memorandum and articles of association or trust deed. This chapter briefly notes the different types of constitution and their general effect; but for a full exposition of the law relating to companies, statutory bodies and charitable trusts reference should be made to standard works on these subjects. The more important provisions of the Charities Act 1993 are, however, referred to here.

A voluntary hospital authority, if a corporate body, may be legally responsible for loss or damage suffered by a third party as a result of the wrongful acts and omissions of its officers, employees or other persons acting on its behalf and with its authority. The position of the trustees or committee of an unincorporated voluntary hospital is discussed at pp. 75–76, below.

3.1.1 Chartered hospitals

The general effect of the grant of a Royal Charter is to confer on the hospital the status of a corporate body which may hold land and other property and investments, enter into contracts and sue and be sued in its corporate name. The Trustee Investments Act 1961 sets out the range of authorised investments. The members of the governing body of the hospital are under no personal liability otherwise than for any breach of trust to which they may be parties or for their own personal acts and omissions (such as in the case of a surgeon on the governing body who is negligent when operating on a patient in hospital).

A Royal Charter, granted on petition to the Privy Council, usually provides for the making of bye-laws, subject to the sanction of the Privy Council the first bye-laws being normally annexed as a schedule to the Charter. The Charter is broadly comparable with the memorandum of association of a hospital incorporated under the Companies Act and the bye-laws to the articles of association.

3.1.2 Hospitals incorporated by private Act of Parliament

The constitution, powers and functions of a hospital incorporated by Act of Parliament are all wholly governed by the relevant Act together with any bye-laws or rules properly made under it. A hospital so incorporated can hold land, investments and other property, make contracts and sue and be sued in its corporate name, subject to restrictions contained in the Act. The members of the governing body are usually free of any personal liability whatever in respect of the affairs of the corporation except as regards any breach of trust to which they may be parties, including any loss of trust property due to their personal negligence.

Some private Acts to which reference might be made by anyone in search of precedents are the Birmingham United Hospitals Act 1934, the Liverpool United Hospital Act 1937, and the Royal Sheffield Infirmary and Hospital Act 1938. These Acts were repealed by the National Health Service Act 1946; but the corporations created by these Acts may not actually have been dissolved.[1]

In any modern Act incorporating a charity the powers of the High Court and of the Charity Commissioners in respect of the charity are usually expressly preserved and power is also usually conferred on them to authorise amendments in the sanctioned scheme and bye-laws subject only to the overriding provisions of the Act. Hence it should seldom be necessary to go back to Parliament for an amending Act. Further powers in relation to alteration of provisions of a private Act relating to an incorporated charity are conferred on the Charity Commissioners by section 17 of the Charities Act 1993, which provides for amending schemes to be approved by resolution of both Houses of Parliament without going through the troublesome and expensive private bill procedure.

3.1.3   Hospitals incorporated under the Companies Act

Application under the Companies Act 1985 is now the simplest, cheapest and most expeditious way of obtaining the advantages of incorporation with limitation of the liability of the members and the most frequently adopted. A hospital so incorporated may take, hold and use land, investments and other property, make contracts and sue and be sued in its corporate name in the same manner as hospitals incorporated by Royal Charter or by special Act of Parliament.

Formation of a company limited by guarantee rather than one limited by shares is the method appropriate to a hospital or other charitable organisation. The subscribers to the memorandum, that is those co-operating in the formation of the company, and all subsequent members of the company (often called 'governors' in the case of a voluntary hospital) undertake to find a nominal amount, usually one pound, towards meeting any outstanding liabilities of the company on its being wound up.

The objects clause of the memorandum should be in the widest possible terms but there are certain limitations. For example, if it is an existing hospital which is being incorporated, the Charity Commissioners will have to be satisfied that the objects as set out do not allow the possibility of existing endowments and other trust funds being diverted from the purposes for which they were given or subscribed unless the circumstances are such that the Commissioners authorise application *cy-près* under sections 13 or 14 of the Charities Act 1993.

3.1.4   Unincorporated hospitals

Such unincorporated hospitals and similar institutions as may still exist will generally be carried on under the provisions of a trust deed providing for the responsibility of administering the trust to be exercised by a committee or board of management. The method of appointment of the committee, except in the case of certain hospitals carried on by religious orders, was at one time almost invariably by election by and from amongst the subscribers either generally or on a franchise restricted to say, annual subscribers of a certain minimum amount who might be designated 'governors'. In the years immediately prior to the taking over of most of the voluntary hospitals by the Minister of Health in 1948, representatives of the medical staff, of contributory scheme subscribers, of local authorities and of other interests may transpire to have been added. There is no prevailing pattern among surviving voluntary hospitals or among any which may have been established since 1948.

Unless transferred into the name of the Official Custodian for Charities as custodian trustee, the real property and investments of an unincorporated hospital must ordinarily be held in the names of a small number of trustees, usually elected by the subscribers or governors, unless the trust deed vests the powers of appointment in the committee of management or there are other provisions for their nomination. The trustees may themselves have discretionary power as to selection of investments within the limits laid down in the Trustee Investments Act 1961, or may be mere custodian trustees obliged to carry out the instructions of the committee of management so long as those instructions are in accordance with the provisions of the trust deed and are not otherwise contrary to law.

The essential disadvantages of an unincorporated hospital, even with a well drawn up trust deed, are: first, that there is considerable trouble and expense when a trustee dies or resigns or when the removal of a trustee is imperative and a new trustee or trustees have to be appointed; second, that the absence from England or the illness of a trustee may create difficulties; third, that the extent of the personal liability of the members of the committee of management in respect of hospital affairs and even of members of the general body of subscribers who take an active interest by attending meetings for the election of members of the committee and so forth is by no means clear and could well be extremely onerous.

Property and investments may be held by the Official Custodian for Charities as custodian trustee. It is not possible to say dogmatically that the personal liability of the members of the committee of management would in all circumstances be limited to the amount of the charity funds under their control. For example, if the committee were sued in respect of negligence in their management of hospital affairs leading to loss or injury to a patient (such as, for instance, their negligent appointment of an incompetent or unqualified medical practitioner to the staff) they might be personally liable in damages.

There have in the past been in existence a few unincorporated charitable hospitals not having a constitution embodied in a trust deed. Probably none survived the coming into operation of the National Health Service Act 1946. In such cases there may have been a set of rules which will certainly have provided for some sort of committee of management and there must have been trustees of property and investments.

3.1.5 Hospitals administered under a scheme established by the Court or the Charity Commissioners

In any of the circumstances set out in sections 13 and 14 of the Charities Act 1993, the court or the Charity Commissioners or, in the case of an educational charity, the Secretary of State for Education and Science may make a scheme for the administration of a charity. This matter is more fully discussed in Chapter 21.

3.1.6 Effect of Health Service Acts on voluntary hospitals

As from 5 July 1948, all existing voluntary hospitals other than hospitals excluded by the Minister of Health under section 6(3) of the National Health Service Act 1946 were transferred to the Minister and placed under the control of governing bodies constituted in accordance with the provisions of the Act. By section 78 (1)(c) of the Act, the governing bodies of the voluntary hospitals so transferred, whose functions wholly ceased in consequence of the passing of the Act, were dissolved as from the appointed day, the Minister being empowered to make any necessary regulations for the winding-up of their affairs. The National Health Service Act 1977, Schedule 14, paragraph 6 provides for the case of a hospital constituted or whose affairs are regulated under a private Act or charter. The Secretary of State has power by order to alter, amend or repeal such provisions of the private Act or charter as may be inconsistent with those of the National Health Service Act 1946.

Any voluntary hospitals not taken over under the Act on the appointed day retained their existing constitution. The law relating to such hospitals and to any new voluntary hospitals is unaffected by the legislation relevant to the National Health Service.

A transferred hospital still remains a charity, as to which see Chapter 21, pp. 610–621, below.

For a discussion of the position of charitable corporations which formerly owned hospitals transferred to the Secretary of State under the Act of 1946, see *Re Kellner's Will Trusts* (1949).[1]

3.2 POWERS OF VOLUNTARY HOSPITALS

3.2.1 Limits of powers of incorporated hospitals

A general outline of the powers of voluntary hospital governing bodies has already been given, above. The general powers of a hospital incorporated by Royal Charter or by Act of Parliament are in the Charter or Act and detailed rules of procedure in bye-laws, rules or regulations made thereunder. Hospitals incorporated under the Companies Acts have a memorandum of association which indicates the limits of the powers of the incorporated body by defining its objects and the articles of association determine the detailed rules of procedure. The Companies Acts contain provisions regarding meetings, audit and also as to annual and other returns to the Registrar of Companies.

Acts in excess of powers

If a chartered hospital does anything which is outside the objects of powers specified in its Charter, such acts would not appear to be necessarily invalid, but would constitute grounds for revocation of the Charter. If abuse of power amounted to a use of trust funds for objects other than those for which they had been provided, members of the governing body would apparently be personally liable to make restitution.

Generally speaking, if the Board of a hospital incorporated otherwise than by Royal Charter acts outside the limits of the objects of the incorporated body as set out in the special Act or in the memorandum of association, the wrongful act is invalid and is incapable of ratification. If, however, an act done is not *ultra vires* the corporation or company but exceeds the powers delegated to the Board it is still invalid but is usually capable of ratification by a general meeting of governors or other body to which the Board is responsible.

Indemnity for Board members

If the members of the Board of an incorporated hospital exceed their powers causing a third party loss, they may be personally liable for breach of warranty of authority; though with exercise of ordinary prudence this risk is far more remote than the risk of personal liability for a possibly technical breach of trust. Modern incorporations by special Act normally provide blanket cover against personal liability for purely technical breaches of trust.

Similar cover for reasonable actions in the course of carrying out their duties is usually given by the articles to members of the Board of a hospital incorporated under the Companies Acts. Such cover does not confer the same immunity as when embodied in a special Act, for a clause is always inserted in the memorandum of association saving the jurisdiction of the court and of the Charity Commissioners and reserving the personal liability of the managers and trustees of the hospital as answerable for their own acts, receipts, neglects and defaults, *and for the due administration of its property* in the same manner and to the same extent as they would have been had there been no incorporation. The words in italics apparently preserve the full liability of the Board as trustees subject always to the power of the court to excuse a breach of trust under section 61 of the Trustee Act 1925.

3.2.2   Powers of unincorporated hospitals

Limits on the powers

The powers of the trustees or committee of management of an unincorporated hospital are strictly limited by the terms of the trust deed, if any, and except so far as expressly therein duly varied, under the provisions of the Charities Act 1993. It is beyond the scope of this work to discuss the position where there is no trust deed nor other written constitution; reference may be made however, to pp. 598–600, below, as to the powers of the Charity Commissioners to make a scheme for such a charity.

Indemnity for trustees and committee

Trustees of unincorporated charities as well as persons concerned with administration of an incorporated charity may in respect of any breach of trust apply to the court to be relieved of personal liability under the provisions of section 61 of the Trustee Act 1925, on the grounds that they have acted honestly reasonably and ought fairly to be excused, and the court may make an order relieving them wholly or partly of personal liability. If, however, charity trustees (for the definition of which see Chapter 21, pp. 593–594) have doubt of the lawfulness of any action they propose to take and they act on the advice of the Charity Commissioners given under section 29 of the Charities Act 1993, they are protected against any personal liability. The power of the Commissioners under section 26 to sanction action otherwise outside the powers of the trustees is noted in Chapter 21, p.598, below.

3.3   LOANS AND OVERDRAFTS

The borrowing power of voluntary hospitals varies according to the constitution. Voluntary hospitals incorporated by Act of Parliament in modern times frequently had unrestricted borrowing powers coupled with wide powers of pledging hospital property as security. Similarly wide powers were apparently contained in modern charters.

Apparently unlimited borrowing powers including the right to secure the loan on hospital property or investments may be taken in the memorandum of a hospital incorporated under the Companies Act but these apparently unlimited powers have ordinarily been found to be limited by a standard proviso on the following lines:

'Provided that in case the Hospital shall take or hold any property subject to the jurisdiction of the Charity Commissioners for England and Wales or the Secretary of State for Education and Science, the Hospital shall not sell, mortgage, charge or lease the same without such authority, approval or consent as may be required by law, and as regards any such property the Managers or Trustees of the Hospital shall be chargeable for such property as may come into their hands, and shall be answerable and accountable for their own acts, receipts, neglects and defaults, and for the due administration of such property in the same manner and to the same extent as they would as such Managers and Trustees have been if no incorporation had been effected and the incorporation of the Hospital shall not diminish or impair any control or authority exercisable by the Chancery Division, the Charity Commissioners or the Secretary of State for Education and Science over such Managers or Trustees, but they shall as regards such property be subject jointly and severally to such control or authority as if the Hospital were not incorporated. In case the Hospital shall take or hold any property which may be subject to any trusts, the Hospital shall only deal with the same in such manner as allowed by law, having regard to such trusts.'

The general effect of such a proviso, apart from preserving the personal responsibility of members of the Board and others dealing with the hospital property, is to make dealings, whether by way of sale, mortgage, exchange or otherwise, with real property (land and buildings) being *permanent endowments*[2] of the hospital subject to consent of the Charity Commissioners or of the Court or, in the case of an educational charity (such as a medical school or, possibly, a nurses' training school), of the Secretary of State for Education and Science.

Furthermore, the powers of any charity other than an exempt or an excepted charity to borrow money against property forming part of the permanent endowment, or to deal with land, whether part of its permanent endowment or not, were formerly subject to the provisions of section 29 of the Charities Act 1960 requiring official consent.

Wide exceptions are now made to the requirement of consent of the court or the Commissioners in the case of sale, lease or other disposal of land, and of mortgages, by sections 36 and 38 of the Charities Act 1993. These provisions have no application to exempt[3] charities. The provisions relevant for present purposes are extracted as follows:

'36.—(1) Subject to the following provisions of this section . . . no land held by or in trust for a charity shall be sold, leased or otherwise disposed of without an order of the court or of the Commissioners.

(2) Subsection (1) above shall not apply to a disposition of such land if—
  (a) the disposition is made to a person who is not—
        (i) a connected person (as defined in Schedule 5 to this Act), or
        (ii) a trustee for, or nominee of, a connected person; and
  (b) the requirements of subsection (3) or (5) below have been complied with in relation to it.

(3) Except where the proposed disposition is the granting of such a lease as is mentioned in subsection (5) below, the charity trustees must, before entering into an agreement for the sale, or (as the case may be) for a lease or other disposition, of the land—
  (a) obtain and consider a written report on the proposed disposition from a qualified surveyor instructed by the trustees and acting exclusively for the charity;
  (b) advertise the proposed disposition for such period and in such manner as the surveyor has advised in his report (unless he has there advised that it

would not be in the best interests of the charity to advertise the proposed disposition); and

(c) decide that they are satisfied, having considered the surveyor's report, that the terms on which the disposition is proposed to be made are the best that can reasonably be obtained for the charity . . .

(5) Where the proposed disposition is the granting of a lease for a term ending not more than seven years after it is granted (other than one granted wholly or partly in consideration of a fine), the charity trustees must, before entering into an agreement for the lease—

(a) obtain and consider the advice on the proposed disposition of a person who is reasonably believed by the trustees to have the requisite ability and practical experience to provide them with competent advice on the proposed disposition; and

(b) decide that they are satisfied, having considered that person's advice, that the terms on which the disposition is proposed to be made are the best that can reasonably be obtained for the charity.'

'**38.**—(1) Subject to subsection (2) below, no mortgage of land held by or in trust for a charity shall be granted without an order of the court or of the Commissioners.

(2) Subsection (1) above shall not apply to a mortgage of any such land by way of security for the repayment of a loan where the charity trustees have, before executing the mortgage, obtained and considered proper advice, given to them in writing, on the matters mentioned in subsection (3) below.

(3) Those matters are—

(a) whether the proposed loan is necessary in order for the charity trustees to be able to pursue the particular course of action in connection with which the loan is sought by them;

(b) whether the terms of the proposed loan are reasonable having regard to the status of the charity as a prospective borrower; and

(c) the ability of the charity to repay on those terms the sum proposed to be borrowed.

(4) For the purposes of subsection (2) above proper advice is the advice of a person—

(a) who is reasonably believed by the charity trustees to be qualified by his ability in and practical experience of financial matters; and

(b) who has no financial interest in the making of the loan in question;

and such advice may constitute proper advice for those purposes notwithstanding that the person giving it does so in the course of his employment as an officer or employee of the charity or of the charity trustees.'

If there is any doubt as to the validity of borrowing powers which it is desired to exercise, the advice of the Charity Commissioners under section 29 of the Charities Act 1993 should be sought. The measure of cover afforded to trustees acting on such advice is discussed in Chapter 21.

NOTES

1. See, for instance *Re Kellner's Will Trusts* [1949] 2 All ER 774.
2 For the definition of 'permanent endowment' see Ch. 21, p. 595.
3 See Charities Act 1993, section 3(5)(a).

CHAPTER 4

Nursing homes: registration, conduct and inspection

The discussion of legal provisions relating to institutions and facilities delivering personal health care would be incomplete without also giving a brief survey of regulations relating to nursing homes and mental nursing homes, as well as residential care homes, established and maintained outside the National Health Service. The meaning of 'hospital' was examined in Chapter 1 (pp. 1–4) and Chapter 3 examined legal provisions relating to the status and conduct of voluntary hospitals. By definition, nursing homes (including mental nursing homes) and residential care homes are not a part of the National Health Service; but their registration, inspection and conduct are appropriately examined in this book for a number of reasons. First, the registration and inspection of nursing homes and mental nursing homes is one of the functions of health authorities established under the National Health Service legislation.[1] Second, mental nursing homes which are specifically registered to take detained patients under the Mental Health Act 1983 are legally able to exercise most (but not all) of the powers and functions set out in Chapter 30 of this book. Third, the law relating to injury to a patient, injury at work, consent to treatment, access to documents and records, health and safety, and much of the law relating to employment and professional qualifications, applies equally to residential and nursing homes as it does to facilities within the National Health Service.

Previous editions of this book have concentrated exclusively on legal provisions relating to nursing homes and mental nursing homes, there having been no need until 1984 to discuss residential homes in any detail. However, since the Registered Homes Act 1984 it has become necessary to cross-reference the registration and inspection provisions laid down in that Act, respectively, for residential care homes on the one hand and for nursing homes and mental nursing homes on the other. Large institutions and facilities established and maintained outside the National Health Service can be, and often are, called hospitals even though for the purposes of the Mental Health Act 1983 and the detention of patients under that Act they are in law classified as mental nursing homes. It is even possible, though unlikely in practice, that such an institution or facility might require to be registered as a residential care home as well as a mental nursing home in certain limited circumstances which are briefly explained below.

Legal provisions relating to nursing homes, including mental nursing homes, and to residential care homes were formerly contained in separate legislation resulting in both cases from processes of amendment and consolidation. Since the enactment of the Registered Homes Act 1984 all homes, of whichever type, have been governed by a single piece of legislation, and regulations made under it. Part I of the Registered Homes Act 1984 provides for the registration, inspection and conduct of residential care homes; and Part II of the Act provides for the registration, inspection and conduct of nursing homes and mental nursing homes. Given the occasional relevance, to nursing homes and mental nursing homes, of additional registration under Part I of the Act, the requirements of Part I and II are now dealt with respectively.

4.1 REGISTRATION AND CONDUCT OF RESIDENTIAL CARE HOMES

The definition, for the purposes of the Act, of a residential care home is set out in section 1 of the Act, which provides as follows:

'**1.**—(1) Subject to the following provisions of this section, registration under this Part of this Act is required in respect of any establishment which provides or is intended to provide, whether for reward or not, residential accommodation with both board and personal care for persons in need of personal care by reason of old age, disablement, past or present dependence on alcohol or drugs, or past or present mental disorder.

(2) Such an establishment is referred to in this Part of this Act as a 'residential care home'.

(3) Registration under this Part of this Act does not affect any requirement to register under Part II of this Act.

(4) Registration under this Part of this Act is not required in respect of an establishment which provides or is intended to provide residential accommodation with both board and personal care for fewer than 4 persons, excluding persons carrying on or intending to carry on the home or employed or intended to be employed there and their relatives.

(5) Registration under this Part of this Act is not required in respect of any of the following—

    (a) any establishment which is used, or is intended to be used, solely as a nursing home or mental nursing home;

    (b) any hospital as defined in section 128 of the National Health Service Act 1977 which is maintained in pursuance of an Act of Parliament;

    (c) any hospital as defined in section 145(1) of the Mental Health Act 1983;

    (d) any voluntary home or community home within the meaning of the Child Care Act 1980;

    (e) any children's home to which the Children's Homes Act 1982 applies;

    (f) subject to subsection (6) below, any school, as defined in section 114 of the Education Act 1944;

(g) subject to subsection (7) below, any establishment to which the Secretary of State has made a payment of maintenance grant under regulations made by virtue of section 100(1)(b) of the Education Act 1944;

(h) any university or university college or college, school or hall of a university;

(j) any establishment managed or provided by a government department or local authority or by any authority or body constituted by an Act of Parliament or incorporated by Royal Charter.

(6) An independent school within the meaning of the Education Act 1944 is not excluded by subsection (5) above if the school provides accommodation for 50 or less children under the age of 18 years and is not for the time being approved by the Secretary of State under section 11(3)(a) of the Education Act 1981.

(7) An establishment to which the Secretary of State has made a payment of maintenance grant under regulations made by virtue of section 100(1)(b) of the Education Act 1944 is only excluded by subsection (5) above until the end of the period of 12 months from the date on which the Secretary of State made the payment.'

Concern about establishments providing board and personal care for fewer than four people, the standards of which may be called in question if run by persons declared unfit, but organised in multiple small units to avoid the registration requirement, led to the enactment of the Registered Homes (Amendment) Act 1991. Section 1 of the 1991 Act provides, relevantly, as follows:

'Registration in respect of small residential care homes

1.—(1) Part I of the Registered Homes Act 1984 (residential care homes) is amended as follows.

(2) In section 1 (requirement of registration), for subsection (4) (exemption for small homes) substitute

"(4) Registration under this Part of this Act is not required in respect of a small home—

(a) if the only persons for whom it provides or is intended to provide residential accommodation with both board and personal care are persons carrying on or intending to carry on the home or employed or intended to be employed there or their relatives, or

(b) in such other cases as may be prescribed by the Secretary of State.

(4A) In this Part a 'small home' means an establishment which provides or is intended to provide residential accommodation with both board and personal care for fewer than 4 persons, excluding persons carrying on or intending to carry on the home or employed or intended to be employed there and their relatives.

(4B) The references in subsections (4) and (4A) to the persons for whom residential accommodation is or is intended to be provided relate only to persons who are in need of personal care by reason of old age, disablement, past or present dependence on alcohol or drugs, or past or present mental disorder."'

The remaining provisions of section 1 of this Act relate to optional registration of small homes registered as nursing homes under Part II of the Act (see pp. 89–97 of this chapter); general provisions as to registration;

registration fees; annual returns in respect of small homes, as defined by section 4A of the 1984 Act, as amended; and grounds for refusal or cancellation of registration. The new Regulations relating to small homes came into effect on 1 April 1993.[2]

The key expression in the legal definition of residential care home is 'personal care'. Any institution, facility or establishment which provides such personal care must be registered as a residential care home even if it is known as, and trades under the name of, a rest home, hostel or other such description. Section 20 of the 1984 Act, providing for general interpretation of terms within it, defines 'personal care' as meaning 'care which includes assistance with bodily functions where such assistance is required'. Apart from that, no further definition or description of the term 'personal care' is given. It is an expression which lies at the root of many practical problems and disputes relating to the requirement of registration of, respectively, residential and nursing homes.

Section 20 states that personal care includes such care as is there described, but falls distinctly short of an exhaustive definition of the term. The Act gives no guidance as to what other forms of assistance and support constitute personal care. 'Personal care' certainly cannot be defined by reference merely to section 20 of the Act. Some assistance is derived from a Circular issued by the Department of Health and Social Security in 1987[3] which suggests the following by way of a guide:

'Residential Homes are primarily a means of providing a greater degree of support for those elderly people no longer able to cope with the practicalities of living in their own homes even with the help of the domiciliary services. The care provided is limited to that appropriate to a residential setting and is broadly equivalent to what might be provided by a competent and caring relative able to respond to emotional as well as physical needs. It includes for instance help with washing, bathing, dressing; assistance with toilet needs; the administration of medicines and, when a resident falls sick, the kind of attention someone would receive in his own home from a caring relative under guidance of the general practitioner or nurse member of the primary health care team. However, the staff of a Home are not expected to provide the professional kind of health care that is properly the function of the primary health care services. Nor should residential Homes be used as nursing homes or extensions of hospitals.'

While this guidance is helpful it, too, is illustrative and not exhaustive. The reference to a 'professional kind of health care' should not divert attention from the fact that professional nursing (as well as associated) experts will no doubt furnish personal care in addition to their specialist expertise.

It has been suggested[4] that a distinction could be drawn between 'household nursing' and 'professional nursing'. Household nursing, permissible in residential care homes, would describe those tasks which a caring relative could reasonably be expected to perform, perhaps with guidance from a general medical practitioner. These tasks might include the taking of temperatures, changing simple dressings, the management of incontinence and the dispensing of medication prescribed by a general medical practitioner. By contrast, 'professional nursing', which can be given only in a registered nursing home or mental nursing home (see below) would cover all other types of nursing including any technical procedures such as injections, using specialised equipment and therapeutic procedures beyond the competence of a caring relative. 'Personal care' could also include counselling and general community and social work support, for instance in a rehabilitation hostel.

The definition will take on considerable significance when the small homes become registered, for many small client groups and particularly adults with a variety of learning difficulties live in hostels which should be classified as small homes if one interprets personal care in the broadest way. This has great significance in relation to the supply of public funds to support placement in such units with the transfer of care provision from central government to local authorities; and this means that such units if registered should be the subject of contracting between home owner and local authority (and possibly resident) so that the principal financial obligation will be undertaken by the local authority, whereas if they are regarded as residential hostels the funding will be through government sponsored but local authority administered housing benefit schemes. The very practical difference is that the individual will choose a residential hostel place and then seek payment of housing benefit as a matter of right; whereas social services placements, although in principle selected and selectable by the client, will be much more controlled by the local authority and in practice that local authority will be a county council and not the district council who will be paying housing benefit.

Section 1(4) excluded the requirement of registration in the case of an establishment providing personal care, board and lodging for fewer than four persons (excluding staff); but see now the provisions of section 1 of the Registered Homes (Amendment) Act 1991 (pp. 84–85, above). Furthermore, section 4 of the 1984 Act allows a nursing home or mental nursing home registered under Part II of the Act and providing personal care, board and lodging for *fewer* than four persons the option to register under Part I of the Act as a residential home.

Section 2 provides that if any person carries on a residential care home without being registered under this Part of the Act in respect of it, he shall be guilty of an offence. The expression 'carried on' is explained further by section 3. Where the manager or intended manager of a residential care home is not in control of it (whether as owner or otherwise) both the manager or intended manager and the person in control are to be treated as carrying on or intending to carry on the home; and, accordingly, they require to be registered under Part I of the Act. It is, however, not easy to ascertain the practical meaning of this latter provision, given the difficulty of conceiving what sort of manager is not in fact in control of the home in question. It is not correct to argue, as some local authorities do, that every home must have a separate manager; and section 3 neither expresses nor implies any such requirement.

If only one person is registered under this Part of the Act in respect of a residential care home and that person dies, section 6 provides that his personal representative or his widow, or any other relative of his, may for a period not exceeding four weeks from his death (or for such long a period as the registration authority may sanction) carry on the home without being registered in respect of it.

A person carrying on a unregistered residential care home is committing an offence, and a registration authority which has reasonable cause to suspect that such a home is operating in its area has a legal power to enter and inspect the establishment.

Registers kept by a registration authority for the purposes of Part I of the Act shall be available for inspection at all reasonable times and any person inspecting any such register is entitled to make copies of entries in the register on payment of such reasonable fee as the registration authority may determine.[5] The Secretary of State may by Regulations[6] require persons registered in respect of residential care homes to pay an annual fee and may specify the amount and the time when it is to be paid. Such provision is made by the Residential Care Homes Regulations 1984.[7]

A registration authority must (under section 5 in respect of residential homes, mirrored by section 23 for nursing homes) register the home unless lawful reasons exist for refusing to do so.

Section 9 provides that a registration authority 'may' refuse to register an applicant for registration in respect of a residential care home if it is satisfied that he or any other person concerned or intended to be concerned in carrying on the home is not a fit person to be concerned in carrying on a residential care home; *or* that for reasons connected with their situation, construction, state of repair, accommodation, staffing, or equipment, the premises used or intended to be used for the purposes of the home, or any other premises used or intended to be used in connection with it, are not fit to be used for such purpose; *or* that the way in which it is intended to carry on the home is such as not to provide services or facilities reasonably required.

These provisions are mirrored in section 25 of the Act which provides, in greater detail, for the decision to refuse to register a nursing home. 'Fit' appears to mean, simply, suitable in all the circumstances of the case, and a particularly bad standard of conduct is unnecessary to justify failure to register. The word 'may' in sections 9 and 25 is no doubt directory and not merely permissive; it would be surprising if a registration authority should identify such a defect and then proceed to exercise a discretion to register.

Section 12 provides that when a registration authority proposes to refuse a registration application it must give the applicant notice of this proposal and of the reasons for it. The applicant then has 14 days to inform the authority whether he wishes to make representations about the proposed refusal. The right to make representations is governed by section 13, as follows:

'**13.**—(1) A notice under section 12 above shall state that within 14 days of service of the notice any person on whom it is served may in writing require the registration authority to give him an opportunity to make representations to them concerning the matter.

(2) Where a notice has been served under section 12 above, the registration authority shall not determine the matter until either—

    (a) any person on whom the notice was served has made representations concerning the matter; or

    (b) the period during which any such person could have required them to give him an opportunity to make representations has elapsed without their being required to give such an opportunity; or

    (c) the conditions specified in subsection (3) below are satisfied.

(3) The conditions mentioned in subsection (2) above are—

    (a) that a person on whom the notice was served has required the registration authority to give him an opportunity to make representations to them concerning the matter;

    (b) that the registration authority have allowed him a reasonable period to make his representations; and

    (c) that he has failed to make them within that period.

(4) Representations may be made, at the option of the person making them, either in writing or orally.

(5) If he informs the registration authority that he desires to make oral representations, they shall give him an opportunity of appearing before and of being heard by a committee or sub-committee of the registration authority.'

Section 14 of the Act sets out the procedure to be followed by a registration authority when it decides to adopt a proposal to grant or refuse an application for registration, or to cancel or amend a registration. Such notice shall, by section 14(2), be accompanied by a notice explaining the right of appeal in the event of refusal, cancellation or amendment. Unless the authority decides to grant an application for registration subject to conditions,[8] or refuses an application for registration, the decision of the authority comes into effect (in the absence of any appeal) 28 days from the notification of the decision. In the event of an appeal, the registration authority's decision comes into effect when such an appeal is either determined or abandoned. An appeal lies against the decision of the registration authority to a Registered Homes Tribunal. The appeal must be in writing and may not be brought more than 28 days after service on the applicant of the notice of the decision or order of the authority. On appeal, the Tribunal may confirm the decision or direct that it shall not have effect; and it may vary any condition for the time being in force in respect of the home to which the appeal relates; or it may direct that any such condition shall cease to have effect; or that any such condition as it thinks fit shall have effect in respect of the home. A registration authority is under a legal duty[9] to comply with any direction given by a Tribunal pursuant to section 15 of the Act.

A consequence of the fact that an application for registration may be granted by a registering authority subject to conditions is that (subject to an appeal) it is not possible without the authority's permission to apply to vary conditions only if the registration, once granted, is to continue.

Section 17 provides for inspection of residential care homes, as follows:

'**17.**—(1) Any person authorised in that behalf by the Secretary of State may at all times enter and inspect any premises which are used, or which that person has reasonable cause to believe to be used, for the purposes of a residential care home.

(2) Any person authorised in that behalf by a registration authority may at all times enter and inspect any premises in the area of the authority which are used, or which that person has reasonable cause to believe to be used, for those purposes.

(3) The powers of inspection conferred by subsections (1) and (2) above shall include power to inspect any records required to be kept in accordance with regulations under this Part of this Act.

(4) The Secretary of State may by regulations require that residential care homes shall be inspected on such occasions or at such intervals as the regulations may prescribe.

(5) A person who proposes to exercise any power of entry or inspection conferred by this section shall if so required produce some duly authenticated document showing his authority to exercise the power.

(6) Any person who obstructs the exercise of any such power shall be guilty of an offence.'

Where an establishment is registered both as a residential care home and as a nursing home or mental nursing home, the two registration authorities (the local social services authority, and the health authority, respectively) should work closely together and should carry out joint inspections where they feel this to be appropriate. Good and co-operative working procedures should therefore be established at local level between the relevant registration authorities.

4.2 NURSING HOMES AND MENTAL NURSING HOMES

Given that the Registered Homes Act 1984 distinguishes between residential care homes, on the one hand, and nursing and mental nursing homes on the other, by way of the type of care offered and given, and by distinguishing between 'personal care' and 'nursing care', the meanings of 'nursing home' and 'mental nursing home' under Part II of the Act are now set out. Section 21 defines and describes the meaning of 'nursing home' in the following terms:

'**21.**—(1) In this Act "nursing home" means, subject to subsection (3) below—

   (a)   any premises used, or intended to be used, for the reception of, and the provision of nursing for, persons suffering from any sickness, injury or infirmity;

   (b)   any premises used, or intended to be used, for the reception of pregnant women, or of women immediately after childbirth (in this Act referred to as a "maternity home"); and

   (c)   any premises not falling within either of the preceding paragraphs which are used, or intended to be used, for the provision of all or any of the following services, namely—

      (i)   the carrying out of surgical procedures under anaesthesia;

      (ii)   the termination of pregnancies;

      (iii)   endoscopy;

      (iv)   haemodialysis or peritoneal dialysis;

      (v)   treatment by specially controlled techniques.

(2) In subsection (1) above "specially controlled techniques" means techniques specified under subsection (4) below as subject to control for the purposes of this Part of this Act.

(3) The definition in subsection (1) above does not include—

   (a)   any hospital or other premises maintained or controlled by a government department or local authority or any other authority or body instituted by special Act of Parliament or incorporated by Royal Charter;

   (b)   any mental nursing home;

   (c)   any sanatorium provided at a school or educational establishment and used, or intended to be used, solely by persons in attendance at, or members of the staff of, that school or establishment or members of their families;

   (d)   any first aid or treatment room provided at factory premises, at premises to which the Offices, Shops and Railway Premises Act 1963 applies or at a sports ground, show ground or place of public entertainment;

   (e)   any premises used, or intended to be used, wholly or mainly—

      (i)   by a medical practitioner for the purpose of consultations with his patients;

      (ii)   by a dental practitioner or chiropodist for the purpose of treating his patients; or

      (iii)   for the provision of occupational health facilities, unless they are used, or intended to be used, for the provision of treatment by specially controlled techniques and are not excepted by regulations under paragraph (g) below;

   (f)   any premises used, or intended to be used, wholly or mainly as a private dwelling; or

   (g)   any other premises excepted from that definition by regulations made by the Secretary of State.

(4) The Secretary of State may by regulations specify as subject to control for the purposes of this Part of this Act any technique of medicine or surgery (including cosmetic surgery) as to which he is satisfied that its use may create a

hazard for persons treated by means of it or for the staff of any premises where the technique is used.

(5) Without prejudice to the generality of section 56 below, regulations under subsection (4) above may define a technique by reference to any criteria which the Secretary of State considers appropriate.

(6) In this section "treatment" includes diagnosis and "treated" shall be construed accordingly.'

Section 22 defines and describes 'mental nursing home' as follows:

'**22.**—(1) In this Act "mental nursing home" means, subject to subsection (2) below, any premises used, or intended to be used, for the reception of, and the provision of nursing or other medical treatment (including care, habilitation and rehabilitation under medical supervision) for, one or more mentally disordered patients (meaning persons suffering, or appearing to be suffering, from mental disorder), whether exclusively or in common with other persons.

(2) In this Act "mental nursing home" does not include any hospital as defined in subsection (3) below, or any other premises managed by a government department or provided by a local authority.

(3) In subsection (2) above, "hospital" means—
(a)   any health service hospital within the meaning of the National Health Service Act 1977; and
(b)   any accommodation provided by a local authority and used as a hospital by or on behalf of the Secretary of State under that Act.'

It is an offence under section 23 of the Act to carry on an unregistered nursing home, and (under section 24) to call an establishment a nursing home when it is not registered as such. The distinction between personal care and nursing care was examined above (pp. 85–86). Nursing homes and mental nursing homes will of course offer and give personal care as well as expert professional and, possibly technical, nursing care. It has been a frequent cause for complaint by proprietors of nursing homes that residential care homes can tend to keep their clients much longer than they should as dependency increases.

Section 23(2) provides that registration under Part II of the Act does not affect any requirement to register under Part I. A nursing home which provides both personal care and board and lodging for people in the categories set out in section 1(1) of Part I of the Act must register with the local social services authority as a residential care home (or small home) under that Part of the Act. (If such board and care is provided for fewer than four persons, section 4 offers the *option* to apply for registration of the *whole* home as a residential care home.) In practice it is most unlikely that clients of a nursing home would be perceived as being in need of personal care only, given nursing care requirements. A nursing home considering registration, additionally, as a residential care home would no doubt be doing so on the basis of a plan to provide a full, dual, service to the different categories of client. Any registered nursing home offering abortion facilities (termination of pregnancy) must obtain the prior approval of the Secretary of State pursuant to section 1(3) of the Abortion Act 1967.

The expression, in section 22(1) relating to mental nursing homes, 'care, habilitation and rehabilitation under medical supervision' replicates the identical expression in section 145(1) of the Mental Health Act 1983, for the purposes of 'treatment' falling within the provisions of Part IV of that Act. The expression 'mental nursing home' does not include any hospital, nor does it include any other premises managed by a government department or provided by a local authority social services department.[10] Nor does it cover establishments which provide day care only.

It may in practice be difficult to know whether a registered home is providing general nursing care for the elderly, in which case it should be registered as a nursing home only; or whether it is providing specialist mental health care of the elderly confused, in which case it may have to be registered as a mental nursing home. Departmental Circular HC(81)(8) provides the following guidance to registration authorities:

'Private nursing homes catering for elderly people may often accommodate some people who are mentally confused, but this need not necessarily involve registration as a mental nursing home. In such cases the authority will need to keep under consideration the number of such patients and the seriousness of their condition. Where the possibility of additional registration as a mental nursing home arises this should be fully discussed with those responsible for the home.'

It is suggested that great caution be exercised by proprietors of general nursing homes who care for, or propose to care for, clients clearly suffering from one form or other of mental disorder, and that registration authorities be equally watchful.

Section 55 of the Registered Homes Act 1984 defines 'mental disorder', for the purposes of the Act, as meaning 'mental illness, arrested or incomplete development of mind, psychopathic disorder and any other disorder or disability of mind'. This definition is identical in terms to that set out in section 1(2) of the Mental Health Act 1983. The powers given to psychiatrists and other health care professionals under that Act are set out in detail in Chapter 30. The term 'mental disorder' for the purpose of admission for assessment, or assessment followed by treatment, under section 2 of the Mental Health Act 1983 is sufficiently wide to encompass mental confusion as well as other more specific disorders. Elderly confusional states can frequently result from physical infection, and equally frequently cease to exist when the infection is successfully treated. It could be argued to be unduly onerous for nursing homes catering for elderly residents who are prone to such interludes to register as mental nursing homes, though the final decision rests with the registration authority. On the other hand, if a nursing home offers and gives nursing care for elderly persons suffering from intellectual deterioration and impairment of memory, having an ongoing and organic basis, registration as a mental nursing home will be required.

While there has recently been a rise in the number of general nursing homes caring for elderly mentally infirm (EMI) patients, it appears to be the prudent course to register also as a mental nursing home, a sensible and practical view being taken by the registering authority of the expertise and levels of staffing required in a particular case.

Section 23(5) requires, in respect of patients liable to be detained under the Mental Health Act 1983:

'(5) Where a person is registered in pursuance of an application stating that it is proposed to receive in the home such patients as are described in subsection (3)(c) above—
(a) that fact shall be specified in the certificate of registration; and
(b) the particulars of the registration shall be entered by the Secretary of State in a separate part of the register.'

Section 23(6) requires:

'(6) The certificate of registration issued under this Part of this Act in respect of any nursing home or mental nursing home shall be kept affixed in a conspicuous place in the home, and if default is made in complying with this subsection, the person carrying on the home shall be guilty of an offence.'

Refusal of registration is governed by section 25 of the Act:

'25.—(1) The Secretary of State may refuse to register an applicant in respect of a nursing home or a mental nursing home if he is satisfied—
(a) that the applicant, or any person employed or proposed to be employed by the applicant at the home, is not a fit person (whether by reason of age or otherwise) to carry on or be employed at a home of such a description as that named in the application; or
(b) that, for reasons connected with situation, construction, state of repair, accommodation, staffing or equipment, the home is not, or any premises used in connection with the home are not, fit to be used for such a home; or
(c) that the home is, or any premises used in connection with the home are, used, or proposed to be used, for purposes which are in any way improper or undesirable in the case of such a home; or
(d) that the home or any premises to be used in connection with the home consist of or include works executed in contravention of section 12(1) of the Health Services Act 1976;[11] or
(e) that the use of the home or any premises used in connection with the home is in contravention of any term contained in an authorisation under section 13 of the said Act of 1976;[11] or
(f) that the home is not, or will not be, in the charge of a person who is either a registered medical practitioner or a qualified nurse or, in the case of a maternity home, a registered midwife; or
(g) that the condition mentioned in subsection (3) below is not, or will not be, fulfilled in relation to the home.
(2) In subsection (1) above "qualified nurse", in relation to a home, means a nurse possessing such qualifications as may be specified in a notice served by the Secretary of State on the person carrying on or proposing to carry on the home.

(3) The condition referred to in subsection (1) above is that such number of nurses possessing such qualifications and, in the case of a maternity home, such number of registered midwives as may be specified in a notice served by the Secretary of State on the person carrying on or proposing to carry on the home are on duty in the home at such times as may be so specified.

(4) In preparing any notice under subsection (2) or (3) above, the Secretary of State shall have regard to the class and, in the case of a notice under subsection (3) above, the number of patients for whom nursing care is or is to be provided in the home.'

The registration authority is required to ensure that both the applicant for registration and any person employed or proposed to be employed by the applicant at the home are not unfit to carry out their respective functions under the Act. If the applicant for registration is incorporated (that is, a legal as distinct from a natural person) the authority is required to consider the fitness of the persons who control the company to perform those functions. It would be possible for the authority to refuse registration under section 25(1)(a) on the grounds that those who control the company are not fit for the specific purposes provided for by the 1984 Act. The directory as distinct from merely permissive nature of the power to refuse registration, explained in respect of section 9 as it applies to residential homes, applies equally to section 25 in respect of nursing homes (see p. 88, above).

If a nursing home provides both nursing care, and board and lodging and personal care, for persons in the categories mentioned in section 1(1) of Part I of the Act, registration with the local social services authority as a residential care home will be required. If it provides such care for fewer than four persons the home has an option (under section 4 of the Act) to register the whole home as a residential care home.

Mental nursing homes need not be registered to admit patients detained pursuant to powers under the Mental Health Act 1983 (for which see Chapter 30, generally); but where it is proposed to detain such patients in the home, that fact shall be specified in the certificate of registration, and the particulars of registration shall be entered in a separate part of the register. Section 145(1) of the Mental Health Act 1983 provides that the managers (for the purposes of that Act) of a mental nursing home are the persons registered in respect of that home. These persons have the power to discharge a patient from detained status pursuant to section 23 of the Mental Health Act 1983 (for which see Chapter 30, pp. 776–780, below). Section 12(5)(d) and (e) of the Mental Health Act 1983 provide that a medical practitioner on the staff of a mental nursing home, or any medical practitioner who has a financial interest in that home, is not entitled to provide a supporting medical recommendation for the purpose of an application for detention of a patient under Part II of that Act.

Section 23(3) of the Mental Health Act 1983, noted also in Chapter 30, pp. 780, provides that, where the patient is liable to be detained in a mental nursing home in pursuance of an application for admission for assessment or for treatment, an order for his discharge may be made by the Secretary of State and, if the patient is maintained under a contract with an NHS trust, Regional Health Authority, District Health Authority or Special Health Authority, by that trust or authority.

Section 24 prohibits holding out unregistered premises as a nursing home, maternity home or mental nursing home, as follows:

'**24.**—(1) A person who, with intent to deceive any person,—
    (a) applies any name to premises in England or Wales; or
    (b) in any way so describes such premises or holds such premises out,
as to indicate, or reasonably be understood to indicate, that the premises are a nursing home or maternity home, shall be guilty of an offence unless registration has been effected under this Part of this Act in respect of the premises as a nursing home.

    (2) A person who, with intent to deceive any person,—
    (a) applies any name to premises in England or Wales; or
    (b) in any way so describes such premises or holds such premises out,
as to indicate, or reasonably be understood to indicate, that the premises are a mental nursing home, shall be guilty of an offence, unless registration has been effected under this Part of this Act in respect of the premises as a mental nursing home.'

Section 28 of the Act provides for the cancellation of registration of a nursing home or mental nursing home. Section 32 provides a right to make representations to the registering authority and section 34 provides for machinery to make appeals against the decision of the registering body pursuant to section 33 of the Act.

4.2.1 Imposition of conditions on nursing home registration

Section 29 of the Act provides for mandatory and discretionary conditions imposed upon registration. Subsection (1) makes it mandatory that the number of people cared for in a nursing home shall be limited. Subsection (2) provides for discretionary conditions:

'(1) It shall be a condition of the registration of any person in respect of a nursing home or mental nursing home that the number of persons kept at any one time in the home (excluding persons carrying on, or employed in, the home, together with their families) does not exceed such number as may be specified in the certificate of registration.

    (2) Without prejudice to subsection (1) above, any such registration may be effected subject to such conditions (to be specified in the certificate of registration) as the Secretary of State may consider appropriate for regulating the age, sex or other category of persons who may be received in the home in question.

    (3) The Secretary of State may make regulations—
    (a) as to the variation of any condition for the time being in force in respect of a nursing home or mental nursing home by virtue of this Part of this Act; and
    (b) as to the imposition of additional conditions.

(4) If any condition for the time being in force in respect of a home by virtue of this Part of this Act is not complied with, the person carrying on the home shall be guilty of an offence.'

These provisions are mirrored by section 5 in respect of residential care homes.

No order has to date been made by the Secretary of State pursuant to the power given by subsection (2). In consequence, as was made clear in *McSweeney v Warwickshire County Council* (1988),[12] a registration authority has no power to impose conditions on a matter other than those specifically contemplated by the Act. The same consideration applies to the powers of Registered Homes Tribunals (see below, in this chapter). The decision in *McSweeney* is both important and restrictive in that it clearly curtails the exercise of discretion by registration authorities and tribunals. It might even be doubted whether questions of 'age, sex or other category of persons' would permit the imposition of a condition indirectly connected with such matters, for instance against non-ambulant patients being located on an upper floor in a particular building. While the types of conditions which may be imposed are thus limited, it was decided in *Isle of Wight County Council v Humphreys* (1991)[13] that there is no restriction upon the discretion of an authority in respect of the material which it may legitimately take into account when deciding whether or not to impose conditions on a particular registration. Its own policies and guidelines could, for instance, be reflected in the conditions imposed.

4.2.2 Urgent procedure for cancellation of registration

Section 30 provides for urgent cancellation procedure and, in effect, closure of the home:

'(1) If—
  (a) the Secretary of State applies to a justice of the peace for an order—
      (i) cancelling the registration of a person in respect of a nursing home or mental nursing home;
      (ii) varying any condition for the time being in force in respect of a home by virtue of this Part of this Act; or
      (iii) imposing an additional condition; and
  (b) it appears to the justice of the peace that there will be a serious risk to the life, health or well-being of the patients in the home unless the order is made,
he may make the order, and the cancellation, variation or imposition shall have effect from the date on which the order is made.

(2) An application under subsection (1) above may be made ex parte and shall be supported by a written statement of the Secretary of State's reasons for making the application.

(3) An order under subsection (1) above shall be in writing.

(4) Where such an order is made, the Secretary of State shall serve on any person registered in respect of the home, as soon as practicable after the making of the order,

(a) notice of the making of the order and of its terms; and
(b) a copy of the statement of the Secretary of State's reasons which supported his application for the order.'

This is a truly draconian power which in practice means that a home can be closed as a matter of urgency even without the knowledge of the owner and without warning. Accordingly, magistrates should not make such an order without very careful deliberation. In practice, however, in the absence of opposition to such an application the cancellation (and therefore closure) order is almost bound to be obtained.

It was held in *East Sussex County Council v Lyons* (1988)[14] that it does not matter whether the emergency order is sought before or after a decision to close by ordinary procedures. Nevertheless, it would appear that if the order by magistrates is first made there remains nothing upon which the ordinary procedure could operate.

It was held in *Martine v South East Kent Health Authority* (1993)[15] that there is no cause of action in negligence against a health authority for alleged careless investigation into a registered nursing home resulting in an urgent application for cancellation under section 30.

4.3 INSPECTION OF HOMES

Section 35 provides for the inspection of mental nursing homes and also for the visiting of patients and the investigation of complaints by residents:

'**35.**—(1) Subject to the provisions of this section, any person authorised in that behalf by the Secretary of State may at any time, after producing, if asked to do so, some duly authenticated document showing that he is so authorised, enter and inspect any premises which are used, or which that person has reasonable cause to believe to be used, for the purposes of a mental nursing home, and may inspect any records kept in pursuance of section 27(b) above.

(2) A person authorised under subsection (1) above to inspect a mental nursing home may visit and interview in private any patient residing in the home who is, or appears to be, suffering from mental disorder—

(a) for the purpose of investigating any complaint as to his treatment made by or on behalf of the patient; or
(b) in any case where the person so authorised has reasonable cause to believe that the patient is not receiving proper care;

and where the person so authorised is a medical practitioner, he may examine the patient in private, and may require the production of, and inspect, any medical records relating to the patient's treatment in that home.

(3) Regulations made under section 26 above may make provision with respect to the exercise on behalf of the Secretary of State of the powers conferred by this section, and may in particular provide—

(a) for imposing conditions or restrictions with respect to the exercise of those powers in relation to mental nursing homes which, immediately before 1 November 1960, were registered hospitals as defined in subsection (4) below, and

(b)   subject as aforesaid, for requiring the inspection of mental nursing homes under subsection (1) above to be carried out on such occasions, or at such intervals, as the regulations may prescribe.

(4) In subsection (3)(a) above, "registered hospital" means a hospital registered as mentioned in section 231(9) of the Lunacy Act 1890.

(5) Any person who refuses to allow the inspection of any premises, or without reasonable cause refuses to allow the visiting, interviewing or examination of any person by a person authorised in that behalf under this section or to produce for the inspection of any person so authorised any document or record the production of which is duly required by him, or otherwise obstructs any such person in the exercise of his functions, shall be guilty of an offence.

(6) Without prejudice to the generality of subsection (5) above, any person who insists on being present when requested to withdraw by a person authorised as aforesaid to interview or examine a person in private shall be guilty of an offence.'

Both the relevant registration authority (or authorities, if there is dual registration under Parts I and II of the Act)[16] and the Mental Health Act Commission[17] have the power to visit mental nursing homes. The health authority, as registration authority of a nursing home, has the power to examine patients and to require the production of relevant documents; and the Mental Health Act Commission has the power to visit and interview in private patients who are detained under the provisions of that Act. The power to investigate complaints from, or in some cases on behalf of, patients detained in mental nursing homes is vested in the Mental Health Act Commission by virtue of section 120(1) of the Mental Health Act 1983. The ambit of that power, together with the precise function of the Mental Health Act Commission in relation to its exercise, are examined in Chapter 30, pp. 844–847, below. Certain other ancillary provisions of the Mental Health Act 1983 are applicable to mental nursing homes under the Registered Homes Act 1984. Section 38 of the 1984 Act provides:

'**38.** So far as section 125 (inquiries), 126 (forgery, false statements, etc.) or 139 (protection for acts done) of the Mental Health Act 1983 applied immediately before the commencement of this Part of this Act in relation to any provision re-enacted by this Part of this Act, those sections shall apply in relation to the corresponding provision of this Act.'

4.4   REGISTERED HOMES TRIBUNALS

4.4.1   Constitution and functions

Part III of the Registered Homes Act 1984 establishes a system of Registered Homes Tribunals having responsibility for hearing appeals relating to the registration of residential care homes, nursing homes and mental nursing homes. Appeals can be heard in respect of a registration authority's decision to refuse a registration application; to grant a registration subject to certain conditions; or to cancel or amend a registration. Part III provides for the constitution of such tribunals and panels to hear particular appeals and for the special constitution of tribunals for the hearing of appeals relating to nursing homes (including maternity homes) and mental nursing homes. In the latter cases, the tribunal, in addition to an appointed lawyer, shall include a registered medical practitioner as well as a registered midwife, if the appeal relates to the registration of a maternity home and, in any other case, a qualified nurse.[18]

4.4.2 Limitation on the power of the Registered Homes Tribunal

The Divisional Court of the Queen's Bench Division ruled in *Coombs v Hertfordshire County Council* (1991)[19] that, under the Registered Homes Act 1984, the owner of a registered residential home has no right of appeal against the refusal by a local authority to agree to a variation in the conditions of registration.

In so ruling they dismissed an appeal by the applicant for registration against the decision of a Registered Homes Tribunal that it had no jurisdiction to hear his appeal against the refusal by Hertfordshire County Council to agree to a proposed variation in the conditions of registration of his residential homes.

Section 15 of the 1984 Act provides as follows:

'(1) An appeal against—
  (a) a decision of a registration authority . . . shall lie to a registered homes tribunal.'

The applicant and his wife were the registered joint proprietors of a residential home for 11 elderly residents. Application was made to increase the number of residents to 12, but the local authority refused permission.

When the applicant appealed, the Registered Homes Tribunal decided that it had no jurisdiction to hear the appeal, as it related to variations rather than to registration, under the Act. The Council argued that, when read in context, the right of appeal in section 15 of the Act applies only to decisions relating to registration and not to applications to vary conditions of registration. It is the registration as a whole, and not merely the conditions attaching to it, which must be appealed.

In Mr Justice Kennedy's opinion, that argument was conclusive in the present case. The court was obliged to construe section 15 in its context in the Act. On this basis it was clear to his Lordship that there is no provision under the Act for going to the tribunal to test the refusal of a local authority to agree to a variation. As he went on to explain, while it may not have been the true intention of the legislature in 1984 specifically to exclude from appeal those dissatisfied with a refusal to vary (as distinct from a refusal to register), Acts of Parliament can only accomplish what the legislature and the parliamentary draftsman have drawn them up to achieve.

Thus a registration authority has discretion to refuse to entertain an application for variation. It is not, however, entitled to consider an application for variation of conditions and refuse that application, and thereafter to argue that no appeal exists against its decision to refuse. It is submitted that the decision in *Coombs* does not mean that there is no appeal against a decision not to vary conditions once an authority has entertained an application to vary, but simply that there is no means of testing (appealing against) the authority's refusal to entertain such an application.

4.5   OFFENCES

Part IV of the Act provides for fines on the commission of certain offences under the Act. These offences include: failure to register (section 46); failure to affix a certificate of registration pursuant to section 5(6) of the Act (section 47); breach of conditions as to registration; contravention of regulations (for which see below); contravention of the prohibition in section 24 of holding out premises as a nursing home, maternity home or mental nursing home if registration requirements and conditions are not met; and the offence of obstructing a person authorised, under respective sections of the Act, to visit and inspect a registered home. Proceedings in respect of an offence under section 23(1), above, or section 23(6) above relating to a nursing home shall not, without the written consent of the Attorney-General, be taken by any person other than a party aggrieved or by the Secretary of State.[20]

Prosecutions may only be brought after a warning notice (see the Residential Care Homes Regulations 1984, regulation 20 and the Nursing Homes and Mental Nursing Homes Regulations 1984, regulation 15, below). That notice should specify the regulation which is alleged to have been broken, the manner in which it is alleged to have been broken and what is required to remedy the situation together with a time limit for the remedy. Such notices need to be carefully considered but the service of such a notice is a useful warning to an owner and a tool for the authority's regulatory responsibilities. The owner will know that a prosecution is coming and may avoid the damaging consequences. Conviction under the 1984 Act entails a complete and irreversible ban on the offender's being awarded a community care contract as a care provider to a social services authority.

4.6 NURSING HOMES AND MENTAL NURSING HOMES REGULATIONS 1984[21]

The Regulations make specific provision for the following matters:

'Specially controlled techniques

3. Any technique of medicine or surgery (including cosmetic surgery) involving the use of a class 3B laser product or a class 4 laser product (being a technique of medicine or surgery as to which the Secretary of State is satisfied that its use may create a hazard for persons treated by means of it or for the staff of any premises where the technique is used) is hereby specified as subject to control for the purposes of the Act.

["Class 3B laser product" and "class 4 laser product" have the meanings assigned to them in Part 1 of British Standard 4803:83 (Radiation safety of laser products and systems) as effective on 31st March 1983]

Registration

4.—(1) An application shall be made to the Secretary of State in writing and sent or delivered to the health authority and shall be accompanied by a fee provided for in Schedule 1.

(2) In making an application an applicant shall furnish the particulars specified in Schedule 2 and such other information, including details of any comments made by the fire authority in relation to the home, as the Secretary of State may reasonably require.

Annual fees

5. An annual fee of an amount calculated in accordance with Schedule 3 shall be paid by a person registered, within the appropriate time specified in that Schedule, for each home in respect of which he is registered.

Variation of conditions of registration

6.—(1) The Secretary of State may vary any condition for the time being in force in respect of a home by giving notice in writing to that effect to the person registered.

(2) A notice given under paragraph (1) shall specify a date, which shall be reasonable in the circumstances, on which the variation specified in the notice shall have effect.

(3) Where it is a condition that the number of persons kept at any one time in the home shall not exceed a specified number ("the original maximum") and the Secretary of State varies that condition by specifying a lower number, he shall specify that the original maximum shall continue to apply so long as all the patients in the home are patients who were resident there at the date on which notice of the variation was given under paragraph (1).

Records

7.—(1) The person registered shall keep a record in the form of a register of all patients, which register shall, in respect of each patient, and as from the date when the patient enters the home, include the particulars specified in Part I of Schedule 4, and, in the case of a maternity home, the additional particulars specified in Part II of Schedule 4.

(2) The person registered shall keep a separate record in the form of a register of—

(a)   all surgical operations performed in the home which register shall include the name of the medical practitioner or dentist who performed the operation and the name of the anaesthetist in attendance;

(b) where the home is a nursing home, any occasion on which a specially controlled technique is used, the nature of that technique, the name of the person using it and, where that person is not a medical practitioner or dentist, the name of the medical practitioner or dentist in accordance with whose directions the technique was used.

(3) Any record in the form of a register kept under paragraph (1) or (2) shall be retained for a period of not less than one year beginning with the date on which the last entry was made in the register.

(4) The person registered shall keep a case record in the home in respect of each patient which shall include the following particulars:—

(a) an adequate daily statement of the patient's health and condition; and

(b) details of any investigations made, surgical operations carried out and treatment given.

(5) In the case of a maternity home, in addition to the register and case records kept under paragraphs (1), (2) and (4), the person registered shall keep a case record of each child born to a patient in the home which shall include the particulars specified in Part III of Schedule 4.

(6) The case records kept under paragraphs (4) and (5) shall be retained for a period of not less than one year beginning with the date on which the patient to whom, or to whose child, they relate ceases to be a patient in the home.

(7) The person registered shall keep a record of the staff employed at the home which shall include the name, date of birth and details of position and dates of employment at the home of each member of staff and, in respect of the nursing staff, details of their qualifications.

(8) The person registered shall keep a record of—

(a) all fire practices which take place at the home;

(b) all fire alarm tests carried out at the home together with the result of any such test and the action taken to remedy defects; and

(c) the procedure to be followed in the event of fire.

(9) The person registered shall keep a record of maintenance carried out on medical, surgical and nursing equipment in the home.

(10) Any records which are required to be made under the Mental Health (Hospital, Guardianship and Consent to Treatment) Regulations 1983 and which relate to the detention or treatment of a patient in a mental nursing home shall be kept for a period of not less than five years beginning with the date on which the person to whom they relate ceases to be a patient in that home.

Notices in respect of deaths

8.—(1) If a patient, or a child born to a patient, dies in the home, the person registered shall give notice in writing of the death to the health authority not later than twenty four hours after it occurs.

(2) For the purposes of paragraph (1), no account shall be taken of any part of a period of twenty four hours which falls on a Saturday, Sunday, Christmas Day, Good Friday or on a bank holiday in England and Wales within the meaning of the Banking and Financial Dealings Act 1971.

Absence of person in charge from the home

9.—(1) The person registered shall give notice to the health authority in writing of any period of more than four weeks during which he or, if he is not in charge of the home, the person who is in charge of it, proposes to be absent from the home.

(2) The notice referred to in paragraph (1) shall be given not later than a month before the beginning of the proposed absence except—

(a)   where the health authority agrees to a shorter period, in which case notice shall be given not later than the beginning of that period, or

(b)   in an emergency, in which case the notice shall be given not later than one week after the start of the absence unless it is impracticable to do so, in which case it shall be given as soon as possible thereafter.

(3) The person registered or the person in charge as the case may be shall within one week from the date of his return to the home after an absence of which notice was required to be given in accordance with paragraph (1), give notice to the health authority in writing that he has returned.

(4) The notice referred to in paragraph (1) shall contain the following information—

(a)   the length or expected length of the proposed absence from the home;

(b)   the arrangements which the person registered will make or has made for the running of the home during the proposed absence, including the name, address and qualifications of the person in charge of the home during that absence.

Inspection of nursing homes

10.—(1) Subject to the following provisions of this regulation any person authorised, on producing (if asked to do so) a duly authenticated document showing that he is so authorised, may enter and inspect any premises which are used, or which he reasonably believes to be used, as a nursing home, and in the course of such inspection may require the production of records.

(2) Subject to paragraph (3), a person authorised may require the person registered to furnish such information in relation to the nursing home as may reasonably be required for the purposes of inspection.

(3) Nothing in this regulation authorises any person other than a medical practitioner in the service of the Crown or of a health authority to inspect a clinical record relating to a patient in a home.

Frequency of inspection of homes

11. Inspection of a home pursuant to section 35 of the Act or to regulation 10 may be made on such occasions and at such intervals as the Secretary of State may decide but he shall cause every home to be inspected not less than twice in every period of twelve months.

Provision of facilities and services

12.—(1) The person registered shall, having regard to the size of the home and the number, age, sex and condition of the patients therein—

(a)   provide adequate professional, technical, ancillary and other staff;

(b)   provide for each patient in the home adequate accommodation and space, including, where appropriate, day-room facilities;

(c)   provide adequate furniture, bedding, curtains and where necessary adequate screens and floor covering in rooms occupied or used by patients;

(d)   provide and maintain adequate medical, surgical and nursing equipment and adequate treatment facilities;

(e)   provide for the use of patients adequate wash basins and baths supplying hot and cold water and adequate water closets and sluicing facilities;

(f)   provide adequate light, heating and ventilation in all parts of the home occupied or used by patients;

(g) keep all parts of the home occupied or used by patients in good structural repair, clean and reasonably decorated;

(h) take adequate precautions against the risk of fire, including the provision of adequate means of escape in the event of fire and make adequate arrangements for detecting, containing and extinguishing fires, for the giving of warnings and for the evacuation of all persons in the home in the event of fire and for the maintenance of fire fighting equipment;

(i) make adequate arrangements to secure by means of fire drills and practices that the staff in the home and, so far as practicable, patients know the procedure to be followed in the case of fire including the procedure for saving life;

(j) provide adequate kitchen equipment, crockery and cutlery and adequate facilities for the preparation and storage of food;

(k) supply adequate food for every patient;

(l) arrange adequate laundering facilities;

(m) make adequate arrangements for the disposal of swabs, soiled dressings, instruments and similar substances and materials;

(n) make adequate arrangements for patients in the home where necessary to receive medical and dental services, whether under Part II of the National Health Service Act 1977 or otherwise;

(o) make adequate arrangements for the recording, safe keeping, handling and disposal of drugs;

(p) provide adequate arrangements for the prevention of infection, toxic conditions, or spread of infection at the home;

(q) make adequate arrangements where appropriate for the training or occupation and recreation of patients and play and education facilities for children;

(r) provide adequate facilities for patients to receive visitors in private;

(s) take adequate precautions against the risk of accident;

(t) provide adequate facilities for any person authorised to interview in private any patient in the home.

(2) The person registered shall—

(a) provide for the home to be connected to a public telephone service;

(b) where the home is a maternity home or a home in which surgical operations are undertaken or life support systems used, provide such electrical supply as during interruption of public supply is needed to safeguard the lives of the patients;

(c) at such times as may be agreed with the fire authority, consult that authority on fire precautions in the home;

(d) make adequate arrangements either with the health authority or otherwise for the care of patients, and children born to patients, in medical emergencies;

(e) make adequate arrangements for the running of the home while he, or if he is not in charge of the home, the person who is in charge of it is absent from the home.

Conduct of nursing homes using specially controlled techniques

13. The person registered shall ensure that any treatment (including diagnosis) by specially controlled technique in a nursing home is carried out only by a person who is, or who is acting in accordance with the directions of, a medical practitioner or a dentist.

Transitional provisions

14.—(1) This regulation applies where an applicant or person registered is

aggrieved by a decision of the Secretary of State made under regulation 5(4) of the Nursing Homes and Mental Nursing Homes Regulations 1981 ("the 1981 Regulations") before 1 January 1985 and before that date—
 (a) he has appealed to a magistrates' court under regulation 5(5) of the 1981 Regulations and the appeal has not been determined, or
 (b) he has not so appealed and the period referred to in regulation 5(5) of the 1981 Regulations has not expired.
 (2) Where paragraph (1)(a) applies the appeal shall be determined as though regulation 5 of the 1981 Regulations were still in force.
 (3) Where paragraph (1)(b) applies an appeal against a decision of the Secretary of State made under regulation 5(4) of the 1981 Regulations shall be to a Registered Homes Tribunal and shall be made within the period of twenty-one days beginning with the date on which the decision was received.

Offences

15.—(1) Any person who fails without reasonable cause—
 (a) to keep or retain any record which he is required to keep or retain under regulation 7 or Schedule 4; or
 (b) to give to a health authority any notice which he is required to give under regulation 8 or 9; or
 (c) to furnish any information which he is required to furnish under regulation 10(2),
shall be guilty of an offence against these regulations.
 (2) Any person who without reasonable cause refuses to allow a person authorised to inspect any premises or any record under regulation 10(1) shall be guilty of an offence against these regulations.
 (3) Any person who fails to comply with any provision of regulation 12, other than regulation 12(2)(c), shall be guilty of an offence against these regulations.
 (4) Subject to paragraph (5), the Secretary of State shall not bring proceedings against a person in respect of any failure referred to in paragraph (1) or (3) unless—
 (a) he has served on that person a notice in writing specifying—
  (i) the provision of these regulations with which that person, in the Secretary of State's opinion, has failed or is failing to comply,
  (ii) the respect in which, in the Secretary of State's opinion, that person has failed or is failing to comply with that provision,
  (iii) the action which, in the Secretary of State's opinion, should be taken by that person so as to comply with that provision, and
  (iv) the period within which such action should be taken; and
 (b) the period referred to in sub-paragraph (a)(iv) of this paragraph has expired.
 (5) Paragraph (4) shall not apply where, at the time proceedings relating to a home are brought—
 (a) the Secretary of State has applied to a justice of the peace for an order under section 30(1) of the Act (urgent procedure for cancellation of registration etc.) relating to that home and that application has not yet been determined; or
 (b) such an order is in force.
 (6) Any person who fails to comply with regulation 13 shall be guilty of an offence against these regulations.'

Schedule 1 to the Regulations provides for fees to accompany applications for registration; Schedule 2 for particulars to be furnished by an applicant for registration; Schedule 2 for annual fees; Schedule 4, Part I for particulars to be included in the register of patients at the home; Schedule 4, Part II for additional particulars to be included in the register of patients in a maternity home; and Schedule 4, Part III for particulars to be included in the case record of a child born in a maternity home.

NOTES

1. See the National Health Service Functions (Direction to Authorities and Administration Arrangements) Regulations 1991, SI 1991/554.
2. Registered Homes (Amendment) Act 1991 (Commencement) Order 1992, SI 1992/2240.
3. Circular LAC(77)13.
4. Richard Jones 'The Registered Homes Act 1984' *Current Law Statutes Annotated Reports* (London, Sweet & Maxwell, 1984).
5. Registered Homes Act 1984, section 7.
6. See the Residential Care Homes Regulations 1984, SI 1984/1345.
7. Residential Care Homes Regulations 1984, regulation 5.
8. For which see the Registered Homes Act 1984, section 12(2).
9. Registered Homes Act 1984, section 15(7).
10. See the Registered Homes Act 1984, section 22(2) and (3); and the National Health Service Act 1977, section 128.
11. Repealed, with savings, by the National Health Service and Community Care Act 1990, section 63.
12. QBD, Mr Justice Roch, 8 December 1988, unreported.
13. QBD, Mr Justice Hutchison, 6 December 1991, unreported.
14. (1988) 152 JP 488, CA.
15. The Times, 8 March 1993, CA.
16. For dual registration, see pp. 86, 91 above, of this chapter.
17. Mental Health Act 1983, section 120(1).
18. Registered Homes Act 1984, section 42(2).
19. The Times, 26 April 1991.
20. Registered Homes Act 1984, section 53.
21. SI 1984/1578.

CHAPTER 5

Legal proceedings against health authorities and trusts

5.1 VICARIOUS LIABILITY

Vicarious liability is the liability of an employer (including a health authority or trust) for injury caused to a third party by the wrongdoing of its employee. While the doctrine of vicarious liability consists of rules from decided cases, as well as certain principles, it is in essence a *doctrine*. It is intended to provide an injured person with a better or more efficient opportunity to obtain compensation for injury caused by wrongdoing. The fact that an employer (including an authority or trust) may, on the basis of certain rules and principles discussed in this section, be liable to compensate the injured third party does not remove the responsibility – and with it the responsibility to pay damages – from the individual wrongdoer. The legal relations between the wrongdoer and his employer are discussed later in this section.

5.1.1 Employee distinguished from independent contractor

The doctrine of vicarious liability depends fundamentally on the existence of an employment relationship between the wrongdoer and the employer against whom liability is sought to be established via this doctrine. While certain (now fairly ancient) legal decisions on the relationship between professionals and their authorities presented difficulties which will be briefly examined in this section, it is not difficult to establish that those working in and for the National Health Service have a contract of employment with an agency or authority within that service. Trusts apart, consultants' contracts are generally held by Regional Health Authorities; and the employment contracts of other doctors are held by District Health Authorities. Nurses and paramedical staff, as well as auxiliary and manual staff, are employed by their District. The structure of health authorities and ancillary bodies was examined in Chapter 2. By contrast with National Health Service employees, general medical practitioners, general dental practitioners, pharmacists and opticians are classed in law as 'independent contractors.' This means that, while they have a contract with the health authority, which through one of its agencies (the Family Health Services Authority in the case of GPs) acts as paymaster, they are not employees of the health authority. There is nevertheless a standard form of contract between such independent contractors who contract their services to the health service and the authority which pays them. The standard terms of contract for general medical practitioners, for instance, are contained in the National Health Service (General Medical and Pharmaceutical) Regulations 1974, in its first schedule. Analysis of the contract for engagement of general medical practitioners and other independent contractors is beyond the immediate scope of this book. However, general practitioners may be employed, in another capacity, within a unit or trust, for instance as clinical assistants in a hospital. For that purpose they would be employees of the health authority or trust, but for purposes of the remainder of their business they would not be employees but contractors.

The point of distinguishing between employees and independent contractors is that the doctrine of vicarious liability does not apply in the latter case. If a principal who engages an independent contractor establishes or maintains a faulty system of working conditions and someone, for instance a patient, is injured in consequence, there may well be liability on the principal wrongdoer; but this is not an example of vicarious liability, rather of direct liability on the person or authority responsible for the faulty working conditions.

5.1.2   The course of employment

Vicarious liability depends not only on the employment relationship but, having established that, upon an act which is referable to the course of employment. Clearly, no employee is employed to injure third parties. Any such contract would be unenforceable and would probably amount to a criminal conspiracy. The attitude taken by the law is that a negligent way of doing a job is still doing the job. So if any employee of a health authority, trust or other healthcare body were to injure a third party, including either a patient or another member of staff, or indeed a member of the public, the injury would be regarded for the purposes of the doctrine of vicarious liability as a negligent way of carrying out the task to be done. Remarkably, even fraud and criminal damage have in some cases[1] been held to fall within the immensely wide 'course of employment' notion. There is no doubt, therefore, that not only a negligent act injuring a patient but also assault and battery could fall within the course of employment so as to make the employing authority liable for the injury caused by the member of staff. The relationship between negligent injury and trespass to the person (battery) where there has been no consent to treatment is explained in Chapter 7. If the patient did not give consent this may amount to battery (a criminal offence as well as a civil wrong); but this does nothing to alter the employer's legal obligation to pay damages by way of compensation to the injured person.

There is even a line of cases which clearly establishes that acts done in the face of express prohibitions by an employer or employing authority may nevertheless constitute acts within the course of employment such as to make an employer liable to the injured third party. In the context of hospital management, there may well be express prohibitions issued to nurses about lifting patients in certain ways (emergencies excepted). Injury to a patient, or (as is frequent) to another employee resulting from breach of instructions not to lift except in a certain manner, will not detract from the employer's liability to compensate an injured party by way of damages.

5.1.3 Vicarious and direct liability distinguished

The vicarious liability of an employer for injuries caused by the wrong of an employee is a very strict liability. All proper care may have been taken in the selection and training of the wrongdoing employee, but this will have no effect on the liability of the employer vicariously for the employee's wrongs. If, however, the employer or employing authority has itself been careless either in the selection, or the training, or in some other vital aspect of the tasks given to the employee who then injures a third party, liability may fall upon the employer as a principal wrongdoer. Such liability is direct, and not vicarious.

With specific reference to allegations of injury caused by medical negligence, the comments of Sir Nicolas Browne-Wilkinson in the case of *Wilsher v Essex Area Health Authority* (1986)[2] are instructive. Even counsel in the case were thought by the judges to have blurred the distinction between vicarious liability and direct liability of the health authority. It was a case in which a young baby had been negligently catheterised and as a result, it was alleged, contracted RLF (retrolental fibroplasia). The main point of the case (discussed in Chapter 6, pp. 196–197, below) was whether or not the established negligence actually caused the damage complained of. But in relation to the question of whom to sue, Sir Nicolas Browne-Wilkinson said:

'I agree with the comments of Mustill LJ as to the confusion which has been caused in this case both by the pleading and by the argument below which blurred the distinction between the vicarious liability of the health authority for the negligence of its doctors and the direct liability of the health authority for negligently failing to provide skilled treatment of the kind that it was offering to the public. In my judgment, a health authority which so conducts its hospital that it fails to provide doctors of sufficient skill and experience to give the treatment offered at the hospital may be directly liable in negligence to the patient. Although we were told in argument that no case has ever been decided on this ground and that it is not the practice to formulate claims in this way, I can see no reason why, in principle, the health authority should not be so liable if its organisation is at fault.'

An example of organisational problems which may lead to injury to a patient is found in the report of the Health Service Commissioner (Ombudsman) for the period April–October 1986. A health authority was criticised for 'cumulative failings' after the death of an elderly woman who fell over in hospital. The woman, who was admitted to hospital suffering from a depressive illness, died of head injuries which followed three falls after she got out of her hospital bed at night.

After taking up the case, health ombudsman Mr Anthony Barraclough concluded that night nursing staff levels were unsatisfactory. It was unreasonable, he concluded, that patients had to shout for help because there was no nurse-call system on the ward. The health authority concerned assured the Commissioner that his recommendations would be passed to nursing staff in all hospitals and that the night nursing establishment would be 'reviewed'.

It should be noted that the National Health Service Act 1977[3] excludes the Commissioner's jurisdiction in cases where litigation is anticipated or probable in respect of such a problem. The powers of the Health Service Commissioner are detailed in Chapter 8, pp. 302–315.

5.1.4   Health authority staff as employees

The decision in *Hillyer v St Bartholomew's Hospital* (1909)[4] was at one time authority for the view that hospital authorities were not liable for the acts of their medical staff, but only for failure to take due care in making appointments. In later years *Hillyer's* case had been distinguished most decisively by a majority in *Cassidy v Ministry of Health* (1951)[5] so that the apparent non-liability of a hospital authority was limited to consultants employed under a contract for services, it being held in that case that a hospital authority would be liable for the negligence or incompetence of a whole-time officer employed under a contract of service even though qualified as a specialist and working as a surgeon. The majority judgments in the Court of Appeal in *Cassidy's* case appeared to make liability or non-liability of the hospital authority depend on the nature of its contract with the surgeon or physician concerned, a most unreal distinction. This left the patient's recourse against the hospital for negligent injury to be determined by reference to a contract to which he was not a party and of the terms of which he could know nothing. The difficulties in *Cassidy's* case now seem to have been largely removed by the judgments delivered in the Court of Appeal in *Roe v Minister of Health, Woolley v Same* (1954).[6]

In *Roe's* case two patients in a voluntary hospital, before that hospital became part of the NHS, suffered serious injury by reason of injection with a spinal anaesthetic contaminated with phenol which was alleged to have seeped through molecular flaws or microscopic cracks in the ampoules. The injured men alleged negligence on the part of the anaesthetist and sued the Minister as successor to the liabilities of the former voluntary hospital. It was eventually decided that the anaesthetist had not been negligent. The trial judge, Mr Justice McNair, had also held, on the authority of *Gold v Essex* CC (1942)[7] and of the majority judgments in *Cassidy's* case, that the hospital authority was not liable for the wrongful acts and omissions of the anaesthetist, whom he compared to the consulting physicians and surgeons referred to by Lord Greene in *Gold's* case.

Lord Justice Denning, consistently with his judgment in the *Cassidy* case, said:[8]

'I think that the hospital authorities are responsible for the whole of their staff, not only for the nurses and doctors, but also for the anaesthetists and the surgeons. It does not matter whether they are permanent or temporary, resident or visiting, whole-time or part-time. The hospital authorities are responsible for all of them. The reason is because, even if they are not servants, they are the agents of the hospital to give the treatment. The only exception is the case of consultants or anaesthetists selected and employed by the patient himself.'

The concluding sentence of this extract from the judgment of Lord Justice Denning is his reconciliation of his decision in this and in *Cassidy's* case with *Hillyer v St Bartholomew's Hospital*.

Although Lord Justice Morris determined in favour of the vicarious liability of the voluntary hospital authority for the work of a visiting anaesthetist he left open the question of liability for visiting surgeons saying:

'If a patient in 1947 entered a voluntary hospital for an operation it might be that if the operation was to be performed by a visiting surgeon the hospital would not undertake, so far as concerned the actual surgery itself, to do more than to make the necessary arrangements to secure the services of a skilled and competent surgeon. The facts and features of each particular case would require investigation.'

That a health authority under the National Health Service legislation being under a duty to provide hospital accommodation and medical and nursing treatment is vicariously liable for the negligence of its staff in the performance of their duties, whether in respect of treatment of patients or otherwise, has never been in doubt, save only in the case of the specialists whose title in the hierarchy is 'consultant'. Many consultants are also in private practice and are by the terms of their contract committed only to a specified number of hospital, clinic or health centre sessions per week. In the early days of the National Health Service, many of them tended to regard themselves as outside experts distinguishable from other hospital medical staff in the nature of their relationship both to the patient and to the hospital authority with whom they were in contract.

That specialists might be in a fundamentally different position from other hospital medical staff received some slight support from the wording of section 3(1) of the National Health Service Act 1946 which, until repealed and replaced by section 2(2) of the National Health Service Reorganisation Act 1973,[9] set out the hospital and specialist services which it was the duty of the Secretary of State to provide. They included:

'(a) hospital accommodation;
(b) medical, nursing and other services required for the purposes of the hospitals;
(c) the services of specialists, whether at a hospital, a health centre . . . , or a clinic, or, if necessary on medical grounds at the home of the patient . . .'

However, in *Razzel v Snowball* (1954)[10] the Court of Appeal firmly rejected the contention that specialists within section 3(1)(c) of the 1946 Act were not public servants within the protection of section 21 of the Limitation Act 1939[11] although other medical practitioners employed by hospital authorities and falling within section 3(1)(b) were. In the course of his judgment Lord Justice Denning said:[12]

'An attempt was made to distinguish between doctors and nurses under paragraph (b) and specialists under paragraph (c). It was conceded that doctors and nurses were carrying out the duty of the Minister but it was said that specialists were not. I cannot see any justification for this distinction. All of them, doctors, nurses and specialists, are carrying out the Minister's duty to treat the sick. . . . [W]hatever may have been the position of a consultant in former times, nowadays, since the National Health Service Act 1946, the term "consultant" does not denote a particular relationship between a doctor and a hospital. It is simply a title denoting his place in the hierarchy of the hospital staff. He is a senior member of the staff but nevertheless just as much a member of the staff as the house surgeon. Whether he is called specialist or consultant makes no difference.'

The basis of the Minister's agreement with the medical defence societies, embodied in Circular HM(54)32, acknowledged the fact that hospital authorities are vicariously liable for the acts and omissions of medical staff, including consultants, to the like extent to which they are vicariously liable for the acts and omissions of nurses and other members of the staff of their hospitals who may be concerned with the treatment of patients.

5.1.5 Financial aspects of liability: National Health Service indemnity arrangements

Since the National Health Service Act 1946 health authorities have been responsible for the acts of their employees carrying out the duty of the Minister to provide all necessary services at the hospitals: see *Razzel v Snowball* (1954)[10] (above). If, however, the health authority only was sued it would have been open to it to bring into the proceedings, by way of third party notice, all those employees whose faults it was thought had caused the injury. To avoid this, in respect of doctors and dentists working within the National Health Service, arrangements were made with the three medical defence organisations to share any damages or settlement monies by way of agreement rather than fighting the matter out in court. Doctors and dentists working within the National Health Service were, until 31 December 1989, required as a condition of hospital appointment to subscribe to one of the medical defence organisations.

The rapidly increasing number and amount of claims put severe strains upon the medical defence organisations, culminating in one defence society proposing differential subscriptions for higher risk specialties. Financial responsibility within the National Health Service was subsequently radically altered. Circular HC(89)34, which effectively replaces the former HM(54)32 (above), provides as follows:

'Health authorities are asked, with effect from 1 January 1990, to:

(i)   assume responsibility for new and existing claims of medical negligence;
(ii)   ensure a named officer has sufficient authority to make decisions on the conduct of cases on the Authority's behalf;
(iii)   cease to require their medical and dental staff to subscribe to a recognised professional defence organisation and cease to reimburse two-thirds of medical defence subscriptions;
(iv)   encourage their medical and dental staff to ensure they have adequate defence cover as appropriate;
(v)   distribute urgently to all their medical and dental staff, including those with honorary NHS contracts, copies of a leaflet explaining the new arrangements (which will be sent separately).

Handling claims of medical negligence

Claims lodged on or after 1 January 1990

1. Health authorities, as corporate bodies, are legally liable for the negligent acts of their employees in the course of their NHS employment. From 1 January 1990

health authorities will also be formally responsible for the handling and financing of claims of negligence against their medical and dental staff. With regard to claims lodged on or after 1 January 1990, it is for each health authority to determine how it wishes claims against its medical or dental staff to be handled. Health authorities may wish to make use of the services of the medical defence organisations (at rates to be agreed), but they may also put the work out to other advisers or deal with it in-house, provided they have the necessary expertise.

Claims notified to an MDO before 1 January 1990

2. Subject to final agreement with the medical defence organisations (MDOs) on the detailed financial arrangements, health authorities will take over financial responsibility for cases outstanding at 1 January 1990. The medical defence organisations have been asked to inform health authorities of the cases in which they may have a substantial liability.

3. Health authorities are entitled to take over the management of any cases outstanding, since they will become liable for the costs and damages arising. However, they are strongly advised to employ the MDOs to continue to handle such claims, in consultation with them and on their behalf, until completion. This is essential not only because of the amount of work in progress, but mainly because the re-insurance cover of the MDOs for claims initiated before 1990 would remain valid only if the MDO currently handling the case continued to do so. If required, health authorities should co-operate with an MDO's re-insurers in the conduct of a claim. Since some of the cover is on an aggregate basis the advice in this paragraph applies to both large and small claims. Health authorities are asked to give prior notice to the Department where they wish to adopt a different approach in the handling of claims notified before 1 January 1990.

General handling principles

4. Health authorities should take the essential decisions on the handling of claims of medical negligence against their staff, using MDOs or other bodies as their agents and advisers. Authorities should particularly ensure that authority is appropriately delegated to enable decisions to be made promptly, especially where representatives are negotiating a settlement, and are asked to give such authority to a named officer.

5. In deciding how a case should be handled, and in particular whether to resist a claim or seek an out-of-court settlement, health authorities and those advising them should pay particular attention to any view expressed by the practitioner(s) concerned and to any potentially damaging effect on the professional reputation of the practitioner(s) concerned. They should also have clear regard to:

(i)   any point of principle or of wider application raised by the case; and
(ii) the costs involved.

6. Where a case involves both a health authority and a general medical practitioner (or any other medical or dental practitioner in relation to work for which a health authority is not responsible), the health authority should consult with the practitioner(s) cited or their representative to seek agreement on how the claim should be handled. Where a health authority (or its employees) alone

is cited, but there is reason to believe that the action or inaction of a practitioner outside the health authority's responsibility was a material factor in the negligence concerned, the health authority should similarly consult with a view to obtaining a contribution to the eventual costs and damages. Conversely, in cases where such a practitioner alone is cited, there may be circumstances in which an MDO asks the health authority to make a similar contribution, as if it were a defendant. In any such circumstances, health authorities should co-operate fully in the formulation of the defence and should seek to reach agreement out of court on the proportion in which any costs and damages awarded to the plaintiff should be borne.

7. It is open to the practitioner concerned to employ at his or her expense an expert adviser, but the practitioner can be represented separately in court only with the agreement of the Court. The plaintiff and the health authority may agree to separate representation for the practitioner, but under normal circumstances the health authority should not do so if it considers that this would lead to additional costs or damages falling on the health authority.

Coverage of the scheme and practical arrangements

8. The Health Departments' views on some of the questions that have arisen about the coverage and practical operation of the new arrangements are at Annex A. The indemnity scheme applies to all staff in the course of their HCHS employment, including those engaged through private agencies. The Annex is to be reproduced as a leaflet, which the Health Departments will shortly be making available to health authorities who should distribute them to all their medical and dental staff, including those with honorary NHS contracts.

9. Since authorities will be taking financial responsibility in cases of medical negligence it will no longer be necessary for them to require employed staff to subscribe to a recognised professional defence organisation, for example, as in the recommended form of consultant contract at Annex D of PM(79)11. Authorities should inform their medical and dental staff that the provision no longer applies, but they should encourage such staff to ensure that they have adequate defence cover as appropriate.

Financial arrangements

Pooling arrangements for major settlements

10. Where they have not already done so RHAs are strongly recommended to introduce arrangements (for both medical and non-medical negligence) so as to share with Districts the legal costs and damages of individual large settlements or awards, whose incidence can be quite random. The Department will be making arrangements for Authorities without an RHA, for example the London SHAs, to limit the financial effects on them of substantial settlements.

Funding of claims

11. Subject to final agreement with the MDOs, the public sector will have access to a share of the MDOs' reserves in respect of the hospital and community health services. It is expected that the MDOs will each establish a fund to be drawn on according to criteria set by the Health Departments. The Health Departments will be introducing a transitional scheme under which these reserves will be made available to assist health authorities to meet the costs of particularly large settlements. These will usually, but not necessarily, be cases which arose from incidents before 1 January 1990. The Departments propose to set a threshold,

initially £300,000 in England and Wales; 80 per cent of the costs of a settlement above this threshold, including the legal costs, would be met from this source, until the identified funds are exhausted. Detailed information on the means of access to the funds [was] given in the December 1989 edition of "Financial Matters".

NHS trusts

12. NHS trusts will be responsible for claims of negligence against their medical and dental staff.' [Guidance on financing liability from the date when trusts become operational is in EL(90)195, EL(91)19 and EL(92)8.]

Who is covered by the health authority indemnity scheme?

An Annex to the Circular gives some practical guidance as to the particular incidence of liability in an assortment of cases. The following extracts from the Annex are relevant to the liability of medical and dental practitioners employed by health authorities and trusts.

'Health authorities as employers are liable at law for the negligence (acts or omissions) of their staff in the course of their NHS employment. The legal position is the same for medical and dental staff as for other NHS employees, but for many years doctors and dentists have themselves taken out medical defence cover through the three medical defence organisations (MDOs). Under the indemnity scheme, health authorities will take direct responsibility for costs and damages arising from medical negligence where they (as employers) are vicariously liable for the acts and omissions of their medical and dental staff.

Does this include clinical academics and research workers?

Health authorities are vicariously liable for the work done by university medical staff and other research workers under their honorary contracts in the course of their NHS duties, but not for pre-clinical or other work in the university.

Is private work in NHS hospitals covered by the indemnity scheme?

Health authorities will not be responsible for a consultant's private practice, even in an NHS hospital. However, where junior medical staff are involved in the care of private patients in NHS hospitals, they would normally be doing so as part of their contract with the health authority. It remains advisable that any junior doctor who might be involved in any work outside the scope of his or her employment should have medical defence (or insurance) cover.

Is Category 2 work covered?

Category 2 work (eg reports for insurance companies) is by definition not undertaken for the employing health authority, and will therefore not be covered by the indemnity scheme; medical defence cover would be appropriate.

Are GMC disciplinary proceedings covered?

Health authorities should not be financially responsible for the defence of medical staff involved in GMC disciplinary proceedings. It is the responsibility of the practitioner concerned to take out medical defence cover against such an eventuality.

Is a hospital doctor doing a GP locum covered?

This would not be the responsibility of the health authority, since it would be general practice. The hospital doctor and the general practitioners concerned should ensure that there is appropriate medical defence cover.

Is a GP seeing his own patient in hospital covered?

A GP providing medical care to patients in hospital under a contractual arrangement, eg where the GP was employed as a clinical assistant, will be covered by the health authority indemnity. On the other hand, if the health authority is essentially providing only hotel services and the patient(s) remain in the care of the GP, the GP would be responsible and medical defence cover would be appropriate.

Are clinical trials covered?

The new arrangements do not alter the current legal position. If the health authority was responsible for a clinical trial authorised under the Medicines Act 1968 or its subordinate legislation and that trial was carried out by or on behalf of a doctor involving NHS patients of his, such a doctor would be covered by the indemnity scheme. Similarly, for a trial not involving medicines, the health authority would take financial responsibility unless the trial were covered by such other indemnity as may have been agreed between the health authority and those responsible for the trial. In any case, health authorities should take steps to make sure that they are informed of clinical trials in which their staff are taking part in their NHS employment and that these trials have the required Research Ethics Committee approval.

Would a doctor be covered if he was working other than in accordance with the duties of his post?

Such a doctor would be covered by the health authority indemnity for actions in the course of NHS employment, and this should be interpreted liberally. For work not covered in this way the doctor may have a civil, or even in extreme circumstances criminal, liability for his actions.

Are retired doctors covered?

The health authority indemnity will apply to acts or omissions in the course of NHS employment, regardless of when the claim was notified. Health authorities will thus cover doctors who have subsequently left the Service, but they may seek their co-operation in statements in the defence of a case.

Will a health authority provide cover for a locum hospital doctor?

A health authority will take financial responsibility for the acts and omissions of a locum doctor, whether 'internal' or provided by an external agency.

Are private sector rotations for hospital staff covered?

The medical staff of independent hospitals are responsible for their own medical defence cover, subject to the requirements of the hospital managers. If NHS staff in the training grades work in independent hospitals as part of their NHS training, they would be covered by the health authority indemnity, provided that such work was covered by an NHS contract.'

5.1.6 Other relationships involving care and treatment

An inadequate system of working or inadequate rules for correlating the work and responsibilities of different persons may be evidence upon which a finding of negligence may be made against a health authority or trust even though no single individual had been demonstrably negligent in carrying out his duties. Failure to take precautions advised by the Secretary of State in an official Circular might well invite a finding of negligence.

The question of vicarious liability in respect of injuries to patients making a strictly limited payment towards cost of accommodation in a single room or a small ward (the so-called amenity bed) does not call for special consideration. Such patients do not pay for treatment nor do they (or can they) make a separate contract for medical or surgical attendance as can patients received as private in-patients under section 65 of the National Health Service Act 1977 or treated as private out-patients under section 66 of that Act. In all other respects their position is identical with that of the normal National Health Service patient. The position would be different in the case of a patient paying charges designed to cover full cost of hospital accommodation and services under sections 65 or 66 of the National Health Service Act 1977. The liability of a hospital would depend on whether the alleged negligence were that of a medical practitioner (usually a consultant) with whom the patient had made a private contract and for whose acts and omissions the authority was, therefore, not liable, or of some employee or agent of the authority (whether medical or otherwise) for whose acts and omissions in the course of duty it was responsible.

It is in theory possible for a patient to have pay-bed accommodation without being attended by a consultant with whom he has made a private contract. In such case the patient would pay the hospital at a higher daily rate than would a patient who was receiving privately arranged specialist treatment, to take into account all necessary medical and surgical services, including the cost of the necessary services of hospital consultants who would not receive any extra remuneration for attending him. The additional charge made is usually much below what the patient would have had to pay a consultant with whom he made a private contract; but it must be borne in mind that such a patient would have no greater right than a general ward patient to the services of any particular consultant and that, not being bound by a private contract, any consultant attending him could delegate responsibility for the care of the patient to such extent as he thought proper. Some degree of delegation is also proper when there is a private contract but then there still remains the contractual obligation on the consultant who, for example, could not properly delegate his obligation to perform an operation. In such circumstances the authority would be undertaking the whole treatment of the patient and doing so for reward. The authority would then be vicariously liable for the negligence of any professional (including consultants) who actually treated the patient on its behalf.

A private patient is usually admitted under the care of a consultant on the staff of the hospital with whom the patient has made a direct contract to pay for specialist services. The patient may, in fact, have contracted privately for the services of more than one consultant, e.g., a surgeon, a radiologist and a pathologist. Alternatively he might rely on the hospital for such supporting services of the hospital staff. But even when a private patient makes his own arrangements with one or more consultants, he still has the services of junior professional medical or surgical staff of the hospital, as well as of nursing staff and of hospital facilities generally. Everything, except what the patient has arranged for his own consultant to do, is taken into account in calculating the charge to be made. The Secretary of State or trust decides the charge.

A hospital will not ordinarily be liable for the negligence of a consultant chosen and employed by the patient or his relatives; but it will be liable for the negligence of members of the hospital staff of whatever kind and grade whose services are meant to be covered by the charge made by the hospital. Hence the hospital would not be liable for the negligence of the consultant surgeon (although a member of its staff) because he would be treating the patient not by virtue of his contract of employment but by virtue of his contract with the patient. But the hospital would be liable for the negligence of a registrar or house surgeon who looked after the patient between visits of the consultant and for whose services the hospital was being paid, as well as for the negligence of nurses, physiotherapists and other members of the staff.

The distinction between those for whose actions the hospital is liable and those for whose actions it is not liable is reasonably clear. The practical possibility of a successful claim against the hospital by a private patient in hospital attended by a consultant under a separate contract made by him or on his behalf or for his benefit is much smaller than in the case of the normal type of health service patient. The reason is clear from *Cassidy's* case (1951).[13] The plaintiff left hospital in a worse state than he entered it. He went in with two crippled fingers and left with four. He could not say who had been negligent. It might have been the specialist, a houseman, a sister, a nurse, or any two or more of them. In these circumstances, he therefore relied on the doctrine *res ipsa loquitur* and won his case against the hospital. But had the consultant been employed not by the hospital but by the patient, to substantiate his claim against the hospital the patient would ordinarily either have had to prove positively that some one person or more for whom the hospital was responsible had been negligent, or at least bring evidence to prove that the circumstances were such as to show that someone on the hospital staff other than the consultant or consultants had been negligent. In short, where a private patient who has employed his own consultant or consultants suffers harm as a result of alleged negligent treatment and brings an action for damages, he will as a rule be unable to rely on *res ipsa loquitur* given that the matters complained of as having caused the injury were not under the exclusive control of the defendant hospital or authority.

That doctrine can be of assistance in a case as *Urry v Bierer and another* (1955)[14] where both the operating surgeon and the proprietor of the nursing home were sued on grounds of alleged negligence for harm suffered by a patient through a swab being left in after an operation. The surgeon was sued for his own alleged negligence in failing to remove the swab, and the nursing home on grounds of the alleged negligence of the theatre sister who had miscounted and told the surgeon that all the swabs and packs were accounted for. The action succeeded against both defendants, the plaintiff apparently having the benefit of the doctrine of *res ipsa loquitur* against both. The Court of Appeal held that the surgeon should have known what swabs and packs he had put in and where, and was negligent if he failed to remove them; but that the nurse had been at fault in telling him all the swabs and packs were accounted for. Her negligence had therefore contributed to the mistake. The nursing home was vicariously liable for her negligence. Each defendant was liable for half the damages.

Liability of negligent employee to indemnify his employer

It is generally accepted that an employer is entitled to indemnity from the employee whose negligence had resulted in damages being awarded against the employer. The decision in *Jones v Manchester Corporation and others* (1952)[15] cast doubt on that proposition and was some authority for the view that the employer's right of indemnity was restricted to apportionment of liability at the discretion of the court under the Law Reform (Married Women and Tortfeasors) Act 1935.

In *Jones'* case a patient suffered harm as a result of the negligence of an anaesthetist of house officer status and little experience. On grounds that they had allowed a doctor of such slight experience to administer pentothal, the trial judge ordered the Regional Hospital Board to indemnify the doctor fully against the damages under the Act of 1935. The Board successfully appealed. The Hospital Board was negligent not merely vicariously, and the doctor was negligent not only through inexperience but also in some degree in not carrying out what she had been taught. The court, by a majority of two to one, apportioned responsibility as to 20 per cent on the doctor and 80 per cent on the Board. Lord Justice Hodson, who dissented, would have granted full indemnity to the Board.

Lord Justice Denning, referring to the suggestion made on behalf of the Board that an employer who was made liable for the negligence of an employee was entitled to indemnity, said that he knew of no case in which that had actually been decided and he could see no contractual basis for such indemnity. The issue was entirely a matter for the discretion of the court exercised under the 1935 Act whether it should order any, and if so what, contribution or indemnity between them.

In *Lister v Romford Ice and Cold Storage Co Ltd* (1957)[16] the House of Lords rejected Lord Justice Denning's *dictum* and asserted an implied contractual obligation of an employee to indemnify his employer against the vicarious liability for his negligence. Viscount Simonds and Lord Morton of Henryton said that the employer was also entitled to recover contribution from the servant under the Law Reform (Married Women and Tortfeasors) Act 1935. In the course of their opinions both Viscount Simonds and Lord Somervell cited with approval and in support of the proposition that a servant impliedly undertakes to exercise due skill, carrying with it the duty of reasonable care, the judgment of Mr Justice Wiles in *Harmer v Cornelius* (1858)[17]:

> 'When a skilled labourer, artisan or artist is employed, there is on his part an implied warranty that he is of skill reasonably competent to the task he undertakes – *Spondes peretiam artis*. Thus, if an apothecary, a watch-maker or an attorney be employed for reward, they each impliedly undertake to possess *and exercise* reasonable skill in their several arts.'

Lord Somervell added that the learned judge was saying that the skilled labourer of the first sentence is under the same contractual obligation to his master as those mentioned in the second sentence are to their customers and clients. This serves to underline the point that it matters not whether a member of the medical or surgical staff of a hospital is employed under a contract of service or a contract for services. He will in either case be liable contractually to the employing health authority for any loss occasioned by his failure to use reasonable skill, unless such implied term is expressly excluded. In practice, however, an action for indemnity under the employment contract is most unlikely, given the policy of HM(54)32 as now replaced by HC(89)34 (for which see pp. 113–117, above).

Vicarious liability of nursing home proprietor

Powell v Streatham Manor Nursing Home (1935)[18] decided that the proprietors of a private hospital or nursing home are liable for injury caused to a patient by the negligence of nurses or others employed by the nursing home for the treatment of a patient. In that case a patient's bladder was punctured by the negligence of two trained nurses using a catheter and the proprietors of the nursing home were held liable.[19]

Vicarious liability when hospital services are provided for the Secretary of State under contractual arrangements

In a voluntary hospital

A corporate or unincorporated body responsible for the administration of a voluntary hospital is vicariously liable for the negligence of any member of the staff of the hospital in the course of his duties if that negligence causes injury or loss to a National Health Service patient treated in the hospital under contractual arrangements entered into with it by a health authority acting on behalf of the Secretary of State. (As to voluntary hospital governing bodies and the extent of any personal liability of their members, see Chapter 3. When in this part of this chapter reference is made to the liability of voluntary hospitals it is shorthand for the liability of trustees, board or committee responsible for the institution.)

The health authority is itself responsible on behalf of the Secretary of State for providing hospital care and treatment to National Health Service patients, and that authority will also be vicariously liable for negligent injury to such a patient suffered in the voluntary hospital.[20] This is so, not because it is directly answerable for the negligence of members of the staff of the voluntary hospital, but because it is vicariously liable for the failure of its agent, the voluntary hospital, to provide proper care and treatment for the injured National Health Service patient.

If, in respect of such negligent injury to a National Health Service patient in a voluntary hospital, the contracting health authority alone were sued, of course, it would have a right of indemnity against its agent, the voluntary hospital, unless any such right were excluded by contract. But it would have no right of indemnity against the negligent member of the staff of the voluntary hospital, there being no contractual connection between them and also no duty of care owing by him to the authority. If, however, the health authority claimed indemnity from the voluntary hospital, that hospital in turn could join in the action any member of the staff whose negligence had given rise to the claim. Ordinarily a health authority desirous of claiming indemnity against a voluntary hospital would bring it in as a co-defendant in any action for damages brought against it. If so brought in, the voluntary hospital could similarly bring in any allegedly negligent person for the consequences of whose conduct it might be held responsible.

The position would be different if a National Health Service patient being treated in a voluntary hospital suffered injury in consequence of the negligence of a visiting medical practitioner (say a consultant) in contract with the health authority and not with the voluntary hospital. Clearly the health authority would be vicariously liable for the consequences of his negligence. The voluntary hospital, with which the negligent practitioner had no contractual connection, could also be so liable. The hospital would probably be responsible because, so far as the injured patient was concerned, it would have been the voluntary hospital which had taken immediate responsibility for his treatment. If in such circumstances the voluntary hospital were sued, it could look for indemnity not only to the negligent practitioner but also to the health authority as being vicariously responsible for him. But should it transpire that the voluntary hospital was not vicariously liable for the acts of such a visiting practitioner and the facts were such that, as in *Cassidy v Ministry of Health*,[21] the plaintiff could not establish exactly who had been negligent though seemingly someone must have been and so sought to rely on *res ipsa loquitur* to shift the burden of proof to the defendant, his chance of doing so successfully would be much diminished. The injured patient would be advised to make the health authority as well as the voluntary hospital a defendant.

In a nursing home
For this purpose 'nursing home' means any institution, large or small, receiving patients, not being a charitable institution. Vicarious liability and rights of indemnity of a nursing home proprietor in respect of the negligent injury of any National Health Service patient received for treatment by virtue of contractual arrangements with a health authority is the same as that of a voluntary hospital in the same circumstances.

Vicarious liability of agency supplying nurse to hospital

An agency which undertakes to supply nurses is not as a rule the employer of the nurse supplied and will not ordinarily therefore be liable either to the patient or to the employing health authority for her wrongful acts and omissions. But if an agency has agreed either expressly or by implication to supply, say, a registered nurse and the nurse was not so qualified, an action for breach of contract and indemnity would lie against the agency.

5.1.7 Personal liability of members of governing body or proprietors

Where liability falls on a hospital or nursing home under any of the foregoing heads it means that the liability falls on the proprietors or responsible authority. The nature and extent of *personal* responsibility of members is discussed fully under appropriate heads. See p. 49, above, as to members of health authorities under the National Health Service Act 1977 and pp. 77–78, above, as to members of governing bodies of voluntary hospitals.

The extent of any personal responsibility may be summed up as follows:

1. *A public authority* such as a health authority or trust is liable in its corporate capacity only. The members, as such, are under no personal liability to the injured party.
2. *If a voluntary hospital or a nursing home is incorporated* with limited liability either by Royal Charter, or special Act of Parliament, or under the Companies Act the members of the governing body are under no personal liability unless they have exceeded the powers they are entitled to exercise under the Charter, Act, or memorandum of association of the hospital or nursing home and the injury has arisen therefrom and they are sued personally. Hence any judgment awarding damages against an incorporated hospital or nursing home can be enforced only against the assets of the incorporated body.
3. *If a nursing home is unincorporated* the proprietor or proprietors are *personally* answerable in damages, when the employer is under a vicarious liability for the acts of his servants or for the dangerous state of the premises.
4. *If a charitable hospital is unincorporated* it appears that the subscribers, even though they may have voting rights as regards the appointment of the members of the governing body, are under no personal responsibility for the liabilities of the institution. It may, however, be relevant in deciding the question of liability of subscribers in any particular case to consider whether the voting power is conferred only as a result of formal application to become a 'governor' or whether it is a right automatically conferred by virtue of subscription and possibly even without the knowledge of the subscriber. In the latter case it might also be relevant to consider whether the right had ever been exercised and how recently.

   The members of the governing body are probably personally responsible for the liabilities of the hospital but if they have acted properly they are entitled to indemnity out of the available assets of the hospital, which can then be used directly to satisfy the liability.

5.1.8 Addition of defendants

If a health authority is sued for damages for injury due to alleged negligence of a member of its staff it may have that person joined as co-defendant and, if the plaintiff succeeds, the court will apportion liability for damages or give one or other co-defendant full indemnity under the provisions of the Law Reform (Married Women and Tortfeasors) Act 1935. This is without prejudice to the plaintiff's right to recover in full from either co-defendant. Similarly, a member of the hospital staff who is sued personally, if he alleges that the health authority or some other member of the staff is blameworthy in the matter, can have the authority or such other person joined as a co-defendant. Then, as in the former case, if damages are awarded the court will either apportion liability, in accordance with what it considers just and equitable, or give one co-defendant the right of full indemnity against the other or others.

5.2 LIMITATION OF ACTIONS

5.2.1 Generally

Under the Limitation Acts an action must be brought within a specified period from the date on which the cause of action accrues. The day itself on which a cause of action occurs is not included in computing the period of limitation.[22] Since the passing of the Law Reform (Limitation of Actions) Act 1954 actions in tort against public authorities and public officials must be brought within the same period of time as would be applicable in the case of any other defendant. The effect of the expiry of the limitation period is to bar the remedy but not the right to it and accordingly a defendant who wishes to rely on the Limitation Acts must specially plead it in his defence.

The period for actions founded in tort and simple contract is generally six years.[23] However, where the claim is for damages for negligence, nuisance or breach of duty (whether the duty exists by virtue of a contract or of provision made by or under a statute or independently of any contract or any such provision) where the damages claimed by the plaintiff for the negligence, nuisance or breach of duty consist of or include damages in respect of personal injuries to any person, the period is reduced to three years. Personal injuries for the purpose of the subsection include any disease and any impairment of a person's physical or mental condition.

In *Letang v Cooper* (1965)[24] the Court of Appeal held that these words were wide enough to include all tortious breaches of duty, including trespass to the person. An action in trespass, no less than an action for negligence, is statute-barred after three years if the substance of the action is for damages for personal injuries caused by breach of duty. In *Stubbings v Webb* and another (1993)[25] the House of Lords held that a plaintiff claiming damages for the psychiatric effects of alleged sexual abuse as a minor was limited to six years from the time at which her minority (legal disability) ended. They further held that the extension of the primary limitation period, discussed in the following pages, was unavailable in the case of an intentional assault as distinct from injury caused by 'breach of duty' (negligence). The decision will affect hospitals only in the admittedly rare event of intentional injury on the part of a member of staff. The normal case of an action for damages for negligence, and the limitation periods which apply, are now discussed.

The three-year limitation period applies whether it is the injured person himself suing or someone else who may have suffered loss through his injury. Moreover, if a plaintiff couples in a single action a claim in respect of personal injuries to himself or another, being an injury caused by negligence, nuisance or breach of duty, and therefore within the section, and also a claim in respect of some other damage suffered as a result of the same negligence, nuisance or breach of duty, the period of limitation in respect of the whole cause of action is three years, not six. As to the possible effect of concealed fraud[26] on the period of limitation, and the possibility of an action being commenced out of time where facts of a decisive character were outside the knowledge of the plaintiff, reference should be made to later sections of this chapter.

If an injured plaintiff dies before the end of the three-year limitation period, the cause of action survives for the benefit of the estate by virtue of section 1 of the Law Reform (Miscellaneous Provisions) Act 1934. Such a claim may include loss of income between injury and death, medical and other necessary expenses, and damages for pain, suffering and loss of amenity suffered by the deceased before death.

An action under section 1 of the 1934 Act, as amended by section 11(5) of the Limitation Act 1980, may be brought by or on behalf of the estate of an injured person who dies within three years from either (a) the date of his death, or (b) the date of knowledge of his personal representative, whichever is the later.

Subsection 8 provides that 'personal representative' includes any person who is or has been a personal representative of the deceased. As regards the personal representative's knowledge, subsection (6) provides that the court shall have regard to any knowledge acquired by any such person either while a personal representative or previously.

5.2.2   The 'date of knowledge' period

The general rule in personal injury cases is to limit the period of limitation to three years. It was held in *Cartledge v Jopling and Sons Ltd* (1963)[27] that where a plaintiff did not know and could not have known even with proper medical advice that he had been injured, nevertheless time ran against him under the 1939 Act. This was generally felt to be an injustice. Accordingly Parliament provided a remedy by statutes in 1963, 1971, 1975 and 1980.

Section 14 of the Limitation Act 1980 gives the definition of 'date of knowledge' for the purposes of sections 11 and 12. It covers the case where a plaintiff suffers an injury which shows no symptoms for many years as, for instance, a victim of asbestosis, whose action would otherwise be statute-barred as being possibly well outside the normal limitation period.

Under section 14 of the 1980 Act, time runs from either the date of the accrual of the cause of action or, if it is later, the date when the plaintiff first had knowledge of the cause of action. Section 14 then goes on to define what this means, in subsection (6). It will be noted that the mischief disclosed in *Cartledge v Jopling* (1963, above) is dealt with by the section. In that case the plaintiff had no reason even to consult medical advisers about any industrial injury until after three years from the date when, by his employer's negligence, he had in fact been injured. However, even if he had consulted them they would not have been able to link his physical state with damage done to him by dust getting into his lungs.

Section 14(1) provides that, in sections 11 and 12 of the Act, references to a person's date of knowledge are references to the date on which he first had knowledge of the following facts: (a) that the injury in question was significant; (b) that the injury was attributable in whole or in part to the act or omission which is alleged to constitute negligence, nuisance or breach of duty; (c) the identity of the defendant; and (d) if it is alleged that the act or omission was that of a person other than the defendant, the identity of that person and the additional facts supporting the bringing of an action against the defendant. Knowledge that any acts or omissions did or did not, as a matter of law, involve negligence, nuisance or breach of duty is irrelevant.

It is irrelevant that the plaintiff has not taken legal advice; indeed, it may not assist a plaintiff that he consulted a solicitor, but received incorrect advice that there was no legal cause of action.[28] In such a case the injured person may have an action in negligence against the solicitor.

Section 14(2) defines what the Act means by a 'significant injury'. This is defined as follows:

'(2) For the purposes of this section an injury is significant if the person whose date of knowledge is in question would reasonably have considered it sufficiently serious to justify his instituting proceedings for damages against a defendant who did not dispute liability and was able to satisfy a judgment.'

Therefore, the test is whether the injury is sufficiently serious for a plaintiff to bring an action which will require the minimum of effort. Such an injury probably need not be very serious at all. In *McCafferty v Metropolitan Police District Receiver* (1977),[29] Lord Justice Geoffrey Lane explained:

'It is partly a subjective test, namely: Would this plaintiff have considered the injury sufficiently serious? And partly an objective test, namely: Would he have been reasonable if he did *not* regard it as sufficiently serious? It seems to me that section 14(2) is directed at the nature of the injury as known to the plaintiff at that time. Taking *that* plaintiff, with *that* plaintiff's intelligence, would he have been reasonable in considering the injury not sufficiently serious to justify instituting proceedings for damages?'

Section 14 (3) defines the scope of the 'knowledge' required under the Act:

'(3) For the purposes of this section a person's knowledge includes knowledge which he might reasonably have been expected to acquire:
    (a) from facts observable or ascertainable by him; or
    (b) from facts ascertainable by him with the help of medical or other
        appropriate expert advice which it is reasonable for him to seek.
But a person shall not be fixed under this subsection with knowledge of a fact ascertainable only with the help of expert advice so long as he has taken all reasonable steps to obtain (and where appropriate, to act on) that advice.'

An exception to this rule is the case in which incorrect expert advice prevents the plaintiff bringing the action until after the primary limitation period. In *Scuriaga v Powell* (1979),[30] the plaintiff received incorrect medical advice in 1972 that her injury was not attributable to any negligence. It was not until 1975, outside the limitation period, that the correct position became known. She succeeded in her action for medical negligence following a failed abortion.

More than one injury

The situation where more than one type of injury is sustained by a plaintiff was considered in *Bristow v Grout* (1986).[31] The plaintiff suffered facial injuries, and settled the claim. However, he subsequently discovered a far more serious hip injury, allegedly caused by the same accident. Mr Justice Jupp held that the limitation period began to run when the plaintiff first knew that the *facial* injuries were significant. The claim brought in respect of the hip injury outside the primary limitation period, though within three years of discovering that injury, was held to be statute-barred.

Misleading medical advice

In *Wilkinson v Ancliff* (1986)[32] the plaintiff had been employed by the defendants to drive tankers containing chemicals. In April 1981 he suffered chest congestion and in August stopped work. On 2 November he attended hospital to have his symptoms investigated. He was diagnosed as suffering from bronchial asthma, as a result of inhaling chemical fumes. He consulted solicitors in either late 1982 or early 1983 and a writ was issued on 7 March 1984 against the defendants, claiming damages for personal injury. The writ was not served until 29 March 1985.

The Court of Appeal held that the date that the plaintiff first knew that his injury was 'attributable . . . to the act or omission' of the defendants was when he either first knew that the injury was capable of being, or ought to have known that it was capable of being, so attributed. Section 14(3)(b) provides that he was deemed to know facts which he could ascertain from expert medical or legal advice which it was reasonable for him to seek. However, they added that mere reasonable belief or suspicion that the injury was attributable to the defendants' act or omission was *not* enough to constitute 'knowledge' within section 14(1). Time began to run from the date of the visit to hospital on 2 November.

In *Stephen v Riverside Health Authority* (1989)[33] a patient who suspected that her symptoms were caused by over-exposure to radiation after a mammography in 1977, but was told by many medical experts that the mammography could not have caused the symptoms, did not have knowledge of significant injury attributable to negligence, within the Limitation Act 1980. Mr Justice Auld said that knowledge was required under section 14(1) and the plaintiff's belief or suspicion that she had received an overdose in the mammography sufficient to cause the erythema, the moist spots and increased risk of cancer, was not enough.

The plaintiff would have been entirely reasonable in considering that the early symptoms, such as the erythema and moist spots and anxiety about those symptoms, were not sufficiently serious to justify instituting proceedings for damages. It could not be said that the plaintiff knew before examination in February 1985 that the symptoms she suffered immediately after the mammography were capable of being attributed to excessive exposure to radiation caused by an improperly conducted mammography. She did not have the critical piece of knowledge that she had, or could have received, a sufficiently high dose of radiation to cause the symptoms.

Her past experience in radiography did not characterise her suspicion as knowledge, or attributability, to set off against the 'chorus of highly qualified experts' who told her that the exposures were well below any level that could cause the symptoms. The turning point was in February 1985 when the reliability of the recorded level of 34 Roentgen was questioned. Before that date she knew neither that she had suffered significant injury nor that such injury as she knew of was capable of being attributed to the mammography. Her case was therefore not statute-barred.

5.2.3 Extension of the limitation period: persons 'under a disability'

Section 28(1) and (6) of the Act of 1980 provide that if a plaintiff is under a disability at the time his cause of action arises, the limitation period is extended in order that an action may be brought at any time before the expiration of three years from the date when the plaintiff ceased to be under the disability or died, or whichever was the earlier.

Section 38(2) of the Act provides that a person shall be treated as under a disability if he is an infant (that is, a minor, for which see Chapter 7) or is of unsound mind. A person is of unsound mind if he has a mental disorder within the meaning of the Mental Health Act 1983 and is, accordingly, unable to manage or administer his own property and affairs: section 38(3). A person is conclusively presumed to be of unsound mind if (a) he is liable to be detained or subject to guardianship under the Mental Health Act 1983; and (b) he is receiving treatment as an in-patient in any hospital or mental nursing home within the meaning of the Mental Health Act 1983 (although he is not liable to be detained under that Act) that being treatment which follows without any interval a period during which he was liable to be detained or subject to guardianship under that Act or by virtue of any enactment repealed or excluded by that Act.

It follows that, in the case of a minor, action may be brought during the three-year period following his reaching majority, notwithstanding that the cause of action may have accrued many years previously. In the case of any other disability, action may be brought during the three-year period following the date when such disability ceases. The 'date of knowledge' rules also apply (pp. 126–129, above).

5.2.4　Discretionary exclusion of time limits

Section 33(1) of the 1980 Act creates an exception to the above provisions and is of great practical importance:

'33.—(1) If it appears to the court that it would be equitable to allow an action to proceed having regard to the degree to which—
- (a)　the provisions of section 11 or 12 of this Act prejudice the plaintiff or any person whom he represents; and
- (b)　any decision of the court under this subsection would prejudice the defendant or any person whom he represents;
the court may direct that those provisions shall not apply to the action, or shall not apply to any specified cause of action to which the action relates.'

The discretion of the court in disallowing the defence plea that an injured plaintiff's action is barred by lapse of time is unfettered; but some guidance is given in the Limitation Act 1980, as to the circumstances in which the overriding discretion can be used. They are:

1. the length of, and reasons for, delay on the part of the plaintiff;
2. the extent to which, having regard to the delay, the evidence adduced or likely to be adduced by the plaintiff or the defendant is or is likely to be less cogent than if the action had been brought within the time allowed by section 11 or (as the case may be) by section 12;
3. the conduct of the defendant after the cause of action arose, including

the extent (if any) to which they responded to requests reasonably made by the plaintiff for information or inspection for the purpose of ascertaining facts which were or might be relevant to the plaintiff's cause of action against the defendant;

4. the duration of any disability of the plaintiff arising after the date of the accrual of the cause of action;

5. the extent to which the plaintiff acted promptly and reasonably once he knew whether or not the act or omission of the defendant, to which the injury was attributable, might be capable at that time of giving rise to an action for damages; and

6. the steps, if any, taken by the plaintiff to obtain medical, legal or other expert advice and the nature of any such advice he may have received.

The wide discretion given under section 33 to disapply normal limitation periods is vividly illustrated by the decision in *Harris v Newcastle-upon-Tyne Health Authority* (1989),[34] discussed at pp. 136–137 of this chapter in the context of pre-action discovery of health authority case notes.

5.2.5 Fraud of the potential defendant

If the reason why the plaintiff could not reasonably have obtained knowledge of his right of action earlier was the fraud of the defendant, the plaintiff's cause of action is deemed to arise when he could with reasonable diligence have become aware of his right.

The word *fraud* does not imply any degree of moral turpitude. What is referred to is *equitable fraud* which covers conduct which, having regard to some special relationship between the parties concerned, is an unconscionable thing for the one to do towards the other. In *Gerber v Pines* (1935)[35] Mr Justice du Parcq held that as a general rule a doctor who found that he had left some foreign substance in a patient's body should tell the patient at once, though there were exceptions. Concealment, unless justified, would therefore amount to equitable fraud.

What is the position when a surgeon has negligently injured a patient or has performed the wrong operation, for instance through two patients getting mixed up and the wrong one taken to the operating theatre, and the patient is not told what has happened? Although it is known to the surgeon and, possibly, to other hospital officers, the injury is one of which the patient could not be aware unless informed. Dr Speller was once credibly informed of a case in which two female patients were mixed up. One, who needed only minor surgical treatment, was subjected to a major gynaecological operation which inevitably resulted in her being unable to have children. She was not informed, apparently on the ground that the surgeon, having consulted her family doctor, concluded that she should not be told because of the possible adverse effect on her mental and physical health. In such a case, is a claim to damages statute-barred after the normal period of three years?

The answer seems to be that if the surgeon had no valid and special reason for his reticence the patient would have her right of action on grounds of concealed fraud at any time within three years of the time when, with reasonable diligence, she could have discovered the wrong.

5.2.6 Time limit for claiming contribution between joint tortfeasors

A tortfeasor (wrongdoer) who has become entitled to a right to recover contribution from a joint tortfeasor must bring his action within two years from the date on which the right accrued to him, being either the date on which the tortfeasor had judgment given against him or an award made on any arbitration; or, he having admitted liability, the date on which the amount to be paid to discharge that liability was agreed.

5.2.7   Limitation periods and retention of records

Circular HC(89)20 recommends the minimum periods for retention of personal health records as well as records which may affect a hospital's legal liability as a producer of defective products. The recommendations of the Circular do not extend to Family Health Service Authorities or to Community Health Councils. The guidance takes account of the provisions of the Limitation Acts, the Congenital Disabilities (Civil Liability) Act 1976 and the Consumer Protection Act 1987. The Circular also advises on the requirements of the Public Records Acts, for which see Chapter 15. The requirements and recommendations of the Circular in respect of possible litigation against health authorities are contained in the following paragraphs:

'Legal actions or complaints about hospital or community health services

9. Any documents (other than personal health records – see para 12) relating to legal actions or to complaint, including accident reports, should be kept for a minimum of ten years after the incident or matter complained of, or, when an action has been commenced, as legally advised.

Product records

10. The Consumer Protection Act 1987 covering the liability of producers for defective products came into force on 1 March 1988. Health authorities are affected by those provisions as producers of products and equipment. They may also be liable in certain circumstances as suppliers and users of products. Full details are contained in health notice HN(88)3.

11. A health authority's capacity to avoid liability or defend an action brought

under the Act for damages resulting from a defect in a product depends upon its keeping comprehensive records relating to the procurement, use, modification and supply of products. An obligation arising from liability lasts for ten years after the product was supplied by the producer and up to one year is allowed for serving a writ. Those records must therefore be kept for 11 years.

Personal health records

12. Personal health records need to be retained for minimum periods to take account of the Limitation Act [1980] and the Congenital Disabilities (Civil Liability) Act 1976. The Limitation Act [1980] amends the law on the time limits within which actions for personal injuries, or arising from death, may be brought. The Congenital Disabilities (Civil Liability) Act 1976, clarifies the right of a child born disabled, as distinct from the right of his mother, to bring civil action for damages in respect of that disability. The limitation period for bringing such actions remains 3 years, but this now runs from when it is first realised that a person has suffered a significant injury that may be attributable to the negligence of a third party. The lapse between the "injury" and "knowledge" of it is without limit of time. For a minor the limitation period runs from the time he attains the age of 18 years and may be extended where material facts are not known.

13. A person of 'unsound mind'* can, as long as he remains under the disability in question, bring an action without limit of time through his "next friend". After the person's death, the period of limitation will run against his personal representative(s). Authorities will appreciate that, in the context of current practices in the care and treatment of mentally disordered persons, discharge from hospital can no longer be regarded as implying that the person has ceased to suffer from the disability.

* The definition of "unsound mind" was not, when HC(89)20 was issued, defined in law. The Department's advice was that "a court would be likely to find that a person suffering from any of the forms of a mental disorder within the meaning of section 2 of the Mental Health Act 1983 . . . would be treated as being under a disability". [This should have read "section 1(2)". See now Limitation Act 1980, section 38(2), above.]

14. The limitation period of three years applies only to actions which include a claim for damages in respect of personal injuries. In the case of other claims, e.g. a claim by a mentally disordered patient that he has been falsely imprisoned, the appropriate limitation period prescribed by section 2 of the Limitation Act [1980] is six years from the date when the patient ceases to be under a disability or dies.

15. Personal health records may now be required as evidence in legal actions for considerably longer than hitherto. The Department's advice is that the minimum periods proposed are likely to be regarded as acceptable by the courts. It is not necessary however to keep every single piece of paper received in connection with patients. Health authorities should determine in consultation with their health professionals their policy with regard to the elements which should be regarded as a permanent constituent of the record and those elements of a transitory nature which may be discarded as their value ceases.

16. Special considerations apply to records relating to children, young people and mentally disordered people. In most other cases a person or his representatives might be expected to know whether he has a cause of action

within five years of the alleged negligence, from which time the limitation period should be taken to run. It is recommended that the following minimum retention periods should be observed:

(i)   Obstetric records: 25 years.

(ii)   Records relating to children and young people (including paediatric, vaccination and community child health service records): until the patient's 25th birthday, or 26th birthday if an entry was made when the young person was 17.

(iii)   Records relating to mentally disordered persons within the meaning of the Mental Health Act 1983: 20 years from the date at which, in the opinion of the doctor concerned, the disorder has ceased or diminished to the point where no further care or treatment is considered necessary.

Except that such records need only be retained for a minimum of 8 years after the death of a patient (or, in the case of obstetric records, death of the child – but not of the mother). [Obstetric records of stillbirths need to be kept only for 8 years.]

(iv)   All other personal health records: 8 years after the conclusion of treatment.

17. After the appropriate minimum period has expired the need to retain them further for local use should be carefully, and if necessary periodically, reviewed. Because of the sensitive and confidential nature of such records and the need to ensure that decisions on retention balance the interests of professional staff, including any research in which they are or may be engaged, and the resources available for storage, some health authorities have established committees to oversee the procedures for the retention and destruction of these records. Others may wish to consider if it would be helpful to do so.

18. As records could be required in litigation virtually without limit of time, the Department recognises that some records may be destroyed that might otherwise subsequently have been required for litigation. The Department's view, however, is that the cost of indefinite retention of records would greatly exceed the liabilities likely to be incurred in the occasional case where defence to an action for damages is handicapped by the absence of records. If a hospital doctor involved in litigation claims that prior disposal of relevant medical records has prejudiced the outcome, this should be considered by the health authority along with all other factors when the apportionment of any liability as between the doctor and health authority is being contemplated.'

5.3   ACCESS TO RECORDS, REPORTS, NOTES AND DATA

Patients already enjoy a general right of access to their computerised medical records under the Data Protection Act 1984 and, as from 1 November 1991, to their manually held notes under the Access to Health Records Act 1990. However, it is doubtful that either the Data Protection Act 1984, or the Access to Health Records Act 1990, will have any significant effect on the use of pre-action discovery.

First, the Access to Health Records Act 1990 only applies to those records compiled after 1 November 1991, and as such will clearly be inappropriate in cases where the treatment under scrutiny was administered prior to this.

Second, both the Data Protection Act 1984 and the Access to Health Records Act 1990 contain various exemptions. These permit information to be withheld if, for example, disclosure would be likely to cause the patient serious harm. No such exemptions apply to pre-action discovery, although the court may limit disclosure to the patient's legal and medical advisers, if appropriate.

Third, pre-action discovery is not limited to the patient's notes. An application may, for example, be made for the disclosure of accident reports relating to the incident or events complained of.

5.3.1 Access to medical records prior to the commencement of legal proceedings

The nature of clinical medicine is such that is frequently difficult, if not impossible, to assess whether a patient has received negligent treatment without first obtaining access to his notes. Yet, until 1971, patients' legal and medical advisers were required to do that, disclosure of the notes only being obtained at the trial itself. Section 31 of the Administration of Justice Act 1970 introduced the process known as 'pre-action discovery' whereby the High Court could order that a patient suspecting medical negligence be given access to his notes to enable him to receive proper legal advice before incurring the expense of commencing formal proceedings against the hospital or doctor. Pre-action discovery represents probably the most important way to access medical records. For other forms of access under statutory entitlement see Chapters 13 and 14.

Section 31 of the Administration of Justice Act 1970 has now been replaced by section 33(2) of the Supreme Court Act 1981 which provides that:

'(2) On the application, in accordance with the rules of Court, of a person who appears to the Court to be likely to be a party to subsequent proceedings in that Court in which a claim in respect of personal injuries to a person, or in respect of a person's death, is likely to be made, the High Court shall, in such circumstances specified in the rules, have the power to order a person who appears to the court to be likely to be a party to the proceedings and to be likely to have in his possession, custody or power any documents which are relevant to an issue arising or likely to arise out of that claim—

(a) to disclose whether those documents are in his possession, custody or power; and

(b) to produce such of those documents as are in his possession, custody or power to the applicant, or on such conditions as may be specified in the order. . . .'

'Likely to be a party to subsequent proceedings'

The applicant will in the vast majority of cases be the patient. However, all that is required is that he be a likely party to subsequent proceedings.

Dunning v Board of Governors of the United Liverpool Hospitals (1973)[36] demonstrates that the applicant does not have to show that at the time of the application he has a good cause of action making proceedings 'likely'. In 1963, Mrs Dunning, who had enjoyed good health all her life, developed a persistent cough and was admitted to hospital for investigations. After two or three weeks her condition became dramatically worse, and when she was finally discharged from hospital some 17 weeks after her admission, her illness had not cleared up. Her illness was initially diagnosed as undulant fever and finally as periarteritis nodosa, but her family took the view that it had been caused by one of the drugs given to her whilst in hospital. Even so, no action was taken against the hospital within the limitation period, probably because Mrs Dunning's doctor had told her that her condition would clear up. Any action therefore became statute-barred unless the court granted leave to sue out of time because of absence of knowledge of material facts.

In 1969 Mrs Dunning's medical adviser, Dr Evans, sought access to the hospital case notes. However, the Board was unwilling to make them available unless they received an assurance that no action would be commenced, an assurance which Mrs Dunning's solicitors were unable to give.

In May 1970, without having seen the notes, Dr Evans formed the opinion that, on the evidence available to him, the hospital had not acted negligently.

The Board was ordered by Mr Justice Caulfield to make the records available to Dr Evans but appealed to the Court of Appeal.

Counsel for the Board argued that the plain wording of the section only enabled the court to order discovery if the applicant could show at the time of the application that she was likely to bring a claim in respect of her illness. The report of Dr Evans, however, had advised that there was no foundation for making such a claim. Disclosure was therefore sought not for the purposes of providing evidence on which a claim could be based, but allaying the anxieties of Mrs Dunning and her family. Accordingly, he argued, an order for discovery should be refused.

The Court of Appeal (Lord Justice Stamp dissenting) rejected the submission. Lord Denning and Lord Justice James stated that one of the objects of the section was to enable plaintiffs to find out before they start proceedings whether they have a good cause of action or not. The purpose of the legislation would therefore be frustrated if the applicant had to show in advance that she had already got a good cause of action before seeing the documents. An order for discovery was accordingly granted.

In *Harris v Newcastle upon Tyne Health Authority* (1989)[37] Lord Justice Kerr accepted that in its ordinary and sensible meaning the word 'likely' involves something which is not unlikely, which in turn is something more probable than not. However, his Lordship added:

'On the authority of this Court in *Dunning v United Liverpool Hospital Board of Governors* . . . I have come to the conclusion that we are bound by that authority to construe the word "likely" . . . as having the meaning which James LJ gave to it when he said: "I would construe 'likely' . . . as meaning 'reasonable prospect'." You can have a reasonable prospect even though you may fall considerably short of more than a 50% chance. Another phrase which might be used to describe the same effect is . . . "on the cards".'

However, pre-action discovery does not permit an aggrieved patient to simply go on a 'fishing expedition' for evidence of negligence. He must disclose the nature of the claim he intends to make. 'Illfounded, irresponsible and speculative allegations based merely on hope would not provide a reasonable basis for an intended claim in subsequent proceedings', said Lord Justice James in *Dunning*.

The facts of *Dunning v Board of Governors of United Liverpool Hospitals* suggest that the occurrence of something untoward during a course of treatment will often constitute a reasonable basis for disclosure, particularly if a satisfactory explanation of the patient's condition is not forthcoming.

The claim must be 'in respect of personal injury or death'

'Personal injuries' is defined in section 35 of the Act as including 'any disease and any impairment of a person's physical or mental condition'. 'Personal injuries' therefore includes a claim for nervous shock, in the sense of an actual psychiatric disorder as opposed to mere upset or distress: see *McLoughlin v O'Brian* (1983).[38] A claim may involve medical negligence, or injury to a visitor or to an employee.

There is no reason why a patient involved in such a claim should not be given access to his notes voluntarily, providing that:

1. A written assurance is given that he will pay any costs incurred by the health authority and that no proceedings are contemplated against the health authority.
2. A letter of authority from the patient consenting to the disclosure is included with any request.
3. Where the information sought is of a medical nature (occasionally the information sought may be entirely unrelated to medical matters, for example, the date of the patient's admission to, or discharge from hospital) the doctor or dentist in charge of the patient's treatment, or his successor, is appropriately consulted. This is to ensure that the notes do not contain information which may harm the patient, and that, where the request is only for extracts from the case notes, any extracts which are made are not misleading. Failure to ensure that the notes do not contain information which might harm the patient

could result in a claim being brought against the health authority for nervous shock. Where the patient is legally represented, this problem may usually be overcome by requiring an undertaking from his representative that he will not communicate the contents of the notes to the patient. Providing that the reason for seeking to restrict access is explained, such an undertaking will usually be forthcoming.

4. Information about anyone other than the patient will not be disclosed, other than where the individual concerned has consented in writing to the disclosure. Failure to obtain the requisite consent may result in a claim for breach of confidence, or, if the notes are stored on computer, for the unauthorised disclosure of data (see Chapters 16 and 13, respectively).

5. Disclosure will not reveal the identity of a third party who has provided information about the patient, unless the third party is a health professional who has provided the information in a professional capacity, or has consented in writing to the disclosure. Again, failure to obtain the requisite consent might result in damages being sought for breach of confidence or breach of the Data Protection Act 1984.

It is unlikely that a court will refuse an application for pre-action discovery on the grounds that it is unnecessary, particularly where an allegation of medical negligence may be made. Sir John Donaldson in *Lee v South West Thames Regional Area Health Authority* (1985)[39] said:

'It should never be forgotten that we are here concerned with a hospital patient relationship. The decision of the House of Lords in *Sidaway v Bethlem Royal Hospital Governors* (1985)[40] affirms that a doctor is under a duty to answer his patient's questions as to the treatment proposed. We see no reason why there should not be a similar duty in relation to hospital staff . . . Why, we ask ourselves, is the position any different if the patient asks what treatment he has in fact had?'

What documents are covered by the section?

The section refers to 'any documents which are relevant to an issue arising or likely to arise out of the claim'. All medical, nursing, anaesthetic, and surgical notes, laboratory test reports, X-ray films, consent forms, clinical and other correspondence, and accident reports may be subject to pre-action discovery.

However, there are two important limitations on the court's power to order disclosure. First, the court is not empowered to order the disclosure of documents which would attract privilege from disclosure, had proceedings actually commenced. Second, the court is prohibited by section 35(1) of the Supreme Court Act 1981 from making an order under section 33(2) if it considers that 'compliance with the order, if made, would be likely to be injurious to the public interest' (see p. 144 of this chapter).

Legal professional privilege

The courts consider that they have an overriding obligation to ensure full and candid disclosure by clients to their lawyers. This would be impossible if clients were aware that their confidences could be broken. Any direct communications between lawyer and client are therefore privileged from disclosure, irrespective of whether or not legal proceedings have begun or are even contemplated. The principle applies equally to communications between employers and salaried solicitors employed directly by them.

However, documents other than these will enjoy privilege from disclosure only where:

1. litigation was contemplated when they were written; and
2. the documents were drawn up for the immediate communication to legal advisers; and
3. where the report in question was prepared for more than one reason, the dominant reason was so that it could be referred to a solicitor to assist in defending a claim or potential claim.

It is this aspect of legal professional privilege that can create problems, particularly in relation to accident reports. The attitude of the courts to accident reports, and whether or not they may be privileged against disclosure, is best illustrated by the decision in *Waugh v British Railways Board* (1980).[41] The case concerned a report on a fatal accident which occurred in a railway goods yard; but the principle which it established is equally applicable to accidents concerning health services, whether to a patient or to an employee.

In the *Waugh* case, an employee of the British Railways Board had been killed in an accident while working on the railways. In accordance with the Board's usual practice a report on the accident, called an internal enquiry report, was prepared by two of the Board's officers two days after the accident. The report was headed 'For the information of the Board's solicitor'. However, it appeared from an affidavit produced on behalf of the Board that the report was prepared for two purposes: to establish the cause of the accident so that appropriate safety measures could be taken, and to enable the Board's solicitor to advise in the litigation that was almost certain to ensue. Although the first purpose was more immediate than the second, they were described in the affidavit as being of equal importance. The report contained statements by witnesses and was probably the best evidence available as to the cause of the accident.

The plaintiff (widow of the deceased) commenced an action against the Board under the Fatal Accidents Acts 1846–1959 and applied for discovery of the report to assist in preparing and conducting her case. The Board resisted discovery on the ground that the report was protected by legal professional privilege. The master ordered disclosure but on appeal the judge reversed the order. The plaintiff appealed to the Court of Appeal which held, on authority, that a report which came into existence or was obtained for the purpose of anticipated litigation was privileged from production even though it might serve some other even more important purpose, and dismissed her appeal. The plaintiff appealed to the House of Lords.

The court was faced with two competing principles, namely that all relevant evidence should be made available for the court and that communications between lawyer and client should be allowed to remain confidential and privileged. In reconciling those two principles the public interest was, on balance, best served by rigidly confining within narrow limits the privilege of lawfully withholding material or evidence relevant to litigation. Accordingly, a document was only to be accorded privilege from production on the ground of legal professional privilege if the dominant purpose for which it was prepared was that of submitting it to a legal adviser for advice and use in litigation. Since the purpose of preparing the internal enquiry report for advice and use in anticipated litigation was merely one of the purposes and not the dominant purpose for which it was prepared, the Board's claim of privilege failed and the report would have to be disclosed.

An accident report cannot be protected from disclosure merely by writing on it that it is intended solely for legal defence purposes. The court will examine the true substance of the document. In *Lask v Gloucester Health Authority* (1985)[42] the Court of Appeal held that a confidential accident report, which National Health Service Circulars require to be completed by health authorities both for the use of solicitors in the event of litigation consequent upon the accident, and also to enable action to be taken to avoid a repetition of the accident, is not subject to legal professional privilege. This is because the dominant purpose of its preparation has not been the submission to solicitors in anticipation of litigation, even though both the health authority and the solicitors had deposed that it had, and the form itself referred only to that purpose. According to the report in *The Times* of the above case, both the authority and its solicitors attempted to alter the substance by changing the name. The attempt deservedly failed.

To whom may disclosure be ordered?

There is no legal basis for seeking to limit disclosure to a nominated medical adviser only in the case of a legally represented plaintiff. Section 33(2) of the Act expressly states that the court may order disclosure:

'to the applicant or, on such conditions as may be specified in the order—
  (i) to the applicant's legal advisers; or
  (ii) to the applicant's legal advisers and any other medical or professional adviser of the applicant; or
  (iii) if the applicant has no legal adviser, to any medical adviser or other professional adviser of the applicant.'

While an order for pre-action discovery may exclude the applicant from being permitted access to his notes, so long as he has retained a lawyer his lawyer must be permitted to examine the notes.

As the result of increasing specialisation and experience of medical negligence litigation, few solicitors are now prepared to accept disclosure to a nominated expert only and will state so when requesting discovery. However, where the request for discovery does not contain any statement to this effect, health authorities may wish to take the opportunity of gaining a tactical advantage over the patient's solicitor by offering to disclose the notes to a nominated medical adviser only.

In what circumstances will an order for pre-action discovery be restricted to the applicant's professional advisers?

A court will rarely restrict an order for discovery to an applicant's professional advisers. A restrictive order may be appropriate in circumstances where, for example, the notes contain information concerning a third party, such as a spouse, or where disclosure of the notes is likely to cause the applicant serious harm.

However, the fact that the notes contain confidential information about a third party, or even potentially harmful information, will not necessarily result in the court refusing the applicant access to his notes. The court has to approach each case on a 'case by case' basis, balancing the principle that confidentiality should be preserved or that the applicant should be protected from harm, against the principle that potential litigants should be able to comment on their notes in order that they may receive proper legal advice. The court has power to order that part only of the notes be disclosed if confidentiality would otherwise be inappropriately offended.

Order for discovery in an action for personal injuries made on persons who are not themselves parties

Section 34 of the Supreme Court Act 1981 provides:

'(2) On the application, in accordance with rules of court, of a party to any proceedings to which this section applies, the High Court shall, in such circumstances as may be specified in the rules, have power to order a person who is not a party to the proceedings and who appears to the court to be likely to have in his possession, custody or power any documents which are relevant to an issue arising out of the said claim—

(a) to disclose whether those documents as are in his possession, custody or power; and

(b) to produce such of those documents as are in his possession, custody or power to the applicant or, on such conditions as may be specified in the order—

    (i) to the applicant's legal advisers; or

    (ii) to the applicant's legal advisers and any medical or other professional adviser of the applicant; or

    (iii) if the applicant has no legal adviser, to any medical or other professional adviser of the applicant.'

In *Paterson v Chadwick, Paterson v Northampton and District Hospital Management Committee* (1974)[43] the plaintiff suffered a serious and permanent disability to her left arm allegedly caused by the negligent injection of an anaesthetic for the purpose of dental treatment at the Northampton and District General Hospital. She consulted solicitors with the object of obtaining damages, but before they started proceedings her claim became statute-barred. She alleged this had been due to the fault of the solicitors. She commenced an action alleging professional negligence against them. She needed the hospital notes in support of her claim. Section 32 of the Administration of Justice Act 1970 (now replaced by section 34(1) of the 1981 Act) would only help her if the action against the solicitors was 'in respect of personal injury'. Mr Justice Boreham held that the words *in respect of* in section 32(1) conveyed the need for some connection or relation between the plaintiff's claim and the personal injuries sustained. He found also that there was in this case such a connection or relation because the nature and extent of the plaintiff's injuries were an essential element in the proof of her claim against her former solicitors, and that accordingly the plaintiff was 'a party to proceedings in which a claim in respect of personal injuries to a person is made' within the meaning of section 32(1), and so entitled to an order for discovery of the medical records.

Production and protection of property relevant to actual or intended civil proceedings

Inspection and preservation may be ordered by the court in relation to both actual and anticipated proceedings. The Supreme Court Act 1981 provides:

'**33.**—(1) On the application of any person in accordance with rules of court, the High Court shall, in such circumstances as may be specified in the rules, have power to make an order providing for any one or more of the following matters, that is to say—

(a) the inspection, photographing, preservation, custody and detention of property which appears to the court to be property which may become the subject-matter of subsequent proceedings in the High Court, or as to which any question may arise in any such proceedings; and

(b) the taking of samples of any such property as is mentioned in paragraph (a), and the carrying out of any experiment on or with any such property.

34.—(3) On the application, in accordance with rules of court, of a party to any proceedings to which this section applies, the High Court shall, in such circumstances as may be specified in the rules, have power to make an order providing for any one or more of the following matters, that is to say—

(a) the inspection, photographing, preservation, custody and detention of property which is not the property of, or in the possession of, any party to the proceedings but which is the subject-matter of the proceedings or as to which any question arises in the proceedings;

(b) the taking of samples of any such property as is mentioned in paragraph (a) and the carrying out of any experiment on or with any such property.'

It has been held that this power does not apply to the taking of a blood sample or to the carrying out of any surgical undertaking on a living body: *W v W* (1964).[44]

Charging for the supply of information relating to legal proceedings

Departmental Circular HC(87)13 states:

'1. This Circular clarifies the Department's policy on charging for the supply of information about patients engaged in legal proceedings.

Background

2. The Department's current advice is contained in HM(59)88 paragraph 7 which states:

"No hospital charge should be made for the supply of information . . . unless significant additional expenditure has to be incurred specifically for the purpose of providing it."

3. The Health Service Commissioner has brought to our attention that health authorities are interpreting in different ways what are significant costs and whether charges can be made. The Department has undertaken to clarify the policy – see paragraph 4, below.

Policy on charging

4. i.   Health Authorities are not required to provide information for litigation purposes free of charge unless they are satisfied that no cost has been incurred.

ii.   Where the cost of providing a service can be calculated each authority should decide whether such cost should be recovered or waived.

iii.   There is no nationally recommended scale of fees as the amount of work will vary. It is open to an authority to calculate the cost and seek payment in respect of each application or to introduce a standard fee for the service.

iv.   Any charges made for the service should be limited to recovery of costs incurred and should not include an element of profit.

Action

5. Authorities are asked to consider this guidance and to determine their own policies in accordance with it.'

Public interest immunity

Section 35(1) of the Supreme Court Act 1981 provides that:

'**35.**—(1) The High Court shall not make an order under section 33 or 34 if it considers that compliance with the order, if made, would be likely to be injurious to the public interest.'

Discovery will not be ordered if it would be injurious to the public interest to allow it. It used to be thought that this only applied to what may be termed *Crown information* and hence non-production of information on this ground came to be called Crown privilege. It is now more accurately called 'public interest immunity', given that it is clear that the prohibition does not depend on the source of the information but on the conclusion of the courts that having regard to (a) the public interest in the full disclosure in the interests of the administration of justice, and (b) to the damage to the public interest by the disclosure of this information, on balance the information ought not to be disclosed.

It is for the court to decide whether or not a claim to immunity has been made out. The various views advanced by the judges as to the balance of the public interest are neither a model of clarity nor of consistency. However, it is clear that where the documents are ordinary documents collected or compiled in the ordinary way and that normally documents of their type are admitted in litigation, the claim will not lie. Where, however, the information has some special confidentiality about it a claim may be allowed. In one case, for example, reports of child welfare officers were protected not only by regulations but also by the court. In another case, the House of Lords allowed a claim made by the National Society for the Prevention of Cruelty to Children to refuse disclosure of the name of an informant.[45]

The health authority's response

It will usually be in the health authority's interests to respond to a proper request for discovery (that is, where the specified grounds are satisfied) by agreeing to disclose the patient's notes voluntarily. Unreasonable refusal or delay may result in the health authority being ordered to pay the costs incurred by the applicant.

Even where an application for pre-action discovery is successful it is by no means certain that proceedings against the defendant will ensue, the applicant merely having to establish that there is a reasonable prospect of subsequent proceedings.

Irrespective of whether or not the application is successful, the defendant will usually be entitled to costs.

However, the court may refuse to grant an order for costs where the health authority has been dilatory in complying with a proper request for discovery. A period of six weeks within which to consent to disclosure, and a further 14 days within which to produce the notes, was approved of in *Hall and others v Wandsworth Health Authority* (1985).[46]

Where there is no reasonable basis for refusing discovery the court may order the health authority or trust to pay the applicant's costs (see *Hall and others v Wandsworth Health Authority* (1985), above, and *Jacob (a minor) v Wessex Regional Health Authority* (1984)).[47]

5.3.2   Department's guidance on voluntary disclosure

Circular HC(82)16 draws attention to the 1981 legislation concerning the powers of the High Court to order disclosure of documents before and in proceedings for personal injury or death and sets it in the context of existing guidance on voluntary disclosure of information about hospital patients contemplating or engaged in civil legal proceedings:

'Existing guidance and practice
1. Guidance on the voluntary release of information about patients contemplating or engaged in civil legal proceedings is contained in HM(59)88. Paragraphs 3 and 4 [see below] advise on the action to be taken by health authorities when a request for case notes or information from them is received from the patient concerned or his representative. This advice remains applicable, in particular that authorities should not stand on their strict rights in these circumstances and that the doctor concerned must always be consulted where medical matters are in any way involved.

2. It has since become a widely accepted practice for disclosure in these circumstances to be made to the applicant's medical adviser. This practice is commended as a means of ensuring that case notes are correctly interpreted for the applicant's benefit.'

The relevant extract from HM(59)88 states:

'3. Where a request for records or reports is made on what are manifestly insubstantial grounds, the hospital cannot be expected to grant it, but where information is being sought in pursuance of a claim of prima facie substance against the Board or Committee or a member of their staff or both, the decision is more difficult and each request must be examined on its own merits, in the light of legal advice, and of course in consultation with any member of their medical or dental staff directly concerned in the outcome of the claim . . . the Minister does not feel that Boards and Committees, especially as they are public authorities, would either wish or be well advised to maintain their strict rights . . . except for some good reason bearing on the defence to the particular claim or on the ground that the request is made without substantial justification.

4. Where the information is required in a matter which has nothing to do with the hospital or any member of its staff, for example in litigation between the patient and a third party, hospital authorities should be prepared to help by providing, as far as possible, the information asked for subject always to the consent of the patient. Sometimes the information sought may be entirely unrelated to medical matters – for example the date of the patient's admission or discharge; whether he was a private patient and signed the appropriate form of

undertaking; and if so, the amount paid by way of hospital charges. Such information may properly be given by the Secretary of the Board or Committee without reference to the medical staff. But in all cases – and they will undoubtedly be the majority – where medical matters are in any way involved (for example, where information is wanted about the diagnosis made on admission, details of treatment, conditions on discharge, or prognosis) the doctor or dentist who was in charge of the patient's treatment at the hospital, or his successor, should be consulted. It is self-evident that this must be done when a medical or dental report is being asked for. But the principle is equally important when the request is only for extracts from the case notes, since it is necessary for the doctor or dentist to ensure that any extracts which are made are not misleading, and also that their disclosure to the patient cannot in any way be harmful medically to him – it would no doubt often be undesirable to let the patient himself have so detailed a report or such full extracts from the medical records as it would be proper to give to his general practitioner. This decision is one which can be made only by a professionally qualified person. At the same time it is imperative that no material information which can in any way be relevant to the matter should be withheld in such a way as to convey a wrong picture.'

NOTES

1. *Lloyd v Grace, Smith Co* [1912] AC 716 (fraud); *Photo Production v Securicor Transport* [1980] AC 827 (arson).
2. [1986] 3 All ER 801.
3. Section 116.
4. [1909] 2 KB 820.
5. [1951] 2 KB 343.
6. [1954] 2 QB 66.
7. [1942] 2 KB 293.
8. [1954] 2QB 66 at 82.
9. Now the National Health Service Act 1977, section 3(1).
10. [1954] 1 WLR 1382.
11. Section 21 has since been repealed.
12. [1954] 1 WLR 1382 at 1385–1386.
13. [1951] 2 KB 343.
14. The Times, 15 July 1955.
15. [1952] 2 QB 852.
16. [1957] AC 555.
17. (1858) 5CB(NS) 236.
18. [1935] AC 243.
19. And see *Urry v Bierer and another* The Times, 15 July 1955 (note 14).
20. See *Razzel v Snowball* [1954] 1 WLR 1382.
21. [1951] 2 KB 343.
22. *Kaur v Russell* [1973] 1 All ER 617.
23. Limitation Act 1939, section 2(1).
24. [1965] 1 QB 232.
25. [1993] 1 All ER 322.
26. Limitation Act 1939, section 26.
27. [1963] AC 758.
28. Such an action could be founded on inadequate attention to, or expert scrutiny of, medical or nursing notes.

29. [1977] 1 WLR 1073.
30. (1979) 123 Sol Jo 406.
31. The Times, 3 November 1986.
32. [1986] 1 WLR 1352.
33. The Times, 29 November 1989.
34. [1989] 1 WLR 96.
35. (1935) 79 Sol Jo 13.
36. [1973] 2 All ER 454.
37. [1989] 1 WLR 96.
38. [1983] AC 410.
39. [1985] 1 WLR 845.
40. [1985] AC 871.
41. [1980] AC 521.
42. The Times, 13 December 1985.
43. [1974] 1 WLR 891.
44. [1964] P 67.
45. *D v NSPCC* [1978] AC 171.
46. (1985) 129 Sol Jo 188.
47. The Times, 11 September 1984.

CHAPTER 6

Injury to the patient

6.1. INTRODUCTORY

This chapter briefly examines the criminal law relating to injury to a patient but principally concerns the nature and extent of civil liability resulting from negligent care and treatment. Injury to the patient may be caused by negligent, incompetent treatment, wrong diagnosis and frequently by failure of communication. As Chapter 8 explains, the jurisdiction of the Health Service Commissioner (Ombudsman) does not extend to complaints involving allegations of medical negligence or other clinical judgment. Nevertheless, as a former deputy Health Service Commissioner was once heard to say: 'Although we cannot go through the door marked clinical judgment, we can go right up to it and knock on it very hard.' The regular reports of the Health Service Commissioner to Parliament frequently refer to instances of injury caused not by incompetence in treatment or diagnosis but by simple failure of communication. Litigation in the courts is increasingly the avenue chosen by victims of poor communication between health care professionals, provided they can prove that the deficiency in communication caused their injury.

Negligence as a tort, or civil wrong, does not also amount to a criminal offence except when 'gross' negligence causes death and the crime of manslaughter is committed. Treatment of a patient without consent, constituting assault and battery, may also amount to a criminal offence. Various forms of assault and battery are crimes under the Offences Against the Person Act 1861. As is explained in Chapter 7, one reason why judges in this country are unwilling to find that a doctor has committed battery is that the practitioner might also be open to a criminal charge resulting from the same actions. Criminal prosecutions relating to treatment without consent are, in fact, extremely rare in this country.

This chapter is principally concerned with injury to patients which may generally be described as resulting from medical or other professional negligence. Injury to patients, as well as their visitors and even to staff, may be caused for other reasons, for instance lack of safety of premises, or of working conditions. Injury to patients, or to staff, resulting from these other causes (including injury resulting from defective products) are discussed respectively in Chapters 9 and 20.

Earlier editions of this book did not examine the amounts of money awardable by way of damages in cases of medical and other professional negligence. For the first time, the present edition includes a brief discussion, for two reasons. First, recent high awards have led health care professionals and their managers to fear that the delivery of health care is coming to be threatened by adverse influences of American-style litigation. There is in fact no legal or economic basis for such fears. Second, given the real and sometimes serious financial implications of large awards against health authorities who have to balance their books from year to year, a substantial award in a medical negligence case is discussed and broken down into its constituent elements so that the reader may understand precisely why the awards in this field of litigation are often so high. While specific advice on risk management is beyond the scope of this book, health care professionals and managers may wish to weigh the opportunities for, and financial consequences of, legal liability in the balance when advising on local policies and practices. Procedural aspects of litigation against health authorities, health services and agencies, and their employees are examined in Chapter 5 It is worth recalling, however, in the present context that a finding of *vicarious* liability on the part of a health authority or trust does nothing to remove individual personal liability from an individual staff member found liable for having negligently injured a patient.

6.2 CRIMINAL LIABILITY FOR INJURY

6.2.1 Introduction

At this stage, the reader will require only a brief summary of criminal liability for personal injuries to patients. In the somewhat rare event of a prosecution being brought in respect of criminal injury, it will be the police and the Crown Prosecution Service, and not health care professionals or their managers, who are primarily concerned with the details of criminal liability. Certain criminal offences involving injury to the person, or potentially involving such injury, are examined in other chapters. These include: illegal operations for abortion (Chapter 27); misuse of drugs, causing injury (Chapter 29); and breach of statutory health and safety requirements (Chapter 20).

Broadly speaking, any person who wilfully commits a wrongful act injuring or killing another is liable to prosecution in respect of the injury or death provided that a relationship of cause and effect can be proved.

Criminal liability may also arise in respect of injury caused recklessly though not intentionally. An example is death or injury caused by reckless driving of a car. Criminal liability may also be incurred if a person is killed or injured in the course of the commission of another offence, such as illegal abortion or attempted abortion. In all these cases, neither the prior consent of the victim of the offence, nor his subsequent unwillingness for criminal charges to be brought against the wrongdoer, is a bar to prosecution. The victim in such cases will usually be a compellable witness in the criminal trial and may be compelled to give evidence. Illegal abortion or attempted abortion is an exception to this, given that the victim, having been a consenting party to the offence, could herself be charged with participation in it. Such a person cannot be compelled to give what would be self-incriminatory evidence in criminal proceedings brought against the abortionist. Anyone who knowingly assists in preparations for committing an offence or in carrying it out, even though not the principal wrongdoer and even though deriving no benefit from the crime, will normally be criminally liable.

Anyone assisting in the concealment of a crime, or who actively helps the wrongdoer to escape, may commit a criminal offence. However, in the absence of a positive duty to disclose information to the authorities (such as the police), no criminal liability is incurred by a person who merely omits or chooses not to volunteer information relating to a threatened or criminal offence. Legal duties relating to disclosure of information and the maintenance of confidentiality are examined in Chapter 16.

Although rare, criminal prosecutions have been brought against medical and other staff of hospitals where, for instance, negligence has affected the performance of an operation or other procedure, a massive overdose of a drug has been negligently administered, or the practitioner at the time was so much influenced by drink or drugs that his judgment was substantially impaired. It is irrelevant to a conviction for manslaughter that the practitioner concerned did not intend to cause death. The standard of proof in a civil case (where the victim of wrongful injury sues for damages) being proof on the balance of probabilities, falls clearly short of the criminal burden of proof, namely proof beyond reasonable doubt. But in a case alleging wrongful death of a patient the proof beyond reasonable doubt of the following type of conduct will be a sufficient basis for criminal conviction. In *R v Bateman* (1925)[1] a doctor was convicted of manslaughter. He had attended the deceased patient in childbirth, the child being stillborn. The evidence of negligence against the doctor involved ignorance of medical technique and failure to cause the deceased to be conveyed to hospital as soon as he should. In fact, the doctor successfully appealed against his conviction for manslaughter because the Court of Appeal held that the judge at the trial had not correctly directed the jury as to the degree of negligence which must be proved for a finding of manslaughter. The Court of Appeal ruled that:

'in order to establish criminal liability the facts must be such that, in the opinion of jury, the negligence of the accused went beyond the mere matter of compensation between subjects and showed such disregard for the life and safety of others as to amount to a crime against the State and conduct deserving punishment'.

The nineteenth century case of *R v Spiller*[2] was a case in which a charge of manslaughter was based on an allegation of failure of a medical practitioner to exercise due care. In that case, Baron Bolland in his summing up said:

'If any person, whether he be a registered or licensed medical man or not, proposes to deal with the life or health of his Majesty's subjects he is bound to have competent skill to perform the task that he holds himself out to perform, and he is bound to treat his patients with care, attention and assiduity.'

Alternatively, as stated in *R v Long* (1830, 1831 – two separate cases)[3]:

'A person acting as a medical man, whether licensed or unlicensed, is not criminally responsible for the death of a patient, occasioned by his treatment, unless his conduct is characterised either by gross ignorance of his art or gross inattention to his patient's safety,'

and

'Where a person undertaking the cure of a disease (whether he has received a medical education or not) is guilty of gross negligence in attending his patient after he has applied a remedy, or a gross rashness in the application of it, and death ensues in consequence of either, he is liable to be convicted of manslaughter.'

Further, in cases of manslaughter by neglect, a reckless breach of an assumed duty to care for a patient rather than mere inadvertence is required: *R v Stone* (1977).[4]

The question of possible criminal liability of those helping a surgeon to perform an operation when he is under the influence of drink or drugs would be likely to arise only if it were obvious before he began that he was unfit to perform it. In that case those assisting, especially those medically qualified, might also lay themselves open to prosecution. If the fact that something was wrong became apparent only after the operation had started, one can only suggest that those assisting should do what they consider is in the best interest of the *patient* at the time. Conceivably that could mean that, if practicable, someone present who was competent to do so should take over.

The fact of a criminal conviction may be used as evidence in civil proceedings, for instance for negligence. The common law rule used to be that a criminal conviction could not be used as evidence in civil proceedings. That rule was reversed by the Civil Evidence Act 1968 which provides that if a person is proved to have been convicted of a criminal offence, he shall be taken to have committed that offence unless the contrary is proved. A plaintiff in an action for negligence may therefore be entitled to succeed simply by proving that the defendant has been convicted of an offence relating to the conduct now complained of in the civil proceedings, unless the defendant can prove that he was not in fact negligent. The burden of proof is therefore on the defendant once the criminal conviction is proved.

6.2.2 Manslaughter and failure of care: liability of others

In *R v Senior* (1899)[5] a parent belonged to a sect whose beliefs did not permit him to seek aid. He failed to get help for his child, who died. He was convicted of manslaughter. In *R v Lowe* (1973)[6] parents of low intelligence so neglected a baby that it died. The father was charged under the Children and Young Persons Act 1933 and with manslaughter. His conviction on the first charge was affirmed. The sole question was whether the failure to get a doctor was deliberate (wilful) and caused the child suffering. However, the conviction for manslaughter was quashed. Mere neglect, even though deliberate, which resulted in death did not (as the trial judge had told the jury) necessarily constitute manslaughter where, as here, the accused failed to foresee the consequences of his neglect.

The Court of Appeal said:

'If I strike a child in a manner likely to harm it it is right that if the child dies I may be charged with manslaughter. If I omit to do anything with the result that it suffers injury to health which results in its death, we think that a charge of manslaughter should not be an inevitable consequence, even if the omission is deliberate.'

However, the court gave leave to appeal on this point to the House of Lords. Lord Justice Phillimore said:

'This court feels there is something inherently unattractive in a theory of constructive manslaughter. It seems strange that an omission which is wilful solely in the sense that it is not inadvertent, the consequences of which are not in fact foreseen by the person who is neglectful should, if death results, automatically give rise to an indeterminate sentence instead of the maximum of two years which would otherwise be the limit imposed [namely for the offence of ill-treatment under section 1 of the 1933 Act].'

While it is necessary to prove more than mere neglect which happens to result in death, a decision in 1977 shows that the prosecution, in order to secure a conviction for manslaughter, does not have to go as far as to prove the accused's foresight of the likelihood or the possibility of death or serious injury. All that need be proved is gross negligence in the sense of a *reckless disregard* of danger to the health and welfare of an infirm person under the care of the accused: *R v Stone* (1977).[7]

This decision is of interest to those involved in the health services for the following reason. A relative of a family which lived in very poor circumstances (an old man who was almost blind and deaf, his mistress and the man's 34-year-old mentally handicapped son) came to live with them. She had, or developed, anorexia nervosa which stopped her eating properly and, in her last days, at all. She became helplessly infirm, and from that time onwards the law regarded the relatives with whom she lived as having assumed the duty of caring for her. The decision that they (man and mistress) were guilty of manslaughter seems less harsh when it is remembered (as the Court of Appeal pointed out) that this was a duty which they could have discharged not only by looking after her properly themselves, but also by summoning help, which the neighbours (knowing the filthy conditions of the woman) had urged.

6.3   CLAIMS FOR DAMAGES ARISING FROM ALLEGED NEGLIGENCE

6.3.1   Statutory duty to provide health services, and individual legal action

Section 1 of the National Health Service Act 1977 imposes the duty of the Secretary of State to continue the provision in England and Wales (there is separate legislation for Scotland and Northern Ireland) of a comprehensive health service designed to secure improvement in the physical and mental health of the people of those countries, and in the prevention, diagnosis and treatment of illness; and for these purposes to provide or secure the effective provision of health services. Such services are expressed by section 1 to be free of charge except so far as the law otherwise provides.

Section 2 empowers the Secretary of State to provide such services as he considers appropriate for the purpose of discharging his duties, and also to do anything else which is calculated to facilitate, or to be conducive or incidental to, the discharge of his duties.

Section 3 obliges the Secretary of State to provide throughout England and Wales, to such extent as he considers necessary to meet all reasonable requirements, hospital accommodation; other accommodation for the purpose of any service provided under the 1977 Act;

medical, dental, nursing and ambulance services; such other facilities for the care of expectant and nursing mothers and young children as he considers appropriate as part of the health service; such facilities for the prevention of illness, the care of persons suffering from illness and the after-care of persons who have suffered from illness as he considers are appropriate as part of the health service; and such other services as are required for the diagnosis and treatment of illness.

In *R v Secretary of State for Social Services, ex parte Hincks* (1979)[8] four patients commenced legal proceedings against the Secretary of State alleging failure in the duty to provide an adequate health service. All four were orthopaedic patients who had waited for treatment and had consequently endured further pain and suffering. Their wait was caused by a shortage of facilities arising in part from a decision by Region not to extend a facility on grounds of cost.

The action was brought against the Secretary of State, the Regional Health Authority and the (then) Area Health Authority. It alleged they were in breach of their duty under the National Health Service Act 1977, and in particular of the duty under section 3 to provide the accommodation, facilities and services appropriate to the health care which those authorities should provide.

The complainants desired a ruling whether patients have a legal right to bring such proceedings; if so, a declaration that the specified authorities had failed to discharge their statutory duties; and an order to compel the health authorities to perform their duties, as well as an award of damages for pain and suffering caused by the delay in treatment resulting from non-performance.

The judge concluded: 'I have come to the conclusion that it is impossible to pinpoint anywhere a breach of statutory duty on the part of the Secretary of State . . . it all turns on the question of financial resources. If the money is not there then the services cannot be met in one particular place.' The Act provides, added the judge, that the statutory duty of health authorities is to provide services 'to such extent as is necessary'.

The court will interfere only if health authorities have acted so as to frustrate the policy of the National Health Service legislation, or as no reasonable authority would have acted. Even, he ruled, if such a breach of statutory duty had been proved (which was not the case), the cause of action must be distinguished from that of a duty of care owed as between individuals and breach of which, by carelessness, is an integral part of a negligence action.

On appeal, the Court of Appeal upheld the judge's decision. It added that if no limits in respect of longer term financial planning were to be read into public statutory duties such as those in question, the duty to provide health care would increase and expand in line with all available facilities and techniques.

The Court of Appeal expressly reserved the right to declare a decision over resource allocation to be illegal if it were so manifestly irrational that no reasonable health authority could have reached it.

In *Re Walker's application* (1987),[9] the Court of Appeal ruled that the decision of a health authority to postpone operating immediately on a baby with a hole in his heart was not a matter for judicial review. Judicial review of administrative (including health services) action is not an appeal on the merits of a particular decision. It is, rather, an examination of the legality of what the body whose decision is complained about has or has not done. Sections 1 and 3 of the 1977 Act impose on the Secretary of State a duty to provide a wide variety of health services, and to provide resources for their continued availability.

It was the repeated postponement of the proposed operation on baby Walker which was the subject of the complaint to the courts. On 24 November 1987 Mr Justice Macpherson stressed that the baby was at no immediate risk and was in fact being treated and cared for with full medical attention. Other more urgent cases had to be dealt with, he said, and he pointed to a shortage of human resources and of necessary equipment. On the facts, the judge decided the health authority's decision had not been irrational.

6.3.2 Personal liability for negligence: breach of duty

Negligence consists of a breach of a duty of care causing injury or damage. This simple definition of the tort (or civil wrong, actionable in damages) of negligence contains four separate elements, all of which need to be proved if a successful action is to be brought by an injured patient. First, there must be a duty of care. Second, that duty must be broken. Third, the breach of duty must cause injury or damage. Fourth, the connection between the breach of duty and the injury or damage must be proved to be one of cause and effect. In litigation concerning negligence by doctors and other health care professionals these elements are not always kept completely separate and proof of one or more elements may present little difficulty in some cases. However, absence of proof (on the balance of probabilities) of any one of these elements will defeat the plaintiff's claim.

The principal difficulties in claims for negligence against health authorities and other health services occur in relation to the elements of breach of duty and causation. These elements are separately discussed in this chapter. Certain difficulties may, however, arise in relation to the question of duty, as well as that of damage or injury. It is commonplace that a hospital and a doctor owe a duty of care to a patient whom they have accepted into their care. But does a doctor owe a duty not to cause financial loss to a patient (or client) who is examined and given a prognosis for the purposes of an insured injury claim? While pain and suffering in childbirth is a foreseeable consequence of a negligently failed abortion followed by subsequent pregnancy, do the damages for upbringing of such a child when born include damages for private education? The examining doctor may be liable depending on the particular duty assumed. Damages for upbringing may be awarded if a foreseeable outcome of that child's birth.

In certain cases of injury caused by defective products the suppliers of such a product (which could include a health authority) may be strictly liable (without proof of fault) for the injury. That subject is discussed in detail in Chapter 20 on injury at work to which reference should be made in appropriate cases.

The liability in negligence which is discussed in this chapter in various forms and situations excludes, for the sake of convenience, reference to the consequences of breach of a legal duty to inform a patient, or prospective patient, of risks and adverse consequences inherent in a proposed procedure or treatment. Frequently referred to as 'informed consent', this duty and its extent are reserved for discussion in Chapter 7 on consent to medical and associated treatment.

Personal responsibility of medical practitioners and of others

There is no liability for injury to person or property due to an accident *not* arising from incompetence or carelessness, unless someone assumes such a liability by contract. If a patient is injured or dies as a result of a diagnosis, made with proper care and skill but which transpires to be incorrect,[10] or of an operation or other medical treatment performed with such skill as in all the circumstances was reasonable, no liability is incurred by the medical practitioner, nurse or other health care professionals concerned.[11] For instance, a patient may die under anaesthetic, all normal precautions having been taken by the surgeon and the anaesthetist; or a sudden, violent and unexpected movement by a patient who is being catheterised may cause injury to the patient, the nurse having warned him not to move and all due precautions having been taken; or again, a drug for injection is wrongly labelled by the manufacturers and a patient suffers harm in consequence. In such cases there is no liability on the professional person or on any hospital or other authority or person by whom he may be employed unless something ought reasonably to have put the user on inquiry, such as the appearance or smell of the drug, or the level or dosage prescribed. Any employee of an authority, trust other medical enterprise, whether medical, nursing, paramedical or otherwise, must exercise the skill and care appropriate to his respective calling. If he fails to do so, and harm results, he may personally be answerable in damages. In practice, if such a health care employee causes injury by his negligence, he is not likely to be sued personally, either because he is not worth suing, not having the money to satisfy a judgment or, as is normally the case, because any action is brought against the health authority or trust as employer.

A person who undertakes work for which special skill (including, for present purposes, professional health care) is needed must exercise the requisite degree of care and skill, even though he undertakes the work gratuitously and for the benefit of that other person. Incompetence or lack of care by his own standards makes the expert liable in damages.[12] The skill to be demonstrated is (at least) that which ordinary professional opinion would regard as the minimum acceptable. It is no defence to show that an incompetent person (or a person with an incompetent method) behaved normally and according to his own (too low) standards.

The measure of the responsibility of the professional person, with special reference to a surgeon, was clearly stated in *Mahon v Osborne*[13] by Lord Justice Scott:

'It is desirable to recall the well-established legal measure of a professional man's duty. If he professes an art he must be reasonably skilled in it. There is no doubt that the defendant surgeon was that. He must also be careful, but the standard of care the law requires is not insurance against accidental slips. It is such a degree of care as a normally skilful member of the profession may reasonably be expected to exercise in the actual circumstances of the case in question. It is not every slip or mistake which imports negligence and, in applying the duty of care to the case of a surgeon, it is peculiarly necessary to have regard to the different kinds of circumstances that may present themselves for urgent attention.'

This principle applies to anyone whose work requires some special skill. It is applicable to the work of a medical practitioner,[14] a nurse or a paramedical practitioner such as a radiographer[15] or physiotherapist. If any such person fails to exercise reasonable skill and competence and the patient suffers injury, he will be personally liable in negligence, even though he may be working as a whole-time salaried officer for a hospital or health authority. The question of the extent of the concurrent liability of the health authority or turst is examined in Chapter 5.

The significance of expert evidence

The importance of expert evidence in any case involving an allegation of medical negligence causing injury to a patient is illustrated by *Moore v Lewisham Group Hospital Management Committee* (1959),[16] being a case in which the judgment and skill of an anaesthetist came into question. The patient had been anaesthetised by means of spinal anaesthesia (for the purpose of an operation for the removal of her gall bladder) as a result of which she suffered paralysis of the left leg. The plaintiff's case was that, having regard to the risks of spinal anaesthesia, the operation should have been performed under one of the relaxant drugs. The judge, giving judgment for the defendant hospital authority, referred to the very great assistance given to the court by expert evidence of eminent anaesthetists, and said:

> 'No one suggested that Dr Piney was anything other than a highly competent anaesthetist or that he failed to acquaint himself with up-to-date techniques. . . . On the whole of the evidence it would not be difficult to find that on balance it might have been better for this operation to be performed under one of the relaxant drugs. But it was impossible to hold that Dr Piney's decision was a negligent one: it was one which could have been made by a competent and properly informed anaesthetist exercising a proper degree of skill and care.'

Moore's case may be contrasted with *Smith v Lewisham Group Hospital Management Committee* (1955).[17] Negligence was alleged in respect of injury to a woman of 86 years of age who fell off a hospital trolley whilst left unattended for a few minutes. A surgeon gave evidence that in his hospital (not a general hospital) there was one attendant per trolley night and day: he said that in his opinion it was unwise (though he did not say improper) to leave the patient unattended. Counsel for the injured patient admitted that if the plaintiff had only been left unattended for 30 seconds, they might find it difficult to say there was negligence.

Counsel for the defendant hospital asked that the court should hold as a matter of law that to say that hospital staff must always, at all times, have an attendant upon a trolley was too high, and that there was no such duty. There was in fact evidence that the plaintiff had been left inattended for four or five minutes. It was open to the jury to accept the evidence of the plaintiff's medical expert, speaking of leaving such a patient for four or five minutes, that 'it was unwise, it was a mistake, and it did cause serious injury'. He had given as his reason, in the first place, that an elderly lady of 85 or 86 should not be left unattended and, taking that and other factors into account, he considered that the plaintiff should not have been left. The hospital was accordingly liable for the injury.

Despite the vital role played by expert medical or other appropriate expert evidence in cases where the professional judgment of a practitioner is called in question in a claim alleging negligence, the courts will not allow themselves to be dictated to by such evidence. It is explained elsewhere in this chapter that a judge's preference for expert evidence on one side or the other is no basis for a finding of negligence. Furthermore a 'school of thought' sufficient to answer an allegation that some practitioners would not have done as the defendant did is not established merely by getting a couple of doctors together to agree that what they did was acceptable. Nevertheless it is only very rarely that a court will be bold enough to rule that a practice established across a profession (or at least a significant part of it) is not acceptable and forms the basis of an action in negligence if injury to the patient results.

Such a case is *Clarke v Adams* (1950)[18] in which the treatment given to the plaintiff by a physiotherapist was called in question. The patient was being treated by the defendant physiotherapist for a fibrositic condition of the left heel. In the process of diathermy the patient suffered burning which was so bad that the leg had to be amputated below the knee. Before applying the treatment the physiotherapist gave the patient the following warning: 'When I turn on the machine I want you to experience a comfortable warmth and nothing more; if you do, I want you to tell me.' Expert evidence was given by the chief examiner for the Chartered Society of Physiotherapy that the warning was entirely proper.

Mr Justice Slade said that in physiotherapy the co-operation of the patient was vital. The instrument which the physiotherapist used was dangerous because burns caused by it could lead to serious consequences. The apparatus was not in any way defective and the sole question to be decided was whether the warning given by the physiotherapist was adequate. There must in such circumstances, said the judge, be a warning of the danger as it would appear to a hypothetically reasonable person.

Would the words used here, he asked, warn such a person that his safety depended on informing the physiotherapist the moment he felt more than a comfortable warmth? The warning, he added, must make it abundantly clear that it was a warning of danger. In the circumstances of this particular case the judge was not satisfied that the warning given, although the very warning which the defendant physiotherapist had been taught to give, was adequate. For this reason he awarded the plaintiff damages in respect of his severe personal injuries.

Extent of medical practitioner's duty to keep up to date

What is reasonable care and skill is determined in accordance with the evidence in the particular case and may vary from time to time as knowledge increases. Thus in *Roe v Ministry of Health and others; Woolley v Same*[19] which reached the Court of Appeal in 1954, the two plaintiffs had been given a spinal anaesthetic in 1947. The ampoules containing the anaesthetic were said to have become contaminated with phenol and in consequence the two patients suffered very serious and permanent incapacity. From the evidence it appeared that the ampoules had been kept in phenol as an antiseptic precaution, it not being then appreciated that there was any danger of the phenol seeping in through molecular flaws not visible on ordinary inspection. It was held by the Court of

Appeal that in the state of medical knowledge in 1947 neither the anaesthetist nor any other member of the hospital staff had been guilty of negligence. It was said that 'we must not look through 1954 spectacles at what happened in 1947', in other words, be too wise after the event which was unavoidable at the time.

Lord Justice Somervell said in his judgment in *Roe's* case that the attention of the profession was first drawn to the risk in this country only by the publication of Professor Mackintosh's book *Lumbar Puncture and Spinal Anaesthesia* in 1951. The defence on the facts in *Roe's* case would therefore not succeed nowadays; indeed, it was this decision which drew the relevant risk of the procedure to the attention of the medical profession.

On the other hand, members of the medical profession are not placed under the impossible duty of reading every technical paper as soon as it appears, still less of agreeing with the suggestions of every contributor to a medical journal. In *Crawford v Board of Governors of Charing Cross Hospital*[20] the plaintiff had suffered permanent injury, brachial palsy, as a consequence of the position of his arm during an operation during which blood transfusion to that arm had been necessary. An article had appeared in *The Lancet* some six months before the operation was performed in which the writer condemned the positioning of the arm which had given rise to Mr Crawford's injury. The anaesthetist agreed that he had seen letters in *The Lancet* commenting on the article but had not, in fact, referred back to it. The plaintiff patient alleged that he had been negligent in not knowing that the position should never be adopted. The Court of Appeal rejected that contention. Lord Denning summarised the obligation of a medical practitioner thus:

'It would, I think, be putting too high a burden on a medical man to say that he has to read every article appearing in the current medical press; and it would be quite wrong to suggest that a medical man is negligent because he does not at once put into operation the suggestions which some contributor or other might make in a medical journal. The time may come in a particular case when a new recommendation may be so well proved and so well known and so well accepted that it should be adopted. But that was not so in this case.'

As an example of technical writings which medical practitioners in hospital as well as other officers of hospital authorities may disregard at their peril are advisory Circulars and Guidelines, often supported by Memoranda prepared by appropriate working parties, issued by the Department of Health. For instance, Departmental Circular HM(72)37 concerned precautions for the avoidance of surgical accidents. In that Circular hospital authorities were asked to review the procedures at their hospitals to ensure that the precautions against operations on the wrong patient, side, limb or digit and against swabs and suchlike being left in a patient after an operation were as closely as possible in line with those recommended in the joint memoranda of the Medical Defence Union and the Royal College of Nursing as revised in 1969. The Circular also required authorities to investigate any such accidents which might occur in their hospitals and to take steps to avoid a recurrence. The results of such investigations were to be reported to the Department which, in turn, would circulate to all hospital authorities any recommendations arising which might be of general interest and application. Other illustrations are Circulars on provision of safe cots for babies, on anaesthetic explosions in operating theatres and on control of staphylococcal infections in hospitals. Some specifically indicate a hazard, usually relating to equipment which has been discovered to be dangerous or unreliable. Circular HM(73)9 requires untoward incidents to be reported to Department immediately, so that other hospitals can be advised or warned against possible harm to patients and staff. This Circular relates to incidents caused by defects in medicinal products or in other medical supplies and equipment. The possible liability of the Secretary of State if, such a report of an incident having been received by the Department, a second incident causes harm at a different hospital and one which has not received any warning from the Department, is discussed below at p. 178. What is said there about reports under HM(73)9 applies equally to failure of the Department to issue any warning or advice which might be appropriate after receiving a report under any other Circular.

Such publications do not afford conclusive proof that anyone who, without good reason, falls short of the standard of care suggested in them has been negligent. However, they afford some (possibly strong) evidence of the appropriate standard of care, especially if it were proved that precautions advised were generally taken as a matter of accepted practice and there was no reason why they should not have been in the particular instance. Such evidence might be against a defendant medical practitioner if the fault were alleged to be his but, as in the matter of provision of safe cots, the responsibility might rest squarely on the health authority if, for example, it had refused to authorise expenditure on necessary alterations or replacements. Any such liability might rest on the authority as occupier of the premises by virtue of the Occupiers' Liability Act 1957 which is examined in Chapter 9.

If through Departmental Circulars and official reports the desirability of particular precautions being taken for the safety of patients becomes known to, and adopted by, most of the medical and nursing profession, it is highly likely that private hospitals and nursing homes and those who work in them could be held liable if they failed to take such precautions and harm results.

The degree of skill and the standard of care required of a medical practitioner to avoid civil liability in negligence is not static but is conditioned by the level of knowledge and skill current among those with whom the defendant practitioner may fairly be compared at the time of the accident. The acts or omissions of a person who practises as an anaesthetist will be judged by the current knowledge and skill of ordinarily competent anaesthetists at the time of the act or omission; and similarly in the case of other specialities. He will, for instance, be bound to recognise known, if very rare, phenomena such as ether convulsions.[21] In none of these cases will the standard of skill and competence achieved by the practitioner be judged against that of the most eminent specialist in the relevant field. But insofar as the leaders in a speciality make known better techniques which can be adopted by others, and so far as those techniques have become accepted by competent practitioners in the speciality, a defendant practising that speciality will invite a finding of negligence if he does not follow that accepted technique, and the harm it was designed to avoid occurs. A practitioner allows his knowledge and techniques to become out of date at his peril. An example of the necessity of keeping up to date is the need to be aware of the possible ill-effects of new drugs as they come into common use, from penicillin to the contraceptive pill.

Duty of practitioner where there is more than one school of thought on the treatment to be given

In *Bolam v Friern Hospital Management Committee*[22] the plaintiff failed in a claim for damages for injury in the course of administration of ECT (electroconvulsive therapy). He alleged that his injuries caused by an unrestrained convulsion were due to negligence. He also alleged negligent failure to warn him of the risk of injury. Mr Justice McNair in his summing up to the jury adopted substantially the same approach as the Court of Appeal in *Crawford v Board of Governors of Charing Cross Hospital* (1953).[23] In *Bolam's* case the plaintiff patient was given electroconvulsive therapy in 1954 by a member of the professional staff who, following his normal practice and that of his clinical superior, a consultant psychiatrist attached to the hospital, gave the treatment 'unmodified', that is, without the prior administration of a relaxant drug and without applying any form of manual restraint. The plaintiff sustained bilateral 'stove-in' fractures of the acetabula and brought an action for damages against the hospital alleging negligence in the failure to administer a relaxant or the provision of manual control; also in failing to warn him of the risks which he was running when he consented to the treatment, in particular, failing to warn him that it was proposed to carry out the treatment without relaxant drugs being previously administered and without manual control being available. Mr Justice McNair said:

'Where you get a situation which involves the use of some special skill or competence . . . the test . . . is the standard of the ordinary skilled man exercising and professing to have that special skill. A man need not possess the highest expert skill; it is well-established law that it is sufficient if he exercises the ordinary skill of an ordinary competent man exercising that particular art. In a . . . Scottish case, *Hunter v Hanley* [1955][24] Lord President Clyde said:

"In the realm of diagnosis and treatment there is ample scope for genuine difference of opinion and one man clearly is not negligent merely because his conclusion differs from that of other professional men, nor because he has displayed less skill or knowledge than others would have shown. The true test for establishing negligence in diagnosis or treatment on the part of a doctor is whether he has been proved to be guilty of such failure as no doctor of ordinary skill would be guilty of, if acting with ordinary care."

If that statement of the true test is qualified by the words "in all the circumstances", Mr Fox-Andrews [the barrister for the plaintiff] would not seek to say that that expression of opinion does not accord with the English law. It is just a question of expression. I myself would prefer to put it this way, that he is not guilty of negligence if he has acted in accordance with a practice accepted as proper by a responsible body of medical men skilled in that particular art. I do not think there is much difference in sense. It is just a different way of expressing the same thought.'

In so saying his Lordship referred with approval to the decision in *Roe v Minister of Health* (1954),[25] 'a not dissimilar case'.

The test of an 'ordinary competent practitioner exercising a particular art or skill' was approved by Sir Hugh Wooding, delivering the judgment of the Privy Council in *Chin Keow v Government of Malaysia and Another* (1967).[26] In *Chin Keow's* case, a young woman had been given an injection of procaine penicillin by a clinic doctor and had died within an hour. The death occurred as a result of a reaction due to the patient's having at some previous time been given an injection of penicillin, such reaction being known to be a remote risk in such circumstances. In an action for damages Mr Justice Ong had found for the plaintiff, the mother of the deceased, on grounds that the doctor had been negligent in failing to enquire whether the patient had ever previously been injected with penicillin before administering the drug. The Privy Council, applying the test approved from the summing up of Mr Justice McNair in *Bolam's* case, and reversing the Malaysian Court of Appeal, restored the judgment of Mr Justice Ong.

The decided cases clearly demonstrate that if a medical or other healthcare practitioner in his dealings with a patient, whether by way of diagnosis, warning or treatment, acts in a manner which would find favour with a significant number (albeit a minority) of competent colleagues, he will not, in the absence of unnecessary deviations from standard and accepted practice, be found negligent. 'Competent' here means competent in the particular branch or (if relevant) sub-branch of professional practice concerned.

The effect of Bolam in practice

Following the basic principle enunciated in *Bolam v Friern Hospital Management Committee* (1957) that what the law expects, if a practitioner is to avoid liability in negligence, is the ordinary skill and competence of the type of practitioner whose professional conduct is in question, the decision of the House of Lords in *Maynard v West Midlands Regional Health Authority* (1984)[27] is instructive as to its practical effect. A consultant physician and a consultant surgeon, while recognising that the most likely diagnosis of the plaintiff's illness was tuberculosis, considered that Hodgkin's Disease, carcinoma and sarcoidosis were also possibilities. Given that Hodgkin's Disease is fatal unless remedial steps are taken in its early stages they therefore decided that, rather than await the result of a sputum test which would involve some weeks' delay, the procedure of mediastinoscopy should be performed to provide them with a biopsy. This procedure involves a risk of damage to the left laryngeal recurrent nerve even if properly performed. Although this procedure was correctly performed, the damage in fact occurred causing considerable neurological damage to the plaintiff.

The biopsy proved negative and it was subsequently confirmed that the plaintiff was indeed suffering from tuberculosis and not from Hodgkin's Disease. She brought an action in negligence against the defendant health authority and was awarded damages by the trial judge. On appeal, the Court of Appeal reversed his decision and this was confirmed by the House of Lords.

The House of Lords held that, in the medical profession, as in others, there is room for differences of opinion and practice and a court's preference for one body of opinion to another is no basis for a conclusion of negligence. Accordingly, where it is alleged that a fully considered decision by two consultants in their own special field was negligent, it is not sufficient to establish negligence for the plaintiff to show that there is a body of competent professional opinion which considers that the decision was wrong, if there is also a body of professional opinion, equally competent, supporting the decision as having been reasonable in the circumstances. The House of Lords held that the Court of Appeal had been correct in treating the issue of negligence as open to consideration by them and in consequently holding that the judge had applied the wrong test.[28] The burden on a plaintiff patient is onerous, given that judicial preference for one body of opinion over another is an insufficient basis to find a defendant practitioner negligent. What must be proved at the end of the day is that no reasonable practitioner would have behaved in the way the defendant in fact did: see the principle as enunciated in *Hunter v Hanley* (1955),[29] above.

Failure to observe ordinary precautions

One of the principles for which *Bolam v Friern Hospital Management Committee* (1957)[30] is authority is that an action is not to be judged negligent merely because other professionals of skill and competence would not perform a procedure in the way in fact adopted, and may even disagree strongly with the approach taken, if there is nevertheless a school or body of thought, again of ordinary skill and competence in the particular field, which considers that the approach taken is a reasonable course to take. While this ruling, and its application in practice in such cases as *Maynard v West Midlands Regional Health Authority* (1984),[31] can place a heavy burden on an injured plaintiff to prove fault of a medical or other healthcare practitioner, any other decision would effectively serve to stagnate professional and scientific progress in practice. If, however, a medical or other healthcare practitioner fails to observe an accepted precaution and damage or injury results from this failure, such failure cannot be defended by the *Bolam* principle. In *Clark v MacLennan* (1983)[32] the plaintiff, soon after the birth of her first child, began to suffer from stress incontinence, a not uncommon post-natal condition whereby normal bladder control is lost when the sufferer is subjected to mild physical stress. Her diasability was particularly acute and the defendant, a gynaecologist, performed an anterior colporrhaphy operation on her. It was normal practice among gynaecologists not to perform such an operation until at least three months after birth so as to ensure its success and to prevent the risk of haemorrhage. The operation was unsuccessful and haemorrhage caused the repair to break down. Two further such procedures were necessary, neither successful, and the stress incontinence from which the plaintiff suffered became a permanent disability.

In her action for negligence it was held that, although the burden of proof normally rests on the plaintiff to prove negligence, nevertheless in a case where a general duty of care arises and there is a failure to take a recognised precaution and that failure is followed by the very damage which the precaution is designed to prevent, the burden of proof is transferred to the defendant. It is then up to the defendant, if he can, to show either that he was not in breach of any duty or, if he fails to prove that, that the damage suffered by the plaintiff did not result from his breach.

In other words, a doctor owes a duty to his patient to observe the precautions which are normal in the course of the treatment which is given.

Where a patient suffers damage following a departure from orthodox treatment the courts must enquire whether the doctor took all proper factors into account prior to taking action in order to determine whether that departure was in fact justified. If it was not justified, the departure is a breach of duty to the patient. On the facts of this case, it was held to be a general precautionary practice amongst gynaecologists that an anterior colporrhaphy should not normally be performed on a patient until at least three months after the birth of a child. The defendant's departure from that general practice was unjustified and the plaintiff therefore succeeded in a negligence action against the defendant.

Res ipsa loquitur: *'the matter speaks for itself'*

In certain situations assistance is given to an injured plaintiff when an accident has occurred in circumstances about which the defendants are much better placed to comment or explain than the plaintiff. While it is always at the end of the day for the injured plaintiff to establish a case of negligence on the balance of probabilities against the defendant, the device of *res ipsa loquitur* may assist the plaintiff to succeed in proving negligence. Even the judiciary can disagree over the precise application of the device, as the following cases show.

Where the thing giving rise to an accident such as performing a surgical operation or giving other medical treatment is shown to be under the management of the defendant or his employees and the accident is such as in the ordinary course of things does not happen if those who have the management use proper care, the injury itself affords reasonable evidence that the accident arose from lack of care in the absence of explanation by the defendant. In *Lloyd* v *West Midlands Gas Board* (1971)[33] Lord Justice Megaw said:

'I doubt whether it is right to describe *res ipsa loquitur* as a "doctrine". I think that it is no more than an exotic, although convenient, phrase to describe what is in essence no more than a common sense approach, not limited by technical rules to the assessment of the effect of evidence in certain circumstances. It means that a plaintiff *prima facie* establishes negligence where: (i) it is not possible for him to prove precisely what was the relevant act or omission which set in train the events leading to the accident; but (ii) on the evidence as it stands at the relevant time it is more likely than not that the effective cause of the accident was some act or omission of the defendant or of someone for whom the defendant is responsible, which act or omission constitutes a failure to take proper care for the plaintiff's safety.'

A classic case for guidance on the correct approach to be taken to the application of *res ipsa loquitur* is *Cassidy v Ministry of Health* (1951).[34] The plaintiff entered a hospital for an operation on his left hand, which necessitated post-operational treatment. While undergoing that treatment he was under the care of the surgeon who performed the operation, who was a whole-time assistant medical officer of the hospital, the house surgeon and members of the nursing staff of the hospital, all of whom were employed under contracts of service. At the end of the treatment it was found that his hand had been rendered useless. The trial judge dismissed his action for damages for negligent treatment which he brought against the hospital on the ground that he had failed to prove any negligence. On appeal it was held that, in the circumstances, the doctrine of *res ipsa loquitur* applied, and the onus lay on the hospital authority to prove that there had been no negligence on its part or on the part of anyone for whose acts or omissions it was liable, and that onus had not been discharged.

Lord Justice Denning said:

'If the plaintiff had to prove that some particular doctor or nurse was negligent, he would not be able to do it. But he was not put to that impossible task: he says, "I went into the hospital to be cured of two stiff fingers. I have come out with four stiff fingers, and my hand is useless. That should not have happened if due care had been used. Explain it, if you can."'

Disagreement has arisen even in the Court of Appeal as to the circumstances in which the device should properly apply. In *Mahon v Osborne* (1939),[35] at the end of an abdominal operation a swab which had been used by the surgeon to pack off adjacent organs from the area of the operation was left in the patient's body, with the result that three months later he died. By a majority of two opinions to one the Court of Appeal held that *res ipsa loquitur* was applicable to this occurrence. The dissenting judgment of Lord Justice Scott is nevertheless instructive on the general conditions for the applicability of the device:

'It is difficult to see how the principle of *res ipsa loquitur* can apply generally to actions of negligence against a surgeon for leaving a swab in a patient, even if in certain circumstances the presumption may arise. If it applied generally, plaintiff's counsel, having by a couple of answers to interrogatories proved that the defendant performed the operation and that a swab was left in, would be entitled to ask for judgment, unless evidence describing the operation was given by the defendant. Some positive evidence of neglect of duty is surely needed. It may be that a full description of the actual operation will disclose facts sufficiently indicative of want of skill or care to entitle a jury to find neglect of duty to the patient.

It may be that expert evidence in addition will be requisite. But to treat the maxim as applying in every case where a swab is left in the patient seems to me an error of law. The very essence of the rule when applied to an action for negligence is that on the mere fact of the event happening, for example, an injury to the plaintiff, there arise two presumptions of fact: (1) that the event was caused by a breach by somebody of the duty of care towards the plaintiff, and (2) that the defendant was that somebody. The presumption of fact only arises because it is an inference which the reasonable man knowing the facts would naturally draw, and that is in most cases for two reasons: (1) because the control over the happening of such an event rested solely with the defendant, and (2) that in the ordinary experience of mankind such an event does not happen unless the person in control has failed to exercise due care. The nature even of abdominal operations varies widely, and many considerations enter it – the degree of urgency, the state of the patient's inside, the complication of his disorder or injury, the condition of his heart, the effects of the anæsthetic, the degree and kind of help which the surgeon has (for example, whether he is assisted by another surgeon), the efficiency of the theatre team of nurses, the extent of the surgeon's experience, the limits of wise discretion in the particular circumstances (for example, the complications arising out of the operation itself, and the fear of the patient's collapse). In the present case, all the above considerations combined together to present a state of things of which the ordinary experience of mankind knows nothing, and therefore to make it unsafe to beg the question of proof. I cannot see how it can be said that the first essentials of the rule, if it can be called a rule, apply.'

Lord Justice Goddard, representing the majority view, said:

'The surgeon is in command of the operation, it is for him to decide what instruments, swabs and the like are to be used, and it is he who uses them. The patient, or, if he dies, his representatives, can know nothing about this matter. There can be no possible question but that neither swabs nor instruments are ordinarily left in the patient's body, and no one would venture to say that it is proper, although in particular circumstances it may be excusable, so to leave them. If, therefore, a swab is left in the patient's body, it seems to me clear that the surgeon is called on for an explanation, that is, he is called on to show not necessarily why he missed it but that he exercised due care to prevent it being left there. It is no disparagement of the devoted and frequently gratuitous service which the profession of surgery renders to mankind to say that its members may on occasion fall short of the standard of care which they themselves, no less than the law, require, and, if a patient on whom had befallen such a misfortune as we are now considering were not entitled to call on the surgeon for an explanation, I cannot but feel that an unwarranted protection would be given to carelessness, such as I do not believe the profession itself would either expect or desire.'

In *Fish v Kapur* (1948)[36] the plaintiff claimed damages from the defendants, dental surgeons, on the ground that the second defendant had been negligent in extracting one of her teeth as a result of which part of the root of the tooth was left in and her jaw was fractured. Mr Justice Lynskey held that the doctrine of *res ipsa loquitur* did not apply and that there was no evidence of negligence. He explained his decision as follows:

'No suggestion has been made, either by the plaintiff herself or by any of the medical or dental witnesses called for her, of any improper act on the part of the defendant. He has chosen, through his counsel, to submit that there is no evidence of negligence and to stand on that submission, with the result that I have not seen him in the witness box and he has not given any explanation of what took place. All I have in the shape of evidence of negligence in the operation of extracting the tooth, if I have anything at all, is that, after the extraction there was a fracture of the jaw. I am asked by the plaintiff's counsel to say that, where you have a qualified dentist who extracts a tooth and, after the extraction, the jaw is found to be fractured, that of itself is *prima facie* evidence of negligence on the part of the dentist. In other words, it is sought to apply to a case of that sort the doctrine of *res ipsa loquitur*.

There have been many cases in which actions have been brought against dentists, or claims made against them, for fractures occasioned in the course of the extraction of teeth. Counsel for the plaintiff has not been able to refer me to any authority where any court has held that the fact that a fracture of the jaw is found after a tooth has been extracted is of itself *prima facie* evidence of negligence. Counsel for the defendants has referred me to *Warner v Payne* [1935, unreported] where one of the questions which arose was whether the fact that a fracture of the jaw had occurred in the course of the extraction of a tooth was *prima facie* evidence of negligence. The learned judge, giving judgment, said:

"I think that both the plaintiff and her husband had in mind all along that, provided they could prove that there was a fracture or that the fracture was caused in the extraction of the tooth, they had good ground for complaint about the dentist. I should certainly not hold that the mere fact that the jaw was fractured in the course of an extraction would be of itself any evidence of negligence against the dentist at all."

In my view, that statement of the law is correct.'

In *Brazier v Ministry of Defence* (1965)[37] an injection was given to the plaintiff, a diver, by a sick berth attendant on the ship on which they were serving. Part of the needle broke off and remained in the plaintiff's right buttock. The plaintiff relied on *res ipsa loquitur* in his claim for negligence against the defendant. The ruling of Mr Justice McNair is instructive:

> 'At that state of the evidence or on those findings, it seems to me that the position lies in this way: That I reject, without any criticism of the plaintiff, his direct evidence that the injection was done by means of a sudden stab with the cylinder held in the closed fist like a dagger, but there remains the fact that he was left, after this comparatively simple operation, with a needle in his buttock. That evidence, it seems to me, is sufficient for the defendants to be called upon to give some explanation. I do not think it is necessary for them, when such a case is made, to establish affirmatively that there was no negligence. It is sufficient, I think, if they give an explanation "how it could happen without negligence". I take that expression from the judgment of Lord Justice Denning in the case of *Cassidy v Ministry of Health* (1951). . . . On the evidence which I have reviewed and on which I have stated my findings, I think that the defendants have clearly given an explanation of how this accident could have happened without negligence, namely, by a latent defect in the shaft of the needle.'

Risk of injury to patient due to infirmity or disability of staff

Circular HC(82)13 advises health authorities to request appropriate medical and dental committees to introduce procedures to help prevent harm to patients resulting from physical or mental disability, including addiction, of all medical and dental staff employed by health authorities. These comprise medical and dental staff, including honorary staff, in hospitals, in community medicine and dentistry and in the community health service. General medical and dental practitioners are included only in connection with health authority appointments they may hold in hospitals or community clinics. The relevant paragraphs are as follows:

'1. The Secretary of State has considered with representatives of the professions precautionary measures which can be taken to protect patients from harm which might arise from incapacity of medical or dental staff, including locum staff, due to physical or mental disability, including addiction. It is recognised that when members of medical or dental staff have reason to suspect such circumstances it is their clear duty to do what they can to ensure that the safety and care of patients is not threatened. Authorities are asked to request the appropriate professional staff committees to consider this circular and to institute arrangements based on the recommended procedure (paragraphs 3–11, below) which represents the agreed views of the Secretary of State and the professions.

2. The Secretary of State fully appreciates the difficulty and delicacy of the position of medical and dental staff in the circumstances dealt with in this circular. For this reason Authorities should recognise the essentially professional nature of the responsibilities of a sub-committee set up in accordance with the recommended procedure and should rely on a sub-committee to act appropriately. If exceptionally any question concerning a sub-committee's procedure arises it should be referred by the Authority to the Special Professional Panel (see paragraph 3) which set it up. The medical and dental professions fully agree that a collective responsibility for the safety of patients rests upon the professional staff as a whole and that the professions should continue to co-operate in providing appropriate safeguards. Accordingly the professional staff as a whole has a duty to do all in its power to see that the arrangements made for dealing with these rare but potentially dangerous circumstances are fully effective.'

The Circular recommends the following procedure:

'3. For each District Health Authority, there should be a panel, the Special Professional Panel, set up by the District Hospital Medical Committee or Medical Executive Committee or other appropriate medical or dental committees, consisting of members of the senior medical/dental staff, from which in each case a small sub-committee should be appointed. The sub-committee should receive, and take appropriate action on, any report of incapacity due to physical or mental disability including addiction. It does not have a duty to report back to the Panel.

4. The composition of the special professional panel will need to take into account the particular pattern of services in the District but the most suitable pattern would usually be provided by the annual election of four or five consultants from the hospital staff of the Authority (chosen so that one or more was accessible to each of the units in the District), one member of the Local Medical/Dental Committee (LMC/LDC) preferably one with a hospital appointment, one Community Physician serving in the District, and one member of the senior clinical community dental staff nominated by the appropriate Dental Committee. There should be named deputies for the member of the local Medical/Dental Committee, the Community Physician and the community dentist. One member should be elected Chairman, and another nominated to act should the Chairman be unavailable.

5. In a hospital under the management of a Preserved Board or a Special Health Authority the arrangements should be considered by the Medical Executive Committee, or, where none exists, by the Medical or Dental staff Committee, and a panel appointed from the consultant staff. For clinical support services directly managed by Regional Health Authorities such as the Blood Transfusion service, the arrangements should be considered by the Regional Medical Advisory Committee.

6. Information would normally be given in the first instance to one of the members of the panel but sometimes to the Chairman of a clinical division. It may come from a variety of sources and may relate to medical or dental staff of

any grade. It will usually be given by a colleague but may be from another discipline or from a general medical or dental practitioner. Staff other than medical or dental should normally first approach the most senior member of their discipline in the unit or department.

7. The person receiving such information should immediately consult the Chairman of the panel (or his deputy if the Chairman is unable to act). The Chairman should at once call together three members of the panel, of which if he wishes he may be one, to form a sub-committee to consider the information which has been received. If the subject of the inquiry is a member of hospital staff the three members should be consultants. If he is also a gp/gdp the LMC/LDC member should be added. If the subject is a community doctor or dentist one member should be the community physician or the community dental officer who is a member of the panel as appropriate. A member of the panel who is in any way involved in a case should not serve on the sub-committee which considers it. If immediate action in the interests of patient safety seems to the panel member who received the information to be necessary and other members are not available he should be prepared to take informal action on his own responsibility; the information received and the action taken should be reported to the Chairman of the panel as soon as possible.

8. The sub-committee should make such confidential enquiries as are necessary to verify the accuracy of any report. Whilst they are not required to establish positively that the possibility of harm to patients exists or to make a clinical diagnosis, nevertheless if they are satisfied that the report has substance the practitioner should be told of its contents, but not necessarily of its source, and be given the opportunity to be interviewed by the sub-committee. If the practitioner is interviewed he may, if he wishes, ask for a professional colleague of his choice to be present, and the sub-committee must make it clear to the practitioner that they are interviewing him under the terms of this circular. If the sub-committee feel that the possibility of harm to patients cannot be excluded by the exercise of their influence with the practitioner concerned, they should bring the circumstances to the notice of the Regional Medical Officer and the Medical Officer (or Dental Officer if a dental practitioner is concerned) of the employing authority, or in the case of an employee of a Board of Governors, of the Secretary of the Board.

9. It is the responsibility of the officer of the employing authority (normally a medical or dental officer) who receives a report from a sub-committee under this procedure to decide what further investigations are necessary, whether the information should be passed to the authority or discussed with the Chairman, and what further action should be taken, including informing the medical officer of any Authority for which services are provided by the relevant practitioner. If it appears that a question arises that the doctor's fitness to practise may be seriously impaired by reason of his physical or mental condition consideration should be given to whether the circumstances might justify a report to the Registrar of the General Medical Council for consideration in accordance with the procedures of the Council's Health Committee. In considering this it will be relevant to bear in mind that the Council's procedures are specifically designed to encourage a sick doctor to accept treatment. A note on these procedures, and on reports to the GMC, is attached as an Annex.

10. Where a practitioner who is the subject of a report is employed or in contract with more than one Authority the officer of the Authority who receives the

report should communicate its substance to the appropriate officer of the other Authority so that they can act in concert.

11. Medical and dental committees concerned are asked to include in their arrangements after consultation with appropriate clinical divisions, provision for immediate action to secure the safety of the patient should the incapacity of a practitioner become apparent in the course of an operation or other clinical procedure.'

Failure of communication

In *Crichton v Hastings* (1972)[38] plaintiff had a tendency to phlebitis. The defendant operated and prescribed an anti-coagulant drug which when taken in overdose could cause a haemorrhage. He gave no warning because he did not think the plaintiff would be discharged from the hospital whilst taking the drug. This was held to be negligent.

In *Chapman v Rix* (1960)[39] Mr Chapman, a butcher, when boning a rump of beef, slashed his abdomen. He was taken to Brentwood District Hospital, a 'cottage hospital' where, there being no resident medical staff, he was dealt with by a local general practitioner, Dr Rix, who happened to be there. Dr Rix concluded that, though the deep fascia had been cut, the wound had not penetrated the peritoneum, and ordered that the wound be stitched (the report does not say by whom) and dressed. He then sent Mr Chapman home, giving him emphatic instructions to see his own doctor, Dr Mohr, that evening. Mr Chapman told Dr Mohr that the hospital had told him that the wound was 'superficial'. Dr Mohr, not appreciating that the hospital was a cottage hospital and that Dr Rix was not a casualty officer, examined the patient and diagnosed a digestive disorder. The patient died and a post mortem revealed that the wound had penetrated the small intestine. In an action by the widow Mr Justice Barry found that Dr Rix had been negligent in failing to communicate directly by telephone or letter with the man's own doctor after he had dealt with him. The judgment was reversed by the Court of Appeal. The plaintiff's further appeal to the House of Lords, which turned solely on the question whether the failure of the defendant to communicate directly was negligent, was also dismissed.[40]

Dismissing the appeal, Lord Goddard (with whom Lord Morton agreed) said that it was true that Dr Rix did not communicate directly with Dr Mohr, but he had emphatically warned the patient to call in his own doctor (which he in fact did) and to tell him exactly what had happened and what had taken place at the hospital (which was done). It was easy to say after the event: 'Well, Dr Rix might have told him more.' But if he had written or spoken directly to his fellow practitioner, his Lordship doubted whether he would have told him more than that after observation and probing he had formed the opinion there was no penetration. He might have added: 'He needs watching', but that he might well assume Dr Mohr would understand without being told.

Lord Hodson, also dismissing the appeal, said that the patient would be expected to pass on to his own doctor the reassuring statement that the wound was, in the opinion of Dr Rix, superficial. That did not, said his Lordship, cancel out the main sense of the message, which was emphatic. An object of that message must have been to guard, by observation, against what Dr Rix thought an outside chance, that penetration of the peritoneal cavity had occurred.

In his dissenting speech Lord Keith said that Mr Chapman had fallen between two stools and that was due chiefly to the failure of communication. The patient himself was made the medium of communication. The question was, was that communication adequate; and, if not, was Dr Rix responsible for the inadequacy; and did his failure amount to negligence? Dr Mohr would have acted differently had he known of the observed penetration through the deep fascia down to the muscles of the abdomen. A doctor who was expected to look after a patient with an abdominal wound, which had already been diagnosed and treated by another doctor who had decided that the injury did not require operative or observational treatment in a hospital, should be put in possession of information on what had been observed and done by the first doctor. The question had to be dealt with in relation to the risks run by the patient in the absence of proper medical and surgical treatment. The non-communication, in his Lordship's view, amounted to negligence in law.

Lord Denning, also dissenting, said that misleading information is a dangerous thing to throw about; there is no telling where it will finish up. A medical man may sometimes feel justified in giving misleading information to a patient so as not to worry him. But if he does, he must be very careful to give the true information to his relatives and those about him, and most important of all, to the patient's own doctor who has to treat him. It was the failure of Dr Rix to observe that rule, which his Lordship would regard as elementary, which was his mistake here.

The striking division of judicial opinion both in the Court of Appeal and in the House of Lords on the somewhat unusual facts of *Chapman v Rix* leave the impression that a slight variation of the facts (or even their presentation) might have produced a different result. The case is certainly not authority for the proposition that a practitioner treating a person who has met with an accident, without admitting him as an in-patient is never under a duty to communicate directly with the patient's own doctor.

If in a later case it could be shown that since *Chapman v Rix* it had become common practice for a medical practitioner treating an accident victim at a hospital, without admitting him as an in-patient, to communicate directly with the patient's own doctor (even if the injury appeared superficial), *Chapman v Rix* would be no obstacle to a finding of negligence.

The judgment of Lord Justice Romer in the Court of Appeal included an interesting passage on the criteria for establishing medical negligence.

Having referred to evidence of eminent medical men in support of the course Dr Rix had taken, his Lordship said that he knew of no case in which a medical man had been held guilty of negligence when eminent members of his own profession had expressed on oath their approval of what he had done. He adopted the views of Lord Clyde in *Hunter v Hanley* (1955)[41] when he said that to establish liability by a doctor where deviation from normal practice was alleged, it must be proved 'that there was a usual and normal practice; that the defendant had not adopted that practice; and that the course the doctor had adopted was one which no professional man of ordinary skill would have taken if he had been acting with ordinary care'. However, in the House of Lords, Lord Goddard issued a caution about putting the matter in that way:

'I desire to add that if Lord Justice Romer meant that if a doctor charged with negligence could find two other doctors to say they would have acted as he did that of itself entitled him to a verdict I could not agree with him if there was evidence the other way. But this is not to say that if some doctors think one course should be followed while others prefer another, a judge may not say without actually deciding in favour of one view over the other that he is not prepared to find negligence. . . . If there are two recognised schools of thought on a subject, to follow one cannot be negligent, and this is what I prefer to think Lord Justice Romer really meant.'

Failure of communication by hospital staff and negligent treatment by general practitioner

In *Coles v Reading and District Hospital Management Committee and another* (1963)[42] the facts, though similar, were sufficiently different to have justified the trial judge in distinguishing the case before him from the decision of the House of Lords in *Chapman v Rix*. The plaintiff in *Coles'* case was the father of the deceased and sued on behalf of the estate for damages on the ground that his son's death had resulted from negligent failure of communication by the staff of the hospital where he had first been seen, and from negligent treatment by the general practitioner who had attended him thereafter. At 8.40 a.m. on 5 November 1959, the deceased (who afterwards died of tetanus) was shovelling coal from a railway truck when a large lump of coal fell on his hand, causing a crush injury to his left index finger. The wound was covered with dust and dirt, such that the deceased should have been given an anti-tetanus injection at the first reasonable opportunity. Immediately after the accident the deceased received first aid and went to Wallingford Hospital, a cottage hospital, at about 9.00 a.m. where he was examined by a nurse. After further examination by a sister, the nurse obtained instructions from the duty doctor by telephone, and cleansed and covered the wound. The deceased was instructed by the sister to go immediately to Battle Hospital at Reading for further examination and treatment. A friend who had accompanied him said he would drive him there.

But the deceased did not then, or at any time, attend Battle Hospital. Instead, he went home, where he was seen by the second defendant, his general practitioner who told him to call the following day, 6 November. The deceased was seen again by the general practitioner at his surgery on 6 and 11 November, and at the deceased's home on 21 and 22 November. The wound became infected and the deceased was admitted to the Park Hospital, Reading, where he died of tetanus on 25 November. The judge found against both defendants on grounds of negligence. He said that it was manifestly clear that tetanus infection had entered through the wound on the occasion of the accident and also that if an appropriate anti-tetanus injection had been given on 5 or 6 November, or within a couple of days, the deceased would probably still have been alive.

The finding of negligence against the hospital authority was based on failure of proper communication. His Lordship defined 'proper communication' as 'that which was reasonably necessary for safeguarding a patient's interests'. He said that the responsibility for a proper system of communication rested on whomever was in charge of a hospital. It should not be left to individual sisters or nurses to decide without any guidance. There were apparently many difficulties of 'proper communication' but the witnesses were reluctant to say what was reasonably necessary. The deceased was not given to understand either the importance of going to Battle Hospital or that there was any risk involved in not going. When transferring a patient from one hospital to another there ought to be some communication. Any system which fails to provide for adequate communication of the type in question is negligently wrong. None of the potentially appropriate steps relating to anti-tetanus precautions were taken and that resulted from the breakdown in communications.

The judge also found the general practitioner negligent because he took the case 'too lightly'. Having learnt that the deceased had come from the hospital, the doctor assumed that all that was necessary had been done. He should have made some inquiries, and had he done so, he would have been put on the right track and the deceased would still have been alive. Even taking the doctor on his own evidence that he had considered anti-tetanus and decided that no precautions were necessary, he was clearly neglecting elementary precautions.

The judge's criticism of the sister and the nurse having been left responsible for communication invites the further question whether, in the case of an injury of the kind in question, it is reasonable for the duty doctor to give directions on the telephone without having seen the patient. That might appear to be leaving responsibility for diagnosis to the nursing staff. In this particular case it might have made no difference had the duty doctor seen the patient. However, if a patient suffered harm through not having been seen by a doctor at a hospital (even at a community hospital) a finding of negligence against the authority or trust would be highly likely.

A doctor who attempted to deal with a hospital casualty case by telephone might also be liable unless neither he nor any other practitioner could attend, or it was most unlikely that he could have reached the hospital in time to be of any use.

The giving of instructions by telephone for the immediate treatment of a patient in an emergency pending the arrival of the doctor on the scene is an altogether different matter, whether such instructions were given to someone looking after the patient at home or to a member of the nursing staff of a hospital where the patient may be. That it would have been very inconvenient for a general practitioner on call as a member of the staff of a community hospital to deal with accident and emergency cases, or for any other practitioner similarly on call as a member of the staff of a hospital to have attended on a particular occasion, would not, in itself, be sufficient justification for relying entirely on the telephone for diagnosis and for instructions for treatment. If it is reasonably practicable in a larger hospital to obtain the attendance of a more senior member of the staff, even though at some inconvenience, a case should not be dealt with at night by a junior houseman which, at any other time, would certainly be seen by a specialist. However, a doctor might still exercise proper competence in not attending a patient if he could show that on the information available to him it was not necessary. To this extent communication by telephone is allowed.[43]

Coles' case differed from *Chapman v Rix* in that the patient's own general practitioner was sued in *Coles'* case and not in *Chapman v Rix*. In *Coles* the hospital doctor, who advised the nursing staff on the telephone, was not a party to the action; and the case involved also the question of communication between one hospital and another.

Failure to communicate warning

Under some Departmental Circulars, it is required that if a specified type of incident occurs which causes, or might have caused, harm to a patient or to a member of staff the authority or one of its officers report the incident to the Department. The Department is then a position to advise or warn other health and associated authorities. A question which has not yet been determined by the courts is whether, if harm to a patient or member of the staff in a National Health Service hospital is caused by an incident of a kind which has already been reported to the Department as having happened in another hospital, the Secretary of State would be liable for negligence had there been a failure by the Department to warn or advise the hospital where the second incident occurred. A Departmental Circular[44] issued to health authorities in 1973 requires immediate report to the Department of any incidents arising from defects in medicinal products and other medical supplies and equipment which lead to injury, however slight, and also of incidents where harm was avoided but potential danger suggested. Suspicion is also to be reported.

The Circular requires immediate reporting so that warnings can be issued simultaneously when necessary to all authorities concerned and appropriate action taken under the Medicines Act 1968 where medicinal products are affected. The great importance the Department attaches to the requirements of the Circular being observed is stressed in paragraph 18:

'No arrangements can be effective unless hospital staffs at all levels have in mind that untoward incidents may have a significance going far beyond their own hospitals and that there is a duty in the interests of all patients and staff to see that they are reported even in some cases of suspicion only. Therefore doctors and hospital authorities should do everything within their power to see that all staff, both senior and junior, are conscious of their responsibilities in this respect. It may be that action on these lines is what is needed above all else. Without it, the reporting system will never be fully effective.'

It appears that a negligent failure of the Department to give to authorities concerned any warning or other advice which ought to have been given following report of an incident within the terms of the Circular, could form the basis of an action for damages by anyone who suffered harm as a result.

But there would probably be no such liability if the failure in communication had been between the authority managing the hospital where the first incident had occurred and the Department, and not between the Department and the authority managing another hospital where subsequently someone suffers harm for want of the warning which ought to have been given. There seem to be no grounds on which the injured person could claim from the authority where the breakdown in communication occurred, since there is no relationship between that person and such authority and the chain of causation is too tenuous.

Failure to protect patient from risk of harm (including self-harm)

The duty includes, in the case of a suicidal patient, such supervision as is reasonably practicable to prevent his making an attempt on his life. In *Selfe v Ilford and District Hospital Management Committee* (1970)[45] a 17-year-old youth was admitted to hospital after taking an overdose of sleeping pills. He was placed in a ground floor ward with an open window at the back of his bed, and his bed was grouped at one end of the ward with those of three other suicidal patients. He escaped through the window and climbed some steps to a roof, from which he threw himself, as a result suffering serious injuries. His claim against the hospital authority on grounds of negligence succeeded. The judge said that the degree of care which was reasonable was proportionate to the degree of risk and to the magnitude of the mischief which might be occasioned. It was accepted that reasonable care demanded adequate supervision, which included continuous observation by duty nurses in the ward. There had been a breach of that duty by the hospital. To leave unobserved a youth of 17 with suicidal tendencies and an unlocked window behind his bed was asking for trouble.

There had been three nurses on duty in Mr Selfe's ward and each knew that he was a suicide risk and had to be kept under constant supervision. Besides the charge nurse there was another nurse who, just before the occurrence giving rise to the action, and without a word to the charge nurse, had gone to the lavatory. The third, a nursing auxiliary, went to the kitchen, neither of those nurses being able to see into the main ward. The charge nurse answered a call for assistance by a patient and went to him. Thus, no one had an eye on Mr Selfe, who was able to get out of bed. The judge thought that the charge nurse had been let down by the other two nurses. The incident should never have been allowed to happen, should not have happened, and would not have happened if three, or even two, nurses had been in the ward keeping Mr Selfe under observation. The case may be contrasted with one in which a patient suffering from mental disability ate a lavatory freshener and died of the consequent poisoning. In this case, which was not litigated, the Coroner found that no one was to blame.[46]

In *Thorne v Northern Group Hospital Management Committee* (1964)[47] an action by the husband of the deceased failed. While awaiting transfer from a general ward to a psychiatric ward the deceased left the ward, went home and took her own life. It was held that there was nothing in her behaviour to put staff on enquiry as to that risk.

The trial judge concluded that later events showed,

'the patient was set upon making her escape for the purposes of self-destruction, and it was highly conceivable that she kept a wary eye on the nurses and seized her opportunity immediately their backs were turned and they had absented themselves temporarily. That did not connote negligence on the part of the nurses.'

The hospital was not liable.

In *Hyde v Tameside Area Health Authority* (1981)[48] the plaintiff, in a general ward, became obsessed with a fixation that he was suffering from cancer. He threw himself from a hospital window causing himself severe multiple injuries.

Lord Denning, Master of the Rolls, asked:

'What made this man do this thing? It looks as if it was because he had got it into his head that he had cancer and was going to die in the next hour or so. Shortly before he jumped out of the window, he wrote moving letters to his wife and to his mother and father and to his cousin. He left the letters to be opened after his death. But he did not die. And he did not have cancer. Instead he is kept alive by all the aids which medical skill provides nowadays. He is, I fear, a burden to himself and his family and to the community.'

Burden or not, the Court of Appeal held that his action for negligence against the hospital nursing staff failed. Nevertheless, in a case[49] involving the death of a depressive alcoholic remanded in custody, for whose suicide the police were held liable in negligence, Mr Justice Tudor Evans cited the words of Lord Justice O'Connor in *Hyde* when he said in that case:

'I do not think that the fact that a patient commits suicide or attempts suicide will necessarily break the chain of causation if breach of duty is established against the hospital. It all depends on the circumstances of an individual case.'

Emergency treatment given in the absence of normal facilities or qualified staff

A general practitioner or some other medical practitioner acting outside his own speciality or normal sphere of work in an emergency who has done his best will be judged not according to the more exacting standards by which the work of a specialist would be judged but by what, in the circumstances, it is reasonable to expect of a practitioner who is not a specialist. Hence a general practitioner who undertook a surgical procedure beyond his competence when he could have referred the case to a surgeon would be liable. He would not, however, be liable, if, in an emergency, he did his best which, although inadequate, did not fall short of what could reasonably be expected of a general practitioner.

Take the case of a patient who came to harm through failure in aseptic technique. If something had to be done on the spot for victims of a road accident it can be imagined that the risk inevitably and therefore legitimately taken would be greater than it would be if a general practitioner tackled an emergency operation or put in stitches in his own surgery, or even at the patient's home. But even then, with the limited resources available, he could not be judged by the same standards as if he were working in hospital. His major risk is a claim that, without necessity, he had attempted something which he ought to have known was beyond either his capacity or his resources.

Casualty officer: negligent failure to see and examine patient

Barnett v Chelsea and Kensington HMC[50] concerned the duty of a hospital with a casualty department, and of a medical casualty officer and of nurses working in such a department, towards a patient presenting himself there and complaining of illness or injury. The patient in this case, having been referred from the hospital casualty department to his own doctor without having been seen by the duty medical casualty officer, died a few hours later of arsenical poisoning. The circumstances were as follows. Three nightwatchmen presented themselves at eight o'clock in the morning at the casualty department of a hospital for which the defendant hospital authority was responsible, complaining that they had been vomiting since drinking some tea three hours earlier. The nurse to whom they spoke reported their complaints *by telephone* to the duty medical casualty officer who told her to tell the men to go home and call in their own doctor. She did and the men left. Some five hours later one of them died from poisoning by arsenic which had been introduced into the tea. The deceased's widow claimed that his death had resulted from the defendant's negligence in not diagnosing or treating her husband's condition when he presented himself at the casualty department. Mr Justice Nield held that since the defendants ran the casualty department to which the deceased had presented himself complaining of illness or injury, such a close and direct relationship existed that they owed him a duty to exercise the skill and care expected of a nurse and medical casualty officer acting reasonably. The medical casualty officer was clearly negligent in not seeing and examining the deceased, in not admitting him to the wards and in not treating him or causing him to be treated. Despite this clear breach of duty, the plaintiff failed in her action because she failed to establish on the balance of probabilities that the negligence of the defendants had caused her husband's death, the judge accepting the view put forward by the witnesses for the defence that the poisoned man would have died even had he been promptly admitted to hospital. The importance of proving that the breach of duty caused the injury complained of is examined on pp. 195–197, below.

The judge stressed that he was not suggesting that a duty casualty officer at a hospital is obliged to see everyone who presented himself. 'If a receptionist, for example, discovers that the visitor is already attending his own doctor and merely wants a second opinion, or if the caller has a small cut which the nurse can perfectly well dress herself, then the casualty officer need not be called.' The second example given by his Lordship may be open to question, since for a nurse to decide that the cut is so trifling that a doctor need not be called involves a diagnosis as well as a decision on what treatment is necessary. Take the case of a small wound covered in dirt and dust for which, perhaps, an antitetanus injection should be given as well as a dressing applied. The treatment would surely be for a medical practitioner to decide, and if an anti-tetanus injection had to be given it should be given by him or under his supervision, having regard to the patient's possible adverse reaction to it.

The Department now appears to accept that every patient who presents himself at a National Health Service hospital, at whatever time of the day or night, should be seen by a doctor. Paragraph 18 of the memorandum sent to hospitals under cover of Departmental Circular HM(68)11, dated 25 March 1968, reads as follows:

> 'The hospital out-patient clinics for the treatment of addicts are therefore not planned to operate on a 24-hour basis, nor is it intended to provide facilities for addicts to obtain a prescription for heroin at any time of the day or night. But, as in the case of all other patients, it is important that an addict presenting himself at a hospital at any time should not be turned away by non-medical staff without being seen by a doctor on duty and, if the doctor considers it necessary, being given emergency treatment.'

There seems to be the inference that, except by way of 'first aid' pending the arrival of a duty doctor, no treatment should be given by a nurse until the patient has been seen by a doctor and that even if the nurse's first aid may, in fact, appear to have met the patient's need, he should not be sent away until a duty doctor has satisfied himself that that is so. This would be a major obstacle to a successful defence by an authority in a negligence action where a patient had been sent away without being seen. Anyone on the hospital staff who was involved in sending the patient away might be open, if harm resulted, to an action in negligence.

Acting reasonably under instructions

Junor v McNicol and others (1959),[51] a Scottish case, a boy had lost his arm because of inadequate treatment. It was decided that a house officer is not personally liable for negligence if the treatment he gives a patient on the instructions of the consultant is faulty or inadequate, the house officer not being in charge of the case. Lord Kilmuir stated that there was no doubt that a mistake had been made in letting the boy out of hospital; but the question was whether the house officer, Dr McNicol, was negligent. There was no doubt that she had a duty to exercise the care and skill of a prudent qualified house surgeon, as well as a duty to carry out the instructions of the consultant unless those instructions were manifestly wrong.

The house officer's duty was to follow instructions. There are certainly cases which state that where instructions are manifestly wrong, duty and common sense combine to say that they must not be followed. However, in view of the opinion which the consultant in this particular case gave in respect of the child's wound, the judge could not say that Dr McNicol should have disregarded what she believed her instructions to be. On these facts the plaintiff patient had failed to show that the house officer was 'in charge' of the case in the sense of being fully answerable for it.

Liability of medical staff senior to house officer, acting on instructions or advice of a consultant

Presumably, the *Junor* principle applies to all hospital medical and surgical staff below the consultant grade when working on the instructions of a medical practitioner in a higher grade than themselves, even though that senior officer is not the consultant ultimately in charge. For example a house officer, in the absence of the consultant, is expected to accept instructions from a registrar who is working under the general supervision of the consultant on his cases. And it applies also even to the senior registrar who carries out the instructions of his chief. But in this case, his own qualifications often being the same as those of his senior and his experience very much greater than that of a house officer, he will presumably be held liable for negligence in carrying out instructions which he ought to have known were wrong.

Medical practitioners in the hospital hierarchy: extent of liability

Generally, in a hospital, between the specialist of consultant rank and the newly qualified house officer come various grades of medical and surgical officer. Senior registrars are high up the professional ladder, standing in for consultants and carrying out operations and treatment unsupervised. Below them are registrars, practitioners of some experience – or gaining experience – in a particular specialty, who have either obtained, or are preparing for, a higher qualification. Below them again are the various grades of house officer, the most junior in many hospitals being newly qualified medical practitioners, still only conditionally registered. In any action for injury to a patient in which negligence is alleged, all these will be judged according to the skill they hold themselves out as possessing. Thus a senior registrar in any specialty would ordinarily have to accept the full responsibilities of a specialist. A house officer if he had failed to use the skill of a specialist, when such skill was called for would, like a general practitioner, have to justify his having undertaken something beyond his competence, for instance by pleading that in an emergency it had been impossible to obtain the help of a better qualified person.

The range of responsibilities that a house officer is qualified to undertake is more limited than that which senior members of the staff can perform, especially if the houseman is only conditionally registered and is still engaged in serving the 12 months in approved hospital posts, a prerequisite of full registration. Consequently, the house officer is more likely to err not by negligently doing something he is qualified to do but by failing to seek the aid of a senior member of the staff when he should, and tackling something for which he had neither the skill nor the experience. Unless he has acted in an emergency, there being no more experienced practitioner available in time, he will have no defence if harm results, for by his very actions he has claimed the requisite skill and will be judged as if he had it. If a house officer, on grounds of emergency, does escape personal liability for harm done to a patient by reason of his lack of special skill, it by no means follows that the hospital will also escape liability. As to the position of a houseman following the instructions of the consultant, the treatment ordered being inappropriate or inadequate, see *Junor v McNicol*, above.

Nurses, midwives and paramedical staff

The general principles of liability for medical practitioners apply equally in the case of nurses,[52] radiographers,[53] physiotherapists, pharmacists and any other professionally qualified persons. Any such professionally qualified person is liable in damages if the patient suffers harm as a result either of his negligence or of his failing to exhibit that degree of skill which he had held himself out as possessing.

It can be difficult to predict the outcome of a situation in which a nurse assumes a primary role in diagnosis or treatment. Complex questions may be raised by the emergent concept 'nurse practitioner' who acts independently of medical instruction or direct supervision. Generally speaking a professional person is judged according to the ordinary skill and competence of one who professes a given expertise. In any such treatment or diagnosis the requisite standard of care would in all probability be that of a medical practitioner doing the same thing, though perhaps with appropriate allowance for lack of specialism in a particular medical field if the task were fairly routine, for instance suturing an uncomplicated wound or prescribing painkilling drugs within medically accepted limits.

Until June 1992 the concept of the 'extended role of the nurse' remained prevalent in health care practice. Broad general guidance on the question was given in Circular HC(77)22, which contained the following statements:

'In considering legal aspects of the relative responsibilities of doctors and nurses the Committee concluded that though there were no apparent legal objections to continuing the existing practice of dividing work between the professions nurses should be required to undertake only those duties for which they had been educated and trained . . .

The role of the nurse is continually developing as changes in practice and training add new functions to her normal range of duties. Over and above this, however, the clinical nursing role in relation to that of the doctor may be extended in two ways, viz. by delegation by the doctor and in response to emergency. Where delegation occurs, the doctor remains responsible for his patient and for the overall management of treatment, and the nurse is responsible for carrying out delegated tasks competently. A case in point is the involvement of nurses in immunisation procedures which was the subject of Health Circular (76)26, issued in May 1976.

In an action for damages, a nurse may be held legally liable if it can be shown either that she has failed to exercise the skills properly expected of her, or that she has undertaken tasks she was not competent to perform. The doctor may be held to be guilty of negligent delegation if it can be shown that he conferred authority on a nurse to perform a task which was either outside the scope of the duties she was normally expected to perform, or for which she had no special qualification. Work which has hitherto been carried out by doctors ought therefore to be delegated to nurses only when:

    a. The nurse has been specifically and adequately trained for the perform-ance of the new task and she agrees to undertake it;
    b. this training has been recognised as satisfactory by the employing authority;
    c. the new task has been recognised by the professions and by the employing authority as a task which may be properly delegated to a nurse;
    d. the delegating doctor has been assured of the competence of the individual nurse concerned.'

In June 1992 the Department of Health issued Professional Letter PL/CNO(92)4 to the effect that the concept of 'extended role is no longer appropriate' to current professional conditions in the delivery of per-sonal health care, and made (amongst others) the following comments:

'Nursing, Midwifery and Health Visiting practice takes place in the world of constant change and development. Such change and development may result from advances in health care technology, research and new approaches to care and treatment. Practice therefore must be dynamic, relevant and responsive to the changing needs of individual patients, clients and their families.

Members of the professions will endeavour to take on new techniques and practices, in the interest of serving the patient or client. Each practitioner is personally accountable for their own practice and for the maintenance and development of their knowledge and competence. Decisions concerning professional practice should be based upon the UKCC's Code of Professional Conduct for the Nurse, Midwife and Health Visitor and related documents referred to in the annex of the letter. Practitioners should note that these documents are regularly revised and added to. The current list can be obtained from the Central Council.

Pre-registration education prepares practitioners to accept the responsibilities of professional practice. Any widening of that practice traditionally became an extended role. However, the present concept of the extended role is no longer appropriate as it may serve to limit rather than extend the parameters of practice.

The UKCC's documents referred to in the annex will provide a clear framework for the logical development of practice. The framework promotes greater flexibility and reflects the dynamic nature of nursing, midwifery and health visiting practice. The framework also reflects the personal responsibility and accountability of individual practitioners to protect and improve standards of care.

The UKCC's position statement *The Scope of Professional Practice* (1992) outlines the Council's position concerning the scope of professional practice and draws attention to the practitioner's personal accountability to maintain and improve their knowledge and competence. It also points out that principles of practice rather than certificates for tasks should form the basis for the scope of practice and any adjustments to it.'

The legal liability of the nurse remains effectively the same after the issuing of the Professional Letter, the legal standard of competence being based on the substantive question of the nurse's actual ability rather than on the more procedural question of a certificate. There is, of course, nothing to prevent an authority or trust awarding certificates of competence as a useful adjunct to their staff development practices.

A staff nurse may be promoted to sister of a ward or department if the appointing authority is satisfied that the duties are within her competence. If a nurse were promoted sister in a ward for which post her instruction as a junior nurse might not have fitted her, that would not in itself prove that anything which went amiss with a procedure which she carried out was due to her incompetence. She might have learned by experience in such a ward after qualification as a nurse.

What is the legal position of student and pupil nurses? It would be unhelpful to try to decide what each should be allowed to do, either under supervision or unsupervised, and the role of legal standards of care is not to dictate what shall be done, rather that whatever is done is done with care and competence and is part of an adequate working system. While, in law, if a nurse undertook some task beyond her competence and caused harm to a patient, she might be personally liable if she knew or ought to have known that the order was wrong even though she had been ordered by her superior to do the task, it is fairly certain that the authority for which she worked would, in such circumstances, give full indemnity against legal liability if her behaviour was reasonable in all the circumstances.

What has been said about nurses is true of radiographers, physiotherapists, student radiographers and student physiotherapists and of
any other paramedical staff such as a pathological laboratory technician
who may undertake a procedure in connection with the treatment of a
patient.

Medical and other students

Except for *Collins v Herts CC* (1947)[54] in which, unusually a senior
medical student under war conditions was employed as a house officer,
there appears to be no case in which a claim has been made alleging
negligence of a medical student or, for that matter, of a student
radiographer or physiotherapist. But the principles would be substantially the same. The student acts carelessly, or attempts something
beyond his competence, at his peril; but the law looks equally at the
adequacy or otherwise of the system of working which placed the
medical (or other) student in such a position as to make an unsupervised
judgment.

The legal effect of inexperience

In the case of *Nettleship v Weston* (1971)[55] an inexperienced driver whose
negligence resulted in injury to her amateur instructor was held to be
judged according to the standards of an experienced driver. Effectively,
the defendant was subjected to a compliance with a standard which she
could not in fact attain. Nevertheless, given that the law of negligence
concerns the distribution of risks and allocation of liability if those risks
materialise, even that is a fairer result than an injured plaintiff having to
take his chances (of recovery or non-recovery of damages) according to
the ability or otherwise of the particular defendant. If this principle were
to be directly applied to inexperienced staff in hospitals, no doubt the
ability of injured patients to recover damages for negligence would be
preserved. Liability of relatively inexperienced staff, possibly doing their
best but falling short of the desired result, would nevertheless create
considerable professional concern. The leading decision on the question
is far from straightforward.

In *Wilsher v Essex Area Health Authority* (1986)[56] a premature baby was
placed in a special care unit which was staffed by a team of two
consultants, a senior registrar, several junior doctors and trained nurses.
While the plaintiff was in the unit a junior and inexperienced doctor
monitoring the oxygen in the plaintiff's bloodstream mistakenly inserted
a catheter into a vein rather than an artery but then asked the senior
registrar to check what he had done. The registrar failed to see the
mistake and some hours later, when replacing the catheter monitor,
failed to register correctly the amount of oxygen in the plaintiff's blood
with the result that the plaintiff was given excess oxygen. The plaintiff
subsequently brought an action against the health authority claiming

damages and alleging that the excess oxygen in his bloodstream had caused an incurable condition of the retina resulting in near blindness.

By a majority of two to one the Court of Appeal held that the standard of care required of staff in the special care unit was that of the ordinary skilled professional exercising and professing to have the appropriate special skill; but the standard, they added, was to be determined in the context of the particular posts in the unit rather than according to the general rank or status of those occupying the posts. The duty, said two members of the Court of Appeal, ought to be tailored to the acts which the doctor in question chose to perform rather than to the (relatively inexperienced) doctor himself. However, this potentially harsh standard applicable to staff who are learning their way into special skills was tempered by Lord Justice Glidewell (one of the majority of the court) who held that an inexperienced practitioner who is called upon to exercise a specialist skill and who makes a mistake nevertheless satisfies the necessary standard of care if he seeks the advice and help of his superior when necessary. On the facts of this case, negligence was found to have been committed by one of the senior registrars who failed adequately to interpret readings on monitoring equipment, while the more junior doctor who had instituted the process leading to over-oxygenation was found not to have been negligent.

Even though Sir Nicolas Browne-Wilkinson dissented on the question as to the appropriate standard of care to be required, his judgment contains a formulation not very distant from that of Lord Justice Glidewell:

> 'In my judgment, if the standard of care required of such a doctor is that he should have the skill required of the post he occupies, the young houseman or the doctor seeking to obtain specialist skill in a special unit would be held liable for shortcomings in the treatment without any personal fault on his part at all. Of course, such a doctor would be negligent if he undertook treatment for which he knows he lacks the necessary experience and skill. But one of the chief hazards of inexperience is that one does not always know the risks which exist. In my judgment, so long as the English law rests liability on personal fault, a doctor who has properly accepted a post in a hospital in order to gain necessary experience should only be held liable for acts or omissions which a careful doctor with his qualifications and experience would not have done or omitted.'

6.3.3   Injuries to unborn children

Common law

In *Burton v Islington Health Authority*[57] it was held that a plaintiff born with injuries caused by the pre-natal neglect of the defendant has a cause of action in negligence against the defendant in respect of those injuries. The fact that the plaintiff is undefined in law, and without status, when the train of events which results in that damage is set in motion, was held to be irrelevant.

In 1966 the plaintiff's mother underwent a dilatation and curettage (D and C) at a hospital managed by the defendant health authority, at a time when she was in fact pregnant with the plaintiff to whom she gave birth some months later. On a preliminary point of law, namely as to whether such a plaintiff has a right of action in negligence, it was alleged that the plaintiff was born with numerous disabilities; in particular, she would be unable to conceive in later life, and was greatly embarrassed by her appearance. She had undergone surgery with a resulting scar extending from her back underneath her shoulder-blade to below her diaphragm. The cosmetic deficit was such that it is likely to impair her relationships with the opposite sex and also to impair her earning capacity.

The hearing was not a trial of the merits of the plaintiff's claim, but only a trial of the preliminary point in issue whether the plaintiff had an action in such a case. No evidence as to the merits, namely as to negligence or its absence, was produced by either side. The application proceeded on the basis that the allegations in the statement of claim would be made out.

It was held that the damage done to the embryo during the D and C procedure was an 'evidentiary fact in relation to causation' using the wording adopted in the Australian case of *Watt v Rama* (1972).[58] If there had been neglect in the D and C procedure in breach of proper medical practice, the risk of injury on birth to a child then being carried by the patient's mother was reasonably foreseeable. The circumstances were held to create a contingent or potential duty on the defendants, which crystallised on the birth of the injured child. At that time, the wrong to the child became complete, she having been born alive but physically damaged as a result of the defendants' earlier neglect. On birth, it was held, the child acquired legal status and legal rights. Her cause of action in negligence was therefore complete and accrued to her when she was a legal person who could, as such, sue or be sued.

Legislation

The Congenital Disabilities (Civil Liability) Act 1976 clarifies a number of important points as regards possible liability for pre-natal injury. It follows closely the Law Commission's Report on Injuries to Unborn Children[59] which was provoked by the thalidomide tragedy but goes further than providing for that type of case alone. The principal sections likely to affect the law relating to hospitals are sections 1 and 4:

'1.—(1) If a child is born disabled as the result of such an occurrence before its birth as is mentioned in subsection (2) below, and a person (other than the child's own mother) is under this section answerable to the child in respect of the occurrence, the child's disabilities are to be regarded as damage resulting from the wrongful act of that person and actionable accordingly at the suit of the child.

(2) An occurrence to which this section applies is one which—
(a) affected either parent of the child in his or her ability to have a normal, healthy child; or
(b) affected the mother during her pregnancy, or affected her or the child in the course of its birth, so that the child is born with disabilities which would not otherwise have been present.

(3) Subject to the following subsections, a person (here referred to as "the defendant") is answerable to the child if he was liable in tort to the parent or would, if sued in due time, have been so; and it is no answer that there could not have been such liability because the parent suffered no actionable injury, if there was a breach of legal duty which, accompanied by injury, would have given rise to the liability.

(4) In the case of an occurrence preceding the time of conception, the defendant is not answerable to the child if at that time either or both of the parents knew the risk of their child being born disabled (that is to say, the particular risk created by the occurrence); but should it be the child's father who is the defendant, this subsection does not apply if he knew of the risk and the mother did not.

(5) The defendant is not answerable to the child, for anything he did or omitted to do when responsible in a professional capacity for treating or advising the parent, if he took reasonable care having due regard to then received professional opinion applicable to the particular class of case; but this does not mean that he is answerable only because he departed from received opinion.

(6) Liability to the child under this section may be treated as having been excluded or limited by contract made with the parent affected, to the same extent and subject to the same restrictions as liability in the parent's own case; and a contract term which could have been set up by the defendant in an action by the parent, so as to exclude or limit his liability to him or her, operates in the defendant's favour to the same, but no greater, extent in an action under this section by the child.

(7) If in the child's action under this section it is shown that the parent affected shared the responsibility for the child being born disabled, the damages are to be reduced to such extent as the court thinks just and equitable having regard to the extent of the parent's responsibility.

4.—(1) References in this Act to a child being born disabled or with disabilities are to its being born with any deformity, disease or abnormality, including predisposition (whether or not susceptible of immediate prognosis) to physical or mental defect in the future.

(2) In this Act—
(a) "born" means born alive (the moment of a child's birth being when it first has a life separate from its mother), and "birth" has a corresponding meaning;

(3) Liability to a child under section 1 . . . of this Act is to be regarded—
(a) as respects all its incidents and any matters arising or to arise out of it; and

(b) subject to any contrary context or intention, for the purpose of construing references in enactments and documents to personal or bodily injuries and cognate matters,

as liability for personal injuries sustained by the child immediately after its birth.

(4) No damages shall be recoverable under [that section] unless the child lives for at least 48 hours.

(5) This Act applies in respect of births after (but not before) its passing, and in respect of any such birth it replaces any law in force before its passing, whereby a person could be liable to a child in respect of disabilities with which it might be born; but in section 1(3) of this Act the expression "liable in tort" does not include any reference to liability by virtue of this Act, or to liability by virtue of any such law.'

Effect of the legislation for health services

The effect of this is to ensure that a child who is born disabled by pre-natal injury has a cause of action against the person responsible. The Act applies to children born after 22 July 1976. The Law Commission was anxious in proposing this statute to ensure that it was harmonious with the common law (and other sources of liability) and that it went no further than the probable or possible scope of already existing causes of action. It is partly for this reason that the Act avoided creating a direct legal duty between the child *in utero* and the tortfeasor (wrongdoer). The other reason for this is also reflected in section 1(6) which, in effect, applies the doctrine of *volenti non fit injuria* so that the mother can consent to run a known risk not only on her own behalf but also on the behalf of her child. The purpose of this provision is to ensure that women are not discriminated against in the course of their normal lives. The effect of section 1(3) is to make the child's right of action dependent on the breach of legal duty to one of its parents. It is also for this reason that section 1(1) and section 4(2)(a) give the right of action to a child born alive (thus a foetus which is not born alive or a child which is stillborn has no cause of action) and not to an embryo or foetus. Indeed section 4(4) goes further and only allows damages to be recovered where the child survives for at least 48 hours. The question as to when the action may be brought is subject to the general law of limitation of actions in personal injury cases, for which see Chapter 5.

Section 1(3) requires the injury to be to one of the child's parents. an injury to a parent, e.g. through genetic changes, which is only manifested in a grandchild does not give a cause of action.

The occurrences giving rise to the liability can take place either to the father (before conception) or to the mother. These occurrences may be by way of a physical injury to the person of either parent or by way of some medication taken by the mother which has no permanent affect on her but which affects the child *in utero* or by way of some advice perhaps offered by a doctor which adversely affects the child *in utero*. The medical profession expressed its concern about this possible extra liability and section 1(5) is intended to allay these fears. It gives effect to *Roe v Minister of Health*.[60] A doctor is not bound to read every article in the medical press nor to apply current orthodoxy as if it were an eternal truth. It suffices that the doctor takes reasonable care having regard to the received professional opinion at the time he is treating his patient. If it is later shown that the received professional opinion was wrong, that does not give rise to liability. The date at which the reasonableness is to be judged is the date of the treatment, not that of the legal action.

The Law Commission recognised two further problems which worried the medical profession. First, a doctor might be concerned about a conflict of interest of the mother and her child. It took the view that the reference to 'received medical opinion' would suffice to deal with any medical or ethical problems associated with such conflicts. Also, what should happen to a doctor who departs from the received medical opinion perhaps because he is in advance of his time? It is perhaps justifiable for the law to require of a doctor who wishes to depart from received professional opinion that he has confidence in the reasonableness of his judgment.

6.3.4 Negligent abortion or sterilisation: claim for birth and upbringing of child

If an abortion or sterilisation procedure is carried out negligently, and the plaintiff remains or becomes pregnant, that outcome is a perfectly foreseeable result of negligence. In *Chaunt v Hertfordshire Area Health Authority* (1982)[61] a negligent sterilisation and unwanted pregnancy resulted in the award of damages to the plaintiff. In that case, the plaintiff's pregnancy was terminated; but it is, or should be, no surprise that damages may also be awarded for the pain and suffering occasioned by the subsequent birth of a child, together with damages for the child's upbringing. In relation to pain and suffering, the courts have had no difficulty in awarding damages.

In *Scuriaga v Powell* (1979)[62] the plaintiff's termination of pregnancy was carried out negligently by the doctor. By the time the procedure was found to have been unsuccessful it would have been too late for the plaintiff to undergo an abortion. Her child was born, and she was awarded damages in respect of pain and suffering, together with damages for past and future loss of earnings. No claim was made in the case for damages for upbringing, a maintenance order being in force at the relevant time.

In the Canadian case of *Doiron v Orr* (1978)[63] damages were claimed for the upbringing of a child following a negligent sterilisation. The judge rejected the plaintiff's claim for damages to cover upbringing of the child in emphatic terms:

'Mrs Doiron said that she would not consider an abortion when she found out she was pregnant, nor would she consider giving the child up to adoption. She wished to keep the child, but she wishes to have the doctor maintain the child until aged 21 because of what she considers to be the doctor's mistake. Personally, I find this approach to a matter of this kind which deals with human life, the happiness of the child, the effect upon its thinking, upon its mind when it realises that there has been a case of this kind, that it is an unwanted mistake and that its rearing is being paid for by someone other than its parents, is just simply grotesque.'

Nevertheless, the Court of Appeal in this country subsequently awarded damages to the mother of a child, in fact born handicapped, there having been negligence in performing an unsuccessful sterilisation procedure upon her. In *Emeh v Chelsea & Kensington & Westminster AHA* (1984)[64] the health authority, as defendants, contended that, assuming it is contrary to public policy for damages to be recoverable were the child to have been born normal and healthy, the cost of bringing up a normal child ought to be deducted from any damages awarded to the plaintiff for having to bring up a disabled child. Rejecting this contention, the Court of Appeal held that there is no rule of public policy preventing a plaintiff from recovering in full the financial damage sustained by her as a result of the negligent failure to perform the sterilisation operation properly, regardless of whether the child is born healthy or disabled.

Since the avoidance of a further pregnancy and birth was the object of the sterilisation operation, the loss suffered by the plaintiff resulting from the negligence was held to extend to any reasonably foreseeable financial loss directly caused by her unexpected pregnancy. It was held that her decision not to have an abortion did not break the chain of causation, nor did it amount to a failure to mitigate her damage. The health authority, by the negligence for which it was responsible, had in fact confronted the plaintiff with the very dilemma of whether to have the child or an abortion which she had sought in the first place to avoid by having herself sterilised. The health authority could not legitimately expect that, if its doctors did not perform the operation properly, the plaintiff would undergo an abortion with all its attendant risks, pain and discomfort. It was held to be reasonably foreseeable that if, as a consequence of the negligent sterilisation, the plaintiff found herself again pregnant she might decide to keep the child. The fact that she exercised that particular option did not mean that it was an option she wished to have. She was accordingly entitled to damages for loss of future earnings, maintenance of the child up to date of trial, and maintenance of the child in future. Her own pain and suffering up to the time of the trial and future loss of amenity and pain and suffering, including the extra care that the child would require, were also compensated by way of damages. It was added by Lord Justice Slade that, except in the most exceptional circumstances, it cannot be right for a court to declare it unreasonable for a woman to decline to have an abortion where there is no evidence that there are medical or psychiatric grounds for terminating the pregnancy.

So far as concerns the birth of healthy or 'normal' children, it was held by Mr Justice Jupp in *Udale v Bloomsbury Area Health Authority* (1983)[65] that it is contrary to public policy to award damages to a mother whose (normal) child was conceived after the mother had undergone a negligently performed sterilisation operation to cover the cost of carrying out necessary extensions to the home and of bringing up the child. As in the Canadian case *Doiron v Orr* (1978) he held that it is undesirable for a court to declare that the birth was a 'mistake' and that the child was unwanted or rejected. He added that the birth of a healthy, normal baby is a beneficial, and not a detrimental, event. In the slightly later case of *Thake v Maurice* (1984)[66] Mr Justice Peter Pain declined to follow the ruling in the *Udale* case and awarded damages to the parents of a healthy baby born in consequence of a negligently performed sterilisation. He held that, having regard to the policy of the state as expressed in legislation and social provision for family planning and abortion, it cannot be said that the birth of a healthy baby is always a blessing, nor that it is necessarily against public policy to award damages for the unwanted birth of a healthy child. He effectively held that, while the birth of a child may indeed be a 'blessing' or beneficial event, the upbringing of a child costs money, and that requires compensation by way of damages to support the resulting cost. Mr Justice Peter Pain declined to award damages for the distress, pain and suffering undergone respectively by the plaintiffs by the pregnancy, birth and upbringing of the child because that was cancelled out by the joy they received from the child. They were nevertheless awarded damages for the birth and upkeep of the child, but on a moderate basis 'in view of the humble household into which the child had been born'. His ruling was upheld by the Court of Appeal in respect of damages for upbringing; and the Court of Appeal restored the damages for distress, pain and suffering. The pre-natal distress of both plaintiffs and the pain and suffering of the birth were separate heads of claim not cancelled out by the relief and joy felt after the birth of a healthy baby. The court held that there is no reason in principle why damages cannot be recovered for the discomfort and pain of a normal pregnancy and delivery.

The same approach has been taken by the courts of this country in cases where there is a contract between doctor and patient as in the situation of private treatment. In *Eyre v Measday* (1986)[67] the plaintiff and her husband decided that they did not wish to have any more children and the plaintiff consulted the defendant gynaecologist privately with a view to undergoing a sterilisation operation. The defendant told the couple that the operation he intended to perform was 'irreversible'. He stated that the operation 'must be regarded as a permanent procedure', but did not inform the plaintiff that there was a very small risk (less than 1 per cent) of pregnancy occurring following the operation. The plaintiff subsequently became pregnant and gave birth to a child. In an action for damages against the doctor, the Court of Appeal held that the contract undertaken by the defendant was a contract to carry out a particular type of operation, rather than to render the plaintiff absolutely sterile. The defendant's statement to the plaintiff that the operation was 'irreversible' did not, the court held, amount to an express guarantee that the operation was bound to achieve its object of sterilising the plaintiff. The court added that where a doctor contracts to carry out a particular operation on a patient and a particular result is expected, the court will imply a term into the contract that the operation will be carried out with reasonable care but will be 'slow to imply a term that the expected result will actually be achieved'. It is probable, said the court, that no responsible medical practitioner would intend to give such a warranty. On the facts, it was held, no intelligent bystander could reasonably have inferred that the defendant practitioner was intending to give the plaintiff a guarantee that after the operation she would be absolutely sterile. The fact that she believed this would be the result was, it was held, irrelevant. Her claim for damages failed.

The judicial attitude to such a statement as 'the procedure is irreversible' is equally applicable to cases where there is a private contract between practitioner and patient, and to those where there is no such contract, as in the ordinary National Health Service case. While no doubt a fair result for the practitioner, one is left to wonder whether the ordinary patient could reasonably be taken to understand that irreversible does not in fact mean irreversible, but simply that the procedure cannot be reversed by medical means.

6.3.5 Causation

Even if a breach of the professional duty of care is established, and even if injury or harm to health occurs, no liability in negligence is made out unless the breach of duty is proved to have caused the injury. As with other aspects of civil liability, proof on the balance of probabilities is what is required. If it is for the plaintiff to establish the causal connection. A clear case in which such proof was lacking is *Barnett v Chelsea and Kensington Hospital Management Committee* (1969),[68] the facts of which are set out on p. 181 of this chapter. Medical evidence showed that the deceased would have died of the poisoning (which was due to the act of an unknown third party) even in the event of a timely admission to the appropriate ward in the hospital. The plaintiff, his widow, had therefore failed to establish on the balance of probabilities that the defendant's negligence had caused the death.

There are some cases in which the courts are prepared to give a degree of assistance to injured plaintiffs in the matter of proving a causal connection between breach of duty and injury. In *McGhee v National Coal Board* (1972)[69] the plaintiff's job involved cleaning out brick kilns, in consequence of which brick dust and perspiration gathered on his hands. In breach of a statutory duty, the defendants failed to provide adequate washing facilities for such employees after work. The plaintiff developed dermatitis and sued the Board for his injury. In response to a contention by the defendants that it could not be proved whether his injury resulted from the brick dust not being washed off (which was a tort, there being no washing facilities) or simply getting on in the first place (which disclosed no liability, this being part of his ordinary job) the House of Lords refused to draw any such distinction. They held that a finding that the defendants' breach of duty had materially increased the risk of injury to the plaintiff amounted for practical purposes to a finding that their breach of duty had materially contributed to his injury. Put simply, the plaintiff had come 'near enough' to proving his case on the balance of probabilities, and therefore was awarded damages.

The principle of *McGhee* is not applicable to a case in which injury may be attributable to one of two causes, only one of which (as in *McGhee*) discloses liability, but where the alleged wrongdoing has not been scientifically established to be capable of producing the injury complained of. In *Kay v Ayrshire and Arran Health Board* (1987)[70] a two-year-old boy was admitted to a hospital by the respondent authority with pneumococcal meningitis and was negligently given an overdose of penicillin. Following recovery from the meningitis he was found to be suffering from deafness. Evidence established that while deafness commonly results from meningitis, in no recorded case had an overdose of penicillin caused deafness.

It was decided by the House of Lords that where two competing causes of damage exist (such as, in this case, meningitis, and penicillin overdose) the law cannot presume in favour of the plaintiff that the wrongful act caused the damage in the absence of proof that it is an accepted fact that the wrongful act is capable of causing or at least aggravating such damage. Given that the expert medical evidence in this case indicated that penicillin overdose had never caused deafness, the boy's deafness had to be regarded as resulting solely from the meningitis. His claim therefore failed.

A subsequent decision of the House of Lords has established that where an injury is attributable to a number of possible causes, only one of which is the negligence of the defendant, the fact that injury to the plaintiff happens to be combined with negligence by the defendant does not give rise to a presumption that the defendant caused the injury. In

Wilsher v Essex Area Health Authority (1988)[71] the infant plaintiff was born prematurely suffering from various illnesses including oxygen deficiency. While in a special baby unit at the hospital where he was born a catheter was twice inserted into a vein of the plaintiff rather than an artery and on both occasions the plaintiff was given excess oxygen. The plaintiff was later discovered to be suffering from an incurable condition of the retina resulting in near blindness. The plaintiff's retinal condition could have been caused by excess oxygen but it also occurred in premature babies who were not given oxygen but who suffered from five other conditions common in premature babies and all of which had afflicted the plaintiff. The plaintiff brought an action against the health authority claiming damages for negligence and alleging that the excess oxygen in his bloodstream had caused his retinal condition. At the trial the medical evidence was inconclusive as to whether the excess oxygen had caused or materially contributed to the plaintiff's retinal condition. The Court of Appeal upheld the trial judge's decision that the hospital's breach of duty and the plaintiff's injury were such that the hospital was to be taken as having caused the injury even though the existence and extent of the contribution made by their breach of duty could not be ascertained. Reversing this decision, the House of Lords ruled that where a plaintiff's injury is attributable to a number of possible causes, one of which being admitted or established negligence, the plaintiff must still establish, on the balance of probability, that the defendant's negligence caused his injury. Since, in the particular case, the plaintiff's condition could have resulted from any one of a number of different causes, it had not been proved on the balance of probabilities that the cause was the failure to prevent excess oxygen being given, the plaintiff had not discharged the burden of proof as to causation. His claim therefore failed. A retrial on the question of causation was ordered; in such a retrial it would be for the plaintiff to establish on the balance of probabilities that it was the hospital's negligence, amongst all the possible causes of his injury, which actually caused it.

Loss of the chance of a better medical result?

In *Hotson v East Berkshire Area Health Authority* (1987)[72] the question arose whether loss of the chance of a better medical result, had appropriate and timely treatment been given, which was in fact lost owing to a hospital's negligence gave the injured plaintiff a cause of action. The thirteen-year-old plaintiff injured his hip when he fell from a tree. His injury was incorrectly diagnosed by the defendant's hospital and he was sent home. Only after five days of severe pain was he re-examined and a correct diagnosis made. The delay left him with a major permanent disability of the hip joint. The trial judge found that even if the authority's medical staff had correctly diagnosed and treated the plaintiff when he first attended the hospital there was still a 75 per cent risk of the plaintiff's disability developing, but that the medical staff's breach of duty had turned that risk into an inevitability, thereby denying the plaintiff a 25 per cent chance of a good recovery.

The case reached the House of Lords, where the plaintiff's action failed. The trial judge had held that, given the plaintiff's condition when he was first taken to hospital, even correct diagnosis and treatment would not on the balance of probabilities (that is, more likely than not) have prevented the disability occurring. He nevertheless awarded the plaintiff one quarter (25 per cent) of the damages which would have been awarded on a full liability basis, namely if the injury had been caused wholly by the negligent failure in treatment. The House of Lords disagreed. Quite simply, a 25 per cent chance falls distinctly short of proof on the balance of probabilities.

6.3.6   The level and heads of damages

In view of the anxiety often felt about the large sums which are apt to be awarded in cases of personal injury caused by medical negligence, it is appropriate to quote briefly from the judge's decision in the first case in this country in which the damages resulting from medical negligence exceeded £1 million. Mr Justice Hirst clearly felt under some obligation to set out the precise approach to reaching this large figure.

In *Samer Aboul-Hosn v Trustees of the Italian Hospital and Grant and Crawford and Nouri* (1987),[73] general damages in respect of pain, suffering and loss of amenities were fixed by the trial judge at £85,000. That was the 'tariff' in respect of an accident happening on the relevant date in this case. Almost three quarters of the award comprised future care in all its aspects and loss of earnings. The level of these heads of award is readily explained by the fact that the plaintiff was at the time of the accident a very promising student aged just under 19 years. Liability was in due course admitted on behalf of the second, third and fourth defendants. Despite the title by which the case will be known, judgment was entered in favour of the first defendants, the trustees of the Italian Hospital, who denied liability.

After detailed consideration of the precedents relevant to the heads of damage claimed, his Lordship concluded his judgment with the following summary of the award made to the plaintiff. In so doing, he was emphatic that the element of general damages to reflect pain, suffering and loss of amenities constituted but a small fraction of the total award.

'The amounts I have awarded under the various headings are conveniently summarised as follows:

Pain, suffering and loss of amenities	£85,000
Parents' past care and expenditure	£100,700
Future care in all its aspects	£400,800
Housing needs	£48,100
Future loss of earnings (including car)	£331,000
Court of Protection fees	£34,500

To this must be added interest, which is agreed at £31,550.

Samer's award including interest therefore amounts to £1,032,000 (rounded).

This is an enormous sum, and it may be useful if, in conclusion, I explain very briefly how it is made up.

Less than 10 per cent is in respect of pain and suffering and loss of amenity. The figure is fixed in accordance with awards in comparable cases, and only a fraction of the amount he would recover under this head in some other jurisdictions (e.g. USA).

Well over 50 per cent is attributable to care, rehabilitation and housing needs past and future.

The great bulk of the remainder is attributable to loss of earnings.

Future care, rehabilitation and housing needs and future loss of earnings together absorb nearly 80 per cent of the award. These are estimates based on the evidence as to Samer's expectation of life.

If he dies sooner, they will be too much. If he outlives his expectation of life, the money for care will probably have run out, since it is calculated on the footing that both capital and income would be exhausted by the end of that period.'

6.3.7 Contributory negligence

In any case in which damages for injury (including death) or loss due to negligence are claimed and the person or body satisfies the court that the plaintiff was himself guilty of negligence which contributed to those injuries or losses (namely, that had he taken due care and acted reasonably he could have avoided or reduced the loss or injury caused by the defendant's negligence) the court may reduce the award of damages in proportion to the plaintiff's share of the responsibility.[74]

A defendant's legal advisers would do well to consider whether such a defence may apply. A doctor may be negligent not only in his diagnosis or the treatment he prescribes but also in failing to give adequate information to a patient about the future steps the patient should take. A doctor cannot reduce the extent of his responsibility to compensate for injury resulting from inadequate information by being 'wise after the event' of his patient's inadequately advised actions. What may be obvious, by way of care or precaution, to a medical or other health care expert may not be obvious to a patient.

A related though separate question is the duty on any person who suffers injury or loss at the hand of another to take reasonable steps to limit the extent of the injury or loss and hence the damages. While a defendant must take a plaintiff as he finds him, he is not bound to take the plaintiff's unreasonableness.[75]

NOTES

1. [1925] 19 Cr App Rep 8.
2. 5 C and P 333 at 336.
3. 4 C and P 398 at 423.
4. [1977] 2 WLR 169.
5. [1899] 1 QB 283.
6. [1973] QB 702.
7. [1977] QB 354.
8. (1979) 123 Sol Jo 436.
9. The Times, 26 November 1987.
10. *Whiteford v Hunter* (1950) 94 Sol Jo 758.
11. Lord Justice Scott in *Mahon v Osborne* [1939] 2 KB 14.
12. *Coggs v Bernard* (1704) 2 Ld Raym 909, Salk 26.
13. [1939] 2 KB 14.
14. *R v Bateman* (1925) 19 Cr App Rep 8.
15. *Gold v Essex CC* [1942] 2 KB 293.
16. The Times, 5 February 1959.
17. The Times, 21 June 1955.
18. (1950) 94 Sol Jo 599.
19. [1954] 2 QB 66.
20. The Times, 8 December 1953.
21. *O' Donovan v Cork CC and others* [1967] IR 173 (Eire).
22. [1957] 1 WLR 582.
23. The Times, 8 December 1953.
24. [1955] SLT 213 at 217.
25. [1954] 2 QB 66.
26. [1967] 1 WLR 813.
27. [1984] 1 WLR 634.
28. See *Hughes v Waltham Forest HA* The Times, 9 November 1990.
29. [1955] SLT 213 at 217.
30. [1957] 1 WLR 582.
31. [1984] 1 WLR 634.
32. [1983] 1 All ER 416.
33. [1971] 1 WLR 749 at 755.
34. [1951] 2 KB 343.
35. [1939] 2 KB 14.
36. [1948] 2 All ER 176.
37. [1965] 1 Lloyd's Rep 26.
38. (1972) 29 DLR (3rd) 692.
39. The Times, 19 November 1959.

40. The Times, 21 December 1960.
41. [1955] SLT 213.
42. The Times, 31 January 1963.
43. *Cavan v Wilcox* (1973) 44 DLR (3rd) 42, New Brunswick Sup Ct.
44. HM(73)9.
45. The Times, 26 November 1970.
46. Medical Defence Union Annual Report 1971, p. 46.
47. (1964) 108 Sol Jo 484.
48. The Times, 15 April 1981.
49. See *Kirkham v Chief Constable of the Greater Manchester Police* [1990] 3 All ER 246.
50. [1969] 1 QB 428.
51. The Times, 25 March 1959.
52. *Collins v Herts CC* [1947] 1 All ER 639.
53. *Gold v Essex CC* [1942] 2 KB 293.
54. [1947] 1 All ER 639.
55. [1971] 2 QB 691.
56. [1986] 3 All ER 801, Court of Appeal.
57. [1992] 3 All ER 833, Court of Appeal, affirming [1991] 1 All ER 825 (Potts J.).
58. [1972] VR 353 (State of Victoria, Australia).
59. Cmnd 5709 (1974).
60. [1954] 2 QB 66.
61. (1982) 132 NLJ 1054.
62. (1979) 123 Sol Jo 406.
63. (1978) 86 DLR (3d) 719.
64. [1984] 3 All ER 1044.
65. [1983] 2 All ER 522.
66. [1984] 2 All ER 513.
67. [1986] 1 All ER 488.
68. [1969] 1 QB 428.
69. [1972] 3 All ER 1008.
70. [1987] 2 All ER 417.
71. [1988] 3 All ER 871.
72. [1987] 2 All ER 909.
73. Unreported, QBD, Mr Justice Hirst, 10 July 1987.
74. Law Reform (Contributory Negligence) Act 1945 section 1.
75. *Morgan v Wallis* [1974] 1 Lloyd's Rep 165; *Steel v George* [1942] AC 497.

CHAPTER 7

Consent to medical and associated treatment

7.1 INTRODUCTORY

This chapter examines the extent of the duty of a medical or other health care practitioner not to undertake any medical, dental or surgical procedure without the consent of the patient. On some occasions, whether for legal reasons (such as the minority of the patient) or factual reasons (such as in the case of an unconscious patient) it may be necessary to seek the consent, or the agreement or approval, of some other person in his stead.

Also discussed is the extent of the obligation to give the patient (or other person) some explanation about the nature and consequences of the proposed procedure. A signature on a 'consent form' is evidence of consent but no more than that. The 'signature' of a pre-medicated or delirious patient is most unlikely to constitute any evidence of real consent and will therefore be of no legal effect. The legal question is whether the consent was full and free and not whether a form was signed. Decided cases show clearly that, irrespective of a signature on a consent form, valid consent is not induced by misleading information. The same principles apply equally to things done by any medical practitioner or health care practitioner, such as a physician undertaking an investigation or treatment involving risk to the patient, including diagnostic procedures; a physiotherapist applying heat treatment; and a nurse turning a patient with bedsores. So far as concerns the consent requisite to provide a defence (or justification) against a legal action for assault and battery, the law is concerned only with those methods of treatment or investigation that involve a physical touching of the person. Generally, no action lies for a psychiatric examination carried out without consent. However, in a case in which such an examination was carried out on an infant ward of court without the consent of either the court or the Official Solicitor, the court condemned this practice.[1]

7.2 PATIENTS OF FULL AGE AND UNDERSTANDING

7.2.1 General principles

An operation, or any other surgical or medical procedure or examination, carried out without the express or implied consent of the patient will normally amount to actionable trespass to the person. It is a direct, unauthorised interference with the patient's body for which the surgeon or other responsible medical practitioner and those helping him may be held personally liable. As to vicarious liability of health authorities trusts and other employers, see Chapter 5.

While in criminal law, relating to offences against the person, 'assault' normally signifies unlawful physical contact, the civil law (damages actions by individuals) distinguishes between assault, which is the apprehension of immediate physical contact (or 'force'), and battery, which is its infliction. In *Fowler v Lanning* (1959)[2] Mr Justice Diplock ruled that an action for trespass to the person does not lie if the injury to the plaintiff has been caused unintentionally and without negligence on the defendant's part. Does this help if the surgeon honestly believes that the patient's consent to an operation has been obtained, if for instance, he is so informed by another member of the hospital staff? And does it if, through another's carelessness, the wrong patient is brought into the theatre and the surgeon performs what in fact is an unauthorised operation? The answer is 'No' in both instances.

In the first (absence of consent) it might be argued that the surgeon was entitled to rely on other members of the hospital staff to obtain consent and could reasonably have accepted the assurance of, say, the theatre sister or house officer that consent had been obtained; and that therefore, in operating in reliance on such assurance, he had not been negligent. He might, however, be under a duty to ensure that there was a duly signed consent form in the patient's notes. But to bring himself within the protection of *Fowler v Lanning*, the surgeon must not only have acted without negligence but must also have acted *unintentionally*. In fact, he has performed the operation on the patient by way of an intentional act (as distinct from inadvertence). But if sued the surgeon could join as third parties other hospital staff who, by their negligence, had misled him. The surgeon could also bring in the hospital authority, either as being vicariously liable as employers for the negligence of those other members of the staff, or as answerable for a negligent system of working.

In the second instance (operation performed on the wrong patient) the trespass to the person is again intentional and therefore the defence that he had acted without negligence would not be open to the surgeon. In this case his position may be weaker since the court might take the view that he ought to have known his own patient and what procedure he intended to perform.

Exceptions to the rule that a patient's own consent to an operation or analogous procedure must be obtained are children up to the age of 16 and persons suffering from mental disorder if that disorder be of such a nature and degree as to render them incapable of giving real consent. In the case of a minor it is the parent or guardian who ordinarily gives the necessary consent. The case of a patient who is mentally disordered is less clear.

7.2.2   Potential restrictions on consent

The Mental Health Act 1983 provides for the imposition of medical treatment for mental disorder on certain (longer term) detained patients and in consequence of certain requisite procedures, even in the absence of comprehending consent. These statutory powers extend also to an express refusal of treatment (see Chapter 30). The present chapter (pp. 268–75, below) also examines the circumstances in which treatment for physical ailments may lawfully be given in the absence of consent. Such circumstances do not extend to an express and comprehending refusal, the case of blood transfusion being specifically discussed (see pp. 238–240, below). The powers given by the Mental Health Act 1983 apply to hospitals and mental nursing homes but do not extend to the treatment of prisoners (unless transfered to hospital under statutory powers). The question arises whether a prisoner (including a resident in a remand centre or borstal) may fully and freely consent to proposed treatment even though a refusal might adversely affect prison privileges or even parole. The point is addressed in the case of *Freeman v Home Office* (1984).[3]

In 1973, while serving a term of life imprisonment, the plaintiff had administered to him certain drugs. In 1979 the plaintiff brought an action against the Home Office claiming damages for trespass to the person, on the grounds that a medical officer employed by the prison authorities, together with other prison officers, had administered the drugs to him by force against his consent. He contended (a) that the drugs prescribed by the medical officer were not for the relief of any recognisable mental illness or disorder but were purely to control him, and that a prisoner could not, in law, give consent to treatment by a prison medical officer where the medical officer was not acting in his capacity as a doctor but as a disciplinarian; and (b) that for a patient's consent to be operative in law it had to be informed, i.e. the patient had to be told (i) what he was suffering from, (ii) what was the precise nature of the treatment being proposed and (iii) what, if any, were the adverse effects and risks involved in the treatment. The judge found that the plaintiff had consented to the administration of the drugs and he accordingly dismissed the action. The plaintiff appealed. The Court of Appeal ruled that the sole issue was whether on the facts the plaintiff had consented to the administration of the drugs and on that issue the trial judge had found that the plaintiff had so consented. Furthermore, the judge was right to hold that in the circumstances the plaintiff was not incapable in law of giving his consent to the treatment by the prison medical officer.

While the decision is practical in legal terms, otherwise no prisoner would be able to consent because agreement to proposed treatment could not be entirely uninfluenced by conditions of incarceration, the decision by the trial judge on the facts is remarkable. The plaintiff in evidence said: 'I threshed (sic) around on the bed and shouted . . . I was terrified.'

The argument of 'fettered' and therefore invalid consent might also be significant in the context of treatment, especially medical treatment for mental disorder, proposed to inmates or residents of secure (locked) accommodation in psychiatric hospitals. Particular care will be needed in such circumstances to avoid too hasty a conclusion that such a person's apparent agreement to proposed treatment is genuine. In such a situation, powers given by Part IV of the Mental Health Act 1983 are an alternative safeguard (see Chapter 30, pp. 813–814, below).

Another decided case in which the validity of consent in restricted conditions was challenged is *R v Apicella* (1985).[4] In this case the Court of Appeal (Criminal Division) held that there is no rule of law to prevent the admission of evidence of anything taken from a defendant unless he consented to the taking.

The Court of Appeal (Criminal Division) so held when dismissing an appeal by the accused, Alfred Robert Apicella, against his conviction on three counts of rape and one count of possessing an imitation firearm. The Central Criminal Court had sentenced him to 15 years' imprisonment.

The appellant, posing as a minicab driver, had raped three girls. Several items of evidence pointed to the appellant as being the rapist. Probably the strongest of these was the fact that each of the girls, as a result of the attack, had contracted an unusual strain of gonorrhoea. It had been for the Crown to prove that the appellant was suffering from the same strain of the disease, and this appeal concerned their attempt to do so.

While the appellant was awaiting trial, the prison doctor, suspecting that he was suffering from gonorrhoea, called a consultant physician. His object in doing so was solely therapeutic. The consultant examined the appellant and took from him a sample of body fluid in order to proceed to a diagnosis of his condition.

The consultant who had been called in by the prison doctor assumed that the appellant was consenting to this procedure. The appellant was, in fact, only submitting and not consenting. He had been told by a prison officer that, as a prisoner, he had no choice in the matter.

When tested, the sample of body fluid showed that the appellant was suffering from the same strain of gonorrhoea as the three victims. The prosecution called evidence to that effect at the trial. Giving the judgment of the court, Lord Justice Lawton said that it was accepted that the evidence derived from the appellant's body fluid was relevant. There was no rule of law, he said, which states that evidence of anything taken from a suspect, be it a body fluid, a hair or an article hidden in an orifice of the body cannot be admitted unless the suspect consented to the taking.

It is, he said, well-established law that the way in which evidence has been obtained has no relevance to its admissibility as such, though its intended use in a trial by the prosecution may call for the exercise of judicial discretion to exclude it in certain cases. The evidence in the present case was, therefore, admissible. The only question was, was its intended use likely to make the trial unfair?

In the circumstances, the Court of Appeal held it was not and the judge had been right, in the exercise of his discretion, not to exclude it.

The decision in *R v Apicella* is unaffected by the Police and Criminal Evidence Act 1984, section 78(1), which came into force on 1 January 1986 and provides as follows:

'78.—(1) In any proceedings the court may refuse to allow evidence on which the prosecution proposes to rely to be given if it appears to the court that, having regard to all the circumstances, including the circumstances in which the evidence was obtained, the admission of the evidence would have such an adverse effect on the fairness of the proceedings that the court ought not to admit it.'

Certain (generally speaking, longer term) detained patients can be treated in certain circumstances and subject to certain statutory procedures without their consent. The relevant provisions of the Mental Health Act 1983 relate only to treatment for mental disorder. Physical treatment of detained patients, or mental or physical treatment of informal (non-detained) patients, is often thought to require the 'consent' of someone else. This may take the form of the approval of the patient's consultant or other doctor in charge of the patient's treatment (responsible medical officer) if the patient is liable to detention in hospital or, possibly, the patient's guardian if one has been appointed. Not infrequently the 'consent' of the patient's nearest relative or next-of-kin is relied on.

In reality, treatment (whether for physical or mental disorder, but normally the former) of a person unable to consent – by reason of unconsciousness, or of severe learning disability, or due to a non-lucid psychotic interval – must depend on a principle other than consent. That principle is examined later in this chapter. One thing is clear. Whether 'necessity' or 'best interests' or someone else's agreement or approval is in issue, what is being relied on is *not* 'consent'. That state of mind is personal and peculiar to the recipient of treatment; and in the case of physical or mental incapacity to consent, that state of mind is absent.

The consent of the husband may be necessary in the case of a proposed operation on his wife if the operation may or will result in sterility.

If a person presents himself for treatment as a patient at a hospital his unquestioning or willing co-operation is ordinarily sufficient to signify his consent to ordinary external physical examination. In the case of such presentations as a severe cut manifestly needing stitches, a broken arm requiring setting, or an eye with a piece of metal in it, the pressing need for attention may sufficiently indicate consent to necessary treatment. But it can be difficult to say in particular circumstances whether the patient's consent may reasonably be inferred (implied) or not. What if the broken arm does not set properly and needs resetting to make a satisfactory job of it? Or if the patient's trouble is internal and for purposes of diagnosis the surgeon wishes an internal examination with the aid of instruments? Prudence would indicate that even if the patient's formal (express) consent had not already been obtained it should not be neglected at this stage.

While it is not, strictly, legally necessary in every case, even of in-patients, to obtain the patient's consent in writing, it is advisable to do so in order to have a record of valid consent in respect of any surgical and anaesthetic procedures, as well as in the case of any medical or radiological procedures where there is more than a minimum degree of risk and where the proposed treatment is truly elective. Such, for instance, would be the case where the patient might have the choice, say, between having an operation entailing considerable risk which, if successful, would result in a complete cure, or of not having the operation and going on living subject to a disability and all its consequences. The kind of case in which written consent might be dispensed with is that of a pregnant woman who had been having ante-natal care before entering hospital for what was expected to be a normal delivery. But if it were known at the time of the woman's admission, or became known before the onset of labour, that surgical intervention such as a Caesarian section would be necessary, then it would be desirable to obtain consent in writing. Whether consent in writing might usefully be sought after the onset of labour would depend on whether the patient was in a condition meaningfully to consent and without undue distress. If she were under any degree of sedation when she signed the form its value would be significantly diminished, if not entirely negated. In such circumstances, being in the nature of an unforeseen emergency, whether a form is signed or not matters little, provided that what is best is done for the patient.

It is wise to avoid the practice, encountered from time to time, of regarding a pre-natal patient as 'impliedly' consenting to any ward practice which happens to be routine. An example would be 'routine' episiotomies to train midwives.

It is equally unwise (as well as equally devoid of legal effect) to obtain a signature on a consent form framed in very general terms, at the very outset of a patient's stay in hospital, with the object of 'covering' anything the staff treating the patient may do.

It is doubtful how effective would be a general consent given by a patient on entering hospital in ignorance of what was proposed to be done and of any possibility of choice. It is preferable that, in all cases, the patient's consent should be sought only when the surgeon (or other health care practitioner) has decided to advise a particular operation (or other procedure) and in the case of surgical operations that the appropriate explanation be given to the patient by the responsible surgeon or other senior member of the surgical team (alternatively by other health care professionals in the case of treatments proposed directly and appropriately by them).

7.2.3   The nature of the required explanation

What explanation is necessary? In most instances of elective (chosen) treatment where there is no question of balancing the advantage of a beneficial outcome against the adverse consequences materialising from a risk inherent in even careful treatment it will be sufficient to give a simple, non-technical explanation which concentrates attention more on the object sought to be attained by the proposed operation than on the precise surgical or clinical procedure to be adopted. The patient may simply want reassurance. But is there any obligation on the doctor or other practitioner in any circumstances to warn the patient of particular risks, or personal consequences adverse to the patient, arising even from careful treatment? In answering that question it may once have been appropriate to distinguish statements made in answer to a question asked by the patient the volunteered statements, whether or not there is a truly elective element in the decision the patient has to make. Since the decision of the Court of Appeal in *Blyth v Bloomsbury Health Authority* (1987)[5] there has been no such distinction. The removal of any distinction as may have been discernible from cases discussed in previous editions of this book does not mean that doctors have a legal duty to recite to their patient all the clinical and associated data in their possession; nor to give *all* patients the same information whatever their psychological state, but merely that whatever is properly accepted as good professional practice should draw no distinction between patients who happen to enquire about possible adverse consequences to them ('risks') and patients who do not. It is nevertheless worth examining the case-law specifically on enquiring patients for an impression of the sort of explanation, or information, which should be imparted generally.

If a patient asks a question about the risk involved in a proposed operation or procedure (such as a clot causing gangrene and amputation, following aortography) or about the possible consequences (such as the effect on the voice of thyroidectomy), may the question be answered untruthfully or evasively, or just avoided by a contrived turn of conversation? Or must the surgeon answer frankly? *Smith v Auckland Hospital Board* (1965)[6] is strong persuasive authority from the New Zealand Court of Appeal, and the answer is that the medical practitioner should ordinarily answer accurately. This has since been confirmed by the House of Lords in *Sidaway v Bethlem Royal Hospital Governors* (1985)[7] (pp. 216–221, below) in which their Lordships held that a patient's question requires a truthful and full answer. The New Zealand decision indicated that there is no legal duty to volunteer information beyond that positively asked for by the patient, it being for the patient to ask supplementary questions if the answer to his original question, being a truthful answer, has not told him all he wanted to know. This must now be read subject to the decision of the English Court of Appeal in *Blyth v Bloomsbury Health Authority* (above). Their Lordships in that case held that the standards of proper explanation and information are governed in the case of both enquiring and non-enquiring patients by the test of accepted proper practice laid down in the case of *Bolam v Friern HMC* (1957).[8] Lord Justice Kerr said:

'The question of what a plaintiff should be told in answer to a general enquiry cannot be divorced from the *Bolam* test, any more than when no such enquiry is made. In both cases the answer must depend upon the circumstances, the nature of the enquiry, the nature of the information which is available, its reliability, relevance, the condition of the patient, and so forth. Any medical evidence directed to what would be the proper answer in the light of responsible medical opinion and practice (that is to say, the *Bolam* test) must in my view equally be placed in the balance in cases where the patient makes some enquiry, in order to decide whether the response was negligent or not.'

The surgeon may not be at risk by refraining from answering provided it should have been clear to the patient that he was deliberately not answering and provided also that such a practice would be accepted as proper in the particular circumstances by a responsible body of professional opinion in the particular branch of the art (or science) in question. It is rarely, if ever, permissible to answer so evasively as to mislead the patient. There might be the exceptional case in which an untruthful or evasive answer could be justified; but the onus would then be on the defendant to satisfy the court that the circumstances were exceptional and the untruth or evasion in the patient's own interest. This exception in fact asserts the validity of 'consent' to an operation obtained by deceit.

In *Hatcher v Black* (1954)[9] Lord Justice Denning said, of untruths by even well-meaning doctors:

> 'What should the doctor tell his patient? [The doctor] admitted that on the evening before the operation he told the plaintiff that there was no risk to her voice, when he knew that there was some slight risk, but that he did it for her own good because it was of vital importance that she should not worry. In short, he told a lie, but he did it because he thought in the circumstances it was justifiable. If this were a court of morals, that would raise a nice question on which moralists and theologians have differed for centuries. Some hold that it is never permissible to tell a lie even for a just cause: a good end, they say, does not justify a bad means. You must not do a little wrong in order to do a great right. Others, however, hold that it is permissible, if the justification is strong enough, and they point to the stratagems used in war to deceive the enemy. This, however, is not a court of morals but a court of law, and the law leaves this question of morals to the conscience of the doctor himself – though I may perhaps remark that if doctors have too easy a conscience on this matter they may in time lose the confidence of the patient, which is the basis of all good medicine. But so far as the law is concerned, it does not condemn the doctor when he only does that which many a wise and good doctor so placed would do.'

Any analogy between the doctor-patient relationship, based as it is on information and trust, and 'stratagems used in war to deceive the enemy' belongs to a different era of medical-legal relations and can now safely be ignored.

However, even if a patient's consent to a procedure or operation were given after the surgeon had made an untrue or evasive statement about the risk involved, the patient would not succeed in an action for damages unless the court were satisfied that he would have been likely to refuse consent had a truthful answer been given. That is because the statement would not have *caused* the outcome, which resulted from the patient's own choice in the event. Presumably the position would be the same if the untruthful statement had been made after the consent had been given and the patient nevertheless refrained from withdrawing his consent.

The facts of *Smith v Auckland Hospital Board* (above) were these. The plaintiff suffered from an aortic aneurism and a surgeon in one of the defendant Board's hospitals sought his consent to a preliminary exploratory procedure, aortography, before deciding on the next step. Aortography involved passing a catheter through the femoral artery to the aorta to inject an opaque fluid to outline the aorta for photography. In answer to a question by the patient whether there was any risk, the surgeon gave an answer which was so evasive as to mislead the plaintiff into the belief that there was no risk, although he was aware that there was a slight risk of the mishap which unfortunately did occur, a gangrenous condition of the right leg consequent upon the formation of a clot necessitating amputation of the leg below the knee. The evasive answer was given only to reassure the patient.

The plaintiff claimed damages alleging that the surgeon, employed by the Board, had been negligent in answering his question whether there was any danger in aortography and that the answer had misled him into giving his consent. The plaintiff failed in his action in the lower court, Mr Justice Woodham setting aside a finding by the jury that the Board by its servants or agents had been negligent.

He ruled that there was no evidence on which the jury could find any breach of duty; and alternatively that even if there had been such evidence the answer given by the surgeon could not reasonably be found causative of the damage suffered by the plaintiff. Both these conclusions were attacked in the Court of Appeal where the court allowed the plaintiff's appeal.

Applying *Hedley, Byrne & Co Ltd v Heller & Partners Ltd* (1964)[10] the court held that the particular relationship of doctor and patient is sufficient to impose upon a doctor a duty to use proper care in answering a question put to him by the patient where the patient, to the knowledge of the doctor, intends to place reliance on that answer in making a decision as to a treatment or procedure to which he is asked to consent. Strictly speaking, this reference to the *Hedley Byrne* principle was unnecessary. That case concerned the question whether a legal duty is owed by one who volunteers or gives in response to an enquiry information (in the particular case, as to the creditworthiness of a third party) upon which the recipient of the information might rely and thereby incur financial loss. But in the doctor-patient relationship there is no doubt about the duty to inform and explain; the only question being how, and to what extent. If in answering such a question the doctor fails to use proper care and, as a result of submitting to the treatment or procedure the patient suffers injuries, the doctor will be liable to the patient in tort if the evidence shows that, had a proper answer been given, the patient would probably have refused to undergo the treatment or procedure, either immediately or after further questions.

In the course of his judgment, Sir Harold Barrowclough (the Chief Justice) said:

'I do not think that it will be disputed, and I cannot imagine [the surgeon] disputing that he had not answered truthfully in this case.

Of course I do not mean that he acted mendaciously. He meant only to be reassuring and he avoided a real answer, and one can understand his reasons for that. But what he said was so reassuring as to be capable of the construction that there was no risk. That would not have been the truth: at least it fell short of the truth.'[11]

The plaintiff had not only to establish that the surgeon had not answered him frankly but also that his injury resulted in consequence. In other words, that the breach of the legal duty to give a proper and acceptable answer caused the damage or injury complained of, causation being an essential ingredient of the tort (or wrong) of negligence. The jury in the lower court had found as a fact that the plaintiff had indeed proved that he would have refused the proposed operation had his question been answered truthfully.

So far as concerns information and explanation given to patients otherwise than in answer to a specific or general enquiry, case law was relatively lacking until quite recently. In principle and practice it is generally accepted that if a patient's consent to an operation or other procedure is to be relied on he must have been given, even without asking, such reasonable explanation of the nature and effect of what is proposed to be done as is appropriate and practicable in the circumstances, taking into account such things as the patient's level of understanding and his physical and mental condition. But the question arose: Should information be volunteered about *any* risk involved? The line generally taken by members of the medical profession of not volunteering information about a slight but inevitable risk involved in undergoing a 'necessary' operation or procedure (for instance, an operation or procedure which affords the only reasonable chance of saving the patient's life or of curing the condition from which he is suffering) was (and perhaps is) taken to be no more than common sense. Any interference with the human body must, it is argued, entail some risk of danger to life or at least ill-effects, however remote that risk may be. To warn a patient of such minimal risk without the patient himself raising the question could not but be unsettling to even the most level-headed patient (it is argued), for such a patient would inevitably assume that the risk was much greater than it really was, and that by being referred to as a slight risk it was being played down. This view gains some support in the summing up of Mr Justice McNair in *Bolam v Friern HMC* (1957).[12]

The plaintiff had agreed to undergo electro-convulsive therapy (ECT) and, in the course of that treatment, sustained serious injury, namely bi-lateral stove-in fractures of the acetabula. In his action against the hospital management committee he alleged not only negligent treatment but also that he should have been warned of the risk involved in the operation to which his consent had been sought and obtained. In other words, that there was also negligence in failing to warn. On the question of whether a warning should have been given, Mr Justice McNair told the jury that they should consider two questions: first, does good medical practice require a warning to a patient before he undergoes ECT treatment; and, second, if a warning had been given, what difference would it have made? He continued:

'Having considered the evidence on this point you have to make up your minds whether it has been proved to your satisfaction that when the defendants adopted the practice they did (namely, the practice of saying very little and waiting for questions from the patient), they were falling below a proper standard of competent professional opinion on this question of whether or not it is right to warn. Members of the jury,[13] though it is a matter entirely for you, you may well think that when dealing with a mentally sick man and having a strong belief that his only hope of cure is ECT treatment, a doctor cannot be criticised if he does not stress the dangers which he believes to be minimal involved in that treatment.'[14]

On the question whether a warning, if given, would have had any effect, his Lordship suggested that unless the plaintiff had satisfied the jury that he would not have taken treatment if he had been warned, there was really nothing in that point.

If then we leave aside the case of the operation or procedure in respect of which any sensible person, as a potential patient, would feel that there was a true choice and restrict attention to the operation which is the *only* course reasonably practicable if *anything* is to be done for a patient whose condition is grave, it would seem that what was said by Mr Justice McNair in his summing up in *Bolam's* case (1957) gives reasonable guidance.

One is, however, left to speculate on whether the lead given in the summing-up in this case would have been quite so strong, had the patient's disability been not mental but physical, bearing in mind that his life was not apparently in danger.

Mr Justice McNair carefully left on one side what the position might have been, had the patient asked questions. There is no conflict between *Bolam's* case and the later decision of the New Zealand Court of Appeal in *Smith* v *Auckland Hospital Board* (1965)[6] which concerned only the surgeon's duty to answer questions frankly. Nor does the summing-up in *Bolam's* case give blanket cover to the surgeon even where no questions are asked, for he was addressing himself properly only to the case in hand where the surgeon himself reasonably believed not only that the operation was the patient's only hope of cure but also that the risk was minimal. This belief, though not universal among practitioners in his speciality, was shared at the date of the injury by his clinical senior and also by others of similar standing in his field. The case where the risk is more than slight, and the question as to what explanation is called for in the case of the truly elective operation, are both left open by the decision in *Bolam*.

If the risk involved in a proposed operation is more than slight and the patient's life is not in immediate danger if he does not undergo it, though possibly if he does not do so his expectation of life may be shortened or he may have to live the rest of his days under some serious disability, it would seem only proper that such operation should be regarded as an elective procedure involving free choice; and that the patient be given a simple and straightforward explanation of risks and consequences.

Where there is an immediate danger to life if the operation is not done, it might well be in keeping with medical practice and common sense not unduly to emphasise or, perhaps, even mention the risk. But it may equally be desirable, from an ethical and humane point of view, to explain sufficient to a patient who may be near death to give him opportunity of putting his affairs in order.

Duty to inform patient of risks in treatment: the modern law

Often referred to, unhelpfully, as a duty 'to obtain the patient's informed consent to treatment' is the duty of medical and other health care practitioners to explain to patients risks inherent even in careful treatment. The expression 'informed consent' has found its way into the medical and health care professional terminology of this country, largely owing to the adoption of a name given to a doctrine adopted by many states in the United States but which is unlikely to find its way into medicolegal relations in this country. The so-called obligation to obtain the 'informed consent' of a patient to medical or other treatment which is proposed is an obscure way of stating a duty incumbent on medical and other practitioners to explain to patients the risks or danger of adverse consequences of treatment, even if that treatment is given in the absence of such negligence as has been discussed in preceding chapters of this book. The duty to inform of inherent risks in careful treatment is as much a part of the doctor-patient relationship, and indeed of the relationship between patients and other health care professionals, as the duty to diagnose, advise and treat with reasonable care. It is the particular content of that duty, in terms of what should, and what need not, be explained by way of risks in proposed treatment which presents practical problems. It is only relatively recently that the English courts have addressed the question of what consequences of, or risks naturally occurring in, proposed treatment should be explained to a patient if the duty to take reasonable care in giving such information is to be discharged.

As recently as 1954 it was possible for Lord Justice Denning to say, in the case of *Hatcher v Black* (1954),[15] that deliberate misinformation given in order to reassure a patient before treatment was a legitimate course of action for a medical practitioner. He said: 'Some hold that it is never permissible to tell a lie even for a just cause: a good end, they say, does not justify a bad means. You must not do a little wrong in order to do a great right. Others, however, hold that it is permissible, if the justification is strong enough, and they point to the stratagems used in war to deceive the enemy.' In that case, a singer who was in fact contracted to the British Broadcasting Corporation was to undergo an operation to her thyroid, and was gratuitously assured prior to the operation that there was no risk to her vocal chords. In fact such a risk did exist, and in her particular case materialised in the form of injury to her voice. In a jury trial (such cases being conducted before juries in those days, but no longer) the doctor who volunteered to the patient the erroneous information was held not to have been in breach of a duty to take reasonable care.

The point of information-giving was raised in *Bolam v Friern Hospital Management Committee* (1957)[12] which was discussed earlier, in the context of acceptable practices. In another case involving a jury, Mr Justice McNair directed: 'Members of the jury, though it is a matter entirely for you, you may well think that when a doctor is dealing with a mentally sick man and has a strong belief that his only hope of cure is submission to electro-convulsive therapy, the doctor cannot be criticised if he does not stress the dangers, which he believes to be minimal, which are involved in that treatment.' No doubt this statement continues to represent English law as to the limits of the duty to inform of inherent risks in care and careful treatment, for two reasons. First, the patient in that particular case was mentally disordered, and this might (but would not necessarily) have affected his capacity to understand what was proposed. Second, the medical evidence in *Bolam v Friern Hospital Management Committee* was that the risk which in fact materialised was 'minimal' and would probably not now fall within the duty to explain the inherent risks in the treatment offered.

Even though other cases on the duty to inform of risks ('informed consent') have reached the Court of Appeal, and one has reached the House of Lords, the most useful and frequently quoted judicial authority on the duty to explain risks is the case of *Chatterton v Gerson* (1981).[16] The plaintiff who, after a hernia operation, suffered chronic and intractable pain in the area surrounding the operation scar was referred to the defendant, a specialist in the treatment of her condition. It was the defendant's practice to explain to patients the risks inherent in the treatment proposed. There was a conflict of evidence between the plaintiff patient and the doctor as to what precisely was explained prior to the treatment.

The plaintiff claimed damages from the defendant, alleging that he had not given her an explanation of the procedures to be performed and their implications so that she could make an informed decision whether to risk them. She alleged that the defendant had committed a trespass to her person (battery) since her consent to the operations was vitiated by the lack of prior explanation; and had been negligent in not giving an explanation as he was required to do as part of his duty to treat a patient with the degree of professional skill and care expected of a reasonably skilled medical practitioner.

The plaintiff failed in her action for the following reasons. First, it was held that in an action against the medical practitioner for trespass to the person (battery) based on alleged lack of consent to the treatment administered by the practitioner, the plaintiff must show that there has been a lack of real consent. Mr Justice Bristow held that once a patient has been informed in broad terms of the nature of the intended treatment and has consented, the patient cannot then say that there has been a lack of real consent. In such circumstances, an action in trespass to the person (battery) is not tenable.

Furthermore, the court ruled that a doctor is also required, as part of his duty of care to the patient, to explain what it is intended to do and the implications involved, in the way in which a responsible doctor in similar circumstances would do. If there is a real risk of misfortune inherent in the procedure, however well it is carried out, then the doctor's duty is to warn of the risk of such misfortunes.

Although this ruling was sufficient to dispose of the issue before the court in the particular case, two questions remained to be answered. First, what is a 'real risk'? And second, whose responsibility is it in law to decide upon the answer to that question?

In the case of *Sidaway v Bethlem Royal Hospital Governors* (1985)[17] the House of Lords addressed this question. Lord Scarman was alone in wishing to move from the test of duty and breach of duty laid down in *Bolam v Friern Hospital Management Committee* (1957) to the substitution of the 'prudent patient' test. He said:[18]

> 'I think that English law must recognise a duty of the doctor to warn his patient of risks inherent in the treatment which he is proposing; and especially so if the treatment be surgery. The critical limitation is that the duty is confined to material risks. The test of materiality is whether in the circumstances of the particular case the court is satisfied that a reasonable person in the patient's position would be likely to attach significance to the risk. Even if the risk be material, the doctor will not be liable if on a reasonable assessment of his patient's condition he takes the view that a warning would be detrimental to his patient's health.'

However, the other four Law Lords preferred a test of liability based squarely on the *Bolam* principle. They held that liability in respect of a doctor's duty to warn his patient of risks inherent in treatment recommended by him is the same as the test applicable to diagnosis and treatment, namely that the doctor is required to act in accordance with a practice accepted at the time as proper by a responsible body of medical opinion. Their decision means that English law does not recognise the American doctrine of informed consent based on the 'prudent patient' test. They nevertheless emphasised that although a decision as to what risks should be disclosed to a particular patient to enable him to make a rational choice whether to undergo the particular treatment recommended by a doctor is primarily a matter of clinical judgment, the disclosure of a particular risk of adverse consequences may be so obviously necessary for the patient to make an informed choice that no reasonably careful doctor would fail to disclose that risk.

The basis of the decision in *Chatterton v Gerson* (1981)[16] was that the real risks inherent in careful treatment ought to be revealed, under all normal circumstances, to a patient. The House of Lords in *Sidaway v Board of Governors of the Bethlem Royal Hospital* (1985)[17] took the principle a stage further by reference to factors which may weigh with a patient in wanting to know and with a doctor in choosing not to disclose. There is discernible in the speeches in the House of Lords in the *Sidaway* case, as well as in the arguments addressed to their Lordships in that case, a tension between the claim that the patient is entitled to know and therefore to choose and the necessity, in the interests of the patient and of the practitioner alike, that the proper treatment of the patient will not be complicated by taking his or her view upon matters on which the patient will or may not be able to form a proper view. The conclusion might be drawn from the judgments of the majority of their Lordships that the guiding principle is that of the acceptability of professional practice, though qualified in clear cases by matters of patient choice.

This tension came to a head in the New South Wales case of *Rogers v Whittaker* (1991).[19] The plaintiff, then aged 48, had been almost totally blind in her right eye from the age of nine, due to a penetrating injury which she received at that age. Her left eye was normal. The defendant, an ophthalmic surgeon, advised her that he could operate on her right eye to remove scar tissue and improve the sight in that eye. Given, no doubt, the fact that the plaintiff was well used to living with her condition, and that the proposed treatment was in all the circumstances clearly elective, she made clear to the doctor her desire for information. In particular, she said that she wanted to be warned of the possible consequences of the operation. She did not specifically ask the doctor whether the operation might damage the sight in her good eye. There was in fact a 1 in 14,000 chance of sympathetic ophthalmia consequent on the operation, but the defendant practitioner did not mention its existence. Had he done so, the plaintiff would not have accepted the risk and would not have consented to the proposed procedure. In the event, the plaintiff agreed to surgery and the operation was competently carried out. Sympathetic ophthalmia resulted, and she lost the sight of her left eye. Within two years she had become virtually totally blind.

The Supreme Court of New South Wales held, on appeal, that the trial judge had been correct in finding that the defendant had failed to exercise reasonable skill and care in answering the plaintiff's general question about possible complications when he failed to mention the admittedly low risk of sympathetic ophthalmia occurring in her good eye, leading to possible blindness. Mr Justice Mahoney summed up the patient's entitlement and the obligation of the doctor, as follows:[20]

> 'For myself, I think it should be clear that if a patient makes it plain to her medical practitioner that she desires to be told or warned of a particular thing, it is in principle a breach of duty by the medical practitioner not to tell her. There are, of course, obvious limits and qualifications to this. There are some questions to which the answer may be: "I do not know". There may be cases in which the condition of the patient, for example, in the emotional or the psychiatric sense, is such that there is a compelling medical reason why the answer should not be given. It is not necessary to pursue the circumstances in which this may be so. And there may be other reasons why it would not be a breach of duty for the answer not to be given, for example, the urgent need of treatment, the real likelihood of misunderstanding or failure to understand, and matters of that kind. But, in my opinion, the position remains in principle that subject to appropriate qualifications, the patient is entitled to be told what she asks to be told.'

The decision gives support to the view that a patient is not so much concerned with real risks as meaning the statistically assessed clinical risks involved in proposed treatment, as with the consequences to himself or herself from a particular treatment. If statistical risks tend to be associated with judicial expressions of the duty of medical practitioners to disclose real risks in treatment, then particular consequences to the individual are more closely connected with a right, or entitlement, to patient self-determination and the doctor's legal duty to recognise it. Particular support for this view is to be found in the judgment of Mr Justice Mahoney:

> 'I am conscious that other possible complications might involve serious consequences: she might, for example, die under a general anaesthetic. But, in the end, the reasonable person whose response is the test in law of these matters . . . would, I think, have expected that the response of her medical practitioner to her persistent enquiries would be to warn her of the complication apt to send her blind. That was the kind of complication which was peculiarly likely

to influence her judgment whether to undergo the procedures. The possibility of blindness was, in my opinion, peculiar and was something of which she, as a reasonable person, would have expected to be told.'

In the same case, Mr Justice Handley referred to the decision of the House of Lords in the *Sidaway* case, recalling that the opinions of the majority were that the question whether an omission to warn a patient of inherent risks in proposed treatment constitutes a breach of a doctor's duty of care is determined by the *Bolam* test. He pointed out, however, that in the *Sidaway* case itself there was no evidence that the patient asked a single question of the surgeon. He held, in consequence, that the view taken of the *Bolam* principle by the majority of their Lordships in the *Sidaway* case 'can have no direct application in the present case where the patient did ask questions and demonstrated a keen interest in the outcome of the suggested procedures'.

In effect, the decision of the Supreme Court of New South Wales in *Rogers v Whittaker* adds a necessary gloss to the interpretation of the *Bolam* principle in *Sidaway* similar to that added by *Blyth v Bloomsbury Health Authority* (1987) to the duty, expressed in *Sidaway*, to answer questions honestly and truthfully. The patient's entitlement to information should not, in other words, depend on asking the doctor the right questions. In this respect, Mr Justice Handley stated in *Rogers v Whittaker*:[21]

'I confess to being quite unable to appreciate how the respondent's request for information about possible complications did not require the appellant to advise her of this particular complication. I cannot accept that the standard of care required of the appellant by the law can be conclusively determined by the evidence given by some of the experts that only a direct question about possible complications to the good eye could call for any mention of the risk of sympathetic ophthalmia.'

Lord Templeman said in *Sidaway* that, when advising a patient about proposed or recommended treatment, a doctor is under a duty to provide the patient with the information necessary to enable that patient to make a balanced judgment in deciding whether to submit to the proposed treatment. That information includes a requirement to warn the patient of any dangers which are special in kind or magnitude, or special to the patient. The duty is, nevertheless, subject to the doctor's overriding duty to have regard for the best interests of the patient. It is therefore, according to Lord Templeman, for the doctor to decide what information should be given to the patient and the terms in which that information should be couched. It is suggested that Lord Templeman cannot be taken to have meant that 'ordinary' dangers, not 'special in kind or magnitude', need not be disclosed; for such dangers may be the most obvious of which warning should be given.

Furthermore, although Lord Templeman refers to a requirement to warn the patient of any dangers which are special to that patient, he nevertheless concludes that it is for the doctor to decide what information shall be given to the patient.

On the facts of the *Sidaway* case itself there was little or no conclusive evidence as to information or warning, if any, given by the doctor to the patient. For one thing, the matter had taken so long to come to trial that the doctor had in the interim died. As Lord Scarman pointed out, the lack of knowledge of the doctor's assessment of his patient reduced to some extent the guidance which the House of Lords could give for the assistance of judges in future cases. The plaintiff's allegations in the instant case could not be proved on the balance of probabilities simply by conjecture; and their Lordships were therefore left to generalise upon various hypotheses which may arise in communications between doctor and patient. Lord Bridge pointed out that, although the issue did not strictly arise in the instant appeal, when questioned specifically by a patient of apparently sound mind about risks involved in a particular treatment proposed, the doctor's duty must be to answer both truthfully and as fully as the questioner requires. This formulation apparently draws a dichotomy between the enquiring and the non-enquiring patient. Quite apart from ethical and social difficulties which this dichotomy may produce, it is a view from which the Court of Appeal decisively departed in *Blyth v Bloomsbury Health Authority* (1987) (p. 209, above). Although the House of Lords in the *Sidaway* case was not dealing with an enquiring patient, the refusal in *Blyth* to draw a distinction between enquiring and non-enquiring patients, and the duty expressed by Lord Bridge in *Sidaway* to answer questions both truthfully and as fully as the questioner requires, go a long way to explaining the statement in the Department of Health's Patient's Charter (1991)[22] on risks. Stating that 'every citizen has the following established National Health Service Rights' (the precise meaning of which is unclear, given that it is legal rights in general which are under consideration), the Patient's Charter states that there is a right 'to be given a clear explanation of any treatment proposed, including any risks and any alternatives, before you decide whether you will agree to the treatment'. Nevertheless, the position in English law appears to fall short of the wide statement in the Patient's Charter. Precisely how 'truthfully' a particular questioner requires the answer, or volunteered explanation, to be, appears still to be at least conditioned by the *Bolam* standard. It is suggested that, putting even the most favourable interpretation on the combined effect of *Sidaway* and *Blyth*, the categorical statement in the Patient's Charter appears to be somewhat in advance of the present state of English law.

Information and the doctor-patient relationship

There must be a balance between judicial regulation and professional independence. In professional standards, not least in the medical and other health care professions, the balance is struck by the *Bolam* principle: 'A doctor is not guilty of negligence if he has acted in accordance with a practice accepted as proper by a responsible body of medical men skilled in that particular art'.

A central point is whether the application of the *Bolam* principle involves the court handing over to the medical profession the whole question of what is acceptable, and thereby the whole question of what amounts to breach of duty in law. Nowhere has the fear that this might occur been more clearly expressed than in the judgment of CJC Laskin in the Canadian case of *Reibl v Hughes* (1981).[23] Instead, the court in that case robustly ruled that the matter of acceptable practice in disclosure and non-disclosure was in the final analysis a question for the 'trier of fact' (the court). In *Sidaway*, Lord Bridge, with whose judgment Lord Keith concurred, said that he did not understand how the *Bolam* test amounted to handing over questions of acceptability and therefore of standards of care to the medical profession. When two such eminent judges disagree on an elementary proposition, the only possible conclusion is that they have different perceptions of it.

In *Sidaway* Lord Bridge said: 'Broadly, a doctor's professional functions may be divided into three phases: diagnosis, advice and treatment'. He was speaking in the context of a case involving a particular condition and a particular treatment for it. He was therefore speaking of a case in which the doctor-patient relationship was already firmly established and well advanced into a state of patient dependence. He was not speaking of a case in which the doctor-patient relationship was hardly, if at all, advanced.

Clearly, there are a great many stages of a great many types of doctor-patient relationship.

The doctor-patient relationship advances by negotiation. The precise form taken by that negotiation will be affected by many factors. These include: the nature of the treatment, the gravity of the patient's condition, the intellect, understanding and resilience of the patient, the urgency of treatment, the availability of treatment, and alternatives within the range of treatment. The doctor-patient relationship is, as with all questions of the delivery of personal health care, a co-operative or at least reciprocal process.

Special skill, and the reliance which can reasonably be expected to be placed on it, assume increasing proportions as the relationship between doctor and patient (or individual aspects of it) advance. It is not so much a question of the doctor's duty of care not being divisible or susceptible of 'dissection'. It is, rather, a question of the weight to be given at each stage and in each aspect of the doctor-patient relationship to the expertise of the doctor, on the one hand, and the autonomy and choice of the patient, on the other. There is nothing in the *Bolam* decision itself to contradict this proposition.

Protecting the consenting patient

Given that a breach of duty to inform as to inherent risks is actionable in negligence, and given that liability in negligence requires that the breach of duty caused the injury or damage complained of, an important point relating to causation affects the outcome of the cases under discussion. The plaintiff must prove that he would not have agreed to the treatment, which has resulted in injury due to its inherent risk, being carried out had appropriate information about risk or consequences been given to him. In other words, if the patient would have elected to proceed with the treatment in any event, regardless of knowledge of the risk involved, then the plaintiff cannot show that the alleged breach of duty to inform was the cause of the injury. The injury, or adverse outcome of the treatment, will in such cases have been directly caused by the plaintiff patient's choice to proceed with the treatment.

However, damages have been awarded in cases where a patient would have proceeded with treatment involving a risk, but information or counselling relating to the possible adverse outcome of treatment has been improperly withheld. In the case of *Smith v Barking Havering and Brentwood Health Authority* (1988)[24] the plaintiff had undergone an operation to drain a cyst in her spinal cord and claimed damages for the failure of the health authority, through its employees, to warn of the risks inherent in the procedure or to afford her any opportunity to reach an informed decision as to whether to submit to it. On the particular facts of the case, the need for treatment being pressing, Mr Justice Hutchison concluded that the strong possibility was that the plaintiff would have agreed to the operation in any case. He held, however, that the plaintiff was entitled to damages of £3,000 for the shock and depression attributable to the failure by her doctors to warn her of the possible immediate onset of tetraplegia, which was a risk in the treatment and which in fact occurred.

Negligence and battery

Judges in this country have demonstrated a marked reluctance to hold a defendant medical practitioner liable in battery when what is alleged by an injured plaintiff is that risks or adverse consequences inherent even in careful treatment have not been disclosed. The cases establish that an alleged failure to volunteer, or to respond to an enquiry with, appropriate information as to risks and consequences, will be actionable in negligence and not battery. This is unsurprising, given the small risks in decided cases, and the fact that battery is also a crime. In the Canadian case of *Reibl v Hughes* (1981)[23] the risk of a stroke inherent in the proposed procedure (such risk being withheld from the patient) was no more than about 10 per cent. In the *Sidaway* case (1985)[17] the risk of the neurological damage, which in fact materialised, was between 1 and 2 per cent.

While in practical terms it is most unlikely that a practitioner would withhold from either an enquiring or non-enquiring patient a very substantial risk of, say, 20 or 30 per cent or even higher, the question arises: would inappropriate failure to disclose such a substantial risk be actionable in negligence only, or might an action in battery be appropriate as a form of action, either as well as or instead of the action in negligence? No doubt because of the practical unlikelihood of such a situation, there is no judicial decision in this country on the point. Were an action in battery to be appropriate, then the basis of liability would be that explained earlier in this chapter, in the discussion of the legal consequences of medical and other treatment given unwarrantedly and in the absence of consent.

7.2.4 Consent forms

The giving of consent to any proposed procedure or treatment involving physical contact prevents that contact from amounting to an unlawful battery. It thus avoids both civil liability to pay damages for trespass to the person, as well as a criminal offence against the person. It is the reality, or genuineness, of the consent which produces this legally requisite result. Nevertheless the practice has developed (and now predominates) that written evidence be obtained in respect of what may clinically be regarded as the more major or intrusive procedures. Surgery, anaesthetics and gynaecological procedures are the commonest and clearest examples. If a patient to whom a procedure involving physical contact is proposed cannot in fact genuinely consent, for whatever reason (including the effects of pre-medication) any written signature purporting to evidence consent is worthless and has no legal significance. It happens not to be clinical practice in most cases to obtain formal written consent to a great variety of lesser procedures, such as innoculation and the manipulation of limbs. Nevertheless, any treatment involving physical contact with the patient, however trivial, requires real consent. In very many cases the real agreement of the patient to treatment offered will be clearly implicit by conduct. Care must be taken in situations where the doctor or other practitioner regards a given treatment as 'routine', but the patient is not made sufficiently aware of this routine (which may be far from routine for him).

In its advice to members *Consent to Treatment* the Medical Defence Union[25] states that any doubt whether consent was truly given to a procedure occurring perhaps years ago may be resolved in favour of a plaintiff patient's evidence if no written independent evidence of consent can be produced in court. It is no disrespect to say that this advice (and indeed the very institution of consent forms) is defensive in nature. The Medical Defence Union states:

'The primary purpose of the consent form is to provide evidence that the patient gave consent to the procedure in question and that this was obtained with due care and formality.

The form should specify precisely the procedure envisaged. The defence societies have agreed with the Department of Health the wording of the multi-purpose consent form set out in the appendix to this booklet.

The form should be countersigned and dated by a medical practitioner who has explained the nature and purpose of the procedure. His name should also be identified in block capitals. If a junior countersigns the consent form, he must be someone who knows the hazards involved.

In general the MDU does not advise that it is necessary to record specific hazards on consent forms; but if an operation carries with it a material risk which the surgeon has expressly mentioned to the patient, it is prudent to record the fact in the clinical notes and in correspondence with the patient's GP. There is then a record of the explanation given to the patient should a query arise later.'

The consent forms should be kept in the patient's medical and nursing notes. A particular person in the treatment team should have the task of ensuring that a consent form has been completed in respect of any patient in the ward upon whom it is proposed to operate or to undertake any other procedure for which it is the practice to obtain consent in writing.

Exceptions, such as accident cases, will arise. Such exceptions should always be brought to the notice of the operating surgeon as a matter of course and, if there is any grave doubt as to the advisability of proceeding, referred to the most senior manager available. Failure to observe these elementary precautions might involve the surgeon and all who collaborated with him, as well as the health authority and the hospital, in a civil action for assault. If there were any unfortunate sequel to the operation, substantial damages might be awarded.

In September 1990 the Department of Health issued a guidance booklet entitled *A Guide to Consent for Examination or Treatment*, containing specimen forms of consent which are reproduced below, under cover of Circular HC(90)22.

The introduction in the Circular draws attention to a patient's fundamental right to grant or withhold consent prior to examination or treatment.

The guide covers important aspects of obtaining consent including the rights of the patient, the role of the health professional, some examples of treatments which have raised concern, and consent in cases where a patient is suffering from a mental disorder. An appropriately defensive note is struck by the Circular when it states:

'The guidance in the handbook reflects the common law rights of patients. Doctors and/or Health Authorities may face an action for damages if a patient is treated without consent. Where treatment carries substantial risks the patient must be advised of this by a doctor so that consent may be well-informed, and the doctor's advice must be formally recorded.'

Introducing the new forms the Minister for Health said:

'No longer do patients wish to be treated as passive recipients of health care: they are partners with the professionals in the promotion of their own health and well being. They expect to be involved in decisions about their own treatment.

These new forms are in plain English. Together with the guidance for health professionals that we have issued today, they emphasise patients' rights. The old consent forms, focusing on the legal and defensive aspects of obtaining consent, are out of date; they were too remote from the concerns of the patient.

Patients should feel confident that their wishes about their treatment will be respected. We want patients to understand the nature and purpose of their proposed treatment. Health professionals must realise that the signature on the consent form is *not* an end in itself.

These new forms are well laid out and easy to understand. They bring out the importance of the communication of information between health professional and patient. Obtaining a signature is relegated to its proper function as confirmation that this vital communication has taken place.'

There are four model consent forms: a general form for medical or dental investigations, treatment or operation; a form for use where a patient is undergoing sterilisation or vasectomy; a form for use by a health professional other than a doctor or dentist; and a form to record the decision taken when a patient suffering from mental disorder is unable to give consent. The first three of these will be available in a number of ethnic minority languages. The Department can supply translations of consent forms for copying locally, in the following languages: Bengali, Gujerati, Hindi, Punjabi, Urdu, Cantonese, Vietnamese, Turkish and Greek. The forms were slightly amended by HSG(92)32, for added clarity in practice.

CONSENT FORM   APPENDIX A (1)

For medical or dental investigation, treatment or operation

Health Authority . . . .   Patient's Surname . . . .

Hospital . . . .   Other Names . . . .

Unit Number . . . .   Date of Birth . . . .

                                            Sex: *(please tick)*   Male ☐   Female ☐

DOCTORS OR DENTISTS *(This part to be completed by doctor or dentist. See notes on the reverse)*

TYPE OF OPERATION INVESTIGATION OR TREATMENT FOR WHICH WRITTEN EVIDENCE OF CONSENT IS CONSIDERED APPROPRIATE

I confirm that I have explained the operation investigation or treatment, and such appropriate options as are available and the type of anaesthetic, if any (general/local/ sedation) proposed, to the patient in terms which in my judgement are suited to the understanding of the patient and/or to one of the parents or guardians of the patient

Signature . . . .   Date . . . ⁄ . . . . ⁄. . . .

Name of doctor or dentist . . . .

PATIENT/PARENT/GUARDIAN

1. Please read this form and the notes overleaf very carefully.
2. If there is anything that you don't understand about the explanation, or if you want more information, you should ask the doctor or dentist.
3. Please check that all the information on the form is correct. If it is, and you understand the explanation, then sign the form.

I am the patient/parent/guardian *(delete as necessary)*

I agree	■	to what is proposed which has been explained to me by the doctor/ dentist named on this form.
	■	to the use of the type of anaesthetic that I have been told about.
I understand	■	that the procedure may not be done by the doctor/dentist who has been treating me so far.
	■	that any procedure in addition to the investigation or treatment described on this form will only be carried out if it is necessary and in my best interests and can be justified for medical reasons.
I have told	■	the doctor or dentist about the procedures listed below I would *not* wish to be carried out without my having the opportunity to consider them first.

Signature   . . . .

Name   . . . .

Address   . . . .
(if not the patient)

CONSENT FORM   APPENDIX A (2)

For sterilisation or vasectomy

Health Authority . . . .   Patient's Surname . . . .

Hospital . . . .   Other Names . . . .

Unit Number . . . .   Date of Birth . . . .

                                            Sex: *(please tick)*   Male ☐   Female ☐

DOCTORS *(This part to be completed by doctor. See notes on the reverse)*

TYPE OF OPERATION: STERILISATION OR VASECTOMY

Complete this part of the form
I confirm that I have explained the procedure and any anaesthetic (general/local)
required, to the patient in terms which in my judgement are suited to his/her
understanding.

Signature . . . .   Date . . . *l* . . . . *l* . . .

Name of doctor . . . .

PATIENT

1. Please read this form very carefully.
2. If there is anything that you don't understand about the explanation, or if you want more information, you should ask the doctor.
3. Please check that all the information on the form is correct. If it is, and you understand the explanation, then sign the form.

I am the patient

I agree	■	to have this operation, which has been explained to me by the doctor named on this form.
	■	to have the type of anaesthetic that I have been told about.
I understand	■	that the operation may not be done by the doctor who has been treating me.
	■	that the aim of the operation is to stop me having any children and it might not be possible to reverse the effects of the operation.
	■	that sterilisation/vasectomy can sometimes fail, and that there is a very small chance that I may become fertile again after some time.
	■	that any procedure in addition to the investigation or treatment described on this form will only be carried out if it is necessary and in my best interests and can be justified for medical reasons.
I have told	■	the doctor about the procedures listed below I would *not* wish to be carried out straightaway without my having the opportunity to consider them first.
		. . . .
For vasectomy I understand	■	that I may remain fertile or become fertile again after some time.
	■	that I will have to use some other contraceptive method until 2 tests in a row show that I am not producing sperm, if I do not want to father any children.

Signature   . . . .

For treatment by a health professional other than doctors or dentists

Health Authority . . . .   Patient's Surname . . . .

Hospital . . . .   Other Names . . . .

Unit Number . . . .   Date of Birth . . . .

                                              Sex: *(please tick)*   Male □   Female □

HEALTH PROFESSIONAL *(This part to be completed by health professional. See notes on the reverse)*

TYPE OF TREATMENT PROPOSED FOR WHICH WRITTEN EVIDENCE OF CONSENT IS CONSIDERED APPROPRIATE

Complete this part of the form.

I confirm that I have explained the treatment proposed and such appropriate options as are available to the patient in terms which in my judgement are suited to the understanding of the patient and/or to one of the parents or guardians of the patient.

Signature . . . .   Date . . . *l* . . . . *l* . . . .

Name of health profesional . . . .

Job title of health professional . . . .

PATIENT/PARENT/GUARDIAN

1. Please read this form and the notes overleaf very carefully.

2. If there is anything that you don't understand about the explanation, or if you want more information, you should ask the health professional who has explained the treatment proposed.

3. Please check that all the information on the form is correct. If it is, and you understand the treatment proposed, then sign the form.

I am the patient/parent/guardian *(delete as necessary)*

I agree   ■   to what is proposed which has been explained to me by the health professional named on this form.

Signature   . . . .

Name   . . . .

Address   . . . .
(if not the patient)

Medical or dental treatment of a patient who is unable to consent because of mental disorder

Health Authority . . . .   Patient's Surname . . . .

Hospital . . . .   Other Names . . . .

Unit Number . . . .   Date of Birth . . . .

Sex: *(please tick)*   Male ☐   Female ☐

NOTE: It is the personal responsibility of any doctor or dentist proposing to treat a patient to determine whether the patient has capacity to give a valid consent.

It is good practice to consult relatives and others who are concerned with the care of the patient. Sometimes consultation with a specialist or specialists will be required.

The form should be signed by the doctor or dentist who carries out the treatment.

DOCTORS/DENTISTS

Describe investigation, operation or treatment proposed.

(Complete this part of the form)

In my opinion . . . .
is not capable of giving consent to treatment. In my opinion the treatment proposed is in his/her best interests and should be given.

The patient's next of kin have/have not been so informed. *(delete as necessary)*

Date: . . . .

Signature

. . . .

Name of doctor or dentist who is providing treatment:

. . . .

Further notes for guidance on the above Forms read:

Doctors

A patient has a legal right to grant or withhold consent prior to examination or treatment. Patients should be given sufficient information, in a way they can understand, about the proposed treatment and the possible alternatives. Patients must be allowed to decide whether they will agree to the treatment and they may refuse or withdraw consent to treatment at any time. The patient's consent to treatment should be recorded on this form (further guidance is given in HC(90)22 (*A Guide to Consent for Examination or Treatment.*)

Patients

■ The doctor is here to help you. He or she will explain the proposed procedure, which you are entitled to refuse. You can ask any questions and seek further information.

■ You may ask for a relative, or friend, or a nurse to be present.

■ Training health professionals is essential to the continuation of the health service and improving the quality of care. Your treatment may provide an important opportunity for such training, where necessary under the careful supervision of a senior doctor.

■ You may, however, decline to be involved in the formal training of medical and other students without this adversely affecting your care and treatment.
(Similar notes for dentists and other health professionals are given.)

On the standard form of consent the patient acknowledges that 'any procedure in addition to the investigation or treatment described on this form will only be carried out if it is necessary and in my best interests and can be justified for medical reasons'. Explaining this, the guidance booklet states:

'Consent given for one procedure or episode of treatment does not give any automatic right to undertake any other procedure. A doctor may, however, undertake further treatment if the circumstances are such that a patient's consent cannot reasonably be requested and provided the treatment is immediately necessary and the patient has not previously indicated that the further treatment would be unacceptable.'

If it is known or suspected at the outset that two or more procedures will be necessary, the form originally used might be appropriately amended. If requisite treatment involves two or more procedures separated in point in time the original consent form might suffice if the position is properly explained to the patient. Nevertheless, the patient is free at any time after the first part of the procedure has been carried out to withdraw consent to any further treatment. In such a case it would no doubt be part of the duty of care owed by the doctor or other practitioner in charge of the patient's treatment to explain any particular risks incurred or exacerbated by withdrawal of consent. It would also be prudent to obtain the patient's signed acknowledgment of this explanation. What the standard form of consent certainly does not refer to is any further treatment known or believed to be necessary but not found to be so during the course of the first procedure.

A somewhat more difficult situation from the hospital's point of view would arise, if say, valuable radium needles had been implanted and the patient would not submit to the procedure necessary for withdrawal. It would not be lawful to compel the patient to submit but it is suggested that, provided the patient had understood the nature of the implantation when he accepted it, he could be sued for damages if he refused to allow the hospital to recover the needles.

7.2.5 Removal of male organs and fashioning of artificial vagina

The removal of a patient's male organs and the fashioning of an artificial vagina, for therapeutic reasons, i.e. for the sake of his mental health and done with the consent of the patient is not illegal but the patient does not thereby become a female and subsequent 'marriage' will be null and void.

If the patient were married at the time he sought surgical intervention, it is questionable whether the operation should be undertaken without the consent of his wife: see *Bravery v Bravery* (1954)[26] even though for the sake of his mental health unless evidence of a psychiatrist were available that the effect on the patient's mental health of his not having it would be grave. *Corbett v Corbett* (1971)[27] was the first case in which an English court has been called on to pronounce on the sex of a male who has undergone such an operation. Mr Justice Ormrod, himself medically qualified, having referred to the various possible factors taken into account in determining sex in doubtful cases and which should be taken into account in deciding whether a 'sex-change' operation should be undertaken, reached the common sense conclusion that a person who has male primary sex organs is in law a male and does not become a female by having them removed and an artificial vagina substituted. The report is also interesting because a form of consent for such a 'sex-change' operation is there referred to. It reads as follows:

'I . . . of . . . do consent to undergo the removal of the male genital organs and the fashioning of an artificial vagina as explained to me by . . . (name of surgeon).

I understand it will not alter my male sex and that it is being done to prevent deterioration of my mental health.'

7.2.6   Hypnotism

Hypnotism not involving physical contact with the patient does not therefore attract the application of the law relating to assault and battery. The practice is, however, regulated by statute.

The Hypnotism Act 1952, which regulates the use of hypnotism for the purpose of entertainment, places no restriction on its use for medical and scientific purposes, section 5 providing as follows:

'Nothing in this Act shall prevent the exhibition, demonstration or performance of hypnotism (otherwise than at or in connection with an entertainment) for scientific or research purposes or for the treatment of physical or mental disease.'

Consequently it is lawful, with the patient's consent (which for evidential purposes should be obtained in writing), to use hypnotism for producing anaesthesia or otherwise for the purpose of treatment. Whether or not it is lawful to use hypnotism for any such purpose without the patient's consent remains an open question.

The question of when consent to an operation or other procedure is unnecessary or when the consent of some person other than the patient is required or suffices is discussed elsewhere in this chapter. The position would be the same in respect of use of hypnotism if, ordinarily, the patient's consent is necessary.

7.2.7   Breath tests and samples of blood and urine under the Police and Criminal Evidence Act 1984

Under section 62(II) of the Act, preserving sections 7 and 8 of the Road Traffic Act 1972, a constable in uniform may require a driver in hospital after a road accident to take a breath test and to provide a specimen of blood or urine. 'Hospital' here means an institution which provides medical or surgical treatment for in-patients or out-patients. It does not include an ambulance: *Hollingsworth v Howard* (1974).[28] See further Chapter 1, pp. 1–4, above on the meaning of 'hospital'.

The doctor in immediate charge of the case, including an out-patient case[29] must be told of the procedure and its consequences[30] and must agree to the tests being carried out.[31] This applies where a police officer makes a request for a breath test before the patient reaches the hospital but the request is not complied with until after he gets there. This would include, e.g., a houseman treating a patient in 'casualty' or on admission to a ward at night, even though – in hospital parlance – it would probably not be 'his' patient but rather the patient of the consultant under whom he worked. There is no objection to his agreeing to both tests at once[32] and a *pro forma* is available from the police for this purpose.[33]

If the patient is discharged from the hospital, the 'hospital' procedure does not apply and the police must follow normal practice.[34] This applies even if the motorist absconds from the hospital before being asked to provide the specimens. But if he absconds deliberately he may be guilty of obstructing the police in the execution of their duties.[35] It also applies where, although the patient is still in the hospital, the treatment has been given and he is leaving.[36]

If the doctor objects to the procedure as prejudicial to the proper care or treatment of the patient it may not be carried out. Tests themselves may not be made on a patient, nor any specimen taken from him, without his consent; nor may they be made on or taken from an unconscious patient. If a constable erroneously but honestly and reasonably believes that the patient (driver) can hear and understand he can be convicted.[37] 'Consent', in the true sense, is a matter entirely between the patient and the constable. Hospital staff are not required to take part in taking specimens nor is hospital equipment to be used in the tests. A patient in hospital is not liable to arrest without warrant under the 1984 Act, nor can he be required to go elsewhere to give specimens of breath, blood or urine.

Circular HM(67)64 advised on procedures to be adopted by hospitals and their staff in respect of blood specimens following an accident. The advice still holds good under the current legislation relating to blood specimens and is as follows:

'[The Act] makes it an offence to drive with a proportion of alcohol in the blood exceeding the prescribed limit and enables the police in certain circumstances to require drivers to provide specimens of breath for breath tests and of blood or urine for laboratory tests. When following a road accident a driver is at a hospital as a patient the Act enables the police to require him to provide specimens for these tests while he is at the hospital, provided the doctor in immediate charge of the case does not object on the grounds that this would be prejudicial to the proper care or treatment of the patient. It is not intended that the police should seek to invoke these provisions of the Act in every case of a driver suspected of having been drinking who is at a hospital as a patient after an accident, for example a patient who is seriously injured or ill; on the other hand, a driver who has an accident after he has been drinking should not necessarily escape the provisions of the Act simply because he is at a hospital.

2. The procedure, so far as it may affect a driver who is at a hospital as a patient, whether an in-patient or an out-patient, following an accident, is given in greater detail in the following paragraphs. Apart from the need for the hospital doctor in immediate charge of the patient to be notified of the proposal to require provision of a specimen and his power to object, hospital staff will not be involved in the taking of the specimens or their evaluation for the purposes of the Act. Specimens of breath and urine will be taken by a police constable and specimens of blood by a police doctor and the laboratory tests will be carried out in forensic science laboratories. The necessary equipment for breath tests and for the taking of specimens of blood and urine will be provided by the police. There is no provision in the Act for the taking of urine specimens by catheter.

Breath test
3. Section [8(2)(b)] of the Act provides that where a driver is at a hospital as a patient following a road accident a constable in uniform may require him to take

a breath test at the hospital, but the requirement is not to be made if the doctor in immediate charge of the case is not first notified of the proposal to make the requirement or if he objects on the grounds that the provision of a specimen of breath or the requirement to provide it would be prejudicial to the proper care or treatment of the patient. Tests may not be made on a patient without his consent, nor on an unconscious patient.

4. The notification by the constable and any objection by the doctor would both normally be given orally.

5. The doctor in immediate charge of the case would be the doctor attending the patient. If he is in any doubt whether or not to object he can consult his senior. The grounds on which he can object are wide enough to enable him to object on the grounds that the test would interfere with the examination, diagnosis or treatment of the patient as well as that it would be likely to be detrimental to the patient's health.

6. The doctor may object on the above grounds at the beginning or at a later stage, having first not objected; if he objects at any stage before the specimen has been provided, the constable may not proceed. The breath test will be taken at the hospital and a person at a hospital as a patient may not be required to go elsewhere to take the test, nor under the provisions of section [8(4) or 8(5)] of this Act will he be subject to arrest without warrant, unless and until he is no longer at hospital as a patient.

Laboratory tests

7. Section [9(2)] provides that a person at a hospital as a patient may be required by a constable to provide a specimen for a laboratory test if he has been required to take a breath test after an accident, whether at the hospital or elsewhere, and either the test is positive or he fails or refuses to take it and the constable has reasonable cause to suspect him of having alcohol in his body. On making the requirement the constable must, in accordance with section [9(7)], warn the person that failure to provide a specimen may make him liable to a penalty.

8. As in the case of a breath test, the constable must first notify the doctor in immediate charge of the case of the proposal to require a person to provide a specimen and the doctor has the same power to object on the same grounds as in the case of a breath test, and also on the grounds that the warning would be prejudicial to the proper care or treatment of the patient.

9. If the doctor offers no objection to the taking of specimens for a laboratory test the procedure will be as follows:

    i.   the person will first be requested to provide a specimen of blood. This may be taken only with his consent and by a police doctor, and will be a very small quantity of capillary blood;

    ii.   if he refuses to provide a specimen of blood he will be asked to provide two specimens of urine within an hour;

    iii.   if he refuses or fails to provide two specimens of urine within an hour he will be offered another chance to provide a specimen of blood.

10. What is said in paragraphs 4, 5 and 6 above applies also to laboratory tests.

Specimens may not be taken from a patient without his consent nor from an unconscious patient.

General

11. The Home Office will be advising Chief Police Officers that they may consider it useful to discuss the arrangements generally with the hospital authorities in their areas in advance of the Act coming into force, approaching Regional Hospital Boards and Boards of Governors in the first instance. Detailed discussions will be needed between the police and individual hospitals. Hospital authorities are asked to co-operate in these discussions and to bring into them such administrative, medical and nursing staff as may be appropriate.

12. The following points should be made known to all medical staff concerned:

i.   Under the Act a patient at a hospital is not liable to arrest without warrant, nor can he be required to go elsewhere to give the specimens of breath, blood or urine.

ii.   Specimens may not be taken from a patient without his consent, and a specimen may not be taken from an unconscious patient or by catheterisation.

iii.   The constable must notify the doctor in immediate charge of the case of the intention to require a patient to provide a specimen and the doctor may object at any stage before a specimen has been provided if he considers that such action would be prejudicial to the proper care or treatment of the patient. He may also object to the patient being told of the requirement to provide a specimen, or warned of the penalty.

iv.   Members of the hospital staff are not required to take part in the taking of specimens or in their evaluation, although the hospital is requested to arrange conditions of privacy under which patients may provide specimens.

v.   Hospital equipment will not be used in the tests.

Subject to the overriding consideration of the medical interest of patients the Minister trusts that hospital authorities and staff will co-operate with the police when action is taken under the Act.

13. Hospital authorities are asked to bring this memorandum to the notice of all staff likely to be concerned, particularly the medical staff of accident and emergency departments.'

7.2.8   Accident cases and other emergency patients: views of relatives

Sometimes it is possible in these cases to obtain the usual consent before commencing treatment. But sometimes the patient is either unconscious or so affected by his physical condition as to be unable either to consent or to object. Then, if the operation is urgently necessary to save the patient's life or to reduce grave pain, or for his ultimate well-being (in cases such as the saving of a limb), it is ordinarily carried out with the consent of the husband or wife or of the nearest relative immediately available. But if even that consent is unobtainable there is no alternative but to operate. If what is done is reasonable in the circumstances, no legal action against the surgeon or the hospital is likely to succeed.

What if the spouse or nearest relative refuses to sign a form of consent? Such refusal may well be accompanied by what purports to be a positive prohibition on the proposed procedure being carried out. The refusal may be more limited but still fundamental (relating, for instance, to a blood transfusion). Such refusals are sometimes on religious grounds and may or may not include an assertion that it is the patient's view which is being expressed.

There are no established legal grounds on which any relative has the right to refuse to allow an adult patient to receive necessary medical treatment. Therefore if, on refusing consent, the spouse or near relative of the patient does not purport to be expressing the patient's own wishes, the refusal or purported prohibition might safely be ignored. But if the spouse or near relative purports to be conveying what he believes to be the patient's own wishes, a more difficult situation arises.

If a procedure is necessary in order to attempt to save life, or similarly, to prevent serious disablement or suffering, it should probably still be carried out despite objection by a spouse or relative, even if he purports to be expressing what he believes would be the patient's wishes. This is because there is no certainty that if the patient were told, 'Either you have this procedure carried out or you will be in danger of almost certain death', he would refuse his consent to the advised procedure.

Cases of express refusal, or known objection, to treatment on the part of a competent adult patient are discussed below.

7.2.9 Objection to blood transfusion

Clear and unequivocal wishes expressed by a patient should be heeded. Although there may well be a duty on the doctor to rehearse the possible outcome of an operation potentially involving transfusion so that the patient can make a fully informed choice about an elective procedure, it is not the function of a doctor to seek to impose moral attitudes on a patient. Doctors should remember that an unconsented-to transfusion may also constitute a criminal assault on the patient.

In its advice to members entitled *Consent to Treatment* (1989) the Medical Defence Union specifically addresses the question of refusal of blood transfusion in the case of Jehovah's Witnesses:

'**Adults**

A doctor has a duty to treat to the best of his ability all patients for whom he has a contractual or ethical responsibility. If a patient imposes certain conditions on the recommended treatment, the doctor can refuse to treat the patient, provided either that no harm results to the patient or that there is a colleague available to take over the patient's care.

Although a surgeon may be restricted by the refusal of a

Jehovah's Witness to permit a blood transfusion, the surgeon cannot refuse essential treatment, for instance the removal of a malignant tumour, if he is the only suitably qualified person available. If another practitioner willing to treat the patient cannot be found, the following procedure should be adopted.

1. The patient should be interviewed by the physician or surgeon in the presence of a witness and, if felt desirable, a close relative or the religious adviser. He should be given an account of the benefits of the treatment or operation as well as the hazards which may be encountered if he refuses a blood transfusion. An attempt should be made to help him to understand the reasoning behind the physician's or surgeon's recommendation.
2. If the patient remains adamant, he should be asked to acknowledge in writing the fact that, although he has been warned that during the course of his treatment or operation he may require a blood transfusion, he is nevertheless unwilling to give his consent.
3. The patient's signature to the statement should be witnessed by the doctor and by the witness who was present at the interview.
4. If the patient cannot sign a written statement, his oral refusal should be recorded in the clinical notes and countersigned by the witness.

Children

Although the administration of a blood transfusion to a child in opposition to the parents' wishes may constitute in law a technical assault, a doctor should not allow this to override his duty of care to the child. If a blood transfusion is deemed necessary to save the life of, or prevent harm to a child, a doctor should act in the best interests of the child.

The following precautions are advisable:

1. The doctor should obtain a supporting opinion in writing from a colleague.
2. If time permits he should, in the presence of a medical colleague, discuss the situation fully with the parents, explaining as clearly and precisely as possible the nature and purpose of the treatment proposed and the risks to the child if it is not given.
3. If the parents still refuse, a record of their refusal should be made in the case notes and this should be signed by the doctor and his colleague. If the doctor does administer the blood transfusion, the note recording the parents' refusal is evidence that they were warned of the danger to their child.

It is not generally considered necessary to apply to a magistrate to remove the child from its parents' custody so that necessary consent can be given by the person to whom the child's care is entrusted.'

Despite the fact that treatment such as an emergency blood transfusion may be necessary to save life or to prevent grave permanent injury, treatment in the face of a clear and known refusal may amount to a battery against the patient. In the Canadian case of *Malette v Schulman* (1990)[38] it was held to be an assault to administer a blood transfusion to a Jehovah's Witness who carried a donor card stating clearly that no transfusion was to be administered.

The plaintiff, a Jehovah's Witness aged 57, was seriously injured in a road accident and was admitted unconscious to hospital. A card was found in her purse requesting that no blood be administered 'under any circumstances'. Although aware of the card, the doctor in charge of her emergency care personally administered blood transfusions which he considered therapeutically necessary to save her life. It was held by the Ontario Court of Appeal that the card imposed a valid restriction on the emergency treatment which could lawfully be provided to the plaintiff. So far as concerns society's interest in the preservation of life, Mr Justice Robins said:[39]

'The state's interest in preserving the life or health of a competent patient must generally give way to the patient's stronger interest in directing the course of her own life . . . there is no law prohibiting a patient from declining necessary treatment or prohibiting a doctor from honouring the patient's decision. To the extent that the law reflects the state's interest, it supports the right of individuals to make their own decisions. By imposing civil liability on those who perform medical treatment without consent even though the treatment may be beneficial, the law serves to maximise individual freedom of choice. Recognition of the right to reject medical treatment cannot, in my opinion, be said to depreciate the interest of the state in life or in the sanctity of life. Individual free choice and self-determination are themselves fundamental constituents of life. To deny individuals freedom of choice with respect to their health care can only lessen, and not enhance, the value of life. This state interest, in my opinion, cannot properly be invoked to prohibit Mrs Malette from choosing for herself whether or not to undergo blood transfusions.'

Referring to the legitimate interest of the medical profession in upholding its own professional ethic to care and to treat, Mr Justice Robins added:

'Safeguarding the integrity of the medical profession is patently a legitimate state interest worthy of protection. However, I do not agree that this interest can serve to limit a patient's right to refuse blood transfusions. I recognise, of course, that the choice between violating a patient's private convictions and accepting her decision is hardly an easy one for members of a profession dedicated to aiding the injured and preserving life. The patient's right to determine her own medical treatment is, however, paramount to what might otherwise be the doctor's obligation to provide needed medical care.

The doctor is bound in law by the patient's choice even though that choice may be contrary to the mandates of his own conscience and professional judgment. If patient choice were subservient to conscientious medical judgment, the right of the patient to determine her own treatment . . . would be rendered meaningless. Recognition of a Jehovah's Witness' right to refuse blood transfusions cannot, in my opinion, be seen as threatening the integrity of the medical profession or the state's interest in protecting the same.'

In the English case of *Re T* (*adult: refusal of medical treatment*) (1992),[40] Lord Justice Staughton made it clear that English law on the point is exactly the same:

'An adult whose mental capacity is unimpaired has the right to decide for herself whether she will or will not receive medical or surgical treatment, even in circumstances where she is likely or even certain to die in the absence of treatment. Thus far the law is clear. The difficulty arises when it is uncertain whether or not the competent adult (as I call her for brevity) does or does not consent to the proposed treatment.'

On the particular facts of *Re T*, there existed some doubt as to the precise views and intentions of the patient. She had been injured in a car accident when 34 weeks pregnant. She was admitted to hospital, and the possibility arose of her requiring a blood transfusion. The patient's mother was a Jehovah's Witness, but the patient herself was not a member of that sect. Following a private conversation with her mother, the patient told the staff nurse that she used to belong to a religious sect which believed blood transfusion to be a sin and a bar to eternal salvation, and that she still maintained some beliefs of the sect and did not want a blood transfusion. Shortly afterwards she went into labour, and because of her distressed physical condition it was decided that a Caesarian section should be performed. Following a further conversation, alone, with her mother the patient again informed medical staff that she did not want a blood transfusion. She was told that other solutions to expand the blood could be used in such a procedure and that blood transfusions are not often necessary following an operation for Caesarian section. The patient then blindly signed a form of refusal of consent to blood transfusion, but it was not explained to her that it might be necessary to give a blood transfusion to save her life. After undergoing an emergency Caesarian section operation, her condition deteriorated and she was transferred to an intensive care unit. The consultant anaesthetist in the unit would normally have unhesitatingly administered a blood transfusion, but felt inhibited in doing so in the light of the patient's expressed wishes.

Her father and boyfriend applied to the court for assistance and, following an emergency hearing, the judge authorised the administration of a blood transfusion, declaring that despite the absence of her consent such transfusion appeared manifestly to be in her best interests. At a second hearing, the judge held that she had neither consented to, nor refused, a blood transfusion in the emergency that had arisen; and that it was accordingly lawful for doctors to treat her in whatever way they considered, in the exercise of their clinical judgment, to be in her best interests. Concluding the matter, the Court of Appeal held that, on the facts, the doctors had been justified in disregarding the patient's instructions and administering a blood transfusion to her as a matter of necessity to save her life.

The evidence showed that she had not been fit to make a genuine decision because of her medical condition, and in particular that she had been subjected to the undue influence of her mother, which in the circumstances vitiated her decision to refuse a blood transfusion. As to the role of close relatives and next of kin, the Court of Appeal said that to seek the consent of the next of kin is not an undesirable practice, provided the interests of the patient will not be adversely affected by any consequential delay. Nevertheless, the next of kin of a patient who is normally physically and mentally capable of exercising a choice, but who is not in a position to make such a decision because, for instance, of unconsciousness, have no legal right either to consent or to refuse to medical treatment on behalf of the patient. Their Lordships ruled that if, in a potentially life-threatening situation or one in which irreparable damage to the patient's health can be anticipated, doctors or provider units are faced with a refusal by an adult patient to accept essential treatment and they have real doubts as to whether that refusal is valid, they should seek a judicial declaration as to the lawfulness of the proposed treatment. It should not, said the court, be left to the patient's family to take action. In passing, the court advised that the standard forms of refusal to accept a blood transfusion used by hospitals should be redrafted in order to separate the disclaimer of legal liability on the part of the hospital from the declaration by the patient of his decision not to accept a blood transfusion. The object of this would be to bring the possible consequences of refusal of a transfusion forcibly to the attention of the patient.

The case of *Re S (adult: refusal of medical treatment)* (1992)[41] involved significantly different, and additional, considerations. A 30-year-old woman had been admitted to hospital with ruptured membranes and in spontaneous labour with her third pregnancy. She was six days overdue beyond the expected date of birth, but refused on religious grounds to consent to an emergency Caesarian section operation which was advised.

The surgeon in charge of the patient was emphatic that the operation was the only means of saving the life of the patient and that of her unborn child, who could not be born alive if the operation was not performed. The health authority applied for a declaration to authorise the surgeons and staff of the hospital to carry out the emergency Caesarian section operation. Sir Stephen Brown, President of the Family Division, held that the court would exercise its inherent jurisdiction to authorise the surgeons and staff of the hospital to carry out the operation on the patient, given that the operation was vital to protect the life of the unborn child.

The court granted a declaration that such an operation, together with any necessary consequential treatment which the hospital and its staff proposed to perform on the patient, was in the vital interests of the patient and of her unborn child; and that such treatment could be lawfully performed in spite of the patient's refusal to consent to the operation. His Lordship said that the evidence showed that the court was concerned with a question of 'minutes rather than hours' and that it was a situation of life and death.

Given the extreme urgency with which the court considered the question, the report of *Re S* contains little by way of critical argument or detailed factual circumstances underlying such argument. Nevertheless, accepting the capacity of the patient to refuse the Caesarian section operation, the words of Lord Justice Donaldson in *Re T* (above) are instructive, albeit from a rather different context:[42]

'It is well established that in the ultimate the right of the individual is paramount, that this merely shifts the problem where the conflict occurs and calls for a very careful examination of whether, and if so the way in which, the individual is exercising that right. In case of doubt, that doubt falls to be resolved in favour of the preservation of life, for if the individual is to over-ride the public interest he must do so in clear terms.'

By analogy, the 'public interest' in the life of the unborn child in *Re S* was no doubt taken by the court in that case to be a valid object of attention in the public interest. Sadly, in the event, the child of S was stillborn.

7.3 MINORS

A person reaches full age at 18. For legal reasons it is necessary to distinguish minors who have attained the age of 16 from those who have not. Section 8 of the Family Law Reform Act 1969 provides that a minor who has reached 16 can, to the same extent as a person of full age, give real consent to surgical, medical and dental treatment. Section 9 states that a particular age is reached at the start of a birthday.

7.3.1 Minors who have reached 16

Any doubt whether a person who had attained the age of 16 and who needed surgical, medical or dental treatment may himself give consent thereto was finally removed by section 8 of the Family Law Reform Act 1969:

'8.(1)—The consent of a minor who has attained the age of sixteen years to any surgical, medical or dental treatment which, in the absence of consent, would constitute a trespass to his person, shall be as effective as it would be if he were of full age; and where a minor has by virtue of this section given an effective consent to any treatment it shall not be necessary to obtain any consent for it from his parent or guardian.

(2) In this section "surgical, medical or dental treatment" includes any procedure undertaken for the purposes of diagnosis, and this section applies to any procedure (including, in particular, the administration of an anaesthetic) which is ancillary to any treatment as it applies to that treatment.'

This provision covers any necessary medical or surgical attention to a pregnant unmarried girl who has reached the age of 16, whether or not such help is in respect of a normal delivery.

The question whether, in such a case or any other, it is permissible without the consent of the patient to communicate with the parents of a patient between the ages of 16 and 18 is raised in Chapter 16.

What the section apparently does not cover is consent by the minor to the use of his body for purposes of experimentation or research. As to the use of patients and others, including minors, whether patients or volunteers, and on the general question of consent to any such use, see later in this chapter.

The possibility of parental consent as an alternative to consent by the minor himself is preserved by the Act. Section 8(3) provides:

'(3) Nothing in this section shall be construed as making ineffective any consent which would have been effective if this section had not been enacted.'

If treatment to which a minor had himself refused consent were such that his co-operation, or willing submission, were necessary to its success, parental consent would be practically useless. But there are other circumstances in which such consent would afford cover for a procedure to which the minor had refused his consent or to which he was unable to give it, e.g. the administration of a blood transfusion during an operation or a therapeutic abortion to save the life of a young girl or any other operation necessary to attempt to save life or prevent permanent disability. There could also be circumstances, such as an elective operation, not being a matter of extreme urgency, when the surgeon might think it desirable that the minor should have the advice of a parent or guardian in reaching a decision and so might indicate to the minor that (assuming the parent or guardian were available) their consent was required. But the absence of such consent would not be a defence in an action by a minor who had suffered harm because necessary treatment which he was willing to undergo had been withheld. In any case in which parental consent might be appropriate, either mother or father could ordinarily give that consent without the other.

Another interpretation of subsection (3) is that it does no more than to preserve the right of a minor under 16 years of age, if capable of understanding what he is doing, himself to give consent to operative or other treatment. Read literally, section 8(3) is apt to cover both cases.

What is clear is that no parent of a minor who has reached the age of 16 can veto any treatment, whether necessary or only desirable, which the minor is willing to accept.

The case of *Re W (a minor) (medical treatment)* (1992)[43] concerned a 16-year-old girl who was under local authority care. She suffered from anorexia nervosa so severely that she was admitted to a specialist adolescent residential unit, where her condition so deteriorated that the consultant psychiatrist in charge of the unit proposed to move her to a hospital specialising in the treatment of eating disorders. W, the patient, wished to stay where she was and to cure herself when she decided it was right to do so. She refused to move to the hospital. The local authority applied to the court under section 100(3) and (4) of the Children Act 1989 for a direction that it be at liberty to place W in the hospital for treatment, and that W be given medical treatment for her condition without her consent if that became necessary. The judge at first instance exercised the inherent jurisdiction of the court over a minor and made the order which the local authority sought. Upholding the order, the Court of Appeal stated that the court may, in the child's own best interests objectively considered, override the wishes even of a child who has sufficient intelligence and understanding to make an informed decision but who refuses treatment which may lead to death or severe injury. Neverthless, before exercising that jurisdiction, the court should carefully examine the specific wishes of the minor in question.

Making a point of general application, Lord Donaldson said that the effect of section 8 of the Family Law Reform Act 1969, enabling a minor aged 16 or over to consent to treatment, is only one way in which consent may validly be given. The court may itself give permission for the treatment to be administered, either in wardship proceedings or in proceedings such as those involved in the instant case; or consent may be given by a parent or someone with parental responsibility for the minor.

It is therefore apparent that the general principle used by the courts in relation to the treatment of minors is that consent will somehow be found: if not from the minor, then from a parent or someone with parental responsibility, and if not from a parent, then by the court, either in wardship proceedings or in the exercise of its inherent jurisdiction over minors.

7.3.2 Minors who have not reached 16

A child who is not yet 16 is subject to 'parental responsibility' within the meaning of the Children Act 1989. The term 'parental responsibilities' is defined broadly in the Act as meaning 'all the rights, duties, powers, responsibility and authority which by law a parent of a child has . . .'. Any interference with the child's body by medical or surgical treatment without parental consent or other lawful justification may give grounds for an action for trespass to the person of the child. Section 8(3) of the Family Law Reform Act 1969 may reasonably be interpreted as preserving the right of a child under the age of 16 who understands the nature and likely effects of the proposed treatment to consent to it. The more complex or serious the proposed procedure, the greater the degree of understanding that is required.

If by 'treatment' is meant treatment immediately necessary for relieving present pain and suffering; for preventing or alleviating pain and suffering foreseen as an immediate consequence of the child's condition; for averting or minimising any permanent disability; for reducing the prospect of a shortened life; for saving life, or attempting to do any of those things, it can be accepted that if the child has sufficient understanding of what he is doing, his consent is sufficient. But if the child objected to having such treatment and it were practicable to give it without his active co-operation, a medical or dental practitioner, whether in hospital or elsewhere, could probably lawfully undertake that treatment on the basis of the duty of care owed by a practitioner to his patient. But treatment which, though necessary, was not immediately necessary or which, although desirable, was not necessary (such as, for instance, certain cosmetic surgery) should ordinarily be undertaken only with parental consent.

For this purpose parental consent includes that of a lawfully appointed guardian (for which see sections 5 and 6 of the Children Act 1989). It would be under all normal circumstances most unwise to proceed with treatment of a child mature enough to give a comprehending refusal to be treated. Thus if a girl under 16 refuses an abortion, her parents cannot compel her to have it, provided she understands the nature of the operation which she is refusing and also the consequences of bearing the child. The comments made earlier on blood transfusions and other treatments attracting moral or other personal objections should be recalled here also (see pp. 237–238).

The law relating to parental responsibility for children is governed by section 2 of the Children Act 1989, the relevant parts of which, for present purposes, are as follows:

2.—(1) Where a child's father and mother were married to each other at the time of his birth, they shall each have parental responsibility for the child.

(2) Where a child's father and mother were not married to each other at the time of his birth—

(a) the mother shall have parental responsibility for the child;

(b) the father shall not have parental responsibility for the child, unless he acquires it in accordance with the provisions of this Act.

(5) More than one person may have parental responsibility for the same child at the same time.

(6) A person who has parental responsibility for a child at any time shall not cease to have that responsibility solely because some other person subsequently acquires parental responsibility for the child.

(7) Where more than one person has parental responsibility for a child, each of them may act alone and without the other (or others) in meeting that responsibility; but nothing in this Part shall be taken to affect the operation of any enactment which requires the consent of more than one person in a matter affecting the child.

(8) The fact that a person has parental responsibility for a child shall not entitle him to act in any way which would be incompatible with any order made with respect to the child under this Act.

(9) A person who has parental responsibility for a child may not surrender or transfer any part of that responsibility to another but may arrange for some or all of it to be met by one or more persons acting on his behalf.

(10) The person with whom any such arrangement is made may himself be a person who already has parental responsibility for the child concerned.

(11) The making of any such arrangement shall not affect any liability of the person making it which may arise from any failure to meet any part of his parental responsibility for the child concerned.'

It is not apparently necessary for the hospital or practitioner to inquire whether the other parent, whether father or mother, knows what is proposed to be done, though one can envisage circumstances in which, unless the treatment were urgently necessary, it would be sensible to make sure that both parents were in the picture. This could be so in the case of an elective operation not immediately necessary, being one of which a successful outcome was by no means certain, even leaving aside unforeseen accidents. The position which might arise if the father and mother were known to disagree on a particular course of action, one consenting, the other objecting, is discussed later.

Under section 8 of the Children Act 1989 the court may make a variety of orders with respect to children. One such order is called a 'specific issue order', meaning an order giving directions for the purpose of determining a specific question which has arisen, or which may arise, in connection with any aspect of parental responsibility for a child. A 'child' is defined generally for the purposes of the Act as a person under the age of 18. Section 9, however, specifically provides that:

'(6) No court shall make any section 8 order which is to have effect for a period which will end after the child has reached the age of sixteen unless it is satisfied that the circumstances of the case are exceptional.

(7) No court shall make any section 8 order, other than one varying or discharging such an order, with respect to a child who has reached the age of sixteen unless it is satisfied that the circumstances of the case are exceptional.'

A specific issue order could be made in order for a particular doctor to decide whether a particular proposed treatment was indicated, or to determine how certain treatment should be carried out. It would be for the court to decide how specific or otherwise to make the question put to such a practitioner; but it is unlikely that a specific issue order would fetter the exercise of professional judgment as to the technique to be adopted.

When a child is in the care of a local authority that authority assumes parental responsibility (Children Act 1989, section 33) and may give consent for appropriate treatment. A lawful guardian may also consent to medical treatment on a minor in his charge. As to a child under 16 who, at the time when treatment is considered to be required, is in the care of an adult other than a parent, and parental consent is either unobtainable or at least not obtainable in time for treatment to be given, the consent of such other person should, if practicable, be obtained. Section 3(5) of the Children Act 1989 provides as follows:

'(5) A person who—
    (a)   does not have parental responsibility for a particular child; but
    (b)   has care of the child,
may (subject to the provisions of this Act) do what is reasonable in all the circumstances of the case for the purpose of safeguarding or promoting the child's welfare.'

It will no doubt be reasonable for a person caring for a child whose parents are away to arrange emergency medical or other treatment, though not elective treatment at least which is of any major kind. No doubt the requirement of reasonableness would indicate the involvement of the natural parents if they were known or thought to hold particular views on medical treatment or certain types of treatment. It is questionable whether even a foster parent would have the authority to refuse to hand over to natural parents a sick child to whose treatment an objection is raised; but such a problem is beyond the scope of this book.

Child under 16 years of age: refusal of parental consent

There are circumstances in which, if there is to be any hope whatever of saving the life of a child, the necessary treatment must be given without delay. A clear example is that of a new-born baby whose only hope of survival (for instance, because of rhesus factor incompatibility) is that his blood should be wholly and speedily replaced by blood transfusion.

Parents holding particular religious or otherwise deeply-held personal views may sometimes refuse consent to that procedure. In such circumstances there is no time for an order to be obtained by the local social services authority for an authorised officer of the authority to consent in place of the parents. Consequently, either the blood transfusion has to be given despite parental objection or, although the child is in the care of the hospital staff who have available means whereby its life might be saved, it must be left to die. The choice is the same whatever may be the age of any child urgently needing a blood transfusion.

Ordinarily a child in hospital will be under the care of the consultant surgeon or physician into one of whose beds he has been admitted and under whose general or specific guidance treatment may be given by other members of his team. Nevertheless, if, say, an emergency admission has to be dealt with without reference to him, then the immediate responsibility will be on the practitioner who has to deal with the situation, e.g. a registrar or – especially at night – a house officer. Also, if the consultant instructed a registrar to perform an operation to which parents had objected, it is then the registrar who, as well as the hospital authority, might be sued if the parents thought that they had a case. Medical practitioner must also here be understood to include dental practitioner.

It would be the same if the practitioner, on good medical grounds, believed that without the recommended treatment the child's chance of survival would be significantly less.

Assuming, in a case within the above general description, that the child is in hospital under the care of a medical practitioner, is that practitioner justified in doing what is necessary to attempt to save the child's life, despite parental objection? It seems beyond doubt that he is justified, since in doing all he can to try save the child's life the medical practitioner is doing no more than it is the duty of the parents to have had done. It is inconceivable that an action against the hospital or against any member of its staff for trespass to the person, solely on the ground that parental consent had not been obtained, could succeed unless a comprehending child unequivocally refused.

The position of a medical practitioner who feels obliged to disregard objection by one parent, say, the child's father, is strengthened if he has obtained the consent of the other parent. This is because of section 1(1) and (3) of the Guardianship Act 1973, there being no time for the parents to resolve their differences by an application to the court. The above arguments (pp. 236–240) on blood transfusions and similar procedures carried out in elective operations do not hold here, save in the case of minors of particularly mature and independent understanding. While this is a legal question, its outcome is determined for all practical purposes by medical judgment.

A parent's duty to provide necessary medical aid for his child and his liability to prosecution for manslaughter if he wilfully fails to do so and the child dies in consequence, upon which the above statement is based, are brought out in *R v Senior* (1899).[44] He might also be convicted of manslaughter if the failure to provide medical aid had been reckless, though not deliberate as in *R v Senior*.[45]

In *R v Senior*, the father of a child suffering from pneumonia, being a member of a sect known as the Peculiar People, omitted on religious grounds to supply the child with medical aid or medicine although he was aware of the danger to the child's life. The child died. Medical evidence was given that the child's life would have been prolonged and might have been saved if a doctor had been allowed to treat it. The father was convicted of manslaughter. On appeal it was held that the defendant had been rightly convicted. But in *R v Spencer and Spencer* (1958)[46] on somewhat similar facts in an unreported case tried at the Nottingham Assizes in 1958 the defendants were acquitted. In this case the defendants belonged to the Jehovah's Witnesses and, on religious grounds, had refused to allow their newborn child to be given the blood transfusion which offered the only hope of saving its life. Under cross-examination the family doctor, who had attended the patient and had been called by the prosecution, admitted that, although he had told the father that the child should go into hospital for a transfusion, he might have omitted to warn the parents that failure to give a transfusion would result in the child's death. At that point in the trial the prosecution offered no further evidence and, on the direction of Mr Justice Paull, the defendants were acquitted. But in discharging them the judge said memorably: 'If after all you have learned in this court anything like this happens again, the position may be quite different. Just remember that.'

If a medical practitioner withheld treatment he believed to be necessary and the child died, it is unlikely that, if he were charged with manslaughter, the parents' refusal of consent would constitute a defence, the parents themselves being under a duty to provide for the child the very care which had been withheld. If such defence were available the life of the child in hospital would be less protected by the criminal law than that of a child at home since neither medical practitioner nor parent would be answerable; for a parent would surely never be convicted of manslaughter for refusing to sign a form, especially as it is reasonably clear that, in case of dire need, parental objection can be ignored, the more so if it is apparently unreasonable.

What about a child in hospital whose life is not in immediate danger but who, unless appropriate treatment is given without undue delay, will suffer, or be very likely to suffer, some permanent disability or degree of ill-health, and have a shorter expectation of life, and parental consent to such treatment is refused? What about the case where failure to carry out promptly the necessary treatment would subject the child to a period of otherwise avoidable pain and suffering, though without foreseeable long-term consequences?

Oakey v Jackson (1914)[47] is authority for the view that the unreasonable refusal by a parent to the carrying out on a child of an operation which ought to be done may constitute wilful neglect, while *R v Hayles* (1969)[48] supports the view that a parent not providing a child with necessary medical aid may be convicted of ill-treatment under section 1(1) of the Children and Young Persons Act 1933.

A conviction for neglect or ill-treatment may be obtained whenever a parent fails to provide medical aid for the child when a reasonable parent, similarly placed, would have done so and the child suffers in any way in consequence. Except in extreme cases parental failure or wrong-headedness seldom results in prosecution. More likely, the local social services authority would obtain a care and protection order and would then authorise whatever was necessary for the child's welfare, for instance the provision of spectacles or of a hearing aid or the carrying out of a tonsillectomy.

In the case of a child in hospital needing immediate treatment for present pain and suffering or to avert permanent disability or shortened life, obtaining a care and protection order may be just as impracticable as where the operation is to save life. It can be argued that if the necessary treatment is given despite parental objection, the parents will have no cause of action either against the hospital or against those members of its staff who actually gave that treatment, for they will have done no more for the child than the parents were under a legal duty to have done. If, in any action alleging trespass to the person of the child, the parents' case was supported by medical experts who satisfied the court that a significant body of medical practitioners qualified to express an opinion would not have considered the disputed treatment necessary, then assault and battery may have been committed. A court will not, however, readily find against a medical practitioner who, in a case in which prompt action was required, has taken a course approved by a substantial body of professional opinion, even though some other practitioners might have done otherwise.[49]

The success of a challenge on medical grounds (for which see Chapter 6) is remote especially if the member of the hospital staff who believes it urgently necessary to treat a child in a manner not approved by the parents obtains a second opinion before doing so and that second, concurring, opinion is recorded in the patient's case notes.

The case of *Re P (a minor)* (1982)[50] concerned the question of an abortion to be performed on a girl aged 15, already with one young child, and in the care of the local authority.

In July 1979, the girl then aged 13, having been convicted of theft, was committed to the care of the local authority under the provisions of the Children and Young Persons Act 1969. In November 1980 she gave birth to a boy. Mother and child were placed in a mother and baby unit with educational facilities. During school hours the boy was in the nursery but outside school hours the mother had to care for the child. In August 1981 the minor became pregnant for the second time. Her parents refused to consent to an abortion. The local authority made the minor a ward of court and invited the court to make an order directing that her pregnancy be terminated. The court held that it was appropriate for the local authority to have invoked the wardship jurisdiction and that it would be appropriate to continue the wardship.

It was held that since, on the evidence, the risk to the minor's mental health and to that of her year-old child were greater than if the pregnancy were terminated the proposed termination came within section 1 of the Abortion Act 1967; further, that since it was in the girl's best interests to direct that the pregnancy be terminated notwithstanding the wishes of the parents, their wishes must be overridden and the court would direct that the termination should take place forthwith.

Mrs Justice Butler-Sloss commented in her judgment on this and associated problems in the following manner:

> 'I must take into account in considering the welfare of Shirley – and her welfare is what is paramount in my mind because she is the ward of court – and through her the effect on her son of having this unwanted child, the important aspect of her parents . . . These parents are in certain difficulties in that they do not have the day to day care of Shirley since she is in care, and they are not able to offer to take over the day to day care of Shirley. In the circumstances, although I must give weight to their feelings as a factor in the case to be taken into consideration, and I must take into account their deeply and sincerely held religious objection, in considering the best interest of the minor as to whether she should have her pregnancy terminated, I draw to some extent an analogy with Jehovah's Witnesses and blood transfusions; nevertheless, if I am satisfied, as I am, that there is a risk of injury to the mental health of this minor, the factors raised by the grandfather on behalf of himself and his wife – which I have taken into account – cannot weigh in the balance against the needs of this girl so as to prevent the termination which I have decided is necessary in her best interests.'[51]

Medical and surgical treatment of disabled neonates

A particular problem is apt to arise in the case of parental attitudes to a newborn child affected by substantial disability or abnormality. The question may be one of parental objection to treatment; but it may go further into the relationship between law and medical ethics. Two contrasting situations faced by the courts in recent years are these. In *Re B (a minor) (wardship; medical treatment)* (1981)[52] a baby girl who was born suffering from Down's syndrome also had an intestinal blockage which could be cured without great difficulty. However, if she did not have the operation she would die within a few days. If she had the operation her life expectancy would be about 20 to 30 years. Her parents, believing that it was not in her best interests to have the operation because she would be very handicapped both mentally and physically if she survived, refused their consent to the operation. Although it could not be said to what extent her mental and physical defects would be apparent if she lived, the probability was that she would not be a person whose faculties were entirely destroyed. The local authority made her a ward of court and applied to the court to authorise it to direct that the operation be carried out. The judge held that the parents' wishes should be respected and that it was not in the child's best interests that the operation be performed. He accordingly refused to authorise the operation. The local authority appealed.

It was held by the Court of Appeal that the question which the court had to determine was whether it was in the child's best interests to have the operation and live as a mongoloid (sic.) child or to die within a week, and not whether the parents' wishes should be respected. Since there was evidence that if the operation took place and was successful the child would live the normal life span of a mongoloid child with the handicaps and defects and life of such a child, and since it had not been demonstrated that a life of that description ought to be extinguished, the court would authorise the local authority to direct the operation to be carried out.

On the other hand the case of *Re J (a minor) (wardship; medical treatment)* (1990)[53] the baby involved was a ward of court who had been born very prematurely. He suffered very severe and permanent brain damage at the time of his birth, the brain tissue then lost being irreplaceable. He was epileptic and the medical evidence was that he was likely to develop serious spastic quadriplegia, would be blind and deaf and was unlikely ever to be able to speak or to develop even limited intellectual abilities, but it was likely that he would feel pain to the same extent as a normal baby. His life expectancy was uncertain but he was expected to die before late adolescence, although he could survive very few years. He had been ventilated twice for long periods when his breathing stopped, that treatment being both painful and hazardous. The medical prognosis was that any further collapse which required ventilation would be fatal. However, he was neither on the point of death nor dying. The question arose whether if he suffered a further collapse the medical staff at the hospital where he was being cared for should reventilate him in the event of his breathing stopping. The judge, exercising the court's *parens patriae* jurisdiction, made an order that J should be treated with antibiotics if he developed a chest infection but should not be reventilated if his breathing stopped unless the doctors caring for him deemed it appropriate given the prevailing clinical situation. The Official Solicitor appealed against the order, contending that except where a child was terminally ill the court could never be justified in approving the withholding of life-saving treatment from a ward of court whatever the quality of the life being preserved or, alternatively, that it ought to do so only if it was certain that the child's life was going to be so intolerable that such a drastic conclusion was justified, but that that had not been shown in the case of J.

It was held that where a ward of court suffered from physical disabilities so grave that his life would from his point of view be so intolerable if he were to continue living that he would choose to die if he were in a position to make a sound judgment, the court could direct that treatment without which death would ensue from natural causes need not be given to the ward to prolong his life, even though he was neither on the point of death nor dying. However, the court would never sanction positive steps to terminate the life of a person. In deciding whether to authorise that treatment need not be given the court had to perform a balancing exercise in assessing the course to be adopted in the best interests of the child, looked at from his point of view and giving the fullest possible weight to his desire, if he were in a position to make a sound judgment, to survive, and taking into account the pain and suffering and quality of life which he would experience if life was prolonged and the pain and suffering involved in the proposed treatment. Having regard to the invasive and hazardous nature of reventilation, the risk of further deterioration if J was subjected to it and the extremely unfavourable prognosis with or without the treatment, it was in J's best interests that authority for reventilation be withheld.

In so deciding, Lord Donaldson emphasised two important points. First, that a child who is a ward of court should be treated medically in exactly the same way as one who is not, the only difference being that the doctors will be looking to the court rather than the parents for any necessary consent; and second, that in allocating limited resources to particular patients the fact that a child is or is not a ward of court is irrelevant.

By way of guidance on the approach to be taken in such a severe case, Lord Justice Taylor explained[54]

'At what point in the scale of disability and suffering ought the court to hold that the best interests of the child do not require further endurance to be imposed by positive treatment to prolong its life? Clearly, to justify withholding treatment, the circumstances would have to be extreme . . .

I consider that the correct approach is for the court to judge the quality of life the child would have to endure if given the treatment and decide whether in all the circumstances such a life would be so afflicted as to be intolerable to that child. I say "to that child" because the test should not be whether the life would be tolerable to the decider. The test must be whether the child in question, if capable of exercising sound judgment, would consider the life tolerable . . .

It takes account of the strong instinct to preserve one's life even in circumstances which an outsider, not himself at risk of death, might consider unacceptable. The circumstances to be considered would, in appropriate cases, include the degree of existing disability and any additional suffering or aggravation of the disability which the treatment itself would superimpose. In an accident case, as opposed to one involving disablement from birth, the child's pre-accident quality of life and its perception of what has been lost may also be factors relevant to whether the residual life would be intolerable to that child.

Counsel for the Official Solicitor argued that, before deciding against treatment, the court would have to be *certain* that the circumstances of the child's future would comply with the extreme requirements to justify that decision. Certainty as to the future is beyond human judgment. The courts have not, even in the trial of capital offences, required certainty of proof. But, clearly, the court must be satisfied to a high degree of probability.

In the present case, the doctors were unanimous that in his present condition, J should not be put back on to a mechanical ventilator. That condition is very grave indeed. I do not repeat the description of it given by Lord Donaldson MR. In reaching his conclusion, the judge no doubt had three factors in mind. First, the severe lack of capacity of the child in all his faculties which even without any further complication would make his existence barely sentient. Second, that, if further mechanical ventilation were to be required, that very fact would involve the risk of a deterioration in [J]'s condition, because of further brain damage flowing from the interruption of breathing. Third, all the doctors drew attention to the invasive nature of mechanical ventilation and the intensive care required to accompany it. They stressed the unpleasant and distressing nature of that treatment. To add such distress and the risk of further deterioration to an already appalling catalogue of disabilities was clearly capable in my judgment of producing a quality of life which justified the stance of the doctors and the judge's conclusion.'

In *Re J (a minor) (wardship: medical treatment)* (1992),[55] the question before the Court of Appeal was whether extraordinary measures should be taken to prolong the life of a severely mentally and physically disabled child aged 16 months. J had a fall when he was one month old, and was as a result microcephalic, and he suffered from a severe form of cerebral palsy. He had cortical blindness and severe epilepsy. Medical opinion was unanimous that he was unlikely to develop much beyond his present level of functioning, and that level might well deteriorate. His expectation of life, though uncertain, would inevitably be short. On application to the court, the judge below made an order requiring the health authority to use intensive therapeutic measures, including artificial ventilation, for so long as these measures were capable of prolonging the life of the child. On appeal, the Court of Appeal held that the court will not exercise its inherent jurisdiction over minors by ordering a medical practitioner to treat the minor in a manner contrary to the practitioner's clinical judgment. To do so would be to require the practitioner to act in a way contrary to the fundamental duty owed to his patient, namely to treat the patient (subject to obtaining any necessary consent in cases to which that is relevant) in accordance with his own best clinical judgment. The consultant paediatrician in charge of the child considered that it would not be medically appropriate to intervene with intensive therapeutic measures such as artificial ventilation. The child's mother, relying on an expert report by a specialist in child health at another hospital, had taken a more optimistic view of the child's prognosis. The decision is of particular interest on account of the court's refusal to make an order interfering with the judgment of the paediatrician in charge of J's care, despite the fact that other expert practitioners (not themselves involved in the treatment of the patient) might have formed a quite different judgment as to the measures which might appropriately be taken in the particular case.

Whether the child's condition is terminal or non-terminal, the decision in *Re C (a minor) (wardship: medical treatment)* (1989)[56] is instructive as to correct procedures and as to the form of direction which it is appropriate for the court to make.

A baby was made a ward of court shortly after her birth because the local authority's social services department considered that her parents would have great difficulty in looking after her. Soon after being made a ward it was discovered that the baby had been born seriously brain damaged, that she was severely handicapped and was terminally ill. The question arose as to the appropriate treatment for the baby, the extent to which the medical staff looking after her should seek to prolong her life and whether the baby should receive treatment appropriate to a child who was not handicapped or treatment appropriate to her condition. The local authority applied to the court for directions in the wardship proceedings. The Official Solicitor, as the baby's guardian *ad litem*, obtained a specialist's report which stated that the aim of treatment of the baby should be to ease her suffering rather than achieve a short prolongation of her life. The judge directed that leave be given to the hospital authorities to treat the ward in such a way that she ended her life peacefully with the least pain, suffering and distress and that the hospital authorities were not required to treat any serious infection which the baby contracted or to set up any intravenous feeding system for her. The Official Solicitor appealed against the terms of the order, contending, *inter alia*, that the judge had been wrong to direct that treatment of serious infections and intravenous feeding were not necessary.

The Court of Appeal ruled that where a ward of court was terminally ill the court would authorise treatment which would relieve the ward's suffering during the remainder of his or her life but would accept the opinions of the medical staff looking after the ward if they decided that the aim of nursing care should be to ease the ward's suffering rather than achieve a short prolongation of life; and in such circumstances it would be inappropriate to include in the court's directions any specific instructions as to how the ward was to be treated. Accordingly, the Official Solicitor's appeal would be allowed to the extent that the judge's direction that treatment of serious infections and intravenous feeding were not necessary would be deleted.

In applications for directions concerning the medical treatment of terminally ill wards of court the court, in giving judgment, should make clear what it is doing and why, what are the reasons leading to the court's decision, and may say what kind of treatment is to be followed or not, as the case may be.

Child under 16 years of age: operation or other treatment not immediately necessary

Where an operation or other treatment can be deferred without immediate adverse consequences to the child, it should not be performed against the wishes of the parents. If, however, it is considered necessary in the child's interest, the position should be brought to the attention of the appropriate medical officer of the health authority or of the appropriate officer of the social services authority for the area in which the child lives, leaving it for that officer to consider what steps it might be desirable for his authority to take for the child's welfare. This could include the obtaining of a care and protection order. If the parents refuse the recommended treatment, the child may properly be discharged from hospital unless to do so would plainly and seriously be detrimental to his health.

In *Re D (a minor) (wardship: sterilisation)* (1976)[57] a girl of 12 was suffering from Sotos Syndrome, a disability which might have led her to give birth to an abnormal child. Both the mother and a consultant paediatrician considered sterilisation advisable. This view was challenged by an educational psychologist on the staff of the local social services authority. She applied to make the girl a ward of court with a view to preventing the operation. Mrs Justice Heilbron held that since the right of a woman to reproduce is a basic human right and since the girl was likely to be able to appreciate the nature of the operation when she was 18, she should be a ward of court. In respect of the likely understanding, and therefore capacity to consent, in years to come the case of *Re D* therefore differs fundamentally from that in *Re F* (1989)[58] discussed later in this chapter in the context of patients who will never, because of their mental incapacity, be able to understand and therefore consent to treatment. She also held that a decision to carry out a sterilisation operation on a minor for non-therapeutic purposes was not solely within a doctor's clinical judgment. She pointed to the fact that there is no regular machinery for reviewing proposed operations where the parents and the doctors are agreed. The position of those who are, or are likely to be, permanently mentally incompetent is now clarified by the Official Solicitor's Practice Note, relating to proposed sterilisation, issued in October 1989 (see pp. 266–267 below).

In the context of provision of contraception for a girl under 16, Mr Justice Woolf expressed the following opinion in *Gillick v West Norfolk and Wisbech Area Health Authority* (1984):[59]

'In the absence of binding authority, the position seems to me to be as follows. The fact that a child is under the age of 16 does not mean automatically that she cannot give consent to any treatment. Whether or not a child is capable of giving the necessary consent will depend on the child's maturity and understanding and the nature of the consent which is required. The child must be capable of making a reasonable assessment of the advantages and disadvantages of the treatment proposed, so the consent if given can be properly and fairly described as a true consent. If the child is not capable of giving consent, then her parents can do so on the child's behalf. If what is involved is some treatment of a minor nature, and the child is of normal intelligence and approaching 16, it will be easier to show that the child is capable of giving the necessary consent; it will be otherwise if the implications of the treatment are long-term. Taking an extreme case, I would have thought it is unlikely that a child under the age of 16 will ever be regarded by the courts as being capable of giving consent to sterilisation.'[60]

In the subsequent appeal to the House of Lords[61] on what were effectively different issues in this case (see pp. 257–259, below) Lord Scarman referred with approval to this statement by the trial judge and repeated a passage from a leading medico-legal textbook published in 1957:

'Like Woolf J, I find illuminating and helpful the judgment of Addy J of the Ontario High Court in *Johnston v Wellesley Hospital* (1970):[62]

"But, regardless of modern trend, I can find nothing in any of the old reported cases, except where infants of tender age or young children were involved, where the courts have found that a person under 21 years of age was legally incapable of consenting to medical treatment. If a person under 21 years were unable to consent to medical treatment, he would also be incapable of consenting to other types of bodily interference. A proposition purporting to establish that any bodily interference acquiesced in by a youth of 20 years would nevertheless constitute an assault would be absurd. If such were the case, sexual intercourse with a girl under 21 years would constitute rape. Until the minimum age of consent to sexual acts was fixed at 14 years by a statute, the courts often held that infants were capable of consenting at a considerably earlier age than 14 years. I feel that the law on this point is well expressed in the volume on *Medical Negligence* (1957) by Lord Nathan (p. 176): 'It is suggested that the most satisfactory solution of the problem is to rule that an infant who is capable of appreciating fully the nature and consequences of a particular operation or of particular treatment can give an effective consent thereto, and in such cases the consent of the guardian is unnecessary; but that where the infant is without the capacity, any apparent consent by him or her will be a nullity, the sole right to consent being vested in the guardian'."

(The age of consent to medical and dental treatment was reduced by the Family Law Reform Act 1969 to 16 years: see p. 242, above.)

These statements and quotations are taken from the *Gillick* case which concerned provision of contraception, but are relevant to the law relating to consent to treatment insofar as such provision may involve physical contact between the provider and the under-16 girl.

Provision of contraception: whether to involve parent

The case of *Gillick v West Norfolk and Wisbech Area Health Authority* (1986)[61] concerned much wider legal, social and ethical issues than simply the question of consent to medical procedures involving physical contact.

The Department of Health and Social Security issued a Circular to health authorities containing advice that a doctor consulted at a family planning clinic by a girl under 16 would not be acting unlawfully if he prescribed contraceptives for the girl, so long as in doing so he was acting in good faith to protect her against the harmful effects of sexual intercourse. The Circular stated that, although a doctor should proceed on the assumption that advice and treatment on contraception should not be given to a girl under 16 without parental consent and that he should try to persuade the girl to involve her parents in the matter, nevertheless the principle of confidentiality between doctor and patient applied to a girl under 16 seeking contraceptives and therefore in exceptional cases the doctor could prescribe contraceptives without consulting the girl's parents or obtaining their consent if in the doctor's clinical judgment it was desirable to prescribe contraceptives. The plaintiff, who had five daughters under the age of 16, sought an assurance from her local health authority that her daughters would not be given advice and treatment on contraception without the plaintiff's prior knowledge and consent while they were under 16. When the authority refused to give such an assurance the plaintiff brought an action against the authority and the Department seeking (a) as against both the Department and the health authority a declaration that the advice contained in the Circular was unlawful, because it amounted to advice to doctors to commit the offence of causing or encouraging unlawful sexual intercourse with a girl under 16, and (b) as against the health authority a declaration that a doctor or other professional person employed by it in its family planning service could not give advice and treatment on contraception to any child of the plaintiff below the age of 16 without the plaintiff's consent, because to do so would be unlawful as being inconsistent with the plaintiff's parental rights. The judge held (a) that a doctor prescribing contraceptives to a girl under 16 in accordance with the advice contained in the Circular would not be committing an offence of causing or encouraging unlawful sexual intercourse with the girl, and (b) that a parent's interest in his or her child did not amount to a 'right' but was more accurately described as a responsibility or duty, and accordingly giving advice to a girl under 16 on contraception without her parents' consent was not unlawful interference with parental 'rights'. He accordingly dismissed the plaintiff's action. The plaintiff appealed to the Court of Appeal, which allowed her appeal and granted the declarations sought, on the grounds that a child under 16 could not validly consent to contraceptive treatment without her parents' consent and that therefore the circular was unlawful. The Department appealed to the House of Lords against the grant of the first declaration. The health authority did not appeal against the granting of the second declaration.

By a majority of four to one the House of Lords ultimately held that, having regard to the reality that a child became increasingly independent as it grew older and that parental authority dwindled correspondingly, the law did not recognise any rule of absolute parental authority until a fixed age. Instead, parental rights were recognised by the law only as long as they were needed for the protection of the child and such rights yielded to the child's right to make his own decisions when he reached a sufficient understanding and intelligence to be capable of making up his own mind. Accordingly, a girl under 16 did not, merely by reason of her age, lack legal capacity to consent to contraceptive advice and treatment by a doctor. By a majority of three to two they ruled that a doctor had a discretion to give contraception advice or treatment to a girl under 16 without her parents' knowledge or consent provided the girl had reached an age where she had a sufficient understanding and intelligence to enable her to understand fully what was proposed, that being a question of fact in each case. It also followed that the Department's guidance could be followed by a doctor without involving him in any infringement of parental rights or breach of the criminal law.

7.3.3   Child assessment order: refusal of examination

Under section 43 of the Children Act 1989 a court may, by means of a child assessment order, authorise an assessment including a medical examination. The Act responds specifically to the need to tackle sexual abuse of children in an effective way. Section 43 of the Act provides:

'(7) A child assessment order authorises any person carrying out the assessment, or any part of the assessment, to do so in accordance with the terms of the order.

(8) Regardless of subsection (7), if the child is of sufficient understanding to make an informed decision he may refuse to submit to a medical or psychiatric examination or other assessment.'

7.3.4   Blood test on child for purpose of matrimonial proceedings in which paternity of child questioned

The circumstances in which the court should permit a blood test on a young child for the purpose of matrimonial proceedings in which the paternity of the child is in question were summarised and explained by Lord Reid in *S v McC and M* (1972)[63] as follows:

'The court ought to permit a blood test of a young child to be taken unless satisfied that it would be against the child's interest. I say a young child because as soon as a child is able to understand these matters it would generally be unwise to subject it to this operation against its will. The court must protect the child, but it is not really protecting the child to ban a blood test on some vague conjecture that it may turn out to be to its disadvantage; it may equally well turn out to be for its advantage or at least do it no harm.'

The court's power to permit a blood test on a child does not place any doctor under any obligation to undertake the procedure. Even if so requested by both 'parents' a doctor would be unwise to undertake a blood group test on a young child without a court order if he knew or had reason to suspect that matrimonial proceedings had been or were likely to be commenced. If he did, he might find himself in contempt of court. There is, however, nothing to prevent a doctor at any time doing a blood test on a child for therapeutic reasons, whatever the state of relations might be at that time between the parties.

Lord Reid stated clearly in *S v McC and M* (1972), above that it would generally be unwise to subject the child to such a test against his/her will. By inference, the court will be slow to compel a child to submit to a test. It would therefore be wrong for a medical practitioner, even at the request of both parents, to carry out blood tests on the child against his will, otherwise than for therapeutic purposes. Nor should he do so, for other than therapeutic purposes, if the child appears to be acquiescing under parental pressure. Nor should an older child, though perfectly willing, be subjected to a blood test in relation to matrimonial proceedings or possible proceedings, at the request of either or even both parents, since his interests should be under the protection of the court. If a medical practitioner does undertake a blood test on a child, he may be called to give evidence about it in any subsequent matrimonial proceedings. Also, had he been a party to a blood test, in circumstances when it ought not to have been done without an order of the court, he might be open to criticism and, had he acted knowingly, possibly to contempt proceedings.

7.4   MARRIED PERSONS

This part of the chapter deals with problems specifically concerning married persons as such. As to the refusal of consent by a spouse or relative in cases of emergency, see pp. 246–249, above.

7.4.1   Married women: operative treatment on medical grounds

A married woman has the right to decide for herself whether or not to undergo operative or other treatment advised on medical grounds. This applies to gynaecological operations, including abortion, and to any other medical or surgical procedure. Therapeutic abortion may now be carried out only in accordance with the provisions of the Abortion Act 1967 as amended by the Human Fertilisation and Embryology Act 1990, as to which see Chapter 27. The Act does not alter the position as regards consent of the patient.

What is necessary for preserving a woman's life or health need not, and should not, be withheld because her husband refuses his consent. No English case gives the husband a power of veto. In *Paton v Trustees of BPAS* (1979)[64] (a case involving a proposed abortion, consented to by a woman) it was held that a husband had no legal right to veto the abortion. It is, however, most important that the woman should herself understand both the effect of the operation and equally the consequences of not having it, so that she may not afterwards be able to allege that her consent was given under a misapprehension induced by the surgeon. This is particularly important given that some patients may have religious or deeply held personal reservations about proposed treatment. In *Devi v West Midlands Regional Health Authority* (1980)[65] a woman with religious objections to sterilisation underwent a gynaecological procedure with consent. During the operation doctors found a condition which they reasonably considered would put her at risk were she to become pregnant, and without reviving her and affording her an opportunity to consent to, or refuse, the sterilisation they performed it forthwith. The patient sued the health authority successfully in battery (trespass to the person).

The gravest complication that one can imagine is in the case of a young married woman who has not had sexual intercourse with her husband up to the time when an operation is performed resulting in sexual incapacity. Such incapacity might possibly afford grounds for a decree of nullity. This would not seem to impose any legal responsibility on the surgeon, but in view of its grave effect on the woman's position should not be overlooked. An informal explanation to the husband *with the patient's consent* may be useful.

If a suitably qualified registered medical practitioner exercising a reasonable degree of care and skill advises a married woman to have an operation on medical grounds, the woman's own consent to that operation is all that is necessary even though it is a gynaecological operation which may result in sterility or hinder sexual intercourse. If, however, such advice were given negligently, the operation being unnecessary, then the husband, as well as the wife, might have a cause of action. The position would be no different had the husband's consent been obtained, were it shown that the advice that the operation was necessary or desirable had been given negligently. But although in respect of some gynaecological operations it may be desirable to seek the husband's consent whenever (with the woman's consent) the position can be explained to him, a surgeon in charge of a patient who refused to operate solely because the husband's consent was not forthcoming might be liable in damages to the husband under fatal accidents and associated legislation if he had failed for such reason to give the appropriate treatment and the patient either died or suffered ill-health, disability or pain in consequence.

Position if patient refuses to allow advice to terminate pregnancy to be discussed with her husband: confidentiality

In *Consent to Treatment* (1986) the Medical Defence Union recommended that:

'the written consent of a patient whose pregnancy is to be terminated should always be obtained. The consent of the husband or putative father is not a legal requirement (*Paton v Trustees of BPAS* (1978)) but it is sound practice to discuss a proposed termination with the father, provided the mother agrees.'

What is not clear is what should happen if the wife refuses to allow the proposed termination of pregnancy to be *discussed* with her husband. The answer may depend upon the purpose for which the question is asked. If it was for the sake of the woman's own life or health the practitioner's duty is clear: with the woman's consent, to do what is necessary for her well-being.

But suppose termination of pregnancy had been advised because the practitioner was of the opinion that, if it continued to term, a child was likely to be born with grave physical or mental abnormalities. If the woman either refused her consent to her husband's being consulted or, on his being consulted with her consent, he was unwilling to agree to the abortion, the abortion may nevertheless lawfully proceed. If, with the patient's consent, the practitioner did terminate the pregnancy, the husband not having been consulted or, having been consulted and refused his consent, the husband would have no legal action, provided that the practitioner had acted in good faith.

If the reason for the proposed abortion were potential risk to the health of existing children of the family, it might be less wise for the practitioner to go ahead without having heard the husband. Even where the husband is consulted, there is no question of the decision resting with him in law. It still remains the practitioner's reponsibility, subject only to the patient's consent, though in reaching his decision the practitioner may properly take into account information from the husband or from any other source.

In respect of girls under 18 the Medical Defence Union (*Consent to Treatment*, above) advises its members as follows:

'It is unnecessary in law to obtain the consent of the parents to terminate the pregnancy of an unmarried girl who has attained the age of 16. If the girl is living with her parents, it would be prudent for the practitioner, with the girl's agreement, to obtain their approval.

The MDU has been advised that when the girl is under 16, her parents should be consulted, unless the girl forbids the practitioner to do so. The written consent of the parents should be obtained, but their refusal should not be allowed to prevent a lawful termination to which the patient herself consents and which is considered to be clinically necessary. Conversely, a termination should never be carried out in opposition to the girl's wishes even if the parents demand it.'

Married persons: operations on generative organs

It was said in *Bravery v Bravery* (1954)[66] that an operation for sterilisation should not be performed on the one spouse (in that case the husband) without the consent of the other. That opinion is not legally binding (inasmuch as it was not central to the question to which the case gave rise) though in the particular case the operation was not medically necessary. An operation or procedure on either spouse without medical need (e.g. on eugenic or social grounds) without the consent of the other spouse, being an operation or procedure which took away or suspended the capacity for procreation or child-bearing, *might* lay the medical practitioner open to action by an aggrieved spouse. Where the operation is medically necessary *Bravery* is of little guidance. Where it is not medically necessary but is merely desirable (perhaps on social grounds) attitudes have changed so much since 1954 that the position is difficult to predict. The agreement of one spouse may be required for a surgical operation (even a minor one) which either permanently or possibly permanently takes away the capacity for child-bearing or procreation. It is very probably not required for other medical procedures such as the prescription of an oral contraceptive or the fitting of an intra-uterine contraceptive device. A husband cannot by withdrawing his 'consent' compel a doctor to restore the fertility of his wife.

The Annual Report of the Medical Defence Union 1971 reports the case of a husband who was in prison and wanted an intra-uterine device removed from his wife. To do this without the consent of the wife would be an assault.

7.5 MENTALLY DISORDERED PERSONS

The Mental Health Act 1959 offered no guidance as to who should permit medical treatment of a person suffering from mental disorder, even in the case of a patient lawfully detained under that Act. The Mental Health Act 1983 leaves the legal position on treatment for physical disorder unaffected, even in the case of a detained patient. Powers to impose treatment under the Act for mental disorder extend beyond mere incapacity and apply also to the imposition of such treatment even in the face of a patient's comprehending refusal of treatment. These powers are explained in Chapter 30, pp. 813–814.

Some guidance, though not very specific or extensive, on the question of the treatment, for a physical condition, was given by the House of Lords in *Re F* (1989).[67] In that case a severely mentally handicapped informal patient in a mental handicap hospital was having sexual relations with a male patient at the same hospital. Staff at the hospital neither discouraged nor encouraged her relations. Following a proposal by her doctor and parents to sterilise her in order to avoid a pregnancy, and perhaps birth, which she would certainly not be able to cope with, the Official Solicitor intervened and the case went to the House of Lords. The decision of their Lordships focused almost exclusively on the specific question of sterilisation. In the Code of Practice published by the Department of Health pursuant to section 118 of the Mental Health Act 1983 to accompany and amplify that Act, Chapter 15 includes this summary entitled 'Incapacity and Medical Treatment':

> 'The administration of medical treatment to people incapable of taking their own treatment decisions is understandably a matter of continuing concern to professionals and others involved in the care of such people. It is the personal responsibility of professionals to ensure that they understand the relevant law.
>
> The House of Lords' decision in *Re F* (1989)[67] helped to clarify the common law in relation to general medical and surgical treatment of people who lack the capacity to give consent. It held that a doctor may lawfully operate on or give treatment to a person who lacks the capacity to give consent provided that it is in the best interests of the patient, being necessary to save life, or to prevent a deterioration, or ensure an improvement, in his physical or mental health. However, as a matter of practice, an operation for sterilisation should not be performed on an adult who lacks the capacity to give consent without first obtaining the opinion of the court that the operation is, in the circumstances, in the best interests of the person concerned. The means of doing this is by seeking a declaration that the operation is lawful. The standard of care required of the doctor concerned in all cases is that laid down in *Bolam v Friern Hospital Management Committee* (1957),[12] namely, that he must act in accordance with a responsible and competent body of relevant professional opinion.'

In the guidance booklet *A Guide to Consent for Examination or Treatment* issued by the Department of Health under cover of HC(90)22 the following comments are offered:

'In many cases, it will not only be lawful for doctors, on the ground of necessity to operate or give other medical treatment to adult patients disabled from giving their consent, it will also be their common law duty to do so.

In the case of the mentally disordered, when the state is permanent or semi-permanent, action properly taken may well transcend such matters as surgical operation or substantial medical treatment and may extend to include such (humdrum) matters as routine medical and dental treatment and even simple care such as dressing and undressing and putting to bed.

In practice, a decision may involve others besides the doctor. It must surely be good practice to consult relatives and others who are concerned with the care of the patient. Sometimes, of course, consultation with a specialist or specialists will be required; and in others, especially where the decision involves more than a purely medical opinion, an inter-disciplinary team will in practice participate in the decision.'

Specifically on the question of sterilisation the guidance reads:

'In *Re F* it was said that special features applied in the case of an operation for sterilisation. Having regard to those matters, it was stated to be highly desirable as a matter of good practice to involve the court in the decision to operate. In practice an application should be made to a court whenever it is proposed to perform such an operation. The procedure to be used is to apply for a declaration that the proposed operation for sterilisation is lawful, and the following guidance was given as to the form to be followed in such proceedings:

i.   applications for a declaration that a proposed operation on or medical treatment for a patient can lawfully be carried out despite the inability of such patient to consent thereto should be by way of originating summons issuing out of the Family Division of the High Court;

ii.   the applicant should normally be those responsible for the care of the patient or those intending to carry out the proposed operation or other treatment, if it is declared to be lawful;

iii.   the patient must always be a party and should normally be a respondent. In cases in which the patient is a respondent the patient's guardian *ad litem* should normally be the Official Solicitor. In any cases in which the Official Solicitor is not either the next friend or the guardian *ad litem* of the patient or an applicant he shall be a respondent;

iv.   with a view to protecting the patient's privacy, but subject always to the judge's discretion, the hearing will be in chambers, but the decision and the reasons for that decision will be given in open court.'

The principle of the best interests of the patient was earlier used by the House of Lords in permitting the sterilisation of a 17-year-old girl who suffered from severe learning disabilities and epilepsy. In *Re B (a minor) (wardship: sterilisation)* (1987)[68] a local authority had the care of the 17-year-old girl who had a mental age of five or six years. She had no understanding of the connection between sexual intercourse, pregnancy and birth, and would not be able to cope with birth, nor care for a child of her own. She nevertheless exhibited normal sexual inclinations for someone of her own physical age. The local authority, which had no wish to institutionalise the patient, applied to have her made a ward of court and for leave to be given for her to undergo a sterilisation operation. The House of Lords held that the paramount consideration for the exercise of its wardship jurisdiction was the welfare and best interests of the ward in question. On the facts of this case, sterilisation was held to be in the best interests of the minor and permission was given to perform the operation. Lord Templeman made it clear that, in the case of proposed sterilisation of a minor aged under 18, the decision should be made only by a High Court judge; and that it would appear that a doctor who performed the sterilisation on such a minor without leave of a court exercising the wardship jurisdiction will, in spite of the fact that the child's parents consent to the operation, be liable in criminal, civil or professional proceedings.

The Official Solicitor issued the following Practice Note in October 1989 concerning applications to the High Court involving proposed sterilisations:

'1. The sterilisation of a minor or a mentally incompetent adult ("the Patient") will in virtually all cases require the prior sanction of a High Court judge: *Re B* (*a minor*) (wardship: sterilisation) [1988] AC 199; *Re F* [1989] 2 WLR 1025.

2. Applications in respect of a minor should be made within wardship proceedings in the Family Division of the High Court which, if the minor is not already a ward, should be commenced for the purpose. The Originating Summons or Notice of Application should seek an order in the following or broadly similar form:

"It is ordered that there be leave to perform an operation of sterilisation on the minor [X] [if it is desired to specify the precise method of carrying out the operation add, e.g., by the occlusion of her fallopian tubes] and to carry out such post-operative treatment and care as may be necessary in her best interests."

3. Applications in respect of an adult should be by way of Originating Summons issuing out of the Family Division of the High Court for an order in the following or broadly similar form:

"It is declared that the operation of sterilisation proposed to be performed on [X] [if it is desired to specify the precise method of carrying out the operation add, e.g., by the occlusion of her fallopian tubes] being in the existing circumstances in her best interests can lawfully be performed on her despite her inability to consent to it.
It is ordered that in the event of a material change in the existing circumstances occurring before the said operation has been performed, any party shall have liberty to apply for such further or other declaration or order as may be just."

4. The Plaintiff or Applicant should normally be a parent or one of those responsible for the care of the Patient or those intending to carry out the proposed operation. The Patient must always be a party and should normally be a Defendant or Respondent. In cases in which the Patient is a Defendant or Respondent the Patient's guardian *ad litem* should normally be the Official Solicitor. In any case in which the Official Solicitor is not either the next friend or the guardian *ad litem* of the Patient or a Plaintiff or Applicant he shall be a Defendant or Respondent.

5. Prior to the substantive hearing of the application there will in every case be a summons for directions which will be heard by a High Court judge.

6. The purpose of the proceedings is to establish whether or not the proposed sterilisation is in the best interests of the Patient. The judge will require to be satisfied that those proposing sterilisation are seeking it in good faith and that their paramount concern is for the best interests of the Patient rather than their own or the public's convenience.

7. The Official Solicitor acts as an independent and disinterested guardian representing the interests of the Patient. He will carry out his own investi-

gations, call his own witnesses and take whatever other steps appear to him to be necessary in order to ensure that all relevant matters are thoroughly aired before the judge, including cross-examining the expert and other witnesses called in support of the proposed operation and presenting all reasonable arguments against sterilisation. The Official Solicitor will require to meet and interview the Patient in private in all cases where he or she is able to express any views (however limited) about the legal proceedings, the prospect of sterilisation, parenthood, other means of contraception or other relevant matters.

8. Without in any way attempting either to define or to limit the factors which may require to be taken into account in any particular case the Official Solicitor anticipates that the judge will normally require evidence clearly establishing:

(1)   That (a) the Patient is incapable of making his or her own decision about sterilisation and (b) the Patient is unlikely to develop sufficiently to make an informed judgment about sterilisation in the foreseeable future. (In this connection it must be borne in mind (i) that the fact that a person is legally incompetent for some purpose does not mean that he or she necessarily lacks the capacity to make a decision about sterilisation and (ii) that in the case of a minor his or her youth and potential for development may make it difficult or impossible to make the relevant finding of incapacity.)

(2)   That the condition which it is sought to avoid will in fact occur, e.g., in the case of a contraceptive sterilisation, that there is a need for contraception because (a) the Patient is physically capable of procreation and (b) the Patient is likely to engage in sexual activity, at the present or in the near future, under circumstances where there is a real danger as opposed to mere chance that pregnancy is likely to result.

(3)   That the Patient will experience substantial trauma or psychological damage if the condition which it is sought to avoid should arise, e.g., in the case of a contraceptive sterilisation that (a) the Patient (if a woman) is likely if she becomes pregnant or gives birth to experience substantial trauma or psychological damage greater than that resulting from the sterilisation itself and (b) the Patient is permanently incapable of caring for a child even with reasonable assistance, e.g., from a future spouse in a case where the Patient has or may have the capacity to marry.

(4)   That there is no practicable less intrusive alternative means of solving the anticipated problem than immediate sterilisation, in other words (a) sterilisation is advisable at the time of the application rather than in the future, (b) the proposed method of sterilisation entails the least invasion of the Patient's body, (c) sterilisation will not itself cause physical or psychological damage greater than the intended beneficial effects, (d) the current state of scientific and medical knowledge does not suggest either (i) that a reversible sterilisation procedure or other less drastic solutions to the problem sought to be avoided, e.g., some other contraceptive method, will shortly be available or (ii) that science is on the threshold of an advance in the treatment of the Patient's disability, and (e) in the case of a contraceptive sterilisation all less drastic contraceptive methods, including supervision, education and training, have proved unworkable or inapplicable.'

In a case in which the mental state of a ward of court casts doubt upon the competency to decide whether to consent to medical treatment, the Court of Appeal decided, in *Re R (a minor) (wardship: medical treatment)* (1991),[69] that the court will resolve the issue so as to reflect the best interests of the child. Two difficulties are presented by the decision in this case. First, Lord Donaldson expressed the view that a doctor may lawfully administer treatment to a child who is not a ward of court and who is competent to, and does, refuse consent if the parent nevertheless consents to such treatment. While the case concerned medication for psychiatric disorder, and not sterilisation as in the case of *Re B* (1987) (above), Lord Donaldson's view appears to be inconsistent with that expressed by Lord Templeman in the latter case. Furthermore, the judge in the lower court in *Re R* found that the minor, aged 15 years 10 months at the time of his judgment, was not (as it is put) 'Gillick competent', because of her fluctuating mental state.

The Court of Appeal agreed with him that the fact of the fluctuating mental state of the girl, who was a ward of court, meant that it would be dangerous for the ward if her competence were to be judged purely on her state of mind during a period when her mental illness was in recession. If by this the judge meant that the girl's mental state was so fluctuating that she could never really form a view one way or another, then the finding of fact is readily understandable. If, however, she genuinely objected to the medication which was proposed for her, during a lucid or relatively lucid period, the approach of the judge (which was approved by the Court of Appeal) is not easy to reconcile with the existence of procedures under Part IV of the Mental Health Act 1983 (as discussed in Chapter 30, pp. 813–814). Even a long-term detained psychiatric patient has the lawful opportunity to consent to proposed medication, as an alternative to it being imposed in the absence of consent and even in the face of a refusal.

7.6   WHAT MAY BE DONE IF THE PATIENT IS INCAPABLE OF CONSENT?

While in no way having the force of law, the occasional paper *Consent to Treatment*, prepared and published by the Mental Health Act Commission in 1985, offers useful practical guidance on the probable approaches to a variety of cases (in which the capacity to consent is lacking) which would be taken by a court if an otherwise unresolved dispute about treatment were to go that far. While limited guidance on the application of such principles to the particular case of sterilisation of a mentally incompetent woman was given in *Re F* (above), the Mental Health Act Commission's paper is more detailed, and likely to be of more practical assistance in cases of proposed treatment short of the highly invasive sterilisation or abortion of a woman.

'The problem

Any patient who needs physical treatment – whether for mental disorder or a physical ailment – but is incapable of consenting to it presents a problem for his therapist.

The law presents a conflict between the basic requirement of consent and the principle that a practitioner is under a duty to take reasonable care for his patient and to enable him to receive treatment which he needs. That conflict has not been resolved in relation to incapable patients.

There are many thousands of incapable patients in need of treatment, who are not detained and in some cases are not detainable. Some are informal patients in hospital, but many more are at home or in other types of residential care, such as Part III accommodation, old people's homes, or local authority or voluntary hostels. Many suffer from mental handicap or dementia.

Part IV of the Mental Health Act 1983 is society's attempted answer to at least part of that problem. If the patient is detainable, the process of detaining him and giving him treatment under the compulsory powers will ensure that his incapacity to consent does not prevent him receiving treatment for his mental disorder.

The MHA has statutory protections for the detainable patient. The main protections are:

(a) the involvement of two doctors and an "applicant" in the detaining procedures;

(b) the involvement of medical and lay "certifiers" before certain special treatments can be given to a detained patient;

(c) the right of the patient to apply to a Tribunal for his discharge.

On the other hand, detention under the MHA has four substantial limitations for the patient:

(i) it carries a stigma, which attaches to the patient for the rest of his life;

(ii) it does not enable treatment to be given for a physical condition which does not cause or at least contribute to the mental disorder;

(iii) it is restrictive and may conflict with the principle of the least restrictive measure;

(iv) it may militate against a good relationship between patient and staff.

The choice for good practice is, therefore, between the following courses:

(a) formally detaining all the present and future incapable patients who are detainable and need treatment. This carries both the protections and the limitations above; or

(b) employing some other method, which avoids the limitations but gives as much protection comparable with the statutory protections as is feasible.

A pre-requisite of the second method would be that it should not conflict with the known law. But even if a principle of good practice conflicts with the form which the Common Law might be expected to take in the future, it should be stated, so that it can be accepted or rejected, and if accepted, can (as a practice approved not merely by one profession but by society) help to shape the Common Law.

To each alternative, there are advantages and disadvantages which are directly related to the patient's interests, but in addition to the limitations for the patient which detention involves, there is also the pragmatic consideration that to detain all the present and future incapable patients would:

(a) dramatically change the climate of opinion which has encouraged the increase of informality in the patient/staff relationship; and

(b) lead to great practical problems, which cannot be dismissed or diminished as "resource problems".

Treatments in circumstances of "necessity"

The law relating to treatment without consent in cases of 'necessity' has grown up in the context mainly of patients temporarily deprived of their ability to consent by physical unconsciousness. It has not focussed on the problem of the mentally disordered patient who is conscious but incapable. But at least similar limited principles should, it is thought, apply to the latter case, as in the former:

(i) life-threatening or seriously disabling conditions of mental disorder should be treated without consent and without having to resort to statutory detention, where the threat to life or health is immediate and a "necessity" thereby arises;

(ii) similarly, purely physical conditions of such patients should be treated under the same circumstances;

(iii) if a condition (whether mental disorder or purely physical) is a continuing one, which if not treated will become life-threatening or seriously disabling not immediately but at some time in the future, the treatment may be deferred until the "point of no return", i.e. where (within a reasonable safety margin) the future threat to life or health cannot be stopped, if treatment is not started. If at that point, the patient is still incapable, the treatment would be justified even without consent or detention;

(iv) if however there is no real prospect of the patient ever becoming capable of giving a consent, or if the condition is causing suffering which should be alleviated the treatment may properly be given without waiting for the "point of no return";

(v) if treatment is deferred, and by the "point of no return" the patient recovers his capacity and gives his consent, the treatment can be given [subject only to the protection provided by section 57 of the Mental Health Act, see Chapter 30, pp. 805–813;

(vi) if, however, after recovering his capacity the patient refuses a treatment which he needs for mental disorder, he may have to be detained formally for the purposes of treatment;

(vii) but if the treatment refused by a patient who has recovered his capacity is a treatment only for a physical condition (not causing or contributing to mental disorder), then the patient's refusal has to be respected, like the refusal of any other capable patient.

Good practice should embrace the above principles (which have not yet been declared as law, and until so declared, must remain predictions).

Since the aim must be to afford to any incapable informal patient, if he is treated without detention or a positive consent, as much as possible of the protection afforded to detained patients in respect of their treatment, certain safeguards should, where it is possible, be employed, even if the law would not require them.

In the case of "necessity" treatments it may be difficult to employ the safeguards set out below. But the principle should be to use as many of them as is feasible and appropriate to the particular circumstances in which the necessity arises.

Safeguards

The general safeguards which can be employed for the purpose of affording protection to a patient may be summarised as follows:

(1) It will always be good practice for the doctor to discuss the proposed treatment with one or more close relatives or friends of the patient, and to evaluate their views and information, including their knowledge of any past attitudes of the patient to the proposed treatment. Records of such interviews should be kept.

(2) At all times the doctor proposing treatment should give due weight to the observations and opinions of other persons, of any discipline, who are involved in the medical treatment. But the ultimate responsibility will nevertheless remain his.

(3) In appropriate cases the doctor should invite a written second opinion from a consultant in an appropriate speciality, or sometimes from an established G.P.

(4) In exceptional cases the Mental Health Act Commission should be consulted with a view to an appointed doctor being sent to interview the patient, and to consult others in the manner

required by section 58 in the case of detained patients, and to issue a certificate in the same form as Form 39, as though the patient were detained.

(5) When a surgical treatment is being considered, there should always be consultation between the senior professionals, e.g. G.P. or psychiatrist and surgeon, after discussion with near relatives or friends. . . .

Treatments other than "necessity" treatments

As regards other treatments for incapable patients, the law is even more difficult to predict. But it is likely that the principles of practice set out below would not conflict with the form which the law might take.

The deciding factor should be the attitude of the patient. An incapable patient may, in spite of his incapacity, express an attitude to the proposed treatment. He may purport to "consent", either expressly in words, or impliedly by his conduct in presenting himself willingly for the treatment without any unfair pressure from person, place or relationship. Alternatively he may purport to "refuse" the treatment; again either expressly in words, or impliedly by his conduct in resisting or avoiding the treatment. Another course which he may take is to remain totally "neutral" i.e. neither "consenting" by word or conduct, nor "refusing".

The 'refusing' patient

If the patient's initial attitude is one of "refusing" (whether expressly or by conduct) the treatment should be temporarily deferred in the hope that he will agree later. If he persistently refuses and the proposed treatment is one which he really needs "for" his mental disorder, he should, if he is detainable, be detained formally under section 2 or section 3 of the Mental Health Act 1983 as appropriate, and given the treatment under the powers in Part IV of the Act. This would include cases in which the treatment is for a physical condition which is either causing or contributing to the mental disorder (so that the treatment for the physical condition would be treatment "for" the mental disorder within Part IV of the Act).

If there are difficulties in properly detaining him (as may be the case in some instances where the patient is mentally handicapped but not "impaired" within the meaning of the Mental Health Act 1983), then good practice would require that the patient should not go untreated, but should have as much protection as possible. The treatment should be given but with the protection of Safeguards (1) (2) and (4) [above].

If however the proposed treatment for a "refusing" patient is for a physical condition which is neither causing nor contributing to the mental disorder (even if it is itself caused by, or contributed to by, the mental disorder), the following principles of good practice should be observed:

(a) no treatment can be given under the Mental Health Act 1983 because the treatment is not "for" mental disorder;

(b) if the treatment can properly be deferred, an opportunity or opportunities should be given for the patient to change his mind:

If the treatment cannot be deferred, or if the patient does not change his mind, the following principles should apply:

(a) if the physical condition is a serious one, or is causing, or is likely within the near future to cause, pain or distress, *and* if the doctor's view is that the patient's "refusal" to have the treatment is the result of his mental disorder, the treatment should be given, with the safeguards referred to [above].

(b) if however it is clear that the patient's "refusal" is not the result of his mental disorder, but is the result of e.g. religious or cultural views, the "refusal" should be respected and the treatment not given.

The "consenting" or "neutral" patient

Where instead of "refusing", the patient's attitude is either "consenting" or "neutral" towards treatment for either mental disorder or a physical condition (or any kind), the following principles should be observed:

(a) if the treatment is ECT [electroconvulsive therapy], the treatment may be given without detention but with the use of Safeguards (1), (2) and (4);

(b) where the treatment, in relation to the particular patient, is likely to give rise to significant risks to his physical or mental condition; or where there are doubts about the plan of treatment; or where surgery is proposed, such treatments may be given, but with the use of Safeguards (1), (2), (3) and where appropriate (5);

(c) if the treatment does not fall into any of the above categories, it may be given, but with the use of Safeguards (1) and (2).

Conclusion

All the above principles recognise:

(a) that treatment of the incapable patient is in a special category with which the law has not yet expressly dealt;

(b) that if possible he should not have to be detained if protection comparable to the statutory protection can be provided.'

7.6.1   Withdrawal of treatment from an incompetent adult

Until the case of *Airedale NHS Trust v Bland* (1993),[70] English courts had not been faced with the question whether it may be lawful to withdraw treatment from an incompetent living adult. The patient, who was in the care of the applicant health authority, had been in a persistent vegetative state for three-and-a-half years after suffering a severe crushed chest injury in a catastrophic accident prior to a football match which he had gone to watch. He suffered irreversible damage to the higher functions of his brain, and the unanimous opinion of all the doctors who examined him was that there was no hope whatsoever of recovery or improvement of any kind in his condition. Nor was there any reasonable possibility of his ever emerging to a cognitive sapient state from his existing condition. Nevertheless, the patient continued to breathe unaided, and his digestion continued to function. He could not see, hear, taste, smell, speak or communicate in any way; he was incapable of involuntary movement, could feel no pain and had no cognitative function.

The question arose whether the nasogastric tube used for artificial feeding could be withdrawn from him, and whether antibiotic drugs could lawfully be withheld from him in the event of infection developing. The House of Lords held that medical treatment, in the form of artificial feeding and the administration of antibiotic drugs, could lawfully be withheld from an insensate patient with no hope of recovery, provided responsible and competent medical opinion took the view that it would be in the best interests of the patient not to prolong his life by futile medical treatment. On the Official Solicitor's appeal to the House of Lords, contending that the withdrawal of life support was both a breach of the doctor's duty to care for his patient, indefinitely if need be, and a criminal act, their Lordships held that discontinuance of life support by withdrawal of artificial feeding did not amount to a criminal act. If the continuance of an intrusive life-support system is not in the best interests of the patient, the doctor in charge of the patient is no longer under a duty to maintain the patient's life; he is simply allowing his patient to die of the pre-existing condition, and the law would regard the patient's death as caused exclusively by the injury or disease to which his condition was attributable. The House of Lords chose not to follow the path taken by many American courts in such cases, namely to base their decision on the 'substituted judgment' test of what the patient may be taken to have chosen had he, hypothetically, been in a position to make a prospective choice.

Instead, the majority of their Lordships based their opinions on one form or other of the 'best interests' principle, upon which their Lordships' opinions in the case of *Re F* (1989) (see pp. 263–265 of this chapter) were centrally based. Nevertheless, Lord Mustill found difficulty with both approaches:

'To postulate a patient who is in such a condition that he cannot know that there is a choice to be made, or indeed know anything at all, and then ask whether he would have chosen to terminate his life because that condition made it no longer worth living is surely meaningless.'

And in relation to the 'interests' argument, his Lordship concluded:

'The distressing truth which must not be shirked is that the proposed conduct is not in the best interests of Anthony Bland, for he has no best interests of any kind.'[71]

At the time of writing, the matter is to be referred to Parliament for detailed consideration. In the interim, the courts are in a difficult position. As Lord Browne-Wilkinson stated:

'Unless, as I very much hope, Parliament reviews the law, the courts will be faced with cases where the chances of improvement are slight, or the patient has very slight sensate awareness. I express no view on what should be the answer in such circumstances; my decision does not cover such a case. I therefore consider that for the foreseeable future, doctors would be well-advised in each case to apply to the court for a declaration as to the legality of any proposed discontinuance of life-support where there has been no valid consent by or on behalf of the patient to such discontinuance.'[72]

Their Lordships therefore resolved that doctors should for the time being, as a matter of practice, seek the guidance of the court in all cases before withholding life-prolonging treatment from a patient in a persistent vegetative state. The appropriate means of seeking such guidance is by way of an application for declaratory relief. It is to be hoped, said their Lordships, that with the passage of time a body of experience and practice will build up which will enable the President of the Family Division to relax that requirement so as to limit applications for declarations to those cases in which there is a special need for the procedure to be invoked.

7.7 USE OF PATIENTS FOR CLINICAL TEACHING OR AS CONTROLS, OR OTHERWISE FOR RESEARCH, OR AS DONORS OF ORGANS

7.7.1 Use of patients for clinical teaching

It is necessary to consider the lawfulness of the use of patients in connection with the clinical teaching of medical and dental students, as when a student takes a patient's history or makes a physical examination; or when a clinical teacher demonstrates on a patient, whether to a single student or to a group of students large or small, whether in the ward, the operating theatre or elsewhere and whether by closed circuit television or video-tape or by the use of still photographs. The scenario may involve the similar use of patients in postgraduate courses for medical practitioners and refresher courses for general practitioners as well as the similar use of patients in connection with the clinical teaching of student and pupil nurses, pupil midwives and of those training for other paramedical professions, as well as in post-qualification courses for members of such professions. The actual *treatment* of a patient by a medical student or by a medical practitioner being trained in a particular speciality, or by a student nurse, a pupil midwife or other paramedical student, is considered in Chapter 6. In so far as it is customary to use student grades, most notably student and pupil nurses, in the treatment of patients and for medical students to carry out procedures on them, e.g. when serving as dressers, their proper dealings with the patient by way of treatment are fairly covered if any necessary consent to treatment has been obtained. Such consent, while safeguarding the student from an action for trespass to the person, would not protect against a claim based on negligence. As to that and the vicarious liability of the health (or hospital) authority, as well as the possibility of liability of the practitioner in charge of the treatment of the patient for negligent delegation, see Chapter 5. The use of a patient for purposes of research, as for example, by using him as a control or (otherwise than primarily in his own interest) subjecting him to a method of treatment still in its experimental stage, is examined on pp. 283–288, below.

Any physical contact or interference with the patient's body otherwise than in the ordinary course of treatment, done without consent, would be actionable as trespass to the person. So, too, would the use of a patient for demonstration purposes if it involved touching him in any way without consent. It is important that no patient should be used in connection with clinical teaching without his consent.

If something for which the patient's consent was necessary were done without that consent but no harm resulted the probability of an action for trespass to the person being brought is very remote; and, were such action brought, the likelihood of more than nominal damages being awarded no less remote unless what had been done had been done wilfully in the face of the patient's objection. But if some harm had been done, then the patient could claim substantial compensatory damages without proving negligence. Had what was done been done with the patient's consent, he could succeed in an action for damages only if he could establish negligence.

It is arguable that the communication of information about a patient to a group of medical students in the course of a demonstration could be a breach of professional confidence and for this the patient *might* have a remedy in damages had he sustained any material loss or loss of reputation as a consequence. If what had been done had been done with the patient's consent, such remote risk would have been avoided.

If a patient is to be used for clinical teaching, it should be only with his consent. Consent in the case of children and other persons under a disability is discussed separately (see pp. 241–260; 263–275, above). It is unsafe to rely on the patient's having not in any way indicated his unwillingness to be so used. The patient should be given a reasonable opportunity to object if they so wish.

Useful guidance for making the position abundantly clear to patients in National Health Service hospitals is given in a Circular, *Teaching on Patients*, the 1973 version of which[73] incorporates, by reference, the recommendations contained in paragraphs 287–293 of the Royal Commission on Medical Education[74] which is set out as an Appendix to the circular. When they first attend hospital, it should be made known to patients, out-patients and in-patients alike, that they may refuse to be used for teaching, without this prejudicing their treatment. There should be a personal explanation by the clinical teacher to the patient when the patient is to be used for demonstration purposes. The Circular warns:

'The Secretary of State would deprecate any attempt to overpersuade an unwilling patient to participate in teaching and the provision of necessary treatment available at a hospital should, of course, never be prejudiced by the patient's attitude in this respect.'

On the presence of students when emergency procedures are being carried out, the patient being unconscious or otherwise unable to give consent, the departmental advice is as follows:

'while it may be impossible to seek the consent of a patient or his next of kin to the presence of students at emergency procedures this should be done whenever possible and when it is not possible the teacher should remember that the students are present without the patient's consent, and should keep their numbers to a minimum.'

The model paragraphs on information to patients set out in Appendix II to HM(73)8 were criticised on the ground that they contained no explicit reference to a patient's right to decline to take part in teaching procedures without prejudice to treatment, even though this right was recognised in paragraph 3 of that Circular. The revised version (Circular HC(77)18) is based on a clarified philosophy:

'The distribution of explanatory literature should, however, be regarded as no more than an insurance that a patient has been made aware that the hospital he is to attend is engaged in teaching; it should not be looked upon as an acceptable substitute for personal explanation by the teacher.

On the first occasion that a student is present during the examination or treatment of a patient, or himself attends the patient, his status and the reason for his attendance should be explained to the patient whose co-operation should be sought. When practicable, this explanation should be given by the teacher but may be given by the student or a member of the nursing staff. Whenever a teacher proposes to discuss a patient's condition with a student in the presence of the patient, or to demonstrate the condition to a group of students or doctors, he should ensure that the patient understands the situation and consents. He should also ensure that patient's consent and co-operation where the demonstration is to be given wholly or partly by means of closed-circuit television or is to be recorded on videotape or still photographs for later showing to students.'

The current recommended information to patients reads:

'In-patient

We are sure you will realise that it would be impossible to train future members of the health professions without the help and co-operation of patients. This is a hospital where such staff are trained. A few students will normally be attached to the medical team which will be treating you; one of them may be allocated to take a personal interest in your case. They will usually accompany the other members of the team on their rounds. One or two may assist in other ways in looking after you. During your stay in hospital you may also be asked whether you would be willing to take part in a teaching session attended by a number of medical students.

Patients therefore play a very important part in the teaching work of the hospital. We hope you will agree to co-operate in this work if we need your help. If, however, you do not wish to take part in any teaching work, it is open to you to refuse without your treatment being affected in any way. In this case you should, as soon as possible, inform the Ward Sister, or the doctor.'

'Out-patient

We are sure you will realise that it would be impossible to train future members of the health professions without the help and co-operation of patients. This is a hospital where such staff are trained. Instruction takes place in the out-patients department as well as in the wards. This means that a small number of students may be present during consultations with patients, which form a most valuable part of their training.

Patients, therefore, play a very important part in the teaching work of the hospital. We hope you will co-operate in this work if we need your help. If, however, you do not wish to take part in any of this teaching work it is open to you to refuse, without your treatment being affected in any way. In this case you should let your general practitioner know so that he can make other arrangements with the hospital.'

In the case of children, and in that of patients who are mentally disordered, the departmental advice is as follows:

'Consent for child patients to participate in teaching should be secured from their parents and for mentally handicapped patients from parents or next of kin as appropriate.'

There seems no reason for *parents* in the plural in the first place and *parent* in the singular in the other. Presumably it is meant that, whether in the case of a child patient or of one who is mentally handicapped, the consent of either parent would be regarded as sufficient unless it were known that the other parent objected. 'Mentally handicapped' appears to refer to a patient who, by reason of mental disorder or disability, cannot appreciate the implications of the (proposed) teaching situation.

Presumably, also 'parents' here includes 'guardians' and 'custodians' and might also include persons in actual control. In the case of a mental patient under statutory guardianship who might be admitted to hospital otherwise than for treatment of his mental disorder, e.g. admitted for treatment of a physical injury or acute physical illness, the consent of the statutory guardian would be appropriate. Also see Chapter 30, pp. 770–773, on the treatment of mental disorder under the Mental Health Act 1983.

Although any such consent to the use of a child or mentally disordered patient for use in connection with clinical teaching within the limits discussed in the departmental circular would ordinarily suffice, it would not be effective to authorise the use of the patient for purposes of research, by using him as a control or subjecting him to experimentation.

7.7.2 Use of patients as controls, or otherwise for research, or as donors of organs

Patients may reasonably be expected to understand that in a teaching hospital (or possibly in any other hospital) they may, incidentally to their treatment, serve as material for the teaching of medical and other students. This is ordinarily brought to their notice by an explanatory leaflet, and even in a non-teaching hospital they may possibly serve an analogous purpose in practitioner refresher courses. Medical students, student nurses, student physiotherapists and other trainee health care professionals may, under proper supervision and subject to suitable safeguards, take a part in their treatment. But patients cannot be held, by merely attending hospital, to have agreed to submit to any procedures or the administration of any drugs not directed towards the treatment of their condition. Also, having regard to the statutory obligations of health services to provide care, it would appear that if a hospital which in any way committed itself to the treatment of a patient, (by having had him on a waiting list and then calling him in when a bed was available) but (because the patient was unwilling to be used for teaching) refused to give or continue any treatment necessary, it would be liable for any adverse consequences suffered by the patient unless satisfactory alternative arrangements had been made for treatment at another hospital. This could apparently be done since there is no statutory right to treatment at any particular hospital. It has, however, to be added that refusal to treat or continue treatment in these circumstances, even if coupled with reference to another hospital, would be contrary to official policy, the Secretary of State for Social

Services having stated clearly in Parliament that the minority of patients who refuse to be taught on should not, on that account, be denied treatment at a teaching hospital.

No experimental treatment of the disease involving risk to the patient is permissible when a well-tried treatment involving less risk to the patient or with greater degree of probability of a successful outcome is available. The only obvious cases justifying experimental treatment are when the patient's condition is not serious (e.g. the common cold) or when it is virtually hopeless and the proposed experiment is the only hope of either saving his life or restoring or partially restoring his health. Even so, the position should be explained to the patient or, if he is not in a fit condition to understand, to the appropriate relative, and assent obtained. Even if the patient were not in a condition to give or withhold consent, the 'consent' of a relative on his behalf to any experimental procedure involving unnecessary pain, suffering or discomfort to the patient would be valueless.

If experimental treatment which, at the time of its use, had not gained any acceptance among members of the relevant sector of the profession caused injury to the patient, the practitioner would be open to a claim for damages based on negligence if injury were to ensue, unless the patient had been made aware of the experimental nature of the treatment and of the risk involved and had fully consented. In *Slater v Baker and Stapleton* (1767)[75] damages were awarded against an eminent surgeon and an apothecary for negligently causing injury. The surgeon, Baker, had been called in by the apothecary, Stapleton, to set Slater's broken leg. Things did not go well and the surgeon tried out a new instrument, apparently to straighten the leg. The leg broke again at the point of the original fracture and this led to Slater's successful claim against both practitioners for 'unskilfully disuniting the callous of the leg after it had set'. In the judgment in appeal proceedings by the defendants when the judgment in favour of the plaintiff was upheld, it was said:

> 'For any thing that appears to the court this was the first experiment made with this new instrument and, if it was, it was a rash action and he who acts rashly, acts ignorantly: and although the defendants in general may be as skilful in their respective professions as any two gentlemen in England, yet the court cannot help saying, that in this particular case they acted ignorantly and unskilfully, contrary to the known rules and usages of surgery. . . .'

It is to be doubted whether today the courts would use quite that language but it is certain that they would still hold a practitioner liable for experimental treatment which caused injury, unless it could in some way be justified, for example, by showing that it had been the only chance of saving the patient's life or limb. Furthermore, it seems unlikely that if today a general practitioner called in a surgeon to his patient and remained in attendance while the surgeon dealt with a fracture or other condition needing skilled surgical attention, the general practitioner as well as the surgeon would be held liable for the negligence of the latter. From the report, the evidence against the apothecary in *Slater's* case seemed slight.

If it is desired to use a patient of full age and understanding as a control or otherwise for research, involving procedures or administration of drugs not directed primarily to the treatment of his disease, or perhaps deprivation of some substance normally included in his diet, his full and express consent should be obtained. He should be told quite clearly what is involved in terms of discomfort, pain and risk, if his consent is to be regarded as genuine and to be relied on. The obligation to disclose risks known to the researcher no doubt increases in relation to the lack of benefit likely to be gained by the 'patient'. But lawful consent may not be given for any surgical procedure or the administration of any drug or to any deprivation involving danger to life or limb.

What is the position where an organ, such as a kidney, is removed from a living person with his consent to try to save the life of another person? Could such procedure result in either a criminal charge or in civil proceedings if the donor died or suffered serious injury? Authority is lacking on both these points. But it is suggested that provided that the operation is not one which must inevitably result in the death or serious impairment of the health of the donor and that the surgeon has reasonable grounds for believing that the donor will not be subjected to grave risk of death or serious impairment of health, there would be no risk of a prosecution if (of course, without criminal negligence) the donor suffered harm. If a donor, even with full knowledge, consented to, or requested a procedure necessarily resulting in his death or serious disability, even if the object were to save the life of another, the surgeon who performed the procedure would probably be liable for manslaughter, if not murder, if the donor died, and for causing grievous bodily harm if he lived. Consent, freely given, would even in this case almost certainly be a defence in civil proceedings.

Apart from circumstances in which death or injury to the donor *must* result from the procedure, it is reasonable to assume that a responsible surgeon will be willing to effect such operations as transfer of a kidney from a donor to a dangerously ill patient only when he is satisfied that the operation does not involve an unnecessary risk to the donor. If he has explained the position to the donor, making it plain that there must be some risk in the procedure, with any relevant long-term risk of the donor's relying on one kidney only for the future, then it would seem that, provided the procedure is properly carried out and any necessary after-care properly given, there can be no civil liability either for bodily harm to the donor or even for his death.

The position as regards persons under a disability, notably children and mentally disordered patients, is different. They clearly cannot themselves consent to be controls or subjects of research nor can anybody else, such as a parent or guardian, do so on their behalf.[76] No medical procedure involving the slightest risk or accompanied by the slightest physical or mental pain may be inflicted on a child for experimental purposes unless there is a reasonable chance, or at least a hope, that the child may benefit.[77]

In the case of a child, treatment is paramount and nothing must be done which cannot be justified as treatment. Perhaps the use of young people between 16 and 18 (who are in full possession of their faculties) and mentally disordered persons as controls or for research with their own consent, as well as with the consent of their parent or guardian, is not entirely ruled out. But the greatest care must be exercised, and only the very clearest explanation of the nature and likely consequences of the proposed procedure is likely to suffice in law. Section 8(3) of the Family Law Reform Act 1969 refers only to consent to *treatment* and makes no reference to the use of minors for research or as controls.

The MRC (below) states that 'it may be safely assumed that the courts would not regard a child of 12 years or under . . . as having the capacity to consent to any procedure which may involve him in an injury'. Although of no legal authority the report of a committee of the Royal College of Physicians of London on the supervision and ethics of clinical investigations in institutions, circulated to National Health Service hospitals under cover of Departmental Circular HM(68)33 states:

'The design and conduct of clinical investigation should be guided by a code of clinical practice and the Code of Ethics of the World Medical Association ("Declaration of Helsinki") is accepted throughout the civilised world. The Medical Research Council has also issued a statement on "Responsibility in Investigation on Human Subjects" . . . The Committee accepts that these statements define the ethical situation and considers that all clinical investigators should be familiar with their recommendations.'

The legal position is probably as stated in the Canadian decision of *Johnston v Wellesley Hospital*, quoted with approval in *Gillick v West Norfolk and Wisbech Area Health Authority* (1985) pp. 256–257 above), namely that a minor may properly consent to treatment involving some pain or suffering but which is ultimately of benefit to the minor himself. The extent of suffering and the size of benefit must be weighed with the greatest care and doubt should result in a decision not to proceed.

The basis of the view that a parent or guardian cannot lawfully consent to or permit the use of a child under 16 years of age or of a mentally disordered person as a control or for purposes of research, if it involves any pain, discomfort or risk, is that the authority of the parent or guardian[78] exists only for the protection and well-being of the child or of the person under the disability. So he may consent to something involving pain, discomfort or even risk for the good of the child or other such person himself, but not for any other purpose, not even the good of other children or of other sick persons.

7.8 RESPONSIBILITY IN INVESTIGATIONS ON HUMAN SUBJECTS: STATEMENT BY THE MEDICAL RESEARCH COUNCIL IN ITS ANNUAL REPORT FOR 1962–63

'During the last fifty years, medical knowledge has advanced more rapidly than at any other period in its history. New understandings, new treatments, new diagnostic procedures and new methods of prevention have been, and are being, introduced at an ever-increasing rate; and if the benefits that are now becoming possible are to be gained, these developments must continue.

Undoubtedly the new era in medicine upon which we have now entered is largely due to the marriage of the methods of science with the traditional methods of medicine. Until the turn of the century the advancement of clinical knowledge was in general confined to that which could be gained by observation, and means for the analysis in depth of the phenomena of health and disease were seldom available. Now, however, procedures that can safely, and conscientiously, be applied to both sick and healthy human beings are being devised in profusion, with the result that certainty and understanding in medicine are increasing apace.

Yet these innovations have brought their own problems to the clinical investigator. In the past, the introduction of new treatments or investigations was infrequent and only rarely did they go beyond a marginal variation on established practice. Today, far-ranging new procedures are commonplace and such are their potentialities that their employment is no negligible consideration. As a result, investigators are frequently faced with ethical and sometimes even legal problems of great difficulty. It is in the hope of giving some guidance in this difficult matter that the Medical Research Council issue this statement.

A distinction may legitimately be drawn between procedures undertaken as part of patient care which are intended to contribute to the benefit of the individual patient, by treatment, prevention or assessment, and those procedures which are undertaken either on patients or on healthy subjects solely for the purpose of contributing to medical knowledge and are not themselves designed to benefit the particular individual on whom they are performed. The former fall within the ambit of patient care and are governed by the ordinary rules of professional conduct in medicine; the latter fall within the ambit of investigations on volunteers. Important considerations flow from this distinction.

Procedures contributing to the benefit of the individual

In the case of procedures directly connected with the management of the condition in the particular individual, the relationship is essentially that between doctor and patient. Implicit in this relationship is the willingness on the part of the subject to be guided by the judgment of his medical attendant. Provided, therefore, that the medical attendant is satisfied that there are reasonable grounds for believing that a particular new procedure will contribute to the benefit of that particular patient, either by treatment, prevention or increased understanding of his case, he may assume the patient's consent to the same extent as he would were the procedure entirely established practice. It is axiomatic that no two patients are alike and that the medical attendant must be at liberty to vary his procedures according to his judgment of what is in his patients' best interests. The question of novelty is only relevant to the extent that in reaching a decision to use a novel procedure the doctor, being unable to fortify his judgment by previous experience, must exercise special care. That it is both considerate and prudent to obtain the patient's agreement before using a novel procedure is no more than a requirement of good medical practice.

The second important consideration that follows from this distinction is that it is clearly within the competence of a parent or guardian of a child to give permission for procedures intended to benefit that child when he is not old or intelligent enough to be able himself to give a valid consent.

A category of investigation that has occasionally raised questions in the minds of investigators is that in which a new preventive, such as a vaccine, is tried. Necessarily, preventives are given to people who are not, at the moment, suffering from the relevant illness. But the ethical and legal considerations are the same as those that govern the introduction of a new treatment. The intention is to benefit an individual by protecting him against a future hazard; and it is a matter of professional judgment whether the procedure in question offers a better chance of doing so than previously existing measures.

In general, therefore, the propriety of procedures intended to benefit the individual – whether these are directed to treatment, to prevention or to assessment – are determined by the same considerations as govern the care of patients. At the frontiers of knowledge, however, where not only are many procedures novel but their value in the particular instance may be debatable, it is wise, if any doubt exists, to obtain the opinion of experienced colleagues on the desirability of the projected procedure.

Control subjects in investigation of treatment or prevention

Over recent years, the development of treatment and prevention has been greatly advanced by the method of the controlled clinical trial. Instead of waiting, as in the past, on the slow accumulation of general experience to determine the relative advantages and disadvantages of any particular measure, it is now often possible to put the question to the test under conditions which will not only yield a speedy and more precise answer, but also limit the risk of untoward effects remaining undetected. Such trials are, however, only feasible when it is possible to compare suitable groups of patients and only permissible when there is a genuine doubt within the profession as to which of two treatments or preventive regimes is the better. In these circumstances it is justifiable to give to a proportion of the patients the novel procedure on the understanding that the remainder receive the procedure previously accepted as the best. In the case when no effective treatment has previously been devised then the situation should be fully explained to the participants and their true consent obtained.

Such controlled trials may raise ethical points which may be of some difficulty. In general, the patients participating in them should be told frankly that two different procedures are being assessed and their co-operation invited. Occasionally, however, to do so is contra-indicated. For example, to awaken patients with a possibly fatal illness to the existence of such doubts about effective treatment may not always be in their best interest; or suspicion may have arisen as to whether a particular treatment has any effect apart from suggestion and it may be necessary to introduce a placebo into part of the trial to determine this. Because of these and similar difficulties, it is the firm opinion of the Council that controlled clinical trials should always be planned and supervised by a group of investigators and never by an individual alone. It goes without question that any doctor taking part in such a collective controlled trial is under an obligation to withdraw a patient from the trial, and to institute any treatment he considers necessary, should this, in his personal opinion, be in the better interests of his patient.

Procedures not of direct benefit to the individual

The preceding considerations cover the majority of clinical investigations. There remains, however, a large and important field of investigations on human subjects which aims to provide normal values and their variation so that abnormal values can be recognised. This involves both ill persons and 'healthy' persons, whether the latter are entirely healthy or patients suffering from a condition that has no relevance to the investigation. In regard to persons with a particular illness, such as metabolic defect, it may be necessary to know the range of abnormality compatible with the activities of normal life or the reaction of such persons to some change in circumstances such as an alteration in diet. Similarly it may be necessary to have a clear understanding of the range of a normal function and its reaction to changes in circumstances in entirely healthy persons. The common feature of this type of investigation is that it is of no direct benefit to the particular individual and that, in consequence, if he is to submit to it he must volunteer in the full sense of the word.

It should be clearly understood that the possibility or probability that a particular investigation will be of benefit to humanity or to posterity would afford no defence in the event of legal proceedings. The individual has rights that the law protects and nobody can infringe those rights for the public good. In investigations of this type it is, therefore, always necessary to ensure that the true consent of the subject is explicitly obtained.

By true consent is meant consent freely given with proper understanding of the nature and consequences of what is proposed. Assumed consent or consent obtained by undue influence is valueless and, in this latter respect, particular care is necessary when the volunteer stands in special relationship to the investigator as in the case of a patient to his doctor, or a student to his teacher.

The need for obtaining evidence of consent in this type of investigation has been generally recognised, but there are some misunderstandings as to what constitutes such evidence. In general, the investigator should obtain the consent himself in the presence of another person. Written consent unaccompanied by other evidence that an explanation has been given, understood and accepted is of little value.

The situation in respect of minors and mentally subnormal or mentally disordered persons is of particular difficulty. In the strict view of the law parents and guardians of minors cannot give consent on their behalf to any procedures which are of no particular benefit to them and which may carry some risk of harm. Whilst English law does not fix any arbitrary age in this context, it may safely be assumed that the courts will not regard a child of 12 years or under (or 14 years or under for boys in Scotland) as having the capacity to consent to any procedure which may involve him in an injury. Above this age the reality of any purported consent which may have been obtained is a question of fact and as with an adult the evidence would, if necessary, have to show that irrespective of age the person concerned fully understood the implications to himself of the procedures to which he was consenting.

In the case of those who are mentally subnormal or mentally disordered the reality of the consent given will fall to be judged by similar criteria to those which apply to the making of a will, contracting a marriage or otherwise taking decisions which have legal force as well as moral and social implications. When true consent in this sense cannot be obtained, procedures which are of no direct benefit and which might carry a risk of harm to the subject should not be undertaken.

Even when true consent has been given by a minor or a mentally subnormal or mentally disordered person, considerations of ethics and prudence still require that, if possible, the assent of parents or guardians or relatives, as the case may be, should be obtained.

Investigations that are of no direct benefit to the individual require, therefore, that his true consent to them shall be explicitly obtained. After adequate explanation, the consent of an adult of sound mind and understanding can be relied upon to be true consent. In the case of children and young persons the question whether purported consent was true consent would in each case depend upon facts such as the age, intelligence, situation and character of the subject and the nature of the investigation. When the subject is below the age of 12 years, information requiring the performance of any procedure involving his body would need to be obtained incidentally to and without altering the nature of a procedure intended for his individual benefit.

Professional discipline

All who have been concerned with medical research are aware of the impossibility of formulating any detailed code of rules which will ensure that irreproachability of practice which alone will suffice where investigations on human beings are concerned. The law lays down a minimum code in matters of professional negligence and the doctrine of assault. But this is not enough. Owing to the special relationship of trust that exists between a patient and his doctor, most patients will consent to any proposal that is made. Further, the considerations involved in a novel procedure are nearly always so technical as to prevent their being adequately understood by one who is not himself an expert. It must, therefore, be frankly recognised that, for practical purposes, an inescapable moral responsibility rests with the doctor concerned for determining what investigations are, or are not, proposed to a particular patient or volunteer. Nevertheless, moral codes are formulated by man and if, in the ever-changing circumstances of medical advance, their relevance is to be maintained it is to the profession itself that we must look, and in particular to the heads of departments, the specialised Societies and the editors of medical and scientific journals.

In the opinion of the Council, the head of a department where investigations on human subjects take place has an inescapable responsibility for ensuring that practice by those under his direction is irreproachable.

In the same way the Council feel that, as a matter of policy, bodies like themselves that support medical research should do everything in their power to ensure that the practice of all workers whom they support shall be unexceptionable and known to be so.

So specialised has medical knowledge now become that the profession in general can rarely deal adequately with individual problems. In regard to any particular type of investigation only a small group of experienced men who have specialised in this branch of knowledge are likely to be competent to pass an opinion on the justification for undertaking any particular procedure. But in every branch of medicine specialised scientific societies exist. It is upon these that the profession in general must mainly rely for the creation and maintenance of that body of precedents which shall guide individual investigators in case of doubt, and for the critical discussion of the communications presented to them on which the formation of the necessary climate of opinion depends.

Finally, it is the Council's opinion that any account of investigations on human subjects should make clear that the appropriate requirements have been fulfilled and, further that no paper should be accepted for publication if there are any doubts that such is the case.

The progress of medical knowledge has depended, and will continue to depend, in no small measure upon the confidence which the public has in those who carry out investigations on human subjects, be these healthy or sick. Only in so far as it is known that such investigations are submitted to the highest ethical scrutiny and self-discipline will this confidence be maintained. Mistaken, or misunderstood, investigations could do incalculable harm to medical progress. It is our collective duty as a profession to see that this does not happen and so to continue to deserve the confidence that we now enjoy.'

Though this well-considered statement was propounded in 1963 and had not been updated by the Medical Research Council, the statements contained in it remain to this day applicable, as critically argued principles, to current problems.

7.8.1 Clinical trials

If patients and other volunteers are to be used in clinical trials additionally the provisions of sections 31–39 of the Medicines Act 1968 must be complied with (see Chapter 29, pp. 703–5).

NOTES

1. *Re R (PM)* [1968] 1 WLR 358. See also *Re D (a minor) (wardship: sterilisation)* [1976] Fam 185.
2. [1959] 1 QB 426.
3. [1984] 1 All ER 1036.
4. The Times, 5 December 1985.
5. The Times, 11 February 1987.
6. [1965] NZ 191.
7. [1985] AC 871.
8. [1957] 1 WLR 582.
9. The Times, 2 July 1954.
10. [1964] AC 465.
11. [1965] NZ 191 at 198.
12. [1957] 1 WLR 582.
13. Juries were at the time (but are no longer) used in civil actions for personal injuries.
14. [1957] 1 WLR 582 at 590.
15. The Times, 2 July 1954.
16. [1981] QB 432.
17. [1985] AC 871.
18. [1985] AC 871 at 889–890.
19. [1992] 3 Med LR 331.
20. [1992] 3 Med LR 331 at 334.
21. [1992] 3 Med LR 331 at 339.
22. Department of Health, 1991; HMSO 51–1003, 10/91.
23. [1981] 114 DLR (3d) 1.
24. Unreported; QBD, Mr Justice Hutchison; 27 July 1988.
25. Medical Defence Union (1986), p. 4.
26. [1954] 1 WLR 1169.
27. [1971] P 83.
28. [1974] RTR 58.
29. *MacNeil v England* [1972] Crim LR 255.
30. *Burke v Jobson* [1972] RTR 59.
31. *R v Crowley* [1977] RTR 153.
32. *Routledge v Oliver* [1974] RTR 394.
33. *Taylor v Armand* [1975] RTR 225.
34. *R v Porter*, The Times, 6 December 1972.
35. *Cunliffe v Bleasdale* [1973] RTR 90.
36. *AG's Reference (No. 1 of 1976)* The Times, 29 March 1977.
37. *R v Nicholls* [1972] 1 WLR 502.
38. [1991] 2 Med LR 162.
39. At 166 et seq.
40. [1992] 4 All ER 649 at 668.
41. [1992] 4 All ER 671.
42. [1992] 4 All ER 649 at 661.

43. [1992] 4 All ER 627.
44. [1899] 1 QB 283.
45. *R v Lowe* [1973] QB 702.
46. The Times, 1 March 1958.
47. [1914] 1 KB 216.
48. [1969] 1 QB 364.
49. *Bolam v Friern HMC* [1957] 1 WLR 582 (for which see also Chapter 6, pp. 162–165.
50. (1982) 80 Loc Gov R 301.
51. At 311.
52. [1981] 1 WLR 1421.
53. [1990] 3 All ER 930.
54. At 945.
55. [1992] 4 All ER 614.
56. [1989] 3 WLR 240 at 252.
57. [1976] 1 All ER 326.
58. [1989] 2 WLR 1025.
59. [1984] 1 All ER 365.
60. At 373, 374.
61. [1986] AC 112.
62. [1970] 17 DLR (3d) 139.
63. [1972] AC 24 at 45.
64. [1979] QB 276; and see *C v S* [1987] 1 All ER 1230.
65. (1980) 80 Current Law 687.
66. [1954] 1 WLR 1169.
67. [1989] 2 WLR 1025.
68. [1987] 2 All ER 206.
69. [1991] 4 All ER 177.
70. [1993] 1 All ER 821.
71. At 892, 894.
72. At 884.
73. HM(73)8.
74. 1965–68; Cmnd 3569.
75. (1767) 95 ER 860. See now *Haluska v University of Saskatchewan* (1963) 53 DLR (2d) 436 (Sask. CA).
76. See Skegg 'Consent to Medical Procedures on Minors' (1973) 36 MLR 370.
77. See Fisher (1953) *The Lancet* 993.
78. See Children Act 1989, section 3.

CHAPTER 8

Complaints in the National Health Service

8.1 HOSPITAL COMPLAINTS PROCEDURE ACT 1985

In order to give statutory force to the availability to patients of proper complaints mechanisms the Hospital Complaints Procedure Act was enacted in 1985 and came into force on 11 July 1989. The interval of time was to enable appropriate procedures to be evolved at local level, through the various draft stages which can take much time. The Act simply obliges health authorities and trusts in England and Wales, and health boards in Scotland to establish a complaints procedure for hospital patients and to draw such a procedure to the attention of patients. The Act has no relevance to complaints by staff in relation to employment conditions; for that area reference should be made to Chapter 20. The Act provides as follows:

'1.—(1) It shall be the duty of the Secretary of State to give to each health authority in England and Wales and to each Health Board in Scotland such directions under section 17 of the National Health Service Act 1977 or section 2(5) of the National Health Service (Scotland) Act 1978 (directions as to exercise of functions) as appear to him necessary for the purpose of securing that, as respects each hospital for the management of which that authority or Board is responsible—

    (a) such arrangements are made for dealing with complaints made by or on behalf of persons who are or have been patients at that hospital; and

    (b) such steps are taken for publicising the arrangements so made, as (in each case) are specified or described in the directions.

(2) No right of appeal, reference or review conferred under this section shall preclude an investigation under Part V of the said Act of 1977 or Part VI of the said Act of 1978 (investigations by Health Service Commissioners) in respect of any matter.

(3) In this section—

    (a) in its application to England and Wales, expressions which are also used in the said Act of 1977 have the same meaning as in that Act;

    (b) in its application to Scotland, expressions which are also used in the said Act of 1978 have the same meanings as in that Act.'

The Act itself says nothing about any particular type of procedure which should be adopted at local level, still less what any particular policy should contain. Annex A to Circular HC(88)37 is entitled 'Directions on Hospital Complaints Procedures' and implements the Secretary of State's duty in section 1 of the Act (above):

'The Secretary of State for [Health], in exercise of the powers conferred on him by section 17 of the National Health Service Act 1977, hereby directs:

(i)   each district health authority in England or Wales; [and each NHS trust responsible for a hospital, from 1 July 1993]

and each of the following special health authorities:
Each of the Authorities for the London Postgraduate Teaching Hospitals;
The Board of Governors of the Eastman Dental Hospital;
Broadmoor Hospital Board;
Moss Side and Park Lane Hospitals Board [now Ashworth Hospital];
Rampton Hospital Board;
to make arrangements, as specified or described in the following paragraphs of these directions, for dealing with complaints made by, or on behalf of, persons who are or have been patients at any hospital for the management of which that authority is responsible and for monitoring the effectiveness of, and for publicising, the arrangements made for dealing with such complaints; . . .

1. In these Directions:

"authority" means any district health authority or special health authority [or trust] to whom these directions are given;
"complainant" means a person who is or who has been a patient at a hospital or the person acting on behalf of any such patient in making a complaint in relation to such hospital;
"designated officer" means a person who has been designated by a health authority as having responsibility for dealing with complaints made in relation to that hospital or group of hospitals.

2. (1)   For each hospital or group of hospitals for which an authority has responsibility, there must be an officer designated by the authority as having responsibility for dealing with complaints made in relation to that hospital or group of hospitals.
(2)   The duties of a designated officer must include responsibility for receiving, and seeing that action is taken upon, any formal complaint made at the hospital or hospitals for which he is given responsibility and, where the complainant had indicated a wish for him so to do, assisting in dealing with a complaint that is likely to be able to be dealt with informally.
(3)   Except to the extent that the subject matter of a complaint falls within any of the categories specified in the next sub-paragraph of these directions the duties of the designated officer must include responsibility for investigating and reporting on the investigation of any formal complaint to the complainant, to any person involved in the complaint, and to such other persons as the authority may require.
(4)   To the extent that the subject matter of any complaint made at a hospital or group of hospitals for which a designated officer is responsible:
(a)   concerns the exercise of clinical judgment by a hospital doctor or dentist and cannot be resolved by discussion with the consultant concerned; or

(b)   relates to what the authority is satisfied constitutes a serious untoward incident involving harm to a patient; or

(c)   relates to the conduct of hospital medical or dental staff which the authority considers ought to be the subject of disciplinary proceedings; or

(d)   gives reasonable grounds for inviting a police investigation as to whether a criminal offence may have been committed;

the duties of the designated officer in accordance with arrangements made pursuant to these directions shall not involve responsibility for investigating the complaint but the designated officer shall be required to bring the matter to the attention of his authority who shall, in the case of a matter specified in (a), (b) or (c) of this sub-paragraph, secure that the matter is promptly dealt with in accordance with the appropriate procedure laid down in guidance issued to authorities by the Department of Health and Social Security in respect of England and by the Welsh Office in respect of Wales.

(5)   Arrangements made may include provision for a designated officer to have the assistance of other officers of the authority in carrying out his duties under those arrangements and, with the agreement of the designated officer, such other officers may act on his behalf in the performance of those duties.

3. Each authority shall secure that arrangements are made for staff at any hospital for which that authority is responsible to seek to deal informally to the satisfaction of the complainant with any complaint made at that hospital and to advise any complainant, whose complaint cannot be so dealt with to his satisfaction, to make a formal complaint to the designated officer for that hospital.

4. Arrangements for making formal complaints should secure that such complaints are made or recorded in writing. Such complaints should normally be made within three months of the matter complained of arising although the designated officer ought to have a discretion to allow a longer period if satisfied that the complainant had good cause for not having made the complaint earlier. Arrangements made should secure that formal complaints are investigated promptly and that both the complainant and any hospital staff involved are afforded an opportunity to bring to the attention of the designated officer any information or comments they wish to make that are relevant to his investigation of the complaint.

5. Each authority must monitor arrangements made for dealing with complaints at hospitals for which it is responsible. Arrangements must be made for reports to be prepared at quarterly intervals for use by the authority in monitoring progress on the procedure for dealing with complaints, for considering trends in complaints and for taking remedial action on complaints as appropriate.

6. Each authority shall take such steps as are necessary to ensure that any patients at, or visitors to, any hospital for which the authority is responsible, as well as the staff working at the hospital, and any Community Health Council covering an area served by that hospital, are fully informed of the arrangements for dealing with complaints made at the hospital and are informed of the identity and location of the designated officer for such hospital.'

The real substance of the Circular so far as concerns the projected content of complaints procedures is contained in the following paragraphs. It is to be noted that, while the Circular states that the guidance contained in HC(81)5 is withdrawn, paragraph 12 of the following maintains in existence the 'clinical judgment' procedures.

'Procedural requirements

6. The basis of any complaints procedure is good communication. Problems of communication between patients and staff can generate misunderstandings which can result in complaints. Good communications may help defuse awkward situations. However, not all complaints can be dealt with on the spot and in this informal way. Some complaints will be of such concern to the patient that they warrant consideration and a formal response by a senior officer of the authority or it may be that the complaint is comparatively trivial but the patient feels unwilling or unable to discuss the matter with the staff who are directly involved. Again, good communications will be necessary to ensure that the complainant can give full expression to his concerns and that the full facts about the complaint are obtained.

7. The directions outline the mandatory requirements which health authorities must adopt in establishing complaints procedures. They involve

i. *A designated officer.* Each health authority must designate a senior officer for each hospital or group of hospitals for which it is responsible. The designated officer should be located in the hospital for which he is responsible and his whereabouts made known to facilitate contact by patients or those acting on a patient's behalf. The Unit General Manager might be the appropriate person for this task. The designated officer will be the recipient of formal complaints made by or on behalf of patients and will be accountable for the investigation of complaints other than those involving clinical judgment, serious untoward incidents, disciplinary proceedings, physical abuse of patients or criminal offences. Where the designated officer is also the Unit General Manager he may well be directly involved in these particular complaints. But investigation of these may also involve other senior officers, e.g. the Regional Medical Officer (RMO) or the equivalent or the District General Manager (DGM), or members of the authority (see sub-paragraph iv, below). The designated officer should not be denied access to relevant records which are essential for the investigation of a complaint. The designated officer should normally be available to assist in cases of minor grievances which the patient feels unable to discuss with e.g. ward staff.

ii. *Who may complain.* Any person who is or has been a patient at the hospital (either as an inpatient or outpatient) is eligible to make a complaint. If the person concerned has died or is otherwise unable to act for himself the complaint should be accepted from a close relative, or friend, or a body or individual suitable to represent him. The designated officer must be satisfied that where the patient is capable, the complaint is being made with his knowledge and consent.

iii. *Investigating the complaint.* In investigating the complaint, the designated officer must ensure that he has a full picture from the complainant of the events complained about. This may involve a preliminary interview to clarify the nature of the complaint or to obtain further information. It may be possible at this stage to resolve the issue to the complainant's satisfaction without taking the matter further. Care must be taken not to prejudice the outcome of any further investigation.

The designated officer, in liaison with other appropriate senior officers, should circulate details of the complaint to the staff concerned for their comments and seek to agree a reply. General complaints about, for example, the hotel services would be sent to the Head of the Department concerned for advice on a reply. Care must be taken not to introduce delays into the system by allowing excessive periods for comment. The aim should be to process the complaint speedily and thoroughly at all stages. The complainant must be kept informed of progress and where appropriate interim replies or holding letters must be sent.

Where the designated officer considers that a complaint carries a threat of litigation he should seek legal advice on whether and in what form an investigation might proceed to minimise the risk of prejudicing any civil proceedings. The possibility of legal proceedings should not prevent the officer undertaking the investigations necessary to uncover faults in procedures and/or prevent a recurrence.

    a. *Admission booklets.* Information about making a complaint should be given in the hospital booklet issued to patients on or prior to admission to hospital and available in hospital outpatient departments. It is essential for the location of the designated officer to be included.

    b. *Leaflets.* A leaflet explaining the complaints procedure and including a reference to the Health Service Commissioner's role in investigating complaints should be available for all patients. In addition to explaining the procedure in straightforward terms, the leaflet should give the location of the designated officer. Authorities should consider the need to make leaflets available in ethnic minority languages.

    c. *Notices.* These should be displayed in health authority premises including reception areas. Notices should give the location of the designated officer to whom appropriate comments, suggestions and complaints should be addressed.

    d. *CHCs.* Publicity material should be available to CHCs for information and issue to the public.

    e. *Staff training.* All staff will need to be made aware of the complaints procedure and to know the name and location of the designated officer to enable them to refer patients. Training will be needed to ensure that staff attitudes are positive and do not deter legitimate complaints.

Additional procedures

8. In considering their procedures health authorities are asked to take the following elements, which are not requirements under the directions, into account.

    i. *Form of complaint.* It is not a requirement that a complaint should be in writing. But it is important that a note be made in cases where the complaint is not readily settled and where a dispute as to the precise nature of the complaint might arise. This is particularly so when a formal investigation is likely. Where the complainant is unable to put the formal complaint in writing the designated officer should ensure that a record of the complaint is made and ask the complainant to sign it. A refusal to sign by the complainant should not delay investigation of the complaint.

    ii. *Time limits.* Complaints should be made and dealt with as quickly as possible. The longer the delay the more memories fade and less fruitful the investigation of the complaint. It is reasonable to expect that complaints should be made within three months of the incident giving rise to the complaint and publicity should encourage this. However there may be circumstances in which this recommended time limit may not be appropriate and the directions provide the designated officer with the discretion to extend the period if it is considered that the complainant has good reason for delay.

    iii. *Complaints about the Community Health Services.* Complaints about the

Community Health Services do not come within the scope of the procedures to be laid down in the directions under the Hospital Complaints Procedure Act 1985. Health authorities are asked to consider that the procedure directed for the handling of general complaints about hospital services should also be adopted in respect of the Community Health Services.

iv.   *Further action to certain complaints*
     Where the complaint concerns:
     a.   the exercise of *clinical judgment* which cannot be resolved by discussion with the consultant concerned;
     b.   what the authority is satisfied constitutes *a serious untoward incident* involving harm to a patient;
     c.   the conduct of hospital medical or dental staff which the authority considers ought to be the subject of *disciplinary proceedings*;
     d.   the alleged *physical abuse of patients*;
     e.   a possible *criminal offence*;
the designated officer should bring the matter to his senior officers' attention (or if appropriate the RMO) without delay so that appropriate action can be taken to ensure that the complaint is dealt with promptly in accordance with the Department's guidelines and local procedures.

v.   *Conclusion of an investigation*
When an investigation into a complaint has been completed the designated officer must complete a report and send a letter detailing the results of the investigation to the person who made the complaint, to any person who is involved in the complaint and where appropriate to the manager of any Department or service concerned. The letter should be informative both as to the reasons for any failure in service and any steps taken to prevent a recurrence and should contain an apology where appropriate. If the complainant remains dissatisfied he should be advised to refer the matter to the Health Service Commissioner unless the complaint is clearly outside the Health Service Commissioner's jurisdiction or the complainant proposes to take further action through the courts.

vi.   *Monitoring complaints*. Health authorities must monitor the arrangements. The purpose of this requirement is to ensure that health authorities monitor trends in complaints and can direct that appropriate action is taken. The designated officer should therefore provide summaries of complaints for the health authority. These summaries should be anonymised to preserve confidentiality of patients. The monitoring role must be undertaken by the authority itself, a committee of the authority or specified authority members. Progress in dealing with complaints should be kept under review by the District General Manager who should report to the authority at quarterly intervals about any cases outstanding.

vii.   *Publicity*. Publicity must be given to the procedure. This is an essential part of improving the public perception of the complaints procedure. [*Authorities and trusts should derive their own publicity procedures.*]

Investigation by statutory authorities

The Health Service Commissioner

9. Section 1(2) of the Hospital Complaints Procedure Act provides that nothing in the procedure promulgated in the directions shall preclude investigation by the Health Service Commissioner. The Health Service Commissioner may therefore investigate a complaint about health authority services or maladministration if a complainant is not satisfied with the conduct or outcome of the health authority's own investigations. The Health Service Commissioner cannot

investigate complaints relating to actions taken solely in consequence of the exercise of clinical judgment. Whether the action is taken solely in consequence of the exercise of clinical judgment will be determined by the Health Service Commissioner.

The Mental Health Act Commission

10. Section 120(1) of the Mental Health Act empowers the Mental Health Act Commission to investigate any complaint which a detained patient thinks has not been dealt with satisfactorily by the hospital managers. Nothing in the directions preclude such investigation by the Mental Health Act Commission.

The police

11. The District General Manager must be consulted where it appears that a criminal offence may have been committed. Where the allegation is serious and substantial the police must be notified immediately.

Complaints about clinical judgment

12. The current procedures for dealing with complaints relating to the exercise of clinical judgment by hospital medical and dental staff are subject to an agreement with the medical profession. The procedures were outlined in Circular HC(81)5, Annex, Part III (a copy is attached as Annex B).

13. The procedures provide for the complainant to be accompanied by a relative or personal friend. It is for the complainant to decide who the friend is. Such a person is there to help and support the complainant and not to act as an advocate nor in a way which detracts from the clinical nature of the consultation. The friend may sometimes help a less articulate complainant explain their concerns but this should not be allowed to create an adversarial situation.'

Part III HC(81)5 broke new ground by recommending as follows:

'Complaints relating to the exercise of clinical judgment by hospital medical and dental staff

First stage

18. As explained in paragraph 5 of Part I, a complaint may initially be made, and dealt with, orally or in writing. Complaints concerning clinical matters may be made direct to the consultant concerned, or to a health authority or one of its officers. In either case it is the responsibility of the consultant in charge of the patient to look into the clinical aspects of the complaint. This must be the first step in handling the complaint at the *first stage*.

19. If another member of the medical staff is involved, the consultant should discuss the complaint with the doctor concerned, at the outset and at all later stages in this procedure. It may be helpful to discuss the complaint with the patient's general practitioner. [In this Memorandum the terms "medical" and "doctor" include "dental" and "dentist" in appropriate cases.] The consultant should try to resolve the complaint within a few days preferably by offering to see the complainant to discuss the matter and seek to resolve his anxieties. If there is any delay, he should get in touch with the complainant and explain the reason. When the consultant sees the complainant, he should make a brief, strictly factual, record in the hospital notes. [The doctor's first responsibility is to the patient, hence this Memorandum is concerned with complaints made by patients. It applies also to complaints made by parents or guardians of minors,

and relatives of those patients with physical or mental disability limiting their competence to deal with the matter themselves, and of deceased patients. The term "complainant" is used to cover all such cases.]

20. Where a complaint is made which involves hospital medical staff other than consultants, the consultant in charge of the patient and the doctor concerned should both be involved in the handling of the complaint at all stages.

21. If the consultant feels the risk of legal action is significant, he should at once bring the matter to the notice of the district administrator. Where there are non-clinical aspects to a complaint made direct to a consultant, the consultant should inform the district administrator, who will arrange for these aspects of the complaint to be considered by an appropriate member of staff.

22. Where a complaint which has a clinical element is made to the authority or one of its officers, the district administrator should show the complaint to the consultant concerned and refer the clinical aspects to him.

23. The normal practice will be for the district administrator to send a written reply to the complainant on behalf of the authority. Any reference to clinical matters in the reply, whether interim or final, should be agreed by the consultant concerned. Sometimes it may be appropriate to confine this to mentioning that the clinical aspects had been discussed between the consultant and the complainant. On occasion, the consultant may wish to send the complainant a written reply direct covering the clinical aspects.

Second stage

24. Where a complainant is dissatisfied with the reply he has received at the first stage, he may renew his complaint either to the authority, one of its administrators or to the consultant. In any case, if he has not so far put his complaint in writing, he should now be asked to do so before his complaint is considered further. The next step, *in this second stage*, is for the Regional Medical Officer (RMO) to be at once informed; this should be done by the consultant, informing the district administrator that he has done so. The RMO will discuss the matter with the consultant.

25. At this point, the consultant may indicate to the RMO that he also wishes to discuss the matter with his professional colleagues. After these discussions, he may consider that a further talk with the complainant might resolve the complaint. If this fails, or if the consultant feels that such a meeting would serve no useful purpose, the RMO should discuss with the consultant the value of offering to the complainant the procedure – outlined more fully below – whereby the RMO would arrange for two independent consultants to see the complainant jointly to discuss the problem. If in the light of his discussion with the consultant and – where necessary – the complainant, the RMO considers it appropriate, the procedure of the *third stage* should be set in motion.

Third stage – independent professional review

26. The procedure at the third stage is intended to deal with complaints which are of a substantial nature, but which are not prima facie (and in the light of legal advice where appropriate) likely to be the subject of more formal action either by the health authority or through the courts. The procedure is intended for use in suitable instances as an alternative to the inquiry procedures provided in HM(66)15, though these will remain available for use when necessary. It would

not be appropriate if legal powers such as subpoena seem likely to be required. Nor is it intended that the new procedure should be invoked for complaints of a trivial nature.

27. Arrangements should be made by the RMO for all aspects of the case to be considered by two independent consultants in active practice in the appropriate specialty or specialties. They should be nominated by the Joint Consultants Committee. At least one should be a doctor working in a comparable hospital in another Region. These "second opinions" should have the opportunity to read all the clinical records. They should discuss the case with the consultant concerned and any other member of the medical staff involved as well as with the complainant. The meeting between the two independent consultants and the complainant should be in the nature of a medical consultation. The consultant who had been in charge of the patient at the time of the event giving rise to the complaint should not be present at the meeting, but should be available if required. The complainant should, if he wishes, be accompanied by a relative or personal friend and might wish to ask the general practitioner to be present.

28. "Second opinions" should discuss the clinical aspects of the problem fully with the complainant. In cases in which it is their view that the clinical judgment of the medical staff concerned has been exercised responsibly, they should endeavour to resolve the complainant's anxieties. The view they have reached and the outcome of the discussion with the complainant should be reported to the RMO on a confidential basis.

29. In other cases the "second opinions" might feel that discussion with the medical staff concerned would avoid similar problems arising in the future. When they had held such a discussion they would inform the complainant and would explain to him, as far as appropriate, how it was hoped to overcome the problems which had been identified. They should not provide a detailed report for the complainant but they should report the action they had taken to the RMO. The "second opinions" would also consider whether there were any other circumstances which had contributed to the problems in the case and on which they could usefully make recommendations, which they would include in their report to the RMO. These might include matters requiring action by the health authority, for example the workload carried by the medical or nursing staff.

30. In exceptional cases it may appear to the "second opinions", at any stage of an investigation, that the particular case is not appropriate to the second opinions procedure and that the complaint would be best pursued by alternative means. In this event they should report to the RMO accordingly.

Concluding action by the health authority

31. The district administrator will, on completion of the review by the "second opinions", write formally to the complainant on behalf of the authority, with a copy to the consultant. The district administrator will, where appropriate, explain any action the authority has taken as a result of the complaint but, where clinical matters are concerned, he will follow the RMO's advice regarding the comment which would be appropriate. So far as the authority is concerned the matter will remain confidential unless previous or subsequent publicity makes it essential for the authority to reply publicly, in which case comment on clinical matters will be confined to the terms of the district administrator's letter.

The Health Service Commissioner

32. Complaints relating to clinical judgment remain outside the responsibility of the Health Service Commissioner. However, it will be possible for him to advise complainants whose complaints contain elements of clinical judgment of the availability of the procedure described in this part of the Memorandum.'

The functions and jurisdiction of the Health Service Commissioner, or 'Ombudsman', are examined elsewhere in this chapter. A statutory limitation on the Ombudsman's jurisdiction prevents the investigation by his officers of the 'clinical judgment' aspect of complaints. The view taken by the Ombudsman of the operation of the clinical complaints procedure is nevertheless instructive and for convenience is discussed now.

In a periodical report by the Health Service Commissioner in 1984, attention was drawn to the need for greater clarity at the second stage, in the following terms:

'Interpretation of paragraph 25 of clinical complaints procedure

During my investigation the RMO said it was accepted by RMOs, the DHSS and the profession, that an RMO could not initiate an IPR if the consultant who is complained against did not agree to it. I disagreed with this interpretation and, although it was not directly relevant to the complaint I sought clarification from DHSS. The Department told me that it would be unacceptable for a consultant complained about to have a "veto" over the second opinions procedure and they agreed to my recommendation that the interpretation of paragraph 25 of HC(81)5 should be clarified.'

The breadth of discretion given under Part III of the Circular to Regional Medical Officers as to whether or not to refer a complaint to 'second opinions' is illustrated by a case briefly commented on by the Health Service Commissioner in a periodical report in 1984:

'Summary of case

The complainant had previously complained to the district health authority about her son's medical treatment. She then asked, through her Member of Parliament, that her complaint be dealt with under that part of DHSS health circular HC(81)5 which deals with complaints about clinical judgment. The RMO subsequently told the complainant and her Member that he had decided not to obtain opinions on the case from two independent consultants. The complainant then complained to me, again through her Member, that the RMO's grounds for refusing her request were neither proper nor adequate.

Findings

The provisions of DHSS health circular HC(81)5 give RMOs a wide discretion when deciding whether or not to refer a complaint to "second opinions", and I may not question such a decision if it is taken without maladministration. In this case I found that the reasons given by the RMO for not seeking "second opinions" were neither proper nor adequate and I upheld the complaint.

Remedy

I asked the regional health authority if I might convey their apologies to the Member and the complainant and if they would give me an undertaking to review the action that had been taken on the complaint. The health authority did not agree to this and I have therefore reported the matter to the Parliamentary Select Committee on the Health Service Commissioner.'

A problem can come to be regarded as one which involves 'maladministration', in the example given, at the point of the procedure which marks the interface with clinical judgment – in this case, that of the Regional Medical Officer himself. It is reminiscent of the limited power of the courts, in their judicial review of administrative action, to challenge the legality and reasonableness of the way an administrative decision was reached, but not to make a judgment on the merits of that decision.

8.2   COMPLAINTS AND INQUIRIES IN PSYCHIATRIC HOSPITALS

The guidance and recommendations contained in the Circulars and other material set out above should be followed in any hospital, including generally in hospitals providing care and treatment for mental disorder. The three special hospitals have their own specially agreed complaints procedure. Under section 120 of the Mental Health Act 1983 the Mental Health Act Commission has the duty to investigate complaints of the types set out and distinguished in that section. The Commission's exercise of its responsibilities relating to complaints from detained patients are discussed at pp. 845–847 of Chapter 30.

Under section 125 of the Mental Health Act 1983 the Secretary of State has the power to 'cause an inquiry to be held in any case where he thinks it advisable to do so in connection with any matter arising under this Act'. As is the case with inquiries caused to be held under section 84 of the National Health Service Act 1977 (below), such an inquiry has the power to compel the attendance and testimony of required witnesses.

8.3   FORMAL INQUIRIES

Section 84 of the National Health Service Act 1977 provides:

'**84.**—(1) The Secretary of State may cause an inquiry to be held in any case where he deems it advisable to do so in connection with any matter arising under this Act or Part I of the National Health Service and Community Care Act 1990.

(2) For the purpose of any such local inquiry (but subject to subsection (3) below), the person appointed to hold the inquiry—
(a) may by summons require any person to attend, at the time and place stated in the summons, to give evidence or to produce any documents in

his custody or under his control which relate to any matter in question at the inquiry; and

(b) may take evidence on oath, and for that purpose administer oaths, or may, instead of administering an oath, require the person examined to make a solemn affirmation:

(3) Nothing in this section—

(a) requires a person, in obedience to summons under the section, to attend to give evidence or to produce any such documents, unless the necessary expenses of his attendance are paid or tendered to him or;

(b) empowers the person holding the inquiry to require the production of the title, or of any instrument relating to the title, of any land not being the property of a local authority.

(4) Any person who refuses or deliberately fails to attend in obedience to a summons issued under this section, or to give evidence, or who deliberately alters, suppresses, conceals, destroys, or refuses to produce any book or other document which he is required or is liable to be required to produce for the purposes of this section, shall be liable on summary conviction to a fine not exceeding level 3 on the standard scale [currently up to £2000] or to imprisonment for a term not exceeding six months, or to both.

(5) Where the Secretary of State causes an inquiry to be held under this section:—

(a) the costs incurred by him in relation to the inquiry (including such reasonable sum not exceeding £30 a day as he may determine for the services of any officer engaged in the inquiry) shall be paid by such local authority or party to the inquiry as he may direct, and

(b) he may cause the amount of the costs so incurred to be certified, and any amount so certified and directed to be paid by any authority or person shall be recoverable from that authority or person by the Secretary of State summarily as a civil debt.

No local authority shall be ordered to pay costs under subsection (4) of that section in the case of any inquiry unless it is a party to that inquiry.

(6) Where the Secretary of State causes an inquiry to be held under this section he may make orders—

(a) as to the costs of the parties at the inquiry, and

(b) as to the parties by whom the costs are to be paid,

and every such order may be made a rule of the High Court on the application of any party named in the order.'

The power under subsection (1) now extends to any matter arising under the National Health Service and Community Care Act 1990, Part I.

8.4   THE HEALTH SERVICE COMMISSIONER

8.4.1   Introductory

Health Service Commissioners, one for England and one for Wales, are appointed under Part V of the National Health Service Act 1977 for the investigation of complaints of injustice or hardship allegedly caused by maladministration or by some failure in the provision of health services by a 'relevant body', or by an officer of a relevant body responsible for providing such services, or caused by an action taken by or on behalf of a relevant body. Under section 109, as amended, 'relevant body,' includes health authorities and trusts; and section 120 provides that, unless the context otherwise requires, the definition includes an officer of such body.

The terms and conditions under which Health Service Commissioners hold office are dealt with in sections 106–107 of the 1977 Act, which provide for salary and employment terms of the office-holder. Provision is also made for the appointment of officers who, if so authorised by him, may perform any functions of a Commissioner. A Commissioner may also authorise an officer of another Commissioner to act for him. The duty is placed on the Health Service Commissioner for Wales of including among his officers such persons having a command of the Welsh language as he considers are needed to enable him to investigate complaints in Welsh. To assist him in any investigation a Commissioner may obtain advice from any person who in his opinion is qualified to give it and may pay such fees and allowances to any such person as he may determine with the approval of the Minister for the Civil Service. So far both offices have been held by the same person; when held by different persons, the authority of each to investigate complaints is restricted to matters which are the responsibility of a relevant body within the country for which he had been appointed.

8.4.2 Matters subject to investigation

Matters which may be subject to investigation are to be found in section 115, which provides that:

'15. A Commissioner may investigate—
  (a) an alleged failure in a service provided by a relevant body; or
  (b) an alleged failure of a relevant body to provide a service which it was a function of the body to provide; or
  (c) any other action taken by or on behalf of a relevant body,
in a case where a complaint is duly made by or on behalf of any person that he has sustained injustice or hardship in consequence of maladministration connected with the other action.'

With section 115 must be read section 120(2) as follows:

'(2) It is hereby declared that nothing in this Part of this Act authorises or requires a Commissioner to question the merits of a decision taken without maladministration by a relevant body in the exercise of a discretion vested in that body.'

(Sections 110, 113 and 116 below should be read with section 115.)

8.4.3 Matters in respect of which a person aggrieved has or had some other right or remedy

If the matter complained of is one in respect of which the person aggrieved has or had some other right or remedy within section 116(1), a Commissioner may conduct an investigation only if satisfied that in the particular circumstances it is not reasonable to expect him to resort or to have resorted to it. The subsection says:

'(1) Except as hereafter provided, a Commissioner shall not conduct an investigation under this Part of this Act in respect of any of the following matters—
  (a) any action in respect of which the person aggrieved has or had a right of appeal, reference or review to or before a tribunal constituted by or under any enactment or by virtue of Her Majesty's prerogative, or
  (b) any action in respect of which the person aggrieved has or had a remedy by way of proceedings in any court of law;
but a Commissioner may conduct an investigation notwithstanding that the person aggrieved has or had such a right of remedy, if satisfied that in the particular circumstances it is not reasonable to expect him to resort or have resorted to it.'

Many complainants are reluctant to sue but anxious that a similar untoward occurrence happens to nobody else. In such a case the Commissioner should not refuse to investigate since such an attitude, if genuine, is reasonable.

8.4.4 Matters expressly excluded from investigation by Commissioner

By section 116(2) and Schedule 13, there are a number of matters which a Commissioner has no authority to investigate. Section 116(2) reads as follows:

'(2) Without prejudice to subsection (1) above—
  (a) a Commissioner shall not conduct an investigation under this Part in respect of any such action as is described in Part II of Schedule 13 to this Act; and
  (b) nothing in sections 110, 113 and 115 above shall be construed as authorising such an investigation in respect of action taken in connection with any general medical services, general dental services, general ophthalmic services or pharmaceutical services by a person providing the services.'

The following matters are listed in Schedule 13 as not subject to investigation. They are in addition to those mentioned in section 116:

1. action taken in connection with the diagnosis of illness or the care or treatment of a patient, being action which, in the opinion of the Commissioner in question, was taken solely in consequence of the exercise of clinical judgment, whether formed by the person taking the action or by any other person;
2. action taken in respect of appointments or removals, pay, discipline, superannuation or other personal matters in relation to service under this Act;
3. action taken in matters relating to contractual or other commercial transactions, other than in matters arising from arrangements between a relevant body and another body which is not a relevant

body for the provision of services for patients by that other body; and in determining what matters arise there shall be disregarded from such arrangements any arrangements for the provision of services at an establishment maintained by a Minister of the Crown for patients who are mainly members of the armed forces of the Crown; and

4. action which has been, or is, subject to an inquiry under section 84 of the 1977 Act (above).

8.4.5   Failure in treatment of patient

A question arises as to whether the negligence of medical or other staff causing injury to a patient may be subject of investigation by the Commissioner. Because of the limiting provisions of section 116(1) and (2) of the Act and of sub-paragraph (1) of paragraph 19 of Schedule 13, it will be rarely that harm to a patient allegedly attributable to the negligence of a medical or dental practitioner or of a nurse or midwife or of others assisting in providing treatment will be accepted for investigation by a Commissioner. Section 116(2) excludes from investigation any action whatever taken or not taken ('action' including, by Schedule 13, failure to act) or thing done in connection with any general medical, general dental etc. services by a person providing those services. If, however, the general practitioner, besides providing general practitioner services for National Health Service patients, is also in contract with a health authority for providing services for patients in hospital for an agreed number of sessions per week, whatever he does or fails to do in that capacity will not be excluded from investigation under section 116(2), though it may be under sub-paragraph (1) of paragraph 19 of Schedule 13, even though the person aggrieved may also be one of the practitioner's own 'list' patients. If, however, the general practitioner had been treating a 'list' patient in hospital not because of a contractual obligation to the health authority but because the authority provided accommodation and nursing care in a 'cottage' hospital to which general practitioners had the privilege of access to treat their own patients, what the doctor did or did not do would be within section 116(2) and outside the investigatory jurisdiction of the Commissioner. That would also be the position if a general practitioner attended one of his National Health Service list patients in a local nursing home.

Despite the wide terms of sub-paragraph (1) of paragraph 19 there are acts and omissions by medical practitioners and by nurses and others assisting them in the care and treatment of the patient which would not be within its scope. The decision whether action falls within that paragraph is whether or not that action had been taken solely in consequence of exercise of *clinical judgment*. If the action, or inaction, had been solely in consequence of an exercise of clinical judgment, it would be within the paragraph; otherwise not. A wrong diagnosis and consequently wrong treatment, however harmful, cannot be subject of investigation by a Commissioner, nor can an otherwise proper operation negligently performed. The difficulties inherent in the exclusion of complaints about clinical judgment and the Commissioner's own role are evident from the 1979/80 Report:

> 'I am particularly concerned about the difficulties which appear to me to be inherent in a parallel jurisdiction between my office and the courts with respect to medical negligence. There is an obvious danger that if my jurisdiction were to be extended to include clinical judgment then a person dissatisfied with some aspect of the medical treatment he has received might take advantage of my office to obtain a "free" investigation into the merits of a possible case against a health authority. If I issue a report in his favour, this report might then be used as the basis for obtaining legal aid for a subsequent action and generally as a means of bringing pressure to bear. While I would see this, in itself, as an abuse, unintended by Parliament, of the service I provide, there is the further – and, in my view, more fundamental – danger that if such an action were subsequently decided against the plaintiff, perhaps on different evidence, the standing of my reports, and hence of my office as a whole, might be diminished. Conversely, if the courts decided for the plaintiff, there might be the equally undesirable suspicion that my report had somehow prejudiced the trial against the health service and its employees. And, last, but not least, the co-operation and frankness which I enjoy in my investigations might be seriously lessened if National Health Service staff thought that my reports might somehow be used to found legal actions against them.'

A borderline case is that of the patient in need of operative or other treatment not believed to be immediately necessary, who because of a shortage of beds has been placed on the waiting list. If such a patient is not admitted as soon as all the patients before him in the list have been dealt with, and patients lower in the list being treated before him cause a serious and possibly permanent deterioration in his condition, such a patient would be a 'person aggrieved'. But would paragraph 19(1) 'prevent his grievance being investigated'? This depends on the reason for the delay. If it were that the consultant concerned had believed on the basis of his clinical judgment that patients lower in the waiting list had been more urgently in need of treatment than the patient whose operation had been deferred on their account, the matter would not be open to investigation by a Commissioner. But if the failure to call the patient in for treatment at the proper time had been due, say, to his records having been mislaid and overlooked or being misfiled, whether by the consultant himself or by any other member of the hospital staff, the matter would be one which could be subject of such investigation, because the failure to act was not the consequence of the exercise of clinical judgment. Even more clearly outside sub-paragraph (1) of the paragraph, and therefore open to investigation, are the following instances.

A wrong operation performed on a patient, not because of faulty diagnosis but because other patient's notes have been referred to, cannot be said to be something done in consequence of the exercise of clinical judgment and is therefore not caught by sub-paragraph (1) of the paragraph. Examples of this are: the performance of a total hysterectomy on a woman admitted to hospital for no more than an internal examination under anaesthetic; the performance of a sterilising operation on a patient of either sex in hospital for examination only; an appendicectomy performed on a child patient admitted to hospital overnight for no more than attention to a whitlow; and, disturbingly, amputation of the wrong limb or digit. All the above are cases of operations without consent and usually the consequence of the patient not being properly identified as being the person to whom the accompanying medical notes relate.

In such investigable cases the patient (or, if he died, his personal representatives and dependants) might be able to claim damages for negligence or for trespass to the person against both the person who committed the wrong, and vicariously against the employing health authority (or possibly against the authority directly as a principal wrongdoer operating a faulty system). If so, investigation of the matter by a Commissioner would still be barred, unless the Commissioner were satisfied that in the particular circumstances it would not have been reasonable to expect the aggrieved person to resort or to have resorted to his right of action. Given increased patient awareness these days of their legal rights, the consideration of the likelihood or otherwise of litigation relating to the injury will require care and prescience by the Commissioner.

'Mixed' cases involving matters which bear on clinical judgment and matters which do not require such a discretion to guide action, are provided for by section 113:

'(1) In determining whether to initiate, continue or discontinue an investigation under this Part of this Act, a Commissioner shall, subject to section 110 above and sections 115 and 116 below, act in accordance with his own discretion.

Any question whether a complaint is duly made to a Commissioner under this Part of this Act shall be determined by the Commissioner.'

8.4.6 Handling clinical and non-clinical complaints

That an initially 'clinical' matter can develop non-clinical and therefore investigable aspects is illustrated by the following case reported by the Commissioner in 1984 (numbered W4/83–84; W158/83–84):

'Following hospital treatment a lady wrote in December 1981 to a consultant, not directly concerned with her case, expressing dissatisfaction with her treatment. He did not reply and she then wrote in January and June 1982 to the consultant who had been responsible for her care. He did not reply either and therefore she complained about this, and her treatment, to the district administrator (DA). He told her that her treatment had been appropriate to her condition and that if she wanted further attention she should consult her family doctor. Thereupon she wrote to the RMO [Regional Medical Officer] on 20 July asking for an independent opinion. He began to deal with her clinical complaint and asked the regional administrator to deal with her non-clinical complaints. Nine months later, in April 1983, the complainant wrote to me expressing her dissatisfaction with the way her complaints had been dealt with by the health authorities.

Findings

I upheld her complaint against the DHA. The two consultants failed to deal with her letters in accordance with the guidance in Part III of HC(81)5. The DA's letter to the complainant was woefully inadequate – thus non-clinical aspects were added to what essentially had been a clinical complaint. The RMO was responsible for dealing with the clinical complaint but he was not prepared even to consider initiating an independent professional review (IPR) of her case mainly because he was not satisfied that the possibility of settling her complaint by discussion at local level (the first stage) had been exhausted. I found that the RMO failed to appreciate soon enough that the first stage was unsuccessful and that in doing so he acted maladministratively. To that limited extent I upheld the complaint that he did not deal adequately with the matter.

Remedy

Both the DHA and the RHA apologised for the shortcomings which I found. The DHA have also reminded medical staff of the action they should take when they receive a written complaint direct from a patient. The RMO also apologised to the complainant and said that he was prepared to offer her an IPR subject to its main purpose being accepted by her as not being designed to provide evidence in support of a claim for compensation.'

This illustration clearly demonstrates that a matter does not become for all purposes a question exclusively of clinical judgment simply because it is a doctor who decides on what action, if any, shall be taken.

8.4.7 Who may make a complaint?

Although section 111(1) provides for complaints not only by natural persons but also by bodies of persons, whether incorporated or not, a complaint must still be made by or on behalf of a person who has suffered injustice or hardship within the provisions of section 109. In the context in which the word 'person' is used in section 115 it can mean no other than an individual natural person. Hence, a body of persons, whether incorporated or not, cannot themselves have a cause of complaint and their authority to make a complaint can only be on behalf of the person aggrieved.

Exceptionally, in certain circumstances, a complaint may be made on behalf of another person, or in respect of a deceased person, pursuant to section 111(2). It is even possible for an officer of a body against which a complaint is made to make the complaint to the Commissioner on behalf of the complainant, for investigation, subject to section 112(b), below. Or the relevant body itself might refer a complaint to the Commissioner under section 117, below, though not when actually making a complaint on behalf of the aggrieved person.

There must in any event be a complaint; and the person by whom, or on whose behalf, or in respect of whom if deceased, the complaint is made must have suffered hardship or injustice as a result of the alleged maladministration. The Commissioner cannot initiate an investigation, as a case discussed in the Annual Report for 1979–80 illustrates:

'Inability to initiate investigations

Under section 115 of the National Health Service Act 1977 I may investigate a complaint from someone who claims to have suffered injustice or hardship as a result of alleged failures or maladministration on the part of a Health Service Authority. So before I can accept a complaint for investigation I must, besides being shown evidence of a *prima facie* failure in the service, be satisfied on two counts: first, that the person making the complaint is the person who has suffered the alleged injustice (unless, as provided by section 111(2) of the Act, he is for some reason unable to act for himself); and secondly, that I am provided with *prima facie* evidence that injustice has resulted from the maladministration complained of. In the great majority of complaints I receive, and which I could otherwise investigate, these two conditions are met. But in the course of the year I received one complaint where I considered that an investigation by me would have been in the public interest but which I was forced to reject because neither of these statutory requirements was met.

The complaint arose from the employment by an Area Health Authority of a bogus doctor who operated on a number of patients during the latter part of 1977. Following his discovery and subsequent conviction by the courts, the Authority concerned reached the decision that it would be in the best interests of the patients involved *not* to tell them that their operations had been performed by the "doctor" concerned. This decision led the Patients' Association to refer the case to me as a possible instance of maladministration, on the grounds that the patients concerned had a right to be informed of the circumstances surrounding their medical treatment.

After carefully considering the complaint I had to conclude, however, that, as presented to me, it failed to comply with the two provisions of the Act I refer to above and that consequently it was outside my present jurisdiction. For while I was in no doubt that the reasons which led the AHA to decide not to tell the patients concerned were investigable by me, the legislation makes it quite clear that the complainant must have been personally aggrieved by the action taken. I could not conclude that the Patients' Association met this requirement, nor was I given any evidence to indicate that the Association had been asked to refer the complaint on behalf of any of the patients involved in the belief that they had suffered injustice or hardship. As the law stands the only way an investigable complaint about the AHA's actions could have reached me (other than if by chance one of the patients concerned had become suspicious), was if one of them had suffered hardship and the facts of the case were subsequently revealed to him. I could take no action to initiate an investigation into the AHA's action prior to being asked to do so by one of the individuals involved – despite the fact that the AHA's action had the effect of securing that the people who were affected by it remained ignorant of their involvement. Whether or not that action was sound I was of course not in a position to determine. The only step I could, and did, take was to obtain an assurance that the patients involved had subsequently been seen by medically qualified staff of the Authority.

The circumstances of this case highlight the fact that I can only investigate cases where there is *prima facie* evidence of injustice to a named individual. This limitation on my jurisdiction, which appears to conflict with the public interest, has caused me some concern and I believe it is one which deserves to be examined closely and critically, with a view to considering whether I should be empowered to *initiate* investigations where in my discretion I think that an investigation would be in the public interest, and to report my findings to Parliament.'

Prior opportunity for investigation by relevant body

Section 112 provides:

'112. Before proceeding to investigate complaint—
  (a) a Commissioner shall satisfy himself that the complaint has been brought by or on behalf of the person aggrieved to the notice of the relevant body in question and that that body has been afforded a reasonable opportunity to investigate and reply to the complaint; but
  (b) a Commissioner shall disregard the provisions of paragraph (a) in relation

to a complaint made by an officer of the relevant body in question on behalf of the person aggrieved if the officer is authorised by virtue of section 117(2) above to make the complaint and the Commissioner is satisfied that in the particular circumstances those provisions ought to be disregarded.'

The importance, from the Commissioner's own point of view, of resolution (if possible) at local level is evident from the Annual Report for 1983/84:

'When Parliament considered the National Health Service Reorganisation Bill which led to the Act establishing the Offices of Health Service Commissioner for England and for Wales it recognised that the Commissioners would not and should not investigate all the complaints which arose in the National Health Service. It regarded the handling of complaints as an important duty of National Health Service managers and the function of my Office as the provision of a safety net for those complaints for which the normal procedures proved inadequate. I believe that that approach was entirely right. All complainants require a rapid solution to their difficulties and this is usually possible only if their grievances are considered as close as possible to the point at which they were given the relevant service. Local consideration of complaints also helps the managers of the service because it enables them to monitor standards and alerts them to the views of the community on their work. I am therefore in no doubt that Parliament was right to provide that in the normal course of events my investigation into complaints should not begin until I have evidence that the responsible health authority has had a suitable opportunity to consider and respond to the matters raised. I am therefore not dismayed that a substantial proportion, 20 per cent in the year under review, of complaints cannot be accepted when they first reach me because they have not been submitted to the appropriate health authority. In many cases I hear nothing further after I refer the authors of such complaints to their health authorities and I hope and believe that they have been given satisfaction. If they have not and return to me and the complaint is otherwise within my jurisdiction I can then investigate.'

Complaints to be in writing within one year, with discretion to investigate complaints out of time

Section 114 (1) provides:

'(1) A Commissioner—
    (a) shall not entertain a complaint under this Part of this Act unless it is made in writing to him by or on behalf of the person aggrieved not later than

one year from the day on which the person aggrieved first had notice of the matters alleged in the complaint, but

(b) may conduct an investigation pursuant to a complaint not made within that period if he considers it reasonable to do so.'

Reference to Commissioner by a relevant body of complaint made to it

Section 117 provides:

'**117.** Notwithstanding anything in sections 111 and 112 and section 114(1) above, a relevant body—

(a) may itself (excluding its officers) refer to a Commissioner a complaint that a person has, in consequence of a failure of maladministration for which the body is responsible, sustained such injustice or hardship as is mentioned in section 115 above if the complaint—

    (i) is made in writing to the relevant body by that person, or by a person authorised by virtue of section 111(2) above to make the complaint to the Commissioner on his behalf, and

    (ii) is so made not later than one year from the day mentioned in section 114(1) above, or within such other period as the Commissioner considers appropriate in any particular case, but

(b) shall not be entitled to refer a complaint in pursuance of paragraph (a) after the expiry of [twelve] months beginning with the day on which the body received the complaint.

A complaint referred to a Commissioner in pursuance of this section shall, subject to section 113 above, be deemed to be duly made to him under this Part of this Act.'

The effect of section 113 (for which see also p. 307, above) is to give the Commissioner discretion whether to commence, continue or discontinue the investigation of a complaint so referred. As a referred complaint is deemed to be a complaint duly made, it follows that all the provisions of Part V of the Act so far as relevant apply to it. Reference of a complaint by a relevant body under section 117 is to be distinguished from the making of a complaint by one of its officers on behalf of an aggrieved person, as to which see section 111(2).

8.4.8 Procedure, evidence, obstruction and contempt; secrecy of information

Section 114(2) in effect applies the provisions of the Parliamentary Commissioner Act 1967 relating to procedure, evidence, obstruction and contempt and secrecy of information to the Health Service Commissioners. These matters are now contained in Part I of Schedule 13 of the 1977 Act.

'Procedure in respect of investigations
1. Where the Commissioner proposes to conduct an investigation pursuant to a complaint under Part V of this Act, he shall afford to the relevant body concerned, and to any other person who is alleged in the complaint to have

taken or authorised the action complained of, an opportunity to comment on any allegations contained in the complaint.

2. Every such investigation shall be conducted in private, but except as aforesaid the procedure for conducting an investigation shall be such as the Commissioner considers appropriate in the circumstances of the case.

3. Without prejudice to the generality of paragraph 2 above, the Commissioner may obtain information from such persons and in such manner, and make such inquiries, as he thinks fit, and may determine whether any person may be represented, by counsel or solicitor or otherwise, in the investigation.

4. The Commissioner may, if he thinks fit, pay to the person by whom the complaint was made and to any other person who attends or furnishes information for the purposes of an investigation under Part V of this Act—
    (a) sums in respect of expenses properly incurred by them;
    (b) allowances by way of compensation for the loss of their time,
in accordance with such scales and subject to such conditions as may be determined by the Minister for the Civil Service.

5. The conduct of an investigation under Part V of this Act shall not affect any action taken by the relevant body concerned, or any power or duty of that department or authority to take further action with respect to any matters subject to the investigation.

6. Where the person aggrieved has been removed from the United Kingdom under any Order in force under the Immigration Act 1971, he shall, if the Commissioner so directs, be permitted to re-enter and remain in the United Kingdom, subject to such conditions as the Secretary of State may direct, for the purposes of the investigation.

Evidence

7. For the purposes of an investigation under Part V of this Act the Commissioner may require any employee, officer or members of the relevant body concerned or any other person who in his opinion is able to furnish information or produce documents relevant to the investigation to furnish any such information or produce any such document.

8. For the purposes of any such investigation the Commissioner shall have the same powers as the Court (which in this Schedule means, in relation to England and Wales, the High Court, in relation to Scotland, the Court of Session, and in relation to Northern Ireland, the High Court of Northern Ireland) in respect of the attendance and examination of witnesses (including the administration of oaths or affirmations and the examination of witnesses abroad) and in respect of the production of documents.

9. No obligation to maintain secrecy or other restriction upon the disclosure of information obtained by or furnished to persons in Her Majesty's service, whether imposed by any enactment or by any rule of law, shall apply to the disclosure of information for the purposes of an investigation under this Act; and the Crown shall not be entitled in relation to any such investigation to any

such privilege in respect of the production of documents or the giving of evidence as is allowed by law in legal proceedings.

10. No person shall be required or authorised by Part V of this Act and this Schedule to furnish any information or answer any question relating to proceedings of the Cabinet or of any committee of the Cabinet or to produce so much of any document as relates to such proceedings.

For the purposes of this paragraph a certificate issued by the Secretary of the Cabinet with the approval of the Prime Minister and certifying that any information, question, document, or part of a document so relates shall be conclusive.

11. Subject to paragraph 9 above, no person shall be compelled for the purposes of an investigation under Part V of this Act to give any evidence or produce any document which he could not be compelled to give or produce in civil proceedings before the Court.

Obstruction and contempt

12. If any person without lawful excuse obstructs the Commissioner or any officer of the Commissioner in the performance of his functions under Part V of this Act and this Schedule, or is guilty of any act or omission in relation to an investigation under that Part which, if that investigation were a proceeding in the Court, would constitute contempt of court, the Commissioner may certify the offence to the Court.

13. Where an offence is certified under paragraph 12 above, the Court may inquire into the matter and, after hearing any witnesses who may be produced against or on behalf of the person charged with the offence, and after hearing any statement that may be offered in defence, deal with him in any manner in which the Court could deal with him if he had committed the like offence in relation to the Court.

14. Nothing in paragraphs 12 and 13 above shall be construed as applying to the taking of any such action as is mentioned in paragraphs 5 and 6 above.

Secrecy of information

15. The Commissioner and his officers hold office under Her Majesty within the meaning of the Official Secrets Act 1911.

16. Information obtained by the Commissioner or his officers in the course of or for the purposes of an investigation under Part V of this Act shall not be disclosed except—
   (a) for the purposes of the investigation and of any report to be made in respect of the investigation under that Part,
   (b) for the purpose of any proceedings for an offence under the Official Secrets Acts 1911 to 1939 alleged to have been committed in respect of information obtained by the Commissioner or any of his officers by virtue of that Part or for an offence of perjury alleged to have been committed in the course of an investigation under that Part or for the purposes of an inquiry with a view to the taking of such proceedings, or
   (c) for the purposes of any proceedings under paragraph 12 and 13 above, and the Commissioner and his officers shall not be called upon to give evidence in any proceedings (other than those mentioned in this paragraph) of matters

coming to his or their knowledge in the course of an investigation under that Part.

[16A.—(1) Where the Commissioner also holds office as a relevant commissioner and a person initiates a complaint to him in his capacity as such a commissioner which relates partly to a matter with respect to which that person has previously initiated a complaint to him in his capacity as the Commissioner, or subsequently initiates such a complaint, information obtained by the Commissioner or his officers in the course of or for the purposes of the investigation under Part V of this Act may be disclosed for the purposes of his carrying out his functions in relation to the other complaint.

(2) In this paragraph "relevant commissioner"—

(a) in relation to the Health Service Commissioner for England, means the Parliamentary Commissioner, the Health Service Commissioner for Wales and the Health Service Commissioner for Scotland; and

(b) in relation to the Health Service Commissioner for Wales, means the Parliamentary Commissioner, the Health Service Commissioner for England and the Health Service Commissioner for Scotland.]

17. A Minister of the Crown [or the Welsh Assembly] may give notice in writing to the Commissioner, with respect to any document or information specified in the notice, or any class of documents or information so specified, that in the [opinion of the Minister or Assembly] the disclosure of that document or information, or of documents or information of that class, would be prejudicial to the safety of the State or otherwise contrary to the public interest.

18. Where a notice under paragraph 17 above is given nothing in this Schedule shall be construed as authorising or requiring the Commissioner or any officer of the Commissioner to communicate to any person or for any purpose any document or information specified in the notice, or any document or information of a class so specified.'

CHAPTER 9

Liability for premises

9.1 INTRODUCTORY

The Occupiers' Liability Act 1957 imposes upon the occupier of premises the duty to exercise a 'common duty of care' for the reasonable safety of all 'visitors' (persons lawfully on the premises). The duty is owed also to the property of such persons.

The Defective Premises Act 1972 concerns the extent of the responsibility of landlords and contractors for personal injury when the state of the premises causing or contributing to personal injury is attributable to the fault of any such landlord or contractor. The Health and Safety at Work etc. Act 1974 sets out a broad range of duties owed by employers to their employees and to the general public and by the occupiers of premises to those using plant or substances provided for their use there. The provisions of these Acts are considered in this chapter only so far as is necessary to understand their application to hospital patients and their visitors. The position of employees and contractors' men on hospital premises is no different from what it would have been had they been working elsewhere, and liability for injury at work is discussed more fully, and generally, in Chapter 20.

This chapter also examines the related questions of injury to persons or property not on the premises where the cause of injury originates from the hospital, and interference with quiet enjoyment and normal use of other premises in the neighbourhood (nuisance) as well as with interference with easements such as rights of light enjoyed by prescription or agreement.

9.2 INJURIES TO PERSONS LAWFULLY ON HOSPITAL PREMISES

9.2.1 Occupiers and visitors

The former distinction between invitees and licensees, now no longer significant, was that invitees were on the premises for a purpose in which the occupier had a material interest while licensees were not.

Now, under the Occupiers' Liability Act 1957, all who would have been either invitees or licensees at common law are included in a single category as 'visitors', the invitee being no longer specially favoured, nor the licensee discriminated against. It is also expressly provided that for the purposes of section 2, which sets out the duty of an occupier to visitors, that persons who enter premises for any purpose in the exercise of a right conferred by law are to be treated as persons permitted by the occupier to be there for that purpose, whether or not they in fact have his permission.

9.2.2   Extent of occupier's ordinary duty

The occupier's ordinary duty to lawful visitors under the 1957 Act is laid down in section 2(1) as follows:

'(1) An occupier of premises owes the same duty, the "common duty of care" to all his visitors, except in so far as he is free to and does extend, restrict, modify or exclude his duty to any visitor or visitors by agreement or otherwise.'

Such freedom, or otherwise, on the part of a health authority or similar occupier is discussed on pp. 323–324 below.

Common duty of care

The definition and extent of the 'common duty of care' is contained in sections 2(2)–(5) of the Act. Section 2(2) provides:

'(2) The common duty of care is a duty to take such care as in all the circumstances of the case is reasonable to see that the visitor will be reasonably safe in using the premises for the purpose for which he is invited or permitted by the occupier to be there.'

This means that the decision in any particular case will usually turn on matters of fact rather than on points of law. An example, of particular relevance to hospitals, of failure to exercise 'such care as in all the circumstances of the case is reasonable' is afforded by *Marshall v Lindsey County Council* (1937)[1] in which case a patient was negligently admitted to a local authority maternity home when there was danger of infection from puerperal fever and did in fact contract the disease. In *Weigall v Westminster Hospital* (1935)[2] a visitor enquiring about a paying patient suffered injury as the result of slipping and falling on an unsecured mat on a polished floor. He was awarded damages because there was a concealed danger of which he was not warned and therefore had no opportunity of avoiding. In *Slade v Battersea and Putney Hospital Management Committee* (1955),[3] the plaintiff was a wife who was invited by the hospital to visit her dangerously ill husband in a general ward at any time. Having visited him out of normal visiting hours, she fell and injured herself whilst leaving the ward, an area round the door of the ward having been rendered dangerous by being covered with floor polish prior to final polishing. Seemingly, knowledge of the state of the floor and the question of warning were equally immaterial in *Slade's* case, since it was reasonable for someone confronted with such slippery floor and having no other way out, to walk over it, taking reasonable care in so doing (see now section 2(4)(a) of the Occupiers' Liability Act 1957, below).

An authority or trust is also, of course, liable to visitors in the same way as other occupiers of premises for more common dangers such as defective or badly lit stairs, defective gutterings and the like.

Quite apart from the provisions of section 2(3), discussed below, the duty on the occupier of premises to take reasonable care to make the premises 'reasonably safe for the purposes for which [the visitor] is invited or permitted . . . to be there' means that in the case of both in-patients and out-patients it is the duty of the occupier (such as the health authority) to take all reasonable precautions for their safety, taking into account their physical and mental condition. Mentally disordered patients and those whose faculties have been impaired by age or illness will also be within section 2(3) (below). Hence, what precautions it may be necessary for an authority to take for the reasonable safety of patients may well be greater than would be expected of an occupier whose premises were not for the care and treatment of the sick. It seems likely, however, that occupiers of premises to which the public may have access, e.g. offices and shops, no less than hospitals, must foresee and guard against injury to blind persons through unusual hazards. This is illustrated by *Haley v London Electricity Board* (1965)[4] which, though not decided as falling within the provisions of the Occupiers' Liability Act 1957, concerned an ineffectively guarded excavation in a public thoroughfare, resulting in injury to a blind man using that thoroughfare.

Section 2 also provides:

'(5) The common duty of care does not impose on an occupier any obligation to a visitor in respect of risks willingly accepted as his by the visitor (the question whether a risk was so accepted to be decided on the same principles as in other cases in which one person owes a duty of care to another).'

In other words, wide as the section is, it does not affect the common law defence of consent to the risk of injury.

Subsections (3) and (4) of the Act offer greater guidance on the meaning of the common duty of care. Subsection 2(3) says:

'(3) The circumstances relevant for the present purposes include the degree of care, and of want of care, which would ordinarily be looked for in such a visitor, so that (for example) in proper cases:

   (a) an occupier must be prepared for children to be less careful than adults; and

   (b) an occupier may expect that a person, in the exercise of his calling, will appreciate and guard against any special risks ordinarily incident to it, so far as the occupier leaves him free to do so.'

The duty of an occupier to exercise care to see that the premises are safe for visitors extends to things in those premises which may have been provided for the use of visitors, or which visitors might reasonably be expected to use such as lifts or even chairs. The case of *Baxter v St Helena Group Hospital Management Committee* (1972)[5] is not more than a persuasive authority on this point, since it related to an accident which occurred to a member of the staff and could have been decided solely on the basis of the employer's duty to provide safe plant and equipment. A nurse was injured because a chair in the nurses' changing room had collapsed under her. The collapse had been due to extensive infestation with woodworm which would have been apparent on reasonable examination. It was admitted that the defendant hospital authority had no system of inspection of furniture at all. Giving judgment in the Court of Appeal, Lord Justice Davies said that it was the duty of every employer to take reasonable care to provide and maintain proper plant and equipment, and it seemed to him that chairs, *whether sat on by nurses or patients* [italics supplied] came within that context and therefore the hospital authorities should have had some system of inspection. They had none.

Section 2(3) says that the relevant circumstances include the degree of care, or lack of care, to be expected of the visitor himself. An occupier must be prepared for children to be less careful than adults but may expect that a person, in the exercise of his calling, will appreciate and guard against any special risks ordinarily incident to it. These examples, by being embodied in the definition, have become part of the law. But if other circumstances were relied on, by either plaintiff or defendant, as 'circumstances' within section 2(2), the judge would have to consider whether they were circumstances appropriate to be taken into account. The guidance given in section 2(3) does not restrict the meaning of the term to 'the degree of care of want of care' to the examples given.

The degree of care for the safety of a child to be expected of hospital staff was subject to judicial comment in *Gravestock and another v Lewisham Hospital Management Committee* (1955).[6] The case concerned a child of nine years of age who, when running down the ward and swinging on the doors, tripped on a stud and ran into one of the glass-panelled swing doors, suffering injury from broken glass. What the child had been doing at the time of his injury was contrary to the rules. Mr Justice Streatfield dismissed the claim against the hospital authority, not being prepared to hold that there had been any lack of proper supervision, even though the accident had happened whilst the orderly was absent for a few minutes. He said that the duty of the hospital towards a child of nine was no greater than that of a schoolmaster, which is that of an ordinary prudent parent.

In his judgment in *Gravestock's* case Mr Justice Streatfield also referred to the judgment of Lord Justice Denning in *Cox v Carshalton Hospital Management Committee* (1955)[7] and which also concerned the adequacy of supervision in a hospital ward. A child in bed suffering from a certain degree of disability had been left to manage a jug of hot inhalant on a tray, something which she had done quite successfully before. While the nurse was out of the room attending to another patient the jug tipped over and the child was injured. It was held that there had been no failure in supervision, regard being also had to the fact that it was in the child's own interests to have been encouraged to do things for herself.

While *Gravestock* concerned the use of premises, *Cox* was rather more concerned with matters incidental to treatment. Furthermore, while the cases are authority for the statement that the standard of care required in a hospital is that of an ordinary prudent parent, it does not follow that another case where the facts were similar to those in *Cox* or in *Gravestock* would necessarily be decided the same way. It might, indeed, be questioned whether a reasonably prudent parent would have left so disabled a child unattended to manipulate a jug of water so hot that injury would result if it overturned; or whether, having regard to the provisions of section 2(3) of the Occupiers' Liability Act 1957, standard glass in the door of the children's ward in *Gravestock* would be regarded as satisfactory. In two cases decided some years after *Gravestock* local education authorities were liable for injury to a child when the injury was caused by breaking of a thin glass panel in a school door, on the ground that thin glass, instead of reinforced glass, constituted a forseeable danger. Today, in the circumstances of *Gravestock*, thin glass in the door of a children's ward might also be held to be a no less foreseeable danger, though the naughtiness of an injured child in running about and swinging on the door might (but only in a clear and perhaps extreme case) be found to constitute contributory negligence.[8]

Section 2(3) provides that the common duty of care is to take such care as *in all the circumstances of the case* is reasonable . . .'. Hence a hospital, through its staff, must have regard to the nature of the physical disabilities of its patients, even of patients exercising ordinary adult care, and make the premises reasonably safe. A patient walking upon a crutch, especially if just learning to use it after an amputation, is much more at risk of a fall than a person who is firm on his legs. So also greater care ought to be taken for a person who uses a walking stick and is walking on a highly polished floor. What might not constitute a danger to a person of normal sight might well be a danger to a blind or poorly-sighted person. Omission to cater for such a person would be likely to render the hospital liable if any person under such disability suffered injury as a result.

Section 2 continues:

'(4) In determining whether the occupier of premises has discharged the common duty of care to a visitor, regard is to be had to all the circumstances, so that (for example)—

(a) where damage is caused to a visitor by a danger of which he had been warned by the occupier, the warning is not to be treated without more as absolving the occupier from liability, unless in all the circumstances it was enough to enable the visitor to be reasonably safe; and

(b) where damage is caused to a visitor by a danger due to the faulty execution of work of construction, maintenance or repair by an independent contractor employed by the occupier, the occupier is not to be treated without more as answerable for the danger if in all the circumstances he had acted reasonably in entrusting the work to an independent contractor and had taken such steps (if any) as he reasonably ought in order to satisfy himself that the contractor was competent and that the work had been properly done.'

For a health authority or other occupier to take advantage of the possibility of escape from liability provided by section 2(4)(b) it will have to show that the delegation to an independent contractor was reasonable and that it had done whatever it ought to do to satisfy itself that the contractor was competent and that the work had been properly done. *Clayton v Woodman & Son (Builders) Ltd* (1962)[9] illustrates this exception for health authorities. Some alterations were being made by a contractor, the first defendant, in an old building of which the Hospital Board were occupiers, the Board having also engaged a firm of architects to supervise the work. In the course of the work the plaintiff, a workman, was injured as the result of the fall of a gable wall rendered unsafe by reason of a chase having been cut in the gable on the instructions of the architect. On the facts, the Board, who were the second defendants, were held not liable either under the Occupiers' Liability Act 1957 or for the negligence of the architects whom they rightly believed to be of high repute and who were independent contractors.

Effect of contract on occupier's liability to third party

Section 3 of the Act provides as follows:

'3.—(1) Where an occupier of premises is bound by contract to permit persons who are strangers to the contract to enter or use the premises, the duty of care which he owes to them as his visitors cannot be restricted or excluded by that contract, but (subject to any provision of the contract to the contrary) shall include the duty to perform his obligations under the contract, whether undertaken for their protection or not, in so far as those obligations go beyond the obligations otherwise involved in that duty.

(2) A contract shall not by virtue of this section have the effect, unless it expressly so provides, of making an occupier who has taken all reasonable care answerable to strangers to the contract for dangers due to the faulty execution of any work of construction, maintenance or repair or other like operation by

persons other than himself, his servants and persons acting under his direction and control.

(3) In this section "stranger to the contract" means a person not for the time being entitled to the benefit of the contract as a party to it or as the successor by assignment or otherwise of a party to it, and accordingly includes a party to the contract who has ceased to be so entitled.

(4) Where by the terms or conditions governing any tenancy (including a statutory tenancy which does not in law amount to a tenancy) either the landlord or the tenant is bound, though not by contract, to permit persons to enter or use premises of which he is the occupier, this section shall apply as if the tenancy were a contract between the landlord and the tenant.

(5) This section, in so far as it prevents the common duty of care from being restricted or excluded, applies to contracts entered into and tenancies created before the commencement of this Act, as well as to those entered into or created after its commencement; but, in so far as it enlarges the duty owed by an occupier beyond the common duty of care, it shall have effect only in relation to obligations which are undertaken after that commencement or which are renewed by agreement (whether express or implied) after that commencement.'

While the primary object of section 3 is apparently to make landlords liable to visitors for the safety of such parts of the premises (such as forecourts, and staircases of blocks of flats) as the landlord might have retained under his own control, it will also, when read with section 2(4)(a), protect (among others) employees of persons in contractual relations with the occupier. And since by section 3 it is provided that 'the duty of care . . . shall include the duty to perform his obligations under the contract . . .' an employee of a contractor who is injured on hospital premises as the result of the failure of the hospital to perform its obligations under the contract will have a direct right of action against the hospital even though there has been no failure in respect of the common duty of care as laid down in section 2.

Implied terms in contracts

By section 5 of the Act, whenever a contract with the occupier of premises confers on another party to the contract the right to enter or use, or bring or send goods to, the premises, the duty on the occupier implied by the contract will be the common duty of care. Like section 2, this section also applies to fixed and movable structures.

There is nothing in the Act which would prevent a health authority, as is usual, disclaiming liability for safe keeping of a patient's belongings not handed over for the purpose (see Chapter 10 below and as regards property belonging to members of the staff, see Chapter 20, below).

9.2.3   Landlord's liability

Section 4 of the Defective Premises Act 1972 replaces section 4 of the Occupiers' Liability Act 1957 and makes a landlord liable in damages if, having an obligation or a right to do so, he fails to keep the premises let in a reasonably safe condition and that failure leads to an injury to anyone whom he might reasonably expect to be affected.

The section is not likely to have any relevance to most premises used as hospitals within the National Health Service because such premises are almost invariably owned by the Secretary of State and administered for him by the appropriate authority, the relationship between the Secretary of State and the authority not being that of landlord and tenant. An authority might, however, be using property leased from a private landlord, such as accommodation for nurses.

9.2.4 Warning notices and signs excluding liability

The Occupiers' Liability Act 1957 imposes a common duty of care except in so far as the occupier of premises is lawfully able, by way of contract or otherwise, to restrict or limit this liability or avoid it altogether. The Act does not specifically mention the circumstances in which the person seeking to alter, restrict or avoid his liability is so lawfully able. That question is dependent on further principles of both common law and statute. Soon after the passing of the Occupiers' Liability Act it was judicially decided that an occupier was at liberty lawfully to avoid the liability he would otherwise be under to a lawful visitor by the placing of a notice at the boundaries of the premises in question saying that persons entering the premises did so at their own risk. This judicial decision aroused a great deal of hostile criticism and was even hailed by some as a kind of charter for careless occupiers. However, the decision was legally correct within the bounds of the common law principle of consent, or the voluntary acceptance of risk.

In 1977, however, the full force of that decision was reduced very considerably by statute, namely the Unfair Contract Terms Act. This statute renders null and void any contract terms, or any 'notice' (a term which is clearly meant to include the sign which was in issue in the earlier decision) purporting to restrict or avoid personal liability for personal injury or death to another resulting from negligence. Thus, while the earlier decision is still authority for the proposition that damage to property may be lawfully avoided by an appropriately displayed notice at the edge of the property or premises, the more important and more usual complaint of personal injuries caused to a lawful visitor will not be hindered by an alleged consent to risk – the law no longer allows it.

In the case of loss or damage other than personal injury or death a person cannot, since the 1977 Act, exclude or restrict this liability for negligence except in so far as the term or notice satisfies the requirement of 'reasonableness'. The definition of negligence expressly includes the breach of the common duty of care imposed by the Occupiers' Liability

Act, but the prohibition of the 1977 Act on exclusion of liability applies only where the duty arises from things done in the course of a business or from the occupation of premises used for business purposes of the occupier. By section 14 'business' includes a profession and also the activities of any government department or local or public authority. The 1977 Act applies generally, therefore, to health services premises both within and outside the public sector.

If, in any case, a hospital relied on a notice disclaiming liability or warning of a danger as answer to an action for failure to exercise the common duty of care under section 2 of the Occupiers' Liability Act 1957, the question of fact would then arise whether (a) the notice had been seen by the injured person; and (b) if it had not, whether it was adequate to limit or exclude liability; and (c) whether or not it was reasonable.

The Unfair Contract Terms Act 1977 does not abolish the defence of consent to risk, but provides that a person's agreement to or awareness of an exempting condition or notice is not of itself to be taken as indicating his voluntary acceptance of the risk. All depends, in the final analysis, on the construction put by a court of law on the contractual condition or the notice in question, and in particular on the general point as to whether, in all the circumstances, it can be considered fair.

9.2.5 Personal liability of staff for accidents on premises

Even if, under the Occupiers' Liability Act 1957, a health authority or trust had been able effectively by warning notice or contract to disclaim liability for the safety of the premises, or if such authority had, by contract, effectively disclaimed liability for injury or loss to persons on the premises arising, for instance, by reason of the negligence of medical, nursing or other staff when performing their duties, that would not protect staff from actions for negligence against them personally.

9.3 DUTY OF OCCUPIER OF PREMISES TO TRESPASSERS

9.3.1 Common law

A trespasser is not a 'visitor' within the meaning of the Occupiers' Liability Act 1957 and accordingly the liability of an occupier to a trespasser injured on his land used to be a matter of the application of common law principles. Until the House of Lords' decision in *British Railways Board v Herrington* (1972)[10] the only duty of an occupier was not to act with reckless disregard for a trespasser's safety. In that case, however, the House of Lords condemned this rule as harsh and outmoded and substituted a new rule. Lord Denning in *Pannett v McGuiness and Co* (1972)[11] summarised the rule in *Herrington* thus:

'The long and short of it is that you have to take into account all the circumstances of the case and see then whether the occupier ought to have done more than he did. (1) You must apply your common sense. You must take into account the gravity and likelihood of the probable injury. Ultra-hazardous activities require a man to be ultra-cautious in carrying them out. The more dangerous the activity, the more he should take steps to see that no one is injured by it. (2) You should take into account also the character of the intrusion by the trespasser. A wandering child or a straying adult stands in a different position from a poacher or burglar. You may expect a child when you may not expect a burglar. (3) You must also have regard to the nature of the place where the trespass occurs. An electrified railway line or a warehouse being demolished may require more precautions to be taken than a private house. (4) You must also take into account the knowledge which the defendant has, or ought to have of the likelihood of trespassers being present. The more likely they are, the more precautions may have to be taken.'

It is worth noting some of the factors the courts have indicated they will take into account. In *Herrington* Lord Reid suggested that an impecunious occupier with little assistance at hand would often be excused from doing something which a large organisation with ample staff would be expected to do; Lord Morris of Borth-y-Gest said that it was a matter of what common sense or common humanity would dictate; Lord Pearson said that with the progress of technology there are more and greater dangers and there is considerably more need for occupiers to take reasonable steps to deter persons, especially children, from trespassing in dangerous places.

Accordingly, where in *Herrington* it was a six-year-old child who had trespassed on a railway line by going through a gap in a fence, liability was imposed on the Board because one of their employees (a stationmaster) knew both of the gap and the general tendency of children to trespass there. In *Pannett* a five-year-old child defied both his mother and the employees of the defendants and trespassed on a demolition site. The site, however, was near a children's playground, the time of the trespass was just after school; and perhaps conclusively the danger on the site was enhanced by a fire burning waste.

In *Davies v British Railways Board* (1984)[12] the plaintiff was a 12-year-old boy. He was playing on a housing estate abutting a railway line. He kicked a football over a six foot high fence separating the housing estate from the railway embankment. To retrieve his ball he went through a hole in the fence. He received severe burns when he tripped and fell near the railway tracks and landed on the conductor rail. He brought an action for damages against the British Railways Board on the grounds that the Board had negligently failed properly to guard the tracks.

The plaintiff's claim was unsuccessful. Through its employees the Board knew that children came onto the railway line and that special vigilance was therefore required. The Board had been slow in putting temporary repairs on a more permanent basis. The type of fence was, however, suitable for the purpose of barring entry onto the railway line although, like most such barriers, it could be penetrated by those determined enough to do so. The system of checking the fence and effecting repairs could be improved; but it could not in all the circumstances be said that the Board had failed in its duty to deter intruders from entry onto the line.

It was further held that, had the court found in the plaintiff's favour, his damages would have been reduced by 25 per cent on account of his own contributory negligence.

Mr Justice Farquharson also considered *Titchener v British Railways Board* (1983).[13] The unsuccessful plaintiff in that case was aged 15 and was crossing the railway line between two suburban stations in Glasgow. Access to the line could readily be obtained by climbing an embankment and passing through gaps in the Board's fencing. The Board knew the spot was used as a short cut, and had effected no repairs for years. In finding for the Board, the House of Lords held that the duty owed by the occupier under the Occupiers' Liability (Scotland) Act 1960 (which does not exclude trespassers from those to whom a duty is owed) is to the particular person who enters the premises in question. The existence and extent of the duty of care in Scotland, and by analogy of the duty of humanity in England, depends on the age and intelligence of the person entering the premises in question, upon the nature of the location and upon the obviousness or otherwise of the risk.

There was no suggestion in *Titchener v British Railways Board* that the train which hit the plaintiff was being driven negligently. *Slater v Clay Cross Co Ltd* (1956)[14] in which a negligently operated train on the defendant's land injured the plaintiff, was therefore distinguished.

9.3.2 Occupiers' Liability Act 1984

While decided cases prior to May 1984 are guides to judicial views on the practicability of precautions against injury to trespassers, the position is now governed by the Occupiers' Liability Act 1984. The Act came into force in May 1984 and applies to actions proceeding from facts occurring on or after that date. The Act brings English law affecting liability to trespassers substantially into line with existing Scots law (see *Titchener*, above) but goes further and protects also those who enter under rights of way, whether public or private, and who are not 'visitors' within the

Occupiers' Liability Act 1957. The 1984 Act also amends the Unfair Contract Terms Act 1977.

Section 1, affecting the legal duty of an occupier of premises to persons other than his visitors, provides as follows:

'**1.**—(1) The rules enacted by this section shall have effect, in place of the rules of the common law, to determine:

(a) whether any duty is owed by a person as occupier of premises to persons other than his visitors in respect of any risk of their suffering injury on the premises by reason of any danger due to the state of the premises or to things done or omitted to be done on them; and

(b) if so, what that duty is.

(2) For the purposes of this section, the persons who are to be treated respectively as an occupier of any premises (which, for those purposes, include any fixed or movable structure) and as his visitors are:

(a) any person who owes in relation to the premises the duty referred to in section 2 of the Occupiers' Liability Act 1957 (the common duty of care), and

(b) those who are his visitors for the purposes of that duty.

(3) An occupier of premises owes a duty to another (not being his visitor) in respect of any such risk as is referred to in subsection (1) above if:

(a) he is aware of the danger or has reasonable grounds to believe that it exists;

(b) he knows or has reasonable grounds to believe that the other is in the vicinity of the danger concerned or that he may come into the vicinity of the danger (in either case, whether the other has lawful authority for being in that vicinity or not); and

(c) the risk is one against which, in all the circumstances of the case, he may reasonably be expected to offer the other some protection.

(4) Where, by virtue of this section, an occupier of premises owes a duty to another in respect of such a risk, the duty is to take such care as is reasonable in all the circumstances of the case to see that he does not suffer injury on the premises by reason of the danger concerned.

(5) Any duty owed by virtue of this section in respect of a risk may, in an appropriate case, be discharged by taking such steps as are reasonable in all the circumstances of the case to give warning of the danger concerned or to discourage persons from incurring the risk.

(6) No duty is owed by virtue of this section to any person in respect of risks willingly accepted as his by that person (the question whether a risk was so accepted to be decided on the same principles as in other cases in which one person owes a duty of care to another).

(7) No duty is owed by virtue of this section to persons using the highway, and this section does not affect any duty owed to such persons.

(8) Where a person owes a duty by virtue of this section, he does not, by reason of any breach of the duty, incur any liability in respect of any loss of or damage to property.

(9) In this section:

"highway" means any part of a highway other than a ferry or waterway;

"injury" means anything resulting in death or personal injury, including any disease and any impairment of physical or mental condition; and

"movable structure" includes any vessel, vehicle or aircraft.'

Section 1 (3)(a) and (b) impose a legal duty to those on the occupier's premises whose presence is or should be known, and section 1(3)(b) specifically provides for trespassers. Factors relevant in *Davies, Herrington* and *Titchener* (above) will continue to be relevant. Both the forseeability of the plaintiff and the extent of duty to such a person depends on all the circumstances of the case. In *Herrington* the House of Lords allowed a subjective element in balancing magnitude of risk with the particular defendant's resources. The Law Commission[15] recommended the elimination of the subjective element from the equation. It remains to be seen whether the courts will so interpret section 1 of the 1984 Act.

Section 2 provides as follows:

'**2.**—At the end of section 1(3) of the Unfair Contract Terms Act 1977 (which defines the liability, called "business liability", the exclusion or restriction of which is controlled by virtue of that Act) there is added: "but liability of an occupier of premises for breach of an obligation or duty towards a person obtaining access to the premises for recreational or educational purposes, being liability for loss or damage suffered by reason of the dangerous state of the premises, is not a business liability of the occupier unless granting that person such access for the purposes concerned falls within the business purposes of the occupier".'

9.4   NUISANCE ETC.

9.4.1   Private nuisance

For an occupier of land to allow things, such as smells, smoke, noise or vibration, to interfere with the material enjoyment of other land in the vicinity or to cause loss or injury may constitute actionable private nuisance if the interference is, given the nature of the locality and all the surrounding circumstances, unreasonable. Other things which have been subject of actions for nuisance are electricity, heat, fumes and noxious vegetation, also pollution of water and apparently 'germs'[16] as well as wild animals and water in an artificial reservoir. Nor is the class of such things closed. Instances that might concern hospitals would be spread of infection or escape of radiation. Roots of trees encroaching on neighbouring property, if they cause damage for instance by drying out the soil and so causing cracks in a building on that property, may constitute nuisance.[17] Also actionable as private nuisance is any interference with an easement or other servitude appurtenant to land, such as a right of way or right to light.

A hospital or nursing home may be liable for nuisance committed, if any department such as a maternity block is inconveniently near residential property so that noises unpleasant either by reason of their nature, volume, continuance, or the time at which they are heard, reach neighbouring residential or business premises. Or again, the risk of disease germs may be a nuisance,[18] though the case in which this was decided, which concerned the erection of a smallpox hospital, might today be decided differently because knowledge of the control of infection has increased.[19] The noise from an engine room may equally be a nuisance,[20] as may the close proximity of a mortuary[21] so that distressing sights, sounds and obnoxious smells, reach the adjoining property. In *Bone v Scale* (1975)[22] the smells came from a pig farm. It was also said in this case that in assessing damages for loss of amenity caused by a nuisance a parallel may be drawn with the loss of amenity caused by personal injury but there is no rigid standard of comparison.

The test of reasonable standards applies also to claims for nuisance based on partial obstruction of ancient lights. The occupier of the dominant tenement is entitled only to a reasonable amount of light through the window which, by grant or prescription, has become an ancient light. He is not entitled to continue to receive the same amount of light as at the time the status of an ancient light was acquired, should that exceed what is reasonable judged by ordinary standards. There is no prescriptive right to a view, however attractive or however beneficial that might be to the patients of a private nursing home and, therefore, lucrative to the proprietor.

The same kind of standard of reasonableness is applicable in all actions for nuisance. Hence, if a hospital were using delicate electrical apparatus it would not have a remedy in nuisance merely on account of the fact that vibration from adjoining premises interfered with the use of that apparatus. The test is whether the vibration interferes with normal use or enjoyment, not extraordinary use, and an occupier of premises cannot rely on abnormal sensitivity or peculiar activities.

9.4.2 Public nuisance

Public nuisance is a criminal office; but it is also actionable as a tort by anyone who suffers loss or injury beyond the inconvenience suffered by the public at large, for instance, a shopkeeper, access to whose shop is blocked by an unlawful trench in the road.

Another example of privately actionable public nuisance is injury caused by the fall of a gutter or overhanging lamp which is out of repair, or of the bough of a tree which has become rotten and the state of which should have been known to the responsible person. Whether the action will lie against the owner or the occupier will depend on the extent of their respective responsibilities for external repairs under the tenancy agreement. That point will usually be academic so far as health authorities within the National Health Service are concerned, for hospital premises are usually owned by the Secretary of State and occupied, not by tenants, but by an authority or trust on his behalf. Moreover, so far as hospital houses let on service tenancies are concerned, the standard agreement provides that the health authority remains responsible for external repairs and so would be liable for any injury or damage due to failure to carry out the duty. Reference should now also be made to the Defective Premises Act 1972, section 4. It will, however, be a defence to a claim for damages in such circumstances to show that the accident was due to some latent defect not discoverable by reasonably careful inspection.[23]

9.4.3   The Clean Air Acts

The emission of smoke, grit, dust or fumes[24] is subject to the provisions of the Clean Air Acts 1956 and 1968, the purpose of the Acts being to vest in local authorities the power to control and ultimately to forbid the emission of dark smoke, grit or dust into the atmosphere and to forbid the emission of smoke, whether dark or not, in a smoke control area, as well as to control the emission of fumes. Enforcement of the Acts is by way of prosecution of offenders by the local authority in whose area the emission has taken place.

The Health and Safety at Work etc. Act 1974[25] created a duty under section 5 to use the best practicable means for preventing the emission into the atmosphere from any premises of noxious or offensive substances and for rendering harmless and inoffensive such substances as may be so emitted. 'Substance' is defined is section 53(1) as 'any natural or artificial substance, including micro-organisms, whether in solid or liquid form or in the form of a gas or vapour'. It is unclear whether noise is included or not. As stated above this Act specifically excludes any civil liability (section 47). Breach of the duties under it is a criminal offence (section 33). These provisions apply to National Health Service hospitals, under section 48.

In the case of emission of smoke, grit or dust contrary to the provisions of the Clean Air Acts, from premises such as a National Health Service hospital,[26] the local authority for the area in which the premises are situate may report the matter to the responsible Minister,[27] who shall inquire into the circumstances and, if the inquiry reveals that there is cause for complaint, shall employ all practicable means for preventing or minimising the emission of the smoke, grit, dust or fumes or for abating the nuisance and preventing its recurrence.

Notwithstanding the passing of the Clean Air Acts 1956 and 1968, the civil remedy of an action for nuisance in respect of emission of smoke, grit, dust or fumes, if such as to constitute actionable nuisance at common law, remains available against health authorities constituted under the National Health Service Act 1977, in respect of hospitals under their administration, no less than against occupiers of other hospitals and nursing homes, though one would not expect that an injunction would readily be granted against such authority in any but exceptional circumstances.

In the case of a voluntary hospital the local authority can launch a prosecution under the Clean Air Act 1956, and such hospital may also be made defendant in a civil action for damages for smoke nuisance as for any other common law nuisance.

9.4.4 Fire Precautions Act 1971

The Fire Precautions Act 1971 is applicable to health authorities and trusts and breach would afford strong evidence of negligence in any action for damages arising from injury to or the death of any person, or loss of or damage to personal property, by a fire.

NOTES

1. [1937] AC 97.
2. [1935] 51 TLR 554.
3. [1955] 1 WLR 207.
4. [1965] AC 778.
5. The Times, 15 February 1972.
6. The Times, 27 May 1955.
7. The Times, summary for 24 March 1955, published on 21 April.
8. *Lyes v Middlesex County Council* (1963) 61 LGR 448; *Reffell v Surrey County Council* [1964] 1 WLR 358.
9. [1962] 2 QB 533.
10. [1972] AC 877.
11. [1972] 2 QB 599 at 606–607.
12. (1984) 134 New LJ 888.
13. [1983] 1 WLR 1427.
14. [1956] 2 QB 264.
15. Cmnd 6428, 1976.
16. *Metropolitan District Asylum Board v Hill* (1881) 6 AC 193, 50 LJ (QB) 353.
17. *Davey v Harrow Corporation* [1958] 1 QB 60.
18. *Metropolitan District Asylum Board v Hill* (1881) 6 AC 193, 50 LJ (QB) 353.
19. See *Marshall v Lindsey County Council* [1937] AC 97. This case involved puerperal fever and turned on the safety of the premises.
20. *Allison v Merton, Sutton and Wandsworth AHA* [1975] CL 2450. But in *Nottingham Area No 1 HMC v Owen* [1958] 1 QB 50 it was held that an injunction did not lie to order the abatement of a nuisance.
21. A case on this point is understood to have been settled on terms in 1939.
22. [1975] 1 WLR 797.
23. *Noble v Harrison* [1926] 2 KB 332, a case concerning the bough of a tree which fell onto a motor coach on a public highway.
24. The emission of fumes is the subject of the 1968 Act, the powers and responsibilities of local authorities under the 1956 Act being widened accordingly.
25. The Act is further discussed in Chapter 20 on injury at work. Many of its provisions apply equally to visitors as well as employees.
26. *Pfizer Corporation v Ministry of Health* [1965] AC 512.
27. For the National Health Service, the Secretary of State for Health or the Secretary of State for Wales.

CHAPTER 10

Patients' property: loss or damage

10.1   WHETHER GOODS DEPOSITED

Claims may be made by patients and others in respect of valuables and other belongings which have been lost or damaged on hospital premises. The legal principles applicable to these two types of situation are examined separately, given that they differ. No liability is incurred if goods which are deposited are damaged, destroyed or stolen without negligence on the part of the hospital or its staff. What is proper care depends on all the circumstances of each case. It is clear that the lowest duty that might be imposed is to look after property as if the hospital were itself the owner. In such a case, no liability would be incurred where loss was suffered through dishonesty of an employee so long as there were no grounds for suspecting wrongdoing.

Liability in respect of property not given to the hospital management for safe custody is governed by the Occupiers' Liability Act 1957, which lays down a 'common duty of care' to take such care of the property as is reasonable in all the circumstances of the case. For the application of that Act to personal injuries, reference should be made to Chapter 9. Where, however, there is a duty to look after goods it is no excuse to seek to blame either the carelessness or even dishonesty of an employee.[1]

In *Martin v London County Council* (1947)[2] the defendant health authority was sued for loss of a patient's property. The plaintiff was awarded damages on the basis that the defendants had been bailees for reward.

10.2   DISCLAIMER OF LIABILITY

Hospitals are legally entitled to disclaim responsibility for the loss of, or damage to, patients' personal effects, except when the hospital staff take the property in question into safe custody on the admission of the patient to the hospital.

The common if not invariable practice of hospitals to take steps to disclaim responsibility for patients' property not handed over for safe custody strongly suggests that hospitals hold themselves out as having reasonable facilities for looking after property handed over by patients and that money, unless banked, as well as jewellery and other valuables, would be kept in a safe.

One should not overlook the importance of reasonable care during the period before which valuables handed in for safe custody reach the safe and also after they have been taken out of the safe to be handed back to the patient. It may be suggested that the standard of care expected to be taken of a patient's property immediately on reception might well be higher if the patient were not an emergency case, because it is then reasonably practicable to carry out properly whatever precautionary procedure might have been laid down; whereas if the patient were being received in an emergency, say, by the necessarily depleted night staff, the circumstances might well warrant what would otherwise be negligence.

Despite any disclaimer of responsibility on the lines indicated in departmental circulars, it is suggested that if, say, a patient's wrist-watch, jewellery, spectacles or dentures, of which he had retained physical control while in hospital, had been taken from him when he went to the theatre for an operation, the hospital authority at that point in time, and until the patient was again volitional and could exercise effective control, would have to be regarded as having accepted responsibility as bailee. Yet another case in which that would probably be true is that of the out-patient who was not allowed to have personal possessions with him when going for examination or treatment, but was compelled to leave them in a cubicle. It is to be doubted very much whether in such circumstances a notice disclaiming responsibility would be effective, at all events in a hospital within the National Health Service.

In respect of disclaimer of responsibility for other items, the effectiveness of any notice of disclaimer which might be exhibited in the reception area, whether for in-patients or for out-patients, is doubtful for it seems that unless a patient making a claim for loss of property can be proved to have read the notice he will not be bound by it. It would be a more reliable practice for the hospital to draw the patient's attention to the disclaimer when the letter of appointment or admission is sent out.

If any article, such as a dressing gown, which the patient had kept in the ward for necessary use was stolen, damaged or destroyed in circumstances attributable to negligence of any member of the hospital staff, the patient would not be able to claim against the hospital in the face of an effective disclaimer. It does not follow, however, that a member of the hospital staff through whose negligence property was damaged, lost or destroyed which belonged to a patient and has been kept by him in the ward (e.g. watch, fountain pen, spectacles) could not be made personally liable. Insofar as theft is concerned, this view is supported by *Tinsley v Dudley* (1951),[3] part of the judgment in which was cited with approval in the Court of Appeal in *Edwards v West Herts Group Hospital Management Committee* (1957):[4]

> 'There is no warrant at all on the authorities so far as I know, for holding that an invitor, where the invitation extends to the goods as well as the person of the invitee, thereby by implication of law assumes a liability to protect the invitee and his goods, not merely from physical dangers arising from defects in the premises, but from the risk of the goods being stolen by some third party. That implied liability, so far as I know, is one unknown to the law.'

'*Edwards*' case concerned the property of a resident medical officer, stolen from his quarters; but the principle is equally applicable to patients' property.

The common law has, over the years, imposed special duties of property safekeeping on innkeepers and persons keeping guesthouses and boardinghouses, but not on hospitals. Even if, in respect of patients received under section 65 of the National Health Service Act 1977, a hospital were in the position of a boardinghouse keeper, those responsible for it could still, by notice, disclaim responsibility for theft by third parties, even if caused by lack of care of its employees. Any such disclaimer notice would have to be 'fair' under the Unfair Contract Terms Act 1977 (see Chapter 9, pp. 323–324, above). Unless the common duty of care under the Occupiers' Liability Act 1957 has been expressly disclaimed in respect of the patient's belongings which he keeps in the ward, it is possible that by section 1(3) of the Act of 1957, the hospital would be liable for damage to, or destruction of, such belongings caused by the negligence of its employees.

10.3   VOLUNTARY HOSPITALS AND NURSING HOMES

Except for references to official Circulars and to National Health Service legislation, this chapter applies equally to voluntary hospitals and to nursing homes. These may make whatever conditions or disclaimers they like concerning patients' property and, provided they do so before the patient is accepted for treatment (or at any rate draw it to the attention of the patient before such time as it is sought to rely on the disclaimer), any disclaimer of liability is effective provided that it is in all the circumstances fair. In the absence of an effective disclaimer, paying patients would be entitled to expect of the hospital staff the same degree of care in relation to their property as a prudent owner would take of his own property. Such was the standard of care which in *Dansey v*

Richardson (1854)[5] it was held that a boardinghouse keeper owed to his guests. The standard applicable to a hospital would be at least as high, if not actually higher, on account of the dependent nature of many patients.

10.4 DEPOSIT OF VALUABLES: FORMALITIES

When valuables are deposited by a patient it is customary, for the avoidance of disputes, for a list of the articles deposited to be made and acknowledged as correct by the patient's signature. It is wise to avoid describing any article such as an item of jewellery in such way that the hospital may (possibly after the patient's death) be committed as to its quality or the material of which it is made. It is desirable to include with the list to be signed by the patient a form of authority to the hospital to dispose of any articles unclaimed within a certain time of the patient's leaving hospital and to be accountable only for the proceeds.[6] If some such expression as 'ceased to be an in-patient at the hospital' were used, the authority might also cover disposal after the patient's death.

If a patient is brought in as an accident or emergency case and therefore cannot sign the form, the correctness of the list made may conveniently be certified by the signature of any accompanying responsible relative or friend, but if there is none such, it is advisable that two members of the staff together remove money and valuables from the patient and both certify the correctness of the list.

If, because a patient is unconscious or too ill to sign when he is received, no form is signed, it is reasonable to assume that the liability of the hospital is not increased, the only doubt being as to whether the goods could, without express authority, be sold if unclaimed after the patient had left the hospital even though the form of deposit and authority ordinarily in use so authorised. If, by inadvertence, no form is signed, the respective rights and duties of the patient and the hospital would have to be determined on the evidence, taking into account any general practice or hospital policy, notices exhibited and any agreement by word of mouth.

10.5 HANDING OVER PATIENT'S PROPERTY TO THIRD PARTY

A patient admitted otherwise than as an emergency case is often accompanied by a friend or relative who, with his knowledge and consent, takes away any valuables and clothing not required in hospital. Then no difficulty arises. When a seriously ill patient is brought into hospital (maybe unconscious as the result of an accident) and clothing, money or valuables are handed to a person accompanying the patient, there is the risk of a civil action for the tort of conversion against the hospital if the patient loses his property thereby. In practice, provided the value of the property handed over is regarded as falling within reasonable limits, that risk is usually taken.

10.6 PROPERTY OF DECEASED PATIENTS

Property of a deceased patient should not normally be handed over to anyone other than the patient's legal personal representative (for instance, the executor of his will who has obtained probate, or the administrator of his estate under letters of administration), or to a person duly authorised by the personal representative. Hospitals do in fact exercise some discretion and it is customary to hand over to the deceased patient's widow, widower or next of kin (against a letter of indemnity) property of the deceased patient, provided that property is not of very high value and provided it is not known that there are competing claimants.

If a person dies intestate and without lawful kin (for illegitimacy see later in this section) his estate passes to the Crown as *bona vacantia* and is administered by the Treasury Solicitor. If the deceased person had been ordinarily resident in the Duchy of Cornwall then it is administered by the Solicitor to the Duchy or, if in the County Palatine, by the Solicitor to the Duchy of Lancaster. If a patient dies in hospital leaving in possession of the hospital property (such as money or jewellery) of substantial value and he is not known, after reasonable inquiry, to have made a will or to have left any relatives entitled to his estate on intestacy, the Treasury Solicitor (or the Solicitor to the Duchy of Cornwall or of Lancaster as appropriate) should be informed. While the hospital should make reasonable inquiries before communicating with the Treasury Solicitor, that is not a legal obligation and a hospital is under no obligation to go to trouble and expense in pursuing inquiries. The Treasury Solicitor might, however, in any particular case refuse to accept responsibility for the property if he were not satisfied that the patient had died intestate and without lawful next of kin. All that the hospital could do then would be to retain the property until claimed by someone having a lawful right to it or until any such claim were statute-barred. A claim by the Crown could not be so barred.

In relation to the rights of illegitimate children on the intestacy of a natural parent and of natural parents on the intestacy of an illegitimate child, section 14(1) and (2) of the Family Law Reform Act 1969 formerly provided that, where either parent of an illegitimate child died intestate as respects all or any of his or her real or personal property, the illegitimate child was entitled to take any interest therein to which he or such issue would have been entitled if he had been born legitimate; and that where an illegitimate child died intestate in respect of all or any of his real or personal property, each of his parents, if surviving, was entitled to take any interest therein to which that parent would have been entitled if the child had been born legitimate.

These provisions were repealed by section 33(4) of, and Schedule 4 to, the Family Law Reform Act 1987. Section 18 of that Act, dealing with the rights of succession to property on intestacy, removes illegitimacy as a point to be taken into consideration when determining rights of succession to the estate of an illegitimate person, or traced through an illegitimate relationship.

The possible effect of the provisions of the Act on the position of a hospital finding itself left in possession of property belonging to a deceased patient should be noted in the formulation of practice and policy.

Where there is near illegitimate kin as well as legitimate kin of a deceased patient who has died intestate, it is unsafe to hand over property without the production of letters of administration in his favour on the assumption that his claim to the estate would prevail.[7] Although to take a letter of indemnity from a relative to whom property of moderate value is handed over without production of letters of administration is a sensible precaution, it has to be recognised that the value of such a letter as security against loss is largely dependent on the solvency and integrity of the giver.

10.7   PROPERTY LEFT IN HOSPITAL

Property left behind by a patient, whether deposited as valuable or not, is a problem unless the patient has given written authority for disposal of any such property. It is usually reasonable to treat property not deposited as valuables as abandoned by the patient if not speedily claimed after his discharge and to dispose of it accordingly. But if an article left behind in hospital, even though not deposited as valuable, is in fact valuable, precipitate action to dispose of it would be unwise and might lead to an action for the tort of conversion, the measure of damages ordinarily being the value of the article at the time of conversion, of which the price obtained on sale would be evidence.

Deposited valuables present a more difficult problem. Apart from authority for disposal contained in the form signed by the patient at the time of deposit, such articles could not be treated as abandoned but should, in principle, be held until claimed. The patient's claim would probably not be barred until six years after his demand for return of the deposited article which would mean that however long after disposal by the hospital such demand were made 'conversion' would be regarded as having taken place only at that date.[8]

10.8   PROPERTY FOUND ON HOSPITAL PREMISES

Lost property may have been found either in a part of the hospital to which the members of the public are admitted or in some other part of the premises and may have been found by any person, possibly a member of the staff or possibly by a 'visitor' within the meaning of the Occupiers' Liability Act 1957 or possibly by a trespasser. If the owner of any such object so found did not claim it and could not be traced, to whom would it belong?

The finder has good title against all the world except the true owner. If the article were found by someone other than a member of the staff in a part of the hospital to which the public had access, that person would be entitled to keep it unless the owner could be traced. Indeed a person who found a lost article in a part of the hospital in which he was a trespasser *might* still have a good title except against the rightful owner,[9] though there is a legal presumption that the owner of land is the owner of chattels found there.[10] The position of an employee of the hospital who finds an article of value depends on the circumstances of the case and on his conditions of employment. If the finding is in the course of his duties and on behalf of his employing authority, then the hospital will have good title except against the true owner.[11] Conditions of employment might include an obligation to hand over to the hospital any article he might find on the premises, and much would depend on the wording of the relevant term of the agreement. Consideration would have to be given to whether it referred only to things found on hospital premises while the employee was on duty, or to whatever he might find there at any time – an important distinction, particularly in the case of a resident officer. Failing any such agreement, the position of an officer who found any money or chattels on hospital premises, otherwise than in the course of his duties, and otherwise than in a part of the hospital to which he had access only because of his status as an officer, would seem to be indistinguishable from that of a member of the public who did so.

10.9   PROTECTION OF PROPERTY OF PERSONS TAKEN TO HOSPITAL OR LOCAL AUTHORITY HOME ETC.

Section 48 of the National Assistance Act 1948 imposes on local social services authorities the duty of protecting the movable property (a term which includes money and cheques) of (amongst others) persons admitted as patients to any hospital. The section reads:

'**48.**—(1) Where a person—
   (a)   is admitted as a patient to any hospital, or
   (b)   is admitted to accommodation provided under Part III of this Act, or
   (c)   is removed to any other place under an order made under subsection (3) of the last foregoing section,
and it appears to the council that there is danger of loss of, or damage to, any

moveable property of his by reason of his temporary or permanent inability to protect or deal with the property and that no other suitable arrangements have been or are being made for the purposes of this subsection, it shall be the duty of the council to take reasonable steps to prevent or mitigate the loss or damage.

(2) For the purpose of discharging the said duty the council shall have power at all reasonable times to enter any premises which immediately before the person was admitted or removed as aforesaid were his place of residence or usual place of residence, and to deal with any moveable property of his in any way which is reasonably necessary to prevent or mitigate loss thereof or damage thereto.

(3) A council may recover from a person admitted or removed as aforesaid, or from any person who for the purposes of this Act is liable to maintain him, any reasonable expenses incurred by the council in relation to him under the foregoing provisions of this section.

(4) In this section the expression "council" means in relation to any property [the council which is the local authority for the purposes of the Local Authority Social Services Act 1970 and][12] in the area of which the property is for the time being situated.

For the purposes of this provision a person is admitted as a patient to a hospital if he is admitted for treatment of mental disorder. Under section 99 of the Mental Health Act 1983 the Court of Protection may appoint a receiver of the patient's property. An approved social worker or other appropriate officer of the local social services authority may apply to the Court of Protection and be appointed receiver of the patient's property in appropriate cases. By section 49 of the National Assistance Act 1948, as amended, the authority has power to reimburse his expenses. There are no provisions for reimbursement by a hospital of the expenses of an officer of such authority making application or being appointed receiver of a patient's property.

Persons admitted to accommodation provided under Part III of the Act are those admitted to accommodation provided by a local authority under section 21, namely (a) residential accommodation for persons who by reason of age, infirmity or any other circumstances including mental disorder are in need of care and attention which is not otherwise available to them, and (b) temporary accommodation for persons who are in urgent need thereof, being need arising in circumstances which could not reasonably have been foreseen or in such other circumstances as the authority may in any particular case determine.

The third class of person in respect of whose property section 48 may apply is those removed under an order made under section 47 (as to which see Chapter 30, p. 870, below).

NOTES

1. See *Houghland v R R Lowe (Luxury Coaches) Ltd* [1962] 1 QB 694 at 697–698; *Morris v C W Martin and Sons Ltd* [1966] 1 QB 716; and *Transmotors v Robertson, Buckley* [1970] 1 Ll Rep 224.

2. [1947] 1 All ER 783.
3. [1951] 2 KB 18 at 31, per Jenkins, J.
4. [1957] 1 WLR 415.
5. (1854) 3 E & B 144.
6. *Beaman v ARTS Ltd* [1949] 1 KB 550 illustrates the risks of a bailee who disposes of the bailor's property otherwise than in accordance with his authority even after a long interval of time.
7. See also HM(62)2, HM(71)90.
8. See also *Beaman v ARTS Ltd* [1949] 1 KB 550.
9. This would appear to follow from *Bridges v Hawksworth* (1851) 21 LJ (QB) 75; *Hannah v Peel* [1945] KB 509.
10. *City of London Corporation v Appleyard* [1963] 1 WLR 982 and *Moffatt v Kazana* [1969] 2 QB 152.
11. See *City of London Corporation v Appleyard* [1963] 1 WLR 982 and the cases there referred to.
12. Words in brackets substituted by the Local Government Act 1972.

CHAPTER 11

Visitors who refuse to leave

Patients' visitors are in law 'lawful visitors' being expressly or impliedly allowed to enter the premises. The nurse in charge of a ward acts on the managers' behalf and can exercise their lawful right to exclude a person from the premises. Subject to the rules of the hospital, that nurse will have the authority to decide how many visitors are permitted, and for how long.

A person entering or remaining on premises such as a hospital or nursing home without the consent, express or implied, of the occupier or his representative becomes a trespasser, and if he refuses to leave when ordered to do so can be removed provided no more force is used than the occasion requires. (The limited duty of care to trespassers in respect of premises safety is considered in Chapter 9.) If a trespasser resists such removal he commits an assault and a person lawfully moving him, if attacked, is justified in reasonable self-defence.

An attempt should first be made to persuade a trespasser to leave quietly. If he refuses he should be clearly and unambiguously ordered to go, if possible in the presence of at least one witness; then and then only may force be used to eject him. Police attendance may be useful on such occasions, for a show of resistance by the trespasser in the presence of a police officer to the use of reasonable force to remove him would constitute a breach of the peace in respect of which the police officer would have power of arrest.

The problem of dealing with trespassers on hospital premises is usually practical rather than legal, though it is not always easy to determine whether a person has become a trespasser, and still less to decide whether to treat him as such. Two examples are therefore useful. First, there is the in-patient who declines to leave on the completion of his treatment. Legally he becomes a trespasser if he refuses to leave when discharged. If by reason of some incapacity, such as blindness, unconnected with the illness for which he was treated in hospital, he is not fully able to take care of himself elsewhere, there is a problem. Accommodation offered by the local social services authority is not within section 47 of the National Assistance Act 1948. Consequently the patient cannot be compulsorily removed to a welfare institution under that section and hospital accommodation may be more attractive than that provided in a social services facility and it is also provided free, while social services accommodation is subject to payment according to means.

Persons who are a nuisance in a ward, whether by their conduct or by their effect on the patient, can be required to leave and may be removed. It makes no difference that a visitor excluded at the request of a patient is the husband or wife, the patient's wishes being a sufficient justification for exclusion of any person in all but the most exceptional circumstances.

What if the patient is under the age of 16 and a parent were insistent on access? Refusal might well result in the parent with custody and control claiming to exercise the right to remove the child. While there is a lack of legal guidance, it is highly unlikely that any court would uphold the right to do so if removal would imperil the child's life or health or subject him to immediate suffering. Perhaps the parent of a young child could be refused access to the child if that were urgently medically necessary. Parental objection to treatment might be disregarded in a very urgent and dangerous case. So long as the parent remains unobtrusive he may have a right to remain with his child, and it is only where he actually interferes with the doctor's duty to take proper care of the patient's treatment that he may be excluded. While Circular HC(76)5 requires District Health Authorities to provide facilities for parental and other visiting, such requirement gives no guide to the decision as to when, in difficult circumstances such as those just discussed, the right to use the facilities should be permitted.

Visitors, so far as allowed, enter the wards (to use the common law term) as licensees and the ward sister, having full responsibility for her ward may, on behalf of the health authority, withdraw the licence at any time. She is not strictly obliged to give a reason for her decision. When, for example, a patient has visitors in excess of such number as may be authorised, the sister can, in her absolute discretion, require such of the visitors to leave as she thinks fit. A person who does not do so becomes a trespasser and, if thought desirable, reasonable force may then be used to remove him.

CHAPTER 12

Search and arrest of suspected persons

From time to time thefts occur in most hospitals and similar institutions and a patient or member of staff may be suspected. Sometimes, too, conclusive proof is very hard to come by, especially in respect of a regular course of petty theft as, for example, of comparatively small quantities of foodstuffs. The question then arises as to whether there is any right of search either of the individual or, in the case of a resident, of his or her quarters. Also, there is the question of what justifies the making of a formal charge against a suspected person, and of the circumstances in which anyone who is not a policeman may have the right of arrest in respect of theft or of other offences.

12.1 POWERS OF SEARCH

Leaving aside the right of the police to search and detain a person suspected of a particular offence, it can be said that noone has the right to search either a person or his quarters except with his consent. This statement of general principle will be further analysed and explained in succeeding paragraphs.

12.1.1 Search of the person

Any wrongful act infringing a person's right to his personal liberty, i.e. freedom from restraint, generally falls under the head of false imprisonment, which expression covers any infliction of bodily restraint which is not expressly or impliedly authorised by law[1]; or, put another way, the act of arresting or imprisoning any person without lawful justification or otherwise preventing him without lawful justification from exercising his right of leaving the place in which he is. Similarly any act infringing the right of liberty of the person by direct application of force, or even threat of force, amounts to battery if force is used and to assault if it is effectively threatened.

From this it follows that to detain a person for search, when he has not freely consented to remain for that purpose, may lay those responsible for so doing open to legal actions both for false imprisonment and for assault and battery. If, in the course of an unlawful search, stolen property were found on the person searched so as to justify his being handed over to the police and charged, those responsible are nevertheless not exempted from liability in respect of the original wrong of false imprisonment and of assault and battery. In such a case, however, it can be said with some confidence that there would then be little risk of any action by the wrongdoer, or of such action resulting in the award of substantial damages, provided the charge leading to their search had been substantiated. If, however, an illegal search did not lead to the discovery of any stolen property, or if, stolen property having been found, the person searched had been able to give a good account of his possession of it, whether at once or to the satisfaction of the criminal court hearing any charge preferred against him, then he would be likely to obtain substantial damages in any action he might bring.

The only effective line of defence to search without lawful authority is consent, and it sometimes happens that an employing authority makes the right of search a condition of employment; but even this gives the employer no right of forcible search should an employee, in the event, refuse to be searched. The right of the employer would then be no more than to treat the refusal as a breach of contract.[2]

In order to be an effective defence consent at the time of the search must be genuine consent, real acquiescence in the search with full opportunity to refuse. In particular it is not true consent if a person, although he objects, submits to what he conceives to be authority or force. If he feels that he will be searched whether he likes it or not he does not consent by passively submitting to it. On the other hand, in refutation of a suggestion of theft, a person may demand to be searched and unless he withdraws that invitation, 'leave and licence' to proceed with the search may be implied.

Intimate searches, or 'body orifice' searches, should always be accompanied by the greatest care for both the civil liberties and the safety and wellbeing of the person whom it is proposed to search, as well as for the safety and wellbeing of other persons including, for this purpose, both other patients and members of staff. Depending on the urgency with which it is professionally considered advisable or necessary to conduct an intimate search, persuasion should be attempted to produce the desired outcome of safety and wellbeing. Particular questions relating to the degree of risk and the reality or otherwise of any apparent consent to search may be raised in the care and treatment of patients suffering from mental disorder and who are judged to present a risk to themselves or others (including staff), or both.

12.2 MENTALLY DISORDERED PATIENTS

The Mental Health Act Code of Practice, issued by the Department of Health in 1990, makes the following recommendations on search of patients:

'25.1 Authorities should ensure that there is an operational policy on the searching of patients and their belongings. Such a policy should be checked with the health authority's legal advisers.

25.2 It should not be part of such a policy routinely to carry out searches of patients and their personal belongings. If, however, there are lawful grounds for carrying out such a search, the patient's consent should be sought. In undertaking such a search staff should have due regard for the dignity of the person concerned and the need to carry out the search in such a way as to ensure the maximum privacy.

25.3 If the patient does not consent to the search, staff should consult with the Unit General Manager (or such other delegated senior staff (e.g. senior nurse manager) when he is not available) before undertaking any lawful search. The same principles relating to the patient's dignity and the need for maximum privacy apply. Any such search should be carried out with the minimum force necessary and in the case of a search of a patient's person, unless urgent necessity dictates otherwise, such a search should be carried out by a staff member of the same sex.

25.4 If items belonging to a patient are removed, the patient should be informed where these are being kept.'

12.2.1 Police powers to conduct intimate body search

Specific powers are given to police, subject to closely defined conditions and safeguards, by section 55 of the Police and Criminal Evidence Act 1984. Section 55, so far as relevant to the context of hospital practice, provides as follows:

'55.—(1) Subject to the following provisions of this section if an officer of at least the rank of superintendent has reasonable grounds for believing—
  (a) that a person who has been arrested and is in police detention may have concealed on him any thing which
      (i) he could use to cause physical injury to himself or others; and
      (ii) he might so use while he is in police detention or in the custody of a court; or
  (b) that such a person—
      (i) may have a Class A drug concealed on him; and
      (ii) was in possession of it with the appropriate criminal intent before his arrest,
he may authorise such a search of that person.

(2) An officer may not authorise an intimate search of a person for anything unless he has reasonable grounds for believing that it cannot be found without his being intimately searched.

(3) An officer may give an authorisation under subsection (1) above orally or in writing but, if he gives it orally, he shall confirm it in writing as soon as is practicable.

(4) An intimate search which is only a drug offence search shall be by way of examination by a suitably qualified person.

(5) Except as provided by subsection (4) above, an intimate search shall be by way of examination by a suitably qualified person unless an officer of at least the rank of superintendent considers that this is not practicable.

(6) An intimate search which is not carried out as mentioned in subsection (5) above shall be carried out by a constable.

(7) A constable may not carry out an intimate search of a person of the opposite sex.

(8) No intimate search may be carried out except—

(a)   at a police station;

(b)   at a hospital;

(c)   at a registered medical practitioner's surgery; or

(d)   at some other place used for medical purposes.

(9) An intimate search which is only a drug offence search may not be carried out at a police station.'

Class A drugs, referred to in section 55(1)(b)(i) as objects for which an intimate search may be proposed, are defined by section 2(1)(b) and Schedule 2, Part I, of the Misuse of Drugs Act 1971. Class A drugs include cocaine, heroin, methadone, morphine and pethidine, but do not include cannabis.

12.2.2   Search of quarters

For search of residential accommodation occupied by a member of the staff of a hospital to be lawful, the consent of the occupant is necessary. In practice the issue may be confused (but not altered in law) by the fact that the right of entry to staff quarters by senior officers may be at least impliedly reserved, for the purpose of supervision, particularly for seeing that the domestic staff are carrying out their duties and that the quarters are being kept clean and used in a proper manner. But such a general right of entry and inspection cannot be expanded into a right of search. Any prying into the personal belongings of a member of staff, feeling amongst the folds of clothing and in the pockets and inspecting the contents of bags and handbags, is far beyond any such right of general inspection and, if to be justified at all, must be justified as what it truly is, namely, a search. Whether in any instance there had been consent sufficient to justify such search would be a matter of fact, relevant factors being substantially the same as in respect of consent of a search of the person. If there has been no effective consent, the search will be actionable as trespass to goods. 'The wrong of trespass includes any unpermitted contact with or impact upon another's chattel . . .

probably the courts will hold that direct and deliberate interference is trespass even if no damage [to the goods] ensues.'[3]

12.2.3 Search of staff lockers

What has been said about the search of staff quarters applies equally to staff lockers intended to be used exclusively for personal belongings. The existence of a master key in the hands of a senior officer makes no difference.

12.2.4 Search of patient's lockers etc.

What has been said in this section of the chapter about searching staff quarters would no less apply to the deliberate searching of a patient's possessions, though this is less likely to be at issue. Certainly the bona fide tidying up of a patient's locker would not be unlawful.[4]

12.3 ARREST

The power of arrest, both by the police and ordinary citizens, is now governed by Part III of the Police and Criminal Evidence Act 1984. The Act draws a distinction between arrest during the commission of an offence and arrest after an offence has been committed.

12.3.1 Arrest during the commission of an offence

Section 24(4) provides:

'(4) Any person may arrest without a warrant—
  (a) anyone who is in the act of committing an arrestable offence;
  (b) anyone whom he has reasonable grounds for suspecting to be committing such an offence.'

The section enables any person to arrest anyone who is, or whom he or she has reasonable grounds for suspecting to be, committing an arrestable offence.[5] It is therefore important to be able identify an arrestable offence. In the present context the most important arrestable offences include: theft; robbery; burglary; handling stolen goods, knowing or believing them to be stolen goods; going equipped for burglary or theft; obtaining property by deception; obtaining a pecuniary advantage by deception; false accounting; blackmail; and attempting or conspiring to commit any of the above offences.

If the person arrested was not in fact committing an arrestable offence, then the person making the arrest must have reasonable grounds for suspecting that such an offence was in fact being committed. The test is objective but account must be taken of the circumstances of the arrest. A leading judge has stated that reasonable suspicion may take account of matters which could not be put in evidence, or matters which, though admissible, could not form part of the case against the suspect.[6] The circumstances of the case should be such that a reasonable man acting without passion or prejudice would have suspected the person of committing the offence.

The suspicion must also be that the offence is being committed at the moment of arrest. This can cause difficulties with theft. If theft is a single act, an arrest could not be justified under section 24(4) unless it took place at the moment of the dishonest appropriation, which is notoriously difficult to pinpoint.[7]

12.3.2   Arrest after the commission of an offence

Section 24(5) provides:

'(5) Where an arrestable offence has been committed, any person may arrest without a warrant—
   (a)   anyone who is guilty of the offence;
   (b)   anyone whom he has reasonable grounds for suspecting to be guilty of it.'

For an arrest under section 24(5) to be lawful the offence must actually have been committed. If the arrested person is acquitted because they lack the necessary intention, the arrest will be unlawful.

If a hospital officer detained someone for theft it seems, on the basis of *Tims v John Lewis & Co Ltd* (1952),[8] that the arrest would not be invalidated, nor the detention support an action for false imprisonment, merely because the person arrested had been detained a reasonable time for reference to be made to a senior officer in accordance with hospital rules, for him to decide whether a charge should be made. It must be observed, however, that in the *Tims* case there was justification for the charge being made although, in the event, the accused person was acquitted. Consequently the *Tims* case will not help if the arrest was unjustified *ab initio*. But the prompt release of the arrested person without his being charged might go in mitigation of damages in an action for wrongful arrest and false imprisonment.

12.4   LIABILITY FOR WRONGFUL SEARCH AND ARREST

Should a member of staff or a patient be searched in circumstances giving rise to an action for assault or for false imprisonment, or should quarters or possessions be searched so as to result in an action for trespass to goods, who may be made the defendants?

Certainly the individual officer concerned could be made a defendant as well as any other members of staff who might have assisted him; and 'superior orders' does not exonerate from such liability. But the aggrieved person would, if possible, usually prefer to sue the defendant authority or trust, either alone or jointly with the officer or officers concerned, since any judgment in his favour would then be more likely to be effective than if solely against individuals who might be insolvent. And in most cases it is probably safe to say that the defendant employer could be made liable, the test being whether the officer concerned acted in the course of his employment.

The practical conclusion to draw from this outline of the law as to arrest is that only in absolutely clear-cut cases of manifest and serious wrongdoing should a private person, such as a hospital officer, take the responsibility of arresting another person. Otherwise, unless the situation is one of extreme urgency, he should seek advice and instructions.

NOTES

1. In the case of a mentally disordered patient liable to detention it may be said that insofar as those in charge of him may do whatever is necessary for his wellbeing or for the safety of others, a search without his consent, e.g. for a knife or for drugs, would clearly be justified. But it is open to some doubt whether, if the patient were volitional, a search for some other purpose (e.g. money or valuables which have been stolen) without his consent would be lawful. The position in the case of an informal patient suffering from a mental disorder is more obscure. It is questionable whether, if volitional, he should be searched, even for drugs or weapons, against his will.
2. See Annual Report of the Medical Defence Union for 1972 at p. 50.
3. Clerk and Lindsell *Torts* (16th edn, 1989) pp. 972–975; also Salmond & Heuston, *Law of Torts* (20th edn, 1992) pp. 128–131.
4. Those treating a patient in hospital may sometimes have the strong suspicion that he has a supply of and is using dangerous drugs. Such suspicion does not in law justify any member of the hospital staff searching possible hiding places such as wallets, purses and handbags. The hospital may, however, be in a position to exercise some control over what a patient may keep with him in the ward and could possibly find a reason for having a suspect container removed from the ward for safe custody. Also, as ordinarily a hospital has power to exclude visitors, it could on occasion consider use of that power to exclude visitors who might be possible sources of drugs, giving no more than a conventional reason to anyone excluded. As to giving information to the police see Chapter 16.
5. See section 24(1)–(3).
6. Lord Devlin in *Shaaban Bin Hussein v Chong Fook Kam* [1969] 3 A11 ER 1626.
7. See Hargreves *A Practitioner's Guide to the Police and Criminal Evidence Act 1984* (1985), Legal Action Group, p. 69.
8. [1952] AC 676.

CHAPTER 13

Data protection

The extensive use of computers in the field of health care, for patient and associated data, makes a working knowledge of the Data Protection Act 1984 essential to hospital managers.

Legislation was needed because of the threat posed to privacy by the rapid growth in computer use. By January 1981 the Council of Europe had completed a convention aimed at securing protection of privacy in the face of this threat. The convention, when it came into effect, would enable party states to refuse to allow personal information to be sent to other countries which did not have comparable safeguards.

The Data Protection Act 1984 places legal obligations on those who record and use 'personal data'. They must register their use of personal data with the Data Protection Registry and comply with the Data Protection Principles which require that data be obtained and processed fairly and lawfully. The Act confers new rights on those about whom personal data are recorded. These include certain rights of access to the data, and a right to compensation for damage caused by any inaccuracy found to exist in it.

13.1 TO WHAT DOES THE ACT APPLY?

It is essential to achieve a working knowledge of the definitions in the Act, referring to concepts which interact with each other in a complex way. The Act is only concerned with regulating the use of 'personal data'.

13.1.1 Data

'Data' is defined as

'information recorded in a form in which it can be processed by equipment operating automatically in response to instructions given for that purpose'.[1]

Any information is thus capable of constituting data, provided it is in a form in which it can be *processed* automatically. The definition of 'data' is in therefore turn dependent upon the meaning given to the term 'processing'.

13.1.2 Processing

' "Processing", in relation to data, means amending, augmenting, deleting or re-arranging the data or extracting the information constituting the data . . .'[2]

This wide definition is subject to three qualifications.

First, the definition must be read in conjunction with the definition of 'data'. An example is useful. Information stored on microfilm may either be in a form in which it can be extracted manually or by microprocessor. But 'processing' is defined in relation to data, and information only constitutes data if it can be processed automatically; therefore only in the latter instance does the Act apply.

Second, the data must be processed '. . . by reference to the data subject',[3] that is the person whom the data concerns. This is an important qualification: since the data needs to be processed by reference to the data subject, processing which incidentally reveals personal data will not fall within the scope of the Act.

Third, any operation performed solely for the purpose of preparing the text of documents does not constitute processing as defined in the Act.[4]

13.1.3 Personal data

'Personal data' is defined as

'information which relates to a living individual who can be identified from that information (or from that and other information in the possession of the data user), including any expression of opinion about the individual but not any indication of the intentions of the data user in respect of that individual'.[5]

'Personal data' therefore do not include information about persons who are not living individuals. The definition excludes statements of intent from the provisions of the Act, but not statements of opinion. There might thus have been an opportunity of avoiding the provisions of the Act by disguising opinions as intentions. However, the Registrar has warned that in determining whether what is recorded is opinion or intention, regard will be had not only to the written form of the information, but also to how the information is recorded and used.[6]

13.2 WHO IS AFFECTED BY THE ACT?

The Act identifies three categories of person affected by its provisions. These are 'data users', 'persons who carry on a computer bureau' and 'data subjects'.

13.2.1 Data users

A 'data user' is a person who 'holds' data, and a person 'holds' data if three criteria are satisfied:

(a) the data form part of a collection of data processed or intended to be processed by or on behalf of that person . . .; and

(b) that person (either alone or jointly with other persons) controls the contents and use of the data comprised in the collection; and

(c) the data are in the form in which they have been or are intended to be processed as mentioned in paragraph (a) above or (though not for the time being in that form) in a form into which they have been converted after being so processed and with a view to being further so processed on a subsequent occasion.'[7]

Control over the contents and use of the data is central to the concept of holding. The data user must contribute, at least partly, to control of both the contents of the data and its use, although he need not actually process the data himself.

In practice decisions as to the contents and use of data will normally be made by individual employees. Employees will not normally, however, be data users themselves, since they will be merely exercising control on behalf of the employer.

The third criterion is designed simply to cover data converted into another form after being processed where it is intended to process the data on some subsequent occasion. For example, data which is only processed occasionally may be processed on a disc but be stored on magnetic tape when not in use. Such data continue to be 'held', despite not being in the form in which they were processed. This simply plugs what would otherwise be a loophole in the Act.

Hospitals themselves are not in law 'legal persons', and therefore cannot be data users. But health authorities and trusts are legal persons and are therefore capable of holding data. Accordingly, the District Health Authority will hold the data within its authority, as the person having control over the contents and use of the data, while the Regional Health Authority will hold the data controlled at regional level. It is quite possible for two people, or here authorities, to hold the same data. National Health Service trusts will hold their own data.

In the private health sector, the company controlling the contents and use of the data will be the data user. A partnership is not a legal person and therefore each partner will 'hold' the data held by the partnership.

13.2.2 A person who carries on a computer bureau

A person carries on a computer bureau if he provides other persons with services in respect of data.[8] There is no requirement that a person be in business as a bureau to fall within the definition and the Act is therefore equally applicable to health care facilities in the public and private sectors. A person provides such services in two situations. First, if 'as [an] agent for other persons he causes data held by them to be processed . . .';[9] or second, 'he allows persons the use of equipment in his possession for the processing . . . of data held by them'. If a health service body processes another such body's data on its behalf, it will be carrying on a computer bureau.[10]

13.2.3 Data subjects

A 'data subject' is 'an individual who is the subject of personal data'.[11] This means a living individual. There is no minimum age requirement or other qualification and therefore everyone is potentially a 'data subject'. In both the National Health Service and the private health sector, data subjects will be predominantly patients and employees, but may also include voluntary workers, medical students, self-employed contractors and other individuals.

13.3   EXEMPT DATA

Certain processed data do not attract the requirements of the Data Protection Act at all. 'Exempt data' must be differentiated from the more limited concept of 'non-disclosure exemption' discussed at pp. 360–363, below.

There are several categories of data to which the Act does not apply, but only the following are relevant in the context of health care facilities.

13.3.1 Data 'held' for payroll, pension and account purposes[12]

The exemption applies to data held for the purpose either of calculating amounts payable by way of remuneration or pension,[13] or of keeping accounts relating to the business or other activity of the data use.[14] This includes keeping records of purchases or other transactions for ensuring that requisite payment is made and for making financial or management forecasts.

The exemption will be lost if the data are 'disclosed' except where permitted by the Act. There is only a disclosure of personal data if the data, either alone or in conjunction with other information disclosed, identify the individual to whom they relate. There are several situations in which the disclosure of data is permitted under the Act.[15] In addition to these exemptions of general application, data held for payroll or account purposes may be disclosed in order to enable an audit to be made, or to give information solely about the data user's financial affairs.[16]

Data held purely for the purpose of calculating amounts payable by way of remuneration or pension may be disclosed:

1. to any person by whom the remuneration or pensions in question are payable;
2. for the purpose of obtaining actuarial advice;

3. for medical research into occupational diseases or injuries;
4. the data subject (or a person acting on his behalf) has requested or consented to either the *specific* disclosure or disclosure of data *generally*; or
5. the person making the disclosure has reasonable grounds for believing that the data subject has requested or consented to the disclosure as in paragraph 4, above.[17]

The payroll and accounts exemption will not be lost by any improper disclosure if the data user can show that he took such care as in all the circumstances was reasonably required to prevent the disclosure.[18] The 'reasonable care' defence places the burden of proof on the person relying on the defence to show that it is more probable than not that he took reasonable care to prevent the improper disclosure. Relevant factors will include the likelihood of improper disclosure, the cost of steps to prevent improper disclosure, and established practice.[19]

13.3.2 Data concerned solely with the distribution of articles or information[20]

The exemption is particularly narrow in scope. The data may consist solely of the names and addresses of data subjects, or any other particulars necessary for effecting distribution. The data subject must also have been asked by the data user whether he objects to the data relating to him being held and has not objected.[21]

The exemption will be lost if the data are disclosed except where permitted by the Act. In addition to those instances of general application, the data may be disclosed where the data subject (or a person acting on his behalf) has requested or consented to either the specific disclosure or disclosure of data generally or the person making the disclosure has reasonable grounds for believing that the data subject has requested or consented to the disclosure. Again the exemption will not be lost by any unauthorised disclosure if the data user can show that he took such care as in all the circumstances was reasonably required to prevent the disclosure.[22]

13.3.3 The effect of the exemptions

Only data falling exclusively within one or more of the definitions are exempt from the whole of the Act; it is therefore extremely unlikely in the field of health care that the exemption will exempt data users from registering altogether. The exemption is, however, important in three respects. First, when registering under the Act exempt data need not be included in the description of the personal data held. Second, certain rights conferred on data subjects by Part II of the Act are not applicable to the exempt data. Third, the Registrar has no powers of enforcement in respect of exempt data.

13.4 REGISTRATION

The Data Protection Registrar is required to maintain a register of data users who hold, and of persons carrying on a computer bureau who provide services in respect of, personal data.[23] The register can be inspected at the Registrar's office or at most major libraries and provides the public with a record of the persons who hold personal data, what data are held, and the purposes for which they are held.

13.4.1 Who must register?

Every person who holds personal data not wholly exempt from the Act, or who carries on a computer bureau, must register.[24] Any person who holds personal data when not registered to do so commits a criminal offence.[25]

Registration occurs when either the application is received by the Registrar, or if posted by recorded delivery, on posting.[26]

13.4.2 Applications for registration

An application for registration should be made on form DPR1 obtainable from the Registrar's office.[27] Other forms of registration exist but are unsuitable for use by health authorities and trusts. At the time of writing the fee for registration is £75.00. There are three categories of registration: data user only; computer bureau only; and data user who also carries on a computer bureau. As already noted, it is easy for a health authority or trust to fall within the definition of a person carrying on a computer bureau and it is therefore prudent to register as a data user who also carries on a computer bureau. This involves no extra fee or paperwork.

The form comes in two parts: Part A, to be completed by all applicants, and Part B, to be completed by data users, whether they are solely data users or also persons who carry on a computer bureau. Part A is concerned purely with simple details about the applicant, such as the category of registration applied for and the address where subject access requests can be received. Part B is concerned with the data held by the data user. The applicant is required to give a description of the data held and other information about the data, such as the purposes for which they are held.

13.4.3 Acceptance or refusal of application

The Registrar must notify the applicant of the result of the application as soon as is practicable, or at the latest within six months of his receipt of the application.[28] The Registrar may only refuse an application where:

'(a)   he considers that the details provided for registration . . . [do] not give
      sufficient information as to the matters to which they relate; or
 (b)   he is satisfied that the applicant is likely to contravene any of the data
      protection principles; or
 (c)   where he considers that the information available to him is insufficient to
      satisfy him that the applicant is unlikely to contravene any of the data
      protection principles.'[29]

If any discrepancy is found in the application the Registrar will normally
try to resolve the problem by informal correspondence before refusing
an application.[30] If an application is refused, the Registrar must notify
the applicant in writing of the reasons for the refusal and of his rights of
appeal to the Data Protection Tribunal.[31] The refusal will not take effect
until 28 days have elapsed from the date of notification;[32] or, if by reason
of special circumstances the Registrar considers that the refusal should
take effect as a matter of urgency, seven days after the notification.[33]

13.4.4   Rights of appeal

Any person whose application is refused has a right of appeal to the
Data Protection Tribunal.[34] A notice of appeal must be served on the
Tribunal within 28 days of the refusal being notified to the applicant,
although the Tribunal may in its discretion extend the limitation period
where there are special circumstances for doing so.[35] Unless the
Registrar has ordered that the refusal should take effect as a matter of
urgency, the lodging of an appeal suspends the refusal until the appeal
is either determined or withdrawn.[36]

13.4.5   Renewal of registration

Every register entry has a limited maximum life of three years[37] which
obviously necessitates renewal of the entry. An application for renewal
must be made within the six months prior to the date on which the
current register entry expires and is a simple procedure. The Registrar
has no powers to refuse an application for renewal. If, however, an
application for renewal is not made within the prescribed period, a fresh
application must be made.

13.5   THE DATA PROTECTION PRINCIPLES

The first Schedule to the Act contains the Data Protection Principles,
which are incorporated into the Act by section 2(2). The Principles are
based upon the provisions of the Council of Europe Convention on Data
Protection, and are intended to protect the rights of individuals about
whom personal data are held.

(i) *'The information to be contained in personal data shall be obtained, and personal data processed, fairly and lawfully.'*

Part II of Schedule 1 gives guidance to interpreting the principle.

'1.—(1) Subject to sub-paragraph (2) below, in determining whether the information was obtained fairly regard shall be had to the method by which it was obtained, including in particular whether any person from whom it was obtained was deceived or misled as to the purpose or purposes for which it is to be held used or disclosed.'

The Guidelines pose several questions which the Registrar may ask in order to determine whether information has been fairly obtained.[38] These are:

1. Could the person supplying the information reasonably be expected to appreciate, without explanation, the identity of the data user and the purposes for which the information would be used or disclosed? If not, why did the data user not explain them to the person?
2. Did the data user explain why the information was required and why it might be used or disclosed? If so, was the explanation complete and accurate?
3. Did the person ask about uses and disclosures of the information and, if so, what reply was made?
4. Was he under the impression that the information would be kept confidential by the data user? If so, was that impression justified by the circumstances and did the data user intend to preserve that confidence?
5. Was any unfair pressure used to obtain the information? Were any unjustified threats made, or inducements offered?
6. Was he improperly led to believe that he must supply the information, or that failure to provide it might disadvantage him?

The Act gives a special dispensation from the first Principle to personal data held for historical, statistical or research purposes. Information is not to be regarded as obtained unfairly merely because its use for those purposes was not disclosed when the information was obtained. However, the dispensation only applies if the personal data are not used in such a way that damage or distress is, or is likely to be, caused to any data subject.[39]

(ii) *'Personal data shall be held only for one or more specified and lawful purposes.'*

Part II, paragraph 2, of the Schedule adds:

'Personal data shall not be treated as held for a specified purpose unless that purpose is described in particulars registered under this Act in relation to the data.'

(iii) *'Personal data held for any purpose or purposes shall not be used or disclosed in any manner not compatible with that purpose or those purposes.'*

In relation to the third Principle Part II, paragraph 3, of the Schedule states that:

'Personal data shall not be treated as used or disclosed in contravention of this principle unless:
  (a) used otherwise than for a purpose of a description registered under this Act in relation to the data; or
  (b) disclosed otherwise than to a person of a description so registered.'

The third Principle is reinforced by section 5(2) of the Act which operates, *inter alia*, to prevent a data user from holding personal data for any purpose not described in his entry in the register, or from disclosing data to any person not described in the entry. These restrictions apply equally to the data user's employees and agents.[40] Any person, including the data user's servants and agents, who knowingly or recklessly contravenes these restrictions commits an offence.[41]

(iv) *'Personal data held for any purpose or purposes shall be adequate, relevant and not excessive in relation to that purpose or those purposes.'*

Part II of the Schedule provides no guidance as to the interpretation of the principle. Guideline 4 states that in trying to comply with this principle, data users should first consider their policies for collecting information about individuals. They should seek to identify the minimum amount of information about each individual which is required in order to give effect to their purpose. Data should not be recorded merely because there is a slight possibility that this will become one of the special cases where the extra information might become useful. The Guideline warns that the Registrar will not accept that information is relevant merely because the data user considers it to be relevant.[42]

(v) *'Personal data shall be accurate and, where necessary, kept up to date.'*

Part II, paragraph 4, of the Schedule states that:

'Any question whether or not personal data are accurate shall be determined as for the purposes of section 22 of this Act but, in the case of such data as are mentioned in subsection (2) of that section, the principle shall not be regarded as having been contravened by reason of any inaccuracy in the information there mentioned if the requirements specified in that subsection have been complied with.'

For the purposes of section 22, data are defined as 'inaccurate' if they are incorrect or misleading as to any matter of fact. Subsection (2) applies where the data accurately record information received or obtained by the data user from either the data subject, or a third party, provided that it is apparent that the information was so received whenever extracted from the data. If the data subject has notified the data user that he regards the information as incorrect or misleading, this also must be apparent whenever the information is extracted from the data.

The Guideline adds that the Registrar, when considering formal action to remedy a breach, will not merely seek to establish that there is a factual inaccuracy, but will also wish to see whether the data user has taken all reasonable steps to prevent the inaccuracy. The matters he may wish to consider include:

1. the significance of the inaccuracy and whether it caused or is likely to cause damage or distress to the data subject;
2. the source from which the inaccurate information was obtained, and whether it was reasonable for the data user to rely on that source;
3. any steps taken to verify the information;
4. the procedures for data entry and for ensuring that the system itself does not introduce inaccuracies into the data;
5. the procedures followed when the inaccuracies came to light. Were the data corrected as soon as the inaccuracy became apparent? Was the correction passed on to any third parties to whom the inaccurate data may already have been disclosed?[43]

(vi) *Personal data held for for any purpose or purposes shall not be kept for longer than is necessary for that purpose or those purposes.'*

Part II of the Schedule provides no guidance as to how the Principle is to be interpreted. However, the Guideline states that in order to comply with the Principle, data users will need to review their personal data regularly and to delete the information which is no longer required for their purposes.[44] Recommended retention periods for health records are set out in Chapter 5 (pp. 132–134) and Chapter 15 (pp. 385–389).

If the personal data have held been on account of a relationship between the data user and the data subject, the need to keep the information should be considered when that relationship ceases to exist; for example, where the data subject is an employee who has left the data user's employment.

(vii) *'An individual shall be entitled—*
    (a) *At reasonable intervals and without undue delay or expense—*
        (i) *to be informed by any data user whether he holds personal data of which that individual is the subject; and*
        (ii) *to access to any such data held by the data user; and*
    (b) *where appropriate, to have such data corrected or erased.'*

Part II, paragraph 5, of the Schedule adds that, in determining whether access to personal data is sought at reasonable intervals, regard shall be had to the nature of the data, the purposes for which it is held and the frequency with which the data is altered.

The seventh Principle is specifically enacted by sections 21 and 24 of the Act, for which see pp. 364 and 370 of this chapter.

(viii) *'Appropriate security measures shall be taken against unauthorised access to, or alteration, disclosure or destruction of, personal data and against any loss or destruction of personal data.'*

Part II, paragraph 6, of the Schedule adds that regard shall be had:

'(a) to the nature of the personal data and the harm that would result from such access, alteration, disclosure, loss or destruction as are mentioned in this principle; and

(b) to the place where the personal data are stored, to security measures programmed into the relevant equipment and to measures taken for ensuring the reliability of staff having access to the data.'

Factors such as whether passwords are necessary to gain access to equipment, and whether the password gives access to all levels of the system, will be relevant in determining whether sufficient security measures have been taken. Strict security measures will be demanded where the data include medical records.

13.6 NON-DISCLOSURE EXEMPTIONS

The 'non-disclosure' exemptions operate to excuse compliance with the restrictions on disclosure imposed by the Act. This prevents the Registrar from taking any action in respect of breach of any of the Data Protection Principles, provided that the data in question fall within one or more of the exemptions.[45] Furthermore, no offence is committed by disclosing exempt data to a person who is not described in the data users entry in the register.[46] It is important to note, however, that the exemptions do not restrict the courts' powers to award compensation for damage and distress suffered as a result of unauthorised disclosure.

13.6.1 National security

Personal data which are not generally exempt from the Act in the interests of national security are nevertheless exempt from the non-disclosure provisions where the exemption is required for safeguarding national security.[47] A certificate signed by a Minister of the Crown certifying that personal data are or have been disclosed in the interests of national security is conclusive evidence of the fact.[48]

13.6.2 Crime and taxation

Section 28 provides that:

'(3) Personal data are exempt from the non-disclosure provisions in any case in which—
  (a) the disclosure is for any of the purposes mentioned in subsection (1) above; and
  (b) the application of those provisions in relation to the disclosure would be likely to prejudice any of the matters mentioned in that subsection.'

The purposes mentioned in subsection (1) are: (a) the prevention or detection of crime; (b) the apprehension or prosecution of offenders; and (c) the assessment or collection of any tax or duty.

In any proceedings for contravention of the non-disclosure provisions, it is a defence to prove that the defendant had reasonable grounds for believing that failure to make the disclosure in question would have been likely to prejudice any of the matters mentioned above.[49] This exemption simply enables the relevant data to be disclosed without contravening the Act. The separate issue of what confidential information may, or must, be disclosed is considered in Chapter 16.

13.6.3 Disclosure required by law

Personal data are exempt from the non-disclosure provisions in any case in which the disclosure is 'required by any enactment, by any rule of law or by the order of a Court'.[50]

Discovery (disclosure) of records and documents which may be relevant to the conduct of civil litigation is discussed in Chapter 5.

13.6.4 Disclosure in order to obtain legal advice

Exemption from the non-disclosure provisions also applies when 'made for the purpose of obtaining legal advice for the purposes of, or in the course of, legal proceedings in which the person making the disclosure is a party or a witness'.[51]

The exemption applies to disclosures made in order to obtain advice in non-contentious business as well as in connection with legal proceedings, providing that in the latter instance the person making the disclosure is a party or witness to proceedings.[52]

13.6.5 Disclosure to or at the request of the data subject

Section 34 provides, relevantly:

'(6) Personal data are exempt from the non-disclosure provisions in any case in which—
  (a) the disclosure is to the data subject or a person acting on his behalf; or

(b) the data subject or any such person has requested or consented to the particular disclosure in question; or . . .

(d) the person making the disclosure has reasonable grounds for believing that the disclosure falls within any of the foregoing paragraphs of this subsection.'

Guideline 6 notes that it has been suggested that this prevents data users from discussing an individual's affairs with a third party, for example an advice worker. The Guideline notes this to be incorrect; providing the data user has reasonable grounds for believing that the third party is acting on the data subject's behalf, disclosures of personal data may be made if the data user wishes to make them. However, the data user should have some system of checking the enquirer's identity and authority before disclosing any personal information; particularly, notes the Guideline, if discussions take place over the telephone. The precautions required will vary according to the sensitivity of the information and the likelihood and the harm that might result from its disclosure to somebody falsely claiming to be the data subject or somebody acting on his behalf.[53]

13.6.6 Disclosures to employees or agents

Section 34(6) provides that:

'(6) Personal data are exempt from the non-disclosure provisions in any case in which—

(a) . . .

(b) . . .

(c) the disclosure is by a data user or a person carrying on a computer bureau to his servant or agent for the purpose of enabling the servant or agent to perform his functions as such; or

(d) the person making the disclosure has reasonable grounds for believing that the disclosure falls within any of the foregoing paragraphs of this subsection.'

The Registrar's Guideline 6 warns that the exemption does not cover all disclosures to employees.[54] For example, a disclosure to an employee in his capacity as a trade union representative would not fall within the exemption because it would not be made in order to enable him to perform his duties as an employee.

13.6.7 Emergency disclosures

Section 34 provides that:

'(8) Personal data are exempt from the non-disclosure provisions in any case in which the disclosure is urgently required for preventing injury or other damage to the health of any person or persons; and in proceedings against any person for contravening a provision mentioned in section 26(3)(a) above it shall be a defence to prove that he had reasonable grounds for believing that the disclosure in question was urgently required for that purpose.'

The provisions mentioned in section 26(3)(a) are subsection 5(2)(d) and section 15. Subsection 5(2)(d) makes it an offence for any data user knowingly or recklessly to disclose data held by him to any person not described in the entry on the register. Section 15 contains similar provisions in relation to computer bureaux. The 'reasonable grounds' defence therefore applies to criminal but not civil proceedings.

13.6.8 Consequences of breaching the Data Protection Principles

In order to secure compliance with the Principles the Registrar can serve three types of notice, two of which are relevant in the present context.

Enforcement notices

An enforcement notice may be served on a data user if the Registrar is satisfied that the user has broken or is breaking one or more of the Data Protection Principles.[55] The notice will contain the Registrar's reasons for believing that a breach has occurred or is occurring, the steps which he requires to take in order to comply with the principle, and the time within which those steps are to be taken.[56] The notice will normally allow 28 days to take the steps required. However, if the Registrar requires the steps to be taken urgently, the notice need only allow seven days in which to take them.[57] There is a right of appeal against a decision to serve an enforcement notice[58] which the data user will be informed of when he is served the enforcement notice.[59]

Failure to comply with an enforcement notice is a criminal offence, but it is a defence to show that all due care was exercised to comply with the notice.[60]

De-registration notices

In order to serve a de-registration notice the Registrar must be satisfied that serving an enforcement notice will not ensure compliance; and in deciding whether to serve a de-registration notice the Registrar is obliged to consider whether the contravention has caused, or is likely to cause, any person damage or distress.[61] The effect of a de-registration notice is that the registered data user can no longer legally undertake the activities covered by the notice.

13.7 RIGHTS OF DATA SUBJECTS

Under Part III of the Act, new rights and remedies are given to data subjects. Data subjects have a right of access to data held about themselves and in certain circumstances are entitled to claim compensation if the data are inaccurate or if appropriate security measures have not been taken to prevent unauthorised destruction or disclosure of the data. A data subject may apply to the High Court or county court for an order that any inaccurate personal data held about him be erased or amended.

13.7.1 Access to personal data

Of the new rights created by the Act, probably the most important is the right of access to personal data.

'21.—(1) Subject to the provisions of this section, an individual shall be entitled—
  (a) to be informed by any data user whether the data held by him include personal data of which that individual is the data subject; and
  (b) to be supplied by any data user with a copy of the information constituting any such personal data held by him.'

The information disclosed must carry an explanation if it is otherwise unintelligible.

The right of access created by section 21(1) is not activated until three criteria are satisfied.

First, a request under paragraph (a) or (b) must be in writing.[62] In the absence of any indication to the contrary, a request for information under paragraph (a) must be treated as also including a request for information under paragraph (b). Similarly a request for information under both paragraphs (a) and (b) must be treated as one application.[63] Where a data user has separate entries in the register in respect of data held for different purposes, a separate application must be made in respect of each entry.[64] A health authority may, for example, make separate entries in respect of medical and employment records. In such a case, an employee of the health authority seeking to gain access to both his employment and medical records, would have to make two separate requests, one in relation to his employment records and another in relation to his medical records.

Second, the application must provide the data user with sufficient information as he may reasonably require to identify the person making the request and to locate the information he seeks.[65]

Third, a data user is entitled to charge a fee, up to a prescribed maximum,[66] for processing the request. Where the data user makes such a charge, the appropriate fee may be required in advance of access being granted.[67]

As a part of the obligation of confidence, the data user must be able to comply with the request without disclosing information relating to another identifiable individual, unless he is satisfied that the individual concerned has consented to the disclosure.[68] 'Information relating to another individual' includes references to information identifying that individual as a source of the information sought by the request.[69] However, the provision does not excuse the supply of information which can be supplied without disclosing the identity of the other individual concerned, whether this be by omission of the name or other identifying particulars of the individual or otherwise.[70]

The information to be supplied in response to a subject access request is to be supplied by reference to the data in question at the time when the request is received.[71] There is an exception where the data is amended or deleted between the time the request is received and the time the information is supplied, provided the amendment or deletion would have been made regardless of the request. The data user is thus prevented from amending the data in order to cover up an inaccuracy, for example, or from erasing data he does not wish to be disclosed, but not from updating his records.

The data user has 40 days with which to comply with the request.[72] Ordinarily the 40 days run from the date on which criteria 1 and 2 (above) are satisfied; however, in relation to data identifying another individual, the 40 days run from the date on which the data user receives the requisite consent to the disclosure.[73]

Failure to comply with the provisions of section 21 does not entitle the data subject to compensation. However, an aggrieved data subject may either seek to enforce his right of access directly by seeking a court order requiring the data user to comply with his obligations under the Act,[74] or indirectly by reporting the data user to the Registrar, who may then serve an enforcement notice.

Safeguards and exemptions

There are in all eleven classes of exemption to the right of subject access of which only five are relevant in the present context. Where the exemptions apply, data subjects have no right of access to personal data concerning them, nor can the Registrar order the data user to grant access in accordance with paragraph (a) of the seventh Data Protection Principle. However, unless exempt under Part IV of the Act (see pp. 353–355, above), data are still required to be registered and are subject to the powers of the courts and Registrar in all other respects.

Guideline 6 advises that the data user need not inform the data subject that information is being withheld in reliance on one of these exemptions. Indeed, if all the personal data held about an individual who has made an access request are covered by one of the exemptions, the data user could properly reply 'I do not hold any personal data which I am required to reveal to you'.[75]

Health and social work
On 9 November 1987, the Home Secretary, exercising his powers under

section 29(1) of the Data Protection Act 1984, made the Data Protection (Subject Access Modification) (Health) Order 1987.[76] The Order applies to personal data consisting of information as to the physical or mental health of the data subject, provided that the data are held by a health professional; or are held by a person other than a health professional, but the information constituting the data was first recorded by or on behalf of a health professional.[77]

The term 'health professional' is defined in Schedule 1 of the Order as follows:

'Registered Medical Practitioner; Registered Dentist; Registered Optician; Registered Pharmaceutical Chemist or Druggist; Registered Nurse, Midwife, or Health Visitor, Registered Chiropodist, Dietician, Occupational Therapist; Orthoptist or Physiotherapist; Clinical Psychologist; Child Psychotherapist or Speech Therapist; Art or Music Therapist employed by a health authority, health board or health and social services board; and scientists employed by such an authority or board as head of department.'

Subject access may be withheld under the Order only where access would be likely:

'(a) . . . to cause serious harm to the physical or mental health of the data subject; or

(b) . . . to disclose to the data subject the identity of another individual (who has not consented to the disclosure of the information) either as a person to whom the information or part of it relates or as the source of the information or enable that identity to be deduced by the data subject either from the information itself or from a combination of that information and other information which the data subject has or is likely to have.'[78]

However, the Order does not excuse the data user from

'(a) supplying the information sought where the only individual whose identity is likely to be disclosed is a health professional who has been involved in the care of the data subject and supplied that information in a professional capacity; or

(b) from supplying so much of the information as can be supplied without causing serious harm to the data subject or enabling the identity of another to be disclosed (or deduced), whether by omission of names, or other particulars, or otherwise.'[79]

Where the data is not held by a health professional, but for example by a health authority, the data user must consult the person appearing to him to be the most appropriate health professional to determine whether the criteria for withholding subject access are satisfied.[80]

The term 'appropriate health professional' is defined in paragraph 4(6) of the Order as being:

'(a) the medical practitioner or dental practitioner who is currently or was most recently responsible for the clinical care of the data subject in connection with the matters to which the information which is the subject of the request relates; or

(b) where there is more than one such practitioner, the practitioner who is the most suitable to advise on the matters to which the information which is the subject of the request relates; or

(c) where there is no practitioner available falling within sub-paragraph (a) or (b) above, a health professional who has the necessary experience and qualifications to advise on the matters to which the information which is the subject of the request relates.'

Statistical or research data

Personal data held for the purpose of preparing statistics or carrying out research are exempt from the subject access provisions, providing that the data are not used or disclosed for any other purpose. Furthermore the results of the research must not be available in a form which identifies any of the data subjects. But the exemption will not be lost where:

'(a) the disclosure is to the data subject or a person acting on his behalf; or

(b) the data subject or any such person has requested or consented to the particular disclosure in question; or

(c) the disclosure is by a data user or a person carrying on a computer bureau to his servant or agent for the purpose of enabling the servant or agent to perform his functions as such . . . .'.[81]

Prohibited disclosure

The Secretary of State has the power under section 34(2) of the Act to order exemption from the subject access provisions of personal data consisting of information the disclosure of which is prohibited or restricted by or under any enactment if he considers that the prohibition or restriction ought to prevail over those provisions in the interest of the data subject or of any individual.

To date only one such Order has been made under the provision. The Order applies to adoption records and reports, and statements and records of the special educational needs of children.

Back-up data

In certain situations the data subject has a right to compensation for damage suffered as a result of the loss or impairment of personal data concerning him. Retaining 'back-up' copies of data is therefore good policy. Such back-up copies are exempt from the subject access provisions providing they are kept solely for the purpose of replacing other data in the event of it being lost, destroyed, or impaired.[82] The purpose of the exemption is to avoid the need for what would effectively be double access to the same information. Guideline 6 warns that if the data are kept so that they may be consulted whether or not the original files have been damaged, the exemption will be lost.[83]

Data incriminating the data user

The right against self-incrimination is an established principle of the common law. The principle is preserved to an extent by section 34(9) which provides that:

'(9) A person need not comply with a notice, request or order under the subject access provisions if compliance would expose him to proceedings for any offence other than an offence under this Act; and information disclosed under by any person in compliance with such a notice shall not be admissible against him in proceedings under this Act.'

Although not strictly a subject access exemption, its practical effect is the same.

13.7.2 Compensation for inaccuracy

If an individual suffers damage as the result of inaccurate data held by a data user, he is entitled to compensation from the data user for the damage and for any distress suffered as a consequence of the inaccuracy.[84] However, the provision is of a fairly limited application. The right to compensation does not extend to persons who are not individuals, such as registered companies, nor does it extend to individuals who are not themselves the subject of the inaccurate data. Furthermore, as a condition precedent to the right to compensation for distress, the inaccuracy must have caused the data subject to suffer damage. Damage is not defined in the Act and accordingly must be given its ordinary natural meaning. In the Registrar's view, damage includes financial loss or physical harm, but does not include distress suffered by the individual.[85]

For the purposes of the section, data are defined as 'inaccurate' if they are incorrect or misleading as to any matter of fact.[86] A mere opinion which does not purport to be a statement of fact cannot therefore be the subject of an action for compensation, even though an individual may dispute the opinion recorded about him.

The right to compensation is subject to an important qualification. There is no right to compensation where the data accurately record information received or obtained by the data user from either the data subject, or a third party, provided that: (a) it is apparent that the information was so received whenever extracted from the data; and (b) if the data subject has notified the data user that he regards the information as incorrect or misleading; again this must be apparent whenever the information is extracted from the data.[87]

The Registrar considers that the exemption is not easy to understand. However, in his view, it is clear that whenever received information is displayed on a screen, or is printed out, then some indicator of the above criteria must also appear.[88] At the time of writing it has not been made clear what type of 'indicator' the courts will require. However, according to the Guideline, an indicator which expressly states 'this item of information was received by X from the data subject or a third party' will be sufficient, though of course in practice it may prove difficult to repeat this on each screen or page of printout. Accordingly it has been suggested that displaying the letter 'R' beside an item of information might suffice to indicate that the information was obtained from the data subject or a third party. However, the Registrar warns that this may be difficult to sustain unless the meaning of 'R' has been explained to the person seeking the information. Unfortunately the Guideline gives no advice beyond this. It is therefore left to the data user wishing to rely on the exemption to devise his own system.

The data user has a legal defence if he can show that he had taken such care as in all the circumstances was reasonably required to ensure the accuracy of the data at the material time.[89] Whether reasonable steps were taken to ensure the accuracy of the data is a question of fact to be determined in each individual case. Factors such as the likelihood of damage, and the cost of taking additional steps to ensure its accuracy, will be relevant.

13.7.3   Compensation for unauthorised loss or disclosure

Individuals may claim compensation for a breach of security on the part of either a data user who holds personal data about them, or a computer bureau which is involved in the processing of personal data which relates to them. Section 23 provides that:

'**23**—(1) An individual who is the subject of personal data held by a data user or in respect of which services are provided by a person carrying on a computer bureau and who suffers damage by reason of—
  (a) the loss of the data;
  (b) the destruction of the data without the authority of the data user or, as the case may be, of the person carrying on the computer bureau; or
  (c) subject to subsection (2) below, the disclosure of the data, or access having been obtained to the data, without such authority as aforesaid,
shall be entitled to compensation from the data user, or as the case may be, the person carrying on the bureaux for that damage and for any distress which the individual has suffered by reason of the loss, destruction, disclosure or access.'

Subsection (2) of section 23 provides that in the case of a registered data user subsection (1)(c) does not apply to disclosure to, or access by, any person falling within section 4(3)(d). Section 4(3)(d) relates to the description in the register of the person or persons to whom it is intended to disclose data.

In all other respects the provisions of section 23 mirror the provisions of section 22. Compensation is again available only to the subject of the personal data. Other individuals who suffer loss as a result of a breach of security would have to prove negligence, breach of confidence, breach of contract, or defamation on the part of the data user or his employees.

Damage is a condition precedent to compensation for distress and the statutory 'reasonable care' defence applies.[90]

13.7.4 Rectification and erasure

The fourth and final right conferred upon data subjects by Part III of the Act is the right to apply to the court for rectification and erasure of inaccurate data. The right, which is created by section 24 of the Act, reflects the fifth and seventh Data Protection Principles. Section 24(1) provides that:

'**24**—(1) If a court is satisfied on the application of a data subject that personal data held by a data user of which the applicant is the subject are inaccurate within the meaning of section 22 above, the court may order the rectification or erasure of the data and of any data held by the data user and containing an expression of opinion which appears to the court to be based on the inaccurate data.'

Where the data accurately record information received or obtained by the data user from the data subject or a third party, the court may, instead of making an order under subsection 1, make an order requiring the data to be supplemented by a statement of the true facts relating to the matters dealt with by the data.[91] If the requirements of section 22 have not been complied with, the court may make such an order as it thinks fit for securing compliance with those requirements as well as having the discretion to make an order requiring the data to be supplemented by a statement of the true facts.[92]

The court's power to order erasure is much more limited than its power to order rectification. The discretion to order erasure may be invoked only when two strict criteria are satisfied. First, the data subject must have suffered damage by reason of the personal data, or of access being obtained to personal data, in circumstances entitling him to compensation under section 23. Second, there must be a substantial risk of further unauthorised disclosure of, or access to, the data in question.[93]

NOTES

1. Section 1(2).
2. Section 1(7).
3. Section 1(7).
4. Section 1(8).
5. Section 1(3).
6. Guideline 2 at 3.4.
7. Section 1(5).
8. Section 1(6).
9. Section 1(6)(a).
10. Section 1(6)(b) and see NHS and Community Care Act 1990, section 4(2).
11. Section 1(4).

12. Section 32.
13. Section 32(1)(a).
14. Section 32(1)(b).
15. See 'Non-disclosure exemptions' at p. 360, below.
16. Section 32(4)(a).
17. Section 32(3).
18. Section 32(2).
19. The nature, including the possible sensitivity, of much data relating to medical care, treatment and research may in some cases require very clear and cogent proof of reasonable care, going beyond the standard of 'more likely than not' in particular cases.
20. Section 33(2)(b).
21. Section 33(3).
22. Section 33(4).
23. Section 4(1).
24. Sections 5(1) and 5(4).
25. Section 5(5).
26. Section 7(9).
27. Office of the Data Protection Registrar, Springfield House, Water Lane, Wilmslow, Cheshire SK9 5AX.
28. Section 7(1).
29. Section 7(2).
30. See Guideline 3 at 6.4–6.5.
31. Section 7(4).
32. Section 7(6)(b).
33. Section 7(7).
34. Section 13.
35. Data Protection Tribunal Rules 1985, SI 1985/1568 at paragraph 4.
36. Section 7(6)(b).
37. Section 8(2).
38. Guideline 4 at 1.1.
39. Schedule 1, Part II, paragraph 7(a).
40. Section 5(3).
41. Section 5(5).
42. Guideline 4 at 4.4.
43. Guideline 4 at 5.3.
44. Guideline 4 at 6.1.
45. Section 26(3)(b).
46. Section 26(3)(a).
47. Section 27(3).
48. Section 27(4).
49. Section 28(3).
50. Section 34(5)(a). Notification of abortions to the Chief Medical Officer is, for instance, required by law.
51. Section 34(5)(b).
52. Section 34(5)(b).
53. Guideline 6 at B.2.3.
54. Guideline 6 at B.3.3.
55. Section 10(1).
56. Sections 10(5) and 10(6).
57. Section 10(7).
58. Section 13(1)(b).
59. Section 10(5)(b).
60. Section 10(9).

61. Section 11(2).
62. Section 21(2).
63. Section 21(2).
64. Section 21(3).
65. Section 21(4)(a).
66. Section 21(2): currently £10.
67. Section 21(2).
68. Section 21(4)(b).
69. Section 21(5).
70. Section 21(5).
71. Section 21(7).
72. Section 21(6).
73. Section 21(6).
74. Section 21(8), see also section 3.5 on the Data Protection Principles, at pp. 356–360, above.
75. Guideline 6 at C.1.2.
76. SI 1987/1903.
77. Paragraph 3(1).
78. Paragraph 4(2).
79. Paragraph 4(3).
80. Paragraph 4(5).
81. Section 34(7).
82. See Section on compensation for unauthorised loss or disclosure at pp. 369–370, below.
83. Guideline 6 at what is now C.6.3.
84. Section 22(1).
85. Guideline 5 at 3.3.
86. Section 22(4).
87. Section 22(2).
88. Guideline 5 at 3.6.
89. Section 22(3).
90. Section 23(3).
91. Section 24(2)(a).
92. Section 24(2)(b).
93. Section 24(3).

CHAPTER 14

Access to medical records and reports

The subject of access to medical records is covered by no less than four separate pieces of legislation. These are the Supreme Court Act 1981, the Data Protection Act 1984, the Access to Medical Reports Act 1988 and the Access to Health Records Act 1990. An understanding of the inter-relationship between these pieces of legislation is therefore essential.

Since 1970 the High Court and the county court have had certain powers to order the disclosure of a patient's medical records during the course of litigation, or where litigation is contemplated. The power to order disclosure is now contained in the Supreme Court Act 1981 and was examined in detail in Chapter 5.

Until 1987, when the Data Protection Act 1984 came into practical operation, patients had no general right of access to their medical records. That Act gave patients a limited right of access to personal data stored on computer only, thus creating a difference between manually held and computerised records.

14.1   ACCESS TO MEDICAL RECORDS

The Access to Health Records Act 1990 confers on patients a right of access to their non-computerised 'health records'. These are defined in section 1(1) as records which:

'(a) consist of information relating to the physical or mental health of an individual who can be identified from that information, or from that and other information in the possession of the holder of the record; and
(b) has been made by or on behalf of a health professional in connection with the care of the individual . . . .'

14.1.1   The essential definitions

'Health professional' is defined in section 2 as any of the following, namely:

'(a) a registered medical practitioner;

(b) a registered dentist;
(c) a registered optician;
(d) a registered pharmaceutical chemist;
(e) a registered nurse, midwife or health visitor;
(f) a registered chiropodist, dietician, occupational therapist, orthoptist or physiotherapist;
(g) a clinical psychologist, child psychotherapist or speech therapist;
(h) an art or music therapist employed by a health service body; and
(i) a scientist employed by such a body as head of a department.'

'Care' is defined in section 11 of the Act as including: 'examination, investigation, diagnosis and treatment.'

There is no requirement that the examination, investigation, or diagnosis be made with a view to providing treatment. Reports compiled for insurance purposes, for example, may therefore fall within the scope of the Act. These may also come within the scope of the Access to Medical Reports Act 1988, which is explained later in this chapter.

There are two important limitations on the scope of the Act. First, the Act applies only to those records compiled after 1 November 1991 other than to the extent that access to an earlier record is necessary to make intelligible any part of the record to which the applicant is entitled to have access.[1] This means that although the Act did not come into force until 1 November 1991, notes made during an earlier period of treatment may still be subject to patient scrutiny.

Second, the definition of 'health record' provided by section 1(1):

'does not include any record which consists of information which the individual is, or but for any exemption would be, entitled to be supplied with a copy under section 21 of the Data Protection Act 1984 (right of access to personal data)'.

14.1.2 Who may apply for access?

1. *The patient.*[2] Where the patient is a child (i.e. under the age of 16)[3] he must, in the opinion of the record holder, be capable of understanding the nature of the application.[4]
2. *A person authorised in writing to make the application on the patient's behalf.*[5]
3. *Where the patient is a child, a person having parental responsibility for the child.*[6] An application may only be made by a person having parental responsibility for the child where:
   (a) the child has consented to the application; or
   (b) the child is incapable of understanding the nature of the application and giving access would be in the child's best interest.[7]
4. *Where the patient is incapable of managing his own affairs, any person appointed by a court to manage those affairs.*[8]
5. *Where the patient has died, the patient's personal representative and any*

person who may have a claim arising from the death.[9] Where the patient has died, an application for access may be made only in respect of information relevant to any claim that may arise out of the patient's death.[10] Furthermore, access may not be given to any part of the patient's record if it includes a note, made at the patient's request, that he did not wish access to be given on such an application.[11]

Section 11 provides that any application must be made in writing; and section 3(6) implicitly requires that it must contain sufficient information to enable the patient to be identified. Where the application is made otherwise than by the patient, the applicant must also establish that he is entitled to make the application.

14.1.3   How to make the application

Section 3(1) provides that the application must be made to the 'holder' of the records to which access is sought, which:

'in the case of a record made by a health professional for purposes connected with the provision of health services by a health service body, [is] the health service body by which or on whose behalf the record is held . . .'.[12]

The 'health service body' is defined in section 11 as:

'(a) a health authority within the meaning of the National Health Service Act 1977
(b) [applies to Scotland only];
(c) [applies to Scotland only]; or
(d) a National Health Service trust first established under section 5 of the National Health Service and Community Care Act 1990 . . .'

Although the health service body 'holds' the patient's records, it is under an obligation to take advice from 'the appropriate health professional' when deciding how to respond to an application for access.[13] The 'appropriate health professional' is defined in section 7(12) as follows:

'(a) where . . . one or more medical or dental practitioners are currently responsible for the clinical care of the patient, that practitioner or, as the case may be, such one of those practitioners as is most suitable to advise the body on the matter in question;
(b) where paragraph (a) above does not apply but one or more medical or dental practitioners are available who, for the purposes connected with the provision of such services by the body, have been responsible for the clinical care of the patient, that practitioner or, as the case may be, such one of those practitioners as was most recently so responsible; and
(c) where neither paragraph (a) or paragraph (b) above applies, a health professional who has the necessary experience and qualifications to advise the body on the matter in question.'

14.1.4   The health service body's responsibilities

The period within which access must be given depends upon the information to which access is sought. Where the application relates to a record, or part of a record, made during the 40 days immediately preceding the date of the application, access must be given within 21 days of the application.[14] In any other case access must be given within 40 days of the date of the application.[15]

Access is to be given by allowing the applicant to inspect the record to which the application relates. Where access to part of the record is withheld, access is to be given by allowing the applicant to inspect an extract setting out the relevant part or parts of the record. In either case, should the applicant so require, he must be provided with a copy of the record or extract.[16]

With an eye to practicality, the Act also provides that:

'Where any information . . . contained in a record or extract . . . is expressed in terms which are not intelligible without explanation, an explanation of those terms shall be provided with the record or extract, or supplied with the copy.'[17]

14.1.5 Safeguards and exemptions

It is important for the holder of the record to bear in mind that access must not be given under the Act to any part of a health record which in the opinion of the holder of the record

1. would be likely to cause serious harm to the physical or mental health of the patient or of any other individual;[18] or
2. relates to or has been provided by a third party who could be identified from that information, unless the individual concerned consents to the application, or the information has been provided by a health professional who has been involved in the care of the individual;[19] or
3. would disclose any part of the record which was made prior to 1 November 1991, unless necessary to make any part of the record to which the applicant is entitled to have access intelligible.[20]

Where the applicant is neither the patient nor the patient's authorised representative, further exemptions apply. Access must not be given to any part of a record which in the opinion of the holder would disclose

4. information provided by the patient in the expectation that it would not be disclosed to the applicant; or information obtained as a result of any examination or investigation to which the patient consented in the expectation that the information would not be disclosed.[21]

The Act envisages that regulations may be required to make further exemptions in relation to particular records or classes of health records.[22] No such regulations have been made at the time of going to press.

14.1.6 Correction of inaccurate health records

Where the applicant considers any information to which he has been given access to be incorrect, misleading or incomplete, he may request in writing that the record be corrected.[23]

On receiving a request for correction, the holder of the record shall

'(a) if he is satisfied that the information is inaccurate, make the necessary correction;
(b) if he is not so satisfied, make in the part of the record in which the information is contained a note of the matters in respect of which the information is considered by the applicant to be inaccurate; and
(c) in either case, without requiring a fee, supply the applicant with a copy of the correction or note.'[24]

14.1.7 Charges for granting access

No charge may be made for granting access under the Act other than

1. where access is given to information, none of which was recorded during the 40 days immediately preceding the application, in which case a fee not exceeding the maximum prescribed under section 21 of the Data Protection Act 1984 may be charged;[25] or
2. where a copy of a record or extract is supplied to the applicant, in which case a fee not exceeding the cost of making the copy and (where applicable) the cost of posting it to him may be charged.[26]

14.1.8 Enforcement

Compliance with the Act may be enforced by courts under section 8(1), which provides that:

'where the court is satisfied, on an application made by the person concerned within such period as may be prescribed by the rules of court, that the holder of a health record has failed to comply with any requirement of this Act, the court may order the holder to comply with that requirement'.

The Act also confers on the Secretary of State the power to issue regulations requiring the holders of health records to make such arrangements for dealing with complaints that they have failed to comply with any requirements of the Act.[27] At the time of writing no such regulations have been made. If the Secretary of State should in future issue such regulations:

'The Court shall not entertain an application under subsection (1) above unless it is satisfied that the applicant has taken all such steps to secure compliance with the requirement as may be prescribed by regulations made by the Secretary of State.'[28]

14.2 ACCESS TO MEDICAL REPORTS

The Access to Medical Reports Act 1988 confers on patients a right of access to certain medical reports compiled for 'external consumption'. The scope of the Act is restricted in two ways.

First, the Act applies only to those reports compiled for 'employment purposes or insurance purposes'. 'Employment purposes' are defined as:

'the purposes in relation to the individual of any person by whom he is or has been, or is seeking to be, employed (whether under a contract of service or otherwise)'.[29]

'Insurance purposes' are defined as:

'the purposes in relation to the individual of any person carrying on an insurance business with whom the individual has entered into, or is seeking to enter into, a contract of insurance, and 'insurance business' and 'contract of insurance' have the same meaning as in the Insurance Companies Act 1982'.[30]

Second, the Act applies only to those reports prepared by a registered medical practitioner who is, or has been responsible for, the 'clinical care' of the person about whom the report is made. 'Care' is defined in section 2(1) of the Act as including:

'examination, investigation or diagnosis for the purposes of, or in connection with, any form of medical treatment'.

This specifically excludes reports based upon an examination by an independent doctor who is not subject to the same doctor–patient relationship. In the former case the doctor will have been acting exclusively to further the patient's health and will have access to confidential information provided on the basis of that relationship. On preparing a report for an employer or insurer, the doctor also assumes a duty to that third party, which not only alters the nature of the relationship between himself and the patient but also creates a potential conflict of interests. A patient may nevertheless be able to obtain access to such a report under the Access to Health Records Act 1990 (see pp. 373–377, above).

14.2.1 Dealing with applications for access

No person may apply to a medical practitioner for a medical report (for employment or insurance purposes) about a patient without first obtaining the patient's written consent.[31] Sensibly, the Act also requires the potential applicant to inform the patient (in writing) of his rights under the Act when seeking the requisite consent.[32]

If the patient consents to the application he may, should he wish to do so, inform the potential applicant that he wishes to have access to the report. The applicant must then both inform the doctor concerned of this when requesting the report,[33] and at the same time notify the patient that he has requested the report.[34]

The doctor may not then release the report unless: either the patient has been given access to the report[35] by making the report available for his inspection, or by providing him with a copy of it;[36] or

'the period of 21 days beginning with the date of the making of the application has elapsed without his having received any communication from the patient concerning arrangements for the individual to have access to it'.[37]

Should a patient inform the applicant that he does not wish to be given access to the report, the Act does cater for a subsequent change of mind, provided the patient notifies the practitioner (in writing) of his wish to be given access before the report is supplied. The practitioner may not release the report until either the patient has been given access to it, or 21 days have elapsed (from the date of the notification of the change of mind rather than from the date of the application) without his having received any communication from the patient concerning arrangements for access.[38]

Finally, the patient has a right of access to the report during the six months following the report being supplied to the applicant.[39] A copy of the report must therefore be kept for at least six months.

14.2.2 Exceptions to the disclosure duty

The Act contains exemptions parallel to those contained in the Data Protection Act 1984 (as amended by the Data Protection (Subject Access Modification) (Health) Order 1987.[40]

A doctor is not obliged to disclose any part of a report to the patient if he believes that to do so would be likely to cause serious harm to the physical or mental health of the patient or others.[41] Nor is he obliged to do so if disclosure would reveal information about a third party or the identity of another person who has supplied information about the patient;[42] but this exemption does not apply if the person concerned either consents to the patient having access to the information;[43] or is a health professional who has been involved in the care of the patient and has provided the information in a professional capacity.[44] Finally, information which indicates the doctor's intentions in respect of the patient is also exempt from the provisions of the Act.[45]

Where any of the relevant exemptions apply to any part of the report the practitioner must inform the individual (in writing) of that fact.[46] Where this applies to the whole of the report the practitioner is also prevented from supplying the report unless the individual consents to it being supplied.[47]

14.2.3 Charges

No charge may be made for making a copy of the report available for the patient's inspection. However, where the patient is provided with a copy of the report, either at his request or with his consent, a reasonable fee may be charged to cover the cost of *supplying* it.[48]

14.2.4 Enforcement of the legal obligation

The Act is silent on the issue of whether failure to comply with its provisions will give rise to criminal or civil liability. The means of enforcement is provided by section 8 which states that:

'**8.** If a court is satisfied on the application of an individual that any person, in connection with a medical report relating to that individual, has failed or is likely to fail to comply with any requirement of this Act, the court may order that person to comply with that requirement.'

If records are stored on computer, breach of the obligations just examined could amount to a breach of the Data Protection Act 1984 (for which see Chapter 13).

NOTES

 1. Section 5(1)(b) and section 5(2).
 2. Section 3(1)(a).
 3. Section 11.
 4. Section 4(1).
 5. Section 3(1)(b).
 6. Section 3(1)(c).
 7. Section 4(2).
 8. Section 3(1)(e).
 9. Section 3(1)(f).
10. Section 5(4).
11. Section 4(3).
12. Section 1(2)(b).
13. Section 7(1).
14. Section 3(5)(a).
15. Section 3(5)(b).
16. Section 3(2).
17. Section 3(3).
18. Section 5(1)(a).
19. Section 5(1)(a) as qualified by section 5(2).
20. Section 5(1)(a) as qualified by section 5(2).
21. Section 5(3).
22. Sections 5(5) and 10(1).
23. Section 6(1).
24. Section 6(2).
25. Section 3(4)(a): currently £10.
26. Section 3(4)(b).
27. Section 8(3).
28. Section 8(2).
29. Section 2(1).
30. Section 2(1).

31. Section 3(1).
32. Section 3(2).
33. Section 4(1)(a).
34. Section 4(1)(b).
35. Section 4(2)(a).
36. Section 4(4).
37. Section 4(2)(b).
38. Section 4(3).
39. Section 6(2).
40. Section 7.
41. Section 7(1).
42. Section 7(2).
43. Section 7(2)(a).
44. Section 7(2)(b).
45. Section 7(1).
46. Section 7(3)(a).
47. Section 7(4)(b).
48. Section 4(4).

CHAPTER 15

Medical records: ownership and preservation

15.1 OWNERSHIP OF MEDICAL RECORDS

Generally speaking, notes made by an independent professional person remain the property of that person irrespective of the use to which he may properly put the information which they contain. However, most doctors, other than specialists in private practice, do not nowadays work single-handed; and the specialist who, as a member of the staff, treats patients not in direct contractual relationship with him does not own the medical notes relating to such patients. The legal position as to ownership of medical notes and records is not wholly clear either in the case of National Health Service patients or that of private patients. It should be stressed, however, that questions of ownership of notes and records are by no means conclusive, nor often even relevant, as to questions of access to records (Chapters 13 and 14), disclosure of documents in legal proceedings (Chapter 5) or confidentiality relating to the information which they contain.

15.1.1 General ward and amenity patients in National Health Service hospitals

Medical notes taken by a member of the staff in respect of a general ward patient in a hospital, or of a patient in an amenity bed, do not become the property of the medical practitioner taking them but remain under the ownership and control of the hospital for use by any medical practitioner who may treat the same patient at the hospital subsequently. There is ordinarily no legal obligation to make the notes accessible, even at the patient's request, to any medical practitioner outside the hospital save in legal proceedings and then only where the appropriate steps have been taken to compel disclosure (for which see Chapter 5, pp. 135–143). It is, however, customary and prudent on discharge of a patient for a member of the hospital professional staff to communicate to the patient's general medical practitioner such information as is necessary to acquaint him with the patient's case and to give him advice on such further treatment as might be necessary. Failure of adequate communication might be negligent (for which see Chapter 6, pp. 175–177).

15.1.2   Private patients in National Health Service hospitals

Schedule 1 to the Public Records Act 1958, which makes records generally of National Health Service hospitals public records, excludes records of private patients admitted under section 5 of the National Health Service Act 1946, subsequently sections 65 and 66 of the National Health Service Act 1977 and, since the enactment of section 7(10) of the Health and Medicines Act 1988, now simply section 65 of the 1977 Act. This lends support to the suggestion that all medical records of a private patient belong to the consultant in charge of his treatment. It must be remembered, however, that, although it is rare, a private patient might be treated under section 65(1) of the 1977 Act, in which case the hospital would provide specialist as well as other services at an inclusive charge and there is no contract between patient and consultant.[1] The records would clearly belong to the hospital in the same way as those of a National Health Service patient; but, because of the provisions of Schedule 1 of the Public Records Act 1958, they would not be public records.

Almost invariably, however, the patient, or a relative of the patient, makes a contract with a consultant for medical or surgical treatment under section 65(2) of the National Health Service Act 1977. Then it can properly be argued that that consultant's notes are his own property and not that of the hospital. Do nursing records or records of tests, X-rays or other treatment provided by the hospital belong to the hospital? The hospital may be sued in respect of alleged negligence of members of its staff and should have the records necessary to respond to allegations. (Questions of discovery of documents by court order are examined in detail in Chapter 5.) Although these records do belong to the hospital, they are not 'public records'. Moreover, should a radiologist's or other report be made in respect of a private patient by virtue of a private arrangement with the patient or, as likely as not, with the consultant on his behalf then, even though the radiologist or other specialist concerned is on the staff of the hospital, the hospital is not the owner of the record of such report. In saying this, it is of course assumed that the hospital appointment of the radiologist or other consultant concerned is one under which he is permitted to undertake private work.

Insofar as a specialist attending a patient in hospital under a private contract enters information and instructions in the hospital case notes relating to that patient, for direction and guidance to nursing staff as well as to medical staff having oversight of the patient in his absence, those notes will remain the property of the hospital although not public records.

15.1.3   Patients in voluntary hospitals

Unless a patient in a voluntary hospital has a contract with, for instance, a consultant or general medical practitioner for treatment as a private patient, all records of his treatment are hospital records. Notes made by a medical practitioner about a private patient will normally be the property of that specialist, but the position will depend on the conditions under which the practitioner had been afforded facilities for attending private patients in the particular hospital. Notes made for the direction and guidance of hospital medical and nursing staff in respect to the patient's care and treatment and in the patient's case notes will belong to the hospital.

Should a National Health Service patient be treated at a voluntary hospital under contractual arrangements with a health authority, any communication concerning the patient sent to the authority by the voluntary hospital or by a member of its staff would become a public record. The position in respect of case notes etc. made by members of the staff of a voluntary hospital concerning a particular patient treated under contract with the health authority would depend on the terms of the agreement made for treatment of National Health Service patients in that hospital. In the absence of agreement to the contrary, they would probably be the property of the hospital where the patient was treated.

15.1.4   Patients in nursing homes

Since a patient in a nursing home usually has a direct agreement with a medical practitioner for medical or surgical treatment, the nursing home providing only nursing care, ancillary services and accommodation, the position as to medical records is substantially the same as in the case of a private patient in a voluntary hospital, save insofar as a voluntary hospital is likely to be providing not only nursing care but also medical care between visits of the patient's own doctor. When medical support as well as nursing care is provided in a nursing home, the position in respect of ownership of medical records is the same as in the case of a private patient treated in a voluntary hospital.

15.2   RADIOLOGISTS' REPORTS, X-RAY FILMS AND PRINTS

If a patient has paid the radiologist's fee, the question of ownership of developed X-ray films of a particular patient, and prints, is problematic.

If, as appears to be the case, what the patient pays for is not a photograph but the expert interpretation of the films by the radiologist, the films and prints would appear to remain the practitioner's own.

Nor do films or prints become the property of a medical practitioner who refers a patient for X-ray or scan, simply because that practitioner requires further detail for diagnostic or treatment purposes. However if, in private practice, a consultant radiologist makes or obtains an X-ray film relating to a private patient and sends a print to the patient's general practitioner or to another specialist dealing with the patient, it would appear that while the print becomes the property of the recipient doctor, the copyright would ordinarily remain vested in the radiologist who had made the X-ray photograph or had paid for it to be made in accordance with his directions.

The question of the rights and duties in respect of X-ray films and prints is chiefly of interest to hospitals and to their staff in respect of paying patients having a direct contract with the specialist(s) concerned. Paying patients who elect not to make separate arrangements with specialists will be charged inclusive fees by the hospital, pursuant to section 65 of the National Health Service Act 1977 (references in which do not include references to a hospital vested in an NHS trust[2]). A patient would not appear to have any legal claim to possession of an X-ray photograph taken. The photographs and radiologists' reports will no doubt be available as a matter of practice for the use of medical practitioners at other hospitals within the National Health Service where the patient may later be treated.

15.3   PUBLIC RECORDS ACT 1958

A duty is now placed by the 1958 Public Records Act on every person responsible for public records of any description which are not in the Public Record Office or a place of deposit appointed by the Lord Chancellor to make arrangements for the selection of those records which ought to be permanently preserved and for their safe-keeping and this duty is to be performed under the guidance of the Keeper of Public Records.[3] After thirty years such records have to be deposited with the Keeper or at another appointed place unless needed for administrative purposes.[4] Categorisation of records, transfer between categories, destruction of formerly preserved records and associated functions are subject to the jurisdiction of the Lord Chancellor.[5]

In effect that means that each government department is primarily responsible for its own records and by section 10, paragraph 3(1) of Schedule 1 to the Act, and Part I of the Table annexed thereto, it is provided that the departmental and administrative records of the National Health Service hospitals, whether or not records belonging to

Her Majesty, should be public records for which the Department of Health is responsible.

Records of property passing to Regional or (formerly) District Health Authorities or to Special Health Authorities under sections 24–26 of the National Health Service Reorganisation Act 1973 as well as records of property held by a Regional or Area Health Authority or by a Special Health Authority under section 90 or 91 of the 1977 Act are also public records.[6] Since, between them, it can be said that sections 21–26 of the 1973 Act and 90 and 91 of the 1977 Act cover all the modes by which a health authority might come into possession of property substantially corresponding, so far as the hospital side of its work is concerned, with acquisitions under sections 7, 59 and 60 of the National Health Service Act 1946, it follows that records of charitable funds of all kinds at the disposal of any health authority are public records for the purposes of the 1958 Act. These sections were repealed by the National Health Service Act 1977 but remain in the text of this chapter on account of the fact that the 1977 Act is not yet 30 years old. But where, in the case of a District (formerly Area) Health Authority (Teaching), such property has passed to, or is receivable by Special Trustees under section 95 of the 1977 Act, records relating thereto are not public records. It would be otherwise in any case in which, pursuant to a request under section 24(2) of the 1973 Act, Special Trustees had not been appointed, so that such property would have passed to or be receivable by the authority itself.

In August 1989 the Department of Health sent a circular[7] to hospital authorities giving them instructions as to what records are to be permanently retained and what may be destroyed and after what interval. The point is expressly made that if documents have been selected for permanent preservation the original documents must be preserved; it is rarely permissible to preserve microfilm copies in their place.

Clinical records of individual patients will not normally be preserved permanently under the Public Records Act 1958, other than by way of samples. That is best done by hospitals who are prepared to select and deposit samples in agreement with local record offices which have suitable facilities and are prepared to house such records.

Appendix A to Circular HC(89)20 further provides relevantly as follows:

'Extended closure

5. Section 5 of the Public Records Act 1958 as amended makes provision for the Lord Chancellor to prescribe periods of closure in excess of 30 years. A 100 year closure period was prescribed in 1961 [by Lord Chancellor's Instrument No. 3 of 7 January 1961] for medical records of individual patients; it applies only to records then in existence. Health authorities are reminded that other sensitive material may exist among records selected for permanent preservation and that

they are responsible for identifying such material and for applying to the Lord Chancellor, through the Keeper of Public Records, for an extension of closure beyond 30 years. The criteria for extended closure are:

(i) Exceptionally sensitive papers, the disclosure of which would be contrary to the public interest whether on security or other grounds (including the need to safeguard the Revenue);

(ii) Documents containing information supplied in confidence the disclosure of which would or might constitute a breach of goodfaith; and

(iii) documents containing information about individuals, the disclosure of which would cause distress to, or endanger, living persons or their immediate descendants.

6. Under section 5(4) of the 1958 Act records of health authorities which are not yet open to public inspection may not be examined without the express permission of those authorities or their successors. In exercising such discretion, health authorities should observe the following conditions:

(i) Permission should be restricted to the specific applicant.

(ii) For medical records, the consent of the patient or his next of kin and the agreement of the appropriate health professional should be sought [if practicable].

(iii) A signed undertaking must be obtained from the applicant not to identify any patient or member of staff in any work resulting from his research.

(iv) Any text concerning transcripts from or reference to material not open to public inspection should accordingly be submitted to the health authority before publication, to verify that the undertaking has been kept.

Place of deposit

7. Public records selected for permanent preservation are normally transferred to the Public Record Office. However, under section 4 of the 1958 Act public records may be held locally in a place of deposit appointed by the Lord Chancellor, if the authority responsible for records deposited in that place so agrees. In general, NHS records are appropriate for local deposit. Records created or inherited by District and Regional Health Authorities should usually be deposited in the approved place of deposit nearest to their administrative headquarters. Those places of deposit are normally local authority record offices maintained by county and district councils. In a very few instances individual hospitals have made suitable arrangements for care of their own records and have been appointed as places of deposit to hold them; certain libraries of medical institutions have also been appointed as places of deposit for records of hospitals, particularly personal health records.

8. The storage accommodation provided for the records must conform as nearly as possible to the British Standards Institution's *Recommendations for the Storage and Exhibition of Archival Documents* (BS 5454: 1977). In particular the accommodation must be secure, with proper environmental controls and adequate protection against fire and flood. Members of the public wishing to consult those records which are open to inspection must be able to do so in a properly supervised search room, where finding aids to the records must be available. There should be a guarantee of continued existence and commitment on the part of the authority maintaining a place of deposit. Ideally, the records there should be in the care of a professionally qualified archivist.

9. Whether records are held in the Public Record Office or a Place of Deposit, the transferring authority has the right, under section 4(6) of the 1958 Act, to have its records temporarily returned to it.

Exempt records

10. The following records, although technically exempt from the provisions of the Public Records Acts, contain information which meets the criteria for retention for the purposes of statutory audit or civil proceedings.

(i)   Records of non-Exchequer funds.
(ii)   Records of private patients admitted under section 65 of the National Health Service Act 1977 or section 5 of the National Health Service Act 1946.

Authorities should consider treating such records as if they were not so exempt. Advice on this point may be obtained from the Liaison Officer.

Retention of records: general

11. Permission to retain records for a period longer than 30 years, under section 3(4) of the 1958 Act, must be sought in respect of *all* records which are so retained, whether or not they have been selected for permanent preservation. Health authorities are responsible for identifying records which are already or within the next ten years will become 30 years old and for applying to the Lord Chancellor, through the Keeper of Public Records, if they need to be retained by the authority rather than transferred to a place of deposit or destroyed.

Administrative retentions

12. Administrative records may, with the approval of the Lord Chancellor, be retained by health authorities for more than 30 years if they are required for the day-to-day conduct of business. It should however be rare for administrative records in which the last entry was made 31 years previously to be still required for the day-to-day conduct of business. Before giving that approval, the Lord Chancellor will require to be informed whether arrangements can be made for members of the public to have access to the retained material. No approval of this kind will be given for a period in excess of 5 years.

Retention of records for other reasons

13. Health authorities may need to retain administrative records and personal health records for other purposes after these are no longer required for administrative or operational use, e.g. for research or for use as evidence in litigation. The minimum period for retention of personal health records (other than FBC records) no longer required for clinical purposes should take account of the provision of the Limitation Act 1980 and the Congential Disabilities (Civil Liability) Act 1976 and the Consumer Protection Act 1987. In the event of their retention for a period longer than 30 years, the same considerations apply as with retention for administrative purposes (see paragraph 12 above).'

Appendix B to the Circular sets out criteria for the selection of National Health Service records for permanent preservation. Recommendations for minimum retention periods are contained in Appendix C. Minimum retention periods are recommended in the case of financial records; records of legal value; building and engineering works records; legal actions or complaints about hospital or community services; product records, relevant to product liability claims (for which see

Chapter 20); and personal health records, relevant to possible legal proceedings against hospitals and health authorities (which are set out in detail, with specific reference to HC(89)20, in Chapter 5, pp. 132–134).

When public records have been deposited permanently in the Public Record Office or other place of deposit appointed under the Act, the Keeper of Public Records may nevertheless authorise their destruction or disposal subject to the approval of the Lord Chancellor and of the Minister or other person who appears to the Lord Chancellor to be primarily concerned.[8]

It is provided in section 9 that the legal validity of any record shall not be affected by its removal under the Act or under the Public Record Office Acts of 1838 to 1898 now repealed or by the provisions in those Acts with respect to its legal custody. A copy of or extract from a public record in the Public Record Office purporting to be examined and certified as true and authentic by the proper officer and to be sealed or stamped with the seal of the Public Record Office is admissible as evidence in any proceedings without any further or other proof thereof if the original record would have been admissible as evidence in those proceedings.[9]

NOTES

1. Schedule 9, paragraph 18(4) of the National Health Service and Community Care Act 1990 provides that references in section 65 of the National Health Service Act 1977 do not include references to a hospital vested in an NHS trust.
2. National Health Service and Community Care Act 1990, Schedule 9, paragraph 18(4).
3. Public Records Act 158, section 3(1),(2).
4. Public Records Act 1958, section 3(4).
5. Public Records Act 1958, section 3(4)–(7).
6. These were added to the list in Schedule 1 of the Public Records Act 1958 by Schedule 4, paragraph 82 of the National Health Service Reorganisation Act 1973. See now National Health Service Act 1977, Schedule 15, paragraph 22.
7. HC(89)20.
8. Public Records Act 1958, section 6.
9. Public Records Act 1958, section 9(2).

CHAPTER 16

Professional confidence

16.1 INTRODUCTORY: NATURE OF OBLIGATION OF PROFESSIONAL CONFIDENCE

Confidentiality is considered as a value, in which deep and important interests may be held or claimed. Indeed, the profession of medicine is itself a valued interest of any civilised community. Duty to patient and duty to the community, of which the patient is one member, may be coterminous; but equally, they may not. Varying interests and disparate values are apt to create tensions, tensions which are themselves conditioned by the very way in which basic interests and values are expressed. The tension, often experienced within the area under discussion, between pragmatism and principle creates a multitude of problems for both theorist and practitioner.

There is a moral obligation on doctors and other health care professionals to exercise great discretion not only concerning the nature of a patient's illness and attendant circumstances but also about all else which might come to their knowledge concerning the patient, his family and his affairs in the course of such a professional relationship. The obligation is independent of contract and arises whoever (if anyone) may be paying for the services. The obligation, though weighty, is not an absolute obligation and may be conditioned by circumstances. There may be circumstances in which the patient knows, or should know, that the doctor's medical records are, or may be, available to a third party, such as for instance a person in one of the armed forces attended by a Service doctor. *R v Kent Police Authority, ex p Godden* (1971)[1] ruled that the decision of a medical member of a Police Pension Tribunal is judicial and not medical in nature and must conform to rules of natural justice; and *Watts v Monmouthshire CC* (1967)[2] decided that a pre-employment medical was available to, but confidential to, the employers.

The Hippocratic Oath, which can be traced to the fifth century BC, was intended to be affirmed by each doctor on entry to the medical profession. The Oath begins:

> 'I swear by Apollo the physician, and Aesculapius and Health, and All-heal, and all the gods and goddesses, that, according to my ability and judgment, I will keep this stipulation . . .'

and continues later with the subject of our discussion:

'Whatever, in connection with my professional practice, or not in connection with it, I see or hear, in the life of men, which ought not to be spoken of abroad, I will not divulge, as reckoning that all such should be kept secret.'

The Oath ends with this sentiment:

'While I continue to keep this Oath unviolated, may it be granted to me to enjoy life and the practice of the Art, respected by all men, in all times. But should I trespass and violate this Oath, may the reverse be my lot.'

Is this moral duty also a legal obligation? In one sense it is, insofar as any breach of it renders a practitioner liable to disciplinary proceedings by the General Medical Council on a charge of serious professional misconduct. Such proceedings, if the charge were substantiated, might result in suspension or erasure of the practitioner's name from the Medical Register.

But is it also a legal obligation in the sense that any improper disclosure to a third party would render the practitioner legally liable for any consequential loss? Would an injunction lie against threatened disclosure? A case sometimes quoted in support of the proposition that breach of confidence is civilly actionable, *Kitson v Playfair* (1896),[3] is not precisely in point, the claim against the doctor having amounted to a claim for libel and slander and not simply for breach of professional confidence. In that case the judge assumed that a medical practitioner is under a duty of secrecy concerning his patient's illness and the circumstances surrounding it and summarised the exceptions to the obligation of secrecy. The decisions in *A–G v Mulholland* and *A–G v Foster* (1963)[4] are not binding authority since the defendants in those two cases were journalists. Even so Lord Denning referred to the medical practitioner's duty to respect his patient's confidence.

The courts might find that the medical practitioner's obligation not to disclose anything about his patient or his patient's affairs save on proper occasion was a legal duty no less than a moral obligation and may give a remedy (damages, or injunction, or both) to a patient who had suffered loss or damage to reputation, or even embarrassment, as a result of a breach of that duty. But there has so far been no such decision, and any such legal action would be highly speculative. What can be said for certain is that following a breach of confidence causing an already recognised head of legal damage, such as negligently caused psychiatric injury, an action for damages could confidently be brought under such an identified head of legal liability, such as psychiatric injury caused by negligence, as in *Furniss v Fitchett* (1958) (pp. 413–414, below).

16.2   HOSPITALS AND THEIR STAFF

The same obligation to treat information about patients and their affairs as confidential and not to be disclosed (except on proper occasion) is accepted by hospitals of all types, as well as nursing homes.

The obligation rests with the health authority and therefore on its employees, and breach by an employee may incur the authority in liability in an appropriate case. In any event, some types of staff, e.g. nurses, medical social workers, and paramedical staff accept the duty of discretion about patients and their affairs as part of their own professional code and their position would be the same as that of medical practitioners.

A patient entering or attending for treatment at a National Health Service hospital may reasonably assume that the hospital authority undertakes in respect of all its staff that proper discretion will be observed concerning the patient's illness and affairs.

The preservation of a patient's privacy and confidence is a privilege of the patient. That privilege may, legally and ethically, be waived by the genuine consent of the patient to the relay of certain information to certain other people (or bodies). Precisely what information is sought to be relayed, and to whom and for what purpose, must be understood and agreed to by the patient.

If the privilege of confidentiality may be waived by a patient's agreement that information be relayed, so much more pressing is the case of an actual request or instruction that certain information be passed to others. Failure to comply with an apparently reasonable request to relay information could in fact be unlawful: in a private contractual relationship for the delivery of health care, inaction could amount to a simple breach of contract actionable as such; and in the absence of a contractual relationship, injury or harm suffered in consequence of failure to implement a reasonable instruction to relay information could constitute actionable negligence to the person harmed.[5]

16.3   INFECTIOUS DISEASES

16.3.1   Information to District Medical Officer

This chapter concerning professional confidence as such, the separate topic of notifiable diseases is not discussed, being left to Chapter 28. It is nevertheless relevant to mention the following Regulations, giving their specific requirement of confidentiality.

There is a statutory obligation on medical practitioners to notify the District Medical Officer of cases of certain infectious diseases and he may use or disclose information concerning individual patients only so far as is required or authorised by statute. In particular, the District Medical Officer, as an officer of the District Health Authority, receives information concerning the identity of persons suffering from sexually transmitted diseases subject to the provisions of Regulation 2 of the National Health Service (Venereal Diseases) Regulations 1974,[6] which reads:

'Every Regional Health Authority and every District Health Authority shall take all necessary steps to secure that any information capable of identifying an individual obtained by officers of the Authority with respect to persons examined or treated for any sexually transmitted disease shall not be disclosed except—
(a) for the purpose of communicating that information to a medical practitioner, or to a person employed under the direction of a medical practitioner in connection with the treatment of persons suffering from such disease or the prevention of the spread thereof, and
(b) for the purpose of such treatment or prevention.'

The expression 'sexually transmitted disease' used in regulation 2, being apt to include any disease so transmitted, is wider in scope than the expression 'venereal disease', applied only to syphilis, gonorrhoea and soft chancre. It was suggested by Mr Justice Rose in *X. v Y.* (1988)[7] that AIDS is within the scope of these Regulations.

When the National Health Service (Venereal Diseases) Regulations 1968 were made, hospital authorities and their staff were sent a departmental memorandum including the following paragraph:

'The Minister is advised that the Regulations do not absolve any person from the existing obligation to give evidence in a court of law if required to do so, or to prevent them (*sic*) from giving information about a patient when asked by that patient preferably in writing.'

The position of a medical practitioner or other member of the staff of a health authority required to give evidence in court or asked by a patient to give information to a third party about him is apparently the same under the 1974 Regulations as under those of 1968.

16.3.2 Other disclosures

Apart from disclosure under compulsion of law there should broadly speaking (otherwise than with the consent of the patient or client) be no disclosure save when the life or health of some other person or persons is put in jeopardy, or in greater jeopardy, by silence; for example, the case of the patient who despite warnings, persists in exposing others to the risk of contracting an infectious disease in circumstances which do not give grounds for action by the District Medical Officer. If danger to the health or life of another or others were sufficiently grave, communication to an appropriate person of information necessary to afford opportunity for steps to be taken to prevent or minimise the danger normally would surely be justifiable.

The position is more complicated if what the patient is suffering from is a sexually transmitted disease, because any communication concerning the identity of a patient beyond what is authorised in regulation 2 of the National Health Service (Venereal Diseases) Regulations 1974 would contravene the Regulations. Any medical or other officer of a health authority who, say, warned any third person that a patient was suffering from such disease, or who authorised anyone else to do so, would be in breach of duty to his employing authority and a health authority which permitted such disclosure would be in breach of its duty to the Secretary of State.

If such improper disclosure were made, would either the officer who made the disclosure or his employing authority be liable to the patient in damages?

Having regard to the terms of the 1974 Regulations and to the fact that it has been publicly advertised that treatment for venereal disease is obtainable in hospitals under conditions of secrecy and against the background of the Regulations, it is reasonable that the patient should assume that he has an enforceable right to secrecy about his disease. But there would be no enforceable right unless he were a paying patient in which case such a right might be enforceable contractually. If, therefore, any such right exists, it can only be a variant of the more general obligation of discretion about the patient and his affairs which has already been discussed. Probably in this instance the obligation undertaken by the hospital and its staff would be construed more strictly than in others, but the obligation is not absolute. If disclosure were made to protect third parties against the risk of infection to which the patient had been wilfully exposing them, it is not conceivable that any court would award him damages. But if disclosure had been made for no good reason and the court were satisfied that what had been done constituted an actionable wrong, it is possible that damages would be awarded (on proof of actual loss or damage), even if what had been said was in fact true.

16.4 DISCLOSURE UNDER COMPULSION OF LAW

16.4.1 Generally

A medical practitioner or other member of the staff of a hospital is a compellable witness on *subpoena* or witness summons and may be obliged to produce his own or hospital records such as case notes, if in his possession, custody or control. And when in the witness box, a medical practitioner or other member of the staff of a hospital may not refuse to answer a question on grounds of professional privilege. Nevertheless, the court has some discretion and will generally compel a breach of confidence only when it is considered necessary in the interests of justice. The position of the medical witness and the attitude of the court towards him was stated in *A–G v Mulholland* and *Foster* (1963).[8] Lord Denning, the Master of the Rolls, said, in the course of his judgment:

> 'The only profession that I know which is given a privilege from disclosing information to a court of law is the legal profession, and then it is not the privilege of the lawyer but of his client. Take the clergyman, the banker or the medical man. None of these is entitled to refuse to answer when directed to by a judge. Let me not be mistaken. The judge will respect the confidences which each member of these honourable professions receives in the course of it, and will not direct him to answer unless not only it is relevant but also it is a proper and, indeed, necessary question in the course of justice to be put and answered. A judge is the person entrusted, on behalf of the community, to weigh these conflicting interests – to weigh on the one hand the respect due to confidence in the profession and on the other hand the ultimate interest of the community in justice being done . . .'

It must be appreciated, however, that the reference to the position of the medical practitioner as a witness was not the subject of the cases. Consequently this statement is not of binding authority. It was, however, substantially in line with what had for a very long time been understood to be the position. The only doubt left in one's mind is whether Lord Denning did not, perhaps, overemphasise the extent to which the judge could properly protect a medical witness. Certain it is that the court may compel disclosure by a medical practitioner of matters concerning his patient if those matters are regarded as essential to the case.

The 16th Report of the Law Reform Committee[9] dealt with privilege in civil actions. The Committee, having summed up the position of the medical practitioner called as a witness, substantially – but not precisely – in line with what Lord Denning said in *A–G v Mulholland* and *Foster*, recommended that no change be made in the existing law.

Perhaps the most controversial statement in the Report is that where its authors say that where a doctor is called not in his capacity as a medical adviser to testify as to the physical or mental condition of his patient, any judge would protect him from being questioned upon information obtained by him from his patient in his capacity of medical adviser. This statement, by inference founded in the judge's present discretion to disallow questions, implies that he has the right to disallow them without paying any regard either to 'all the circumstances of the case' or to 'the overriding claims of the interests of justice', which elsewhere in the Report is apparently regarded as paramount. Lord Denning's more cautious words on the subject in *Mulholland* and *Foster* would appear to be a more accurate statement of the present law. If the view of the Committee is indeed that a judge would protect a doctor from being questioned upon information obtained by him from his patient, save in exceptional cases that is tantamount to saying that the doctor – on behalf of his patient – has absolute privilege. Yet earlier in the Report the Committee in the statement of what the law is, stopped short of saying any such thing. The House of Lords left the point open in *D v NSPCC* (1977).[10]

By way of contrast when one looks at what they said as to confidences between priest and penitent or between any other minister of religion and a person who seeks his help in exercise of his spiritual duties, the Committee is content rather to rely on the fact that, *ex hypothesi*, a confession is known only to priest and penitent and that it is unlikely that any fishing questions would be put or allowed to be put about such confession. This would seem the reasonable line to take in respect of communications between doctor and patient as well, since only if either the doctor or the patient has already talked about it would there be any solid ground for questioning the doctor on what had passed between them.

The Criminal Law Act 1967 abolished the common law offence of misprision of felony, namely, having knowledge of the commission of a felony but failing to inform the police. Hence no member of staff of a hospital will longer be even remotely at risk of prosecution for simply not telling the police about, for example, an illegal abortion or attempted abortion, which may possibly have become known to him because of the woman's account of the matter on admission to hospital – such account amounting in law to a confession. If, however, for some compensation – otherwise than allowed by section 5 of the Criminal Law Act 1967 – anyone withholds information about the commission or the attempted commission of an arrestable offence, e.g. criminal abortion or attempted abortion, he will be committing an offence. Moreover, irrespective of such considerations, there remains the duty of giving information to the police in specific circumstances, such as under the Road Traffic Acts. But apart from such exceptional statutory obligation and subject to the provisions of section 5 of the Criminal Law Act 1967, there is not a legally enforceable obligation voluntarily to tell the police of any offence known to one or to do so on being questioned, though it could be an offence to give the police false or misleading information. In *Rice v Connolly* (1966)[11] it was held that preserving silence alone did not amount to obstructing the police, though undoubtedly it made their duties more difficult. Nor, at common law, is it obstruction to refuse to accompany a policeman to a police station unless arrested. But there are numerous local statutory exceptions.

16.4.2   Duty to give information to a police officer in road traffic cases

By section 168 of the Road Traffic Act 1972 (now section 112 of the Road Traffic Regulation Act 1984) if the driver of a mechanically propelled vehicle or the rider of a cycle who is alleged to have committed an offence under the Act has not been identified, any person if required to do so by or on behalf of a chief officer of police must give any information which it is in his power to give and which may lead to the identification of the driver. In *Hunter v Mann* (1974)[12] it was held that the words 'any . . . person' in section 168(2) of the Act had their ordinary unrestricted meaning and that, accordingly, a medical practitioner may be required to give information to the police under the subsection notwithstanding that to give the information otherwise than under compulsion of law might be a breach of professional confidence.

Under the section the information must be 'required by or on behalf of the chief officer of police'. Proof must therefore be offered by a policeman that he requires it in that behalf but this may be implied by his rank.

On the evening of 3 January 1973, Dr Hunter, a registered medical practitioner, treated a man at his surgery. The patient asked him to visit his girl friend who mentioned that she had been in a car accident. The doctor advised both patients to inform the police but he did not seek their consent to disclose their identity if asked to do so. Three weeks later a police officer requested him to divulge the name and address of either or both patients or to give information that would lead to their identification. The facts were that a stolen car had been involved in an accident, the driver and passenger having run away immediately afterwards; it was alleged that the driver was guilty of dangerous driving. The doctor refused, both at the time and later in writing, to divulge this information on the ground that this would be a breach of professional confidence. He was prosecuted in the local magistrates' court under section 168(2)(b) of the Road Traffic Act 1972 which states 'any other person . . . shall if required . . . give any information which it is in his power to give and may lead to the identification of the driver'. He was fined.

On the advice of the Medical Defence Union he appealed against the conviction on the ground that he was not within the words 'any other person' which were not to be construed as having an unrestricted meaning so as to cause a doctor to act in breach of the duty of confidence on which the patient was entitled to rely, and not within the words 'in his power' because power must include a legal right and he had no legal right to disclose. The Divisional Court dismissed the appeal stating that a doctor acting within his professional capacity and carrying out his professional responsibility was within the words 'any other person'. As to 'power' the court decided that there was no doubt that a practitioner in the circumstances in which the doctor found himself had the power. The doctor had only to disclose information which might lead to identification and which was not otherwise confidential. The appeal was dismissed with a certificate that a point of law of general public importance was involved in the decision. Leave to appeal to the House of Lords was refused. Although the member was found guilty of failing to give information to the police about his patients he maintained professional secrecy.

It will have been noticed that Dr Hunter was faced, not with an order from a judge to disclose information, but with the stipulations of a statutory provision of the Road Traffic Act. Breach of the stipulation is punishable by fine, which was accordingly imposed on Dr Hunter.

While leave to appeal was refused by the Divisional Court, such leave might have been sought independently from the House itself. But this approach was not made. Like as not, the same sort of result would have followed. One can, however, have more than a degree of sympathy with Dr Hunter and with anyone faced with the same problem. Courts of law are not always at their strongest when they seek to rely on 'the ordinary meaning' of words, especially when such words might constitute terms of art and not just terms of reference, still less ordinary verbiage. The doubtful point of the Divisional Court's judgment, delivered by Mr Justice Boreham reads:

'I am not going to attempt to define "power". It seems to me a word of fairly common understanding and reading it in its ordinary way I have no difficulty in coming to the conclusion that a doctor in the circumstances in which the appellant found himself had the power. It may be that but for the section in the Act he would not have exercised that power because of his duty to his patient, but that seems to me to beg the question, for that would have been in accordance with his duty not to make voluntary disclosure. Once it is decided that the appellant is a person to whom the statutory duty imposed by section 168 applies, then I have no doubt that he had the power. I think it would be no injustice to counsel for the appellant to say that this was the least strenuously argued of his points and I find it a point without substance.'

The particular point in issue – the meaning of one phrase (indeed, one word) in a statutory stipulation – may seem insignificant. But any apparent insignificance is overborne by the evidence we find here of a judicial unwillingness to admit legal consequences of a medical practitioner's ethical duty. The judge argued: the doctor had a 'power' (in the 'ordinary meaning' – presumably, 'all he could, all within his memory or intellectual capacity'); then said 'that' power would not, but for the statutory stipulations, have been exercised by the doctor because of his duty to his patient. But one may then ask: what power? The argument in defence of Dr Hunter begged the question only if the judge refused outright to attach any ethical significance to 'in his power'. And that, apparently, is precisely what the judge did.

This was not a case of a judicial order to divulge, merely of a statutory requirement, the breach of which attracted a fine. Dr Hunter was accordingly fined. But during the court proceedings he was not called upon to disclose the information sought by the police.

16.5 JUSTIFIABLE DISCLOSURE

16.5.1 Generally

Even when there is no legal compulsion on a medical practitioner or other member of the staff of a hospital to give information to the police, there may still be a public or social duty to do so. Such public duty would in law be a sufficient justification for disclosure to the police of information which ought normally to remain confidential. Nor could a hospital treat as a breach of discipline such disclosure to the police by one of its staff even though against the hospital rules.

Since there is no compulsion to perform the public or social duty of giving information to the police, whether there should be disclosure falls to be decided largely as a matter of conscience and with regard to the balance of social advantage.

Suppose a person attends hospital who, whether as regards injuries from which he is suffering or in appearance, answers the description of someone suspected of being concerned with murder, rape, robbery with violence or other serious crime. There may very well be a public duty to tell the police. But what about a minor offence? At least some staff may think their public duty is not the apprehension of criminals but rather the curing of the sick and the alleviation of suffering, in which case they might take the view that it is certainly not their job to volunteer information to the police and possibly not even to answer questions.

The question of the giving of confidential information in order to prevent medical harm to others has already been discussed.

If a health authority or trust, or its staff are sued by the patient, or, after his death, by his personal representatives or relatives, in respect of loss or injury he suffered or is alleged to have suffered by the fault of the authority or its staff, it is proper that all relevant information should be communicated to the solicitors acting for the hospital or its staff. Where a request for information comes from a solicitor acting for the patient in a claim against the hospital or its staff, even though production of case notes and similar documents was not obligatory before the stage of discovery in the actual proceedings was reached, the Minister of Health in 1959 advised hospital authorities that he did not feel that boards and committees, especially as they were public authorities, would either wish or be well-advised to maintain their strict rights in this connection except for some good reason bearing on the defence to the particular claim or on the ground that the request was made without substantial justification.[13]

It will usually be reasonable to agree to produce medical notes, before an action is commenced, to the legal adviser of the person seeking disclosure, leaving him to seek an order of the court if he wants more. A similar restriction might also be imposed if medical notes were voluntarily produced instead of by order under the Supreme Court Act 1981 in an action to which the hospital or the medical practitioner who made the notes was not a party. The approach of the Department of Health to disclosure relevant to possible legal proceedings is set out in Circular HC(82)16, for which see Chapter 5, p. 145.

Reports by hospital staff made after an accident in hospital has caused some injury to the patient, if they are reports prepared following a request by the solicitor to the hospital that such reports be prepared for his use, are less likely to be produced as they are privileged against discovery by virtue of legal professional privilege.[14]

Disclosure about a patient with his consent, express or implied, or reasonably assumed, is also justifiable. A simple example of consent being reasonably assumed is the customary giving of information to the patient's spouse or to a near relative about his condition, always provided that the patient has not forbidden such communication. But consent to informing even a near relative that a patient was suffering from a sexually transmitted disease could certainly not be assumed.

If a solicitor asks a hospital for information about a patient, stating in writing that he is acting for the patient and has the patient's authority for his request the hospital, and its staff within the limits of their authority, may properly and without further assurance give such information to the solicitor as they are willing to give, on such terms as to payment for extra work involved as they think proper. But if a solicitor who does not claim to be acting for the patient or his personal representatives or, perhaps, not a solicitor but an insurance company, seeks information about the patient or deceased patient, even with his or his personal representatives' consent as the case may be, it does not necessarily follow that it is always in the best interests of the patient or of his dependants that the inquiry should be answered especially when it is borne in mind that the circumstances may have been such that the patient or his personal representatives would have found it exceedingly difficult to withhold consent. Then the hospital authority and its staff may consider it more appropriate not to give the required information, being under no legal obligation to do so.

It is made clear in Departmental Circular RHB(53)93 to hospital authorities that the patient's right to have his hospital record treated as confidential is to be respected even as against the Ministry of Pensions and National Insurance (now the Department of Health) Medical Boards and Medical Appeal Tribunals. All these were to be supplied with such records to assist in assessing claims, for disablement benefit or war disability pension, only if the Ministry of Pensions and National Insurance had first obtained the consent of the patient in writing. The procedure was that the Department when applying to the hospital for information gives an assurance that the patient's written consent has been obtained. The Department indicated that this would suffice. It is, however, suggested that nonetheless the hospital might be under a liability for improper disclosure if consent had not in fact been obtained. If not, it is difficult to see how this could fail to be maladministration within the jurisdiction of either the Parliamentary Commissioner for Administration or the Health Service Commissioner. Only such extracts as are essential are to be made and they are to be treated as confidential. They are, however, communicated to the claimant or, if containing information which might be harmful to the claimant, to his doctor or, as appropriate, to his trade union or legal representative.

In the same Circular hospital authorities were told that so far as treatment reports on service pensions cases are concerned which by another Circular they are required to furnish to the War Pensions Office of the Ministry, no question of consent arises because they are required only for the clinical records of the medical staff of that Ministry to enable them to act on recommendations from the hospital, to follow up the case and to take such action as is indicated on the pensioner's behalf. That argument is unconvincing: unless it can be shown that the patient consented to such disclosure or it was a condition of his treatment as a Service pension case that such disclosure was permitted, it would not appear to be proper.

The then Ministry of Health gave the British Medical Association an assurance that in the event of proceedings for defamation against a doctor arising out of his entries on a hospital patient's case papers by reason of their loan to and use by the Department, the Minister will indemnify the doctor against any damages that may be recovered and against all reasonable costs that he may incur in defending proceedings. The indemnification of medical practitioners called upon to disclose confidential information before tribunals is also covered by this assurance. This indemnity is understood to be subject to the Minister being informed at once of any threatened proceedings and having complete control over the conduct of the defence. Circular HM(61)110 gives guidance on disclosure of information relating to psychiatric patients.

Doctors are often asked to give evidence in court about the medical history of a patient. If the patient or his solicitor makes the request consent is implicit, but if a third party seeks evidence of his medical state, even if it be the husband or wife of a patient, in divorce or custody proceedings, he must first provide the doctor with the written consent of the patient. This rule applies to a preliminary medical report and to attendance in court. Without the consent of the patient a report cannot be given, but a doctor can still be compelled to attend court by a witness summons. Having taken the oath, the doctor is still not free to give medical evidence about his patient unless he is so directed by the judge, coroner or magistrate. The doctor is free to say, after taking the oath, that he has not had his patient's permission to speak about him and that he would welcome the court's direction whether he is to answer questions which involve a breach of professional secrecy. There is an instructive instance cited in the Annual Report of the Medical Defence Union (1970):

'A general practitioner had treated a man of 21 who was addicted to amphetamine and was prosecuted for stealing drugs. He was immature and irresponsible and the general practitioner considered that since there was no ground under the Mental Health Act for his compulsory admission to hospital the only way in which he could be helped would be for him to be committed to gaol. The Union advised him that before giving such evidence in the magistrates' court at the request of the police, he should insist upon a witness summons being served upon him and should ask the magistrates whether he was directed to answer questions. The patient could not then object to him giving a frank opinion to the court.'

So the doctor may not only be compelled by order of the court to make disclosure, he may actually prefer this procedure to be put in train, so that he will be given a legitimate reason to provide the court with details which would otherwise be available only on the definite initiative of the court. Is there any wider duty on a doctor, deriving from the requirements of 'due process of law', to volunteer information which he thinks may lead to the prevention of a crime or the apprehension of a criminal? A comment in the Report of the Medical Defence Union (1977) is instructive, but less than conclusive:

'Doctors frequently have to decide whether to notify the police of confidential medical facts which suggest that a crime may have been committed. Even though not legally obliged to report a suspected crime, a doctor may feel bound in a given case to disclose what he knows about a patient as a means of preventing foreseeable harm to the public. The possibility that drugs may be sold to members of the public has sometimes influenced doctors to disclose information about patients whom they know to have drugs in their possession.'

It may be that in such cases the doctor's 'overriding duty to society' dictates or at least argues in the direction of disclosure. In any event, neither of the two instances just mentioned gives any credence to the view that disclosure should be made whenever the likelihood of crime, to be committed or already committed, presents itself. Indeed, in the former case, relating to mental disorder detention or alternatives to it, the requisite procedure for legitimate disclosure was put in hand so that the patient himself could be helped, and thus better treated – in the doctor's opinion.

In the sort of clash between judge and medical practitioner which normally seems to be avoided, at least in the extreme form of a contempt of court, the relationship between the obligations of law and ethics is worthy of comment. Chapter 3 of the British Medical Association's *Philosophy and Practice of Medical Ethics* is instructive:

'Court orders

In the UK there is no legal privilege for communications between patient and doctor; a court can therefore compel a doctor to give evidence, and direct him to disclose confidential information when giving it. A refusal to comply with such a direction could constitute a contempt of court, punishable by fine or imprisonment. When asked by a court to disclose information without a patient's consent, the doctor should first refuse on the grounds of professional confidence, and explain why he feels that the disclosure should not be made. The court will normally take such a statement into consideration, but if it nonetheless orders the doctor to answer the questions, he will have to decide as a matter of conscience whether he should comply.'

16.5.2 Alternative courses to agreement to disclose

If a patient will not agree that his tendency to fits, fainting or impaired muscle power or control be notified to the licensing authority, it is to this quarter rather than to the police that Medical Defence Union members have been advised to give information. Where the risk lies in the nature of the patient's employment, the medical officer of the employing body may be appropriately contacted in the interests of the patient and of the public. Although a family doctor is naturally reluctant to inform the licensing authority, against the wishes of his patient, that a tendency to fits is being concealed, particularly when the livelihood of the individual depends on driving, public safety is paramount.

In one case, two general practitioners were advised by the Union that their patients, each employed as a police officer and driving a police car, should report their tendency to fits to their employers, but that, if they refused to agree to this, the doctors should contact the senior police surgeons.

The family doctor of a British Rail engine driver who became subject to fits and wished to conceal the fact was advised by the MDU to inform the principal medical officer for the region. Similar advice was given to the doctor of a colour-blind signalman. In each case the patient was given the opportunity to take this step himself or to authorise his doctor to disclose it in the public interest.

If all else fails, open disclosure might be made, and in a way which might directly attract the possibility of legal process. Such open disclosure could be considered a matter of last resort, but in some situations the 'last resort' may occur very early. In any event, the doctor must be mindful of the general exhortation in Chapter 3 of *Philosophy and Practice of Medical Ethics*:

'Occasions may arise which persuade the doctor that confidential information acquired in the course of his professional work should be disclosed. In such cases, the doctor should wherever possible seek to persuade the patient to disclose the information himself, or to consent to the doctor's disclosing it. Failing this, it will be for the doctor to decide on his next course of action in accordance with his conscience, bearing in mind that he may be called to justify what he does.

In the course of their professional work, doctors will often receive requests from the police for access to personal medical information. When considering the balance between the public interest and his duty to the individual patient, the doctor should start from the premise that information obtained by him about a patient in the course of a professional relationship must be kept secret. There may well be occasions when the public interest will clearly outweigh the doctor's duty to an individual patient – for instance where the enquiries relate to a crime so grave that the safety of the doctor's other patients, or of the public at large, is at risk. On other occasions the balance may be finely drawn. The doctor must be aware that if, after the most careful consideration, he decides to disclose to the police information which he has obtained in confidence, he may later be called upon to justify his action, either before the GMC or in a court. Before a doctor decides to make such a disclosure, he should satisfy himself:

1. about the gravity of the crime concerned;
2. that the prevention or detection of the crime will be seriously prejudiced or delayed if the information is not disclosed; and
3. that the information will not be used for any other purpose, and will be destroyed if no prosecution is brought, or if it does not lead to a conviction.

Doctors who have difficulty in reaching a decision, having considered the facts presented to them by the police, are advised to discuss such requests with the BMA, or their defence body.'

Sometimes the doctor himself may be endangered, either singly or with others. The *British Medical Journal* of 1973 cites the example of a doctor who was about to catch a train and happened to walk past the engine, only to realise that the man who was about to drive him 450 miles was a patient suffering from syphilitic aneurysm of the aorta which was eroding his sternum and liable to perforate at any minute. The reaction of the doctor contained more than a degree of compromise:

'I went on the train and later sent for him. He hadn't told us he was a train driver, but I persuaded the patient to go to see his general practitioner and the railway doctor. The authorities were most reasonable about it and gave him another job. But if he hadn't stopped it would have been my duty as a citizen to communicate not with the authority – but with the doctor concerned.'

Thus, as in the other cases, every attempt was made to keep the communication between doctors: the information remains within the medical circle.

16.6 RELAY TO PARENTS OF INFORMATION CONCERNING A MINOR

In Chapter 7 the legal position on consent to treatment involving contraceptive procedures on minors was examined. The case of *Gillick v West Norfolk and Wisbech AHA* (1985)[15] established that there is no legal duty either to disclose or to refuse to disclose information to parents. In addition to the question of consent, questions of confidentiality clearly also present in such a context. A disciplinary hearing reported in 1971[16] is to an extent instructive in illustrating medical opinion relating to an allegedly improper disclosure. The case concerned a disciplinary hearing before the Disciplinary Committee of the General Medical Council. Dr Browne was charged with improperly disclosing to the father of a girl then aged 16 that she had been prescribed an oral contraceptive by Birmingham Brook Advisory Centre. In the *British Medical Journal* editorial[17] the dismissal of the charges against Dr Browne by the General Medical Council Disciplinary Committee was hailed as a reaffirmation of 'the principles of medical practice that the doctor has an obligation to act in the way he judges to be in the best interests of his patient'. Given the fact that Dr Browne thought it medically inadvisable for his patient to be given the particular oral contraceptive in question, it is argued that he was acting properly to inform the girl's father.

The case certainly falls far short of constituting anything like a precedent for future action; indeed, the Disciplinary Committee was at pains to stress that the issue was decided very much on its own merits. In particular, the Committee (so far as can be judged from the report) was impressed by Dr Browne's insistence that he, as the family doctor, was most familiar with the girl's medical history. Furthermore, in the event of any adverse reaction, it would be likely, he thought, to be he who would be called in to offer treatment.[18]

16.7   DISCLOSURE OF INFORMATION CONCERNING THE PATIENT'S WILL; DISPOSAL OF WILL

Greater caution has to be exercised in discussing a patient's affairs with a relative without his express approval than in so discussing his state of health. For example, should a patient have made a will while in hospital, the fact that he has done so should not ordinarily be disclosed to any relative, nor even the fact that he may have requested the attendance of a solicitor for that or any other purpose. Further, if a patient's will is in the possession of the hospital for safe-keeping, it should not, while he is alive, be handed over to any other person without his consent, save in the case of one made by a psychiatric patient whose affairs are subject to the Court of Protection, when an order of the court, or of a receiver appointed by the court, as to its disposal, must be complied with. If a patient, not being able to take care of his own property, is transferred from one hospital to another, his will should also be passed over to the receiving hospital for safe custody.

If a patient whose will is in possession of the hospital for safe custody dies or if, after the death of a patient in hospital, a will is found with the effects he kept in the ward, it should ordinarily be handed over only to or on the instructions of a person named therein as executor or, if no executor is named or none able and willing to act, then to someone to whom letters of administration could be granted, such as a residuary legatee. If, however, the name of a solicitor who prepared it is endorsed on the will, it would be reasonable especially in case of real doubt, to ascertain whether that solicitor was in a position to accept custody on behalf of whomever might be concerned.

16.8   CONFIDENTIALITY OF INFORMATION RELATING TO AIDS

The case of *X (Health Authority) v Y and others* (1988)[19] is instructive on the balance of interests, private and (allegedly) public to be struck in maintaining appropriate confidence of persons who have contracted the disease AIDS.

In February 1987 one or more employees of the plaintiffs, a health authority, supplied the first defendant, a reporter on a national newspaper owned and published by the second defendants, with information obtained from hospital records which identified two doctors who were carrying on general practice despite having contracted the disease AIDS. The second defendants made one or more payments of £100 for the information. On 28 February the plaintiffs obtained an order restraining the defendants from 'publishing . . . or making any use whatsoever of any confidential information' which was the property of the plaintiffs and contained in their hospital records. On 15 March the second defendants published an article written by the first defendant, under the headline 'Scandal of Docs with AIDS', which implied that there were doctors in Britain who were continuing to practise despite having contracted AIDS and that the Department of Health and Social Security wished to suppress that fact. The defendants intended to publish a further article identifying the doctors.

The health authority, who were the plaintiffs, sought (a) an injunction restraining the defendants from publishing the identity of the two doctors, (b) disclosure by the defendants of their sources, and (c) committal of the defendants on the grounds that the article of 15 March constituted a contempt of the order of 28 February. The questions arose (a) whether the second defendants were justified in the public interest in publishing and using the information disclosed to the first defendant; (b) whether the defendants should be ordered to disclose the source of their information, having regard to section 10 of the Contempt of Court Act 1981, which provides that the court should not order disclosure of a source unless it is necessary for, *inter alia*, the prevention of a crime; and (c) whether the second defendants' article on 15 March constituted a contempt of court.

In setting out the problem facing the court, the judge said:

'On the one hand, there are the public interests in having a free press and an informed public debate: on the other, it is in the public interest that actual or potential AIDS sufferers should be able to resort to hospitals without fear of this being revealed, that those owing duties of confidence in their employment should be loyal and should not disclose confidential matters and that, prima facie, no one should be allowed to use information extracted in breach of confidence from hospital records even if disclosure of the particular information may not give rise to immediately apparent harm.'

Mr Justice Rose held, in favour of the health authority, that the public interest in preserving the confidentiality of hospital records identifying actual or potential AIDS sufferers outweighed the public interest in the freedom of the press to publish such information, because victims of the disease ought not to be deterred by fear of discovery from going to hospital for treatment, and free and informed public debate about AIDS could take place without publication of the confidential information acquired by the defendants. Accordingly, the plaintiffs were entitled to a permanent injunction restraining the defendants from publishing that information in any form.

16.9   VOLUNTARY REVELATION BY EXAMINING PSYCHIATRIST OF PERCEIVED DANGER TO PUBLIC PRESENTED BY MENTAL PATIENT

The balance between maintaining confidentiality and the voluntary, unprompted relay of information gained from a private examination of a patient's mental state and presentation, on grounds of 'public interest', is illustrated by the decision of the Court of Appeal in *W. v Egdell and others* (1990).[20]

W was detained as a patient in a secure hospital without limit of time as a potential threat to public safety after he shot and killed five people and wounded two others. Ten years after he had been first detained he applied to a Mental Health Review Tribunal to be discharged or transferred to a regional secure unit with a view to his eventual discharge. His responsible medical officer, who had diagnosed him as suffering from schizophrenia which could be treated by drugs, supported the application but it was opposed by the Secretary of State. (The law relating to the addition of further restrictions to hospital detention orders on grounds of danger is set out in Chapter 30, pp. 785–6, 790–791, below.)

His solicitors instructed a consultant psychiatrist, Dr Egdell, to examine W and report on his mental condition with a view to using the report to support W's application to the Tribunal. In his report Dr Egdell strongly opposed W's transfer and recommended that further tests and treatment of W would be advisable, and drew attention to W's longstanding interest in firearms and explosives. Dr Egdell sent the report to W's solicitors in the belief that it would be placed before the Tribunal but, in view of the contents of the report, W through his solicitors withdrew his application. When Dr Egdell learnt that the application had been withdrawn and that neither the Tribunal nor the hospital charged with W's clinical management had received a copy of his report he contacted the medical director of the hospital, who, having discussed W's case with Dr Egdell, agreed that the hospital should receive a copy of the report in the interests of W's further treatment. At Dr Egdell's prompting the hospital sent a copy of his report to the Secretary of State, who, in turn, forwarded the report to the Tribunal when referring W's case to them for consideration.

When W discovered that the report had been disclosed he issued a writ against Dr Egdell and the recipients of the report seeking (a) an injunction to restrain them from using or disclosing the report, (b) delivery up of all copies of the report, and (c) damages for breach of the duty of confidence. The judge held that the duty of confidentiality owed by Dr Egdell to W as his patient was subordinate to Dr Egdell's public duty to disclose the results of his examination to the authorities responsible for W because such disclosure was necessary to ensure that the authorities were fully informed about W's mental condition when making decisions concerning his future. The judge accordingly dismissed W's claim against Dr Egdell and the recipients of the report. W appealed against the dismissal of his action against Dr Egdell, contending that the public interest in the duty of confidentiality owed by Dr Egdell to W should override any public interest considerations in disclosing the report to the authorities responsible for W.

The Court of Appeal upheld the trial judge's ruling against W and held that, as between the competing public interest in the duty of confidentiality owed by Dr Egdell to W and the public interest in disclosure of the report, the balance came down decisively in favour of disclosure because the number and nature of the killings committed by W were such that decisions leading directly or indirectly to his release from a secure hospital should not be made unless the authorities responsible for W were properly able to make an informed judgment that the risk of repetition of the killings was so small as to be acceptable. Accordingly, since Dr Egdell had highly relevant information about W's condition he had been justified in passing it on to those responsible for making decisions concerning W's future because the suppression of that information would have deprived the hospital and the Secretary of State of information which was relevant to questions of public safety. It followed that W's claim against Dr Egdell had properly been dismissed. W's appeal was accordingly dismissed.

As a starting-point the trial judge, Mr Justice Scott (with whose decision the appeal court agreed but not precisely for the judge's own reasons), turned to 'Advice on Standards of Professional Conduct and of Medical Ethics' contained in the General Medical Council's 'Blue Book' on professional conduct and discipline.[21] The judge said:

> 'These rules do not provide a definitive answer to the question raised in the present case as to the breadth of the duty of confidence owed by Dr Egdell. They seem to me valuable, however, in showing the approach of the General Medical Council to the breadth of the doctor/patient duty of confidence.'

These rules do not themselves have statutory authority. Nevertheless, the General Medical Council in exercising its disciplinary jurisdiction does so in pursuance of the provisions of the Medical Act 1983. Under the heading 'Professional Confidence', rules 79–82[21] provide as follows:

'79. The following guidance is given on the principles which should govern the confidentiality of information relating to patients.

80. It is a doctor's duty, except in the cases mentioned below, strictly to observe the rule of professional secrecy by refraining from disclosing voluntarily to any third party information about a patient which he has learnt directly or indirectly in his professional capacity as a registered medical practitioner. The death of the patient does not absolve the doctor from this obligation.

81. The circumstances where exceptions to the rule may be permitted are as follows:

(a) If the patient or his legal adviser gives written and valid consent, information to which the consent refers may be disclosed.

(b) Confidential information may be shared with other registered medical practitioners who participate in or assume responsibility for clinical management of the patient. To the extent that the doctor deems it necessary for the performance of their particular duties, confidential information may also be shared with other persons (nurses and other health care professionals) who are assisting and collaborating with the doctor in his professional relationship with the patient. It is the doctor's responsibility to ensure that such individuals appreciate that the information is being imparted in strict professional confidence.

(c) If in particular circumstances the doctor believes it undesirable on medical grounds to seek the patient's consent, information regarding the patient's health may sometimes be given in confidence to a close relative or person in a similar relationship to the patient . . .

(d) If in the doctor's opinion disclosure of information to a third party other than a relative would be in the best interests of the patient, it is the doctor's duty to make every reasonable effort to persuade the patient to allow the information to be given. If the patient still refuses then only in exceptional cases should the doctor feel entitled to disregard his refusal.

(e) Information may be disclosed to the appropriate authority in order to satisfy a specific statutory requirement, such as notification of an infectious disease.

(f) If the doctor is directed to disclose information by a judge or other presiding officer of a court before whom he is appearing to give evidence, information may at that stage be disclosed. Similarly, a doctor may disclose information when he has been summoned by authority of a court in Scotland, or under the powers of a Procurator-Fiscal in Scotland to investigate sudden, suspicious or unexplained deaths, and appears to give evidence before a Procurator-Fiscal. Information may also be disclosed to a coroner or his nominated representative to the extent necessary to enable the coroner to determine whether an inquest should be held. But where litigation is in prospect, unless the patient has consented to disclosure or a formal court order has been made for disclosure, information should not be disclosed merely in response to demands from other persons such as another party's solicitor or an official of the court.

(g) Rarely, disclosure may be justified on the ground that it is in the public interest which, in certain circumstances such as, for example, investigation by the police of a grave or very serious crime, might override the doctor's duty to maintain his patient's confidence.

(h) Information may also be disclosed if necessary for the purpose of a medical research project which has been approved by a recognised ethical committee.

82. Whatever the circumstances, a doctor must always be prepared to justify his action if he has disclosed confidential information. If a doctor is in doubt whether any of the exceptions mentioned above would justify him in disclosing information in a particular situation he will be wise to seek advice from a medical defence society or professional association.'

In the Court of Appeal's view, expressed by Sir Stephen Brown,

'the two interests which had to be balanced in this case were both public interests. The judge was wrong to refer to W's "private" interest. The judge was also in error, said counsel for W, in saying: "The case seems to me to fall squarely within para (b) of rule 81" (of the General Medical Council's rules). Dr Egdell did not have any clinical responsibility for W and accordingly that particular rule could not be relied on by Dr Egdell in the present circumstances.'

And to this he added:

'In so far as the judge referred to the "private interest" of W, I do not consider that the passage in his judgment accurately stated the position. There are two competing public interests and it is clear that by his reference to *X v Y* [1988] the judge was fully seised of this point. Of course W has a private interest, but the duty of confidence owed to him is based on the broader ground of public interest described by Rose J in *X v Y* [above].'

On European implications for human rights Lord Justice Brigham stated:

'No reference was made in argument before us (or, so far as I know, before the judge) to the European Convention on Human Rights (Convention for the Protection of Human Rights and Fundamental Freedoms) . . . but I believe this decision to be in accordance with it. I would accept that article 8(1) of the convention may protect an individual against the disclosure of information protected by the duty of professional secrecy. But article 8(2) envisages that circumstances may arise in which a public authority may legitimately interfere with the exercise of that right in accordance with the law where necessary in a democratic society in the interests of public safety or the prevention of crime. Here there was no interference by a public authority. Dr Egdell did, as I conclude, act in accordance with the law. And his conduct was in my judgment necessary in the interests of public safety and the prevention of crime.'

16.10   UNJUSTIFIABLE DISCLOSURE

Disclosure of information about a patient and his affairs without the express or implied consent of the patient and not falling within any of the exceptions mentioned above is unjustifiable. If actual damage could be established, a claim for damages might ensue though there is no decided English case directly on the point. *Kitson v Playfair* (1896)[22] is sometimes quoted as authority for the proposition that damages are awardable for breach of confidence in the sphere of medicine and health care treatment. There was in that case a breach of confidence, and there was an award of damages. But the point was that damages were awarded for the particular way in which confidence was breached, which constituted actionable defamation.

Although, in the case of near relatives, the consent of the patient to such disclosures as are normal in the circumstances will readily be implied, it would ordinarily be quite unjustifiable to give information to a spouse or near relative contrary to the express prohibition of the patient. And even though there has been no express prohibition by a married patient on communication of medical information to the other spouse there may still be circumstances in which it should not be given without the patient's express permission, notably if it might be made use of by the other spouse in matrimonial or custody proceedings between the parties. Should it be known to the attendant medical practitioner, or has been recorded by a social worker, in a note or report available to a member of staff of the hospital, that the relationship of the parties is hostile or unusual, that would be an added danger signal.

An example of this given on p. 21 of the Annual Report 1968 of the Medical Defence Union is that of a doctor-husband who asked to be provided with the pathologist's report of the blood group of the foetus, his wife having been admitted to hospital for termination of pregnancy on psychiatric grounds. In the same report (p. 22) it is recorded that a psychiatrist who had treated the estranged wife of a general practitioner for two years, otherwise than under compulsion of law, had made an affidavit about the wife's condition for use of the husband's solicitors in custody proceedings between the parties and that his doing so had been subject of complaint to the General Medical Council. The complaint had been dismissed only after the psychiatrist, through his solicitors, had expressed regret. That a similar complaint against the husband's partner, who had also made an affidavit, had been rejected, apparently on the ground that he had used only his general knowledge of the wife, raises alarming possibilities in custody proceedings for wives who do not get on very well with their general practitioner husbands.

In particular, a doctor having the care of a mentally disordered patient, or who has had the care of such a patient during that patient's stay in hospital, should not disclose information about the patient's condition and treatment to a spouse contemplating divorce proceedings. This applies even though it is with the object of protecting the patient from being unduly bothered about such proceedings.

Even in the case of a minor over 16 years of age it may be appropriate to follow the minor's wish that his/her parents should not be told, though the hospital or responsible member of its staff would be justified in ignoring the minor's express wish if it was thought to be in his/her interests to do so. If, however, as has been known to happen in the case of a pregnant young woman, a minor over 16 years of age were willing to enter hospital for necessary treatment only on assurance that her parents would not be communicated with, the responsible member of the medical staff giving such assurance would doubtless feel obliged to honour his undertaking in any but the gravest emergency; nor do there appear to be any grounds of liability to the parents for so doing.

A rare instance of a reported case in which breach of confidence led to an action for damages in the tort of negligence is the decision of the Supreme Court of New Zealand (whose reasoning would no doubt be adopted by a court faced with a similar problem in this country) in *Furniss v Fitchett* (1958).[23]

On 21 May 1956, and for some time previously, Dr Fitchett (the defendant) was and had been the regular medical attendant of both Mrs Furniss (the plaintiff) and her husband. Dr Fitchett was still being consulted by Mrs Furniss as late as April 1957. It appears that Mrs Furniss entertained suspicions that her husband was doping her and that he was insane. She told her doctor that her husband was cruel to her and occasionally even violent. These suspicions and charges were quite without foundation; but they naturally engendered a certain amount of domestic discord which in turn affected the health of the husband. A separation of husband and wife, temporarily at all events, would probably have been in the interest of the health of both of them and a separation had been discussed, but down to 21 May 1956 this had not been arranged. Dr Fitchett had been asked by Mr Furniss's solicitor whether he could arrange for Mrs Furniss to be 'certified'. Had she been committed to a mental institution that would, of course, have brought about at least a temporary separation and would have relieved Mr Furniss from the anxieties which were adversely affecting his health. Dr Fitchett said in evidence that he was 'deeply worried over the suggestion of certification'. Although he thought that Mrs Furniss showed symptoms of paranoia, he did not think that committal to a mental institution would be in her best interest. As family doctor, he was faced with a problem that presented many difficulties. He was attempting to give medical advice to two persons – husband and wife – whose interests, even if they were not, from a medical point of view, really in conflict, may well have seemed to his patients to be in conflict. That was the situation which existed on 21 May 1956.

On that date Mr Furniss saw the defendant. The defendant's evidence was that his patient was then almost desperate, that he was in a distraught state and that he said: 'You must do something for me, doctor – give me a report for my lawyer'. After deep thought, the defendant out, signed, and gave to Mr Furniss a document which was worded as follows:

'Mrs Phyllis C. L. Furniss   21.5.56
  32 Mornington Road

The above has been attending me for some time and during this period I have observed several things:
(1) Deluded that her husband is doping her.
(2) Accuses her husband of cruelty and even occasional violence.
(3) Considers her husband to be insane and states that it is a family failing.
On the basis of above I consider she exhibits symptoms of paranoia and should be given treatment for same if possible. An examination by a psychiatrist would be needed to fully diagnose her case and its requirements.

                                                 Yours faithfully,
                                                 A. J. Fitchett.'

The evidence does not reveal what was immediately done with this document. Mrs Furniss continued to see the defendant professionally down to the month of April 1957. From 3 June 1956, to 7 August 1956 Mrs Furniss was away from her home. She then returned for a short period, but left again on 4 October 1956. Later, she took proceedings against her husband for separation and maintenance orders. The application was heard in the magistrates' court on 29 May 1957. During the hearing, and in the course of cross-examination of Mrs Furniss, Mr Furniss's solicitor produced to her the above quoted document of 21 May 1956. It was a little more than a year old; but it was only then that Mrs Furniss learned of its existence.

Mrs Furniss then commenced proceedings against the doctor.

Chief Justice Barrowclough held that, in the particular circumstances of this case, Dr Fitchett should reasonably have foreseen that the contents of his certificate were likely to come to his patient's knowledge, and that his patient would be likely to be injured as the result of his action in giving to her husband such a certificate as he gave, knowing that at the time his patient and her husband were estranged, and in giving it to him without placing any restriction on its use. Further, that in such circumstances, there arose a duty of care on his part, notwithstanding that the certificate was true and accurate; and that duty extended also to the exercise of care in deciding whether it should be put in circulation in such a way that it was likely to cause physical harm to his patient; and in consequence that the showing of the certificate to her by her husband's solicitor was forseeable and was the very thing which the law required the doctor to take care to avoid: and the damages resulting from the production of the certificate to Mrs Furniss were not too remote even though their immediate cause was the act of the husband's solicitor and not of the defendant.

In the course of his judgment his Lordship explained:

'I do not hold that the doctor ought to have foreseen the precise manner in which the contents of his certificate did in fact come to Mrs Furniss's knowledge; though I think that, in the circumstances disclosed by the evidence, he ought to have foreseen that the certificate could be expected to be used in some legal proceedings in which his patient would be concerned and thus come to her knowledge. It is sufficient to say that, in my view of the evidence in the special circumstances of this case, Dr Fitchett should have foreseen that his patient would be likely to be injured as the result of his action in giving to her husband such a certificate as he did give, and in giving it to him without placing any restriction on its use. In these circumstances, I am of opinion that, on the principle of *Donoghue v Stevenson* [1932] there arose a duty of care on his part. I have not forgotten that the certificate was true and accurate, but I see no reason for limiting the duty to one of care in seeing that it is accurate. The duty must extend also to the exercise of care in deciding whether it should be put in circulation in such a way that it is likely to cause harm to another.'

In so ruling, the judge reserved his opinion (that is, did not express one) as to whether, apart from any question of defamation (for which see *Kitson v Playfair* (1896), above), a duty of care is owed by every professional person in respect of what is said or written of a client if that person suffers injury or harm in consequence of its being divulged.

NOTES

1. [1971] 2 QB 662.
2. [1967] 66 LGR 171.
3. The Times, 28 March 1896.
4. [1963] 2 QB 477.
5. See Chapter 6.
6. SI 1974/29, as amended by SI 1982/288.
7. [1988] 2 All ER 648.
8. [1963] 2 QB 477.
9. Cmnd 3472.
10. [1977] 1 All ER 589.
11. [1966] 2 QB 414.
12. [1974] QB 767. The relevant section of the Road Traffic Regulation Act 1984 is section 112(2)(b).
13. HM(59)88.
14. *Patch v Bristol United Hospitals* [1959] 1 WLR 955; HM(55)66.

15. [1985] 3 All ER 402.
16. (1971) 1 BMJ (Supplement) 79.
17. (1971) 1 BMJ 620.
18. (1971) 1 BMJ (Supplement) 79, 80.
19. [1988] 2 All ER 648.
20. [1990] 1 All ER 835.
21. General Medical Council *Professional Conduct and Discipline: Fitness to Practice*, republished February 1991.
22. The Times, 28 March 1896.
23. [1958] NZLR 396.

CHAPTER 17

Employment law

17.1 THE CONTRACT OF EMPLOYMENT

17.1.1 Introductory

This chapter gives an overview of employment law generally, together with an indication of particular conditions of employment affecting employees of the National Health Service specifically. More detail is included in what follows than was contained in previous editions of this work on the subject of health care services outside the public sector. Furthermore, while until April 1990 some substantial differences existed between certain aspects of employment law as affecting the National Health Service and health care agencies outside the service, in particular the parts of general employment legislation which did and which did not bind the Crown, the removal by section 60 of the National Health Service and Community Care Act 1990 of Crown status for health authorities has largely removed those differences. Certain different, in the sense of extra, rights and entitlements in respect of non-medical health authority employees continue to apply on account of the implementation of Whitley Council agreements. These include, in particular, rights on redundancy and entitlements relating to the resolution and settlement of employment disputes. While NHS trusts are for most purposes independent of the general guidance operating across the rest of the National Health Service, at the time of going to press the experience has been that the trusts already established have found it at least temporarily convenient to operate the rights and entitlements applicable under Whitley Council agreements.

17.1.2 Employee and independent contractor: the question of status

It is essential to distinguish between an employee and one who is not an employee but an independent contractor whose services are engaged by a person or authority who pays for those services but who for a variety of reasons is not that person's employer. A distinction must correspondingly be drawn between an employment contract, which is a contract of service, and a contract for services by which an independent contractor is engaged. The relevance of this distinction was emphasised in Chapter 5, in relation to differing civil liabilities of an employer and an engager of services, respectively.

In order to qualify for the statutory and other benefits enjoyed by an 'employee', the person claiming them must (subject to certain exceptions affecting the definition in discrimination cases) show that a contract of service exists. It may happen that an employee, so qualifying, enters into a contract for services with another, but he will nevertheless remain, for the purposes of employment law rights, the employee of the person (or body) with whom a contract of service exists. The law relating to vicarious liability in tort, discussed in Chapter 5, follows the same general principle.

A person doing a piece of work for another, whether it be painting a picture, building a house or attending a sick person, must ordinarily be acting in one of two capacities. Either he is an independent contractor, or he is an employee either of the person on whose order the work is being done or of an independent contractor who has undertaken it. The distinction is important, for the independent contractor is not subject to control as regards the method of carrying out the work except so far as the contract may stipulate. An employee is always subject to some degree of supervision and obliged to obey lawful orders in accordance with his contract of employment, and ordinarily at least a certain portion of his time is at the exclusive disposal of his employer. His duties to the employer are also far more comprehensive.

The physician or surgeon attending a patient in private practice is acting as an independent contractor exercising professional skill in advising and treating his patient. The patient has no control over him. His only remedy if dissatisfied is to call in another medical adviser and, if he thinks he has grounds for it, to bring an action for negligence or breach of contract alleging failure to exercise proper skill. If, however, a medical practitioner is on the salaried staff of a hospital his position is different for, although he has discretion as regards treatment of patients, he is subject to rules and regulations imposed by the employer as regards such matters as administration and the general framework of his clinical duties; and even in his professional work, unless he is of consultant status, may be subject to the general oversight or even the specific instructions of a more senior member of the medical or surgical staff, and is an employee of the hospital.

The position of so-called 'honorary staff' in a voluntary hospital is somewhat more obscure, but there is an increasing tendency for such hospitals to give consultants emoluments, and even a purely nominal payment might suffice as evidence that the contract was one of service. On the other hand it might be held to be a contract for services. Elaborate discussion of the point hardly seems called for having regard to the judgments in *Roe v Minister of Health* (1954)[1] indicating that a voluntary hospital authority would be liable for the negligence of a part-time consultant working under a contract for services and *Razzel v Snowball* (1954)[2] from which the inference may be drawn that the Secretary of State, through his agents, the Regional and District Health Authorities, is liable for the acts of part-time consultants in the National Health Service.

General practitioners, who are independent contractors to Family Practitioner Committees, are subject to normal employers' obligations in respect of the employment rights of such people as medical secretaries and also ancillary staff such as cleaners and gardeners.

In the context of normal activities within the National Health Service it is rarely, if ever, that the distinction between employee and independent contractor presents any difficulty. The question might, however, arise in the context of relations between a health authority or unit and an agency for the supply, for instance, of extra nursing staff. The precise terms of the engagement (or employment, as the case may be) would need to be studied in order to ascertain the legal relationship between all the contracting parties.

The decided cases on the distinction are complex, but the broad definition of an employment contract or contract for services is found in the judgment of Mr Justice Mackenna in the case of *Ready-Mixed Concrete v Minister of Pensions etc.* (1968),[3] as follows.

A contract of service exists if the following three conditions are fulfilled:

> '(i) The servant agrees that in consideration of a wage or other remuneration he will provide his own work and skill in the performance of some service for his master. (ii) He agrees, expressly or impliedly, that in the performance of that service he will be subject to the other's control in a sufficient degree to make that other master. (iii) The other provisions of the contract are consistent with its being a contract of service.
>
> As to (i). There must be a wage or other remuneration. Otherwise there will be no consideration, and without consideration no contract of any kind. The servant must be obliged to provide his own work and skill. Freedom to do a job either by one's own hands or by another's is inconsistent with a contract of service, though a limited or occasional power of delegation may not be:
>
> As to (ii). Control includes the power of deciding the thing to be done, the way in which it shall be done, the means to be employed in doing it, the time when, and the place where it shall be done. All these aspects of control must be considered in deciding whether the right exists in a sufficient degree to make one party the master and the other his servant. The right need not be unrestricted.'

The third, and negative condition, is difficult to define without reference to the circumstances in any particular case, and indeed such reference is essential. At the end of the day the courts have the right to pronounce on the nature of the contract in question, on the basis of a broad general impression though with the above considerations in mind. In the case mentioned above the judge was no more specific than this:

'An obligation to do work subject to the other party's control is a necessary, though not always a sufficient, condition of a contract of service. If the provisions of the contract as a whole are inconsistent with its being a contract of service, it will be some other kind of contract, and the person doing the work will not be a servant. The judge's task is to classify the contract (a task like that of distinguishing a contract of sale from one of work and labour). He may, in performing it, take into account other matters besides control.'

While an employer is liable in a very wide variety of circumstances for wrongs (e.g. negligence) of an employee causing injury to another (e.g. a patient in hospital), such liability exists in relation to independent contractors (under contracts for services) only under very restricted circumstances. While, on the one hand, an employer may be liable for negligent injury even by an employee who is disobeying express instructions, liability will fall upon the engager of an independent contractor only if certain highly hazardous acts (such as handling fire or explosives, or activities near the highway) or carelessness on the part of the engager of services himself are involved. The distinction between an employer and one who engages the services of an independent contractor in relation to injury to a third party is explained at pp. 107–123 of Chapter 5. So, too, is the situation in which an employee of one party is seconded or 'lent' to another and injury to a third party occurs. That chapter also explains the practical incidence of legal liability for professional negligence in the delivery of personal health care services following the introduction of National Health Service indemnity arrangements on 1 January 1990.

17.1.3 More than one employer

There is no legal reason why an employee may not have more than one employer, with the result that legal remedies may be pursued in any case where there is an alleged breach of contractual duties or infringement of status produced by the contract of employment. Two types of situation may be distinguished by way of example. On the one hand, the contractual and employment relations between a health authority or nursing home, a nursing agency, and the individual nurse, will normally resolve themselves into a situation in which there is employment by one or other, but not by both. On the other hand if, as is not uncommon in these days, a person has a day job and an evening or night-time job, there may perfectly well be two quite separate employers.

17.1.4   Temporary employees

A temporary employee has the same legal entitlements under employment law as a full-time employee, provided that he can show the appropriate length of service and works the necessary hours per week to qualify for them. An exception to the availability of such rights is provided by section 61 of the Employment Protection Consolidation Act 1978 which provides that if an employee is employed on a temporary basis to replace a woman who has been given maternity leave, or replace another employee suspended on medical grounds, and the latter returns to work, the temporary employee does not benefit from the full range of rights in respect of unfair dismissal. To constitute the exception to normal protection, however, it must be shown that the contract by which the temporary employee is taken on specifically points out the temporary nature of the employment. However, since the raising of the qualifying period of employment for unfair dismissal to two years,[4] section 61 of the 1978 Act has ceased to have any real importance in practice. Allegations of unfair discrimination are subject to a legal time limit, though the requirement that the employee should have a qualifying period of employment in order to make a claim does not apply.

17.1.5   Part-time employees

Temporary employees must be distinguished from part-time employees who may, depending upon the following factors, have full rights in respect of employment protection against dismissal. 'Part-time employee' is a very wide term; but in the context of employment protection it can be said that if a contract of employment exists, anyone who is employed for more than 16 hours per week for more than two years, or who has been continuously employed for between 8 and 16 hours per week for the previous five years, has full legal protection.

17.1.6   Trainees and learners

The legal position relating to trainees can differ according to the nature of the employment in question. A contract of employment is defined by section 153(1) of the Employment Protection Consolidation Act 1978 as a contract of service or apprenticeship, whether express or implied, and (if it is express) whether it is oral or in writing. Apprentices to a tradesman and trainee solicitors (articled clerks) are clearly employees within this definition. However, in *Wiltshire Police Authority v Wynn* (1981)[5] it was held that police cadets are not employees but rather persons who are training to become policemen. Even though they are paid by the police authority during their training, the court held that they are not employed under a contract of employment. A similar result was reached in the case of alleged racial discrimination in *Daley v Allied Supplies Ltd* (1983)[6] which concerned a girl working on a Youth Opportunities Scheme and who was held not to be a 'person employed' within the meaning of sections 4 and 78 of the Sex Discrimination Act 1975. So far as medical, paramedical and nursing training within the National Health Services is concerned, there is no doubt that such trainees are employees of their health authority. Indeed, it is the frequent experience of psychiatric hospitals that nurse trainees make up the complement of nurses on the ward for the purpose of adequate staffing ratios.

17.1.7 'Employee' distinguished from 'worker'

It will have been noticed from the above definitions of employee and contract of employment that the law tends to define the relationship in terms of 'master and servant'. Although somewhat antiquated, these terms have a clear legal meaning and, like the term 'worker', have no pejorative intention. The most recent statutory definition of 'worker' appears in section 8 of the Wages Act 1986 (See pp. 470–471 of this chapter). This provides that a worker is an individual who has entered into, or works under (a) a contract of service; (b) a contract of apprenticeship; or (c) any other contract whereby the individual undertakes to do or personally perform any work or services for another party to the contract whose status is not by virtue of the contract that of client or customer of any profession or business undertaking carried on by the individual, and whether the contract is in writing or only oral. The provisions of the Sex Discrimination Act 1975 (see pp. 452–456 of this chapter) apply to 'workers' and not just to employees. For certain statutory purposes, therefore, the term worker is found to have a wider meaning than the term employee.

17.1.8 Employment and status

It is not merely contractual rights and entitlements which flow from the existence of an employment contract or contract of service. Certain employees also have further rights in respect of job security over and above what is either expressly or impliedly provided for in the contract of employment. Important rights and privileges have been granted by legislation in respect of continuity of employment and freedom from unfair dismissal, on the basis of the status enjoyed by an employee. Nevertheless, the individual contractual relationship still remains relevant. Remedies for dismissal are thus available in respect of status, as an employee, and by way of an ordinary action in the courts for wrongful dismissal resulting from a breach of contract.

A particular status resulting from a contract of employment is demonstrated by the decision in *McClelland v Northern Ireland General Health Services Board* (1957).[7] The plaintiff was appointed to a permanent pensionable post, her contract stating that the Board could dismiss her only for a gross misconduct, inefficiency or unfitness for work. The Health Services Board attempted to terminate her employment on the ground of redundancy. The legal action brought by the plaintiff employee established that the Board's action did not constitute a valid termination of employment, given that the dismissal terms of her contract were exhaustive and that no other ground for dismissal could be implied into them.

In *University of Aston, Birmingham v Malik* (1984)[8] the applicant was employed on yearly contracts. In July 1981 the University did not renew her contract due to lack of funds. She nevertheless continued to work unpaid until her contract was once again renewed, in October 1981. It was held by the Employment Appeal Tribunal that her continuity of employment was not broken during the period between July and October 1981. The fact that the University could not pay for the work that was in fact available did not affect the applicant's continuity of employment just because there was no paid work for her to do.

Entitlements flowing from status and affecting dismissal and redundancy have certain restrictions, principally in terms of length of service and hours worked. Nevertheless, employees outside these restrictions may have status advantages flowing from a contract, in particular the existence of a public law remedy. This may, for instance, take the form of an application to the Divisional Court of the Queen's Bench Division for a declaration that a public body (which term would appear to include health authorities within the National Health Service pursuant to the National Health Service Act 1977, as amended) has acted unreasonably or unfairly in decisions taken relating to employment. The procedure for making such an application falls under Order 53 of the Rules of the Supreme Court. Such an application is not generally possible if a legal remedy based on rights and entitlements under the contract itself would be sufficient. There must, in other words, exist a further and additional element of a public right or the enforcement of a public duty. The public body, including for this purpose a health authority, is effectively being asked (through the court) to do its job properly following the undoing of decisions already allegedly improperly taken. Judicial decisions on the question of contract and status are discussed in detail on pp. 443–446 of this chapter.

17.1.9 The contract of employment

The basic requirement for an enforceable contract is that there must be an agreement supported by consideration. The law of contract relating to the concept 'consideration' is quite complex, but it can generally be described as 'the price of a bargain'. A promise to pay wages is 'bought' either by the actual performance of work or, more often, by a promise to work. Mutual promises, here one to pay and the other to work, are necessarily assumed in law to be 'good consideration' for each other. The promises on each side may be express or implied and the exchange of promises can be analysed in terms of offer and acceptance. In an employment situation the offer is usually made by the prospective employer, but there is no reason in law why it should not be made by the prospective employee.

The agreement must be sufficiently certain for the courts to give it a meaning for the purposes of attaching legal consequences to the employment relationship which is sought thus to be created. However, recent judicial decisions have leaned in favour even of ambiguous terms, provided the lack of clarity or of certainty is not too great. The requirement of consideration, the 'price of the bargain', means that a promise to perform gratuitous services is not legally enforceable. This principle also extends to volunteers who actually do work or perform services on another's behalf and who have thus no legal claim to be paid for them. Thus voluntary workers in the health and care services do not have a legal claim to be paid for their assistance even in the highly unlikely circumstances of changing their minds and deciding that they now want to be paid for what they have done.

Work rules

Among the contractual terms which may either expressly or impliedly become part of the employment agreement are work rules. Many employers issue their employees with a book of rules, or some other such document, either at the time of engagement or subsequently. Some employers display notices at the place of work. Some such rules result from collective bargaining pursued by and on behalf of the workforce or larger groups, but more often these work rules are drawn up by the employer without the aid of collective bargaining. These rules are frequently of a disciplinary nature, such as the right to suspend without pay or summarily dismiss the employee for a wide variety of offences or misdeeds such as bad timekeeping, drunkenness, gambling or other misconduct likely to be prejudicial to the employer. The rules may lay down methods of payment or mention restrictions, such as a duty to wear clean overalls or protective clothing, to work overtime as required, and not to engage in spare-time work. Grievance and disciplinary procedures may also be set out. The incorporation of disciplinary procedures can have important practical consequences including the availability, against an employer's proposed action, of an injunction in favour of an aggrieved employee.

It is a matter of interpretation in each case whether or not work rules, notices, collective agreements and the like are sufficiently certain to be construed as terms of the contract, and whether or not they have actually been incorporated into the contract of employment by the parties either expressly, or impliedly by conduct or by custom.

Written particulars of employment

The general rule of the law of contract is that an agreement supported by good consideration need not be in writing to be legally enforceable. If a contractual agreement is in writing it may, of course, be easier to prove in any dispute as to terms and conditions. But that is a procedural point and does not affect the substance of the issue, which is that an agreement supported by consideration, the price of the bargain, has been reached.

However, the Employment Protection (Consolidation) Act 1978 obliges an employer to provide an employee with a written statement identifying the parties to the agreement, specifying the date when the employment began. This is not a written contract of employment. It is merely strong evidence as to what the terms of the contract are. These necessary written particulars must also state whether any employment with a previous employer counts as a part of the employee's continuous employment with him and, if so, specifying the date on which the continuous period of employment began and giving particulars of certain terms of employment which are listed in a moment. The written statement must be given to the employee not later than 13 weeks after the beginning of his period of employment with the employer and must represent the terms of his employment as at a specified date not more than one week before the statement is given. This means, in other words, that the statement of written particulars must contain details of terms which formed part of the contract before notice of the terms was given. But a practical problem arises if the written particulars differ from the original agreed terms. In this event the original terms take precedence.

The specific terms of which the 1978 Act says that particulars must be given, if they are to form part of the employment agreement, are these:

1. the scale or rate of remuneration, or the method of calculating remuneration;
2. the intervals at which remuneration is paid (that is, whether weekly or monthly or other specified intervals);

3. any terms and conditions relating to hours of work (including any terms and conditions relating to normal working hours);
4. any terms and conditions relating to:
    (a) entitlement to holidays, including public holidays, and holiday pay (the particulars given being sufficient to enable the employee's entitlement, including any entitlement to accrued holiday pay on the termination of employment, to be precisely calculated);
    (b) incapacity for work due to sickness or injury, including any provisions for sick pay;
    (c) pensions and pension schemes; and
5. the length of notice which the employee is obliged to give and entitled to receive to terminate his contract of employment;
6. the title of the job which the employee is employed to do.

Such a statement may refer the employee to some document which he has reasonable opportunities of reading in the course of his employment or is otherwise reasonably accessible. Certain further particulars, including those concerning fixed-term employment, the place of work, work outside the UK and collective agreements, will be required when Schedule 4 of the Trade Union Reform and Employment Rights Act 1993 comes into force.

If there are no job particulars to be given either expressly or by implication, this fact must be stated. An employer who states that there are no particular terms of employment, express or implied, under one or other of the headings listed above, must be careful. Widespread or general practices in relation to many of the listed matters will often provide employees with an opportunity to point to the existence of some understood practice, such as those habitual and customary practices relating to sick pay or holidays. For instance, if an employer states in the notice to the employee of the terms and conditions of the contract that there are no agreed terms relating to holidays, this is quite different from telling an employee that there are no holidays. The latter statement is quite categorical, while the former leaves the way open for the employee to point to customs, habits and practices which indicate that some sort of provision for holidays is to be made.

The 1978 Act requires any such statement given to the employee to include a note:

1. specifying any disciplinary rules applicable to the employee, or referring to a document which is reasonably accessible to the employee and which specifies such rules;
2. specifying, by description or otherwise:
    (a) a person to whom the employee can apply if he is dissatisfied with any disciplinary decision relating to him; and

(b) a person to whom the employee can apply for the purpose of seeking redress of any grievance relating to his employment; and the manner of making any such application;
3. where there are further steps consequent upon any such application, explaining those steps or referring to a document which is reasonably accessible to the employee and which explains them;
4. stating whether a contracting-out certificate (under the Social Security Pensions Act 1975) is in force for the employment in respect of which the statement is given.

To obtain a correct statement of terms and conditions an employee may complain to an industrial tribunal if a question arises as to whether the correct particulars, and any changes in them, have been given. Since, however, the tribunal has no powers to enforce its determination of what the correct terms are, the employee who wants convincing evidence of his employment terms must first go to the tribunal and then, if he complains of a breach of those terms, to the ordinary courts.

Both employers and employees should take care to have an accurate statement, and the actual conduct of either in appearing by conduct to accept a change from the original agreed terms may prevent later denial of those terms in the event of legal proceedings on the contract. For instance, an employee who receives a written statement requiring him to give a minimum of four weeks' notice when the original agreement was for one week may, if his conduct indicates acceptance (at least, no rejection) of those terms, be precluded from raising the original agreed term in legal proceedings; and see Sched. 4, para. 4 of the 1993 Act.

It was held in *Scally v Southern Health and Social Services Board* (1991)[9] that where the terms of an employee's contract of employment had not been negotiated with the individual employee but resulted from negotiation with a representative body or were otherwise incorporated by reference, and a particular term of the contract made available to the employee a valuable right contingent upon his taking action to avail himself of its benefit and the employee could not, in all the circumstances, reasonably be expected to be aware of the term unless it was drawn to his attention, it was an implied term of the contract of employment that the employer was under an obligation to take reasonable steps to bring the term of the contract in question to the employee's attention, so that he was in a position to enjoy its benefit.

Time off work for recognised activities

Little major practical change has been made in this field because the legislation has broadly placed what used to be good employment practice on a statutory footing. Briefly, section 168 of the Trade Union and Labour Relations (Consolidation) Act 1992 requires an employer to permit an employee of his who is an official of an independent trade union a reasonable amount of time off during working hours to enable him to carry out his duties or to undergo relevant training in industrial relations with the employer. The employee is to be paid during this time off.[10] By section 170 of the Act, any employee who is a member of an appropriate trade union is entitled to reasonable time off work but without pay for trade union activities that do not constitute industrial action. The right in both cases is to ask for time off, not to take it, the remedy lying with the tribunal.

Under section 168 of the Act time off will be given only for duties concerned with negotiations with the employer that are related to or connected with any matters which fall within section 178(2) of the Act (collective bargaining) and in relation to which the trade union is recognised by the employer, and duties concerned with the performance of any functions for which the union is not recognised but which the employer has agreed the union may perform. The Act thus restricts in respect of duties for which time off would be available in three ways. First, the duties must be concerned not merely with industrial relations but with negotiations with the employer. Second, the duties must be concerned with the negotiations with the employer related to or connected with matters within section 178(2) of the Trade Union and Labour Relations (Consolidation) Act 1992. This covers terms and conditions of employment or the physical conditions in which any workers are required to work; engagement and non-engagement; termination and suspension of employment; allocation of work; disciplinary matters; the membership or non-membership of a trade union by an employee; facilities for trade union officials; and negotiation and consultation machinery. Third, the duties must be connected with matters in respect of which the union is recognised by the employer, for which specific reference will need to be made to the terms of the recognition agreement. The duty to allow time off for training applies only to training which is relevant the redefined list of duties.

Under section 29 of the 1978 Act the employer must permit an employee to take reasonable time off work for specified public duties. The duties include those of a justice of the peace, a member of a local authority, or any statutory tribunal or the managing or governing body of an educational establishment maintained by a local authority or a water authority. Of particular interest in the field of hospital law the duties also include those of the members of a Regional or District Health Authority, in addition to those of the members of a Special Health Authority including, for instance, the Mental Health Act Commission for England and Wales. The Secretary of State for Employment has power by order to add to or subtract from this list of offices and bodies. Particular arrangements for such matters are extracted from Whitley Council agreements later in this chapter.

Termination of the contract of employment

Either side to a contract of employment may legally terminate the contract by giving notice of the length required in the agreement upon which the employment relationship is based. Termination without notice is normally a breach of contract which will give grounds for an action for damages (unless there is a specific right to do so in the contract, with payment in lieu of notice), in the absence of grounds which a court would regard as sufficient to justify termination without notice. Unjustifiable termination without notice by an employer or employing authority would amount to wrongful dismissal and form the basis for an action for damages.

The agreements in respect of notice must be read subject to the statutory requirements now generally affecting contracts of employment, and subject to exception only in occasional cases specified in the Employment Protection (Consolidation) Act 1978. Section 49 of the Act, as amended, provides as follows:

'(1) The notice required to be given by an employer to terminate the contract of employment of a person who has been continously employed for [one month] or more—
  (a) shall be not less than one week's notice if his period of continuous employment is less than two years;
  (b) shall be not less than one week's notice for each year of continuous employment if his period of continuous employment is two years or more but less than twelve years; and
  (c) shall be not less than twelve weeks' notice if his period of continuous employment is twelve years or more.
(2) The notice required to be given by an employee who has been continuously employed for [one month] or more to terminate his contract of employment shall be not less than one week.
(3) Any provision for shorter notice in any contract of employment with a person who has been continuously employed for [one month] or more shall have effect subject to the foregoing subsections, but this section shall not be taken to prevent either party from waiving his right to notice on any occasion, or from accepting a payment in lieu of notice.
(4) Any contract of employment of a person who has been continuously employed for [three months] or more which is a contract for a term certain of four weeks or less shall have effect as if it were for an indefinite period and, accordingly, subsections (1) and (2) shall apply to the contract.
(5) It is hereby declared that this section does not affect any right of either party to treat the contract as terminable without notice by reason of such conduct by the other party as would have enabled him so to treat it before the passing of this Act.'

Section 4A of the 1978 Act, added by the Employment Act 1982, provides that subsections (1) and (2) above do not apply to a contract made in contemplation of the performance of a specific task which is not expected to last for more than three months, unless the employee has been continuously employed for a period of more than three months.

Health authority and health service employees, generally, are covered by these provisions in just the same way as those working in the private sector of health care.

It is not at all easy to specify the grounds upon which a contract might be held to have been justifiably terminated without notice. In the case of *Wilson v Racher* (1974)[11] Lord Justice Edmund Davies said:

'Reported decisions provide useful, but only general guides, each case turning upon its own facts. Many of the decisions which are customarily cited date from the last century and may be wholly out of accord with current social conditions. What would today be regarded as almost an attitude of Czar-serf, which is to be found in some of the older cases where a dismissed employee failed to recover damages, would, I venture to think, be decided differently today. We have by now come to realise that a contract of service imposes upon the parties a duty of mutual respect.'

While hard and fast rules as to justifiability of summary dismissal are therefore impossible to give, a number of propositions may usefully be made by way of generalisation from judicial decisions on this matter. The modern test is basically whether the conduct complained of by the employee is a breach of an important term of the contract of employment. On the relative importance of such contractual terms the conduct of the parties and the words of their employment agreement are the best guides. However, certain terms and in particular implied terms will always be given a special prominence in judges' deliberations. Such obligations as those not to steal the employer's property, or to damage it deliberately, and to obey reasonable and lawful instructions, are examples. Single acts of misconduct are less likely to provide justification for summary dismissal than a persistent pattern of misconduct. And misconduct inside the place of work is more likely to give rise to breach of an employment obligation entitling the employer summarily to dismiss than misconduct outside the workplace or outside working hours. Whether misconduct is sufficient to justify summary dismissal is not dependent on proof that the misconduct has in fact had serious consequences. The test adopted by the courts in seeking a justification of the employer's action is the nature of the misconduct itself.

While procedural fairness must in all cases be maintained, the following are typical illustrations of summary dismissal without notice:

1. *Wilful disobedience* to a lawful and reasonable order or neglect of duty in a serious matter, or in less serious matters if habitual. Neglect includes forgetfulness.
2. *Serious misconduct* whether in the course of employment or not, if of a kind likely to be prejudicial to the employer. The following may be cited as examples:

(a) dishonesty which, in some circumstances, may not amount to an offence;

(b) insolence or violence, though here there is a question of degree;

(c) receipt of secret commissions.

When misconduct *outside his employment* justifies dismissal of an employee without notice is not always easy to determine. It is, of course, easy to decide that a man who has to handle money in the course of his duties and has been convicted of theft or misappropriation, even outside the scope of his employment, is liable to dismissal without notice. But what of other forms of misconduct? In the case of a doctor, nurse or other person engaged by virtue of a registerable qualification, presumably any action which would be grounds for erasure from the register would justify dismissal without notice. A man may be dismissed for immorality with a fellow employee, but apart from express agreement it would be difficult to justify similar action in respect of sexual irregularity with outsiders unless

(a) the man's suitability for his employment is seriously diminished by his reputation; or

(b) his reputation is such that it would be seriously harmful to his employer's interests to retain him.

3. *Incompetence.* If a person is engaged for a post requiring skill, for instance, on the medical, nursing or administrative staff of a hospital, and in spite of having held himself out as skilled has proved incompetent, the authority may be entitled to dismiss without notice. Even more clear is the right of dismissal if it is found that the employee had falsely laid claim to a particular qualification, for instance, that of state registered nurse or chartered physiotherapist. If a man is engaged for, entrusted with or promoted to work for which he claims no special competence or qualifications then his incompetency is no grounds for immediate dismissal.

4. *Illness.* Temporary illness is not generally a ground for dismissal without notice. Indeed in *Hardwick v Leeds Area Health Authority* (1975)[12] a dismissal was held unfair when a night nurse had exhausted her sick pay entitlement of four months and was dismissed. The National Health Service booklet on sick pay only laid down normal practice and since the nurse would probably have been able to return to work ten days later it was unreasonable to apply normal practice as a strict rule. It is very risky to treat the employment contract as being frustrated in such circumstances, and dismissal may take place only after a fair procedure has been followed. Among other matters, such procedure will involve consultation, the consideration of medical reports and an attempt to secure suitable alternative employment with due notice.

Suspension from employment

It seems that suspension with pay, even though not expressly provided for in the agreement or in rules accepted by the officer, is probably justified in law and is usually not likely to lead to any difficulty if, in the circumstances, the suspension is reasonable, for instance pending the hearing in court of a charge against the officer, either concerning something criminal alleged to have been done in relation to hospital matters or otherwise being of a nature which, if proved, would be strong evidence of the officer's unfitness for his post. The decision to suspend must be based on reasonable grounds, such as the need to investigate an incident, or the safety of patients. The skill of a surgeon may, for instance, decline with age or illness.

Sending an officer off duty, whether by his immediate superior or by some more senior officer, because for some reason he is unfit for duty, or because he has been guilty of some misconduct such as insolence or refusal to obey a lawful order, is a particular case of suspension, the validity of which could hardly be open to question, being often the only practicable course to be taken in the ward situation. On the other hand, the suspension would not be lawful if it were, in all the circumstances, unreasonable. Accordingly, in these cases the suspension might amount to a constructive dismissal and the employee might then be entitled to damages and to an order for reinstatement or re-engagement. Disciplinary proceedings might also be prejudiced.

If a medical practitioner were for any reason to be suspended by the General Medical Council's Professional Conduct Committee from the medical register, employment as a medical practitioner in the National Health Service used automatically to terminate, it being a condition of employment as a medical practitioner in the National Health Service that the practitioner be included on the medical register.[13] Section 47(3) of the Medical Act 1983 now provides[14] that suspension of the registration of a fully registered practitioner shall not terminate a hospital appointment, but the person suspended shall not perform the duties of such an appointment during the suspension.

17.2 UNFAIR DISMISSAL

17.2.1 Rules and principles

Subject to certain important restrictions set out on pp. 442–443, every 'employee' (as statutorily defined) has the right not to be unfairly dismissed by his employer. This right is not dependent on the contractual terms, express and implied, of agreement between employer and employee. Indeed, it really represents a right in job security, according to which employees have a sort of proprietary right in their jobs. The concept of unfair dismissal is certainly, for legal purposes, not just a 'common sense' concept capable of being judged and operated according to what the man in the street thinks to be fair or unfair. The law of this country on the matter of unfair dismissal does not yet go as far as the recommendation adopted by the International Labour Conference in 1963 would have it go.

In the case of *W. Devis and Sons Ltd v Atkins* (1977),[15] relating to dismissal for misconduct, the judge mentioned four principal matters involved in an inquiry into an allegedly unfair dismissal. First, was there a dismissal and, if so, when, and what was its nature? The burden of proving that there was a dismissal (and, for instance, that the employee did not suddenly and for no apparent reason walk out) lies on the employee. Second, what was the reason for the dismissal? The burden of proving the reason (or if there was more than one, the principal reason) for dismissal is on the employer. The reason must be one which falls within a number of specified categories, including capability or qualifications, conduct, redundancy, statutory requirements, or 'some other substantial reason of a kind such as to justify dismissal of an employee holding the position which the employee held'.

In so demonstrating the employer must show the existence of a set of facts, known to him, or of beliefs held by him, which caused him to dismiss the employee. The implication of this is that, in establishing the reason, or principal reason, for the dismissal, evidence of events which have occurred subsequent to the dismissal, or of events occurring before the dismissal of which the person taking the decision to dismiss was not aware at the time of dismissal, is neither relevant nor admissible as evidence in proceedings for an alleged unfair dismissal. So, for instance, if an employee of a hospital or trust were to be for no reason regarded by its officers or by superiors as untrustworthy, with no specific evidence to back up the suspicion; and if that person were dismissed and it were only later shown that there was in fact evidence to link that person with thefts or dishonesty, the dismissal might nevertheless be held to have been unfair. The lesson for employers within the health services here is that the person effecting the dismissal must be sure of his ground before proceeding. Furthermore, in a claim in respect of unfair dismissal, the employer can rely only on the reason in fact for which he dismissed the employee, and not the label which he attached to those facts.

In *W. Devis & Sons Ltd. v Atkins* (above) the House of Lords upheld the tribunal's ruling that fraud could not be taken into account in assessing contributory fault in the employee because it was not known to the employer at the time of the dismissal. Lord Diplock described the legislation which required the tribunal to ignore such misconduct as a 'veritable rogue's charter', saying:

'The tribunal would be bound to award a fraudulent employee, because he had successfully concealed his fraud, a basic compensation which might well amount to a substantial sum.'

Section 9(4) of the Employment Act 1980 amended section 73 of the Employment Protection (Consolidation) Act 1978 with the effect that the tribunal may now reduce the basic award where the complainant was guilty of misconduct before he was dismissed, or before he was given notice of dismissal, even though such misconduct only comes to light after the employer has taken action to dismiss him. Furthermore, by section 9(5), in any case where the tribunal is empowered to reduce the basic award, it may now reduce it to a nil amount – nothing.

Third, not just the particular event or events which led to the dismissal should be examined but also reasons why such event or events in fact led to the dismissal. Fourth, and as a consequence of the third question, it must be asked: Did the employer act reasonably? Unless the dismissal was for one of the reasons, discussed shortly, which are automatically unfair, the employer's reaction by way of dismissal must be a reasonable reaction in the circumstances of the particular case.

The test of 'reasonableness' itself depends upon the application of a number of criteria. Some valuable general guidance as to appropriate approaches by an employer to the possibility of misconduct was given by Mr Justice Arnold in *British Home Stores Ltd v Birchell* (1978).[16] He said:

'What the Tribunal have to decide every time is, broadly expressed, whether the employer who discharged the employee on the ground of the misconduct in question (usually, though not necessarily, dishonest conduct) entertained a reasonable suspicion amounting to a belief in the guilt of the employee of that misconduct at that time. That is really stating shortly and compendiously what is in fact more than one element. First of all, there must be established by the employer the fact of that belief; that the employer did believe it. Secondly, that the employer had in his mind reasonable grounds upon which to sustain that belief. And thirdly, we think, that the employer, at the stage at which he formed that belief on those grounds, at any rate at the final stage at which he formed that belief on those grounds, had carried out as much investigation into the matter as was reasonable in all the circumstances of the case. It is the employer who manages to discharge the onus of demonstrating those three matters, we think, who must not be examined further. It is not relevant, as we think, that the Tribunal would itself have shared that view in those circumstances. It is not relevant, as we think, for the Tribunal to examine the quality of the material which the employer had before him, for instance to see whether it was the sort of material, objectively considered, which would lead to a certain conclusion on the balance of probabilities, or whether it was the sort of material which would lead to the same conclusion only upon the basis of being "sure" as it is now said more normally in a criminal context, or, to use the more old-fashioned term, such as to put the matter "beyond reasonable doubt". The test, and the test all the way through, is reasonableness; and certainly, as it seems to us, a conclusion on the balance of probabilities will in any surmisable circumstance be a reasonable conclusion.'

17.2.2   Constructive dismissal

An employee may prove that he was dismissed, for statutory purposes, if he terminated the contract 'in such circumstances that he is entitled to terminate it without notice by reason of the employer's conduct', as provided by section 55(2)(c) of the Employment Protection (Consolidation) Act 1978. Decided cases indicate that the employee is presented with no less than four hurdles before he can be said to have satisfied this test:

1. The nature of the employer's breach of contract must be such as to entitle him to terminate the contract without notice. He may in fact leave without giving notice or he may leave after giving notice and working out the period of notice, but in either event the nature of the breach must have justified summary termination.
2. He must show that the employer's breach was the reason why he left.
3. He must not have terminated the contract *before* the breach of contract has taken place.
4. He must not have waived his right to terminate the contract by delaying for an unreasonable period *after* the breach.

The employee must establish a causal link between his termination of the contract and his employer's breach. Thus, if an employee told his employer that he intended to leave to go to a better job, and if the employer then behaved in such a way as to break the employment agreement, the employee could not *then* assert that he had been constructively dismissed.

17.2.3   Reasons for dismissal

The test of fairness, or otherwise, of dismissal in a particular case which arises in dispute is a highly circumstantial question. Decided cases, both by tribunals and by the Employment Appeals Tribunal, cannot therefore be expected to yield anything very definite in the way of precedents for future cases. The decision in each case is largely dependent on its own individual merits. Nevertheless, it can be said by way of generalisation that there should have been a reasonable investigation by the employer; that there must be an adequate factual basis for the employer's knowledge or beliefs; that a reasonable procedure was followed prior to the sanction of dismissal being imposed; and, very importantly, that the sanction of dismissal was in fact the better course in the particular circumstances.

The test of the reasonableness, in all the circumstances of a particular case, of the employer's reaction and decision to dismiss, is further qualified and rendered somewhat less strenuous by the Employment Act 1980. Section 6 of the 1980 Act provides that, in deciding the fairness or unfairness of a dismissal, an individual tribunal is to take into account the size and the administrative resources of the employer's undertaking or enterprise. It also amends the requirement of the 1978 Act in relation to the standard of proof. In this way, more subjective reasons for the action taken by the employer or employing authority may properly be considered. These reasons are stated by the 1980 Act to include the size and the administrative resources of the employer's undertaking, but are not restricted to those factors alone. The eventual test is whether, given these factors among all the other factors which an industrial tribunal considers relevant and material to the issue before it, the dismissal was 'in accordance with equity [meaning, simply, fairness and justice] and the substantial merits of the case'.

17.2.4 Potentially fair reasons for dismissal

Potentially fair reasons for dismissal, now examined, give considerable substance in law to employers' responses to allegations of unfair dismissal. It should be stressed that these reasons are only *potentially* fair reasons for dismissal; they are not automatically fair in any circumstances.

As to capability and qualifications, an employer may fairly expect certain standards and degrees of suitability for the job to be present. Capability is to be assessed by reference to skill, aptitude, health, or any other physical or mental quality. Qualifications include any degree, diploma or other academic, technical or professional qualification relevant to the position which the employee held. For instance, a failure to pass aptitude tests reasonably imposed during the course and time of employment may relate both to capability and to qualifications. The most usual example of capability is the question of ill health. Nevertheless, all the relevant circumstances must be considered in deciding whether the dismissal (as distinct from the employer's reaction to the events and occurrences leading up to it) was reasonable.

In the case of a prolonged absence from work, the question must be asked whether the employer can be expected to wait any longer and, if so, how much longer. The nature of the illness, physical or mental, the likely and past length of the continual absence, and the employer's need to have the work done, must all be considered. However, before an ill employee is dismissed it is essential to give him an opportunity to state his case. This is a necessary reasonable step in order to ascertain the true medical position and to allow the employee to throw light on the problem. It will in most cases be appropriate for the employer to seek an independent medical opinion, with the employee's participation and co-operation, so as to clarify any doubt about the illness, its probable length and its probable and possible consequences in terms of job capability.

In cases of ineptitude, where the reason relates to the unsatisfactory work performance of the employee, questions to be asked will include, for instance, whether it might not have been partly the fault of management or superiors that things went wrong; whether or not a suitable warning and a suitable explanation of what was thought to be unsatisfactory had been given (indeed, a warning is imperative except, perhaps, in the case of a very senior employee); whether or not the employee showed signs of improving, or at least could reasonably be thought to have the capability of improving; the standard of work; and, in the case of probationary employees, whether or not the employer took reasonable steps to keep up the appraisal of the employee's behaviour and job efficiency, giving guidance by advice and warning when this was likely to be useful and fair to the employee.

A second reason for a potentially fair dismissal is the conduct of the employee. Rules as to what is right and what is wrong should be carefully brought to the notice of employees, so that they can know what to expect. A common example of misconduct leading to dismissal is disobedience to disciplinary rules or orders. The fairness of such rules themselves may properly be questioned, for the mere imposition of a rule will not justify a dismissal on the basis of its existence alone; the rule may be arbitrary, oppressive or unjust, and may be even immoral. Here again, cases turn very much on their own facts, but it may generally be said that: first, the employer must show the genuineness of his belief that the offence, wrong or other misconduct had been committed; that, at the time of the dismissal, he had reasonable grounds upon which to base that belief; that he carried out as much investigation as was reasonable in all the circumstances; and, in the case of minor offences, whether warning should have been given to the employee. It is in practice harder to rely on such rules if they have not been incorporated into the contract. In *Atkin v Enfield Group Hospital Management Committee* (1975)[17] the tribunal upheld the dismissal of a ward sister, after adequate warnings had been given, for her failure to wear the prescribed uniform, despite the fact that in all other respects her work was exemplary.

A third reason for potentially fair dismissal is redundancy. Generally speaking, the normal tests of reasonableness will be applied to determine whether the dismissal in issue is fair or unfair. Among the circumstances which may render the selection of a particular employee for redundancy unfair are: failure to consult an employee or his trade union before selection; failure to give reasons for his selection for redundancy; and failure to find the employee suitable alternative employment in the undertaking or, if need be, with an alternative employer. If the selection of a particular employee is found by a tribunal to have been unfair, it is legally possible for the employee to be awarded both a redundancy payment and compensation for unfair dismissal; but some adjustment in the amount of the award will be made.

There are two situations in which dismissal by reason of redundancy is never potentially fair. First, if the reason for selecting this particular employee for redundancy in preference to other employees, or the principal reason, was inadmissible. So, for instance, if the reason for the selection of the particular employee related to his trade union membership or activities, this will be automatically unfair. Otherwise redundancy could be used to effect ends which are legally excluded by the law relating to unfair dismissal. Second, if the employee was selected for redundancy in contravention of a customary arrangement or agreed procedure relating to redundancy, and there were no special reasons justifying a departure from that arrangement or procedure in the particular case of the employee in question. Such a 'customary arrangement' must, it appears from decided cases on the matter, be fairly specific. It is not sufficient that the aggrieved employee simply states what can often be taken to be the normal practice of 'last in, first out'. On the contrary, the custom must be established to be well-known, certain and clear in the undertaking in which the employee worked. If a definite 'last in, first out' practice did indeed clearly and certainly exist, this would advance the employee's case.

17.2.5 Automatically unfair reasons for dismissal

The following reasons given by an employer for dismissal can never be fair under the test of 'reasonableness'. In other words, the test of reasonableness in all the circumstances of the particular case is totally inapplicable here. The only saving condition is, as explained shortly, entirely dependent for existence on a specific and exceptional statutory provision, to which itself there is an exception which has been widened by the Employment Act 1980, and so back to the basic concept of unfairness.

First, the Rehabilitation of Offenders Act 1974 provides that a spent conviction shall not be a proper ground for dismissing a person from an office, profession, occupation or employment.

The 1974 Act does not actually specify what is to happen if an employee with a spent conviction is dismissed for that reason; but it appears that this would normally be an unfair dismissal. Most importantly, however, Statutory Instrument 1975/1023 provides that none of the provisions of that Act in relation to questions which may be asked in order to assess suitability shall apply in relation to admission to the professions of medical practitioner, dentist, dental hygienist, dental auxiliary, nurse, midwife, ophthalmic optician, dispensing optician, pharmaceutical chemist or any profession to which the Professions Supplementary to Medicines Act 1960 applies and which is undertaken following registration under that Act.

The instrument provides that the Act shall not apply, in relation to any question asked in relation to suitability for employment, in respect of 'any employment which is concerned with the provision of health services and which is of such a kind as to enable the holder [of the office or employment] to have access to persons in receipt of such services in the course of his normal duties'.

Second, a female employee is to be treated as having been unfairly dismissed if the reason or the principal reason for her dismissal is that she is pregnant, or is any other reason connected with her pregnancy. Since the relevant provision of the Employment Protection (Consolidation) Act 1978 is not specifically limited to medical reasons, it might be that absence from work for social and family reasons connected with pregnancy are also included as unfair reasons. Certainly, however, if a female employee proves to be physically or mentally incapable of carrying on her employment properly, the dismissal might be fair. However, the employer must, again, act reasonably in the circumstances in dismissing the woman, and must in any event have taken the prior step of offering a new contract of employment if there is a suitable alternative vacancy. Failure to do so, even if the aggrieved employee did not actually ask for an alternative job if one were available, will automatically make the dismissal unfair. If the woman is dismissed in circumstances which are in fact fair she retains her right to maternity pay. If a woman is unfairly dismissed for reasons of pregnancy or confinement, she may include her loss of maternity pay in her claim for compensation.

The meaning attached to the words 'dismissed for any other reason connected with her pregnancy' are construed widely by the courts. Section 60 of the Employment Protection (Consolidation) Act 1978 provides:

'(1) An employee shall be treated for the purpose of this Part as unfairly dismissed if the reason or principal reason for her dismissal is that she is pregnant or is any other reason connected with her pregnancy.'

In *Clayton v Vigers* (1990)[18] the plaintiff (the respondent in this appeal case) was a dental nurse and the defendant (the appellant in the present case) a dentist employer. In February 1986 the employee told her employer that she wished to return to work after maternity leave. Her baby was born on 16 May and her proposed date of return was 26 June. On 22 May she received a letter stating that the employer had not been able to employ anyone on a temporary basis and had therefore been obliged to take on a permanent assistant.

The employee complained to an industrial tribunal which held that she had been dismissed and that the reason for her dismissal was automatically unfair under section 60 of the 1978 Act. The issue before the Employment Appeal Tribunal was therefore whether the tribunal had been properly able to find that the employee had been dismissed for a reason connected with her pregnancy. The choice of meanings lay between 'causally connected with' and 'associated with'. The Employment Appeal Tribunal considered the 'mischief' (that is, the wrongful situation) at which section 60 of the 1978 Act was aimed. They decided that the background to the statutory provision envisaged both the pregnancy and the after-effects of it. It had therefore been open to the tribunal in the present case to look at the circumstances and decide what was the reason for the dismissal. There was clear evidence, the Appeal Tribunal held, upon which the industrial tribunal could rightly be satisfied that the applicant had proved her case. Her dismissal had therefore been a dismissal for a reason connected with her pregnancy within the meaning of section 60.

A further situation in which dismissal may be an unfair consequence of a woman's pregnancy or confinement arises in respect of the woman's right to return after work. An employee who has been absent for reasons due wholly or partly to pregnancy or confinement may be entitled to return to work with her original employer or with the successor of that person. Altering the previous position, the Employment Act 1980 placed limitations on the employee's right to return to work in certain cases and it achieved these by introducing two new defences. Under certain circumstances specified in sections 11 and 12 the employer may avoid the obligation to facilitate return to work where such is not reasonably practicable and alternative employment has been offered and either accepted or unreasonably refused. The other defence is available in circumstances where a small concern of five or less employees cannot reasonably practicably re-employ or offer suitable alternative employment.

It cannot be fair to dismiss an employee for his membership of an independent trade union, or for participation in union activities, save in one specific situation. Where there is a union membership agreement (which, incidentally, no employer is legally bound to agree to if he does not want to), dismissal may be not automatically unfair. No contractually binding agreement need be proved in order for dismissal for this specific reason to be considered fair; an 'arrangement' or definite practice is enough. This is an exceptional case of the fairness of a dismissal for reasons connected with trade union membership and activities and it can be seen that the workforce or general body of employees is, to say the least, no less advantaged by this legal exception than the employer.

In cases where a union membership agreement can, exceptionally, render a dismissal fair even though connected with union membership or activities, an exception to that very exception exists and thus back to the rule that the dismissal is unfair. The Employment Protection (Consolidation) Act 1978 withheld the right fairly to dismiss an employee who remained a non-union member in the face of a union membership agreement if the employee genuinely objected, on grounds of religious belief, to being a member of any trade union whatsoever. This exception was regarded by many as either too narrow, far-fetched or simply unrealistic. The Employment Act 1980 extended the immunity of non-members in these respects to cases in which there is a deeply held personal belief. Section 7 of the 1980 Act also amended the 1978 Act in other important respects relating to existing and future closed shops.

Palmer v Inverness Hospitals Board of Management (1963)[19] involved a claim by a house officer who had been dismissed for alleged misconduct to have the resolution of the Board sustaining his dismissal by a senior officer set aside. The claim was based on the ground that the principles of natural justice and fair play had not been observed by the Board when considering the appeal in accordance with the procedure laid down in a Circular from the Department of Health to Scottish Hospital Authorities in 1953. In that Circular the Department had set down the procedure to be followed by hospital employing authorities when representations were made to them on behalf of an employee who was aggrieved by any disciplinary action including dismissal taken or proposed to be taken against him. The Circular further provided that the authority should establish an appeals committee to hear each appeal; that the officer should have the right to appear before the committee; and that the report of the committee should be submitted to the authority for a final decision on the case.

On 22 December 1960, the house officer, Dr Palmer, was told by the deputy medical superintendent that, because of incidents in which he had been involved earlier that day regarded as breaches of duty and proper behaviour, it had been decided to dismiss him. He was paid up to 24 December 1960. Early on 25 December 1960, after a series of incidents, he was removed physically from the hospital.

On 29 December 1961 the house officer submitted to the defenders an appeal against his dismissal. The Board, purporting to act in accordance with the circular, appointed a special committee to hear the appeal and report to them at a special meeting. The committee held an inquiry and heard statements from various witnesses including the house officer and a friend of his who addressed the committee on his behalf. The medical superintendent was also heard. The committee reported to the special meeting of the Board that their unanimous conclusion was that the dismissal was *not* justified. When the report of the committee came before the Board for consideration the chairman allowed to be present the medical superintendent, his deputy, two representatives of the Regional Board and the legal adviser to the Scottish Hospital Service. A resolution that the dismissal of the house officer was justified was carried by the casting vote of the chairman.

The house officer in his action challenged the resolution on the ground that the principles of natural justice and fair play had not been observed by the Board in considering the appeal. The defenders contended that the Circular from the Department of Health was advisory and not obligatory. Lord Wheatley, finding in favour of the pursuer, held that the Circular was indeed obligatory and was incorporated in the pursuer's contract of service; that in considering the report of the special committee the Board were acting in a quasi-judicial capacity in view of the appeals procedure set out in the Circular; that in permitting two senior officers who were involved in the pursuer's dismissal and the legal adviser to the Scottish Hospital Service to be present in the absence of the pursuer or his representative the Board transgressed the basic principles of natural justice.

In certain cases an injunction to restrain dismissal may be granted by a court if that is the appropriate method of rendering the employer's obligations under the employment contract practically effective. In *Robb v Hammersmith and Fulham London Borough Council* (1991)[20] the applicant was purportedly dismissed by the defendant employer following abandonment of disciplinary procedures. An injunction to restrain dismissal since the defendants were in breach of contract and a resumption of the disciplinary procedure was necessary to allow the applicant an opportunity to defend his conduct. In *Irani v Southampton and South West Hampshire Health Authority* (1985)[21] an injunction was granted to restrain dismissal with notice prior to Whitley Council procedures being exhausted.

17.2.6 Status and unfair dismissal

The concept of unfair dismissal takes the law of employment beyond the terms and conditions expressly or impliedly contained in an employment contract or agreement and into the area of status, from which rights flow in respect of job security. It is not, however, any and every employee who qualifies for the legal privileges implicit in the protection of employees against unfair dismissal.

To qualify, an employee shall have been continuously employed for a period of two years at the date of termination of the employment. In ascertaining the effective date of termination, the statutory minimum period of notice, laid down by the Employment Protection (Consolidation) Act 1978, must be added to the employee's period of continuous employment. This is so whether or not the employee actually receives this notice. This means in effect that the qualifying period of an employee not given one week's notice is 51 weeks. Section 8(2) of the 1980 Act provides that failure to renew a fixed term contract of more than one year (previously two years) will not amount to a dismissal.

The rules and principles of unfair dismissal do not apply in the case of an employee who has reached, on or before the date of termination of the employment, the normal retiring age fixed by his or her conditions of service. This is the age at which the employee should retire unless service is extended by mutual agreement. This age may be above or below pensionable age. The rules do not apply to persons employed by their husbands or wives. So, for instance, the wife of a general medical practitioner who is employed by her husband as a medical secretary cannot, if they have a difference, claim any remedy from her husband in respect of unfair dismissal.

The Employment Act 1980 reduces from two years to one year the minimum length of a fixed term contract in which employees may agree to waive their right to complain of unfair dismissal if they are not re-engaged on the expiry of the contract. The unfair dismissal provisions will still apply to dismissal before the contract expires. Those working less than 16 hours per week are excluded from the definition of 'employee', as are those who have not worked for at least 8 hours per week over a period of at least five years, and this remains unchanged under the 1980 Act.

17.2.7 Employment and status: the question of judicial review

Given that certain status is now recognised as arising from the employment contract, and given also that employees of National Health Services agencies are in a sense 'public' employees (though they are not, since 1 April 1991, employees of Crown agencies[22]), the question has occasionally arisen whether aggrieved employees can appeal to the courts alleging that their employing agency has fallen down in its public law duties. In two leading cases the result has been determined by asking whether the authority in question truly fell down in the exercise of its public duties as a health authority, or whether the complaint was, rather, simply one of employer–employee relations.

In *R v East Berkshire Health Authority, ex parte Walsh* (1984)[23] the aggrieved nurse complained to the High Court, and then to the Court of Appeal, about the legality of dismissal by his employing authority, requesting judicial review of the dismissal and an order that the health authority act properly in the exercise of its public law duties. He was employed as a senior nursing officer by the East Berkshire Health Authority under a contract of employment which incorporated terms and conditions negotiated by a recognised negotiating body and approved by the Secretary of State for Social Services (namely, the relevant Whitley Council). In August 1982 the district nursing officer suspended the applicant from duty and on 27 September she purported to terminate his employment with the health authority. The applicant sought judicial review of this dismissal on the ground that the district nursing officer had acted beyond the scope of her statutory powers (*ultra vires*) in dismissing him, and also that there had been breaches of the rules of natural justice in the procedures leading up to his dismissal. The health authority objected to the application by raising the preliminary point of law as to whether it was appropriate at all for the applicant to question his dismissal by bringing proceedings for judicial review to the High Court. A judge of the High Court held that the applicant's rights were of a sufficiently public nature to entitle to seek public law remedies, but the East Berkshire Health Authority successfully appealed to the Court of Appeal. The grounds for the Appeals Court's decision were as follows.

Whether a dismissal from employment by a public authority is subject to public law remedies depends on whether there are special statutory restrictions on dismissal underpinning the employee's position and not on the fact of employment by a public authority as such, or the employee's seniority, or the interest of the public in the functioning of the health authority. Where the authority is required by law to contract with its employees on specified terms (via the Whitley Council machinery) with a view to the employee's acquiring private law rights, a breach of that contract of employment is not a matter of public law and does not give rise to any administrative law remedies. It would be only if the authority failed or refused to contract on the specified, statutorily based, terms that the employee might have public law rights to compel the health authority to comply with its statutory obligations. The fact that the applicant in the present case was employed on conditions of service negotiated by a negotiating body, approved by the Secretary of State and imposed on the applicant and the authority by the 1974 Regulations, was not sufficient to give the applicant public law remedies relating to his dismissal. Since, in the present case, the applicant had been engaged on the proper conditions of service, and his complaint was that he had been dismissed in breach of those conditions, his contract was a simple and straightforward contract of employment and the appropriate remedy in such a case should have been the ordinary private law remedy of a complaint to an industrial tribunal.

Reinforcing the decision of the Court of Appeal, Sir John Donaldson, Master of the Rolls, said:

'I therefore conclude that there is no "public law" element in Mr Walsh's complaints which could give rise to any entitlement to administrative law remedies. I confess that I am not sorry to have been led to this conclusion since a contrary conclusion would have enabled all National Health Service employees to whom Whitley Council conditions of service apply to seek judicial review. While it is true that the judge seems to have thought that this right would be confined to senior employees, I see no grounds for any such restriction in principle. The most that can be said is that only senior employees could complain of having been dismissed in the exercise of a delegated authority, because it is only senior employees who are protected from such dismissal. All employees would, however, have other rights based on the fact that Parliament had intervened to specify and, on this view, protect those conditions of service as a matter of "public law".'

And Lord Justice May put the same point more simply when he said:

'At one time it was contended before us that Mr Walsh was entitled to seek judicial review because of the seniority of his post, but if the judge's statement is taken in his ordinary meaning it would follow that every nurse employed by a health authority is entitled to judicial review of his or her dismissal.'

This is now clearly not the case.

In *R v Secretary of State for Social Services, ex parte Guirguis* (1989)[24] the applicant for judicial review of the health authority's action was a consultant radiologist appointed to the Worksop and Radford district and employed by the Trent Regional Health Authority. Standard terms and conditions were incorporated into his contract of employment. In February 1985 he applied for unpaid leave to go and work in Saudi Arabia, but this was refused. In March he asked for seven weeks' leave in order to go to Egypt because his father was ill and that request was agreed to. He left at the end of March and returned on 20 May. The health authority believed that he had not been to see his father but had in fact been working at a hospital in Saudi Arabia. Disciplinary proceedings were instituted and, on 23 September 1985, the sub-committee set up under the terms and conditions of service recommended that the applicant's contract be terminated and wrote to him accordingly. The letter ended: 'If you are aggrieved with this decision you have a right to appeal to the Regional Health Authority, and that right should be exercised within three weeks of the receipt by you of this letter.' That right of appeal was exercised and the appeal was dismissed.

On 27 November 1985 the applicant wrote to the Secretary of State to intervene, but the latter decided that he had no jurisdiction to entertain representations from the applicant. The applicant then instituted proceedings for judicial review of the health authority's action, claiming that it had fallen down in the exercise of its public law duty and applying for reinstatement.

The application failed, on the ground that judicial review of a health authority's action is appropriate, if at all, only in cases where what is being considered is not something that has already happened, but is something which is presently happening; namely, something which is presently continuing, rather than something which has ceased (in the present case, the applicant's employment). Mr Justice Popplewell added that it was clear in any case that an application for judicial review of a health authority's actions in 'public law', being a discretionary remedy, could not possibly apply to a case where there has already been summary dismissal. He explained: 'The procedure plainly cannot be completed before the authority's decision to terminate the appointment is carried into effect.'

As to the choice between an ordinary action and proceedings by way of judicial review, Lord Justice Woolf observed in *McClaren v Home Office* (1990)[25] that 'problems are being experienced as to when proceedings have to be taken by way of judicial review by employees . . . who wish to bring proceedings against their employer who is a public body'. Certain misunderstandings had, he said, arisen in interpreting the decided cases. In *Roy v Kensington and Chelsea Family Practitioner Committee* (1992)[26] the Committee had reduced the basic practice allowance of the respondent doctor, who commenced civil proceedings by way of a writ for reimbursement of moneys which he claimed were wrongly withheld. The Committee contended that his proper route should have been through judicial review, which involves a different judicial procedure from that applicable to the private contractual action brought by the doctor. The House of Lords held that the doctor's form of proceedings were appropriate even though their Lordships were uncertain whether an ordinary contactual relationship existed between the doctor and the Committee, given the 'public' aspect, namely the statutory National Health Service structure under which his relationship with the Committee (his paymasters) existed. The contention, unsuccessful in the event, that the doctor's proper approach would have been by way of an application for judicial review, was precisely the opposite of the health authority's (successful) contention in the *Walsh* case, above. But, speaking generally, Lord Lowry said that:

'it seems to me that, unless the procedure adopted by the moving party is ill-suited to dispose of the question at issue, there is much be said in favour of the proposition that a court having jurisdiction ought to let a case be heard rather than entertain a debate concerning the form of the proceedings.'

17.2.8 Remedies for unfair dismissal

The Employment Protection (Consolidation) Act 1978 provides for three types of remedy following a finding of unfair dismissal by way of application to an industrial tribunal. These are: reinstatement, re-engagement and compensation. While reinstatement and re-engagement are the primary remedies, intended as they are to make for security and continuity in employment, the statistics show that these remedies are ordered in less than 2 per cent of the disputes which go for a hearing to an industrial tribunal. This is not surprising since, despite their being the 'primary' remedies, the dismissal and the dispute will normally have soured relations between employer and employee beyond the point at which they could reasonably be expected to continue to work together.

Reinstatement requires the employer to treat the employee in all respects as if he had not been dismissed. So the employee's pay, pension, and seniority rights must be restored to him and he will also benefit from any improvement in terms and conditions which came into operation while he was dismissed. Re-engagement differs from reinstatement in that the employee may be re-engaged in a different job from the one which he formerly held, so long as the new job is comparable with the old or is otherwise suitable employment. Re-engagement need not be by the same employer; it may instead be with the successor of an employer or an associated employer. An industrial tribunal should consider re-engagement only if reinstatement is not suitable.

If neither reinstatement nor re-engagement is suitable, the tribunal will award compensation for dismissal which has been shown to have been unfair. Such compensation can consist of a basic award together with a further compensatory award. There may be an additional award where an employer refuses to comply with the tribunal's order for reinstatement or re-engagement. Subject to a current maximum of £5,330, the basic award is calculated in the same way as the amount of redundancy payment under Part VI of the Employment Protection (Consolidation) Act 1978 (discussed below). Based on a maximum of 20 years' service, the basic award is, for each year of continuous employment, from 18 to 22, half a week's pay; from 22 to 41 one week's pay; and from 41 to 65, one-and-a-half weeks' pay; in each case subject to a maximum figure for weekly pay, currently £205.

The additional, or compensatory, award will be either between 13 and 26 weeks' pay, or between 26 and 52 weeks' pay in the case of a 'discriminatory' dismissal, that is, dismissal based on reasons of sex, race or trade union membership or activity. The actual amount of money awarded will be, in the words of section 74(1) of the 1978 Act:

'such amount as the tribunal considers just and equitable in all the circumstances having regard to the loss sustained by the complainant in consequence of the dismissal in so far as that loss is attributable to action taken by the employer.'

The current maximum compensatory award is £10,000.

Both the basic award and the compensatory award are liable to be
reduced in certain cases. Any redundancy payment must be deducted,
and deduction may also be made on account of the contribution of the
employee's conduct to the dismissal, albeit the latter was in the event
unfair. Further, in the case of the compensatory award (but not the basic
award) a reduction should be made equivalent to the earnings of the
employee in new employment since his dismissal, or to the extent that
he would have had such earnings had he taken reasonable steps to
mitigate his loss (that is, by getting a job). Reduction may also be made
in respect of the extent to which the employee has contributed to his
own dismissal. Ex gratia payments, and payments in lieu, are usually
taken into account.

17.2.9   Transfer of undertakings

The Transfer of Undertakings (Protection of Employment) Regulations
1981[27] provide that, if there is a relevant transfer of an undertaking from
one person or body to another by sale or other disposition, the contracts
of employment of affected employees will be transferred automatically
from the transferor to the transferee. With such transfer will go all
rights, powers, duties and liabilities connected with such a contract of
employment. This has the effect of creating continuity of employment
for the employee and the preservation of other contractual and statutory
rights. Qualifying periods for protection against unfair dismissal are
therefore themselves protected. It is unfair to dismiss a person on
account solely of a relevant transfer, but the new employer may show
that the dismissal was fair if it was for an economic, technical or other
organisational reason entailing workforce changes which amounts to a
substantial reason for dismissal, to be judged by ordinary standards of
fairness (for which see pp. 432–442 of this chapter). It is emphasised that
the Regulations are highly complex, and specific reference should be
made to the Regulations themselves when dealing with any particular
case.

17.2.10   Continuity of employment and transfer of staff to
National Health Service trusts

Under the provisions of the National Health Service and Community
Care Act 1990 staff who are employed solely at, or for the purposes of, a
unit which is to become an NHS trust will automatically transfer to trust
employment on the operational date with all their employment rights
intact. Other staff, for example those employed at more than one unit,
will have their employment rights protected on transfer to a trust as a
result of being designated in a 'scheme' made by the health authority
specified in the establishment order.

The Secretary of State has delegated to Regional Health Authorities his functions, under section 6(2) of the National Health Service and Community Care Act 1990, of approving schemes for the transfer of staff to NHS trusts where the scheme is made by a health authority in its region. Circular HC(91)8 sets out the new legal position and at Annex A explains the practical effects of transfer:

'Automatic transfer

Under the provisions of the National Health Service and Community Care Act 1990 staff employed solely at, or for the purposes of, a unit which is to become a NHS Trust will automatically transfer to Trust employment on the operational date with all their employment rights intact.

Staff who work at more than one unit

Other staff, for example those employed at more than one unit, will have their employment rights protected on transfer to a Trust as a result of being designated under a "scheme" made by the health authority specified in the establishment order.

Drawing up a scheme

The health authority specified in the establishment order will be responsible for drawing up the scheme. A scheme should identify beyond doubt which staff are to transfer and (where appropriate) for what part of their work. It should be drawn up in a simple schedule/list form and identify:

i.   staff to be transferred, either collectively (e.g. by location or function) or individually;
ii.   their location; and
iii. their new employer.

Transfer of staff by means of a scheme will not be a simple change of employer and in many cases will involve staff having "split" (i.e. separate) contracts of employment. In such cases individual consultation between employer and employee will be appropriate. For example where an employee works at more than one hospital, only one of which is to become a Trust, he will need to need to be informed of how this affects his original contract and discussions will need to take place between all parties (employee, Trust and current employer) to determine the details of the contracts (i.e. location of work, hours etc).

Medical and dental staff

In general, NHS Trusts will want to employ their own senior medical staff (i.e. Consultants, Associate Specialists and Staff Grade Practitioners). However, where, for instance, the Consultant will be working only a small number of sessions with the NHS Trust, the parties concerned (i.e. Trust, employing RHA and Consultant) may agree that "split" contracts are inappropriate and that alternative arrangements should be made. For example, that the RHA should remain the employer and that the Consultant should be made available to the NHS Trust under a service agreement.

Junior medical (and dental) staff in training will continue to have national pay and terms and conditions of service and have their contracts held as at present. Senior registrars and registrars contracts will continue to be held by RHAs and made available to NHS Trusts under training agreements for the relevant part of their training programme. The contracts of employment for senior house officers and pre-registration house officers will also continue to be held locally (i.e. by the NHS Trust or the directly managed unit). Precise arrangements for SHOs will depend upon the nature of their training rotations and should be agreed between NHS Trusts, HAs and Units.

It is important to note that under such arrangements the employer will remain responsible for all contractual issues – including, for example, variations in contract and disciplinary action.

Special care will be needed to ensure that staff who, for whatever reason, are not at work during the transfer period, and new staff who have yet to take up post, are properly consulted and informed about the transfer.

The contracts of employment of people employed by a health authority will not be terminated by the transfer, but will have effect as if originally made between employees and the NHS Trust, and all of the health authority's rights, powers, duties and liabilities will transfer to the NHS Trust. Moreover, anything done by the health authority in relation to employees or their contracts before the transfer is deemed to have been done by or in relation to the NHS Trust.

Of course, this does not prejudice the right of an employee to terminate his contract of employment if a substantial change is made to his detriment in his working conditions; but no such right shall arise by reason only of the change in employer.

Approval of schemes

The direction attached to this Circular delegates to Regional Health Authorities the responsibility for approving staff transfer schemes in all cases except those where the RHA currently has direct management responsibility for the establishment or function being transferred.

As far as approving schemes is concerned RHAs should ensure that:

— all staff affected by the transfer have been properly identified and informed;
— staff who will have split contracts have been told how this will affect their original contracts and that the contracts are being correctly separated.

At the same time RHAs may also wish to satisfy themselves that consultation has been properly carried out.'

Regional Health Authorities transferring staff from an establishment or function which they manage directly should obtain Department of Health approval for their scheme.

Circular HC(91)8 makes particular provision for transfer of employment to more than one trust, and provides also for statutory maternity pay and sick pay, and national insurance.

Redundancy pay arrangements in Part VI and Schedule 4 of the Employment Protection (Consolidation) Act 1978 do not apply to employment in the Health Service. The National Health Service scheme in section 45 of the General Whitley Council Conditions of Service is recognised as an equivalent scheme under section 111 of the 1978 Act. This scheme is contractual and its benefits continue for the transferred employees.

In relation to staff transferred to a trust from a directly managed unit, the obligations of the trust relating to redundancy payments fall within the Whitley scheme. While trusts are free to offer Whitley Conditions to their staff there is no legal obligation to do so, in which case staff entitlements would be governed by the statutory scheme under the 1978 Act.

Conversely, an employee's previous service with an NHS trust constituted under the National Health Service and Community Care Act 1990 shall count as reckonable service with an employing authority in respect of each appropriate agreement made by negotiating bodies and Whitley Councils for the Health Services.[28]

17.3 UNFAIR DISCRIMINATION

The Race Relations Act 1968 prohibited discrimination on racial grounds. The Equal Pay Act 1970 requires equal terms of employment between men and women workers. The Sex Discrimination Act 1975 prohibits discrimination on grounds of sex or marital status in the employment field which falls outside the scope of the Equal Pay Act. The model of the Sex Discrimination Act was used to frame a new Race Relations Act 1976, repeating and replacing the 1968 Act.

17.3.1 Varieties of discrimination

First, and most generally, discrimination may be either direct or indirect. Second, whether the discrimination is direct or indirect, it may be based on sex, or race, or marital status, or on a combination of such factors. Discrimination on racial grounds is defined in the 1976 Act as grounds of 'colour, race, nationality or ethnic or national origin'. Nationality was added by the 1976 Act to the list of factors contained in the Race Relations Act 1968. The law applies more widely than merely to employees, but it is employees who are our present concern. Direct discrimination is simply 'less favourable' treatment on grounds of sex, marital status or race. A single act of discrimination is sufficient to establish a case of direct discrimination. The act must have been committed with a discriminatory motive, although the motive may be inferred from the employer's conduct. The concept of indirect, or 'effects', discrimination is different.

To make out a case of indirect discrimination an employee must establish the following. First, that the person about whose conduct the complaint is made applied a 'requirement or condition' which he applies, or which would equally apply, to persons of the other sex, or to single persons, or to persons of another racial group. Examples of the expression 'requirement or condition' in decided cases include those relating to an age barrier to job entry and a seniority rule. Second, that the proportion of the complainant's sex, or of married persons or of the complainant's racial group is considerably smaller than the proportion of persons of the other sex, or of single persons, or of persons not of that racial group, as the case may be, who can comply with it. An example of a discriminatory requirement would be a prohibition on the wearing of turbans or saris, or a beard, unless the employer could show this to be justifiable, for instance on grounds of safety or health.

The Sex Discrimination Act 1975 and the Race Relations Act 1976 make it unlawful for a person, in relation to employment by him at an establishment in Great Britain, to discriminate on any of the above grounds against applicants in selection arrangements and job offers, and against those employed in access to promotion, training and any other benefits, facilities or services. The legislation also makes unlawful discrimination on the above grounds by partnerships, by organisations of workers or employers and by professional and trade associations, as well as by bodies which can confer an authorisation or qualification needed for or facilitating engagement in a particular trade or profession. Discrimination by vocational training bodies, employment agencies and the Manpower Services Commission is also made unlawful. Health services applications of these rules are plentiful, especially in respect of professional qualifications and organisation and society membership.

In *Noone v North West Thames Regional Health Authority* (1988)[29] the important question of an inference of discrimination arose. Dr Noone, a Sri Lankan candidate for a job, had superior qualifications to all the other applicants. An industrial tribunal was held to have been justified in inferring that she had been discriminated against on racial grounds. But in *Webb v EMO Air Cargo (UK) Ltd* (1992)[30] it could not be inferred that a pregnant woman had been discriminated against on grounds of sex, even though her unavailability during a period in which she had been engaged to cover for the maternity leave of another employee was caused by her pregnancy. The House of Lords held that the same treatment (dismissal by the employer) would have been accorded to a man who, having been taken on as temporary cover, became unavailable during the period of cover. The case has been referred to the European Court of Justice.

It is also unlawful to publish, or to cause to be published, an advertisement which indicates or which might reasonably be understood as indicating an intention to do an unlawful discriminatory act. This does not apply if the intended act would actually have been lawful after all. The use of a sexual connotation, for instance, 'stewardess' or 'waiter' is taken to indicate an intention to discriminate unless the advertisement contains an indication to the contrary. It is unlawful to instruct or to pressurise another to discriminate improperly.

17.3.2 Sex discrimination

Part II of the Sex Discrimination Act 1975, as amended by the Sex Discrimination Act 1986 prohibits unlawful discrimination in employment. The protection against discrimination is wide enough to cover those who do not fall within the definition of 'employee' (see pp. 417–420, above). Employment, for the purposes of sex discrimination, is defined as 'employment under a contract of service or apprenticeship or a contract personally to execute any work or labour'. Section 6(1)(A) of the 1975 Act provides for arrangements which a person makes for the purpose of determining who shall be employed. These arrangements must ensure that job opportunities are available to all, irrespective of sex. In *Brindley v Tayside Health Board* (1976)[31] it was held that an individual may complain if he or she feels that he or she has been discriminated against in relation to a way in which a job was advertised, given that advertisements form a part of the arrangements for determining who shall be employed.

The Sex Discrimination Act 1975 was amended in 1986 in order to comply with the ruling of the European Court of Human Rights in the case of *Marshall v Southampton and South West Hampshire Area Health Authority* (1986).[32] It was held that the European Community Equal Treatment Directive (76/207) is directly enforceable against a state organisation (though not a private employer). It was held that a woman's right to bring a claim for unfair dismissal after she had reached the age of 60 was discriminatory, given that a man could bring a claim up to the age of 65.

17.3.3 Exceptions to unlawful discrimination

Any exception to anti-discrimination legislation tends to weaken the basic principles, but there are now relatively few exceptions to the unlawfulness of discrimination. In health services contexts, the 'small employer' exception is likely to apply only to small general practices, on account of the larger numbers necessarily involved in most other personal health service enterprises.

A number of circumstances are listed in section 7 of the Sex Discrimination Act 1975 in which being a man or a woman, as the case may be, is a 'genuine occupational qualification' and is therefore not unlawful. Toilet attendants are an obvious inclusion. Personal welfare counsellors are also included. Importantly, those employed in single sex health care institutions are also included. But not all employees in a single sex hospital or clinic are within the scope of this exception to the unlawfulness of discrimination. The exception is restricted to single sex provision in respect of special care, supervision or attention. So hospital kitchen staff, gardeners and cleaners would not come within the exception, and any discrimination against them would stand to be unlawful according to the normal principles.

It is possible for a man to train, qualify and be employed as a midwife. But until 1983 it was lawful, under section 20 of the Sex Discrimination

Act 1975, to discriminate against a man in the employment, promotion, transfer and training as a midwife. It was said that this effected a compromise between the principle of equality between the sexes and the preservation of midwifery as a female profession. This exception was removed by statutory instrument[33] in 1983, with the effect that the provisions of the Act apply normally from that date to male midwives. From 1 January 1984 men have been legally able to train and to practise as midwives on equal terms with women.[34]

It is permissible to discriminate in the filling of a vacancy if a particular employer already has a sufficient number of employees of one sex who are capable of carrying out 'single sex' duties of the types described above. Furthermore, an employer is permitted to train members of one sex for a job which has previously been performed exclusively, or virtually exclusively, by members of the other sex during the preceding 12 months. However, in such a case, discrimination in selection and recruitment for such a post is not permissible.

17.3.4 Enforcement

Two principal methods of enforcement are used in the anti-discrimination legislation. The first method is by way of individual civil action before industrial tribunals (and, in cases other than those relating to employment, the county courts). The other method is by strategic enforcement in the public interest by the Equal Opportunities Commission and the Commission for Racial Equality. Under the first method a complainant may be awarded one of three remedies if unlawful discrimination is proved: an order declaring the rights of the parties; compensation by way of money; or a recommendation that the person whose conduct is the subject of the complaint take steps to obviate or reduce the adverse effects of the discrimination. Unlike unfair dismissal, there is no power to award the remedies of reinstatement or re-engagement. If those are what a complainant wants he should frame his claim in unfair dismissal, based on grounds of race or sex. The maximum compensation awarded is from time to time prescribed by legislation, currently £10,000. Compensation may be reduced on account of the contributory fault of the complainant, or increased (by up to 26 weeks' pay) if the person whose conduct is complained of refuses without lawful justification to comply with an order for reinstatement or re-engagement.

17.3.5 Race and health services

In addition to its brief summary of the purposes and effects of the Race Relations Act 1976, Circular HC(78)36 is instructive in relation to the application of the letter and spirit of the law to health services. In relation to 'genuine occupational qualifications' the Circular reads:

'Under the Act, an employer may offer a job to a member of a particular racial group if membership of that group is a genuine occupational qualification for the job. Membership of a racial group could be a genuine occupational qualification in cases where the job holder provided personal welfare services for a racial group whose needs could most effectively be met by a member of the same group. This provision could be used to justify the recruitment of new staff only if the employer did not already have a sufficient number of suitably qualified members of that racial group among his existing staff whom it would be reasonable to employ on that work. Authorities may wish to take advantage of this provision in some cases where there are particular problems relating to the language or cultural background of clients of the health services, for example in the health education or health visiting field.

In discharging their general duties under the Act, authorities may wish to bear in mind the following points:

(a) In recruiting staff, and in making decisions about promotion and training opportunities, care should be taken to ensure that the criteria employed are genuinely related to the nature of the job concerned and, in particular, that any tests which may be applied do not contain elements which are likely to place members of minority groups at a disadvantage but which cannot really be justified by reference to the requirements for the job itself. For example, a test of general knowledge for a comparatively junior post should reflect the standards required for that post so that artificially high standards do not affect the chances of some racial groups.

(b) A review of staff structures may suggest that members of minority groups are not enjoying full equality of opportunity. Members of such groups may be unduly concentrated in jobs which carry lower pay or status, or may be under-represented in supervisory posts. There may also be informal patterns of segregation where members of minority groups are concentrated in particular sections or departments or on particular shifts.

(c) There may be evidence to suggest that members of minority groups fail to apply for more senior posts in their field because of fears of discrimination. It may be desirable to take steps to encourage applications for promotion by members of these groups who, it is felt, would be well qualified for it but have been reluctant to put their names forward.

It should be emphasised that employing authorities should do more than seek to secure bare compliance with the provisions of race relations legislation; and employment policies and practices should therefore include effective positive procedures to ensure equality of opportunity for members of minority groups. This can best be achieved by developing a policy which is clearly stated, known to all employees, has, and is seen to have the backing of senior management, is effectively supervised, provides a periodic feedback of information to senior management, and is seen to work in practice. Guidance on the formation and monitoring of such a policy is given in two booklets published by the Commission for Racial Equality, "Equal Opportunity in Employment" and "Monitoring an Equal Opportunity Policy".'

17.3.6   Equal pay

The matter of equal pay for 'equal' work is governed principally by the Equal Pay Act 1970. This short but important statute sought to eliminate, by 19 December 1975, discriminatory treatment as between men and women in pay and other terms and conditions of employment. The Act represented the culmination of a long campaign for the equal treatment of men and women in employment, not only by feminist organisations but also by the TUC which first advocated the principle in 1888. While the objectives of the Act met with a considerable degree of success in changing the attitudes of employers and potential employers, a not insubstantial amount of regret was voiced in many quarters that employers had five years to find ways of avoiding the spirit of the Act by altering, in time for the commencement date in December 1975, job descriptions and specifications so that the letter of the law would be complied with. Although the Act applies also to men, it is women who are normally in practice affected, though complaints from men in respect of terms and conditions of work have also occasionally been made.

The title of the Act is something of a misnomer since the statute aims to achieve equal treatment not only in respect of pay, but also in respect of other terms and conditions of employment such as holidays, hours, provision of clothing and sick pay (but only where such terms are *contracted*). Pensions are probably excluded. Section 1 provides for equality of treatment regarding terms and conditions of employment as between men and women employed on like work or on work rated as equivalent as the result of a job evaluation exercise. The requirement of equal pay and equal treatment is, importantly, implied into individual contracts; the consequences of this for enforcement will be mentioned in a moment. Section 2 confers jurisdiction upon industrial tribunals to determine claims arising out of the contractually implied term just mentioned. The Sex Discrimination Act 1975 adds to section 2 a further power, that where a dispute arises in relation to the effect of an equality clause the employer may apply to an industrial tribunal for an order declaring the rights of the employer and employee in relation to the matter in question. Section 3 provides for the elimination of discrimination on grounds of sex in collective agreements and employers' pay structures.

A woman has a right to equal treatment when employed on work of the same or a broadly similar nature to that of men in the same employment. The tribunal should look at the respective contracts of the man and woman and see how they are carried out in practice. Mere job titles are of little importance but job specifications may be useful. The tribunal should consider whether the work done by each is of a broadly similar nature, or whether differences exist and, if there are differences, whether these are of any practical importance for the purposes of the issue of equal treatment.

The individual may enforce her right to equal treatment through a statutory term of the contract of employment, the so-called 'equality clause'. The claim will be due either for arrears of pay, if remuneration is the matter in issue, or for damages for breach of the duty to accord equal treatment.

Section 1(3) of the Equal Pay Act 1970 provides that an employer may be able to resist an equal pay claim on the grounds that the variation in pay 'is genuinely due to a material factor which is not the difference of sex'. In deciding whether or not there exists a genuine material factor between cases of allegedly light work and work rated as equivalent, an industrial tribunal is entitled to have regard to extrinsic economic and labour forces which lead to a man being paid more than a woman or vice versa. In the case of *Rainey v Greater Glasgow Health Board* (1987)[35] a health authority decided to establish its own prosthetic fitting service. Rates of pay for qualified prosthetists were to be on the same scale as for medical physics technicians. In order to attract a sufficient number of qualified persons to get the service off the ground the employing authority found itself needing to make a higher pay offer to those who came from the private sector. The applicant, who came into the Health Board's service directly from her training, sought equal pay with a man on a higher salary who had been recruited from the private sector. The tribunal held that the difference in pay was due to a genuine material factor having nothing to do with sex. The reason why the man was paid more than the female applicant was because of the need to attract qualified persons, their sex being immaterial to the economic question, from the private sector in order to establish the new service.

There are certain circumstances in which only the Sex Discrimination Act, and not the Equal Pay Act, will apply. Such will be the case if the less favourable treatment relates to a matter which is not included in a contract, either expressly, or impliedly by way of the Equal Pay Act; or if the less favourable treatment relates to a matter (other than the payment of money) in a contract, and the comparison is with workers who are not doing the same or broadly similar work, or work which has been given an equal value under a job evaluation exercise by the employer; or if the complaint relates to a matter (other than the payment of money) which is regulated by an employee's contract of employment but is based on an allegation that an employee of the other sex *would* be treated more favourably in similar circumstances (that is, it does not relate to the actual treatment of an existing employee of the other sex).

Article 119 of the Treaty of Rome, as interpreted by EEC Directive 75/117 (1975), acts as an aid to the interpretation of UK equal pay legislation in both the tribunals and the courts. Under the Directive it *may* be possible to claim, in a High Court case, for equal pay for work of equal value, even where no job evaluation scheme has been conducted.

The decision of the Employment Appeal Tribunal in January 1991 indicated circumstances in which salary differentials may be justified. In the case of *Enderby v Secretary of State for Health* (1991)[36] the Employment Appeal Tribunal held that health service employers are entitled to pay higher salaries, agreed through collective bargaining, to pharmacists and clinical psychologists who are predominantly male than to speech therapists who are predominantly female, where the latter are assumed to be engaged on work of equal value. In so doing, the Employment Appeal Tribunal rejected the applicant's argument that a *prima facie* case of unintentional indirect discrimination on the ground of sex was established where an applicant who is a member of a predominantly female group is doing work of equal value, but is paid less than chosen comparators belonging to a predominantly male group, even where access to the two groups is available to all without discrimination.

Mr Justice Wood said that the case raised a principle of fundamental importance. The industrial tribunal had held that it was satisfied that the Whitley Council collective bargaining arrangements do not have embedded in them any element of sex discrimination and that the differences in pay objected to in the present case related to matters which at the relevant time were properly taken into account by the employers, such as hours, nature of work involved and responsibilities.

The applicant's principal argument was that the European Court of Justice has developed in European Community law a concept of 'unintentional indirect discrimination'. This term refers to a neutral practice which in fact adversely affects a group composed exclusively or predominantly of women and which the employer cannot show to be objectively justifiable by reference to the test of need or necessity. The response of the health authority employer was that, before the *prima facie* case of unintentional discrimination can be established (which would subsequently require justification on the evidence), it is necessary to analyse the pay practice and identify the term or condition which has to be satisfied by the applicant before she can achieve equal pay and show that she would be unable or less able to comply with it than a man in a similar position.

Mr Justice Wood said that it is clear from UK statutory provisions on discrimination that before an applicant can succeed the law requires discrimination to be established. It is only if a woman is paid less because she is a woman that she suffers discrimination. Without such discrimination, a woman is not entitled to equal pay for equal work or work of equal value. The purpose of the Equal Pay Act 1970 is to prevent discrimination, not to provide equal pay, he said.

A person is not, he decided, entitled to equal pay for work of equal value with a comparator of the opposite sex. The mere numerical comparison adds nothing. The Employment Appeal Tribunal could not accept that a purely numerical basis on a given day is a sound legal foundation for establishing rights and liabilities between parties in cases of alleged discrimination. Indeed, if the applicant's argument in the present case were to have been correct, no employer could conduct collective bargaining with different groups with any confidence unless at all times the groups consisted of equal proportions of men and women.

In seeking to identify a *prima facie* case of unintentional indirect discrimination, the law requires identification of a factor causing the disparate impact. If that factor is not gender-tainted, it does not require justification. If it was gender-tainted, the applicant could then bring herself within section 1(1)(b)(i) and (iii) of the Sex Discrimination Act 1975. Sex discrimination would then have to be justified.

17.4 REDUNDANCY

17.4.1 The concept

In the case of employees covered by the Employment Protection (Consolidation) Act 1978, a right to receive compensation is given to those who are dismissed, laid off or placed on short time by reason of redundancy. Compensation is assessed according to the length of continuous employment with the particular employer. The employer who makes a statutory redundancy payment is entitled to claim a rebate, currently fixed at 41 per cent of the payment, from the Redundancy Fund to which all employers contribute as part of their national insurance contributions. Employees whose employers have failed or refused to pay after all reasonable steps have been taken, or whose employers are insolvent, may claim in full from the Redundancy Fund.

An employee who is dismissed is taken as having been dismissed for redundancy if the dismissal is attributable wholly or mainly to either: the fact that the employer has ceased, or intends to cease, to carry on the business for the purpose of which the employee was employed by him, or has ceased, or intends to cease, to carry on that business in the place where the employee was so employed; or to the fact that the requirements of that business for employees to carry out work of a particular kind, or for employers to carry out work of a particular kind in the place where he was so employed, have ceased or diminished, or are expected to cease or diminish. It is not necessary that the sole reason for dismissal be redundancy – but it must be the main reason.

A distinction has been drawn in the decided cases between redundancy, on the one hand, and on the other the need of an employee to adapt to new methods and techniques with developing technology. This situation is quite likely to arise in a number of health service contexts. While health services of all types are often understaffed, the dismissal of an employee for his failure to adapt himself to technological advances is not a dismissal for redundancy, whatever other reason it may be based upon. The same may apply to the reorganisation of business in the interests of efficient, effective and economic management of services.

17.4.2   Conditions for redundancy payment

If an employee is dismissed because of misconduct no entitlement to redundancy payment can arise, since such entitlement is dependent upon the dismissal being wholly or mainly attributable to redundancy. Furthermore, an employee dismissed for redundancy shall be disqualified from receiving redundancy payment if he unreasonably refuses an offer from his employer to renew the contract on the same terms as before, such renewal to take place no later than four weeks after the dismissal. And an employee loses his right to redundancy compensation if he unreasonably refuses an offer of re-engagement in suitable alternative employment, such re-engagement to take place no later than four weeks after the dismissal. The concepts of *suitability* of employment and *reasonableness* of refusal are separable, but they are frequently dealt with together by industrial tribunals. As in the case of decisions on unfair dismissal, each one tends to relate solely to its own particular facts.

Certain categories of employee are excluded from eligibility for redundancy payments. These categories generally follow those excluded in respect of remedies for unfair dismissal. Excluded categories include men and women aged 65 or more; domestic servants who are close relatives working in a private household; the husband or wife of the employer; employees who are employed under a contract of employment for a fixed term of one year or more who have agreed in writing to exclude any right to a redundancy payment in the event of non-renewal of that contract. Also excluded is any employee who has been continuously employed for less than two years. In computing the number of weeks of continuous service for the purpose of eligibility for redundancy payments, reckonable weeks are those in which the employee has worked for 16 hours or more, or for eight or more hours weekly over a period of at least five years.

Differential redundancy payments under statute (65 for men, 60 for women) were removed by the Employment Act 1989.

17.4.3 Compensation

The amount of compensation to be received by an employee who is eligible for it under the rules just stated is based on the same principles which underline the 'basic' award in respect of unfair dismissal. Thus, for each year of continuous employment between the ages of 18 and 21 the employee is to receive half a week's pay; for each week of completed employment between 22 and 40, one week's pay; and for each year of employment between the ages of 41 and 64, one-and-a-half weeks' pay, up to a maximum weekly pay of £205.

17.5 NATIONAL HEALTH SERVICE EMPLOYMENT CONDITIONS

17.5.1 Health service employment conditions

The requirements in respect of written particulars of employees' remuneration and conditions of service which have just been outlined did not until recently apply to the Crown. Certain sections of the Employment Protection (Consolidation) Act 1978 which relate to security in employment, and which are considered in a moment, are specifically stated to apply to the Crown, and that includes, for our purposes, employees of National Health Service authorities. The above provisions as to pay and conditions of service in the 1978 Act represent an expanded version of what had earlier been laid down by the Contracts of Employment Act 1972. And in 1974 the case of *Wood v United Leeds Hospitals*[37] decided that the 1972 Act did not apply to the contracts made by a health authority with its employees. Since the removal of Crown status by the National Health Service and Community Care Act 1990, section 60,[38] there is now no difference in these respects between National Health Service employees and others.

Health authorities under the National Health Service Act 1977 are governed by Part III of Schedule 5 together with regulations which are either made under its powers, or which are preserved from an earlier date, including principally regulations made by statutory instrument under powers given by the National Health Service Reorganisation Act

1973. It is desirable not only that all contracts be in writing (even though, as earlier explained, this is a matter of procedural convenience rather than one of legal requirement), but also that they should make specific reference to such national conditions of employment as may be applicable to the particular group or groups of National Health Service employees in question and to the fact that such conditions may from time to time be altered. The only circumstances in which any such alterations may validly be made to an agreement as to remuneration or conditions of employment, once concluded, are either by a recommencement of formal negotiating machinery, the results of which are subject to the approval of the Secretary of State for Social Services; or, in exceptional instances, by the direct intervention of the Secretary of State himself.

In certain circumstances where there is in existence a written contract, section 5 of the Employment Protection (Consolidation) Act 1978 provides that there is no need for the supply of written particulars in addition. While, as a matter of law, the terms of the contract are offered by the employing authority to the employee, as a matter of practice they are settled by the Whitley Council's machinery. This standing negotiating machinery includes provision for consultation in respect of remuneration and conditions of service with trade unions and other bodies representing the staff side.

By paragraph 10 of Schedule 5 of the 1977 National Health Service Act regulations may be made as regards the terms of employment, the qualifications of persons who may be employed, and the manner in which they are to be employed. Paragraph 11(1) provides that, before the regulations are made, the Secretary of State shall consult 'such bodies as he may recognise as representing persons who in his opinion are likely to be affected by the regulations'.

The National Health Service (Appointment of Consultants) Regulations 1982[39] provide that, with certain exceptions, consultants may be appointed only after advertisement of the vacancy in the manner required by the Regulations and that no one may be appointed unless recommended to the appointing authority as suitable by an advisory appointments committee formed *ad hoc* in accordance with the Regulations. The duty of the advisory committee is to select from the list of applicants all those they consider suitable and to forward them to the appointing body with any comments they wish to make. They may forward one name only if they consider one applicant only to be suitable, but they would be exceeding their powers if, there being more than one suitable candidate, they forwarded one name only because they considered him best. If the advisory committee considers none of the applicants suitable and so makes no recommendation, the appointing authority may not make an appointment without re-advertisement nor until one or more suitable applicants have been approved by the advisory appointments committee. Other medical and dental appointments are made with less formality by the relevant appointing authority.

Further regulations which have been made under paragraph 10 are the National Health Service (Remuneration and Conditions of Service) Regulations 1991,[40] the National Health Service (Professions Supplementary to Medicine) Regulations 1974[41] and the National Health Service (Speech Therapists) Regulations 1974.[42] The general effect of the National Health Service (Remuneration and Conditions of Service) Regulations 1991 is to prohibit any health authority from paying more or less remuneration to any class of officer than may be laid down for that class of officer in nationally negotiated agreements approved by the Secretary of State. Similarly, if other conditions of service (e.g. hours, sick pay, holidays) have been nationally negotiated for any class of officer and approved by the Secretary of State, 'the conditions of service of any officer belonging to that class shall include the conditions so approved'. The Secretary of State, however, retains the right to vary the remuneration or other conditions of service so approved in the case of an individual officer or of officers of a particular description. This, of course, gives effect to the Whitley Council procedure within the health service.

By paragraph 10(3) of Schedule 5 of the Act directions may be given to a lower authority to place the services of any of its officers at the disposal of another authority. However, normally before this can be done, the officer or his negotiating body must be consulted. There is, however, a temporary emergency power which allows the Secretary of State or the Regional Health Authority to give effect to previously negotiated procedures.[43] The powers of direction reserved to the Secretary of State by the Schedule and the Regulations appear to exclude, in respect of matters covered by them, the general power of direction he has under section 13 of the 1977 Act.

17.5.2 Conditions not in accordance with National Health Service Regulations

The number of possibilities of unauthorised variation of conditions of employment is so great that it is impossible to deal with them exhaustively here. But one or two major problems may usefully be mentioned.

First, as to hours of duty. If an officer has been engaged on terms that he is to work for, say, three hours less per week than is required under a relevant national agreement approved by the Secretary of State under the Regulations, but for the same pay as for the full number of hours, it seems that it is the duty of the employing authority on discovering the irregularity to terminate the agreement by notice and offer new conditions in accordance with those authorised. If an officer is found to have been employed on terms which required him to undertake longer hours than are authorised under the Regulations but for the same pay as for the lesser number of hours to which the standard week's pay is related, and he is in an overtime grade, it is suggested that the excess hours worked should count for overtime payment; and that is probably what would happen. The case is analogous to underpayment of wages, though not precisely the same.

Other conditions which might, by mistake, have varied from those under the Regulations are as to sick pay and holidays. The factors governing the position regarding the claiming back of overpaid sick pay, or of the making up of sick pay wrongfully withheld or insufficient in amount, would be the same as in respect of overpayment or under-payment of remuneration generally. The granting, by mistake, of too long a holiday presents no problem. The officer has had it; no court would be likely to entertain a claim by the employing authority in respect thereof. If, on the other hand, owing to a mistake and without protest on his part, an officer had not been granted all holidays to which under the Regulations he was entitled, it is possible that the court might award him damages in respect of the advantage lost, though this is most doubtful. After all, in most cases, an officer of a health authority is likely to find out the correct holiday from others working with him and he could, therefore, easily be held to have acquiesced in the wrong which he had suffered.

17.5.3　Gifts to officers on retirement or otherwise; superannuation payments, or supplementary superannuation payments, by employers

The questions here posed are whether a hospital under the National Health Service Act 1977, may (a) make any gift to an officer in its service; (b) make a retiring gift to any such officer; (c) make any periodic or other payment to a former officer by way of superannuation.

Gifts to or for the benefit of serving officers

A gift to an officer which was in the nature of remuneration for his service beyond what had been authorised under the National Health Service (Remuneration and Conditions of Service) Regulations 1991,[40] could not be justified whether or not paid out of Exchequer funds, as it would contravene the express terms of those Regulations which forbid payment of remuneration in excess of that authorised, whether or not paid out of moneys provided by Parliament.[44] And this would be so whether it was a single payment or periodic.

But payments to officers for special purposes may nevertheless be justified and, indeed, may be authorised by the Secretary of State. For example, subject to conditions set out in the relevant circulars to health authorities, officers may be paid expenses of attendances at conferences and residential courses. Also, any officer undertaking a course of study for a qualification likely to increase his usefulness may receive financial aid within approved limits, in both cases out of Exchequer funds. Similarly, payment by way of ex gratia compensation may be made out of Exchequer funds to an officer who, say, has had his spectacles broken or his clothing damaged in an accident on duty for the consequences of which the health authority are not responsible in law, for instance damage caused by a patient having an epileptic fit, there being no question of the damage having been caused or contributed to by inadequate staffing, by the negligence of a fellow employee or by anything else which might import liability on the employer's part.

There are many gifts which may be made out of non-Exchequer funds which the Secretary of State would not authorise out of Exchequer funds; for example, financial aid beyond that authorised in departmental Circulars for officers studying for approved qualifications, or paying for time off work for trade union activities under section 169 of the Trade Union and Labour Relations (Consolidation) Act 1992, or payment of convalescent home charges for a nurse who had been seriously ill. The tests to be applied to ascertain whether a payment to or for the benefit of an officer out of a trust might be justifiable are (a) to ask whether, in all the circumstances, the payment proposed is for purposes relating to health services or to the functions of the authority with respect to research; and (b), if the trusts on which the fund out of which the payment is proposed to be made is held are for more specific purposes, to ask whether the proposed payment can fairly be regarded as for those purposes. Whether a payment can be regarded as 'for purposes relating to health services' is a question of fact. If it were of a kind designed, even indirectly, to advance the efficiency of the authority or to promote research, then it might be so regarded. Payments to assist officers improve their qualifications in particular fields of work clearly would;[45] so would ex gratia compensation for, say, spectacles broken in carrying out duties such as restraining an epileptic patient, because it would encourage staff to do their utmost in such circumstances without worrying about possible loss to themselves. In *Re White's Will Trust, Tindall v United Sheffield Hospitals and others* (1951)[46] a gift for provision of a rest home for nurses was held to be a charitable trust which a hospital authority could accept and affords strong evidence that payment for a nurse at a convalescent home would in appropriate circumstances be within the powers of a health service employer.

However, even though a payment to or for the benefit of a serving officer may on the face of it be within the powers of a health service employer as charitable trustees, it must also be reasonable in amount. An excessively large payment would be a breach of trust, because any possible benefit to the health service would be so disproportionately small that no prudent trustee could regard the money as spent for the purposes of the service.

A gift for the benefit of officers generally or of a particular class of officer, whether on a single occasion or periodic, for instance provision of additional amenities for nurses or other resident staff, must be judged on the same principles. The purposes of the health service are the provision of care and treatment for the sick and medical and similar research. Extras for the staff out of monies provided for such purposes generally are justified only if the authority authorising the expenditure has grounds for belief that such expenditure is likely significantly to forward those purposes; for example, within common sense limits, improvement of accommodation and provision of extra amenities for resident nursing staff, especially in a hospital where the basic accommodation and amenities so far provided out of Exchequer funds are poor, is justifiable because it may be expected to help the hospital obtain and keep the nurses it needs. It must, however, be reasonable in amount, having regard to all the circumstances, including the size of the fund available and other calls on it.

Retirement gift and payments in the nature of superannuation

The legality of a retirement gift (other than a very small gift of money or goods) by a hospital has to be tested by the same yardstick as a gift to a serving officer. Does it offend against any National Health Service regulation? If not, is the payment permissible out of Exchequer funds? Or, may it be paid out of trust funds at the disposal of the health authority? Let us deal with the first question.

Any payment or payments to an officer on retirement otherwise than payments he has a right to under the Act or regulations, if of substantial amount, must either be regarded as remuneration or as superannuation. If such payment or payments were in the nature of remuneration, they would be unlawful, whether out of Exchequer funds or out of trust monies, for reasons we have already seen. If regarded as in the nature of superannuation different considerations apply.

On balance, it seems that any lump sum payment to an officer on retirement, as well as any periodic payments to him after retirement, would be in the nature of superannuation rather than remuneration, and that view is strengthened by the fact that superannuation benefits provided for in the National Health Service (Superannuation) Regulations[47] include not only a pension but also, and in addition, lump sum retiring allowances.

If, then, one regards either a lump sum payment to an officer on retirement or periodic payments to him thereafter as in the nature of superannuation, such payments would not be rendered unlawful by the

National Health Service (Remuneration and Conditions of Service) Regulations 1991.[40] They could not, however, be made out of Exchequer monies since the superannuation of officers is provided for in regulations made under section 10 of the 1972 Superannuation Act and such payments are not a proper purpose for use of Exchequer monies by a health authority.

Would it then be permissible to make such payments out of trust funds not impressed with more than the broad trusts 'for purposes relating to health services . . . or in respect of research'? The test is whether such payment, or payments of the particular kind, are designed and likely to advance the efficiency of the hospital or hospitals or other services for which the body is responsible, or further research. The larger the amount involved, either in one sum or in aggregate, the clearer should be the evidence if such payment is reasonably to be justified. The provisions of the National Health Service (Superannuation) Regulations, substantially in line with the provisions for superannuation in public services generally, will ordinarily be regarded as appropriate. It would not be likely to further the work of the authority to make any payments in excess of that to which the retiring officer is entitled; but there may be exceptional circumstances when such payments are reasonable. One example is an officer whose employment was transferred either in 1948 or in 1974 and who would otherwise be worse off than officers in similar grades with similar total length of employment. Of course, if at any time an employee had exercised an option and lost, he cannot claim to have been prejudiced in this way.

The limitation on the use of Exchequer monies or of trust funds for making substantial retirement gifts in money or payments in the nature of superannuation to officers in the health service applies equally to gifts in kind, although a gift of comparatively small value, for long service or retirement, might be justifiable if out of trust funds but not out of Exchequer monies.

17.5.4 Qualifications for employment prescribed by Regulations under the National Health Service Act 1977

The National Health Service (Professions Supplementary to Medicine) Regulations 1974,[41] lay down that no officer shall be employed by a Regional or District or Special Health Authority in the capacity of a chiropodist, dietician, medical laboratory technician, occupational therapist, orthoptist, physiotherapist, radiographer or remedial gymnast unless in effect he is registered under the Professions Supplementary to Medicine Act 1960, in respect of the profession appropriate to the work for which he is employed or was employed in such capacity by a local authority or voluntary organisation immediately before 1 April 1974.

The National Health Service (Speech Therapists) Regulations 1974,[42] lay down the prescribed qualifications for speech therapists in the service of a health authority.

If a health service body engaged a person who, being a member of one of the professions covered by the National Health Service (Professions Supplementary to Medicine) Regulations 1974, was not registered or, being a speech therapist, was not qualified for employment under the relevant regulations and the authority had not been deceived by that person as to his qualifications, it could even so be argued that the contract was a nullity because both the body and that person must be taken to have known the relevant regulations. But so far as services had been rendered there would be no question of obtaining a refund of remuneration paid. If, however, one assumes the contract to be a nullity and the person's employment were terminated summarily on realisation that he was not qualified under the regulations, it seems that the dismissed person would, strictly, have no claim to remuneration accruing due nor, possibly, even to that already accrued due under the void contract. In practice, no health service body would be likely to be so unreasonable as to refuse payment and an employer wishing to act fairly might also make an ex gratia payment of salary in lieu of notice to the person whose service had been terminated.

If the employing body retained the unqualified person longer, allowing him to work his notice under the void agreement, they would continue in breach of the Regulations. That would not be a very serious matter unless in flat defiance of a direction from the Secretary of State, since it would constitute neither a criminal offence nor a civil wrong. If a health service body wilfully ignored the Regulations or deliberately disobeyed a direction, the Secretary of State might have recourse to default powers under section 85 of the National Health Service Act 1977. To retain a person lacking the prescribed qualification either for the appropriate period of notice or, possibly, until a qualified substitute had been found, would usually be most inadvisable because the fact that the person lacked a recognised qualification for the work he was doing might make it considerably harder for the body to defend an action for damages based on an allegation of the unqualified person's negligence or incompetence in treating a patient, unless it could be shown that the person was qualified for registration.

If a person obtained an appointment by claiming to hold a particular qualification which they did not possess, the employing body, on discovering the deception, would have the right summarily to dismiss.

17.5.5　Appointments in excess of authorised establishment

If the maximum establishment for a particular grade of staff employed by a health service body had been fixed either by itself or by direction of a higher authority that would not invalidate the contract with a person engaged in excess of establishment since that person could know nothing of the limitation nor, if he did, whether the body had a full establishment. Moreover, the fault consists in having in aggregate too large an establishment of practitioners, not in having engaged a particular one.

17.5.6   Student nurse and pupil nurse training agreements

Formerly it was customary in the agreement with a student nurse to create an obligation for the full three or four years training and to include a clause that an agreed sum was to become payable as liquidated damages if he or she left voluntarily before the completion of training. Today such conditions have vanished; and student and pupil nurses, like other staff, can leave at any time on giving the agreed notice or, if no notice has been agreed, reasonable notice. Although the agreement is expressed to be for training and the remuneration is called a training allowance the contract is, in substance, a contract of employment analogous to apprenticeship, though not for a fixed term. Contracts of employment and national conditions of service apply equally to all trainee nurses. Indeed, their 'training allowances' and conditions of service are negotiated, as are the salaries and conditions of service of other nursing staff, by the Nurses and Midwives Whitley Council, and observance of the agreed conditions made obligatory on the approval of the Secretary of State being given under regulation 3 of the National Health Service (Remuneration and Conditions of Service) Regulations 1991.[40]

17.5.7   Contracts of employment of persons in special hospitals

Special hospitals provided by the Secretary of State under section 4 of the National Health Service Act 1977 for persons suffering from mental disorder, being persons who, in the opinion of the Secretary of State, require treatment under conditions of special security on account of their dangerous, violent or criminal propensities, are under the control and management of the Secretary of State and not of health authorities established under the National Health Service Act. Consequently the staff of those hospitals are civil servants and hold their appointments during the pleasure of the Crown. In practice, as is the case with other civil servants, remuneration and conditions of service of the different grades are subject of negotiation and, in most cases, on disagreement, may be referred to the Civil Service Arbitration Tribunal, though not as of right.

17.5.8 Contracts of employment outside the National Health Service

Hospitals and nursing homes outside the national hospital service, whether carried on for private profit or not and whether or not providing accommodation or other services for health service patients under contractual arrangements with a health authority, do not fall within the National Health Service employment conditions so far discussed.

The above limitations on the powers of health service bodies to pay what remuneration they like and engage staff on whatever other conditions they think fit does not apply to these independent employers. But those of them who are responsible for hospitals which are in law charities have to remember their obligations as charity trustees; squandering trust monies would be a breach of trust.

As the scales of salaries and conditions of service for different grades of health service staff approved or determined under the Regulations are not automatically written into contracts of employment made by those controlling private hospitals or nursing homes it is important that due care should be taken to cover such matters as are there dealt with, holiday entitlement being a case in point. Sometimes an attempt is made to deal with the matter by a statement that National Health Service Whitley conditions shall apply to the post. Most scales and conditions are settled in Whitley Councils and approved under Regulation 3 of Statutory Instrument 1991/481. This may not, however, always be entirely appropriate and may even be ambiguous. As an example of this it may be said that what past service in the grade may be counted for incremental purposes and what past service is to count for sick leave entitlement may be obscure, because the nationally negotiated terms are being applied without amplification or modification to a situation for which they were not intended. Unless specially exempted by order made by the Secretary of State for Employment, employment in charity hospitals will fall within the provisions of the Employment Protection (Consolidation) Act 1978.

17.6 PAYMENTS AND DEDUCTIONS

17.6.1 Payment of wages

The Truck Act 1831 provided that the wages of manual workers had to be paid in the current coin of the realm. That Act was repealed by the Wages Act 1986, and now 'cashless pay' is lawful for all classes of employee. The actual mode of payment of wages is left to agreement between employer and employee.

The Wages Act does, however, itself impose certain restrictions on deductions. Section 1 of the Act provides that an employer must not make any deductions from the wages of any worker employed by him, or receive any payments from him, unless:

1. the deduction is required to be made or is authorised by statutory provision (for instance, national insurance contributions); or
2. the deduction is authorised by a relevant provision in any worker's contract (for instance, in respect of contributions taken from pay towards an occupational pension scheme); or
3. the worker has in writing in advance signified his agreement to the deduction being made (for instance, in respect of payment of a loan advanced for travel purposes).

In this last instance, the deduction must not relate to any event which happened before this agreement is effected in writing. An aggrieved employee may complain to an industrial tribunal that the employer has made a deduction or demanded payment in contravention of section 1 of the Wages Act. Such a complaint is not, however, available in the case of a deduction by the employer designed to reimburse the employer for an overpayment of wages or expenses paid to the worker. In such a case, the worker retains his normal remedy in the county court, based on an argument that the employer acted in breach of contract in making the deduction. Any such dispute falls to be resolved in the county court on the basis of normal principles of the law of contract relating to mistakes of law or/and mistakes of fact. The question of overpayment and workers' rights attracted considerable attention in previous editions of this book and an updated summary of the law is given in the following section of this chapter.

17.6.2 Miscalculations and remuneration not in accordance with the National Health Service (Remuneration and Conditions of Service) Regulations 1991

What would be the effect in law of an engagement not in accordance with the National Health Service (Remuneration and Conditions of Service) Regulations 1991?[40] First, what is the position if the rate of remuneration agreed is otherwise than as authorised under the Regulations? Could either party, discovering before the person engaged had commenced work that the contract was not in accordance with the Regulations, regard it as a nullity and refuse to be bound by it? Or, suppose the mistake were discovered after the employee had commenced work but at or before the end of the first regular period for which, under the agreement, the employee would be entitled to remuneration. Could the employing authority then refuse to pay more than the remuneration authorised under the Regulations if it were that the agreed remuneration had been in excess thereof, or could the employee refuse to accept the agreed remuneration, being less than that to which he would have been entitled under the Regulations? Suppose, finally, that the fact that the agreement had not been in accordance with the Regulations was discovered after the contract of employment had been in force some time.

Could the health authority then claim repayment of any remuneration paid under the agreement in excess of that authorised under the Regulations? Or could the employee whose agreed remuneration had been less than that laid down under the Regulations claim as a debt due to him the difference between the remuneration he had received and that which he ought to have received thereunder? In all the foregoing possible cases mistake or oversight has been assumed. The position would be different if one or both parties had wilfully ignored the effect of the Regulations and is a matter which will be discussed separately.

As a preliminary to consideration of the different situations outlined above it must be observed that a contract entered into, not in accordance with the Regulations, cannot be dismissed as a nullity as being contrary to law. This is because the Regulations do not themselves contain the authorised scales of salary. Those authorised under regulation 3(1) are to be found only in agreements entered into in the various Whitley Councils for the Health Services which, on approval by the Secretary of State under the Regulations, are almost invariably transmitted to health authorities under cover of a circular (or otherwise, by individual letter) signifying that approval and given instructions for action thereon. The Whitley and departmental circulars are not publications purchasable by the public, though there is no obstacle to the dissemination of their contents in newspapers, staff magazines and textbooks. From time to time salary scales and conditions are collected into handbooks which, although so far as available are purchasable from the Department of Health and Social Security – being mainly bought by trade unions and professional societies – are not, in the ordinary sense, freely on sale, as are publications obtainable from Her Majesty's Stationery Office. Consequently, information about the generally authorised rates and scales of remuneration is not very accessible. In practice, persons accepting a first appointment with a health authority must, in the nature of things, rely on what they are told by their prospective employer about pay and conditions of service. Further, since the Secretary of State has power under regulation 3(3) to authorise a board or committee to vary the nationally agreed and approved remuneration in the case of an individual officer, or of officers of a particular description, and such authorisation may be known only to the particular employing authority and the Department, it can be argued that even if a person knew of the existence of nationally approved scales of remuneration he would be under no obligation to check that what he was offered was in accordance with those scales since he could fairly assume that, if what he was offered varied from the approved national rate, the variation had been authorised by the Secretary of State. This assumption is the more reasonable since seemingly the Secretary of State is not obliged to give his authorisation to a variation under regulation 2 in writing.

Moreover, even had any such authorisation been in writing, it would most probably have been in a letter to the health authority, the contents of which would not ordinarily be within the knowledge of any candidate for a post or of any officer whose pay or conditions of service had been varied.

Against that background, what is the position in law if the agreed remuneration exceeds the national rate approved by the Secretary of State under regulation 2 and no approval has been given to a variation, the mistake being discovered before the commencement of the relationship of employer and employee?

It is unlikely that, in practice, any health authority would seek to avoid its obligations under a contract of employment in the manner discussed or that the Secretary of State would expect it to do so. What it would certainly be expected to do would be to terminate the agreement by proper notice as soon as the mistake was discovered, offering the employee, as an alternative to dismissal, continued engagement on the proper remuneration. Even this might cause real hardship to an employee who had altered his position on the assurance that in his new employment he would receive a particular rate of pay, but it would probably not constitute an actionable wrong.

Consequences of overpayment

What if the fact that the rate of remuneration contracted to be paid exceeds that approved or directed under the Regulations is discovered only after the agreement has been in force for some time and there has in fact been overpayment? Is any part of the remuneration already paid, maybe over a long period, recoverable?

A distinction must be made between errors of law and errors of fact which lead to the overpayment. The decision in *Holt v Markham* (1923)[48] is authority for the proposition that overpayment made as the result of an error of law is not generally recoverable by the employer or employing authority, unless the employee were aware of the error and it would be in all the circumstances of the case inequitable to allow him to keep the overpaid money. A typical example of an error of law in health services management would be a misinterpretation of Whitley Council pay scales, given that Whitley terms and conditions owe their legal status to regulations made under National Health Service regulations.

The legal position relating to overpayment as the result of an error of fact can be more difficult. An error of fact consists of an erroneous impression by an employer that certain facts were true, and the payments in question would not have been made had the employer known the true facts. It was decided in the case of *Avon County Council v Howlett* (1983)[49] that if the overpayment resulted from an error of fact, and not of law, the sum in question will generally be recoverable by the employer. There are, however, three conditions which, if all present, will prevent (estop) the employer from reclaiming the sum. First, if the employer made a representation of fact which led the employee to believe that he was entitled to treat the overpaid money as his own; second, that the employee in good faith and without notice of the mistake changed his position in reliance on the payment; and third, that the overpayment was not caused by the fault of the employee. The court has an overriding power to reject the overpaid employee's plea to keep the sums in question if in all the circumstances of the case it would be inequitable to allow him to do so.

It is for the employer or employing authority seeking to recover an overpayment to demonstrate whether the error was one of law or of fact, and it is not possible to generalise in advance of each case as it arises whether the mistake is exclusively of one type or the other, or is a combination of the two.

A case of overpayment which is apt to be troublesome, and which one suspects is much more common, is in respect of miscalculation of remuneration of an existing officer who is on the right scale, or a mistake in principle in the calculation of overtime payments or rates of deduction for emoluments or, maybe, a miscalculation on the addition of an increment on a scale or on the application of a new scale by approved national agreement.

Appendix B to Circular HC(78) 42 gives advisory guidance to health service employers as to appropriate action to be taken following the overpayment of salaries, wages, fees and allowances:

'Take steps to end overpayment immediately on discovery. Where necessary the contract of service should be varied forthwith by agreement in writing with the employee who should be informed of his right to consult his union or staff organisation. Failing such agreement, at the earliest possible date the employee must be given a notice of termination of his contract at the expiration of his entitled period of notice and offered a new contract on the correct terms from that date (see also paragraph 9 of Appendix C).'

Further specific advice on policy relating to overpayment is given in Appendix C of the Circular, paragraph 9, as follows:

'9. Where an overpayment concerns one person only, repayment terms should minimise hardship. Normally the rate of recovery should not exceed the rate of overpayment. Failing agreement by the person overpaid:

1. in cases of wilful misrepresentation, all possible steps to effect recovery should be taken. Legal and disciplinary action should be considered;

2. in cases of misconstruction of regulations, agreements etc., recovery should not be pursued unless the person overpaid might reasonably have been expected to be aware of the correct application;
3. in cases of genuine mistakes all practicable steps should be taken to effect recovery with minimum hardship;
4. in cases of collective overpayment arising from the same mistake, repayment would not be expected unless there were good grounds for recovery from all concerned, or all had agreed to make repayment;
5. In cases where recovery would involve expenditure disproportionate to the overpayment, recovery need not normally be pursued;
6. in all cases, except 9.1 above, recovery should be limited to the last 12 months of overpayment.'

17.7   CONTRACTS OF CONSULTANTS AND OTHER HOSPITAL MEDICAL AND DENTAL STAFF

These are set out in detail in Personnel Memorandum PM(79)11 and its annexes, to which specific reference should be made in particular cases. The principal provisions of the Memorandum itself are as follows:

'Whole time contract

a. Private practice

5. The obligations of the whole-time consultant will remain as at present in respect of commitment and work done. It has been agreed however that from the effective date whole time consultants should be able to undertake a limited amount of private practice, receiving professional fees up to a limit in gross annual earnings from it of 10% of their gross whole time salary (including any distinction award, if applicable) for that financial year. The calculation of the 10% shall exclude any charge payable by a patient to a health authority for the use of NHS facilities.

6. The private practice may be undertaken, within the agreed limit,

  i.   in the NHS hospitals at which they are contracted to provide a service, on the same terms as those applying to part-time consultants; and
  ii.   outside those hospitals but in such a way that significant amounts of the consultant's time will not be taken up in travelling to and from private commitments.

7. Whole-time consultants who undertake private practice will accept that their NHS work should receive priority at all times (subject to the consultant's ethical obligation to all his patients when emergencies arise) and that health authorities are entitled to expect no diminution in the level of service to NHS patients as a result of this arrangement. The representatives of the professions have accepted that this extended right to private practice should not be exercised in such a way as to damage working relationships with other NHS staffs. They have formally accepted that the agreed changes relating to whole-timers and maximum part-timers should not bring about any reduction overall in the commitment of consultants to the NHS or in the work done.

8. At the end of each financial year, whole-time consultants will be asked to

submit a return indicating that their annual gross income from private practice has not exceeded the 10% limit in that year. Detailed accounts will not normally be required since such a system will work most satisfactorily on the basis of a large measure of trust and confidence between employing authorities and consultants. Exceptionally, however, an employing authority considering that they have grounds for seeking fuller information will be entitled to call for and to receive fully audited accounts.

9. Whole-time consultants exceeding the 10% limit for two consecutive financial years will be automatically regraded as maximum part-time at the end of the third year unless, by that time, they can show that they have taken effective steps to reduce their private practice commitments, and this is confirmed by the next earnings return. When a consultant has been regraded in this way he will not be able to exercise an option to return to whole-time status until two consecutive years have passed in which he can show that his private practice earnings have not exceeded the 10% limit. A consultant so regraded will not be eligible to contract for an extra paid session (paragraphs 10–11 below) and if he holds a contract for such a session at the time of regrading it shall be terminated in accordance with paragraph 10 below.

b. Extra paid session

10. Whole-time consultants may be contracted for not more than one extra non-superannuable session, paid at the rate of 1/11 of their whole-time salary (excluding merit award if any), the session to be offered at the discretion of the authority in the light of service needs and to be the subject of a separate letter of appointment, subject to review not less often than annually and terminable at three months notice on either side without formality (ie without recourse to paragraph 190 of the Terms and Conditions of Service).

11. The extra session should be available only in exceptional circumstances and should be in respect of work which is not part of a consultant's normal contractual duties (including his obligations under paragraph 110(a) of the Terms and Conditions of Service) and can be clearly distinguished from them. Examples of such exceptional circumstances might include covering part of the workload arising from the prolonged and unexpected absence of a colleague or a sudden increase in the overall workload. The cover of annual and study leave of colleagues would not count as an exceptional circumstance.

Part-time contract

a. 9-session contract

12. Following the revised definition of the maximum part-time commitment . . . it has been agreed that authorities should be able to offer part-time contracts up to and including a total of 9 notional half-days.

b. Extra paid sessions

13. The part-time consultant with a contract or contracts for nine sessions or fewer may take on extra paid sessions, permanently up to a total of nine and exceptionally a further session to a total of 10 on the same basis as would apply to a whole-time consultant.

Advertisement of consultant posts

14. From the effective date, consultants posts should be advertised in such a way that candidates unable for personal reasons to work full-time should be able to apply.

Starting salaries

15. In addition to existing provisions, authorities may advertise a consultant post at the maximum of the consultant scale if it has been vacant for at least a year and has been unsuccessfully advertised at least twice. Other consultants whose principal commitment is in the same hospital and specialty as the principal commitment of the advertised post will be entitled when such an appointment is made to be placed upon the maximum of the consultant scale (if they have not yet reached it) from the date of the relevant appointment.

Other career grades

16. Whole-time staff in the grades of medical assistant, assistant dental surgeon and senior hospital medical and dental officer may (i) engage in private practice up to the limit of 10% (paragraphs 5–8 above) and (ii) contract for an extra paid session, on the same basis as whole-time consultants (paragraphs 10–11 above). If in any financial year a practitioner has exceeded the 10% limit he will be required thereupon to take effective steps to reduce his private practice commitments to within the 10% limit. Part-time staff in these grades with a contract or contracts for 9 sessions of fewer may take on extra paid sessions, permanently up to a total of 9 and exceptionally a further session to a total of 10 on the same basis as whole-time staff (cf. paragraph 13 above).

Distinction awards

17. From the effective date, a number of modifications to the distinction awards system will be introduced. Details are at Annex C, but the main provisions are:

i.   Awards will in future be known as distinction and meritorious service awards for consultants, and community physicians.
ii.   Awards will be made in such a way as to acheive a more equitable distribution both between regions and specialities.
iii.   The criteria for making awards will be clarified, and they will make it clear that outstanding service contributions alone can be sufficient reason for recommending an award.
iv.   The Central Advisory Committee on distinction awards will be enlarged by the inclusion of additional members representing the general body of consultants.
v.   The Chairman of the Advisory Committee will consult regional health authorities to ensure that employing authorities are able to put forward recommendations for the consideration of his Committee.
vi.   The confidentiality of the system will be modified to allow the names of holders to be made available to consultants generally within their region.

Maximum part-time and 9 session part-time consultant contracts: consultative machinery

18. The Department consider that employing authorities may find it helpful to establish a joint consultative group to consider and give guidance to employing authorities and consultants on any contentious matters of fact or interpretation arising in the changes . . . affecting holders of maximum part-time and 9-session part-time contracts. This group should be available as an informal point of reference for consultants and the authority, and will not be an appeal body, for which see paragraphs 20–21 below.

19. The group should consist of broadly equal numbers of representatives of the

employing authority and the Regional Committee for Hospital Medical Services. It will be for employing authorities to decide who should represent them, but there is clear merit in using the expertise of their medically qualified staff as far as possible.

Appeals

20. Where consultation has been exhausted and disagreement persists between the authority and the consultant on the work commitment of a contract, the consultant may use the appeals machinery provided for in Section XXII of the General Whitley Council Terms and Conditions of Service if there is dispute as to whether his existing work commitment satisfies the revised criterion . . . for a maximum part-time contract.

21. If on appeal the consultant establishes that his workload satisfies the revised criterion for a maximum part-time contract, the authority will pay the 10/11 salary. If he does not establish this point, the authority will pay the 10/11 salary provided he is prepared to make an appropriate additional work commitment. If he was a maximum part-time contract holder on 31 December 1979 he may change to a 9-session part-time contract, or retain a personal 9/11 maximum part-time contract, as provided in paragraph 3 above.'

Model forms of contract and job description are attached to the Memorandum and health service bodies are asked to follow these closely in drawing up particular contracts. Also attached is a model form of job description which such bodies may find useful in advertising a vacant consultant post.

The agreement has the approval of the Secretary of State under the National Health Service (Remuneration and Conditions of Service) Regulations 1991.[40]

17.7.1　Consultants' contracts and job plans: management of the consultant's contract of employment

Circular HC(90)16 advises Regional Health Authorities on the devolution of the day-to-day management of consultants' contracts to their districts and requires all health service bodies responsible for the management of consultants' contracts to introduce a system of job plans for all hospital consultants.

'Regional and District General Managers are requested:

    i.　to devolve the day-to-day management of consultants' contracts to District Health Authorities (DHAs), subject to certain functions remaining with the RHA where it is the employing authority (paragraphs 1–4).

Regional, District and SHA General Managers are requested:

    ii.　starting as soon as is practicable, to ensure that by 1 April 1991 all hospital consultants have job plans setting out their main duties and responsibilities and including a work programme for the "typical" week (paragraphs 5–15);
    iii.　to consider, in the course of agreeing job plans, which consultants may be eligible for additional notional half-day(s) (or fractions thereof) in

recognition of their significant additional management responsibilities (paragraphs 16–17).

Management of consultants' contracts

1. Where a District Health Authority does not already hold the contracts of the consultants working in the District, the RHA should appoint the DHA as its *managing agent* in relation to the arrangement of consultants' duties and the day-to-day management of their contracts. This does not require any legislative action and is fully consistent with the terms of consultants' existing contracts, e.g. the model contract at Annex D of PM(79)11. Such agency arrangements will not be required in the case of teaching Districts and Special Health Authorities, which already directly employ their hospital consultants and hold their contracts. However, *all* health authorities are required to follow the guidance in paragraph 4 onwards.

2. Most functions related to the day-to-day management of consultants' contracts should be devolved at least to District level. Examples of such functions include payroll, the organisation of leave (including study leave) and the organisation of locums. RHAs should review all functions affected by this approach and, following consultation with representatives of the profession locally including the Regional Consultants and Specialists Committee, develop action plans for their devolution. Such devolution should take effect as soon as possible.

3. Certain functions will, for legal and other reasons, need to be retained at employing authority level. These include the formal appointment process for a new consultant (including issuing the contract itself) and formal disciplinary matters. Manpower planning functions, including consideration of early retirement proposals, should continue to be carried out by the RHA.

4. Where a consultant provides services for more than one District/SHA, responsibility for the day-to-day management of the various aspects of the contract will rest with the District/SHAs concerned. In these circumstances the authority (District or SHA) with the greater proportion of the consultant's contractual commitment should normally have the lead responsibility. Exceptionally, the RHA may take a co-ordinating role in the arrangement of the consultant's duties.

Consultants' job plans

5. In both the White Paper and Working Paper 7, the Government noted the heavy workload which the majority of consultants carry, and the key role which they play in the organisation of the work of hospitals. The arrangement of consultants' work has, of necessity, to be flexible and consultants need to be free to take clinical decisions within the boundaries of accepted professional standards. The Department and the profession have re-affirmed their commitment to the agreements on the consultant contract set out in PM(79)11, which continues to apply. However, for their part, general managers need to have a clear understanding of the work which is being undertaken by consultants and to be in a position to make changes following discussion and agreement with them. Under the recommended form of contract for hospital consultants, the health authority and the consultant are responsible for agreeing the consultant's duties. A job plan (called a 'job description' in Working Paper 7) – and its integral

work programme – will henceforth be part of every such contract. The Terms and Conditions of Service of hospital medical and dental staff are amended to reflect this provision.

6. Starting as soon as practicable, health authorities should ensure that, by 1 April 1991, all hospital consultants (whether newly-appointed or already in post and whether whole-time, maximum part-time, part-time or honorary) have job plans agreed with local management for their National Health Service work. Such job plans should include as a minimum the following elements:

— the main duties and responsibilities of the post, including information on the clinical, teaching, research and administrative elements;
— a work programme, including the fixed commitments of the consultant;
— requirements to participate in medical audit under local arrangements (in the light of relevant Departmental guidance);
— details of out-of-hours responsibilities, including rota commitments;
— budgetary and other management responsibilities, where appropriate.

7. Job plans should include certain general provisions such as that consultants would be expected to observe the policies and procedures of the hospital and/or health authority, drawn up in consultation with the profession where they involve clinical matters, e.g. admissions procedures.

8. A model outline of a job plan is at *Annex A*. A model outline of a work programme – which forms part of the overall job plan – is at *Annex B*.

Job descriptions

9. Where a consultant has a job description drawn up under Annex F of PM(79)11 for the purpose of advertising the post, and the consultant took up that post within the previous 3 years, this may replace part of the job plan as set out at paragraphs 5 and 6 of *Annex A*. Nevertheless, such a consultant's job plan will have to be supplemented by a work programme including the fixed commitments of the post-holder (see paragraph 12 below). Where the original job description is at least 3 years old, it will be open to the two parties to agree at an annual review either to continue to use the existing job description or to replace it with a full job plan as set out in *Annex A*.

Drawing up of job plans

10. District or SHA General Managers (or other general managers acting on their behalf) may either (with appropriate medical advice) draw up draft job plans for each consultant or ask consultants to draw up their own, allowing them 3 months to do so. Where a consultant provides services for more than one District/SHA, the general managers concerned shall agree which general manager will have the lead responsibility for the consultant's job plan. This will normally be the general manager in the authority with the greater proportion of the consultant's contractual commitment. Each job plan, including its work programme, shall then be agreed between the general manager and the individual consultant.

11. The assessment of duties should be made in accordance with the new paragraph 30A and the revised paragraph 61 of the Terms and Conditions of Service (see *Annex C*). The general manager may seek the advice of the Director of Public Health and make use of any other appropriate source of medical or dental advice (including any relevant College or Faculty guidelines) when

drawing up or evaluating a proposed job plan or work programme, in order to facilitate agreement between the consultant and the general manager.

Fixed commitments

12. For a consultant on a whole-time or maximum part-time contract, *between 5 and 7 notional half-days*, depending on specialty, should normally be allocated in the work programme to fixed commitments. For consultants on other part-time contracts, including honorary contracts, *at least half* of the notional half days should normally be allocated to fixed commitments (but see paragraph 13 below). The number of fixed commitments may be varied with the agreement of the consultant and the general manager. A fixed commitment (e.g. out-patient clinics, operating lists) is a commitment which a consultant must fulfil, except by agreement with local management or in emergency, because otherwise the use of other Health Service resources would be adversely affected.

Honorary contract-holders

13. Health authorities should recognise the particular needs and responsibilities of clinical academic staff. They should be prepared to allow more flexibility in the way in which National Health Service commitments are fulfilled by members of academic departments, e.g. where necessary – for the purpose of a research programme, for instance – agreeing temporary variations to the number and timing of any such fixed commitments. The number of fixed commitments to be included in each job plan should be agreed by the consultant and the general manager in consultation with the Dean or the head of the academic department in the context of the overall service commitments of university staff.

Review of a job plan

14. Each consultant's job plan (including the work programme) is subject to review each year. This annual review should provide an opportunity for the consultant and the general manager to discuss any problems which may have arisen and to settle any changes which need to be made to meet new circumstances or service priorities. It is likely that in many cases job plans will need to be amended only occasionally and even then will be subject to minimal alteration.

Where agreement is not reached

15. Where the consultant and the general manager are unable to reach agreement on the content of the consultant's job plan, either initially or at an annual review, they should follow local procedures which provide for the resolution of grievances or differences relating to an individual practitioner's duties. These procedures culminate in a right of appeal to the employing authority. When an appeal is made in relation to a job plan, the authority should set up an appeal panel in the form described in the new paragraph 30B of the Terms and Conditions of Service (*Annex C*).

Consultants' management responsibilities

16. Where a consultant takes on significant additional management responsibilities in one or more of the following roles:

   i.   in co-ordinating the development and the operation of medical audit in a hospital or District;
   ii. as a clinical director (or equivalent e.g. consultant in administrative charge);

iii.   in leadership of the Resource Management Initiative;

the health authority, in reviewing the job plan of the consultant, may enter into a contract for up to one temporary additional notional half-days (or fraction thereof) or, where appropriate, up to two temporary additional notional half-days (or fraction thereof), as provided for in paragraph 14 (as amended) of the Terms and Conditions of Service. Alternatively, a consultant who takes on additional clinical duties as a result of a consultant colleague dropping some clinical duties to take on such additional management responsibilities may, instead, qualify for one temporary additional notional half-day (or fraction thereof).

17. General managers of DHAs and SHAs should consider, when drawing up and agreeing job plans, which consultants may qualify for additional notional half-day(s) (or fractions thereof). Regional Health Authorities should monitor the operation of this new arrangement, including recording the numbers agreed, to ensure consistency across the Region. The amendments to paragraph 14 of the Terms and Conditions of Service are shown in *Annex C*.

NHS trusts
18. Subject to the passage of the necessary legislation, NHS trusts will be responsible for arranging the duties of the consultants they employ, whether under existing contractual provisions or under such arrangements as the parties may agree.'

17.7.2   Junior hospital medical and dental staff

The pay and conditions of service of junior hospital medical and dental staff are regulated by Circular HC(PC)(76)15, which contains detailed amendments to the relevant Whitley Council terms and conditions. For full detail reference should be made to the Circular, which contains a recommended form of model contract and a recommended model claim form for payments as on a locum basis.

Of particular relevance to the scope of this book is the amended form of paragraph 110 of the Whitley Council terms and conditions of service in respect of such staff, given the attention which has recently been paid to long hours worked by junior hospital staff:

Paragraph 110
Senior Registrar, Registrar, Senior House Officer and House Officer
(b) Subject to paragraphs 112 and 113 and sub-paragraphs (c) to (e) below, practitioners in the grades of Senior Registrar, Registrar, Senior House Officer and House Officer shall be expected in the normal run of their duties, and within their contract and job description, to cover for the occasional brief absence of colleagues as far as is practicable.

(c) Account should as necessary be taken in their job description of the need for them to provide cover for annual or study leave of colleagues, provides always that the resulting increase in duties is reasonable in the circumstances.

(d) In addition, they will be prepared to perform duties in occasional emergencies and unforeseen circumstances without additional remuneration in accordance with the provisions of circular DS 378/75. Commitments arising under these provisions are however exceptional and practitioners should not be required to undertake work of this kind for prolonged periods or on a regular basis.

(e) In circumstances other than those in (b) to (d) above, the employing authority (and not the practitioner) shall be responsible for the engagement of a locum tenens to undertake work which in their view must be carried out, but the practitioner shall have the responsibility of bringing the need to their notice. The practitioners involved shall assess the number of units of medical time required and shall recommend accordingly to the employing authority. Practitioners may be employed as on a locum basis by their own employing authority in their own hospitals but not within the hours for which they are already contracted.

(f) Arrangements for engaging locums should, wherever practicable, be made in advance of need.'

For the question of over-long hours and the effect on a health service employer, see Chapter 20, pp. 559–560.

17.8 TERMINATION OF THE CONTRACTS OF HOSPITAL MEDICAL AND DENTAL STAFF

Annex C of Circular HC(90)9, which relates principally to disciplinary procedures, sets out a revised version of paragraph 190 of the terms and conditions of service for hospital medical and dental staff, as follows:

'Paragraph 19.
a. Subject to sub-paragraph (c), a consultant, SHMO, SHDO, AS, child psychiatrist appointed to a personal substantive grade under circular HC(79)7 or hospital practitioner who considers that his appointment is being unfairly terminated may appeal to the Secretary of State against the termination by sending to him a notice of appeal at any time during the period of notice of termination of his appointment.

b. A practitioner appealing under sub-paragraph (a) shall also send a full statement of the facts of his case to the Secretary of State within—

i.   the period of 4 months beginning with the date on which he received notice of termination of his contract, or
ii. where the Secretary of State is satisfied that it was not reasonably practicable for a statement of facts to be presented before the end of that period of 4 months, such further period as the Secretary of State may permit.

If he fails to do so, the appeal shall be treated as having been determined by a decision confirming the termination of his appointment.

c. There is no right of appeal under sub-paragraph (a) where—

i.   the practitioner is ordinarily required to work in the hospital and community health service (HCHS) for no more than 5 NHDs and he has income from other NHS medical or dental work equal to or greater than the income from the appointment being terminated,* or

ii.   subject to sub-paragraphs (d) and (e), where the termination is on the sole ground of personal misconduct.*

* Section 40 of the General Whitley Council Terms and Conditions provided a mechanism for appeal where a practitioner is excluded by this provision from an appeal under paragraph 190. Where such an appeal is made, the panel set up by the employing authority should include one professional member appointed from outside the Authority at the same grade and in the same (or related) specialty as the practitioner concerned.

"**Personal misconduct**": for the purposes of this paragraph shall mean "performance or behaviour of practitioners due to factors other than those associated with the exercise of medical or dental skills".

d. A practitioner who considers that his appointment is being unfairly terminated on the sole ground of personal misconduct and who does not agree that his conduct could reasonably be described as personal misconduct may, within the period of 1 month beginning with the date on which he received notice of termination of his employment, require the Secretary of State to refer to a panel the question whether his appointment is being terminated on the sole ground of personal misconduct.

e. The panel shall comprise the Chief Medical Officer or Chief Dental Officer of the Department (as appropriate), the Chairman of the Joint Consultants Committee, or their deputies, and a barrister or solicitor not in the employment of the government legal service or any Health Authority. The panel shall decide whether or not the termination is on the sole ground of personal misconduct and notify the practitioner and the Authority terminating the appointment ("the Authority") accordingly. If the panel decides that the termination is not on the sole ground of personal misconduct, the practitioner may (if he has not already done so) appeal in accordance with sub-paragraph (a) within the period of one month beginning with the date of the notification to him of the panel's decision and the time allowed for the purposes of sub-paragraph (b) shall be two months from the date of such notification.

f. On receipt of a notice of appeal from a practitioner entitled under sub-paragraph (a) and (c) to appeal the Secretary of State shall—

i.   request the Authority to give its written views on the case;
ii.   refer the case for advice to a professional committee consisting of representatives of the Secretary of State and representatives of the practitioner's profession and chaired by the Chief Medical Officer or Chief Dental Officer of the Department or their deputies.

g. The Authority shall send to the Secretary of State its written views ("the Authority's views") within the period of 2 months following the date of the request made in accordance with sub-paragraph (f)(i) ("the request date"). If the Authority fails to do so and unless the Secretary of State extends the period for such further period as he thinks reasonable in a case where he is satisfied that it was not reasonably practicable for the Authority's views to be presented within 2 months from the request date, the appeal shall be treated as having been determined by a decision to direct that the practitioner's appointment be continued.

h. The professional committee—

i.   shall be assisted by a barrister or solicitor;
ii.   may, if it thinks fit, interview the practitioner and representatives of the Authority;
iii. shall, so far as is reasonably practicable, hold any such interview no earlier than one month, and no later than three months, after receipt by the Secretary of State of the Authority's views;
iv.   shall give its advice to the Secretary of State.

i. Where it appears to the professional committee that a solution other than confirmation of termination or continuance of the appointment may be appropriate, it shall:

i.   ascertain as far as possible the extent to which such a solution is likely to be acceptable to the practitioner and the Authority, and
ii.   include in any advice given to the Secretary of State to arrange such a solution its assessment of the extent to which it would prove acceptable to the practitioner and the Authority.

j. In the light of the professional committee's advice, the Secretary of State shall, as far as is reasonably practicable, within the period of 3 months of the date of the professional committee having considered the case—

i.   confirm the termination of the practitioner's appointment;
ii.   direct that the practitioner's appointment continue; or
iii. arrange some other solution agreeable to the practitioner and the Authority.

k. The termination of the practitioner's appointment shall not have effect while an appeal duly made in accordance with sub-paragraph (a) or a matter duly referred in accordance with sub-paragraph (d) is under consideration. Where a decision is not given before the expiry of the period of notice of termination of the appointment, the notice shall be extended by the Authority until the decision is given (and, in the case of a referral under sub-paragraph (d) until any time allowed by sub-paragraph (e) for appealing has expired). If the Secretary of State so directs, the period of notice shall be further extended as he may direct in a case where he gives a decision to arrange a solution other than confirming the termination of the practitioner's appointment or directing that his appointment continue.'

17.9   DISCIPLINARY PROCEEDINGS IN CASES RELATING TO HOSPITAL MEDICAL AND DENTAL STAFF

Guidance is given in Circular HC(90)9 on the procedure to be followed in serious disciplinary cases involving hospital, public health and community health doctors or dentists.

'This Annex B replaces HM(61)112 and outlines the procedures which Health Authorities should use when handling serious disciplinary charges, for example, where the outcome of disciplinary action could be the dismissal of the medical or dental practitioner concerned. For such cases Authorities should also apply the guidance contained in Section 40 of the General Whitley Council Terms and Conditions. The lines of procedure proposed are designed to ensure that justice is done and seen to be done and injustice avoided in respect of all the parties concerned (patient, practitioner and employer).

The arrangements described are without prejudice to the right of the Authority to take immediate action (e.g. suspension from duty) where this is required in cases of a very serious nature.

There are broadly three types of case which may involve medical or dental staff:

— cases involving personal conduct;
— cases involving professional conduct;
— cases involving professional competence.

It is for the Authority to decide under which category a case falls. Guidance on the definition of each category is given in paragraph 3 of the Circular.

Cases involving personal conduct

In cases involving personal conduct, the position of a doctor or dentist is no different from that of other health service staff. Accordingly, provisions from time to time applicable to health service staff generally (at present those set out in Section 40 of the General Whitley Council Terms and Conditions) also apply in such cases.'

17.9.1 Cases involving professional conduct and professional competence

Circular HC(90)9 provides:

'Preliminary investigation – Establishment of prima facie case

The first step when an incident occurs or a complaint is made involving the professional conduct or competence of a medical or dental officer should be for the Chairman of the Health Authority to decide whether there is a prima facie case which, if well founded, could result in serious disciplinary action such as dismissal. Such preliminary inquiries if any as are necessary before this decision is reached should be in the hands of the Regional or District Director of Public Health (DPH) on behalf of the Regional or District Health Authority, whichever is the appointing authority. In appropriate cases, the legal adviser or solicitor to the Authority should be called in to assist. Where the matter arises from an incident for which an accident report has been made in accordance with HM(55)66, the Chairman, before reaching his decision, should have regard to the accident report, but normally no subsequent use should be made of the report in the proceedings, except insofar as it is used by the appointing authority's solicitors in preparing the case to be presented to the investigating panel (see paragraph 8 below).

6. Unless the Chairman decides forthwith that there is no prima facie case, the doctor or dentist should be warned in writing immediately of the nature of the incident which has been alleged, or of the complaint which has been made, and that the question of an inquiry, which might lead to serious disciplinary action, is under consideration. Copies of all relevant correspondence should be sent to the practitioner, and he should be informed that any comments made by him

will be placed before the Chairman and any investigating panel which may be appointed. The practitioner should be given reasonable time to make representations and to seek advice if he so wishes before any final decision is taken on whether an inquiry is necessary.

7. If, on considering the allegation or complaint made and the practitioner's comments, if any, in reply to the written warning given in accordance with paragraph 6, the Chairman decides that a prima facie case exists, and that there is a dispute as to the facts, the Authority should proceed to an inquiry, as in paragraphs 8–15. If the Chairman decides that a prima facie case exists, but there is no substantial dispute as to the facts, any subsequent disciplinary action which the Authority may take should comply with the guidance contained in GWC [General Whitley Council] Section 40. An inquiry on the lines laid down in paragraphs 8–15 below would normally be unnecessary also where, in a matter affecting the practitioner's professional conduct or competence, the facts in question have been the subject of a criminal charge on which he has been found guilty in a court of law or have been established by a public inquiry set up by the Government. Where the facts have been established by a public inquiry and there is a dispute as to whether further facts need to be established or as to the conclusion to be drawn from the facts, an investigating panel set up in accordance with paragraphs 8 and 9 below will consider if a further inquiry is required (in which case they will proceed in accordance with paragraphs 10–15 below). Where the panel consider that no further inquiry is required they will proceed in accordance with paragraphs 14–18 below.

Inquiry

8. An investigating panel, the composition of which should differ with the type of inquiry, should be set up by the Authority responsible for appointing the practitioner. No member of the panel should be associated with the hospital(s) in which he works, or, in the case of a doctor in Public Health Medicine or the Community Health Service, in the Authority in which the practitioner concerned works. In all cases the panel should be small, normally of three persons, including a legally qualified Chairman, not being either an officer of the Department of Health or a member or officer of the Authority concerned, who will be nominated in each case which arises by the Secretary of State from a panel appointed by the Lord Chancellor. In cases involving professional conduct, the members other than the Chairman should contain an equal proportion of professional and lay persons, unless the charges relate only to relationships between a doctor or a dentist and his professional colleagues, when it would clearly be appropriate to have a panel wholly of predominantly of professional members, apart from the Chairman. In cases involving solely professional competence, all the other members should be professionally qualified, and it will probably be appropriate that at least one of their number should be in the same specialty as the practitioner whose professional competence has been called in question; it may also be appropriate that one of them should be a practitioner from another hospital in the same grade. Before the professional members are chosen, there should be consultation with the Joint Consultants Committee (JCC) or Community Medicine Consultative Committee (CMCC) as appropriate. In the case of a dental officer, the appointment of the professional member should be made after consultation with the appropriate group of the British Dental Association.

9. Payment should be made by the Authority to the Chairman and members of

the panel at a rate determined from time to time. This fee covers any preparatory work required and any time spent on preparation of reports. Travelling and subsistence expenses of both the Chairman and members of the panel should be payable in accordance with the National Health Service and English and Welsh National Boards for Nursing, Midwifery and Health Visiting (Travelling) Allowances etc. Determination 1983.

10. The terms of reference of the panel should include the nature of the incident or complaint against the practitioner, who should be informed of the setting up of the panel and its terms of reference and given not less than 21 days' notice in order to prepare his case. He should be provided as soon as possible with any copies of correspondence or written statements made. A copy of the list of witnesses referred to in paragraph 11, and the main points on which they can give evidence, should be furnished to the practitioner as long as possible before the hearing if he so requests, unless for any exceptional reason the Chairman of the panel gives authority for the names of the witnesses not to be provided in advance of the hearing.

11. The investigating panel should be held in private, and should establish all the relevant facts of the case. To that end, the panel should ensure, as far as possible, that colleagues of the practitioner should be asked to give factual evidence, rather than personal impressions or opinions. A list of witnesses should be drawn up with the main points on which they are to give evidence; in the case of a Regional Health Authority, this task might with advantage be undertaken by the legal adviser or solicitor to the Authority, assisted by the Regional Director of Public Health. Subsequently at the hearing, the case should be presented by the legal adviser or solicitor, who should conduct an examination of the witnesses before the investigating panel. In the case of other Authorities, these tasks would no doubt be undertaken by the Authority's solicitor acting on the instructions of the Authority. The Authority and/or the practitioner may be represented before the panel by a lawyer, although both sides should make efforts to reduce the formality of the proceedings and the consequent time they take.

12. The practitioner should have the right to appear personally before the investigating panel and to be represented (either by a lawyer in accordance with paragraph 11 above, or otherwise), and to hear all the evidence presented to the panel. He should have the right to cross-examine all witnesses and to produce his own witnesses, and they and he may also be subjected to cross-examination. The question of what is to happen upon any application for adjournment in the event of the illness or unavoidable absence of the practitioner, or any witness, should be a matter for the Chairman to decide in accordance with the normal procedures for similar inquiries.

13. The procedure and rules as regards the admission of evidence before the investigating panel should be determined by the Chairman who may, if he wishes, hold a preliminary hearing with the parties (or their representatives) for the purpose.

14. The report of the investigating panel should be presented in 2 parts. The first part should set out the committee's findings and all the relevant facts of the case, but contain no recommendations as to action. The second part should contain a view as to whether the practitioner is at fault, and may, at the request of the Authority appointing the panel, contain recommendations as to disciplinary action. In no circumstances should the investigating panel itself be given disciplinary powers.

15. The panel should send the practitioner a copy of the first part of their report, and should allow a period of 4 weeks for the submission to them of any proposals for corrections of fact, or for setting out in greater detail the facts on any particular matter which has arisen. It would be for the panel to decide whether to accept any proposed amendments and whether any further hearing was necessary to enable them thus to decide. Subject to this procedure, the facts as set out in the panel's report should be accepted as established in any subsequent consideration of the matter.

16. The Authority should then receive the full report of the investigating panel and decide what action to take. In the event of the investigating panel finding that the practitioner is at fault, the substance of their views on the case and recommendations in the second part of their report should be made available to him in good time before the meeting of the Authority, and he should be given the opportunity to put to them any plea which he may wish to make in mitigation before they reach any conclusion as to action.

17. The Departments and the professions are concerned at the length of time some hearings take before conclusion. In all cases, it has been agreed with the professions that the following time limits will apply to each stage, and in all cases, the time taken from the decision that there is a prima facie case to referral to the Health Authority should not exceed 32 weeks:

a.	Chairman decides that there is a prima facie case and informs the practitioner		
b.	Practitioner comments on the case	–	within 4 weeks
c.	After receipt of comments, Health Authority decides to follow this procedure	–	within 2 weeks
d.	Health Authority appoints Chairman and rest of inquiry panel; and panel meets	–	within 3 months
e.	Hearing is concluded	–	within 1 week
f.	Report is produced and factual part sent to practitioner	–	within 4 weeks
g.	Practitioner makes comments	–	within 4 weeks
h.	Report goes to Health Authority	–	within 4 weeks

18. These provisions are without prejudice to the provisions of paragraph 190 of the Terms and Conditions of Service of Hospital Medical and Dental Staff and Doctors in Community Medicine and the Community Health Service (England and Wales).'

An employee may appeal pursuant to paragraph 190 against the decision of an authority to terminate the contract of employment with notice; but no such right exists in the case of the summary dismissal.[50]

17.9.2 Professional review machinery

Circular HC(90)9 introduces for the first time, in Annex D, an informal professional review procedure to review the conduct of hospital consultants who are alleged to have failed repeatedly to honour their contractual commitments. The procedure is in addition to, and does not replace, either health authorities' existing powers to take disciplinary action or the arrangements for dealing with sick doctors outlined in HC(82)13. This procedure applies from the date of the Circular (namely

March 1990) and may include the investigation of acts or omissions which occurred before that date.

17.9.3 Intermediate procedure

Annex E introduces a new procedure for dealing with cases of professional misconduct and professional incompetence which warrant disciplinary action short of dismissal. This procedure also applies from the date of the Circular and may include the investigation of acts or omissions which have occurred before that date.

In practical terms, as Annex E explains, the new procedure involves the use of independent professional assessors, nominated by the Joint Consultants Committee, who would be invited by the Director of Public Health (on behalf of the employing authority) to investigate and advise him on matters involving professional conduct or competence. The assessors themselves would have no disciplinary powers. The procedure could be used both in cases where there is a specific disciplinary allegation against a consultant or consultants and where there are problems arising from differing professional views within a department.

17.10 THE WHITLEY COUNCILS FOR THE HEALTH SERVICES

17.10.1 The Whitley Councils

A great many aspects of the terms, conditions and incidents of employment within the National Health Service are governed by non-statutory arrangements and agreements which, however, have the approval of the Secretary of State for Health under enabling powers set out in the National Health Service Act 1977. There is a General Council as well as ten functional Councils which deal with particular groups of persons engaged in the health services, namely: administrative and clerical; ancillary staffs; dental (local authorities); medical and (hospital) dental; nurses and midwives; optical; pharmaceutical; professional and technical (divided into A and B); and ambulance.

Under the earlier structure of the National Health Service, the Secretary of State for Social Services, the Secretary of State for Wales and the Secretary of State for Scotland have approved the General Council agreements incorporated in the Handbook under the National Health Service (Remuneration and Conditions of Service) Regulations 1991[40] and under paragraph 11 of Schedule 3 of the National Health Service Act 1977 and the corresponding Scottish Regulations 1991.[51]

The General Council deals with National Health Service staff conditions of service of general application and other than those allocated to functional Councils. The General Council's scope and membership are set out in the Main Constitution for the Whitley Councils for the Health Services (Great Britain), which is reproduced as an Appendix to the Handbook.

General Council agreements apply to all employees within the purview of the Whitley Councils for the Health Services (Great Britain), except where provision is made to the contrary. National Health Service Works Maintenance Staff (Craftsmen and Assistants) are not within the purview of the Whitley Councils for the Health Services (Great Britain) but by agreement with the unions concerned the terms of a number of General Council agreements are applied to them. A list of the agreements which are applied to them is set out as an Appendix to the *Pay and Conditions of Service Handbook* applicable to those trades.

General Council agreements apply to hospital medical and dental staff only if the Staff Side representatives of Committee B of the Medical and (Hospital) Dental Whitley Council on the General Council so agree. A list of the agreements which apply to hospital medical and dental staff, and in what way, is set out as an Appendix to the *Hospital Medical and Dental Staff (England and Wales) Terms and Conditions of Service Handbook* and the *Hospital Medical and Dental Staff (Scotland) Terms and Conditions of Service Handbook*. For doctors in community medicine and the community health services, and for administrative dental and community clinical dental officers, General Council agreements apply with the agreement of the Joint Negotiating Body for Doctors in Community Medicine and the Community Health Services, and the Joint Negotiating Forum for the Community Dental Services respectively.

The functions of the ten individual Councils are as follows:

1. To secure the greatest possible measure of co-operation between the management and staff of the health services with a view to increasing efficiency and ensuring the well-being of those employed in the services.
2. To provide machinery for the consideration of remuneration and conditions of service of persons within the ambit of paragraph 10 of Schedule 5 to the National Health Service Act 1977 as amended, section 66 of the National Health Service Act 1946 as amended and having effect pursuant to the provisions of section 15 of the National Health Service Reorganisation Act 1973 or paragraphs 7 and 8 or Schedule 5 to the National Health Service (Scotland) Act 1978 as amended.
3. To provide machinery for the consideration of the remuneration of persons with whom arrangements may be made pursuant to Part II of the National Health Service Act 1977 or Part II of the National Health Service (Scotland) Act 1978.
4. To provide machinery also for the consideration of the remuneration and conditions of employment of any persons whom the General Council may from time to time decide to admit within its scope.

Scope of each Council

Paragraph 10 of the Main Constitution provides:

'10.1 Subject to 10.2 and 10.3 below, each of the functional Councils specified in

Clause 1.2 above shall determine remuneration and all conditions of service requiring national decision affecting directly only those persons comprised within its group.

10.2 Where conditions of service other than remuneration affect more than one functional Council and less than ten, those conditions of service may be determined by the functional Councils concerned acting together.

10.3 Where conditions of service and remuneration are of general application they shall be determined by the General Council.'

17.10.2 Legal status of Whitley terms and conditions

It is to be noted that, in respect of each of the provisions which are set out in this section, any Whitley agreement approved by the Secretary of State becomes a statutorily binding condition of employment of all officers to which it applies.

17.10.3 Joint consultation machinery

Joint Staff Consultative Committees are not local Whitley Councils and are not empowered to make recommendations which conflict with or override any decision of a Whitley Council. Nor may the recommendations of Joint Staff Consultative Committees cover matters which are properly the subject of national negotiations. Nevertheless, the General Council reaffirms in the *Handbook* that joint consultation between management and representatives of recognised staff organisations benefit both sides and is essential to the smooth working of the National Health Service. The General Council have therefore agreed that joint consultative machinery should be set up at all the appropriate levels in the National Health Service. In so reaffirming, the General Council recognises that in many places joint consultative machinery already exists, and where management and representatives of recognised staff organisations agree that existing arrangements are satisfactory, these should be left alone unchanged.

Joint consultative machinery provides an opportunity for representatives of National Health Service employees and to members of recognised staff organisations to meet management representatives to discuss matters of common interest. Nothing in the joint consultative machinery should prejudice the right of any recognised staff organisation to negotiate directly with a recognised Whitley Council on an appropriate matter.

17.10.4 Selected terms and conditions relating to leave from the Whitley Council's *General Handbook*

The following are the principal provisions of the terms and conditions selected as relating to leave. Reference should be made to the *Handbook* for the full details of each provision.

Special leave: Section 3

1. Employing authorities shall make available special leave with pay to staff required to be absent from duty for essential civic and public duties of the kinds listed in Section 29 of the Employment Protection (Consolidation) Act 1978 and as required by other legislation. In determining the maximum amount of such paid leave employing authorities shall have regard to existing practice as informed by Section 29(4) of the Employment Protection (Consolidation) Act 1978. Examples of the duties listed in Section 29 of the Employment Protection (Consolidation) Act 1978 are attached in an Annex to this agreement.

2. In addition to these provisions, special leave with pay shall be made available in the following circumstances.

- Absence from duty following contact with a case of notifiable disease;
- attendance at court as a witness;
- training with the reserve and cadet forces;
- attendance at Whitley Council meetings;
- attendance as a witness at appeal hearings;
- attendance at meetings of community health councils or, in Scotland, local health councils.

3. Special leave for any other circumstances may be granted (with or without pay) at the discretion of the employing authority.

Procedures

4. Each health authority should provide clear guidelines in consultation with staff and local staff representatives on the length of special leave which would normally be available, whether it should be paid or unpaid and on the procedures for applying for such leave. The application of these guidelines will have to take account of the particular needs and circumstances of each individual.

Examples of the public duties for which special paid leave shall be given, under the terms of Section 29 of the Employment Protection (Consolidation) 1978 (as amended):

(a) serving as a justice of the peace;
(b) membership of a local authority;
(c) membership of the Broads Authority;
(d) membership of any statutory tribunal;
(e) membership of a Board of Prison Visitors (England and Wales) or a prison visiting committee (Scotland);
(f) membership of a National Health Service Trust, a Regional or District Health Authority, or Family Health Services Authority or (in Scotland) a Health Board;
(g) membership of, in England and Wales, the managing or governing body of an educational establishment maintained by a local education authority or, in Scotland, a school or college council or the governing body of a designated or central institution;
(h) membership of the governing body of a grant-maintained school, further or higher education corporation, or of a school board or board of management of a college of further education or self-governing school;
(i) membership of, in England and Wales, the National Rivers Authority or, in Scotland, a river purification board.

For further details please see the text of the Act [and see SI 1990/1870: Time Off for Public Duties Order].

Special leave for domestic, personal and family reasons: section 12

1. The General Whitley Council attaches considerable importance to each health authority drawing up clear policies for the consideration and approval of special leave for domestic, personal and family matters. The objective of such leave is to help staff balance the demands of domestic and work responsibilities at times of urgent and unforeseen need through the provision of paid or unpaid leave according to circumstances. Leave granted under these arrangements is not intended for long term domestic and family needs which may be provided, for example, by the retainer scheme arrangements (Section 10).

Range of leave provision

2. Examples of special leave under this heading may be:

Carer leave

The aim of such leave is to provide a compassionate response to immediate needs. The leave will be essentially short term and normally with pay. The needs covered will be those arising from the many and varied domestic situations which from time to time arise, e.g. bereavement; illness of a child, close relative or dependant; breakdown of normal carer arrangements; making arrangements for longer term coping with a care problem.

Adoption leave

The nature and period of this leave will be largely determined by (1) the requirements of the formal adoption procedures, (2) when the child first comes under the adoptive parents full time care and attention, (3) the age of the child and any special home care needs. There may be other special and particular needs to be taken into account.

Paternity leave

Such leave may be made available at the time of the birth, or if more helpful to the family, in the weeks following the birth, e.g. when the mother and baby leave hospital.

Procedures

3. Each health authority should provide clear guidelines in consultation with staff and local staff representatives on the length of special leave which would normally be available, whether it should be paid or unpaid and on the procedures for applying for such leave. The application of these guidelines will have to take account of the particular needs and circumstances of each individual.

Appeals

4. Any appeals arising from the application of this agreement will be for resolution through local grievance procedures, and shall not be appealable beyond employing authority level.

Entitlement to maternity leave with pay: Section 6

3. An employee working full-time or working part-time under arrangements which entitle her to paid leave in respect of normal sick absence shall be entitled to maternity leave with pay, provided that she:

3.1   continues to be employed by the employing authority until immediately before the beginning of the eleventh week before the expected week of confinement;

3.2   has completed at that time, without a break in service, 12 months' service in the employment of one or more employing authorities or local authorities;

3.3   notifies the employing authority in writing not less than 21 days before the commencement of maternity leave (or if this is not possible, as soon as is reasonably practicable) that she intends to take maternity leave and return to work, after her confinement, for the same or another employing authority for a minimum period of three months;

3.4   submits a statement from a registered medical practitioner or practising midwife not less than 21 days before the commencement of maternity leave indicating the expected date of confinement, or if this is not possible, as soon as is reasonably practicable.

Entitlement to maternity leave only

4. A woman employee who does not satisfy the conditions in paragraph 3.2 shall be entitled to unpaid maternity leave for a period not exceeding eighteen weeks.

Timing of leave and related matters

5. Maternity leave shall normally commence at the beginning of the eleventh week before the expected week of confinement. However, an employee may, with the agreement of her employing authority, which shall not be unreasonably refused, and subject to the production of written evidence from a registered medical practitioner or a practising midwife of her capacity to continue in her normal employment, postpone the commencement of her maternity leave for such period as the medical practitioner or practising midwife considers appropriate.

6. Where a confinement occurs prior to the eleventh week before the expected week of confinement, Maternity Leave shall commence from the beginning of the actual week of confinement. Prior absence supported by a medical statement of incapacity for work, or a self-certificate, shall be treated as sick leave in accordance with the sick leave agreement to which the employee is conditioned. If the employee has worked in the actual week of confinement and is therefore entitled to payment in respect of the work done, the Maternity Leave shall commence from the first day of absence in the week of confinement. With the agreement of her employing authority, an employee whose confinement has occurred prior to the eleventh week before the expected week of confinement and whose child is in hospital may choose to split her Maternity Leave entitlement, taking a short period of leave immediately after confinement and then returning to work to take the balance of leave following the child's discharge from hospital.

7. Where in the period prior to the eleventh week before the expected week of confinement an employee is, in the opinion of a registered medical practitioner, incapable of carrying out all or part of her duties, or where the employing authority or the registered medical practitioner consider that she or the unborn child would be at risk were she to continue in her normal duties but the employee is not advised to refrain from work by a registered medical practitioner, the employing authority shall, except where it is not reasonably practicable, provide alternative work for which she should receive her normal

rate of pay even though the work done might normally attract a lower rate of pay. This provision shall only continue after the eleventh week before the expected week of confinement by mutual agreement between the employee and her employing authority.

8. An employing authority shall be entitled to receive written confirmation of the actual date of confinement, and this shall be provided on written request, as soon as is reasonably practicable.

Sick absence during pregnancy and maternity leave

9. Where an employee is absent on sick leave during the period from the beginning of the eleventh week before the expected week of confinement until the date in paragraph 11 below, her absence shall be treated as Maternity Leave and entitlement under the normal sick leave provisions shall be suspended during this period.

10. Where an employee has chosen to work beyond the eleventh week before the expected week of confinement, absence on account of sickness after the eleventh week which is certified as unrelated to pregnancy shall be dealt with in accordance with the normal provisions for paid sick absence. Such absence shall be treated as sick leave until the date previously agreed that she should commence Maternity Leave. If the illness is attributable to pregnancy then Maternity Leave shall commence from the fourth day of such absence, the first three days being dealt with in accordance with the normal sick leave provisions.

11. Where an employee submits a medical statement from a registered medical practitioner, or a self-certificate, to cover absence from:

11.1   the date she has notified her employing authority that she will return to work following confinement; or

11.2   the date she and the authority have agreed that she will return; or

11.3   where no date has been notified or agreed, the first day following the maximum period of Maternity Leave to which she is entitled,

she will be entitled to sick leave in accordance with the normal sick leave provisions.

Return to work

19. An employing authority shall be entitled to send a written request to the employee, not earlier than 49 days from the date of the expected week of confinement or the date of confinement, asking the employee to confirm in writing that she intends to return. If the authority does write asking for confirmation and in the course of the request explains to her the effect of this provision on her right to return, she must give the written confirmation asked for within 14 days of receiving the request (or, if this is not possible, as soon as is reasonably practicable).

20. An employee must inform her employing authority of the date she proposes to return, in writing, at least 21 days before that date.

21. An employee who has notified her intention to return to work has the right to return to her job under her original contract and on no less favourable terms and conditions. However, she may return to work on any basis agreed with the employing authority, including part-time working and job sharing, and the General Whitley Council believes that authorities should wherever possible meet the expectation of women wanting to return under more flexible working arrangements. Authorities should ensure that, following maternity leave, women returning part-time or as a job share return at a grade commensurate with their leaving grade and to work of similar status.

Failure to return to work

22. If an employee who has notified her authority of her intention to return to work does not do so or, where she has notified her intention to return to another authority, fails to submit to her former authority a copy of her letter of appointment to another authority within 15 months of the beginning of her Maternity Leave, she shall be liable to refund the whole of the Maternity Pay received, less any Statutory Maternity Pay to which she is entitled. However, in the case of an employee who has title to the six weeks' pay under paragraph 16 above, the six weeks' pay shall be deducted from the sum due for repayment. In cases where an employing authority considers that to enforce this provision would cause undue hardship or distress the authority shall have discretion to waive their right to recovery.

Miscellaneous provisions

Employees on fixed-term or training contracts

23. Employees subject to fixed-term or training contracts which expire after the eleventh week before the expected week of confinement and before six weeks after the expected week of confinement shall, subject to satisfying the conditions in paragraph 3 above, have their contracts extended so as to enable them to receive the eighteen weeks' paid Maternity Leave.

24. The contract will not be extended to cover a period of unpaid leave, but in the case of employees who have two or more years' continuous service of sixteen or more hours a week, or five or more years' service of between eight and sixteen hours a week, an absence prior to their return to work in their next appointment for up to 29 weeks commencing with the week in which the confinement occurs will not constitute a break in service for the purposes of this section.

25. Where a medical practitioner or other employee is participating in a planned rotation of appointments as part of an agreed programme of training, she shall have the right to return to work in the same post or in the next planned post with the same or another employing authority, irrespective of whether the contract would have ended if pregnancy and confinement had not occurred. In such circumstances, the contract will be extended to enable the practitioner to complete the agreed programme of training.

26. If there is no right of return to be exercised because the contract would have ended if pregnancy and confinement had not occurred, paragraph 22 above shall not apply unless the employing authority can demonstrate that the declaration of intent to return to work was not signed in good faith.

Compassionate leave

27. Employing authorities have discretion to grant special leave for domestic, personal and family needs in accordance with Section 12 of the General Council Handbook.

Annual leave

29. Only a period of paid Maternity Leave shall count towards the calculation of annual leave entitlement. Unpaid Maternity Leave shall count as service for the purpose of satisfying the service qualification for entitlement to additional annual leave based on years of service in accordance with functional Council agreements.

Ante-natal care

31. The employee has the right to leave and pay for ante-natal care as set out in Section 31A of the Employment Protection (Consolidation) Act.

Position of employees elected to Parliament: section 52

1. No special facilities shall be accorded to employees who become Members of Parliament. Such employees are not by reason of their office rendered incapable of being elected to Parliament or of sitting and voting as a Member of the House of Commons, and their position in regard to remaining in Health Service employment will therefore be governed by their ability or inability to continue to render the services appropriate to their posts.

2. It is recognised that full-time employees who are elected to Parliament will inevitably have to resign their Health Service appointments. In such cases the resignation must be unconditional and the employees, if they should seek re-employment on ceasing to be a Member of Parliament, shall have no claim to reinstatement either in their old posts or in any other post in the National Health Service.

Membership of local authorities: section 53

1. As the bodies constituted under the National Health Service and Health Services Acts are not in direct relationship with local authorities, there need be no objection as a general rule to National Health Service employees contesting local elections or taking part in local government activities, provided always that in the discharge of any local authority functions which impinge on the functions for which their Health Service employing authorities are responsible, due regard is had by the employees to the circumstances of their dual position.

2. Employees should seek the consent of their employing authorities before standing for election, but this consent should not be withheld except in cases where special circumstances make membership of the local authority undesirable.'

17.11 PROCEDURE FOR SETTLING DISPUTES RELATING TO CONDITIONS OF SERVICE

17.11.1 The disputes procedure

The principles and procedures contained in the Whitley Councils' *Handbook* include an agreed procedure for settling employment disputes, including disputes relating to grading, which is as follows:

'The agreed procedure for settling differences between employing authorities and individual employees within the purview of the Whitley Councils for the Health Services (Great Britain), where the difference relates to a matter affecting the employees' conditions of service, including questions of grading, is as follows:

1.1 Employees who are aggrieved in any matter affecting their conditions of service (other than dismissal or any disciplinary action) shall have the right of appeal to their employing authority (i.e. the authority by whom they were appointed) and of appearing personally before the authority, either alone, or with a representative of their professional organisation or trade union, or with a friend not appearing in a professional capacity. Without prejudice to the right of appeal to the authority thus conferred, the employee may first bring the subject of the appeal before any committee or sub-committee of the authority, or joint committee of the authority with their employees, appointed either generally or specially for the purpose of dealing with appeals.

1.2   Where, following such an appeal, an employee remains aggrieved, it shall be open to his or her professional organisation or trade union (being represented on the Whitley Councils for the Health Services (Great Britain) or otherwise a nationally recognised negotiating body) to appeal on his or her behalf to a Regional Appeals Committee, and no appeal received from any other body or direct from an individual employee shall be entertained.

The agreed terms of reference, constitution and procedure of Regional Appeals Committees are as follows:

2.1   *Terms of reference*   The function of a Regional Appeals Committee is to decide appeals on the local application of national conditions of service and of Whitley Council decisions, and in particular, on questions of grading, in cases where there is an unresolved dispute between an employing authority and any of their employees whose conditions of service are within the scope of the Whitley Councils for the Health Services (Great Britain). Regional Appeals Committees are not local Whitley Councils and are not competent to consider any appeals outside the scope of their terms of reference. Regional Appeals Committees have no power to deal with appeals against dismissal or any disciplinary action.

2.2   *Constitution*   The committee shall consist of not more than 6 members (8 members when appeals relating to employees within the purview of the Ancillary Staffs Council are being heard) appointed in equal numbers by the Management Side and the Staff Side. The members shall be chosen ad hoc for each meeting of the Committee in accordance with the procedure set out in 2.3 below, and shall appoint a chairman from their number.

2.3   The Management Side members shall be selected from a panel representative of the Regional Health Authority, the District Health Authorities in the area of the Regional Health Authority, Special Health Authorities, Family Health Service Authorities, the Department of Health and Social Security, the Scottish Home and Health Department, the Welsh Office, Health Boards and, where appropriate, the Common Services Agency, Scotland, the Welsh Health Technical Services Organisation, the Dental Estimates Board or the Prescription Pricing Authority.

   The Staff Side members shall be selected from representatives of the professional organisations and trade unions represented on the Whitley Councils for the Health Services (Great Britain) and having members employed by the authorities concerned, in such a manner as the Staff Side of the General Council of the Whitley Councils for the Health Services (Great Britain) may determine.

   The members selected shall in neither case include any member or employee of the authority directly concerned in the appeal.'

The procedure on receipt of an appeal is as follows:

'3. An appeal to the Regional Appeals Committee shall be lodged with the Management Side Secretary of the Committee within 3 months of the receipt by the employee of notice of the decision on the appeal made to the employing authority, and any appeal lodged after the expiry of the period shall not be considered unless the Management Side Secretary of the Regional Appeals Committee and the Staff Side Secretary of the appropriate Council of the Whitley Councils for the Health Services (Great Britain) so agree. If, however, the employing authority, having notified its decision, thereupon continues in discussion or negotiation in the matter with the employee or the employee's trade union or professional organisation, the period of 3 months shall not commence to run until a final decision has been communicated.

4. All appeals shall on receipt be reported forthwith by the Management Side Secretary of the Regional Appeals Committee to the appropriate Council through the Joint Secretaries of the Council.

5. The appropriate Council shall decide whether a particular appeal shall be dealt with by the Council as a matter of principle instead of by the Regional Appeals Committee.

6. Whenever the question of the competence of the Regional Appeals Committee to hear an appeal arises and cannot be resolved by the Management Side Secretary of the Regional Appeals Committee and the Staff Side Secretary of the Council concerned, the matter shall be referred to that Council.

7. If the two sides of a Council are unable to agree on a question of competence the appeal itself shall not be referred to the Regional Appeals Committee. It will be for the appellant organisation to take whatever steps it deems appropriate.

8. On receiving notice of an appeal, the Management Side Secretary of the Committee acting also on behalf of the Staff Side, shall invite both parties to the dispute to submit as soon as possible a written statement of case.

9. When both statements have been received, a copy of each statement shall be sent to each member of the Committee and to the Staff Side Secretary of the appropriate Whitley Council. Three copies of each statement shall also be sent to the two parties to the dispute together with a notification of the date and place of the hearing. At least 7 days' notice of the hearing shall be given.

Hearing of appeals

10. An appeal shall be heard by the Regional Appeals Committee as soon as possible, and shall in any event be heard within a period of 2 months from the date on which the appeal is received by the Management Side Secretary of the Committee unless an extension of this period is agreed upon by the Staff Side Secretary of the appropriate Council and the Management Side Secretary of the Committee.

11. The case for the employee shall be presented by a representative of the appellant organisation and the case for the employing authority shall be presented by a representative of the authority, but neither party shall be represented by a barrister or solicitor appearing in a professional capacity.

12. The two parties to the dispute shall be entitled to bring before the Committee such witnesses as they deem necessary to support their case.

13. If either party to the dispute fails to send a representative to the hearing, the Committee shall consider the appeal in the absence of that party, except where there is an adjournment by consent or the Committee in their discretion decide that in all the circumstances it would be reasonable to adjourn the appeal. In the event of any such adjournment, the Committee in fixing a new date should as far as practicable have regard to the convenience of the party who appeared for the original hearing.

Procedure at hearing

14. At the hearing of an appeal before the Committee, the following procedure shall be observed:

14.1 The representative of the appellant organisation shall state the case for the employee and call any witnesses.

14.2 The members of the Committee and the representative of the employing authority shall be entitled to question any witnesses called.

14.3 The representative of the appellant organisation may re-examine his or her witnesses on any matters referred to in their examination by members of the Committee or the representative of the employing authority.

14.4 The representative of the employing authority shall state the case for the authority and call any witnesses.

14.5 The members of the Committee and the representative of the appellant organisation shall be entitled to question any witnesses called.

14.6 The representative of the employing authority may re-examine his or her witnesses on any matters referred to in their examination by members of the Committee or the representative of the appellant organisation.

14.7 The representative of the appellant organisation shall be entitled to reply to the employing authority's case.

14.8 Nothing in the foregoing procedure shall prevent the members of the Committee from inviting the representative of either party to elucidate or amplify any statement he or she may have made; or from asking the representatives such questions as may be necessary to ascertain whether or not they propose to call any evidence in respect of any part of their statements, or, alternatively, whether they are in fact claiming that the matters are within their own knowledge, in which case they will be subject to examination as witnesses under 14.2 or 14.5 above.

14.9 The Committee may at their discretion adjourn an appeal in order that further evidence may be produced by either party to the dispute.

14.10 The Regional Appeals Committee shall fully consider the appeal in the light of any relevant condition of service determined by the Whitley Councils for the Health Services (Great Britain). It shall be open to the Committee to seek guidance from the appropriate Council of the Whitley Councils for the

Health Services (Great Britain) on any question of interpretation of the Councils' recommendations.

14.11   The Committee shall consider their decision in private and reach it by agreement of both sides. If an immediate decision cannot be given it shall be communicated in writing to both parties within 7 days of the hearing by the Management Side Secretary of the Committee acting also on behalf of the Staff Side. If the Committee fail to reach a decision, the fact shall be communicated to both parties in the same manner.

14.12   In the event of the Committee failing to reach a decision, it shall be open to either party to the dispute to refer the matter for consideration by the appropriate Council of the Whitley Councils for the Health Services (Great Britain).

Procedure when no decision is reached by the Regional Appeals Committee

15. A reference to the appropriate Whitley Council shall be made within 3 months of the receipt by the parties of notice of the failure of the Regional Appeals Committee to reach a decision on the appeal, and any reference made after the expiry of that period shall not be considered unless the Joint Secretaries of the Council so agree.

16. An appeal referred to the appropriate Whitley Council shall be heard as soon as possible, and shall in any event be heard within a period of 2 months from the date on which the reference is received by the Joint Secretaries of the Council unless an extension of this period is agreed upon by the Joint Secretaries.

17. The appropriate Council of the Whitley Councils for the Health Services (Great Britain), or any Committee of the Council which the Council may designate for the purpose, shall fully consider an appeal referred to the Council under these provisions. In the event of a failure to reach a decision on the appeal, it shall be open to either party to the dispute to refer the matter to arbitration in accordance with the terms of any arbitration agreement which may be made by the General Council of the Whitley Councils for the Health Services (Great Britain).'

The two parties to the dispute shall be responsible for meeting their own expenses and those of their witnesses.

What has never been tested in the courts is the effect of a decision of a regional or national appeals committee that an officer is entitled to be upgraded, because of the nature of his duties. One view is that, recourse having been had to the appeals machinery in accordance with the Whitley agreement, the decision of the appeals committee is binding on both parties and could be enforced by the court; the other is that the decision is advisory only and not binding on the respondent health authority unless accepted by that authority or unless it is directed by the Secretary of State. It would only be if on some occasion the Secretary of State refused to see that effect was given to the decision of an appeals committee that this question could arise in practice.

17.11.2 Machinery for the resolution of otherwise unresolved disputes

Some disputes may remain unresolved by the procedures which have just been described. In a general statement the *Handbook* says:

'The General Whitley Council attaches great importance to the establishment of clear procedures for settling disputes between employing authorities and employees and which cannot be resolved through the existing Whitley appeals machinery which is designed to deal with the local application of national Whitley agreements. In determining the content of local procedures, employing authorities and recognised staff organisations should take account of the following provisions.

Disputes procedures

The levels to which a dispute should be referred should be spelt out clearly in agreements and the General Whitley Council confirms the principle that disputes should be settled at the lowest possible operational level. The General Council recommends the following stages:

3.1 referral to the immediate local manager responsible for the staff who are in dispute;

3.2 referral to the next-in-line manager (i.e. the officer to whom the immediate local manager is responsible);

3.3 referral to the responsible Chief Officer of the employing authority who should, as necessary, consult other members of the management team (Executive Group in Scotland);

3.4 referral to the employing authority.

Appeals procedure

If the procedures outlined in paragraph 3 have been exhausted, it shall be open to either party to refer the dispute to a locally convened panel. The location of the panel should be settled by agreement between representatives of staff and management.

The panel should consist of an independent person in the Chair acceptable to both Sides and two members on each Side, appointed by the employing authority and the recognised staff organisation(s) concerned. In the case of a dispute involving more than two recognised staff organisations, not more than four members should be appointed from each Side. Only one on each Side may be drawn from members or employees of the authority concerned in the dispute. Persons directly involved in the dispute should not be members of the appeals panel.

The role of the independent person in the Chair would be that of a conciliator. He or she would be expected, with the assistance of other members of the panel, to explore the various issues giving rise to the dispute with a view to an agreed settlement. Recommendations would be made as a result of an agreement of both Sides of the panel.

Should the panel be unable to resolve the dispute, it may be referred to ACAS, by either party to the dispute for conciliation, or by joint agreement of the parties to the dispute for arbitration.'

Where there is failure to agree, either in negotiations in a NHS Whitley Council or in a national appeals committee, the matter is sometimes referred to the ACAS; but this can be done only if, in the case of disagreement in a Whitley Council, both sides agree to the reference or, in the case of failure of a national appeals committee to reach a decision, both parties to the dispute agree to such reference. If, in the latter case, reference to the ACAS is not agreed, the aggrieved officer is without remedy, save where there are grounds for the claim that there has been a breach of contract or a failure of the employing authority to observe terms and conditions of service binding under the provisions of the NHS (Remuneration and Conditions of Service) Regulations 1991[40], when the officer could have recourse to the courts. Indeed, in such case he could have had sought to enforce his rights through the courts without first having had recourse to the Whitley disputes machinery.

'Status quo working

The status quo (i.e. the working and management arrangements which applied before the dispute) should operate until the agreed disputes procedures have been exhausted. If the dispute arises from the suspension or dismissal of an employee, the disciplinary procedures should apply.

Time limits

It is in the interest of both employing authorities and employees that disputes should be resolved quickly. The General Council believes that a dispute should be resolved within two months of the date when it was first brought to the attention of the employee's immediate local manager.

Implementation of agreement

The General Council recognises that some employing authorities have established procedures which have been agreed locally with recognised staff organisations. Where such procedures are consistent with the principles outlined in this agreement and continue to command the support of the parties to the local agreement, the General Council would not wish to see them disturbed.'

17.12   DISCIPLINARY PROCEDURES

The Whitley Councils' *Handbook* sets out procedures for the discipline of National Health Service staff other than doctors and dentists, who are covered by separate arrangements set out in section 17.9, above.

In the case of all other staff Section 40 provides as follows:

'2. In serious matters likely to involve disciplinary action the disciplinary procedures of an authority shall provide that, except in cases justifying immediate suspension from duty or, exceptionally, summary dismissal, employees shall, subject to any further enquiries that may be required, first be reprimanded and given a formal warning in writing signed by a senior officer of the employing authority that any repetition by the employee might result in dismissal.

3. In the case of employees whose employment can be terminated only by a decision of the full employing authority, power of dismissal shall not be delegated to any officer or committee of officers. These employees will include the authority's more senior grades, e.g. senior professional, administrative or technical staff. Employees should be informed in writing on appointment or as soon as possible thereafter whether they can be dismissed only by a decision of the full employing authority or by an officer or committee of officers. In those cases where an employee can be dismissed by an officer or committee of officers the employee should also be informed which officer(s) have the power of dismissal delegated to them by the employing authority.

4. Employees of an authority who are aggrieved by disciplinary action, which results in the issue of a reprimand and formal warning in writing referred to in paragraph 2 above or in their dismissal, shall have the right of appeal against such action to their employing authority. Employing authorities should set up appeals committees consisting of not less than 3 members of the authority to hear appeals. If possible at least one member of the committee should have a special knowledge of the field of work of the employee. Where this is not possible in cases of an appeal against dismissal the committee shall at the request of the employee or the employee's representative appoint an assessor, who is experienced in the particular discipline of the employee, and who has not been directly involved in the circumstances leading to disciplinary action. The assessor may only advise the committee on any matter arising during the course of the hearing which the assessor feels may be related to the professional conduct or professional competence of the employee.

5. Employees should have the right of appearing personally before the appeal committee either alone or accompanied by a representative of their trade union, professional organisation or staff association. Appellants may elect to be legally represented but if so they shall be responsible for such costs as they may incur, and in these circumstances the employing authority may also elect to be legally represented.

6. The members of the appeal committee shall not include any member of the authority or committee or sub-committee of the authority who has been directly involved in the circumstances leading to disciplinary action. No officer of the authority who has been directly involved in the circumstances that appeared to indicate the need for disciplinary action at an earlier stage of the disciplinary procedure shall be present at the appeal hearing as Secretary of the appeals committee or in any other capacity except as a witness or as the representative of the employing authority. The report of the appeal committee should be submitted to the full employing authority who should thereupon reach a decision on the case.

7. It is important that the appeals should be made and heard quickly. Employees who are the subject of any disciplinary action, including dismissal, should be provided if practicable within 7 days with a notice in writing stating the nature of the disciplinary action, the reasons for the disciplinary action together with a summary of the alleged facts on which the disciplinary action is based and the employee's right of appeal. It is recommended that any appeal by the employee should be lodged within 3 weeks of the receipt of the written notice. The hearing of the appeal by the appeal committee should take place within 5 weeks of the receipt of the appeal by the employing authority although employing authorities may in exceptional circumstances be entitled to extend this period. The employee shall be given at least 14 days notice of the date of the hearing.

8. At the hearing of an appeal before the appeal committee the following procedure shall be observed:

1. The authority's representative shall state the authority's case in the presence of the appellant and the appellant's representative and may call witnesses.
2. The appellant or the appellant's representative shall have the opportunity to ask questions of the authority's representative and witnesses.
3. The members of the appeal committee shall have the opportunity to ask questions of the authority's representative and witnesses.
4. The authority's representative shall have the opportunity to re-examine his or her witnesses on any matter referred to in their examination by members of the appeal committee, the appellant or the appellant's representative.
5. The appellant or the appellant's representative shall put his or her case in the presence of the authority's representative and may call witnesses.
6. The authority's representative shall have the opportunity to ask questions of the appellant and the appellant's representative and witnesses.
7. The members of the appeal committee shall have the opportunity to ask questions of the appellant, and the appellant's representative and witnesses.
8. The appellant or the appellant's representative shall have the opportunity to re-examine his or her witnesses on any matter referred to in their examination by members of the appeal committee or the authority's representative.
9. The authority's representative and the appellant or the appellant's representative shall have the opportunity to sum up their cases if they so wish. The appellant or the appellant's representative shall have the right to speak last. In their summing-up neither party may introduce any new matter.
10. Nothing in the foregoing procedure shall prevent the members of the committee from inviting either party or a representative to elucidate or amplify any statement they may have made, or from asking them such questions as may be necessary to ascertain whether or not they propose to call any evidence in respect of any part of their statement, or, alternatively, whether they are in fact claiming that the matters are within their own knowledge, in which case they will be subject to examination as witnesses under 8.2 or 8.6 above.
11. The committee may at its discretion adjourn the appeal in order that further evidence may be produced by either party to the dispute or for any other reason.
12. The authority's representative, the appellant, the appellant's representative and witnesses shall withdraw.
13. The committee with the officer appointed as Secretary to the committee and where appropriate the assessor shall deliberate in private only recalling both parties to clear points of uncertainty on evidence already given. If recall is necessary both parties shall return notwithstanding only one is concerned with the point giving rise to doubt.
14. No statement of previous acts of misconduct by the employee or the issue of a formal warning or warnings unrelated to the alleged offence(s) on which the disciplinary action is based shall be made until after the committee has reached a decision on the appeal.

9. An employee shall only be summarily dismissed in exceptional circumstances and only by an officer who has been delegated power of dismissal by the employing authority in accordance with the provisions of paragraph 3 and where the action has been approved by the Senior Officer responsible for the

function in which the employee is engaged or in his or her absence the Senior Officer who is deputising.

10. If an aggrieved employee after exhausting the appeal procedures within his or her employing authority seeks to appeal to a higher authority, namely the appropriate Secretary of State or, in the case of District Health Authority employees in England, the Regional Health Authority, it shall be at the discretion of the Secretary of State or Regional Health Authority what action they shall take in respect of the application. Further consideration would depend upon the merits of each case; it would be for the Secretary of State or the Regional Health Authority to decide and their intervention cannot be claimed as a matter of right by the individual employee. In exercising its discretion in such circumstances a Regional Health Authority should ensure that any application be considered by persons who have not taken part in the original decision against which the appeal is made. In the event that the Regional Health Authority agrees to a hearing the relevant provisions of paragraphs 5–8 shall apply.'

17.13   NATIONAL HEALTH SERVICE REDUNDANCY PAYMENTS

17.13.1   Particular arrangements

Employees in the National Health Service are specifically excluded from the provisions of the Employment Protection (Consolidation) Act 1978 in respect of redundancy compensation. However, special schemes exist independently of the 1978 Act for many excluded categories of employee, and indeed the conditions of service negotiated through the Whitley Councils for the health service contain provisions in respect of redundancy which are more beneficial than the scheme under the 1978 Act. One condition which is equally beneficial is that the qualifying period of two years' reckonable service (that is, the minimum 104 weeks which count for eligibility to receive redundancy compensation) is based on whole-time or part-time working weeks of not less than 16 hours per week, or 8 hours per week for five years continuously.

An exclusion from eligibility parallel to that provided for in the Employment Protection (Consolidation) Act 1978, in respect of unreasonable refusal of suitable alternative employment, is examined in some detail in the *Conditions of Service* published by the Whitley Councils for the health services. For exclusion purposes, 'suitable alternative employment' refers both to the place and to the capacity in which the employee would be employed. The following considerations shall be applied in deciding whether a post is suitable alternative employment and whether it was unreasonably refused:

1. *Place.* A post is normally suitable in place if it involves no additional travelling expenses or is within six miles of the employee's home. If the new post is at a greater distance, the fact that assistance will be

given with the extra travelling expenses will normally outweigh any added difficulties in travel, but exceptionally an employee's special personal circumstances will be considered in comparison with the travel undertaken by other employees in comparable grades. If the post is too far for daily travel, it will be reasonable, since removal expenses will be payable, to require staff (other than those who can be expected to seek employment in their neighbourhood) to move home unless they can adduce special circumstances such as age.

2. *Capacity*. Suitable alternative employment may not necessarily be in the same grade; the employment should be judged in the light of the employee's qualifications and ability to perform the duties. Nor need it be at exactly the same pay. A post carrying salary protection for the employee should on that fact alone be treated as suitable in capacity.

For the purposes of this scheme any suitable alternative employment must be brought to the employee's notice before the date of termination of contract and with reasonable time for him to consider it, and the employment should be available not later than four weeks from that date. Where this is done, but he fails to make any necessary application, he shall be deemed to have refused suitable alternative employment.

The redundancy payment shall be paid by the employing authority subject to the employee submitting a claim which satisfies the conditions before he ceases to be employed or within six months thereafter. Before payment is made he shall provide a certificate that he has not obtained or been offered or refused to apply for or accept suitable alternative health service employment and he understands that the payment is made only on this condition and undertakes to refund if this condition is not satisfied.

Special arrangements are provided by section 45 of the *Whitley Council's General Handbook* for National Health Service employees. The Secretary of State having approved these arrangements by way of Statutory Instrument, the redundancy provisions form a binding term of National Health Service employment in the usual way.

Section 45 of the *Handbook* is set out in full, as follows:

'Scope

1. These arrangements apply to employees who, having been employed for the minimum qualifying period of reckonable service (as defined in paragraph 2.2) in the National Health Service in Great Britain (or previously in Northern Ireland), are dismissed by reason of redundancy, which expression includes events described in section 81(2) of the Employment Protection (Consolidation) Act 1978, and premature retirement on organisational change under paragraphs 1(iii), 6, 7 and 8 of the agreement on Premature Payment of Superannuation and Compensation Benefits (see Section 46). The minimum qualifying period is:

1.1   104 weeks continuous service whole-time or part-time of 16 or more hours a week, or

1.2   5 years continuous service of 8 or more hours a week in each case after attaining age 18.

Definitions

2. For the purpose of these arrangements, the following expressions have the meanings assigned below:

2.1   "Health Service authority" means a Regional Health Authority, a District Health Authority, the Dental Practice Board, a Special Health Authority, a Family Health Service Committee, the Public Health Laboratory Service Board, a Health Board and the Common Services Agency in Scotland, the Northern Ireland Health and Social Services Board and its Central Services Agency, and any predecessor or successor authority.

2.2   "Reckonable service", which shall be calculated up to the date on which the termination of the contract takes effect, means continuous employment as defined in 1.1 or 1.2 above with the present or any previous Health Service authority, after attaining age 18 years.
A period (which may include the aggregate of shorter periods) not exceeding 12 months beginning on or after 1 April 1985 spent as a GP trainee in the employment of a Principal GP trainer under the Trainee Practitioner scheme shall, notwithstanding that it is not employment with a Health Service authority, also count as "reckonable service".
Periods of employment prior to a break of more that 12 months at any one time in employment with a Health Service authority shall not count as "reckonable service", except that any period of employment as a GP trainee counted as "reckonable service" shall not count as part of any period of more than 12 months constituting a break in employment with a Health Service authority.
Service which qualifies under section 58 of this *Handbook* shall also count as reckonable service. The following previous employment shall not so count:

2.2.1   employment which has been the subject of terminal payments under HM(60)47 or HM(62)12 (in Scotland, SHM(60)38 or SHM(62)14);

2.2.2   employment which has been the subject of redundancy payment under this agreement or under any similar redundancy arrangements in Northern Ireland;

2.2.3   employment which has been the subject of compensation for loss of office under the National Health Service (Transfer of Officers and Compensation) Regulations 1948 and 1960, the National Health Service (Transfer and Compensation) (Scotland) Regulations 1948 and 1960, the Local Government (Executive Councils) (Compensation) Regulations 1964 and 1966, the National Health Service (Compensation) Regulations 1971, the National Health Service (Compensation) (Scotland) Regulations 1971, or Regulations made under section 24 of the Superannuation Act 1972, or any orders made under sections 11(9) or 31(5) of the National Health Service Act 1946 or sections 11(10) or 32(5) of the National Health Service (Scotland) Act 1947 or sections 13(3) or 19(6) of the National Health Service (Scotland) Act 1972, or under sections 28(6) and 60 of the Health Service Act (Northern

Ireland) 1948 or article 78 of the Health and Personal Social Services (Northern Ireland) Order 1972 or Regulations made under section 44 of the National Health Service Reorganisation Act 1973, or section 34A of the National Health Service (Scotland) Act 1972.

2.2.4 employment in respect of which the employee was awarded superannuation benefits.

2.3 "Superannuation benefits" means the benefits, or part of the benefits (other than a return of contributions) payable under a superannuation scheme in respect of the period of the employee's reckonable service.

2.4 "Week's pay" means either:

2.4.1 an amount calculated in accordance with the provisions of Schedule 14, Part II of the Employment Protection (Consolidation) Act 1978 except that paragraph 8 of Schedule 14, Part II shall not apply, or

2.4.2 an amount equal to 7/365ths of the annual salary in payment at the date of termination of employment, or

2.4.3 the weekly wage calculated as at the date of termination of employment, to which the employee would be entitled under the agreements of the Ancillary Staffs Council or the Ambulance Council of the Whitley Councils for the Health Services (Great Britain) during absence on annual leave,

whichever is more beneficial to the employee.

Benefits

3. The redundancy payment shall take the form of a lump sum dependent on the employee's age and reckonable service at the date of ceasing to be employed. This shall be:

3.1 for all employees aged 41 or over who are not immediately after that date entitled to receive payment of benefits provided under the NHS Superannuation Scheme, the lump sum shall be assessed as follows:

3.1.1 2 weeks' pay for each complete year of reckonable service at age 18 or over with a maximum of 50 weeks' pay, PLUS

3.1.2 an additional 2 weeks' pay for each complete year of reckonable service at age 41 or over with a maximum of 16 weeks' pay.

(Overall maximum, 66 weeks' pay)

[In all cases the redundancy payment will need to be recalculated, and any arrears due paid, if a retroactive pay award is notified after the date of cessation of employment.]

3.2 For other employees, a maximum of 20 years reckonable service may be counted, assessed as follows:

3.2.1 For each complete year of reckonable service at age 41 or over – 1½ weeks' pay;

3.2.2 For each complete year of reckonable service at age 22 or over but under 41 – 1 week's pay;

3.2.3 For each complete year of reckonable service at age 18 or over but under 22 – ½ week's pay.

(Overall maximum, 30 weeks' pay)

4. Fractions of a year cannot count except that they may be aggregated under 3.2.1, 3.2.2 and 3.2.3 to make complete years. These must be paid for at the lower appropriate rate for each complete year aggregated.

5. If the 64th birthday has been passed, the sum calculated under paragraph 3 above shall be reduced by one twelfth for each complete month between the date of the 64th birthday and the last day of service.

6. Redundant employees who are entitled to an enhancement of their superannuation benefits on ceasing to be employed will, if the enhancement of service is less than 10 years, be entitled to receive redundancy payments. Where the enhancement of service does not exceed 6⅔ years they will be paid in full; where the enhancement of service exceeds 6⅔ years they will be reduced by 30% in respect of each year of enhanced service over 6⅔ years with a pro rata reduction for part years.

Exclusion from eligibility

7. Employees otherwise eligible shall not be entitled to redundancy payments under these arrangements if they:

7.1 are dismissed for reasons of misconduct, with or without notice; or

7.2 are age 65 or over; or

7.3 have reached the normal retiring age in cases where there is a normal retiring age of less than 65 for employees holding the position which they held and the age is the same for men and women; or

7.4 at the date of the termination of the contract have obtained without a break or with a break not exceeding 4 weeks suitable alternative employment with the same or another Health Service authority in Great Britain; or

7.5 unreasonably refuse to accept or apply for suitable alternative employment with the same or another Health Service authority in Great Britain; or

7.6 leave their employment before expiry of notice except as described at paragraph 10; or

7.7 are offered a renewal of contract (with the substitution of the new employer for the previous one) where the employment is transferred to another public service employer not being a Health Service authority.

Suitable alternative employment

8. "Suitable alternative employment", for the purposes of paragraph 7, refers to both the place and to the capacity in which the employee would be employed. The following considerations shall be applied in deciding whether a post is suitable alternative employment and whether it was unreasonably refused:

8.1 *Place*. A post is normally suitable in place if it involves no additional travelling expenses or is within 6 miles of the employee's home. If the new post is at a greater distance, the fact that assistance will be given with extra travelling expenses (see paragraph 6 of section 23) will normally outweigh any added difficulties in travel, but exceptionally an employee's special personal circumstances will be considered in comparison with the travel undertaken by other employees in comparable grades. If the post is too far for daily travel, it will be reasonable, since removal expenses will be payable, to require staff (other than those who can be expected to seek employment in their neighbourhood) to move home unless they can adduce special circumstances such as age.

8.2 *Capacity*. Suitable alternative employment may not necessarily be in the same grade; the employment should be judged in the light of the employee's qualifications and ability to perform the duties. Nor need it be at exactly the same pay. A post carrying salary protection for the employee should on that fact alone be treated as suitable in capacity.

9. For the purposes of this scheme any suitable alternative employment must be brought to the employee's notice in writing before the date of termination of contract and with reasonable time for the employee to consider it; the employment should be available not later than 4 weeks from that date. Where this is done, but the employee fails to make any necessary application, the employee shall be deemed to have refused suitable alternative employment. Where an employee accepts suitable alternative employment the "trial period" provisions in section 84(3) to (7) of the Employment Protection (Consolidation) Act 1978 shall apply.

Early release of redundant employees

10. Employees who have been notified of their cessation of employment on account of redundancy, and for whom no suitable alternative employment in the NHS is available may, during the period of notice, obtain other employment outside the NHS and wish to take this up before the period of notice of redundancy expires. In these circumstances the employing authority shall, unless there are compelling reasons to the contrary, release such employees at their request on a mutually agreeable date and that date shall become the revised date of redundancy for the purpose of calculating any entitlement to a redundancy payment under the other terms of this agreement.

Claim for redundancy payment

11. Subject to the employee submitting a claim which satisfies the conditions and is made either before or within 6 months after cessation of employment, the redundancy payment shall be paid by the employing authority. Before payment is made, employees shall provide a certificate that at the date of termination of

the contract they had not obtained or been offered or unreasonably refused to apply for or accept suitable alternative Health Service employment commencing without a break or with a break not exceeding 4 weeks from the date of termination and that they understand that the payment is made only on this condition and they undertake to refund it if this condition is not satisfied.

Disputes

12. Employees who disagree with the employing authority's calculation of the amount of redundancy payment or rejection of a claim for such payment should in the first instance make representation to the employing authority who should allow the employees to discuss the matter with them with the assistance, if they wish, of a recognised staff organisation. If the employee is still dissatisfied and so wishes, the matter shall be referred to the tribunal provided in section 112 of the Employment Protection (Consolidation) Act 1978. Any such references must be made either before or within 6 months after cessation of employment. However, this time limit can be extended by the tribunal for a further six months, as provided for in section 101(2) of the Employment Protection (Consolidation) Act 1978, if it appears to the tribunal to be just and equitable to do so. The tribunal shall decide the question and its decision whether or not the whole or any part of the calculated payment should be made shall be implemented by the employing authority. This replaces the normal channels of regional and national appeal.'

17.13.2   Eligibility and access to the courts

The terms of paragraph 7 of section 45 of the *Handbook* were amended in consequence of judicial proceedings in 1989 relating to a claim for equal pay. The upper age limit was altered from 60 to 65 for women (it having been 65 already for men) in consequence of the decision of the Employment Appeal Tribunal in *Stevens and others v Bexley Health Authority* (1989).[52] That case also had significant effects upon the legal relationship between claims made for redundancy payment under the terms of section 45 itself, and claims (effectively, complaints) made in respect of and arising out of the provisions of that section.

The appellant women were health service employees who were made redundant. They were not given contractual redundancy payments under the Whitley Council Agreement because they were over age 60.

The women brought complaints to an industrial tribunal under three different headings. They referred the contractual dispute over the redundancy payment to the tribunal under section 112 of the Employment Protection (Consolidation) Act 1978. They also brought complaints under the Equal Pay Act 1970. Third, they claimed that they were entitled to redundancy payments by virtue of EEC law, in that men over age 60 employed on like work received redundancy payments. This was said to contravene the equal pay provisions of article 119 of the EEC Treaty and/or the EEC Equal Treatment Directive.

An industrial tribunal held that it did not have jurisdiction to hear the complaints because they were out of time. An issue arose as to whether the complaint under section 112 was out of time. The industrial tribunal in this case held that, by virtue of the provisions of clause 45 of the Whitley Agreement, an Originating Application under section 112 for a redundancy payment had to be brought by a health service employee within six months of the date of cessation of employment. The tribunal went on to hold that this time limit applied also to claims under EEC law.

On behalf of the appellants it had been conceded at the tribunal by a member of the Free Representation Unit that the claim could not be brought by reason of the provisions of section 6 of the Equal Pay Act 1970. Section 6(1A)(b) excludes terms relating to death or retirement or any provision made in relation to death or retirement.

On appeal from the tribunal the Employment Appeal Tribunal made the following rulings.

The industrial tribunal had erred in law in finding that the appellant employees were precluded from referring a dispute about a contractual redundancy payment under the terms of a collective agreement to the tribunal in accordance with section 112 of the Employment Protection (Consolidation) Act because their complaints were referred more than six months after the cessation of their employment. There was no requirement for the appellants to issue an Originating Application under section 112 within a time limitation of less than six years.

The industrial tribunal had erred in law in finding that the appellant employees were precluded from claiming a redundancy payment under EEC law because their complaints were made more than six months after the cessation of their employment. Although the appellants' original claim was for a redundancy payment under the Whitley Agreement, based in contract, their claims under article 119 and the Equal Treatment Directive, as well as their claim under the Equal Pay Act, were distinct and separate heads of claim and were not based on the right to bring proceedings under section 112 of the Employment Protection (Consolidation) Act by reason of the Whitley Agreement.

The appellants' representative had wrongly conceded before the industrial tribunal that the appellants' redundancy payment claim could not be brought under the Equal Pay Act by reason of the exclusion in section 6 of that Act relating to provision made in relation to retirement. Section 6 was not a bar to the appellants' claim and the industrial tribunal had jurisdiction to hear the appellants' claims under the Equal Pay Act.

NOTES

1. [1954] 2 QB 66.
2. [1954] 1 WLR 1382.
3. [1968] 2 QB 497.
4. Employment Protection (Consolidation) Act 1978, section 64(1)(a) as amended by the Unfair Dismissal (Variation of Qualifying Period) Order 1985, SI 1985/782. The previous qualifying period was one year.

5. [1981] QB 95.
6. [1983] ICR 90.
7. [1957] 1 WLR 594.
8. [1984] ICR 492.
9. [1991] 4 All ER 563.
10. See *London Ambulance Service v Charlton*, Independent, 28 October 1992 (EAT).
11. [1974] ICR 428.
12. [1975] IRLR 319.
13. *Tarnesby v Kensington, Chelsea and Westminster Area Health Authority (T)* [1981] 1 IRLR 369.
14. The change having originally been made by the Health and Social Services and Social Security Adjudications Act 1983, Schedule 6, paragraph 1.
15. [1977] AC 931.
16. [1978] IRLR 379.
17. [1975] IRLR 217.
18. [1990] IRLR 177.
19. [1963] SLT 124.
20. [1991] ICR 514.
21. [1985] ICR 590.
22. National Health Service and Community Care Act 1990, section 60.
23. [1984] 3 All ER 425.
24. [1989] 1 MLR 17.
25. [1990] ICR 824.
26. [1992] 1 All ER 705.
27. SI 1981/1974.
28. Whitley Council General Handbook, section 59.
29. [1988] IRLR 195.
30. [1992] 4 All ER 929.
31. [1976] IRLR 364.
32. [1986] QB 401 on compensation, see The Times, 4 August 1993.
33. Sex Discrimination Act 1975 (Amendment of section 20) Order 1983, SI 1983/1202.
34. Sex Discrimination (Midwives) (Specified Date) Order 1983, SI 1983/1841.
35. [1987] AC 224.
36. [1991] IRLR 44.
37. [1974] ICR 535.
38. Came into operation 1 April 1991, SI 1990/1329.
39. SI 1982/276, in Wales SI 1983/1275.
40. SI 1991/481.
41. SI 1974/495; amended by SIs 1978/1090, 1982/288.
42. SI 1974/495; amended by SIs 1982/288, 1985/47.
43. Schedule 1, paragraphs 11(2), 11(3).
44. Regulation 3(1).
45. Medical Defence Union Annual Report 1971, p. 67.
46. [1951] 1 All ER 528.
47. SI 1961/1441; 1966/1523;1972/1339 and 1537; 1973/242, 731 and 1649; 1974/223 and 1047.
48. [1923] 1 KB 504.
49. [1983] 1 All ER 1073.
50. *R v Secretary of State for Health, ex parte Guirguis* [1989] 1 MLR 17.
51. SI 1991/537.
52. [1989] IRLR 240.

CHAPTER 18

Nurses agencies

The establishment and conduct of agencies for the supply of nurses is regulated by the Nurses Agencies Act 1957, as amended. For the purposes of the Act the term 'agency for the supply of nurses' is defined by section 8 as meaning:

'the business (whether or not carried on for gain and whether or not carried on in conjunction with another business) of supplying persons to act as nurses, or of supplying persons to act as nurses and persons to act as midwives, but does not include the business carried on by any county or district nursing association or other similar organisation, being an association or organisation established and existing wholly or mainly for the purpose of providing patients with the services of a nurse to visit them in their own homes without herself taking up residence there'.

18.1 NURSES AGENCIES ACT 1957

18.1.1 Conduct of agencies

Section 1 of the Act[1] provides for the conduct of such agencies:

'**1.**—(1) A person carrying on an agency for the supply of nurses shall, in carrying on that agency, only supply —
   (a) registered nurses and registered midwives; and
   (b) such other classes of persons as may be prescribed.
   (2) A person carrying on an agency for the supply of nurses shall, at the prescribed time and in the prescribed manner, give to every person to whom he supplies a nurse, midwife or other person a statement in writing in the prescribed form as to the qualifications of the person supplied.
   (3) No person shall carry on an agency for the supply of nurses unless the selection of the person to be supplied for each particular case is made by or under the supervision of a registered [and qualified] nurse or a registered medical practitioner.
   (4) A person carrying on an agency for the supply of nurses shall keep such records in relation thereto as may be prescribed.'

The intention here is to provide, so far as is considered desirable, for keeping an agency for the supply of nurses separate from any other employment agency business, as distinct, for instance, from an employment agency for purely domestic staff. The Secretary of State may, by regulation, add to the classes of persons or agencies for supply of nurses they supply and he has, in fact, used that discretion in regulation 3 of the Nurses Agency Regulations 1961,[2] to permit any such agency to supply the following (though these are today of little, if any, practical significance):

'(a) persons on the list maintained under section 5 of the Nurses Act 1957;
(b) persons who hold the certificate of proficiency in mental nursing or the certificate of proficiency in the nursing of mental defectives formerly granted by the Royal Medico-Psychological Association;
(c) persons who hold the tuberculosis nursing certificate granted by the British Tuberculosis Association;
(d) persons who hold the orthopaedic nursing certificate granted by the Central Council for the Care of Cripples or the Joint Examination Board of the British Orthopaedic Association and the said Central Council;
(e) persons who are entitled, under the Nurses Regulations 1957, to use the name or title of "service-trained nurse";
(f) persons, being persons to whom none of the preceding paragraphs of this regulation applies, of any class prescribed for the purposes of paragraph (d) of subsection (1) of section 27 of the Nurses (Scotland) Act 1951, or of paragraph (d) of subsection (1) of section 7 of the Nurses Act (Northern Ireland) 1946.'

The selection of the person to be supplied in each particular case is to be made by or under the supervision of a registered and qualified nurse or a registered medical practitioner.[3] By section 1(2) a person carrying on an agency for the supply of nurses is obliged, at the prescribed time and in the prescribed manner, to give to every person to whom he supplies a nurse, midwife or other person a statement in writing in the prescribed form as to the qualifications of the person supplied. Regulations may also be made under section 1(4) of the Act as to the keeping of records by agencies.[4]

18.1.2 Licensing of agencies

No one is permitted to carry on an agency for the supply of nurses on any premises in the area of any licensing authority without a licence from such authority. The licensing authorities are: for premises within the City of London, the Common Council; in Greater London, the London Borough Council for the area in which the agency is situate, and elsewhere in the country the Social Services Authority.[5]

Any application for a licence to carry on an agency must give the information and be made in the form and manner and at the time prescribed by the Secretary of State, the prescribed fee being payable.[6] Any licence applied for in accordance with the Act must be granted unless statutory grounds for refusal are established to the satisfaction of the licensing authority, but the licensing authority when granting a licence may impose such conditions as they think fit for securing the proper conduct of the agency, including conditions as to the fees to be charged by the person carrying on the agency, whether to the nurses or other persons supplied, or to the persons to whom they are supplied.[7]

Ordinarily, but not necessarily, applications for licences will be dealt with at an annual meeting of the licensing authority or an authorised committee of the authority and when granted will be valid until 31 December in the year next following that in which the licence is granted.[8] On the death of the holder of a licence, the licence enures for the benefit of his personal representatives.[9] The Nurses Agencies Amendment Regulations 1981[10] require records to be kept, in the case of a nurse or other person who trained outside the United Kingdom, of that nurse's or other person's knowledge of English.

Refusal or revocation of licence

Any application for a licence may be refused, or a licence already granted revoked, on any of the following grounds:[11]

1. that the applicant or, as the case may be, the holder of the licence is an individual under the age of twenty-one years or is unsuitable to hold a licence; or
2. that the premises are unsuitable; or
3. that the agency has been or is being improperly conducted; or
4. that offences against the Nurses Agencies Act 1957 have been committed.

No licence may be revoked or renewal application refused unless the holder of the licence has been given an opportunity of being heard by the licensing authority or by a committee thereof.[12]

Appeals against refusal or revocation of licence or conditions imposed

The applicant for or holder of a licence may within 21 days from receipt by him of notice of the refusal or of the revocation of a licence or of the grant of a licence subject to conditions appeal to a court of summary jurisdiction who may make such order as they think just. The licensing authority must within seven days of demand in writing by the applicant or holder send or deliver to him particulars in writing of the grounds of the refusal, revocation or attachment of conditions.[13]

18.1.3 Enforcement of rules as to the conduct and licensing of agencies

The responsibility for enforcing the provisions of the Nurses Agencies Act 1957 is placed upon the licensing authorities and qualified.[14] Any registered nurse *or other officer* duly authorised by the licensing authority may at all reasonable times on producing, if so required, some duly authenticated document showing his authority:

1. enter the premises specified in any licence or application for a licence or any premises which are used, or which that officer has reasonable cause to believe are used, for the purposes of or in connection with an agency for the supply of nurses; and
2. inspect those premises and the records kept in connection with such agency as aforesaid carried on at those premises. Obstruction of such officer in the execution of his duty is an offence under the Act.[15]

By section 4 of the Act penalties are provided for breaches of its provisions. It is further provided that where any such offence by a corporation (which term includes a limited company) is proved to have been committed with the consent or connivance of any director, manager, secretary or other officer of the corporation he, as well as the corporation, shall be deemed to be guilty of that offence and shall be liable to be proceeded against and punished accordingly.[16]

18.1.4 Exemptions

The provisions as to the licensing and conduct of agencies for the supply of nurses do not apply to agencies for the supply of nurses carried on in connection with any hospital maintained or controlled by a government department or local authority or combination of local authorities, or by any body constituted by special Act of Parliament or incorporated by royal charter. Nor do they apply to the Manpower Services Commission, the Employment Service Agency or the Training Services Agency.[17]

Nurses agencies are exempt from the provisions of the Employment Agencies Act 1973, and from any provisions relating to employment agencies or servants registries contained in any local Act.

NOTES

1. As amended by the Nurses, Midwives and Health Visitors Act 1979, section 23(4) and Schedule 7, paragraph 8.
2. SI 1961/1214. The amounts of fees payable under the Regulations have been successively altered, see now SI 1986/1414.
3. Nurses Agencies Act 1957, section 1(3), as amended by the Nurses, Midwives and Health Visitors Act 1979, Schedule 7, paragraph 8.
4. See the Nurses Agencies Regulations, SI 1961/1214, regulation 6.
5. Nurses Agencies Act 1957, section 2(1) as amended by the Local Government Act 1972, Schedule 29, paragraph 30.
6. Nurses Agencies Act 1957, sections 2(2) and 7; Nurses Agencies Regulations 1961, SI 1961/1214.
7. Nurses Agencies Act 1957, section 2(2).

8. Nurses Agencies Act 1957, section 2(6).
9. Nurses Agencies Act 1957, section 2(7).
10. SI 1981/1574.
11. Nurses Agencies Act 1957, section 2(3).
12. Nurses Agencies Act 1957, section 2(5).
13. Nurses Agencies Act 1957, section 2(4).
14. Nurses Agencies Act 1957, section 2(1).
15. Nurses Agencies Act 1957, section 3.
16. Nurses Agencies Act 1957, section 4(7).
17. Manpower Services Commission (Exemption) Order 1974, SI 1974/1571, article 2, Schedule, Part I.

CHAPTER 19

Professional qualifications

This chapter briefly outlines the qualifications, statutory and otherwise, for medical, dental, nursing and midwifery staff, and for pharmacists, opticians and professions supplementary to medicine. The formal question of qualifications, and the substantive question of actual ability and experience to do a particular job of work or to carry out a particular task requiring expertise, must be carefully distinguished. It is most unlikely that any hospital could escape liability for the negligence of a member of its medical or other professional staff on the grounds that it had done its duty in appointing a statutorily qualified person. It may be observed that even if circumstances did arise in which such defence could conceivably avail, it would be useless merely to show that a person with, say, the minimum registrable qualification in medicine had been appointed. In making senior hospital appointments, full regard is paid to the applicant's postgraduate experience, as well as to appropriate higher qualifications. Given the distinction just indicated, relegating the question of formal qualifications to a subsidiary role in the overall question of a hospital's responsibilities to patients as well as to other staff, this chapter simply draws attention to the broad features of the relevant legislation.

Strictly speaking, the practice of few health care professions is limited to those who are on a statutory register, the most notable being veterinary surgery, dentistry, midwifery, pharmacy and practice as an optician. The right to practise medicine is not strictly limited to registered medical practitioners, though the disabilities of the unregistered are such that normal practice is closed to them.

19.1 MEDICAL PRACTITIONERS

Registration, removal and restoration etc. is now dealt with in the Medical Act 1983 (consolidating the Medical Act 1956 which had been substantially amended, particularly by the Medical Acts 1969 and 1978).

19.1.1 Registration of medical practitioners

Medical practitioners entitled to fully registered status

Persons qualifying in the United Kingdom

By virtue of section 3 any person who:

'holds one or more primary United Kingdom qualifications[1] and has passed a qualifying examination[2] and satisfies the requirements of . . . [the] Act as to experience;[3]'

is entitled to be registered as a fully registered medical practitioner.

Persons qualifying elsewhere in the EEC
Again by virtue of section 3, any person who:

'being a national of any member State of the Communities, holds one or more primary European qualifications,[4]'

is entitled to be registered as a fully registered medical practitioner. Section 17 of the Act provides for 'primary qualifications' obtained in other member states of the Communities:

'17.—(1) A primary European qualification for the purposes of this Part of this Act is—
- (a) any European qualification listed in Schedule 2 to this Act which is acquired in a member State of the Communities on or after the date on which it implemented the second Medical Directive and is not evidence of training commenced by the holder before that date;
- (b) subject to compliance with subsection (2) below, any qualification obtained in a member State of the Communities before the date on which it implemented the second Medical Directive or on or after that date where training of which that qualification is evidence commenced before that date.

(2) For compliance with this subsection in the case of any qualifications, either—
- (a) they must be such that the Registrar is satisfied with respect to them (by means of a certificate of the medical authorities of the member State of the Communities in which they were acquired or otherwise) that they accord with the standards laid down by the second Medical Directive; or
- (b) evidence of them must be accompanied by a certificate of the medical authorities of any member State of the Communities that the holder has lawfully been engaged in actual medical practice for at least 3 consecutive years during the 5 years preceding the date of the certificate.

(3) In subsection (2) above, references to the medical authorities of a member State of the Communities are references to the authorities and bodies designated in accordance with the first Medical Directive or the second Medical Directive.

(4) In this Act—
"the first Medical Directive" means Council Directive No. 75/362/EEC concerning the mutual recognition of diplomas, certificates and other evidence of formal qualifications in medicine, and

"the second Medical Directive" means Council Directive No. 75/363/EEC concerning the co-ordination of provisions in respect of activities of doctors;

and for the purposes of subsection (1) above a member State [other than Spain or Portugal] is to be regarded as having implemented the second Medical Directive on the date notified to the Commission of the European Communities as that on which it did so [and Spain and Portugal are to be regarded as having implemented it on 1 January 1986].'

The specific 'primary qualifications' referred to in section 17 are listed in Schedule 2 of the Act, in alphabetical order of member States, as follows:

'Belgium

"Diplôme légal de docteur en médecine, chirurgie et accouchements/Wettelijk diploma van doctor in de genees-, heel-en verlos-kunde" (diploma of doctor of medicine, surgery and obstetrics required by law) awarded by the university faculties of medicine, the Central Examining Board or the State University Education Examining Board.

Denmark

"Bevis for bestaet lægevidenskabelig embedseksamen" (diploma of doctor of medicine required by law) awarded by a university faculty of medicine and "dokumentation for gennemført praktisk uddannelse" (certificate of practical training issued by the competent authorities of the health service).

France

1. "Diplôme d'Etat de docteur en médecine" (State diploma of doctor of medicine) awarded by the university faculties of medicine, the university joint faculties of medicine and pharmacy, or by the universities.
2. "Diplôme d'université de docteur en médecine" (university diploma of doctor of medicine) where the diploma certifies completion of the same training course as that laid down for the State diploma of doctor of medicine.

Germany

1. "Zeugnis über die ärztliche Staatsprüfung" (the State examination certificate in medicine) awarded by the competent authorities and the "Zeugnis über die Vorbereitungszeit als Medizinalassistent" (certificate stating that the preparatory period as medical assistant has been completed) in so far as German law still requires such a period to complete medical training.
2. The certificates from the competent authorities of the Federal Republic of Germany stating that the diplomas awarded after 8 May 1945 by the competent authorities of the German Democratic Republic are recognised as equivalent to those listed in point 1 above.

Greece

"πτυχίο ἰατρικῆς Σχολῆς" (degree awarded by the Faculty of Medicine) awarded by a University Faculty of Medicine, and
"πιστοποιητικό πρακτικῆς ἀσκήσεως" (certificate of practical training) issued by the Ministry for Social Services.

Republic of Ireland

A primary qualification granted in the Republic of Ireland after passing a qualifying examination held by a competent examining body and a certificate of experience granted by that body which give entitlement to registration as a fully registered medical practitioner.

Italy

"Diploma di abilitazione all'esercizio della medicina e chirurgia" (diploma conferring the right to practise medicine and surgery) awarded by the State Examining Commission.

Luxembourg

1.   "Diplôme d'Etat de docteur en médecine, chirurgie et accouchements" (State diploma of doctor of medicine, surgery and obstetrics) awarded by the State Examining Board, and endorsed by the Minister of Education, and "certificat de stage" (certificate of practical training) endorsed by the Minister for Public Health.
2.   Diploma conferring a degree in medicine awarded in a member State of the Communities and—
    (a)   giving the right to take up training but not to practise the profession, and
    (b)   officially recognised by the Minister of Education in accordance with the law of 18 June 1969 on higher education and recognition of foreign degrees and diplomas,
if the diploma is accompanied by a certificate of practical training endorsed by the Minister for Public Health.
3.   Diploma conferring a degree in medicine awarded elsewhere than within the area of the Communities and accorded official recognition—
    (a)   by the Minister of Education in accordance with the law of 18 June 1969 above-mentioned, and
    (b)   by the Education Committee,
if the holder is a Luxembourg national and the diploma is accompanied by a certificate of practical training endorsed by the Minister for Public Health.

The Netherlands

"Universitair getuigschrift van arts" (university certificate of doctor).

Portugal

"Carta de curso de licenciatura em medicina" (diploma confirming the completion of medical studies) awarded by a University and the "Diploma comprovativo da conclusao do internato geral" (diploma confirming the completion of general internship) awarded by the competent authorities of the Ministry of Health.

Spain

"Titulo de Licenciado en Medicina y Cirugia" (University degree in medicine and surgery) awarded by the Ministry of Education and Science.'

This gives effect to the United Kingdom's obligations under Community law, specifically the first and second medical Directives (Council Directives 75/362/EEC and 75/363/EEC). The former concerns the mutual recognition of diplomas, certificates and other formal medical qualifications. The latter seeks to lay down certain minimum criteria regarding the requirements for training.

The Directives have been considered by the European Court of Justice on two occasions. In *Knoors v Secretary of State for Economic Affairs* (Netherlands) (1979)[5] it was held that a member state generally may not impose on its own nationals more stringent provisions than those applicable to the nationals of other member states seeking to exercise the right of establishment. In *Brockmeulen v Huisarts Reg
istatie Commissie* (1981)[6] it was held that a state may not unilaterally seek to raise the minimum requirements in the Directives.

Visiting EEC practitioners

A person who is a national of any member state and is lawfully established in medical practice in a member state other than the UK may render medical services while here temporarily without being registered either under section 3 or section 19 (registration of persons qualifying overseas) providing that he complies with the provisions of section 18:

'**18.**—(1) If he complies with the requirements of this section it shall be lawful for a person who is a national of any member State of the Communities and lawfully established in medical practice in a member State of the Communities other than the United Kingdom on visiting the United Kingdom to render medical services there temporarily without first being registered under the foregoing provisions of this Part or under Part III of this Act.

(2) Such a person intending so to render services shall provide the Registrar with—
- (a) a declaration in writing giving particulars of the services to be rendered and the period or periods in which he expects to render them; and
- (b) a certificate or certificates issued by the competent authority or body and bearing a date not less recent than 12 months prior to the date on which it is provided, which shows—
  - (i) that he is lawfully practising medicine in a member State other than the United Kingdom, and
  - (ii) that he holds medical qualifications which member States are required by the first Medical Directive to recognise;

and for the purposes of this subsection 'the competent authority or body' means the authority or body designated by the member State concerned as competent for the purposes of article 16(3) of that Directive.

(3) In an urgent case the declaration to be provided under paragraph (a) of subsection (2) above may be provided after the services have been rendered, but where it is so provided it shall be provided as soon as possible thereafter and in any event not more than 15 days after the date on which the practitioner first rendered such services.

(4) Where a person complies with the requirements of subsection (2) above, the Registrar shall register him under this section in the register of medical practitioners as a visiting EEC practitioner for such period or periods as, having regard to the particulars given in the declaration referred to in subsection (2)(a) above, he considers appropriate.

(5) Registration of a person as a visiting EEC practitioner shall cease if—
(a) he becomes established in medical practice in the United Kingdom; or
(b) he renders, save in a case of urgency, medical services in the United Kingdom otherwise than in accordance with a declaration made by him under subsection (2)(a) above.'

A practitioner complying with the requirements of subsection (2) is entitled to be registered as a visiting EEC practitioner for such a period(s) as the Registrar considers appropriate. By virtue of section 55, registration under this section renders a person 'fully registered'.

Persons qualifying overseas

By virtue of section 19(1):

'**19.**—(1) Where a person satisfies the registrar—
(a) that he holds one or more recognised overseas qualifications;[7]
(b) that he has the necessary knowledge of English;[8] and
(c) that he is of good character,[9] and satisfies the requirements . . . as to experience,[10] that person shall, if the General Council think fit so to direct, be registered under this section as a fully registered medical practitioner.'

Temporary full registration for visiting overseas specialists

Section 27 provides that a person who is or intends to be in the UK temporarily for the purpose of providing medical services of a specialist nature may be registered temporarily (for a period not exceeding 12 months) as a *fully registered* practitioner if the Council is satisfied—

'(a) that he holds one or more recognised overseas qualifications or acceptable overseas qualifications;
(b) that he possesses special knowledge of and skill in a particular branch or branches of medicine; and
(c) that the medical services he is to provide lie within that branch or one or more of those branches of medicine, they may, if they think fit, direct that he shall be registered under this section as a fully registered medical practitioner for such period as they may specify in the direction.'

Section 27(2) provides that no person shall be fully registered under this section for more than 12 months, and by virtue of section 27(3) the period of temporary full registration may be less than 12 months if so specified by the General Medical Council.

Professional misconduct and criminal offences

The effects on registration of professional misconduct or the commission of a criminal offence are the business of the Professional Conduct Committe of the General Medical Council and are mostly beyond the scope of this book. Section 36 of the 1983 Act is nevertheless set out for information, with the addition of some comments likely to be of relevance to hospital managers.

'36.—(1) Where a fully registered person—

(a) is found by the Professional Conduct Committee to have been convicted in the British Islands of a criminal offence, whether while so registered or not; or

(b) is judged by the Professional Conduct Committee to have been guilty of serious professional misconduct, whether while so registered or not;

the Committee may, if they think fit, direct—

(i) that his name shall be erased from the register;

(ii) that his registration in the register shall be suspended (that is to say, shall not have effect) during such period not exceeding twelve months as may be specified in the direction; or

(iii) that his registration shall be conditional on his compliance, during such period not exceeding three years as may be specified in the direction, with such requirements so specified as the Committee think fit to impose for the protection of members of the public or in his interests.

(2) Where a fully registered person whose registration is subject to conditions imposed under subsection (1) above by the Professional Conduct Committee or under section 42(3)(c) below by the Preliminary Proceedings Committee is judged by the Professional Conduct Committee to have failed to comply with any of the requirements imposed on him as conditions of his registration the Committee may, if they think fit, direct—

(a) that his name shall be erased from the register; or

(b) that his registration in the register shall be suspended (that is to say, shall not have effect) during such period not exceeding twelve months as may be specified in the direction.

(3) Where the Professional Conduct Committee have given a direction for suspension under subsection (1) or (2) above, the Committee may—

(a) direct that the current period of suspension shall be extended for such further period from the time when it would otherwise expire as may be specified in the direction;

(b) direct that the name of the person whose registration is suspended shall be erased from the register; or

(c) direct that the registration of the person whose registration is suspended shall, as from the expiry of the current period of suspension, be conditional on his compliance, during such period not exceeding three years as may be specified in the direction, with such requirements so specified as the Committee think fit to impose for the protection of members of the public or in his interests;

but the Committee shall not extend any period of suspension under this section for more than twelve months at a time.

(4) Where the Professional Conduct Committee have given a direction for conditional registration, the Committee may—

(a) direct that the current period of conditional registration shall be extended for such further period from the time when it would otherwise expire as may be specified in the direction; or

(b) revoke the direction or revoke or vary any of the conditions imposed by the direction;

but the Committee shall not extend any period of conditional registration under this section for more than twelve months at a time.

(5) Subsection (2) above shall apply to a fully registered person whose registration is subject to conditions imposed under subsection (3)(c) above as it applies to a fully registered person whose registration is subject to conditions imposed under subsection (1) above, and subsection (3) above shall apply accordingly.

(6) Where the Professional Conduct Committee give a direction under this section for erasure, for suspension or for conditional registration or vary the conditions imposed by a direction for conditional registration the Registrar shall forthwith serve on the person to whom the direction applies a notification of the direction or of the variation and of his right to appeal against the decision in accordance with section 40 below.

(7) In subsection (6) above the references to a direction for suspension and a direction for conditional registration include references to a direction extending a period of suspension or a period of conditional registration.

(8) While a person's registration in the register is suspended by virtue of this section he shall be treated as not being registered in the register notwithstanding that his name still appears in it.

(9) This section applies to a provisionally registered person and to a person registered with limited registration whether or not the circumstances are such that he falls within the meaning in this Act of the expression "fully registered person".'

The expression 'serious professional misconduct' was introduced by the Medical Act 1969, replacing the expression, used in earlier legislation, 'infamous conduct in any professional respect'. A single act or mistake, even in the absence of 'moral censure', can amount to professional misconduct.[11] The Professional Conduct Committee must require a higher standard of proof of an allegation of serious professional misconduct than merely proof on the balance of probabilities.[12]

In 1978 the Health Committee of the General Medical Council was for the first time given the power to suspend a medical practitioner, or to make a practitioner's registration conditional, on the ground of fitness to practise being 'seriously impaired' on account of the practitioner's physical or mental condition. The present form of the power is provided for in section 37 of the 1983 Act:

'Unfitness to practise through illness etc.

37.—(1) Where the fitness to practise of a fully registered person is judged by the Health Committee to be seriously impaired by reason of his physical or mental condition the Committee may, if they think fit, direct—

    (a)   that the registration in the register shall be suspended (that is to say, shall not have effect) during such period not exceeding twelve months as may be specified in the direction;

    (b)   that his registration shall be conditional on his compliance, during such period not exceeding three years as may be specified in the direction, with such requirements so specified as the Committee think fit to impose for the protection of members of the public or in his interests.

(2) Where a fully registered person whose registration is subject to conditions imposed under subsection (1) above by the Health Committee or under section 42(3)(c) below by the Preliminary Proceedings Committee is judged by the Health Committee to have failed to comply with any of the requirements imposed on him as conditions of his registration the Committee may, if they think fit, direct that his registration in the register shall be suspended (that is to say, shall not have effect) during such period not exceeding twelve months as may be specified in the direction.

(3) Where the Health Committee have given a direction for suspension under subsection (1) or (2) above, the Committee may—

    (a)   direct that the current period of suspension shall be extended for such further period from the time when it would otherwise expire as may be specified in the direction; or

    (b)   direct that the registration of the person whose registration is suspended shall, as from the expiry of the current period of suspension, be conditional on his compliance, during such period not exceeding three years as may be specified in the direction, with such requirements so specified as the Committee think fit to impose for the protection of members of the public or in his interests;

but the Committee shall not extend any period of suspension under this section for more than twelve months at a time.

(4) Where the Health Committee have given a direction for conditional registration, the Committee may—

    (a)   direct that the current period of conditional registration shall be extended for such further period from the time when it would otherwise expire as may be specified in the direction; or

    (b)   revoke the direction or revoke or vary any of the conditions imposed by the direction;

but the Committee shall not extend any period of conditional registration under this section for more than twelve months at a time.

(5) Subsection (2) above shall apply to a fully registered person whose registration is subject to conditions imposed under subsection (3) (b) above as it applies to a fully registered person whose registration is subject to conditions imposed under subsection (1) above, and subsection (3) above shall apply accordingly.

(6) Where the Health Committee give a direction under this section for suspension or for conditional registration or vary the conditions imposed by a direction for conditional registration the Registrar shall forthwith serve on the person to whom the direction applies a notification of the direction or of the variation and of his right to appeal against the decision in accordance with section 40 below.

(7) In subsection (6) above the references to a direction for suspension and a direction for conditional registration include references to a direction extending a period of suspension or a period of conditional registration.

(8) While a person's registration in the register is suspended by virtue of this section he shall be treated as not being registered in the register notwithstanding that his name still appears in it.

(9) This section applies to a provisionally registered person and to a person registered with limited registration whether or not the circumstances are such that he falls within the meaning in this Act of the expression "fully registered person".'

The criminality of pretending to be a registered medical practitioner when such is not the case, and of misuse of professional name or title, is an essential part of the professionalising framework legislated by the 1983 Act. Section 49 provides:

'Penalty for pretending to be registered

49.—(1) Subject to subsection (2) below, any person who wilfully and falsely pretends to be or takes or uses the name or title of physician, doctor of medicine, licentiate in medicine and surgery, bachelor of medicine, surgeon, general practitioner or apothecary, or any name, title, addition or description implying that he is registered under any provision of this Act, or that he is recognised by law as a physician or surgeon or licentiate in medicine and surgery or a practitioner in medicine or an apothecary, shall be liable on summary conviction to a fine not exceeding level 5 on the standard scale (as defined in section 75 of the Criminal Justice Act 1982); and for the purposes of this subsection—

(a) section 37 of that Act; and

(b) an order under section 143 of the Magistrates' Courts Act 1980 which alters the sums specified in subsection (2) of the said section 37,

shall extend to Northern Ireland and the said section 75 shall have effect as if after the words "England and Wales" there were inserted the words "or Northern Ireland".

(2) Subsection (1) above shall not apply to anything done by a person who is a national of any member State of the Communities for the purposes of or in connection with the lawful rendering of medical services by him without first being registered under this Act if he has previously complied with the requirements of subsection (2) of section 18 above or subsequently complies with its requirements as modified in respect of urgent cases by subsection (3) of that section.

(3) Any penalty to which a person is liable on summary conviction under subsection (1) above may be recovered in Scotland by any person before the sheriff or the district court who may, on the appearance or the default to appear of the accused, proceed to hear the complaint, and where the offence is proved or admitted the sheriff or court shall order the accused to pay the penalty as well as such expenses as the sheriff or court shall think fit.

(4) Any sum of money arising from conviction and recovery of penalties as mentioned in subsection (3) above shall be paid to the treasurer of the General Council.'

For a claim to be made 'wilfully and falsely' for the purpose of subsection (1) above it must be proved by the prosecution beyond reasonable doubt that there was a real subjective intention to deceive the person or body to whom or to which the representation in question was made.[13]

Privileges of fully registered medical practitioners

No one is entitled to recover any charge in any court of law for any medical or surgical advice or attendance, or for the performance of any operation, or for any medicine which he has prescribed and supplied, unless he is fully registered.[14] But this does not permit a fellow of a college of physicians prohibited by the bye-laws of the college from suing for fees to do so.[15]

Section 46(2) of the Medical Act 1983 introduced the following exception to the general rule as to fees:

'(2) Subsection (1) above shall not apply to fees in respect of medical services lawfully rendered in the United Kingdom by a person who is a national of any member State of the Communities without first being registered under this Act if he has previously complied with the requirements of subsection (2) of section 18 above or subsequently complies with those requirements as modified in respect of urgent cases by subsection (3) of that section.'

A registered medical practitioner, if in practice, is exempt from jury service[16] (as are also nurses and midwives, if practising).

Certain appointments are not to be held except by fully registered medical practitioners. Section 47(1) of the Act provides as follows:

'**47.**—(1) Subject to subsection (2) below, no person who is not fully registered shall hold any appointment as physician, surgeon or other medical officer—
  (a) in the naval, military or air service,
  (b) in any hospital or other place for the reception of persons suffering from mental disorder, or in any other hospital, infirmary or dispensary not supported wholly by voluntary contributions,
  (c) in any prison, or
  (d) in any other public establishment, body or institution, or to any friendly or other society for providing mutual relief in sickness, infirmity or old age.'

Subsection (2) of section 47 provides for the following exception to this general requirement:

'(2) Nothing in this section shall prevent any person who is not a Commonwealth citizen from being and acting as the resident physician or medical officer of any hospital established exclusively for the relief of foreigners in sickness, so long as he—
  (a) has obtained from a foreign university a degree or diploma of doctor in medicine and has passed the regular examinations entitling him to practise medicine in his own country, and
  (b) is engaged in no medical practice except as such a resident physician or medical officer.'

Special provision is made in section 47(3) for cases in which a practitioner has been suspended from practice by reason of unfitness through illness (the provisions relating to which are set out in detail above):

'(3) Suspension of the registration of a fully registered person by a direction of the Health Committee under section 37(1) or (2) above, an order of that Committee under section 38(1) above or an interim order of the Preliminary Proceedings Committee under section 42(3)(b) above shall not terminate any appointment such as is mentioned in subsection (1) above, but the person suspended shall not perform the duties of such an appointment during the suspension.'

Provisional registration

Persons qualifying in the United Kingdom and elsewhere in the EEC

As noted above, in order to obtain registration under section 3(a) of the Act the practitioner must, after passing a qualifying examination, have been engaged for a prescribed period in employment in a resident medical capacity in one or more approved hospitals or approved institutions and have obtained a certificate under section 10(2), which provides for the necessary 'requirements as to experience' required by section 3.

To enable the requisite experience to be gained, section 15(2) entitles a person who, apart from any requirement as to experience, would be entitled to be registered under section 3, to be registered provisionally. A person provisionally registered under the section is *deemed* to be fully registered under section 3 so far as is necessary to enable him to be engaged in employment in a resident medical capacity in one or more approved hospitals or approved institutions, but not further.

Persons qualifying overseas

Section 21 provides that where a person who has qualified overseas and satisfies criteria (a), (b) and (c) of section 19 (above) but lacks the requisite in-service experience, the Council may register that person provisionally. Section 19 makes the 'requirement of experience' which is further specified in section 20 requiring experience no less extensive than that required by section 10 in the case of practitioners qualifying in the United Kingdom. The practitioner will then be *deemed* to be fully registered under section 19 so far as is necessary to enable him to be engaged in employment in a resident medical capacity in one or more approved hospitals or approved institutions, but not further. Section 21 effectively reiterates the facility provided for in section 15 and applies it to non-EEC overseas practitioners.

Limited registration of persons by virtue of overseas qualifications

Section 22 of the Medical Act 1983 provides for the status, introduced for the first time by the Medical Act 1978, of 'limited registration':

'22.—(1) Subject to sections 23(5) and 24 below, where a person satisfies the Registrar—
- (a) that he has been selected for employment in the United Kingdom or the Isle of Man as a medical practitioner in one or more hospitals or other institutions approved by the General Council for the purposes of this section;
- (b) that he holds, has held, or has passed the examination necessary for obtaining some acceptable overseas qualification or qualifications;
- (c) that he has the necessary knowledge of English;
- (d) that he is of good character; and
- (e) that he has the knowledge and skill, and has acquired the experience, which is necessary for practice as a medical practitioner registered under this section and is appropriate in his case,

he shall, if the General Council think fit so to direct, be registered under this section as a medical practitioner with limited registration.

(2) In this Act "limited registration" means registration under this section limited in accordance with subsection (5) below in respect of the period for which and the employment for the purposes of which it has effect.

(3) No person shall be registered under this section for a period, or for periods which amount in the aggregate to a period, exceeding five years; and in this Act

the "permitted period", in relation to an applicant for registration under this section, means—

    (a) if he has not previously been registered under this section, five years;

    (b) if he has previously been so registered, the amount by which five years exceeds the period or aggregate of periods for which he has been so registered.

(4) In this Act an "acceptable overseas qualification" means any qualification granted outside the United Kingdom and for the time being accepted by the General Council for the purposes of this section as furnishing a sufficient guarantee of the possession of the knowledge and skill requisite for the practice of medicine under the supervision of a person who is registered as a fully registered medical practitioner.'

'(5) The limits of a person's registration under this section shall be defined in the direction by virtue of which he is registered in accordance with the following provisions that is to say—

    (a) the direction shall specify a period, not exceeding his permitted period, as the period for which his registration is to have effect; and

    (b) the direction shall specify the particular employment or the descriptions of employment for the purposes of which he is registered under this section;

and, subject to subsection (6) below and to section 24(1) and (2) below, that person's registration shall have effect for the period and for the purposes of the particular employment or the descriptions of employment specified in the direction.

(6) Where a direction specifies a particular employment as the employment for the purposes of which a person is registered under this section and that employment terminates before the end of the period specified in the direction by virtue of subsection (5)(a) above, the registration of the person under this section shall cease to have effect when that employment terminates.'

The practitioner in question is treated for specified limited purposes as being fully registered, and this is made conditional on supervision by a fully registered medical practitioner:

'(7) A person registered under this section shall be treated as registered under section 19 above as a fully registered medical practitioner in relation to the following matters, namely—

    (a) any employment in which he is engaged during the currency of his registration, being the particular employment or employment of a description for the purposes of which he is registered; and

    (b) things done or omitted in the course of that employment; and

    (c) any other thing incidental to his work in that employment which, by virtue of any enactment, may not lawfully or validly be done except by a fully registered medical practioner;

but in relation to other matters he shall be treated as not so registered.

(8) A person registered under this section shall not, while engaged in the particular employment or in employment of a description for the purposes of which he is registered, work otherwise than under the supervision of a person who is registered as a fully registered medical practitioner.'

The status of 'limited registration' replaced the former (pre-1978 Act) status called 'temporary registration'.[17] This latter status had been renewable, and prior to the Medical Act 1978 it had been possible to develop a medical career in the United Kingdom on that basis. Limited registration under the 1983 Act is not renewable with that effect, as section 22(3) makes clear. However, section 25 of the 1983 Act provides for the conversion of limited registration into full registration:

'25. A person who is or has been registered with limited registration may, on satisfying the Registrar that he is of good character, apply to the General Council to be registered fully by virtue of this section; and if the Council think fit so to direct, having regard to the knowledge and skill shown and the experience acquired by the applicant, he shall be registered under section 19 above as a fully registered medical practitioner.'

19.2   DENTISTS AND AUXILIARY DENTAL WORKERS

19.2.1   Dentists

The law relating to the training and registration of dentists, restrictions on the practice of dentistry and for the control of dental auxiliaries by the General Dental Council are contained in the Dentists Act 1984. Disciplinary powers are vested in the Council but, as in the case of the General Medical Council, subject to appeal to the Privy Council.

Only a registered dentist is entitled to take and use the description of dentist, dental surgeon or dental practitioner[18] and it is an offence for anyone other than a registered dentist or registered medical practitioner to practise or hold himself out as practising dentistry.[19]

What constitutes the practice, or 'business', of dentistry for the purposes of the Act is set out in section 40:

'40.—(1) For the purposes of this Act a person shall be treated as carrying on the business of dentistry if, and only if, he or a partnership of which he is a member receives payment for services rendered in the course of the practice of dentistry by him or by a partner of his, or by an employee of his or of all or any of the partners.
   (2) Notwithstanding subsection (1) above, the receipt of payments—
   (a)   by an authority providing national health services, or
   (b)   by a person providing dental treatment for his employees without a view to profit, or
   (c)   by a person providing dental treatment without a view to profit under conditions approved by the Secretary of State or the Department of Health and Social Services for Northern Ireland,
shall not constitute the carrying on of the business of dentistry for the purposes of this Act.'

Sections 41–44 deal with the business of dentistry and corporate bodies practising dentistry. They are subject to the control of the General Dental Council.

19.2.2 Dental auxiliaries

Generally

Under sections 45–48 of the 1984 Act, provision is made for the establishment of a roll or record of ancillary dental workers by the General Dental Council. Disciplinary authority may be exercised through the Dental Auxiliaries Committee of the Council.

The Council may not in its regulations authorise any ancillary dental worker to undertake:

(a) the extraction of teeth other than deciduous teeth; or
(b) except in the course of provision of national health services, the filling of teeth or the extraction of deciduous teeth; or
(c) the fitting, insertion or fixing of dentures or artificial teeth.

Section 45 of the Act enables the General Dental Council to make regulations relating to dental auxiliaries and for their classification; and section 47 provides for the use of titles and descriptions:

'**47.**—(1) Regulations under section 45 above may authorise members of a class of dental auxiliaries established by the regulations to use a title indicating their membership; and any person who wilfully uses that title when he is not authorised under the regulations to use that title shall be liable, on summary conviction, to a fine not exceeding the third level on the standard scale.

(2) Any member of a class of dental auxiliaries who uses any title or description reasonably calculated to suggest that he possesses any status or qualification connected with dentistry other than a status or qualification which he in fact possesses and which is indicated by particulars entered in the roll or record of the class in respect of him shall be liable, on summary conviction, to a fine not exceeding the third level on the standard scale.

(3) Where in the case of any class of dental auxiliaries regulations under section 45 above do not provide for a roll or record of the class in which particulars of status and qualifications may be entered, subsection (2) above shall have effect as if the words "and which is indicated by particulars entered in the roll or record of the class in respect of him" were omitted.'

Under these powers, the General Dental Council has made the Dental Regulations 1986[20] under which separate rolls of dental hygienists and of dental therapists are kept, with provision for penal erasure, as in the case of dentists.

Dental hygienists

The work which may be undertaken by a dental hygienist and the conditions under which it may be undertaken are laid down in regulation 23, reading as follows:

'**23.**—(1) Subject to the provisions of this regulation, a dental hygienist shall be permitted to carry out dental work (amounting to the practice of dentistry) of the following kinds:

(a) cleaning and polishing teeth;

(b) scaling teeth (that is to say, removal of deposits, accretions and stains from those parts of the surfaces of teeth which are exposed or which are directly beneath the free margins of the gums, including the application of medicaments appropriate thereto);

(c) the application to the teeth of such prophylactic materials as the Council may from time to time determine;

but shall not be permitted to carry out dental work amounting to the practice of dentistry of any other kind, except that the scaling of teeth under sub-paragraph (b) above may be carried out by a dental hygienist under local infiltration analgesia administered by the dental hygienist or under any local or regional block analgesia administered by a registered dentist.

(2) A dental hygienist shall not be permitted to carry out such dental work authorised as aforesaid except under the direction of a registered dentist and after the registered dentist has examined the patient and has indicated in writing to the dental hygienist the course of treatment to be provided for the patient.

(3) A dental hygienist shall administer local infiltration analgesia authorised as aforesaid only under the direct personal supervision of a registered dentist who is on the premises at which the hygienist is carrying out such work at the time at which it is being carried out.'

Dental therapists

The work which may be undertaken by a dental therapist, and the conditions under which it may be undertaken, are laid down in regulations 27:

'27.—(1) Subject to the provisions of this regulation, a dental therapist shall be permitted to carry out dental work (amounting to the practice of dentistry) of the following kinds:

(a) extracting deciduous teeth;

(b) undertaking simple dental fillings;

(c) cleaning and polishing teeth;

(d) scaling teeth (that is to say, the removal of deposits, accretions and stains from those parts of the surfaces of the teeth which are exposed or which are directly beneath the free margins of the gums, including the application of medicaments appropriate thereto);

(e) application to the teeth of such prophylactic materials as the Council may from time to time determine;

(f) giving advice within the meaning of section 37(1) of the Act, such as may be necessary to the proper performance of the dental work referred to in this regulation;

but shall not be permitted to carry out dental work amounting to the practice of dentistry of any other kind except that (a), (b), (d) and (e) above may be carried out by a dental therapist under local infiltration analgesia administered by the dental therapist or under any local or regional block analgesia administered by a registered dentist.

(2) A dental therapist shall not be permitted to carry out such dental work authorised as aforesaid except

(a) in the course of providing national health services;

(b) under the direction of a registered dentist; and
(c) after the registered dentist has examined the patient and has indicated in writing to the dental therapist the specific treatment to be provided for the patient by the said therapist.'

19.3 PHARMACISTS

The registration of pharmacists by the Pharmaceutical Society dates back to the Pharmacy Act 1852. Now, however, the powers and responsibilities of the Pharmaceutical Society in the matter are to be found in the Pharmacy Act 1954. The Society itself conducts qualifying examinations though, under the examination regulations, a candidate who has obtained a degree in pharmacy of a university in Great Britain is deemed to have satisfied the Society's examiners in the subjects taken in his degree examinations. The Society has statutory disciplinary powers.

19.3.1 Evidence of registration

Section 6(1) of the 1954 Act provides:

'**6.**—(1) Any document purporting to be a print of the Annual Register of Pharmaceutical Chemists printed and published by authority of the registrar in any year shall, at any time before the publication of the said Annual Register for the succeeding year, be admissible in any proceedings as evidence that any person named therein is, and that any person not named therein is not, a registered pharmaceutical chemist.

(2) Any such certificate as is mentioned in the last foregoing section shall be admissible in any proceedings as evidence that the person named therein as a registered pharmaceutical chemist is a registered pharmaceutical chemist.'

19.3.2 Restriction on use of certain titles

The provisions of section 78 of the Medicines Act 1968 restricting the use of certain titles, such as pharmacy and pharmacist, replace those of section 19 of the Pharmacy and Poisons Act 1933. To be noted here are (a) that the use of the description *pharmacy* in respect of the pharmaceutical department of a hospital, clinic, nursing home or similar institution, or a health centre, is authorised; and (b) that, in connection with his work at a hospital, clinic, nursing home or similar institution, or at a health centre, as well as in retail pharmacy, a pharmacist may use any of the following titles, viz. pharmaceutical chemist, pharmaceutist, pharmacist, member of the Pharmaceutical Society and, if so entitled, Fellow of the Pharmaceutical Society.

In so far as a medical practitioner may become directly involved in the dispensing of, or similar dealing with, medicines and drugs, special provision is made by section 54 of the Medical Act 1983:

'**54.** Nothing in this Act shall prejudice or in any way affect the lawful occupation, trade, or business of chemists and druggists and dentists, or the rights, privileges or employment of duly licensed apothecaries in Northern Ireland, so far as the occupation, trade or business extends to selling, compounding or dispensing medicines.'

So far as hospitals and similar institutions are concerned the position in law of pharmacists in relation to the control of medicines, poisons and dangerous drugs is set out in Chapter 29.

19.4   OPTICIANS

19.4.1   Registration of opticians

The qualification and registration of opticians and the keeping of a list of corporate bodies carrying on business as opticians is dealt with in the Opticians Act 1989. Under it the General Optical Council is constituted with powers, including disciplinary powers, analogous to those of the General Medical Council.

Two registers of ophthalmic opticians are kept, one register of those engaged or proposing to engage both in the testing of sight and in the fitting and supply of optical appliances (defined in section 36 of the Act as 'an appliance designed to correct, remedy or relieve a defect of sight'), and the other for the registration of persons engaged or proposing to engage in the testing of sight but not the fitting and supply of optical appliances.[21] There is also a register of dispensing opticians, i.e those engaging in the fitting and supplying of optical appliances but not the testing of sight.[22]

19.4.2   Restrictions on the testing of sight[23]

A person who is not a registered medical practicioner or registered ophthalmic optician may not test the sight of another person, the only exceptions to this rule being medical students and, under rules of the General Optical Council, persons training as ophthalmic opticians.[24]

19.4.3   Restrictions on sale and supply of optical appliances

No one may sell any optical appliance unless the sale is effected by or under the supervision of a registered medical practitioner or an optician and this also applies to supply of such appliances under arrangements with the Minister or a health authority. It does not, however, apply to sales to medical practitioners, opticians, hospitals and government departments.[25]

19.4.4 Penalty for pretending to be registered

Section 28 of the Act creates offences related to unregistered practice and wrongful use of title:

'**28.**—(1) Any individual—

- (a) who takes or uses the title of ophthalmic optician or the title of optometrist when he is not registered in either of the registers of ophthalmic opticians; or
- (b) who takes or uses the title of dispensing optician when he is not registered in the register of dispensing opticians; or
- (c) who takes or uses the title of registered optician or enrolled optician when he is not registered in any of the registers; or
- (d) who takes or uses any name, title, addition or description falsely implying that he is registered in any of the registers; or
- (e) who otherwise pretends that he is registered in any of the registers,

shall be liable on summary conviction to a fine of an amount not exceeding level 4 on the standard scale.'

A specific defence is, however, provided by section 28(2):

'(2) On any prosecution for an offence under subsection (1)(d) or (e) above the taking or use of the title of optician by a person to whom this subsection applies is to be taken to imply that he is registered in one of the registers, but the implication may be rebutted if the defendant proves that he took or, as the case may be, used the title in circumstances where it would have been unreasonable for people to believe, in consequence of his taking or, as the case may be, use of it, that he was in fact registered in one of the registers.'

19.5 PROFESSIONS SUPPLEMENTARY TO MEDICINE

19.5.1 Generally

The Professions Supplementary to Medicine Act 1960 provides for the establishment of the Council for Professions Supplementary to Medicine with the general function of co-ordinating and supervising the activities of the boards established under the Act and the additional functions assigned to it by the Act.[26] Further, for each of the following professions – chiropodists, dieticians, medical laboratory technicians, occupational therapists, physiotherapists, radiographers, remedial gymnasts and orthoptists[27] there has been established under the Act a body called the Chiropodists Board, the Dieticians Board, and similarly for the other professions, having the general function of promoting high standards of professional education and professional conduct among members of the relevant profession and the additional functions assigned to it by the Act. The Privy Council on the recommendation of the Council and subject to the provisions of section 10 of the Act may, by order, extend the provisions of the Act to other professions and may order that the provisions of the Act shall cease to apply to any profession. Modification of the list to take account of any amalgamation or proposed amalgamation of professions is also provided for as is any consequential amendment of the constitution of the Council.

19.5.2 Registration of members of the supplementary professions

This is the responsibility of the several boards, provided for by section 2 of the Act, subject to the Registration Rules 1962.[28] Initially, any person qualified in relation to the relevant profession, as mentioned in regulation 3 of the National Health Service (Medical Auxiliaries) Regulations 1954[29] was entitled to registration, subject to the provisions of section 3(1).[30] Disciplinary powers are vested in the boards substantially similar to those vested in the General Medical Council.[31]

19.5.3 Use of title

A person who is registered is entitled to use the title state registered chiropodist or state registered dietician (and similarly for the other professions mentioned in section 1 of the Act or to which the provisions of the Act may subsequently be extended under the provisions of section 10) according to the profession in respect of which he is registered.[32]

Any person who:

1. takes or uses either alone or in conjunction with any other words, the title of state registered chiropodist, state chiropodist or registered chiropodist (and similarly as regards the other professions) when his name is not on the register established under the Act in respect of that profession; or
2. takes or uses any name, title, addition or description falsely implying, or otherwise pretends that his name is on a register established under the Act,

is on summary conviction liable to a fine not exceeding level 3 on the standard scale.[33] The comparatively moderate maximum penalties compared with those under the Acts relating to medical practitioners, pharmacists and opticians is probably related to the fact that while those belonging to the three latter professions have certain exclusive privileges in relation to the practice of their respective professions, persons belonging to professions within the provisions of the Professions Supplementary to Medicine Act 1960, are given no such exclusive privileges. Furthermore, anyone may describe himself as a chiropodist etc. provided he does not infringe section 6(2). Hence, a physiotherapist who was not registered under the Act could still call himself a physiotherapist or, if a member of the Chartered Society of Physiotherapists, a chartered physiotherapist in accordance with the rules of that society, but generally unless he is registered he may not be employed by a health authority.[34]

19.5.4 Approval of courses, qualifications and institutions

The responsibility for the approval of courses, qualifications and institutions, as well as for keeping the register, rests with the relevant Board.[35]

19.6 NURSES, MIDWIVES AND HEALTH VISITORS

Earlier legislation governing the registration and conduct of nurses and midwives was substantially altered by the Nurses, Midwives and Health Visitors Act 1979. This section of the chapter of professional qualifications examines only those provisions of the Act, and regulations made thereunder, as are likely directly to affect the management of hospitals and their staff.

The 1979 Act was substantially amended by the Nurses, Midwives and Health Visitors Act 1992 which made major changes to the structure of the professions in question. In particular the relationship between the United Kingdom Central Council and the four National Boards was changed, concentrating greater powers relating to the regulation of the professions in the UKCC. Provisions relating to registration remain largely unaffected, but two additional powers in respect of professional discipline are given to the UKCC. These are mentioned briefly at the conclusion of the present section.

19.6.1 Registration

General provisions

The Central Council for Nursing, Midwifery and Health Visiting is obliged to maintain a register of qualified nurses, midwives and health visitors.[36] The professional register is divided[37] into 15 parts, which are as follows:

Part 1 First level nurses trained in general nursing.
Part 2 Second level nurses trained in general nursing (England and Wales).
Part 3 First level nurses trained in the nursing of persons suffering from mental illness.
Part 4 Second level nurses trained in the nursing of persons suffering from mental illness (England and Wales).

Part   5 First level nurses trained in the nursing of persons suffering from mental handicap.

Part   6 Second level nurses trained in the nursing of persons suffering from mental handicap (England and Wales).

Part   7 Second level nurses (Scotland and Northern Ireland).

Part   8 Nurses trained in the nursing of sick children.

Part   9 Nurses who are trained in the nursing of persons suffering from fever and who either were registered as such on 1 July 1983, or are not registered in, and cannot be admitted to, any other Part of the Register.

Part 10 Midwives.

Part 11 Health visitors.

Part 12 Nurses qualified following a course of preparation in adult nursing.

Part 13 Nurses qualified following a course of preparation in mental health nursing.

Part 14 Nurses qualified following a course of preparation in mental handicap nursing.

Part 15 Nurses qualified following a course of preparation in children's nursing.

Admission to the Register

A person is entitled to admission to the Register on making an application to the Council in accordance with the Council's rules[38] if he satisfies the Council that:

1. he is of good character; and
2. he has the appropriate professional qualifications.[39]

The term 'appropriate professional qualifications' is defined in section 11(3) (a)–(c), as follows:

'(3) He is to be regarded as having those qualifications if—
   (a) he has in the United Kingdom undergone the training, and passed the examinations, required by the Council's rules for admission to that part of the register; or
   (b) being a national of any member State of the European Communities, he has professional qualifications, obtained in a member State other than the United Kingdom, which the Secretary of State has by order designated as having Community equivalence for purpose of registration in that part; or
   (c) he has, elsewhere than in the United Kingdom, undergone training in nursing, midwifery or health visiting (as the case may be) and either—
      (i) that training is recognised by the Central Council as being to a standard sufficient for registration in that part; or
      (ii) it is not so recognised, but the applicant has undergone in the United Kingdom or elsewhere such additional training as the Council may require.'

Further provision is made by subsections 3A, 4 and 4A[40] of section 11 for the recognition of qualifications having 'Community equivalence', as follows:

'(3A) An order under subsection (3)(b) may provide that a professional qualification designated by the order is to be regarded as having Community equivalence for the purposes of registration in a part of the register only if prescribed conditions [required by a directive issued by the Council of the European Communities] are fulfilled; and different conditions may be prescribed with respect to the same qualification for different circumstances; and

(4) In the case of an applicant within subsection (3)(c), the rules may either—
(a) make it an additional condition of his being registered that he has the necessary knowledge of English; or
(b) require him to have that knowledge within a period specified by the rules (failing which his registration will lapse at the end of the period).

(4A) In any case where—
(a) an application for admission to a part of the register is made by an applicant within subsection (3)(b), and
(b) the Council has received all the documentary evidence as to his character and qualifications required to enable him to be registered, he shall be registered in that part within 3 months of the date on which the Council was in receipt of that evidence.

(5) "National" in relation to a member State of the European Communities, means the same as it does for the purposes of the Community Treaties.'

Qualifications having Community equivalence for registration purposes

In relation to paragraph (b) of section 3(2) above, the EEC Nursing and Midwifery Qualifications Designation Order 1983[41] provides for the mutual recognition of qualifications, the co-ordination of provisions relating to the practice of midwifery, and general nursing, in accordance with the First and Second Midwifery Directives[42] and the Second Nursing Directive.[43]

The Regulations provide, relevantly, as follows:

'Qualifications having community equivalence for registration purposes

3. Subject to Articles 4 to 6 below, a European nursing or midwifery qualification in respect of which a certificate or other document specified in Part I (nursing qualifications) or Part II (midwifery qualifications) of the Schedule to this Order is hereby designated as having Community equivalence for the purposes of registration, in the case of a nursing qualification, in Part 1 of the professional register and, in the case of a midwifery qualification, in Part 10 of that register.

Further certificates required in certain cases

4. A certificate or other document—
(a) specified in Part I of the Schedule to this Order and obtained in respect of training which does not comply with the requirements of article 1 of the Second Nursing Directive (minimum standard of training for nurses)—
(i) before the date on which the member State in which it was obtained had implemented that Directive, or
(ii) on or after that date in respect of a course of training begun before that date; or

(b) specified in Part II of that Schedule and obtained at any time before 23 January 1986 in respect of training which does not comply with the requirements of Article 1 of the Second Midwifery Directive (minimum standards of midwifery training),

shall not have Community equivalence for the purposes of any person's registration in the professional register unless it is accompanied by a competent authority certificate relating to that person.

5. A certificate or other document specified in Part II of the Schedule obtained in a member State by any person in respect of training which is not required to be recognised by other member States in pursuance of article 2 of the First Midwifery Directive unless it is followed by professional practice for which a certificate complying with article 4 of that Directive is issued shall not have Community equivalence for the purposes of registration in the professional register unless—

(a) if it was obtained before the date on which that member State implemented that Directive, it is accompanied by a competent authority certificate relating to that person;

(b) in any case, if it is accompanied by an Article 4 certificate relating to that person.'

The Schedule to the Regulations[44] provides specifically for the EC qualifications which may be recognised for the purposes of professional practice in the United Kingdom. These are as follows:

'EUROPEAN NURSING QUALIFICATIONS

Belgium

1.—(1) The certificate of "hospitalier(ère)/verpleegassistent(e)" awarded by the State or by schools established or recognised by the State.

(2) The certificate of "infirmier(ère) hospitalier(ère)/ziekenhuisverpleger (-verpleegster)" awarded by the State or by schools established or recognised by the State.

(3) The diploma of "infirmier(ère) gradué(e) hospitalier(ère)/gegradueerd ziekenhuisverpleger (-verpleegster)" awarded by the State or by higher paramedical colleges established or recognised by the State.

Denmark

2. The diploma of "sygeplejerske" awarded by nursing schools recognised by the "Sundhedsstyrelsen" (State board of health).

France

3. The State diploma of "infirmier(ère)" awarded by the Ministry of Health.

Germany

4.—(1) The certificates awarded by the competent authorities as a result of the "staatliche Prüfung in der Krankenpflege" (State nursing examination).

(2) The certificates from the competent authorities of the Federal Republic of Germany stating that the diplomas awarded after 8 May 1945 by the competent authorities of the German Democratic Republic are recognised as equivalent to those listed in sub-paragraph (1) above.

Greece

5.—(1) The diploma of 'Ανωτέρυς Σχολῆς Αδελψῶν Νοσοκόμων' (college of nurses responsible for general care), recognised by the Ministry for Social Services or the diploma of "τῶν παραϊατρικῶν σχολῶν τῶν Κέντρων' Ανωτέρας

Τεχνικῆς καὶ Ἐπαγγελματικῆς Ἐκπαιδευσεως" (paramedical schools of the Higher Technical and Vocational Education Centres) awarded by the Ministry for National Education and Religious Affairs; and

(2) The "πιστοποιητικό πρακτικῆς ασκήσεως τον επαγγέλματος τῆς ἀδελφῆς νοσοκόμου" (certificate of practical training for the nursing profession) awarded by the Ministry for Social Services.

Ireland

6. The certificate of "Registered General Nurse" issued by "An Bord Altranais" (the Nursing Board).

Italy

7. The "diploma di abilitazione professionale per infermiere professionale" awarded by State-recognised schools.

Luxembourg

8. The following diplomas awarded by the Ministry of Public Health on the strength of an examining board decision—
  (a) the State diploma of "infirmier";
  (b) the State diploma of "infirmier hospitalier gradué".

The Netherlands

9. The following diplomas awarded by one of the examining boards appointed by the public authorities—
  (a) the diplomas of "verpleger A", "verpleegster A" or "verpleegkundige A";
  (b) the diploma of "verpleegkundige MBOV (Mid-delbare Beroepsopleiding Verpleegkundige)" (intermediate nursing training);
  (c) the diploma of "verpleegkundige HBOV (Hogere Beroepsopleiding Verpleegkundige)" (higher nursing training).

Portugal

9A. Diploma do curso de enfermagem geral (diploma in general nursing) awarded by State recognised educational establishments and registered by the competent authority.

Spain

9B. Título de Diplomado universitario en Enfermeria (university diploma in nursing) awarded by the Ministry for Education and Science.

Part II

European Midwifery Qualifications

Belgium

10. The "diplôme d'accoucheuse/vroedvrouwdiploma" awarded by schools set up or approved by the State or by the "Jury central".

Denmark

11. The "bevis for bestàet jordemodereksamen" awarded by "Danmarks Jordemoderskole".

France

12. The "diplôme de sage-femme" awarded by the State.

Germany

13.—(1) The "Hebammenprüfungszeugnis" awarded by the State-appointed examining board.

(2) The certificates issued by the competent authorities of the Federal Republic of Germany, stating that the diplomas awarded after 8 May 1945 by the competent authorities of the German Democratic Republic are recognised as equivalent to those specified in sub-paragraph (1) above.

Greece

14.—(1) The πτυχιο μάιαδ authenticated by the Ministry of Social Services.

(2) The πτυχιο Ανωτέρας Σχοληγς Στελεχῶν 'Υγέιας κάι Κοινωνικης Προωο ιαδ Τμήματος Μαιῶν' issued by the KATEE.

Ireland

15. The certificate in midwifery awarded by "An Bord Altranais".

Italy

16. The "diploma d'ostetrica" awarded by schools approved by the State.

Luxembourg

17. The "diplôme de sage-femme" awarded by the Minister for Health following a decision by the examining board.

The Netherlands

18. The "vroedvrouwdiploma" awarded by the examining body designated by the State.

Portugal

19. The diploma of "enfermeiro especialista em enfermagem de saúde materna e obstétrica".

Spain

20. The diploma of "asistencia obstétrica" awarded by the Ministero de Educación y Ciencia.'

Linguistic requirements

Rule 8(4) of the Nurses, Midwives and Health Visitors Rules Approval Order 1983[45] provides for proficiency in the understanding and use of English, as follows:

'(4) Any person applying for admission to the register under section 11(3)(c) of the Act shall satisfy the Council that she has the necessary knowledge, understanding and use of the English language for effective and safe practice of nursing, midwifery or health visiting as the case may be.'

As pointed out in Chapter 20,[46] 'Injury at work', legal liability for accidental injury may fall upon an employer through failure to see to it that staff working in a team have sufficient linguistic and communication skills to be safe colleagues.

Visiting EEC nurses and midwives

Any nurse or midwife satisfying the criteria laid down in section 22B may practise as a nurse responsible for general care or as a midwife and while doing so shall be deemed to be registered either as a nurse responsible for general care or midwife, as the case may be.[47]

19.6.2   Attendance by unqualified persons at childbirth

One of the restrictions consequent upon professional registration as a midwife under the Act is that unqualified persons are prohibited from attending a woman during childbirth. Section 17 provides:

'**17.**—(1) A person other than a registered midwife or a registered medical practitioner shall not attend a woman in childbirth.

(2) Until the day appointed by the Secretary of State by an order[48] under paragraph 3(1) of Schedule 4 to the Sex Discrimination Act 1975, a man who is a registered midwife shall not attend a woman in childbirth except in a place approved in writing by or on behalf of the Secretary of State.

(3) Subsections (1) and (2) do not apply—

(a)   where the attention is given in a case of sudden or urgent necessity; or

(b)   in the case of a person who, while undergoing training with a view to becoming a medical practitioner or to becoming a midwife, attends a woman in childbirth as part of a course of practical instruction in midwifery recognised by the General Medical Council or one of the National Boards.

(4) A person who contravenes subsection (1) or (2) shall be liable on summary conviction to a fine [not exceeding level 4 on the standard scale].'

In an unreported case in 1982[49] a father was successfully prosecuted under section 9 of the Midwives Act 1951 for delivering his partner of their child.

19.6.3   False claims of professional qualification

Section 14 of the Nurses, Midwives and Health Visitors Act creates offences of false representation of possessing professional registration, as follows:

'**14.**—(1) A person commits an offence if, with the intent to deceive (whether by words or in writing or by the assumption of any name or description, or by the wearing of any uniform or badge or by any other kind of conduct)—

(a)   he falsely represents himself to possess qualifications in nursing, midwifery or health visiting; or

(b)   he falsely represents himself to be registered in the register, or in a particular part of it.

(2) A person commits an offence if—

(a)   with intent that any person shall be deceived, he causes or permits another person to make any representation about himself which, if made by himself with intent to deceive would be an offence in him under subsection (1); or

(b)   with intent to deceive, makes with regard to another person any representation which—

(i)   if false to his own knowledge, and

(ii)   if made by the other with that intent would be an offence in the other under that subsection.

(3) A person guilty of an offence under this section shall be liable on summary conviction to a fine [not exceeding level 4 on the standard scale].'

19.6.4 Removal from, and restoration to, the Register

Matters of professional misconduct and discipline are provided for in section 12 of the 1979 Act, as amended and supplemented by the Nurses, Midwives and Health Visitors Act 1992, and rules made thereunder. In addition to the power to remove from the Register there is also a power, provided by section 7 of the 1992 Act, to suspend. The power to caution created by section 9 of the 1992 Act does not include the power, contained in the relevant section[50] of the Medical Act 1983, to make continued professional registration conditional on compliance with standards or conditions set down by the Council for the particular case.

NOTES

1. Defined in section 4(3), as amended by the Medical Qualifications (Amendment) Act 1991, section 1.
2. Section 4(1) defines a qualifying examination as an examination held by any of the bodies or combination of bodies specified in subsection (2).
3. Section 10 lays down the requirements as to experience. The main provision is subsection (2) which states that: 'A person must, after passing a qualifying examination, have been engaged for the prescribed period in employment in a resident medical capacity in one or more approved hospitals or approved institutions and have obtained a certificate under this section.' 'Approved' is defined in section 11(4).
4. A primary European qualification is defined in section 17.
5. Case 115(78) [1979] ECR 399.
6. Case 246(80), European Court, 6 October 1981.
7. Defined in subsection (2).
8. Defined in section 55. An improperly administered test may give rise to a complaint of racial discrimination, see *GMC v Goba* [1988] IRLR 425.
9. 'Good character' is not defined.
10. See the Medical Act 1983, section 20.
11. *R v Pharmaceutical Society, ex parte Sokoh* The Times, 4 December 1986.
12. *Bhandari v Advocates Committee* [1956] 3 All ER 742.
13. *Hunter v Clare* [1897] 1 QB 635.
14. Medical Act 1983, section 46(1).
15. Medical Act 1983, section 46(3).
16. Juries Act 1974, section 9 and Schedule 1, Part III.
17. Not to be confused with the temporary full registration of visiting overseas specialists pursuant to section 27.
18. Dentists Act 1984, section 26(1); and see also section 39, 'Prohibition on use of practitioners' titles by Laymen'.
19. Dentists Act 1984, section 38(1) and (2).
20. SI 1986/887, as amended by SI 1991/1706.

21. Opticians Act 1989, section 7(a).
22. Opticians Act 1989, section 7(b).
23. Opticians Act 1989, section 24.
24. See the General Optical Council (Rules on the Testing of Sight by Persons Training as Ophthalmic Opticians) Order, SI 1974/1329; these remain in force following the National Health Service Act 1977 (see the Interpretation Act 1978, section 17).
25. Opticians Act 1989, section 27.
26. Professions Supplementary to Medicine Act 1960, section 1(1).
27. Orthoptists were added by the Professions Supplementary to Medicine (Orthoptists Board) Order in Council, SI 1966/990.
28. Professions Supplementary to Medicine (Registration Rules), SI 1962/1765, as amended by SIs 1966/1111, 1967/266, 1968/1973 and 1975/1691, 1979/365, 1980/968, 1981/178, 1986/660 and the (Registration (Appeals) Rules) Orders in Council, SI 1962/2545.
29. SI 1954/55.
30. Professions Supplementary to Medicine Act 1960, section 3(2).
31. See also the Professions Supplementary to Medicine (Disciplinary Committees) (Procedure) Rules Order in Council, SI 1964/1203 and the Professions Supplementary to Medicine (Disciplinary Proceedings) Legal Assessor Rules, SI 1964/951.
32. Professions Supplementary to Medicine Act 1960, section 6(1).
33. Professions Supplementary to Medicine Act 1960, section 6(2).
34. See the National Health Service (Professions Supplementary to Medicine) Regulations 1974, SI 1974/494.
35. Professions Supplementary to Medicine Act 1960, section 4.
36. Nurses, Midwives and Health Visitors Act 1979, section 10(1) (unaffected by the amendments in the Nurses, Midwives and Health Visitors Act 1992).
37. Schedule 1 of the Nurses, Midwives and Health Visitors (Parts of the Register) Order 1983, SI 1983/667), as amended by SI 1989/104 and SI 1989/1456.
38. See the Nurses, Midwives and Health Visitors Rules Approval Order 1983, SI 1983/873, as amended by SIs 1989/109, 1989/1456, 1990/1624, 1991/135 and 1991/766.
39. Nurses, Midwives and Health Visitors Act 1979, section 11(2).
40. Subsections 3A and 4A were inserted by the Nursing and Midwifery (EEC Recognition) Order 1983, SI 1983/884, as amended by the Nursing and Midwifery (EEC Recognition) Amendment Order 1984, SI 1984/1975.
41. SI 1983/921.
42. EC Council Directives 80/154/EEC and 80/155/EEC.
43. EC Council Directive 77/453/EEC and see HC(91)32 for EEC 89/48 (other professions).
44. As amended, in the case of Portugal and Spain following the accession of those countries to the EEC, by SI 1985/1852.
45. SI 1983/873, as amended (see note 38, above).
46. At p. 554
47. Nurses, Midwives and Health Visitors Act 1979 (as amended by the Nurses, Midwives and Health Visitors Act 1992), section 11A.
48. 1 January 1984 (Sex Discrimination (Midwives) (Specified Date) Order SI 1983/1841), that being the date from which men may train and practise as midwives on equal terms with women.
49. See Finch 'Paternalism and Professionalism in Childbirth' (1982) 132 New Law Journal 995–996, 1011–1012.
50. Medical Act 1983, section 36(1)(b)(iii).

Injury at work

20.1 LIABILITY FOR INJURY TO EMPLOYEES

The liability of an employer, including an employing health authority, to an injured employee is to be found in both common law and statute. This chapter addresses both sources of such liability and examines the grounds on which compensation may be awarded for injury at work, not only against a negligent employer, but also against other employees, from social security sickness benefits and from the Criminal Injuries Compensation Board. Furthermore, wherever a statute or regulations impose duties on an employer and provide criminal penalties (such as a fine) for the breach of such duties, there may in certain cases be an additional civil liability (individual action for damages) in favour of a person injured by the breach of duty. In all such cases, proof by the defendant of contributory negligence on the part of the person injured is no bar to compensation in any of these cases, though it may reduce the damages awarded in respect of breach of a common law duty, or in breach of a statutory duty causing personal injury to an employee.

Section 125 of the National Health Service Act 1977 (formerly section 72 of the National Health Service Act 1946 and originally section 265 of the Public Health Act 1875) affords no defence to an action in tort (civil liability) against a health authority or one of its officers in respect of injury to a member of staff. Section 265 of the 1875 Act provides:

'**265.** No matter or thing done, and no contract entered into by any local authority . . . and no matter or thing done by any member . . . or by any officers of such authority or other person whomsoever acting under the direction of such authority, shall, if the matter or thing were done or the contract were entered into *bona fide* for the purpose of executing this Act, subject them or any of them personally to any action liability claim or demand whatsoever; and any expense incurred by any such authority member officer or other person acting as last aforesaid shall be borne and repaid out of the fund or rate applicable by such authority to the general purposes of this Act. . . .'

Schedule 2, Part III, paragraph 25 of the National Health Service and Community Care Act 1992 provides that the same legal position applies to NHS trusts. It has been held[1] that this section protects an authority only against an action for breach of its *public* duties, and not negligence as an employer towards an injured employee. A health authority or trust employer, as defendant in a personal injuries action, is equally open to the judicial procedures for discovery of documents relating to the accident (such as investigation reports) as is any defendant. For such procedures, reference should be made to Chapter 5.

A health authority, trust hospital, or private institution, as occupier of the premises used for its purposes as such, has the responsibilities of an occupier to lawful visitors to the premises in respect of their safety. The term 'lawful visitors' in the Occupiers' Liability Act 1957 includes employees as well as patients and those visiting them, in the most literal sense of the word. Particular regard should be had to the provisions of section 2 of the Occupiers' Liability Act 1957, the subject of the liability of an occupier to lawful visitors being discussed in detail in Chapter 9.

Until the coming into operation of the National Health Service and Community Care Act 1990 health authorities, as Crown operations, did not insure on the commercial market against the risk of liability of injuries to members of their staff. That risk was carried by the Exchequer. Section 60(1) of the 1990 Act effectively provided that, from 1 April 1991, 'no health service body shall be regarded as the servant or agent of the Crown or as enjoying any status, immunity or privilege of the Crown . . .'.[2] While there are certain saving provisions, noted later in this chapter,[3] Crown status and any immunities attaching to that status are once and for all removed by section 60. Certain enactments, orders and regulations relating to food and health and safety in respect of certain health service bodies and premises had already been applied to the National Health Service by the National Health Service (Amendment) Act 1986.[4] Nevertheless, by an Executive Letter[5] of October 1990, general managers of health service units and facilities were instructed in the following terms:

'The general principle to be applied to insurance is that the public sector should generally carry it own risks unless greater value for money is obtained by alternative arrangements. Authorities should not enter into commercial insurance arrangements in respect of any of their insurable risks unless Departmental approval has been granted (and this requires Treasury agreement). At present approval has been given only for income generation activities and for a very limited number of specific schemes for the business use of Crown cars.'

The Executive Letter gives a more general approval in respect of NHS trusts and sets up the arrangements to be used for certain specific risks, in particular clinical negligence. This matter is dealt with in Chapter 5, 'Legal proceedings against health authorities and trusts'.

Executive Letter EL(90)195 left some doubt as to who should meet the costs of litigation and claims made by former employees of health authorities whose contracts of employment transferred to an NHS trust by virtue of section 6 of the National Health Service and Community Care Act 1990. That section deals with the transfer of rights, powers, duties and liabilities in connection with contracts of employment from health authorities to newly formed NHS trusts. To remove this doubt a further Executive Letter, EL(92)8 provides, relevantly, as follows:

'2. *NHS trusts are not expected to meet the cost of claims for periods before their operational date even though the legal liability under the contract of employment has transferred. These costs remain the responsibility of the former employing health authority.* Exceptionally, where a claim bridges the operational date of the NHS trust there will be joint financial responsibility and an appropriate apportionment will need to be agreed between the health authority and the trust.

3. Claims for any period before the trust's operational date should normally be handled by the former employing health authority, although the exact arrangements are for local determination. NHS trusts and health authorities should cooperate to the maximum extent possible so that cases are brought to a rapid and satisfactory conclusion.

4. We expect that the total cost to the National Health Service of employers' liability claims will be very small by comparison with total National Health Service expenditure. In recent years expenditure by the National Health Service on claims arising from civil litigation has been of the order of £10 to £12 million yearly, excluding medical negligence. Most of this is probably accounted for by clinical negligence claims against nurses and other professional groups.

5. Health authorities remain both legally and financially liable for claims from employees whose contracts of employment have not transferred under section 6 of the Act to an NHS trust.'

If any voluntary organisation, such as a league of hospital friends or other such group, undertakes any activity on hospital premises, such as the provision of canteen facilities for patients, the risk of liability for injury to a member or employee of that organisation, or indeed to anyone else, would appear to lie on the organisation itself and not upon the Secretary of State or health authority or trust. In the case of joint ventures pursuant to section 7 of the Health and Medicines Act 1988, the critical question to be answered would be which organisation, the health authority (or trust) or the collaborating organisation, was the employer (if any) of the injured person at the material time. For the precise relationship between employer and employee, and the circumstances in which the courts have been prepared to hold that such a relationship does and does not exist, reference should be made to Chapter 5.

In the case of National Health Service employees, even when an employing health authority is for some reason under no liability in tort in respect of an injury to a member of staff on duty, the injured person may have a contractual entitlement to sick pay and other benefits for a limited period, in accordance with the terms of nationally negotiated

Whitley Council agreements,[6] where such arrangements apply. Employment conditions are discussed in detail in Chapter 17.

20.2 EMPLOYER'S LIABILITY TO PROVIDE SAFE SYSTEM OF WORK

An employer is under a legal responsibility to provide a safe system of working conditions for all employees. The duty falls distinctly short of a guarantee of safety; but it has been the subject of close judicial attention on account of the fact that employers not only owe a duty to take care in creating and maintaining safe working conditions, but also a more onerous duty to see to it that care is taken and that such provision is made. It was once the case that an employer was not vicariously liable[7] for injury by one employee to another employee. This 'doctrine of common employment' was gradually reduced in scope until it was finally abolished by the Law Reform (Personal Injuries) Act 1948.[8] While the former doctrine is now of historical interest only, the steps taken by the courts to reduce its scope have created significantly greater responsibilities of an employer over and above 'ordinary' negligence.

Any employer, including a health authority, hospital, NHS trust and health services employer in the private sector, owes a duty to all employees to provide competent staff, safe plant, tools and equipment, safe premises and a generally safe system of working practices and communications, for the establishment and maintenance of employee safety. While the safe system of work is an overall responsibility, it is possible to cite judicial decisions specifically concerned with each of these separate elements of an employer's responsibility.

The employment and training of competent and reliable staff is so elementary that few judicial decisions have concerned the question. Such judicial decisions as there are have focused on the question of 'practical jokes' and the question of whether the employer is, or is not, liable to a third party (including another member of staff) injured in consequence. In *Hudson v Ridge Manufacturing Co* (1957)[9] one of the defendants' employees had been making a nuisance of himself to his fellow employees, including the plaintiff who was disabled, by persistently engaging in horseplay such as tripping them up. He had been reprimanded on many occasions by the foreman at the factory and had been warned that one day he would hurt someone, but with no effect. No further steps were taken by the employers to check this conduct, whether by dismissal or otherwise. On one occasion, the employee tripped up a fellow employee and injured him. It was held that, as this potentially dangerous behaviour had been known to the employers for a long time, and as they had failed to prevent it or remove the source of it, they were liable to the plaintiff to failing to take proper care of his safety. By contrast, in *Smith v Crossley Brothers* (1951)[10] an apprentice employed in the defendants' apprentice training school was seriously injured by a practical joke played upon him by two fellow apprentices. The Court of Appeal held that the defendant employers were not liable to the plaintiff in negligence because his injury had occurred through an act of wilful behaviour which the defendants could not, on the facts, have reasonably foreseen.

An employer is under a common law duty to provide adequate training to all employees such that other employees will be reasonably safe in working alongside them, and jointly with them. In *Hawkins v Ian Ross Castings (Ltd)* (1970)[11] the plaintiff employee was injured when a seventeen-year-old labourer, who spoke very poor English, took one end of the shank of a container carrying molten metal, the plaintiff taking the other. The employee whose English was poor misunderstood an instruction to stop walking with the container, in a situation of danger, and the plaintiff consequently lost his balance and fell over the mould. The molten metal was spilled and some of it went on his foot, causing a severe injury. It was held that the presence of an unskilled labourer with an imperfect knowledge of English who was employed to carry molten metal imposed a higher standard of care on the defendant employers, both in the layout of the work and in the steps to be taken to avoid accidents. It follows from this decision that an authority, trust or any agency providing health care services should not only take reasonable steps to avoid accidents in a situation where employees are less reliable than they might otherwise be, but also that such employers should take particular care in the training of employees (whether by way of practical experience, or linguistically) even before such employees are placed in a working situation where their inexperience or inability may create a foreseeable risk.

An employer is under a duty to establish and maintain a safe working place. This responsibility is apt to cover not only the working premises themselves, but the immediate access to them such as pathways, driveways, steps and ladders. There is, however, no duty to guarantee the safety of premises and the responsibility stops short at seeing to it that all reasonable steps are taken to avoid injury. In *Latimer v AEC Ltd* (1953)[12] an unusually heavy rainstorm had flooded the floors of a large factory and an oily cooling mixture, normally contained in a channel in the floor, along which it was pumped to machinery as a cooling agent, rose and mixed with the flood waters so that, when they subsided, the whole floor became slippery. So far as supplies permitted, sawdust was spread on the floor but some areas were left untreated. A workman working in a gangway which had not been treated with sawdust was attempting to load a heavy a barrel onto a trolley when he slipped and injured his ankle. In an action against his employers for failing to provide safe premises, it was held that the employers were not negligent as they had done all which a reasonable employer could be expected to do for the safety of employees, having regard to the degree of risk balanced against the practicability of precautions to avoid the risk.

The application of responsibilities to maintain safe working premises is unproblematic so far as hospitals, including out-patients departments, and other health services premises are concerned. While the legal principle is equally clear, the case of 'outworkers' including, for instance, community psychiatric nurses and other staff working away from a central base or health authority premises, may present certain difficulties. The general principle of employers' liability to see to it, so far as reasonably practicable, that injury does not occur on working premises, applies equally to the premises which may be visited on a domiciliary or similar basis by health authority and hospital employees. It has been held[13] that there is considerable difference in degree between the performance of the duty to maintain safe premises when those premises are in the employer's own control and the situation in which they are in the control of a stranger or third party. Nevertheless, a health authority whose community outworkers were asked to visit premises, the condition of which, or even the occupier of which, was known or could reasonably be anticipated to present a danger to the employee, could be liable in damages in the event of injury caused by the materialisation of such known or foreseeable risk. Following the principle of *Holgate v Lancashire Mental Hospitals Board* (1937),[14] in which a mentally disordered patient with a serious criminal record was released from a secure institution without proper steps to ensure supervision, and in which the plaintiff who was injured in an attack by this patient succeeded against the hospital authorities on the ground of breach of duty, a community psychiatric or other health care professional could maintain an action against the allegedly negligent health authority or hospital concerned. In *Partington v Wandsworth London Borough Council* (1989)[15] it was accepted as 'common ground' by the court that both the mother of a seventeen-year-old mentally handicapped girl, and the local authority who shared her care, were jointly under a duty to take reasonable care to prevent her injuring other people, and that duty would no doubt have extended to health care professionals in appropriate circumstances. On the facts of the case itself, the duty was held not to have been broken by taking the seventeen year old out for a walk, during which she suddenly and unpredictably pushed over an old lady, the plaintiff.

The general responsibility to maintain a safe system of work encompasses all aspects of communications and instructions, which should be adequate to avoid injury in consequence of relying on them. The case mentioned above, of an employee who spoke imperfect English in consequence of which the plaintiff was injured, is an example also of the failure to maintain safe communications between employees.

So, too, is the case of apprentices, pupils or trainees upon whom reliance is being placed by the health authority, hospital or other employer to form an integral and reliable part of a working team. Such, for instance, would be the case of injury to a nurse caused in a lifting accident on account of the inexperience of a trainee colleague for which the employer should have made provision. There may even be tasks where, according to circumstances, it would be unreliable and unsafe, and in consequence actionable, to allow the involvement of a trainee at all before a certain stage of experience or development. The decision by the employer would rest on the circumstances of each particular case, balancing the importance of the object to be attained with the practicability of precautions against injury.

Finally, an employer is under an obligation to provide safe plant, tools and equipment to employees. Employees should be instructed in proper ways of using tools and equipment and failure to give such proper instructions and training may result in breach of the employer's legal responsibility under the principles set out above. If, however, a tool or piece of equipment is used properly but nevertheless causes injury, the question arises whether the employer can be liable even if reasonable care has been taken to obtain the equipment from a reputable supplier and to put it into commission after having followed reasonable safety precautions. Given that the responsibility of an employer for the safety of employees falls short of a duty to guarantee such safety, it was formerly the law[16] that an employee injured by a piece of apparently reliable equipment had no action against an employer who had purchased it from a reputable supplier. The loss fell on the injured employee and was not transferred by law to the employer. This situation, which was capable of injustice to the relatively more vulnerable employee, was reversed by statute in 1969. The Employers' Liability (Defective Equipment) Act 1969 provides that even if a piece of equipment is apparently reliable, the employer will be *deemed* to have been negligent, thus allowing an action by the employee against the employer; the employer being left to recover an indemnity, if he can, against the supplier of the equipment. The significance of the Act in practical terms, so far as concerns employee safety and compensation for injury, is that the negligence of the employer is presumed, or 'deemed', to have occurred, leaving the injured employee simply with the task of proving that the breach of duty caused the injury in question.

Such causation will not normally present any difficulty to an injured employee. Even when causation is in doubt, the principle of *McGhee v National Coal Board* (1972)[17] favours the injured plaintiff in the following way. In breach of regulations, the defendant employers failed to provide adequate shower and washing facilities for their employees, one of whom was the plaintiff. The plaintiff, who had been cleaning out a brick kiln and whose hands were covered in brick dust, regularly left work in a hot and dusty condition and contracted dermatitis. The defendants alleged that his skin condition resulted simply from the fact that he had been doing a dirty job, and denied liability. The House of Lords held the defendant employers liable, saying that if competing causes existed, namely brick dust getting onto his skin (which was part of his job, and no legal wrong), and brick dust not being washed off owing to the lack of washing facilities in breach of regulations, the law would presume the wrongful cause to have been the actual cause of the injury. The plaintiff therefore succeeded in his claim against the National Coal Board for the skin disease which he had contracted. This principle of causation is to be carefully distinguished from the significantly different situation which arose where the wrongful cause was only one among a number of allegedly competing causes, and in which the principle of *McGhee* failed to benefit the plainfiff.[18]

Not only complex equipment but also the simplest of items may constitute a danger to employees. In *Baxter v St Helena Group Hospital Management Committee* (1972)[19] the plaintiff nurse went into a changing room to change her uniform and sat down on a chair which collapsed underneath her. Examination of the chair showed that it was riddled with woodworm and must, to be in such a state, have been infested for a considerable time. The employers were liable for the injury on the basis that they had not inspected the chair properly at regular intervals.

In *Smith v St Helier Hospital Group Hospital Management Committee* (1956)[20] the plaintiff, a theatre orderly, alleged that dermatitis had been caused by the constant use by her in her work of a solution of Dettol and soap in hot water, and resulted from the defendant authority's negligence in allowing this to occur. It was found that she was more sensitive to Dettol than most people. In giving judgment against her, Mr Justice Devlin said:

'It was not suggested that the defendants were aware that the plaintiff was one of those sensitive people – perhaps if they had been, some duty might have been put on them in law . . . It was impossible for the plaintiff to establish any case against the defendants based on negligence in the absence of any proof that they knew of particular sensitivity, nor could it be suggested that they ought to have taken any particular precautions as regards the use of Dettol by her.'

An employer is under no legal duty to refuse to employ an adult employee on work he is willing to do merely because the employer thinks it is not in the employee's best interests. In *Withers v Perry Chain Co Ltd* (1961)[21] the plaintiff had been employed for some years on bicycle hub assembly work in the defendants' factory and contracted dermatitis from constant contact with grease. She was moved to another, less greasy, job but her dermatitis continued. In ruling in favour of the defendant employers it was said that, if the common law was otherwise, it would be imposing a restriction on the freedom of the individual and would be oppressive to the employee by limiting his ability to find work rather than beneficial to him. There is, said the court, no duty at common law requiring an employer to dismiss an employee rather than to retain him in employment and allow him to earn his wages, simply because there may be some risk to health. If there is such a risk, it is for the employee to weigh it against the desirability or necessity of the employment. The duty of the defendant employers in that case was to take reasonable care of the plaintiff in the employment in which she was engaged, having regard to the fact that she was prone to dermatitis.

As to the legal responsibility of an employer proposing to take on a member of staff who is likely to work in situations presenting danger, the decision of the Court of Appeal in *White v Holbrook Precision Castings* (1984)[22] is instructive. Lord Justice Lawton formulated the test of what an employer should tell a prospective employee in the following terms:

> 'Generally speaking, if the job has risks to health and safety which are not common knowledge but of which the employer knows or ought to know and against which he cannot guard by taking precautions, he should tell anyone to whom he is offering the job what those risks are if, on the information then available to him, knowledge of those risks would be likely to affect the decision of the sensible, level-headed prospective employee about to accept the offer.'

A duty to take reasonable steps to maintain the safety of employees may be owed if a particular personal risk is presented in an employment which it is otherwise perfectly reasonable to ask the employee to pursue. In *Paris v Stepney Borough Council* (1951)[23] a workman employed as a garagehand had, to the knowledge of his employers, only one good eye. When working on the back axle of a vehicle, which he struck with a hammer, a metal chip flew off a bolt seriously injuring his good eye. He was not wearing goggles. In an action for damages against his employers on the grounds that they were negligent in failing to provide and require the use of goggles as part of the system of work it was held that in the case of an employee suffering, to the employer's knowledge, from a disability, special considerations apply. Although the disability did not *itself* increase the risk of an accident occurring, it did increase the risk of serious injury in the event of an accident occurring. That special risk was held to be a relevant consideration in determining the precautions which employers should have taken in fulfilling the duty of care owed to the employee. Each case will depend on its own particular facts, and the decision as to whether or not the employer is liable may be fine. In *Paris v Stepney Borough Council* itself, the House of Lords gave a majority decision of three to two in the plaintiff's favour.

Where a person's employment regularly involves him in tasks of which a reasonably foreseeable and potentially frequent result is the risk of personal injury, and which the employee may be called upon to perform at any time, it is not sufficient that the employer makes safety provision such as protective clothing or equipment and simply informs the employee of its existence. In *Crouch v British Rail Engineering Ltd* (1988)[24] the Court of Appeal held that it was not sufficient for the defendant employers to have made goggles available in the store and to have informed the employee of the need to wear them. An eye injury, sustained during the course of welding as part of the employee's employment, was held to have been caused by the negligence of the defendants who should, held the court, have taken steps actually to hand the goggles directly to the employee. In the event, in that case, the court assessed the contributory negligence of the plaintiff in failing to wear the goggles, which were in fact available in the defendant's store, at 50 per cent.

The decision of the House of Lords in *Winter v Cardiff Rural District Council* (1950)[25] is instructive in relation to systems of any difficulty or complexity. It was held that the duty of an employer is to act reasonably in all the circumstances. One of those circumstances is that competent employees should be taken on and supplied with adequate plant and equipment, together with adequate directions as to the system of work or mode of operation. This does not mean, however, that the employer must decide upon every single detail of the system of work or mode of operation. When the system or mode of operation is complicated or highly dangerous or prolonged, or involves a number of employees performing different functions, it is naturally a matter for the employer to take the responsibility of deciding what system shall be adopted. On the other hand, where the operation is simple and the decision how it should be done has to be taken frequently, it is natural and reasonable that it should be left to the employees together with such senior staff as foremen, nursing officers or the like, on the spot. The House of Lords held that the giving of proper instructions may well be a part of a proper system of working, and the omission to give them may constitute a defect in the system of working or a breach of the employer's obligation to take reasonable steps for the safety of those employed on the task.

In *Johnstone v Bloomsbury Health Authority* (1991)[26] a senior house officer employed by the defendant health authority sought a declaration that he could not lawfully be required by the authority to work under his contract of employment for so many hours in excess of his standard working week as would reasonably and foreseeably injure his health. He also sought from the court a declaration that his contract was contrary to section 2 of the Unfair Contract Terms Act 1977 which provides that a term of a contract cannot in law exclude or restrict a person's liability for death or personal injury resulting from negligence. This was not a trial of the action on its facts, but rather litigation surrounding a preliminary point of law which required to be clarified if the matters complained of were to proceed further. The applicant succeeded on his preliminary point. Counsel for the health authority had suggested that if a potential house officer thought that he could not perform the hours required, he should not take the job. To this, Lord Justice Stuart-Smith responded that:

> 'although the principle that if you cannot stand the heat in the kitchen you should get out, or not go in, may often be a sound one, it would have serious implications if applied in these circumstances. Any doctor who wishes to practise has to serve at least one year as a house officer in a hospital. The National Health Service is effectively a monopoly employer. Is the aspiring doctor who has spent many years in training to this point to abandon his chosen profession because the employer may exercise its power to call on him to work so many hours that his health is undermined? . . . I fail to see why he should not approach the matter on the basis that the employer will only exercise that power consistently with its duty to have proper regard to his health and safety. The fact that one doctor may have less stamina and physical strength than another does not mean that he is any less competent at his profession.'

An employer owes a duty at common law to his employees to take reasonable care for their safety, but does not generally owe these duties in respect of independent contractors. There are, however, exceptions to this principle. In *McArdle v Andmac Roofing Co* (1967)[27] the plaintiff worked for one of several sub-contractors employed on converting a building at a holiday camp under the direction of Pontins (Contractors) Ltd. The main contractors had made no arrangements for safety precautions with sub-contractors and in consequence the plaintiff suffered severe injuries when he fell from a roof. It was held that the main contractors (Pontins Contractors Ltd) had assumed the responsibility of co-ordinating the work and were therefore under a duty to ensure legal safety precautions were put in place for all those working on the job, even though the main contractors were not the employers of those who were working for the sub-contractors. The case will be of particular importance, not only in relation to outside contractors brought in to do work on or in connection with National Health Service premises, or indeed the premises of any hospital or other facility in the private sector, but also on account of the fact that many young people on work experience courses are not in law employees. Given the limitation of the employer's duties in maintaining a safe system of work to those who are employees, the decision in *McArdle* extends the employer's common law duties in relation to safe systems of work to such people also.

20.3 LIABILITY FOR BREACH OF STATUTORY DUTY

An alternative, and additional, ground for an employer's liability may be that the employee has been injured as a result of the breach by the employer of a duty imposed by statute or regulations. Not all such breaches of duty will result in civil liability for injury and the courts look to the general intention of the regulation or statute in question in order to ascertain whether an individual action should proceed. Certain cases are regulatory only and therefore result in no action for personal injury. Other cases, however, are so clearly concerned with the class of plaintiffs to which the plaintiff belongs that it would be unjust to deny a civil action, as well as the (quite separate) criminal prosecution which may follow from a breach of the duty.

Although resulting from breach of a statute or regulation, the action by an injured employee for personal injury resulting from breach of such duty is an action at common law and is an alternative to the type of action described above. There may be cases in which the breach of a statutory or regulatory duty exists as an additional ground of liability (though the plaintiff will recover damages only once); or as an alternative, in case common law negligence cannot be established. There may also be cases in which common law negligence can be established, on the balance of probabilities, against an employer even though the specific terms of the statute or regulation have not in fact been broken. Such a case was *Chipchase v British Titan Products Ltd* (1956)[28] in which regulations provided for platforms above six feet six inches from the ground to be of a minimum width of 34 inches. The plaintiff was working at a height slightly lower than that envisaged by the regulation, on a platform much narrower than would have been required at a greater height. He failed in his action for breach of statutory duty, the regulation being interpreted literally; but his action for breach of the employer's duty to provide a safe system of working succeeded.

20.4 CONDUCT OF THE EMPLOYEE

There is no doubt that the plea of contributory negligence, which if successful results in a reduction in the damages payable by the defendant to the injured plaintiff, applies equally in the case of breach of the employer's common law duty to provide safe working conditions as to an action for personal injury resulting from breach of a statutory duty. In consequence of section 1(1) of the Law Reform (Contributory Negligence) Act 1945 which provides that the court shall, in the event of the plaintiff's own carelessness having contributed to the injury, reduce the damages to such extent as is fair and equitable, there can never be a finding of 100 per cent contributory negligence. That is because the careless actions of both parties have contributed as a matter of cause and effect to the injury complained of. Nevertheless, if the only wrong committed by an employer is a technical breach of regulations, in a case in which an employee foolishly shows complete disregard for his own safety, a finding of 100 per cent contributory negligence is possible. In *Jayes v IMI (Kynoch) Ltd* (1985)[29] the plaintiff was an experienced production supervisor at the defendants' factory. Problems developed in a power press machine and its guard was removed for the faults to be corrected. The machine had to be started for testing, and while it was unguarded the plaintiff attempted to wipe off spreading grease with a rag. The rag caught up in the machine and as the plaintiff tried to pull it out the tip of his finger was severed. The plaintiff contended that, in such a case as this relating to the breach of a statutory duty, one of the purposes of fencing regulations was to guard against employees' acts of folly and that consequently a finding of 100 per cent contributory negligence against an employee is inappropriate. The Court of Appeal held, however, that there is no principle of law which states that, where there is breach of a statutory duty in circumstances such as in this case, even though the intention of the statute is to protect against (among other things) folly by employees, there cannot be a case where the folly is of such a degree that there may be a finding of 100 per cent contributory negligence. Lord Justice Goff said that the plaintiff, a man of complete frankness and openness, had admitted to the judge at first instance that what he did was a foolish and 'crazy thing to do'. There may come a time, said the court, when it can be said that the fault is entirely that of the employee. Where, by contrast, the complaint by the injured employee relates to the failure by the employer to establish and maintain a safe system of working conditions, a finding of liability on the part of the employer will never be consistent with a finding of 100 per cent contributory fault on the employee for the simple reason that the employer is in such a case, in point of fact, at least partly at fault for the accident and resulting injury.

20.5 EMPLOYER'S OBLIGATION TO INSURE AGAINST PERSONAL INJURY TO EMPLOYEES

A complementary statute which was passed at the same time as the Employers' Liability (Defective Equipment) Act 1969 (p. 556, above) was the Employers' Liability (Compulsory Insurance) Act 1969, designed to insure compensation in the event of injury. The Act places an obligation on employers to be covered by an approved policy of insurance against liability for bodily injury or disease sustained by an employee and arising out of and in the course of employment. By section 3(1) of the Act, its provisions are inapplicable to the Crown, or to 'any body corporate established by or under any enactment for the carrying on . . .

of any undertaking and the national ownership or control'. Hence, were health authorities to be regarded either as Crown activities, or as 'body corporate' activities, the Act had no application to those authorities. Since 1 April 1991, on which section 60 of the National Health Service and Community Care Act 1990 came into effect, health authorities have ceased to enjoy any immunity of the Crown, and their status ceased on that date to be that of a Crown activity. Nevertheless, by Schedule 8, paragraph 1, of the 1990 Act, a health service body, and an NHS trust established under Part I of that Act, are exempt from the requirement of insurance in section 1 of the Employers' Liability (Compulsory Insurance) Act 1969. For practical recommendations relating to insurance cover for liability to injured employees, reference should be made at this point to the recommendations contained in Executive Letter EL(90)195 and the further explanation and clarification given in Executive Letter EL(92)8, set out on pp. 551–552, above. Unless exempted by regulations made under section 3(1)(e) of the 1969 Act, its provisions will apply to voluntary hospitals and to all hospitals and nursing homes in the private sector.

It was held by the Court of Appeal in *Reid v Rush Tompkins Group plc* (1989)[30] that an employer is under no duty to insure an employee against the special risk posed by the employment in question. While the point will not, for reasons explained in the preceding paragraph, apply at the time of going to press to facilities within the National Health Service, facilities within the independent sector and perhaps also NHS trusts will wish to note this decision. The Court of Appeal held that the duty of care in tort cannot extend so far as to require an employer to procure third party insurance for the benefit of employees other than in situations in which the employer is legally liable for failure to provide a safe system of working conditions. In such circumstances, the Employers' Liability (Compulsory Insurance Act) 1969 applies only to the system of working provided by the employer and not to wrongful acts against employees by independent third parties. Nevertheless, for reasons explained above (p. 555) the 'system of work' established and maintained by a health service or similar employer may involve activities and care on a variety of premises, perhaps on a domiciliary basis, and provision for unpredictable or even dangerous behaviour by third parties, including clients, is apt to constitute part of the overall working system for the employee.

20.6 INJURY INCURRED OR DISEASE CONTRACTED AT WORK

20.6.1 The state insurance scheme

The Social Security Contributions and Benefits Act 1992, as amended, provides for cash benefits payable to persons suffering injury or contracting specified diseases at work. This is not the place to enter into a full discussion of social security benefits and reference should be made in appropriate cases to standard works on that subject. Section 94 of the 1992 Act provides for four principal benefits for personal injury to an employed earner arising by accident out of and in the course of his employment. Those benefits are: disablement benefit, reduced earnings allowance, retirement allowance and industrial death benefit. By section 1(1) of the Social Security Contributions and Benefits Act 1992 industrial injuries benefits are paid out of funds provided by Parliament, having been formerly drawn from the National Insurance Fund.

A claimant is eligible for industrial injuries benefit of one of the above types if he suffers a personal injury caused by accident arising out of and in the course of his employment. That employment must be the employed earner's employment, as defined in section 2(1) of the 1992 Act. That section defines 'employed earner' as meaning 'a person who is gainfully employed . . . under a contract of service, or in an office (including elective office) with emoluments chargeable to income tax under Schedule E . . .'. The concept of 'employed earner' has caused difficulty, but it appears that it refers to cases where there is an obligation by an employer to pay remuneration to an employee for tasks which the employee is bound to perform for the employer under the contract of employment.[31]

Claims which have been determined to fall within the expression 'out of and in the course of employment' include a nurse while sleep walking at a nurses' home in which she was obliged to live; a member of a blood collection unit injured at an hotel where he was obliged by his contract of employment to stay; and a nurse injured while playing football with patients at a mental hospital as part of their therapy. By contrast, a claim made by a nurse at a psychiatric hospital, injured playing football for the hospital team which he was not required to do (despite having been given time off to do so), was unsuccessful. It must be determined in every case whether the claimant's condition was caused by the alleged accident or was due to some previous accident or pre-existing condition. In one case, a railway engine driver was awarded industrial injury benefit in respect of a hernia caused by the continual operation of a stiff lever. It was held that each strain would have successively widened the tear constituting the hernia. By contrast, a railway worker suffering from heart disease, who suffered an attack of angina pectoris while lifting steel sleepers, was held on the facts of the particular case not to have suffered injury by accident.

Amongst prescribed diseases, tuberculosis has been the subject of particular provision and is a prescribed disease in one of the following occupations: medical treatment or nursing of one or more persons suffering from tuberculosis, or in a service ancillary to such treatment or nursing; attendance upon one or more persons suffering from tuberculosis where attendance is needed because of some physical or mental infirmity; employment as a research worker engaged in research connected with tuberculosis; and employment as a laboratory worker, pathologist or person taking part in, or assisting at, post mortem examinations of human remains where the occupation involves working with material which is a source of tuberculosis infection.

Industrial injuries benefits of the type provided in section 94 of the Social Security Contributions and Benefits Act 1992 are contributory benefits and a claim based on that section could fail unless requisite contributions have been made. However, section 102(1) of the 1992 Act provides that sickness benefit in respect of industrial injury is available to an employed earner who is rendered incapable of work as a result of personal injury of a kind mentioned in section 94(2) of the Act, despite the contributions not being satisfied. The test of incapacity is vital to the availability of the benefit under section 102(1). It may be necessary to decide whether short-term incapacity (namely, an incapacity lasting less than the 50-week qualifying period for disablement benefit under the Act) results from an industrial accident where the claimant has a defective contribution record and can establish his entitlement to sickness benefit only with the assistance of this section.

20.6.2 National Health Service injury benefits

In addition to the types of sickness benefit just described, it is open to any employer to provide benefits to an individual employee or employees generally in respect of sickness or incapacity for work. Specific benefits are incorporated by way of standard form into National Health Service employment conditions by the National Health Service (Injury Benefits) Regulations 1974.[32] These Regulations (as amended) provide in detail for benefits to National Health Service employees, including assistant and trainee practitioners, in respect of: injuries in the course of employment; injuries attributable to the duties of employment; or disease to which the employee is exposed by nature of his employment. To this extent the Regulations overlap with the provisions of the legislation. The Regulations do not, however, apply to any person in relation to an injury or disease wholly or mainly due to, or seriously aggravated by, the employee's own culpable negligence or misconduct. Benefits are payable under the Regulations in accordance with reduction of earning capacity of more than 10 per cent caused by reason of the injury or disease. The Regulations provide for a widow's or widower's allowance, child's allowance, dependent relative's allowance and for lump sum payment on death. Reference should be made to the detailed provisions of the Regulations in the resolution of a specific case.

Any uncertainties of the common law relating to the right to receive pay during sickness, when the matter is not covered by express contract, are removed in respect of most if not all grades of officer within the National Health Service by national agreements approved by the Secretary of State under the National Health (Remuneration and Conditions of Service) Regulations 1991.[33] This entitlement ordinarily covers accidents as well as illnesses. If a superannuable officer becomes permanently incapacitated before reaching retirement age, that officer may qualify for a pension or gratuity under the national agreements.

In the event of absence from work following contact with a case of notifiable disease, section 7.1 of the General Whitley Council's Agreement formerly provided:

'Employees who are required to absent themselves from duty following contact with a case of notifiable disease shall be granted special leave with full pay subject to an adjustment of pay [in the circumstances there set out].'

The matter is now provided for in section 3, 'Special Leave', alongside leave for a variety of other reasons (for which see Chapter 17):

'1. Employing authorities shall make available special leave with pay to staff required to be absent from duty for essential civic and public duties of the kinds listed in section 29 of the Employment Protection (Consolidation) Act 1978 and as required by other legislation. In determining the maximum amount of such paid leave employing authorities shall have regard to existing practice as informed by section 29(4) of the Employment Protection (Consolidation) Act 1978. Examples of the duties listed in section 29 of the Employment Protection (Consolidation) Act 1978 are attached in an Annex to this agreement.

2. In addition to these provisions, special leave with pay shall be made available in the following circumstances.

• absence from duty following contact with a case of notifiable disease; . . .

4. Each health authority should provide clear guidelines in consultation with staff and local staff representatives on the length of special leave which would normally be available, whether it should be paid or unpaid and on the procedures for applying for such leave. The application of these guidelines will have to take account of the particular needs and circumstances of each individual.'

20.6.3 Sick pay to victims of crimes of violence

Following recommendations by the General Council of the Whitley Councils for the Health Services, provision has been inserted in the pay schemes of all the functional Health Service Whitley Councils to the effect that employing authorities in aggregating periods of an officer's absence due to illness, for the purpose of ascertaining his entitlement to full or half pay during any period of 12 months, shall not take into account any absence due to an injury resulting from a crime of violence not sustained on duty but connected with or arising from the officer's employment, where the injury has been subject of payment by the Criminal Injuries Compensation Board, or if due to such injury for which the Board has not paid compensation on the ground that it did not give rise to more than three weeks loss of earnings or was not one for which compensation of more than £400 would be given. The Whitley agreements also provide that the employing authority may at its discretion take no account of the whole or part of any periods of absence due to injury – not on duty – resulting from a crime of violence not arising from or connected with the officer's employment.

In a brief explanation of the above arrangements issued by the General Council (10 May 1967) it was stated that an officer who felt that an employing authority had decided wrongly that the circumstances were not connected with his employment or profession could appeal through the normal channels (i.e. the normal National Health Service Whitley appeals machinery.) There appears to be nothing in the agreement, however, to prevent an aggrieved officer from having such issues determined in the courts.

The right of access to the courts could be important in two cases: (a) where the officer has had recourse to the Whitley appeal machinery and there has been a failure to reach an agreed decision first by regional appeal committee and then by a national appeal committee; and (b) where the officer was not a member of a trade union or professional society represented on a National Health Service functional Whitley council, through which alone an appeal by an officer may be submitted, or where the body of which he is a member has failed or refused to submit his appeal. But seemingly, if an employing authority has rightly decided that the circumstances of an officer's injury were not connected with his employment, then its refusal to allow the officer's sick leave to be aggregated or to allow only a part to be disregarded would not be referable to the courts, being a matter which – by the terms of the agreement – is within the discretion of the authority.

20.6.4 Criminal injuries compensation

A further possibility of obtaining compensation for an injury caused by a mentally disordered person, which may be open to members of the staff of a psychiatric or other hospital in common with other persons, is an application to the Criminal Injuries Compensation Board. The Board may pay compensation to anyone who suffers a criminal injury which for the purposes of the Scheme extends to any personal injury directly due to a crime of violence (including arson and poisoning), any immunity at law of the offender, attributable to his youth or insanity or other condition being left out of account.[34]

An award rests at the date when it is made and not at the date when the claimant receives his notification. His estate is therefore entitled to the whole of an award when he dies between the two dates: *R v Criminal Injuries Compensation Board, ex parte Tong* (1976).[35] A widow may also make an application in respect of the death of her husband: *Re Lancaster's Application* (1977).[36]

A requirement of any application is that the circumstances of the injury have been the subject of criminal proceedings or were reported to the police without delay. The Board may waive this requirement at their discretion. Circumstances in which the Board will waive it in respect of injuries to staff and, more doubtfully, to patients injured by another patients in a mental hospital and steps to be taken by health authorities are the subject of a Circular[37] from the Department of Health and Social Security to hospital administrators in 1971. The relevant paragraphs read:

'Reports to the police

4.　　We have been in touch with the Criminal Injuries Compensation Board and explained the complications which would arise, particularly in psychiatric hospitals, if we were to ask hospital authorities to make it the invariable rule to report to the police every instance where a member of the staff has been assaulted by a mentally disordered patient under treatment. The Board states that while the Scheme requires that the circumstances of the injury be reported to the police without delay they have always recognised that in certain situations different considerations may apply and it would be appropriate in these to waive the requirement of a report to the police. An example is where the full circumstances of an injury inflicted in a prison are reported to the Governor without delay.

5.　　The Board recognise that a similar situation may exist in mental hospitals and that hospital authorities must have some discretion to decide whether to call the police in or not. They have asked us to make it clear accordingly that it is not their practice to reject applications from staff in mental hospitals simply because the incident has not been reported to the police. Provided the Board are satisfied that the full circumstances of the injury has (*sic*) been reported to the hospital authorities without delay, the Board will waive the requirement. The Board stress, however, that the manner of reporting must be such as to enable a proper decision to be made by the hospital authority whether or not police intervention is appropriate: a mere note in an accident or occurrence book may not, therefore, be sufficient.'

It is assumed that in the Circular the expression *mental hospitals* is used in its widest sense, as including psychiatric hospitals for patients suffering from any form of mental disorder, including impaired and severely impaired and psychopathic patients, as well as the mentally ill. What was not clear is whether what is said in paragraph 5 as to waiver will also apply to injuries caused by psychiatric patients being treated in general hospitals or in a psychiatric observation ward of such a hospital. With the development, since the date of issue of the Circular, of psychiatric units within general hospitals there can today be no doubt that the spirit of the Circular would apply to such units.

'Action required by hospital authorities

6.   Hospital authorities are asked to take note of this guidance, to review their arrangements for reporting of any assault by a patient involving injury to a member of the staff or to another patient in light of it and to ensure that all such reports are appropriately investigated.'

Although there is a reference in paragraph 6 of the Circular to the reporting and investigation of an assault by a patient on a patient, as well as of an assault by a patient on a member of the staff, there is no assurance in paragraph 5 that waiver of the requirement of prompt report to the police extends to attacks on patients, though it would seem unlikely that the Board would seek to draw any distinction between the two cases.

Whatever may be the understanding between the Department and the Criminal Injuries Compensation Board on waiver of the requirement of prompt report to the police where a proper report has been made within the hospital, that understanding does not take away the right of any injured person, or of any friend or relative of his or, indeed, of any disinterested observer of reporting the circumstances of the injury to the police. Nor, it is suggested, would a hospital authority be within its rights if it sought to enforce by disciplinary action any rule to the effect that injuries caused by patients should not be reported to the police.

On 8 December 1989, the Home Office announced measures to widen the scheme substantially, still on a non-statutory basis.[38]

Rape victims who keep a child born as a result of the attack may now be awarded £5,000 under the scheme. Common-law wives and husbands whose partners are killed as the result of violent crime will be entitled to cash payments. Train drivers who suffer shock because of railway suicides are entitled to compensation.

In *R v Criminal Injuries Compensation Board, ex parte Webb and others* (1986)[39] the claimant failed in an application for judicial review of a decision of the Criminal Injuries Compensation Board that suicide is not a 'crime of violence' for the purpose of compensation by the scheme. The Court of Appeal held that it is the nature of the crime and not its likely consequences which determine whether it is a crime of violence for the purposes of the Criminal Injuries Compensation Scheme.[40] The new scheme reverses the decision on those facts alone.

20.6.5   Liability for defective products

Part I of the Consumer Protection Act 1987 imposes strict liability (that is, liability without fault) for damage caused by defective products. It is possible for both injury at work, to employees, and injury to patients to result from defective products under the Act. While the present chapter is referred to in Chapter 6, 'Injury to the patient', the subject of defective products is dealt with in the present chapter on account of the greater likelihood, in practice, of injury at work resulting from such defects.

Part I of the Consumer Protection Act implements the European Product Liability Directive[41] which was the culmination of commissions, reports and discussions resulting from the Thalidomide tragedy in the late 1960s and early 1970s. For the reasons which have been pointed out in relation to negligence actions, in Chapter 6, 'Injury to the patient', it may be difficult to prove that a product is defective as a result of the fault or carelessness of the manufacturer or other supplier. Part I of the Consumer Protection Act accordingly reduces the difficulties of an injured plaintiff. Part I of the Act applies not only to personal injury but also to damage to property, there being a minimum level for which a strict liability claim is allowed under Part I of the Act.[42] Liability for defective products under Part I of the Act does not supplant the common law relating to injury caused by another's fault (including the manufacturer, producer or supplier of a defective product) but rather eliminates the need to prove fault in the cases where damage or injury resulting from defective products is most likely to cause difficulties for an injured plaintiff.

Section 2 of the Act, which is the central provision of Part I, imposes strict liability for defective products if the plaintiff can prove (on the balance of probabilities, that is, more likely than not) the following requirements:

1. that a product, as defined in section 1 of the Act, contained a defect, as defined in section 3;
2. that the plaintiff suffered damage, as determined by section 5:
3. that the damage was caused by the defect, on which point the ordinary principles of common law causation will apply (Chapter 6, pp. 195–197); and
4. that the defendant was either the producer of the product (both these terms being defined by section 1 of the Act) or was someone else falling within section 2(2) of the Act as being liable for such damage.

Part I of the Act defines all these terms, as follows. Section 1(2) defines 'producer' in relation to a product as:

(a) the person who manufactured it;
(b) in the case of a substance which has not been manufactured but has been won or abstracted, the person who won or abstracted it;
(c) in the case of a product which has not been manufactured, won or abstracted but central characteristics of which are attributable to an industrial or other process having been carried out (for example, in relation to agricultural produce), the person who carried out that process.

'Product' means any goods or electricity and (subject to subsection (3)) includes the product which is comprised in another product, whether by virtue of being a component part or raw material or otherwise. Subsection (3) provides an exception to the above, and states that for the purposes of Part I of the Act a person who supplies any product in which products are comprised, whether by virtue of being component parts or raw materials or otherwise, shall not be treated by reason only of his supply of that product as supplying any of the products so comprised.

The significance of the terms 'producer' and 'supplier' becomes apparent from an examination of section 2 of Part I of the Act, which provides the principal basis for strict liability for defective products. Section 2(1) provides that, subject to exceptions mentioned below, where any damage is caused wholly or partly by a defect in a product, every person to whom subsection (2) applies shall be liable for the damage. Subsection (2) applies to: the producer of the product; any person who, by putting his name on the product or using a trademark or other distinguishing mark in relation to the product, has held himself out to be the producer of the product; and any person who has imported the product into a member state from a place outside the member states in order, in the course of any business of his, to supply it to another.

The relationship between 'producer' and 'supplier' is made clear by section 2(3) of the Act, in the following terms:

'(3) Subject as aforesaid, where any damage is caused wholly or partly by a defect in a product, any person who supplied the product (whether to the person who suffered the damage, to the producer of any product in which the product in question is comprised or to any other person) shall be liable for the damage if—
  (a) the person who suffered the damage requests the supplier to identify one or more of the persons (whether still in existence or not) to whom subsection (2) above applies in relation to the product;
  (b) that request is made within a reasonable period after the damage occurs and at a time when it is not reasonably practicable for the person making the request to identify all those persons; and
  (c) the supplier fails, within a reasonable period after receiving the request, either to comply with the request or to identify the person who supplied the product to him.'

Neither subsection (2) nor subsection (3) of section 2 applies to a person in respect of any defect in any game or agricultural produce if the only supply of the game or produce by that person to another was at a time when it had not undergone an industrial process. Section 2(6) states that liability under section 2 shall be 'without prejudice to any liability arising otherwise than by virtue of this Part'. This means that liability according to ordinary common law principles (for which see Chapter 6) exists concurrently with, and independently of, Part I of the

Act; and that there may be liability according to ordinary common law principles of damage caused by fault, even in the event of the requirements of Part I of the Act not being met in a particular claim.

The liability of a 'producer' of a product is very wide insofar as the definition of producer encompasses any person who puts his name or trademark, or other distinguishing mark, on the product and holds himself out thereby to be the producer. A hospital, health authority or trust would therefore be the producer, under the Act, of goods sold by it in the hospital shop, or bought wholesale and marked with the name or other distinguishing feature of the hospital. It would not, however, be the producer of food supplied to it by an outside supplier and passed on by it to an associated or affiliated institution without any 'industrial processing'. Given, however, that the processing of food is apt to cover a wide range of processes in relation to it, a hospital may very easily find itself the producer of food when any process has been carried out in relation to it. The addition of preservatives or sanitisation could amount to such a 'process'.

Section 2(1) requires proof (on the balance of probabilities) that the defective product *caused* the damage, either wholly or in part. The ordinary principles of causation at common law will therefore be applicable to an action taken under Part I of the Consumer Protection Act, and for these reference should be made to Chapter 6, pp. 195–197.

The meaning of 'defect' is central to the strict liability under Part I of the Act. Defining this meaning, section 3 provides as follows:

'3.—(1) Subject to the following provisions of this section, there is a defect in a product for the purposes of this Part if the safety of the product is not such as persons generally are entitled to expect; and for those purposes "safety", in relation to a product, shall include safety with respect to products comprised in that product and safety in the context of risks of damage to property, as well as in the context of risks of death or personal injury.

(2) In determining for the purposes of subsection (1) above what persons generally are entitled to expect in relation to a product all the circumstances shall be taken into account, including

(a) the manner in which, and purposes for which, the product has been marketed, its get-up, the use of any mark in relation to the product and any instructions for, or warnings with respect to, doing or refraining from doing anything with or in relation to the product;

(b) what might reasonably be expected to be done with or in relation to the product; and

(c) the time when the product was supplied by its producer to another; and nothing in this section shall require a defect to be inferred from the fact alone that the safety of a product which is supplied after that time is greater than the safety of the product in question.'

Defects in manufacture will normally be easy to identify because there will usually be criteria or measures of comparison by which the standard or quality of the product may be judged. Design defects are apt to present more difficulty and whether or not a product was defective for the purposes of the Act may depend on a number of factors including: whether the risk was known at the time of production; how long development would have taken to eliminate the risk; whether the cost of the risk-elimination would have reduced any element of profitability in the product; whether the cost would have been prohibitively expensive from the consumer's viewpoint; the utility or usefulness of the product; and whether the product was produced to meet emergency conditions. At the time of going to press there is no case law on the interpretation of defect under section 3 of the Act. Section 3(2)(c), however, makes clear that a product is not retrospectively to be regarded as defective simply because a better or safer product has been manufactured subsequent to the manufacture of the product complained of. In making such provision, the Act is reminiscent of the judicial approach in negligence cases, as evidenced in *Roe v Minister of Health* (1954)[43] in which Lord Justice Denning said 'nowadays it would be negligence not to realise the danger, but it was not then'.

A number of defences protect against strict liability under the Act. Section 4(1) provides as follows:

'**4.**—(1) In any civil proceedings by virtue of this Part against any person ("the person proceeded against") in respect of a defect in a product it shall be a defence for him to show—

(a) that the defect is attributable to compliance with any requirement imposed by or under any enactment or with any Community obligation; or

(b) that the person proceeded against did not at any time supply the product to another; or

(c) that the following conditions are satisfied, that is to say—
(i) that the only supply of the product to another by the person proceeded against was otherwise than in the course of a business of that person; and
(ii) that section 2(2) above does not apply to that person or applies to him by virtue only of things done otherwise than with a view to profit; or

(d) that the defect did not exist in the product at the relevant time; or

(e) that the state of scientific and technical knowledge at the relevant time was not such that a producer of products of the same description as the product in question might be expected to have discovered the defect if it had existed in his products while they were under his control; or

(f) that the defect
(i) constituted a defect in a product ("the subsequent product") in which the product in question had been comprised; and
(ii) was wholly attributable to the design of the subsequent product or to compliance by the producer of the product in question with instructions given by the producer of the subsequent product.'

It seems likely that hospitals will normally be unable to avail themselves of the defence created by section 4(1)(b), namely that they did not at any time supply the product to another (employee or a patient), for in normal circumstances they will have done precisely that. While there is as yet no judicial decision on the meaning of 'in the course of business', as that expression appears in section 4(1)(c)(i), it seems unlikely that a hospital will be able to claim, by way of defence under this subsection, that the supply was not in the course of business. Even directly managed units within the National Health Service are now subject to the market forces of the provider–purchaser dichotomy; and it is probable that a court would hold that products supplied by a directly managed unit within the National Health Service to employees, or to patients, would be supplied in the course of business.

Apart from the possibility of the defence under section 4(1)(d), that the defect did not exist in the product at the time when the injury was caused (which will be a question of proof in all the circumstances), the particular defence on which a hospital is in practice most likely to rely in relation to defective products is that contained in section 4(1)(e), sometimes referred to as the 'state of the art' defence. If the state of scientific and technical knowledge at the time when the injury was allegedly caused by the defective product was not such that the producer of products of the same description as the product in question might be expected to have discovered the defect if it had existed in his products while they were under his control, then strict liability under the Act will not apply. The defence is dependent on reasonable conduct by the producer, and if inadequate production, inspection or other checks allow a defective product to cause damage to an injured plaintiff, the defence will not avail the producer or supplier.

Section 5 defines damage, for the purpose of Part I of the Act, as meaning death or personal injury or any loss of or damage to any property (including land). However, section 5(4) provides that no damages should be awarded to any person by virtue of Part I of the Act in respect of loss or damage to property if the amount which would fall to be so awarded is below £275.[44]

By virtue of section 6 of Part I of the Act, and Schedule 1, the ordinary provisions of section 11 of the Limitation Act 1980 relating to actions in respect of personal injuries (for which see Chapter 5) are altered in the following way. None of the time limits given in that Act shall apply to an action to which Part I of the Consumer Protection Act 1987 applies. An action to which that Part applies shall not be brought after the expiration of the period of ten years from the relevant time (meaning the supply of the product) and this provision operates to extinguish a right of action at the end of ten years in all circumstances. It is for that reason that records relating to the production or supply of products are recommended, in Circular HC(89)20 (see Chapter 5, pp. 132–133), to be kept for 11 years only, after a complaint relating to injury or damage resulting from strict liability under Part I of the Act has been made.

20.7 PARTICULAR INSTANCES OF RISK MANAGEMENT IN HEALTH SERVICES

In previous editions of this book a separate section has been devoted to liability in psychiatric hospitals. While the duty of an employer to provide safe working conditions for employees is a general duty, and is not confined to particular instances of danger or apparent danger, the question of assessment and management of risk is briefly dealt with here, for two reasons. First, considerable attention has been devoted since the publication of the last edition of this book to the management of violence on health service premises and to health service and hospital staff. Second, the view now taken of legal responsibility in relation to situations of particular danger, including not only those in psychiatric hospitals but also in accident and emergency departments of general hospitals, departs from that adopted by the previous editors.

In the case of patients suffering from, and possibly also being treated for, mental disorder, a particular set of practical problems may face those in charge of their care. So far as concerns the legal liability of such an individual to an injured member of staff in the event of injury caused either intentionally or negligently, the decision in *Morriss v Marsden* (1952)[45] establishes that the insanity or other mental disorder of a defendant in an action for damages for injury done by him to the plaintiff whom he had attacked is no defence. The decision creates different bases for civil and for criminal liability in this respect. There does not, however, appear to be a reported case in which damages have been awarded against a patient who has injured a nurse or other member of staff in a psychiatric facility or accident and emergency department of a general hospital. So far as psychiatric hospitals are concerned, it was stated in the previous edition of this book that:

'it seems reasonable to assume that a contractual or quasi-contractual obligation is accepted by the authority and by the staff to take the risk of damage and injury due to the patient's irresponsible conduct caused by his malady. It is submitted that any other view would make nonsense of the purpose of a psychiatric hospital.'

The view now taken is that it would be wrong to assume that members of staff take upon themselves not only the risk of physical injury, but also the risk of remaining uncompensated, simply by working in an environment in which the risk or threat of physical violence or other danger is known to be present. It would be inappropriate to regard all patients in psychiatric facilities, even detained patients, as *necessarily* so disordered that they cannot form an intent or mental state in relation to their actions. For instance, Part IV of the Mental Health Act 1983 admits of the possibility that even a long-term detained patient *may* be in a fit mental state to give real consent to medication or electroconvulsive therapy. Since, however, most mentally disordered patients have small means and are protected against bankruptcy law, there will always be in practice a certain disincentive for the bringing of any such action by a member of staff. More significant in practice may be the staff's professional reasons for not taking any such action against an individual patient.

Despite any difficulties in the way of direct action against a patient, there remains the common law responsibility of employers to provide a safe system of working conditions for all their employees. An employee injured by a patient or client, whether in a psychiatric facility, accident and emergency department or anywhere else in hospital, or community,[46] premises, may have an action against the employing authority for failure to take reasonable precautions against the risk of violence or other harm. A hospital or health authority, like any other employer, is under a legal obligation to take all reasonable precautions for the safety of employees given the particular dangers or risks presented by the particular work involved. Given that there is no guarantee of employee safety, a health authority, hospital or similar employer will not necessarily be liable whenever a member of staff is injured in an attack by a patient. If, however, the staffing of a ward or department were inadequate when judged by reasonable standards, having regard to the type of patient, the conditions, the time of day and so forth, there could be grounds for liability at common law. It could be, for instance, that the possibility of an attack was particularly great given certain staffing or other conditions, and the risk of injury to staff seriously increased because of an inadequate staffing or other system established or maintained by the employer. Similarly, if a particular patient were known to be violent or of uncertain and challenging behaviour, and appropriate additional precautions for his supervision had not been taken, liability might fall upon the employing authority.

On the principle of *Hudson v Ridge* (1957)[47] (p. 553, above) the employing hospital or health authority might be liable as a result of failure by a key member of staff, for instance a nursing officer, charge nurse or similar health care professional, to communicate to senior management the risk which should have been foreseen and anticipated.

In *Michie v Shenley and Napsbury General Hospital Management Committee* (1953)[48] a nurse failed in his action against a psychiatric patient who attacked him. The court apparently came to the conclusion that there had been no negligence on the part of the health authority, and that the plaintiff was aware that the patient was likely to become violent and had not taken proper steps for his own safety, such as by obtaining help. Although each case must be decided on its own special facts, it is suggested that the decision in such circumstances as presented in the

Michie case might well lead to a different outcome today, in view of attention which is now paid to staffing levels and staff safety.

In 1991 a substantial out-of-court settlement was made between a health authority and a patient who alleged failure in adequate psychiatric care leading to the unlawful killing of his mother.

In *Porterfield v Home Office* (1988)[49] the plaintiff, a prisoner, failed in his action against the Home Office concerning the prison authorities' failure to protect him from attack by other prisoners. The assistant governor knew that there had been a fight between the plaintiff and another prisoner resulting in the other prisoner sustaining a broken nose. He also knew that there had been warnings that certain prisoners were out to 'get' the plaintiff. In consequence, the assistant governor warned the prison staff to be alert and to keep an eye on the plaintiff and other prisoners. It was held that, in all the circumstances, the prison authorities had not been negligent in relation to the injured plaintiff. Furthermore, even if it had been found that there had been a breach of duty of care the court was in some doubt whether the failure to warn the plaintiff of a prospective incident played any causative part in the injuries which he sustained. On the facts, had any warning been given to the plaintiff he would probably have ignored it.

Of particular interest in this regard is health circular HC(76)11, relating to the management of violent or potentially violent, hospital patients. This was issued in March 1976 by the Department of Health and Social Security, giving guidance on this difficult subject. The Circular points out that serious acts of violence by patients in hospital are relatively infrequent, but arrangements in general hospitals, as well as psychiatric, should be reviewed in the light of this guidance. The appendix to the circular shows that prevention of a violent incident is the first objective, and the need to ensure that a potentially violent patient is in the most appropriate place for care. Staff attitudes are important in both prevention and management of violent incidents and nursing staff have a particular responsibility in this direction. The number of staff (suitably trained or instructed) allocated to a ward must take account of possible violence and the Circular explains that there should not be other patients at risk with patients who may be violent. It is hoped that most patients who exhibit violence from time to time can be treated in a local hospital, and only in a few cases should it be appropriate to transfer to a regional secure unit, or similar accommodation. The problems arising in accident and emergency departments are recognised and staff should be aware of the difficulties that may be encountered and the occasional need for some form of physical restraint. In some circumstances patients suspected of having offensive weapons may be searched and staff should have means of calling for assistance.

Advice is given on dealing with violent incidents which occur, although it is recognised that the action taken will be a matter for judgment in the recognised circumstances. A patient may be restrained with the degree of force which is necessary and reasonable in the circumstances and staff acting in good faith and in accordance with training received should not be blamed as a result of an incident. However, authorities must not condone or defend actions which appear to be wrong or inappropriate. It is recognised that staff can be vulnerable to unfounded complaints in some situations and membership of trade unions and professional organisations is in the interests of staff needing advice. Each hospital should have an adequate system of reporting incidents which involve violence, restraint, isolation or damage and the report of an incident should be brought to the attention of the authority as well as the officers concerned. The action to be taken as a result of a report must be determined and, generally, relatives should be informed of any incident of violence. If staff are injured as a result of violence, they may have rights under the Criminal Injuries Compensation Scheme, but the incident must have been fully reported to the authority.

In October 1988 the Health and Safety Executive published a report entitled *Preventing Violence to Staff*. The report contains nine detailed case studies showing the action which different organisations have taken to reduce the risks to their employees. It also suggests the framework which all employers can use to tackle the problem of violence and threatened violence. The case studies include community nursing as well as other areas where violence to staff may be a serious problem.

20.8 CONDITIONS AT THE PLACE OF WORK

20.8.1 Factories Act 1961

General scope and limits of application to hospitals

Section 175 of the Factories Act 1961 contains an exhaustive definition of a 'factory' for the purposes of the Act. In the main the provisions of the Act relate mainly to 'factories' carried on by way of trade or for the purpose of gain. However, notwithstanding the references to 'trade' and 'gain' in section 175(1), subsection (9) expressly extends the Act to any premises belonging to or in the occupation of the Crown or of any municipal or other public authority which would otherwise be excluded because the work carried on there is not carried on by way of trade or for purposes of gain. This would clearly bring in hospitals and health authorities under the National Health Service Act 1977.

The principal provisions of section 175(1) are as follows:

'175.—(1) Subject to the provisions of this section, the expression factory means any premises in which or within the close or curtilage or precincts of which, persons are employed in manual labour in any process for or incidental to any of the following purposes, namely:

   (a) the making of any article or of part of any article; or

   (b) the altering, repairing, ornamenting, finishing, cleaning, or washing, or the breaking up or demolition or any article; or

   (c) the adapting for sale of any article; . . .

being premises in which, or within the close or curtilage or precincts of which, the work is carried on by way of trade or for purposes of gain and to or over which the employer of the persons employed therein has the right of access or control. . . .'

Moreover, under section 175(2) of the Act, whether or not within the foregoing definition, the following, inter alia, are also included in the definition of a 'factory'.

   '(b) any premises in which the business of sorting any articles is carried on as a preliminary to any work carried on in any factory or incidentally to the purpose of any factory;

   (c) any premises in which the business of washing or filling bottles or containers or packing articles is carried on incidentally to the purpose of any factory;

   (e) any laundry carried on as ancillary to another business or incidentally to the purposes of any public institution;

   (g) any premises in which printing by letterpress, lithography, photo-gravure, or other similar process, or bookbinding is carried on by way of trade or for purposes of gain or incidentally to another business so carried on;

   (k) any premises in which mechanical power is used in connection with the making or repair of articles of metal or wood incidentally to any business carried on by way of trade or for the purpose of gain;

   (l) any premises in which the production of cinematograph films is carried on by way of trade or for purposes of gain, so, however, that the employment at any such premises of theatrical performers within the meaning of the Theatrical Employers Registration Act 1925, and of attenders on such theatrical performers shall not be deemed to be employment in a factory;

   (m) any premises in which articles are made or prepared incidentally to the carrying on of building operations or works or engineering construction, not being premises in which such operations or works are being carried on. . . .'

Hence, first, laundries in hospitals and institutions, whether voluntary or public authority, are subject to the provisions of the Factories Acts as are departments for the maintenance of equipment.

Second, any activities at a public authority hospital which if carried on in privately owned premises by way of trade or for purposes of gain would make any part of the premises where they are carried on a 'factory' within the meaning of section 175(1)–(8) of the Factories Act 1961, render that part of the institution where they are carried on a factory. This would apparently apply, inter alia, to such places as the tailor's shop in a mental hospital and to the clerk of works department of any public authority hospital where articles are made or prepared incidentally to building or engineering operations. Any line or siding (not being part of a railway or tramway) and used in connection with a factory is deemed part of that factory. The Court of Appeal decided in *Wood v London Country Council* (1940)[50] that a hospital kitchen is not a factory.

The decision in *Wood* was, however, distinguished in *Bromwich v National Ear, Nose and Throat Hospital* (1980).[51] The plaintiff was injured in the course of his employment as a plumber and fitter at the defendants' hospital, while working in a workshop containing two grinding machines, a lathe and a bench drill provided for the use of employees engaged in general maintenance and repair work. The workshop was only used from time to time for mechanical and electrical repairs and minor installation work for the hospital. The plaintiff was injured when he attempted to use one of the grinding machines to trim off a metal strap he was making for a piece of hospital equipment with the rest on the machine not properly adjusted. He brought an action against the defendants for damages for personal injuries, claiming that the defendants were in breach of their statutory duty under regulation 15(1) of the Abrasive Wheels Regulations 1970 in failing to ensure that the rest was properly adjusted. The Regulations only applied to premises which were a factory within the meaning of section 175(1)(a) of the Factories Act 1961, which defined a factory as premises in which persons were employed in manual labour in the making of an article or part of an article, or the altering or repairing of an article. The defendants denied liability, contending that, even if the work done in the workshop did consist of such work as making and repairing articles, the workshop was not a place to which the 1961 Act could have been intended to apply because it was merely used in connection with the maintenance of the hospital and was purely incidental to the functions of the hospital which had to be inspected.

The court held that, in regard to the nature of the workshop and the work carried out there, it was prima facie a factory and there was nothing in the general provisions of the Factories Act 1961, looked at as a whole, to show that those provisions were clearly not applicable to it and the processes carried on there; nor would the application of the Act to the workshop produce a bizarre or ludicrous result. It could not, therefore, be inferred that Parliament had not intended the Act to apply to the workshop and accordingly the 1970 Regulations applied to it. It followed that, the defendants not having satisfied themselves that the plaintiff was competent to use the grinding machine, they were responsible in law for the accident and the plaintiff's claim succeeded.

Third, a voluntary hospital being neither controlled by a public authority nor carried on for gain apparently escapes the provisions of the Factories Act 1961, save in respect of the laundry and of any activities carried on for gain, being activities of any of the kinds mentioned in section 175(1) of the Act. Also, where in any premises forming part of an institution carried on for charitable or reformatory purposes any manual labour is exercised in or incidental to the making, altering, repairing, ornamenting, finishing, washing, cleaning or adapting for sale of articles not intended for the use of the institution, but the premises do not constitute a factory then, nevertheless, the provisions of the Act apply – with certain modifications – to those premises. This might clearly apply to some work done by blind or disabled patients and long-stay patients in some hospitals.

20.8.2   Offices, Shops and Railway Premises Act 1963

The purpose of the Offices, Shops and Railway Premises Act 1963 as set out in the long title is:

'to make fresh provision for securing the health, safety and welfare of persons employed to work in office or shop premises . . . to amend certain provisions of the Factories Act 1961; and for purposes connected with the matters aforesaid'.

The premises to which the Act applies are office premises, shop premises and railway premises, being (in each case) premises in the case of which persons are employed to work therein.[52]
In the Act:[53]

'(a) "office premises" means a building or part of a building, being a building or part the sole or principal use of which is as an office or for office purposes;
(b) "office purposes" includes the purposes of administration, clerical work, handling money and telephone and telegraph operating; and
(c) "clerical work" includes writing, book-keeping, sorting papers, filing, typing, duplicating, machine calculating, drawing and the editorial preparation of matter for publication;
and for the purposes of this Act premises occupied together with office premises for the purposes of the activities there carried on shall be treated as forming part of the office premises.'

In section 1(3) of the Act:

'(a) "shop premises" means—
   (i) a shop;
   (ii) a building or part of a building, being a building or part which is not a shop but of which the sole or principal use is the carrying on there of retail trade or business;
   (iii) a building occupied by a wholesale dealer or merchant where goods are kept for sale wholesale or a part of a building so occupied where goods are so kept, but not including a warehouse belonging to the owners, trustees or conservators of a dock, wharf or quay;
   (iv) a building to which members of the public are invited to resort for the purpose of delivering there goods for repair or other treatment

or of themselves there carrying out repairs to, or other treatment of, goods, or a part of a building to which members of the public are invited to resort for that purpose;

(v) any premises (in this Act referred to as "fuel storage premises") occupied for the purpose of a trade or business which consists of, or includes, the sale of solid fuel, being premises used for the storage of such fuel intended to be sold in the course of that trade or business, but not including dock storage premises or colliery storage premises;

(b) "retail trade or business" includes the sale to members of the public of food or drink for immediate consumption, retail sales by auction and the business of lending books or periodicals for the purpose of gain;

(c) "solid fuel" means coal, coke and any solid fuel derived from coal or of which coal or coke is a constituent.'

From the foregoing definitions it is clear that any parts of a hospital the main purpose of which is the carrying out of office work is an office within the meaning of the Act, but a ward would not be an office simply because nurses did a certain amount of paper work or even if a clerical officer had been assigned to relieve them of that work. Nor, for example, would the pharmacy be an office simply because a considerable amount of paper work were involved in the keeping of records. If, however, a particular part of the pharmacy were given over to clerical staff or even to pharmacists devoting the major part of their time to paper work, it is likely that that part of the pharmacy would be caught by the Act. Besides administrative departments clearly caught by the Act, there might also be mentioned medical records departments and patients' appointments offices as within its provisions.

Hospital shops, including patients' canteens, are also within the Act. But it seems that a hospital staff canteen (unless wholly or mainly for persons employed in office or shop premises) such as a canteen or dining room mainly for medical, nursing or other professional staff,[54] would not be within its provisions.

The Act is comprehensive in scope and its provisions too detailed for treatment here. Although not as exacting in its requirements as the Factories Act 1961, its provisions follow broadly the same lines.

20.8.3 Fire Precautions Act 1971

This Act strengthens and rationalises the law relating to fire precautions. The Act provides that the local fire authority[55] shall issue fire certificates in respect of those premises governed by the Act and fire authorities are placed under statutory duty to enforce the Act. Where premises are occupied by the Crown and the Act applies (see below) the fire certificate is to be issued by the fire inspector (or other authorised person) and not the fire authority or a person authorised by the Home Secretary.[56] Since the removal, by section 60 of the National Health Service and Community Care Act 1990, of the Crown status of health authorities within the National Health Service, this distinction has become irrelevant to National Health Service facilities. A saving clause is nevertheless included in Schedule 8 of the 1990 Act, paragraph 15 providing as follows:

'15.—(1) Without prejudice to the continuing validity on and after the appointed day of any fire certificate issued before that day in accordance with subsection (3) of section 40 of the Fire Precautions Act 1971 (certain functions in relation to premises occupied or owned by the Crown exercisable by a fire inspector instead of by the fire authority), any application made, notice issued or other thing done before the appointed day to or by a fire inspector in relation to premises held, used or occupied by a health service body, shall be treated on and after that day as if made, issued or done to or by a fire authority.

(2) Expressions used in sub-paragraph (1) above have the same meaning as in the Fire Precautions Act 1971.'

The authority is given the power to restrict the use of the premises to those uses specified in the certificate, to specify the means of escape, the means for fighting fire and the means of giving warning of a fire.[57] It may also impose requirements as to the freedom from obstruction of the means of escape, the number of persons who may be in the premises and similar matters. By section 1 of the Act the Home Secretary is required to designate by reference to use to which it is put the premises governed by the Act. By subsection 1(2) he can only do so if the user is at least one of the following classes:[58]

'(a) use as, or for any purpose involving the provision of, sleeping accommodation;
(b) use as, or as part of, an institution providing treament or care;
(c) use for purposes of entertainment, reception or instruction or for purposes of any club, society or association;
(d) use for purposes of teaching, training or research;
(e) use for purpose involving access to the premises by members of the public or otherwise.'

The Health and Safety at Work etc. Act 1974, section 78, has added:

'(f) use as a place of work.'

From 1 January 1977, the Act has been applied generally to factories, offices and shops,[59] including those in the occupation of the National Health Service.

From 1 June 1972, the Act was applied to hotels and boarding houses.[60] It is, however, probable that a hospital or (less clearly) a nursing home is not an hotel or a boarding house within the meaning of the regulations. It is also possible, but unlikely, that although a hospital normally has 'patients' rather than 'guests', if provision is made for, say, the parents of a child patient to stay overnight that might alter the position. This is, however, unlikely since such a provision is ancillary to the ordinary business of a hospital or nursing home rather than being itself in the business of a hotel or boarding-house keeper. If, however, this is wrong, it will be noted that since 1 January 1977 hospitals, nursing homes and their staff premises run by the National Health Service were within the control since on that date section 40 governing the Act's application to the Crown was brought into force.

By section 12, the Secretary of State is given power to make regulations governing fire precautions in any of the premises, the uses of which he may designate under section 1. He need not actually have made an order under section 1 requiring the premises to have a fire certificate. The regulations under section 12 may cover broadly similar matters to those which must or may be in a fire certificate under section 6. As yet the only order under section 12 is the Fire Precautions (Non-Certified Factory, Offices, Shops and Railway Premises) Regulations 1976.

Section 40(2) provides that fire certificates are not required for any premises constituting or forming part of a prison (which would include the prison hospital), special hospitals run by the Secretary of State for mental patients, or any premises occupied solely for purposes of the armed forces of the Crown (which would include any hospital run solely for them).

20.8.4 Health and Safety at Work etc. Act 1974

This is a broadly framed measure passed with a view to the creation of a more unified, integrated system to increase the effectiveness of the state's contribution to health and safety at work. In due course, when the appropriate regulations have been made and the approved codes of practice issued, it will replace many of the previous enactments in the field (including the Factories Act 1961 and the Offices, Shops and Railway Premises Act 1963, and regulations made thereunder); but at present its provisions supplement and do not replace all the earlier legislation. As with other enactments of a general nature, a full discussion of its effects cannot be made in this book for reasons of space.

It will, however, be noted that the main thrust of the Act as regards hospitals is to be found in Part I. Section 1(1) provides as follows:

'1.—(1) The provisions of this Part shall have effect with a view to—
   (a) securing the health, safety and welfare of persons at work;
   (b) protecting persons other than persons at work against risks to health or safety arising out of or in connection with the activities of persons at work;
   (c) controlling the keeping and use of explosive or highly flammable or otherwise dangerous substances, and generally preventing the acquisition, possession and use of such substances. . . .'

Section 2(1) provides:

'2.—(1) It shall be the duty of every employer to ensure so far as is reasonably practicable the health, safety and welfare at work of all his employees.'

Subsection 2(2) provides for a series of matters included within this general duty. Subsection 2(3) requires the employer to issue

'(3) . . . a written statement of his general policy with respect to health and safety at work of his employees and the organisation and arrangements for the time being in force for carrying out that policy, and to bring the statement and any revision of it to the notice of all his employees.'

Subsection 2(4) provides for regulations[61] to be made for the appointment of safety representatives in prescribed cases by recognised trades unions from amongst the employees. Subsection 2(6) provides that such representatives shall be consulted and subsection 2(7) provides that every employer must in prescribed[61] cases establish a safety committee if requested by the safety representatives.

Other sections of the Act deal with the duties to persons other than employees,[62] and the duties of persons in control of premises or parts of premises (which would include, for example, a hospital workshop).[63] Section 7 imposes duties on every employee whilst at work to take reasonable care to look after himself and others and to co-operate with the fulfilment of the statutory duties imposed on his employer and others.

In general, the operation of the Act is supervised by the Health and Safety Commission and the Health and Safety Executive.[64] Inspectors may be appointed.[65] They may enter premises (normally at any reasonable time) with a view to ensuring compliance with the Act and the regulations etc. made thereunder and investigating possible breaches.[66] An inspector may generally issue an improvement or prohibition notice and the employer must comply with it.[67] Breach of the duties under the Act can lead to criminal proceedings.[68]

Of particular relevance to hospital and health care practice are the Control of Substances Hazardous to Health Regulations 1989[69] and the Manual Handling Operations Regulations 1992.[70] The COSHH Regulations provide for the assessment, control and monitoring of toxic, harmful, corrosive and irritant substances apart from asbestos, lead and ionizing radiations. The Manual Handling Operations Regulations require employers to assess and control risks in handling and lifting loads, which in the hospital context includes lifting patients.

Reporting adverse incidents and reactions, and defective products relating to medical and non-medical equipment and supplies, food, buildings and plant, and medicinal products

HSG(93)13, issued on 8 June 1993, provides as follows:

Executive summary

General Managers and Chief Executives are responsible for ensuring prompt reporting of adverse incidents and reactions, and defective products relating to medical and non-medical equipment and supplies, food, buildings and plant.

Adverse drug reactions to medicinal products should be reported to the Medicines Control Agency on specially designed yellow cards.

Prompt action should be taken on receipt of Hazard or other warning notification. Detailed advice on how to notify the Department is annexed.

Action

Managers should ensure that:

- adverse incidents, reactions and defective products are reported promptly;
- procedures for reporting are followed;
- for medical devices, a liaison officer is appointed at unit level to take responsibility for reporting;
- products involved in an adverse incident should be kept until the Department's officers have been given the option of investigating the incident;
- healthcare sector staff, including those in the contracted sector, at all levels, are aware of their responsibilities, and of the procedures to be used with regard to reporting and the isolation and retention of defective items;
- local procedures include regular reminders to all staff, and new recruits have specific induction training;
- warnings issued as a consequence of reports are circulated to all potential users and that prompt action is taken;
- electronic mailboxes are read regularly and details of warnings are passed urgently to those who need to know.

Under their statutory powers, Health and Safety Executive or Local Authority inspectors may identify inadequacies in a product's design, instructions for use or manner of use. They may also make recommendations. Any defective products identified by inspectors, or observations or recommendations made by them which have implications for other users, should be reported.

Reports should be submitted in accordance with the detailed advice given in:

Annex A: Procedures to be followed and information to be supplied.

Annex B: Other actions/responsibilities.

Annex C: Reports relating to all *medical devices*: equipment, hospital laboratory equipment and medical supplies (excluding medicinal products).

Annex D: Reports relating to *food*.

Annex E: Reports relating to *non-medical equipment*, engineering plant, installed services, buildings and building fabrics.

Annex F: Reports relating to *medicinal products*.

Note should be taken that the address for the reporting of food incidents has been amended since the issue of HC(88)51, see *Annex D*.

Purpose of the reporting system

An adverse incident is an event which gives rise to, or has the potential to produce, unexpected or unwanted effects involving the safety of patients, users or other persons. Every healthcare employee has a duty to see that all safety related incidents and potentially harmful products are reported, even if on suspicion only. Adverse incidents occurring in local units may often have implications for the rest of the healthcare services. **Note**: *reports are also welcomed from the private sector*. This allows action to be co-ordinated centrally and other users to be warned, nationally and internationally, about hazardous products and unsafe procedures. (The Department's NHS Estates Agency wishes to be informed not only of safety related defects but also of serious deficiencies in the technical or economic performance of products.)

Notification system

Where the results of investigations have implications for other users, then a Hazard or other warning will be issued.

Contacting the Department

The Department should be notified through the contact points (described in annexes C, D, E and F) as appropriate.

Other related guidance

HC(88)37, HM(66)15 and HM(55)66.

Procedures to be followed and information to be supplied

1. The initial report of an incident should contain as much essential detail as available. However, it should never be delayed on this account and serious cases should be reported by the fastest means available. A written report should always follow without delay.

2. All material evidence should be labelled and kept secure, under the charge of a responsible officer. This includes the products themselves and, where appropriate, packaging material or other means of batch identification.

3. The product should not be interfered with in any way except for safety reasons or to prevent its loss. If necessary, a record should be made of all readings, settings and positions of switches, valves, dials, gauges and indicators, together with any photographic evidence and eye witness reports. In serious cases, this record should be witnessed, and the witness should also make a personal written record.

4. Defective items should not be allowed to be repaired, returned to the supplier or discarded before an investigation has been carried out. (See also paragraphs 6 and 7.) The manufacturer or supplier of a defective product should be informed promptly, and may be allowed to inspect the product if accompanied by a responsible officer. In the case of a large batch, it may be possible to pass sample(s) to the manufacturer if this will facilitate the investigation. However, the manufacturer must not be allowed to exchange, interfere with or remove any part of the product if this would prejudice the investigations of the Department, or other official bodies, but see paragraphs 6, 7 and 8 below.

5. If samples of defective, or possibly defective, medicinal product are required for analysis, attempts should be made to acquire them from another part of the same batch. The material implicated can be used as a last resort only if other samples would not provide the information needed.

6. Where clinical need requires equipment to be kept in use, and defective part(s) are clearly identifiable, they can be removed, secured and labelled for later inspection and the equipment repaired for re-use.

7. Advice on procedures to be followed if healthcare equipment is contaminated is contained in HN(87)22, shortly to be revised.

8. Where a manufacturer wishes to investigate a CE marked medical device (see Annex B, paragraph 4) immediate contact should be made with the Medical Devices Directorate, see Annex C.

Other actions/responsibilities

1.   This reporting system does not affect the duty of staff locally to take other actions, as required legally and/or by line management, as a result of an adverse incident:

(a)   To prevent further use of a product which may be defective.

(b)   To report to particular local NHS officers (eg, radiation hazards to Radiation Protection Adviser).

(c)   To report to Health and Safety Executive when legally obliged to do so (see 2 below).

(d)   To refer to the local Environmental Health Officer incidents/complaints relating to food.

(e)   To refer to the Coroner in the case of unexpected death (see paragraph 3 below).

(f)   To inform the manufacturer of a medical device, to assist him in fulfilling his obligations under EC Directives (see 4 below).

2(1). Some incidents are legally notifiable to the Health and Safety Executive under the Reporting of Injuries, Diseases and Dangerous Occurences Regulations 1985, and the Ionising Radiations Regulations 1985.

2(2). A copy of any such notification should be sent to the Department. Include in the copy a clear note showing that it is a report being made under this HSG and that it is a copy of an official notification to the HSE. Notification to the Department does not count as, or substitute for, any other report which should be sent (eg, in respect of an employee's industrial injury).

3. If a patient dies unexpectedly, the clinician in charge of the case should report the death immediately to the Coroner. Pending the instructions of the Coroner or his officer, any product implicated must not be interfered with in any way unless this is necessary for safety or to prevent loss of samples. Although the manufacturer of a suspect product should be informed immediately, neither he nor his agent should be allowed to inspect the product or remove any part of it without the Coroner's prior agreement. The Department has agreed with the Coroner's Society that, with the permission of the Coroner, the Department's officer can examine suspect products so as not to delay remedial action to protect others.

4. As a result of regulations coming into force, implementing the EC Directives, manufacturers of medical devices will be required by law to report to the UK Competent Authority (Medical Devices Directorate) any death or injuries involving their products. The first Directive applies to Active Implantable Medical Devices (for example implantable cardiac pacemakers), and came into force on 1 January 1993. A further Directive covering a much wider range of medical devices, is under consideration.

NOTES

1. *McGinty v Glasgow Victoria Hospital Board* [1951] SC 200.
2. See SI 1990/1329 (Commencement No. 1 Order).
3. In relation to the Employers' Liability (Compulsory Insurance) Act 1969 and the Fire Precautions Act 1971; see National Health Service and Community Care Act 1990, Schedule 8.

4. National Health Service (Amendment) Act 1986, sections 1 and 2; now repealed by the National Health Service and Community Care Act 1990, Schedule 10.
5. EL(90)195.
6. Validated pursuant to the National Health Service (Remuneration and Conditions of Service) Regulations, SI 1991/481.
7. For the meaning and practical significance of vicarious liability, see Chapter 5 'Legal proceedings against health authorities and trusts'.
8. Law Reform (Personal Injuries) Act 1948, section 1.
9. [1957] 2 QB 348.
10. (1951) 95 Sol Jo 655.
11. [1970] 1 All ER 180.
12. [1953] AC 643.
13. *Wilson v Tyneside Window Cleaning Co* [1958] 2 QB 110.
14. [1937] 4 All ER 19. And see Chapter 30, p. 859.
15. The Independent, 8 November 1989.
16. *Davie v New Merton Board Mills Ltd* [1959] AC 604.
17. [1972] 3 All ER 1008.
18. *Wilsher v Essex Area Health Authority* [1988] 1 All ER 871.
19. The Times, 15 February 1972.
20. The Times, 10 May 1956.
21. [1961] 1 WLR 1314.
22. Current Law 1984/2311.
23. [1951] AC 367.
24. The Times, 10 March 1988.
25. [1950] 1 All ER 819.
26. [1991] 2 All ER 293.
27. [1967] 1 All ER 583.
28. [1956] 1 QB 545.
29. [1985] ICR 155.
30. [1989] 3 All ER 228.
31. See section 2(1); and see Mr. Justice Slade in *Vandyke v Minister of Pensions and National Insurance* [1955] 1 QB 29, 38.
32. SI 1974/1547; as amended by SIs 1982/288, 1985/39 and 1985/1626.
33. SI 1991/481.
34. 1990 Scheme (revised), paragraph 4. The Scheme was given specific statutory status by the Criminal Justice Act 1988, sections 108–117.
35. [1976] 1 WLR 1237.
36. Current Law 1977/59.
37. Circular DS 166/71 dated 22 June 1971.
38. The changes came into effect on 1 February 1990. They were to have been introduced through the Criminal Justice Act 1988, but to avoid delay they were incorporated directly into the non-statutory Scheme.
39. The Times, 9 May 1986.
40. For a full examination and statement of the modern common law of damages for psychiatric injury, see *Alcock and others v Wright* [1991] 4 All ER 907. The Criminal Injuries Compensation Scheme (1990 Revision) now includes the possibility of compensating railway engine drivers for the psychiatric effects of track suicides; but neither the common law nor the Scheme extends any several liability otherwise.
41. Directive 85/374/EEC.
42. Consumer Protection Act 1987, section 5(4).
43. [1954] 2 QB 66.

44. This figure is based on ecu values established by the Directive upon which Part I of the Consumer Protection Act 1987 is based.
45. [1952] 1 All ER 925.
46. For instance, relating to the professional responsibilities of community psychiatric or social work staff.
47. [1957] 2 QB 348.
48. The Times, 19 March 1952.
49. The Times, 9 March 1988.
50. [1941] 2 KB 232.
51. [1980] ICR 450.
52. Offices, Shops and Railway Premises Act 1963, section 1(1).
53. Section 1(2); exceptions provided in sections 2 and 3 of the 1963 Act are not relevant to hospitals.
54. Offices, Shops and Railway Premises Act 1963, section 1(5).
55. Constituted under the Fire Services Act 1947; see section 43 of the 1971 Act.
56. Fire Precautions Act 1971, section 40(3), as and when it comes into force.
57. Fire Precautions Act 1971, section 6(1).
58. There are exceptions relating to single private dwellings which although they may apply to hostel or other accommodation furnished by hospitals for their staff are not further discussed here. See section 2 (as amended by the Health and Safety at Work etc. Act 1974) and section 3.
59. The Fire Precautions (Factories, Offices, Shops and Railway Premises) Order, SI 1976/2009 and the Fire Precautions (Non-Certified Factories, Offices, Shops and Railway Premises) Regulations, SI 1976/2010. These last deal with smaller operations which are not required to have a certificate but which must nevertheless take the specified fire precautions.
60. Fire Precautions (Hotels and Boarding Houses) Order, SI 1972/238. It should be noted that not all the enforcement powers are as yet in operation. Detailed reference should be made to standard works on the law relating to fire precautions.
61. See the Safety Representatives and Safety Committees Regulations, SI 1977/500.
62. Health and Safety at Work etc. Act 1974, section 3.
63. Section 4.
64. Established under sections 10–14 of the 1974 Act.
65. Section 19.
66. Section 20.
67. Sections 21–25.
68. Sections 33–42.
69. SI 1988/1657, amended 1990/2026 and 1992/2382.
70. SI 1992/2793.

CHAPTER 21

Charitable trusts for the benefit of hospitals

This chapter discusses the legal powers and duties of trustees and governing bodies of voluntary hospitals, health authorities and NHS trusts constituted under the National Health Service Act 1977, as amended by the National Health Service and Community Care Act 1990, administering property for charitable purposes. The same rules apply generally to all charity trustees, including for example, leagues of hospitals friends established for helping local hospitals and also the National League of Hospital Friends to which most local leagues are affiliated, though they are quite independent of it. Another example is that of the students' union at a medical school. In *London Hospital Medical College v IRC* (1976)[1] it was held that the union was charitable because its purpose was to advance the purposes of the medical school which was itself charitable. This decision was applied in *Attorney-General v Ross* (1985)[2] in which a students' union was held to have been formed for educational and charitable purposes and that its non-charitable political purposes were merely ancillary to its charitable purpose.

The charitable status of a trust for the benefit of a hospital, either in the National Health Service or the private sector, carries advantages which are explained in this chapter. Section 90 of the National Health Service Act 1977 provides that: 'A health authority has power to accept, hold and administer any property on trust for all or any purposes relating to the health service.' The characteristics of a trust which invest it with charitable status are first explained in general terms in this chapter and the position of hospitals, health authorities and NHS trusts as charitable trustees is then set out in detail. It should, incidentally, he noted that the term 'National Health Service trust' is a specific invention of statute (the National Health Service and Community Care Act 1990) and has nothing as such to do with the law relating to trusts of money and property in general. Nevertheless, National Health Service trusts are, like voluntary hospitals and directly managed units within the National Health Service, legally able to hold funds and property on trust, for charitable purposes of the type discussed in this chapter, for the benefit of their services.

21.1   THE CHARITY COMMISSIONERS

21.1.1   Constitution and general powers

By Section 1 and Schedule 1 of the Charities Act 1993 have the general function of promoting the effective use of charitable resources by encouraging the development of better methods of administration, by giving charity trustees information or advice on any matter affecting the charity and by investigating and checking abuses. They also possess ample powers to appoint and remove charity trustees when necessary but are expressly prohibited from themselves administering a charity.

21.1.2   Relations generally between the Charity Commissioners and charities: registration

There is a distinction between charities obliged to be registered by the Charity Commissioners under section 3 of the Charities Act 1993 and those not so obliged. Exempt charities[3] are not subject to inquiry[4] or audit[5] at the instance of the Commissioners, while all other charities, even charities excepted from registration,[6] are subject to the jurisdiction of the Commissioners. All charities, including exempt charities, are entitled under section 29 of the Act to seek their advice.

Exempt charities are not required to be registered with the Charity Commissioners and the Commissioners cannot exercise any of their powers under the Act except at the request of the charity. The Exempt Charities Order 1962[7] exempts from registration as a charity the London medical schools, the medical Institutes and certain University medical schools.

Neither voluntary hospitals as a class, nor National Health Service hospitals are exempt charities, nor are they excepted from registration under section 3 of the Act. But National Health Service hospitals do not have to send their accounts to the Charity Commissioners annually under section 69(1), being excepted therefrom. For the position of National Health Service hospitals generally under the Charities Act 1993, reference may be made to departmental Circular HM(61)74. In that Circular it is also indicated that an understanding has been reached between the Secretary of State for Social Services (now Health) and the Charity Commissioners to avoid any duplication or clash of jurisdiction where there are concurrent powers of inquiry and of dismissal. Sections 8 and 18 of the Charities Act 1993, respectively providing for these powers, will not be exercised without consultation with the Department of Health. To voluntary hospitals in particular registration is, in fact, an advantage, for so long as a charity is registered, it is recognized for all purposes as a charity. Appeal to the High Court against any decision of the Commissioners to enter or not to enter an institution on the register of charities or to remove or not to remove it is provided for in section 4.

21.1.3 The Official Custodian for Charities

The responsibility for acting on request as custodian trustee of charity property, real and personal, subject to the provisions of the Charities Act 1993, is placed on the Official Custodian for Charities. Sections 21 and 22 of the 1993 Act deal with matters relating to the entrusting of property to the Official Custodian for Charities.

21.2 VISITORS

In the case of an endowed, incorporated charity the founder and his heirs or the person nominated by him became *visitor* with the right to regulate all the internal affairs of the charity, including disputes as to elections and appointment of officers. However, this did not oust the jurisdiction of the court and the Charity Commissioners in respect of proper application of trust property. When there is no other visitor of a charitable corporation the jurisdiction is vested in the Crown either through the Lord Chancellor, the court or the Charity Commissioners. The rules regarding extent and exercise of visitorial jurisdiction are complex and obscure but are not likely to be significant, except possibly in the case of a few old foundations, and even in some of those cases visitorial jurisdiction other than of the court or of the Charity Commissioners may be excluded by virtue of a Charter or special Act of Parliament.

21.3 CHARITY TRUSTEES

21.3.1 Who are charity trustees?

By section 97 of the Charities Act 1993, the expression charity trustees is defined as meaning 'the persons having the general control and management of the administration of a charity' which in turn is defined so as to include a corporate body The 1993 Act generally makes such trustees personally responsible for any breach of trust. Consequently, the responsibilities and liabilities of a trustee generally fall upon any person undertaking the administration of charity funds by whatever name he may be called though, particularly in the case of some older hospitals incorporated by special Act or Charter, there may have been some modifications or exceptions (for which see Chapter 3, pp. 73–74, above). Even in the case of an incoporated hospital the full liabilities of trustees in respect of the administration of its property may generally be taken to fall upon the members of the governing body. Indeed, in the case of hospitals incorporated under the Companies Act 1985 the personal responsibility of members of the board is now invariably expressly preserved in the memorandum of association (for which see Chapter 3, p. 75, above). Also, when, as frequently happens in the case of an unincorporated hospital, there are trustees so-called in whose name investments are made and there is also a committee of management, the members of the latter body, no less than the trustees so-called, have the full responsibilities and liabilities of trustees in respect of the functions entrusted to them.

In some pre-1974 trust instruments, reference is made to bodies which were abolished by the National Health Service Reorganisation Act 1973. Some charity trustees of charities which were not incorporated under the Companies Acts (or by charter) were defined by reference to offices held on Regional Hospital Boards or a Board of Governors.

Under the National Health Service (Amendment of Trust Instruments) Order 1974[8] such references are now to the Regional Health Authority, the District Health Authority and so forth. The Order does not affect the (formerly) preserved Boards. Nor does it affect the trusts themselves, so that although the trustees may now be defined by reference to the Region or District, the trusts remain as they were affecting only the same purposes as they did before the reorganisation.

21.3.2   General duties of trustees

A trustee or member of a health authority or the board of management of a hospital generally avoids all personal liability if he attends with due diligence to the affairs of the trust he has undertaken; if he approves only investments authorised by or under the Trustee Investments Act 1961 or expressly authorised by the trust instrument; if he sees that trust property is not left unreasonably under the control of any fellow trustee or any agent; if he sees that trust funds are spent only on authorised objects, any necessary consents being duly obtained; if he accepts no personal remuneration or profit out of trust funds except as expressly authorised by the trust instrument; and, importantly, ensures that there are no conflicts of interest with the trust.

As to variation of trusts under sections 13 and 14 of the Charities Act 1993, when the original terms of the trust cannot be carried out or, for good reason, it is desired to vary them, see pp. 598–600, below.

21.3.3   Accounts and inquiries

Section 46 of the Charities Act 1993 provides that charity trustees must keep proper books of account with respect to the affairs of the charity, prepare periodical statements of account, and prepare consecutive statements of account consisting on each occasion of an income and expenditure account relating to a period of not more than 15 months, and a balance sheet to the end of that period. Section 1 of the Charities Act 1985 gives the Secretary of State power, in the case of local charities whose sole primary object is the relief of poverty, to prescribe the form in which statements of account shall be made and provides that such statements shall be sent annually by the charity trustees to the appropriate local authority.

A hospital incorporated under the Companies Act 1985 is required to keep proper books and prepare accounts under the provisions of that Act. Similarly, health and hospital authorities under the National Health Service Act 1977 are under the same obligation by section 98(1) of the 1977 Act, and of directions given thereunder.

The books of account and statements of account relating to any charity must be preserved for a period of seven years at least, unless the charity ceases to exist and the Charity Commissioners permit them to be destroyed or otherwise disposed of.[9] However records and accounts of authorities under the National Health Service Act 1977 may be destroyed or disposed of only in accordance with the provisions of the Public Records Act 1958, for which see Chapter 15, pp. 385–389, above.

Statements of account giving the prescribed information about the affairs of a charity must be transmitted to the Commissioners by the charity trustees on request; and in the case of a charity having a permanent endowment such a statement relating to the permanent endowment is to be transmitted yearly without any request, unless the charity is excepted by order or regulations.[10] By the Charities (Excepted Accounts) Regulations[11] charities administered by Regional, District and Special health authorities and (formerly) preserved Boards are exempted charities for the purpose of section 69. Subject to section 24(9) relating to common investment funds, a charity is deemed for the purposes of the charities Act 1993 to have a permanent endowment unless all property held for the purposes of the charity may be expended for those purposes without distinction between capital and income. Permanent endowment means, in relation to any charity, property held subject to a restriction on its being so expended.[12]

It seems most unlikely that any voluntary hospital would not have permanent endowments as so defined and hardly more likely that any health or hospital authority under the National Health Service Act 1977 would escape that net if not an excepted charity. Most if not all voluntary hospitals must therefore make annual returns to the Commissioners. Those returns will be open to public inspection so long as retained by the Commissioners.

The Commissioners under section 69 of the Charities Act 1993[13] may by order require that the condition and accounts of any charity for such period as they think fit be investigated and audited by an auditor possessing one of the qualifications laid down in the Act and appointed by them.

Under section 9 the Commissioners may by order require any person having in his possession or control any books, records, deeds or papers relating to a charity, other than an exempt charity,[14] to furnish them with copies of or extracts from any of those documents or (unless the document forms part of the records or other documents of a court or of a public or local authority) require him to pass the document itself to them for their inspection.

By section 8 the Commissioners may from time to time institute inquiries with regard to charities or a particular charity or class of charities, either generally or for particular purposes. Provision is made for the effectiveness of any such inquiry including compulsory attendance of persons whose evidence is required and for the taking of evidence on oath.

21.3.4   Notice of charity meetings

Section 81 of the Charities Act 1993 provides:

'(1) All notices which are required or authorised by the trusts of a charity to be given to a charity trustee, member or subscriber may be sent by post and, if sent by post, may be addressed to any address given as his in the list of charity trustees, members or subscribers for the time being in use at the office or principal office of the charity.

(2) Where any such notice required to be given as aforesaid is given by post, it shall be deemed to have been given by the time at which the letter containing it would be delivered in the ordinary course of post.

(3) No notice required to be given as aforesaid of any meeting or election need be given to any charity trustee, member or subscriber, if in the list above-mentioned he has no address in the United Kingdom.'

These provisions would presumably not apply to an incorporated charity whether by Royal Charter, Act of Parliament or under the Companies Act. Nor are they relevant to a health or hospital authority under the National Health Service Act 1977.

21.3.5   Manner of executing instruments

Section 82 of the Charities Act 1993, provides:

'(1) Charity trustees may, subject to the trusts of the charity, confer on any of their body (not being less than two in number) a general authority, or an authority limited in such manner as the trustees think fit, to execute in the names and on behalf of the trustees assurances or other deeds or instruments for giving effect to transactions to which the trustees are a party; and any deed or instrument executed in pursuance of an authority so given shall be of the same effect as if executed by the whole body.

(2) An authority under subsection (1) above—

(a) shall suffice for any deed or instrument if it is given in writing or by resolution of a meeting of the trustees, notwithstanding the want of any formality that would be required in giving an authority apart from that subsection;

(b) may be given so as to make the powers conferred exercisable by any of the trustees, or may be restricted to named persons or in any other way;

(c) subject to any such restriction, and until it is revoked, shall, notwithstanding any change in the charity trustees, have effect as a continuing authority given by and to the persons who from time to time are of their body.

(3) In any authority under this section to execute a deed or instrument in the names and on behalf of charity trustees there shall, unless the contrary intention appears, be implied authority also to execute it for them in the name and on behalf of the official custodian for charities or of any other person, in any case in which the charity trustees could do so.

(4) Where a deed or instrument purports to be executed in pursuance of this section, then in favour of a person who (then or afterwards) in good faith acquires for money or money's worth an interest in or charge on property or the benefit of any covenant or agreement expressed to be entered into by the charity trustees, it shall be conclusively presumed to have been duly executed by virtue of this section.

(5) The powers conferred by this section shall be in addition to and not in derogation of any other powers.'

This section appears to have no relevance to incorporated charities.

21.3.6 Employment of agents

The greatest safeguard charity trustees have against being held liable for financial loss to the trust due to unauthorised or ill-advised investment, or to misappropriation or mismanagement of the trust property, is by employing suitably qualified agents and advisers such as bankers, solicitors and others. The employment of agents in no degree excuses them from personal attention to the affairs of the charity. If an agent, other than a banker, is allowed to retain trust property (such as the proceeds of the sale of investments) under his control for an unreasonable time, the trustees or board members may be held personally responsible for any loss due to the agent's fraud or bankruptcy. The occasions when advice should be obtained in respect of investments, and from whom it should be obtained, are dealt with in the Trustee Investments Act 1961.

21.3.7 Precautions against misapplication of trust funds

The gravest risk run by charity trustees is in respect of innocent misapplication of trust funds to objects not within the terms of the trust. Rarely, if ever, can the terms of a trust be varied except for good cause and then only with the consent either of the court or of the Charity Commissioners. If, therefore, the governing body of a hospital is not absolutely certain that a proposed use of trust funds or other property is strictly within the terms of the trust it should not embark on such course of action without legal advice. Unless that advice is clearly in favour of or against the course proposed, the governing body should seek the advice of the Charity Commissioners under section 29 of the Charities Act 1993. Upon such advice being given, any trustee for the charity acting upon it is deemed to have acted in accordance with the terms of the trust and is relieved from any personal liability should a breach of trust in fact have been committed unless he knew or had reasonable cause to suspect that the opinion or advice was given in ignorance of material facts or the decision of the court had been obtained on the matter or proceedings were pending to obtain one.[15]

Under section 26 the Charity Commissioners also have power to sanction action proposed by the trustees if it is action expedient in the interests of the charity even though that action would not otherwise be within the powers of the trustees.

21.3.8 Application of property cy-près

The court or the Charity Commissioners may, on application, make a scheme superseding (to the extent stated in the scheme) the trust deed or other instrument under which a charity has been created and managed. The grounds on which this may be done are set out in sections 13 and 14 of the Charities Act 1993. Sections 15 and 17 provide a simplified procedure for altering charitable trusts established by Royal Charter or Act of Parliament. Sections 13 and 14 of the Act provide:

'13.—(1) Subject to subsection (2) below, the circumstances in which the original purposes of a charitable gift can be altered to allow the property given or part of it to be applied cy-près shall be as follows:
  (a) where the original purposes, in whole or in part,
      (i) have been as far as may be fulfilled; or
      (ii) cannot be carried out, or not according to the directions given and to the spirit of the gift; or
  (b) where the original purposes provide a use for part only of the property available by virtue of the gift; or
  (c) where the property available by virtue of the gift and other property applicable for similar purposes can be more effectively used in conjunction, and to that end can suitably, regard being had to the spirit of the gift, be made applicable to common purposes; or
  (d) where the original purposes were laid down by reference to an area which then was but has since ceased to be a unit for some other purpose, or by reference to a class of persons or to an area which has for any reason since ceased to be suitable, regard being had to the spirit of the gift, or to be practical in administering the gift; or
  (e) where the original purposes, in whole or in part, have, since they were laid down,
      (i) been adequately provided for by other means; or
      (ii) ceased, as being useless or harmful to the community or for other reasons, to be in law charitable; or

(iii) ceased in any other way to provide a suitable and effective method of using the property available by virtue of the gift, regard being had to the spirit of the gift.

(2) Subsection (1) above shall not affect the conditions which must be satisfied in order that property given for charitable purposes may be applied cy-près, except in so far as those conditions require a failure of the original purposes.

(3) References in the foregoing subsections to the original purposes of a gift shall be construed, where the application of the property given has been altered or regulated by a scheme or otherwise, as referring to the purposes for which the property is for the time being applicable.

(4) Without prejudice to the power to make schemes in circumstances falling within subsection (1) above, the court may by scheme made under the court's jurisdiction with respect to charities, in any case where the purposes for which the property is held are laid down by reference to any such area as is mentioned in the first column in the Third Schedule to this Act, provide for enlarging the area to any such area as is mentioned in the second column in the same entry in that Schedule.

(5) It is hereby declared that a trust for charitable purposes places a trustee under a duty, where the case permits and requires the property or some part of it to be applied *cy-près*, to secure its effective use for charity by taking steps to enable it to be so applied.

14.—(1) Property given for specific charitable purposes which fail or become obsolete shall be applicable cy-près as if given for charitable purposes generally, where it belongs—

(a) to a donor who, after such advertisements and inquiries as are reasonable, cannot be identified or cannot be found; or

(b) to a donor who has executed a written disclaimer of his right to have the property returned.

(2) For the purposes of this section property shall be conclusively presumed (without any advertisement or inquiry) to belong to donors who cannot be identified, in so far as it consists—

(a) of the proceeds of cash collections made by means of collecting boxes or by other means not adapted for distinguishing one gift from another; or

(b) of the proceeds of any lottery, competition, entertainment, sale or similar money-raising activity, after allowing for property given to provide prizes or articles for sale or otherwise to enable the activity to be undertaken.

(3) The court may by order direct that property not falling within subsection (2) above shall for the purposes of this section be treated (without any advertisement or inquiry) as belonging to donors who cannot be identified, where it appears to the court either—

(a) that it would be unreasonable, having regard to the amounts likely to be returned to the donors, to incur expense with a view to returning the property; or

(b) that it would be unreasonable, having regard to the nature, circumstances and amounts of the gifts, and to the lapse of time since the gifts were made, for the donors to expect the property to be returned.

(4) Where property is applied cy-près by virtue of this section, the donor shall be deemed to have parted with all his interest at the time when the gift was made; but where property is so applied as belonging to donors who cannot be identified or cannot be found, and is not so applied by virtue of subsection (2) or (3) above—

(a) the scheme shall specify the total amount of that property; and

(b) the donor of any part of that amount shall be entitled, if he makes a claim not later than twelve months after the date on which the scheme is made, to recover from the charity for which the property is applied a sum equal to that part, less any expenses properly incurred by the charity trustees after that date in connection with claims relating to his gift; and

(c)   the scheme may include directions as to the provision to be made for meeting any such claim.

(5) For the purposes of this section, charitable purposes shall be deemed to "fail" where any difficulty in applying property to those purposes makes that property or the part not applicable cy-près available to be returned to the donors.

(6) In this section, except in so far as the context otherwise requires, references to a donor include persons claiming through or under the original donor, and references to property given include the property for the time being representing the property originally given or property derived from it.

(7) This section shall apply to property given for charitable purposes, notwithstanding that it was so given before the commencement of this Act.'

Section 14 provides for the kind of difficulties which arose in *Re Hillier's Trusts, Hillier and another v Attorney-General and another* (1954)[16] and in *Re Ulverston and District New Hospital Building Fund* (1956).[17] It does not however cover the difficulties found in *Re Gillingham Bus Disaster Fund* (1959)[18] where money was collected from a benevolent public for what were eventually held to be non-charitable purposes.

The proper applicant to the Charity Commissioners for a scheme is the charity itself as defined in section 96.[19] As regards application to the court section 33 provides that proceedings may be commenced by the charity, by any of the charity trustees, or by any person interested in the charity, or by any two or more inhabitants of the area of the charity, if it is a local charity, but not by any other person[20] other than the Attorney-General with or without a relator.[21] Except when proceedings are brought by the Attorney-General the consent of the Charity Commissioners is required.[22]

In the case of a 'local charity for the relief of poverty' (held in *Re Clarke* (1923)[23] to include the provision of a nursing home for people of moderate means), section 2 of the Charities Act 1985 provides for the replacement of the original objects of the charity by other objects, provided these are charitable and subject to certain other precautionary obligations relating to the founder's intentions. Section 3 of that Act empowers the trustees of certain charities with a low gross income to transfer the whole charity property to another charity. The position of health authorities and National Health Service trusts, established by the National Health Service Act 1977 as amended, as charity trustees is further discussed on pp. 610–621 of this chapter.

21.3.9   Gifts to hospitals by will or from a trust fund

This section examines some difficulties which have arisen in respect of testamentary gifts to charitable hospitals and gifts from discretionary funds established by will, with reference to relevant judicial decisions.

Gifts by will

Misdescription

In spite of the efforts made by charitable hospitals to acquaint would-be benefactors with their proper names and to suggest a form of words for a legacy, misdescription still causes problems. In a case in which a testator left a legacy to 'Westminster Hospital, Charing Cross', it was decided on the particular facts that the gift should go to Charing Cross Hospital[24]; and 'King's Cross Hospital' has been taken to mean 'Great Northern Hospital, King's Cross'.[25] In such cases, the court will take into account any reliable evidence which may be available to indicate the testator's interest in a particular hospital. If as between two hospitals doubt cannot be removed, the legacy may be divided, not necessarily in equal shares; or one may take the whole if the other assents. In *Re Nesbitt deceased, Dr Barnardo's Home v Board of Governors of the United Newcastle upon Tyne Hospital* (1953)[26] an earlier will was admitted to identify a hospital which had been misdescribed.

Vague description or expression of charitable intention: application of cy-près doctrine

Sometimes the testator's words may be so vague or general that it is not practicable to identify the particular institution he intends to benefit; or, even if the testator's intention is certain, it may be impossible to carry it out; or the institution he names may have ceased to exist; or it may have amalgamated with another before the testator's death. In these and certain analogous cases, if there is a general overriding charitable intention, the court will give effect as nearly as possible (*cy-près*) to the testator's wishes and, if necessary, will order a scheme to be prepared.

In *Ballingall's Judicial Factor v Hamilton* (1973)[27] the residue of the deceased's estate was to be divided equally between 'heart diseases and cancer research'. It was held that there was an intention to benefit charitable organisations dealing with treatment and research in the fields and that accordingly a scheme could be drawn up.

In *Re Smith (deceased); Barclays Bank Limited v Mercantile Bank Limited* (1962)[28] the testator, who made his will in 1931 and died in 1938, left residue after the death of his widow (in 1959) 'upon trust to pay and apply the same and the income thereof to or for the benefit of such hospital and/or hospitals and/or charitable institutions as the chairman for the time being of Barclays Bank Ltd, shall in his absolute and uncontrolled discretion think fit'. Mr Justice Wilberforce held that the expression 'hospital or hospitals' included profit-making nursing homes and that therefore the gift, not being exclusively charitable, failed for uncertainty. The Court of Appeal reversed that judgment, holding that in the context of the will the word 'hospital' had to be given what would have been its ordinary meaning in the context at the time the will was made, namely a charitable voluntary hospital. As Lord Denning put it: 'In short, when people spoke of giving money to a "hospital" or "hospitals" in 1931, they meant, as of course, voluntary hospitals . . .'; or in the words of Lord Justice Upjohn: 'in my judgment (and it is a very short point) in a will such as this the word "hospital" is apt and appropriate to describe what used to be called a voluntary hospital and is not appropriate to describe an institution, however expert medical and surgical services may be available therein, which is run for profit and which is normally and ordinarily described as a nursing home'.

It was held in *Re Slatter's Will Trusts, Turner v Turner* (1964)[29] that where a gift to a hospital for particular charitable purposes is made in a will, if the hospital closes down before the death of the testator, and if the need for its work has gone and the hospital has no funds dedicated to its general work through which it could sustain its existence, the gift must lapse.

Testamentary gifts to discontinued charities: application cy-près

This must be distinguished from cases where the testator designates the object of his benevolence but it ceases to exist by the time the gift comes into effect. If the object *used* to exist but there is no *general* charitable intention the gift will fail.[30] If however, although the object specifically described in the will never existed, there is nevertheless a general charitable intent, the *cy-près* doctrine is applied.[31] Where, however, a gift is intended to be made to a specific charity but the court is unable to ascertain which one of several it may have been, the court is not at liberty to find a 'specialised general charitable intent.'[32]

Where the gift was made contingently on some other event happening then so long as the will had taken effect, it was held in *Re Faraken* (1912)[33] a general charitable intention had been demonstrated.

What evidence is required of general charitable intent? The courts have decided that where the gift is to an unincorporated body which has ceased to exist but its purposes are still being carried out, effect will be given to the gift by way of a scheme; but where it is incorporated and although its purposes are still being carried out but it has ceased to exist then other, strong evidence is required to show the general charitable intent.[34] Where there is an intention to benefit the charitable work of a hospital there is no failure of the gift if the hospital ceases to exist but its work is continued elsewhere.[35]

Conditional gifts and gifts in perpetuity for non-charitable objects

The testator will sometimes attempt to achieve some such object as the permanent maintenance of a family grave by linking the maintenance of the grave with a gift to a charity, such as a hospital. Provided no obligation to maintain the grave is put on the charitable trustees it is lawful to direct a trustee to pay the income of a trust fund to the governing body of a hospital for so long as the grave is in good condition, with a gift over to another charity should the grave cease to be in good condition. The opposite result was reached in *Re Elliott, Lloyds Bank v Burton on Trent Hospital Management Committee and others* (1952)[36] where £100 was left to the hospital to be invested 'for the purpose of maintaining my grave and headstone'. Subject to the hospital accepting that legacy and the condition attached to it, the testator bequeathed the residue of his estate to be applied for the purposes of the hospital. The condition was held to be void as infringing the rule against perpetuities; but being a *malum prohibitum* which could be disregarded, the gift of the residue passed to the hospital authority unfettered by the condition.

Discretionary distribution by executors or trustees

Executors or trustees are often instructed to distribute either a certain sum or the residue of an estate at their discretion among charities generally or among charities of a particular kind such as hospitals, perhaps in a particular locality. If the distribution is limited to hospitals either generally or in a particular locality the definition of *hospital* becomes important. In *Re Alchin's Trusts* (1872)[37] it was laid down that there is a presumption that 'hospital' means a general hospital while in another case it was decided that a free dispensary dealing only with outpatients could not share in a bequest to the hospitals of Birmingham. In *Re Davies's Trusts* (1872),[38] unless the context of the will indicated an intention to benefit institutions supported out of rates, a hospital supported by voluntary contributions was held to be preferred. This ruling effectively became obsolete with the transfer of most hospitals to the Secretary of State for Health and Social Security under the National Health Service Act 1946, and the express power given to governing bodies of such transferred hospitals to receive and administer charitable gifts (sections 59 and 60 of the 1946 Act). An expression such as 'the hospitals of London' is for such purpose ordinarily construed in a popular sense and without definite boundaries.

It is interesting to observe that King Edward's Hospital Fund for London, a charitable trust for the benefit of hospitals of the metropolis, now extends its activities to cover the whole area of the four Regional Health Authorities, an area very substantially larger than even the Metropolitan Police District. Incidentally the four metropolitan regions *are* very specially linked with London because their services are, in a sense, based on the London teaching hospitals. The point is, of course, not now confined to London.

A case of exceptional difficulty is *Chichester Diocesan Fund v Simpson* (1944)[39] in which a testator named Diplock had left the residue of his estate to his executors upon trust with a direction to them to apply the proceeds of sale 'for such charitable institution or institutions or other charitable or benevolent object or objects as my acting executors in their or his absolute discretion select and to be paid to or for such institutions or objects if more than one in such proportions as my executor or executors may think proper'.

Distribution amounting to some £250,000 to many hospitals was made by the executors under that residuary bequest. The validity of the bequest was challenged by relatives of the deceased who would have benefited on an intestacy, on the grounds that a testamentary gift of this kind to unascertained objects is valid only if there is in the will an express overriding charitable intention; and that the residuary bequest in Diplock's will, which permitted an unascertained proportion of the residue to be distributed to *benevolent objects*, as distinguished from *charitable* objects in the legal sense of the term, was therefore invalid.

The House of Lords[40] declared the residuary bequest invalid, the Lord Chancellor (Viscount Simon) saying that the phrase 'charitable or benevolent' in a will must in its ordinary context be regarded as too vague to give the certainty necessary before such a provision could be supported or enforced. There was no context in the will under consideration to justify a different interpretation: the use of the conjunction 'or' in the will appeared to him to indicate a variation rather than an identity between the coupled conceptions. The clause was not a valid testamentary disposition.

A more serious feature of *Re Diplock* was that, a substantial distribution having been made and the sums distributed used in various ways, there arose the possibility of the charitable institutions which had received gifts under the invalid bequest being called upon to refund the estate. An action by the next of kin of the deceased was subsequently commenced for that purpose.[41]

The House of Lords did permit the recovery of some of the money received by the charities, the decision in respect of each charity depending on a consideration of the rules of equity relating to the recovery of money from an innocent trustee who received it in good faith and also as to tracing orders, the application of the rule in *Clayton's Case* (1816)[42] and of several other leading cases. The effect of *Clayton's Case* is that if monies are mixed in an active banking account the first paid in is the first drawn out. But the rule is not without exception. If a trustee has mixed trust funds with his own monies in a banking account he will be presumed to have drawn out his own monies first unless the drawings were for the purposes of the trust.

A mistake of law on the part of the executor-trustees was held not to bar the right of the next of kin of the deceased testator to recovery, in accordance with the rules of equity, from innocent recipients from the executor-trustees of money belonging to the estate.

The House of Lords affirmed that whenever under the provisions of a will (in the present case a discretionary distribution to charities) a wrongful distribution is made by the executors, the sums wrongly paid may be recovered from the recipient by the person or persons who have suffered thereby (next of kin, beneficiaries or creditors), subject only to action being brought within 12 years of the expiry of the 'executor's year', this period of limitation being in accordance with section 20 of the Limitation Act 1939 (for which see now the Limitation Act 1980, section 22). The fact that a charity may have received a monetary gift in good faith and spent it before any claim is made for repayment on grounds of invalidity is apparently no defence to the claim.

Hospitals offered substantial benefits under a will (particularly under discretionary trusts) should therefore take all practicable steps to assure themselves of the validity of the gift; and if in real doubt, not dispose of the fund, even if accepted, until either the doubt is cleared up or the claim statute-barred. Even the absence of grounds for suspicion will not apparently protect the innocent recipient in all cases.

Following the *Diplock* decision it seems unlikely that the decision of the Privy Council in *Re Resch's Will Trusts; Le Cras v Perpetual Trustee Ltd* (1969)[43] on appeal from New South Wales would be followed in this country. A bequest had been made to the Sisters of Charity for the general purposes of St Vincent's private hospital for paying patients, the validity of the bequest depending on whether the hospital was a charity. The Privy Council decided that this gift was valid despite the fact that surpluses from the private hospital had been used not only to contribute to the maintenance of an ordinary general hospital nearby, which was also run by the Sisters of Charity, but also for the general purposes of the Order, which latter purposes were not all necessarily charitable.

Charitable Trusts (Validation) Act 1954

This Act makes it very improbable that further claims on the lines of the *Diplock* case would succeed, in respect of any trust instrument taking effect before 16 December 1952. That Act validated any imperfect trust instrument which took effect before 16 December 1952 and was an instrument under which the trust property could be used for exclusively charitable objects, but could also be used for purposes that were not charitable. Any such trust instrument was validated provided it would have been valid if the declared objects had been restricted to charitable objects and provided that the trust had not before 16 December 1952 been treated as invalid on the ground that its objects were not exclusively charitable. From the commencement, the objects of any trust validated under its provisions are limited to such of its purposes as are charitable.

The case of *Gillingham Bus Disaster Fund* (1958)[44] illustrates both the limits of the Charitable Trusts (Validation) Act 1954 and the importance of there being a clear statement of the objects of any public appeal (or indeed of any trust instrument). Following an accident in which several cadets were killed the mayors of three towns appealed for contributions to a fund 'to be devoted among other things to defraying the funeral expenses, caring for the boys who may be disabled, and then to such worthy cause or causes in memory of the boys who lost their lives as the mayors may determine . . .' The trusts were held void for uncertainty.

Insufficiency or excess of funds for health services

The Health Services Act 1980 introduced a new section 96A into the National Health Service Act 1977. That section, as now amended by the National Health Service and Community Care Act 1990, provides relevantly as follows:

'(7) Where property held by a health [authority, National Health Service trust or Board] under this section is more than sufficient to enable the purpose for which it was given to be fulfilled the excess shall be applicable, in default of any provision for its application made by the trust or other instrument under or in accordance with which the property comprising the excess was given, for such purposes connected with any of the functions of the authority or Board as the authority or Board think fit.

(8) Where property held by a health [authority, National Health Service trust or Board] under this section is insufficient to enable the purpose for which it was given to be fulfilled then—

    (a) the [authority, National Health Service trust or Board] may apply so much of the capital or income at their disposal as is needed to enable the purpose to be fulfilled subject, however, in the case of trust property to any restrictions on the purpose for which the trust property may be applied and, in the case of money paid or payable by the Secretary of State or by a Regional Health Authority under section 97 below, to any directions he or that Authority may give; but

    (b) where the capital or income applicable under paragraph (a) above is insufficient or is not applied to enable the purpose to be fulfilled, the property so held by the health [authority, National Health Service trust or Board] shall be applicable, in default of any provision for its application made by the trust or other instrument under or in accordance with which the property was given, for such purposes connected with any of the functions of the authority or Board as the authority or Board think fit.

(9) Where under subsection (7) or (8) above property becomes applicable for purposes other than that for which it was given the [authority, National Health Service trust or Board] shall have regard to the desirability of applying the property for a purpose similar to that for which it was given.'

21.3.10   Dealings with land

Since the Charities Act 1960 (now 1993), charity trustees (whether incorporated or not) have been free to hold land for the purposes of the charity subject only to the same rules as other persons, provided that the holding of land is in accordance with the terms of the trust. Land is not in fact ordinarily an authorised investment under the Trustee Investment Act 1961, though, subject to proper advice, mortgages on land are authorised.

21.3.11   Investments

Within the limits and subject to the safeguards laid down in the Trustee Investments Act 1961, trustees, including charity trustees, who have not been given wider powers of investment by their trust instrument, may invest part of their trust fund in first class equities, 'wider range securities' as defined in the Act. The remainder still has to be invested in gilt-edged and similar 'narrower range' fixed interest securities etc., somewhat more liberally defined than were trustee securities in section 1 of the Trustee Act 1925.

Charity trustees may also invest in the Charities Official Investment Fund established by the Charity Commissioners by virtue of the authority given in section 24 of the Charities Act 1993. Participation in the Fund, which takes full advantage of the wider investment powers given by the 1961 Act, relieves charity trustees of all responsibility regarding the suitability and legality of their investments. It is understood that the Fund has been given authority to invest a greater proportion of its capital in wider range securities than have trustees generally. In departmental Circular HM(62)80 the attention of National Health Service authorities was drawn to the possibility of investing endowment capital in the Charities Official Investment Fund.

21.3.12   Payments to trustees and Board members

Unless the conditions of the trust clearly provide otherwise, trustees, including members of the board or committee of a hospital, may properly be reimbursed all reasonable expenses, including travelling expenses, actually incurred by them in respect of their duties. Unless the terms of the trust so provide, they are not entitled to any remuneration for their time and trouble nor, while trustees or members of the board, can they properly accept any office or undertake any work for the hospital remunerated in any way whether by salary or fees. In *Re The French Protestant Hospital* (1951)[45] it was held that although the directors of a charitable hospital established by Royal Charter in 1718 were not technically trustees, they were in the same fiduciary position as trustees and that it was therefore improper for them, of their own motion, to introduce a revised bye-law removing the ban on their receiving any payment from the charity for professional services, such a provision being prima facie repugnant to law. The effect of this general rule is not avoided by any form of words, as by calling the payment made an *honorarium*, and it applies to medical practitioners no less than to others.

It is no justification for payments made in contravention of the rule to show that the trustee or member of the board has undertaken work for the hospital far in excess of that undertaken by his fellow trustees, such as solicitor or accountant or as a medical member of the staff of the hospital; nor that he has undertaken a peculiarly onerous office, such as chairman of the Board or as organiser of an appeal. Equally, it is no justification that the payment is small in relation to the work done, and that anyone else would have required higher payment. The general rule against payment for time and trouble would also prevent payment of Board members for loss of earnings while attending board meetings.

Unincorporated hospitals

The Board itself could not vote remuneration to any of its members unless the trust deed expressly conferred that power. Nor does it seem that an annual meeting of subscribers could regularise the position without the sanction of the court or of the Charity Commissioners, which would be given only if the course proposed were manifestly in the interests of the charity and there were no reasonable alternative.

Incorporated hospitals

A general rule cannot be stated as to whether authority to make payment must be embodied in the principal instrument of incorporation or whether it suffices if it is contained in the bye-laws or articles. The *French Protestant Hospital* case (1951), above, illustrates the obstacles in the way of alteration of bye-laws or articles to permit remuneration being paid to directors of an incorporated charity. The approval of the court or of the Charity Commissioners to any provision to that effect in bye-laws or articles or to any amendment to that effect in the principal instrument of incorporation is almost invariably necessary. The following paragraphs afford some practical guidance.

Hospitals incorporated under the Companies Acts
Hospitals incorporated under the Companies Act in order to obtain permission to omit the word 'limited' from the title, have been required to insert in the memorandum of association a clause categorically forbidding any payment to members of the Board or governing body in respect of services rendered. Occasionally, special exception has been made in favour of representatives of the medical staff, subject to stringent safeguards so that such medical members of the Board should, with the other doctors, receive no more than their due share of any amount allocated to the medical staff, as, for example, from a contributory scheme pool. Medical members of the Board of such a

hospital have not been permitted to receive payment for services rendered otherwise than within the narrow limits indicated.

Hospitals incorporated by Royal Charter

There are wide variations in the terms of the Royal Charters incorporating different hospitals (most of which were revoked on the coming into operation of the National Health Service Act 1946) but in not one of several Charters examined by Dr Speller was payment for services rendered by members of the Board expressly or by necessary implication authorised. Nor does it seem that authority for such payment could properly be inferred. Furthermore, where the detailed constitution of the Board was contained in bye-laws annexed as a schedule to the Charter, there was generally in those bye-laws a provision to the effect that no paid officer of the hospital and no governor supplying any article to the hospital (for which he received some consideration) was eligible to serve on the Board. The Charter almost always contained a stipulation that the original bye-laws contained in the schedule could not be altered except with the approval of the Privy Council and it is difficult to imagine approval for any amendment authorising the payment of Board members either for their services as such or otherwise. Such a proposal would have to be proved necessary in the interests of the charity.

Hospitals incorporated by Act of Parliament

No single pattern is detectable. In some modern private Acts relating to hospitals the detailed constitution has been embodied in a scheme set out in a schedule to the Act and alterations to the scheme might be made only with sanction of the Charity Commissioners or of the court. In the specimens examined by Dr Speller not only was no provision made for payment of members of the Board but there was an express prohibition against any Board member being concerned in any bargain or contract with the hospital to any greater extent than as a shareholder in a company. The court or the Charity Commissioners would be unlikely to sanction alterations of the scheme to allow remuneration or personal profit to any members of the governing body. Although other private Acts are not so explicit it is difficult to avoid the conclusion that authority to pay members of the Board was neither sought nor desired by those who promoted those Acts.

Hospital authorities under the National Health Service Act 1977

There is in the National Health Service Act 1977 no prohibition on appointment to membership of any health or hospital authority of a person who is receiving payment for services to that authority. Indeed places on health authorities are reserved for medical practitioners and, in effect, other employees. Health authorities and trusts must draw up standing orders relating to any interest of members in contracts or other matters.[46] Some guidance was given in a former Circular[47] on the measuring of indirect pecuniary interest:

'1. A member of an authority who has any pecuniary interest, direct or indirect, in any contract or proposed contract or any other matter, and is present at a meeting of the authority or of a committee or sub-committee of the authority at which the contract or other matter is the subject of consideration, must disclose the fact at the meeting as soon as practicable after its commencement, and must not take any part in the consideration or discussion of, or vote on any question with respect to, the contract or other matter.

This disqualification does not extend to—

a.　an interest in a contract or other matter which a member may have as a rate-payer or inhabitant of the area or as an ordinary consumer of gas, electricity or water;
b.　an interest in any matter relating to the terms on which the right to participate in any service, including the supply of goods, is offered to the public;
c.　an interest of a member in a contract or other matter which is so remote or insignificant that it cannot reasonably be regarded as likely to influence a member in the consideration or discussion of, or in voting on, any question with respect to that contract or matter;

and in these cases disclosure of the interest is not required.

2. A person is to be treated as having indirectly a pecuniary interest in a contract or other matter if—

a.　he or any nominee of his is a member of a company or other body with which the contract is made or proposed to be made or which has a direct pecuniary interest in the other matter under consideration; or
b.　he is partner, or in the employment, of a person with whom the contract is made or is proposed to be made or who has a direct pecuniary interest in the other matter under consideration.

But a person is not disqualified—

i.　by reason of his being a member of a public body; or
ii.　by reason of his being a member of a company or other body, if he has no beneficial interest in any shares of the company or other body; or
iii.　by reason of a pecuniary interest in a contract or other matter arising by virtue of a connection mentioned in a. or b. of this paragraph, if the interest of the body or person connected with him is so remote or insignificant that it cannot reasonably be regarded as likely to influence a member in the consideration or discussion of, or in voting on, any question with respect to the contract or matter.'

21.4　HEALTH AUTHORITIES AND TRUSTS AS CHARITY TRUSTEES

21.4.1　Introductory

In *Re Frere (deceased); Kidd and another v Farnham Group Hospital Management Committee* (1951)[48] Mr Justice Wynn-Parry said that a hospital did not cease to be a charity merely because of the coming into effect of the National Health Service Act 1946.

In *Re White's Will Trusts; Tindall v Board of Governors of Sheffield United Hospitals and Others* (1951) [49] a gift for the purpose of providing a home of rest for the nurses at a particular hospital was held to be charitable since the purpose of the gift was to increase the efficiency of the hospital for the healing of the sick. Consequently the income passed to the new hospital authority under section 60(1) of the 1946 Act. It appears that subsequent reorganisations of the health service have not affected the charitable status of health service authorities.

21.4.2 Power of health authorities and trusts to accept gifts

Health authorities and NHS trusts have power to accept, hold and administer any property on trust for all or any purposes relating to the health service. Accordingly charitable gifts may be accepted, held and administered by a health authority or trust for any health service purpose.

Such gifts, like any other charitable gifts, are accepted subject to any conditions laid down by the donor or testator, on the enforceability of which specific legal advice should be sought in each case. They can be freed from such conditions, or the conditions relaxed, only by order of the court or, in appropriate cases, of the Charity Commissioners.

All such gifts will be subject to the Trustee Investments Act 1961 as to authorised investments.

21.4.3 Private trusts for hospitals

Section 91 of the 1977 Act provides:

'**91.**—(1) Where—
  (a) the terms of a trust instrument authorise or require the trustees, whether immediately or in the future, to apply any part of the capital or income of the trust property for the purposes of any health service hospital, then
  (b) the trust instrument shall be construed as authorising or (as the case may be) requiring the trustees to apply the trust property to the like extent, and at the like times, for the purpose of making payments, whether of capital or income, to the appropriate hospital authority.'

By section 96(1), any provision made in sections 90–95 for the transfer of property to the appropriate hospital authority includes provision for the transfer of any rights or liabilities arising from that property. Section 96(1) will not apparently apply to what is authorised by section 91, (payments of money). If, however, when offering a payment, trustees of a private trust sought to impose on the authority some liability beyond the requirements of section 91(2), it could refuse to receive the payment on such terms and should indeed do so, if, in its opinion, it was not in the interests of the charity to accept. Section 91(2) provides:

'(2) Any sum so paid to the appropriate hospital authority shall, so far as practicable, be applied by them for the purpose specified in the trust instrument.'

Section 91(2) must be read subject to section 96(2) which provides that nothing in sections 90–95 shall affect the power of Her Majesty, the court (as defined in the Charities Act 1960) or any other person to alter the trusts of any charity. The only problem of interpretation posed by this subsection is the meaning to be attributed to the word 'practicable', a word previously used in subsection (2) of the corresponding sections of the Acts of 1946 and 1973. Its use in section 60(2) of the 1946 Act was not, however, the subject of judicial interpretation. However, in *Re Hayes' Will Trusts, Dobie and others v Board of Governors of the National Hospital and others* (1954),[50] which concerned a gift to a hospital, the word 'impracticable' was held equivalent to 'not able to be done' and from that it might be argued that 'practicable' in section 60(2) meant 'able to be done or possible'. To interpret 'practicable' in that context would imply a rigidity in the interpretation of the section which the use of the word 'practicable' instead of 'possible' seems designed to avoid. There is the same objection to giving the word that meaning in section 91(2) of the 1977 Act.

Distinctions between the meanings of 'practicable' and 'possible' and between 'practicable' and 'reasonably practicable' were considered in *Jayne v National Coal Board* (1963),[51] an industrial injury case in which the two expressions 'practicable precautions' and 'reasonably practicable precautions' used in section 157 of the Factories Act 1937 were considered. Giving judgment in that case, Mr Justice Veale said:

'It is slightly more difficult to show that avoidance of the breach was impracticable than that it was not reasonably practicable . . . The difference of meaning between the two expressions is hard to define and further definitions of words that in themselves express a shade of meaning are not helpful. But the difference, though hard to define, exists and in a borderline case it might produce a difference in the result. The word "reasonably" has a slight tendency to modify the word "practicable". But in my judgment there may well be precautions which it is "practicable" but not "reasonably practicable" to take. . . . The distinction therefore exists but it is slight.'

There was, he said, in his view clearly a difference between 'practicable' and 'possible'. Had the legislature intended to lay down possibility as a test, it would have been simple to have used the word 'impossible' in section 157; but they did not. In his view 'impracticability' as a conception was different from that of 'impossibility'; the latter was absolute, the former introduced some degree of reason and involved some regard for practice. No doubt the same goes for National Health Service legislation and practice.

The meaning of 'practicable' in section 6(4) of the National Health Service (Scotland) Act 1947[52] was considered in *Adams and others v Maclay (Secretary of State) and the South Eastern Regional Hospital Board* (1958).[53] It had been proposed to open to male practitioners a post for a consultant at two former voluntary hospitals which had been established to provide for the treatment of women and children by female practitioners. The hospitals having been taken over under section 6 of the 1947 Act the Secretary of State was bound under section 6(4) 'so far as practicable to secure that the objects for which any such property was used immediately before the appointed day are not prejudiced by the provisions of this section'. It was held that because of that requirement it was the duty of the Secretary of State to see to it that a male medical practitioner was not appointed consulting physician at the two hospitals unless and until, after the advertisement of the post as being open to women medical practitioners only, it should appear that no women suitable for the appointment had applied.

This decision, like that in *Jayne's* case, leaves room for a distinction between the meaning of 'possible' and 'practicable' since, although under the trust instrument relating to the former voluntary hospitals the Board administering those hospitals might have been under an obligation to appoint none but women to the medical staff even though the best they could find at any particular time, although on the medical register, might lack the particular qualifications and experience appropriate to the post to be filled, the Secretary of State or the Board acting for him, having considered women applicants and decided that none was suitable, could appoint a man. In the case of the two former voluntary hospitals the governing condition would have been a 'possibility'; after transfer to the Secretary of State it was a 'practicability'.

After the decision in the Scottish case, the Minister of Health issued fresh instructions to hospital authorities in England and Wales on the procedure to be adopted when it was proposed to close or change the use of a hospital, the new procedure being designed to take particular account of the duty to secure that, as far as practicable, the objects for which a hospital was used immediately before transfer in 1948 would not be prejudiced by the proposed change.[54]

21.4.4 The Hospital Endowments Fund: distribution on winding-up

The Hospital Endowments Fund was established under the 1946 Act and to it were transferred the endowments of all hospitals transferred to the Minister of Health except those which were designated as teaching hospitals. Section 23 of the 1973 Act required the Secretary of State to wind up the Fund and to provide by order for the distribution of its assets to Regional and Area Health Authorities and Special Trustees. This was done by the National Health Service (Hospital Endowments Fund – Distribution of Assets) Order 1974,[55] which provided for the distribution of the Fund in accordance with the responsibility for hospitals as at 1 April 1974. The distribution was based upon the average number of occupied beds during the year 1973 in non-teaching hospitals (with beds such as those used for long-stay patients being counted twice). Subject to this, in England 10 per cent of the apportioned assets were distributed to the Regional Health Authorities and 90 per cent to Area Health Authorities and Special Trustees and in Wales (where there are no Regional Health Authorities or Special Trustees) all the apportioned assets were distributed to Area Health Authorities.

Under section 7(2) of the 1946 Act it had been the duty of the Secretary of State to secure, so far as had been reasonably practicable, that pre-nationalisation objects and conditions were not prejudiced by transfer to the Fund. Section 7 is now repealed but section 93(2) of the 1977 Act imposes a similar obligation. It provides:

'(2) The person holding the property after the transfer or last transfer shall secure, so far as is reasonably practicable, that the objects of any original endowment and the observance of any conditions attached . . . including in particular conditions intended to preserve the memory of any person or class of persons, are not prejudiced by the provisions of this Part of this Act or Part II of that Act of 1973.
In this subsection "original endowment" means a hospital endowment which was transferred under section 7 of that Act of 1946 and from which the property in question is derived.'

Section 93 continues:

'(3) Subject to the preceding subsection, the property shall be held on trust for such purposes relating to hospital services (including research), or to any other part of the health service associated with any hospital, as the person holding the property thinks fit.
(4) Where the person holding the property is a body of special trustees, the power conferred by the preceding subsection shall be exercised as respects the hospitals for which they are appointed.'

21.4.5 Trust property held by abolished hospital authorities

All trust property held by a hospital authority abolished on reorganisation of the National Health Service under the 1973 Act and the National Health Service (Hospital Trust Property) Order 1974[56] was at that time transferred to the corresponding health authority or to Special Trustees, in accordance with the provisions of section 24 of that Act, provision for apportionment, if necessary, being made in section 30. The uses to which such transferred trust property may be put, and the discretion exercisable by the person to whom the property has been transferred, are set out in section 94 of the National Health Service Act 1977. If, however, the trust property was first acquired as an *endowment* under section 7 of the Act of 1946, the stricter provisions of section 93 apply.

21.4.6 Endowments acquired directly or indirectly under section 7 of the 1946 Act, transferred to new health authorities or to Special Trustees under section 24 of the 1973 Act

If any trust property transferred under section 24 from an abolished hospital authority to a health authority or to Special Trustees had originally been received by a hospital authority as an endowment then under the now repealed provisions of section 7 of the Act of 1946, and now as with the assets of the old Hospital Endowments Fund under section 27(2) of the Act of 1973, there is an obligation to secure so far as is reasonably practicable that the objects of the endowment and the observance of any conditions are not prejudiced by the transfer. Subject thereto, health authorities and trusts may hold such 'original endowments' for purposes within section 93(3) and special trustees for purposes within section 93(4).

Section 93 applies (a) to property which is transferred under section 23 of the National Health Service Reorganisation Act 1973 (winding up of hospital endowments funds); and (b) to property which is transferred under section 24 of that Act (transfer of trust property from abolished authorities) and which immediately before the appointed day was, in accordance with any provision contained in or made under section 7 of the National Health Service Act 1946, applicable for purposes relating to hospital services or relating to some form of research and this section shall continue to apply to the property after any further transfer under the preceding section.

The objects and conditions referred to in section 93(2) are those to which the trust property was subject at the time it was transferred to a hospital authority under section 7 of the 1946 Act. Like other property transferred under section 24 of the 1973 Act, original endowments may, if necessary, have been subject to apportionment under section 92 of the 1977 Act or may in future become subject to transfer to another authority or trust under section 92 (below), following the occurrence of any change of a kind mentioned in section 92(1).[57]

21.4.7 Trust property formerly held by local health authorities

By section 25 of the 1973 Act trust property held by the former local health authorities may be transferred to and vest in such health authorities as may be specified by an order made by the Secretary of

State. Such transfers in some cases were made subject to apportionment under section 92 of the 1977 Act. Property transferred under section 25 of the 1973 Act may also be subject to subsequent transfer under section 92 of the 1977 Act.

21.4.8   Power of Secretary of State to make further transfers of trust property

Section 92 of the 1977 Act as amended by section 11 of the National Health Service and Community Care Act 1990, provides for such transfers, as follows:

'(1) The Secretary of State may, having regard to any change or proposed change in the arrangements for the administration of a hospital [or other establishment or facility] or in the area or functions of any health authority, by order provide for the transfer of any trust property from any health authority or NHS trust, special trustees or trustees for an NHS trust to any other health authority or NHS trust, special trustees or trustees for an NHS trust.

(2) If it appears to the Secretary of State at any time that all the functions of any special trustees should be discharged by one or more health authorities or NHS trusts then, whether or not there has been any such change as is mentioned in subsection (1) above, he may by order provide for the transfer of all trust property from the special trustees to the health authority or NHS trust, or, in such proportions as he may specify in the order, to those health authorities or NHS trusts.

(3) Before so acting the Secretary of State shall consult the health authorities or NHS trusts and special trustees concerned.

(4) Where by an order under this section, property is transferred to two or more authorities or NHS trusts, it shall be apportioned by them in such proportions as they may agree or as may in default of agreement be determined by the Secretary of State, and the order may provide for the way in which the property is to be apportioned.

(5) Where property is so apportioned, the Secretary of State may by order make any consequential amendments of the trust instrument relating to the property.

(6) If it appears to the Secretary of State at any time that—

(a)   the functions of any special trustees should be discharged by the trustees for an NHS trust, or

(b)   the functions of the trustees for an NHS trust should be discharged by special trustees,

then, whether or not there has been any such change as is mentioned in subsection (1) above, he may, after consulting the special trustees and the trustees for the NHS trust, by order provide for the transfer of all trust property from or to the special trustees to or from the trustees for the NHS trust.'

21.4.9   Trust funds and trustees for NHS trusts

The powers provided by section 92 (above) of the 1977 Act, as amended, are of particular practical significance in their application to trust property for the benefit of National Health Service trusts once independent status within the National Health Service is granted to hospitals and facilities formerly managed by health authority beneficiaries of trusts. Section 11 of the 1990 Act provides:

'11.—(1) The Secretary of State may by order made by statutory instrument provide for the appointment of trustees for an NHS trust; and any trustees so appointed shall have power to accept, hold and administer any property on trust for the general or any specific purposes of the NHS trust (including the purposes of any specific hospital or other establishment or facility which is owned and managed by the trust) or for all or any purposes relating to the health service.

(2) An order under subsection (1) above may—

(a) make provision as to the persons by whom trustees are to be appointed and generally as to the method of their appointment;

(b) make any appointment subject to such conditions as may be specified in the order (including conditions requiring the consent of the Secretary of State);

(c) make provision as to the number of trustees to be appointed, including provision under which that number may from time to time be determined by the Secretary of State after consultation with such persons as he considers appropriate; and

(d) make provision with respect to the term of office of any trustee and his removal from office.

(3) Where, under subsection (1) above, trustees have been appointed for an NHS trust, the Secretary of State may by order made by statutory instrument provide for the transfer of any trust property from the NHS trust to the trustees so appointed.'

21.4.10   Special Trustees

Under section 29(1) of the 1973 Act Special Trustees were to be appointed for those hospitals which immediately before 1 April 1974 were controlled and managed by any University Hospital Management Committee or Board of Governors (except the preserved Boards under section 15) and anybody on whose request an order was made under section 24(2). These Special Trustees who now operate under section 95 of the 1977 Act hold and administer the property transferred to them. Thus Special Trustees handle property which would otherwise have become the responsibility of the (then) Area Health Authority (Teaching). Likewise the Special Trustees took a share of the Hospital Endowments Fund. By section 95(2) the Special Trustees have the power to accept further gifts relating to hospital services:

'(2) Special Trustees shall have power to accept hold and administer any property on trust for all or any purposes relating to hospital services (including research), or to any other part of the health service associated with hospitals, being a trust which is wholly or mainly for hospitals for which the Special Trustees are appointed.'

21.4.11   Endowment of beds

A bed or cot may be endowed in a hospital within the health service by payment of such conventional sum as the health authority is prepared to accept. It normally now means 'naming' a bed according to the donor's wishes and investing the sum paid as capital, the income to be expended for the purposes of the hospital or perhaps the health service generally. Such is the general effect of *Re Ginger (deceased); Wood Roberts and another v Westminster Hospital Board of Governors and others* (1951)[58] and of *Re Mills and Mills (deceased); Midland Bank Executor & Trust Co Ltd v. Board of Governors of United Birmingham Hospitals* (1953).[59] In the former case, a gift to endow a cot at Westminster Hospital was left by a will made in 1940, the testator dying in November 1948. The continuity of the work of the hospital was not disputed; but although the governors could still agree to name a cot they could not, as had formerly been the custom, give a right to nominate patients to occupy it. It was held that nomination was not a condition of the bequest and therefore the fact that the trustees could not nominate did not invalidate the gift. It was accordingly payable, under section 59 of the National Health Service Act 1946, to the Board of Governors on their undertaking to name in perpetuity a cot in memory of the testatrix's uncle in Westminster Hospital, St John's Gardens or such other building to which the hospital might be removed and on their undertaking to invest the sum in investments for the time being authorised by law and to apply the income for the purposes of the hospital.

In *Re Mills and Mills (deceased)* the bequest was 'of such sum as shall be necessary to endow a bed in the Children's Hospital Birmingham . . . to be known at all times as the "Mills" bed, in memory of my father, mother and brother'. The testator had died in 1929 but, as the bequest had been subject to a life interest which expired only in 1950, the question had to be settled whether the Board of Governors could take the gift.

The Board of Governors said that for thirty years before 1948 the sum of £1000 had been accepted to endow a bed, that they had not considered the matter since nationalisation but were still willing to name a bed for that sum. They conceded that it was a purely conventional amount, having no reference to the sum required to maintain a bed. On the other side it was contended that the testatrix had had in contemplation that there would be a recognised scheme and recognised sum for endowing a bed. It was held (presumably under section 60 of the 1946 Act) that such a scheme was not essential, and that the sum necessary to endow a bed was a conventional sum acceptable to the hospital. The hospital would therefore receive £1000 on undertaking to name a bed as desired by the testatrix.

If a sum received by an authority in return for naming a bed is accepted as capital only the income of which can be spent otherwise than for capital purposes, it constitutes a 'permanent endowment' as defined in section 96(3) of the Charities Act 1993, as also will other amounts resolved by the authority be treated as capital.

21.4.12 Endowment of beds for private patients in National Health Service hospitals

The question of endowment of beds for private patients came before the court in *Re Adams, deceased; Gee and another v Barnet Group Hospital*

Management Committee (1968).[60] Mrs Adams in her will had made bequests for the endowment of beds for paying patients at Barnet General Hospital and at Finchley Memorial Hospital, both hospitals being within the National Health Service. Mr Justice Cross held that the gift to Barnet General Hospital was good as there was a need at that hospital for beds for paying patients; but that the gift to Finchley Memorial Hospital, which already had sufficient pay beds, failed because the words 'endowing beds for paying patients' could not be construed so as to allow the gift to be used to provide a higher standard of maintenance for paying patients than the hospital was already able to provide out of the payments made by paying patients.

On appeal, the judgment in *Re Adams*, so far as it related to Finchley Memorial Hospital, was reversed. Lord Justice Dankwerts said:

'Mr Kelly's affidavit which I earlier mentioned suggests a number of ways in which the income of such a fund . . . would be used and I think I ought to read them— "The following improvements are desirable (a) the provision of better beds, bedding, furniture, crockery, cutlery, floor coverings, curtains and other furnishings and the better maintenance of all such things; (b) the more frequent redecoration of the accommodation; (c) the sound-proofing of rooms; (d) the provision of telephones and television sets for the use of patients; (e) the provision of better food and a wider choice of food; (f) the provision for patients (who are not required to remain in bed) of a day or sitting room and also a dining room." '

Having quoted that list of things which might be done, he continued:

'It appears to me perfectly proper to apply the income of the fund given to Finchley Memorial Hospital for any of those purposes. As regards the idea that paying patients will not have these amenities, there is nothing unlawful in making provision for them in that way. In view of the heavy payments which they have to make, they may well benefit from any provision which may be made for their comfort and welfare in that hospital. Moreover, it is to be remembered that charity in certain respects is not confined to absolute poverty. In the Statute of Elizabeth, which I suppose may be thought of as the fount and origin of most of the law on this subject, there is, I think, a reference to "poor and infirm" persons. That does not mean that such persons must be both poor and infirm or both infirm and poor. Such infirm persons may be any people suffering from sickness or injury and so such as to fall within the ambit of the term "charity".'

Re Adams therefore appears to decide that it is charitable to provide funds not only for providing pay-bed accommodation in a national health service hospital but also for maintaining that accommodation and for providing better food and a wider choice of food, as well as other amenities, without these things being taken into account in determining the charge to be made to patients in that accommodation, without regard to the patient's means and beyond what is reasonably necessary. An authority would apparently, therefore, commit no breach of trust if it used endowment funds held for the general purposes of the hospital under section 90 of the National Health Service Act 1977 for capital expenditure on the provision of pay-bed accommodation, or the income of such endowments for maintenance and for better food, a wider choice of food, and other amenities for paying patients.

21.4.13   Effect on gifts of National Health Service amalgamation

Gifts for charitable purposes are not subject to the rule against perpetuities. In effect, this means that a gift may be made to a charity in terms that the capital is kept intact without limit of time. Also, there is no obstacle to prevent a gift being given so as to pass from one charity to another on, say, the happening of an event, such as the amalgamation or nationalisation of the first charity at any time. Provided the donor, by settlement or will, has expressed a general charitable intention, his intention will be carried out, even though he has not named the charity he wishes to benefit in that event. But the rule against perpetuities is not relaxed otherwise than in favour of charities; nor is uncertainty cured, except in favour of charities. And it has been decided[61] that benevolent objects are not necessarily charitable in the legal sense.

21.4.14   Breaches of trust by health authorities

There appears to be no liability as charitable trustees on individual members of health authorities within the National Health Service, that is Regional and District Health Authorities, Special Trustees and Boards of Governors in respect of technical breaches of trust (such as unauthorised investment in good faith) as distinct from fraudulent breach of trust, since the corporate body is the trustee and not the individuals constituting its membership, members being expressly protected in respect of bona fide acts in the course of their duties by section 125 of the National Health Service Act 1977. There is no power of surcharge on members of health authorities.

21.4.15   Borrowing powers of health authorities as charity trustees

While there is nothing in the National Health Service Act to hinder health authorities from borrowing against the security of property held by way of permanent endowment[62] on charitable trusts, they are, like trustees of other charities, subject to sections 36 and 38 of the Charities

Act 1993, which prohibit the mortgaging or charging of permanent endowments without an order of the court or of the Charity Commissioners, or the disposal of land without such order, unless proper specific advice has been taken.

21.5 VOLUNTARY HOSPITALS AND NURSING HOMES: ENDOWMENTS OF BEDS FOR PRIVATE PATIENTS

21.5.1 General

The provision of pay-beds by voluntary hospitals has been common practice for many years now, having been facilitated by the passing of the Voluntary Hospitals (Paying Patients) Act 1936 which, subject to safeguards, allowed trusts of hospitals established for the sick poor to be amended to include the provision of pay-bed accommodation. The decision in *Re Adams* (above) applies no less to such hospitals than to hospitals within the National Health Service.

The question therefore arises whether that part of the judgment which allows the income of an endowment to be used for current maintenance and, in particular, for the specific purposes referred to by Lord Justice Dankwerts (p. 619, above), allows or requires the hospital to pass on the advantage of the use of the endowment income in the form of reduction of charges to, or increase in amenities of, all paying patients, without regard to means. In the absence of any judicial decisions specifically covering the point, it is perhaps best to avoid a stance so much at variance with common practice and with the spirit of the Voluntary Hospitals (Paying Patients) Act 1936, which ordinarily obliges the Charity Commissioners, when approving a scheme for provision of pay-beds in a voluntary hospital, to see that patients unable to pay full cost, though able to pay something, should be given priority in certain beds.[63] Moreover, to charge less than full cost to anyone to whom it would be no real financial hardship to pay the full cost would in most cases be contrary to the trusts of the institution.

21.5.2 Endowment of beds for private patients in nursing homes

The Charity Commissioners have been willing to recognise as a charity a nursing home taking mostly, if not exclusively, paying patients, most of whom will be expected to pay full cost of maintenance, subject to the Commissioners being satisfied that its objects, as set out in its trust deed or memorandum and articles, are exclusively charitable. In law such a nursing home recognised as a charity would be indistinguishable from a voluntary hospital and *Re Adams* would similarly apply.

NOTES

1. [1976] 2 All ER 113.
2. [1985] 3 All ER 334.
3. Charities Act 1993, section 3(5)(a) and Schedule 2.
4. Charities Act 1993, section 8.
5. Charities Act 1993, section 69.
6. Charities Act 1993, section 3(5)(b) and (c).
7. SI 1962/1341.
8. SI 1974/63.
9. Charities Act 1993, section 46.
10. Charities Act 1993, section 69.
11. SI 1976/929.
12. Charities Act 1993, section 96(3) and 97.
13. Charities Act 1993, section 69(2).
14. Charities Act 1993, section 9(1)–(4). 'Exempt' means exempt from registration under section 3(5)(a).
15. Charities Act 1993, section 29(2).
16. [1954] 1 WLR 700.
17. [1956] Ch 622.
18. [1959] Ch 62.
19. Charities Act 1993, section 16(4).
20. Charities Act 1993, section 33(1).
21. Charities Act 1993, section 33(6).
22. Charities Act 1993, section 33(2).
23. [1923] 2 Ch 407.
24. *Bradshaw v Thompson* (1843) 2 Y & CCC 295.
25. *Re Lycett* (1897) 13 TLR 373.
26. [1953] 1 WLR 595.
27. [1973] SLT 236, Ct. of Session.
28. [1962] 1 WLR 763.
29. [1964] 3 WLR 18.
30. *Re Harwood* [1936] Ch 285.
31. *Re Davis* [1902] 1 Ch 876.
32. *Re Goldschmidt; Commercial Union Assurance Co v Central British Fund for Jewish Relief* [1957] 1 WLR 524.
33. [1912] 2 Ch 488.
34. *Re Finger's Will Trusts* [1971] 3 WLR 775.
35. *Re Hutchinson's Will Trusts* [1953] 1 Ch 387.
36. [1952] Ch 217.
37. (1872) LR 14 Eq 230.
38. (1872) 21 WR 154.
39. [1944] AC 341.
40. [1944] AC 341.
41. *Re Diplock's Estate, Diplock and others v Wintle and others* [1947] 1 All ER 522; *Minister of Health v Simpson and others* [1951] AC 251.
42. *Devaynes and others v Noble and others (Clayton's case)* [1814–23] All ER Rep 1, (1816) 1 Mer 572.
43. [1969] 1 AC 514.
44. [1958] Ch 300.
45. [1951] 1 Ch 567.
46. Regional and District Health Authorities (Membership and Procedure) Regulations 1990, SI 1990/1331.

47. HM(65)67.
48. [1951] Ch 27.
49. [1951] 1 All ER 528.
50. [1954] 1 WLR 22.
51. [1963] 2 All ER 220.
52. Now section 88 of the 1977 Act.
53. [1958] SC 279.
54. HM58(29).
55. SI 1974/1915.
56. SI 1974/103.
57. See, for instance, SI 1985/25, SI 1985/370; and the National Health Service (Determination of Districts) Order 1981, SI 1981/1837.
58. [1951] Ch 458.
59. [1953] 1 WLR 554.
60. [1968] Ch 80.
61. *Chichester Diocesan Fund and Board of Finance v Simpson and others* [1944] AC 341.
62. Charities Act 1993, sections 96(3) and 97; and see pp. 90–91 and p. 595, above.
63. Voluntary Hospitals (Paying Patients) Act 1936, section 3.

CHAPTER 22

Hospital charges

22.1 ROAD TRAFFIC CASES

22.1.1 Emergency treatment

Section 158 of the Road Traffic Act 1988 provides for payment of a fee in respect of emergency medical or surgical treatment or examination of any person suffering bodily injury (including fatal injury) caused by or arising out of the use of a motor vehicle on the road, the fee being claimable from the user of the vehicle involved, irrespective of negligence. The fee is payable to the first registered medical practitioner examining or treating the patient and, if no medical examination or treatment has been given when the patient reaches hospital, the fee is claimable by the hospital in addition to any payment due from any insurance company in respect of further treatment under section 22.1.2, below. Under the Road Traffic Accidents (Payments for Treatment) Order 1990[1], the fee is now £18.20 in respect of each person in whose case the emergency treatment is effected by the registered medical practitioner and a sum in respect of any distance in excess of 2 miles which he must cover to carry out the treatment and to return to his base, equal to 35p per complete and additional part of a mile.

Section 159 provides that a claim on behalf of a hospital in respect of emergency treatment must be made by an executive officer of the health authority or trust responsible for its administration and may be made by word of mouth at the time of the incident or subsequently in writing signed by the officer on behalf of the authority, stating the name and address of the hospital, the circumstances in which the treatment was effected and that it was first effected in the hospital. The demand has to be delivered to the user of the vehicle in person or sent to him by pre-paid registered letter, or a letter sent by the recorded delivery service, to reach him within seven days of the accident. A chief officer of police is bound, if so requested by a person who alleges that he is entitled to claim under section 158 of the 1988 Act, to furnish all the information at his disposal as to the identity of the vehicle and the user.

As to who is the user, the better opinion seems to be that when the vehicle is being driven by an employee for his employer, even though the employer is not present, the employer may be regarded as the user. If a man lends his car to another, however, then the other is the user.

When more than one vehicle is involved it is proper to claim against that which actually struck the injured person or the car in which he was travelling when the accident occurred. In case of doubt it may be desirable to claim against all or both of the vehicles concerned, though acceptance of multiple payments would not be permissible.

22.1.2 Further hospital treatment

Section 157 of the 1988 Act makes important provisions for the recovery of costs by hospitals for treatment given to victims of road accidents where a payment has been made (with or without admission of liability by the insurer or the owner) to the victim.

The essential points to note are that:

1. An insurer is liable to make such payment to a hospital only when he has made payment (whether or not with an admission of liability) under or in consequence of a policy of insurance which satisfies section 45 of the Road Traffic Act 1988, in respect of the death or bodily injury of some person arising out of the use of a motor vehicle; or a motor vehicle owner acting as his own insurer under the Act by security or deposit becomes similarly liable if he makes any payment in respect of death or bodily injury as aforesaid.

   A payment is made under a Road Traffic Act policy even though it is in respect of injury to a person against liability for injury to whom the driver is not obliged to be insured if, in fact, the policy covers injury to such a person: *Barnett Group HMC v Eagle Star Insurance Co Ltd* (1960).[2]

2. The insurer (or the owner) must have knowledge that the person injured has received hospital treatment: *Barnett Group HMC v Eagle Star Insurance Co Ltd* (above). Hence, the owner's insurance company, or under (1) the owner of the vehicle, should promptly be given particulars of patients treated as a result of the accident and notified of the hospital's conditional claim.

3. No claim arises under this head in respect of treatment of injuries caused by an accident in which an uninsured vehicle is involved (not being one the owner of which is exempted from taking out a policy of insurance as aforesaid) but if an insured vehicle is also involved and the insurer of that vehicle makes a payment in respect of death or bodily injury, the hospital can maintain its claim against the insurer. It follows that no claim arises by reason of payment in respect of injuries caused by a vehicle owned by the Crown, nor by vehicles owned by local and certain other public authorities exempted from insurance under the 1988 Act, which also exempts tramcars and

trolley buses, the use of which is authorised by special Act of Parliament. Nor can the hospital claim under the section against the owner or driver of a car which was not insured because the insurance had lapsed, because the car was stolen or being driven by an unauthorised person, or for any other reason. (See further section 22.1.3, below.)

4. The charge for out-patient treatment is 'reasonable expenses actually incurred'. Strictly, this involves accurate costing but insurers and other interested bodies and hospital authorities have largely agreed scales of charges.

5. The provisions of the Road Traffic Act apply to public authority and voluntary hospitals alike, since they both fall within the definition of 'hospital' in section 161(1).

6. It is understood that the Minister has authorised hospital authorities exceptionally to agree to waive their claim under the Road Traffic Act 1988 against an insurer who makes an ex gratia payment in respect of personal injury. There must, however, be special circumstances to justify that course. Ordinarily public hospital authorities, including trusts, enforce their legal rights.

22.1.3 Persons injured by uninsured cars

Insurers transacting compulsory motor vehicle insurance business in Great Britain, under agreements entered into with the Department of Transport, have established the Motor Insurers' Bureau which, subject to the conditions of the Agreements, undertakes to satisfy any unsatisfied judgment in respect of liability for any risk compulsorily insurable under the Road Traffic Act 1988 whether or not the defendant had been insured. The Motor Insurers' Bureau may also make an ex gratia payment in the case of an unidentified driver who has caused injury or death, or a driver who for some reason cannot be sued. Where the Motor Insurers' Bureau makes a payment in a case where the defendant was not insured, the payment not being made under a Road Traffic insurance policy, nothing is payable under section 157 of the 1988 Act to a hospital which has given treatment to the injured person. In 1989, the Bureau received some 15,000 applications under the Agreements and paid some £28 million in compensation.

22.1.4 Charges for treatment of road accident cases apart from the Road Traffic Act 1988

If a hospital, not being a hospital within the National Health Service, has power to charge and a person injured in a road accident is not regarded as a proper object of charity, there is no obligation on the hospital to receive such person as a patient without charge and to rely on the provisions of section 157 of the 1988 Act. The hospital may well choose to look to the patient himself for full payment of charges, leaving the patient to any remedy he might have in law against the owner or user of the vehicle. If it were established that the accident had been due to the fault of the driver of the car (not being the injured person) the full cost of hospital treatment, if reasonable, would be a proper item in the claim for damages. A hospital administered under the provisions of the National Health Service Act 1977 has no power to refuse to receive a patient into a general ward on the ground that he could afford to pay for treatment and to require that accommodation be taken in the pay-bed block.

22.2   FOR OTHER THAN ROAD ACCIDENT CASES WITHIN THE ROAD TRAFFIC ACT 1988

22.2.1   Hospitals administered within the National Health Service

Under section 1 of the National Health Service Act 1977 all hospital and specialist services provided under that Act, as amended, are to be provided free of charge. This general principle is subject, however, to some exceptions which are explained below.

Recovery of expenses of maintenance of in-patient engaged in remunerative employment during the day

Section 64 of the 1977 Act provides for recovery of expenses of maintenance in hospital from in-patients engaged in remunerative employment during the day. No regulations are necessary and the Secretary of State has full discretion to charge what is reasonable, having regard to the amount of the patient's remuneration.

Persons not ordinarily resident in Great Britain

By section 121 of the National Health Service Act 1977, the Secretary of State may make regulations providing for the making and recovery in such manner as may be prescribed, of such charges as the Secretary of State may determine, in respect of such services provided under the Act as may be prescribed, being services provided in respect of persons not ordinarily resident in Great Britain as may be prescribed; and such regulations may provide that the charges are only to be made in such cases as may be determined in accordance with regulations. The relevant regulations for this section are the National Health Service (Charges to Overseas Visitors) Regulations.[3]

Following the amendment made to the 1977 Act by section 7 of the

Health and Medicines Act 1988, the charges to be paid by overseas visitors are now to be determined by health authorities on behalf of the Secretary of State.

Accommodation available on part payment

The making available of hospital accommodation on part payment is authorised within the limits laid down in section 63 of the National Health Service Act 1977. Such accommodation may be made available for patients to such extent as the Secretary of State may determine, and such charges may be recovered as he may determine, calculated at what is considered to be the appropriate commercial basis (see the following paragraph). Amendments by the National Health Service and Community Care Act 1990 clearly state that the making available of accommodation in a trust hospital is not constrained under this section.[4] By virtue of the National Health Service Functions (Directions to Authorities and Administration Arrangements) Regulations 1991[5] the powers under this section are delegated to Regional Health Authorities and District Health Authorities on their behalf.

Accommodation and services for private patients

The provision of hospital accommodation for patients paying full charges, whether resident or non-resident, is governed by section 65 of the 1977 Act. NHS trusts are not constrained under this section (see note 4, above). Section 65 may only be exercised if the District/Special Health Authority is satisfied that to do so will not to a significant extent interfere with the performance by the authority of any function to provide accommodation or services of any kind and will not to a significant extent operate to the disadvantage of persons seeking or given admission or access to accommodation or services at health service hospitals other than private patients.

Section 65(1A), as amended by the National Health Service and Community Care Act 1990, stipulates that before deciding to make any accommodation or services available, a District or Special Health Authority must consult organisations representative of persons likely to be affected by the decision. Costs for accommodation and services are to be calculated on an 'appropriate commercial basis', the level of which is subject to the discretion of the health authority.

Permission for use of facilities in private practice

Section 72 of the National Health Service Act 1977 permits charges to be made for private practice use of facilities or accommodation for the treatment of private out-patients:

'**72.**—(1) A person to whom this section applies who wishes to use any relevant health service accommodation or facilities for the purpose of providing medical, dental, pharmaceutical, ophthalmic or chiropody services to non-resident private patients may apply in writing to the Secretary of State for permission under this section.

(2) Any application for permission under this section must specify—

(a) which of the relevant health service accommodation or facilities the applicant wishes to use for the purpose of providing services to such patients; and

(b) which of the kinds of services mentioned in subsection (1) above he wishes the permission to cover.

(3) On receiving an application under this section the Secretary of State—

(a) shall consider whether anything for which permission is sought would interfere with the giving of full and proper attention to persons seeking or afforded access otherwise than as private patients to any services provided under this Act; and

(b) shall grant the permission applied for unless in his opinion anything for which permission is sought would so interfere.

(4) Any grant of permission under this section shall be on such terms (including terms as to the payment of charges for the use of the relevant health service accommodation or facilities pursuant to the permission) as the Secretary of State may from time to time determine.'

Charges for optical appliances

The National Health Service Act 1977 permits charges to be made for sight tests and for the supply of glasses and contact lenses. The supply of optical appliances (glasses and contact lenses) ceased in 1986 to be part of the general ophthalmic services provided free of charge, as a result of amendments made by the Health and Social Security Act 1984. Optical appliances continue, however, to be supplied under the hospital eye service. Charges in respect of the supply of optical appliances may be made pursuant to powers set out in section 78(1) and Schedule 12, paragraph 2 of the National Health Service Act 1977.

Supply of dentures and other dental appliances

Section 78(1)(A) of the National Health Service Act 1977 and the National Health Service (Dental Charges) Regulations 1989[6] specify the charges to be made for the supply of dental appliances and other general dental services. The charge for the supply of dentures and bridges, whether or not as part of general dental services, is based on a formula of 75 per cent of the fees which would be payable to a dentist providing general dental services for the supply of a denture or bridge of the relevant type. Under regulation 2 no charge shall be made for the supply of a dental appliance as part of the hospital and specialist services to a person who has undergone operative procedures affecting the mandible, the maxilla or the soft tissues of the mouth as part of treatment for invasive tumours. Regulation 5 lays down conditions for exemption from hospital charges for the supply of dentures and dental appliances under the National Health Service Act 1977. No charge shall be made if the patient is under 18 years of age or under 19 years of age and receiving qualifying full-time education. Also exempt are expectant mothers and patients having borne a child in the last 12 months. Paragraph 2 of Schedule 12 of the National Health Service Act 1977 states that no charges shall be made by the Secretary of State for the supply of a denture or bridge to a patient resident in hospital at the time the appliance is supplied.

Any charges under sections 78 and 79 may be varied by the Secretary of State by regulation.[7] The Minister may also make an order under section 78(2) of the National Health Service Act 1977, remitting charges for dentures supplied by a teaching hospital if satisfied that it is in the interests of dental training or education to do so. Moreover, no charges are payable for dental treatment at any hospital under the Act, although by section 79 and paragraph 3 of Schedule 12, charges are made for such treatment (with certain exceptions) if provided elsewhere by a dentist under Part II of the Act.

Charges for drugs, medicines and appliances

Section 77(1) of the National Health Service Act 1977 allows regulations to be made for the making of such charges as may be prescribed, in respect of supply (including repair and replacement) of drugs, medicines and appliances. No such charges may be made in respect of:

1. drugs, medicines or appliances supplied to resident patients;
2. drugs supplied for the treatment of venereal disease;
3. appliances (including contraceptive appliances) supplied to a person under 16 years of age or under 19 years of age and receiving full-time education; or
4. the replacement or repair of any appliance in consequence of a defect in the appliance as supplied.[8]

Regulations may also provide for the remission or repayment of any charge payable thereunder in such other cases as may be prescribed.

Sections 80–82 give further powers to make regulations to charge for the provision of facilities and appliances. Section 80 covers, in effect, facilities for expectant mothers and young children and for prevention of illness and care and aftercare of persons who are or have suffered from illness. Section 81 deals with the supply of any appliance (or its replacement or repair) which is, at the request of the person supplied, of a more expensive type than the prescribed type, whereas section 82 deals with the replacement or repair of appliances generally. Charges may be recovered if it is determined in the prescribed manner that the replacement or repair is necessitated by an act or omission of the person supplied or (if the act or omission occurred when he was under 16 years of age) of the person supplied or of the person having charge of him when the act or omission occurred.

Charges for wigs and fabric supports provided by hospitals

The National Health Service (Charges for Drugs and Appliances) Regulations 1989 (as amended)[9] provide for any out-patient who receives as part of his treatment a wig or fabric support, to pay the prescribed charges. Charges are payable unless the patient is exempt from payment, either by virtue of an exemption certificate under the National Health Service (Charges for Drugs and Appliances) Regulations 1989[10] or is entitled to remission under the National Health Service (Travelling Expenses and Remission of Charges) Regulations 1988.[11]

22.2.2 Voluntary hospitals

Extent of power to charge

A voluntary hospital can enforce payment of charges for maintenance and treatment of a patient only if the hospital has power to make a charge and a contractual obligation to pay has been expressly or implicitly assumed by the patient or by some other person.

The first point to consider, therefore, is whether the hospital has any power to charge for maintenance or treatment and the answer to this question depends on its objects and constitution. It must not be assumed that because a charity for the relief of the sick poor takes in a patient who could not properly be so described, it therefore has a legal right to make a charge in a particular case. Even in the case of a charity 'for the relief of the sick', a power to charge is not implicit, though there is clearly no objection to a patient making a voluntary payment of the full cost of his treatment; nor in the case of a hospital for the relief of the sick poor can there be any legal objection to a voluntary contribution according to means by a person who is a proper object of the charity. This is presumably the position which arises when patients are invited, but not required, to make a payment according to means.

Assuming that a particular hospital has power to make a charge for maintenance and treatment of patients, the next question to ask is whether an enforceable contract has, in fact, been made. Ordinarily, except in the case of accident or other emergency admission, a hospital having power to charge, whether in respect of all admissions or in respect only of admissions to the pay-bed ward or block, can have a routine admission procedure under which the patient, or, in appropriate cases, the spouse, partner, parent, relative, friend or other interested party, signs a form requesting that the patient be admitted and undertaking in consideration thereof to pay for his maintenance and for services on a fixed scale. A request and promise made orally would be valid at law, although there might well be difficulty in proving the promise, especially a promise made by a third party.

If it is desired to hold both patient and third party liable, the ordinary procedure is for the patient to undertake primary responsibility for payment, the third party acting as guarantor. It must be appreciated that unless a guarantee is by deed, it needs consideration to support it. Even if there is consideration, a guarantee, to be enforceable, must be in writing.[12]

Should nothing have been said about payment at the time of the patient's admission to a voluntary hospital, it is fairly certain that, even though the hospital had the power to charge, it could not do so since there is no well-established custom in this country of exacting payment in voluntary hospitals and so no presumption could arise that the patient was accepting services for which a reasonable person would expect to pay.

Non-Road Traffic Act accidents and other emergency cases

An emergency admission from home is ordinarily arranged by the patient's doctor in consultation with the patient, or if the patient is not capable of deciding, with the nearest available relative. If it is arranged that the patient be admitted to a pay-bed there would appear to be some evidence that either he or someone expressly or impliedly authorised by him had made a binding contract on his behalf. Alternatively it could be that there was evidence that a relative authorising the arrangement was acting as principal and accepting personal liability, though such a presumption could hardly ever arise in the case of a doctor who acted simply as a go-between. The only reasonably satisfactory solution, from the point of view of the hospital, is to get the signature of an appropriate relative to a contract on behalf of the patient coupled with an undertaking to be personally liable.

Nowadays, it is seldom that a patient injured in an accident, or taken seriously ill in a public place, would be taken to a voluntary hospital. Presumably, if he were, the old custom would still be followed, viz. of admitting the patient in the first instance to the appropriate general ward for emergency treatment. When that has been done and it has been subsequently ascertained that the patient or responsible relative (e.g. father of a minor or husband) was in a position to pay the maintenance charges in a pay-bed and also the fees of the surgeon or physician in attendance, it has not been unusual, as a condition of continued treatment in a voluntary hospital with pay-beds, to require that the patient be removed to such a bed.

That attitude is entirely proper when the general wards are expressly provided for the sick poor or for persons of more limited means than the patient in question. But, a patient having once been admitted, the hospital should be cautious lest by hasty and ill-advised action it lays itself open to attack and to possible legal action for withdrawing its aid half-way. In the opinion of Dr Speller, if an accident patient or a patient admitted as an analogous emergency case, does not consent to be removed to a pay-bed, it would probably be better to accept the position rather than risk a legal action or charges, even unfounded, against the reputation of the hospital. The only difficulty in following this advice, apart from the comparatively minor one of some loss of revenue is that the member of the senior medical or surgical staff attending the patient may, perhaps, not be able, under the constitution of the hospital and the terms of his contract, to charge for his services to the patient while in a general ward. It is the possibility of abuse of the sometimes, but now less frequently, honorary services of professional staff in the general wards which is one of the main difficulties presented by such cases; but, on balance, it is likely to be as much in the interests of the staff as of the hospital to avoid occasion for dispute on such a question.

Voluntary Hospitals (Paying Patients) Act 1936

Voluntary hospitals established in recent years are likely to have sufficiently wide powers to permit the use of land, buildings and funds of the charity for provision for pay-bed patients, that is patients paying the full cost of maintenance and nursing in hospital including attendance by the resident medical and surgical staff of the hospital.

It is also understood that some nursing homes, wholly for paying patients, have in recent years been established as charities. Apparently the main purpose of such nursing homes is to provide accommodation for patients 'insured' against the cost of hospital treatment by subscription to a provident scheme. Such patients are also usually required to make a private arrangement for attendance by a physician or surgeon of consultant standing and to pay him his fees. Some older voluntary hospitals, however, were limited by their constitution to the treatment of sick poor so that the treatment of persons able to pay full cost was *ultra vires*. But as was stated in a memorandum attached to the Bill which subsequently became the Voluntary Hospitals (Paying Patients) Act 1936, there are

'patients who, in the event of serious illness or operation, cannot afford the cost of private treatment, but are able and willing to pay for treatment in a hospital at charges proportionate to their means. There are also now many modern methods of diagnosis and treatment which cannot be provided without the aid of the specialised equipment and staff of a hospital except at great expense, if at all.'

The Voluntary Hospitals (Paying Patients) Act 1936 was therefore passed to empower voluntary hospitals in pursuance of an order of the Charity Commissioners to provide accommodation and treatment for paying patients.

Under the Act such a hospital, if it has not already power to provide pay-beds, may apply to the Charity Commissioners for an order allowing it to do so and such order may be made notwithstanding the trusts, express or implied, upon which the property and funds of the hospital are held, and notwithstanding any prohibition or restriction imposed by any local Act relating expressly to the hospital. Any such order made must specify the period for which it is to be operative; how many pay-beds may be maintained, and whether in a new or an old building on land in possession of the hospital. Under section 2 of the Act the order must also lay down a scale of charges for accommodation and maintenance (including such medical and surgical attendance and treatment as is given by the resident staff of the hospital). Except when the Charity Commissioners are satisfied that it would be inappropriate in the circumstances to do so, they must include in the scale of charges specified in an order charges fixed with a view to meeting the needs of patients who, though able to make some payment, are unable to pay charges sufficient to meet the full expense to the hospital of their accommodation and maintenance (including such medical and surgical attendance and treatment as is given by the resident staff of the hospital) and must make it a condition of the order that in the use of a specified number of the beds, the maintenance of which is authorised, priority shall be given to such patients. Under section 3 of the Act the order may allow the difference between the full expense to the hospital of such patients and the sum authorised to be charged to them to be defrayed out of the general funds of the hospital.

The Act does not allow any order to be made authorising any use of property or funds which apart from the order would involve a breach of trust except:

1. in the case of land unless they are satisfied that if the order were not made the land would not come into use for the purposes for which the trusts were created or the prohibition or restriction was imposed until after the expiration of a substantial period from the date of application;
2. in the case of buildings either
   (a) that the use of the buildings or part thereof for the purposes for which the trusts were created or the prohibition or restriction was imposed is impracticable, or likely soon so to become, because the committee of management have not at their disposal, and will

be unable to obtain sufficient funds to enable the buildings or that part thereof to be, or to continue to be, so used; or

(b) that the use of the buildings or part thereof for the purposes aforesaid is impracticable, or is likely soon so to become because of a shortage of demand for accommodation on the part of the persons for whose benefit the trusts were created or the prohibition or restriction was imposed; or,

(c) that the committee of management have, or are likely soon to have, at their disposal premises which could be put to the use to which the application applies without breach of any trust upon which those premises are held or contravention of any such prohibition or restriction as aforesaid and that the buildings or part thereof will be used by way of exchange for those premises. In any case such authorisation to use land or buildings must not be given if it would diminish or restrict the accommodation for persons who were intended to benefit by the original trust as at the date of the order and which the hospital would have been able to maintain had the order not been made.[13]

The powers of the Charity Commissioners under the above Act are in addition to any other powers exercisable by them.[14] Consequently, it would in principle be possible for the Charity Commissioners, when the original trusts of a voluntary hospital were no longer capable of being carried out or otherwise within the limits of the Charities Act 1993,[15] to permit the provision of pay-beds as part of a scheme of administration *cy-près* independently of that Act; but it would seem unlikely that circumstances could arise which the Charity Commissioners would feel justified them in authorising provision of pay-beds without regard to the conditions laid down in the Act.

22.3 PROCEEDINGS FOR RECOVERY OF CHARGES AND FEES

22.3.1 Health authorities and National Health Service trusts

Charges to part-paying patients under section 63, or to paying patients under section 65, of the National Health Service Act, and charges by trusts, as well as charges for appliances or their repair, may be recovered by the Secretary of State, authorities and trusts, as the case may be. Charges may, without prejudice to any other method of recovery, be recovered summarily as a civil debt.

22.3.2 Voluntary hospitals

Liability to pay for a patient's treatment in a voluntary hospital or nursing home is contractual. In the event of the patient or other person failing or refusing to pay, the hospital's only recourse will be to ordinary civil proceedings.

In the case of a patient in a pay-bed who has contracted to pay the physician or surgeon for his attendance, or where the circumstances of the attendance of the physician or surgeon on the patient are such as to imply an undertaking by the patient to pay him and although the hospital may have laid down maximum charges, it is probably preferable that it should not undertake to render an account on behalf of the consultant, since that could easily blur the limits of the responsibility of the consultant and of the hospital for the patient's treatment. In any event, if both the hospital and the consultant remain unpaid, the hospital could not properly include in its own claim any amount which might be due to the consultant.

22.3.3   Medical practitioners and dentists

If a medical practitioner or dentist has made a lawful contract with a hospital patient for his treatment as a private patient and the patient does not meet his obligation to pay the agreed fee, the amount owing is an ordinary civil debt. The health authority or trust has no responsibility or interest in the matter.

NOTES

1. SI 1990/1364.
2. [1960] 1 QB 107.
3. SI 1989/306, as amended by SI 1991/438.
4. National Health Service and Community Care Act 1990, section 66(1) and Schedule 9, paragraph 18(3). See Schedule 2, paragraph 14.
5. SI 1991/554.
6. SI 1989/394.
7. National Health Service Act 1977, Schedule 12, paragraph 2(2).
8. National Health Service Act 1977, Schedule 12, paragraph 1.
9. SI 1989/419 as amended with price increases.
10. SI 1989/419, Regulations 6 and 7 as amended with price increases.
11. SI 1988/551 as amended with price increases.
12. Statute of Frauds 1677, section 4.
13. Voluntary Hospitals (Paying Patients) Act 1936, section 4(c).
14. Voluntary Hospitals (Paying Patients) Act 1936, section 6(2).
15. See Chapter 21, pp. 598–600.

CHAPTER 23

Taxation of hospitals

23.1 NON-DOMESTIC RATES

Since the removal of Crown immunity by section 60 of the National Health Service and Community Care Act 1990, health service bodies (as defined in section 60(7) and including for this purpose a health authority together with its directly managed units) are required to pay non-domestic rates. National Health Service trusts are in any event liable to pay such rates since they have never enjoyed any immunity of the Crown other than as specifically (and exceptionally) provided by the 1990 Act. Formerly, hospitals managed under National Health Service legislation were not subject to such rates but, by virtue of section 59 of the Local Government Finance Act 1988, paid contributions in lieu to the charging authority unless regulations were implemented requiring payment to be made to the Secretary of State for the Environment. From 1 April 1991 health service bodies and NHS trusts have had normal rights of appeal against rateable values, and local authorities have been able to pursue them for non-payment.

Land forming part of a charitable trust is not exempt from rates except insofar as it can be brought within the provisions of section 43 and 45 of the 1988 Act, in which case a lower chargeable amount may be calculated in accordance with formulae set out therein. Section 43 applies to liability for occupied hereditaments and section 45 to those which are unoccupied.

Discretionary powers, rebates and reliefs are provided for in section 47 which provides, so far as is relevant to present purposes, as follows:

'(2) The first condition is that one or more of the following applies on the chargeable day—
  (a) the ratepayer is a charity or trustees for a charity, and the hereditament is wholly or mainly used for charitable purposes (whether of that charity or of that and other charities);
  (b) the hereditament is not an excepted hereditament, and all or part of it is occupied for the purposes of one or more institutions or other organisations none of which is established or conducted for profit and each of whose main objects are charitable or are otherwise philanthropic or religious or concerned with education, social welfare, science, literature or the fine arts;

(c)   the hereditament is not an excepted hereditament, it is wholly or mainly used for purposes of recreation, and all or part of it is occupied for the purposes of a club, society or other organisation not established or conducted for profit.

(3) The second condition is that, during a period which consists of or includes the chargeable day, a decision of the charging authority concerned operates to the effect that this section applies as regards the hereditament concerned.

(6) A decision under subsection (3) above may be revoked by a further decision of the authority.

(7) A decision under subsection (3) above is invalid as regards a day if made after the end of the financial year in which the day falls.'

23.2   INCOME TAX AND CORPORATION TAX

23.2.1   Liability for tax

Section 61(1) of the National Health Service and Community Care Act 1990 inserts a new section 519A into the Income and Corporation Taxes Act 1988 exempting health service bodies from income tax in respect of their income and from corporation tax. 'Health service body' includes, for the purposes of this section, NHS trusts established under Part I of the 1990 Act. Charitable trusts enjoy exemption from taxation; but, as indicated in Chapter 21 dealing specifically and in detail with charities for the benefit of hospitals and other health service bodies, the term (in the 1990 Act) 'NHS trust' is simply a name and has nothing intrinsically to do with the charitable status of any of its activities. NHS trusts share with all bodies within the National Health Service the entitlement to benefit from a specifically established trust for the furtherance of 'charitable purposes' as defined in the case law discussed in that chapter.

The law relating to income and corporation tax is such that any full discussion of it here is impracticable, particularly in relation to profit-making activities carried on by a charitable hospital. Therefore all it is proposed to do is to outline the general nature of the exemptions in favour of charitable hospitals and other charities and the apparent limits to such concessions, leaving the reader who needs more to refer to specialist works.

The general effect of section 505 of the Income and Corporation Taxes Act 1988 is to relieve hospitals and other charities of liability to tax under relevant Schedules as follows, subject to the modifications and exceptions indicated.

23.2.2   Bodies to which concessions apply

There is no general exemption from tax. A charity must demonstrate to the Inland Revenue Commissioners its particular claim to exemption. Bodies to which exemptions apply are bodies or funds established under a definite and irrevocable trust for charitable purposes only (*Ex parte Ranks's Trustees* (1922)),[1] although relief may be granted if any non-charitable purposes of the body are purely ancillary to the charitable purpose (*Institution of Civil Engineers v Commissioners of Inland Revenue* (1931)).[2] Furthermore, the various kinds of income exempted from tax under this section are exempt only in so far as they are applied for charitable purposes (*IRC v Educational Grants Association* (1967)).[3]

Land and buildings which either belong to hospitals or are vested in trustees of charities for their benefit

The rents and profits of any land and, in effect, buildings vested in a hospital or other charity trustees are exempt from tax under Schedule A and Schedule D.

In order to qualify for the exemption a hospital must derive its support at least partially from charity (*Cawse v Nottingham Lunatic Hospital* (1891)).[4] Wholly self-supporting hospitals are not within the exemption (*Needham v Bowers* (1888))[5] but some fee-paying patients will not adversely affect the hospital's position provided that it is substantially supported by charity (*Cawse v Nottingham Lunatic Hospital* (1891)).[4]

Dividends, annuities, interest etc.

Exemption from tax may be granted under Schedule C (interest annuities, dividends or shares of annuities), D (yearly interest or other annual payment) or F (any distribution) where the income in question forms part of the income of a charity or is applied to only charitable purposes (*George Drexter Ofrex Foundation Trustees v IRC* (1966)).[6]

Profits of trade or business

The profits of any trade or business carried on by any charity are exempt from tax when such profits are applied solely for the purpose of the charity and either (a) the trade is exercised in the conduct of a main and primary purpose of the charity, or (b) the work in connection with the trade is mainly carried on by the beneficiaries of the charity. There could be little doubt that a pay-bed block established under the terms of the Voluntary Hospitals (Paying Patients) Act 1936 would be regarded as falling under (a) and also any pay-bed block on the same lines but for the establishment of which the powers of the Act had not been invoked, since the provision of accommodation for paying patients by a charity is itself charitable[7] provided that it is within the terms of the trust of the particular charity to help such patients.

In *Colman v Rotunda Hospital* (1921)[8] it was decided by the House of Lords that a hospital which regularly let out rooms for entertainments while retaining control of the premises could not claim the exemption since neither of the above conditions was fulfilled, but in *R v Special Commissioners, ex parte Shaftesbury Homes* (1923)[9] it was held that where a trade of any kind is carried on by separate trustees who hand over the yearly balance of profits to a 'body of persons or trust established for charitable purposes only' that body is entitled to repayment of tax. Hence in the case of any trade in which a hospital is interested liability to or exemption from tax may, failing compliance with conditions (a) or (b), above, depend on the particular organisational arrangements made.

There appears no authority for a hospital owned by the Secretary of State carrying on a trade or business otherwise than as purely incidental to its main purpose, such as farming or market gardening as occupational therapy for patients receiving care and treatment for mental disorder. Also, if a health authority carries on some activity, properly ancillary to the treatment of patients, it would seem properly within its powers to supply the needs of other authorities within the National Health Service and, for accounting purposes, making a charge for so doing. It would not then be liable to tax.

Intermediate income on share of residue of estate of deceased person

If a hospital or other charity is entitled to the whole or any share of the estate of a deceased person, it can recover tax paid by the executors on the income of the residue or proportionate share of the residue from the date of death until the date of distribution. This is now provided by section 696 of the Income and Corporation Taxes Act 1988, under which intermediate income of the estate of a deceased testator is generally deemed the income of the residuary legatees for income tax purposes.

23.3   CAPITAL GAINS TAX

As to exemptions of charities from capital gains tax reference should be made to section 505(3) of the Income and Corporation Tax Act 1988 and section 256 of the Taxation of Chargeable Gains Act 1992.

In summary, health service bodies are specifically exempted from capital gains tax by virtue of section 149(B)(3) and (3A)(b) of the Capital Gains Tax Act 1979, as substituted by the Finance Act 1990. Gains accruing to a charity will not, subject to stated exceptions, be chargeable if applicable and applied for charitable purposes.

23.4   SPIRIT DUTY

By section 7 of the Alcoholic Liquor Duties Act 1979 duty shall not be payable on any spirits contained in an article imported or delivered from a warehouse which is recognised by the Commissioners of Customs and Excise as being used for medical purposes.

Further, the Commissioners have a discretionary power under section 8 (as amended by the Finance Act 1988) to exempt from duty spirits used in the manufacture or preparation of an article recognised by them as being used for medical or scientific purposes. The Commissioners may attach such conditions as they see fit.

23.5 STAMP DUTY

Section 61(3) of the National Health Service and Community Care Act 1990 exempts from stamp duty any conveyance, transfer or lease made or agreed to be made to an NHS trust established under Part I of the 1990 Act on the basis of any of the following headings in Schedule 1 to the Stamp Act 1891: 'conveyance or transfer on sale', 'conveyance or transfer of any kind not hereinbefore described' or 'lease or tack'. Transfers, conveyances or leases to health authorities are exempt from stamp duty by virtue of section 55 of the Finance Act 1987[10].

23.6 VALUE ADDED TAX

In February 1991 HM Customs and Excise (Division VAH 2) published guidelines to health authorities on the incidence of value added tax for health authorities within the National Health Service. The following extracts are taken from that guidance:

'Insofar as Health Authorities have to comply with general VAT procedures (for example in applying the rates of tax or the issue of tax invoices) they should follow the guidance outlined in the Notices or Leaflets issued by Customs and Excise. Notice 700 (The VAT Guide) explains the main rules and procedures of the tax and Leaflet 701/39/90 (VAT liability law) reproduces the zero rate and exemption schedules to the VAT Act 1983. Notice 700/13 which is updated every six months gives a complete list of all extant C&E VAT publications, and VAT Notes, which is issued two or three times a year with the VAT Return form, draws attention to all VAT changes as and when they occur.

The Department of Health also issues guidance on VAT matters, in consultation with Customs and Excise, in their Financial Matters circulars issued monthly.

2 Nature of the tax

2.1 VAT is charged on a wide range of goods and services supplied by way of business in the United Kingdom, and also on importations. It is a principle of the tax that, so far as possible, it should apply in the same way to the public sector as it does to ordinary traders.

Health Authorities are involved with the tax in two basic ways:

a. as purchasers of taxable goods and services, thereby incurring VAT on their expenditure; and
b. as suppliers of taxable goods and services by way of business.

3 VAT terminology

3.1 The following are some of the most commonly used terms:

a. "Non-business" – Activities which are carried out on a statutory basis and/or for no consideration. They are outside the scope of VAT.

b. "Supplies" – Goods, the exclusive ownership of which passes from one person to another, or services for which payment, in money or in kind, is made.

All supplies within the scope of VAT are either taxable or exempt.

c. "Taxable supplies" – Supplies which are liable to VAT at the standard rate (currently 17½%) or the zero rate (0%).

d. "Exempt supplies" – Supplies which are not taxable because the law says that VAT is not to be charged on them.

e. "Input tax" – Tax incurred on the purchase of supplies (including imports) that are to be used for business purposes.

f. "Output tax" – Tax charged on the sale of goods and services.

g. "Tax point" – The time when a supply is treated as taking place. The liability and rate of tax are determined by the supplier at the tax point.

4 Purchases

4.1 With very few exceptions, the liability to VAT of a supply of goods or services is determined by the nature of the supply and not by the status of the recipient. Health Authorities are required to pay tax on many of their purchases and VAT registered traders are instructed to treat Health Authorities in the same way as ordinary customers for VAT purposes. It is the legal responsibility of VAT registered traders to decide the tax liability of the supplies they make and Health Authorities are asked to ensure that when seeking tenders or placing orders nothing is said which might be construed as overriding that obligation.

4.2 In a case where a Health Authority wishes to query the liability determined by its supplier, the first step is to ask the trader to obtain a written ruling on the liability of his supply from his local VAT office. In most cases this will resolve the matter. However, if it still appears that a liability has not been correctly determined, it is open to the Health Authority to seek advice from VAH2. It will usually be necessary for the Health Authority to provide VAH2 with full details of the supplies involved, as well as the name and address of the supplier, copies of contracts and other documents, to enable the issue to be fully reviewed.

4.3 Apart from the special arrangements for certain contracted-out activities (see paragraph 9) Health Authorities cannot reclaim from Customs and Excise the tax that they incur on purchases made for the purpose of undertaking non-business or exempt activities. This is consistent with NHS funding being set at a level which broadly takes account of the impact of indirect taxes such as VAT.

5 Sales

5.1 Section 27(1) of the VAT Act 1983 specifies that the Act shall apply in relation to taxable supplies by the Crown (which includes Health Authorities) as it applies in relation to taxable supplies by taxable persons. The main purpose of this section is to bring within the scope of VAT those supplies made by Health Authorities of a kind which are or might be made by ordinary traders in the course of business.

5.2 Where Health Authorities supply goods or services which do not amount to the carrying on of a business, but it appears to the Treasury that similar supplies are or might be made by ordinary traders in the course of business, then the Treasury may direct under section 27(2) and 27(3) of the VAT Act 1983 that the supplies by the Health Authorities are treated as supplies in the course or furtherance of business.

5.3   Treasury Directions under section 27(2), (3) and (4) were made by Treasury on 3 March 1993 following a complete revision of earlier Directions undertaken by VAH2 in consultation with the Department of Health. The Schedules to the Directions list all activities which are to be treated as business supplies. These Directions are often referred to as the Taxing Directions.

5.4   The Directions and Schedules thereto were published in the London, Edinburgh and Belfast Gazettes on 2 April 1993. The Directions are revised annually and the Department of Health are responsible for notifying health bodies of any changes.

5.5   To assist Health Authorities to apply VAT correctly to their business activities VAH2 has produced a "Working Document" . . . which amplifies the broad categories of supplies listed in the Schedule to the Directions and shows their liability to tax. For the avoidance of doubts, the document also lists some of the activities which are outside the scope of VAT. The Working Document is not meant to replace the various VAT Notices and Leaflets; neither is it a complete and definitive listing of all supplies likely to be made by Health Authorities.

6   Registration

6.1   Ordinary traders making taxable supplies of annual value exceeding the registration threshold are required to register for VAT with Customs and Excise. Normal registration and the registration threshold to not apply to Health Authorities and they are required to charge and account for tax regardless of the annual value of their taxable supplies. It is therefore necessary for all Health Authorities making business supplies to be recorded by Customs and Excise so that tax can be brought to account, returns processed, changes of address and title noted etc. Health Authorities are issued with VAT numbers in the series HA followed by three digits. Health bodies in the UK are registered through the Regional HAs, those in Scotland through the Scottish Home & Health Department, those in Wales through the Welsh Common Services Authority, and those in Northern Ireland through the Department of Health for Northern Ireland. The HA's VAT number should be shown on tax invoices and correspondence relating to taxable supplies made by Health Authorities. VAH2 should be informed of any change of circumstances or activity that could affect their registration or the credibility of the figures declared on their VAT return.

7   Inter and intra-authority sales

Business supplies between health bodies covered by different registrations must bear VAT at the appropriate rate. However sales between bodies covered by the same registration are not supplies for VAT purposes and are not, therefore, liable to tax.

8   Input tax

Input tax (i.e. VAT incurred on purchases for onward business supplies) is reclaimable only when directly attributable to a taxable business supply. The business supply may either be subject to VAT at the standard rate (17½%) or the zero rate (0%). In some instances VAT incurred on purchases may need to be apportioned between business and non-business activities as only the VAT attributable to business activities is reclaimable.

9 Contracting-out of services

9.1 In 1983 the Government decided to encourage Health Authorities to contract-out to the private sector services which had traditionally been performed in-house where it was more cost effective to do so. It was recognised that many of these services would be subject to VAT and that, where they were acquired for non-business purposes, the non-reclaimable VAT could act as a disincentive to contracting-out. It was, therefore, decided to compensate Health Authorities by a direct refund mechanism. This was put on a statutory basis by section 11 of the Finance Act 1984 which inserted section 27(2A) to the VAT Act 1983. The Directions under article 27(2A) (which are sometimes referred to as section 11 regulations), came into force on 7 November 1984 and have been updated since.

9.2 Section 27(2A) empowers Customs and Excise to refund VAT to Health Authorities, to the extent that the Treasury directs, provided that:

a. the goods and services are acquired for non-business purposes;
b. the claim meets any conditions which may be laid down regarding timing, form, and manner.

The Treasury have directed that a claim may be made for refund ". . . of the tax charged on the supply of services of the nature listed in relation to that department . . . or on goods incidental to the supply of those services, if and only if . . . the charge of the tax would raise the price of obtaining those services from outside the department above the cost to the department of providing them itself . . ."

9.3 Thus, to comply with the contracting-out Directions refunds may only be considered for those *services* which have been traditionally performed in house by Health Authorities, or for those where there is an in-house capability but the service can be performed more efficiently by outside contractors. In addition refunds are limited to cases where it is only the VAT that would have to be charged by an outside contractor that raises his price above the in-house cost. If his price including VAT is less than the in-house cost or if his price excluding VAT is more than the in-house cost no refund can be claimed. Section 11 applies to supplies received by one Health Authority registration from another as well as from the private sector. It does not apply to contracted-out activities traditionally done by outside contractors. Nor does it apply to the supply of *goods* on their own, since there is no distortion of competition caused by the application of VAT in these circumstances, and it must be remembered that any goods on which refunds are being claimed must be only an incidental, or minor, part of the service to which they relate.

9.4 These conditions must be strictly applied both to services entered for the first time in the Treasury Directions and to those already included.

9.5 Each June the Treasury will ask the Department of Health for details of any changes (including deletions) to be reflected in the following years contracting-out Directions for Health Authorities. Unless a service has been approved by Treasury under the contracting-out provision, VAT cannot be recovered. From

1 April 1989 services listed in the Treasury Directions will continue to qualify for a period of up to 5 years; after that period they will be automatically deleted from the list unless the Department of Health have requalified them against the above criteria and notified Treasury accordingly.

9.6 The Refund Directions are published each year, normally in April, in the London, Edinburgh and Belfast Gazettes. The current list of contracted-out services eligible for recovery of VAT and covered by Treasury Directions, is reproduced at Appendix A.

10 Refunds

Tax to be claimed back from Customs & Excise, whether as input tax resulting from a business activity or by section 27(2A) refund, should be recorded on the same return as that used to declare output tax on business activities. Health Authorities should obtain VAT tax invoices from their suppliers which clearly describe the supply received and show the VAT charged as a separate item. The tax point date shown on these invoices indicates the tax period in which the refund should be claimed. Health Authorities should arrive at separate amounts of deductible input tax and refunds due under the contracting-out provisions and record these amounts in the appropriate box of the "Certificate of VAT reclaimed under section 27(2A) of the VAT Act 1983" . . . , which must be attached to the VAT return. The deductible input tax and contracting-out refunds are to be totalled on this certificate and the total transferred to Box 2 of the VAT return.

11 VAT returns

11.1 The normal accounting period is a calendar quarter. Any Health Authority wishing to adopt a different period should apply to VAH2 explaining why non-standard treatment is required. VAT return forms (VAT 100) are issued automatically to accounting bodies by the Customs and Excise office in Southend. Health Authorities should reproduce for themselves the Certificate of VAT reclaimed.

11.2 Errors on VAT returns that are discovered after the return has been submitted should be corrected on the next return by adjusting the figures declared thereon to compensate for the error. A covering letter (or form VAT 652 available from local VAT offices) should accompany the adjusted return giving details of the correction that has been made and how the error arose.

12 NHS Trusts[11]

12.1 At present, district health authorities, family health service authorities and most special health authorities are not separately registered for VAT purposes, but are included within the VAT registration of their Regional Health Authority.

12.2 NHS Trusts will automatically remain part of the Regional Health Authority for VAT purposes and will therefore be included within the RHA VAT registration, unless VAH2 has specifically authorised, in writing, an alternative arrangement.

12.3 Should an individual NHS Trust wish to pursue separate VAT registration for itself, written application should be made to VAH2, at the address given [in paragraph 1]. Such applications must *not* be made to local Customs and Excise VAT Offices.

12.4   The Department of Health have requested that individual NHS Trusts who wish to apply for separate VAT registration should also inform them of their intention, at the following address:

NHS Trust Finance Team
Department of Health
Quarry House
Quarry Hill
Leeds
LS2 7UE

12.5   When an NHS Trust is granted separate VAT registration, VAH2 will allocate a VAT number in the HA series. A separately registered NHS Trust will therefore be completely independent for VAT purposes, and will be responsible for ensuring that VAT is correctly accounted for, where applicable, on all its activities. Separately registered NHS Trusts will be required to submit their own VAT returns.'

NOTES

1. (1922) 38 TLR 603.
2. (1931) 47 TLR 466.
3. [1967] Ch 993.
4. [1891] 1 QB 585.
5. (1888) 21 QBD 436.
6. [1966] Ch 675.
7. In *Re Adams* [1968] Ch 80. In this case the Court of Appeal upheld a bequest for 'endowment' of private beds at a hospital even though no additional private beds were needed.
8. [1921] 1 AC 1.
9. [1923] 1 KB 393.
10. Section 55 of the Finance Act 1987 appears to be intended to remain in force, given that section 61(3) of the NHS and Community Care Act 1990 applies the wording used by section 55 verbatim to NHS trusts; this despite the fact that the 1987 Act exempts in the case of conveyance etc. *to a Minister of the Crown*, and section (60)1 of the NHS and Community Care Act 1990 causes land used, held or occupied by a health authority no longer to be Crown land.
11. See the National Health Service and Community Care Act 1990, Schedule 8, paragraph 9 and the Value Added Tax Act 1983, section 27.

CHAPTER 24

Births and deaths in hospital

24.1 BIRTHS

24.1.1 Registration

The main provisions of the law as to registration of births and deaths in England and Wales are contained in the Births and Deaths Registration Act 1953. By section 41 of the Act, 'house' as referring to the place of a birth or death is defined as including a public institution and 'a public institution', rather inelegantly, as a prison, lock-up or hospital, and such other public or charitable institution as may be prescribed, and 'occupier' in relation to a public institution 'includes a governor, keeper, master, matron, superintendent or other chief resident officer'. Regulation 2 of the Registration of Births, Deaths and Marriages Regulations 1968[1] provides that all institutions maintained wholly or mainly from public funds or charitable endowments or subscriptions or any combination thereof are public institutions for the purposes of the Act. The responsibility for registering a birth or death is now, effectively, that of the unit manager or other person nominated by him for the purposes of such registration.

It is the duty of the father or mother to give information of a birth to the Registrar for the sub-district in which the birth takes place within 42 days, and to sign the register. 'Father' or 'mother' in relation to an adopted child means the natural father or mother.[2] In the case of the death or inability of the father and mother, the duty is laid on every other qualified informant,[3] viz., the occupier (as defined above) of the house in which the child was, to the knowledge of the occupier, born; any person present at the birth; any person having charge of the child. The giving of information by any one qualified informant discharges the duty of all.[3] In the case of a still-birth, the informant has to deliver to the Registrar a written certificate that the child was not born alive, signed by a registered medical practitioner or a registered[4] midwife who was in attendance at the birth or who has examined the body; or make the prescribed declaration as to the reason for the absence of a certificate and that the child was still-born.[5] A still-born child is defined by section 41 of the Act as:

'a child which has issued forth from its mother after the twenty-fourth[6] week of pregnancy and which did not at any time after being completely expelled from its mother breathe or show any other signs of life.'

Upon registering a still-birth the Registrar, if so required, will give free of charge a certificate of having registered a still-birth, either to the informant or to the person who has control over, or who ordinarily effects the disposal of, the body, a certificate having to be produced before the body can be buried in a burial ground or churchyard.[7] Relevant certification must be given by the medical practitioner or midwife to the qualified informant.[8] It is an offence to dispose of the body of a still-born child by burning, except in an authorised crematorium.[9] Should such a certificate have been issued but, for some reason, is not available for the purposes of the enactments relating to the disposal of dead persons, the Registrar may issue a duplicate on payment of the prescribed fee.[10]

The obligation to give information to the Registrar of any 'abandoned child'[11] is laid on the person finding the child and on any person in whose charge the child may be placed. The informant is bound to give such information as he has and to sign the register. There is, in this case, no order of responsibility. Any one qualified informant giving information and signing the register discharges the duty of all.[12] If a foundling is being cared for in hospital it would seem reasonable to regard the consultant or the unit manager as the 'person in charge' for this purpose.

If, after the expiry of 42 days, a birth has not been registered, the Registrar, by 7 days notice in writing, can compel any qualified informant to attend to give information and to sign the register within three months of the birth or finding.[13] The registration within three months is free unless, in pursuance of a request in writing, the Registrar registers the birth at the residence of the person making the request or at the house in which the birth took place, not being a public institution. No fee is therefore payable when the Registrar attends a hospital to register births. In any case, however, if the informant wants a certificate of the registration, he must pay for it.

After a lapse of three months, if a birth has not been registered, any qualified informant is compellable by notice in writing to attend within a year before the Superintendent Registrar to make a declaration and to sign the register, when he is obliged to pay a statutory fee to the Superintendent Registrar and also to the Registrar, unless the latter was in default.[14] After 12 months, the birth may be registered only with the written authority of the Registrar-General.[15]

It will be appreciated that the Act does not require the registration of the child's own name (i.e. christian or given name) although provision is made for registration of the name within 12 months of the original entry or for its alteration within that period.[16] Provision made for re-registration of births of persons legitimised by subsequent marriage of their parents is unlikely to concern hospitals.[17]

24.1.2   Notification of births to District Medical Officer

Under section 124 of the National Health Service Act 1977 (formerly section 203 of the Public Health Act 1936) a doctor or midwife attending a woman in childbirth is under an obligation to notify the District Medical Officer[18] of the birth or still-birth within 36 hours and this whether the birth occurred at home or in an institution or elsewhere. It is also permissible to post the notification within the 36-hour period.[19] By section 124(2) the Registrar of births and deaths is required to furnish to the prescribed medical officer of the District Health Authority the area of which includes the whole or part of the sub-district of the Registrar, the particulars of each birth and death which occurs in the area of the authority as entered in the register of births and deaths of the district. At present the manner of communication is not prescribed; but the maximum period of 14 days is prescribed by the National Health Service (Notification of Births and Deaths) Regulations 1982.[20] Under section 203 of the 1936 Act there was no statutory obligation on the former medical officers of health to communicate to the Registrar particulars of births notified under that section, nor has any such statutory obligation now been placed on District Medical Officers, but the Secretary of State has expressed the hope that the common practice of doing this will be continued. By Circular HSC(15)125 the District Medical Officer is required to give the birth weight to the Registrar. Further reference as to administrative detail may be made to Circular HRC(74)3.

24.2   DEATHS

24.2.1   Registration

Before the expiration of five days[21] from the date of the death, the nearest relative, including a relative by marriage and by adoption[22] of the deceased person, present at the death or in attendance during his last illness, is under a duty to give the Registrar the necessary particulars for registration to the best of his knowledge and belief and to sign the register. If there is no such relative, the duty falls on any relative of the deceased residing or being in the sub-district when the death occurred; failing whom, on any person present at the death or on the occupier (as defined on p. 647, above) of the house, if he knew of the death; failing whom, on any inmate of the house who knew of the happening of the death or on the person causing the disposal of the body. The giving of information and signing the register by any one of the above qualified informants acts as a discharge of the duty of every other qualified informant.[23] If an inquest is held, there is no obligation to give information under section 16.

If a person dies elsewhere than in a house, or a dead body is found and no information as to the place of death is available, the duty of giving information to the Registrar within five days[24] is placed on any relative of the deceased who has knowledge of any of the particulars required to be registered concerning the death; failing whom, on any person present at the death, any person finding or taking charge of the body or any person causing the disposal of the body. Section 17 does not apply if there is an inquest and also any qualified person giving information discharges all.

The provisions of section 17 would appear to concern a hospital only if the body, brought in dead, were taken charge of by the hospital. And since there is under that section no reference to the occupier of the house, it cannot be said dogmatically that the responsibility of registration would, as in the case of deaths in the hospital, fall on the general manager, failing responsible relatives. It is presumed, however, that the Registrar would readily take the view that it was the 'occupier' as defined in the Act who would have taken charge of the body and would therefore readily accept information from such person. On the other hand, since the ambulance service is now the responsibility of the health authorities, if the patient died in the ambulance, whether or not the hospital was held to have taken charge of the body, the responsibility would still fall on one of its officers, such as the ambulance officer who was with the patient when he died.

Section 19 contains provisions for compelling any qualified person to attend and give information for registration of a death within 12 months of a death or of a finding of a body. No fee is chargeable for registering a death within 12 months otherwise than for the attendance of the Registrar at the residence of a person making a request or at the place where the deceased died, not being a hospital or other public institution. Hence, if a person dies in hospital and the Registrar attends to register the death, no charge is payable. After 12 months, a death can be registered only with the authority of the Registrar-General.

Under section 24, the Registrar is required to issue to the informant, free of charge, a certificate of registration of the death save when the coroner's disposal order has been issued. If the Registrar does not subsequently in due time receive notice of the disposal of the body, he is to make inquiries of the person to whom he delivered the certificate, who is under the duty of giving information to the best of his knowledge and belief.[25]

Section 22 lays on a registered medical practitioner who has attended a person in his last illness the responsibility of delivering forthwith a certificate of death to the Registrar and, to a qualified informant, of a notice of having done so. Unless there is an inquest, or a post-mortem examination under section 19 of the Coroners Act 1988, the cause of death as shown in the doctor's certificate will be entered in the register.[26] The Registrar is bound to accept the doctor's certificate as to the last illness where there is no inquest or post-mortem.[27] For details as to the matters to be entered on the certificate see *Medical Certification of Cause of Death* published by the World Health Organisation (1968).[28] Section 23 provides for information to be sent to the Registrar by the coroner of findings at an inquest or of the result of a coroner's post-mortem.

In the case of a person dying in hospital the duty of issuing a death certificate ordinarily devolves on the resident medical or surgical officer who attended the patient regularly in between visits of the consultant though, technically, it might be argued that the physician or surgeon actually in charge of the case should be responsible. If the cause of death is known, even though it is such as clearly to call for an inquest, it does not appear to be a legal obligation on the medical practitioner who attended the patient in his last illness to do more than to complete the certificate for the Registrar in the normal way and to deliver the usual notice of having done so to the appropriate person. And the position is the same if, for any reason, a medical practitioner is unable to certify the cause of death; likewise if he is called in to an accident or other case not his own, dying or dead, for which he is unable properly to issue a certificate. But it is now the established practice for medical practitioners to advise the coroner direct of cases in which he is likely to be concerned and this, although not obligatory, is generally to be recommended not only in the interests of justice but as limiting the delay inevitably consequent upon reference of a death to the coroner. The Human Tissue Act 1961 formerly authorised unofficial post-mortem examinations, inter alia, for the purpose of establishing or confirming the cause of death.[29] Since the passing of the Anatomy Act 1984 this has been the case only if the necessary objective is teaching or research within section 1 of the 1961 Act. That is to say, the cause of death must be established as a prior condition of lawful research or experimentation involving the tissue in question. Close co-operation between hospital staff and the coroner is more than ever desirable since no such unofficial post-mortem examination may be carried out without the consent of the coroner if there is reason to believe that an inquest may be necessary or that the coroner may require a post-mortem examination.[30]

NOTES

1. SI 1968/2049.
2. Children Act 1975, section 108(1)(a) and Schedule 3, paragraph 13; see also section 10.
3. Births and Deaths Registration Act 1953, section 2.
4. Substituted by the Nurses, Midwives and Health Visitors Act 1979, section 23(4) and Schedule 7, paragraph 7.
5. Births and Deaths Registration Act 1953, section 11.
6. The earlier period of 28 weeks was reduced to 24 weeks by section 1 of the Still Birth Definition Act 1992.
7. Births and Deaths Registration Act 1953, section 11(2).
8. Section 11(1A).
9. Crematorium Regulations, SI 1930/1016, regulation 3.
10. Births and Deaths Registration Act 1953, section 11(3).
11. Births and Deaths Registration Act 1953, section 3A.
12. Section 3, as amended by the Children Act 1975, section 92.
13. Section 4.
14. Section 6.
15. Section 7.
16. Section 13.
17. For which see the Births and Deaths Registration Act 1953, section 10A, as amended by the Family Law Reform Act 1987, section 25.
18. National Health Service Act 1977, section 124(4) and (5); and the National Health Service (Notification of Births and Deaths) Regulations, SI 1982/286, naming the District Medical Officer as the prescribed medical officer for the purposes of the section.
19. Section 124(5)(a).
20. SI 1982/286.
21. Births and Deaths Registration Act 1953 section 16; but see section 18 for circumstances in which certain particulars may be given up to 14 days.
22. Section 16(3).
23. Section 16(3)(i).
24. Section 17(3).
25. Section 24(5).
26. Births and Deaths Registration Act, 1953, section 22(3), as amended by Coroners Act 1988, section 36(i) and Schedule 3, para. 3.
27. Decision of the National Insurance Commission No. R(1) 4/74.
28. Available from HMSO.
29. Human Tissue Act 1961, section 2(1).
30. Human Tissue Act 1961, section 2(2).

CHAPTER 25

Organ transplants and disposal of the human body

25.1 HUMAN TISSUE ACT 1961

This Act provides for the use of the bodies of deceased persons for therapeutic purposes and purposes of medical examination and research.

Section 1(1) provides that if a person requests, either in writing (made at any time) or orally in the presence of two witnesses during his last illness, that his body or any specified part of it be used for therapeutic purposes or for purposes of medical education or research then the person in lawful possession of his body may – unless he believes that the request was subsequently withdrawn – authorise the removal for the stated purpose(s).

The request may be made orally or in writing and it is to be noted that a written statement does not require to be witnessed, being different in this respect from a will, as well as from the oral statement. It should also be noted that whoever is in lawful possession of the body *may*, not must, authorise the removal.

On the question as to who is 'in lawful possession' there is no authoritative ruling. Where the person dies in hospital, it seems to be the deceased's next of kin, and not the hospital (subject to the 1975 Circular noted below). If this is so, then even if the deceased has made a written request within this subsection the hospital should not use his body for this purpose without first getting the authority of the next of kin who may then authorise the removal unless he believes the request was subsequently withdrawn.

Section 1(4) requires that only a fully registered medical practitioner is to remove parts of a body under the terms of the Act, and he must satisfy himself by personal examination that life is extinct. By the definition in the Medical Act 1956, a fully registered medical practitioner includes a person who has passed his final examinations and who, while doing his year's service in hospital to secure full registration, is required to do the removal in the course of his hospital work. It also includes a person with limited registration under section 22 of the Medical Act 1983, if the removal forms part of the duties of his employment in respect of which he has secured such limited registration.

The authority under sections 1(1) and 1(2) cannot be given by a person having possession of the body for interment or cremation only.

Section 1(7) provides that in the case of a body lying in a hospital or similar establishment the authority can be given by a person designated by the hospital board or committee. However, where a person dies in hospital the person lawfully in possession is normally the deceased's personal representative.

If no such request as is mentioned in section 1(1) is made, section 1(2) provides that the person in lawful possession may permit the body to be used if he has no reason to believe (after having made 'such reasonable enquiry as may be practicable') that the deceased had expressed an objection, or that the surviving spouse or any surviving relative objects to the body being so dealt with. A Departmental Circular of 1975[1] deals with this topic. It says, amongst other things:

'(i) Some uncertainty has been expressed on the interpretation of "the person lawfully in possession of the body". The Secretary of State hopes that the following guidance will be helpful.[2] If a person dies in hospital, the person lawfully in possession of the body, at least until the executors or relatives ask for the body to be handed to them, is the Area Health Authority responsible for the hospital. In the case of a private institution, the person lawfully in possession would be the managers.

If a person dies elsewhere than in hospital the question of who is lawfully in possession should not normally give rise to difficulty. Thus, it may be the husband in the case of a deceased wife, the parent in the case of a deceased child, the executor, if any, or even the householder on whose premises the body lies. If a person is brought into hospital dead the health authority will be lawfully in possession of the body as in the paragraph above, although in such cases the Coroner will normally be involved.

(ii) Whether or not a request has been made (that is, whether removal is under section 1(1) or 1(2) of the Act), authority for the removal of organs or tissue must be given in each case by the person lawfully in possession of the body, and the receiving of such authorisation should be recorded and timed in the patient's notes by the person receiving it. The authority may be given on behalf of the area health authority by any person or persons designated for the purposes. Area health authorities should authorise certain specified persons to exercise this responsibility for them.

Persons so designated will be responsible for ensuring that the necessary enquiries have been made and should be of sufficient seniority to exercise that important function. It would be appropriate to designate senior administrators; doctors or nurses and authorities should bear in mind that it will often be necessary to contact the officer urgently at night and at weekends. Before a person is designated, authorities should be satisfied that he or she is fully conversant with the requirements of the Act. The designation may be by name or by post and may cover more than one person or post.

A person lawfully in possession of the body of a patient who has not requested that his body or parts of it be used (that is, where section 1(2) applies) may only authorise removal of parts if, having made such reasonable enquiry as may be practicable, he has no reason to believe that the donor would have objected or that the surviving spouse or any surviving relative objects to the body or the specified part being so dealt with. Specific consent is not necessary, merely a lack of objection. What enquiry is reasonable and practicable must depend on the facts of each particular case. However, in most instances it will be sufficient to discuss the matter with any one relative who had been in close contact with the deceased, asking him his own views, the view of the deceased and also if he has any reason to believe that any other relative would be likely to object. In certain circumstances it might be necessary for such discussion to take place on the telephone.

Potential organ donors will often have spent some hours or even days in hospital and in such cases hospitals will have sufficient opportunity to take steps to contact relatives. Where after such reasonable enquiry as may be practicable, there is no evidence that the donor has any relatives, authority may be given under section 1(2) in the absence of any other evidence which suggests to the contrary. Where it is known that a potential donor has relatives but it has not been possible to contact any of them, a person giving authority for organ removal must be especially careful to ensure that the requirements of the Act with regard to the making of enquiries have been met. It is not enough to say in a case where organs must be removed very soon after death that no enquiry is practicable. Any objections made by patients or relatives should be noted immediately in the patient's notes. The word "relatives" is not defined in the Act, but there are some circumstances in which it ought to be interpreted in the widest sense, e.g. to include those who although claiming only a distant relationship are nevertheless closely concerned with the deceased.

In cases where the health authority is the person lawfully in possession of the body, and an authorisation under section 1 has been given, the relatives or executors may subsequently ask that the body be handed over to them; but this action does not revoke the authorisation which continues to be legally effective. If the deceased during his lifetime had recorded an appropriate request, then it would be reasonable for the authorisation under section 1(1) to be acted upon. If the authorisation depended on section 1(2) then despite the legal position set out above, the surgeon should be asked not to proceed if it comes to be known that a surviving relative does object to the use of the body or some part of it. Where no authorisation had been given to the surgeon before a request for the body is received from the relatives, the health authority should ask them to give their agreement to the removal of organs.'

25.1.1 Law and practice in transplantation

A code of practice, designed to allay public fears about the circumstances in which organs may be removed from dead patients for the purpose of transplantation, was issued by the Department of Health in December 1979. The code has two principal purposes: to set out the precise procedure which should be followed by doctors in deciding whether a person is clinically dead; and to set out the manner in which doctors should properly approach relatives for permission to remove organs.

A code of criteria for the diagnosis of brain death was drawn up by the Royal Colleges in 1976 and their code for transplants issued in 1978[3] was able to build on the 1976 criteria in the specific application to transplants. The transplant code of 1978 is intended to reassure the public over fears which had been expressed in some quarters that ventilators or life-support machines might be turned off when a doctor knows that a potential recipient is waiting for a vital organ. In fact, one of the greatest problems facing transplant surgeons having the care of a potential recipient is the shortage of suitable organs and tissue available, due in some part to the very natural and quite frequent unwillingness on the part of doctors treating a critically ill patient actually to declare that patient dead. Nonetheless, the code on transplants indicates a proper response to possible fears, if only to confirm assurance.

The procedure to be adopted specifies that two doctors must certify the brain death of a possible donor and each doctor must complete a checklist independently. The code reads:

'When death is determined on the basis of brain death, or where it is proposed to remove organs within an hour after respiration and circulation have ceased, death should be diagnosed by the following combination of doctors:

   a.   a consultant who is in charge of the case, or in the absence of a consultant, his deputy, who should have been registered for five years or more and who should have had adequate previous experience in the care of such cases, and
   b.   one other doctor.'

Neither of these doctors should be a member of the transplant team and the result of the examination and the diagnosis should be recorded in the case notes relating to the deceased patient.

A patient must, states the code, be presumed to be alive until it is clearly established that he is dead. The time of death should be recorded as the time when death was conclusively established and not when artificial ventilation was withdrawn or the heart beat ceased. It states emphatically that any tests or treatment carried out on a patient before death must be for the benefit of the patient and not solely to preserve organs. But after the patient is dead according to the criteria specified in the code (above) there is no *legal* objection to administering any drugs necessary to maintain the condition of organs. The code is right to make the point in this way for two reasons. First, it states that when death is established there is no legal reason to wait to inject organ-maintaining drugs, not that any particular practitioner ought to have no objection or reservations of a non-legal variety.

Second, an injection, or other application, of organ-maintaining drugs into a living patient with the sole or even the primary purpose of maintaining organs for the benefit of a potential recipient would constitute a battery in the absence of the potential donor's consent. And in the circumstances in which critically ill potential donors find themselves, such consent is most unlikely to be decently obtainable. Nor would any such consent by next-of-kin or other relative suffice; while a relative can consent on behalf of an unconscious or emergency patient, or on behalf of a minor under 16, to treatment of that patient, the injection of organ-maintaining drugs could hardly be said to constitute 'treatment' of *that* patient.

25.1.2 Establishment of local procedures for identification of potential donors and compliance with the Act

Annex 1 to Circular HC(88)63 provides guidance for the establishment of local transplant procedures.

'The checklist covers major internal organs, where the donor will be brain stem dead in an intensive care area. However, health authorities are reminded that corneal tissue may be retrieved some hours after death, and that the Corneal Tissue Act 1986 permits their removal by suitably trained health authority employees, whether medical or non-medical. Procedural documents should refer to corneal donation, particularly in the section on seeking relatives' consent.

1 The diagnosis of brain stem death

Documents may either cover this in detail, or refer to published guidance such as the booklet published by the Health Departments in 1983 entitled "Cadaveric Organs for Transplantation: a Code of Practice including the Diagnosis of Brain Death".

2 Donor identification

a. Potential donors will normally be receiving artificial ventilation in intensive care areas. They are likely to be patients suffering from:
  - severe head injury
  - sub-arachnoid haemorrhage
  - other cerebrovascular accidents
  - cardiac arrest with associated brain stem death
  - non-malignant brain tumour

b.   The document will need to define the local policy on the medical criteria for the acceptability of each type of organ. Guidance can be obtained from the Health Departments' booklet mentioned in paragraph 1 and the local transplant co-ordinator.

c.   The document should specify the members of staff responsible for donor identification.

3   Contact with transplant unit or co-ordinator

a.   The document should identify where responsibility lies for notifying the regional transplant unit of a potential donor.

b.   Names and telephone numbers of transplant co-ordinators or other contact points should be given. It is helpful to have a single contact point.

c.   The transplant team will require medical details of the donor. Transplant co-ordinators can provide guidance on the information normally required in respect of each type of organ.

4   Establishing consent of relatives

a.   Clear procedures for approaching relatives are critical to the success of a local organ donation policy. Each hospital should establish whether the lead will be taken by intensive care or by the transplant co-ordinator; if the latter applies, procedures should ensure that the co-ordinator is contacted in *every* suitable case.

b.   Other points to be covered are:
  – timing (normally after first set of tests for brain stem death);
  – written record of request to be kept in patient's notes;
  – need to identify circumstances in which coroner is involved and seek permission.
  – completion of death certificate if second set of tests confirm patient is brain stem dead (this can be suitable time to begin completion of the audit form). The time of death should be recorded as the time when death was conclusively established.

c.   The need to include the question of the donation of corneas in discussions with the relatives should be mentioned.

5   Optional points

The points listed at 1–4 above should be covered in all procedural documents. Other topics may be included at the discretion of health authorities. For example, guidelines on donor maintenance will normally be agreed between the transplant unit and the donating hospital, but some clinicians may find it helpful to have a written statement. Authorities should recognise that counselling the bereaved is always necessary; details of how this might be done are a matter for local decision. Various charitable organisations exist to help bereaved families, such as The Compassionate Friends and the British Organ Donor Society (BODY).

Section 2 makes it clear that post-mortem examinations (other than those directed or required to be made by a competent legal authority) if carried out for the purposes of establishing or confirming the causes of death or of investigating the existence or nature of abnormal conditions will not contravene the provisions of the Anatomy Act 1832 (an Act which gave power to grant licences to practise anatomy and laid down the conditions under which bodies could be used for anatomical examination). Doubts have been expressed as to whether that Act does or does not apply to the examinations described in this section and it removes any uncertainty there may be about the legality of such examinations carried out in accordance with it.

[It is to be noted that the 1832 Act was repealed and replaced by the Anatomy Act 1984; but the sense of the Circular remains unaffected.]

Subsection (2) lays down the conditions under which such post-mortem examinations must be carried out. They must be carried out by, or in accordance with the instructions of, a fully registered medical practitioner. The words "in accordance with" cover the circumstances where a student or attendant acting under the doctor's instructions may assist and do part of the work.

The subsection further provides that except where the post-mortem examination is ordered or requested by the coroner or any other competent legal authority, the person lawfully in possession of the body must give his authority and that the requirements of section 1(2), (5), (6) and (7) will apply with the necessary modifications. That is,

a. reasonable enquiry must be made to ensure that the deceased had not expressed objection in his lifetime and that the surviving spouse or any surviving relative does not object;

b. the coroner's consent must be obtained if there is reason to believe that he may require an inquest or post-mortem examination;

c. an undertaker may not give authority.

d. the governing body of a hospital, nursing home or other institution may designate an officer to authorise on their behalf the examination, subject to the other requirements in regard to consent.'

25.1.3   Post-mortem declaration

Advice from the Department of Health was given in 1977[4] on the obtaining of consent for a post-mortem on the body of the deceased.

While the Act does not require a written declaration to be made by the surviving spouse or other relative, the Department considers it desirable that in appropriate cases that person should be invited to sign a post-mortem declaration form. This would be a precaution against the possibility of unauthorised removal and also would afford evidence, generally sufficient evidence, that the requirements of the Human Tissue Act as to the enquiries to be made have been complied with, although it is accepted that there will be occasions when only verbal enquiry is possible. The model form is included in the HMR series and is available under central supply arrangements with Her Majesty's Stationery Office (see page 660).

25.1.4   Anatomy Regulations 1988

The Anatomy Act 1984 came into force on 14 February 1988[5] and its coming into operation was accompanied by the Anatomy Regulations

---

POST-MORTEM DECLARATION FORM

I do not object to a post-mortem examination being carried out on the body of

. . . .

and I am not aware that he/she had expressed objection or that another relative objects.

I understand that this examination is carried out:

(a) to verify the cause of death and to study the effects of treatment, which may involve the retention of tissue for laboratory study;
(b) to remove amounts of tissue for the treatment of other patients and for medical education and research.

Signed . . . . date . . . .

relationship to deceased

witnessed by

Notes on completion of this form

1. The signature of a relative of the deceased should be witnessed by the member of staff administering the form.
2. A relative of the deceased should not be invited to sign this form if the hospital itself is aware of objections on the part of other relatives.
3. Should a relative agree to paragraph (a) but not to paragraph (b) appropriate deletions may be made to the form.

1988.[6] While in many cases of marginal relevance only to the question of removal and transplantation of human organs, it is convenient here to reproduce the provisions of the Regulations insofar as they may be relevant to any of the situations under discussion in this chapter.

'Records relating to anatomical examinations and anatomical specimens

2.—(1) A person to whom a licence has been granted under section 3(2) of the Act shall compile records in a permanent form in relation to each anatomical specimen which is in his possession or in the possession of another person to whom he has given permission to have possession of the anatomical specimen which records shall contain the particulars specified in paragraph (2) of this regulation.

(2) The particulars referred to in paragraph (1) of this regulations are as follows:

(a) the full names and sex of the deceased person whose body is used for anatomical examination, his date of death, his age at the time of death and the cause of death;

(b) the date and time at which the body is received by him at the premises where the anatomical examination is to be carried out;

(c) whether authority for the anatomical examination of the body was given in pursuance of subsection (2) or (3) of section 4 of the Act and the name and address of the person lawfully in possession of the body who authorised the use of the body in accordance with subsection (2) or (3) of that section, as the case may be;

(d) the name and address of any person to whom he has given permission under section 3(4)(b) of the Act to have possession of the body or any separated part of the body who retains possession of the body or such separated part for a period exceeding one month;

(e) particulars of any wishes expressed by the deceased person or the surviving spouse or any surviving relative of that person in relation to the disposal of the body after the anatomical examination has been concluded;

(f) the date and method of disposal of the body after the anatomical examination has been concluded.

(3) Subject to paragraph (4) of this regulation, a person to whom a licence has been granted under section 3(2) of the Act shall retain records compiled in accordance with paragraph (1) above for a period of 5 years beginning with the date of disposal of the body.

(4) Where a person to whom a licence has been granted under section 3(2)(a) of the Act is licensed under section 5(5) of the Act to have possession of parts of the body and retains parts after the body has been disposed of he shall retain such records compiled in accordance with paragraph (1) of this regulation as are required for the purposes of regulation 3(1) of these Regulations for the period specified in regulation 3(3) of these Regulations.

Records relating to parts of bodies retained after anatomical examinations have been concluded

3.—(1) A person to whom a licence has been granted under section 5(5) of the Act to have possession of parts of bodies shall compile records in a permanent form in relation to parts of bodies in his possession or in the possession of another person to whom he has given permission to have possession of such parts which records shall contain the particulars specified in paragraph (2) of this regulation.

(2) The particulars referred to in paragraph (1) of this regulation are as follows:

(a) a description of the parts of bodies which he has in his possession identifying the bodies from which they were separated;

(b) whether authority for possession of parts of a body whose anatomical examination has been concluded was given in pursuance of subsection (2) or (3) of section 6 of the Act and the name and address of the person who gave authority for possession to be held;

(c) the name and address of any person to whom he has given permission under section (5)(5)(b) of the Act to have possession of a part of the body who retains possession of such part for a period exceeding one month.

(3) A person to whom a licence has been granted under section 5(5) of the Act shall retain records compiled in accordance with paragraph (1) of this regulation in respect of the parts separated from each body until the latest date of the disposal of any part of the body from which the parts were separated.

Examination and disposal of bodies and care of parts of bodies

4.—(1) Except in relation to a body to which paragraph (3) of this regulation applies, a person to whom a licence has been granted under section 3(2) of the Act shall ensure that—

   (a)   as soon as practicable after a body is received at the place where anatomical examination is to take place the body is subjected to a suitable process for its preservation;

   (b)   a body is held in possession only for such period as an adequate state of preservation of the body is maintained;

   (c)   all bodies in his possession are stored in an orderly and hygienic manner in suitably designed rooms equipped with adequate facilities for regulating temperatures;

   (d)   where an anatomical examination is carried out by a person who is authorised to carry out the examination by virtue of section 3(3)(b) of the Act, (in this paragraph referred to as "the authorised person") the authorised person is adequately supervised by a person who is licensed under section 3(2)(a)of the Act unless the authorised person is sufficiently qualified and trained to carry out anatomical examinations in an orderly and efficient manner without such supervision;

   (e)   after anatomical examination of a body has been concluded its disposal shall, so far as practicable, be in accordance with any wishes expressed by the deceased or any surviving spouse or surviving relative of his and that separated parts of the body, other than those parts which are held in possession by virtue of section 6 of the Act, are, so far as practicable, disposed of with the body from which they were removed.

(2) Except in relation to a body to which paragraph (3) of this regulation applies, a person to whom a licence has been granted under section 5(5) of the Act shall ensure that parts of bodies the possession of which is lawful by virtue of section 6 of the Act are stored in an orderly and hygienic manner in suitably designed rooms equipped with adequate facilities for regulating temperatures.

(3) This regulation shall not apply in relation to the body of a person who died before the coming into force of these Regulations.

Offences

5. A person who without reasonable excuse contravenes any provision of regulation 4 above shall be guilty of an offence and shall be liable on summary conviction to a fine not exceeding level 3 on the standard scale or imprisonment for up to 3 months.'

25.1.5   Human Tissue Act 1961 and the jurisdiction of the coroner

The provisions relating to the removal of tissue for therapeutic use and for medical education and research apply when a post-mortem examination is ordered by a coroner as they apply to any other post-mortem examination, save that their removal requires also the consent or approval of the coroner. Where there is reason to believe that the coroner may require an inquest or post-mortem examination to be held, authority to remove parts of the body may not be given nor may a part be removed without the coroner's consent. In law a coroner has no jurisdiction until death has taken place but in cases where organs, such as kidneys, must be removed very soon after death, coroners may wish to be informed of the proposed course of action before death is reported. It is essential that complete confidence exists between the hospital and the coroner and authorities should do all they can to see that this obtains in all cases. Where a coroner has given consent, it remains the responsibility of the person designated by the health authority, not the coroner, to ensure that the provisions of the Act with regard to the making of enquiries, as specified in section 1 of the Act, are complied with.

There is thus an obligation in such a case on the person who can authorise removal to obtain the coroner's consent and also on the doctor, who with that authority proposes to remove parts, to obtain it or see that it is obtained. This is a safeguard to ensure that the coroner is in no way fettered or defeated in any enquiries into the death which he may think necessary. The consents in subsections (1) and (2) of section 1 of the Act, as applicable, will also be necessary in addition to the coroner's consent.

25.2 TRANSPLANTS BETWEEN LIVE PERSONS

The Human Organ Transplants Act 1989 places restrictions and imposes certain criminal offences upon transplants between live persons. The organs covered by the Act are defined in section 7(2) as 'any part of a human body consisting of a structured arrangement of tissues which, if wholly removed, cannot be replicated by the body'. The Department of Health Circular HC(90)7 points out in its guidance notes on the 1989 Act that the Act does not apply to bone marrow transplantation.

Therefore trading in blood and bone marrow, for example, does not fall within the scope of the Act and consequently is not illegal per se. The Government was at pains to stress that although the Act was drafted to deal solely with the immediate problems posed by the trade in organs, that should not be taken as implying that the sale of regenerative tissue is acceptable. However, extending the scope of the Act would raise a wider and more complex range of issues.

25.2.1 Responsibilities of health authorities

It is primarily for clinicians and other members of staff involved in transplantation to ensure that they comply with the requirements of the Act and the Regulations. Under section 4(1) of the Act, District Health Authorities, Special Health Authorities and Health Boards could be held responsible for offences under the Act committed on premises under their control. Health authorities and trusts, and their senior officers should therefore investigate promptly any alleged breach of the legislation.

Section 1 of the Act prohibits the commercial dealing of human organs (whether from dead or living persons) which are intended for transplantation. Section 1(1)(a) creates a criminal offence for the receipt or the making of payment for the supply of, or the offer of supply of, organs which are intended for transplantation in Great Britain or abroad. Section 1(1)(b) makes it an offence to seek to find a person willing to supply an organ for payment or offers to supply such an organ for payment.

To initiate or negotiate any arrangement which involves the making of payment for the supply, or offer of supply, of an organ is also an offence by virtue of section 1(1)(c). Furthermore, taking part in the management or control of a body of persons corporate or unincorporate whose activities consist of or include the initiation of or negotiation of such arrangements is a criminal offence under section 1(1)(d). The meaning of payment in section 1 does not include defrayal or reimbursement of costs incurred for the removal, transportation or preservation of the organ. A living donor may claim reimbursement or defrayal of expenses and loss of earnings that are reasonably and directly attributable to the donor's supplying an organ (section 1(3)).

The penalty for each of these offences is contained in section 1(5) which lays down the maximum penalty of three months imprisonment on summary conviction or a fine not exceeding £5000 (level 5 on the standard scale), or both.

It is a criminal offence under section 1(2) to cause to be published or distributed, or to knowingly publish or distribute in Great Britain, an advertisement inviting persons to supply organs for payment or an advertisement offering the supply of organs for such payment. Publishing, or causing to be published, an advertisement which indicates that the advertiser is willing to initiate or negotiate arrangements which involve the making of payment for the supply of, or offer to supply, an organ is an offence under section 1(2) of the Act. An advertisement is taken to include 'any form of advertising whether to the public generally, to any section of the public or individually to selected persons' (section 1(4)). The offences laid down by section 1(2) apply not only to the person who places such an advertisement with a publisher but extend to the third party which publishes the advertisement. The maximum penalty for an offence under section 1(2) is a fine not exceeding £5000 (level 5 on the standard scale) (section 1(5)). By virtue of section 5 of the Act a prosecution under section 1 may not be brought except by, or with the consent of, the Director of Public Prosecutions.

Section 2 of the Act places restrictions on transplants between those not genetically related and deals solely with transplants between live persons. The Government felt that the threat of abuse was minimal if the parties were in some way related, a fact which is relatively easy to establish. Section 2(1) makes it an offence to remove an organ from a living person which is intended for transplantation or to transplant an organ from one living person to another unless the donee (or potential donee) is genetically related to the donor, unless the approval of the Unrelated Live Transplant Regulatory Authority (ULTRA) has been obtained. The Authority, brought into being by the Human Organ Transplants (Unrelated Persons) Regulations 1989,[7] requires that no payment is to be made in contravention of section 1 of the 1989 Act and that the other conditions set out in regulation 3 are fulfilled.

The extent of genetic relationships specified in section 2(2) of the Act are described in the guidance booklet. The Human Organ Transplants (Establishment of Relationship) Regulations 1989[8] specify the tests which must be carried out to establish the fact of a genetic relationship. The tests described in the regulations were agreed in consultation with the Royal College of Pathologists and the British Transplantation Society.

Under the above Regulations the specified tests may only be carried out by persons approved by the Secretary of State for that purpose. These arrangements parallel those currently in force to establish paternity in civil cases. Separate application must, however, be made by individuals seeking approval to carry out tests for the purposes of this Act.

The penalty for an offence under this section is imprisonment on summary conviction for a term not exceeding three months or a maximum fine of £5000 (level 5 on the standard scale), or both. Again, proceedings may not be brought for an offence under this section except by, or with the consent of, the Director of Public Prosecutions.[9]

25.2.2   Unrelated Live Transplant Regulatory Authority (ULTRA)

Role of ULTRA

In every case where the transplant of an organ within the definition of section 7(2) of the Act is proposed between a living donor and a recipient who are not genetically related, the proposal must be referred to the Unrelated Live Transplant Regulatory Authority – ULTRA. ULTRA is an independent authority whose members are appointed by the Secretary of State. Its statutory function is confined to consideration of cases where no genetic relationship, as defined in the Act, exists or where such a claimed relationship cannot be established. The Human Organ Transplants (Unrelated Persons) Regulations 1989[7] set out the constitution of ULTRA and the conditions which must be satisfied before an exemption from the prohibition in section 2(1) of the Act applies. When an organ becomes available because of the treatment of the donor (e.g. in the case of a domino* transplant), the Authority will only have to be satisfied that section 1 of the Act has not been breached and that the application is made in the prescribed manner.

* A procedure whereby the heart removed from a patient undergoing combined heart and lung transplantation is transplanted into another patient.

Membership

ULTRA began its legal existence on 1 January 1990 and its membership was announced in February. Members are not appointed as representatives of any particular group but as individuals who can contribute either because they have a knowledge of transplantation or because they can bring an ethical or other more general perspective to enable the Authority to form a balanced view of the cases put to them.

The supply of information concerning transplant operations is governed by section 3 of the 1989 Act. Section 3 authorises the Secretary of State to make regulations outlining the information which is to be supplied to particular bodies. The Human Organ Transplants (Supply of Information) Regulations[10] were made for this purpose. Regulation 2 requires a registered medical practitioner who has removed an organ for transplantation, or has received such an organ (whether from a dead or living person), to supply the details outlined in Schedule 1 to the United Kingdom Transplant Support Services Authority (UKTSSA) and either to the District Health Authority (if the operation was performed in England and Wales) or to the relevant Health Board (if the operation was performed in Scotland). If, however the operation was performed in a hospital managed by a Special Health Authority or National Health Service trust, information should be furnished to the UKTSSA and to that authority or National Health Service trust.[11]

The Human Organ Transplants (Supply of Information) Regulations 1989 came into force on 1 April 1990. Details of the information to be supplied are set out in Schedules to the Regulations. Information will be required in all cases of transplantation, including the removal or implantation of kidney, heart, lung, pancreas or liver and, wherever appropriate, parts or combinations of these organs. A registered medical practitioner removing or receiving an organ will be required to supply the information referred to in the Schedules, within seven days of the procedure, to the United Kingdom Transplant Support Services Authority, Southmead Road, Bristol BS10 5ND (Department HOTA), which has the statutory responsibility for the central record. He will also be required to supply the information to the District Health Authority,

Special Health Authority or, in Scotland, the Health Board in which the procedure takes place. This will include procedures taking place in private hospitals licensed by that Authority or Board. Further details of the mechanism for providing the information are given in the guidance booklet.

At regular intervals, UKTS will send to each health authority a printout of notified transplant activity extracted from the information supplied to them to enable officers to keep their records up to date and carry out audit procedures in hospitals within their area. The arrangements outlined therein in no way affect the voluntary collection of research information as set out in EL(89)P/86.

Section (2) of the 1989 Act requires that the UKTSS and the authorities listed above keep such records of the information supplied by the practitioners as are prescribed by the regulations. Failure to comply with the regulations without reasonable excuse is an offence under section (3) liable on summary conviction to a level 3 fine (up to £2000). So, too, is the supply, knowingly or recklessly, of false or misleading information (punishable by a level 5 fine of up to £5000).

25.2.3 Allocation of cadaveric organs procured in National Health Service hospitals

The Appendix to Circular HC(90)7 provides practical guidance as follows:

'1 Cadaveric organs removed from patients in National Health Service hospitals are in the possession of the managing health authority. In the first instance they should be used for transplantation into patients who are eligible for National Health Service hospital treatment.

2 Eligible patients include:

i. those ordinarily resident in the United Kingdom, whether they are treated as National Health Service patients or have opted to be treated privately;
ii. those from overseas who satisfy the criteria for National Health Service hospital treatment laid down in the Manual of Guidance issued with HC(88)4 "National Health Service Treatment for Overseas Visitors". These include nationals from European Community Member States who have an agreed referral to an National Health Service hospital for treatment and who are in possession of Form E112; and those from certain countries with whom the UK has bilateral reciprocal health care agreements who have an agreed referral to an National Health Service hospital for treatment.

3 Category 2.ii includes patients who have come to the UK for a variety of reasons such as to take up employment or to pursue a course of study lasting longer than six months, but not to receive medical treatment. It is important that the eligibility of patients in this category should be properly checked by the health authority concerned.

4 Individuals falling within any of the categories above should be considered

as having equal claim to cadaveric organs removed from patients in National Health Service hospitals. Where there are competing demands organs should be allocated on clinical grounds. If there is no eligible patient for whom an organ is suitable, the United Kingdom Transplant Service (UKTS) may arrange for it to be exchanged through one of the overseas organ exchange organisations with whom it has negotiated arrangements.

5   A cadaveric organ removed from a patient in an National Health Service hospital may be transplanted into a patient who is not eligible for National Health Service hospital treatment only if there is no eligible patient for whom it is suitable. UKTS maintains registers of eligible patients who are awaiting an organ transplant. A cadaveric organ from an National Health Service hospital should *never* be transplanted into a patient who is not eligible for National Health Service treatment *unless* it has first been offered to UKTS.

6   The Directors of all transplant units and of heart and liver transplant units in particular should ensure that all eligible patients awaiting a transplant are registered with UKTS.

7   An organ obtained in a non-National Health Service hospital and retrieved without using National Health Service resources from residents of the UK may either be offered to UKTS or be transplanted into ineligible patients (those outside categories 2.i–ii above) with the agreement of the relatives of the deceased, provided the donor did not express a contrary wish in life. UKTS, however, should still be informed of the event.

8   Directors of transplant units are asked to note that UKTS has entered into contractual arrangements for the transport of organs with the St John's Ambulance Air Wing and a number of other organisations, on the understanding that the organs are for transplantation into eligible patients. UKTS is prepared to make arrangements for the transport of organs that are to be transplanted into patients who are ineligible for National Health Service hospital treatment; but the UKTS Duty Officer must be told the patient's status at the outset. Arrangements may need to be made on a different basis, and the costs will have to be met by the surgeon receiving the organ.'

25.2.4   Notification by the Registrar to the District Medical Officer of particular deaths registered

Under section 124(2) of the National Health Service Act 1977, the Registrar is required to notify the prescribed medical officer (District Medical Officer) of the particulars of all deaths within the area of that authority furnished to him for registration.

25.3   DISPOSAL OF BODY

25.3.1   Responsibility and expenses

In default of other responsible persons such as an executor, spouse or parent, the occupier of the premises on which the death took place is responsible for the disposal of the body. Under the Public Health

(Control of Disease) Act 1984, local authorities are under an obligation to dispose of the body by burial or cremation of any person who has died or been found dead in their area, where no suitable arrangements have been made for the disposal of the body, and those authorities referred to in section 46(2) have permissive power to do so in the case of any deceased person who immediately before his death was being provided with accommodation under Part III of the National Assistance Act 1948 or by agreement with the Council, or was living in a hostel provided by the Council under section 29 of that Act.

A local authority may recover the cost of burial or cremation within the provisions of section 46(5) of the Public Health (Control of Disease) Act 1984 which provides:

'(5) An authority may recover from the estate of the deceased person or from any person who for the purposes of this Act was liable to maintain the deceased person immediately before his death, expenses incurred under subsection (1) or subsection (2) above.'

The right given to a social services authority which disposes of the body of a deceased person to claim reimbursement from any person liable to maintain the deceased does not extend to a health authority or trust under the National Health Service legislation which disposes of the body of a patient dying in a hospital which it administers. If, however, at the request of the hospital, responsibility for disposing of the body is undertaken by the local social services authority, that authority can claim repayment of the cost from any relative liable to maintain the deceased. It is suggested in a departmental Circular to health authorities[12] that if relatives who are thought to be able to afford it refuse to undertake responsibility for burial or cremation, the local social services authority should be asked to do so.

A hospital, whether administered under the National Health Service Act or, in the case of NHS trusts, under the NHS and Community Care Act, or a voluntary hospital, which has incurred expenses in disposing of the body of a deceased patient, as a creditor of the estate of the deceased, may claim reimbursement directly out of any death grant payable out of the national insurance system. Such a claim has to be made to the Department. Any claim must be limited to the amount spent but if the death grant did not cover the cost, the hospital would remain a creditor of the estate for the balance.

Reference should also be made to the provisions of the Public Health (Control of Disease) Act 1984, sections 43–45 and 47(1), which make further provision for the prevention of spread of infection from dead bodies of persons dying of infectious diseases. The proper officer of the local authority for the district in which the dead body lies, or a registered medical practitioner, can forbid the body of a person who has died from a notifiable disease to be removed from hospital, otherwise than to a mortuary or to be forthwith buried or cremated.

25.3.2 Duties of the Registrar

It is the duty of the Registrar who issues a certificate for burial or cremation to make inquiry if he does not receive a notification of disposal within 14 days. Furthermore, he is obliged to report all cases of delayed disposal (except under the Anatomy Act 1984) to the proper officer of the local authority for the district in which the body is lying (Births and Deaths Registration Act 1953, section 24(5)). If part of the body of a deceased person has been retained under section 1 of the Human Tissue Act 1961, the rules as to burial or cremation would apply only to the remainder of the body.

In addition to burial or cremation, it is lawful to dispose of the body of a deceased person in such other manner as may be prescribed in regulations by the Secretary of State under section 47(1) of the Public Health (Control of Disease) Act 1984. No such regulations have been made at the time of going to press.

25.4 POST-MORTEM EXAMINATIONS ETC.

25.4.1 Generally

Post-mortem examination of the body of a deceased person other than by way of purely external examination, whether to ascertain the cause of death or for any other purpose, is lawful only if carried out on the instructions or at the request of the coroner, or if it is within the provisions of the Human Tissue Act 1961 or the Anatomy Act 1984. The Human Tissue Act also authorises (subject to certain provisions in that Act) the removal of parts of the body of a deceased person either for therapeutic purposes or for purposes of medical examination and research. These matters, as well as the law relating to post-mortem examination under these Acts, are examined in succeeding paragraphs.

25.4.2 Coroners' cases

By virtue of section 8 of the Coroners Act 1988, a coroner is required to hold an inquest whenever he is informed that the dead body of a person is lying within his jurisdiction and there is reasonable cause to suspect that such a person has died a violent or an unnatural death, a sudden death of which the cause is unknown, or that such person has died in prison or in such place or under such circumstances as to require an inquest under any other Act. *R v Westminster City Coroner, ex parte Rainer*

(1968)[13] states that the duty of the coroner applies even if a post-mortem would be contrary to the deceased's religious beliefs.

If there is any reasonable possibility of an inquest being necessary or of the coroner requiring a post-mortem examination in order to decide whether an inquest is necessary, no unofficial post-mortem should be undertaken without the coroner's approval, as any unauthorised post-mortem would almost certainly prejudice the inquiry and amount to the offence of obstructing a coroner in the course of his duties. Section 2(2) of the Human Tissue Act 1961 provides that no post-mortem examination shall be carried out otherwise than by or in accordance with the instructions of a fully registered medical practitioner, and no post-mortem examination which is not directed or requested by the coroner or any other competent legal authority shall be carried out without the authority of the person lawfully in possession of the body.

Under section 19 of the Coroners Act 1988, the coroner himself may order any medical practitioner he may summon as a medical witness to make a post-mortem examination, or he may request any other legally qualified medical practitioner to do so even before deciding to hold an inquest. If on result of that examination (such as in the case of a sudden death without any suspicious features) the coroner decides that the cause of death has been sufficiently ascertained, he may issue his certificate to the Registrar accordingly: otherwise he will proceed to hold an inquest.[14]

The Coroners Rules 1984[15] should also be referred to at this stage. Any post-mortem examination ordered or authorised by the coroner is to be made, whenever practicable, by a pathologist with suitable qualifications and experience and having access to laboratory facilities. But if the deceased died in hospital the coroner should not direct or request a pathologist on the staff of, or associated with, that hospital to make a post-mortem examination if (a) that pathologist does not desire to make that examination, or (b) the conduct of any member of the hospital staff is likely to be called into question, or (c) any relative of the deceased asks the coroner that the examination be not made by such a pathologist, unless obtaining another pathologist with suitable qualifications and experience would cause the examination to be unduly delayed. Also, if pneumoconiosis is suspected, no member of the pneumoconiosis panel should make the examination.[16]

If there is to be a coroner's post-mortem, the coroner must, if practicable without undue delay in the examination, inform inter alia the hospital, and the hospital may be represented at the post-mortem by a medical practitioner.[17] Any medical practitioner on the hospital staff who was concerned might request to be permitted to attend. But neither a hospital representative, nor anyone else permitted to be present during the post-mortem, may interfere with the performance of the examination.[18] Except on his authority, no copy of the post-mortem report or special examination report is to be supplied to anyone but the coroner.[19]

If a person dies on hospital premises, there being suitable accommodation at the hospital, the post-mortem, with consent of the hospital, is to be carried out there unless the coroner decides otherwise.[20]

25.4.3   Post-mortem examination and use of parts of a body of a deceased person under the Human Tissue Act 1961

Generally

In the long title of the Human Tissue Act 1961, its purposes are summarised in the following words:

> 'An Act to make provision with respect to the use of parts of bodies of deceased persons for therapeutic purposes and purposes of medical education and research and with respect to the circumstances in which post-mortem examinations may be carried out; and to permit the cremation of bodies removed for anatomical examination.'

The provisions relating to cremation of deceased persons have since been repealed by section 13 of the Anatomy Act 1984.

Removal of parts of bodies for medical purposes

The removal and use of parts of bodies for therapeutic purposes or for purposes of medical education or research is now covered by section 1 of the Act which provides as follows:

'**1.**—(1) If any person, either in writing at any time or orally in the presence of two or more witnesses during his last illness, has expressed a request that his body or any specified part of his body be used after his death for therapeutic purposes or for purposes of medical education or research, the person lawfully in possession of his body after his death may, unless he has reason to believe that the request was subsequently withdrawn, authorise the removal from the body of any part or, as the case may be, the specified part, for use in accordance with the request.'

Further, by virtue of section 1(2), even if the deceased had not expressed any such request, the person in possession of the body may nevertheless authorise the removal of any part of the body for any of the purposes mentioned in section 1(1) if, having made such reasonable enquiry as may be practicable, he has no reason to believe:

1. that the deceased had expressed an objection to his body being so dealt with after his death, and had not withdrawn it; or
2. that the surviving spouse or any surviving relative of the deceased objects to the body being so dealt with.

Section 1(4) provides that the removal of any part of a body, except eyes, under section 1(1) or section 1(2), is not to be effected except by a registered medical practitioner, who must have satisfied himself by personal examination of the body that life is extinct.

Coroner must not be obstructed

Section 1(5) stipulates that where a person has reason to believe that an inquest may be required to be held on any body or that a post-mortem examination of any body may be required by the coroner, he may not, except with the consent of the coroner, give any authority for a body to be dealt with under section 1, nor may he act on such authority given by any other person.

Person lawfully in possession of body

Nowhere in the Act is there any definition of 'the person lawfully in possession' of the body. By inference it appears that the expression means anyone who has possession of the body even for a limited purpose, as in the case of an undertaker, or for a limited time, as in the case of a hospital which normally has possession of the body only until an undertaker receives it on the instructions of relatives. That view is clearly borne out by the prohibition on the giving of any authority under the Act by a person entrusted with the body for the purpose only of its interment or cremation (section 1(6)), without which prohibition an undertaker could have given such authority; and see also the decided cases cited as relevant authority on p. 654 of this chapter.

That the person having the control and management of a hospital, nursing home or other institution has lawful possession of a corpse is implicit in section 1(7) which states that the authority may be given on behalf of that person by any officer or person designated for that purpose by him. It must be appreciated that the expression 'person' here includes a corporate body, so that in the case of a health service hospital the person having the management and control is the District Health Authority or NHS hospital trust, and such bodies should designate an officer to act on their behalf in the matter and can, presumably, designate more than one person. In the case of a local authority institution, the person having control and management is the local social services authority. In the case of a nursing home, while it could be argued that it is the proprietor, whether a limited company, a partnership or a single natural person, who is in possession of the body of a deceased patient, it is probably safe to assume it to be the person in immediate day-to-day charge, usually a resident medical practitioner or a resident registered nurse or, in the case of a maternity home, possibly a registered midwife.

Delegation of authority

Under the NHS Functions (Directions to Authorities and Administrative Arrangements) Regulations 1991,[21] a health authority can delegate its functions to an officer, e.g. its chief administrative officer.

Saving for existing powers

Section 1(8) states that nothing in section 1 shall be construed as rendering unlawful any dealing with, or with any part of, the body of a deceased person which is lawful apart from the Act.

Post-mortem examinations under the 1961 Act

Section 2(2) stipulates that no post-mortem shall be carried out otherwise than by or in accordance with the instructions of a fully registered medical practitioner and no post-mortem examination which is not directed or requested by the coroner or other competent legal authority is to be carried out without the authority of the person lawfully in possession. Furthermore, section 1(2), (5), (6) and (7) apply in respect of the giving of this authority.

Prohibition on commercial dealings

Section 1 of the Human Organ Transplants Act 1989 prohibits commercial dealing in human organs (whether from dead or living persons) intended for transplantation. Anyone found to be involved in such a commercial enterprise will be guilty of an offence liable to a maximum of three months imprisonment or a fine not exceeding £5000 (level 5) or both. Advertising offences are liable to a level 5 fine only.

Supply of information relating to organ transplants

Section 3 of the Human Organ Transplants Act 1989 enables the Secretary of State to make regulations requiring certain information to be supplied in respect of organ transplants. The Human Organ Transplants (Supply of Information) Regulations 1989[22] state that a registered medical practitioner who removes an organ for transplantation, whether from a dead or living person, must supply specified information to the United Kingdom Transplant Support Services Authority and also to the District Health Authority in which the removal was carried out (if the operation was performed in England or Wales) or the relevant Health Board in Scotland. Failure to supply such information may result in a fine not exceeding level 3. Knowingly and recklessly to supply false information leads to a maximum fine at level 5.

25.4.4 Anatomical examination under the Anatomy Act 1984

The principal provisions of the Act, concerning anatomical examination of the body are:

1. That such examination may be undertaken only by a person duly licensed and at a place duly notified to the Secretary of State. Furthermore, no person shall have in his possession an anatomical specimen unless that person is so authorised by licence.[23]
2. The examination is undertaken with the permission or at the request of the person in lawful possession of the body.[24]

Section 4(9) confirms that:

'in the case of a body lying in a hospital, nursing home or other institution, any authorisation under this section may be given on behalf of the person having the control and management of the institution or any officer or person designated for that purpose by the first-mentioned person'.

It should be noted, however, that a person who is simply entrusted with the body for the purpose only of its disposal cannot give such lawful authority despite being in lawful possession.

Permission for examination may be given pursuant to section 4 of the Act, which provides, inter alia:

'Subsection (2) applies if a person, either in writing at any time or orally in the presence of two or more witnesses during his last illness, has expressed a request that his body be used after his death for anatomical examination.

(2) If the person lawfully in possession of the body after death has no reason to believe that the request was withdrawn, he may authorise the use of the body in accordance with the request.

(3) Without prejudice to subsection (2), the person lawfully in possession of a body may authorise it to be used for anatomical examination if, having made such reasonable inquiry as may be practicable, he has no reason to believe—

(a) that the deceased, either in writing at any time or orally in the presence of two or more witnesses during his last illness, had expressed an objection to his body being so used after his death, and had not withdrawn it, or

(b) that the surviving spouse or any surviving relative of the deceased objects to the body being so used.'

3. The death must be registered, in the case of the body concerned, under section 15 of the Births and Deaths Registration Act 1953.
4. A certificate of death must be signed in accordance with section 22(1) of the Births and Deaths Registration Act 1953.
5. Disposal of the body after completion of the examination or upon expiration of authority to carry out examinations is covered by the Anatomy Regulations 1988.[25] Regulation 4(i)(e) requires that the disposal shall, so far as is practicable, be in accordance with any wishes expressed by the deceased or his relatives.

If, however: parts of the body are held in possession under section 5 of the Act, that is, examination was completed before the expiration of authority under section 4; authority had been given for possession of parts of the body after completion of the examination; the part is such that the person from whose body it came cannot be recognised simply by examination of the part; and finally, the Secretary of State has granted a licence for this purpose, those parts will not be disposed of. Regulation 3 of the 1988 Regulations does, however, require the person in possession of the body to keep records relating to those parts. In addition, regulation 4, paragraph (2) states that these parts of bodies must be stored in an orderly and hygienic manner and in suitable storage facilities.

25.4.5   Further consideration of the application of the Anatomy Act 1984 and of the Human Tissue Act 1961

Because the provisions of the Human Tissue Act 1961 are very much less rigid than those of the Anatomy Act 1984, recourse is now likely to be made to the Anatomy Act only when bodies are needed for dissection by medical students, the use of bodies for other purposes being covered by the Human Tissue Act. It should be remembered, however, that removal of any part[26] of a body under the 1961 Act must be carried out by a registered medical practitioner, whereas the 1984 Act permits removal of parts of the body by those authorised by the Secretary of State. As already mentioned, such persons may be medical students.

Although under section 1 of the Human Tissue Act only the removal and in effect the retention of any part of the body of a deceased person is authorised, it seems clear that more than one part may be removed from the same body. But could part after part of the body be removed until nothing remains? On balance it seems that it could, provided each part removed was wanted for an authorised purpose and its removal from the rest of the body was undertaken by a registered medical practitioner. In support of this view, it may be indicated that the skeleton may be properly described as part of the body. That being so, it could be removed from the body to be kept for the purpose of medical education under section 1. At that point it becomes somewhat academic to argue about the fate of the rest of the body and which parts and how much should be retained for disposal.

25.4.6   Specimens retained after operations, stillbirths etc.

There are no legal obstacles concerning the retention as museum specimens or for other purposes of medical education or interest of organs, growths etc. removed from a patient during an operation, save the theoretical issue that whatever is removed from the patient is his property. On rare occasions, on religious grounds, a patient may ask that some part of his body which is being removed during an operation, e.g. a limb being amputated, be disposed of in a particular way or that he have the disposal of it. In such a case, while a hospital would be under no obligation to incur any additional expenditure in order to comply with the patient's request, it would be reasonable for it to do so provided that no risk of infection was foreseeable and no nuisance thereby created.

The position with regard to the retention of a museum specimen of a stillborn child and that in respect of the retention of a complete foetus, or part of a foetus, are quite different, a distinction having to be drawn between a foetus and a stillborn infant.

A child is stillborn which has issued forth from its mother after the twenty-fourth week of pregnancy and which did not at any time after being expelled from its mother breathe or show any signs of life.[27] Notification of the stillbirth has to be given to the Registrar.[28] The better view is that the body should be disposed of by burial in a burial ground or cremation at an authorised crematorium. The body of a stillborn child is probably not within the provisions of the Human Tissue Act 1961.

In the case of delivery of a foetus without signs of life before the end of the twenty-fourth week of pregnancy, no registration is necessary and the foetus may be disposed of without formality in any way which does not constitute a nuisance or an affront to public decency. Hence its preservation for scientific purposes is in order. No foetus which is thus retained should bear any inscription which would identify the patient from whom it was taken, as that would constitute a breach of professional confidence.

25.5 INQUESTS

25.5.1 Generally

The Coroners Rules 1984[29] lay down the correct procedure to be followed at inquests. Some of the points in the 1984 Rules which will be of interest to hospital authorities and their professional staff are set out in the following paragraphs. Reference has already been made to the Rules concerning post-mortems.

Rule 17 stipulates that all inquests are to be held in public, exception to be made only on grounds of national security.

Provision is made for any person whose conduct is likely to be called into question to be summoned to give evidence and for the inquest to be adjourned for him to be summoned if that has not been done.[30] Furthermore, such a person has the right to examine witnesses, whether in person or through his counsel or solicitor, providing that the coroner considers him to be a properly interested person.[31] This right is subject to the coroner's discretion to disallow irrelevant or improper questions.

This applies to the hospital as well as any member of its staff personally concerned, since the word 'person' includes a corporate body.

Witnesses are ordinarily to be examined first by the coroner and, if the witness is represented at the inquest, lastly by his own representative.[32] No witness is obliged to answer incriminating questions and it is the duty of the coroner, if such a question is asked, to tell him that he need not answer.[33] It must be appreciated, however, that the protection extends only to questions which do tend to incriminate (such as those which might establish a charge of manslaughter) and that there is no protection against questions tending to establish solely civil liability.

25.5.2 The purpose of an inquest

Rule 36 explains that the proceedings and evidence at an inquest are to be directed solely to ascertaining who the deceased was, how, when and where the deceased came by his death and the particulars for the time being required by the Registration Acts to be registered concerning death. Neither the coroner nor the jury are to express any opinion on any other matters. The coroner is permitted, however, to take measures to prevent the recurrence of similar fatalities. Rule 43 allows the coroner to announce at the inquest that he is reporting the matter in writing to the person or authority who may have power to take action to prevent similar fatal incidents and to report the matter accordingly.

Furthermore, no verdict is to be framed in such a way as to appear to determine any question of civil liability[34]. This last-mentioned provision would preclude a finding of negligence not amounting to manslaughter, though use of rule 43 for avoiding similar fatalities in future might, by implication, suggest carelessness or negligence.

NOTES

1. HSC(IS) 156; June 1975.
2. This advice is almost certainly legally correct: see *R v Feist* (1858) Dears B 590 and *William v Williams* (1882) 20 Ch D 659.
3. See Code of Practice prepared by a Working Party established by the United Kingdom Health Departments under the chairmanship of Lord Smith of Marlow; Department of Health, 1978.
4. HC(77)28.
5. Anatomy Act 1984 (Commencement) Order 1988, SI 1988/81.
6. SI 1988/44, as amended by SI 1988/198.
7. SI 1989/2480.
8. SI 1989/2017.
9. Human Organ Transplants Act 1989, section 5.
10. SI 1989/2108, as amended by SI 1991/408 and SI 1991/1645.
11. Regulation 2(1)(a)(ii).
12. HM(72)41.

13. (1968) 112 Sol Jo 883.
14. Coroners Act 1988, section 19(3).
15. SI 1984/552, as amended by SI 1985/1414.
16. Rule 6.
17. Rule 7.
18. Rule 8.
19. Rule 10(2).
20. Rule 11(3).
21. SI 1991/554, regulation 10(1)(d).
22. SI 1989/2108, as amended by SI 1991/1645.
23. Anatomy Act 1984, section 2.
24. Anatomy Act 1984, section 4.
25. SI 1988/44.
26. Except eyes, which are separately provided for; see section 1(4A)(b).
27. Births and Deaths Registration Act 1953, section 41, as amended by the Still Birth Definition Act 1992.
28. Births and Deaths Registration Act 1953, section 11.
29. SI 1984/552.
30. Rules 24 and 25.
31. Rule 20.
32. Rule 21.
33. Rule 22.
34. Rule 42.

CHAPTER 26

Patient making a will

26.1 INTRODUCTORY

A will or testamentary disposition is an expression of the maker's wishes as to the disposition of his property after death and may, subject to certain conditions outlined in the Children Act 1989, contain an appointment of testamentary guardians of children under the age of 18. The Children Act 1989 repealed the Guardianship of Minors Act 1971. The power of a child's parents, if married, to appoint testamentary guardians is preserved. If, however, the child's parents are not married at the time of the child's birth, only the mother will have 'parental responsibility' under the Act. This means in effect that only she has power to appoint a testamentary guardian. It is possible for the father to acquire parental responsibility under the Act, subject to the fulfilment of certain conditions. It is not, however, an automatic right. If both parents are married at the time of the child's birth, the father also has parental responsibility and consequently has the power to appoint testamentary guardians.

Usually too, the person or persons the testator desires to carry out the provisions of the will are named as executors. In English law, any person of full age and sound mind, memory and understanding may make a will. Section 9 of the Wills Act 1837 requires that, to be valid, the will must be in writing (including typewriting etc.) and must be signed by the testator in the presence of two witnesses who both subscribe their signatures. Furthermore, it is also necessary that both witnesses are present during the whole time that the testator was signing his name. So, if as in *Re Colling, deceased* (1972),[1] one of the witnesses of a patient's will were a ward sister who, after the testator had started signing his name but before he had finished, went to attend to another patient, the will would be invalid.

If a necessary witness or spouse of a witness is named as a beneficiary under the will, the will is otherwise good but the benefit to the witness or his/her spouse is ordinarily void.[2] If the testator cannot write or is too ill to sign he may make his mark, usually a cross, or in extreme cases when even that is impossible he may, if of full understanding, authorise some third party other than one of the two witnesses to sign for him. If a will has been made by a blind, illiterate or disabled person, whether he signs his name or marks his name or has the will signed for him by another on his instructions, the registrar, on application for probate, will require proof that the testator had knowledge of the contents of the will at the time of execution. Witnesses of such wills ordinarily subscribe their signatures to an appropriately modified attestation clause which, in the case of a person unable to read whether from blindness or other cause, would place on record that the will had been read over to him before execution.

The duty of a hospital authority and of its staff to treat as confidential the fact that a patient has made a will and the circumstances in which a patient's will may be given to a third party are discussed later.

26.2   PATIENTS IN HOSPITAL OTHER THAN THE MENTALLY IMPAIRED

26.2.1   Will drafted by a patient's solicitor

If a patient in hospital expresses the desire to make a will and he has a solicitor of his own, any request he may make to that solicitor should be transmitted with all convenient speed. Facilities should also be provided for the patient's solicitor to visit the patient even outside ordinary visiting hours, subject of course to the medical needs of the patient himself. When such a course of action can be taken the hospital and its staff are relieved of all moral responsibility in the matter. The only other question to consider is whether it is proper to allow members of staff to act as witnesses of a patient's will. There appears to be no good reason forbidding any member of staff witnessing a will, if the patient so desires, bearing in mind that no witness is allowed to take any benefit under the will.

But even to the sound rule of not witnessing a will unless the patient is himself apparently of full understanding when signing it, there may be an exception. There is some authority for suggesting that if a testator is in his full senses when he gives instructions for the drafting of his will, he may validly execute it even if at the time he no longer has full understanding of its terms. Consequently, even though the mental capacity of the patient at the time of execution is doubtful, it is probably reasonable, especially if the patient is unlikely to attend to business again, for a doctor or senior nurse to witness at the solicitor's request a will drafted by the solicitor on the patient's previous instructions. It must be a matter of personal judgment in each case as to whether, before the will is witnessed, the doctor or nurse should advise the solicitor of any doubts concerning the mental capacity of the patient. Even if no member of the hospital staff is allowed or is willing to witness such a will, no obstacles should be placed in the way of the solicitor arranging for other witnesses.

26.2.2 Will drafted otherwise than by patient's solicitor

If a patient, being apparently of full understanding and having prepared a will without the help of a solicitor, simply asks that two members of the hospital staff should witness his will, it would be unreasonable not to comply with his request.

A serious problem arises in the case of a patient who has no solicitor and wishes to make a will in circumstances which admit of no delay, for instance an accident or post-operative patient in a very grave state, or a patient about to undergo a major operation which cannot be deferred. Whenever possible it is desirable that hospitals should have an arrangement with local solicitors to be on call for such emergency cases, subject of course to the understanding that the patient and not the hospital would be responsible for the solicitor's fee. However, cases will certainly arise in which it is not possible to obtain the help of a solicitor and in such circumstances it would seem desirable that some senior member of the administrative staff, or failing that, of the medical or senior nursing staff, or a social worker or chaplain, should assist the patient if so desired in setting down his wishes. It must be stressed that this should only be attempted when the testator is clear about what he wants and the proposed will is simple and straightforward (for instance, leaving the whole of the testator's property to his spouse or children).

26.3 PATIENTS OF UNSOUND MIND

26.3.1 Generally

For a will to be valid, the testator must be of sound mind, memory and understanding. The law states that the testators must fully comprehend the consequences of making such bequests: *Banks v Goodfellow* (1870).[3] In *Harwood v Baker* (1840)[4] it was said:

> 'To constitute a sound disposing mind, a testator must not only be able to understand that he is by will giving his property to objects of his regard but he must also have capacity to comprehend the extent of his property, and the nature of claims of others whom by his will he is excluding from participation in that property.'

That definition is a purely factual one and its application to a particular person does not depend on legal formalities. The will of a person liable to detention in hospital under the provisions of the Mental Health Act, whether under Part II or III, may be valid and effectual, while the will of a person who has either been admitted informally or who has never been under treatment for mental disorder may be upset on grounds of mental incapacity. In short, the assumption sometimes made that persons liable to detention under the Act can never make a will is erroneous. Special precautions are taken as far as possible to prevent such persons making a will unless those responsible for their welfare are satisfied that they are really competent to do so.

26.3.2 Technical safeguards

Section 96 of the Mental Health Act 1983 empowers the Court of Protection to execute a will on behalf of a person who is mentally disordered. 'Patient' in this part of the Act is independent of any connection with admission to, or treatment in, hospital. This power cannot be exercised unless it is reasonably believed that the patient is incapable of making a valid will for himself.[5] To ascertain whether the patient is so capable, it appears that the rule in *Banks v Goodfellow* (1870)[3] (above) still applies. The rule is that if a patient wishes to make a will while still under the jurisdiction of the court, the court, before granting facilities, must be satisfied that the patient is possessed of full testamentary capacity, namely capacity to understand the nature of the document he is executing, the extent of the property to be disposed of and the claims of those he is benefiting by or excluding from his will. Whenever a mentally disordered patient in hospital expresses the desire to make a will and there is reason to believe that the patient is subject to the jurisdiction of the Court of Protection, the court should be notified of the position so that it can decide whether facilities should be granted. Under section 96(1)(e) the court has to seek to make such a will as the actual (as distinct from hypothetical) patient would have made before he lost testamentary capacity.

Apart altogether from any special precautions called for in the case of patients subject to the jurisdiction of the court, it is customarily the rule in psychiatric hospitals that facilities are not given for any patient to make a will, save on the recommendation of the medical practitioner responsible for the patient's treatment. The same rule usually applies to patients in psychiatric wards of other hospitals.

If a patient is thought to be capable of executing a will prepared on professional advice, the medical officer responsible for his treatment in hospital may normally be willing to be one of the witnesses to its execution. In *Re Simpson; Schaniel v Simpson* (1977),[6] it was stated that, in case of an old or infirm testator, a medical practitioner ought prudently to be a witness. Such medical witness is of value as evidence of the patient's testamentary capacity. In addition to this, the preliminary precaution of obtaining the approval of the hospital is the best guarantee against the validity of the will being successfully challenged.

In practice, if a psychiatric patient expresses a serious desire to make a will, the nurse or other member of the staff to whom he expresses his wish should report without undue delay so that the medical practitioner in charge of the treatment of the patient can advise on appropriate action.

Sometimes the patient will himself have communicated with his solicitor who will then doubtless discuss the patient's capacity with the doctor in charge of the treatment and, if necessary, communicate with the Court of Protection. In other cases, where there appears some reasonable possibility of the patient's being competent to make a will, he may properly be advised to consult a solicitor and be given facilities to do so.

26.3.3   Patients admitted informally

Since any mentally disordered patient who does not object to becoming an in-patient may be accepted as an informal patient and it is not necessary that he should be volitional or even of any real understanding, it follows that many informal patients, e.g. patients with severe learning disabilities, will be quite unfit to make a will. But other patients, not compulsorily detained, will be fit.

As has already been indicated, hospital rules against the making of a will by mentally disordered patients otherwise than with the approval of the medical practitioner responsible for his treatment extend to informal patients as well as to those liable to detention. But it has to be appreciated that an informal patient who is volitional may decide to leave the hospital if he is refused facilities to make a will.

Against that background it seems desirable that in the case of a patient admitted informally who might be capable of making a will wishing to see a solicitor about it, obstacles should not ordinarily be put in the way of his doing so, unless he is subject to the jurisdiction of the Court of Protection. The medical practitioner in charge of the patient's treatment should be prepared to advise the solicitor on his client's condition and, if reasonably satisfied as to the patient's testamentary capacity, to be one of the witnesses to the execution of the will.

26.3.4   Will made by mentally disordered patient in hospital without professional advice and without the knowledge of the medical practitioner in charge of their treatment

It sometimes happens that a will is made by a patient in a psychiatric hospital, or in the psychiatric ward of a general hospital, without professional advice and without the knowledge of the medical practitioner responsible for the treatment of the patient. If later, the existence of such will becomes known it should not be destroyed, however unlikely it is that its validity would be upheld by the court if it were challenged, since the wilful destruction of a will is a criminal offence. The will should be taken into the safekeeping of the appropriate officer on behalf of the managers of the hospital and, if the patient is under the jurisdiction of the Court of Protection, the Master notified. If the patient is not under the jurisdiction of the court it is advisable that the will be retained in the custody of the managers until the patient is discharged or dies. If he were transferred to another hospital it would be convenient that the will be also transferred. It is also most desirable, if possible, that a record be made by the medical practitioner in charge of the treatment of the patient of his opinion of the patient's mental state at the time the will was made, or as near to that time as possible.

26.4   ELDERLY SENILE MENTALLY INFIRM PATIENTS

In any hospital, old people's home or similar institution there may be patients suffering from some degree of mental infirmity or failing memory by reason of old age as well as others whose waning mental capacity is due to chronic disease. Unless such a patient's affairs are subject to the jurisdiction of the Court of Protection, when the court should be communicated with if the patient desires to make a will, it would not be appropriate for the hospital in any way to obstruct the patient in making a will and, if the patient wishes to consult his solicitor, the solicitor should be told. If, however, the medical practitioner in charge of the treatment of the patient were not satisfied that he was of sufficiently sound mind and understanding to make a will, it would be proper not to permit any member of the staff of the hospital to act as a witness.

NOTES

1. [1972] I WLR 1440.
2. Wills Act 1837, section 15.
3. [1870] LR 5 QB 549.
4. (1840) 3 Moore PC 282.
5. Mental Health Act 1983, section 96(4).
6. (1977) 121 Sol Jo 224.

CHAPTER 27

Medical termination of pregnancy (abortion)

27.1 ABORTION ACT 1967, AS AMENDED BY THE HUMAN FERTILISATION AND EMBRYOLOGY ACT 1990

A pregnancy may be lawfully terminated only by a registered medical practitioner acting in accordance with the provisions of section 1 of the Abortion Act 1967, as amended. The termination would otherwise be unlawful under the Infant life (Preservation) Act 1929 or the Offences Against the Person Act 1861, depending upon whether the foetus is viable (that is, capable of being born alive: *C v S* (1987)[1]), or not. The provisions of the Act are as follows:

'**1.**—(1) Subject to the provisions of this section, a person shall not be guilty of an offence under the law relating to abortion[2] when a pregnancy is terminated by a registered medical practitioner[3] if two registered medical practitioners are of the opinion, formed in good faith[4]

(a)   that the pregnancy has not exceeded its twenty-fourth week and that the continuance of the pregnancy would involve risk, greater than if the pregnancy were terminated, of injury to the physical or mental health of the pregnant woman or any existing children of her family; or

(b)   that the termination is necessary to prevent grave permanent injury to the physical or mental health of the pregnant woman; or

(c)   that the continuance of the pregnancy would involve risk to the life of the pregnant woman, greater than if the pregnancy were terminated; or

(d)   that there is a substantial risk that if the child were born it would suffer from such physical or mental abnormalities as to be seriously handicapped.[5]

(2) In determining whether the continuance of a pregnancy would involve such risk of injury to health as is mentioned in paragraph (a) or (b) of subsection (1) of this section, account may be taken of the pregnant woman's actual or reasonably foreseeable environment.

(3) Except as provided by subsection (4) of this section, any treatment for the termination of pregnancy must be carried out in a hospital vested in the Secretary of State for the purposes of his functions under the National Health Service Act 1977 or the National Health Service (Scotland) Act 1978 or in a hospital vested in a National Health Service trust or in a place approved for the purposes of this section by the Secretary of State.

(3A) The power under subsection (3) of this section to approve a place includes power, in relation to treatment consisting primarily in the use of such medicines as may be specified in the approval and carried out in such manner as may be so specified, to approve a class of places.

(4) Subsection (3) of this section, and so much of subsection (1) as relates to the opinion of two registered medical practitioners, shall not apply to the termination of a pregnancy by a registered medical practitioner in a case where he is of the opinion, formed in good faith[4], that the termination is immediately necessary to save the life or to prevent grave permanent injury to the physical or mental health of the pregnant woman.

Notification

2.—(1) The Secretary of State in respect of England and Wales, and the Secretary of State in respect of Scotland, shall by statutory instrument make regulations[6] to provide—

    (a) for requiring any such opinion as is referred to in section 1 of this Act to be certified by the practitioners or practitioner concerned in such form and at such time as may be prescribed by the regulations, and for requiring the preservation and disposal of certificates made for the purposes of the regulations;

    (b) for requiring any registered medical practitioner who terminates a pregnancy to give notice of the termination and such other information relating to the termination as may be so prescribed;

    (c) for prohibiting the disclosure, except to such persons or for such purposes as may be so prescribed, of notices given or information furnished pursuant to the regulations.

(2) The information furnished in pursuance of regulations made by virtue of paragraph (b) of subsection (1) of this section shall be notified solely to the Chief Medical Officer of the Department of Health, or of the Welsh Office, or of the Scottish Home and Health Department.

(3) Any person who wilfully contravenes or wilfully fails to comply with requirements of regulations under subsection (1) of this section shall be liable on summary conviction to a fine not exceeding level 5 on the standard scale.

(4) Any statutory instrument made by virtue of this section shall be subject to annulment in pursuance of a resolution of either House of Parliament.

Application of the Act to Visiting Forces etc.

3.—(1) In relation to the termination of a pregnancy in a case where the following conditions are satisfied, that is to say—

    (a) the treatment for termination of the pregnancy was carried out in a hospital controlled by the proper authorities of a body to which this section applies; and

    (b) the pregnant woman had at the time of the treatment a relevant association with that body; and

    (c) the treatment was carried out by a registered medical practitioner or a person who at the time of the treatment was a member of that body appointed as a medical practitioner for that body by the proper authorities of that body,

this Act shall have effect as if any reference in section 1 to a registered medical practitioner and to a hospital vested in the Secretary of State included respectively a reference to such a person as is mentioned in paragraph (c) of this subsection and to a hospital controlled as aforesaid, and as if section 2 were omitted.

(2) The bodies to which this section applies are any force which is a visiting force within the meaning of any of the provisions of Part I of the Visiting Forces Act 1952 and any headquarters within the meaning of the Schedule to the

International Headquarters and Defence Organisations Act 1964; and for the purposes of this section—

(a)   a woman shall be treated as having a relevant association at any time with a body to which this section applies if at that time—

(i)   in the case of such a force as aforesaid, she had a relevant association within the meaning of the said Part I with the force; and

(ii)   in the case of such a headquarters as aforesaid, she was a member of the headquarters or a dependant within the meaning of the Schedule aforesaid of such a member; and

(b)   any reference to a member of a body to which this section applies shall be construed—

(i)   in the case of such a force as aforesaid, as a reference to a member of or of a civilian component of that force within the meaning of the said Part I; and

(ii)   in the case of such a headquarters as aforesaid, as a reference to a member of that headquarters within the meaning of the Schedule aforesaid.

Conscientious objection to participation in treatment

4.—(1) Subject to subsection (2) of this section, no person shall be under any duty, whether by contract or by any statutory or other legal requirement, to participate in any treatment authorised by this Act to which he has a conscientious objection:

Provided that in any legal proceedings the burden of proof of conscientious objection shall rest on the person claiming to rely on it.

(2) Nothing in subsection (1) of this section shall affect any duty to participate in treatment which is necessary to save the life or to prevent grave permanent injury to the physical or mental health of a pregnant woman.

(3) In any proceedings before a court in Scotland, a statement on oath by any person to the effect that he has a conscientious objection to participating in any treatment authorised by this Act shall be sufficient evidence for the purpose of discharging the burden of proof imposed upon him by subsection (1) of this section.'

For the purposes of section 4 conscientious objection extends beyond the medical practitioner effecting a termination, although its precise ambit remains unclear. *Janaway v Salford Area Health Authority* (1988)[7] established that the right of conscientious objection does not extend to clerical staff who merely type the letters of referral, since this does not constitute 'participating in treatment' within the meaning of section 4.

'Supplementary provisions

5.—(1) No offence under the Infant Life (Preservation) Act 1929 shall be committed by a registered medical practitioner who terminates a pregnancy in accordance with the provisions of this Act.

(2) For the purposes of the law relating to abortion, anything done with intent to procure a woman's miscarriage (or, in the case of a woman carrying more than one foetus, her miscarriage of any foetus) is unlawfully done unless authorised by section 1 of this Act and, in the case of a woman carrying more than one foetus, anything done with intent to procure her miscarriage of any foetus is authorised by that section if—

(a)   the ground for termination of the pregnancy specified in subsection (1)(d)

of that section applies in relation to any foetus and the thing is done for the purpose of procuring the miscarriage of that foetus, or
(b) any of the other grounds for termination of the pregnancy specified in that section applies.'

Section 5(1) makes a major alteration to the law as it existed prior to 14 April 1991 by removing the limitation which was hitherto placed on lawful termination by section 1 of the Infant Life (Preservation) Act 1929. That Act supplemented the law of abortion by making it a criminal offence to destroy the life of a child 'capable of being born alive'. Section 5(1) therefore legalises (or at least provides a defence to criminal prosecutions in respect of) terminations of pregnancy on the 'relative risk to health' grounds, which are limited by section 1(1)(a) of the Act, as amended, to 24 weeks into term, despite the modern possibility of children being born alive (and indeed surviving, with intensive care) below that age. More strikingly, no upper limit is now placed on abortions based on grounds of substantial risk of serious handicap, even though a great many (if not most) such children would be capable of being born alive within the meaning of the 1929 Act. Not only may such a child be aborted at any stage of the pregnancy until birth, but so may a healthy child not so affected if the opinions supporting the abortion have been formed in good faith.

27.1.1 Abortion Regulations

The Abortion Regulations 1991[8] provide as follows:

'Certificate of opinion
3.—(1) Any opinion to which section 1 of the Act refers shall be certified—
(a) in the case of a pregnancy terminated in accordance with section 1(1) of the Act, in the form set out in Part I of Schedule 1 of these Regulations, and
(b) in the case of a pregnancy terminated in accordance with section 1(4) of the Act, in the form set out in Part II of that Schedule.
(2) Any certificate of an opinion referred to in section 1(1) of the Act shall be given before the commencement of the treatment for the termination of the pregnancy to which it relates.
(3) Any certificate of an opinion referred to in section 1(4) of the Act shall be given before the commencement of the treatment for the termination of the pregnancy to which it relates or, if that is not reasonably practicable, not later than 24 hours after such termination.
(4) Any such certificate as is referred to in paragraphs (2) and (3) of this regulation shall be preserved by the practitioner who terminated the pregnancy to which it relates for a period of not less than 3 years beginning with the date of the termination.
(5) A certificate which is no longer to be preserved shall be destroyed by the person in whose custody it then is.

Notice of termination of pregnancy and information relating to the termination
4.—(1) Any practitioner who terminates a pregnancy in England or Wales shall give to the appropriate Chief Medical Officer—

(a) notice of the termination, and

(b) such other information relating to the termination as is specified in the form set out in Schedule 2 to these Regulations,

and shall do so by sending them to him in a sealed envelope within 7 days of the termination.

(2) The appropriate Chief Medical Officer is—

(a) where the pregnancy was terminated in England, the Chief Medical Officer of the Department of Health, Richmond House, Whitehall, London, SW1A 2NS; or

(b) where the pregnancy was terminated in Wales, the Chief Medical Officer of the Welsh Office, Cathays Park, Cardiff, CF1 3NQ.

Restriction on disclosure of information

5. A notice given or any information furnished to a Chief Medical Officer in pursuance of these Regulations shall not be disclosed except that disclosure may be made—

(a) for the purposes of carrying out their duties—

(i) to an officer of the Department of Health authorised by the Chief Medical Officer of that Department, or to an officer of the Welsh Office authorised by the Chief Medical Officer of that Office, as the case may be, or

(ii) to the Registrar General or a member of his staff authorised by him; or

(b) for the purposes of carrying out his duties in relation to offences under the Act or the law relating to abortion, to the Director of Public Prosecutions or a member of his staff authorised by him; or

(c) for the purposes of investigating whether an offence has been committed under the Act or the law relating to abortion, to a police officer not below the rank of superintendent or a person authorised by him; or

(d) pursuant to a court order, for the purposes of proceedings which have begun; or

(e) for the purposes of bona fide scientific research; or

(f) to the practitioner who terminated the pregnancy; or

(g) to a practitioner, with the consent in writing of the woman whose pregnancy was terminated; or

(h) when requested by the President of the General Medical Council for the purpose of investigating whether there has been serious professional misconduct by a practitioner, to the President of the General Medical Council or a member of its staff authorised by him.'

27.1.2 Assisting in suspected illegal abortion

A medical practitioner who co-operates with another practitioner who performs an unlawful abortion or other illegal operation will also be guilty of an offence unless the court is satisfied that he had no knowledge of the illegality. The position of a nurse or midwife assisting in an illegal operation is substantially the same as that of a medical practitioner. Should a nurse or midwife assisting in an abortion become suspicious of its legality only after the operation has commenced, it is suggested that he or she is entitled to continue in order to safeguard the life of the patient. But the choice could be a grave one since, by continuing to help, he or she would inevitably be open to some suspicion of being an accomplice. A nurse so involved should should be careful not to make to any third party any statement about the practitioner which he or she cannot fully substantiate since it might easily be defamatory; but would, of course, be allowed to make a statement to the police or to professional superiors, such as a nursing officer or a supervising midwife, to both seek advice and provide some evidence to rebut any suspicion. Such a statement would, if made in good faith, be privileged under the general law of defamation.

A nurse or midwife should in no circumstances procure a miscarriage nor even assist in procuring a miscarriage, except when acting as an assistant to a registered medical practitioner in circumstances falling within the provisions of section 1 of the Abortion Act 1967. Moreover, neither a medical practitioner nor a nurse or midwife should tell a woman requesting to have an abortion what drug or appliance she might use; still less procure for her any such drug or appliance. The only proper course for a nurse or midwife consulted by a woman requesting an abortion is to refer her to a doctor for advice.

27.2 CRIMINAL OFFENCES RELATING TO ABORTION

27.2.1 Administering drugs or using instruments to procure abortion

The Offences Against the Person Act 1861 provides in section 58 that:

'Every woman, being with child, who, with intent to procure her own miscarriage, shall unlawfully administer to herself any poison or other noxious thing, or shall unlawfully use any instrument or other means whatsoever with the like intent, and whosoever, with intent to procure the miscarriage of any woman, whether she be or be not with child, shall unlawfully administer to her or cause to be taken by her any poison or other noxious thing, or shall unlawfully use any instrument or other means whatsoever with the like intent, shall be guilty of felony, and being convicted thereof shall be [guilty of an offence].'

The offence is committed in the latter instance irrespective of whether the woman is in fact pregnant. The word 'unlawfully', in each instance in which it is used in section 58, is now to be understood as meaning that which is not specifically permitted by the Abortion Act 1967, as amended. It should be carefully noted that even medical termination of pregnancy outside those legal parameters (which are admittedly very wide) remains a serious criminal offence.

27.2.2 Procuring drugs etc. to cause abortion

Section 59 of the 1861 Act provides that:

'Whosoever shall unlawfully supply or procure any poison or other noxious thing, or any instrument or thing whatsoever, knowing that the same is intended to be unlawfully used or employed with intent to procure the miscarriage of any woman, whether she be or be not with child, shall be guilty of a misdemeanour, and being convicted thereof shall be [guilty of an offence].'

As in the case of the latter part of section 58, the offence is committed irrespective of whether the woman is in fact pregnant.

NOTES

1. [1987] 1 All ER 1230.
2. 'The law of abortion' refers to sections 58 and 59 of the Offences Against the Person Act 1861. The law makes unlawful abortion a serious criminal offence, though the circumstances under which it may be committed have been drastically reduced by the Acts of 1967 and 1990.
3. 'By a registered medical practitioner' has been held to include nursing staff acting under the direction of a registered medical practitioner: *Royal College of Nursing v DHSS* [1981] AC 800.
4. Although evidence of professional practice and medical probabilities is relevant, the question as to whether a doctor acted in good faith is for the jury to decide on a totality of the evidence: *R v Smith* [1973] 1 WLR 1510.
5. Amendments made by the 1990 Act have removed the time limit for abortion of the handicapped foetus. Prior to this, termination on grounds of handicap was lawful only if carried out before the foetus was capable of being born alive. See section 5(1).
6. The regulations made under this section are the Abortion Regulations 1991, SI 1991/499.
7. [1988] 3 All ER 1079, HL.
8. SI 1991/499.

CHAPTER 28

Notifiable diseases

Notifiable diseases, including food poisoning, will be discussed in this chapter only so far as the subject is likely to concern hospital authorities and medical practitioners attending patients in hospital.

28.1 DEFINITION

Cholera, plague, relapsing fever, smallpox and typhus are all notifiable diseases to which the provisions of the Public Health (Control of Disease) Act 1984 apply.[1] The following diseases have also been made notifiable by virtue of regulation 3 of the Public Health (Infectious Diseases) Regulations 1988:[2] acquired immune deficiency syndrome (AIDS); acute encephalitis; acute poliomyelitis; meningitis; meningococcal septicaemia (without meningitis); anthrax; diphtheria; dysentery (amoebic or bacillary); paratyphoid fever; typhoid fever; viral hepatitis; leprosy; leptospirosis; measles; mumps; rubella; whooping cough; malaria; tetanus; yellow fever; ophthalmia neonatorum; scarlet fever; tuberculosis; rabies and viral haemorrhagic fever. In the case of diseases made notifiable by regulation, however, the provisions of the 1984 Act apply only to the extent specified in column 2 of Schedule 1 of the 1988 Regulations.

By an order made by a local authority, other diseases may be made notifiable in its area, but there must be specified in the order which of the provisions of the 1984 Act are to apply to each disease.[3]

28.2 CASES OF NOTIFIABLE DISEASE AND FOOD POISONING TO BE REPORTED TO THE LOCAL AUTHORITY

The duty of reporting cases – or suspected cases – of infectious disease or food poisoning is placed on medical practitioners by section 11 of the 1984 Act. If a registered medical practitioner becomes aware, or suspects, that a patient whom he is attending within the district of a local authority is suffering from a notifiable disease or from food poisoning, he shall, unless he believes, and has reasonable grounds for believing, that some other registered medical practitioner has complied with the following requirements, forthwith send to the proper officer of the local authority for that district a certificate stating:

1. the name, age and sex of the patient and the address of the premises where the patient is;
2. the disease or, as the case may be, particulars of the poisoning from which the patient is, or is suspected to be, suffering and the date, or approximate date, of its onset; and
3. if the premises are a hospital, the day on which the patient was admitted, the address of the premises from which he came there and whether or not, in the opinion of the person giving the certificate, the disease or poisoning from which the patient is, or is suspected to be, suffering was contracted in hospital.

Notification is to be made in the form set out in Schedule 2 of the 1988 Regulations, or a form substantially to like effect,[4] forms being obtainable from the local authority. Under section 12 of the 1984 Act, the Secretary of State has power to prescribe the fee payable to medical practitioners making notifications. Section 11 requires that the District Health Authority is to be notified by the officer of the local authority within 48 hours of receipt of the certificate. If, however, the certificate relates to a patient in a hospital who came from premises outside the district of the local authority and the certificate states that the patient did not contract the disease in hospital, notification is to be made to the officer for the district where the premises from which the patient came are situated. If the District Health Authority for the district in which those premises are situated is not responsible for the administration of the hospital, it too must be notified. If the premises in question are a ship or hovercraft situated within a port health district, the officer of that port health authority must be notified.

The duties under section 11 of the 1984 Act do not extend to acquired immune deficiency syndrome. The AIDS (Control) Act 1987 provides that reports shall be furnished periodically to each Regional Health Authority and to the Secretary of State, giving details of the number of persons known to the Authority/NHS trust diagnosed as having AIDS during and up to that period. The number of positive results obtained from HIV testing by that Authority must also be disclosed.

28.3 DISPOSAL OF DEAD BODIES – PRECAUTIONS AGAINST SPREAD OF INFECTION

Section 47(1) of the 1984 Act permits the Secretary of State with the concurrence of the Home Secretary to make regulations regarding the disposal of dead bodies, otherwise than by burial or cremation.

Section 48 provides that if retention of a body would endanger lives of inmates of the building or adjoining building, a justice of the peace may on a certificate to that effect from a medical practitioner in the service of the local authority make an order for its removal to a mortuary and for burial within a limited time or immediately.

Section 43 provides that if a person suffering from a notifiable disease dies in hospital and the local social services authority's proper officer or a registered medical practitioner certifies that in his opinion it is desirable, in order to prevent the spread of infection, that the body should not be removed from the hospital except for the purpose of being taken direct to a mortuary or being forthwith buried or cremated, it shall be unlawful for any person to remove the body from the hospital except for such a purpose.

Section 44 makes the person in charge of premises where there is the body of a person who has died of a notifiable disease responsible for preventing anyone from needlessly coming into contact with, or proximity to, the body.

It is an offence to hold a wake over the body of a person who has died of such a disease.

28.4   COMPULSORY REMOVAL TO HOSPITAL OF A PERSON SUFFERING FROM A NOTIFIABLE DISEASE

Section 37 allows a Justice of the Peace, if satisfied on the application of the local authority, that a person is suffering from a notifiable disease and

1. that his circumstances are such that proper precautions to prevent the spread of infection cannot be taken, or that such precautions are not being taken; and
2. that serious risk of infection is thereby caused to other persons; and
3. that accommodation for him is available in a suitable hospital vested in the Section of State or, pursuant to arrangements made by a District Health Authority (whether under an NHS contract or otherwise), in a suitable hospital vested in a NHS trust or other person;

with the consent of the District Health Authority in whose district lies the area, or the greater part of the area, of the local authority, to order him to be removed to it.

Section 38 permits a Justice of the Peace to make an order for the detention of a person suffering from a notifiable disease in a hospital for infectious diseases.

28.5   POWER OF THE SECRETARY OF STATE TO MAKE REGULATIONS GENERALLY

Under section 13 the Secretary of State may make regulations for England and Wales:

1. with a view to the treatment of persons affected with any epidemic, endemic or infectious disease and for preventing the spread of such diseases;
2. for preventing danger to public health from vessels or aircraft arriving at any place; and
3. for preventing the spread of infection by means of any vessel or aircraft leaving any place, so far as may be necessary or expedient for the purpose of carrying out any treaty, convention, arrangement or engagement with any other country.

NOTES

1. Sections 10–13, 35–38, 43–45.
2. S.I. 1988/1546.
3. Section 16.
4. Regulation 7.

CHAPTER 29

Medicines and poisons

The purpose of this chapter is to draw attention to, in outline only, those aspects of the law relating to medicines, poisons, controlled drugs and radioactive substances which are likely to concern hospitals and nursing home proprietors and members of their staffs.

29.1   MEDICINES ACT 1968

29.1.1   Introduction

The Medicines Act 1968 was designed to replace all earlier legislation relating to medicines and was based on the proposals in the White Paper entitled 'Forthcoming Legislation on the Safety, Quality and Description of Drugs and Medicines'.[1] The Act regulates the manufacture, distribution, import, export, sale and supply of medicinal products, whether for animal or human use or for the inclusion in animal feeding stuffs. These activities are controlled through a licensing system operated by Ministers under Part II of the Act and enforced by the Medicines Inspectorate. It is now necessary to interpret the provisions of the Act in the light of the European Pharmaceutical Directives (in particular Directive 65/65/EEC) as the Act, regulations made thereunder, and relevant administrative decisions, implement the Directives in accordance with the United Kingdom's Community obligations.

The 1968 Act also makes provision for the necessary registration and inspection of retail pharmacies, thereby assuring that medicines can be supplied to the public only from registered pharmacies, except such medicines which are considered reasonably safe to be sold otherwise, and are included in the General Sales List.

29.1.2   Definitions

The parts of the Act relevant to hospital and nursing home application are those concerned with supply, storage and manufacture of medicinal products and only so far as relates to such products for the conventional treatment of, and use in clinical trials on, human beings.[2] Consequently, references in the Act to medicinal products for animals and to the position of veterinary surgeons and veterinary practitioners are here generally ignored, though it may be noted that the expression 'practitioner' when used in the Act includes them as well as medical practitioners and dentists. 'Doctor' means a fully registered person within the meaning of the Medical Act 1983[3] and 'hospital' includes a clinic, nursing home or similar institution.

The definition of 'medicinal product' set out in section 130 of the Act applies to any substance which is manufactured, sold, supplied, imported[4] or exported for use, wholly or mainly for administration[4] to human beings or animals for medicinal purposes, or as an ingredient in a substance for such administration.

'Medicinal purpose'[5] means any one or more of the following:

1. treating or preventing disease;
2. diagnosing disease or ascertaining the existence, degree or extent of a physiological condition;
3. contraception;
4. inducing anaesthesia;
5. otherwise preventing or interfering with the normal operation of a physiological function.

Subject to certain exceptions the Act can be applied to any article or substance (not being an instrument, apparatus or appliance) which is not a medicinal product, but is made wholly or partly for a medicinal purpose, including such items as surgical ligatures and sutures, intra-uterine devices, contact lenses and radioactive substances. Medical device legislation will shortly be passed to implement proposed European Directives on the control of such of these related products as are not controlled by medicines legislation.

29.1.3 Application of the Act

The Medicines Act 1968 applies to businesses carried on in Scotland and Northern Ireland in addition to England and Wales and is administered by the Health and Agriculture Ministers of those countries. These Ministers comprise the licensing authority exercising regulatory functions after consultation with organisations which represent bodies likely to be affected. Advice to Ministers is provided by an appointed body, the Medicines Commission, which itself must make recommendations on the membership of four committees under section 4 to monitor the application of the Act.[6]

29.1.4 Licences

Part II of the Act is largely concerned with control of the manufacture, importation, exportation, sale and supply of medicinal products. It also provides for retail dealings by pharmacists at registered pharmacies and retail sales by other persons of medicinal products on the General Sales List.

Without the appropriate licence or certificate it is not lawful for any person, in the course of a business carried on by him, to manufacture, sell, supply, or import into the United Kingdom any of these products, unless exemption is specifically provided. An exemption relating to export applies until further notice.

Prior to 1991 the Act did not bind the Crown and was not applicable to institutions such as National Health Service hospitals which operated within the service of the Crown. However, on 1 April 1991 such Crown immunity was withdrawn and all aspects of the Medicines Act 1968 now apply.[7] This removal of Crown status brings all aspects of National Health Service hospital transactions of medicinal products into line with other businesses. It has been the cause of considerable change in pharmaceutical activity in the National Health Service.

Licences fall into the following categories:

1. product licence;
2. product licence (parallel importing);
3. manufacturer's licence;
4. wholesale dealer's licence;
5. clinical trial and animal test certificate.

Licences are issued by the licensing authority which may grant, refuse, review, suspend, revoke or vary them accordingly. Licences expire at the end of five years or such shorter period as may be specified.[8] Decisions made by the licensing authority are final and cannot be questioned, either on validity or reason by appeal to the Medicines Commission,[9] though there is an appeal to the Medicines Commission prior to the grant of a licence, as well as against subsequent revocation or suspension. Questions of validity can, however, be raised by the person 'interested' in the licence within three months by application to the High Court, but on the restricted ground that the decision is not within the powers of the Act, or that the requirements of the Act have not been satisfied.[10] Any person with locus standi may challenge the action through the courts by means of judicial review, for instance on grounds of incorrect implementation of EC law.

Product licences

Any substance manufactured or imported as a medicinal product is subject to licensing, as is any substance when sold or supplied as such.[11] The current exemption relating to exports was noted above. A product licence is required[12] by any person who:

1. imports or procures the importation of a medicinal product;
2. first sells or supplies a substance or article as a medicinal product;
3. is responsible for the composition of a medicinal product;
4. markets in the United Kingdom a 'proprietary medicinal product' under a special name and in a special pack.

Licences can be issued to:

1. sell, supply or export the product;
2. procure its sale, supply or exportation; or
3. procure its manufacture or assembly.

Application for a licence must be made according to the regulations[13] with the necessary information to assure the safety, quality and efficacy of the product.

Parallel importing

This practice involves the importation of a medicinal product which is an identical, or virtually identical, version of one already sold pursuant to a product licence in the importing country. In the present context it relates to the importation, from a member state of the European Community, of a version of a medicinal product already licensed in the United Kingdom. This has arisen because of the considerable difference in price of preparations in Europe and the allowance of modified forms of licence to cover the importation.

This modified form of licence can be provided for medicinal products which:

1. are covered by a current valid market authorisation granted in a member state;
2. have no differences of therapeutic significance from the product covered by the UK licence; and
3. must be made by, or under licence to, the UK manufacturer, or a member of the same group of companies.

Manufacturer's licence

Any person who manufactures or assembles a medicinal product is required to have a manufacturer's licence. Each product being manufactured or assembled must be the subject of a product licence, unless an exemption is allowed by the Act.[14]

The Act defines 'manufacture' but not 'preparation' and this needs further consideration for the National Health Service with the withdrawal of Crown immunity. The practical implications for the National Health Service are discussed later in this chapter. The term 'manufacture' relates to any process whereby a product is made, but does not include dissolving the preparation in, or diluting or mixing it with, some other substance used as a vehicle for administration.[15] The term 'assembly' relates to the packaging of the products in containers which are labelled before the product is sold or supplied, or the labelling of a product already enclosed in a container before the product is sold or supplied.[16]

In considering applications for the manufacture of medicinal products the licensing authority will consider:

1. the operations planned;
2. the premises to be involved;
3. the equipment to be used;
4. the qualifications of the person who will be in charge of the operations;
5. the arrangements for the maintenance and safe-keeping of necessary records.

Full information must be provided in the prescribed manner when applications are made, with a particular indication whether the licence is to cover manufacture, assembly, or both.[17]

Wholesale dealer's licence

A wholesale dealer's licence is required by any person who, in the course of a business, sells or offers for sale any medicinal products by way of wholesale dealing, or distributes any proprietary medicinal product which has been imported.[18] The term 'business' includes a professional practice and any activity carried on by a body of persons. It follows from this definition that all sales made to practitioners (whether medical or dental) for use in their practices constitute sales by way of wholesale dealing. A person holding a manufacturer's licence is exempt from holding a wholesaler's licence in order to sell those products. Likewise, a group of retailers or practitioners who buy medicinal products in bulk and divide the stock amongst themselves for resale do not normally require a licence.

When making an application for a licence the class of medicinal products to be involved must be declared together with details of premises, equipment to be used, methods of distribution and arrangements for maintenance and safe-keeping of records.[19]

Exemptions from licensing

The following exemptions from the licensing system are provided for by sections 9–17 of the Medicines Act 1968:

Doctors and dentists (section 9)

Where a doctor or dentist prepares a medicinal product for a particular patient, then such a product does not need a licence of any kind. This exemption (the so-called 'named patient' exemption) applies equally to the preparation of a medicinal product at the request of another practitioner for administration to one of his patients. There is a similar exemption from licensing for a single medicinal product (as distinct from stock) imported by a hospital or retail pharmacy business provided the sale or supply is to a doctor or dentist for administration to a particular patient. Stock of such unlicensed medicines, from which 'named patient' supply can take place, may only be imported in limited quantity and following notice to the Licensing Authority.

Nurses and midwives (section 11)

A registered nurse or registered midwife is not required to have a manufacturer's licence in order to assemble medicinal products in the course of his or her profession.

Pharmacists (section 10)

No licence of any kind is required for the following activities, provided that they are carried out by, or under the supervision of, a pharmacist in a registered pharmacy:

1. the preparation or dispensing of a medicinal product in accordance with a prescription given by a practitioner, or preparing a stock of medicinal products for this purpose;
2. the preparation or dispensing of a product for administration to a person when the pharmacist is requested to do so in accordance with his own professional judgment as to the treatment required, and that person is present at the time of the request;
3. the preparation or dispensing of a product in accordance with a specification furnished by the person to whom the product is to be sold for administration to that person, or to a person under his care;
4. the preparation of a medicinal product with a view to retail sale, provided that the sale is made from the registered pharmacy where it is prepared and is not subject to an advertisement;
5. wholesale dealing, where such dealing constitutes no more than an inconsiderable part of the business carried on at that pharmacy. This allows occasional sales to practitioners or to other pharmacists.

Chiropodists etc.

A practitioner who administers medicinal products in the course of a business of chiropody, naturopathy, osteopathy, or similar field does not require a manufacturer's licence to assemble medicinal products for human use which are on general sale. The product must be for administration to a particular patient who has requested the treatment.[20]

29.1.5 Clinical trials

Clinical trials involve an investigation or series of investigations consisting of the administration of one or more medicinal products, where there is evidence that they may be beneficial to a patient or patients by one or more doctors or dentists for the purpose of ascertaining what effects, beneficial or otherwise, are obtainable. A manufacturer's licence or product licence is not required where the product is to be used only for the purpose of the trial. However, any person wishing to carry out a clinical trial must be the holder of a clinical trial certificate (or clinical trial, or doctors and dentists, exemption) or animal test certificate, as appropriate, and the trial or test is carried out in accordance with it.[21]

Subject to certain conditions, no person may in the course of a business carried out by him either sell, procure the sale of, or procure the manufacture or assembly of a medicinal product for the purpose of a clinical trial without a product licence authorising the clinical trial, or unless a clinical trial certificate or animal test certificate, or clinical trial or doctors and dentists exemption, as appropriate, has been issued. Section 31 of the Act provides in detail for clinical trials:

'31.—(1) In this Act "clinical trial" means an investigation or series of investigations consisting of the administration of one or more medicinal products of a particular description—
  (a) by, or under the direction of, a doctor or dentist to one or more patients of his, or
  (b) by, or under the direction of, two or more doctors or dentists, each product being administered by, or under the direction of, one or other of those doctors or dentists to one or more patients of his,
where (in any such case) there is evidence that medicinal products of that description have effects which may be beneficial to the patient or patients in question and the administration of the product or products is for the purpose of ascertaining whether, or to what extent, the product has, or the products have, those or any other effects, whether beneficial or harmful.

(2) Subject to the following provisions of this Act, no person shall, in the course of a business carried on by him,—
  (a) sell or supply any medicinal product for the purposes of a clinical trial, or
  (b) procure the sale or supply of any medicinal product for the purposes of a clinical trial, or
  (c) procure the manufacture or assembly of any medicinal product for sale or supply for the purposes of a clinical trial,
unless one or other of the conditions specified in the next following subsection is fulfilled.

(3) Those conditions, in relation to a person doing any of the things specified in the preceding subsection, are—
  (a) that he is the holder of a product licence which authorises the clinical trial in question, or does it to the order of the holder of such a licence, and (in either case) he does it in accordance with that licence;
  (b) that a certificate for the purposes of this section (in this Act referred to as a

"clinical trial certificate") has been issued certifying that, subject to the provisions of the certificate, the licensing authority have consented to the clinical trial in question and that certificate is for the time being in force and the trial is to be carried out in accordance with that certificate.

(4) Subject to the following provisions of this Act, no person shall import any medicinal product for the purposes of a clinical trial unless either—

(a) he is the holder of a product licence which authorises that clinical trial or imports the product to the order of the holder of such a licence, and (in either case) he imports it in accordance with that licence, or

(b) a clinical trial certificate has been issued certifying as mentioned in subsection (3)(b) of this section and that certificate is for the time being in force and the trial is to be carried out in accordance with that certificate.

(5) Subject to the next following subsection, the restrictions imposed by the preceding provisions of this section do not apply to a doctor or dentist in respect of his selling or supplying, or procuring the sale or supply of, a medicinal product, or procuring the manufacture or assembly of a medicinal product specially prepared to his order, or specially importing a medicinal product, where (in any such case) he is, or acts at the request of, the doctor or dentist by whom, or under whose direction, the product is to be administered.

(6) The exemptions conferred by the last preceding subsection do not apply in a case where the clinical trial in question is to be carried out under arrangements made by, or at the request of, a third party (that is to say, a person who is not the doctor or dentist, or one of the doctors or dentists, by whom, or under whose direction, one or more medicinal products are to be administered in that trial).

(7) The restrictions imposed by subsection (2) of this section do not apply to anything which is done in a registered pharmacy, a hospital or a health centre and is done there by or under the supervision of a pharmacist in accordance with a prescription given by a doctor or dentist; and those restrictions do not apply to anything done by or under the supervision of a pharmacist which consists of procuring the preparation or dispensing of a medicinal product in accordance with a prescription given by a doctor or dentist, or of procuring the assembly of a medicinal product.

(8) The restrictions imposed by subsection (2) of this section also do not apply to anything done in relation to a medicinal product where—

(a) it is done by the person who, in the course of a business carried on by him, has manufactured or assembled the product, where he has manufactured or assembled it to the order of a doctor or dentist who has stated that it is required for administration to a patient of his or is required, at the request of another doctor or dentist, for administration to a patient of that other doctor or dentist, or

(b) it is done by the person who, in the course of a business carried on by him, has manufactured or assembled the product to the order of a pharmacist in accordance with a prescription given by a practitioner, or

(c) it consists of selling the product by way of wholesale dealing where it has been manufactured or assembled in the circumstances specified in paragraph (a) or paragraph (b) of this subsection.

(9) For the purposes of this section a product licence shall be taken to be a licence which authorises a particular clinical trial if—

(a) the trial is to be a trial of medicinal products of a description to which the licence relates, and

(b) the uses of medicinal products of that description which are referred to in the licence are such as to include their use for the purposes of that trial.

(10) A clinical trial certificate may certify as mentioned in subsection (3)(b) of this section without specifying the doctor or dentist (or, if there is to be more

than one, any of the doctors or dentists) by whom, or under whose direction, any medicinal product is to be administered, or the patient or patients to whom any medicinal product is to be administered.'

29.1.6 Retail sales

The retail sale of medicinal products, other than medicinal products on the General Sale List, can only take place in a retail pharmacy business duly registered with the Royal Pharmaceutical Society. Such a business may lawfully be conducted by a pharmacist (or partnership of pharmacists), a body corporate under the management of a superintendent pharmacist, or a representative of a deceased, bankrupt, or mentally ill pharmacist.[22] In effect, the business must be under the personal control of a pharmacist, whether it be the owner or a manager. Registration with the Society must be in accordance with the prescribed regulations[23] and includes payment of the annual retention fee, a separate application being necessary for each set of premises.

Part III of the Act is concerned with the regulation of dealings with medicinal products. Essentially, as set out in section 52, medicinal products may be sold or supplied by retail only from registered pharmacies, unless they are products included in the General Sales List. The provision of services under the National Health Service is regarded as carrying on a 'registered pharmacy' for the purposes of section 74 of the Act and the dispensing of a National Health Service prescription as 'supply in circumstances corresponding to retail sale'.[24] Certain medical products may only be sold or supplied from pharmacies in accordance with a prescription from an appropriate practitioner. These products are 'prescription only medicines' as provided for in section 58 of the Medicines Act 1968 and listed.[25] Other products which are not 'prescription only' or included in the General Sales List are classified as 'pharmacy medicines', in accordance with the Medicines Act 1968.[26] This group includes all medicines not included in the General Sales List or 'prescription only' list, together with certain General Sales List medicines in packs exceeding specified pack sizes.

29.1.7 General Sales List

General sales medicines are those products which are regarded as reasonably safe to be sold other than under the supervision of a pharmacist. Limits are imposed on the pack sizes of certain items when they are sold in premises other than pharmacies. Such medicines are listed pursuant to the provisions of section 51 of the Act.

29.1.8 Prescription only medicines

This group includes those medicinal products which may be sold or supplied by retail only in accordance with a prescription given by an appropriate practitioner. It follows that no person shall administer a prescription only medicine to anyone other than himself unless he is a practitioner or acting on the instructions of a practitioner.[27] There are several exemptions, including insulin, and certain injectable products which may be administered in order to save life in an emergency.

The Medicinal Products (Prescription by Nurses etc.) Act 1992, entitling nurses to prescribe independently (but not to supply medicines) was due to come into force in October 1993; but the anticipated cost of training for the exercise of this function led the Department of Health to decide in May 1993 to delay bringing the Act into force until further notice.

29.2   MISUSE OF DRUGS ACT 1971

The Misuse of Drugs Act 1971 came into operation on 1 July 1973, taking the place of the Dangerous Drugs Act 1965 and 1967 and the Drugs (Prevention of Misuse) Act 1964, all of which were repealed. The Act consolidates and extends previous legislation in controlling the export, import, production, supply and possession of drugs known as 'controlled drugs'. The Act is also designed to deal with the control and treatment of addicts and to promote education and research relative to drug dependence. The classification of controlled drugs falls into three groups (A, B and C) for the determining of penalties for offences, but into five schedules (1–5) for purposes of day-to-day control by practitioners.

29.2.1   Possession

Leaving aside the exceptional cases and classes of persons mentioned in the Misuse of Drugs Regulations 1985[28] it can be said that for all practical purposes a member of the public can be in lawful possession of a controlled drug included in Schedules 2, 3 or 4 only if he has obtained it from a retail pharmacist or from a doctor or dentist on the prescription of a practitioner. But even in accordance with above, such possession is illegal if the practitioner had been misled into doing so by any concealment or false statement.

The drugs included in Schedule 1 are controlled drugs which may not be used for medicinal purposes, their production and possession being limited, in the public interest, to purposes of research or other special purposes. Production, supply, or possession can only be performed legally with the authority of a special licence issued by the Secretary of State. This Schedule includes such drugs as cannabis, mescaline, raw opium, LSD and psilocin.

Schedule 2 includes the opiates (morphine, methadone, diamorphine) and the major stimulants (such as amphetamine). A list of persons who may lawfully possess or supply is included in the Regulations and allows certain groups of persons to possess or supply in the course of their profession or business. Such persons include:

1. a constable when acting in the course of his duty;
2. a person engaged in the business of a carrier when acting in the course of their business;
3. the sister or acting sister in charge of a ward in a hospital or nursing home;
4. a person engaged in conveying the drug to a person authorised to possess;
5. a person in charge or acting person in charge of a hospital or nursing home where there is not a pharmacist employed;
6. registered practising midwives (see below).

Schedule 3 includes barbiturates and a number of minor stimulant drugs, such as benzphetamine, and other drugs which are not thought likely to be so harmful when misused as those drugs in Schedule 2.

Schedule 4 contains the benzodiazepine tranquillisers.

Schedule 5 specifies those preparations of certain controlled drugs for which there is only a negligible risk of abuse. There is no restriction on the import, export, possession or administration of these drugs.

29.2.2 Midwives

A registered midwife may, for the practice of her profession or employment, possess and administer any controlled drug which the Medicines Act 1968 permits her to administer. Supplies may only be made to her, or possessed by her, on the authority of a 'midwife's supply order', duly signed by an appropriate medical officer. She must maintain a register in which she must enter details of each transaction of obtaining or administering the drug.[29] The delay in implementation of nurses' prescribing entitlements was mentioned above.

29.2.3 Supply

A requisition in writing must be obtained by a supplier before he can deliver any controlled drug (other than a prescription or by way of administration). The order must be signed by the recipient, who must be a person authorised to possess, and must state the total quantity of the drug.[30] A wholesale dealer when supplying a pharmacist does not need a written requisition but must be satisfied that the recipient is authorised to possess and is engaged in the profession stated.[31] Where an urgent supply is needed and the practitioner is unable to provide a written requisition, an emergency issue can be made on the understanding that a written requisition is duly provided within 24 hours.[32]

29.2.4 Prescriptions

The form of prescription for controlled drugs or medicines containing them (except those drugs in Schedules 4 and 5) and provisions for supply on prescription are the subject of regulations 15 and 16 as follows:

'**15.**—(1) Subject to the provisions of this Regulation a person shall not issue a prescription containing a controlled drug other than a drug specified in Schedule 4 or 5 unless the prescription complies with the following requirements, that is to say it shall:

- (a) be in ink or otherwise so as to be indelible and be signed by the person issuing it with his usual signature and dated by him;
- (b) in so far as it specifies the information required by subparagraphs (e) and (f) below to be specified, be written by the person issuing it in his own handwriting;
- (c) except in the case of a health prescription, specify the address of the person issuing it;
- (d) have written thereon, if issued by a dentist, the words "for dental treatment only", or if issued by a veterinary surgeon or a veterinary practitioner, a declaration that the controlled drug is prescribed for an animal or herd under his care;
- (e) specify the name and address of the person for whose treatment it is issued or, if it is issued by a veterinary surgeon or veterinary practitioner, of the person to whom the controlled drug is to be delivered;
- (f) specify the dose to be taken and—
  - (i) in the case of a prescription containing a controlled drug which is a preparation, the form and, where appropriate, the strength of the preparation, and either the total quantity (in both words and figures) of the preparation or the number (in both words and figures) of dosage units as appropriate, to be supplied;
  - (ii) in any other case, the total quantity (in both words and figures) of the controlled drug to be supplied;
- (g) in the case of a prescription for a total quantity intended to be supplied by instalments, contain a direction specifying the amount of the instalments of the total amount which may be supplied and the intervals to be observed when supplying.'

Paragraph (1)(b) shall not have effect in relation to a prescription issued by a person approved by the Secretary of State. This provision is used to facilitate the issue of prescriptions from treatment centres for drug addiction.

The requirements that (e) and (f) must be written by the person issuing the prescription in his own handwriting does not apply to a prescription for phenobarbitone or phenobarbitone sodium.

A prescription issued for the treatment of a patient in a hospital or nursing home and written on the patient's bed card or case sheet need not specify the patient's address. Where a drug is issued and administered from stock held on the ward the prescription requirements do not apply.

Regulation 16 provides that:

'**16.**—(1) A person shall not supply a controlled drug (other than those included in Schedules 4 and 5) on a prescription
  (a) unless the prescription complies with the above provisions of Regulation 15;
  (b) unless the address specified in the prescription as the address of the person issuing it is an address in the United Kingdom;
  (c) unless he either is acquainted with the signature of the person by whom it purports to be issued and has no reason to suppose that it is not genuine, or has taken reasonably sufficient steps to satisfy himself that it is genuine;
  (d) before the date specified on the prescription;
  (e) subject to paragraph (3), not later than thirteen weeks after the date specified on the prescription.

(2) Subject to paragraph (3), a person supplying on prescription a controlled drug other than a drug specified in Schedules 4 or 5 shall, at the time of the supply, mark on the prescription the date on which the drug is supplied and, unless it is a health prescription, shall retain the prescription on the premises from where the drug was supplied.

(3) In the case of a prescription containing a controlled drug other than a drug specified in Schedules 4 and 5 which contains a direction that specified instalments of the total amount may be supplied at stated intervals, the person supplying the drug shall not do so otherwise than in accordance with that direction and:
  (a) paragraph (1) shall have effect as if for the requirement contained in sub-paragraph (e) thereof there were substituted a requirement that the occasion on which the first instalment is supplied shall not be later than thirteen weeks after the date specified in the prescription.
  (b) paragraph (2) shall have effect as if for the words "at the time of the supply" there were substituted the words "on each occasion on which an instalment is supplied".'

A person is not in lawful possession of a drug if he obtained it on a prescription which he obtained from the prescriber by making a false statement or by not disclosing to the doctor that he was being supplied with a controlled drug by or on the prescription of another doctor.

29.2.5 Containers

The container in which a controlled drug, other than a preparation, is supplied must be plainly marked with the amount of drug contained. If the drug is in the form of tablets, capsules or other dosage units, the container must be marked with the amount of controlled drug in each unit and the number of dosage units. For any other kind of preparation, the container must be marked with the total amount of the preparation in it and the percentage of controlled drug in the preparation.[33]

29.2.6 Records

All transactions involving controlled drugs included in Schedule 2, covering production or supply (including administration) must be recorded in a register.[34] This requirement applies to any person authorised to supply the drugs except a sister or acting sister in charge of a ward, theatre or other department in a hospital or nursing home. A pharmacist or practitioner need not record[35] any prescribed drug returned to him for destruction. Despite this legal exemption, it is generally accepted as good practice for such records to be maintained. Entries in the register must be made in chronological sequence in the form specified in Schedule 6 of the Regulations for a register (that being a bound book and not loose leaf or card index). A separate register, or separate part of the register, must be used for each class of drugs, but the salts of any drug may be classed with the drug. Separate sections can be used, if desired, in respect of different drugs or different strengths of a drug falling within the same class. The class of drugs must be specified at the head of each page in the register and entries must be made on the day of the transaction or the next following day. No cancellation, obliteration or alteration of any entry may be made, and corrections must be by way of marginal notes or footnotes which must be dated. Every entry must be in ink or be otherwise indelible.

The register must not be used for any other purpose and must be kept at the premises to which it relates. A separate register must be kept on each set of premises.

Regulation 21 requires that a midwife authorised to have any drug specified in Schedule 2 (including pethidine) in her possession must maintain a register in which she must enter the date, name and address of the patient, together with the amount of drug obtained and its form. When administering the drug she must enter in the register the name and address of the patient, the amount administered and the form in which it was administered.

All registers and books kept in pursuance of regulation 19 or regulation 21 must be kept for a period of two years from the date on which the last entry was made, together with all orders, requisitions or prescriptions.

For controlled drugs in Schedules 3 and 5 it is sufficient to keep each invoice for two years from the date on which it was issued.

29.2.7 Destruction of controlled drugs

Persons who are required to keep records in respect of controlled drugs in Schedules 1, 2, 3 or 4 may only destroy them in the presence of a person authorised by the Secretary of State either personally or as a member of a class.[36] Among the classes of authorised persons for this purpose are police officers, inspectors of the Home Office, inspectors of the Pharmaceutical Society and, in hospitals, the Regional Pharmaceutical Officer, or the senior administrative officer of the hospital concerned.[37]

Particulars of the drugs destroyed, quantities and date must be entered in the register and signed by the authorised person witnessing the destruction. Drugs returned by patients can be destroyed without records being kept.

29.2.8 Drug addicts

Generally

The Misuse of Drugs Act 1971 and of the Misuse of Drugs (Notification of and Supply to Addicts) Regulations 1973[38] concern the obligation of doctors to give to the Chief Medical Officer of the Home Office particulars of any drug addicts they attend and restrict the authority to treat certain addicts to doctors licensed for the purpose by the Home Secretary.

The expression 'doctor', not 'medical practitioner', is used in the Act and regulations, being defined in section 37(1) of the Act as meaning 'a fully registered person within the meaning of the Medical Acts 1956 to [1983]'. Hence, a 'medical practitioner', who is not such a fully registered person, has no authority under the Act or regulations in respect of controlled drugs insofar as it depends on his being a 'doctor' within the meaning of the Act. Even where, as in regulation 9 of the Misuse of Drugs Regulations 1985, the expression used is 'practitioner', that is no help since by section 37(1) of the Act, 'practitioner' means 'a doctor, dentist, veterinary practitioner . . .', that is, in the case of a doctor, a doctor as defined in the Act.

The relevant part of section 10 of the Act reads as follows:

'**10.**—(1) Subject to the provisions of this Act, the Secretary of State may by regulations make such provisions as appears to him necessary or expedient for preventing the misuse of controlled drugs.

(2) Without prejudice to the generality of subsection (1) above, regulations under this section may in particular make provision—

(h) for requiring any doctor who attends a person who he considers, or has reasonable grounds to suspect, is addicted (within the meaning of the regulations) to controlled drugs of any description to furnish to the prescribed authority such particulars with respect to that person as may be prescribed.

(i) for prohibiting any doctor from administering, supplying and authorising the administration and supply to persons so addicted, and from prescribing for such persons, such controlled drugs as may be prescribed, except under and in accordance with the terms of a licence issued by the Secretary of State in pursuance of the regulations.'

The word 'addicted' not being defined in the Act it must be read in context as bearing the meaning ordinarily given to it when used by the medical profession. For the purposes of the Misuse of Drugs (Notification of and Supply to Addicts) Regulations 1973[38] its application has been more precisely limited in regulation 2(2) reading as follows:

'2.—(2) For the purposes of these Regulations, a person shall be regarded as being addicted to a drug if, and only if, he has as a result of repeated administration become so dependent upon the drug that he has an overpowering desire for the administration of it to be continued.'

By regulation 2(1) the expression 'drug' in the Regulations means a controlled drug specified in the Schedule thereto, viz. cocaine, dextromoramide, diamorphine, dipipanone, hydrocodone, hydromorphone, levorphanol, methadone, morphine, opium, oxycodone, pethidine, phenazocine, piritramide. Also, any stereoisomeric form of any of the foregoing substances, not being dextrorphan.

Notification of addicts

Regulation 3 of the 1973 Regulations[38] provides as follows:

'3.—(1) Subject to paragraph (2) of this Regulation, any doctor who attends a person who he considers, or has reasonable grounds to suspect, is addicted to any drug shall, within seven days of the attendance, furnish in writing to the Chief Medical Officer at the Home Office such of the following particulars with respect to that person as are known to the doctor, that is to say, the name, address, sex, date of birth and national health service number of that person, the date of the attendance and the name of the drug or drugs concerned.
(2) It shall not be necessary for a doctor who attends a person to comply with the provisions of paragraph (1) of this Regulation in respect of that person if—
  (a) the doctor is of the opinion, formed in good faith, that the continued administration of the drug, or drugs concerned is required for the purpose of treating organic disease or injury; or
  (b) the particulars which, apart from this paragraph, would have been required under those provisions to be furnished have, during the period of twelve months ending with the date of the attendance, been furnished in compliance with those provisions—
    (i) by the doctor; or
    (ii) if the doctor is a partner in or employed by a firm of general practitioners, by a doctor who is a partner in or employed by that firm; or
    (iii) if the attendance is on behalf of another doctor, whether for payment or otherwise, by that doctor; or
    (iv) if the attendance is at a hospital, by a doctor on the staff of that hospital.'

A doctor on the staff of a hospital[39] attends a person each time he sees him as a patient, whether as an in-patient or as an out-patient and so, should he consider a patient he attends on any particular occasion to be a drug addict or has reasonable grounds for suspicion that he is, the practitioner must within seven days notify the Home Office unless he or some other member of the medical staff of the hospital has notified the Home Office within the previous twelve months ending with the date of attendance and unless the drug of addiction is being medically administered or prescribed by way of treatment of organic disease or injury. If, however, the doctor has no reasonable grounds for suspicion at the time he attends him as an out-patient that a person is a drug addict but is given grounds thereafter he is under no obligation to notify the Home Office until he next attends the patient. This view was expressed by the Department of Health and Social Services in a Circular to Hospital Authorities[40] relating to the corresponding regulation under the now repealed Dangerous Drugs Acts. The Circular added: 'In practice the practitioner would no doubt forward the notification as soon as he formed the opinion that the patient was addicted without waiting for a subsequent attendance.' Even in hospital, the obligation of notification of drug addiction rests personally on the medical practitioner who attends the patient provided he or she is a doctor as defined in the Misuse of Drugs Act 1971, namely, a fully registered person within the meaning of the Medical Act 1983. Consequently, a junior doctor who on any occasion sees a patient and considers or has reasonable grounds for suspicion that he is an addict, is not relieved of his personal responsibility for notifying the Home Office by reporting his opinion or grounds for suspicion to his senior. In paragraph 9 of the Circular referred to above the position was put thus: 'Each medical practitioner who considers or has reasonable grounds to suspect that a patient he is attending is addicted within the terms of the regulations comes under a liability to notify'. The following gloss is then added: 'Hospital medical staff below consultant rank would however normally inform the consultant responsible for the patient's treatment before notifying particulars of that patient.'

No standard form of notification having been prescribed, any notification to the Home Office may be given either by letter or in such other form as the doctor sending it thinks fit. It is, however, understood that in National Health Service hospitals a standard form is generally in use.[41]

Supply to addicts

The rules generally relating to the supply of controlled drugs by doctors to patients, or by pharmacists on prescription, are to be found in the Misuse of Drugs Regulations 1985,[42] the administration and supply of the more dangerous drugs of addiction (cocaine and diamorphine and their salts and preparations containing them) by way of treatment of addiction being also subject to the provisions of regulation 4 of the

Misuse of Drugs (Notification of and Supply to Addicts) Regulations 1973, reading as follows:

'**4.**—(1) Subject to paragraph (2) of this Regulation, a doctor shall not administer or supply to a person who he considers, or has reasonable grounds to suspect, is addicted to any drug,[43] or authorise the administration or supply to such a person of, any substance specified in paragraph (3) below, or prescribe for such a person any such substance, except—

  (a) for the purpose of treating organic disease or injury; or
  (b) under and in accordance with the terms of a licence issued by the Secretary of State in pursuance of these Regulations.

(2) Paragraph (1) of this Regulation shall not apply to the administration or supply by a doctor of a substance specified in paragraph (3) below if the administration or supply is authorised by another doctor under and in accordance with the terms of a licence issued to him in pursuance of these Regulations.

(3) The substances referred to in paragraphs (1) and (2) above are—

  (a) cocaine, its salts and any preparation or other product containing cocaine or its salts other than a preparation falling within paragraph 2 of Schedule 1 to the Misuse of Drugs Regulations [1985];
  (b) diamorphine, its salts and any preparation or other product containing diamorphine or its salts.'

Application of the Misuse of Drugs (Notification of and Supply to Addicts) Regulations 1973 to the Crown

Regulation 5 provides as follows:

'**5.** These Regulations and, in relation only to the requirements of these Regulations, sections 13(1) and (3), 14, 16, 19 and 25 of and Schedule 4 to the Misuse of Drugs Act 1971 (which relate to their enforcement) shall apply to servants and agents of the Crown.'

Hence, the regulations are binding on doctors and other staff of Service and prison hospitals and also of special hospitals under section 4 of the National Health Service Act 1977 and on doctors otherwise acting as servants or agents of the Crown. They already applied to the staff of hospitals, clinics and similar institutions and facilities administered by health authorities on behalf of the Secretary of State under the provisions of the 1977 Act, and continue to do so following the removal of Crown status from health authorities by section 60 of the National Health Service and Community Care Act 1990.

29.2.9 Safe custody

In the Misuse of Drugs (Safe Custody) Regulations 1973[44] certain conditions apply to all controlled drugs except those in Schedules 4 and 5 and any liquid preparations except injections. The premises to which the requirements apply are:

1. retail pharmacies;

2. nursing homes;
3. mental nursing homes;
4. private hospitals within the meaning of the Mental Health (Scotland) Act 1960.

Within these premises, all controlled drugs are to be kept in a locked safe, cabinet or room to prevent unauthorised access to the drugs.

Apart from these special requirements, any person having possession of a controlled drug to which the safe custody regulations apply must ensure that they are kept in a locked room or receptacle which can be opened only by him or by a person authorised by him. This requirement does not apply to authorised carriers in the course of their business, or persons in possession of drugs supplied on prescription.

The definitions of 'nursing home' or 'mental nursing home' for the purposes of the Acts specified in regulation 3 are sufficiently wide to comprehend not only nursing homes conducted for profit, including so-called private hospitals, but also voluntary and co-operative hospitals and clinics. Excluded only are National Health Service hospitals and other public authority hospitals.

29.3 POISONS

The Poisons Act 1972, together with the Poisons Rules 1972[45] are concerned with the sale of poisons, which are substances included in Part I or Part II of the Poisons List which are neither medicinal products as defined under section 130 or sections 104 or 105.

29.3.1 Classification of poisons

Part I poisons are substances the sale of which is restricted to retail pharmacies. Part II poisons are substances which can be sold either in retail pharmacies or by a person whose name is entered in a local authority's list.[46] Some substances included in the Poisons List also have medicinal use and when sold as medicinal products they are controlled under the Medicines Act 1968 (for which see above.)

Except in certain circumstances, it is unlawful for a person to sell any substance which is a Part I poison unless:

1. he is lawfully conducting a retail pharmacy;
2. the sale is effected by or under the supervision of a pharmacist;
3. the sale is effected on the premises of a registered pharmacy.

It is unlawful for a person to sell a Part II poison unless:

1. he is lawfully conducting a retail pharmacy business and the sale is effected in a registered pharmacy; or

2. his name is entered in a local authority list in respect of the premises on which the poison is sold.[47]

29.3.2   Storage of poisons

Part I poisons stated on retail premises must be kept either:

1. in a cupboard or drawer reserved for poisons; or
2. in a part of the premises which are partitioned off or separated from the remainder of the premises to which customers have no access; or
3. on a shelf reserved solely for poisons.

Poisons must not be stored directly near food nor transported in a vehicle in which food is also being transported unless there is adequate separation to prevent contamination.[48]

29.3.3   Sales of poisons and records

Where sales of Part I poisons are made the purchaser must be known to the seller or be in possession of a certificate written by a person authorised to give such a certificate in the Poisons Rules.[49] Following a sale the seller must make the necessary entry in the Poisons Book and the purchaser must sign the entry. Details to be recorded include the date, name and quantity of poison sold, the purchaser's name and address, occupation or business, and the purpose for which the poison is required.[50]

The Poisons Book must be retained for two years from the date on which the last entry was made.[51] A signed order may be accepted in lieu of the purchaser's signature in certain conditions.

29.4   REMOVAL OF CROWN STATUS

On 1 April 1991, health service bodies within the National Health Service ceased to be part of the Crown upon the removal of Crown status.[52] As a result, the provisions of the Medicines Act 1968 apply equally to manufacture, preparation, distribution and sale of medicinal products within National Health Service operations. These provisions include requirements to hold product licences, manufacturers' licences, wholesaler dealers' licences, clinical trial certificates and export certificates in order to deal in medicinal products.

The removal of Crown status has caused considerable practical problems within the service and concern about the possible implications. The Medicines Act 1968 was enacted to control the manufacture, distribution and importation of medicinal products in the circumstances obtaining at that time. The manufacture of products within National Health Service hospitals, together with cross-boundary transfer of drugs between hospitals, were two common practices not covered by the Act when it was introduced, but which now come under the control of the Act following the removal of immunity.

At the time of going to press, some two years following the removal of Crown immunity, the practical application of the Medicines Act remains unclear, mainly due to its interpretation of activities within the National Health Service. The legal options for manufacture, preparation and assembly, and supply of medicinal products are therefore now discussed in outline only.

29.4.1 Manufacture

The Medicines Act defines 'manufacture' on p. 7 of the Guidance Notes[53] but not 'preparation', and this distinction is important because while 'preparation' is exempt from licensing requirements, 'manufacturing' is not. When deciding into which category a particular process falls there will be regard to:

1. the location in which the process is carried out;
2. the scale of the operation;
3. the destination of the end product.

Where *licensed* medicinal products are manufactured in a hospital pharmacy a manufacturing licence must be held and the product must be made in accordance with the terms of the product licence, by the persons holding the licence. *Unlicensed* medicinal products can be made on a hospital site for use in their hospital or other hospitals in the same District in small quantities under section 10 exemption, without the need for a manufacturer's licence. Where, however, such items are supplied to other hospitals in the same District in large quantities, a manufacturer's licence for 'specials' is needed. Where products are manufactured and supplied to other hospitals outside the District Health Authority, a manufacturer's licence is required. Where unlicensed medical products are used in a hospital there should be a clear policy, understood by all concerned, for the use of the products. Medical staff, in particular, should be fully aware that the products being used are unlicensed medicinal products.

One possible differentiation in practice between the terms 'preparation' and 'manufacturing' is the scale of preparation activity. The limits which have been suggested for preparations for stock must take account of the batch size, the number of containers in the batch, the annual demand and the shelf-life of the product. These are informal conventions which do not, as such, have legal force. Even though a licence may not be needed, an acceptable level of quality assurance is nevertheless still required and products should be made to contemporary standards of good manufacturing practice, currently contained in the *UK Guide to Good Manufacturing Practice 1983*[54] as superseded by European Directive 91/356/EEC.

Preparing and dispensing medicines for named patients is excluded from these considerations, the limits applying solely to preparing medicines for stock. The preparation for stock of all aseptically prepared products and aseptic additions including TPN, cytotoxics and CIVAS should be restricted to licensed manufacturing units, preparation for named patients being regarded as a dispensing activity and excluded from this requirement.

Suggested limits on maximum batch size for the 'preparation' of any one product made in one day to be exempt from 'manufacturing' are:

1. liquids: not more than 20 packs;
2. creams or ointments: 20 packs;
3. non-sterile topical liquids: 20 packs;
4. solid dose forms: 100 units (tablets etc.);
5. ear drops: 20 packs;
6. terminally sterilised products: 10 packs;
7. sterile topical fluids: 20 packs;
8. repackaging: 100 packs.

The demand for any of the above should not be more than one batch per month per product prepared for stock.

29.4.2 Supply

Since 1 April 1991 hospital pharmacists have been required to review their activities of sale, supply or transfer of drugs to other hospitals, businesses or practitioners, both within their own health authority and across authority boundaries. All sales, supplies or transfers must now comply with the conditions of the Medicines Act 1968 and hospital pharmacists have the opportunity to review their own local activities and obtain the necessary registration or licensing approvals.

Normal supply activities within a health authority are governed by section 55(1)(b) of the Medicines Act 1968 'in the course of the business of a hospital . . .'. Licensing and consequential exemptions from licensing requirements, such as section 10 of the Act (for which see pp. 701–703 of this chapter), regulate activities outside the normal hospital pharmacy work of dispensing to named patients and supplying to wards within the hospital.

Sales or transfer of drugs to other hospitals or practitioners, whether or not employed by the health authority, for use in their private practice, or to members of the general public, necessitate the pharmacy registering with the Royal Pharmaceutical Society as a retail pharmacy. This registration allows sales to other hospitals or practitioners up to the value of 5 per cent of the sterling value of the total of drugs purchased.

Where the sales exceed this 5 per cent value the pharmacy must register with the Royal Pharmaceutical Society to hold a wholesale dealer licence.

This is a simple account only and a number of problems remain to be resolved. One such problem is the supply of vaccines to general practitioners free of charge, this practice being accepted as one of the responsibilities of health authorities. 'Wholesaling' is defined in the Medicines Act 1968 as *selling* a medicinal product to a person who purchases for the purpose of selling, or administering in the course of business.[55] Supplying free of charge does not therefore constitute a wholesale transaction. However, if two hospitals were to *exchange* drugs, such goods could not be regarded as having been supplied free of charge and a wholesale dealer's licence would be necessary if the transfers represented a sum exceeding 5 per cent of the total annual drug turnover value.

29.5   RADIOACTIVE SUBSTANCES

The law relating to the keeping and use of radioactive materials and substances was formerly governed by a number of statutes including the Radioactive Substances Act 1948, the Radioactive Substances Act 1960 and the relevant amending provisions of the Environmental Protection Act 1990. The law so existing was complex and increasingly difficult to follow by those to whose activities it applied, and the consolidating Radioactive Substances Act 1993 was accordingly enacted. The Act, which came into force on 27 August 1993, consolidates the unrepealed sections of the 1948 Act, the amending provisions of the Act of 1990, and consists principally of updated re-enactments of the Radioactive Substances Act 1960.

The Act of 1993 governs the whole area of use and keeping of radioactive substances, and only those provisions which may impinge upon practice in hospitals are hereafter reproduced.

29.5.1   Radioactive Substances Act 1993

Application to the National Health Service

The Radioactive Substances Act 1993 regulates the keeping and use of radioactive material and makes provision for the disposal and accumulation of radioactive waste. For the purposes of the Act section 1 defines 'radioactive material' as anything which, not being waste, is either a substance to which this section applies or an article made wholly or partly from, or incorporating, such a substance. For the very detailed consequent definitions, reference should be made to the details of section 1 of the Act and to Schedule 1 to which section 1 specifically refers. Schedule 1 includes radium.

The Act applies to hospitals and associated and similar bodies which use radioactive material for therapeutic purposes. The legal position of National Health Service hospitals was originally set out in section 14 of the Act of 1960, being since replaced by section 104 of the Environmental Protection Act 1990. The 1993 Act binds the Crown, with the exception of premises occupied for military or defence purposes or for the purposes of visiting forces. The Act is in any case now binding on hospital and associated facilities within the National Health Service since the inception on 1 April 1991 of section 60 of the National Health Service and Community Care Act 1990.

Registration relating to use of radioactive material and mobile radioactive apparatus

Prohibition of use of radioactive material without registration

'6. No person shall, on any premises which are used for the purposes of an undertaking carried on by him, keep or use, or cause or permit to be kept or used, radioactive material of any description, knowing or having reasonable grounds for believing it to be radioactive material, unless either—

(a) he is registered under section 7 in respect of those premises and in respect of the keeping and use on those premises of radioactive material of that description; or

(b) he is exempted from registration under that section in respect of those premises and in respect of the keeping and use on those premises of radioactive material of that description; or

(c) the radioactive material in question consists of mobile radioactive apparatus in respect of which a person is registered under section 10 or is exempted from registration under that section.'

Registration of users of radioactive material

'7.—(1) Any application for registration under this section shall be made to the chief inspector and shall—

(a) specify the particulars mentioned in subsection (2);

(b) contain such other information as may be prescribed; and

(c) be accompanied by the prescribed fee.

(2) The particulars referred to in subsection (1)(a) are—

(a) the premises to which the application relates;

(b) the undertaking for the purposes of which those premises are used;

(c) the description or descriptions of radioactive material proposed to be kept or used on the premises, and the maximum quantity of radioactive material of each such description likely to be kept or used on the premises at any one time; and

(d) the manner (if any) in which radioactive material is proposed to be used on the premises.

(3) On any application being made under this section, the chief inspector shall, subject to directions under section 25, send a copy of the application to each local authority in whose area the premises are situated.

(4) Subject to the following provisions of this section, where an application is made to the chief inspector for registration under this section in respect of any premises, the chief inspector may either—

(a) register the applicant in respect of those premises and in respect of the keeping and use on those premises of radioactive material of the description to which the application relates; or

(b) if the application relates to two or more descriptions of radioactive material, register the applicant in respect of those premises and in respect of the keeping and use on those premises of such one or more of those descriptions of radioactive material as may be specified in the registration; or

(c) refuse the application.

(5) An application for registration under this section which is duly made to the chief inspector may be treated by the applicant as having been refused if it is not determined within the prescribed period for determinations or within such longer period as may be agreed with the applicant.

(6) Any registration under this section in respect of any premises may (subject to subsection (7)) be effected subject to such limitations or conditions as the chief inspector thinks fit, and in particular (but without prejudice to the generality of this subsection) may be effected subject to conditions of any of the following descriptions—

(a) conditions imposing requirements (including, if the chief inspector thinks fit, requirements involving structural or other alterations) in respect of any part of the premises, or in respect of any apparatus, equipment or appliance used or to be used on any part of the premises for the purposes of any use of radioactive material from which radioactive waste is likely to arise;

(b) conditions requiring the person to whom the registration relates, at such times and in such manner as may be specified in the registration, to furnish the chief inspector with information as to the removal of radioactive material from those premises to any other premises; and

(c) conditions prohibiting radioactive material from being sold or otherwise supplied from those premises unless it (or the container in which it is supplied) bears a label or other mark—
  (i) indicating that it is radioactive material, or
  (ii) if the conditions so require, indicating the description of radioactive material to which it belongs,
  and (in either case) complying with any relevant requirements specified in the conditions.

(7) In the exercise of any power conferred on him by subsection (4) or (6), the chief inspector, except in determining whether to impose any conditions falling within paragraph (b) or (c) of subsection (6), shall have regard exclusively to the amount and character of the radioactive waste likely to arise from the keeping or use of radioactive material on the premises in question.

(8) On registering a person under this section in respect of any premises, the chief inspector—

(a) shall furnish him with a certificate containing all material particulars of the registration; and

(b) subject to directions under section 25, shall send a copy of the certificate to each local authority in whose area the premises are situated.'

Mobile radioactive apparatus

Section 3 defines the meaning of 'mobile radioactive apparatus' as follows:

'**3.** In this Act "mobile radioactive apparatus" means any apparatus, equipment, appliance or other thing which is radioactive material and—

(a) is constructed or adapted for being transported from place to place; or

(b) is portable and designed or intended to be used for releasing radioactive material into the environment or introducing it into organisms.'

Section 9 prohibits the use of such apparatus without registration.

Registration is provided for by section 10 in the following terms:

'**10.**—(1) Any application for registration under this section shall be made to the chief inspector and—
  (a) shall specify—
        (i) the apparatus to which the application relates, and
        (ii) the manner in which it is proposed to use the apparatus;
  (b) shall contain such other information as may be prescribed; and
  (c) shall be accompanied by the prescribed fee.
(2) Where an application is made to the chief inspector for registration under this section in respect of any apparatus, the chief inspector may register the applicant in respect of the apparatus, either unconditionally or subject to such limitations or conditions as the chief inspector thinks fit, or may refuse the application.
(3) On any application being made the chief inspector shall, subject to directions under section 25, send a copy of the application to each local authority in whose area it appears to him the apparatus will be kept or will be used for releasing radioactive material into the environment.
(4) An application for registration under this section which is duly made to the chief inspector may be treated by the applicant as having been refused if it is not determined within the prescribed period for determinations or within such longer period as may be agreed with the applicant.
(5) On registering a person under this section in respect of any mobile radioactive apparatus, the chief inspector—
  (a) shall furnish him with a certificate containing all material particulars of the registration; and
  (b) shall, subject to directions under section 25, send a copy of the certificate to each local authority in whose area it appears to him the apparatus will be kept or will be used for releasing radioactive material into the environment.'

The section does not refer to mobile radioactive apparatus for therapeutic or diagnostic purposes.

If, however, a health authority did own mobile apparatus within section 3, seemingly it would be required to register unless exempted by order of the Secretary of State under section 11.

Disposal and accumulation are governed by sections 13 and 14, as follows:

'**13.**—(1) Subject to section 15, no person shall, except in accordance with an authorisation granted in that behalf under this subsection, dispose of any radioactive waste on or from any premises which are used for the purposes of any undertaking carried on by him, or cause or permit any radioactive waste to be so disposed of, if (in any such case) he knows or has reasonable grounds for believing it to be radioactive waste.
(2) Where any person keeps any mobile radioactive apparatus for the purpose of its being used in activities to which section 9 applies, he shall not dispose of any radioactive waste arising from any such apparatus so kept by him, or cause or permit any such radioactive waste to be disposed of, except in accordance with an authorisation granted in that behalf under this subsection.
(3) Subject to subsection (4) and to section 15, where any person, in the course of the carrying on by him of an undertaking, receives any radioactive waste for the purpose of its being disposed of by him, he shall not, except in accordance with an authorisation granted in that behalf under this subsection, dispose of

that waste, or cause or permit it to be disposed of, knowing or having reasonable grounds for believing it to be radioactive waste.

(4) The disposal of any radioactive waste does not require an authorisation under subsection (3) if it is waste which falls within the provisions of an authorisation granted under subsection (1) or (2), and it is disposed of in accordance with the authorisation so granted. . .

14.—(1) Subject to the provisions of this section and section 15, no person shall, except in accordance with an authorisation granted in that behalf under this section, accumulate any radioactive waste (with a view to its subsequent disposal) on any premises which are used for the purposes of an undertaking carried on by him, or cause or permit any radioactive waste to be so accumulated, if (in any such case) he knows or has reasonable grounds for believing it to be radioactive waste.

(2) Where the disposal of any radioactive waste has been authorised under section 13, and in accordance with that authorisation the waste is required or permitted to be accumulated with a view to its subsequent disposal, no further authorisation under this section shall be required to enable the waste to be accumulated in accordance with the authorisation granted under section 13.

(3) Subsection (1) shall not apply to the accumulation of radioactive waste on any premises situated on a nuclear site.

(4) For the purposes of this section, where radioactive material is produced, kept or used on any premises, and any substance arising from the production, keeping or use of that material is accumulated in a part of the premises appropriated for the purpose, and is retained there for a period of not less than three months, that substance shall, unless the contrary is proved, be presumed—

(a) to be radioactive waste; and
(b) to be accumulated on the premises with a view to the subsequent disposal of the substance.'

Further obligations relating to registration or authorisation

Duty to display documents

'19. At all times while—

(a) a person is registered in respect of any premises under section 7; or
(b) an authorisation granted in respect of any premises under section 13(1) or 14 is for the time being in force.

the person to whom the registration relates, or to whom the authorisation was granted, as the case may be, shall cause copies of the certificate of registration or authorisation issued to him under this Act to be kept posted on the premises, in such characters and in such positions as to be conveniently read by persons having duties on those premises which are or may be affected by the matters set out in the certificate.'

Retention and production of site or disposal records

'20.—(1) The chief inspector may, by notice served on any person to whom a registration under section 7 or 10 relates or an authorisation under section 13 or 14 has been granted, impose on him such requirements authorised by this section in relation to site or disposal records kept by that person as the chief inspector may specify in the notice.

(2) The requirements that may be imposed on a person under this section in relation to site or disposal records are—

(a) to retain copies of the records for a specified period after he ceases to carry on the activities regulated by his registration or authorisation; or

(b) to furnish the chief inspector with copies of the records in the event of his registration being cancelled or his authorisation being revoked or in the event of his ceasing to carry on the activities regulated by his registration or authorisation.

(3) In relation to authorisations under section 13 so far as the power to grant or revoke such authorisations is exercisable by the chief inspector and the appropriate Minister, references in subsections (1) and (2) of this section to the chief inspector shall be construed as references to the chief inspector and that Minister.

(4) In this section, in relation to a registration and the person registered or an authorisation and the person authorised—

"the activities regulated" by his registration or authorisation means—

(a) in the case of registration under section 7, the keeping or use of radioactive material;

(b) in the case of registration under section 10, the keeping, using, lending or hiring of the mobile radioactive apparatus;

(c) in the case of an authorisation under section 13, the disposal or radioactive waste; and

(d) in the case of an authorisation under section 14, the accumulation of radioactive waste,

"records" means records required to be kept by virtue of the conditions attached to the registration or authorisation relating to the activities regulated by the registration or authorisation, and "site records" means records relating to the condition of the premises on which those activities are carried on or, in the case of registration in respect of mobile radioactive apparatus, of any place where the apparatus is kept and "disposal records" means records relating to the disposal of radioactive waste on or from the premises on which the activities are carried on, and

"specified" means specified in a notice under this section.'

Apart from the creation of a number of specific offences (for which see below), the 'teeth' of the 1993 Act are contained in sections 21 and 22, which provide respectively for the enforcement and prohibition of the actions and activities prescribed therein.

Enforcement notices, and the conditions of their issue, are provided for by section 21 in the following terms:

'**21.**—(1) Subject to the provisions of this section, if the chief inspector is of the opinion that a person to whom a registration under section 7 or 10 relates or to whom an authorisation was granted under section 13 or 14—

(a) is failing to comply with any limitation or condition subject to which the registration or authorisation has effect; or

(b) is likely to fail to comply with any such limitation or condition,

he may serve a notice under this section on that person.

(2) A notice under this section shall—

(a) state that the chief inspector is of that opinion;

(b) specify the matters constituting the failure to comply with the limitations or conditions in question or the matters making it likely that such a failure will occur, as the case may be; and

(c) specify the steps that must be taken to remedy those matters and the period within which those steps must be taken.

(3) In the case of an authorisation granted by the chief inspector and the appropriate Minister in accordance with section 16(3), the power to issue notices under this section shall be exercisable by the chief inspector or by

that Minister as if references in subsections (1) and (2) to the chief inspector were references to the chief inspector or that Minister.

(4) Where a notice is served under this section the chief inspector or, where the notice is served by the appropriate Minister, that Minister shall—

(a) in the case of a registration, if a certificate relating to the registration was sent to a local authority under section 7(8) or 10(5); or

(b) in the case of an authorisation, if a copy of the authorisation was sent to a public or local authority under section 16(9)(b),

send a copy of the notice to that authority.'

In the event of an enforcement notice being insufficient in a particular case to avoid the risk of environmental pollution or risk of damage to human health, particularly if that risk is imminent in nature, section 22 provides for the issue of prohibition notices by the inspectorate, as follows:

'**22.**—(1) Subject to the provisions of this section, if the chief inspector is of the opinion, as respects the keeping or use of radioactive material or of mobile radioactive apparatus, or the disposal or accumulation of radioactive waste, by a person in pursuance of a registration or authorisation under this Act, that the continuing to carry on that activity (or the continuing to do so in a particular manner) involves an imminent risk of pollution of the environment or of harm to human health, he may serve a notice under this section on that person.

(2) A notice under this section may be served whether or not the manner of carrying on the activity in question complies with any limitations or conditions to which the registration or authorisation in question is subject.

(3) A notice under this section shall—

(a) state the chief inspector's opinion;

(b) specify the matters giving rise to the risk involved in the activity, the steps that must be taken to remove the risk and the period within which those steps must be taken; and

(c) direct that the registration or authorisation shall, until the notice is withdrawn, wholly or to the extent specified in the notice cease to have effect.

(4) Where the registration or authorisation is not wholly suspended by the direction given under subsection (3), the direction may specify limitations or conditions to which the registration or authorisation is to be subject until the notice is withdrawn.

(5) In the case of an authorisation granted by the chief inspector and the appropriate Minister in accordance with section 16(3), the power to issue and withdraw notices under this section shall be exercisable by the chief inspector or by the appropriate Minister as if references in subsections (1) and (3) to the chief inspector were references to the chief inspector or that Minister.

(6) Where a notice is served under this section the chief inspector or, where the notice is served by the appropriate Minister, that Minister shall—

(a) in the case of a registration, if a certificate relating to the registration was sent to a local authority under section 7(8) or 10(5); or

(b) in the case of an authorisation, if a copy of the authorisation was sent to a public or local authority under section 16(9)(b),

send a copy of the notice to that authority.

(7) The chief inspector or, where the notice was served by the appropriate Minister, that Minister shall, by notice to the recipient, withdraw a notice under this section when he is satisfied that the risk specified in it has been removed; and on so doing he shall send a copy of the withdrawal notice to any public or local authority to whom a copy of the notice under this section was sent.'

Rights of entry

Rights of entry and inspection are given by section 31 of the Act, and further provided for in Schedule 2, to appointed inspectors and other authorised persons:

0'31.—(1) Any person who is either an inspector appointed under section 4 or a person authorised in that behalf by the Secretary of State (in this section referred to as an "inspector") may, for the purposes of the execution of this Act,—

(a) enter, at any reasonable time or, in an emergency, at any time, upon any premises to which this subsection applies, with such equipment as the inspector may require;

(b) carry out such tests (including dismantling and subjecting to any process) and inspections and take such photographs on any such premises, and obtain and take away such samples from the premises, as the inspector may consider necessary or expedient;

(c) give directions that the whole or any part of such premises, or anything in them, be left undisturbed for so long as is reasonably necessary for the purpose of any tests or inspections; and

(d) require the occupier of any such premises, or any person with duties on or in connection with the premises, to provide the inspector with such facilities and assistance and such information relating to the use of the premises, or to permit him to inspect such documents relating thereto, as the inspector may require, and in the case of answers to his questions, to sign a declaration of the truth of the answers.

(2) Subsection (1) applies—

(a) to any premises in respect of which a person is for the time being registered under section 7;

(b) to any premises in respect of which a person is exempted from such registration by section 8(1); and

(c) to any premises in respect of which an authorisation granted under section 13(1) or 14 is for the time being in force. . .

(4) Where an inspector has reasonable grounds for believing—

(a) that radioactive material has been or is being kept or used on any premises to which subsection (1) does not apply; or

(b) that radioactive waste has been or is being disposed of or accumulated on or from any such premises,

the inspector may exercise, in relation to those premises, any of the powers which are conferred by subsection (1) in relation to premises to which that subsection applies, but this subsection has effect subject to subsection (6) unless the premises fall within subsection (7).

(5) Any person authorised in that behalf by the Secretary of State may at any reasonable time enter upon any premises for the purpose of disposing of radioactive waste in the exercise of the powers conferred by section 30, but this subsection has effect subject to subsection (6) unless the premises fall within subsection (7).

(6) Subject to subsection (7), no power shall be exercisable by virtue of subsection (4) or (5) in respect of any premises except—

(a) with consent given by or on behalf of the occupier of the premises; or

(b) under the authority of a warrant granted under the provisions of Schedule 2; or

(c) where entry is required in a case of emergency.

(7) Subsection (6) does not apply in respect of—

(a) premises in respect of which—

(i) a person has been (but is no longer) under section 7, or

(ii) an authorisation has been (but is no longer) in force under section 13(1) or 14; or

(b) premises on which there are reasonable grounds for believing that mobile radioactive apparatus has been or is being kept or used.

(8) In England, subject to section 6(3) of the Atomic Energy Authority Act 1954, any person who is either an inspector appointed under section 5 of this Act or a person authorised in that behalf by the Minister of Agriculture, Fisheries and Food may, for the purposes of the execution of this Act in relation to any premises situated on a nuclear site, exercise in relation to any such premises (but not in relation to any other premises) any of the powers conferred by paragraphs (a) to (d) of subsection (1) of this section, as if references in those paragraphs to an inspector included a reference to a person appointed or authorised as mentioned in this subsection.

(9) An inspector appointed under section 4 or 5 shall not be liable in any civil or criminal proceedings for anything done in the purported exercise of his powers under this section if the court is satisfied that the act was done in good faith and that there were reasonable grounds for doing it.

(10) The provisions of Schedule 2 shall have effect for the purposes of this section.

(11) In this section any reference to a case of emergency is a reference to a case where a person requiring entry to any premises in pursuance of this section has reasonable cause to believe—
  (a) that circumstances exist which are likely to endanger life or health; and
  (b) that immediate entry to the premises is necessary to verify the existence of those circumstances or to ascertain their cause or to effect a remedy.

(12) In the application of this section to Northern Ireland—
  (a) references to the Secretary of State shall have effect as references to the Department of the Environment for Northern Ireland; and
  (b) subsection (8) shall apply as it applies in England, but as if the reference to the Minister of Agriculture, Fisheries and Food were a reference to the Department of Agriculture for Northern Ireland.'

Offences

Offences relating to registration or authorisation

'32.—(1) Any person who—
  (a) contravenes section 6, 9, 13(1), (2) or (3) or 14(1); or
  (b) being a person registered under section 7 or 10, or being (wholly or partly) exempted from registration under either of those sections, does not comply with a limitation or condition subject to which he is so registered or exempted; or
  (c) being a person to whom an authorisation under section 13 or 14 has been granted, does not comply with a limitation or condition subject to which that authorisaiton has effect; or
  (d) being a person who is registered under section 7 or 10 or to whom an authorisation under section 13 or 14 has been granted, fails to comply with any requirement of a notice served on him under section 21 or 22,
shall be guilty of an offence.

(2) A person guilty of an offence under this section shall be liable—
  (a) on summary conviction, to a fine not exceeding £20,000 or to imprisonment for a term not exceeding six months, or both;
  (b) on conviction on indictment, to a fine or to imprisonment for a term not exceeding five years, or both.'

Offences relating to ss.19 and 20

'33.—(1) Any person who contravenes section 19 shall be guilty of an offence and liable—

(a)   on summary conviction, to a fine not exceeding the statutory maximum;

(b)   on conviction on indictment, to a fine.

(2) Any person who without reasonable cause pulls down, injures or defaces any document posted in pursuance of section 19 shall be guilty of an offence and liable on summary conviction to a fine not exceeding level 2 on the standard scale.

(3) Any person who fails to comply with a requirement imposed on him under section 20 shall be guilty of an offence and liable—

(a)   on summary conviction, to a fine not exceeding the statutory maximum or to imprisonment for a term not exceeding three months, or both;

(b)   on conviction on indictment, to a fine or to imprisonment for a term not exceeding two years, or both.'

NOTES

1. 1966–67, Cmnd 3395.
2. That is to say, Parts II, III, IV (since the removal of Crown Status from National Health Service bodies by section 60 of the National Health Service and Community Care Act 1990), Part V; Part VIII (miscellaneous provisions).
3. Medicines Act 1968, section 132(1); and see the Medical Act 1983, Part III.
4. Including the administration of a substance containing a 'medicinal product' so defined: Medicines Act 1968, section 130(1)(b). At present administration to healthy volunteers (e.g. to obtain pharmacokinetic data) is not administration for a medicinal purpose and is therefore outside the controls of the Act.
5. Medicines Act 1968, section 130(2).
6. See the Medicines Act 1968, particularly section 4(3)(a) and (b).
7. National Health Service and Community Care Act 1990, section 60.
8. Medicines Act 1968, section 24(1).
9. Medicines Act 1968, section 107(1).
10. Medicines Act 1968, section 107(2).
11. 'Product licence' has the meaning assigned to it in sections 7 and 8 of the Medicines Act 1968: see section 132(1).
12. Medicines Act 1968, section 7.
13. See the Medicines (Application for Product Licences and Clinical Trial and Animal Test Certificates) Regulations 1971, SI 1971/973, as amended by SI 1972/1201, SI 1975/681, SI 1977/1051, SI 1979/1760, SI 1983/1726 and SI 1992/755; and the Medicines (Renewal Applications for Licences and Certificates) Regulations 1974, SI 1974/832, as amended by SI 1977/180, SI 1982/1789 and SI 1992/755.
14. Medicines Act 1968, section 8(1) and (2).
15. Medicines Act 1968, section 132(1).
16. Medicines Act 1968, section 132(1).
17. Medicines (Application for Manufacturer's and Wholesale Dealer's Licences) Regulations 1971, SI 1971/974, as amended by SI 1977/1052, SI 1983/1725 and SI 1978/1140.
18. Medicines Act 1968, section 8(3); see also section 131 (definition of terms).
19. See references in note 17, above.
20. See the Medicines (Exemption from Licences) (Assembly) Order 1979, SI 1979/1114, article 2.
21. Medicines Act 1968, sections 31(3)(b); and see the Medicines (Exemption from Licences) (Clinical Trials) Order 1981, SI 1981/164, and the Medicines (Exemption from Licences) (Special Cases and Miscellaneous Provisions) Order 1972, SI 1972/1200.
22. Medicines Act 1968, sections 70–72; and see SI 1987/2203, article 3.

23. Medicines Act 1968, section 75.
24. Medicines Act 1968, section 131(4).
    25. Medicines Act 1968, section 58.
26. Medicines Act 1968, section 60.
27. Medicines Act 1968, section 58(2)(b). The Medicines (Products Other Than Veterinary Drugs) (Prescriptions Only) Order 1983 (SI 1983/1212, as amended) provides for the injectable exception mentioned (article 5); but also provides (article 7) that the restrictions imposed by section 58(2)(b) shall not apply to the administration to human beings of a prescription only medicine which is not for parenteral use.
28. SI 1985/2066.
29. Misuse of Drugs Regulations 1985 (SI 1985/2066), regulations 11 and 21.
30. Regulation 14(2).
31. Regulation 14(1).
32. Regulation 14(2).
33. Regulation 18.
34. Regulations 19 and 20.
35. Regulation 19(3).
36. Regulation 26(1).
37. The standard and professionally appropriate practice is for the hospital to invite the attendance of inspectors of the Pharmaceutical Society, given their expertise. Senior administrative hospital officers, though authorised, are seldom – if ever – involved in the statutory process of destruction.
38. SI 1973/799, as amended by SI 1983/1909.
39. The expression 'hospital' in respect of England and Wales now has the same meaning as in the National Health Service Acts and includes a nursing home and mental nursing home within the meaning of the Registered Homes Act 1984 and a special hospital within the meaning of the National Health Service Act 1977.
40. HM(68)6, paragraph 6.
41. See HM(68)6, paragraph 7.
42. SI 1985/2066 amended SI 1986/2330, SI 1988/916, SI 1989/1460 and SI 1990/2630.
43. That is, any controlled drug specified in the Schedule to the Regulations; see SI 1973/799.
44. SI 1973/798 as amended by SI 1974/1449, SI 1975/294, SI 1985/2067 and SI 1986/2332.
45. Poisons Rules 1982, SI 1982/218, as amended by the Poisons (Amendment) Rules 1985, SI 1985/1077, SI 1986/10, SI 1986/1704 and SI 1989/112 and see HSG(93)18.
46. Poisons Act 1972, section 3.
47. Poisons Act 1972, section 3.
48. See SI 1982/218, rule 21.
49. Poisons Act 1972, section 3, and SI 1982/218, rule 25.
50. Poisons Act 1972, section 3(2)(b).
51. Regulation 27.
52. National Health Service and Community Care Act 1990, section 60.
53. Medicines Act 1968, section 132(1). See also Medicines Act Leaflet (MAL) 5, ref. B/M272/72 (August 1971), page 7.
54. Good Manufacturing Practice (GMP) was published as the 'orange guide' (*Guide to Good Manufacturing Practice 1983*. HMSO, ISBN 0 11 320832 4), which has not been updated. It is now published as an EC guide: *The Rules Governing Medicinal Products in the European Community. Volume IV: Guide to good manufacturing practice for medicinal products*. Revised 1992. Office for Official Publications of the European Communities, ISBN 92–826–3180–X.
55. Medicines Act, 1968, section 131.

CHAPTER 30

Mental health law

30.1 THE PURPOSE OF THE MENTAL HEALTH ACT 1983

The great majority of people who are treated in hospital for mental disorder receive treatment on an informal, voluntary basis and are just as subject to the ordinary common law as patients receiving treatment for physical disorder. Likewise, the great majority of admissions to psychiatric and other hospitals for the treatment of mental disorder are arranged in an informal and unforced manner. Typical statistics[1] indicate that approximately one in every ten hospital admissions for reasons of mental disorder is arranged on a compulsory basis, and that at any given time only about 6 to 7 per cent of bed occupancy in hospitals for mental illness and learning disability combined is represented by patients detained there under legal powers. Some patients detained in hospital under compulsory powers for the treatment of their mental disorder may have medical treatment for mental disorder imposed on them, if need be by physical force, if they do not or cannot consent to such treatment. Nevertheless the Mental Health Act 1983 provides opportunity for the giving of real consent of even a longer term detained patient to proposed treatment, as the alternative to compulsion.

Given that the great majority of hospital admissions for the treatment of mental disorder, together with such treatment itself, are arranged on an informal, uncompelled basis, it is necessary to consider the legal entitlements of those patients, as well as the legal responsibilities of those caring for them and treating them, under the appropriate headings found elsewhere in this book. In particular, the law relating to consent to treatment, and judicial decisions governing the practical content of the duty of care to give information about risks in treatment, apply equally to patients informally receiving care and treatment for mental disorder as they do to patients receiving treatment and care for physical disorders in general hospitals. Indeed, the entitlement of detained, as well as informal, patients receiving care and treatment for mental disorder to the exercise of proper professional skill and competence, and to reasonable care for the safety of the systems by which, and the premises on which, they are treated are exactly the same in general terms whatever the nature of the treatment and irrespective of detained or informal status.

Much of the law relating to the care and treatment of mental disorder is accordingly to be found elsewhere than in the Mental Health Act 1983, its accompanying Regulations and associated sources. Conversely, even though that minority of patients who are detained under the mental health legislation have certain entitlements of ordinary law taken from them, extra protections in other directions are put in their place. For instance, complaints may be made not only under the ordinary complaints machinery (discussed in Chapter 8), but in addition a special set of entitlements is given under section 120 of the Mental Health Act 1983 to have the complaint investigated by the watchdog body, the Mental Health Act Commission. Moreover, the managers (being the appropriate members of the health authority or trust pursuant to the 1983 Act) of a hospital in which the patient is detained have a statutory obligation to do all they can to make sure that the detained patient knows and understands the nature and consequences in law of that detention. Such is the requirement of section 132 of the Mental Health Act 1983, discussed on pp. 842–844 of this chapter.

It is against this introductory background that the initial provision of the Mental Health Act 1983 (henceforth referred to in this chapter as 'the Act') must be understood. Section 1(1) provides:

'1.—(1) The provisions of this Act shall have effect with respect to the reception, care and treatment of mentally disordered patients, the management of their property and other related matters.'

Lest it be imagined that the Act makes any provision in relation to duties of care, standards of practice or quality of treatment, it is important to note carefully the way in which the words 'care and treatment' are couched in this provision. The Act lays down certain categorical duties, such as the duty upon social services departments to provide a sufficient number of approved social workers to function under powers given by the Act; the duty of managers under section 132 to take all practicable steps to ensure the understanding by a detained patient of the legal status and consequences of detention; the duty of the Mental Health Act Commission to make arrangements to visit and interview detained patients in private, and to investigate complaints; and, in addition, other duties which will be noted and explained in this chapter.

The Act, however, says nothing about standards of practice or quality of service provision. Its overriding objective, in simple terms, is through the understanding and implementation of certain requisite procedures to render lawful that which either would, or might, otherwise be unlawful. To detain a person against his will would, in the absence of either specific statutory powers (for instance, to effect an arrest) or common law powers such as the power to prevent physical harm to oneself or to another, be likely to amount to the actionable wrong of false imprisonment. Likewise, it would as a general principle amount to another form of trespass to the person, namely battery, to administer treatment in the absence of consent.

While the Mental Health Act 1959 presented, in broadly similar form to that contained in the 1983 Act, a system for health professionals, usually in combination with each other, to effect a lawful detention of a person suffering or thought to be suffering from mental disorder, no specific powers to impose treatment were contained in the 1959 Act. Remarkably, legal uncertainty as to the compellability of treatment for mental disorder in the absence of consent persisted for nearly a quarter of a century after the coming into operation of the Mental Health Act 1959. The 1983 Act contains, in Part IV, a system of checks and balances to effect compulsory treatment for mental disorder in the absence of consent. Some major treatments cannot be enforced under any circumstances and depend upon consent for their legality. The requirements and practical implications of Part IV of the Act are discussed at pp. 802–818 of this chapter.

In addition to the provisions of section 131(1) of the Act, which preserves what is in fact the normal case of informal admission to hospitals or mental nursing homes, there is a further provision of the Act which applies not only to mental nursing homes in the private sector but also to any National Health Service hospital providing accommodation for in-patients. That is the holding power provided by section 5(2) of the Act, entitling any registered medical practitioner in charge of the treatment of an in-patient to impose a holding power for up to 72 hours if he or she is of the opinion 'that an application ought to be made' under Part II of the Act for the formal admission of a patient to (that is, detention under section 2 or section 3 in) hospital. Whereas not all medical practitioners in health services other than those catering for mental disorder are aware of the existence of this power, it is a power which effectively makes a significant part of the Act applicable in *any* hospital. This is the case, whether or not that hospital has a psychiatric unit attached to it. The conditions for the application of the section 5(2) holding power, together with legal and good practice restrictions on its use, are discussed on pp. 757–761 of this chapter. There is also a short-term holding power given to nurses in the event of such a medical practitioner not being immediately available; but it should be noted that the nurse's holding power applies only to facilities in which the patient in question is being treated as an in-patient for mental disorder. The holding power given by section 5(2) to registered medical practitioners in charge of the treatment of the patient, even in a general hospital, could be a vital adjunct to assessment and management of risk in the type of case (discussed in pp. 179–180 of Chapter 6) in which it becomes advisable or necessary to assess or treat a patient for mental disorder who is already an in-patient on a non-psychiatric ward of a hospital. Legal liability could result from a negligent failure to implement this power.

30.2 LEGAL DEFINITIONS FOR THE PURPOSE OF COMPULSORY POWERS

Not all detained patients are subject to the rules and procedures relating to medical treatment for mental disorder given without consent. Moreover, the holding powers indicated above, together with powers under sections 135 and 136 of the Act to remove a person from the place where they are to a place of safety within the meaning of the Act, are not formal admission (detention) powers at all. They are, rather, powers to effect a particular purpose, namely to translate the immediate situation in which risk is presented into one in which compulsory detention and possibly treatment powers are able to be considered within the statutory entitlements given by the Act to health and social services professionals. It is therefore necessary to have a legal definition of 'mental disorder' in order that the abnormality or difference so described can legitimise actions which might otherwise be actionable wrongs and even criminal offences against the individual considered to be disordered.

'Mental disorder', without the need to be any more specific, may be a ground for the formal admission of a person for assessment for a period of up to 28 days, pursuant to section 2 of the Act. As will be seen in pp. 813–814 of this chapter, a person suffering from no more specific a condition than 'mental disorder' may be subjected to medical treatment in the absence of consent, pursuant to Part IV of the Act. A person who is receiving in-patient treatment for mental disorder is (potentially) subject to the nurse's holding power provided by section 5(4) of the Act; and the expression 'mental disorder' does not even appear in the doctor's holding power provided by section 5(2), it being sufficient that the registered medical practitioner in charge of the treatment of the patient be satisfied that an application ought to be made for admission of the patient to hospital. Of course, if and when such formal admission is decided upon, mental disorder (unspecified) may furnish part of the grounds for such admission. Under sections 135 and 136 of the Act ('place of safety' orders) the fact that a person appears to be (section 136), or is reasonably suspected to be (section 135) suffering from mental disorder is an essential ground for implementing such an order. For the purpose of Part VII of the Act, relating to the management of property and affairs of patients and in particular the Court of Protection, the functions of that court are exercisable where, after considering medical evidence, the court 'is satisfied that a person is incapable, by reason of mental disorder, of managing and administering his property and affairs'.

Section 1(2) of the Act defines (or at least describes) 'mental disorder' as follows:

' "Mental disorder" means mental illness, arrested or incomplete development of mind, psychopathic disorder and any other disorder or disability of mind and "mentally disordered" shall be construed accordingly.'

It is immediately apparent that this 'definition' is incomplete in both the legal and the clinical sense. In law, this broad meaning of mental disorder is simply one (albeit vital) element in the decision of health professionals to consider the exercise of lawful detention powers. It is very much an umbrella term. From the clinical point of view, the 'definition' of mental disorder says nothing about the presentation of any such disorder or set of disorders, and it is a matter of professional judgment whether or not mental disorder exists, as is the decision whether or not to do anything about it under legal powers. The 'definition' is, of course, incomplete from the clinical point of view, given that psychiatric and clinical psychological treatment will define their respective objects in much more specific terms. Nevertheless, the simple concept of mental disorder is sufficient to achieve the various objectives noted above and serves as a basis for the implementation of legal powers if those to whom the powers are given reasonably consider it to be present.

30.3 THE ACT AND THE COMMON LAW: THE 'SPIRIT OF THE ACT'

Although the precise practical meaning of powers, duties and responsibilities under the Act is at times unclear, there is no doubt that the Mental Health Act 1983 is designed in such a way as to permit lawful intervention with personal liberty and freedom only so far as that intervention is specifically permitted by law.[2] While, therefore, the various procedures to be described in this chapter relating to elements of detention and compulsory treatment powers say nothing about the practical content of care standards and quality of service provision, the procedures are required if intervention of the various types provided for is to be lawful. In other words, the substantive legal position of individuals, including both patients and health professionals, is altered by the implementation of legal procedures provided by the Act. While there is no legal duty as much to detain, or to compel the treatment of, any individual the procedures prescribed the Act are essential if either or both objectives are to be lawfully achieved. While the Act provides for certain protections against what would otherwise be legal liability for trespass to the person, namely in the rectification of certain deficient admission documents as well as in various protections given to actions which 'purport' to be done pursuant to the Act, there is no general principle that acting in the best interests of a mentally disordered person is for that reason alone lawful.

In the case of *R v Hallstrom and another, ex parte W (No. 2)* (1986)[3] Mr Justice McCullough said:

> 'There is . . . no canon of construction which presumes that Parliament intended that people should, against their will, be subjected to treatment which others, however professionally competent, perceive, however sincerely and however correctly, to be in their best interests. What there is is a canon of construction that Parliament is presumed not to enact legislation which interferes with the liberty of the subject without making it clear that this was its intention. It goes without saying that, unless clear statutory authority to the contrary exists, no one is to be detained in hospital or to undergo medical treatment or even to submit himself to a medical examination without his consent. That is as true of a mentally disordered person as of anyone else.'

Furthermore, a person who has been detained under the Mental Health Act 1983 must be discharged as soon as he is found no longer to be suffering from mental disorder: *Kynaston v Secretary of State for Home Affairs* (1981).[4]

The expression 'spirit of the Act' is sometimes encountered in discussions of the manner in which legal powers provided for by the Mental Health Act 1983 should be implemented in practice, if at all. If 'spirit of the Act' were to refer to the tension, and compromise, between the preservation of civil liberties and the making available of appropriate treatment, then the expression would be harmless enough. Occasionally, however, the expression is quoted in aid of some such principle as that powers of detention and compulsion should be used according to 'the least restrictive alternative' available in the circumstances. In such a context the expression adds little, if anything, to arguments towards good practice and could in fact lead, in ignorance of decided cases on liability for the assessment and management of risk, to practical difficulties and even to litigation. The expression 'in the spirit of the Act' is apt to be used to draw attention away from cross-professional differences of opinion (in particular, between approved social workers and psychiatrists) when these differences ought more appropriately to be addressed on their own practical and professional merits, as distinct from invoking some spurious justification for professional action which is claimed to lie 'between the lines' of the Act of Parliament.

30.4   FORMAL ADMISSION (DETENTION) UNDER PART II
OF THE ACT

30.4.1   Admission for assessment

Section 2 of the Act provides for the compulsory admission of a person
to hospital for assessment, or for assessment followed by treatment, on
the basis of medical grounds no more specific than the diagnosis of
mental disorder. Section 2 provides as follows:

'2.—(1) A patient may be admitted to a hospital and detained there for the
period allowed by subsection (4) below in pursuance of an application (in this
Act referred to as "an application for admission for assessment") made in
accordance with sub-sections (2) and (3) below.

(2) An application for admission for assessment may be made in respect of a
patient on the grounds that
  (a) he is suffering from mental disorder of a nature or degree which warrants
       the detention of the patient in a hospital for assessment (or for
       assessment followed by medical treatment) for at least a limited period;
       and
  (b) he ought to be so detained in the interests of his own health or safety or
       with a view to the protection of other persons.

(3) An application for admission for assessment shall be founded on the
written recommendations in the prescribed form of two registered medical
practitioners, including in each case a statement that in the opinion of the
practitioner the conditions set out in subsection (2) above are complied with.

(4) Subject to the provisions of section 29(4) below, a patient admitted to
hospital in pursuance of an application for admission for assessment may be
detained for a period not exceeding 28 days beginning with the day on which he
is admitted, but shall not be detained after the expiration of that period unless
before it has expired he has become liable to be detained by virtue of a
subsequent application, order or direction under the following provisions of this
Act.'

It is sometimes forgotten by applicant social workers who are
considering the appropriateness of the formal admission of a client to
hospital for care and treatment, or simply for assessment, that the
'health' ground alone (in addition to the other required factors) can
suffice for admission, independently of any element of 'danger'.

Section 29(4) provides for an extended time limit for the imposition of
lawful detention under section 2 in a particular case, namely when a
county court is considering an application to displace the patient's
nearest relative when an objection is made by that person to longer term
(namely section 3) detention. This being a matter more appropriate for
discussion in relation to the other provisions of admission for treatment
under section 3 of the Act, comment is reserved until p. 748 of this
chapter.

Section 11(1) provides that an application for admission for assessment under section 2 of the Act may be made either by the nearest

relative of the patient (that is, the person whom it is sought to detain) or by an approved social worker. Every such application shall specify the qualification of the applicant to make the application; in the case of the nearest relative, namely that the relationship is indeed the nearest within the meaning of section 26 of the Act, or that the social worker is indeed approved as having special knowledge and experience of the care and treatment of mental disorder.

30.4.2 The nearest relative

In relation to 'nearest relative', section 26 of the Act provides as follows:

'**26.**—(1) In this Part of this Act "relative" means any of the following persons:
    (a) husband or wife;
    (b) son or daughter;
    (c) father or mother;
    (d) brother or sister;
    (e) grandparent;
    (f) grandchild;
    (g) uncle or aunt;
    (h) nephew or niece.
(2) In deducing relationships for the purposes of this section, any relationship of the half-blood shall be treated as a relationship of the whole blood, and an illegitimate person shall be treated as the legitimate child of his mother.
(3) In this Part of this Act, subject to the provision of this section and to the following provisions of this Part of this Act, the 'nearest relative' means the person first described in sub-section (1) above who is for the time being surviving, relatives of the whole blood being preferred to relatives of the same description of the half-blood and the elder or eldest of two or more relatives described in any paragraph of that subsection being preferred to the other or others of those relatives, regardless of sex.
(4) Subject to the provisions of this section and to the following provisions of this Part of this Act, where the patient ordinarily resides with or is cared for by one or more of the relatives (or, if he is for the time being an in-patient in a hospital, he last ordinarily resided with or was cared for by one or more of his relatives) his nearest relative shall be determined—
    (a) by giving preference to that relative or those relatives over the other or others; and
    (b) as between two or more such relatives, in accordance with subsection (3) above.
(5) Where the person who, under subsection (3) or (4) above, would be the nearest relative of a patient—
    (a) in the case of a patient ordinarily resident in the United Kingdom, the Channel Islands or the Isle of Man, is not so resident; or
    (b) is the husband or wife of the patient, but is permanently separated from the patient, either by agreement or under an order of a court, or has deserted or has been deserted by the patient for a period which has now come to an end; or
    (c) is a person other than the husband, wife, father or mother of the patient, and is for the time being under 18 years of age;
the nearest relative of the patient shall be ascertained as if that person were dead.

(6) In this section "husband" and "wife" include a person who is living with the patient as the patient's husband or wife as the case may be (or, if the patient is for the time being an in-patient in a hospital, was so living until the patient was admitted), and has been or had been so living for a period of not less than six months; but a person shall not be treated by virtue of this subsection as the nearest relative of a married patient unless the husband or wife of the patient is disregarded by virtue of paragraph (b) of subsection (5) above.

(7) A person, other than a relative, with whom the patient ordinarily resides (or, if the patient is for the time being an in-patient in a hospital, last ordinarily resided before he was admitted), and with whom he has or had been ordinarily residing for a period of not less than five years, shall be treated for the purposes of this Part of this Act as if he were a relative but —

(a) shall be treated for the purposes of subsection (3) above as if mentioned last in subsection (1) above; and

(b) shall not be treated by virtue of this subsection as the nearest relative of a married patient unless the husband or wife of the patient is disregarded by virtue of paragraph (b) of subsection (5) above.'

30.4.3 Approved social workers

In relation to approved social workers, section 114 of the Act provides:

'**114.**—(1) A local social services authority shall appoint a sufficient number of approved social workers for the purpose of discharging the functions conferred on them by this Act.

(2) No person shall be appointed by a local social services authority as an approved social worker unless he is approved by the authority as having appropriate competence in dealing with persons who are suffering from mental disorder.

(3) In approving a person for appointment as an approved social worker a local social services authority shall have regard to such matters as the Secretary of State may direct.'

For such directions, reference should be made to Local Authority Circular LAC(86)15.

30.4.4 Medical recommendations

In relation to the medical recommendations for detention under section 2 of the Act, section 12 provides:

'**12.**—(1) The recommendations required for the purposes of an application for the admission of a patient under this Part of this Act (in this Act referred to as "medical recommendations") shall be signed on or before the date of the application, and shall be given by practitioners who have personally examined the patient either together or separately, but where they have examined the patient separately not more than five days must have elapsed between the days on which the separate examinations took place.

(2) Of the medical recommendations given for the purposes of any such application, one shall be given by a practitioner approved for the purposes of this section by the Secretary of State as having special experience in the diagnosis or treatment of mental disorder; and unless that practitioner has

previous acquaintance with the patient, the other such recommendation shall, if practicable, be given by a registered medical practitioner who has such previous acquaintance.

(3) Subject to subsection (4) below, where the application is for the admission of the patient to a hospital which is not a mental nursing home, one (but not more than one) of the medical recommendations may be given by a practitioner on the staff of that hospital, except where the patient is proposed to be accommodated under section 65 or 66 of the National Health Service Act 1977 (which relate to accommodation for private patients).

(4) Subsection (3) above shall not preclude both the medical recommendations being given by practitioners on the staff of the hospital in question if—

    (a) compliance with that subsection would result in delay involving serious risk to the health or safety of the patient; and

    (b) one of the practitioners giving the recommendations works at the hospital for less than half of the time which he is bound by contract to devote to work in the health service; and

    (c) where one of those practitioners is a consultant, the other does not work (whether at the hospital or elsewhere) in a grade in which he is under that consultant's directions.

(5) A medical recommendation for the purposes of an application for the admission of a patient under this Part of this Act shall not be given by—

    (a) the applicant;

    (b) a partner of the applicant or of a practitioner by whom another medical recommendation is given for the purposes of the same application;

    (c) a person employed as an assistant by the applicant or by any such practitioner;

    (d) a person who receives or has an interest in the receipt of any payments made on account of the maintenance of the patient; or

    (e) except as provided by subsection (3) or (4) above, a practitioner on the staff of the hospital to which the patient is to be admitted,

or by the husband, wife, father, father-in-law, mother, mother-in-law, son, son-in-law, daughter, daughter-in-law, brother, brother-in-law, sister or sister-in-law of the patient, or of a person mentioned in paragraphs (a) to (e) above, or of a practitioner by whom another medical recommendation is given for the purposes of the same application.

(6) A general practitioner who is employed part-time in a hospital shall not for the purposes of this section be regarded as a practitioner on its staff.

(7) Subsections (1), (2) and (5) above shall apply to applications for guardianship as they apply to applications for admission but with the substitution for paragraph (e) of subsection (5) above of the following paragraph—

"(e) the person named as guardian in the application".'

These provisions relating to the qualifications or status of the applicant, and the qualifications for, and restrictions on, the giving of medical recommendations in support of an application for formal admission, are applicable equally to admission (detention) for treatment under section 3 of the Act. The conditions for, and legal effect of, an application of admission for treatment is considered on pp. 746–750, below.

30.4.5 General provisions as to applications

When, as is the normal case (referred to in the Mental Health Act Code of Practice as the 'preferred' alternative), an approved social worker makes the application for assessment under section 2, section 11(3) of the Act provides:

'(3) Before or within a reasonable time after an application for the admission of a patient for assessment is made by an approved social worker, that social worker shall take such steps as are practicable to inform the person (if any) appearing to be the nearest relative of the patient that the application is to be or has been made and of the power of the nearest relative under section 23(2)(a) below.'

(Section 23 provides for the power of the nearest relative to discharge the patient; see p. 779, below).

The application for admission for assessment differs significantly from the application for admission for treatment in that the latter requires not just information to the person appearing to be the nearest relative but actual consultation with such a person if it is the approved social worker who makes the application. The effects of an objection by the nearest relative in relation to a section 3 application are discussed below, in the context of an examination of section 3 as a whole.

Section 11(2) of the Act provides that 'every application for admission shall be addressed to the managers of the hospital to which admission is sought' and it is therefore in the name of such managers that lawful detention is effected. The term 'managers' is defined in section 145(1) as follows:

'(a) in relation to a hospital vested in the Secretary of State for the purposes of his functions under the National Health Service Act 1977, and in relation to any accommodation provided by a local authority and used as a hospital by or on behalf of the Secretary of State under that Act, the District Health Authority or special health authority responsible for the administration of the hospital;
(b) in relation to a special hospital, the Secretary of State;
(bb) in relation to a hospital vested in a National Health Service trust, the directors of the trust;
(c) in relation to a mental nursing home registered in pursuance of the Nursing Homes Act 1975, the person or persons registered in respect of the home;
and in this definition "hospital" means a hospital within the meaning of Part II of this Act.'

It is for the reason that a patient detained in hospital is detained there in the name of the managers (that is, the responsible health authority or NHS trust) that a panel of managers (now consisting of non-executive members)[5] have the legal power under section 23(4) of the Act to effect the discharge of a patient from detained status even in the face of disagreement from the registered medical practitioner in charge of the patient's treatment for mental disorder. Experience points to the infrequent exercise of this power in cases where the patient's doctor opposes discharge.

The effect of section 2(4) is that an application for admission for assessment enables the patient to be detained for up to 28 days and the power is non-renewable. This is not to say that a further admission for assessment under section 2 may not lawfully follow one which has already expired, there being (even the slightest) interval of time between the two. It should normally, however, be unnecessary in practice to make a further application for admission for assessment, and paragraph 5.3 of the statutory Code of Practice published in 1990 (revised 1993) by the Secretary of State pursuant to section 118 of the Act specifically advises against this course of action. Detention under section 3 need not, of course, last any longer than detention under section 2.

The applicant, whether social worker or nearest relative, must have seen the patient within the period of 14 days prior to admission (section 11(5)), and the applicant, if an approved social worker, must interview the patient before making the application (section 13(2)). Once the application has been completed, with the supporting medical recommendations, the patient must be admitted to hospital within 14 days of the time when he was last medically examined prior to the recommendations which are required by subsection (3) of section 2[6] if the admission is to be lawful. A patient who is already receiving in-patient treatment on an informal basis may be admitted (detained) for assessment under section 2. In considering, under section 2(2)(b), whether the patient 'ought to be so detained in the interests of his own health or safety or with a view to the protection of other persons', the patient's safety, that of others, and the patient's health, should all be viewed as independent alternatives to merit detention.

While it has been suggested[7] that the expression 'the protection of other persons' is 'not limited to protection from physical harm, but could include protection from serious emotional harm', this view appears to stretch the meaning beyond the apparent intention of the Act. The view taken in this book is that the expression 'the protection of other persons' refers more normally to the prevention of danger to such people, in accordance with the corresponding principle of maintaining the safety (in addition to the health) of the person whom it is sought to detain. Indeed, the identical wording is used in section 5(4), providing for a nurses' holding power for up to six hours, in the case of a person who is already receiving in-patient treatment for mental disorder. It is unlikely that the emergency measure, depending also on the presence of other factors (see pp. 757–761, below), was envisaged by the legislators as a protection provided to those outside the hospital in which the patient is receiving in-patient treatment for mental disorder from emotional strain and stress. Despite the assertion in paragraph 2.6 of the statutory Code of Practice that 'the burden on those close to the patient not to admit under the Act' is a 'factor to be taken into account at assessment', it is in any event unthinkable that mere distress or inconvenience could alone be considered as an independent ground for formal admission under the Act.

30.4.6   Detention, discharge and barring orders

In addition to the entitlement to appeal to the managers against the detention, which a patient detained under section 2 possesses in common with all other patients detained pursuant to an application made under Part II of the Act, such a patient has a right of appeal to a Mental Health Review Tribunal. This right is excercisable at any time up to the expiration of 14 days from the formal admission of the patient to hospital, and there is an obligation on the Tribunal Office (see p. 825 of this chapter) to ensure that the tribunal takes place within seven days of the receipt of the application. Additionally, the patient's responsible medical officer (that is, the registered medical practitioner in charge of the patient's treatment) is entitled to discharge the patient from detained status. The patient's relative also has the right to give notice, of 72 hours, to discharge the patient. Such discharge may be barred by the patient's responsible medical officer in accordance with section 25 of the Act, which provides as follows:

'25.—(1) An order for the discharge of a patient who is liable to be detained in a hospital shall not be made by his nearest relative except after giving not less than seventy-two hours' notice in writing to the managers of the hospital; and if, within seventy-two hours after such notice has been given, the responsible medical officer furnishes to the managers a report certifying that in the opinion of that officer the patient, if discharged, would be likely to act in a manner dangerous to other persons or to himself—

(a)   any order for the discharge of the patient made by that relative in pursuance of the notice shall be of no effect; and

(b)   no further order for the discharge of the patient shall be made by that relative during the period of six months beginning with the date of the report.

(2) In any case where a report under subsection (1) above is furnished in respect of a patient who is liable to be detained in pursuance of an application for admission for treatment the managers shall cause the nearest relative of the patient to be informed.'

If such a barring order is furnished to the hospital managers, in respect of a patient detained under section 2 or section 3, the patient's nearest relative has a right of appeal to a Mental Health Review Tribunal (p. 826, below).

The misperception is occasionally encountered that patients detained pursuant to an application made under section 2 of the Act are not amenable to compulsory treatment under Part IV. This is incorrect, given that patients detained under section 2 are expressed by section 56 (see p. 803 of this chapter) to be within the ambit of compulsory treatent powers; and it is also to be noted that the declaration on the application and supporting medical recommendations is that the patient is suffering from mental disorder 'of a nature or degree which warrants the detention of the patient in a hospital for assessment (or for assessment followed by medical treatment)'.

In accordance with the general principle (p. 735, above) that a patient should be discharged from detained status if the conditions for lawful detention have ceased, if it is decided following an assessment pursuant to section 2 of the Act that detention is for any reason no longer required, the patient should be formally discharged from detained status. It may, for instance, be decided following the assessment for which section 2 detention has been implemented, that the patient is not mentally disordered within the meaning of the Act; or that detention pursuant to section 3 is, for one reason or another (discussed below), not legally permissible; or that the patient is genuinely willing to remain in hospital on an informal basis. The practice is sometimes encountered of allowing a section 2 order to 'expire' even though following assessment it has been decided for one of the above reasons not to detain the patient further under the longer term section 3. Given the general principles (p. 735, above) by which the provisions of the Act should be interpreted, it is considered that the practice of allowing a section 2 order to expire, or to lapse, could amount to unlawful detention (false imprisonment) of the patient for that remaining period.

30.4.7 Admission for assessment in cases of emergency

It may happen that a pressing need arises to detain a person for reasons of mental disorder but that it is not possible in all the circumstances to obtain the otherwise requisite medical recommendations in accordance with section 12. The normal rule for the provision of medical recommendations in support of an application is set out in section 12(2), which provides as follows:

'(2) Of the medical recommendations given for the purposes of any such application, one shall be given by a practitioner approved for the purposes of this section by the Secretary of State as having special experience in the diagnosis or treatment of mental disorder; and unless the practitioner has previous acquaintance with the patient, the other such recommendation shall, if practicable, be given by a registered medical practitioner who has such previous acquaintance.'

Section 4 provides for admission for assessment in case of urgent necessity, or 'emergency' as stated in the marginal note to the section.

The applicant may, as in the case of a section 2 application, be either the patient's nearest relative or an approved social worker, the latter being the normal case and indeed the 'preferred applicant' as recommended by the statutory Code of Practice. In the case of 'urgent necessity', one supporting medical recommendation suffices.

Typically, an admission for assessment in case of emergency may be considered by a general medical practitioner who need have no particular experience of psychiatry but who considers as a matter of general medical judgment that mental disorder indicates urgent hospitalisation. Equally typically, the applicant may be a social work member of an out-of-hours (emergency duty) team provided by the local social services authority and it may be impracticable at the time the application is considered necessary to obtain the opinion of an approved doctor, having special experience in psychiatry, under section 12. Every effort should be made by Regional Health Authorities to ensure the availability of an adequate number of section 12 approved doctors, in order to avoid reliance being placed on the powers given by section 4 for reasons only of the lack of such provision. It can therefore be perfectly lawful in such cases to detain a patient, up to a maximum of 72 hours, on the recommendation of a single registered medical practitioner having no special knowledge or experience of psychiatry, despite the fact that it may in certain cases not be good practice to do so.

Section 4 provides as follows:

'**4.**—(1) In any case of urgent necessity, an application for admission for assessment may be made in respect of a patient in accordance with the following provisions of this section, and any application so made is in this Act referred to as "an emergency application".

(2) An emergency application may be made either by an approved social worker or by the nearest relative of the patient; and every such application shall include a statement that it is of urgent necessity for the patient to be admitted and detained under section 2 above, and that compliance with the provisions of this Part of this Act relating to applications under that section would involve undesirable delay.

(3) An emergency application shall be sufficient in the first instance if founded on one of the medical recommendations required by section 2 above, given, if practicable, by a practitioner who has previous acquaintance with the patient and otherwise complying with the requirements of section 12 below so far as applicable to a single recommendation, and verifying the statement referred to in subsection (2) above.

(4) An emergency application shall cease to have effect on the expiration of a period of 72 hours from the time when the patient is admitted to the hospital unless—

   (a) the second medical recommendation required by section 2 above is given and received by the managers within that period; and

   (b) that recommendation and the recommendation referred to in subsection (3) above together comply with all the requirements of section 12 below (other than the requirement as to the time of signature of the second recommendation).'

The Mental Health Act 1959 permitted *any* relative of the patient to make an emergency application for admission, but the 1983 Act restricts such power to the patient's *nearest* relative. The applicant will normally be an approved social worker, such being the 'preferred applicant' under paragraph 2.3 of the Code of Practice.

Once admitted to hospital under section 4, the detention can be translated, retrospectively, into detention under section 2 by the provision of the second (expert) recommendation required in the normal course by section 2, referring as it does to section 12(2) above. That is to say, once the second medical recommendation has been made to detain for assessment a person already admitted to hospital under section 4, the maximum period of detention under section 2 commences at the time the patient was admitted to hospital under section 4. Practical difficulties can arise in obtaining a supporting medical recommendation for formal admission from the (now) patient's own general practitioner. While the GP may frequently be most willing to make a journey to the hospital there is no duty imposed by the Mental Health Act 1983 on such a GP to attend a patient other than in an emergency arising within the practice area.

In addition to providing that the applicant must have personally seen the patient within the 24 hours prior to the time at which the application is made, section 6 provides that a duly completed application for admission for assessment in case of emergency shall be sufficient authority for the applicant, or any person authorised by the applicant, to take and convey the patient to hospital within 24 hours beginning with the time when the patient was examined by the single medical practitioner supporting the application, or within 24 hours from the time when the application is made, whichever of these two times is the earlier. This latter permission appears to be an error of drafting; for it admits of the possibility that an application can be made before the time at which the supporting medical recommendation is obtained. This possibility is inconsistent with the requirements of section 2 and section 4. It is considered that the 24-hour period from the supporting medical recommendation is, consistently with section 6(1)(a) relating to admission for assessment in the ordinary way pursuant to section 2, a safer guide to lawful action.

As stated in paragraph 6.2 of the Code of Practice, admission for assessment in case of emergency should never be used simply as a convenience, but only in a genuine emergency or case of necessity.

An application under section 4 cannot be renewed at the end of the 72-hour period. But if by the addition of the second medical recommendation the section 4 admission is translated into a section 2 admission, this is the one and only case under the Mental Health Act 1983 in which one section is truly 'converted' into another. It is sometimes, erroneously, said that the section 2 order may be 'converted' into a section 3 admission for treatment order (pp. 746–751, below). For instance, when (as frequently happens) an order made under section 3 follows immediately on a section 2 order, this is not an example of 'conversion' but rather of a separate process instituted for the purpose of detention under section 3. If a section 4 order is truly converted into a section 2 order, by the furnishing of the second supporting recommendation, there is no further requirement for formal application by an approved social worker or nearest relative.

Although the situation of a patient already in hospital, whether or not receiving treatment for mental disorder, would more normally be dealt with under the provisions of section 5 (pp. 757–758, below), there appears to be nothing in law to prevent the use of section 4 in relation to an in-patient, especially if the urgency of detention is considered to be similar to that to which the section 5(2) holding power, of equal maximum duration, applies. Nevertheless, paragraph 6.2 of the Code of Practice should be remembered in this context:

'Section 4 is for genuine emergency and should never be used for administrative convenience. Those involved in the process of admission are entitled to expect "second doctors" to be available so that they do not have to consider using section 4 in circumstances otherwise than genuine emergencies.'

Furthermore, paragraph 6.4 of the Code of Practice recommends as follows:

'It is wrong for patients to be admitted under section 4 rather than section 2 because it is more convenient for the second doctor to examine the patient in, rather than outside, hospital. Those assessing an individual's need must be able to secure the attendance within a reasonable time of a second doctor and in particular an approved doctor.'

The use of section 4 in relation to an in-patient in a hospital where psychiatric expertise should be either present or on call will therefore be confined in practice to wholly exceptional circumstances in which such support is for some reason impossible to obtain.

As under ordinary admission for assessment, admission for assessment in a case of emergency should never be allowed to lapse or expire. If for any reason the assessment, once completed, indicates the absence of any ground for further detention of the patient, the patient should be formally discharged from detention under section 4. It is also only under the most extreme circumstances, in which ordinary sources of professional attendance and support are simply unavailable, that detention under section 4 could be repeated. It should be noted that such a repetition, were it to occur, is in no sense a renewal of detention, given that neither section 4 nor section 2 are susceptible to renewal. The only renewable section under Part II of the Act is section 3, providing for admission for treatment. This is now considered.

30.4.8 Admission for treatment

There being no section of the Mental Health Act relating to detention which is not purposive in nature, and there being no detention section of the Mental Health Act which provides purely for lawful custody, as distinct from the ultimate objective of treatment for mental disorder, it is section 3 which, in providing for admission to hospital for treatment, comes to be seen as in a sense the characteristic model for detention and treatment under Part II of the Act. Section 3 provides for the longest periods of detention under Part II of the Act and is renewable. There is no legal limit to the number of occasions on which a section 3 order may be renewed, provided that the requirements of section 20 (below) are present at the requisite time. Mental disorder, as a diagnosis, is insufficient for detention under section 3, and the diagnosis of a more specific form (or forms) of mental disorder or disability, as required in section 3(2) of the Act and as defined by section 1 of the Act, is required to support a lawful application under section 3. Section 3 provides as follows:

'**3.**—(1) A patient may be admitted to a hospital and detained there for the period allowed by the following provisions of this Act in pursuance of an application (in this Act referred to as "an application for admission for treatment") made in accordance with this section.

(2) An application for admission for treatment may be made in respect of a patient on the grounds that—

   (a)   he is suffering from mental illness, severe mental impairment, psychopathic disorder or mental impairment and his mental disorder is of a nature or degree which makes it appropriate for him to receive medical treatment in a hospital; and

   (b)   in the case of psychopathic disorder or mental impairment, such treatment is likely to alleviate or prevent a deterioration of his condition; and

   (c)   it is necessary for the health or safety of the patient or for the protection of other persons that he should receive such treatment and it cannot be provided unless he is detained under this section.

(3) An application for admission for treatment shall be founded on the written recommendations in the prescribed form of two registered medical practitioners, including in each case a statement that in the opinion of the practitioner the conditions set out in subsection (2) above are complied with: and each such recommendation shall include—

   (a)   such particulars as may be prescribed of the grounds for that opinion so far as it relates to the conditions set out in paragraphs (a) and (b) of that subsection; and

   (b)   a statement of the reasons for that opinion so far as it relates to the conditions set out in paragraph (c) of that subsection, specifying whether other methods of dealing with the patient are available and, if so, why they are not appropriate.'

'Mental disorder' being an insufficient mental state to support detention under section 3, it becomes necessary to refer specifically to the definition in section 1(2) which provides relevantly as follows:

' "severe mental impairment" means a state of arrested or incomplete development of mind which includes severe impairment of intelligence and social functioning and is associated with abnormally aggressive or seriously irresponsible conduct on the part of the person concerned and "severely mentally impaired" shall be construed accordingly;

"mental impairment" means a state of arrested or incomplete development of mind (not amounting to severe mental impairment) which includes significant impairment of intelligence and social functioning and is associated with abnormally aggressive or seriously irresponsible conduct on the part of the person concerned and "mentally impaired" shall be construed accordingly; "psychopathic disorder" means a persistent disorder or disability of mind (whether or not including significant impairment of intelligence) which results in abnormally aggressive or seriously irresponsible conduct on the part of the person concerned.'

As is the case elsewhere in Part II of the Act, promiscuity or immoral conduct, sexual deviancy or dependence on alcohol or drugs shall not 'be construed as implying that a person may be dealt with under this Act as suffering from mental disorder or from any form of mental disorder described in this section'. That is, none of these reasons affords a basis for a diagnosis of a general or specific form of mental disorder in the absence of other diagnostic or behavioural evidence. However, any one of these reasons could, possibly in combination with another or others, afford a basis on which 'seriously irresponsible conduct', or possibly in appropriate cases even 'abnormally aggressive' conduct could be identified as an element within the diagnosis of impairment or psychopathy.

Authority for detention under section 3 lasts for an initial period of up to six months, which is renewable in the first instance for a period of up to six months, and thereafter up to one year at a time.[8] As is the case with section 2 admission for assessment, the application for detention under section 3 can be made either by the patient's nearest relative or by an approved social worker.[9] The major difference relating to the application under section 3 is, however, that the applicant, if an approved social worker, must if practicable *consult* with the patient's nearest relative before proceeding with the application.

Any objection by the nearest relative is sufficient to prevent the application proceeding further, although steps may be taken pursuant to section 29 of the Act to displace the nearest relative, by application to the county court. It is not sufficient merely to inform the nearest relative either before or within a reasonable time of the making of the application (such being sufficient for an application under section 2). Section 11(4) provides that no such application

'shall be made by an approved social worker if the nearest relative of the patient has notified that social worker, or the local social services authority by whom that social worker is appointed, that he objects to the application being made'.

Furthermore, section 11(4) goes on to provide that

'no such application shall be made by such a social worker except after consultation with the person (if any) appearing to be the nearest relative of the patient unless it appears to that social worker that in the circumstances such consultation is not reasonably practicable or would involve unreasonable delay'.

The exceptions to the general duty to consult the person appearing to be the nearest relative, namely that such would not be normally reasonably practicable, or would involve unreasonable delay, are alternative and not cumulative; in other words, either will suffice in itself. 'Unreasonable delay' is self-explanatory and is to be judged according to the balance to be struck, within the 'spirit of the Act', between the protection of a person's civil liberties and the making available of appropriate treatment at the earliest reasonable time. Furthermore, it is not sufficient if the consultation is considered to be professionally or personally unreasonable, in the sense of undesirable. The words of section 11(4) are that 'such consultation is not reasonably practicable', meaning that the approved social worker making the application need not, in order to comply with the statutory consultation requirement, go to disproportionate lengths to contact a person with whom the patient has long since ceased contact, or whose whereabouts and perhaps even identity have been forgotten by the patient.

A patient suffering from either mental illness or severe mental impairment may be detained pursuant to section 3 irrespective of whether the condition is amenable to treatment. By contrast, in the case of persons suffering from either psychopathic disorder or mental impairment (not being severe mental impairment, a distinction indicated in practice simply by the exercise of clinical judgment), it is a requirement that 'such treatment is likely to alleviate or prevent a deterioration' of the patient's condition.[10] It is possible in practice for a person to be affected by more than one statutorily defined form of mental disorder, for instance, from mental impairment with a 'psychiatric overlay' of mental illness of one form or another. Given also that psychopathic disorder, as statutorily defined by section 1 of the Act, may (but does not necessarily) include subnormality of intelligence, it is possible that psychopathic disorder and mental impairment reside in one in the same person. In practice, patients suffering from a combination of these disorders, as statutorily defined, are apt to present particularly difficult problems of care and management.

In declaring that a person is suffering from one or other form of mental disorder requisite for detention under section 3, the two medical recommendations supporting the application are required to diagnose at least one form of mental disorder, as statutorily defined, in common. It is, for instance, not sufficient to support a valid application pursuant to section 3 for one medical practitioner to declare that a patient is suffering from psychopathy and the other from mental illness. It may indeed be that a particular person is suffering from both these forms of mental disorder, as clinically diagnosed; but unless one or other is declared in statutory form by both medical recommendations to exist, the application is invalid.[11] Furthermore, in the case of psychopathic disorder or mental impairment, both medical recommendations must agree on the 'treatability' criterion.

An order for discharge of a patient detained under section 3 can be made by: the patient's responsible medical officer, that is the registered medical practitioner in charge of the patient's medical treatment for mental disorder; the managers of the hospital (exercisable, in accordance with section 23(4) of the Act, by a panel of non-executive members of the health authority or NHS trust; by a Mental Health Review Tribunal, normally (but not exclusively) on the application of the patient himself or herself; and by the nearest relative of the patient, by giving 72 hours notice of discharge. In the latter case, as under section 2, discharge may be barred by the responsible medical officer in accordance with the provisions of section 25, if it is unwise or inappropriate for reasons set out in that section (see p. 742, above) for the patient to be discharged. The patient's nearest relative has a right of appeal to a Mental Health Review Tribunal against a barring order by the responsible medical officer. It should be emphasised that discharge in this context means discharge from the legal status of 'liable to be detained' and not necessarily physical discharge from the hospital; though the latter will follow the former when the patient does not wish to remain in hospital informally.

The dominant objective of detention under section 3 being the making available of appropriate treatment to suit the patient's mental condition, a declaration by the applicant (normally an approved social worker) and the two supporting medical recommendations that the treatment is not only necessary for the health or safety of the patient or for the protection of other persons, but that such treatment cannot be provided unless the person is detained in hospital under section 3, is vital to the lawful exercise of detention powers. It used to be common practice for consultants to admit patients to hospital, as in-patients but only overnight, and then send them on leave (under section 17 of the Act) subject to recall if, for instance, the patient did not attend out-patient clinics or take the necessary medication as supervised by a community psychiatric nurse. The element of detention in hospital, as required by section 3(2)(c), was therefore simply a device which purported to comply with the requirements of the Act but which effectively was designed to facilitate treatment 'in the community'. The same device was used also on renewal of section 3, pursuant to powers given by section 20 of the Act, when the same objective was desired either six months or a year, respectively, into detention. These devices, whether on initial admission or on renewal, were declared unlawful by the decision in the *Hallstrom* case (1986)[12] discussed on pp. 752–755, below. The power of renewal of a section 3 order, which the 1986 decision also encompassed, must first be explained.

30.4.9   Renewal of an order for admission for treatment

Section 20(2) provides that the authority for the detention of a patient may, unless the patient has previously been discharged, be renewed for an initial period of six months, following the first period of six months detention, and thereafter for periods of up to one year at a time. The procedures required by section 20 for a valid renewal of authority for detention are as follows:

'**20.**—(3) Within the period of two months ending on the day on which a patient who is liable to be detained in pursuance of an application for admission for treatment would cease under this section to be so liable in default of the renewal of the authority for his detention, it shall be the duty of the responsible medical officer—

(a) to examine the patient; and

(b) if it appears to him that the conditions set out in subsection (4) below are satisfied to furnish to the managers of the hospital where the patient is detained a report to that effect in the prescribed form;

and where such a report is furnished in respect of a patient the managers shall, unless they discharge the patient, cause him to be informed.

(4) The conditions referred to in subsection (3) above are that—

(a) the patient is suffering from mental illness, severe mental impairment, psychopathic disorder or mental impairment, and his mental disorder is of a nature or degree which makes it appropriate for him to receive medical treatment in a hospital; and

(b) such treatment is likely to alleviate or prevent a deterioration of his condition; and

(c) it is necessary for the health or safety of the patient or for the protection of other persons that he should receive such treatment and that it cannot be provided unless he continues to be detained;

but, in the case of mental illness or severe mental impairment, it shall be an alternative to the condition specified in paragraph (b) above that the patient, if discharged, is unlikely to be able to care for himself, to obtain the care which he needs or to guard himself against serious exploitation.

(5) Before furnishing a report under subsection (3) above the responsible medical officer shall consult one or more other persons who have been professionally concerned with the patient's medical treatment. . .

(9) Where the form of mental disorder specified in a report furnished under subsection (3) . . . above is a form of disorder other than that specified in the application for admission for treatment . . ., that application shall have effect as if that other form of mental disorder were specified in it; and where on any occasion a report specifying such a form of mental disorder is furnished under either of those subsections the appropriate medical officer need not on that occasion furnish a report under section 16 above.'

(In other words, subsection (9) avoids the need for a separate re-classification report to managers which would at times other than such renewal be required to note a change in the mental condition of the patient, as defined in section 1(2).)

30.4.10 Restrictions on the lawful use of detention under section 3 and renewal of detention

The rationale behind the powers contained in the Act is that mental disorder may itself prevent an individual from exercising ordinary choice or self-determination over treatment. The mental health legislation is essentially hospital based. But there are many people who, while suffering from mental disorder, may be perfectly well cared for in 'the community' without hospitalisation provided that they keep taking their medication. Problems arise when patients think that they are better than their doctors think they are. The following important case sets down the limits to lawful use of the admission for treatment power under section 3 of the 1983 Act.

The case of *R v Hallstrom, ex parte W and R v Gardner, ex parte L* (1986)[12] concerned events which happened in Banstead Hospital, Surrey, in 1984 and 1985. They concerned the practical operation of section 3 of the Mental Health Act 1983. Section 3 of the Act provides for long-term detention, renewable for a period of up to six months in the first instance, followed by further renewals of up to one year at a time. Section 3 requires that 'it is necessary for the health or safety of the patient or for the protection of other persons that he should receive such treatment and it cannot be provided unless he is detained under this section'.

Sometimes people may feel better than their doctors think they are, feel that they need not be in hospital, and may even feel that they do not need to remain on medication for the treatment of their mental condition. Recognising this fact, which is a common occurrence, two doctors at Banstead Hospital attempted in good faith to operate section 3 of the 1983 Act in the way least restrictive to their patients' liberty.

Miss W had a long history of chronic schizophrenic illness and had been admitted to hospital many times. On 24 July 1984 she was admitted to Banstead Hospital on the joint recommendation of two doctors, purportedly pursuant to section 3 of the 1983 Act. Their joint medical recommendations supporting her admission stated that she had 'limited insight into her condition and denies she was ever ill'. The doctors did not think that she needed to remain in hospital long term, but thought that, because of her limited insight, she should still be subject to some compulsion powers to make her stay on the medication they thought she required.

On 25 July 1984, the day after her admission, her responsible medical officer granted her leave of absence from the hospital under section 17 of the Act. She returned to the hostel whence she came. She had therefore been in hospital for one night only following her admission under the Act. Her responsible medical officer regarded himself as having the authority to insist that she take her medication, given her 'detained' status. He believed that her condition required the taking of medication and that this was the best way to do it.

Lawyers acting for Miss W challenged the lawfulness of this recommendation, arguing that section 3 of the 1983 Act can only be used to admit to hospital patients whose mental condition is believed to require their detention *for treatment in hospital*, whereas doctors had recognised all along that her condition merely required treatment which it was intended to give her while she continued to live in the hostel.

Mr L's case was more complicated. In his case there was no question as to the validity of the initial detention. What was questioned was the validity of the *renewal* of detention following the expiration of the first six months period of detention under section 3. The question was asked whether his detention could be renewed merely in order to take him into hospital for a night and then give him long-term leave of absence.

The judge stated categorically that the doctors' clinical judgment and bona fides were not in question. It was merely the legality of the initial admission of Miss W, and in the case of Mr L his renewal, which was being called in question. The doctors considered that continued medication of these two patients respectively was necessary as part of the duty of care which the doctors had assumed in relation to them. What they did has sometimes been referred to as the 'long-leash' approach to the enforcement of medication.

There is no difficulty about the use of the term 'detained patient' in situations where patients are on leave of absence from hospital. While they are not physically detained in the hospital, by nature of their leave, they remain of the legal status 'liable to be detained'. That liability to be detained attracts the provisions of Part IV of the Act. In the case of (broadly speaking) longer term detained patients, treatment can be insisted upon and indeed be forcibly imposed by medical and nursing staff in the event of a refusal to take it or to submit to it voluntarily. It was therapeutic control over the patients in question which the doctors in all good faith and in the interests of the patients' health wished to retain. The treatment needs, however, to be given in hospital under the Act.

The judge in the court to which the challenge was brought, Mr Justice McCullough, gave a brief and lucid description of the ambit of section 3:

'Section 3 of the 1983 Act is concerned with admission to hospital and detention there. A person "admitted" to hospital becomes an in-patient. This is the sense in which the word is ordinarily used. There are references in section 5 of the 1983 Act to those who are already *in-patients*, which confirms it and all parties in this case accept that.

Detention follows admission. As on admission the patient becomes an in-patient, it must follow that his detention is *as an in-patient*, at any rate initially. It would, no doubt, be theoretically possible to detain someone as an out-patient, but detention in that capacity could last for no more than a matter of hours at the end of which the patient would have either to become an in-patient once more or be granted leave of absence. In either event it is difficult to see what purpose would have been achieved by making him an out-patient. This purely theoretical possibility can be ignored. The definition referred to in the section (section 3) is therefore detention as an in-patient.'

Furthermore, his Lordship explained, the admission is for treatment. The conditions of section 3 include the requirements that treatment is needed and that it cannot be given unless the patient is 'detained in hospital'. The judge had the following comment to make on treatment, and on admission to hospital for that purpose:

'In my judgment, the key to the construction of section 3 lies in the phrase "admission for treatment". It stretches the concept of "admission for treatment" too far to say that it covers admissions for only so long as is necessary to enable leave of absence to be granted, after which the necessary treatment will begin. "Admission for treatment" under section 3 is intended for those whose condition is believed to require a period of treatment as an in-patient. It may be that such patients will also be thought to require a period of out-patient treatment thereafter, but the concept of "admission for treatment" has no applicability to those whom it is intended to admit and detain for a purely nominal period, during which no necessary treatment will be given.'

The judge went on to explain that, in his view, detention under section 3 is designed to cater for those whose mental condition requires in-patient treatment. Treatment in a hospital does not mean treatment at a hospital, as counsel for the doctors in the case contended. If that construction were correct there would, said the judge, be a distinction between the patient who could appropriately be treated at home and the patient who could appropriately be treated at the out-patients' department of a hospital. Such a distinction, he said, would be without reason:

'When it is remembered that the section authorises compulsory detention in a hospital it is at once clear why a distinction should be made between those whom it is appropriate to treat *in* a hospital (i.e. as in-patients) and those whom it is appropriate to treat otherwise (whether at the out-patient department of the hospital or at home or elsewhere).'

Exactly the same reasoning lay behind the judge's ultimate rejection of the similar use of section 20 (the renewal power) chosen by the doctor in this case. The criteria for the renewal of authority to detain a patient originally detained under section 3 are substantially the same as those for the initial authority to detain in that section. Section 3, he held, is concerned with patients whose mental condition is believed to require in-patient treatment. The similarity of language between section 3 and section 20 (the renewal power) suggested to his Lordship that it, too, is concerned with those who are believed to require in-patient treatment. To this the judge added: 'This tends to confirm that Parliament did not intend that the provisions for renewal should embrace those liable to be detained but not in fact detained.'

Section 17 of the Act entitles the responsible medical officer (registered medical practitioner in charge of the treatment of the patient for mental disorder) to permit leave of absence for either a specified or unspecified time. Such leave may cover any number of eventualities from going down to the local shop or to the local hairdresser, to spending a specified or unspecified, and possibly long, time at home as part of a process of rehabilitation. A common condition of long-term leave of absence under section 17 is that the patient who remains 'liable to be detained' (though not in fact detained in the hospital) is subject automatically to recall from leave if a condition is broken, for instance that the patient has fallen down in attendance at treatment clinics or for some other reason is found to have abandoned recommended treatment.

Section 17 provides that once a patient has been on leave of absence for six months his liability to be recalled ends in any case. It is possible to frustrate this provision by the device of recall for one night (which happened in the case of Mr L) for which recall there is no necessity save to attempt a long-leash compulsory power which remains with the patient. Mr Justice McCullough said:

'There can only be two intentions behind this device. One is to extend the period during which a patient may be treated compulsorily in the community. The other is to retain the power to recall him should considerations of his health or safety or protection of others require this at some time in the future.'

In either event, concluded the judge, the use of section 17 was not that which was envisaged by the Act.

The Mental Health Act 1983 accordingly falls distinctly short, in terms, of providing anything approaching a 'community treatment order'. Since its enactment, and certainly since the 1986 decision of Mr Justice McCullough, debates have been pursued as to the desirability and viability of community treatment orders falling short of in-patient hospital detention. Although the Royal College of Psychiatrists have made certain proposals for a 'community *supervision* order', no such alteration of the law exists, even in draft form, at the time of publication of this edition.

30.4.11 Section 2 or section 3?

The statutory Code of Practice published by the Secretary of State for Health pursuant to section 118 of the Mental Health Act 1983 makes the following observations and recommendations as to a choice which has often given rise to professional doubt and difficulty.

'5.1   Which admission section should be used? Professional judgment must be applied to the criteria in each section and *only* when this has been done can a decision be reached as to which, if either section applies. It must be borne in mind that detention under section 3 need not last any longer than under section 2.

5.2   Section 2 pointers:

a.   where the diagnosis and prognosis of a patient's condition is unclear;
b.   there is a need to carry out an in-patient assessment in order to formulate a treatment plan;
c.   where a judgment is needed as to whether the patient will accept treatment on a voluntary basis following admission;
d.   where a judgment has to be made as to whether a particular treatment proposal, which can only be administered to the patient under Part IV of the Act, is likely to be effective;
e.   where a patient who has already been assessed, and who has been previously admitted compulsorily under the Act, is judged to have changed since the previous admission and needs further assessment;
f.   where the patient has not previously been admitted to hospital either compulsorily or informally.

5.3   Section 3 pointers:

a.   where a patient has been admitted in the past, is considered to need compulsory admission for the treatment of a mental disorder which is already known to his clinical team, and has been assessed in the recent past by that team;
b.   where a patient already admitted under section 2 and who is assessed as needing further medical treatment for mental disorder under the Act at the conclusion of his detention under section 2 is unwilling to remain in hospital informally and to consent to the medical treatment;
c.   where a patient is detained under section 2 and assessment points to a need for treatment under the Act for a period beyond the 28 day detention under section 2. In such circumstances an application for detention under section 3 should be made at the earliest opportunity and should not be delayed until the end of section 2 detention. Changing a patient's detention status from section 2 to section 3 will not deprive him of a Mental Health Review Tribunal hearing if the change takes place after a valid application has been made to the Tribunal but before it has been heard. The patient's rights to apply for a Tribunal under section 66(1) (b) in the first period of detention after his change of status are unaffected.

5.4   Decisions should *not* be influenced by:

a.   wanting to avoid consulting the nearest relative;
b.   the fact that a proposed treatment to be administered under the Act will last less than 28 days;

c. the fact that a patient detained under section 2 will get quicker access to a Mental Health Review Tribunal than one detained under section 3.'

30.4.12   Holding powers for patients already in hospital

Sections 5(2) and 5(4) of the Act provide for separate but complementary holding powers in respect of patients already receiving treatment in hospital in on in-patient basis. Section 5(2) provides:

'(2) If, in the case of a patient who is an in-patient in a hospital, it appears to the registered medical practitioner in charge of the treatment of the patient that an application ought to be made under this Part of this Act for the admission of the patient to hospital, he may furnish to the managers a report in writing to that effect; and in any such case the patient may be detained in the hospital for a period of 72 hours from the time when the report is so furnished.'

This power is not confined to psychiatrists, but applies to any registered medical practitioner who is in charge of the medical treatment of any patient. The section thus applies not only to psychiatric and mental handicap (learning disability) hospitals, but also to general hospitals whether or not the latter have a psychiatric department. The Act does not further define who is 'in charge of the treatment of the patient', but it may safely be assumed that in all normal circumstances it will be the consultant in charge of the team looking after the patient at any particular time. The person in charge may change with time and the power to exercise the holding power under section 5(2) will change accordingly. The power given by section 5(2) is not a power of formal admission under Part II of the Act, but rather a holding power designed to facilitate an assessment of the patient who is the subject of the power with a view to detention under another section (namely section 2 or section 3) of Part II of the Act. Furthermore, in restricting the use of this power to one who is already an 'in-patient in a hospital' it is apparent that section 5(2) cannot be applied to a person who shows signs of mental disorder, and possibly even the need for admission under section 2 or section 3 of the Act, while in the accident and emergency department of a general hospital. Except for the most unusual case in which such a casualty department were to have an allocation of its own beds, and for a person admitted to the casualty department to have been 'clerked-in' to such a bed as an in-patient, the section 5(2) holding power is inapplicable to such a hospital department.

Section 5(2) provides no authority for applications to be made in respect of patients who are already in hospital under compulsory powers and the power cannot be used to extend the detention of a patient where authority to detain is about to expire.[13]

It will only be in the most unusual circumstances, involving the unavailability on reasonable grounds, for the full 72 hours of detention authorised by section 5(2), of the registered medical practitioner in charge of the patient's treatment, that this holding power may be followed by an emergency application under section 4. The purpose of the holding power is to prevent a patient from discharging himself or herself from hospital before there is time to arrange for an application to be made under section 2 or section 3.

Once the assessment has been completed, normally involving an approved social worker as well as two supporting medical recommendations, the function of section 5(2) is spent. Either the detention should proceed to a formal basis, following an application supported by medical recommendations under either section 2 or section 3, or it should be declared to cease. It is good practice, as well as no doubt also an implicit legal requirement in the Act, that a decision not to invoke section 2 or section 3, following the implementation of the section 5(2) holding power, should result in the formal discharge (in this sense removal) of the patient from the holding power. In other words, the holding power under section 5(2) should not be allowed to 'lapse' or to expire. For such time as a holding power were to purport still to exist following the decision not to detain further under Part II of the Act, the patient would be unlawfully detained. That is not, however, to say that there is any particular virtue in 'converting' (as it is sometimes erroneously expressed) a section 5(2) holding power to a formal admission, following application, under Part II of the Act. Such virtue as there may be in avoiding 'unconverted' holding powers under section 5(2) is more accurately expressed as ensuring that hospital in-patients do not remain apparently subject to the power when the assessment for which the power is designed is complete and a decision has been taken not to detain under Part II of the Act.

For the sake of practicality and the appropriate use of resources, the holding power under section 5(2) may be exercised also by a nominated deputy of the registered medical practitioner in charge of the patient's treatment in hospital. Section 5(3) provides:

'(3) The registered medical practitioner in charge of the treatment of a patient in a hospital may nominate one (but not more than one) other registered medical practitioner on the staff of that hospital to act for him under subsection (2) above in his absence.'

'Nominate' means precisely that, and it is not sufficient simply to identify the doctor on call at any particular time as being the nominated deputy. Such a person would be described, but not nominated. However, a simple device to avoid wrongful use of the power under section 5(3) is to ensure that nursing and medical staff are aware at all times of the name (hence 'nominate') of the registered medical practitioner on call at any particular time. Section 5(3) merely provides an extra entitlement towards holding powers and there is no duty upon the registered medical practitioner in charge of the hospital treatment of the patient if he or she does not wish to do so.

Complementary to section 5(2) is the nurse's holding power under section 5(4), which provides as follows:

'(4) If, in the case of a patient who is receiving treatment for mental disorder as an in-patient in a hospital, it appears to a nurse of the prescribed class—

    (a) that the patient is suffering from mental disorder to such a degree that it is necessary for his health or safety or for the protection of others for him to be immediately restrained from leaving the hospital; and

    (b) that it is not practicable to secure the immediate attendance of a practitioner for the purpose of furnishing a report under subsection (2) above,

the nurse may record that fact in writing; and in that event the patient may be detained in the hospital for a period of six hours from the time when that fact is so recorded or until the earlier arrival at the place where the patient is detained of a practitioner having power to furnish a report under that subsection.'

There are thus five cumulative conditions to be fulfilled for the lawful exercise of the nurse's holding power under this subsection, each one of which must be present if the power is to be validly exercised. The requirement that the patient be 'immediately restrained from leaving the hospital' must not be confused with a situation in which an in-patient presents as a risk or displays challenging behaviour, but shows no real sign of leaving the hospital. Furthermore, section 5(4) makes the additional requirement that the in-patient in question should be receiving treatment in hospital for mental disorder; and regulations[14] provide that it is only registered mental nurses and registered nurses in mental handicap who may validly exercise the section 5(4) holding power.

Like the power provided by section 5(2), the nurse's holding power is not renewable, though that is not to say that a repeated exercise of the power would necessarily be unlawful. In the case of either section 5(2) or section 5(4) the occasion for repeated use of the holding power would no doubt indicate a lack of professional resource provision which managers would be best advised to avoid as a matter of good practice. In requiring that 'it is not practicable to secure the immediate attendance of a practitioner for the purpose of furnishing a report' under section 5(2), section 5(4) goes further than simply providing for a situation in which the doctor in charge of the patient's hospital treatment considers it unreasonable or inconvenient to attend and requires that it is simply not practicable to get such a doctor to the scene. To avoid difficulty, clear hospital policies should exist for appropriate liaison relating to holding powers between consultants in charge of patients' treatment and nurses in charge of the wards.

Even though not admission sections under Part II of the Act (in the sense that sections 2 and 3 are admission sections), there is no power under section 5(2) or 5(4) simply to place an in-patient in custody to allow a 'cooling off' period, or simply to observe the result on the patient's behaviour. The principal purpose of section 5(4) is to secure the attendance of a doctor entitled to implement section 5(2) during the six-hour period, as well as prevent an at-risk patient from leaving hospital during that period; and the purpose of section 5(2) is to create the circumstances and sufficient time in which an assessment with a view to possible longer term admission under Part II may be effected.

Some practical safeguards on the use of section 5(2) holding power are contained in paragraph 8.14 of the Mental Health Act Code of Practice:

'a.   Where the nominated deputy is a junior doctor, the nominating doctor must be satisfied that his deputy has received sufficient guidance and training to carry out the function satisfactorily.
b.   Wherever possible the nominated deputy must contact the nominating doctor or another consultant (where the nominated deputy is not a consultant) before using section 5(2). The nominated deputy should have easy access to the nominating doctor or the psychiatric consultant on-call.
c.   Only registered medical practitioners who are consultant psychiatrists should nominate deputies.
d.   The nominated deputy should report the use of section 5(2) to his nominator as soon as possible.
e.   All relevant staff should know who is the nominated deputy for a particular patient.'

In relation to hints on the practical use of section 5(4), the Code of Practice is less helpful, even in its amended form. Paragraph 9.8 of the Code states:

'The use of section 5(4) is an emergency measure and the doctor with the power to use section 5(2) in respect of the patient should treat it as such, arriving as soon as possible. The doctor must not wait six hours before attending simply because this is the maximum time allowed. If the doctor has not arrived within four hours the duty consultant should be contacted and should attend. Where no doctor has attended within six hours an oral report (suitably recorded) should be made immediately to the Unit General Manager or the equivalent officer in a NHS trust, and a written report should be submitted to the unit General Manager or the equivalent officer of the NHS trust and the Managers on the next working day. The Unit General Manager or the equivalent officer in a NHS trust should nominate a suitable person to supervise the patient's leaving.'

As already indicated in this chapter, powers under the Mental Health Act simply provide legal entitlements to do that which would, or might, otherwise be an unlawful act such as assault, battery or wrongful detention (false imprisonment). If a patient were indeed to be at risk at or towards the end of the six-hour period for which a nurse may lawfully implement the holding power, it might not only be undesirable to make arrangements for the patient to leave hospital, but might actually be dangerous to do so. It is to be hoped that paragraph 9.8 will not convey the impression that the patient in question should always leave. While paragraph 9.8 of the Code of Practice goes to some lengths in the protection of an informal patient's civil liberties, it overlooks the point that once a duty of care in relation to the health and safety of a patient has been assumed by the staff of a hospital, any act or omission falling below ordinary standards of professional skill and competence and leading to injury or harm to the patient may be actionable negligence. Far from defining the practical content of a hospital's duty of care to a patient, once admitted, the detention provisions of the Mental Health Act 1983 merely provide further and extra facilities for the proper exercise of that duty of care.

Paragraph 9.10 of the Code of Practice is more helpful in this regard, providing:

'A suitably qualified nurse should be on all wards where there is a possibility of section 5(4) being invoked. Although the section is more likely to have to be used on acute admission wards, and wards where there are acutely disturbed patients, or patients requiring intensive nursing care, local management must also assess the potential for its use elsewhere in the hospital or unit. As a result of such assessment they should ensure that suitable arrangements are in place for a suitably qualified nurse to be available should the power need to be invoked.'

30.4.13 Rectification of defective applications and recommendations

As already stated, the Act provides a number of lawful entitlements to interfere with what would otherwise be the civil liberties of a person suffering from mental disorder, or a specific disorder, within the meaning of the Act, provided that the requisite procedures are followed. An application or medical recommendation, purporting to support detention under Part II of the Act, which was lacking in some material detail, might therefore be no defence against a legal action for wrongful detention (false imprisonment). Accordingly, section 15 provides for the rectification of certain deficiencies in applications and supporting medical recommendations:

'**15.**—(1) If within the period of 14 days beginning with the day on which a patient has been admitted to a hospital in pursuance of an application for admission for assessment or for treatment the application, or any medical recommendation given for the purposes of the application, is found to be in any respect incorrect or defective, the application or recommendation may, within that period and with the consent of the managers of the hospital, be amended by the person by whom it was signed; and upon such amendment being made the application or recommendation shall have effect and shall be deemed to have had effect as if it had been originally made as so amended.

(2) Without prejudice to subsection (1) above, if within the period mentioned in that subsection it appears to the managers of the hospital that one of the two medical recommendations on which an application for the admission of a patient is founded is insufficient to warrant the detention of the patient in pursuance of the application, they may, within that period, give notice in writing to that effect to the applicant; and where any such notice is given in respect of a medical

recommendation, that recommendation shall be disregarded, but the application shall be, and shall be deemed always to have been, sufficient if—
  (a) a fresh medical recommendation complying with the relevant provisions of this Part of this Act (other than the provisions relating to the time of signature and the interval between examinations) is furnished to the managers within that period; and
  (b) that recommendation, and the other recommendation on which the application is founded, together comply with those provisions.

(3) Where the medical recommendations upon which an application for admission is founded are, taken together, insufficient to warrant the detention of the patient in pursuance of the application, a notice under subsection (2) above may be given in respect of either of those recommendations; but this subsection shall not apply in a case where the application is of no effect by virtue of section 11(6) above.

(4) Nothing in this section shall be construed as authorising the giving of notice in respect of an application made as an emergency application, or the detention of a patient admitted in pursuance of such an application, after the period of 72 hours referred to in section 4(4) above, unless the conditions set out in paragraphs (a) and (b) of that section are complied with or would be complied with apart from any error or defect to which this section applies.'

The ambit of section 15 is limited in both scope and time: in scope, since rectification cannot be used to remedy deficiencies which would otherwise invalidate the application; in time on account of the 14-day limit on the time taken to accomplish rectification. An unrectifiable error would include an application or medical recommendation signed by a person not empowered under the Act to do so. Unrectifiable errors would also include an omission by the two recommending doctors, in purported support of an omission under section 3, to specify that the patient was suffering from at least one form of mental disorder in common.[15] No doubt, also, an application or medical recommendation which is unsigned is not susceptible to rectification under section 15.

Given that it is in the name of the hospital or nursing home managers that a patient is detained under Part II of the Act, such managers are under a legal duty to ensure that all lawful steps have been taken as a basis for formal admission. Some guiding rules as to action to be taken by managers to structure a system for receipt and scrutiny of documents are set out in paragraph 12.5 of the Code of Practice:

'a. the Managers are responsible for ensuring that patients are detained lawfully; they should therefore monitor the receipt and scrutiny of admission documents on a regular basis;
b. those delegated to scrutinise documents must be clear about what kinds of errors on application forms and medical recommendations can and cannot be corrected (see paras 52–55 of Memorandum). If no original pink forms are available photocopies of an original form can be used;
c. details of defective admission documents, whether rectifiable or not, and of any subsequent action, must be given to the Managers on a regular basis;
d. Managers should ensure that those delegated to receive and scrutinise admission documents understand the requirements of the Act, and if necessary receive appropriate training.'

The Memorandum[16] contains detailed guidance on rectifiable and non-rectifiable errors:

'Faults which invalidate the application

52   Documents cannot be rectified under section 15 unless they are documents which can properly be regarded as applications or medical recommendations within the meaning of the Act. A document cannot be regarded as an application or medical recommendation if it is not signed at all or is signed by a person who is not empowered to do so under the Act. This means that a check should be made to confirm that an application is signed by the patient's nearest relative or the acting nearest relative or an approved social worker; and that each medical recommendation is signed by a practitioner who is not excluded under section 12. In doing so the officer scrutinising the form may take statements at face value; for example, he need not check that the doctor who states he is a registered medical practitioner *is* registered (regulation 3(4)). Another fault which would invalidate the application completely would be if the two medical recommendations did not specify at least one form of mental disorder in common (section 11(6)).

53   If any fault of this sort is discovered there is no authority for the patient's detention. Authority can only be obtained through a new application. If the patient is already in hospital he can only be detained if the medical practitioner in charge of his treatment (or his nominee) issues a report under section 5 of the Act. Any new application must, of course, be accompanied by medical recommendations which comply with the Act, but this does not exclude the possibility of one of the two existing medical recommendations being used if the time limits and other provisions of the Act can still be complied with (sections 11, 12 and 6).

Errors which may be amended under section 15

54   Section 15 allows an application or medical recommendation which is found to be in any respect incorrect or defective to be amended by the person who signed it, with the consent of the managers of the hospital, within the period of 14 days from the date of the patient's admission. Faults which may be capable of amendment under this section include the leaving blank of any spaces on the form which should have been filled in (other than the signature) or failure to delete one or more alternatives in places where only one can be correct. The patient's forenames and surname should agree in all the places where they appear in the application and supporting recommendations.

55   Any document found to contain faults of this sort should be returned to the person who signed it for amendment. When the amended document is returned to the hospital it should again be scrutinised to check that it is now in the proper form. Consent to the amendment should then be given by a senior officer of the hospital or mental nursing home who has been authorised to consent to amendments on behalf of the managers (regulation 4(2)). In the case of mental nursing homes, the managers, if two or more in number, may authorise one of their number to consent to amendments. These officers can also issue notices under section 15(2). Similarly, a local social services authority may authorise in writing an officer or class of officers to carry out these functions (regulation 5(2)). The consent should be recorded in writing and could take the form of an endorsement on the document itself. If this is all done within a period of 14 days starting with the date on which the patient was admitted (or the date when the

documents were received if the patient was already in hospital when the application was made) the documents are deemed to have had effect as though originally made as amended.'

30.4.14 Receipt and scrutiny of applications and recommendations

Chapter 12 of the Code of Practice also explains and differentiates the duties of managers in relation to the receipt and the scrutiny of documents supporting formal admission to hospital, in the following terms:

'12.1 The Managers should formally delegate their duties to receive and scrutinise admission documents to a limited number of officers with an adequate knowledge of the relevant parts of the Act. There must be adequate 24 hour cover. It is best that a general manager should take overall responsibility on behalf of the Managers for the proper receipt and scrutiny of documents.

12.2 There is a difference between "receiving" documents and "scrutinising" them. Although it is desirable that documents should be scrutinised at the same time as they are received, circumstances will often dictate that in order for it to be done properly scrutiny should take place later.

12.3 Some guiding rules:
   a.   where the Managers' obligation to receive documents is delegated to nursing staff, such delegation should be to the nurse in charge of the ward. If the nurse is below the grade of first level nurse, he should seek the advice of a first level nurse when "receiving" documents;
   b.   the hospital should have a check list for the guidance of those delegated to receive documents, to ensure that they do not contain any errors which cannot be corrected at a later stage in the procedure (see section 15);
   c.   when the patient is being admitted on the application of an ASW the person "receiving" the admission documents should check their accuracy with the ASW;
   d.   the "receiving" officer should have access to a manager for advice, especially at night.

12.4 Some guidance rules:
   a.   where the person delegated to receive the documents is not authorised by the Managers to rectify a defective admission document the documents must be scrutinised by a person so authorised immediately on the patient's admission (or during the next working day if the patient is admitted at night, weekends or public holidays when such a person is not available);
   b.   the Managers must arrange for the medical recommendations to be medically scrutinised, to ensure that they show sufficient legal grounds for detention. The clinical description of the patient's mental condition should include a description of his symptoms and of his behaviour, not merely a diagnostic classification. This scrutiny should be carried out at the same time as the administrative scrutiny (see immediately above).'

The scrutiny of medical recommendations given in support of application for formal admission by a member of the medical staff of the admitting hospital should be restricted to such formal scrutiny as is required to ensure that the medical recommendations purporting to support an application fulfil the requirements of either section 2 or, more particularly, section 3 of Part II of the Act. Scrutiny, by a medical practitioner within the admitting hospital, of the content of the medical recommendations supporting an application for formal admission should not, simply to fulfil the requirements of the Act for lawful detention, go further into debates and disagreements relating to clinical judgment and differential diagnosis of the patient's medical condition. If a particular hospital, psychiatric unit or mental nursing home wished to institute such a procedure by way of internal audit, such would be done independently of the requirements of Part II of the Mental Health Act 1983.

30.4.15 Reclassification of patients

The mental condition of a patient may change following admission to hospital, or a different diagnosis of the patient's mental condition may be made following initial admission. In order to avoid the need for a fresh application being made in such a case, section 16 of the Act provides for the reclassification of a patient, initially lawfully detained, into a different category of mental disorder (with possibly different legal consequences). Section 16 provides:

'16.—(1) If in the case of a patient who is for the time being detained in a hospital in pursuance of an application for admission for treatment, or subject to guardianship in pursuance of a guardianship application, it appears to the appropriate medical officer that the patient is suffering from a form of mental disorder other than the form or forms specified in the application, he may furnish to the managers of the hospital, or the guardian, as the case may be, a report to that effect; and when a report is so furnished, the application shall have effect as if that other form of mental disorder were specified in it.

(2) Where a report under subsection (1) above in respect of a patient detained in a hospital is to the effect that he is suffering from psychopathic disorder or mental impairment but not from mental illness or severe mental impairment the appropriate medical officer shall include in the report a statement of his opinion whether further medical treatment in hospital is likely to alleviate or prevent a deterioration of the patient's condition; and if he states that in his opinion such treatment is not likely to have that effect the authority of the managers to detain the patient shall cease.

(3) Before furnishing a report under subsection (1) above the appropriate medical officer shall consult one or more other persons who have been professionally concerned with the patient's medical treatment.

(4) Where a report is furnished under this section in respect of a patient, the managers or guardian shall cause the patient and the nearest relative to be informed.

(5) In this section "appropriate medical officer" means—
(a) in the case of a patient who is subject to the guardianship of a person other than a local social services authority, the nominated medical attendant of the patient; and
(b) in any other case, the responsible medical officer.'

Either the patient or his nearest relative has the right to appeal to a Mental Health Review Tribunal within 28 days of a reclassification report being furnished to the managers.

If the diagnosis of the patient's mental condition is changed, on reclassification, from either mental illness or severe mental impairment to either psychopathic disorder or mental impairment, authority to detain that patient under section 3 terminates unless the patient's responsible medical officer certifies that the 'treatability criterion' under section 3 is satisfied: namely, that further medical treatment in hospital is likely to alleviate, or to prevent a deterioration of, the patient's condition. In consulting 'one or more other persons who have been professionally concerned with the patient's medical treatment', pursuant to subsection 3 of section 16, a particular professional involvement with the patient's care or treatment for mental disorder is required. It is insufficient that the person purported to be consulted is simply working on the same ward or in the same unit.

If the registered medical practitioner furnishing a report under section 20 (pp. 750–751, above) renewing the authority to detain a patient initially detained under section 3, states in his report to the managers that the patient is suffering from a form of mental disorder other than that specified on the original application, section 20(9) provides that the legal effect of this is automatically to reclassify the patient. So, for instance, a patient reclassified from severe mental impairment to mental impairment of a non-severe kind would need to satisfy the treatability requirement in section 20(4)(b), namely that 'such treatment is likely to alleviate or prevent a deterioration of his condition'. It would be insufficient merely to state that the patient would be unlikely to care for himself or to obtain the care needed to guard himself against serious exploitation, which would suffice for renewal of authority to detain in the case of severe mental impairment. The same would apply, pursuant to section 20, if a diagnosis of mental illness were to change to a diagnosis of psychopathic disorder.

30.4.16 Leave of absence from hospital

As part of the process of rehabilitation or resocialisation of a patient detained under Part II of the Act, section 17 entitles the patient's responsible medical officer (that is, the registered medical practitioner in charge of the patient's treatment) to give the patient leave of absence from the hospital from where he or she is detained. Such leave may vary from a very short period, for instance to visit a local shop, to a long period of perhaps many weeks or even months. It should be remembered, however, that the device of detaining a patient in hospital overnight, either on initial detention under section 3 or renewal of section 3 pursuant to section 20 of the Act, with the intention of sending that patient on 'extended leave' was declared unlawful by the decision in *R v Hallstrom* (1986).[12]

Paragraph 20.4 of the Code of Practice reminds that 'The decision (which cannot be delegated to another professional) rests with the patient's RMO after necessary consultation (it is not a decision that can be devolved to another doctor) . . .'. Given the variety of meanings which 'leave' is apt to be given (as indicated in the foregoing paragraph), it may be both sensible in practice and legally appropriate to suggest a 'middle way' in interpreting the power. Namely, that the power to grant leave, and the particular description (broad or narrow according to the facts of each case) of the conditions in which it may be envisaged or planned, is solely that of the responsible medical officer. The particular implementation of leave may, however, be left to other staff (for instance, the nurse in charge of the ward) in suitable cases, especially where the absence is short and the risk (if any) small. The 1993 revision reflects this in 20.4 (ii). Some hospitals regard 'leave' as necessarily involving an overnight absence. There is no legal basis for such a rule of thumb and, indeed, leave granted even for a short period within one and the same day could invite substantial care and precautions. A proper assessment of foreseeable risk should at all times inform local practice.

Leave may be granted with or without conditions, but a normal condition of leave of any length is likely to be that the patient attends at an out-patient clinic for regular medication, or is willing to receive it from community psychiatric nursing services. If the condition is broken, the managers of the hospital, and others authorised by them, are entitled under section 18(1)(a), below, to take the patient back into lawful custody in the hospital. It should be emphasised that treatment cannot be enforced in the absence of consent unless a patient is detained at the material time in hospital.[17]

Paragraph 20.6 of the Code of Practice states that 'A refusal to take medication should not on its own . . . be a reason for revocation' (of leave). Were the prescribed medication to be directed at maintaining a patient on leave in a safe and reliable mental state, then circumstances could be envisaged in which 'refusal' to comply with a prescribed regime of medication would be a very cogent reason for recall in a particular case, rather than as a matter of any general legal principle.[18]

Section 17(3) applies to a kind of 'limited leave', whereby the patient is required to remain in lawful custody at another place. Typically, this will occur when a patient is being granted trial leave from a more to a less secure facility. In relation to such leave, the Memorandum published contemporaneously with the Mental Health Act by the Department of Health states, at paragraph 73:

'This subsection "states explicitly that the RMO may direct that the patient must remain in custody during his leave if it is necessary in the interest of the patient or for the protection of other persons. The patient may be kept in the custody of an officer on the staff of the hospital or of any other person authorised in writing by the managers of the hospital. These kinds of arrangement would allow detained patients to have escorted leave for outings, to attend other hospitals for treatment, or to have home visits on compassionate grounds. If a patient is granted leave of absence on condition that he stays in another hospital, he may be kept in the custody of any officer on the staff of the other hospital. This kind of arrangement can be made for a trial period before a formal transfer from one hospital to another." '

It will be noticed that section 17(4) requires revocation of leave by the responsible medical officer to be made 'by notice in writing given to the patient or to the person in time being in charge of the patient'. The question arises, should the initial grant of leave of absence correspond-ingly be in writing? Paragraph 20.5 of the Code of Practice states that 'The granting of leave and the conditions attached to it should be recorded in the patient's notes . . .'. This again begs the question of the meaning to be assigned to 'leave', as discussed above in the context of the responsible medical officer's non-delegable power. Practice must be informed by good sense and an eye to safety as well as the appropriate use of staff resources. It is suggested that detailed written permission in each and every instance of leave would be unduly onerous to medical and perhaps other staff of a hospital in which a patient is for the time being detained. A more practical approach, apparently in no way at odds with the letter or the spirit of the Act, would be for the responsible medical officer to put in writing in the patient's notes the parameters (whether broad or specific) within which leave might be considered in a particular case, and to leave the particular decision (subject to the overriding criteria) to the nursing staff in charge of the ward at any particular time. This would accord with the approach suggested earlier in the present discussion on granting 'leave'. There is no reason why, in the case of a particular patient, a decision should not be made that leave should be authorised in writing on each and every occasion when it is granted; but such would be dictated by the circumstances of a particular case rather than by any preconceived local policy which could fail to address the particular safety, risk and wellbeing factors involved in any particular instance.

Leave given to patients subject to restriction orders under Part III of the Act is subject to special rules, set out on p. 786 of this chapter.

30.4.17 Patients absent without leave

A patient lawfully on leave may be recalled, either for breach of condition of leave or for any other reason, by notice in writing by the patient's responsible medical officer. However, section 17(5) prevents the lawful recall of a patient on leave who has ceased to be liable to be detained under Part II of the Act by virtue of the section having lapsed or expired.

Section 18 deals more fully with the case of detained patients absent without leave (which for this purpose includes also those who have been lawfully on leave but who have been recalled and not yet returned) and sets out powers of lawful return and readmission of patients absent without leave as follows:

'**18.**—(1) Where a patient who is for the time being liable to be detained under this Part of this Act in a hospital—

(a) absents himself from the hospital without leave granted under section 17 above; or

(b) fails to return to the hospital on any occasion on which, or at the expiration of any period for which leave of absence was granted to him under that section, or upon being recalled under that section; or

(c) absents himself without permission from any place where he is required to reside in accordance with conditions imposed on the grant of leave of absence under that section,

he may, subject to the provisions of this section, be taken into custody and returned to the hospital or place by any approved social worker, by any officer on the staff of the hospital, by any constable, or by any person authorised in writing by the managers of that hospital.

(2) Where the place referred to in paragraph (c) of subsection (1) above is a hospital other than the one in which the patient is for the time being liable to be detained, the references in that subsection to an officer on the staff of the hospital and the managers of the hospital shall respectively include references to an officer on the staff of the first-mentioned hospital and the managers of that hospital.

(3) Where a patient who is for the time being subject to guardianship under this Part of this Act absents himself without the leave of the guardian from the place at which he is required by the guardian to reside, he may, subject to the provisions of this section, be taken into custody and returned to that place by any officer on the staff of a local social services authority, by any constable, or by any person authorised in writing by the guardian or a local social services authority.

(4) A patient shall not be taken into custody under this section after the expiration of the period of 28 days beginning with the first day of his absence without leave; and a patient who has not returned or been taken into custody under this section within the said period shall cease to be liable to be detained or subject to guardianship, as the case may be, at the expiration of that period.

(5) A patient shall not be taken into custody under this section if the period for which he is liable to be detained is that specified in section 2(4), 4(4) or 5(2) or (4) above and that period has expired.

(6) In this Act "absent without leave" means absent from any hospital or other place and liable to be taken into custody and returned under this section, and related expressions shall be construed accordingly.'

Section 18(4) provides that a patient shall not be taken into custody after a period of absence of 28 days beginning with the first day of absence without leave; but the patient can, if returned to hospital within the 28-day period, be detained pursuant to section 21(1)(b) for up to one week in order to enable formalities for renewing the authority to detain to be completed. Just as special conditions apply, outside section 17, in relation to leave of absence for patients subject to a hospital order with a restriction on discharge ('restricted patients'), the special circumstances of such patients mean that the time limit of 28 days does not apply in their case.

While section 18 provides legal powers to take an absconding patient into custody, no provision is made as to the duty of any person or authority to retake a patient absent without leave, nor as to any financial responsibility of the authority from whose hospital the patient has been absent without leave. In the absence of either judicial or legislative guidance on this question, the answer appears to lie in a quasi-contractual claim of *quantum meruit*; that is, that reasonable expenditure on staff and travel should be reimbursed by the health authority or trust from whose hospital the patient has absconded and to which the patient is returned.

While section 18(1) specifically provides that a detained patient who is absent without leave may be taken into custody and returned to the hospital 'by any constable', police powers in this respect do not extend to exercising the power of entry and search of premises under section 17(1)(d) of the Police and Criminal Evidence Act 1984. In *D'Souza v Director of Public Prosecutions* (1992),[19] the appellant's mother, who had a history of mental illness, was formally admitted to hospital for assessment under section 2 of the Mental Health Act 1983. Three days after admission she went home without leave. On the evening of the same day two uniformed police constables, having reason to believe that she was 'unlawfully at large' on account of having returned home without leave, went to the house to which the patient had returned in order to take her back to hospital. The appellant refused to admit them and, purporting to act under section 17(1)(d) of the Police and Criminal Evidence Act 1984, the police constables forced their way into the premises. The appellant thereupon attacked the police officers and was arrested for assaulting them in the execution of their duty. The appellant successfully appealed to the House of Lords against her conviction for assault. Their Lordships held that the power given to police officers by section 17(1)(d) of the 1984 Act to recapture a person who is unlawfully at large and who is being pursued is not validly exercised unless the pursuit is 'almost contemporaneous with the entry into the premises'. It is not enough for police officers to form an intention to arrest and to put that intention into practice by going to the premises where they believe the person whom they are seeking may be found. Consequently, in this case, the police were not acting in the execution of their lawful duty at the time of the 'assaults' on them by the appellant.

30.4.18   Reception into guardianship

Sections 7–10 of the Mental Health Act 1983 provide for the reception into guardianship of any person who has attained the age of 16 years and who satisfies the requirements of section 7, which are as follows:

'7.—(1) A patient who has attained the age of 16 years may be received into guardianship, for the period allowed by the following provisions of this Act, in pursuance of an application (in this Act referred to as "a guardianship application") made in accordance with this section.

(2) A guardianship application may be made in respect of a patient on the grounds that—

(a) he is suffering from mental disorder, being mental illness, severe mental impairment, psychopathic disorder or mental impairment and his mental disorder is of a nature or degree which warrants his reception into guardianship under this section; and

(b) it is necessary in the interests of the welfare of the patient or for the protection of other persons that the patient should be so received.

(3) A guardianship application shall be founded on the written recommendations in the prescribed form of two registered medical practitioners, including in each case a statement that in the opinion of the practitioner the conditions set out in subsection (2) above are complied with; and each such recommendations shall include—

(a) such particulars as may be prescribed of the grounds for that opinion so far as it relates to the conditions set out in paragraph (a) of that subsection; and

(b) a statement of the reasons for that opinion so far as it relates to the conditions set out in paragraph (b) of that subsection.

(4) A guardianship application shall state the age of the patient or, if his exact age is not known to the applicant, shall state (if it be the fact) that the patient is believed to have attained the age of 16 years.

(5) The person named as guardian in a guardianship application may be either a local social services authority or any other person (including the applicant himself); but a guardianship application in which a person other than a local social services authority is named as guardian shall be of no effect unless it is accepted on behalf of that person by the local social services authority for the area in which he resides, and shall be accompanied by a statement in writing by that person that he is willing to act as guardian.'

Guardianship is infrequently used, and the opinion is widely held that powers of guardianship are needed only for a very small number of mentally disordered people who do not require treatment in hospital, either formally or informally, but who nevertheless need close supervision and some control in the community as a consequence of their mental disorder. These include people who are able to cope provided that they take their medication regularly, but who may fail to do so, as well as those who neglect themselves to the point of seriously endangering their health.[20]

Any person who has attained the age of 16 years is amenable to the power under section 7, and may be kept under guardianship for an initial period of up to six months from the day on which the application was accepted (section 20(1)). The authority for guardianship may be renewed for a further period of six months in the first instance, and then for periods of one year at a time.

While guardianship has this feature in common with admission for treatment under section 3 of the Act, and while subsection (2) of section 7 closely emulates the requirements applicable also to patients detained under section 3, the 'treatability' criterion in respect of the so-called 'lesser' disorders (psychopathic disorder and mental impairment) does not figure in subsection (2), the reason for this being that patients subject to guardianship do not in any case fall within the provisions of Part IV of the Act relating to the imposition of treatment without consent.

The statutory Code of Practice sets out the following recommendations as 'Components of Effective Guardianship':

'13.4 A comprehensive care plan is required which identifies the services needed by the patient, including as necessary his care arrangements, appropriate accommodation, his treatment and personal support requirements and those who have responsibilities under the care plan. The care plan should indicate which of the powers given by the guardianship order are necessary to achieve the plan. If no power is considered necessary for achieving any part of the care plan guardianship is inappropriate.

13.5 There will need to be the following components:

a.   A recognition by the patient of the "authority" of the guardian. There must be a willingness on the part of both parties to work together within the terms of the authority which is vested in the guardian by the Act;
b.   the guardian should be willing to "advocate" on behalf of the patient in relation to those agencies whose services are needed to carry out the care plan;
c.   readily available support from the local authority for the guardian;
d.   an appropriate place of residence taking into account the patient's needs for support, care, treatment and protection;
e.   access to necessary day care, education and training facilities;
f.   effective cooperation and communication between all persons concerned in implementing the care plan;
g.   commitment on the part of all concerned that care should take place in the community.'

The effect of a guardianship application under section 7 is set out in section 8 of the Act, as follows:

'8.—(1) Where a guardianship application, duly made under the provisions of this Part of this Act and forwarded to the local social services authority within the period allowed by subsection (2) below is accepted by that authority, the application shall, subject to regulations made by the Secretary of State, confer on the authority or person named in the application as guardian, to the exclusion of any other person—

(a)   the power to require the patient to reside at a place specified by the authority or person named as guardian;
(b)   the power to require the patient to attend at places and times so specified for the purpose of medical treatment, occupation, education or training;
(c)   the power to require access to the patient to be given at any place where the patient is residing, to any registered medical practitioner, approved social worker or other person so specified.

(2) The period within which a guardianship application is required for the purposes of this section to be forwarded to the local social services authority is the period of 14 days beginning with the date on which the patient was last

examined by a registered medical practitioner before giving a medical recommendation for the purposes of the application.

(3) A guardianship application which appears to be duly made and to be founded on the necessary medical recommendations may be acted upon without further proof of the signature or qualification of the person by whom the application or any such medical recommendation is made or given, or of any matter of fact or opinion stated in the application.

(4) If within the period of 14 days beginning with the day on which a guardianship application has been accepted by the local social services authority the application or any medical recommendation given for the purposes of the application, is found to be in any respect incorrect or defective, the application or recommendation may, within that period and with the consent of that authority, be amended by the person by whom it was signed; and upon such amendment being made the application or recommendation shall have effect and shall be deemed to have had effect as if it had been originally made as so amended.

(5) Where a patient is received into guardianship in pursuance of a guardianship application, any previous application under this Part of this Act by virtue of which he was subject to guardianship or liable to be detained in a hospital shall cease to have effect.'

Although section 8(1)(b) gives power to the guardian 'to require the patient to attend places and times . . . specified for the purpose of medical treatment', patients subject to guardianship under section 7 of the Act do not fall within the compulsory treatment provisions of Part IV. Section 8(1)(a) entitles the guardian 'to require the patient to reside at a place specified by the authority or person named as guardian', without actually entitling the guardian to compel such residence by physical force. Section 18(3), however, specifically provides the power to return the subject of guardianship to that place:

'(3) Where a patient who is for the time being subject to guardianship under this Part of this Act absents himself without the leave of the guardian from the place at which he is required by the guardian to reside, he may, subject to the provisions of this section, be taken into custody and returned to that place by any officer on the staff of a local social services authority, by any constable, or by any person authorised in writing by the guardian or a local social services authority.'

30.4.19 Transfer of detained patients between hospitals, or between detention and guardianship

The transfer of informal patients between hospitals will be a matter of their consent and except under conditions of grave emergency such transfer may not lawfully be achieved by force. In the case of detained patients, transfer between hospitals or units under the authority of the same managers (health authority) may be effected without formality and if necessary in the absence of the patient's consent. Section 19 (as amended) provides also for the transfer of a patient between hospital detention and guardianship and vice versa.

'19.—(1) In such circumstances and subject to such conditions as may be prescribed by regulations made by the Secretary of State—

(a) a patient who is for the time being liable to be detained in a hospital by virtue of an application under this Part of this Act may be transferred to another hospital or into the guardianship of a local social services authority or of any person approved by such an authority;

(b) a patient who is for the time being subject to the guardianship of a local social services authority or other person by virtue of an application under this Part of this Act may be transferred into the guardianship of another local social services authority or person, or be transferred to a hospital.

(2) Where a patient is transferred in pursuance of regulations under this section, the provisions of this Part of this Act (including this subsection) shall apply to him as follows, that is to say—

(a) in the case of a patient who is liable to be detained in a hospital by virtue of an application for admission for assessment or for treatment and is transferred to another hospital, as if the application were an application for admission to that other hospital and as if the patient had been admitted to that other hospital at the time when he was originally admitted in pursuance of the application;

(b) in the case of a patient who is liable to be detained in a hospital by virtue of such an application and is transferred into guardianship, as if the application were a guardianship application duly accepted at the said time;

(c) in the case of a patient who is subject to guardianship by virtue of a guardianship application and is transferred into the guardianship of another authority or person, as if the application were for his reception into the guardianship of that authority or person and has been accepted at the time when it was originally accepted;

(d) in the case of a patient who is subject to guardianship by virtue of a guardianship application and is transferred to a hospital, as if the guardianship application were an application for admission to that hospital for treatment and as if the patient had been admitted to the hospital at the time when the application was originally accepted.

(3) Without prejudice to subsections (1) and (2) above, any patient, who is for the time being liable to be detained under this Part of this Act in a hospital vested in the Secretary of State for the purposes of his functions under the National Health Service Act 1977 or any accommodation used under Part I of that Act by the managers of such a hospital or in a hospital vested in a National Health Service trust, may at any time be removed to any other such hospital or accommodation which is managed by the managers of, or is vested in the National Health Service trust for, the first-mentioned hospital; and paragraph (a) of subsection (2) above shall apply in relation to a patient so removed as it applies in relation to a patient transferred in pursuance of regulations made under this section.

(4) Regulations made under this section may make provision for regulating the conveyance to their destination of patients authorised to be transferred or removed in pursuance of the regulations or under subsection (3) above.'

Insofar as section 19 refers to patients detained in hospital, it is limited in scope to patients in respect of whom an application for detention has been made. This includes patients detained pursuant to sections 2, 3 or 4 but excludes patients who are 'detained' in the sense of being in lawful custody, but in respect of whom an application for formal admission has not yet been made. The question is apt to arise whether a patient detained in lawful custody under section 5(2), but in respect of whom an application has not yet been made for formal admission under Part II of the Act, may be transferred in the absence of consent from one hospital to another (whether within the same, or to a different, health authority or trust). Whereas section 19 does not itself authorise such transfer, there may be circumstances outside the formal entitlements of section 19 which make such a transfer necessary in the interests of the health or safety of the patients, or for the protection of others. The position as to the transfer of a patient, who is for the time being held under section 5(2), to another hospital or unit appears to be as follows.

Section 19 allows formal transfer to another authority or trust and informal transfer to a hospital managed by the same managers. It applies to 'a patient who is for the time being liable to be detained in a hospital by virtue of an application under this Part of the Act.' That means normally a section 2 or a section 3. It also includes a section 4 even though based on one recommendation and for up to 72 hours only.

Section 5(2) does not concern an application having been made. Rather it is a holding power to see whether one ought to be made. Therefore, neither the formal nor the informal transfer provision applies (respectively, to another or to the same health authority or trust). Does this mean that there are no circumstances in which a patient can be transferred under a section 5(2) order?

Clearly, transfer can be effected with the consent of the patient; though questions might arise as to how full and free that apparent consent was if the patient was already subject to a section 5(2) holding power.

Even in the absence of any such 'consent' there may be circumstances of pressing need when the transfer of a patient to another hospital is required. For instance, if a patient subject to a section 5(2) order were to self-harm in hospital A it might be necessary to transfer immediately to hospital B, no doubt via the latter's accident and emergency department, in order to give necessary physical treatment. There is no doubt that, independently of the Act, the common law would permit (and even under the duty of care possibly dictate) such a transfer if it were to save life or to prevent serious and possibly permanent suffering. The transfer would no doubt be regarded as part of the treatment to be given in the emergency.

Even in less pressing cases, it is possible that a patient incapable of consenting to treatment could be transferred under common law powers on the analogy of the House of Lords decision in *Re F* (1989)[21] on the principle that it would be wrong to deprive a person of 'treatment' merely on the basis that they were incapable of consenting to it. In the case, however, of a patient capable of consenting but refusing such treatment it is likely that the principle of *Re F* would not apply to the situation and that therefore a transfer could not be regarded as 'treatment'.

As a general principle it is probable that an extra-statutory transfer (that is a transfer which cannot rely on section 19 owing to the status of a patient on section 5(2)) would be permitted by the common law only in circumstances of very pressing need or 'emergency'. The defence of necessity to a charge of battery or false imprisonment (wrongful detention) would no doubt be restricted to what was literally necessary, that is, going beyond that which was merely convenient. The necessity would have to represent a pressing need for the safety or health of the patient. It would not, for instance, be permissible on this view to remove a patient from one hospital to another under section 5(2) merely for administrative or clinical convenience. Removal to another hospital for reasons other than the danger-to-health reasons indicated above would probably be restricted to wholly exceptional circumstances such as dangerous conditions in the hospital in which the section 5(2) order had been imposed.

30.4.20   Discharge of patients

Section 23 provides for the circumstances in which, and the persons by whom, a detained patient can be discharged from the legal status of detention. In the great majority of cases discharge will mean not only legal discharge from section but also discharge from hospital. Nevertheless, it should always be remembered that discharge from detained status under the Act need not necessarily entail physical discharge from hospital and that the formally detained patient may remain in hospital on an informal basis subject to the agreement of the hospital managers and a bed being available. The statutory duty under section 117 of the Act, and associated legal responsibilities relating to transfer to, or care in, the 'community' are discussed in the final section of this chapter.

While under statistics compiled for hospital admissions and discharge under the Körner system of statistical record-keeping, a patient who is absent or on leave for more than 28 days ceases to be an in-patient, this administrative practice has nothing whatever to do with detained status under the Mental Health Act. Although a detained patient absent without leave may not, under section 18(4), be taken into custody after the expiration of 28 days beginning with the first day of the absence without leave, patients who are absent with leave under section 17 may be recalled to hospital even after that period; and for the duration they remain patients 'liable to be detained' (albeit temporarily on leave) within Part II of the Act. The discharge of a patient may be effected by the responsible medical officer without formality; nevertheless, it is advisable that detailed notes be made in the patient's records as to the mental condition of the patient prior to, and at the time of, leave, given especially that the occasional case unfortunately arises in which the patient following discharge causes harm to others or to himself and an allegation of professional negligence is made as to the process prior to discharge.

Neither the Act nor the Regulations, nor indeed the Code of Practice, gives guidance as to when the responsible medical officer's power to discharge should be exercised. It has been pointed out that[22] the Act does not expressly state when a patient must, or may, be discharged and conversely contains nothing to prevent a discharge even though the statutory grounds for detention still exist. Nothing exists in the Act, the Regulations or the Code of Practice to ensure that discharge should take place the moment when statutory criteria for detention cease to exist. It was decided, however, in *Kynaston v Secretary of State for Home Affairs* (1981)[23] that a person who has been detained under the Mental Health Act 1983 should be discharged as soon as he or she is found to be no longer suffering from mental disorder.

Given that neither the responsible medical officer nor the hospital managers (health authority) are under any legal duty to inform a formally detained patient of the change to informal status when the grounds for the original application are found no longer to exist, the question arises whether any continued detention following the decision to discharge would amount to the actionable wrong of false imprisonment. Certainly, if such a patient attempted to leave hospital and an attempt were to be made to stop him leaving, purportedly on the ground of detention under the Mental Health Act, such detention would be unlawful unless justified under the doctrine of necessity at common law (which would be extreme circumstances only), or if a section 5 holding power were legitimately exercised in the circumstances of the case.

A patient detained pursuant to an application under Part II of the Act may at any time during detention appeal to the managers against detention and those managers may at any time during detention review the legal status of the patient without the necessity of such an appeal by the patient himself. Both appeal and review are dealt with together by Chapter 22 of the Statutory Code of Practice in the following terms:

'22.1 Managers' review is the process by which the Managers decide whether a patient can still be detained or can be discharged. It is a different procedure from referral to a Mental Health Review Tribunal and the Managers are responsible for ensuring that patients understand the difference. It is important that no impression is given to patients that any application to a Mental Health Review Tribunal must be preceded by a Manager's review nor that an application for a Manager's review negates the patient's rights to apply to a Mental Health Review Tribunal.

22.2 **Managers should undertake a Review**, at any time at their discretion, but must do so:

    a.   when the patient requests it, unless there has recently been a review and there is no evidence that the patient's condition or other relevant factors have changed. In these latter circumstances the Managers should investigate, and if there is any doubt a review should take place;

b.   when the patient's RMO makes a report to the Managers, in accordance with section 20. It is recommended that such reports should be received not less than two weeks prior to the expiry of relevant periods of detention, to enable patient's detention to be reviewed as close as possible to the expiry date of detention;

c.   where a patient's RMO makes a report to the Managers in accordance with section 25(1), barring a nearest relative's discharge application.

Responsibilities before the review

22.3   The Managers should ensure that they have reports from the patient's RMO and other relevant disciplines (such as social workers, psychologists, occupational therapists and nursing staff involved in the patient's care), and they should consult with those professionals concerned with the patient's care, where they think it necessary after reading these reports.

22.4   If the patient consents, Managers must ensure that the patient's nearest and/or most concerned relatives are informed of the review and asked to comment or to be available for interview in the same way as when the patient is to appear before a Mental Health Review Tribunal. If the patient withholds consent the Managers should ask the appropriate professional concerned with the patient's care to obtain the views of the patient's nearest relative and/or most concerned relatives, and include these in their reports to the Managers.

The review

22.5   It is for Managers to decide how to review bearing in mind that the following are necessary:

a.   to balance informality and the gravity of the task; they are reviewing a patient's continued detention;

b.   to help the patient to explain why he wishes to be discharged;

c.   to allow the patient to be accompanied by a member of staff, friend or representative of their choosing, to help put his point of view;

d.   to ensure that the patient's RMO and other relevant professionals are actively and positively questioned by the Managers;

e.   to ensure (subject to 22.4 above) that the patient's nearest/most concerned relatives are given the opportunity to give their point of view or to have it represented through a ASW, CPN or any other such person. The patient must always be offered the opportunity of speaking to the Managers alone;

f.   if the patient so wishes, to enable the patient and other parties to the review to hear each other's accounts to the Managers and to put questions to each other.

After the review

22.6   The Managers should ensure that their decision and the reasons for it are communicated immediately, both orally and in writing to the patient, to any relative who has expressed views, and to the relevant professionals. At least one of the Managers reviewing the patient's detention should explain to the patient in person the reason for their decision, and copies of the reports prepared for the review together with the Managers' written decision letter should be placed in the patient's records.'

While Mental Health Review Tribunals (discussed in section 30.8, below) have a legal obligation to hear an appeal from a detained patient made in the proper form and within the appropriate time limits, there is no corresponding statutory obligation upon the managers either to hear an appeal, or to review detention at any time. The statement in the Code of Practice that managers must undertake a review in the circumstances specified in paragraph 22.2 appears to have the status of good practice but is not a mandatory legal obligation.

It is sometimes said that managers 'accept' or 'reject' the renewal report made by the patient's responsible medical officer pursuant to section 20. This is incorrect, and the responsible medical officer's report to managers, made in the proper form, constitutes in itself the lawful authority to renew detention, as provided for by section 20(8). The managers on such an occasion are not accepting or rejecting, but rather considering the effect of something which has already legally been done and whether that lawful action should be undone and the patient discharged from legal detention. Furthermore, the statement in paragraph 22.2 of the Code of Practice that managers 'must' undertake a review of detention on the specified occasions should not be allowed to convey the impression that a renewed detention under section 3 (or under section 37 of Part III of the Act, for which see pp. 781–785 of this chapter) which has not been scrutinised or reviewed by managers is in some way invalid or unlawful. It is the responsible medical officer's renewal report, furnished in the proper form to managers pursuant to section 20(8) of the Act, which of itself forms the complete lawful authority to continue detention.

The nearest relative of the detained patient may give 72 hours notice of intention to discharge and during that time the power of the nearest relative may be barred by the responsible medical officer under section 25 of the Act, which provides as follows:

'25.—(1) An order for the discharge of a patient who is liable to be detained in a hospital shall not be made by his nearest relative except after giving not less than 72 hours' notice in writing to the managers of the hospital; and if, within 72 hours after such notice has been given, the responsible medical officer furnishes to the managers a report certifying that in the opinion of that officer the patient, if discharged, would be likely to act in a manner dangerous to other persons or to himself—

   (a) any order for the discharge of the patient made by that relative in pursuance of the notice shall be of no effect; and
   (b) no further order for the discharge of the patient shall be made by that relative during the period of six months beginning with the date of the report.

(2) In any case where a report under subsection (1) above is furnished in respect of a patient who is liable to be detained in pursuance of an application for admission for treatment the managers shall cause the nearest relative of the patient to be informed.'

If the detained patient is resident in a mental nursing home, nothing prevents a doctor on its staff from furnishing a barring report under section 25, despite being legally unable to give a medical recommendation in respect of the patient's initial detention. For managers' discharge from mental nursing homes see Chapter 4, pp. 94–95.

Finally, a power to discharge may, and in some cases must, be exercised by a Mental Health Review Tribunal to whom a detained patient has applied within the appropriate time limits. An outline of the function and procedures of Mental Health Review Tribunals is given later in this chapter. An application by a patient detained under Part II of the Act to a Tribunal may become an appeal against detention under a different section of the Act. For example, if a patient detained under section 2 of the Act were to appeal to a Tribunal within the permitted time (namely within the first 14 days of detention) and the patient came to be detained under section 3 before the Tribunal was held and was therefore a section 3 patient at the time of the Tribunal hearing, there would be no question of such a patient losing any rights. On the contrary, the practice of all the Tribunal offices (in London, Liverpool and Nottingham) is to regard such a patient as having not only the appeal, made from an original section 2 status but being on section 3 at the time of the first hearing, but also a further right of appeal from the position (by now) of a section 3 patient in the remainder of the time which has yet to expire under the section 3 order. It was pointed out above, when considering whether section 2 or section 3 is more appropriate in particular circumstances, that the statutory Code of Practice provides in paragraph 5.3c. that 'where a patient is detained under section 2 and assessment points to a need for treatment under the Act for a period beyond the 28 day detention under section 2 . . . an application for detention under section 3 should be made at the earliest opportunity and should not be delayed until the end of section 2 detention. Changing a patient's detention status from section 2 to section 3 will not deprive him of a Mental Health Review Tribunal hearing if the change takes place after a valid application has been made to the Tribunal but before it has been heard. The patient's rights to apply for a Tribunal under section 66(1)(b) in the first period of detention after his change of status are unaffected.'

30.5   PATIENTS CONCERNED IN CRIMINAL PROCEEDINGS

Part III provides for the hospitalisation, and in one case the reception into guardianship,[24] of people found to be suffering from mental disorder and who come into contact in some way with the criminal law. A variety of powers are set out in Part III in addition to the central provision of a hospital order under section 37, which in many ways is the 'criminal equivalent' of an admission for treatment order under section 3 of Part II of the Act. The further powers include: remand to hospital under section 35 for a report on the mental condition of an accused person; remand of an accused person to hospital under section 36 for treatment; an interim hospital order, made under section 38 by a Crown Court in order to evaluate the likely response of a convicted person to a hospital order, as an interim measure; and the transfer to hospital of persons who are either serving sentences of imprisonment (section 47) or are detained in prison or a remand centre awaiting sentence (section 48).

In the case of both hospital orders under section 37, and transfer orders from prison to hospital under section 47, restrictions may be imposed on entitlements to discharge based on the necessity to protect the public from serious harm. In both cases, such a judgment will depend upon the antecedents of the defendant as well as the risk of the offender committing further offences if set at large. The process of civil commitment under Part II of the Act is, of course, absent in the case of mentally disordered offenders or persons suffering from mental disorder who in some way come into contact with the criminal justice system. In particular, it is not necessary for a social worker to make an application, the committal to hospital being done under powers of the courts. Nevertheless, the requirements for a hospital order to be made pursuant to section 37 are seen to be closely parallel to the requirements of a section 3 admission for treatment order.

Section 37 also authorises, albeit in a minority of cases in practice, the compulsory reception into guardianship of a person brought before the criminal courts.

30.5.1 Hospital order

The scope of section 37 is set out in subsection (1) as follows:

'37.—(1) Where a person is convicted before the Crown Court of an offence punishable with imprisonment other than an offence the sentence for which is fixed by law, or is convicted by a magistrates' court of an offence punishable on summary conviction with imprisonment, and the conditions mentioned in subsection (2) below are satisfied, the court may by order authorise his admission to and detention in such hospital as may be specified in the order or, as the case may be, place him under the guardianship of a local social services authority or of such other person approved by a local social services authority as may be so specified.'

An offence the sentence for which is fixed by law means in practice murder, for which the punishment is a mandatory life sentence. Under section 2 of the Homicide Act 1957 murder may be reduced to manslaughter if, in the opinion of the court, the accused at the time of the killing was suffering from such disorder or disability of mind as substantially impaired his responsibility for his acts. Given that the sentence for manslaughter is infinitely variable, from (in theory) an absolute discharge across to life imprisonment, the sentence is not fixed by law and therefore manslaughter cases involving diminished responsibility may be brought within section 37 of the Mental Health Act 1983.

The conditions for the imposition of a hospital order under section 37 are set out in subsection (2), as follows:

'(2) The conditions referred to in subsection (1) above are that—
 (a) the court is satisfied, on the written or oral evidence of two registered medical practitioners, that the offender is suffering from mental illness, psychopathic disorder, severe mental impairment or mental impairment and that either—
   (i) the mental disorder from which the offender is suffering is of a nature or degree which makes it appropriate for him to be detained in a hospital for medical treatment and, in the case of psychopathic disorder or mental impairment, that such treatment is likely to alleviate or prevent a deterioration of his condition; or
   (ii) in the case of an offender who has attained the age of 16 years, the mental disorder is of a nature or degree which warrants his reception into guardianship under this Act; and
 (b) the court is of the opinion, having regard to all the circumstances including the nature of the offence and the character and antecedents of the offender, and to the other available methods of dealing with him, that the most suitable method of disposing of the case is by means of an order under this section.'

A humane power is given to magistrates' courts by subsection 3 of section 37, which provides that:

'(3) Where a person is charged before a magistrates' court with any act or omission as an offence and the court would have power, on convicting him of the offence, to make an order under subsection (1) above in his case as being a person suffering from mental illness or severe mental impairment, then, if the court is satisfied that the accused did the act or made the omission charged, the court may, if it thinks fit, make such an order without convicting him.'

This provision applies only where the court is satisfied that the defendant actually did the act, or was guilty of the omission charged, and it does not apply to psychopathy or to mental impairment which is not severe. In the case of *R v Lincolnshire (Kesteven) Justices, ex parte O'Connor* (1983)[25] the mental disorder of the accused made him unable to understand what it meant to consent to summary trial (that is, a trial without a jury). The magistrates could not try the case and accordingly refused to make a hospital order. On appeal, the Divisional Court of the Queen's Bench Division held that the magistrates could have made a hospital order without holding a trial at all. Lord Lane, the Lord Chief Justice said:

'In our judgment the words of section 37(3) are clear. It gives the justices power in an appropriate case to make a hospital order without convicting the accused. No trial is therefore called for. The circumstances in which it will be appropriate to exercise this unusual power are bound to be very rare and will usually require . . . the consent of those acting for the accused if he is under a disability so that he cannot be tried.'

In the later case of *R v Ramsgate Justices, ex parte Kazmarek* (1985)[26] Mr Justice Mann reserved judgment on the question whether justices would have jurisdiction to make an order under section 37(3) where the offence with which the accused was charged was triable on indictment only and not by way of summary procedure by magistrates.

In accordance with the general legal maxim that the court 'does nothing in vain', the Crown Court or magistrates' court which is minded to make a hospital order requires evidence that there is a bed available in a hospital to which to send the patient under section 37 of the Act. Subsection 4 of that section provides:

'(4) An order for the admission of an offender to a hospital (in this Act referred to as "a hospital order") shall not be made under this section unless the court is satisfied on the written or oral evidence of the registered medical practitioner who would be in charge of his treatment or of some other person representing the managers of the hospital that arrangements have been made for his admission to that hospital in the event of such an order being made by the court, and for his admission to it within the period of 28 days beginning with the date of the making of such an order; and the court may, pending his admission within that period, give such directions as it thinks fit for his conveyance to and detention in a place of safety.'

Given that there is no legal right, under the Mental Health Act 1983 or indeed under the National Health Service legislation generally, to assign an offender to hospital under a hospital order, the question arises whether staff of the hospital can lawfully obstruct the making of the order by ensuring that the managers cannot undertake to find a bed for the offender. For instance, nursing staff might generally be concerned about the risk presented by the particular offender, in particular if such a patient were already known to the service as presenting particular management problems and facilities did not genuinely exist at local level for the containment of the risk presented. The situation was considered in *R v Harding* (1983)[27] by the Court of Appeal. Lord Justice Lawton said that the time had come for those who in the past had been 'obstructive' to the use of secure units to appreciate that once a court has made an order under this section, anyone who obstructs the execution of that order or who counsels or procures others to obstruction might even be guilty of contempt of court. Such an approach by the court would be a draconian response to 'obstruction', which in reality might be the expression of genuine concern about inability to handle a particular patient within the existing manpower and other resources. The statement by Lord Justice Lawton was in any case confined to 'secure units'; but even regional secure units which provide greater security than most available at local level, though falling short of the security of the three special hospitals, might genuinely feel unable to cope with a particular patient in particular circumstances. It is likely to be only in the most extreme case of manifestly unreasonable obstruction or objection that any such power of the court to commit for contempt of court could in reality be exercised.

In order for a hospital (or guardianship) order to be validly made under section 37, subsection 7 (of section 37) provides:

'(7) A hospital order or guardianship order shall specify the form or forms of mental disorder referred to in subsection (2)(a) above from which, upon the evidence taken into account under that subsection, the offender is found by the court to be suffering; and no such order shall be made unless the offender is described by each of the practitioners whose evidence is taken into account under that subsection as suffering from the same one of those forms of mental disorder, whether or not he is also described by either of them as suffering from another of them.'

For reasons of practicality, a 28-day period is allowed by section 37 for the specified hospital to vacate the bed, evidence of the availability of which has been given prior to the making of the order. Subsection (4) of section 37 empowers the court to give such directions as it thinks fit for the conveyance of the offender patient to, and detention in, a 'place of safety'. Place of safety is defined by section 55(1). 'Place of safety' in relation to a patient who is not a child or young person, means any police station, prison or remand centre, or any hospital the managers of which are willing temporarily to receive him, and in relation to a child or young person the terms have the same meaning as in the Children and Young Persons Act 1933.[28]

Given that no National Service hospital (or indeed private mental nursing home) is under any legal obligation to accept a patient against the wishes of the managers, it is even possible for an undertaking to admit a patient, given prior to a section 37 order, to be subsequently withdrawn. This situation is specifically dealt with in the Home Office Circular 66/90. To prevent the objectives of the hospital order being frustrated by the absence of alternative placement at the expiration of the 28 days of the place of safety, the Crown Court procedures have been augmented by an additional direction, given by the Lord Chief Justice and addressed to the Governor of the prison which is to hold the person pending admission to hospital, in the following terms:

'If at any time it appears to the person in whose custody the defendant is detained in a place of safety the defendant might not be admitted to hospital in pursuance of this order within 28 days of this date, that person shall within 21 days of this date (or at once if it becomes apparent only after 21 days that the defendant might not be admitted to hospital) report the circumstances to the Chief Clerk of the Court and unless otherwise directed by the Chief Clerk shall bring the defendant before the court forthwith so as to enable it within 28 days of this date to make such order as may be necessary.'

Magistrates' courts have analogous re-sentencing powers, and will no doubt follow the same procedure in the event of it being necessary. The Circular, emanating as it does from the Home Office, is not directed also at hospital managers, though it would normally be appropriate to follow it and, indeed, it was copied to the Chairman and General Managers of Regional and District Health Authorities.

An order under section 37 differs, not unnaturally, from the similar order made under section 3 of Part II of the Act insofar as the offender's nearest relative does not have the right to give notice of discharge. Otherwise, unless the order is restricted (see below) the entitlements to discharge of a patient detained under section 37 are almost identical to those under section 3. Both the patient's responsible medical officer and the hospital managers (health authority) have the right to discharge the patient, even though the patient has been sent to hospital by order of a court of law. The rationale for this is simply that the offender, once diverted to the health care system as distinct from the penal system, becomes a patient like any other patient and is entitled to discharge once well. As under Part II of the Act, the managers are legally entitled to override the decision of a responsible medical officer not to discharge a patient from legal detention although, in the circumstances of most section 37 orders, it is inconceivable that this power would be exercised except in the most extreme case of inactivity or error by the responsible medical officer. A patient detained under section 37 may apply to a Mental Health Review Tribunal in the same manner as a patient detained under section 3 of Part II of the Act, save that there is no appeal during the initial six months period of detention. The reason for this is simply that a Mental Health Review Tribunal, being a quasi-judicial body, is superior in powers to the responsible medical officer but not to a court of law, be it Crown Court or magistrates' court. Patients detained under section 37 fall within Part IV of the Mental Health Act 1983 and are subject to treatment in the absence of consent, if certain procedures are complied with. These are discussed in a subsequent section of this chapter.[29]

30.5.2   Hospital order with restriction on discharge

In cases where, on the basis of medical evidence and the past history of an offender, a Crown Court may add to a hospital order an order under section 41 of the Act restricting discharge, such a patient then becomes what is commonly known as a 'restricted patient'. In truth, the restriction is not directly on the patient (though the liberties of the patient are further and indirectly curtailed), but rather on the doctors and managers of the hospital in which the patient is for the time being detained. Not only does the nearest relative have no power of discharge (as also is the case under an unrestricted hospital order), but the responsible medical officer in charge of the patient's treatment, and the managers of the hospital in whose authority the patient is detained, have no power of discharge either. The only power of discharge for a restriction order patient lies with either the Home Secretary, or a specially constituted Mental Health Review Tribunal. Section 41 of the Act provides for restriction orders as follows:

'41.—(1) Where a hospital order is made in respect of an offender by the Crown Court, and it appears to the court, having regard to the nature of the offence, the antecedents of the offender and the risk of his committing further offences if set at large, that it is necessary for the protection of the public from serious harm so to do, the court may, subject to the provisions of this section, further order that the offender shall be subject to the special restrictions set out in this section, either without limit of time or during such period as may be specified in the order; and an order under this section shall be known as "a restriction order".

(2) A restriction order shall not be made in the case of any person unless at least one of the registered medical practitioners whose evidence is taken into account by the court under section 37(2)(a) above has given evidence orally before the court.'

An order may be made restricting the patient's discharge, transfer or leave of absence from hospital for either a specified or unlimited period of time. A restriction order may be made where it is necessary to protect the public from serious harm, given the antecedents of the offender. Whereas magistrates' courts may make a hospital order, sometimes without convicting (section 37(3)), magistrates may do no more than commit a convicted offender to the Crown Court if they consider that a restriction order should be made. A restriction order may be terminated at any time by the Home Secretary under section 42(1). For such time as the restriction order is in force a patient may be transferred or given leave of absence from hospital only by order of the Home Secretary. The rationale of an order restricting discharge from a hospital order is that further and extra safeguards are monitored through the medium of the Home Office (C3 Division) which is involved in the disposal and management of an offender patient. The Home Secretary may recall to hospital: see section 42(3) and HSG(93)20.

In some cases a person may become a hospital order patient with a restriction on discharge, by operation of law. The Criminal Procedure (Insanity) Act 1964, section 5(1)(c) provides that a person charged with an offence before a Crown Court and found unfit to plead to the charge of not guilty to a defence by reason of insanity must be admitted to a hospital specified by the Home Secretary and detained there as if he was subject to a hospital order with a restriction order made under section 41 of the Mental Health Act 1983. The rules as to unfitness to plead have been modified by the Criminal Procedure (Insanity and Unfitness to Plead) Act 1991, in order to remedy earlier injustices.

30.5.3 Mental disorder and unfitness to plead

The Criminal Procedure (Insanity and Unfitness to Plead) Act 1991 (the 1991 Act) came into force on 1 January 1992. The new Act amends a number of Acts including, in particular, the Criminal Procedure (Insanity) Act 1964.

Home Office Circular 93/1991 sets out the principal changes and offers guidance on the operation of the revised procedure. The amendments introduced by the 1991 Act are procedural; no changes have been made to the substantive common law on the defence of insanity or the rules determining when a person is unfit to be tried.

The Circular explains the legal background and the changes thus:

'The 1964 Act makes provision in England and Wales for persons who are found unfit to be tried, or not guilty by reason of insanity ("the special verdict"), in respect of criminal charges. Its principal feature is that in any case where an accused person is found unfit to be tried, or not guilty by reason of insanity, the court must order that he shall be detained in such hospital as may be specified by the Home Secretary, where he will be treated as though he had been made subject to a hospital order and to a restriction order without limit of time.

The main changes introduced by the 1991 Act are:

a. *a trial of the facts*: where an accused person has been found unfit to be tried, there will now be provision for there to be a "trial of the facts" to determine whether the jury is satisfied beyond reasonable doubt that the accused did the act or made the omission charged against him (thus reducing the possibility of a person being made subject to the court's powers in respect of an act or omission which, as a matter of fact, he or she did not commit or make);

b. *a wider range of disposals*: where the accused has been found unfit to be tried (and, following a trial of the facts, to have done the act or made the omission charged against him) or not guilty by reason of insanity, the court will now be able to choose between a range of disposal options;

c. *medical evidence*: under *section 1* of the 1991 Act a jury is not to return a verdict of not guilty by reason of insanity under the Trial of Lunatics Act 1883 except on the evidence of two or more medical practitioners, at least one of whom is duly approved by the Secretary of State under the Mental Health Act 1983. Similar evidence is required before a finding that an accused is unfit to be tried.'

Procedure

The Circular states:

'In cases where a prosecution is brought against a person who it is thought may be unfit to be tried the Crown Court may, before reaching a decision on his fitness, wish to consider the use of its power under section 36 of the Mental Health Act 1983 to remand an accused person to hospital for treatment. It will be necessary for the requirements of section 36 to be met before making such a remand; but having regard to the needs of individual cases, courts may wish to consider whether the treatment provided by virtue of a section 36 remand for treatment might result in the accused person becoming fit for trial, thereby reducing the likelihood of having to find him unfit to be tried.

Where an accused person is found unfit to be tried he should always be legally represented during the trial of the facts. There may be cases where the accused, because of his mental disorder repudiates his legal representative prior to, or during the trial of the facts. The court should appoint, to put the case for the accused, a person whom the court considers may properly be entrusted to pursue the accused's interests (new section 4A(2)(b)). This may be a person who has previously represented the accused (possibly even one whom the accused has sought to repudiate) or any other person whom the court considers appropriate, for example a solicitor known to the court to have experience in such matters.'

Alternative options for disposal

The Circular states:

'Under the 1964 Act the court has been required, following a finding that the accused was unfit to plead or not guilty by reason of insanity, to order his detention in such hospital as the Secretary of State might direct, as though he were subject to a restriction order under section 41 of the Mental Health Act 1983 without limit of time. The court will still be required to do this when the offence charged is one for which the sentence is fixed by law (i.e. murder), but otherwise the court will have a power to order such detention with or without such a restriction (whether without limitation of time or for a specified period). In addition, however, the court is given the option under the 1991 Act to make a different disposal in a case where it thinks this appropriate. The new disposal options are set out in section 3 of the 1991 Act, which substitutes a new section for section 5 of the 1964 Act.

Subsection (1) of the new section 5 provides that this section is to apply where the accused is found not guilty by reason of insanity, or is found unfit to be tried and the jury are satisfied that the accused did the act or made the omission charged.

Subsection (2) provides for the court to make one of a number of orders. Under subsection (2)(a) the court may make an order (an admission order) directing that the accused should be admitted to such hospital as may be specified by the Secretary of State.

Subsection (2)(b) provides for further options, namely a guardianship order within the meaning of the Mental Health Act 1983, a supervision and treatment order within the meaning of Schedule 2, or an order for absolute discharge.

Subsection (3) provides that the further options under subsection (2)(b) are not to be available where the alleged offence is one for which the sentence is fixed by law. It is considered right to preserve the present mandatory hospital disposal, with restrictions, where the alleged offence is that of murder.'

Supervision and treatment orders

Of particular concern to hospital and social services managers are the new powers to make supervision and treatment orders. The detailed provisions relating to the making, effecting, amending and revoking of such orders are set out in Schedule 2. Although the supervision and treatment order is a new form of order provided specifically for the purposes of the 1991 Act, it is modelled along existing statutory provisions, namely sections 2 and 3 of the Powers of Criminal Courts

Act 1973 which provide for probation orders with a condition of psychiatric treatment (section 2 was substituted by a new section 2, and section 3 was replaced by a new Schedule 1A, when sections 8 and 9 of, and Part II of Schedule 1 to, the Criminal Justice Act 1991 came into force on 1 October 1992).

The Circular explains the nature and purpose of the new order thus:

'The order is not a punitive measure: its purpose is to benefit the accused. In the generality of cases, it is envisaged that it will be used where the court is satisfied that release into the community will not pose an unacceptable risk to the safety of the public – for example, in the case of a mentally disordered person who will be able to live independently with the help and support of health and social services, and who has been charged with a relatively minor offence. The aim will be to ensure that such persons receive medical treatment either as in-patients for a short period or as out-patients, and receive social support to help them to lead settled lives. In many cases it is likely to be appropriate for social supervision to be provided by social workers, who should be nominated by the social services department concerned. It may be, however, that in some cases supervision by probation officers will be preferable. This is for the court to decide after taking advice from medical practitioners and consultation with the appropriate social service or probation service. The agency responsible for discharging the order will have a supportive role. The duties which will be undertaken will depend on the individual circumstances of each case. However, in general, the supervising officer will be expected to liaise, as appropriate, with the medical and nursing services and to help the accused cope in the community. Such steps might include finding suitable accommodation, ensuring that the person is kept reasonably occupied, and dealing with day-to-day problems which might arise.

Before making an order the court should seek to satisfy itself as far as possible that the accused is likely to co-operate with the supervision and treatment. But in the final analysis the order should not be conditional on the willingness of the accused to comply since in many cases he might be unable to give meaningful consent because of his mental condition. However, should the accused refuse to co-operate with his supervision or treatment, penal sanctions will not apply. The court will have no power to enforce the order or otherwise intervene in cases of non-compliance. It will be for the accused's medical and social supervisors to decide on the appropriate action: if they believe that compulsory medical treatment is necessary it will have to be under the relevant provisions of Part II [and Part IV] of the Mental Health Act 1983. In cases where supervisors believe the accused poses a risk to others, but does not meet the requirements for detention under the civil powers, they should act in the same way as they would in respect of any other person in this position. This will involve liaising closely with the police to ensure they are aware of any concern about possible danger to others.

The order will require the accused to be under the supervision of a social worker or a probation officer for a period to be specified in the order, not exceeding two years. Before making the order the court should be satisfied on the written or oral evidence of two or more registered medical practitioners, at least one of whom is duly approved by the Secretary of State under the Mental Health Act 1983, that the medical condition of the accused is such as requires and may be susceptible to treatment but is not such as to warrant the making of either an admission order or a guardianship order. The court should not make a supervision and treatment order unless it is satisfied that the proposed supervising officer is willing to undertake the supervision. The proposed supervising officer will clearly need to have regard to the feasibility of what is proposed, and may wish to express a view to the court, orally or in writing. The court must also be satisfied that arrangements have been made for the intended treatment. The order will include a requirement that the supervised person is to undergo, during the whole of the period specified in the order or during such part of that period as may be so specified, treatment by, or under the direction of a registered medical practitioner. The treatment required by the order must be one of the following: treatment as a resident patient in a hospital or mental nursing home; treatment as a non-resident patient at such institution or place as may be specified in the order; and treatment by or under the direction of such registered medical practitioner as may be specified in the order.

Where, on application of the supervised person or the supervising officer, it appears to a magistrates' court acting for the petty sessions area concerned that having regard to circumstances which have arisen since the order was made, it would be in the interests of the health and welfare of the supervised person that the order should be revoked, the court may revoke the order.'

30.5.4 Restriction orders in practice

There is judicial authority to the effect that in some cases a restriction order should be the norm, unless the contrary is indicated. Lord Chief Justice Parker said in the case of *R v Gardiner* (1967):[30]

'It is very advisable that a restriction order should be made in all cases where it is thought that the protection of the public from serious harm is required. Thus in, for example, the case of crimes of violence, and of the more serious sexual offences, particularly if the prisoner has a record of such offences, or if there is a history of mental disorder involving violent behaviour, it is suggested that there must be compelling reasons to explain why a restriction order should not be made.'

It was further held in *R v Birch* (1989)[31] that the relevant test is not merely the degree of risk that the defendant will re-offend, but the consequence that if he did re-offend members of the public would suffer serious harm.

Subsection 3 of section 41 lists the restrictions which are placed upon patients subject to restriction orders, which are: there is no periodic review of the authority to detain under section 20, as there is in the case of an unrestricted hospital order made under section 37; the patient cannot be discharged without the leave of the Home Secretary, except when a specially constituted Mental Health Review Tribunal makes such an order (see pp.830–831, below); nor can the patient be transferred or granted leave of absence without Home Office permission (Tribunals having no power in this respect save to make recommendations); the authority to detain lasts as long as the restriction order remains in force, and the patient cannot obtain his discharge under the provisions of section 17(5), namely six months limit on leave of absence, which apply in the case of an unrestricted hospital order, nor under section 18(4) relating to the non-return of patients without leave. Nor is a patient subject to a restriction order entitled to obtain his discharge by reason of his mental disorder being reclassified pursuant to section 16 of the Act, which is applicable in the normal case of a section 37 patient. Although it is good and indeed standard practice for responsible medical officers to keep in close touch with C3 Division of the Home Office as to the mental condition and progress of patients subject to restriction orders, there is no statutory obligation upon any person or body to consider whether the criteria for either the restriction order, or indeed the detention itself, still apply at any given time.

Subsection (5) of section 41 provides that when a restriction order ceases to have effect, either by lapse of time or by direction of the Home Secretary under section 42(1), the patient is to be treated in law as if he had been admitted to hospital under a hospital order without restrictions, such order being deemed to have been made on the date when the restriction order ceased to have effect. If the patient has in the interim been conditionally discharged from hospital (either by the Home Office or by a Tribunal) before the restrictions end, section 42(5) provides that he will cease to be liable to be detained under the relevant hospital order. A patient may apply to a Mental Health Review Tribunal within six months of the restriction order ceasing to have effect.[32]

Section 41(6) requires that, while a restriction order is in force the responsible medical officer shall, at such intervals (not exceeding one year) as the Home Secretary may direct, examine the patient and send a report to the Home Secretary containing such particulars as may be required.

Section 42, in addition to providing for the legal effect of the removal of the restriction order from a patient subject to a hospital order under section 37, makes further provision for the progress of such a patient. The Home Secretary is empowered to take the following action in respect of patients in respect of whom a restriction order has been made: first, to direct that the order should cease to have effect; second, to discharge the patient from hospital absolutely; and third, to discharge the patient from hospital but subject to certain conditions (for instance, that medication should continue to be taken, or that attendance be maintained at an out-patient clinic of a psychiatric hospital). In considering these matters the Home Secretary receives advice from the patient's responsible medical officer. In the case of restricted patients detained in the special hospitals (on which see Chapter 1), the Special Hospitals Service Authority, as manager of the special hospitals, is consulted on proposals for discharge.

30.5.5 Remand to hospital of accused persons

Sections 35 and 36 of the Mental Health Act 1983 were introduced as new powers and came into force one year after the bulk of the Act came into operation. Magistrates' courts are given a power to remand to hospital for report on the accused's condition, and Crown Courts are given not only that power but also a power to remand an accused person to hospital to receive treatment. The year's delay before these new remand powers came into operation was to facilitate the special conditions under which such patients might be cared for, managed and (in the case of section 36) treated for mental disorder. Section 35 provides:

'35.—(1) Subject to the provisions of this section, the Crown Court or a magistrates' court may remand an accused person to a hospital specified by the court for a report on his mental condition.

(2) For the purposes of this section an accused person is—

(a) in relation to the Crown Court, any person who is awaiting trial before the court for an offence punishable with imprisonment or who has been arraigned before the court for such an offence and has not yet been sentenced or otherwise dealt with for the offence on which he has been arraigned;

(b) in relation to a magistrates' court, any person who has been convicted by the court of an offence punishable on summary conviction with imprisonment and any person charged with such an offence if the court is satisfied that he did the act or made the omission charged or he has consented to the exercise by the court of the powers conferred by this section.

(3) Subject to subsection (4) below, the powers conferred by this section may be exercised if—

(a) the court is satisfied, on the written or oral evidence of a registered medical practitioner, that there is reason to suspect that the accused person is suffering from mental illness, psychopathic disorder, severe mental impairment or mental impairment; and

(b) the court is of the opinion that it would be impracticable for a report on his mental condition to be made if he were remanded on bail;

but those powers shall not be exercised by the Crown Court in respect of a person who has been convicted before the court if the sentence for the offence of which he has been convicted is fixed by law.

(4) The court shall not remand an accused person to a hospital under this section unless satisfied, on the written or oral evidence of the registered medical practitioner who would be responsible for making the report or of some other person representing the managers of the hospital, that arrangements have been made for his admission to that hospital and for his admission to it within the period of seven days beginning with the date of the remand; and if the court is so satisfied it may, pending his admission, give directions for his conveyance to and detention in a place of safety.

(5) Where a court has remanded an accused person under this section it may further remand him if it appears to the court, on the written or oral evidence of the registered medical practitioner responsible for making the report, that a further remand is necessary for completing the assessment of the accused person's mental condition.

(6) The power of further remanding an accused person under this section may

be exercised by the court without his being brought before the court if he is represented by counsel or a solicitor and his counsel or solicitor is given an opportunity of being heard.

(7) An accused person shall not be remanded or further remanded under this section for more than 28 days at a time or for more than 12 weeks in all; and the court may at any time terminate the remand if it appears to the court that it is appropriate to do so.

(8) An accused person remanded to hospital under this section shall be entitled to obtain at his own expense an independent report on his mental condition from a registered medical practitioner chosen by him and to apply to the court on the basis of it for his remand to be terminated under subsection (7) above.

(9) Where an accused person is remanded under this section—

(a) a constable or any other person directed to do so by the court shall convey the accused person to the hospital specified by the court within the period mentioned in subsection (4) above; and

(b) the managers of the hospital shall admit him within that period and thereafter detain him in accordance with the provisions of this section.

(10) If an accused person absconds from a hospital to which he has been remanded under this section, or while being conveyed to or from that hospital, he may be arrested without warrant by any constable and shall, after being arrested, be brought as soon as practicable before the court that remanded him; and the court may thereupon terminate the remand and deal with him in any way in which it could have dealt with him if he had not been remanded under this section.'

As with hospital orders under section 37, so too with remands to hospital for report on the accused's mental condition, the magistrates' court or the Crown Court needs to be satisfied, on the evidence of an approved doctor who would be responsible for making the report, or of some other person representing the hospital managers, that a bed is available for the patient. The remand is for up to 28 days at a time and is subject to an overall limit of 12 weeks, following two renewals. In the interests of practicality, the accused person need not be present when the remand order is so renewed, but it is essential that such person be legally represented and that the legal representative be given an opportunity to be heard by the court.

The 'spirit' of section 35 is that it should be used not as an alternative to remand on bail, but only as an alternative to remand to prison. Whereas a remand on bail, subject to an accused presenting for a medical examination, might sometimes be appropriate, a remand under section 35 would be appropriate where there was a possibility that the accused person might break a condition of bail, such as attending or actually residing in hospital. As with section 37, so with section 35, an order cannot be made if the accused has actually been convicted by the court of murder, the sentence for which is fixed by law (life imprisonment). Nevertheless, the inability of the court in this regard is restricted to a case in which the accused has actually been convicted of murder and sentenced to life imprisonment; a remand under section 35 can be made in a murder trial before conviction.

The accused person has the right under subsection (8) to obtain at his own expense an independent medical report on his mental condition and on the basis of it to apply to the court to end the remand. In practice, this is not a particularly valuable right for the accused person, given that there is nothing in law to prevent the obtaining of such a medical report independently of the statute. Nevertheless, given that the right is now enshrined in statute, nursing and medical staff should be alert to the possibility of an accused person remanded to hospital for report requesting that such an independent medical examination be arranged. It has been known that confusion may occur between this second opinion, in the genuine sense of that term, and a 'second opinion' under Part IV of the Act (pp. 813–816 of this chapter), the term by which medical opinions legalising treatment without consent are generally and confusingly known.

In respect of treatment for any mental disorder found to exist during the currency of section 35 remand, the accused person does not fall within the compulsory treatment provisions of Part IV of the Act and ordinary common law rules as to consent apply. This has led many psychiatrists and others to regard a section 35 order as less than useful, given that they cannot get on with the job of treating for mental disorder under section 35 in the absence of consent. The question has arisen, whether it is lawful, under the Act or according to general constitutional principles, to impose a section 3 order on a patient already subject to a section 35 remand order, in order lawfully to impose treatment in the absence of consent. There is nothing in the Act which specifically prevents a patient being subject to both section 35 and section 3 at the same time, and it is an apparent misconception that the patient who is subject to two sections at the same time, thus enabling treatment without consent to be given, is in some way 'doubly detained'. The situation is simply that legal authority to treat in the absence of consent is added to a power which initially gives no such entitlement to staff, but during the currency of which the need to impose treatment becomes apparent as a therapeutic need. Paragraph 17.3 of the statutory Code of Practice states:

'Where a patient remanded under section 35 is thought to be in need of medical treatment for mental disorder under Part IV of the Act the patient should be referred back to court as soon as possible with an appropriate recommendation and with an assessment of whether the patient is in a fit state to attend court. If there is a delay in securing a court date, for example an order under section 36 can only be made by a Crown Court (and there can be considerable delay before the patient is committed to the Crown Court), and depending on the patient's mental condition, consideration should be given to whether the patient meets the criteria for detention under section 3 of the Act.'

The Code thus regards the imposition of section 3 in addition to section

35 as a fall-back position when, for practical reasons, including the mental condition of the accused person, attendance at court for the purpose of instituting proceedings aimed at securing a section 36 order is impracticable or inadvisable.

Against this position, it is argued that a patient whose rights are explained pursuant to section 35 may feel confused and even affronted if, during the currency of that section, apparently contradictory legal powers are explained, including (under section 3 but not under section 35) about susceptibility to compulsory treatment. Any confusion on the patient's part should satisfactorily be removed by a very clear statement to the patient of the changed legal situation to which he is subject. It is suggested that this represents a lesser disadvantage than the unavailability of treatment pending return (if indeed that be possible in the circumstances) to the Crown Court to request an order under section 36.

Practical concern is apt to arise over whose responsibility it is to escort, convey and accompany a patient remanded for report at given stages of hospitalisation and return to court for renewal within the 12-week period. In this respect, Home Office Circular 71/1984 is helpful and recommends as follows:

'31. The effect of a remand to hospital or an interim hospital order (like that of the transfer of a remand prisoner to hospital by direction of the Home Secretary under section 48 of the Act) is that the patient will remain throughout under the jurisdiction of the court before which he was remanded to appear or committed for trial. It follows that responsibility for complying with any subsequent direction by that court for the production of the patient will rest with the managers of the hospital to which he has been admitted. Normally, therefore, it will fall to hospital staff to escort the patient to court. An exception may arise where the patient is very violent or dangerous, in which case the police may be asked by the hospital managers to assist. It is open to the court to renew a remand or an interim hospital order in the patient's absence provided that the patient is legally represented and that his legal representative is present in court and is given the opportunity of being heard.

32. Once the patient has arrived at court the normal arrangements for the detention there of defendants remanded in custody should apply, and the Home Secretary would be grateful for the co-operation of the courts and of the police with members of hospital staff in this respect.

33. In cases where it appears likely that the accused person's trial may last for some time, the responsible medical officer or the managers of the hospital may advise the court of difficulty over producing him in court from the hospital each day and enquire whether in these circumstances the court would consider remanding the accused person in custody or on bail for the duration of the trial, after his initial production in court by the hospital. At this point the court would have power to order further remands in whatever manner it thinks appropriate.'

30.5.6 Remand for treatment

A Crown Court (but not a magistrates' court) may make an order under section 36 of the Act to remand an accused person to hospital for treatment. Needless to say, such a patient falls within the provisions of Part IV of the Act when admitted to hospital and treatment can be imposed for mental disorder in the absence of consent. Section 36 provides:

'**36.**—(1) Subject to the provisions of this section, the Crown Court may, instead of remanding an accused person in custody, remand him to a hospital specified by the court if satisfied, on the written or oral evidence of two registered medical practitioners, that he is suffering from mental illness or severe mental impairment of a nature or degree which makes it appropriate for him to be detained in a hospital for medical treatment.

(2) For the purposes of this section an accused person is any person who is in custody awaiting trial before the Crown Court for an offence punishable with imprisonment (other than an offence the sentence for which is fixed by law) or who at any time before sentence is in custody in the course of a trial before that court for such an offence.

(3) The court shall not remand an accused person under this section to a hospital unless it is satisfied, on the written or oral evidence of the registered medical practitioner who would be in charge of his treatment or of some other person representing the managers of the hospital, that arrangements have been made for his admission to that hospital and for his admission to it within the period of seven days beginning with the date of the remand; and if the court is so satisfied it may, pending his admission, give directions for his conveyance to and detention in a place of safety.

(4) Where a court has remanded an accused person under this section it may further remand him if it appears to the court, on the written or oral evidence of the responsible medical officer, that a further remand is warranted.

(5) The power of further remanding an accused person under this section may be exercised by the court without his being brought before the court if he is represented by counsel or a solicitor and his counsel or solicitor is given an opportunity of being heard.

(6) An accused person shall not be remanded or further remanded under this section for more than 28 days at a time or for more than 12 weeks in all; and the court may at any time terminate the remand if it appears to the court that it is appropriate to do so.

(7) An accused person remanded to hospital under this section shall be entitled to obtain at his own expense an independent report on his mental condition from a registered medical practitioner chosen by him and to apply to the court on the basis of it for his remand to be terminated under subsection (6) above.

(8) Subsections (9) and (10) of section 35 above shall have effect in relation to a remand under that section.'

As distinct from a remand to hospital for a report on the mental condition of the accused person, a Crown Court is restricted in the making of a remand for treatment order to patients who are already diagnosed as suffering from mental illness or severe mental impairment. The power in section 36 is appropriate for use in cases where, should the defendant receive successful treatment in hospital for a short period, it might then be possible to proceed with the full trial. The section does not apply to a person who has been charged with murder, for which 'the sentence is fixed by law'. Medical evidence is required from two registered medical practitioners, at least one of whom must have been approved by the Secretary of State under section 12 (see pp. 738–739, above).[33] In the case of an order under section 36, there is no prohibition on both of the doctors being on the staff in the same hospital. The rationale for this difference between section 36 and admission under Part II of the Act, where there is a prohibition against both doctors being on the staff of the same hospital except in special cases of emergency, is that an order under Part IV is made not by an applicant based on medical recommendations but by the court itself as a judicial order, albeit motivated by expert medical opinion. The rationale for restricting section 36 orders to mental illness or severe mental impairment has been summed up[34] as follows:

'These forms equate most closely to the medical model of illness and sufferers would be seriously disadvantaged by a long remand in custody whereas those felt to be suffering from psychopathic disorder and mental impairment would not.'

As in the case of section 35 remands, an order made under section 36 is made in the first instance for up to 28 days and thereafter is renewable twice up to a maximum of 12 weeks in all.

30.5.7   Interim hospital orders

In addition to the new powers to remand for report and for treatment, the Mental Health Act 1983 also introduced interim hospital orders. In a sense, the very title of the order is a misnomer – the order is here and now, as distinct from any interim measure – and the very point of section 38 is not to make a hospital order, but to institute a regime in which it is possible under lawful custody, including possible treatment in the absence of consent, to investigate under expert supervision whether a hospital order would, if made, be a successful option. Section 38 of the Act provides:

'38.—(1) Where a person is convicted before the Crown Court of an offence punishable with imprisonment (other than an offence the sentence for which is fixed by law) or is convicted by a magistrates' court of an offence punishable on summary conviction with imprisonment and the court before or by which he is convicted is satisfied, on the written or oral evidence of two registered medical practitioners—

  (a) that the offender is suffering from mental illness, psychopathic disorder, severe mental impairment or mental impairment; and
  (b) that there is reason to suppose that the mental disorder from which the offender is suffering is such that it may be appropriate for a hospital order to be made in his case,

the court may, before making a hospital order or dealing with him in some other way, make an order (in this Act referred to as "an interim hospital order") authorise his admission to such hospital as may be specified in the order and his detention there in accordance with this section.

(2) In the case of an offender who is subject to an interim hospital order the court may make a hospital order without his being brought before the court if he is represented by counsel or a solicitor and his counsel or solicitor is given an opportunity of being heard.

(3) At least one of the registered medical practitioners whose evidence is taken into account under subsection (1) above shall be employed at the hospital which is to be specified in the order.

(4) An interim hospital order shall not be made for the admission of an offender to a hospital unless the court is satisfied, on the written or oral evidence of the registered medical practitioner who would be in charge of his treatment or of some other person representing the managers of the hospital, that arrangements have been made for his admission to that hospital and of his admission to it within the period of 28 days beginning with the date of the order; and if the court is so satisfied the court may, pending his admission, give directions for his conveyance to and detention in a place of safety.

(5) An interim hospital order—
   (a) shall be in force for such period, not exceeding 12 weeks, as the court may specify when making the order; but
   (b) may be renewed for further periods of not more than 28 days at a time if it appears to the court, on the written or oral evidence of the responsible medical officer, that the continuation of the order is warranted;
but no such order shall continue in force for more than six months in all and the court shall terminate the order if it makes a hospital order in respect of the offender or decides after considering the written or oral evidence of the responsible medical officer to deal with the offender in some other way.

(6) The power of renewing an interim hospital order may be exercised without the offender being brought before the court if he is represented by counsel or a solicitor and his counsel or solicitor is given an opportunity of being heard.

(7) If an offender absconds from a hospital in which he is detained in pursuance of an interim hospital order, or while being conveyed to or from such a hospital, he may be arrested without warrant by a constable and shall, after being arrested, be brought as soon as practicable before the court that made the order; and the court may thereupon terminate the order and deal with him in any way in which it could have dealt with him if no such order had been made.'

Where a court with appropriate jurisdiction is considering making a hospital order or interim hospital order it may request the regional health authority for the region in which that person resides or last resided, or any other regional health authority which appears to the court to be appropriate, to furnish the court with such information as that authority has or can reasonably obtain relating to the hospital or hospitals (if any) in its region or elsewhere at which arrangements could be made for the admission of the person in question under the order. Section 39(1) imposes a legal duty upon the regional authority to comply with any such request made to it by the court.

An interim hospital order made in respect of a defendant imposes a positive duty upon any constable or other person directed to do so by the court to convey the offender to the hospital specified in the order within the period of 28 days beginning with the date of the order; and the managers of that hospital are under a legal duty to admit the person within that period and thereafter to detain him in accordance with provisions of section 38 (above). The reference to 'constable' means not just the rank of constable in the police force (though it may well include it) but the office of constable, namely any police officer.[35] It has been suggested[36] that, before proceeding to convey the patient to hospital, the authorised person should confirm with the hospital that it is still willing to accept the patient, as section 39 gives no authority to convey the patient *from* hospital if admission to it is refused. As to the extra-statutory responsibility in relation to conveying the patient to and from court within the period of a hospital order or interim hospital order, reference should be made to Home Office Circular 71/1984, the relevant paragraphs of which are set out above (p. 795) in the discussion of associated powers in Part III of the Act.

30.5.8 Transfer to hospital of prisoners serving sentences of imprisonment and on remand in prison

Section 47 provides for the transfer of a person suffering from mental disorder from prison to hospital in order that treatment may be given. Such a patient, when admitted to hospital, falls within the provisions of Part IV of the Act (pp. 802–818, below) and is susceptible to treatment for mental disorder in the absence of consent. The power so to remove a prisoner to a hospital is given to the Home Secretary, whose transfer direction under section 47 has the same effect as a hospital order made without restrictions under section 37. Section 47 provides:

'**47.**—(1) If in the case of a person serving a sentence of imprisonment the Secretary of State is satisfied, by reports from at least two registered medical practitioners—

(a) that the said person is suffering from mental illness, psychopathic disorder, severe mental impairment or mental impairment; and

(b) that the mental disorder from which that person is suffering is of a nature or degree which makes it appropriate for him to be detained in a hospital for medical treatment and, in the case of psychopathic disorder or mental impairment, that such treatment is likely to alleviate or prevent a deterioration of his condition;

the Secretary of State may, if he is of the opinion having regard to the public interest and all the circumstances that it is expedient so to do, by warrant direct that that person be removed to and detained in such hospital (not being a mental nursing home) as may be specified in the direction; and a direction under this section shall be known as "a transfer direction".

(2) A transfer direction shall cease to have effect at the expiration of the period of 14 days beginning with the date on which it is given unless within that period the person with respect to whom it was given has been received into the hospital specified in the direction.

(3) A transfer direction with respect to any person shall have the same effect as a hospital order made in his case.

(4) A transfer direction shall specify the form or forms of mental disorder referred to in paragraph (a) of subsection (1) above from which, upon the reports taken into account under that subsection, the patient is found by the Secretary of State to be suffering; and no such direction shall be given unless the patient is described in each of those reports as suffering from the same form of disorder, whether or not he is also described in either of them as suffering from another form.

(5) References in this Part of this Act to a person serving a sentence of imprisonment include references—

(a) to a person detained in pursuance of any sentence or order for detention made by a court in criminal proceedings (other than an order under any enactment to which section 46 above applies); [Section 46 provides for cases within the definition "during Her Majesty's pleasure."]

(b) to a person committed to custody under section 115(3) of the Magistrates' Courts Act 1980 (which relates to persons who fail to comply with an order to enter into recognisances to keep the peace or be of good behaviour); and

(c) to a person committed by a court to a prison or other institution to which the Prison Act 1952 applies in default of payment of any sum adjudged to be paid on his conviction.'

Section 48 permits the removal to hospital of prisoners other than those serving a sentence, namely those specified in section 48(2), including principally persons detained in a prison or remand centre while not actually serving a sentence of imprisonment. In making a transfer direction under the provisions of section 47 the Home Secretary may, and in the nature of the offender's antecedents in most cases will, impose additional restrictions under section 49 of the Act. The consequence of such restrictions is that the patient cannot be transferred to another hospital or sent on leave without Home Office permission and cannot be discharged from detention under the Mental Health Act without either order of the Home Secretary or by direction of a specially constituted Mental Health Review Tribunal.[37]

30.5.9 Diversion from custody

The wide and detailed legal powers which have been examined in the foregoing sections should receive particular attention in view of Home Office policy on the diversion of mentally disordered offenders from custody. That policy, set out in detail in Home Office Circular 66/90 may be summarised by reference to its concluding paragraphs, which read as follows:

'25 It is the government's policy to divert mentally disordered persons from the criminal justice system in cases where the public interest does not require their prosecution. Where prosecution is necessary it is important to find suitable non-penal disposals wherever appropriate and the police, courts, and probation service are asked to work together with their local health and social services to make effective use of the provisions of the Mental Health Act 1983 and of the services which exist to help the mentally disordered. They are also asked to ensure that all their officers are aware of this circular, and to consider any training which is necessary to equip them in their contacts with mentally disordered persons.

26 In summary:

    i.   Chief Officers of Police are asked to ensure that, taking account of the public interest, consideration is always given to alternatives to prosecuting mentally disordered offenders, including taking no further action where appropriate, and that effective arrangements are established with local health and social services authorities to ensure their speedy involvement when mentally disordered persons are taken into police custody;

    ii.   Courts are asked to ensure that alternatives to custody are considered for all mentally disordered persons, including bail before sentence, and that persons who are in need of medical treatment are not sent to prison. The attention of court clerks is drawn, in particular, to the desirability of establishing arrangements in co-operation with the probation service and the local health and social services authorities, for speedy access to professional advice for the court to assist it in its decision making;

    iii.   Chief Probation Officers are asked to ensure that effective arrangements are established to provide courts with information and advice to enable them to make use of alternatives to imprisonment in dealing with mentally disordered offenders. Attention is drawn to the need to co-operate with local health and social services authorities to provide professional advice to courts and to facilitate a wider use of treatment and non custodial disposals, including remands on bail before sentence and psychiatric probation orders and guardianship orders, where appropriate, after conviction; and

    iv.   Prison medical officers are asked to ensure that action is taken to arrange transfer to hospital under the provisions of section 48 of the Mental Health Act 1983 in respect of any mentally ill or severely mentally impaired person remanded in custody who appears to require urgent treatment in hospital, and to consider advising the courts of the suitability of any other mentally disordered person on remand for treatment as part of a non-custodial disposal, such as a psychiatric probation order or guardianship order, after conviction. Prison medical officers are asked to ensure that action is taken to arrange the transfer to hospital under the provisions of section 47 of the Mental Health Act 1983 of any sentenced prisoner who appears to require treatment in hospital for mental disorder.'

30.5.10 Police and Criminal Evidence Act 1984:
the 'appropriate adult'

Under Code 'C' issued pursuant to sections 66 and 67 of the Police and Criminal Evidence Act 1984,[38] principles are laid down for the detention, treatment and questioning of persons by police officers. Such persons include persons suffering from mental disorder or affected by learning disability. No interview should take place, and no statement should be signed, in the absence of an 'appropriate adult', except where a police officer of superintendent rank or above considers that delay in obtaining the presence of such a person will cause immediate risk of personal harm or property damage. The appropriate adult is intended to provide protection for the mentally disordered person whom it is intended to interview. The appropriate adult may be a relative, guardian or other person responsible for the care of the disordered person; or a person experienced in dealing with mental disorder or learning disability; or indeed any other responsible adult. The Code of Practice states that it is preferable for an experienced, detached person to act as the appropriate adult. The appropriate adult acts not simply as observer but actively facilitates communication between the police and the person whom it is sought to interview. The necessary 'detachment' of the person whom it is proposed to involve as appropriate adult may be diminished or compromised by other professional involvement with the interviewee. Such might, for instance, occur were an approved social worker involved in the assessment of the mentally disordered person for formal admission to become involved also as the appropriate adult; it also would occur in the case of a nurse involved in the care or treatment of the person concerned, when the relevant interview was proposed to be conducted in a hospital.

30.6 MEDICAL TREATMENT FOR MENTAL DISORDER

The Mental Health Act 1959 permitted the formal admission (detention) of patients suffering from mental disorder, whether from the community or through the courts, by way of a pattern of provisions broadly similar to those which are now contained in the Mental Health Act 1983. Nothing, however, in the 1959 Act authorised the compulsory treatment of a person who had been compulsorily admitted to hospital. It was therefore possible to argue that, even when a mentally disordered person had been detained in hospital, there was no power of any hospital staff to impose treatment for mental disorder in the absence of consent. That such treatment was in fact given, during the 24 years' currency of that Act, was an obvious and no doubt much needed consequence of detention. Nevertheless, the absence of legal guidelines and parameters within which lawfully to treat patients who had been admitted otherwise than informally and with their consent, was apt to cause concern amongst staff, especially in situations where a patient clearly and forcibly refused medication or other treatment.[39]

Whereas there was no provision in the Mental Health Act 1959 similar to that which is found in section 4 of the Abortion Act 1967, namely a conscientious objection clause to participation in the treatment which is authorised by the Act, it was possible to argue under the 1959 Act that no such conscientious objection clause was needed in order to refuse to participate in compulsory treatment. Now that powers are given by Part IV of the Mental Health Act 1983 to administer medication and electro-convulsive therapy, as well as other treatments involving physical contact with the patient, in the absence of consent, no member of staff is legally entitled to decline to participate on grounds of conscientious objection to the proposed treatment. Any refusal to participate in all or any of a patient's plan of treatment would have to be founded on grounds outside the Mental Health Act 1983, for instance that the proposed treatment was professionally considered to be unsafe by the person declining to participate. For participation in treatments recommended by other professionals (for instance, required by doctors of nurses) which might harm the patient and result in legal liability, reference should be made to pp. 182–183 of Chapter 6.

Part IV of the Mental Health Act 1983 applies only to medical treatment for mental disorder, including nursing care, and care, habilitation and rehabilitation under medical supervision.[40]

There is no power under Part IV of the Act to administer treatment for a physical disorder in the absence of consent, unless it can truly be said that treating the physical disorder amounts to treating the mental disorder. Two simple examples may serve to illustrate the distinction between treating for mental disorder and treating for physical disorder alone. On the one hand, treating a heart defect which causes anoxia, leading to mental disorder, would be likely to amount to treatment for that mental disorder; but amputation of the gangrenous toe of a person whose mental disorder prevented genuine insight into the nature of the problem and thus the possibility of real consent, would be treatment only for physical disorder. Treatment for physical disorder in an emergency, to save life or to prevent serious and probably permanent damage to health, would have to be administered outside the Act and under powers given by common law. Such powers, though they certainly exist, are only vaguely defined in law, due in part to the absence of legal precedents in this area. For treatment for physical disorder in the absence of consent, reference should be made to pp. 263–268 of Chapter 7.

It is not every detained patient who is susceptible to treatment in the absence of consent under Part IV of the Act. Section 56 provides:

'**56.**—(1) This Part of this Act applies to any patient liable to be detained under this Act except—
  (a) a patient who is liable to be detained by virtue of emergency application and in respect of whom the second medical recommendation referred to in section 4(4)(a) above has not been given and received;
  (b) a patient who is liable to be detained by virtue of section 5(2) or (4) or 35 above or section 135 or 136 below or by virtue of a direction under section 37(4) above; and
  (c) a patient who has been conditionally discharged under section 42(2) above or section 73 or 74 below and has not been recalled to hospital.'

To put the matter the positive way round, Part IV powers to impose treatment in the absence of consent apply to patients detained under sections 2, 3, 36, 37 and 47. In other words, compulsory treatment does not apply to patients detained under orders for admission for assessment in cases of emergency (section 4) or to patients who have been conditionally discharged from a hospital order with restriction (section 42(2)). Nor do the provisions of Part IV apply to patients subject to holding powers under section 5 (in respect of whom an application for admission under Part II has not yet been made), and who are not therefore detained under Part II of the Act; or to patients remanded to court for report, such report being the sole objective of hospitalisation, unless a section 36 order or, possibly,[41] an additional order under section 3 has been made; or to patients who are in lawful custody under section 135 or 136 of the Act but who are not yet detained in hospital following an application for admission.

Part IV of the Act provides not only for treatments which may be imposed upon a patient, either as an alternative to or instead of consent, but also to certain special cases in which both the real consent of the patient and a statutory 'second opinion' is required for the lawful administration of such treatment. The place and function of the statutory second opinion under Part IV of the Act is explained in the course of the following discussion of the provisions of Part IV. As is explained in the following section, some treatments giving rise to 'serious public concern' may not be given without the consent of the patient in addition to certain statutory formalities of certification and consultation by a doctor appointed by the Mental Health Act Commission. Certain other treatments, namely medication (after a certain period from its commencement under detention) and electroconvulsive therapy may be given either with the patient's genuine consent or, failing that, by way of certification and consultation by an 'appointed doctor'. Such a medical practitioner must be distinguished from the 'approved' doctor who must be involved in applications pursuant to sections 2 and 3 of Part II of the Act and whose professional opinion on the mental condition of an accused person is required for certain orders made under Part III of the Act.

The registered medical practitioners who are appointed for the purpose of sections 57 and 58 of the Act are referred to in the marginal note to Part IV of the Act as 'second opinions', though that expression does not appear in the text of sections 57 or 58 themselves. Given that a doctor who may certify, following consultation, under powers provided by Part IV of the Act, requires to be appointed by the Mental Health Act Commission on behalf of the Secretary of State, the statutory Code of Practice has come to use the compendious expression SOAD, or second opinion appointed doctor. The expression 'second opinion doctor' has entered common parlance in the field of personal health care for mental disorder and for easier reference will be used in the following discussion. It should, however, be noted that the professional opinion certified in writing by an appointed doctor under Part IV of the Mental

Health Act 1983 is not in the true sense a 'second opinion'. A medical practitioner might want a second opinion on the diagnosis or treatment of a patient, whether for mental disorder or not, and might request another medical practitioner to provide such an opinion. Also, a patient might want a second opinion, in the true sense if, for instance, some condition such as cancer, giving rise to particular concern for the patient, were diagnosed by one doctor and a further opinion came to be sought.

'Second opinion' doctors under Part IV of the Act are not required to give a second medical opinion in the sense of starting from basics, independently of the first opinion. What they are required to do is to certify, having consulted certain professionals (see below) who have been professionally involved in a detained patient's medical treatment for mental disorder, that treatment should go ahead in spite of the absence of consent. It is suggested, though in the absence of any guidance in the Act or judicial authority on the question, that the function of an appointed doctor under powers set out in Part IV of the Act is to certify in writing that the proposed treatment is a reasonable treatment. To do this is effectively to declare that a reasonable standard of professional skill and competence in diagnosis and proposed treatment is being displayed by the patient's responsible medical officer (the doctor in charge of the patient's treatment for mental disorder) such as would exonerate the patient's doctor from liability in negligence in the event of harm or injury to the patient resulting from the treatment.

30.6.1 Treatments giving rise to serious concern and requiring both consent and a second opinion

Section 57 of the Act provides for certain forms of very serious, possibly personality-changing treatment, which were singled out by Parliament in the 1983 Act to require special legal provision. Indeed, so far from taking away the rights of the patient, section 57 of the Act goes further than the ordinary common law and provides that it is insufficient simply that a patient has understood and agreed to the proposed treatment. Section 57 provides:

'**57.**—(1) This section applies to the following forms of medical treatment for mental disorder—
   (a) any surgical operation for destroying brain tissue or for destroying the functioning of brain tissue; and
   (b) such other forms of treatment as may be specified for the purposes of this section by regulations made by the Secretary of State.
(2) Subject to section 62 below, a patient shall not be given any form of treatment to which this section applies unless he has consented to it and—
   (a) a registered medical practitioner appointed for the purposes of this Part of this Act by the Secretary of State (not being the responsible medical officer) and two other persons appointed for the purposes of this

paragraph by the Secretary of State (not being registered medical practitioners) have certified in writing that the patient is capable of understanding the nature, purpose and likely effects of the treatment in question and has consented to it; and

(b) the registered medical practitioner referred to in paragraph (a) above has certified in writing that, having regard to the likelihood of the treatment alleviating or preventing a deterioration of the patient's condition, the treatment should be given.

(3) Before giving a certificate under subsection (2)(b) above the registered medical practitioner concerned shall consult two other persons who have been professionally concerned with the patient's medical treatment, and of those persons one shall be a nurse and the other shall be neither a nurse nor a registered medical practitioner.

(4) Before making any regulations for the purpose of this section the Secretary of State shall consult such bodies as appear to him to be concerned.'

Psychosurgery, which is defined in section 57(1)(a) as any surgical operation for destroying brain tissue or the functioning of brain tissue, is provided for within the Act itself; and regulation 16 of the Mental Health (Hospital, Guardianship and Consent to Treatment) Regulations 1983[42] specifies, in addition, 'the surgical implantation of hormones for the purposes of reducing male sex drive' as a form of treatment to which section 57 applies. Section 118(2) of the statutory Code of Practice is also a medium by which treatment may be added to the list to which the provisions of section 57 will apply. In the Code of Practice published by the Department of Health in 1990 (revised 1993), no such treatment was specified, despite the following wording of section 118(2):

'The code shall, in particular, specify forms of medical treatment in addition to any specified by regulations made for the purposes of section 57 above which in the opinion of the Secretary of State give rise to special concern . . .'

Electroconvulsive therapy is not a treatment falling within the requirements of section 57, despite the possibility of its being a hazardous treatment, nor is any form of medication save medication falling within the definition of 'surgical implantation of hormones', even though many forms of medication may have profound effects on the personality of the patient.

By section 56(2), the requirements of section 57 are applicable also to informal patients. Due to the fact that section 56(1), paragraphs (a), (b) and (c) exclude patients there referred to from the provisions of Part IV of the Act, it would appear on the face of the statute that all that is required of such patients is consent and that no statutory second opinion is necessary. In view of the objective of section 57, namely to provide special procedures for the lawful administration of the treatments, giving rise to serious concern, to which it refers, the omission of the patients mentioned in section 56(1) from the safeguards provided by Part IV of the Act appears to have been a legislative oversight. In practice, the requirements of section 57 should be followed in relation to any patient.

Apart from emergencies (which are in the present context inconceivable in practice, given the gravity of the proposed treatment) as provided for by section 62 (below) the procedural requisites to the giving of a treatment falling within section 57 are set out in subsection (2) of that section:

'(2) Subject to section 62 below, a patient shall not be given any form of treatment to which this section applies unless he has consented to it and—
   (a) a registered medical practitioner appointed for the purposes of this Part of this Act by the Secretary of State (not being the responsible medical officer) and two other persons appointed for the purposes of this paragraph by the Secretary of State (not being registered medical practitioners) have certified in writing that the patient is capable of understanding the nature, purpose and likely effects of the treatment in question and has consented to it; and
   (b) the registered medical practitioner referred to in paragraph (a) above has certified in writing that, having regard to the likelihood of the treatment alleviating or preventing a deterioration of the patient's condition, the treatment should be given.'

Section 57(2) states that 'a patient shall not be given any form of treatment to which this section applies' in the absence of both consent and the statutory certification and consultation procedures. If any treatment to which section 57 applies were to be given with the patient's consent, but without the further requisite procedures, there would be no actionable battery (for the relevance of which to medical treatment without consent see Chapter 7, pp. 222–223), given that the patient genuinely consented to the treatment. It is just possible that the criminal misdemeanour of intentional disobedience to the mandatory requirements of a statute would be committed (analogously to the legal situation arising from the removal of cadaver organs in the absence of procedures required by the Human Tissue Act 1961), but apparently no other legal wrong.[43]

The appointed doctor is required to certify under section 57(2)(a) that 'the patient is capable of understanding the nature, purpose and likely effects of the treatment in question and has consented to it'. These two requirements are undoubtedly to be read together, given that genuine consent to treatment involves not only the capability of understanding its nature and purpose but also actual agreement to the prospect of its being given. Whereas at common law[44] the understanding, in broad terms, of the nature and purpose of proposed treatment is sufficient to avoid an action in battery by an aggrieved patient, Part IV of the Mental Health Act goes further than the common law and imports an extra safeguard of capability of understanding the likely effects of the treatment in question.

Given that 'likely effects' is in practice apt to be significantly wider than the 'real risks' which a patient at common law should understand and agree to,[45] the question arises in this particular context whether a failure to take reasonable steps to enable the patient to understand the likely effects of proposed treatment under Part IV of the Act could constitute a battery, even if in broad terms the nature and purpose were to be understood. Despite the reluctance of the judiciary[46] to entertain actions in battery based on lack of information as to the real risks of treatment, it appears to be not out of the question that an action in battery might be open to an aggrieved patient treated compulsorily under Part IV of the Mental Health Act 1983 in the absence of understanding, not only of the nature and the purpose of the proposed treatment, but also of its likely effects. This argument makes the assumption, necessary to the sensible working of Part IV of the Act, that capability of understanding, and actual consent as an historical event, are connected. It would be absurd, despite one judicial aside which is apparently to the contrary,[47] for the safeguards intended to be imported by Part IV of the 1983 Act to be satisfied in this respect by mere intellectual capacity to understand (without actual understanding) coupled with a nod of the head. Support for this interpretation of capability of understanding, and consent, is to be found in the Mental Health Act Commission's second Biennial Report (October 1987):[48]

> 'On each occasion all three Commissioners [meaning the statutory appointees] are concerned with the quality of the patient's consent, that is the degree of understanding and agreement. This in part depends on the quality and the sufficiency of information given to the patient so that s/he can freely agree to proceed in full knowledge of the relevant implications.'

While, again, there is no judicial authority on the point (no case having so far required litigation to resolve a dispute), the requirement that a patient not only understand in broad terms the nature and purpose of proposed treatment for mental disorder but also its likely effects, imports even greater safeguards into the medical treatment of mental disorder under Part IV of the Mental Health Act than are present at common law (for which see Chapter 7, pp. 208–223).

Not only is the appointed medical practitioner required to certify that the patient is capable of understanding the nature, purpose and likely effect of the treatment in question and has consented to it, but this declaration must also be certified in writing (on Form 37) by the two non-medical appointees under section 57(2)(a). Furthermore, the registered medical practitioner appointed for the purpose of section 57 must additionally certify (in this case alone, without the requirement of agreement from the non-medical appointees) that the treatment is likely to alleviate or prevent a deterioration of the patient's mental disorder. Section 57(3) requires the medical practitioner appointee, before giving a certificate under section 57(2)(b), to consult 'two other persons who have been professionally concerned with the patient's medical treatment, and one of those shall be a nurse and the other shall be neither a nurse nor a registered medical practitioner'. 'Professional concern' no doubt requires active involvement in a patient's care or treatment plan, and merely working on the ward or in the unit (for instance, at an out-patient clinic) where the patient has received medical treatment is insufficient to satisfy the requirement of professional involvement.

In fact, a great many cases which have arisen for consideration under section 57 of the Act have involved patients (perhaps the term 'sufferers' would be more appropriate) who are living at home albeit perhaps under circumstances of great stress and perhaps attending an out-patient clinic or receiving domiciliary visits. In such circumstances, difficulties may be experienced in securing the involvement in the consultation required by section 57 of even a professional nurse who has been involved with the patient's treatment, let alone a 'second professional' who is neither a nurse nor a doctor but who has been involved in the treatment or treatment plan. Typically, by way of example only, such a second professional may be a clinical psychologist or a therapist from one of the professions supplementary to medicine such as an occupational therapist or in some cases a physiotherapist. The term is also wide enough to encompass a hospital social worker who has been actively involved in the patient's medical treatment for mental disorder, but would exclude a community psychiatric nurse having responsibility for liaison between a prospective patient for psycho-surgery or under section 57 treatment and (for instance) an out-patient department of a hospital. In one case,[49] the second professional was even a probation officer who had been involved in the management (and in that sense the 'care') of an out-patient who had a history of minor sexual offences and who was apparently a candidate for the surgical implantation of hormones under regulation 16.

Given that it can be difficult in cases where a treatment is proposed which will fall under the requirements of section 57 to obtain a nurse, let alone another professional who is neither a nurse nor a doctor and who has been actively involved in the patient's care, this onerous require-ment of section 57 has been criticised as introducing impracticality into the law. Nevertheless, given that Parliament saw fit to legislate this further and extra safeguard into cases giving rise to serious public concern, it should be the statutory requirement which influences patterns of practice, rather than apparent deficiencies in resource provision and practice causing difficulty with statutory compliance.

It has been suggested[50] that nurse means a qualified nurse whose name appears on the register maintained by the Central Council for Nursing, Midwifery and Health Visiting, as provided by section 10 of the Nurses, Midwives and Health Visitors Act 1979. This would have the effect of excluding not only nursing auxiliaries, who are not qualified, but also enrolled nurses whose names do not appear on that register. The limitation to registered nurses would also have the effect of excluding student nurses, even at an advanced stage of the training course leading to registration. While in all normal circumstances it would undoubtedly be a registered nurse who would in the first instance be approached by the appointed doctor as part of the statutory consultation process, there seems to be no reason in principle why an enrolled nurse or even a student nurse should not be consulted as part of that process, perhaps at the recommendation or invitation of the registered nurse initially consulted. No doubt, however, it would be the name of the qualified nurse-in-charge, or supervisor, which was entered on Form 39 by the appointed doctor. Furthermore, there seems to be no reason in principle why the second consultee ('second professional') could not appropriately in exceptional cases be another health carer who had been actively involved in the patient's medical treatment for mental disorder but did not possess a professional qualification. While there is no statutory or other authority for these propositions, with which some might disagree, the rationale of section 57 (as well as section 58 below) so far as statutory consultation is concerned appears to be the obtaining of good-quality information about the patient's antecedents and condition, prior to a decision of some importance being made.

Code of Practice guidelines

The statutory Code of Practice, as revised, gives some brief guidelines as to attitudes to be adopted to the practical operation of section 57:

'16.6   Section 57 reflects public and professional concern about particular forms of treatment; such treatments need to be considered very carefully in view of the possible long-term effects and the ethical issues that arise. Procedures for implementing this section must be agreed between the Mental Health Act Commission and the hospitals concerned.

16.7   Before the RMO or doctor in charge of treatment refers the case to the Mental Health Act Commission:

   a.   the referring doctor should personally satisfy himself that the patient is capable of giving valid consent and has consented;
   b.   the patient and (if the patient agrees) his family and others close to him should be told that the patient's willingness to undergo treatment does not necessarily mean that the decision to proceed has yet been taken. The patient should be made fully aware of the provisions of section 57;
   c.   for psychosurgery the consultant considering the patient's case should have fully assessed the patient as suitable for psychosurgery;
   d.   for psychosurgery, the patient's case should be referred to the Commission prior to his transfer to the neuro-surgical centre for the operation. The Commission organises the attendance of two appointed persons and a doctor. The appointed persons and the doctor will usually visit and interview the patient at the referring hospital at an early stage in the procedure;
   e.   for surgical implantation of hormones for the purpose of reducing male sexual drive, the relationship of the sexual disorder to mental disorder, the

nature of the treatment, the likely effects and benefit of treatment and knowledge about possible long-term effects require considerable care and caution should be taken.

16.8 It should be remembered that section 57 only refers to the surgical implantation of hormones for the reduction of male sexual drive where it is administered as a medical treatment for mental disorder; and that, if there is any doubt as to whether it is a mental disorder which is being treated, independent legal and medical advice must be sought. The advice of the Mental Health Act Commission should also be obtained about arrangements for implementing section 57 where necessary.'

The two-stage procedure

Given that the requirements of section 57 may lead to the apparent disadvantage that an agreement between doctor and patient that a certain procedure should proceed can be frustrated if the statutory requirements are not fulfilled, the Mental Health Act Commission introduced in 1990, following consultation, a new two-stage procedure through which to give practical and humane implementation to section 57 requirements in the case of psychosurgery. The policy reads as follows:

'This procedure which applies to cases of psychosurgery falling within section 57 of the Mental Health Act 1983 replaces what has hitherto been the practice of the Mental Health Act Commission since September 1983. The new procedure has been formulated in the light of experience over the last seven years and seeks to put into effect the procedural safeguards of the law in a smooth and efficient manner, consistent with ensuring the rights and interests of the patient. The new procedure is devised to take place in two stages. The splitting of the medical aspect from the consensual issue is designed to ensure that patients for whom psychosurgery is being prescribed should not be subjected to more delay and anxiety than is necessary in order to give effect to the legal safeguards in section 57.

The initial steps

The patient's consultant psychiatrist will inform the MHAC that he or she is intending to recommend psychosurgery. Simultaneously, the consultant psychiatrist will consult the neuro-surgeon and, where necessary, any other medical advisor for his or her opinion that the patient is a suitable candidate for psycho-surgery.

Stage I

On being informed by the patient's consultant psychiatrist of the intention to prescribe psychosurgery, the MHAC will appoint a suitable registered medical practitioner, who should be a consultant psychiatrist familiar with the assessment and selection of patients for psychosurgery ("the appointed doctor").

The appointed doctor will discuss with the patient's consultant psychiatrist the proposals for psychosurgery, and make such investigations as he or she considers necessary. The appointed doctor will then notify the MHAC of the desire to proceed to the second stage.

Stage II

The MHAC will appoint the two non-medical members for the purpose of section 57(2)(a). All three members of the section 57 team will visit the patient and the relevant professionals. If all three members decide to certify under subsection (a) of section 57(2) and the appointed doctor decides to certify under subsection (b) of the same section, then the certification will be notified immediately by the team to the patient, his or her relative (if appropriate), the patient's consultant psychiatrist, the neuro-surgeon performing the psycho-surgery and the MHAC.

The MHAC will confirm that a certificate has been issued. One of the non-medical members will submit a report to the MHAC office.

The MHAC under section 61(1)(b) will seek a report from the patient's consultant psychiatrist on the treatment and the patient's condition within twelve months of the operation being carried out.

Certification

The certificates under section 57(2)(a) and (b) are granted or not, as the case may be, by respectively all three appointees and the appointed doctor.

If there is any complaint about the decisions of the appointees or about the decision-making process, there is no procedure for appealing to the Commission. There is however, available to any complainant access to the courts by way of judicial review (see *R v Mental Health Act Commission, ex parte W*, 26 May 1988). If there is any matter affecting the operation of section 57, about which anyone feels concerned the MHAC will want to be informed.'

Where a patient has consented to a treatment to which section 57 applies, such consent may be withdrawn at any time before the administration or completion of the treatment. If, by contrast, consent is not withdrawn but the patient becomes incapable of validly consenting or refusing, or becomes so indecisive as to proposed treatment that a neurosurgeon or other doctor would feel unsafe in proceeding with treatment, the question arises whether the certification of capability of consent under section 57 is a once-for-all process. In the case of a refusing or clearly indecisive patient, treatment should not proceed and it would almost certainly be an actionable wrong at common law to do so, irrespective of the provisions of section 57. In the case of a patient who becomes incapable after the giving and certification of a genuine consent, the problem is more difficult. The Mental Health Act Commission has obtained Counsel's opinion to the effect that a treatment governed by section 57 could still be given within the statute if incapability supervened following the giving and certification of consent. Section 57(2)(a) requires that a patient 'has consented', thus representing consent as an historical event rather than a continuing state (of mind).[51] It should be remembered, however, that section 57 simply adds additional requirements to common law obligations related to consent; and that any treatment purporting to be given legally in the absence of clear consent would have to be justified by some such principle as that enunciated in the case of *Re F* (1989).[52] In the present editor's opinion it is far from clear whether the decision in *Re F* would extend to such a case and the question must therefore be considered open. Whatever the requirements as to certification of the fact that a patient has consented, that could (at least in theory) relate to an historical event only; and consent at common law relates to an ongoing state of mind and decision which could change at any time.

30.6.2 Treatment requiring consent or a second opinion

The very great majority of cases governed by Part IV of the Act relate to treatments falling within the provisions of section 58. These are: electroconvulsive therapy, given at any time to a patient to whom Part IV of the Act applies (see pp. 803–804, above); and medication (whether in tablet or syrup form, or by injection) given at any time after the expiration of three months following the first administration of medication (for any reason related to mental disorder) during a continuous detention period. As distinct from section 57 treatments, those falling within section 58 require consent or a second opinion, in the alternative. The certification of consent is in this case simply the job of the patient's responsible medical officer, though section 58(3)(a) provides also for the possibility (rarely encountered in practice) of a second opinion doctor certifying capability of consent in the event of the responsible medical officer's having expressed a doubt and for that reason implemented the second opinion procedure.

The notion of consent for section 58 purposes is exactly the same as that for section 57 above: namely, that the patient should be capable of understanding the nature, purpose and likely effects of the proposed treatment, and has consented. The comments in relation to capacity and consent under section 57 above apply equally in the case of section 58: namely, that capability of understanding is no mere intellectual capacity but is linked with an actual decision or choice, and that the term 'likely effects' appears to go further than the common law requirement[53] that a patient receive an explanation of 'real risks'. The same comment which was made above in relation to section 57 treatments applies equally, and with much greater frequency in practice, to electroconvulsive therapy and 'medication after three months', namely, that a patient who is unreasonably and therefore wrongly certified as understanding the likely effects of treatment could bring an action in battery against the person administering it. For reasons given above, as well as the reasons set out in Chapter 7, any legal action would probably in practice be limited to negligence as distinct from battery.

The 'three months' rule' enables medication to be administered, by any means, for a period of three months from the date on which medication was first given during a period of continued detention. Typically, such detention would be under a section 3 order, though it could be constituted by a section 2 order followed immediately, by way of a fresh application, by consultation with the nearest relative and so forth, and constituting a continuous detention period. Detention in hospital under sections of the Act not falling within the provisions of Part IV (section 4, or holding powers under section 5) do not constitute part of the continuous detention period for the operation of the three months rule. The period of three months was accepted by Parliament as a compromise representing the period which it would be reasonable to give medical practitioners to assess drugs, their dosage levels and their action in combination. The 'three months rule' means effectively that medication may be given without consent for that period, namely, three months following the initial administration of medication (which may have been for any reason, including emergency sedation). It is normally the practice of medical records departments to assume that medication has been given on the first day of detention under section in hospital, unless and until the contrary is indicated by, for instance, the consultant psychiatrist's medical secretary. This will mean that the three months rule reminder goes out to the consultant of a relevant detained patient three months from the date of admission, unless there has been a positive indication from the doctor or doctor's secretary that medication began only at a later time. There is no 'three months rule' for electroconvulsive therapy and (emergencies apart, for which see pp. 815–816, above), either consent or a second opinion is required from the outset of such treatment. It is in any event good practice to seek the consent even of a patient subject to Part IV of the Act, in respect of whom there is ultimately legal power to impose treatment.

The comments made above in relation to section 57 on consultation and the nurse and second professional consulted by the appointed doctor, apply equally in the case of treatments falling within section 58. As distinct from section 57 treatments, there is no non-medical or lay representation in the certification procedure, the only person statutorily appointed being a registered medical practitioner. Section 59 of the Act provides that any consent or certificate under section 58 (as well as under section 57 above) may relate to a plan of treatment under which the patient is to be given (whether within a specified period or otherwise) one or more of the forms of treatment to which that section applies. The case of a patient aged under 16 years, to whom Part IV of the Mental Health Act may nevertheless apply, and whose capacity to consent is in doubt on account of earlier psychiatric disorder, is discussed on p. 267 of Chapter 7. As is the case in section 57, so also in the case of section 58 the common law entitlement to withdraw consent to treatment at any time is recognised by section 60. An exception, is however, made to the common law position in that withdrawal of consent to treatment falling within Part IV of the Act may lead to the implementation of section 62, which overlaps with the common law justification of necessity (see Chapter 7) but also goes further. The effect of section 62 is explained next.

30.6.3 Urgent treatment

Section 62 provides as follows:

'**62.**—(1) Sections 57 and 58 above shall not apply to any treatment—

(a) which is immediately necessary to save the patient's life; or

(b) which (not being irreversible) is immediately necessary to prevent a serious deterioration of his condition; or

(c) which (not being irreversible or hazardous) is immediately necessary to alleviate serious suffering by the patient; or

(d) which (not being irreversible or hazardous) is immediately necessary and represents the minimum interference necessary to prevent the patient from behaving violently or being a danger to himself or to others.

(2) Sections 60 and 61(3) above shall not preclude the continuation of any treatment or of treatment under any plan pending compliance with section 57 or 58 above if the responsible medical officer considers that the discontinuance of the treatment or of treatment under the plan would cause serious suffering to the patient.

(3) For the purposes of his section treatment is irreversible if it has unfavourable irreversible physical or psychological consequences and hazardous if it entails significant physical hazard.'

While it is inconceivable that such a procedure as psychosurgery or the surgical implantation of hormones would in practice attract the provisions of section 62, is quite common for treatment by way of electroconvulsive therapy, and sometimes by way of medication, to be given under situations of urgency which do not permit sufficient time to put in hand the second opinion procedure in the event of a patient's refusal of treatment or incapacity to consent. Section 62 overlaps with what appears to be the common law in respect of treatments designed to save life or to prevent serious damage to health; but it goes further, in particular in section 62(1)(d), to cover treatment which is regarded as therapeutically desirable to stabilise the patient's condition and 'to prevent the patient from behaving violently or being a danger to himself or to others'. While consent may be withdrawn at any stage during treatment falling within Part IV of the Act, if such treatment is considered urgent it may be continued under section 62(2) 'if the responsible medical officer considers that the discontinuance of the treatment or of treatment under the plan would cause serious suffering to the patient'. In relying on the exceptions created by section 62, the patient's responsible medical officer is not under any statutory obligation to consult any other professional. The absence of specific statutory guidance on the use of section 62 for urgent treatments is remedied by paragraphs 16.18 and 16.19 of the Code of Practice, which provide as follows:

'16.18 Any decision to treat a patient urgently under section 62 is a responsibility of the patient's RMO who should bear in mind the following considerations:

a. treatment can only be given where it is immediately necessary to achieve one of the objects set out in section 62 and it is not possible to comply with the safeguards of Part IV of the Act. It is insufficient for the proposed treatment to be simply "necessary" or "beneficial";

b.   in certain circumstances "hazardous" or "irreversible" treatment cannot be administered under this section even if it is immediately necessary. The patient's RMO is responsible for deciding whether treatment falls into either of these categories, having regard to mainstream medical opinion;

c.   urgent treatment given under section 62 can only continue for as long as it is immediately necessary to achieve the statutory objective(s);

d.   before deciding to give treatment under section 62 the patient's RMO should wherever possible discuss the proposed urgent treatment with others involved with the patient's care;

It is essential that RMOs have a clear understanding of the circumstances when section 62 applies (see paragraph 16.2.d.).

16.19   The Managers should ensure that a form is devised to be completed by the patient's RMO every time urgent treatment is given under section 62. Such a form should require details to be given of the proposed treatment; why it is of urgent necessity to give the treatment; the length of time for which the treatment was given. The Managers should monitor the use of section 62 in their hospitals.'

Medication is from time to time required on a 'PRN' basis, which stands for the latin *pro re nata*, meaning 'as the need arises'. The expression PRN medication is accordingly susceptible of application to two quite separate situations, one being an emergency falling within section 62 and the other as part of the plan of treatment in which the application of PRN medication is actually anticipated. If PRN medication is part of the treatment plan or should in some other way have been anticipated as a likely treatment for a particular patient on particular occasions, then the treatment will not attract the exceptional rules set out in section 62 and will fall within the normal provisions of section 58, if it is a treatment to which Part IV of the Act applies. If, by contrast, the term 'PRN medication' is used loosely to describe urgent or emergency treatment in respect of which it would be clinically inadvisable to wait for section 58 requirements to be implemented, then no harm is done, provided that the two senses are kept clearly distinct.

30.6.4   Treatment not requiring consent

Given that many treatments within the general meaning of 'medical treatment for mental disorder' may involve physical contact, but do not fall within the provisions of either section 57 or section 58 above, legal authority or justification is required in a case where such treatments involve physical contact with a patient who refuses or cannot consent to treatment. For that reason, section 63 provides as follows:

'**63.** The consent of a patient shall not be required for any medical treatment given to him for the mental disorder from which he is suffering, not being treatment falling within section 57 or 58 above, if the treatment is given by or under the direction of the responsible medical officer.'

From the legal point of view, there are two categories of treatment to which section 63 accordingly applies. First, there are treatments which do not in any event fall within the provisions of section 57 or 58, including for instance physiotherapy or occupational therapy which may involve some degree of physical contact. Quite separately, but still falling within section 63 which authorises treatment without consent, are treatments which would fall within section 57 or, much more frequently and realistically in practice, within section 58, but which no longer do so because of the urgency as defined by section 62 above. An example would be electroconvulsive therapy which is suddenly necessary to cause a severely and rapidly dehydrating patient suffering from deep depression to resume eating and drinking, without which severe injury to health or even death might ensue. Such treatment would normally fall within section 58, but owing to the urgency as set out in section 62 no longer does so. It therefore becomes a treatment to which section 58 does not apply.

Although no harm is done by saying, as is common, that such a treatment is given under section 62, the treatment is in fact given under section 63 of the Act. The significance of this distinction is that, in order to be legally justified, treatments given under section 63 require to be given by or under the direction of the responsible medical officer. Thus, even though a life-saving treatment referred in section 62(1)(a) could be given by anybody, to anyone else, treatment covered by section 62 (1)(d), which is necessary to stabilise a patient's condition and prevent violence, may only be given, under section 63, by or under the direction of the responsible medical officer. It is in relation to section 63 that the definition in section 145 of the Act of medical treatment comes to be of particular practical importance. Treatment is defined as including 'nursing, and also includes care, habilitation and rehabilitation under medical supervision'.

30.6.5 Review of treatment

Treatment given under section 57, or under compulsory powers following consultation under section 58(3)(b) (the patient refusing or incapable of consenting), requires to be reviewed from time to time in accordance with section 61 of the Act, which provides:

'**61.**—(1) Where a patient is given treatment in accordance with section 57(2) or 58(3)(b) above a report on the treatment and the patient's condition shall be given by the responsible medication officer to the Secretary of State—
  (a) on the next occasion on which the responsible medical officer furnishes a report in respect of the patient under section 20(3) above; and
  (b) at any other time if so required by the Secretary of State.
(2) In relation to a patient who is subject to a restriction order or restriction direction subsection (1) above shall have effect as if paragraph (a) required the report to be made—

(a) in the case of treatment in the period of six months beginning with the date of the order or direction, at the end of that period;

(b) in the case of treatment at any subsequent time, on the next occasion on which the responsible medical officer makes a report in respect of the patient under section 41(6) or 49(3) above.

(3) The Secretary of State may at any time give notice to the responsible medical officer directing that, subject to section 62 below, a certificate given in respect of a patient under section 57(2) or 58(3)(b) above shall not apply to treatment given to him after a date specified in the notice and sections 57 and 58 above shall then apply to any such treatment as if that certificate had not been given.'

In respect of this review, the report is sent to the Mental Health Act Commission which has a specially constituted review process to audit the use, in particular, of compulsory treatment powers under section 58. The Hospital, Guardianship and Consent to Treatment Regulations 1983[42] provide no particular Form for such a review, and the Commission has therefore designed Form MHAC1 for this purpose. It is now the practice of the Commission to ask, at each review, whether an originally non-consenting patient is now consenting to treatment.

30.7 REMOVAL OF DISORDERED PERSON TO PLACE OF SAFETY

Sections 135 and 136 of the Act provide a variety of powers to take a person considered to be mentally disordered into lawful custody in order that they may be removed to a place of safety within the meaning of the Act. Section 135 provides for two distinct circumstances. Section 135(1) provides:

'**135.**—(1) If it appears to a justice of the peace, on information on oath laid by an approved social worker, that there is reasonable cause to suspect that a person believed to be suffering from mental disorder—
(a) has been, or is being, ill-treated, neglected or kept otherwise than under proper control, in any place within the jurisdiction of the justice, or
(b) being unable to care for himself, is living alone in any such place,
the justice may issue a warrant authorising any constable to enter, if need be by force, any premises specified in the warrant in which that person is believed to be, and, if thought fit, to remove him to a place of safety with a view to the making of an application in respect of him under Part II of this Act, or of other arrangements for his treatment or care.'

Since the Police and Criminal Evidence Act 1984 it has not been necessary to name a particular constable in the warrant.

Subsection (1) simply requires the approved social worker to 'think fit' to remove the person considered to be mentally disordered to a place of safety 'with a view to the making of an application' under Part II of the Act (for instance, a section 2 or section 3 order). No such order need eventually be made for the lawful exercise of section 135. Subsection (2) of section 135 provides for the different situation in which a warrant may be issued to a policeman to enter premises, forcibly if necessary, to take or retake a patient who is already liable to be detained under the Act. Subsection (2) accordingly applies to detained patients who are absent without leave, or who have been recalled for some reason, including breach of a condition. Nevertheless, the view has been expressed[54] that a warrant could not be issued under subsection (1) if the sole cause of concern was that a person was refusing to take his medication. While such refusal might not amount to such a person 'being unable to care for himself', the retaking of a person unwilling either to receive medication or to leave the premises in question, would appear to be authorised by subsection (2) if such refusal put him at risk.

Warrants issued pursuant to section 135 of the Act must comply with the requirements of sections 15 and 16 of the Police and Criminal Evidence Act 1984 in order to be lawful.

'Place of safety' is defined in section 135(6):

'(6) In this section "place of safety" means residential accommodation provided by a local social services authority under Part III of the National Assistance Act 1948 or under paragraph 2 of Schedule 8 to the National Health Service Act 1977, a hospital as defined by this Act, a police station, a mental nursing home or residential home for mentally disordered persons or any other suitable place the occupier of which is willing temporarily to receive the patient.'

'Place of safety' has an identical meaning for the purposes of section 136, which provides:

'**136.**—(1) If a constable finds in a place to which the public have access a person who appears to him to be suffering from mental disorder and to be in immediate need of care or control, the constable may, if he thinks it necessary to do so in the interests of that person or for the protection of other persons, remove that person to a place of safety within the meaning of section 135 above.

(2) A person removed to a place of safety under this section may be detained there for a period not exceeding 72 hours for the purpose of enabling him to be examined by a registered medical practitioner and to be interviewed by an approved social worker and of making any necessary arrangements for his treatment or care.'

In the case of both section 135 and section 136, the place of safety is much less likely in practice to be a police station than a hospital or other more suitable place in which the person concerned can receive care and treatment, or perhaps just assessment, for mental disorder. Neither section 135 nor section 136 is an admission section, meaning that if a patient is detained, for instance, under section 2 or section 3 of Part II of the Act following (physical) admission to hospital, there may be no particular record of the lawful means by which the patient was removed to such a place of safety. If, on the other hand, a person is taken under section 135 or (in practice more frequently) under section 136 to a police station, the record of police detention will in normal circumstances specifically indicate that section 136 has been the lawful authority to apprehend the person in question. If a police station is chosen as the place of safety, the rights to legal representation and other rights under Code 'C' of the Police and Criminal Evidence Act 1984 apply equally to the person 'apprehended' under the Mental Health Act. This has led to the section 136 power, in particular, being referred to in police circles as a power of arrest. This is incorrect and has potentially misleading pejorative implications for the use of section 136 and possibly even an unwillingness to implement it.

The statutory Code of Practice is helpful on the practical implementation of the police power to remove to a place of safety and it is worth setting out Chapter 10 of the Code of Practice in full, as follows:

'Good practice

10.1   This depends on:

a.   the local social services authority, district health authority and the Chief Officer of Police establishing a clear policy for its implementation;
b.   all professionals involved in its implementation understanding the power and its purpose and following the local policy concerning its implementation.

The local policy

10.2   The aim of the policy should be to secure the competent and speedy assessment by a doctor *and* an ASW of the person detained under the power.

10.3   The policy should define, in particular, the responsibilities of:

a.   police officers to remain in attendance, where the patient's health or safety or the protection of others so require when the patient is taken to a place of safety (other than a police station);
b.   police officers, doctors and ASWs for the satisfactory returning to the community of the person assessed under section 136 but not admitted to hospital or immediately placed in accommodation.

10.4   The policy should include provisions for the use of the section to be monitored so that:

a.   a check can be made of how and it what circumstances it is being used, including its use in relation to given categories of people, such as those from particular ethnic or cultural groups;
b.   informed consideration can be given by all parties to the policy to any changes in the mental health services that might result in the reduction of its use.

The place of safety

10.5   The identification of preferred places of safety is a matter for local agreement. Regard should be had to any impact different types of place of safety may have on the person held and hence on the outcome of an assessment.

Good practice points

10.6   Where an individual is detained by the police under section 136 it is desirable that:

a.   where he is to be taken to a hospital as a place of safety *immediate* contact is made by the police with both the hospital and the local social services department;
b.   where the police station is to be used as a place of safety immediate contact is made with the local social services authority and the appropriate doctor.

The local policy for the implementation of section 136 should ensure that police officers have no difficulty in identifying whom to contact.

Record keeping

10.7   A record of the person's time of arrival must be made immediately he reaches the place of safety. As soon as the individual is no longer detained under section 136 he must be so advised by those who are detaining him. It would be good practice for Managers (where the hospital is used as the place of safety) to devise and use a form for recording the end of the person's detention under this section (similar to the form used for section 5(4)).

10.8   Section 136 is not an emergency admission section. It enables an individual who falls within its criteria to be detained for the purposes of an assessment by a doctor and ASW, and for any necessary arrangements for his treatment and care to be made. When these have been completed, within the 72 hour detention period, the authority to detain the patient ceases. Where a hospital is used as a place of safety it may be better for the patient not to be formally admitted although he may have to be cared for on a ward. Where such a policy is adopted it is essential to remember that the patient must be examined by a doctor in the same way as if he had been formally admitted.

Information about rights

10.9   Where an individual has been removed to a place of safety by the police under section 136:

a.   the person removed is entitled to have another person of his choice informed of his arrest and whereabouts (Section 56 of Police and Criminal Evidence Act 1984);
b.   when the person removed is in police detention (that is, a police station is being used as a place of safety) he has a right of access to legal advice (Section 58 of Police and Criminal Evidence Act);
c.   where detention is in a place of safety other than a police station access to legal advice should be facilitated whenever it is requested.

10.10   Where the hospital is used as a place of safety the managers must ensure that the provisions of section 132 (information) are complied with.

10.11   Where the police station is a place of safety, although section 132 does not apply, it would be good practice for the policy referred to above to require that the same information is given in writing on the person's arrival at the place of safety.

Assessment

10.12   The local implementation policy should ensure that the doctor examining the patient should wherever possible be "approved".

10.13   Assessment by both doctor and social worker should begin as soon as possible after the arrival of the individual at the place of safety. Any implementation policy should set target times for the commencement of the assessment and the health authority/NHS trust/local authority should review what happens in practice against these targets.

10.14   The person must be seen by *both* the doctor and the ASW. The local policy should include the necessary arrangements to enable the person wherever possible to be jointly assessed. If the doctor sees the person first and concludes that admission to hospital is unnecessary, or the person agrees to informal admission, the individual must still be seen by an ASW, who must consult with the doctor about any other necessary arrangements for his treatment and care that might need to be made. It is desirable for a consultant psychiatrist in learning disabilities (mental handicap) and an ASW with experience of working with people with learning disabilities to be available to make a joint assessment should there be a possibility that the detained person has a learning disability.

10.15   The role of the ASW includes:

- interviewing the person;
- contacting any relevant relatives/friends;
- ascertaining whether there is a psychiatric history;
- considering any possible alternatives to admission to hospital;
- considering the need to make any other "necessary" arrangements.

Treatment

10.16   Part IV of the Act does not apply to persons detained under section 136. The person can only be treated in the absence of consent in accordance with provisions of the common law.

Necessary arrangements

10.17   Once the assessment has been concluded it is the responsibility of the doctors and ASW to consider if any necessary arrangements for the person's treatment and care have to be made.

10.18   Where compulsory admission is indicated:

a.   where the hospital is the place of safety the person should be admitted either under section 2 or section 3 (whichever is appropriate). Wherever possible where the approved doctor providing one recommendation is on the staff of the hospital (as is usually the case) the second recommendation should be provided by a doctor with previous knowledge of the person (for example their GP). It has to be recognised that many people detained under section 136 are not registered with a GP and in these circumstances as well as where it is not possible to secure the attendance of a GP who knows the person, it would be preferable for the second opinion to be provided by a second approved doctor;

b.   persons detained under section 136 in hospital pending completion of their assessment should not find their detention being continued under section 5(2) or section 5(4);

c.   where the police station is the place of safety then compulsory admission should be under sections 2 or 3 (whichever is appropriate); but there may be exceptional circumstances where there is urgent necessity to remove the person to hospital, in which case section 4 must be considered.

10.19   Section 136 provides the lawful authority for the removal by the police of a person to whom the provision applies, from a place to which the public have access. Where it is necessary to consider gaining access (and possibly removing to a place of safety) to a mentally disordered individual other than in a public place and where access is denied then consideration must be given to invoking the powers of entry under section 135(1) or (2). Local authorities should issue guidance to ASWs on how to invoke the power.'

30.8   MENTAL HEALTH REVIEW TRIBUNALS

In addition to the possibility of discharge by managers (that is, members of the health authority or trust), by the patient's responsible medical officer (registered by the medical practitioner in charge of medical treatment for mental disorder) and by the patient's nearest relative, in each case where applicable, detained patients are entitled to apply within certain defined periods to a Mental Health Review Tribunal for discharge from section (detained status). Just as in the case of all of the other methods of discharge, so too in the case of discharge by a Mental Health Review Tribunal, the legal effect amounts to discharge from detained status only, though in the great majority of cases that will also amount to discharge from hospital unless the patient is willing to stay on an informal basis. In some cases, mentioned in this section, a Mental Health Review Tribunal (hereafter referred to simply as a 'Tribunal') has jurisdiction to discharge at a future specified date and, since the inception of the Mental Health Act 1983, all patients including patients subject to restriction orders under Part III of the Act have the opportunity of applying, at times specified in Part V of the Act, to a Mental Health Review Tribunal for discharge.

Entitlement to apply to a Mental Health Review Tribunal for discharge is independent of the right to appeal to managers against detention, in those cases where managers have the power to discharge. There is a legal obligation on the health authority or trust in whose name any patient is detained to take all possible steps to ensure a detained patient's understanding of the availability, and co-existence, of appeals to managers and appeals to Tribunals. While the provisions of section 23 of the Act are unspecific as regards the time at which, or the occasions on which, a detained patient is entitled to appeal to managers against detained status, good practice[55] requires that whatever procedure is instituted at a particular hospital for managers' appeals, this should not in any way detract from, but in fact should add to, the opportunities to apply to a Mental Health Review Tribunal.

30.8.1   Structure of the Tribunal system

There are now four Tribunal offices to cover England and one for Wales, which together are under the jurisdiction of the Mental Health Act 1983. The Nottingham office covers the Northern, Yorkshire and Trent Regional Health Authorities as well as Rampton Special Hospital; the Liverpool office covers North Western, Mersey and West Midlands

Regions, as well as Ashworth Special Hospital; and the London offices cover the East Anglian, North West Thames, North East Thames, South East Thames, Oxford, Wessex and South Western Regional Health Authorities, as well as Broadmoor Special Hospital. The Welsh tribunal office in Cardiff covers Wales. A Tribunal consists of three people, with a lawyer president and two further experts, one of whom is a psychiatrist.

The Tribunal's function is to enquire into the justification for, in the sense of the merits of, a detained patient's continued detention (or guardianship) as at the time of the hearing. In one sense the word 'review' in the Tribunal's title is misleading. If a patient considers that his initial admission was unlawful he should apply to the High Court for a writ of *habeas corpus* and it is the function of the Mental Health Act Commission, established in 1983, to 'keep under review the operation of powers and discharge of duties conferred or imposed' by the 1983 Act. The function of the Tribunal is to examine whether, on the day of the hearing, the statutory criteria for detention are met. Nevertheless, the distinction between appeal and review is blurred by the fact that there are some cases in which, based on findings of the patient's mental condition and surrounding circumstances, a Tribunal *must* discharge the patient, while in other cases it *may* (as a matter of discretion) discharge a patient if certain conditions are met. These differing outcomes are discussed below. Yet a further opportunity for a person who considers that he has been wrongfully detained is to apply to the High Court for judicial review of the administrative action taken in his detention, such as in the case of *R v Hallstrom and another, ex parte W* (1986) (pp. 752–755, above) though such is rare in practice.

Detained patients who appeal to a Mental Health Review Tribunal may represent themselves, but legal assistance is available under the so-called Green Form Scheme to help patients (as well as other applicants, including nearest relatives in the cases to which that right applies) prepare their case for the Tribunal hearing. Assisted legal representation is also available at the hearing itself under the Assistance by Way of Representation Scheme, now provided under the Legal Advice and Assistance Regulations 1990.[56] The Law Society has established a panel of solicitors with experience of Tribunal work to assist detained patients wishing to appeal to a Tribunal to find suitable legal representation.

It is now convenient to discuss separately applications to Tribunals under Part II and Part III of the Act respectively.

30.8.2 Application to Tribunals from patients detained under Part II of the Mental Health Act 1983

Section 66 of the Act provides opportunities to apply to a Mental Health Review Tribunal against detained status, and specifies the periods within which application may be made.

A patient admitted to hospital in pursuance of an application for admission under section 2 for assessment may appeal to the Tribunal at any time within the 14 days beginning with the day on which the patient is admitted to hospital on section. In the case of such a Tribunal application, the Tribunal hearing must be held within seven days of the Tribunal office receiving the application.[57] Certain rules of Tribunal procedure do not apply in the case of applications by patients detained under section 2 (see p. 833, below).

Admission to hospital under section 4, namely for admission for assessment as a matter of urgency in the absence of a second medical recommendation supporting the application, is not excluded by section 66 of the Act. In practice, however, it would be inconceivable that a Tribunal could be convened in sufficient time to make the application from such a patient worthwhile. An application by a patient detained under section 4 made within the 72 hours detention which that section permits would automatically lapse and be of no legal significance if the second medical recommendation required by section 4(4), to convert the section 4 order into a section 2 order, was not supplied by the end of that period. In such a situation the patient detained under section 4 would not be deprived of a Tribunal, since the occasion for having a Tribunal (namely, detained status) would have lapsed on the expiration of 72 hours following which, in the absence of another order being made under section 2, the patient would be informal and free to leave hospital in any event.

A patient admitted to hospital in pursuance of an application for admission for treatment under section 3 may apply to the Tribunal within six months beginning with the day on which the patient is admitted to hospital under the order. In the event of no appeal being made by such a patient, there is a duty upon managers automatically to refer the patient to a Tribunal after a certain period (see p. 826 of this chapter). A patient received into guardianship under section 7 may apply to the Tribunal at any time in the six months beginning with the day on which the application is accepted by the authority or person supervising the guardianship.

If a patient is reclassified from one mental disorder (as statutorily defined in section 1 of the Act) to another, then given that this may have the effect of changing legal rights under the statute, section 66(1)(d) entitles the reclassified patient to a Tribunal hearing. Such a hearing is not limited in its purpose merely to the clinical or other reasons for reclassification but, in common with all other Tribunal appeals, enables the Tribunal to examine the merits and legal justification of the 'new' detained status. Application is to be made within 28 days beginning with the day on which the applicant is informed that the reclassification report has been furnished to managers. Under section 66(1)(i) the patient's nearest relative has an alternative (but not additional) power to appeal to the Tribunal against the reclassification order, instead of the patient's doing so.

A patient transferred from guardianship to a hospital under section 19 may apply within six months beginning with the day of transfer. Where a renewal report is furnished by the patient's responsible medical officer under section 20 of Part II of the Act, and the managers have not discharged the patient by the date on which the renewal report takes effect, such a patient may apply to a Tribunal within 'the period for which authority for the patient's detention or guardianship is renewed by virtue of the report'. This means, in the case of an order under section 3 and a guardianship order under section 7, within the period of six months following first renewal and within periods of one year at a time upon second and subsequent renewals.

Where a report is furnished under section 25 (namely, a barring order by the responsible medical officer against the nearest relative's notice of discharge) the patient's nearest relative may apply to the Tribunal within 28 days beginning with the day on which the applicant is informed that the report has been furnished. An order made under section 29 of the Act, displacing the patient's nearest relative, may be the subject of an application by such nearest relative within 12 months beginning with the date of the order and in any subsequent period of 12 months during which the order continues in force.

Under section 67 of the Act the Secretary of State may at any time, if he thinks fit, refer to a Mental Health Review Tribunal the case of any patient who is liable to be detained or subject to guardianship under Part II of the Act. To make information available for the purposes of a reference under section 67, any registered medical practitioner authorised by or on behalf of the patient may, at any reasonable time, visit the patient and examine him in private and may require the production of and inspect any records relating to the detention or treatment of the patient in any hospital. Such records are not limited to the hospital records in the hospital in which the patient is currently resident, but may apply to any or all hospitals during the present or even an earlier period of detention.

Some detained patients may lack the insight or the motivation to make an application to a Mental Health Review Tribunal, and to cater for such cases section 68 of the Act imposed a new duty on hospital managers to refer certain cases to the Tribunal.

Where a patient admitted to a hospital in pursuance of an application for admission for treatment, or who is transferred from guardianship to hospital, does not exercise his right to apply to a Tribunal within the initial period specified by section 66 above, the managers of the hospital (namely, the authority or trust, acting through the on-site management) shall at the expiration of the period for making such an application refer the patient's case to such a Tribunal unless an application has been made by the nearest relative in the case to which that applies (above) or a reference has been made under section 67 by the Secretary of State.

Furthermore, section 68(2) provides that if the authority for detention is renewed under section 20 and a period of three years has elapsed since his case was last considered by a Mental Health Review Tribunal, whether on the patient's own application or otherwise, the hospital managers are legally obliged to refer the case to the Tribunal. In the case of a patient who had not at the relevant time attained the age of 16 years, the period is reduced to one year from the date of the last Tribunal. In each case the period dates from the last Tribunal, whether the detained patient made the application or whether it was made on the patient's behalf by the managers. In this way, not only patients lacking insight or motivation to seek review of their detention, but also patients who might be in prospect of becoming institutionalised, have at least some access to regular review, albeit it at fairly long-term intervals.

For the purposes of the managers' duty to refer cases, under section 68(1), to a Tribunal if the patient has not made application within the first six months of detention, a person who applies to a Tribunal but subsequently withdraws the application is to be treated as not having exercised his right to apply at all. Where a detained patient applies to a Tribunal but withdraws the application on a date after that six-month period, the managers are under a legal duty under section 68(5) to refer the patient's case to the Tribunal as soon as possible after the withdrawal date.

For the purpose of furnishing information connected with any managers' reference under this section, any registered medical practitioner who is authorised by or on behalf of the patient may at any reasonable time visit and examine the patient in private. The medical practitioner has the right to demand the production of and inspect any records relating to the detention and treatment of the patient in any hospital, such records not being necessarily restricted to the hospital in which the patient is at present detained.

30.8.3 Applications to Tribunals concerning patients detained under Part III of the Act

By virtue of Schedule 1, Part I of the Act, section 66(1), above, applies with some amendments to patients subject to hospital orders and also to guardianship orders made by a court under section 37. In the case of a patient detained under section 37 the patient's nearest relative may not give notice of discharge and there is no Tribunal appeal during the initial six months of detention. The reason for this latter distinction is that the order, for an initial period of up to six months, is a judicial order which could not be upset by a Tribunal which is a quasi-judicial body; but the quasi-judicial authority of the Tribunal is superior to that of the report which may be furnished to managers at the end of the initial period renewing the detention of a patient detained under section 37. In such a case the Tribunal has jurisdiction to hear an appeal at any time after the expiration of the initial authority. In the case of hospital orders without restriction on discharge (pp. 781–785 of this chapter) the power of discharge lies with both the patient's responsible medical officer and with the managers in exactly the same way as an order under section 3, for admission under Part II of the Act for treatment. As under Part II, so under Part III the managers have the legal authority to override the clinical opinion of the responsible medical officer; but in the very nature of Part III cases, such action will be extremely rare.

Section 70 of the Act provides for application to Tribunals concerning restricted patients:

'70.—A patient who is a restricted patient within the meaning of section 79 below and is detained in a hospital may apply to a Mental Health Review Tribunal—
  (a) in the period between the expiration of six months and the expiration of 12 months beginning with the date of the relevant hospital order or transfer direction; and
  (b) in any subsequent period of 12 months.'

It was decided in *R v Mental Health Review Tribunal, ex parte Secretary of State for the Home Department* (1987)[58] that the Tribunal has no power to adjourn the proceedings to monitor the patient's progress in hospital with a view to eventually discharging the patient if proposed treatment were to be successful. The Tribunal can, however, adjourn for further information if appropriate.

Section 71, in addition to providing that the Secretary of State may at any time refer the case of a restricted patient to a Mental Health Review Tribunal, imposes a duty by subsection (2) on the Secretary of State to refer to a Tribunal the case of any restricted patient detained in a hospital whose case has not been considered by such a Tribunal, whether on his own application or otherwise, within the last three years. When a patient who is treated as subject to a hospital order with restriction on discharge, by virtue of detention under section 5(1) of the Criminal Procedure (Insanity) Act 1964, does not exercise his right to apply to a Tribunal in the period of six months beginning with the date of that order, the Secretary of State shall at the end of that period refer the case to a Tribunal. (Although the options for disposal of a person found unfit to plead are considerably extended by the Criminal Procedure (Insanity and Unfitness to Plead) Act 1991, the option to deal with the accused as if under a restriction order under the Mental Health Act 1983 is preserved and the automatic reference of such a patient to a Tribunal remains unaffected.)

No doubt by way of oversight, the Act does not provide for managers' automatic references to Tribunals in the case of section 37 order patients without restrictions on discharge, even though there is a duty (on the Secretary of State in this case) to refer restricted patients to Tribunals (above). The situation of patients detained in hospital pursuant to a hospital order under section 37 is not covered by either the legislation or the Code of Practice, nor indeed mentioned in the Department of Health Memorandum published contemporaneously with the Act. It is considered to be good practice, however, for managers (through their medical records officers) to refer patients detained under hospital orders at the same intervals of time as are applicable to a patient detained under section 3. Given the very close similarity between the effects of detention under section 3 and section 37, it is suggested that the two should be treated in the same way for Tribunal application purposes. It is understood that medical records officers in some parts of the country arrange automatic references to Tribunals for patients detained under section 37 hospital orders even sooner than the statutory requirements for patients detained under section 3, though there is no legal duty to enhance a hospital order patient's rights in this way.

30.8.4 Powers of Tribunals

Section 72 of the Act empowers a Mental Health Review Tribunal to discharge a detained patient 'in any case'. In so doing, the Tribunal is considering the detention on its merits and does not have power in law to consider the validity of the initial admission.[59] It is in this sense that a Tribunal is in fact a body to which to appeal, rather than one which reviews legality of detention (see pp. 751–755). In certain cases, the Tribunal is under a legal duty to discharge the patient if certain criteria are satisfied. Section 72(1)(a) provides, in relation to patients detained under section 2 for assessment:

'**72.**—(1)(a) the tribunal shall direct the discharge of a patient liable to be detained under section 2 above if they are satisfied—
    (i) that he is not then suffering from mental disorder or from mental disorder of a nature or degree which warrants his detention in a hospital for assessment (or for assessment followed by medical treatment) for at least a limited period; or
    (ii) that his detention as aforesaid is not justified in the interests of his own health or safety or with a view to the protection of other persons.'

In respect of patients detained under section 3, as well as patients detained under a hospital order under section 37 of the Act, section 72(1)(b) provides:

'(b) the tribunal shall direct the discharge of a patient liable to be detained otherwise than under section 2 above if they are satisfied—
    (i) that he is not then suffering from mental illness, psychopathic disorder, severe mental impairment or mental impairment or from

any of those forms of disorder of a nature or degree which makes it
appropriate for him to be liable to be detained in a hospital for
medical treatment; or

(ii) that it is not necessary for the health or safety of the patient or for
the protection of other persons that he should receive such
treatment; or

(iii) in the case of an application by virtue of paragraph (g) of section
66(1) above, that the patient, if released, would not be likely to act in
a manner dangerous to other persons or to himself.'

Section 72(2) provides, in the case of a patient detained under an
admission of treatment order not falling within the criteria set out in
section 72(1)(b) above, that the Tribunal shall:

'have regard to the likelihood of medical treatment alleviating or preventing a
deterioration of the patient's condition; and in the case of a patient suffering
from mental illness or severe mental impairment, to the likelihood of the patient,
if discharged, being able to care for himself, to obtain the care he needs or to
guard himself against serious exploitation.'

This provision is a mirror image of the contents of section 20(4),
providing for the circumstances in which a renewal report may validly
be furnished, in respect of patients detained under section 3 or section
37, by their responsible medical officer.

A new power was introduced by the Mental Health Act 1983 for
Tribunals to discharge a patient from detained status at a specific future
date, in order to make arrangements for the handover of responsibility
for, or next placement of, a detained patient. Section 72(3) provides that
a Tribunal may under subsection (1) of that section direct the discharge
of a patient on a future date specified in the direction. Furthermore,
where the Tribunal do not order discharge they may:

'with a view to facilitating his discharge on a future date, recommend that he be
granted leave of absence or transferred to another hospital or into guardianship;
and further consider his case in the event of any such recommendation not being
complied with.'

Section 72(5) enables the Tribunal to reclassify the form of mental
disorder recorded for the patient, in the original admission application.
The reclassification has the same effect in law as a reclassification by the
patient's responsible medical officer.

Prior to the inception of the Mental Health Act 1983, the Home
Secretary had the sole jurisdiction over the discharge of patients
detained under a hospital order with restriction on discharge. In the case
of X v United Kingdom (1981)[60] it was held by the European Court of
Human Rights that this restriction offended against the principles of the
European Convention on Human Rights and the United Kingdom
Government resolved to incorporate correction of this deficiency. This
was effected by sections 73 and 74 of the Act. Section 73 provides that a
patient who is subject to a restriction order under section 41, who either

applies directly or is referred to a Mental Health Review Tribunal, shall be absolutely discharged if:

'he is not then suffering from mental illness, psychopathic disorder, severe mental impairment or mental impairment or from any forms of disorder of a nature or degree which makes it appropriate for him to be liable to be detained in a hospital for medical treatment; or that it is not necessary for the health or safety of the patient or for the protection of other persons that he should receive such treatment.'

In a case in which the Tribunal is satisfied as to the former question, but not as to the latter, the Tribunal is obliged to direct the conditional discharge of the patient.

A patient who is absolutely discharged under section 72 thereupon ceases to be liable to be detained by virtue of the relevant hospital order, and both the hospital order and the restriction order attached to it cease to have effect. Where, however, a patient is conditionally discharged, he may be recalled to hospital by the Secretary of State and, unless and until recall takes place, the patient is obliged to comply with such conditions, if any, as may be imposed at the time of the discharge by the Tribunal, or imposed at any subsequent time by the Secretary of State (Home Secretary). These latter conditions may be varied from time to time by the Home Office. In the case of a patient in respect of whom a restriction order ceases to have effect subsequent to conditional discharge (that is, where the restriction had been imposed for a limited period) the patient shall, unless previously recalled to hospital, be deemed to be absolutely discharged on the date when the restriction order ceases to have effect. The relevant hospital order also ceases accordingly.

A Tribunal has power, if it so wishes, to defer a direction for the conditional discharge of a patient until necessary arrangements have been made to the Tribunal's satisfaction. Nevertheless, the question of conditional discharge rests solely on the appropriateness of recall, as an option if needed; and not on the need for, nor appropriateness of, a regime of compulsory aftercare.

In the case of patients transferred to hospital from prison, subject to a restriction direction, where application is made to the Tribunal by that person, or by the Home Secretary, the Tribunal shall notify the Home Secretary whether, in their opinion the patient would, were he to be subject to a restriction order, be entitled to be absolutely or conditionally discharged. In the event of the Tribunal notifying the Home Secretary that the patient would be entitled to be conditionally discharged, it may recommend that the patient should continue to be detained in hospital. If the Tribunal notifies the Home Secretary that the patient would be entitled to be absolutely or conditionally discharged, and within 90 days the Home Secretary notifies the Tribunal that the patient may be so discharged, the Tribunal shall direct the absolute or, or as the case may be, the conditional discharge of the patient. If, in the case of a patient who is subject to a transfer direction from remand in prison, the Tribunal notifies the Home Secretary that the patient would be entitled to be absolutely or conditionally discharged, the Home Secretary shall, unless the Tribunal have made a recommendation that he would be entitled to be conditionally discharged if he had been subject to a restriction order, by warrant direct that the patient be remitted to a prison or other institution in which he might have been detained if he had not been removed to hospital, 'there to be dealt with as if he had not been so removed'.

Paragraph 227 of the Memorandum explains the operation of section 72 as follows:

'Patients subject to a restriction given by the Home Secretary are liable to resume serving their sentence of imprisonment or to be brought before a court to stand trial if they no longer require treatment in hospital. Under these circumstances, the Tribunal cannot therefore authorise discharge in the normal way. Instead, it has to notify the Home Secretary if it finds that the patient could otherwise be conditionally or absolutely discharged, and may at the same time recommend that if the patient cannot be discharged he should continue to be detained in hospital rather than being returned to prison. In the case of a patient who was originally a remand prisoner transferred under section 48, the Home Secretary has no discretion; unless the Tribunal has made a recommendation for the patient's retention in hospital, he must return the patient to prison. In the case of a *sentenced* prisoner, however, it may be that the Home Secretary is able to agree to his discharge. The Home Secretary has 90 days from the date of notification of the Tribunal's finding in which to give notice that the patient may be discharged: if he does not, the patient must be returned to prison unless that Tribunal has made a recommendation that in those circumstances he should remain in hospital.'

30.8.5   Procedure of Tribunals

Section 78 of the Act empowers the Lord Chancellor to make rules with respect to the making of applications to Mental Health Review Tribunals and with respect to the proceedings of such Tribunals and matters incidental to or consequential on such proceedings. The Mental Health Review Tribunal Rules 1983[61] came into force at the same time as all but a few sections[62] of the Mental Health Act 1983. The Tribunal rules are lengthy, and this chapter includes some comments on only such rules as are necessary to managers' understanding of their legal powers and duties.

An application must be made to the Tribunal in writing, though there is no particular form on which to do this. Paragraph 3(2) of the Regulations makes the following requirement, in the case of applications other than those from a patient admitted under section 2 for assessment:

'(2) The application shall wherever possible include the following information—
   (a) the name of the patient;

   (b) the patient's address, which shall include—
      (i) the address of the hospital or mental nursing home where the patient is detained; or
     (ii) the name and address of the patient's private guardian; or
   (iii) in the case of a conditionally discharged patient or a patient to whom leave of absence from hospital has been granted, the address of the hospital or mental nursing home where the patient was last detained or is liable to be detained, together with the patient's current address;
   (c) where the application is made by the patient's nearest relative, the name and address of the applicant and his relationship to the patient;
   (d) the section of the Act under which the patient is detained or is liable to be detained;
   (e) the name and address of any representative authorised in accordance with rule 10 or, if none has yet been authorised, whether the applicant intends to authorise a representative or wishes to conduct his own case.'

A modified requirement applies under rule 30, to patients admitted for assessment, as follows:

'**30.**—(1) An assessment application shall be made to the tribunal in writing signed by the patient or any person authorised by him to do so on his behalf.

(2) An assessment application shall indicate that it is made by or on behalf of a patient detained for assessment and shall wherever possible include the following information—
   (a) the name of the patient;
   (b) the address of the hospital or mental nursing home where the patient is detained;
   (c) the name and address of the patient's nearest relative and his relationship to the patient;
   (d) the name and address of any representative authorised by the patient in accordance with rule 10 or, if none has yet been authorised, whether the patient intends to authorise a representation or wishes to conduct his own case.

(3) If any of the information specified in paragraph (2) is not included in the assessment application, it shall in so far as is practicable be provided by the responsible authority at the request of the tribunal.'

When the application is received by the Tribunal office notice must be sent to the responsible authority, meaning the managers of the hospital or mental nursing home in which the patient is detained or liable to be detained, or to the responsible local social services authority in the case of guardianship; to the patient (where the patient is not the applicant); and, if the patient is subject to a restriction order, to the Home Secretary. The information to be contained in the statement by the responsible authority (as above defined) to the Tribunal in respect of the various categories of detained patient who may apply to a Tribunal is detailed in the Schedule to the Regulations, as follows:

'PART A

INFORMATION RELATING TO PATIENTS (OTHER THAN CONDITIONALLY DISCHARGED PATIENTS)

1. The full name of the patient.
2. The age of the patient.

3. The date of admission of the patient to the hospital or mental nursing home in which the patient is currently detained or liable to be detained, or of the reception of the patient into guardianship.

4. Where the patient is being treated in a mental nursing home under contractual arrangements with a health authority, the name of that authority.

5. Details of the original authority for the detention or guardianship of the patient, including the Act of Parliament and the section of that Act by reference to which detention was authorised and details of any subsequent renewal of or charge in the authority for detention.

6. The form of mental disorder from which the patient is recorded as suffering in the authority for detention (including amendments, if any, under section 16 or 72(5) of the Act, but excluding cases within section 5 of the Criminal Procedure (Insanity) Act 1964).

7. The name of the responsible medical officer and the period which the patient has spent under the care of that officer.

8. Where another registered medical practitioner is or has recently been largely concerned in the treatment of the patient, the name of that practitioner and the period which the patient has spent under his care.

9. The dates of all previous tribunal hearings in relation to the patient, the decisions reached at such hearings and the reasons given. (In restricted patient cases this requirement does not relate to decisions before 30 September 1983.)

10. Details of any proceedings in the Court of Protection and of any receivership order made in respect of the patient.

11. The name and address of the patient's nearest relative or of any other person who is exercising that function.

12. The name and address of any other person who takes a close interest in the patient.

13. Details of any leave of absence granted to the patient during the previous 2 years, including the duration of such leave and particulars of the arrangements made for the patient's residence while on leave.

PART B

REPORTS RELATING TO PATIENTS (OTHER THAN CONDITIONALLY DISCHARGED PATIENTS)

1. An up-to-date medical report, prepared for the tribunal, including the relevant medical history and a full report on the patient's mental condition.

2. An up-to-date social circumstances report prepared for the tribunal including reports on the following—
   (a) the patient's home and family circumstances, including the attitude of the patient's nearest relative or the person so acting;
   (b) the opportunities for employment or occupation and the housing facilities which would be available to the patient if discharged;
   (c) the availability of community support and relevant medical facilities;
   (d) the financial circumstances of the patient.

3. The views of the authority on the suitability of the patient for discharge.

4. Any other information or observations on the application which the authority wishes to make.

PART C

INFORMATION RELATING TO CONDITIONALLY DISCHARGED PATIENTS

1. The full name of the patient.

2. The age of the patient.

3. The history of the patient's present liability to detention including details of

offence(s), and the dates of the original order or direction and of the conditional discharge.

4. The form of mental disorder from which the patient is recorded as suffering in the authority for detention. (Not applicable to cases within section 5 of the Criminal Procedure (Insanity) Act 1964.)

5. The name and address of any medical practitioner responsible for the care and supervision of the patient in the community and the period which the patient has spent under the care of that practitioner.

6. The name and address of any social worker or probation officer responsible for the care and supervision of the patient in the community and the period which the patient has spent under the care of that person.

PART D

REPORTS RELATING TO CONDITIONALLY DISCHARGED PATIENTS

1. Where there is a medical practitioner responsible for the care and supervision of the patient in the community, and up-to-date medical report prepared for the tribunal including the relevant medical history and a full report on the patient's mental condition.

2. Where there is a social worker or probation officer responsible for the patient's care and supervision in the community, an up-to-date report prepared for the tribunal on the patient's progress in the community since discharge from hospital.

3. A report on the patient's home circumstances.

4. The views of the Secretary of State on the suitability of the patient for absolute discharge.

5. Any other observations on the application which the Secretary of State wishes to make.'

30.8.6 Notice to other interested persons

Rule 7 provides for notice of the proceedings to other interested persons, as follows:

'7. On receipt of the authority's statement or, in the case of a restricted patient, the Secretary of State's statement, the tribunal shall give notice of the proceedings—

   (a) where the patient is liable to be detained in a mental nursing home, to the registration authority of that home;

   (b) where the patient is subject to the guardianship of a private guardian, to the guardian;

   (c) where the patient's financial affairs are under the control of the Court of Protection, to the Court of Protection;

   (d) where any person other than the applicant is named in the authority's statement as exercising the functions of the nearest relative, to that person;

   (e) where a health authority has a right to discharge the patient under the provisions of section 23(3) of the Act, to that authority;

   (f) to any other person who, in the opinion of the tribunal, should have an opportunity of being heard.'

30.8.7 Appointment to the Tribunal

Tribunal members for each Tribunal panel are appointed by the chairman of the Mental Health Review Tribunal for each region. A member or officer of the responsible authority or of the registration authority concerned in the proceedings, a member or officer of the health authority having a right to discharge the patient under section 23, and any person having a personal connection with the patient or having recently treated the patient in a professional medical capacity, are all disqualified from serving as a member of the Tribunal in the case of that patient.

30.8.8   The Tribunal proceedings

Any party to the proceedings may be represented at the Tribunal by any person authorised for that purpose other than a person who is liable to be detained or subject to guardianship and any such representative must notify the Tribunal of this authorisation and of his postal address. In the absence of such authorisation, the Tribunal may appoint a person to act as the authorised representative for a patient who does not wish to conduct his own case. The authorised representative must receive from the Tribunal copies of all notices and documents required by the Tribunal Rules or authorised to be sent to the person who is being represented. Unless the Tribunal otherwise directs, a patient or any other party appearing before the Tribunal may be accompanied by such other person or persons as he wishes, in addition to any representative he may have authorised.

The medical member of the Tribunal (or one medical member, if there is more than one) must, at any time before the hearing of the application, examine the patient as well as take such other steps as the medical member considers necessary to form an opinion of the patient's mental condition. Such examination may be conducted in private and all the patient's medical records may be examined by the medical member, who may take such notes and copies as are required for this purpose.

Special provision is made by regulation 12 for the disclosure of documents:

'12.—(1) Subject to paragraph (2), the tribunal shall, as soon as practicable, send a copy of every document it receives which is relevant to the application to the applicant, and (where he is not the applicant) the patient, the responsible authority and, in the case of a restricted patient, the Secretary of State and any of those persons may submit comments thereon in writing to the tribunal.

(2) As regards any documents which have been received by the tribunal but which have not been copied to the applicant or the patient, including documents withheld in accordance with rule 6, the tribunal shall consider whether disclosure of such documents would adversely affect the health or welfare of the patient or others and, if satisfied that it would, shall record in writing its decision not to disclose such documents.

(3) Where the tribunal is minded not to disclose any document to which paragraph (1) applies to an applicant or a patient who has an authorised representative it shall nevertheless disclose it as soon as practicable to that representative if he is—

(a) a barrister or solicitor;

(b) a registered medical practitioner;

(c) in the opinion of the tribunal, a suitable person by virtue of his experience or professional qualification;

provided that no information disclosed in accordance with this paragraph shall be disclosed either directly or indirectly to the applicant or (where he is not the applicant) to the patient or to any other person without the authority of the tribunal or used otherwise than in connection with the application.'

Within the parameters permitted by Rules, the Tribunal is entitled to give such directions as it thinks fit to 'ensure the speedy and just determination of the application'. A Tribunal may take evidence on oath and may also subpoena any witness to appear before it or to produce documents. It is specifically provided by rule 14(2) that 'the tribunal may receive in evidence any document or information notwithstanding that such document or information would be inadmissible in a court of law'. The distinction is based on the fact that Mental Health Review Tribunal procedure is more in the nature of a enquiry, as distinct from the adversarial arguments in a court of law which depend upon considerable formality of evidence. Furthermore, rule 15 provides that before or during any hearing the Tribunal may call for such further information or reports as it may think desirable. The Rules provide for adjournment of proceedings (rule 16) and for transfer of proceedings to other members of the Tribunal (rule 17). Rule 19 provides that an application to the Tribunal may be withdrawn in writing at any time provided the Tribunal agrees and that, in any case in which the patient ceases to be liable to be detained or subject to guardianship, any application shall be deemed to be withdrawn.

The Tribunal hearing

Rules 20–22 provide for procedure prior to and at the hearing:

'Notice of hearing

20. The tribunal shall give at least 14 days' notice of the date, time and place fixed for the hearing (or such shorter notice as all parties may consent to) to all the parties and, in the case of a restricted patient, the Secretary of State.

Privacy of proceedings

21.—(1) The tribunal shall sit in private unless the patient requests a hearing in public and the tribunal is satisfied that a hearing in public would not be contrary to the interests of the patient.

(2) Where the tribunal refuses a request for a public hearing or directs that a hearing which has begun in public shall continue in private the tribunal shall record its reasons in writing and shall inform the patient of those reasons.

(3) When the tribunal sits in private it may admit to the hearing such persons on such terms and conditions as it considers appropriate.

(4) The tribunal may exclude from any hearing or part of a hearing any person or class of persons, other than a representative of the applicant or of the patient

to whom documents would be disclosed in accordance with rule 12(3), and in any case where the tribunal decides to exclude the applicant or the patient or their representatives or a representative of the responsible authority, it shall inform the person excluded of its reasons and record those reasons in writing.

(5) Except in so far as the tribunal may direct, information about proceedings before the tribunal and the names of any persons concerned in the proceedings shall not be made public.

(6) Nothing in this rule shall prevent a member of the Council on Tribunals from attending the proceedings of a tribunal in his capacity as such provided that he takes no part in those proceedings or in the deliberations of the tribunal.

Hearing procedure

22.—(1) The tribunal may conduct the hearing in such manner as it considers most suitable bearing in mind the health and interests of the patient and it shall, so far as appears to it appropriate, seek to avoid formality in its proceedings.

(2) At any time before the application is determined, the tribunal or any one or more of its members may interview the patient, and shall interview him if he so requests, and the interview may, and shall if the patient so requests, take place in the absence of any other person.

(3) At the beginning of the hearing the president shall explain the manner of proceeding which the tribunal proposes to adopt.

(4) Subject to rule 21(4), any party and, with the permission of the tribunal, any other person, may appear at the hearing and take such part in the proceedings as the tribunal thinks proper; and the tribunal shall in particular hear and take evidence from the applicant, the patient (where he is not the applicant) and the responsible authority who may hear each other's evidence, put questions to each other, call witnesses and put questions to any witness or other person appearing before the tribunal.

(5) After all the evidence has been given, the applicant and (where he is not the applicant) the patient shall be given a further opportunity to address the tribunal.'

The Tribunal's decision

The decision of a Tribunal may be either unanimous or by a majority, and shall be recorded in writing, giving reasons. It was decided in *Bone v Mental Health Review Tribunal* (1985)[63] that it is insufficient for a Tribunal simply to give the 'statutory' reason, namely that the statutory requirements set out in the section of the Act under which the patient is detained are present or are no longer present. It is the substantive, factual reasons supporting the statutory grounds, which must be given. For instance, it is insufficient to say that 'for the protection of others, the patient requires continued detention in hospital'; rather, the clinical and management reasons for which, based on a factual description of the patient's mental condition, behaviour and prognosis support the decision to continue detention on the statutory basis, need to be stated.

The Tribunal president has discretion to announce the decision of the Tribunal immediately after the hearing, and the Tribunal must in any event communicate the written decision, including reasons, to all parties within seven days (or, in the case of an application from a patient detained for assessment under section 2, within three days). In the case of a restricted patient, this includes the Home Secretary. Where the Tribunal considers that full disclosure of the recorded reasons for its decisions for the patient would adversely affect the health or welfare of the patient or others, it may instead communicate its decision to the patient in such manner as it considers appropriate and may communicate its decision to the other parties subject to any conditions it may think appropriate as to the disclosure of the decision to the patient. For information to be restricted in this way, the applicant or the patient must have been represented at the hearing by a person to whom documents would be disclosed. The Tribunal must disclose the full recorded grounds of its decision to any such person, but may impose conditions as to the disclosure of information to the patient.

If a decision to discharge is announced immediately after the hearing, then the formerly detained patient is apparently free to leave hospital (or free of guardianship, as the case may be) and any further stay in hospital would be on an informal basis. While it appears to be an open point in law, the written communication within seven days of an earlier decision, at the hearing or at some subsequent time, to discharge from legal detention, must be presumed to take effect only on such communication. Otherwise the patient would in the interim have been informal, but would have considered himself, and been considered by others, a detained patient. The tort of false imprisonment could apparently be committed in such circumstances.

30.9   REMOVAL AND RETURN OF PATIENTS

Part VI of the Act provides various powers for the removal of patients to Scotland, Northern Ireland, the Channel Islands and the Isle of Man; for the removal to England and Wales of offenders found insane in the Channel Islands or the Isle of Man; and for the removal of alien patients. It also provides for the return of patients absent without leave.

Section 80(1) provides that if it appears to the Secretary of State that in the case of a patient who is detained otherwise than under section 35, 36 or 38 of the Act, or is subject to guardianship, the patient's interests indicate that he should be removed to Scotland and that arrangements have been made for admitting him to a hospital there (or receiving him into guardianship there), the removal may be authorised by the Secretary of State who may also give any necessary directions for the patient's conveyance to that destination. Section 81(1) makes similar provision in respect of removal to Northern Ireland and section 83 makes similar provision for the removal of patients to the Channel Islands or the Isle of Man. Given that Scotland and Northern Ireland have separate legislation[64] relating to detention and treatment for mental disorder, sections 80 and 81 respectively make provision for the effect of such removal from England and Wales on the detained status of the patient. For specific details of the effect and procedure of such removal, reference should be made to those sections.

Section 82 provides for the removal to England and Wales of patients from Northern Ireland, such powers depending on the decision of the responsible authority that such removal is in the interests of the patient, such authority having power to give any necessary directions for the patient's conveyance to his destination. The remainder of section 82 makes specific provision for the effect of such removal on the detained status of the patient, or which reference should be specifically made in the event of such removal. Section 84 provides for the removal to England and Wales of offenders found insane in the Channel Islands and the Isle of Man. Section 85 provides for the removal of patients from the Channel Islands to the Isle of Man to a hospital (or to guardianship) in England and Wales. Specific provision is made by section 85 for the legal effect on detention of such removal. Section 86, which applies to any patient who is neither a British citizen nor a Commonwealth citizen having the right of abode in the United Kingdom by virtue of section 2(1)(b) of the Immigration Act 1981, provides that the Secretary of State may by warrant authorise the removal of the patient from the place where he is receiving treatment. The Home Secretary may give such directions as are thought fit for the conveyance of the patient to his destination country and for the detention of the patient in any place or on board any ship or aircraft until his arrival at any specified port or place in that country. The Home Secretary must not exercise his powers in this respect except with the approval of a Mental Health Review Tribunal.

Sections 87–89 make provision for the return of patients absent from hospitals in Northern Ireland, England and Wales, the Channel Islands or the Isle of Man respectively. Powers to take into custody, by physical force if need be, are specifically provided by sections 87, 88 and 89, to which detailed reference should be made in the event of any such proposed return.

30.10 OFFENCES CREATED BY THE ACT

While it could be a criminal offence, for instance assault and battery, to impose unwarranted physical restraint unpermitted by the various provisions of the Mental Health Act discussed in this chapter, separate consideration should be given to offences which are specifically created by the Act, as well as an offence created by the Mental Health Act 1959 and not repealed by the Mental Health Act 1983. In the case of actions which are alleged by a claimant to be unlawful, but which purport to be done under powers conferred by the Act itself, special consideration must be given to the effect of section 139 on the liability, if any, of the person or body against whom the complaint is made. This is discussed in the following section of this chapter. The present section concerns only offences which are the specific creature of statute and in respect of which the qualified protection of section 139 (below) does not therefore apply since they are not actions which purport to be done under powers given by the Act.

Section 128 of the Mental Health Act 1959 remained in force after the enactment of the 1983 Act. It is an offence under section 128 for a man on the staff of, or employed by, a hospital or mental nursing home to have sexual intercourse outside marriage with a woman who is receiving treatment for mental disorder at that place; and it is an offence for a man to have such intercourse with a woman who is subject to his guardianship or otherwise in his custody or care. It is a defence to any such charge that the man did not know that the woman was a mentally disordered patient.

Section 126 of the 1983 Act makes provision for forgery and false statements, subsection (1) making it an offence for any person without lawful authority or excuse to have in his custody or under his control any document to which the subsection applies; subsection (2) makes it an offence for any person to have in his custody or under his control, without lawful authority, any documents so closely resembling such a forged document as to be calculated to deceive. The documents to which the section applies are: an application under Part II of the Act, a medical recommendation or report under the Act, and any other document required or authorised to be made for any of the purposes of the Act. Section 126(4) provides that any person who wilfully makes a false entry or statement in any application, recommendation, report, record or other document required or authorised to be made for any of the purposes of the Act, or with intent to deceive makes use of such entry or statement knowing it to be false, shall be guilty of an offence. It is the wilful use or deceitful intention respectively which prevent any such document falling within the limited protection of section 139, the latter depending upon actions which purport genuinely to fall within the Act's powers.

It is an offence under section 127 of the Act for any person who is an officer on the staff of, or otherwise employed in, or is one of the managers of, a hospital or mental nursing home to ill treat or wilfully to neglect a patient who is receiving treatment for mental disorder as an in-patient, or as an out-patient if the unit has such a facility. The offence is committed irrespective of whether the patient is liable to be detained. It is also an offence for any individual to ill treat or wilfully neglect a mentally disordered patient subject to his guardianship under the Act (sections 7 and 8) or otherwise in his custody or care. This latter offence is defined in wide terms and custody or care is further amplified by the expression 'whether by virtue of any legal or moral obligation or otherwise'. The offence is committed even if the 'patient' is not receiving treatment for mental disorder and is committed irrespective of detained or informal status. Section 127(4) provides that no proceedings shall be instituted for an offence under this section except by or with the consent of the Director of Public Prosecutions.

Under section 128 it is an offence to assist patients to absent themselves without leave. Where any person induces or knowingly assists another person who is liable to be detained in hospital within the meaning of Part II of the Act, or is subject to guardianship, to absent himself without leave he shall be guilty of an offence. Furthermore, given that a completed application for formal admission (detention) in due form constitutes the legal authority to take and convey the patient to hospital and that it is provided by section 137 of the Act that the patient is in the interim in lawful custody (therefore subject to physical compulsion if need be), it is an offence under section 128(2) to induce or knowingly to assist another person to escape from legal custody under section 137.

Section 129 provides that any person who without reasonable cause refuses to allow the inspection of any premises; or refuses to allow the visiting, interviewing or examination of any person by a person authorised in that behalf by or under the Act; or refuses to produce for the inspection of any person so authorised any document or record the production of which is duly required; or otherwise obstructs any such person in the exercise of his functions shall be guilty of an offence. Any person who insists on being present when required to withdraw by a person authorised by or under the Act to interview or examine a patient in private shall be guilty of an offence. This offence might, typically, be committed when an interview is required in private with a member or members of the Mental Health Act Commission, the Commission having both the duty and the power under section 120 of the Act to make arrangements to visit and interview detained patients in private.

Section 130 provides that proceedings for any offence under Part IX of the Act may be instituted by a local social services authority, with the exception of the offence of ill treating patients for which the action or consent of the Director of Public Prosecutions is required under section 127.

30.11 INFORMATION TO DETAINED PATIENTS

It is a cardinal principle of the Mental Health Act 1983 not only that rights and safeguards should be made available to detained patients, such as the right to appeal to a Tribunal at stated intervals, and the right to a second opinion for treatment imposed without consent, but also that detained patients should be fully aware of their rights and entitlements and of the legal consequences of their detention. Accordingly, section 132 imposes a duty at the highest level, namely upon the body in whose name a patient is detained, to do everything possible to make sure that the patient possesses such an understanding at the earliest possible stage of detention. Section 132 provides:

'132.—(1) The managers of a hospital or mental nursing home in which a patient is detained under this Act shall take such steps as are practicable to ensure that the patient understands—
- (a) under which of the provisions of this Act he is for the time being detained and the effect of that provision; and
- (b) what rights of applying to a Mental Health Review Tribunal are available to him in respect of his detention under that provision;

and those steps shall be taken as soon as practicable after the commencement of the patient's detention under the provision in question.

(2) The managers of a hospital or mental nursing home in which a patient is detained as aforesaid shall also take such steps as are practicable to ensure that the patient understands the effect, so far as relevant in his case, of sections 23, 25, 56 to 64, 66(1), 118 and 120 above and section 134 below; and those steps shall be taken as soon as practicable after the commencement of the patient's detention in the hospital or nursing home.'

Although good sense should prevail in practice, especially for instance where it will clearly be harmful to insist on explaining legal rights and entitlements to a severely disturbed newly admitted patient, the essence of this obligation of managers is that all practicable steps, not merely all reasonable steps, should be taken to give the requisite explanation. This means, for instance, that although the patient's doctor, or nursing staff, may not wish to worry the patient with particular details in a very difficult period of the patient's life, the legal requirement that practicable steps be taken to explain the consequences of detention is an essential safeguard for detained patients. Given that the legal consequences of detention depend not only upon the provisions of the Act itself, but upon other areas of law such as lawfulness of detention and consent to treatment at common law, it is clear that professional staff having management and care of the patient should receive education and training sufficient to discharge the obligation of managers. The health authority, trust or mental nursing home upon which the obligation under section 132 is directly cast may otherwise find itself in breach of its legal duty.

Section 132(3) requires that these steps towards an explanation of the legal consequences of detention shall include giving the requisite information both orally and in writing; and under subsection (4) the managers of a hospital or mental nursing home in which a patient is detained shall, except where the patient otherwise requests, take practicable steps to give the relevant information, in writing, to the person appearing to be the patient's nearest relative. While there is no statutory obligation positively to ask the patient whether there is any objection to such information being furnished, it is good practice and within the meaning of subsection (4) to give the patient an opportunity to object to such transmission of information to the nearest relative.

The same consideration, of giving the patient an opportunity to object, figures also in the practical implementation of section 133 of the Act. That section requires the managers of the hospital or nursing home to take such steps as are practicable to inform the person appearing to be the patient's nearest relative of the proposed discharge of the patient, at least seven days before the date of discharge. However, this obligation shall not apply if the patient or his nearest relative has requested that information about the patient's discharge should not be given.

30.12   MENTAL HEALTH ACT COMMISSION

The Mental Health Act Commission, a watchdog body, was established to keep under review the exercise of powers and discharge of duties which are respectively conferred, or imposed, by the Mental Health Act 1983 and Regulations made thereunder.[65] On behalf of the Secretary of State, the Commission shall make arrangements for authorised persons to visit and interview in private patients detained under the Act in hospitals and in mental nursing homes, though there is no power to inspect the use of guardianship. The Commission exercises the function of appointing registered medical practitioners for the purposes of Part IV of the Act (pp. 802–818, above) and discharges the function of periodically reviewing treatment under section 61 of Part IV of the Act. Section 120 restricts the Commission's powers to the provisions of the Act so far as they relate 'to the detention of patients or patients liable to be detained under this Act'. Section 121(4) provides that the Secretary of State may, at the request of or after consulting the Commission and after consulting such other bodies appearing to him to be concerned, direct the Commission to keep under review the care and treatment, or any aspect of the care and treatment, in hospitals and mental nursing homes of patients who are not liable to be detained under this Act. At the date of going to press, no such order has been made, and there appear to be no definite plans to extend the jurisdiction to the Commission in this regard. As an altogether separate issue, there are at the time of writing plans to radically reconstruct the Mental Health Act Commission with a smaller number of members, working full time, and with a significantly different practice on hospital visiting.

For the purpose of its general review powers (above), any person authorised by the Commission may at any reasonable time visit and interview the patient and, if the authorised person is a registered medical practitioner, examine in private any patient in a mental nursing home. Such authorised person may also require the production of, and inspect, any records relating to the treatment of any person who is or who has been a patient in a mental nursing home. The Secretary of State already has a power to direct health authorities to make their records and facilities similarly available in respect of detained patients.[66] Section 121(7) imposes a specific duty on the Mental Health Act Commission to review any decision to withhold a postal packet, or anything contained in it, under section 134 of the Act (see pp. 847–848 of this chapter).

In addition to its general power to authorise persons to visit and interview in private detained patients, the Commission has a particularly important duty in the investigation of complaints made by persons who are or who have been detained. Section 120(1)(b) imposes an obligation upon the Commission, on behalf of the Secretary of State:

'to investigate—
  (i) any complaint made by a person in respect of a matter that occurred while he was detained under this Act in a hospital or mental nursing home and which he considers has not been satisfactorily dealt with by the managers of that hospital or mental nursing home; and
  (ii) any other complaint as to the exercise of the powers or the discharge of the duties conferred or imposed by this Act in respect of a person who is or has been so detained.'

In relation to either category of complaint, arrangements made under this section may exclude matters from investigation in specified circumstances, and shall not require any person exercising these investigative functions to undertake or continue with any investigation where it is not considered appropriate to do so.

While complaints do not of course come to the Commission in a neat division between paragraphs (b)(i) and (b)(ii), it is usually clear into which statutory category the complaint falls. A complaint as to the exercise of the powers or discharge of the duties under the Act would include, for instance, alleged misuse, or non-use, of second opinion obligations under Part IV of the Act relating to treatment without consent; to alleged inefficiency by managers in hearing appeals and reviewing detention of detained patients; and to making local arrangements for Mental Health Review Tribunals and communications with the Tribunal Office. A complaint falling under (b)(i) could include anything else which occurred while the patient was detained, not directly connected with powers or duties under the provisions of the Act.

Complaints appearing to relate to powers or duties under the Act are investigable directly by the Commission without the intervention of managers at local level; and such complaints may be made either by the patient or by someone else on the patient's behalf, which could in certain circumstances include a member of the hospital staff. Complaints not relating to powers or duties must be made by the patient himself, though they may relate either to a present or to a past period of detention during which the incident complained of is alleged to have taken place.

It has been the frequent practice of the Mental Health Act Commission, on receipt of complaints not relating to the exercise of powers or discharge of duties under the Act, to refer the matter initially to local management, and only in the event of the patient's remaining dissatisfied with investigation at local level to assume jurisdiction itself. While in many cases this will be a sensible and practical approach, given that certain cases involve only minor matters which can be readily corrected at local level, there is no legal requirement that the Commission should refer such matters to local management in this way.

While complaints seldom in practice come neatly packaged, section 120 of the Mental Health Act 1983 draws a division. Any complaint about powers and duties is immediately investigable by the Commission. First, the Commission is presumed to know about such things; second, if the complaint were that the managers never did anything about their statutory responsibilities (and put all the papers in the bin), the complaint would be prevented from reaching the Commission.

This suggestion addresses the other limb of the complaints jurisdiction of the Commission, contained in section 120(1)(b)(i). It has been assumed hitherto that the detained patient who complains must have given the managers a chance, which he subsequently considers they have unsatisfactorily used, and complains to the Commission. It is equally possible to read this paragraph in a wholly different way. The paragraph relates to 'any complaint made by a person in respect of a matter that occurred while he was detained . . . and which he considers has not been satisfactorily dealt with by the managers . . .'. While the patient's complaint to the Commission will often relate in point of fact to a maladministered complaint made first to the managers, the paragraph appears also to countenance a complaint to the Commission about 'a matter which was not satisfactorily dealt with'. The complaint *to the Commission* relates to 'a matter', which includes many concerns not actually having culminated in an earlier complaint *to the managers*. For instance, in hospital X there is a general malaise about the lack of nutritional value in the food. The managers produce a whitewash report. On the suggested reading of section 120, there is nothing to prevent a detained patient now complaining to the Commission about the alleged whitewash.

Both (i) and (ii) mention complaint only once; consistently, that must mean the complaint to the Commission. The suggested interpretation would serve to enfranchise patients formerly in a psychotic interlude but now able to complain, as well as some patients with a learning disability who are now better than they were (at the time the 'matter' occurred) at self-advocacy. Paragraph 10 of HC(88)37 (p. 297, above) should be read in this light.

30.13   VOTING AT ELECTIONS

Section 7(1) of the Representation of the People Act 1983 provides that patients detained in hospital or in a mental nursing home pursuant to powers under the Mental Health Act 1983 are not entitled to have their names placed on the Register of Electors. The rationale behind this rule is that people who are detained in hospital are not to be treated as resident there for electoral purposes. In the case of patients informally receiving treatment for mental disorder in hospital, a different rule applies. Section 7(4) of the Representation of the People Act 1983 provides that an informal patient may have his name placed on the Register if he has made a valid declaration as provided for in that section. An informal patient is not to be treated as resident of the hospital if, to use the expression in section 7(2) of the Act, it is one which is 'maintained wholly or mainly for the reception and treatment of persons suffering from any form of mental disorder'. The declaration under section 7(4) must give not only the address of the hospital in which the patient is for the time being resident, but also the United Kingdom address where the patient would be resident were he not to be in hospital. If the patient cannot give such an address, any address apart from a mental hospital in the United Kingdom where he has at some time resided will suffice.

The declaration under section 7(4) is required to be made without assistance. In practice this means that the informal patient must be capable of filling in the form and making the requisite declaration in his or her own right as distinct from the form being filled in and declaration made by a member of staff of the patient's behalf. Assistance is, however, permitted in the case of blindness on other physical incapacity not affecting the mental capacity of the informal patient to complete the form and declaration. Practical guidelines as to the completion of this process are given to health authority managers by Circular HC(83)14.

30.14   PATIENTS' CORRESPONDENCE

Certain powers of 'censorship' of mail either to or from a patient detained in hospital under the Act are provided by section 134. A postal packet addressed to any person by a patient detained in a hospital under the Act, and delivered by the patient for dispatch, may be withheld from the Post Office by the hospital if the person to whom it is addressed has requested that communications addressed to him by the patient should be withheld. Section 134(1)(b) provides wider powers of withholding of mail in the case of a patient detained in a special hospital. With the exceptions mentioned below, if the managers of a special hospital consider that the postal packet which the patient proposes to send out of the hospital is likely either to cause distress to the addressee or any person other than a member of the hospital staff, or is likely to cause danger to any person, the managers of the special hospital may withhold that postal packet from the Post Office. Any request for the withholding of communications to an addressee outside the hospital must be made in writing to the managers of the hospital, or to the registered medical practitioner in charge of the patient's treatment, or to the Secretary of State. No special statutory procedure is required in the 'distress or danger' case relating to the special hospitals and the managers of those hospitals are left to make their own practical arrangements for censorship. As to postal packets addressed to patients, section 134(2) restricts powers of censorship to the case of special hospital detainees. Mail may be withheld from them if, in the opinion of the hospital managers, it is necessary to do so in the interests of the safety of the patient or for the protection of other persons.

Mail addressed by or to patients detained in a special hospital may not be withheld if it is addressed by the patient to, or sent to a patient by or on behalf of, any of the following:[67]

'(a) any Minister of the Crown or Member of either House of Parliament;
(b) the Master or any other officer of the Court of Protection or any of the Lord Chancellor's Visitors;
(c) the Parliamentary Commissioner for Administration, the Health Service Commissioner for England, the Health Service Commissioner for Wales or a Local Commissioner within the meaning of Part III of the Local Government Act 1974;
(d) a Mental Health Review Tribunal;
(e) a health authority within the meaning of the National Health Service Act 1977, a local social services authority, a Community Health Council or a probation and after-care committee appointed under paragraph 2 of Schedule 3 to the Powers of Criminal Courts Act 1973;
(f) the managers of the hospital in which the patient is detained;
(g) any legally qualified person instructed by the patient to act as his legal adviser; or
(h) the European Commission of Human Rights or the European Court of Human Rights.'

In the case of all correspondence withheld other than at the request of the addressee, hospital managers will wish to know whether a particular item in fact falls within the censorship powers and its contents may well need to be inspected. Accordingly, section 134(4) provides that hospital managers may inspect and open any postal packet for the purposes of determining whether it is one to which this section of the Act applies and whether or not it should be withheld. The power to withhold either incoming or outgoing mail includes a power to withhold any particular item contained in it.

Any withholding of mail, including withholding at the request of the addressee, must be recorded in writing by managers. In the case of withholding of mail other than at the request of the addressee, the managers of the hospital must within seven days give notice of the withholding to the patient and in the case of incoming mail withheld under section 134(2) on grounds of safety or protection, notice shall within the same period be given to the person (if known) by whom the item was sent. Any such notice to the patient or sender must contain a statement of the right to appeal to the Mental Health Act Commission under section 121(7) of the Act. The Mental Health Act Commission is under a duty to review any decision to withhold a postal packet or anything contained in it under section 134 (other than cases in which the addressee has requested such withholding) provided such appeal is made within six months of the receipt by the applicant of the notice from managers required by section 134(6). Following its review, the Commission has power under section 121(8) of the Act to direct that the postal packet which is the subject of the appeal, or anything contained in it, shall not be withheld. Hospital managers are then under a duty, imposed by section 121(8) of the Act, to comply with such direction from the Commission.

The various cases of censorship provided for by section 134 of the Act thus encompass both safety and protection, as well as personal choice and convenience. Cases may arise, independently of the censorship powers given by section 134 of the Act, in which managers or authorised officers within the staff of a hospital may have reasonable cause to believe that an incoming or outgoing postal packet or similar item could cause danger to the recipient or to others. Such suspicion may not, by experience, be confined to detained patients to whom the provisions of section 134 of the Mental Health Act 1983 are exclusively applicable. In case of suspected danger not falling within the specific powers of section 134, any person on the staff of a hospital is entitled to take reasonable precautions to prevent harm to a third party, or indeed to himself. Thus a suspicion that incoming mail addressed to a detained patient in a hospital which is not a special hospital, or that mail addressed to or from any informal patient, may contain an item which could endanger the recipient or another person (perhaps a member of staff on the ward on which the recipient of a dangerous object is resident), may give grounds at common law to withhold and inspect the item. It is essential for managers and staff to remember in this context, as in others, that the purpose of the Mental Health Act 1983 is to bestow further entitlements upon managers and staff over and above those already existing at common law. Section 134 is not, therefore, to be regarded as the sole means by which a safety policy relating to mail may be implemented.

30.15 PROTECTION FOR ACTS DONE IN PURSUANCE OF THE ACT

Section 139 of the Mental Health Act 1983 provides for both substantive and procedural limitations upon the right of detained patients to commence either civil or criminal proceedings against hospital staff or others who have allegedly committed legal wrongs against them during the course of procedures 'purporting to be done in pursuance of this Act or any regulations or rules made under this Act'. Section 139(1) states that no person shall be liable for such an act, whether on the ground of want of jurisdiction or on any other ground, to any civil or criminal proceedings, unless the act in question was done either in bad faith or without reasonable care. Furthermore, by way of procedural limitation on the entitlement of a detained patient to commence proceedings, section 139(2) provides that no civil proceedings shall be brought against any person in any court in respect of such an act without the leave of the High Court; and that no criminal proceedings shall be brought against any person in any court in respect of such an act except by or with the consent of the Director of Public Prosecutions. The substantive protection (that is, provided there is no bad faith or negligence) of section 139 does not apply to an offence under section 127 of the Mental Health Act 1983, namely ill treatment of patients although, as provided for in section 127(4), no proceedings shall be instituted for such an offence except by or with the consent of the Director of Public Prosecutions.

The rationale of section 139 (formerly section 141 of the Mental Health Act 1959, which provided even greater obstacles to a detained patient) is thought by some to be of doubtful justification. In the case of *Pountney v Griffiths* (1976)[68] Lord Simon commented that 'patients under the Mental Health Act 1959 may generally be inherently likely to harass those concerned with them by groundless charges and litigation, and may therefore have to suffer modification of the general right of access to the courts.' By contrast, he added that detained patients 'are, on the other hand, a class of citizen which experience has shown to be peculiarly vulnerable.' Of the procedural barriers (permission of the High Court, or of the Director of Public Prosecutions) to a detained patient, Hoggett[69] comments:

'Only a minority of patients, even of those compulsorily detained, are suffering from disorders which make it at all likely that they will harass other people with groundless accusations. Rather more of them are suffering from disorders which make it likely that they will not complain at all, even if they have every reason to do so. There is no evidence that the floodgates will open if section 139 were entirely repealed. There is more evidence, from a series of reports and investigations, that mental patients are in a peculiarly powerless position which merits, if anything, extra safeguards rather than the removal of those available to everyone else.'

Nevertheless, the present (1993) Master of the Rolls, Lord Donaldson, commented in *Winch v Jones* (1986)[70] that this section

'is intended to strike a balance between the legitimate interests of the applicant to be allowed, at his own risk as to costs, to seek the adjudication of the courts on any claim which is not frivolous, vexatious or an abuse of the process and the equally legitimate interest of the respondents to such an application not to be subjected to the undoubtedly exceptional risk of being harassed by baseless claims by those who have been treated under the Mental Health Acts (sic).'

It was held in *Winch v Jones* that the correct test to be applied by a court, or by the Director of Public Prosecutions on an application for leave to commence proceedings is

'not whether the applicant has established a prima facie case or even whether there is a serious issue to be tried, although that comes close to it. The issue is whether, on the materials immediately available to the court, which, of course, can include material furnished by the proposed defendant, the applicant's complaint appears to be such that it deserves the fuller investigation which will be possible if the intended applicant is allowed to proceed.'

In other words, the threshold of a detained patient's making out a case is set at a low level. This position contrasts clearly with the earlier section 141 of the Mental Health Act 1959, under which a detained patient had to show 'substantial grounds' for an action to proceed at all.

As regards the substantive protection given by section 139, namely the particular acts and intentions of the person against whom wrongdoing is alleged, the law is rather less clear. Certainly, in the case in which bad faith is alleged, a wrongful act based on such a motive will clearly give ground for legal proceedings, though the standard of proof of bad faith is high.[71] The case of acts done 'without reasonable care' is less clear. In *Richardson v London County Council* (1957),[72] a case decided on section 141 on the 1959 Act but equally applicable to this aspect of section 139, it was decided that the protection is given to acts purporting to be done under the legislation or regulations even though the person proceeded against acted either without jurisdiction or misconstrued the meaning of the Act, provided the misconstruction was one which the Act or regulations were reasonably capable of bearing. In other words, a mistake of law can provide a defence under section 139 of the 1983 Act.

It has been said (see Hoggett, above) that:

'People who are acting without negligence and within their lawful powers will not be liable at all and the section gives no protection against negligence, but it does give protection to people who have made an honest and reasonable mistake, including a mistake about the extent of their powers. If the Act is so clear that even a layman could not have misconstrued it, then he will still be liable, but if it could reasonably be thought to mean what he thought it did, then he will be protected.'

Given, however, that managers are under a duty by means of their staff's understanding and explanation to take 'such steps as are practicable to ensure' that a detained patient knows and understands the legal consequences of detention, it is difficult to resist the conclusion that section 139 of the Act gives only limited protection against acts which 'purport' to be done in pursuance of powers and duties conferred or imposed by the Act. The doubly onerous, and practically important, duty of managers under section 132 of the Act appears to place both them and their staff in a special professional position to which the analogy of 'lay people trying to interpret a difficult Act of Parliament' is hardly appropriate.

While all the protection given by section 139 applies to patients subject to the jurisdiction of the Court of Protection, as well as patients subject to guardianship under section 7 of the 1983 Act, the section does not apply to acts done in respect of informal patients, following the decision in *R v Runighian* (1977).[73] There is as yet no legal ruling on the question whether, for instance, an ambulanceman or other health care professional acting on the instructions of a social worker applicant to take and convey the patient to hospital pursuant to section 6 would have the protection of section 139 if for some reason the application was invalid. On the analogy of section 6(3) it is suggested that the ambulanceman or other person acting under such instruction would have the protection of section 139, under the principle of 'apparent authority'. Section 6(3) provides that any application for the admission of a patient appearing to be duly made and to be founded upon the necessary medical recommendations 'may be acted upon without further proof of the signature or the qualification of the person by whom the application or any such medical recommendation is made or given or of any matter of fact or opinion stated in it'.

30.16   MARRIAGE OF PATIENTS

Although section 128 of the Mental Health Act 1959, which remains unrepealed,[74] makes it an offence for a man on the staff of, or employed by, a hospital or mental nursing home to have extra-marital sexual intercourse with a woman who is receiving treatment for mental disorder, or to have such relations with a woman who is subject to his guardianship or otherwise in his custody or care, the mental health legislation provides no obstacle to the marriage of patients. Such obstacles as exist are to be found, not in the mental health legislation, but in the Matrimonial Causes Act 1973. Section 12 of that Act provides two grounds on which a marriage involving a mentally disordered person might be annulled. First, because of 'unsoundness of mind' under section 12(c), which applies if at the time of the ceremony the bride or groom could not understand the nature of the contract being entered into and appreciate its basic responsibilities. In practical terms, there must be few people who can get through a ceremony of marriage that they are incapable of understanding the nature and purpose of. The second ground is that, though able to understand the nature and purpose of the proceedings and to consent to their legal effect, the bride or groom was suffering (whether continuously or intermittently) from mental disorder within the meaning of the Mental Health Act 1983 'of such a kind or to such an extent as to be unfitted for marriage'. It was decided in *Bennett v Bennett* (1969)[75], a case decided when the Mental Health Act 1959 was still in force, that it is not enough to annul the marriage that one of the spouses is difficult to live with on account of mental disorder and should probably not have got married. The criterion, for the purposes of section 12(d) of the Matrimonial Causes Act 1973, is whether the spouse is incapable of living in the married state and of carrying out the ordinary duties and obligations of marriage. In the particular case, it was decided that the wife of the marriage was not so incapable. Indeed, so far from placing positive obstacles in the way of person suffering from mental disorder getting married the law, by way section 1 of the Marriage Act 1983, makes specific provision to help the marriage of patients who are detained under any of the long-term powers conferred by the Mental Health Act 1983. Under that section they may be married at the hospital, whereas in all other 'normal' cases the marriage must take place in an Anglican church, registered religious building or civil registry office, apart from a few exceptional cases not relevant in the present context.

Apart from the question of annulment, on the grounds of invalidity, based on mental disorder, a question may also arise of the breakdown of a marriage because of one spouse's mental disorder. The fact that the person mentally disordered is in no way to blame for the breakdown of the marriage no longer constitutes an obstacle to matrimonial relief for the parties, as provided by the Matrimonial Causes Act 1973. The subject of divorce for reason of mental disorder being outside the scope of the present work, reference should be made by managers or by the legal representatives of patients or persons mentally disordered to relevant authorities on family law and the law of divorce.

30.17 CONTRACTS OF PERSONS SUFFERING FROM MENTAL DISORDER

It is a question of fact in each case, and not a question of law, whether a person suffering from some form or other of mental disorder is, or is not, capable of understanding the nature, purpose and effects of a contractual agreement in such a way as to be legally bound by its terms. Mental disorder is by no means synonymous with the inability to participate in a legally binding contract. On the one hand, a person need not be detained or even accommodated in hospital in order to fall within the definition of 'patient' for the purposes of Court of Protection jurisdiction (for which see the following section of this chapter); on the other hand, even a longer term detained patient, as well as all other detained patients under the Act, may in fact be perfectly capable, at some time or times, of entering into a legally binding contract. Indeed, this is synonymous with the 'spirit' of Part IV of the Act which allows of the possibility of legally binding consent to treatment even by a patient who is significantly mentally disordered. A person's capacity to enter into a binding contract is governed by much the same principles as those which govern capacity to make a will and depends in each case upon the fact of capability to understand the nature of the contract involved.

Contrasting with the case of a binding agreement being made during a lucid interval in a particular patient's delusional system, or unaffected in any case by the particular mental disorder from which the patient suffers, is the case of mental incapacity to make a contract at all. Such is the case of patients (indeed persons generally) who are sufficiently mentally disabled as not to understand the nature of their actions. The general rule in the law of contract is that a mentally incapable person is bound by a contract that he has made unless he can definitely prove that the other person knew or ought to have known of his incapacity.[76] However, the circumstances of the purported agreement may be such that any reasonable person would have realised that the mentally disordered person was in fact incapable, in which case the agreement would not constitute a binding contract.[77] There is one statutory exception to these general rules, namely in the case of the supply of 'necessaries' under section 3(2) of the Sale of Goods Act 1979. This provides that if necessaries are supplied to a mentally incompetent person, a reasonable price must be paid for them. Necessaries includes goods which are suitable to his condition in life and his actual requirements at the time of the agreement. The rule not only protects suppliers of goods who might otherwise lose money, but also the incapable person who need pay only what is a reasonable price.

As to contractual agreements made between hospitals and nursing homes or mental nursing homes in the private sector of health care, and persons suffering or thought to be suffering from mental disorder, considerable care should be taken to ascertain whether that person is genuinely capable of agreeing to a contract to provide private medical care and to the legal effects of that contract. In the case of patients who are detained under the Mental Health Act 1983 in mental nursing homes in the private sector, the equitable presumption of undue influence would no doubt in all normal cases prevent the managers of the institution from relying upon any purported agreement of such a patient to pay for medical treatment and associated care under detained conditions.

30.18   MANAGEMENT OF PROPERTY AND AFFAIRS OF PATIENTS

30.18.1   Court of Protection: appointment of receiver

Part VII of the Mental Health Act 1983 sets out the very wide powers of the Court of Protection over the management of the property and affairs of a person incapable, by reason of mental disorder, of managing and administering his own property and affairs whether or not that person is liable to detention or placed under guardianship under the provisions of the Act. Such a person is called a 'patient' in Part VII, and not every disordered person is a patient for this purpose, incapability to manage affairs being the essential additional requirement.

Detailed consideration of that part of the Act and of the Court of Protection Rules 1984[78] are largely outside the scope of this book, but in succeeding paragraphs reference is made to one or two aspects of the subject likely to concern hospitals or nursing homes.[79]

Since it is not within the powers of a health authority under the National Health Service Act 1977 to undertake responsibilities in respect of a patient's property, except such property as the patient has brought into hospital with him, and then only doing what is reasonably necessary in the circumstances, it would not normally be a function of any of its officers, as such, to apply for appointment as receiver for a patient; nor is there any statutory authority for reimbursement of the expenses of any such officer if he does so – apart from what he may be authorised to charge against the patient's estate. But section 49 of the National Assistance Act 1948 has been amended to authorise payment of the expenses of an officer of a local social services authority who, with the permission of his authority, applies for appointment under Part VII of the Act of 1983 as receiver for a patient or as a person otherwise having functions in relation to the property and affairs of a patient. This provision, together with that made in section 99 of the Mental Health

Act 1983, for the appointment of the holder of an office for the time being, points to the possibility of a local social services authority giving general authority to a particular officer or class of officer to apply *ex officio* in case of need for appointment as receiver or otherwise to safeguard the property or other affairs of a patient in the area of the authority. Section 99 provides:

'99.— 1) The judge may by order appoint as receiver for a patient a person specified in the order or the holder for the time being of an office so specified.

(2) A person appointed as receiver for a patient shall do all such things in relation to the property and affairs of the patient as the judge, in the exercise of the powers conferred on him by sections 95 and 96 above, orders or directs him to do and may do any such thing in relation to the property and affairs of the patient as the judge, in the exercise of those powers, authorises him to do.

(3) A receiver appointed for any person shall be discharged by order of the judge on the judge being satisfied that that person has become capable of managing and administering his property and affairs, and may be discharged by order of the judge at any time if the judge considers it expedient to do so; and a receiver shall be discharged (without any order) on the death of the patient.'

The Court of Protection may act for the benefit of the patient. The term 'benefit' is much wider than mere material benefit: it includes divorce proceedings and the making of a gift or a will. The full scope of the powers is set out in sections 95 and 96 of the Act:

'95.—(1) The judge may, with respect to the property and affairs of patient, do or secure the doing of all such things as appear necessary or expedient—
  (a) for the maintenance or other benefit of the patient,
  (b) for the maintenance or other benefit of members of the patient's family,
  (c) for making provision for other persons or purposes for whom or which the patient might be expected to provide if he were not mentally disordered, or
  (d) otherwise for administering the patient's affairs.

(2) In the exercise of the powers conferred by this section regard shall be had first of all to the requirements of the patient, and the rules of law which restricted the enforcement by a creditor of rights against property under the control of the judge in lunacy shall apply to property under the control of the judge; but, subject to the foregoing provisions of this subsection, the judge shall, in administering a patient's affairs, have regard to the interests of creditors and also to the desirability of making provision for obligations of the patient notwithstanding that they may not be legally enforceable.

96.—(1) Without prejudice to the generality of section 95 above, the judge shall have power to make such orders and give such directions and authorities as he thinks fit for the purposes of that section and in particular may for those purposes make orders or give directions or authorities for —
  (a) the control (with or without the transfer or vesting of property or the payment into or lodgment in the Supreme Court of money or securities) and management of any property of the patient;
  (b) the sale, exchange, charging or other disposition of or dealing with any property of the patient;
  (c) the acquisition of any property in the name or on behalf of the patient;
  (d) the settlement of any property of the patient, or the gift of any property of

the patient to any such persons or for any such purposes as are mentioned in paragraphs (b) and (c) of section 95(1) above;

(e) the execution for the patient of a will making any provision (whether by way of disposing of property or exercising a power or otherwise) which could be made by a will executed by the patient if he were not mentally disordered;

(f) the carrying on by a suitable person of any profession, trade or business of the patient;

(g) the dissolution of a partnership of which the patient is a member;

(h) the carrying out of any contract entered into by the patient;

(i) the conduct of legal proceedings in the name of the patient or on his behalf;

(j) the reimbursement out of the property of the patient, with or without interest, of money applied by any person either in payment of the patient's debts (whether legally enforceable or not) or for the maintenance or other benefit of the patient or members of his family or in making provision for other persons or purposes for whom or which he might be expected to provide if he were not mentally disordered;

(k) the exercise of any power (including a power to consent) vested in the patient, whether beneficially, or as guardian or trustee, or otherwise.

(2) If under subsection (1) above provision is made for the settlement of any property of a patient, or the exercise of a power vested in a patient of appointing trustees or retiring from a trust, the judge may also make as respects the property settled or trust property such consequential vesting or other orders as the case may require, including (in the case of the exercise of such a power) any order which could have been made in such a case under Part IV of the Trustee Act 1925.

(3) Where under this section a settlement has been made of any property of a patient, and the Lord Chancellor or a nominated judge is satisfied, at any time before the death of the patient, that any material fact was not disclosed when the settlement was made, or that there has been any substantial change in circumstances, he may by order vary the settlement in such manner as he thinks fit, and give any consequential directions.

(4) The power of the judge to make or give an order, direction or authority for the execution of a will for a patient—

(a) shall not be exercisable at any time when the patient is a minor, and

(b) shall not be exercised unless the judge has reason to believe that the patient is incapable of making a valid will for himself.

(5) The powers of a patient as patron of a benefice shall be exercisable by the Lord Chancellor only.'

30.18.2 Lord Chancellor's Visitors

It is provided in section 102 of the Act that there shall continue to be medical and legal visitors of patients, being persons qualified as required by the Act, appointed by the Lord Chancellor, to be known as Lord Chancellor's Visitors.

It is the duty of the Lord Chancellor's Visitors to visit patients in accordance with the directions of the judge (within the parameters of standing directions given by the Master of the Court of Protection) for the purpose of investigating matters relating to the capacity of any patient to manage and administer his property and affairs or otherwise relating to the exercise, in relation to him, of the functions of the judge under Part VII of the Act; and the Visitors are to make such reports on their visits as the judge may direct. The Master of the Court of Protection may also visit any patient for those purposes. For the purposes of section 103 relating to visitation by Lord Chancellor's Visitors or the Master the word 'patients' includes not only patients within the meaning of section 94 but also persons *alleged* to be incapable, by reason of mental disorder, of managing and administering their property and affairs.

A Visitor or the Master making a visit may interview the patient in private and a medical Visitor may carry out in private a medical examination of the patient and may require the production of and inspect any medical records relating to the patient.

A report made by a Visitor under section 103 and the information contained in such a report shall not be disclosed except to the judge and any person authorised by the judge to receive the disclosure. Any wrongful disclosure is a criminal offence.

30.19   RISK MANAGEMENT AND MENTAL DISORDER

30.19.1   Protection of others against dangerous patients

The actions of a great many mental patients are remarkably predictable, and it would be wrong to suppose that, once outside the confines of a mental hospital or institution, such patients are apt to run amok. Some detainees, however, act unpredictably, and if such patients are also violence-impulsed the danger exists that an innocent third party might be harmed.

In *Home Office v Dorset Yacht Company* (1970),[80] damages were recovered against the Home Office on account of the negligence of prison officers at an open Borstal. Officers at the Borstal on Brownsea Island, off the South Coast, failed to exercise adequate supervision with the result that a number of detainees were able to abscond. In their flight they damaged a boat belonging to the Dorset Yacht Company and this damage was held to be a foreseeable result of the original negligence of the supervisors. The Home Office was sued as principal, the actual negligence being that of its agents or employees.

Liability for negligence is based on the foresight of a 'reasonable man' or, simply on reasonably foreseeable consequences. There is no general duty to prevent harm by someone else to a third party; such a duty may, however, exist, if the potential offender is in some way under restraint or supervision. Supervisors may become liable for damages if they do not supervise properly. Clearly, not every error suffices to produce legal liability if damage or injury ensues; but, equally clearly, the greater the degree of risk, the greater the corresponding duty of care. In this respect, violence-impulsed patients present special problems.

The case of *Holgate v Lancashire Mental Hospitals Board* (1937)[81] concerned negligence in releasing on licence a patient who had a criminal record, who had a mental age of nine and who was described as a 'moral imbecile'. Insufficient attention was paid by the officers of the institution to the grant of a licence and they (with the institution as principal) were held liable for damages when the patient caused severe physical injury to a woman whom he visited. This was a case in which the officers had a *discretion* as to how they should act and it was held by the court that they were so negligent as to have failed to act within the proper confines of their discretion. The case was specifically referred to in these terms by Lord Reid in the *Dorset Yacht Company* case.

Some cases – the Borstal case is one – do not involve discretion, for the question is simply one of detention or proper supervision. Lest it be thought that mental institutions admit dangerous or unpredictable patients at their peril, or that it is harsh to attach liability to those to whom Parliament has entrusted a difficult task, the words of Lord Reid should be emphasised: 'Parliament cannot reasonably be supposed to have licensed those who do such things to act negligently in disregard to the interests of others so as to cause them needless damage.' Those acting in pursuance of statutory authority will be liable to compensate victims of their carelessness.

30.19.2 Protection of patients against harm to themselves

The judicial decisions in actions alleging negligence in staff failure to guard against patients harming themselves are of general application and their principles, discussed in Chapter 6, are not confined to patients receiving treatment for mental disorder.

30.19.3 Seclusion and time-out

Neither of these terms has any direct legal counterpart, nor is either likely to be encountered in any legal textbook or guide. It is therefore to specialist publications that attention must be directed for an indication of what the terms mean in practice. Such documents will include those issued by the Royal College of Psychiatrists and the Royal College of Nursing, as well as the Mental Health Act Code of Practice. Such definitions of seclusion and time-out as are used in health care management have no specific legal significance other than to indicate accepted practice in a given area of care and treatment, with particular relevance in the case of complaint or legal action. Beyond that, any professional or other guide to the use of seclusion and time-out is likely to take the form of a statement of good practice, applicable either generally (perhaps nationally) or at local level depending upon particular conditions. Paragraphs 18.15–18.23 (inclusive) of the Code of Practice are statutorily approved guides, at national level, to good practice.

Such is the range of uses, and therefore purposes, to which the term seclusion is put that some psychiatric facilities will regard its use as a custodial or containment reaction to circumstances which cannot otherwise be controlled, while in others (including at least one of the special hospitals), seclusion includes even conditions of solitude which can be requested by a patient. In the latter case, seclusion records cover equally instances of custodial detention for reasons of violence as well as the perhaps frequent occasions when detained patients with insight into their condition and reactions request seclusion to be kept away from other patients and even from staff.

Sometimes the concept of seclusion is made to depend upon the existence of a lock, in others not. Most uses of the term 'seclusion' exclude a situation in which a member of staff is present in the room in which the patient is placed. Some definitions include the word 'alone', meaning that not only other patients but also staff are absent from the place of seclusion or confinement.

There are two broad purposes, possibly in combination, of seclusion. These are: containment, of a situation involving danger (particularly to others); and observation, given the danger to the particular patient concerned. A negative distinguishing feature of seclusion is that it is generally taken to be something which does not form, nor ought to form, part of a predetermined treatment plan. That idea is useful for most purposes, though it does not accord with the practice, just mentioned of patients 'requesting' seclusion. It would be wrong to say that there was confusion amongst those using the term seclusion and much better to say that the term, and the concomitant practice, are susceptible of differing content according to the circumstances and the purposes for which it is used in any given facility (or perhaps even situation).

Time-out is more easily defined, including normally the removal from factors reinforcing 'negative behaviour'.

Paragraph 18.15 of the Code of Practice states: 'Seclusion is the supervised confinement of a patient alone in a room which may be locked for the protection of others from significant harm.' Seclusion, states the Code, should be used as little as possible and for the shortest possible time, though many practitioners might in their own practice substitute the word 'reasonable' for the word 'possible' in this statement in the Code. The Code states that 'seclusion should not be used as a punitive measure or to enforce good behaviour'. The Code further states: 'Although it falls within the definition of medical treatment in the Mental Health Act, (section 145), seclusion is not a treatment technique and should not feature as part of any treatment programme. Its use therefore cannot be foreseen.' The point of saying this is that seclusion may perfectly well fall within the definition of 'medical treatment for mental disorder' as defined in section 145 of the Act where statutory authority under the Act itself is desirable legally to justify physical contact with a patient. In the case of detained patients, the physical contact with a patient consisting in seclusion may therefore be justified on account of the provisions of section 63 which covers treatments not falling within section 57 or 58, and for which consent (to physical contact) is not required if the treatment is given or directed by the RMO.

It would probably be wrong, in practice if not also in law, to put a patient on a section if future seclusion were foreseen as a realistic possibility, solely for that reason. This is because ample common law powers exist to justify proportionate reaction to danger offered, either to the patient himself or to others. If, however, the other requirements (for instance of section 2 or section 3 admission) are fulfilled, then if the patient is for those reasons put on section, and it is one of the longer-term sections making the patient susceptible to Part IV of the Mental Health Act, then probably section 63 can be relied upon for the removal of doubt in the event of seclusion being thereafter employed.

While, therefore, it is broadly true to say that a patient on section may more confidently be secluded by staff than an informal patient, the absence of detained status should not deter the use of appropriate force or firmness where harm is offered by, or expected from, an informal patient. In any event, the end of the emergency should signify the cessation of seclusion.

Time-out is defined, or at least described, in paragraph 19.9. Time-out is a behaviour modification technique which removes a patient for a period (lasting no more than 15 minutes) from opportunities to participate in an activity or to obtain positive reinforcers following (normally immediately) the occurrence of unacceptable behaviour, and which then returns the patient to the original environment.

The Code goes on to explain that time-out should be seen as one of a range of methods of managing a difficult or disturbed patient and not as immediate reaction to such behaviour. This notion of time-out appears to be fairly uncontroversial, save for the restriction to no more than 15 minutes, which is unexplained.

Some practitioners might wish to depart from the Code's statement that the use of seclusion 'cannot be foreseen'. It may in fact be foreseeable that, in violent or otherwise unmanageable interludes which can reasonably be anticipated, advance or anticipatory provision needs to be made for their containment. If the definition of seclusion set out earlier in paragraph 18.15 is still fulfilled, the fact that its use may be quite reasonably anticipated in the case of some patients does not somehow stop the practice being seclusion and change it into time-out.

Code of Practice and common law

The Mental Health Act 1983 contains no duty to detain or to treat, but it provides for duties to act in certain ways if the decision is first of all made to detain or to treat. Put simply, the Act provides for powers to legalise what could otherwise amount to civil wrongs or criminal offences, though if those powers are to be properly exercised there is a duty to comply with certain procedures. In particular, the Act itself does not provide either expressly or by implication any standards of good practice, or care standards fulfilling the legal duty of care. A particular feature of the statutory Code of Practice is that the Code goes much further than the Act and Regulations in making recommendations, and sometimes stipulations, for good practice.

Practitioners, and managers, require reliable and specific information in order to be quite clear about which parts of the Code of Practice refer to specific legal duties and requirements, and which parts refer to recommendations of good practice falling short of such obligations. The interface between legal responsibilities and other professional, social or personal responsibilities may not always be wholly clear in some sections of the Code of Practice. That is not to say that the latter recommendations are unwelcome, but simply that practitioners may usefully be advised which responsibility is being attributed to which legal or other source.

Time-out may perfectly well, and in most cases will, be a part of treatment and therefore part of the care offered by professionals to patients. Given that the legal 'right' to personal freedom effectively takes the form of remedies in the case of wrongful physical contact, the only consent needed in the case of time-out occurs in the situation where physical contact is made by the carer with the patient in order to effect it. No doubt for professional and ethical reasons the consent of a patient ahead of time to a treatment plan involving time-out would be desirable. Except, however, in the most extreme circumstances of medical negligence being committed by the wrongful use of time-out, the absence of consent will not (without physical contact being involved) have any legal significance.

An exclusive definition of both the meaning and purpose of seclusion and time-out is probably impossible. The mental health legislation mentions neither and only by implicit reference refers to either by way of the general definition of medical treatment for mental disorder in section 145. Regulations made pursuant to the Act mention neither term. The Code of Practice, which has statutory force, mentions both terms. The legal significance of the Code of Practice is that, having been approved by Parliament, its stipulations and recommendations are taken to be indications of good practice, unless the contrary can be proved. Therefore it is still open to practitioners and other professionals to argue their case in the event of litigation or other complaint, about the use of either seclusion or time-out or both, even if they depart from or even contradict the recommendations of the Code; it is simply a case of the onus shifting to them to demonstrate good practice in the event of complaint.

So far as the law of trespass to the person is concerned (assault and false imprisonment) departure from or even contradiction of the recommendations of the Code will not by any means necessarily lead to the commission of these wrongs; and even in the event of harm or injury to a patient or a third party, it is a well-established legal rule that simply to depart from or even act in contradiction of a widespread and accepted medical practice is not in itself evidence of negligence if there is an established and respectable school of thought of professionals of ordinary skill and competence who follow the minority practice.

30.20 AFTERCARE FOLLOWING DISCHARGE FROM HOSPITAL

30.20.1 Mental Health Act 1983, section 117

Section 117 of the Mental Health Act 1983 imposes a duty on health authorities (and NHS trusts, following the National Health Service and Community Care Act 1990) to see to the aftercare (sometimes referred to in practice as 'throughcare') of certain formerly detained patients. It goes without saying that, as a matter of common law safety repsonsibilities, health authorities and trusts and local authority social services departments should commence discharge planning in sufficient time for the post-discharge care plan to be effective and reliable once it is put in place in respect of the patient or client.

Section 117 provides as follows:

'**117.**—(1) This section applies to persons who are detained under section 3 above, or admitted to a hospital in pursuance of a hospital order made under section 37 above, or transferred to a hospital in pursuance of a transfer direction made under section 47 or 48 above, and then cease to be detained and leave hospital.

(2) It shall be the duty of the District Health Authority and of the local social services authority to provide, in co-operation with relevant voluntary agencies, after-care services for any person to whom this section applies until such time as the District Health Authority and the local social services authority are satisfied that the person concerned is no longer in need of such services.

(3) In this section "the District Health Authority" means the District Health Authority for the district, and "the local social services authority" means the local social services authority for the area in which the person concerned is resident or to which he is sent on discharge by the hospital in which he was detained.'

The purpose of aftercare is to enable a patient to return to his home or accommodation other than a hospital or nursing home, and to minimise the chances of him needing any future in-patient hospital care. Section 117 of the Act 1983 requires health authorities and local authorities, in conjunction with voluntary agencies, to provide aftercare for certain categories of detained patients. Health and social services authorities should, together with local voluntary organisations, agree procedures for establishing proper aftercare arrangements. These arrangements should be regularly reviewed and it should be the responsibility of an officer from each of the authorities to ensure that the procedures are working properly. In the case of patients detained under section 37/41 or section 47/49 there will be special considerations to be taken into account.

Until 1992 it was widely believed that failure to implement the duty imposed by section 117 of the Act could be enforced only by the exercise of default powers on the part of the Secretary of State, as provided by section 124 of the Act. (By section 66(2) and Schedule 10 of the National Health Service and Community Care Act 1990, section 124 of the 1983 Act is prospectively repealed, and by the same Act a new section 7D of the Local Authority Social Services Act 1970 provides the Secretary of State with a general default power in respect of the social services functions of local authorities, thus anticipating the transfer of functions under the 1990 Act from health authorities to local authority social services.) In the case of the exercise, by the Secretary of State, of statutory default powers, no other remedy is available to a complainant. In the case of *Southwark LBC v Williams* (1971),[82] Lord Denning stated that 'where an Act creates an obligation, and enforces that obligation in a specified manner, we take it to be a general rule that performance cannot be enforced in any other manner'.

Nevertheless, the duty imposed by section 117 of the Mental Health Act 1983 was held in the case of *R v Ealing District Health Authority, ex parte Fox* (1992)[83] to create a right enforceable at the instance of an aggrieved individual. In that case, Mr Justice Otton ruled that a District Health Authority is under a legal duty to provide aftercare services pursuant to section 117 of the Mental Health Act 1983 when a patient leaves hospital (or is in prospect of leaving hospital); and the authority acts unlawfully in failing to make practical arrangements for aftercare prior to that patient's discharge from hospital where such arrangements have been required by a Mental Health Review Tribunal in order to enable the patient to be conditionally discharged from hospital.

In that case, which concerned a patient who had been detained pursuant to sections 37 and 41 of the Mental Health Act 1983 (hospital order with restriction on discharge), the Oxford Mental Health Review Tribunal had directed 'that the patient be conditionally discharged but that such discharge be deferred until the tribunal is satisfied that certain conditions can be met'. When the matter was considered by the District Health Authority whose responsibility the patient was, they concluded that the applicant should be supervised for at least 18 months in a regional secure unit rather than in the community in their locality. The Tribunal in reaching its decision expressly stated that they considered that any delay in discharging the patient would cause greater problems in his rehabilitation.

The case therefore raised the important question of principle, namely where a patient is detained in conditions of maximum security and a Tribunal is prepared to grant conditional discharge but the relevant health authority is unable or unwilling to make available care in the community for reasons other than lack of resources, with the result that the patient is obliged to remain under conditions of maximum security. The submission made to the court by counsel for the applicant (patient) was that the health authority by their decision had effectively refused to refer the patient to a responsible medical officer in its community, the co-operation of whom was a prerequisite to the fulfilment of the conditions of conditional discharge. In the words of his counsel, he was 'thus being prevented from obtaining his conditional discharge by the decision of the health authority'. By contrast, it was contended on behalf of the defendant health authority that the legal remedy is confined to the exercise by the Secretary of State of default powers (for which see above).

Holding that section 117 of the 1983 Act creates an individual right, Mr Justice Otton reached the following conclusion:[84]

'I consider section 117(2) as mandatory. It shall be the duty of the district health authority to provide aftercare services for any person to whom the section applies. The section clearly will apply to the applicant as he falls within subsection (1). Thus, the duty is not only a general duty but a specific duty owed to the applicant to provide him with aftercare services until such time as the district health authority and local social services authority are satisfied that he is no longer in need of such services.'

Specifically in relation to the unwillingness of doctors representing the health authority in its decision to accept the patient in consequence of the Tribunal's decision, Mr Justice Otton said:

'As consultants, in my judgment, they are perfectly free and untrammelled in reaching their opinions and recommendations. It is not suggested that either doctor has acted in bad faith or in order to extricate the health authority from its obligations. I have come to the conclusion that the mere acceptance by the health authority of the doctors' opinions is not of itself a sufficient discharge of their obligations to proceed with reasonable expedition and diligence and to give effect to the arrangements specified and required by the mental health review tribunal.'

Referring to an argument that the duty under section 117 does not come into existence until the actual discharge of a formerly detained patient from hospital, his Lordship said:

'I reject the submission that this duty only comes into existence when the applicant is discharged from [hospital]. I consider a proper interpretation of this section to be that it is a continuing duty in respect of any patient who may be discharged and falls within section 117, although the duty to any particular patient is only triggered at the moment of discharge.'

The breadth of the responsibility of authorities into whose area a patient may prospectively be discharged was underlined by his Lordship in the following terms:

'In my judgment, if the District Health Authority's doctors do not agree with the conditions imposed by the Mental Health Review Tribunal and are disinclined to make the necessary arrangements to supervise the applicant on his release, the District Health Authority cannot let the matter rest there. The District Health Authority is under a continuing obligation to make further endeavours to provide arrangements within its own resources or to obtain them from other health authorities who provide such services so as to put in place practical arrangements for enabling the applicant to comply with the conditions imposed by the Mental Health Review Tribunal or, at the very least, to make enquiry of other providers of such services. If the arrangements still cannot be made then the District Health Authority should not permit an impasse to continue but refer the matter to the Secretary of State to enable him to consider exercising his power to refer the case back to the Mental Health Review Tribunal under section 71(1).'

In respect of the practical operation of responsibilities under section 117 the statutory Code of Practice provides, relevantly, as follows:

'27.4   Proper records should be kept of all those patients for whom section 117 could apply and of those for whom arrangements have been made under section 117. These records could be in the form of a register.

27.5   Managers in the health service, NHS trusts and Directors of Social Services should ensure that all staff are aware of the care programme approach as laid down in Circular HC(90)23/LASSL(90)11 and the principles set out in the Welsh Office Mental Illness Strategy.

27.6   When a decision has been taken to discharge or grant leave to a patient, it is the responsibility of the RMO to ensure that a discussion takes place to establish a care-plan to organise the management of the patient's continuing health and social care needs. This discussion will usually take place in multi-professional clinical meetings held in psychiatric hospitals and units. If this is not possible, administrative support should be available to the RMO to assist in making arrangements.

27.7 Those who should be involved in the discussion are:

- the patient's RMO;
- a nurse involved in caring for the patient in hospital;
- a social worker specialising in mental health work;
- the GP;
- a CPN;
- a representative of relevant voluntary organisations (where appropriate and available);
- the patient if he wishes and/or a relative or other nominated representative.

27.9 Those contributing to the discussion should consider the following issues:

a. the patient's own wishes and needs;
b. the views of any relevant relative, friend or supporter of the patient;
c. the need for agreement with an appropriate representative at the receiving health authority if it is to be different from that of the discharging authority;
d. the possible involvement of other agencies, e.g. probation, voluntary organisations;
e. the establishing of a care-plan, based on proper assessment and clearly identified needs, in which the following issues must be considered and planned for insofar as resources permit: day care arrangements, appropriate accommodation, out-patient treatment, counselling, personal support, assistance in welfare rights, assistance in managing finances, and, if necessary, in claiming benefits;
f. the appointment of a key worker from either of the statutory agencies to monitor the care-plan's implementation, liaise and co-ordinate where necessary and report to the senior officer in their agency any problems that arise which cannot be resolved through normal discussion;
g. the identification of any unmet need.

27.10 The multi-professional discussion should establish an agreed outline of the patient's needs and assets taking into account their social and cultural background, and agree a time-scale for the implementation of the various aspects of the plan. All key people with specific responsibilities with regard to the patient should be properly identified. Once plans are agreed it is essential that any changes are discussed with others involved with the patient before being implemented. The plan should be recorded in writing.

27.11 The care-plan should be regularly reviewed. It will be the responsibility of the key worker to arrange reviews of the plan until it is agreed that it is no longer necessary. The senior officer in the key worker's agency responsible for section 117 arrangements should ensure that all aspects of the procedure are followed.'

Specifically in relation to certain patients who are or have been considered for discharge from hospital, Chapter 27 of the Code of Practice provides:

'28.1 **Conditionally discharged restricted patients – supervision** Those involved in the supervision of a conditionally discharged restricted patient should have copies of and be familiar with "Supervision and After-care of Conditionally Discharged Restricted Patients" (HO/DoH notes of guidance (1987) and Recall of mentally disordered patients subject to Home Office restrictions on discharge (HSG(93)20/LAC(93)9).

30.20.2   The Care Programme Approach

Although still of legal importance to the duties of health authorities and trusts, and local social services departments, the practical effect of section 117 has been subsumed in the much wider duty imposed by Circular HC(90)23, which applies to all patients irrespective of detention or former detained status.

The Circular states:

'By 1 April 1991 District Health Authorities and the Bethlem and Maudsley Special Health Authority were instructed to have drawn up and implemented, in consultation and agreement with social services authorities, local care programme policies to apply to all in-patients considered for discharge, and all new patients accepted, by the specialist psychiatric services they manage from that date. Where a District Health Authority purchases psychiatric services from a self-governing trust or elsewhere, the contractual arrangements should require these organisations to have adopted the care programme approach.

How the Care Programme Approach works

Individual health authorities, in discussion with relevant social services authorities, will have agreed the exact form the care programme approach will take locally. All care programmes should, however, include the following key elements:

    i.   systematic arrangements for assessing the health care needs of patients who could, potentially, be treated in the community, and for regularly reviewing the health care needs of those being treated in the community;

    ii.   systematic arrangements, agreed with appropriate social services authorities, for assessing and regularly reviewing what social care such patients need to give them the opportunity of benefiting from treatment in the community;

    iii.   effective systems for ensuring that agreed health and, where necessary, social care services are provided to those patients who can be treated in the community.

It will be for relevant health and social services staff to decide whether the resources available to them can enable acceptable arrangements to be made for treating specific patients in the community. If a patient's minimum needs for treatment in the community – both in terms of continuing health care and any necessary social care – cannot be met, in-patient treatment should be offered or continued, although (except for patients detained under the Mental Health Act) it is for individual patients to decide whether to accept treatment as an in-patient. Health authorities will need to ensure that any reduction in the number of hospital beds does not outpace the development of alternative community services.'

Maintaining cohesion and contact with, and within, the multi-disciplinary care team is central to the successful implementation of the care programme approach, and paragraphs 15–20 of the Circular provide for the role of the keyworker as follows:

'15. **Key workers**. Where this can be agreed between a health authority and the relevant social services authority, the ideal is for one named person to be appointed as key worker to keep in close touch with the patient and to monitor that the agreed health and social care is given. The key worker can come from any discipline but should be sufficiently experienced to command the confidence of colleagues from other disciplines. When the key worker is unavailable, proper arrangements should be made for an alternative point of contact for the patient and any carer(s).

16. A particular responsibility of the key worker is to maintain sufficient contact with the patient to advise professional colleagues of changes in circumstances which might require review and modification of the care programme.

17. In addition to key worker arrangements, professional staff implementing a care programme may decide that they need a suitable information system as a means of keeping in touch and prompting action. Systems using a micro-computer are available and some relevant information about them is available from Research and Development for Psychiatry, 134 Borough High Street, London SE1 1LB, Tel: 071–403 8790. When establishing such a system, those concerned have a duty to consider how to ensure the proper confidentiality of information about individual patients.

18. Sometimes patients being treated in the community will decline to co-operate with the agreed care programmes, for example by missing out-patient appointments. An informal patient is free to discharge himself/herself from patient status at any time, but often treatment may be missed due to the effects of the illness itself, and with limited understanding of the likely consequence.

19. Every reasonable effort should be made to maintain contact with the patient and, where appropriate, his/her carers, to find out what is happening, to seek to sustain the therapeutic relationship and, if this is not possible, to try to ensure that the patient and carer knows how to make contact with his/her key worker or the other professional staff involved. It is particularly important that the patient's general practitioner is kept fully informed of a patient's situation and especially of his or her withdrawal (partial or complete, see paragraph 20 below) from a care programme. The general practitioner will continue to have responsibility for the patient's general medical care if she/he withdraws from the care programme.

20. Often patients only wish to withdraw from part of a care programme and the programme should be sufficiently flexible to accept such a partial rather than a complete withdrawal. It is important that, within proper limits of confidentiality, social services day care, residential and domiciliary staff (including those from the voluntary and private sectors) are given sufficient information about the situation to enable them to fulfil completely their responsibility of care to the patient. Similarly, relatives and carers should also be kept properly informed.'

30.21 REMOVAL OF SICK ETC. PERSONS FROM PREMISES

While not in law confined to the care of persons suffering from mental disorder, the 'place of safety' powers provided by the National Assistance Acts may be of use.

A person who is suffering from grave chronic disease or, being aged, infirm or physically incapacitated, is living in insanitary conditions, or is unable to devote to himself, or receive from persons with whom he resides, proper care and attention, may be removed to a hospital or to an institution under Part III of the National Assistance Act 1948, on a justice's order under section 47 of that Act when, in either case, the community physician certifies in writing to the appropriate local social services authority that he is satisfied after thorough inquiry and consideration that in the interests of any such person as aforesaid residing in the area of the authority, or of preventing injury to the health of, or serious nuisance to, other persons, it is necessary to remove any such person as aforesaid from the premises in which he is residing. Section 1 of the National Assistance (Amendment) Act 1951, amends section 47 of the 1948 Act by providing means of making an *ex parte* order without 7 days' notice and other formalities: an *ex parte* order is operative for only three weeks.

Section 47 of the National Assistance Act 1948 does not cover the case of the patient in hospital whose treatment is complete but who has nowhere else to go, e.g. the elderly infirm patient whose relatives refuse to have him back. Such a person cannot be moved from a hospital to Part III accommodation under the Act of 1948 without his consent. If, however, it is practicable for the hospital to formally discharge such a patient, if necessary by ejecting him from the premises, it may well be that if he has nowhere else to go, the local social services authority may be able to take steps which result in his being taken to Part III accommodation.

NOTES

1. Department of Health Statistical Bulletin *In-patients Formally Detained in Hospital under the Mental Health Act 1983 and other legislation* (2 January 1991).
2. See Mr Justice McCullough in *R v Hallstrom and another, ex parte W (No. 2)* [1986] 2 All ER 306, 314.
3. [1986] 2 All ER 306.
4. (1981) 73 Cr App Rep 281; by a tribunal, though not (oddly) by managers.
5. Since the National Health Service and Community Care Act 1990, Schedule 9, paragraphs 24(3), 24(9).
6. Mental Health Act 1983, section 6(1)(a).
7. R Jones *Mental Health Act Manual* (3rd edn, 1991), Sweet and Maxwell, London, p. 21. Paragraph 2.8 of the Code of Practice refers to 'serious persistent psychological harm to others' as an 'indicator' of the need for formal admission.
8. Mental Health Act 1983, section 20(2)(a) and (b).
9. In practice the application is normally made by the ASW.
10. Mental Health Act 1983, section 3(2)(b).
11. Mental Health Act 1983, section 11(6).

12. [1986] 2 All ER 306.
13. Mental Health Act 1983, section 5(6).
14. Mental Health (Nurses) Order 1983, SI 1983/891.
15. See the requirement in section 11(6).
16. Department of Health and Social Security *Mental Health Act 1983, Memorandum on Parts I to VI, VII and X* (1987, revised), HMSO, London.
17. See *R v Hallstrom, ex parte W (No. 2)* [1986] 2 All ER 306 and pp. 751–755 of this chapter.
18. As indicated in paragraph 1.1 of the Code of Practice, compliance with its recommendations is not compulsory; and while 'failure to follow the Code could be referred to in evidence in legal proceedings', recommendations as broad and unspecific as those under discussion could, in occasional inauspicious cases, be seriously questioned in legal proceedings for negligence.
19. [1992] 4 All ER 545.
20. Cmnd 8405, paragraph 43.
21. *Re F (Mental patient: sterilisation)* [1989] 2 WLR 1025.
22. B. Hoggett *Mental Health Law* (3rd edn, 1990) Sweet and Maxwell, London, p. 247.
23. (1981) 73 Cr App Rep 281.
24. Mental Health Act 1983, section 37(1).
25. [1983] 1 WLR 335.
26. (1985) 80 Cr App Rep 366, Divisional Court.
27. The Times, 15 June 1983, Court of Appeal.
28. Mental Health Act 1983, section 55(1).
29. See pp. 802–818, below.
30. [1967] 1 WLR 464, 469.
31. The Times, 4 May 1989.
32. Mental Health Act 1983, section 69(2)(a).
33. Mental Health Act 1983, section 54(1).
34. J Higgins, 'Tried and Treated' Social Work Today, Vol. 14, No. 21, p. 11.
35. Mental Health Act 1983, section 40(1)(a) and the Police Act 1964, section 18 and Schedule 2.
36. R Jones *Mental Health Act Manual* (3rd edn, 1991), Sweet and Maxwell, London.
37. Mental Health Act 1983, section 73 and Mental Health Review Tribunal Rules, SI 1983/942, rule 8(3).
38. Originally brought into operation on 1 January 1986 by the Police and Criminal Evidence Act 1984 (Codes of Practice) (No. 1) Order 1985, SI 1985/1937; now revoked and replaced by the Police and Criminal Evidence Act (Codes of Practice) (No. 2) Order 1990, SI 1990/2580, taking account of revisions made in the interim to the Codes.
39. See also the legal argument that the Mental Health Act 1959 permitted involuntary detention but not involuntary treatment: Jacob 'The Right of a Mental Patient to Psychosis' (1976) 39 Mod Law Rev 17.
40. Mental Health Act 1983, section 145(1).
41. For divergence of views relating to such 'dual detention' see p. 794 of this chapter.
42. SI 1983/893.
43. See *R v Lennox-Wright* [1973] Crim LR 529; but see Kennedy (1976) 16 Med Sci Law 49 at 52–54.
44. *Chatterton v Gerson* [1981] QB 432.
45. *Chatterton v Gerson* [1981] QB 432; *Sidaway v Board of Governors of the Bethlem Royal Hospital and the Maudsley Hospital* [1985] AC 871.

46. See, for instance, Mr Justice Hirst in *Hills v Potter* [1984] WLR; and Mr Justice Bristow in *Chatterton v Gerson*, [1981] QB 432.
47. *R v Mental Health Act Commission, ex parte MW* The Times, 27 May 1988; the comment is made by Lord Justice Stuart-Smith on p. 13 of the official report.
48. At p. 21.
49. In case of MW, note 47, above.
50. R. Jones *Mental Health Act Manual* (3rd edn, 1991), Sweet and Maxwell, London, p. 128, citing the recommendation contained in paragraph 7.6(d) of the Mental Health Act Commission's Third Biennial Report, 1987–89.
51. Section 60 permits the competent patient to withdraw consent, once given, at any time thereafter.
52. *Re F (mental patient: sterilisation)* [1989] 2 WLR 1025.
53. *Chatterton v Gerson* [1981] QB 432.
54. R. Jones *Mental Health Act Manual* (3rd edn, 1991), Sweet and Maxwell, London, p. 217.
55. Mental Health Act Code of Practice, paragraph 22(1).
56. SI 1990/486.
57. Mental Health Review Tribunal Rules 1983, SI 1983/942, rule 31(a).
58. The Times, 25 March 1987.
59. See Lord Justice Ackner in *R v Hallstrom, ex parte W* [1985] 3 All ER 775, 784.
60. (1981) 4 EHRR 181 (application 6998/75).
61. SI 1983/942; amended SI 1991/2684.
62. Sections 35, 36 and 38.
63. [1985] 3 All ER 330.
64. Mental Health (Scotland) Act 1984; Mental Health (Northern Ireland) Order 1986.
65. Mental Health Act Commission (Establishment and Constitution) Order, SI 1983/892.
66. The Secretary of State did so by way of direction in HC(83)19.
67. Mental Health Act 1983, section 134(3).
68. [1976] AC 314.
69. B. Hoggett *Mental Health Law* (3rd edn, 1990), Sweet and Maxwell, London, at p. 367.
70. [1986] QB 296.
71. *Hornal v Neuberger Products Ltd* [1956] 2 All ER 970, per Lord Denning at p. 973.
72. [1957] 1 WLR 751.
73. [1977] Crim LR 361.
74. See Mental Health Act 1983, Schedule 6.
75. [1969] 1 WLR 430.
76. *Imperial Loan Co v Stone* [1892] 1 QB 599.
77. *York Glass Co v Jubb* (1925) 134 LT 36.
78. SI 1984/2035; modified SI 1991/2684.
79. Advice to National Health Service hospital authorities on Part VIII of the Act and on the circumstances in which the management of a mentally disordered patient's affairs should be referred to the Court of Protection is given in Departmental Circular HM(60)80.
80. [1970] AC 1004.
81. [1937] 4 All ER 294. See also, now, HSG(93)20, 'Recall of mentally disordered patients subject to Home Office restrictions on discharge.'
82. [1971] Ch 734.
83. [1993] 3 All ER 170.
84. Ibid. at p. 181.

Index